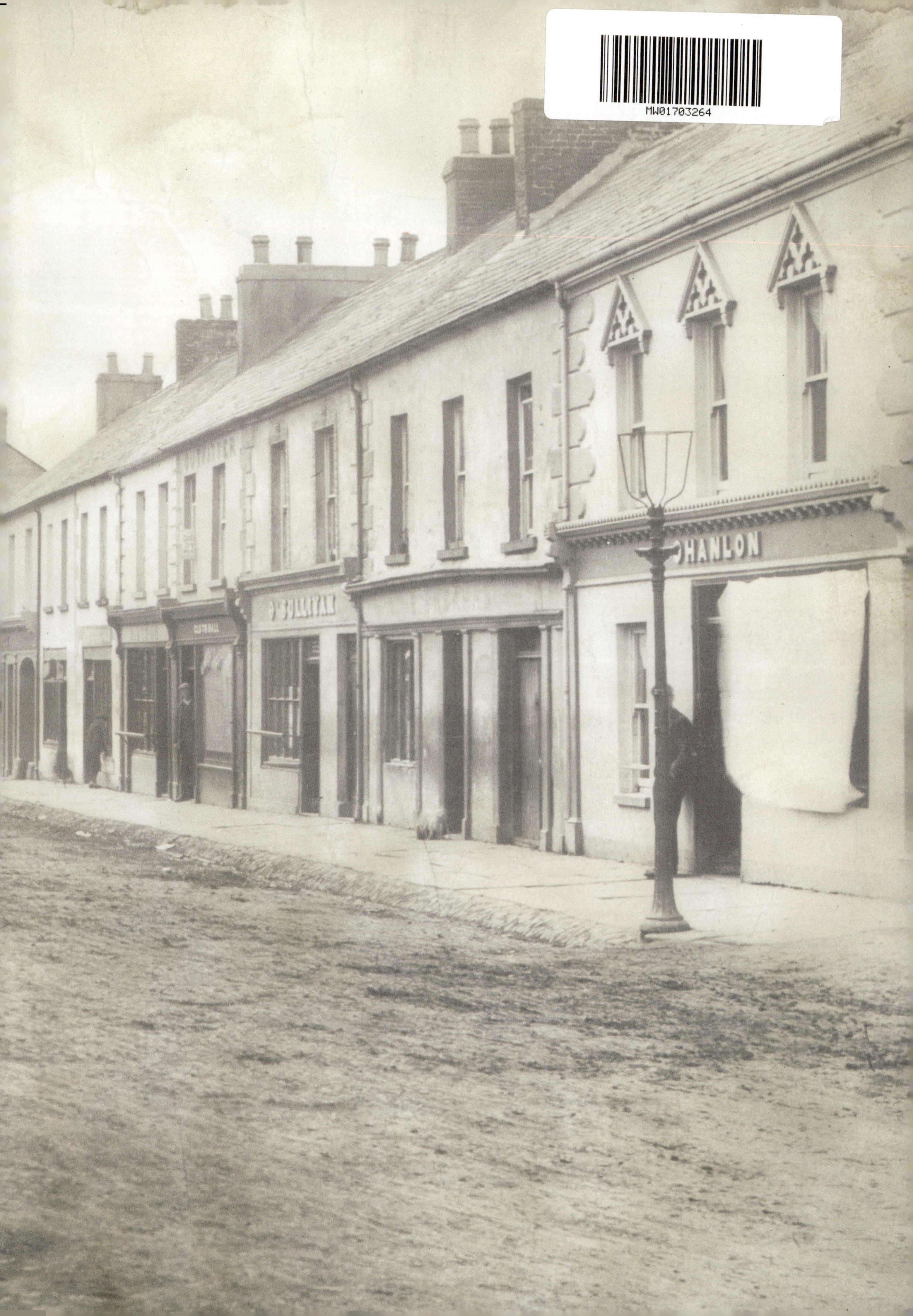
O' SULLIVAN
HANLON

LISTOWEL

SNAPSHOTS OF AN IRISH MARKET TOWN

1850-1950

Best wishes to
a fellow Roundlaner
Michael and Margaret
From
Vincent Carmody
9/12/2012

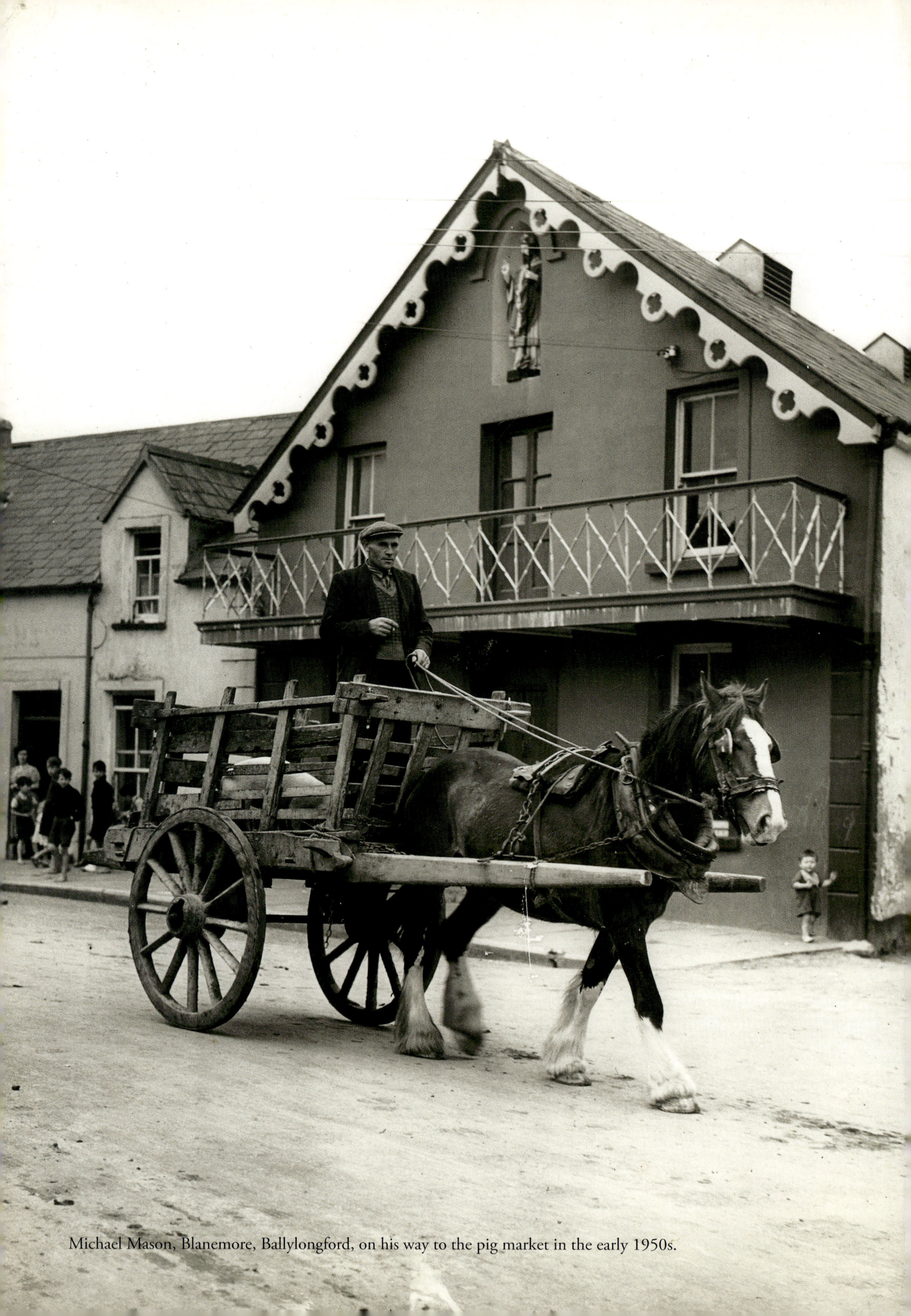

Michael Mason, Blanemore, Ballylongford, on his way to the pig market in the early 1950s.

LISTOWEL

SNAPSHOTS OF AN IRISH MARKET TOWN
1850-1950

Best wishes to
a fellow Poundlaner
Michael and Margaret
from
Vincent Carmody
9/12/2012

VINCENT CARMODY

Published in 2012 by Vincent Carmody.

ISBN: 978-0-9574618-0-2

Design and typesetting by Bright Idea, Killarney.

Typeset in Garamond Pro.

Printed in Spain by Graficas Cems.

CONTENTS

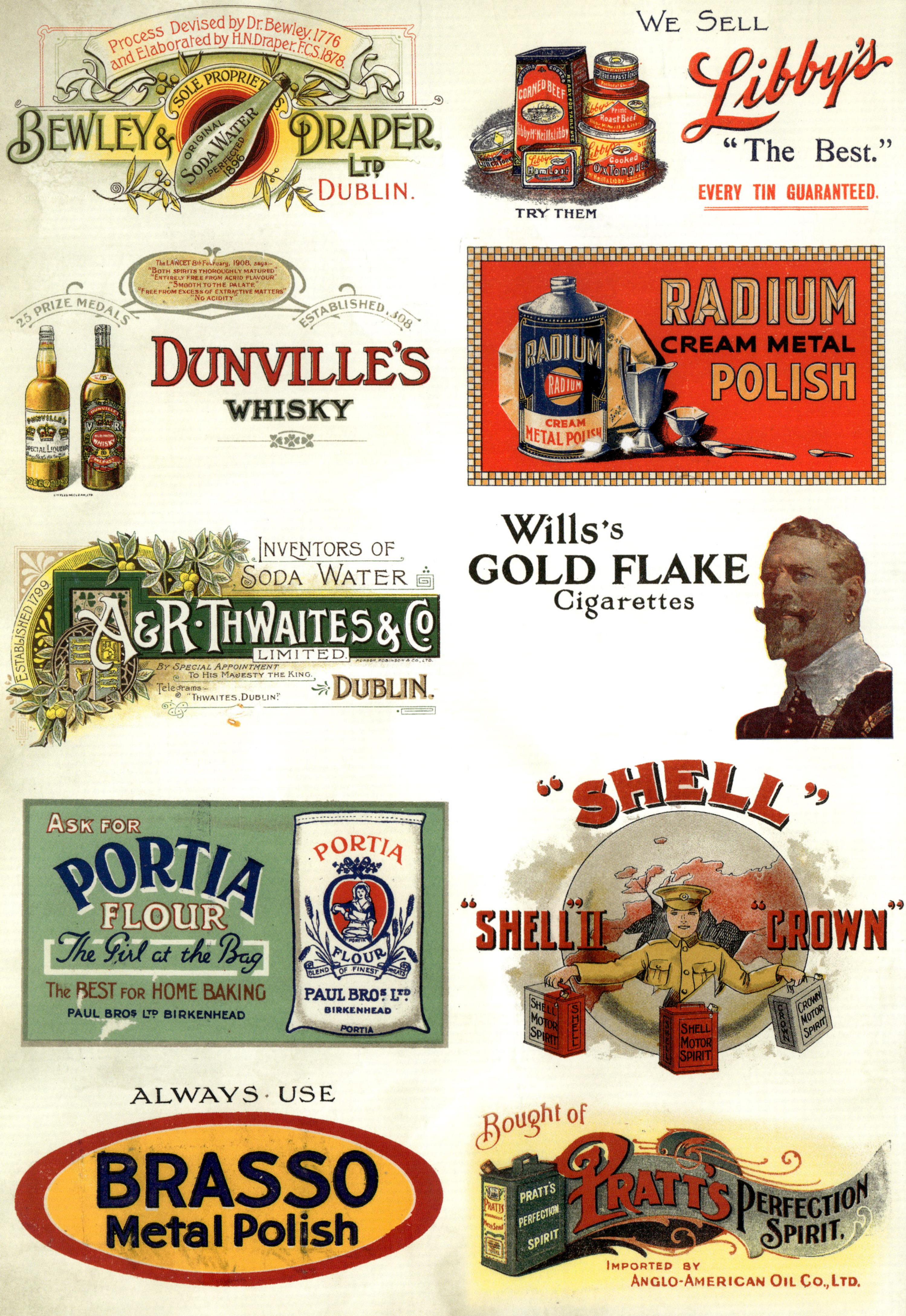
Process Devised by Dr. Bewley. 1776
and Elaborated by H.N. Draper. F.C.S. 1878.
SOLE PROPRIETORS
ORIGINAL SODA WATER PERFECTED 1896
BEWLEY & DRAPER, LTD
DUBLIN.
WE SELL
Libby's
"The Best."
EVERY TIN GUARANTEED.
TRY THEM
The LANCET 8th February, 1908, says:-
"Both spirits thoroughly matured"
"Entirely free from acrid flavour"
"Smooth to the palate"
"Free from excess of extractive matters"
"No acidity"
25 PRIZE MEDALS
ESTABLISHED 1808
DUNVILLE'S
WHISKY
RADIUM
CREAM METAL
POLISH
Wills's
GOLD FLAKE
Cigarettes
INVENTORS OF
SODA WATER
ESTABLISHED 1799
A&R·THWAITES & Co
LIMITED.
BY SPECIAL APPOINTMENT
TO HIS MAJESTY THE KING.
Telegrams:-
"THWAITES, DUBLIN."
DUBLIN.
ASK FOR
PORTIA
FLOUR
The Girl at the Bag
The BEST FOR HOME BAKING
PAUL BROS LTD BIRKENHEAD
PORTIA
FLOUR
PAUL BROS. LTD
BIRKENHEAD
"SHELL"
"SHELL" II
"CROWN"
SHELL MOTOR SPIRIT
CROWN MOTOR SPIRIT
ALWAYS · USE
BRASSO
Metal Polish
Bought of
PRATT'S PERFECTION SPIRIT.
IMPORTED BY
ANGLO-AMERICAN OIL Co., LTD.

FOREWORD

By Seán Lynch

Vincent Carmody's careful study of the history of Listowel is primarily an examination of time. It took time for each receipt and letterhead to be designed and printed. Time is recorded in the details inscribed in each transaction recorded in the growth of Listowel as a market town and commercial centre. Time is seen in the many images of the town gone by, with the shopkeepers' opening hours, with streets full of people going to and fro, maybe in urgent hurry, perhaps on a leisurely stroll. Time is present in the construction of Listowel itself; buildings are renovated, names above shopfronts change, and the fashions and styles of residents evolve. Carmody himself has spent a great deal of time gathering this material together. For several years now he has chased up loose ends, found out who is recorded in each photograph, and often rescued pieces of history that otherwise would be lost or forgotten.

In the resulting pages, we are offered a way of reviving and reinvigorating Listowel's streetscape. We all know that identity is not a stable entity - it changes through the years, traditions are forgotten and remembered, one idea seems fresh as another disappears from public consciousness. As time plays these tricks on our senses, Carmody grasps specific moments, pulls them out of the dustbin of history and allows them to flash in front of us, almost as an apparition from the past. A photograph of the pharmacy on Market Street, today O'Connor's, can be examined in this context. There, a shopfront was designed and rendered by stuccodore Pat McAuliffe in the 1880s for Gerard Leahy-Stack, a chemist and Justice of Peace for Kerry. A close look at the facade reveals McAuliffe executing a type of architectural ornamentation called vermiculation. Here, on pieces of plaster above the building's window, one can see an irregular pattern, intended to represent the tracks of worms who are eating their way through the building itself, reminding us that all that is made manifest will one day turn into dust. Such pieces of symbolism are often obscured by the contemporary, often alienated relationships we have to our surroundings. A publication like this offers an opportunity to begin to break down these barriers, and look at Listowel and its stories with greater detail and attention.

Is such a compilation of material an urgent activity? A common understanding of a book such as Carmody's might be that it exists as a coffee table book, a compendium of years gone by to be leisurely flicked through. One could view its pages as a kind of distraction from the harsh realities of today, a chance to reminisce and look at an era where life seemed more straightforward and simpler to live in. As a reader of these pages, I would suggest to you an alternative. This publication is more like a manual or guidebook, a way of positioning ourselves within today's Listowel. After all, we can still walk down the same streets that Carmody examines in his research, and forensically uncover the construction of a streetscape that is more or less still with us. Carmody has allowed us a way of tracking down physical elements and incidental moments that have accumulated in the development of Listowel. What happened at that location on William Street on market day? Who has walked on the footpath before us? What was sold inside this shop? This book now offers some answers to these questions. It reclaims pieces of history to help us, as an active and engaged audience, to understand our own existence today.

Moyvane native Seán Lynch is a visual artist with a keen interest in the plasterwork of Listowel craftsman Pat McAuliffe (1846-1921). He has exhibited photographs, films and sculptures at venues around the world, and is the author and editor of several publications on Irish art.

For my wife Kathleen,

my three children, Kevin, Norma and Karen

and their families.

ACKNOWLEDGEMENTS

This book would not have been possible without the assistance and kindness of many people. First and foremost, I would like to thank the people of Listowel and the Listowel diaspora who contributed the photos, documents and information contained in this publication. These contributors are numerous but their input was invaluable. The book's sponsors are listed elsewhere but their financial assistance allowed me to complete the book to the standard I wanted. North & East Kerry Development gave grant support under the LEADER/Rural Development Programme. Eamon Ó Murchú read early proofs of the book and his suggestions were most helpful, while Noel Twomey was a great help with the proofreading of the book before publication. Cathal Cudden of Bright Idea is responsible for the excellent layout and design of the finished product. My thanks also to Seán Lynch for his kind foreword. I am grateful to Fr. Tony Gaughan for his permission to use extracts and photographs from his book *Listowel and its Vicinity*. Tommy O'Connor (County Librarian), Michael Lynch (Kerry County Library Archivist) and the staff of Listowel Library were of great assistance when called on and that was often. Among the photographs used in the book are several from the Lawrence Collection. This was assembled by William Lawrence who traversed the country in the early 1900s with his photographer friend Robert French. The Listowel pictures date from 1904 and are taken from a album compiled by Mamie McAuliffe, formerly of Main Street, Listowel, and daughter of Thomas McAuliffe who acted as a guide for French during his visit to North Kerry. I would also like to acknowledge the input of Dr. Pádraig de Brún, Dr. Noel Kissane, John Pierse, Paddy Keane, Kit and Pat Guerin, Professor John Coolahan, Hugh Stancliffe, Dr. Fiona Brennan (George Fitzmaurice Society), Kieran Moloney, Cyril Kelly, Mary Cogan and Cara Trant (Seanchaí Centre, Listowel). Finally, I would like to thank my own family, and particularly my wife Kathleen, for their support and unstinting patience over the many years it took to finish this book.

Vincent Carmody

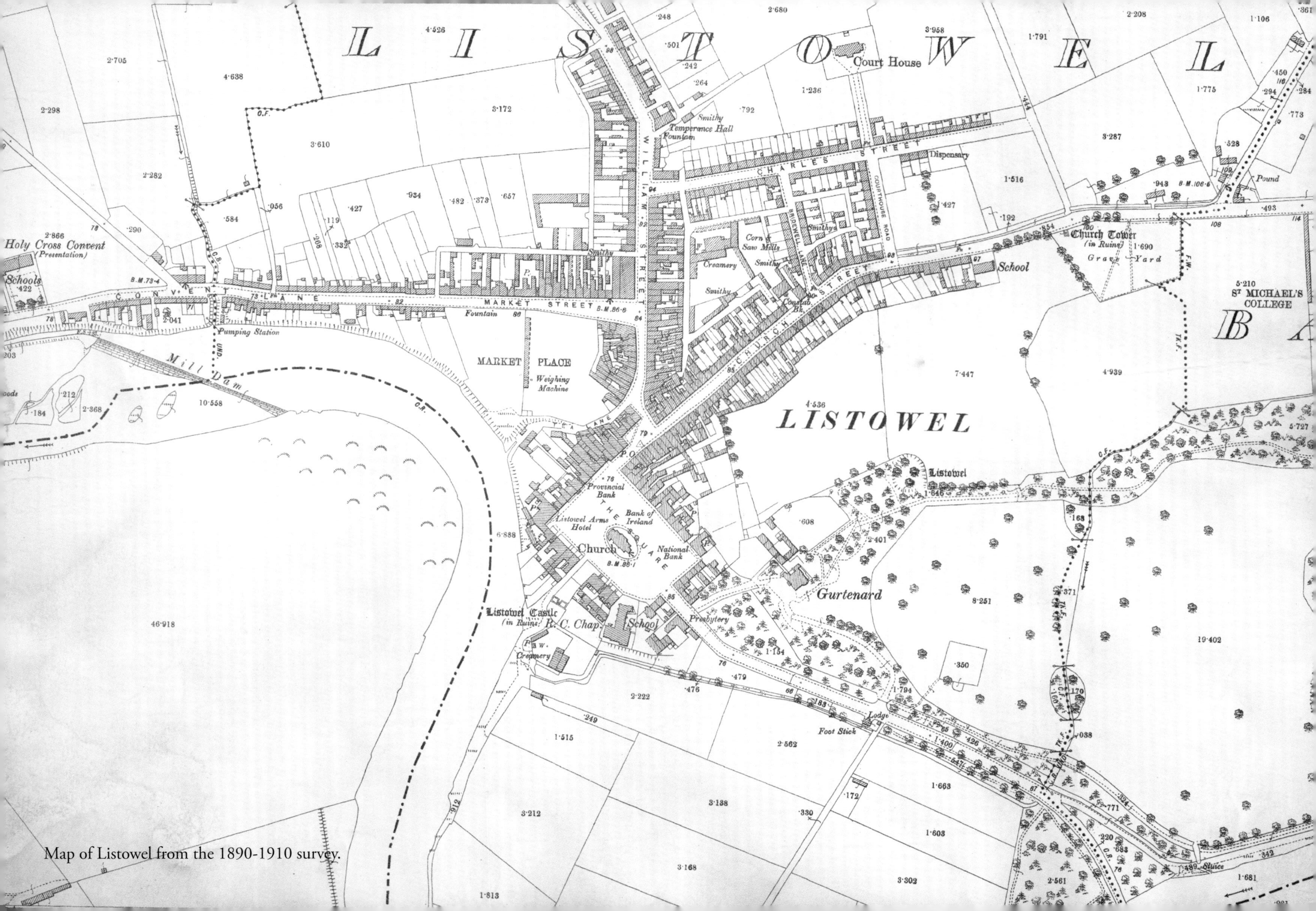

Map of Listowel from the 1890-1910 survey.

INTRODUCTION

Having self-published a book *North Kerry Camera* in 1989 and having experienced the joy and happiness that it brought (the late Bryan MacMahon told me that the euphoria publishing brings was the nearest a man could get to experiencing childbirth), it was always in my mind to publish another one.

It was easier said than done and it has taken me over 20 years to witness the 'birth' of this second book, *Snapshots of an Irish Market Town*. Ideas may come easily but suitable content is not always readily available. But, believe it or not, the genesis of this book was found in a rubbish skip.

Walking down Church Street one day in the early 1990s my attention was drawn to some books lying on the top of the skip which contained discarded items from No. 22 Church Street, then in the process of being refurbished by Paddy and Mary O'Halloran. I took the books home and examined them. One was a notebook containing entries for goods received and leaving Listowel Railway Station and the other an account book with various entries. These had been the property of John Enright whose day job was clerk at the station and his wife Jane had run a public house at No 22 in the 1890s. What made me more intrigued was a sheaf of old billheads stuck inside one of the notebooks. Fascinated by the information that the billheads contained, I quickly decided that documents similar to these could form the basis of an interesting book.

Over time, as I began to seek out the elusive billheads, I kept getting the same answer – "Ah yes, I remember those. Sure they were all thrown out years ago when the place was being done up". When all seemed lost, Jack Flavin of Church Street called me one day and told me he had a large quantity of receipts and billheads dating from the 1920s to the 1950s. Shortly after this, I visited Donovan Hadley, owner of Dromin House at the time, who was a patient in the District Hospital. Mentioning that I was collecting old billheads and documents, Donovan told me of a sizeable collection stored in the attic of Dromin House. These turned out to be a treasure trove of material relating to the commercial history of Listowel and its hinterland, and they form the basis of *Snapshots of an Irish Market Town*. I am grateful to the late Donovan Hadley for his generosity in giving me this material which relates mainly the Raymond family, previous owners of Dromin House.

Other useful material came later from Liam O'Flaherty of the Mermaids bar and nightclub, and from Dermot O'Mahony of Jumbo's fast food restaurant. Liam retrieved old documents from his farmhouse near Ballybunion and wisely didn't throw them out, while Dermot located papers dating back to the 1850s in a cubbyhole in the attic of his premises.

Once I started sifting through the various documents from the businesses around the town, I began to divide them into decades and streets. This approach is reflected in the final book which, starting at Dromin House, takes a street-by-street, address-by-address look at business life in Listowel from roughly 1850 to 1950. Many of the photos and letters that appear in the book were sourced from the albums of the families and descendents of the people who ran those original businesses.

Over time, my collection built up and the idea for publishing it in book form really gained momentum after a conversation with the late Pádraig Kennelly of *Kerry's Eye*. Pádraig gave me a book on letterheads and, in his own inimitable way, told me to look at it, use it as a template and 'do a better book than it'.

Naturally, not every address and business of this period in Listowel's history is covered as I decided to work with what I had. But I hope that the material assembled does the town justice, and hope that the reader will get as much satisfaction from browsing through it as I got from collecting it over two decades.

Vincent Carmody, October 2012

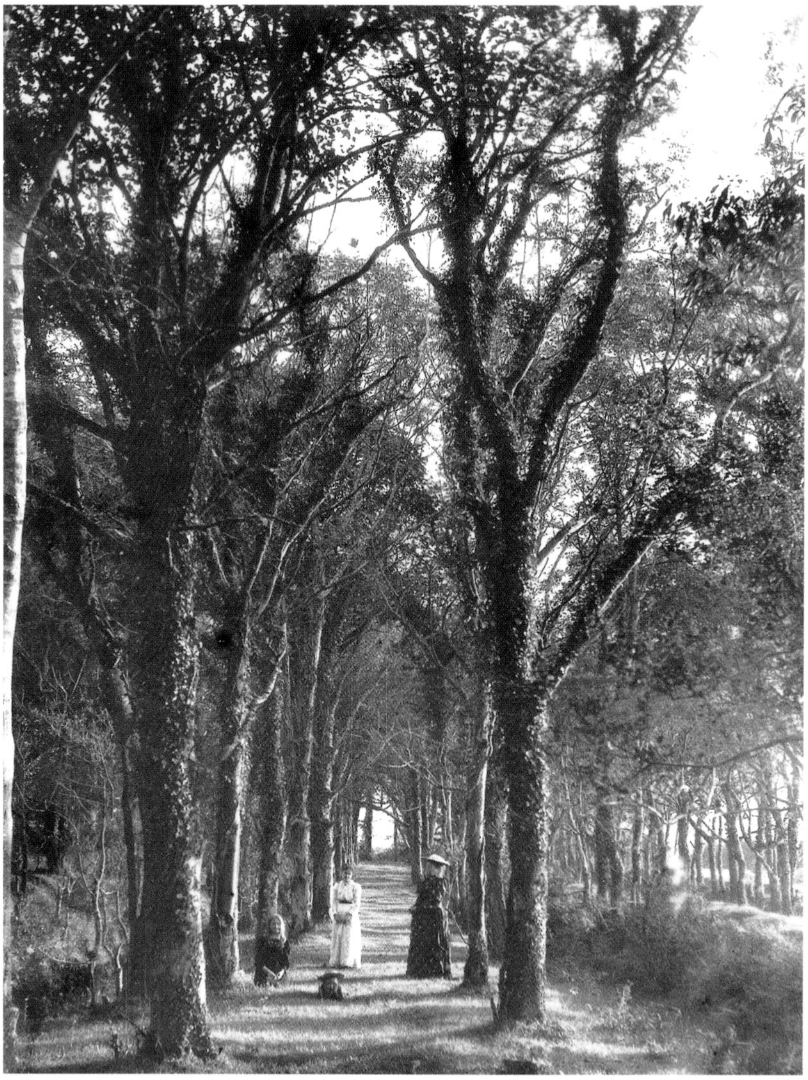

Above: Out for a stroll in the woodlands at Dromin House.
Opposite: Dromin House circa 1890.

Chapter 1

DROMIN HOUSE

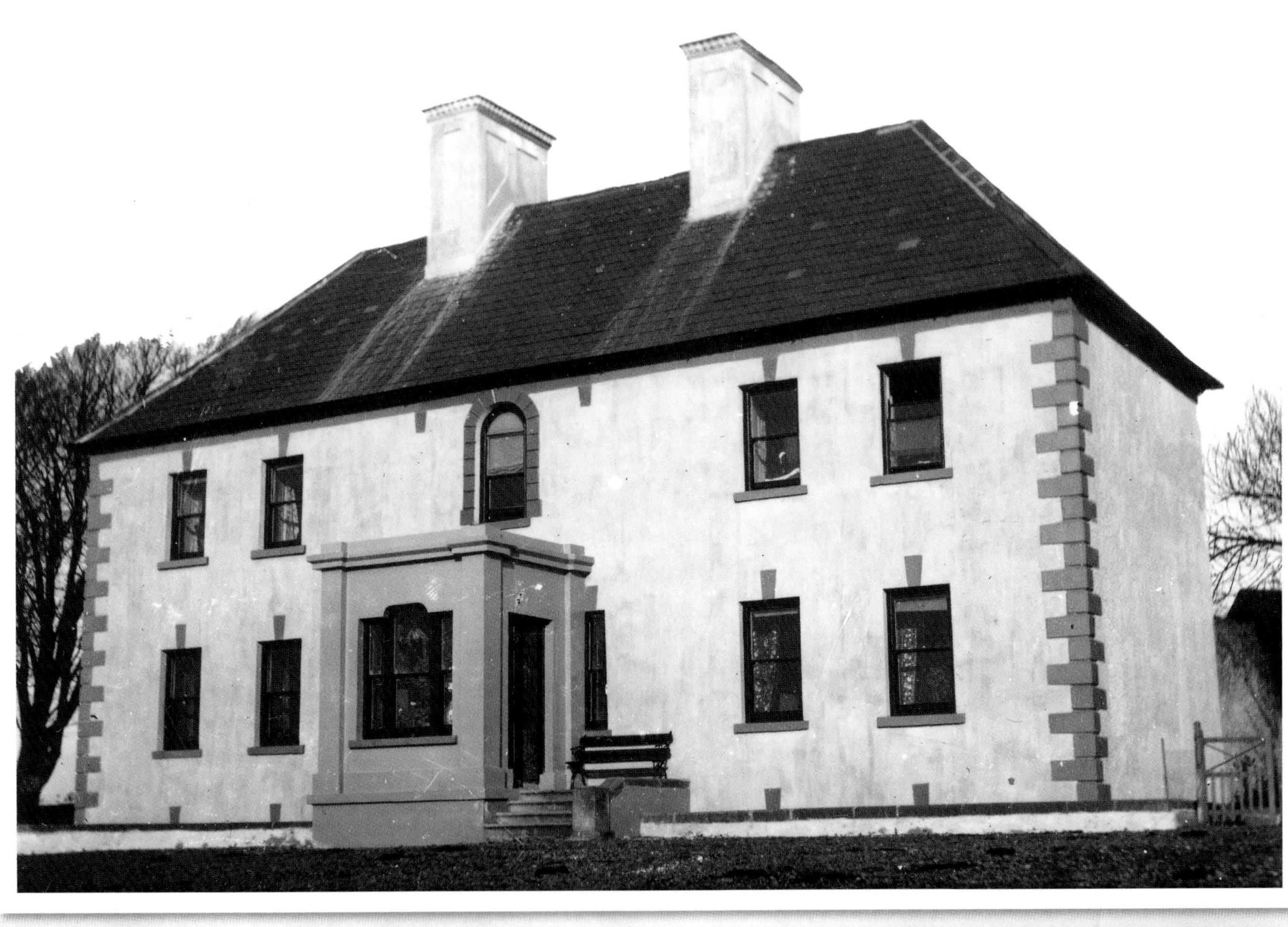

In a brief history of Dromin House from the *Houses of Kerry* by Valerie Bary, she records that building work on Dromin House commenced in 1661 and was completed in 1668 for William Fitzmaurice, 19th Lord Kerry. James, sixth son of Anthony and Elizabeth Raymond of Ballyloughrane, took possession of it and, from the 1800s, the estate was in the hands of this family. In 1812, there was a James W. Raymond in residence. His son was Captain James William Raymond and, in 1892, a James Fitzjames Raymond, Captain Raymond's son and later owner of the property, was born in Dromin. In the 1960s, the house and property passed from the Raymonds to their cousin, Donovan Hadley. Mr. Hadley, a local historian, remained in residence there until his death in 2003. The property has since been bought and refurbished by Sean and Elizabeth Ryan. Many of the billheads and documents included in this book were sourced in Dromin House and they provide us with a snapshot of the commercial and social life of the market town of Listowel over a period of nearly 100 years. The billheads were mainly for goods bought and services rendered to James William Raymond, his wife Anna and their son James Fitzjames.

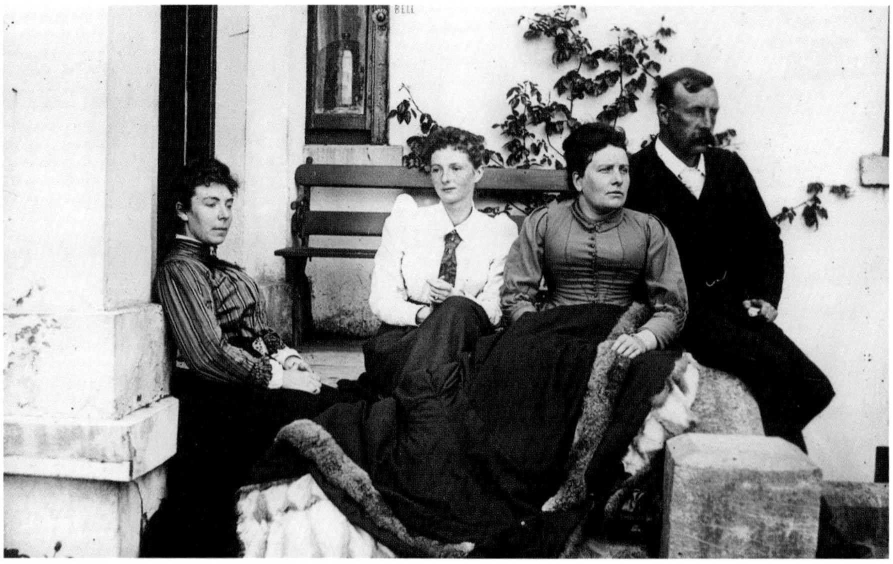

James William Raymond, the son of James and Catherine (née Chute-Mason) Raymond was born at Dromin House in 1858. Following the death of his father in 1870, James William inherited the property. A barrister by profession, he also served as a justice of the peace. As local organiser, he was a member of the local Kerry Militia and the 4th Battalion Royal Munster Fusiliers, first as Lieutenant and afterwards as Captain. A committed Unionist and a member of Lodge 62 Tralee Freemason Society, the Captain, as he was known locally, was nevertheless popular as can be gleaned from the number of local businesses and tradespeople that he supported. He was a enthusiastic fisherman and early photographer and he left a small collection of glass negatives, some recording life in the Great House and a number of Listowel town in the 1880/1890s. The Captain was married to Anna Burke from County Cork. They had two sons, the eldest died at eight years of age; the second, James Fitzjames, subsequently inherited Dromin House and died in 1965. Captain Raymond died on September 4th, 1894 and was buried in the family vault at Lisselton Churchyard.

Above: James William and Anna Raymond relaxing with friends at the porch of Dromin House, circa early 1890s.

Below: Anna Raymond and her youngest son James Fitzjames in their pony and trap with Dan Twomey holding the pony by the head, circa early 1890s.

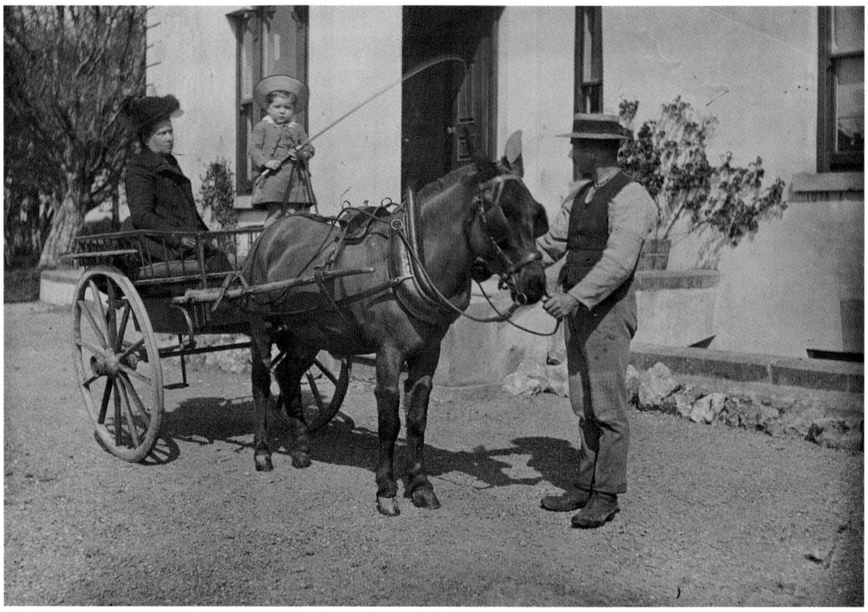

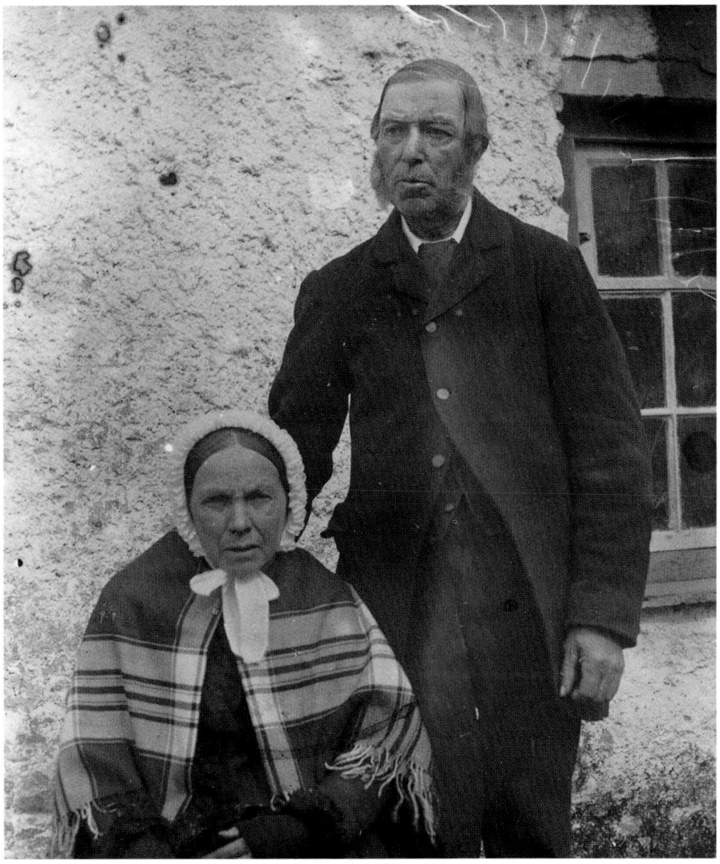

Above: James and Johanna Galvin pictured circa early 1890s outside their cottage in the yard of Dromin House. They had previously been evicted from their small farm in Lisselton. Hearing of their predicament James's old family friend Captain Raymond offered them a cottage at Dromin House. In return, James helped on the farm and Johanna in the house. Their daughter Mary married Dan Twomey who worked as coachman/labourer for the Raymonds. Both of the Galvins lived through the Great Famine, James was born in 1831 and Johanna in 1826. In the 1901 census they were living with their daughter Mary, her husband Dan and their family at their home in Coolatosane, Listowel.

Below: James F. Raymond on left with his co-workers making grass cocks in a meadow at Dromin House, circa 1920s.

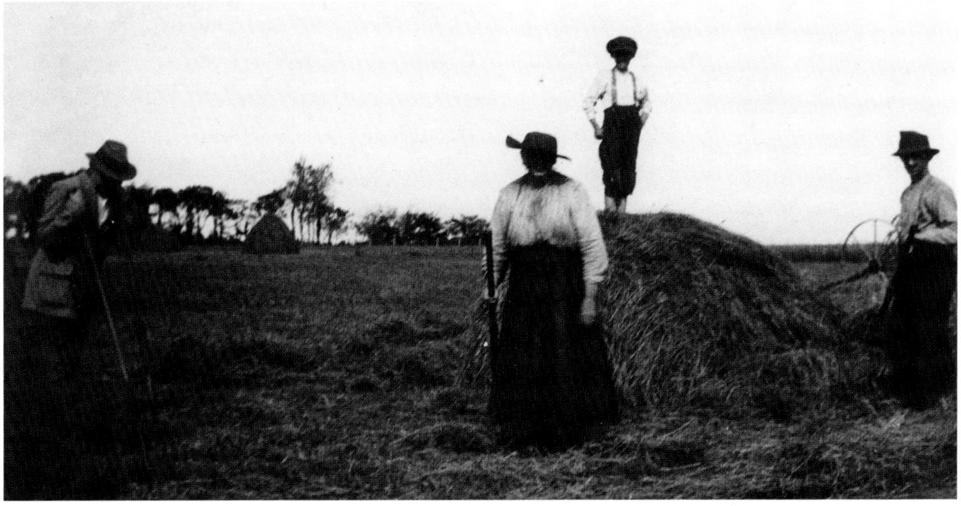

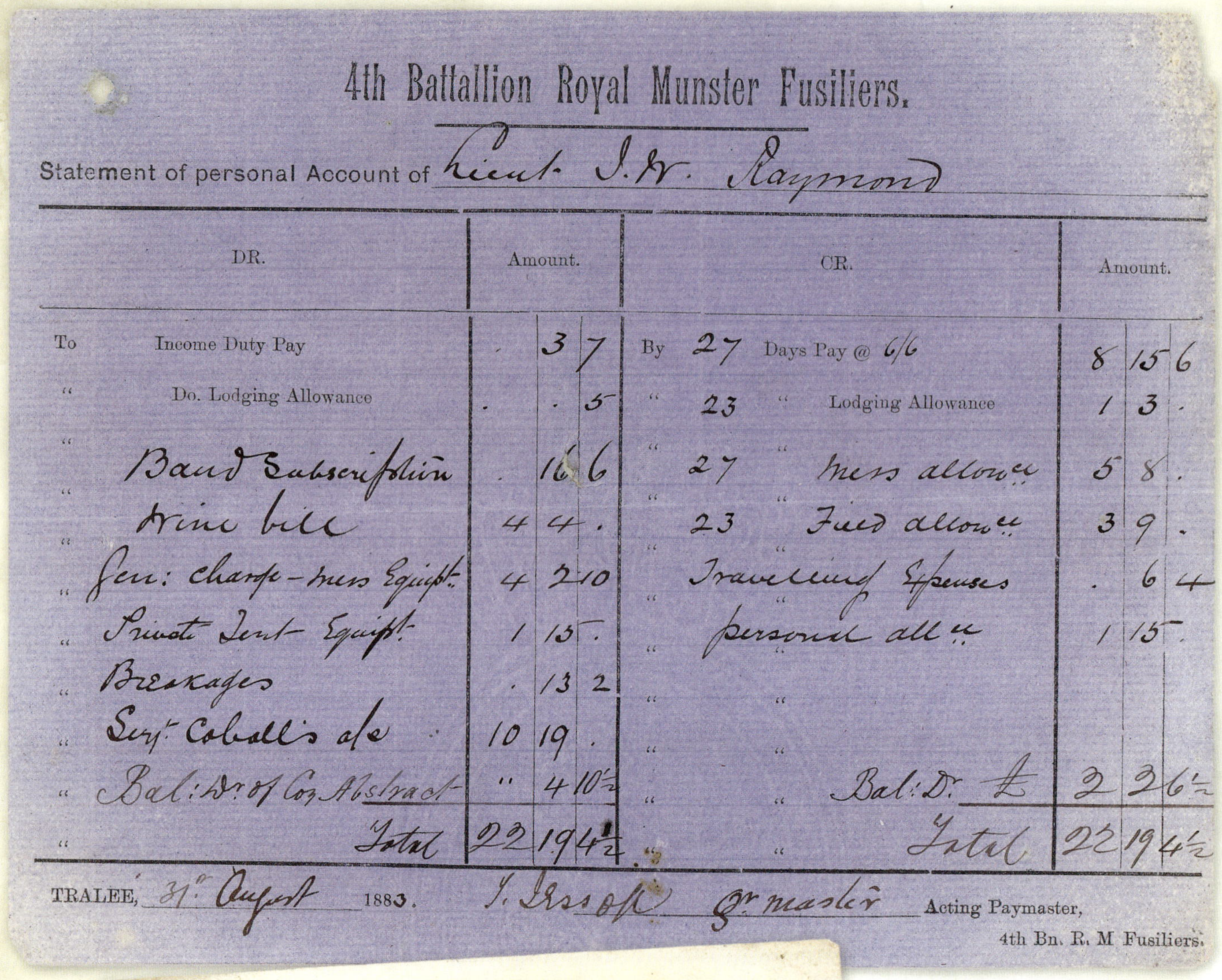

4th Battallion Royal Munster Fusiliers.

Statement of personal Account of Lieut. J.W. Raymond

DR.	Amount.			CR.	Amount.		
To Income Duty Pay	.	3	7	By 27 Days Pay @ 6/6	8	15	6
" Do. Lodging Allowance	.	.	5	" 23 " Lodging Allowance	1	3	.
" Band Subscription	.	16	6	" 27 " Mess allowce	5	8	.
" Wine bill	4	4	.	" 23 " Fuel allowce	3	9	.
" Gen: charge - Mess Equipt.	4	2	10	" Travelling Expenses	.	6	4
" Private Tent Equipt.	1	15	.	" personal allce	1	15	
" Breakages	.	13	2	"			
" Sergt. Cobbell's a/c	10	19	.	"			
" Bal: Dr. of Coy Abstract	"	4	10½	" Bal: Dr. £	2	3	6½
Total	22	19	4½	Total	22	19	4½

TRALEE, 31st August 1883. I. Issott Qr master Acting Paymaster, 4th Bn. R. M Fusiliers.

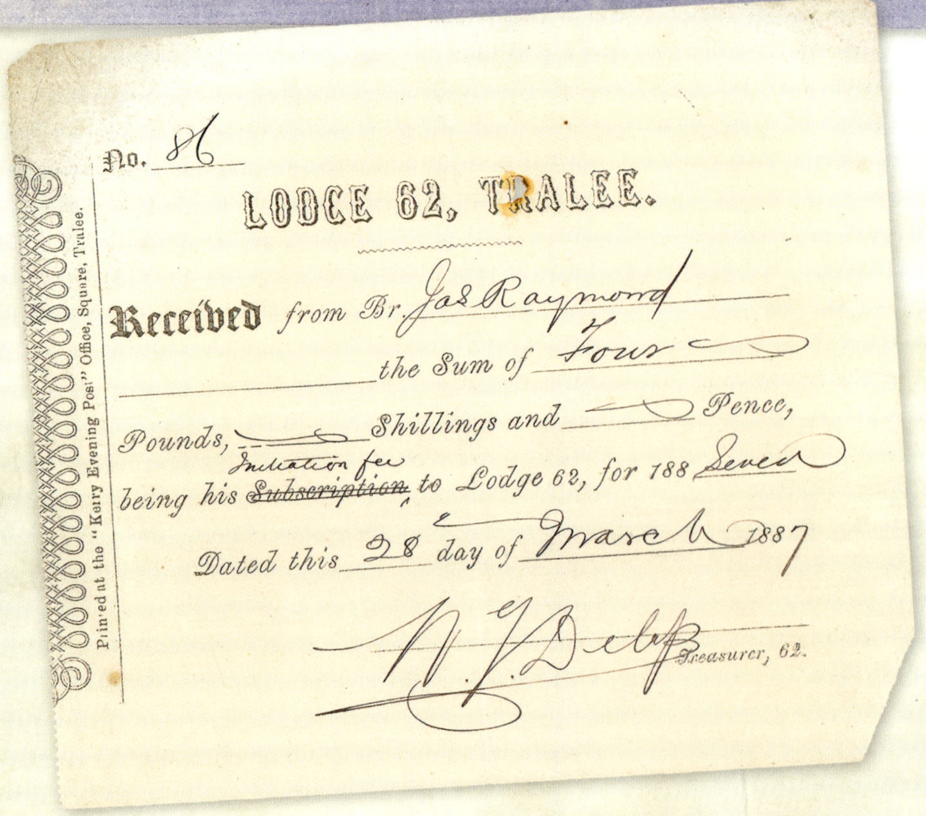

No. 86

LODGE 62, TRALEE.

Received from Br. Jas Raymond the Sum of Four Pounds, — Shillings and — Pence, being his ~~Subscription~~ Initiation fee to Lodge 62, for 188 Seven

Dated this 28th day of March 1887

[illegible] Treasurer, 62.

Printed at the "Kerry Evening Post" Office, Square, Tralee.

Above: Letterhead dated August 31st, 1883 from the 4th Battallion Royal Munster Fusiliers, personal account of Lieut. J.W. Raymond.

Left: Receipt dated March 28th, 1887. Initiation fee to Lodge 62 of the Freemasons, Tralee.

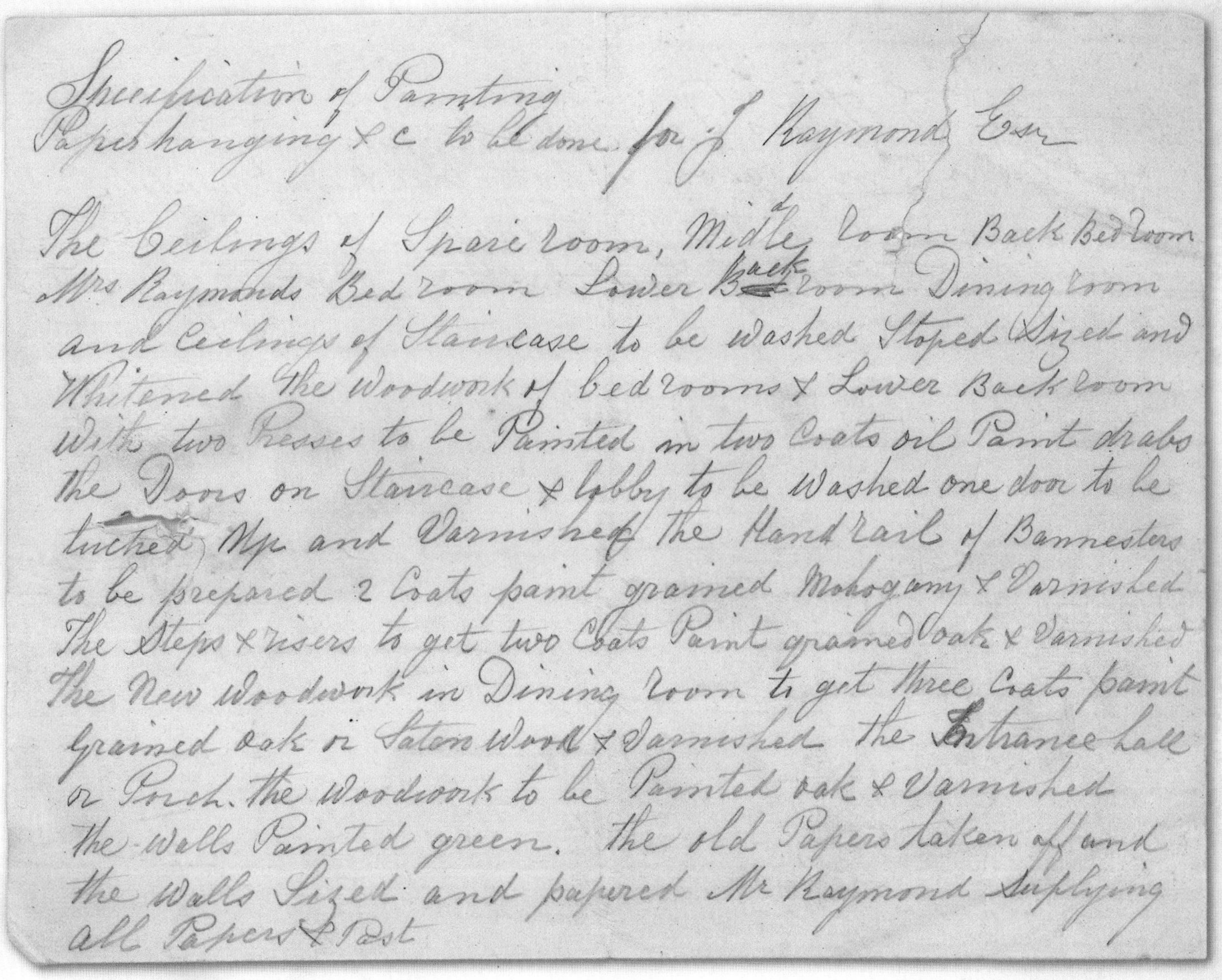

Specification of Painting
Paperhanging &c to be done for J Raymond Esq

The Ceilings of Spare room, Midle room Back Bedroom Mrs Raymonds Bed room Lower Back room Dining room and Ceilings of Staircase to be washed Stoped Sized and Whitened the Woodwork of bed rooms & Lower Back room with two Presses to be Painted in two Coats oil Paint drabs the Doors on Staircase & lobby to be Washed one door to be tuched up and Varnished the Hand rail of Bannesters to be prepared 2 Coats paint grained Mohogany & Varnished The Steps & risers to get two Coats Paint grained oak & Varnished the New Woodwork in Dining room to get three Coats paint grained oak or Saton Wood & Varnished the Entrance hall or Porch the Woodwork to be Painted oak & Varnished the Walls Painted green. the old Papers taken off and the Walls Sized and papered Mr Raymond Supplying all Papers & Past

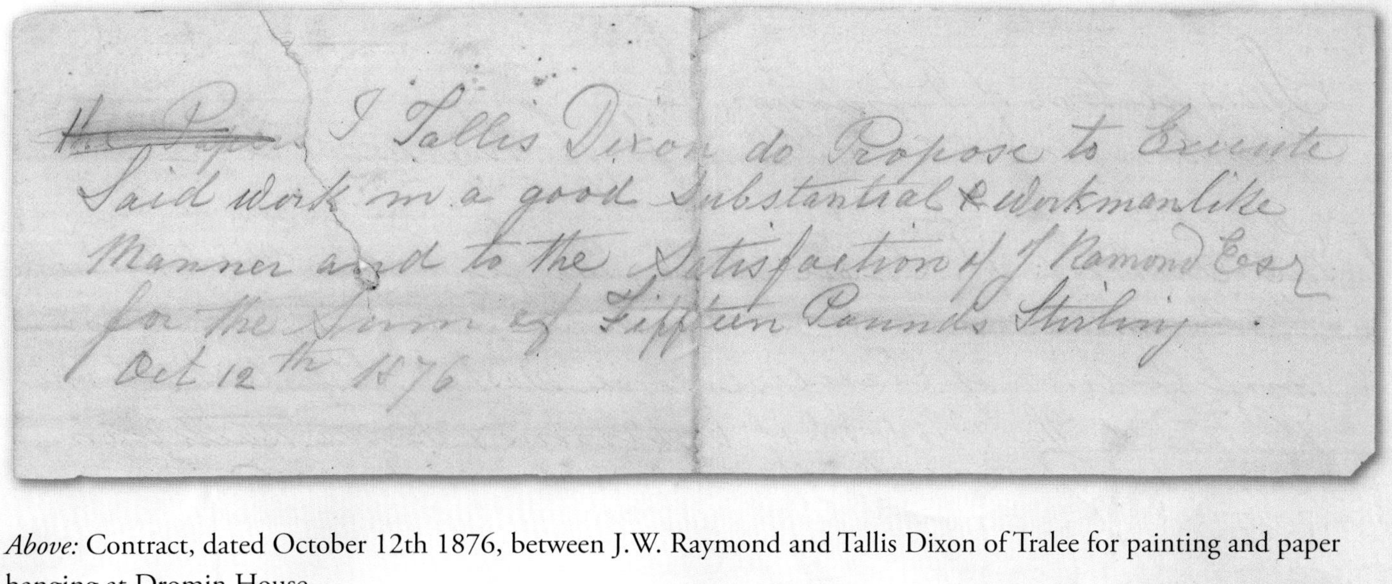

~~H Paper~~ I Tallis Dixon do Propose to Execute Said work in a good Substantial & Workmanlike Manner and to the Satisfaction of J Ramond Esq for the Sum of Fifteen Pounds Sterling.
Oct 12th 1876

Above: Contract, dated October 12th 1876, between J.W. Raymond and Tallis Dixon of Tralee for painting and paper hanging at Dromin House.

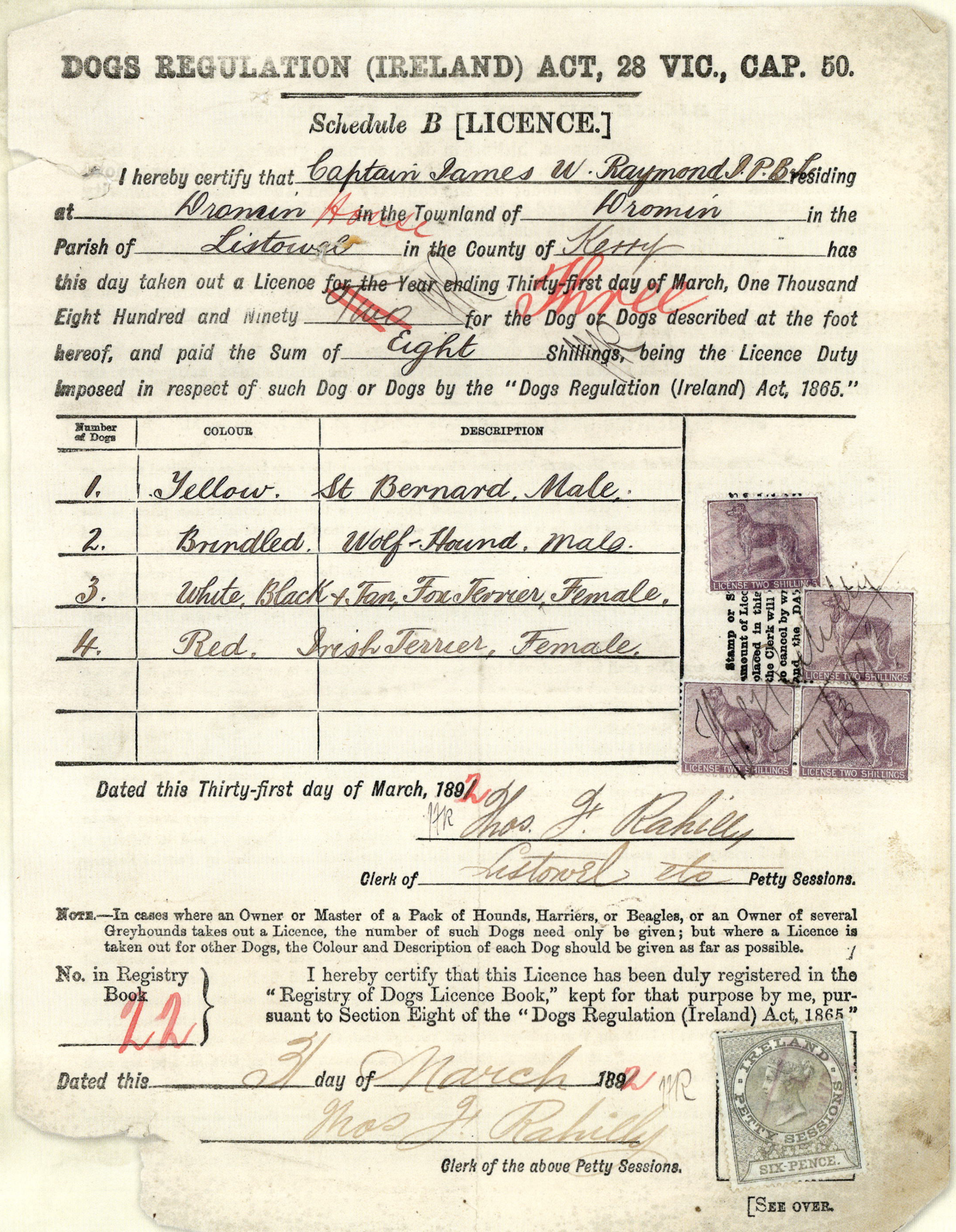

DOGS REGULATION (IRELAND) ACT, 28 VIC., CAP. 50.

Schedule B [LICENCE.]

I hereby certify that Captain James W. Raymond J.P. B.L. residing at Dromin House in the Townland of Dromin in the Parish of Listowel in the County of Kerry has this day taken out a Licence for the Year ending Thirty-first day of March, One Thousand Eight Hundred and Ninety ~~Two~~ Three for the Dog or Dogs described at the foot hereof, and paid the Sum of Eight Shillings, being the Licence Duty imposed in respect of such Dog or Dogs by the "Dogs Regulation (Ireland) Act, 1865."

Number of Dogs	COLOUR	DESCRIPTION
1.	Yellow.	St Bernard. Male.
2.	Brindled.	Wolf-Hound. Male.
3.	White, Black + Tan.	Fox Terrier, Female.
4.	Red.	Irish Terrier, Female.

Dated this Thirty-first day of March, 1892

Thos. F. Rahilly

Clerk of Listowel etc Petty Sessions.

NOTE.—In cases where an Owner or Master of a Pack of Hounds, Harriers, or Beagles, or an Owner of several Greyhounds takes out a Licence, the number of such Dogs need only be given; but where a Licence is taken out for other Dogs, the Colour and Description of each Dog should be given as far as possible.

No. in Registry Book 22

I hereby certify that this Licence has been duly registered in the "Registry of Dogs Licence Book," kept for that purpose by me, pursuant to Section Eight of the "Dogs Regulation (Ireland) Act, 1865."

Dated this 31 day of March 1892

Thos. F. Rahilly

Clerk of the above Petty Sessions.

[SEE OVER.

A dog licence issued on March 31st 1892 for four dogs, a St Bernard, a Wolf Hound, a Fox Terrier and an Irish Terrier, in the ownership of Captain James W. Raymond. The issuing officer was Thos. F. Rahilly, Clerk of Listowel Petty Sessions.

NOTICE TO OWNERS OF DOGS.

SIGNS OF MADNESS IN DOGS.

Change of habits, restlessness, hiding in dark corners, gnawing and eating indigestible substances. Altered voice, uttering the peculiar noise in which the howl predominates. Surly, but not vicious; on the contrary often affectionate. Difficulty in swallowing, but showing no dread of water. Thick spittle hanging from the mouth, which the dog tries to remove with his paws. Frequently snapping.

Dogs showing any of these signs should be at once isolated and kept by themselves till a Veterinary Surgeon can be called in.

In the furious form, the first signs are followed by fits of excitement, with a tendency to attack other animals. The dog wanders, snapping at every animal he meets, until he drops and dies.

In dumb madness the lower jaw drops, rendering the dog unable to bark or bite. The dog remains quiet in some dark place, paralysis of the hind limbs soon sets in, followed by death.

DOGS REGULATION (IRELAND) ACT.—28 Vic., Cap. 50, Secs. 7, 9, 20 and 21.

SEC. 7.—"The Occupier of any House or Premises where any Dog or Dogs are kept or permitted to live or "remain shall be liable to pay the Licence Duty for such Dog or Dogs, and in default of such Payment shall be "liable to the Penalties incurred by Persons keeping unlicensed Dogs, unless the said Occupier can prove to the "Satisfaction of the Justice or Justices that he is not the Owner or has not the Custody of such Dog or Dogs, and "that such Dog or Dogs were kept or permitted to live or remain in the said House or Premises without his Sanction "or Knowledge. Provided always, that where there are more Occupiers than One in any House or Premises let in "separate Apartments or Lodgings or otherwise, the Occupier of that particular Part of the Premises in which such "Dog or Dogs shall have been kept or permitted to live and remain shall be liable to pay the Licence Duty for such "Dog or Dogs."

SEC. 9.—"Where any Dog shall be transferred by Sale or Gift by its Owner to any other Person, it shall not "be necessary for such Person to take out a new Licence for such Dog if such Dog shall have been licensed within "the Year, but such Person shall obtain from the Petty Sessions Clerk of the District where the Licence was issued "a Certificate in the Form in the Schedule (D.) to this Act annexed, to which Certificate a Sixpenny Petty Sessions "Stamp shall be affixed to be paid by the Person requiring the same, and such Person shall, within Fifteen Days "after such Transfer, cause such Certificate to be registered in the "Registry of Dogs Licence Book" for the Petty "Sessions District in which the Person to whom such Transfer shall have been made resides, and the Petty Sessions "Clerk of such District shall, on Application, register such Certificate, and shall certify such Registry at the Foot or "at the Back of the Certificate, and no Fee or Stamp Duty shall be payable on such Registry; and in default of "causing such Registry to be made such Person shall be liable to the Penalties incurred by Persons keeping "unlicensed Dogs."

SEC. 20.—"Any Person who shall, from and after the Thirty-first Day of *March* in each Year after the Commence"ment of this Act, have in his Possession or Custody any Dog or Dogs not duly licensed in accordance with the "Provisions of this Act, shall be liable to a penalty not exceeding Two Pounds, and the Justice or Justices shall "further order such Person forthwith to take out a Licence for such Dog or Dogs, and the Petty Sessions Clerk shall "thereupon issue such Licence upon Payment of the proper Licence Duty by such Person, and such Licence shall be "held to be valid to the Thirty-first day of *March* next following the Date of such Licence; and if after such Order "such Person shall continue to keep any Dog or Dogs without having obtained a Licence, he shall, in addition to "the Penalty imposed for the Second and any subsequent Offence, pay a sum not exceeding One Shilling for each "Day he shall have kept a Dog without Licence."

SEC. 21.—"Every Person having in his Possession or Custody any Dog or Dogs shall produce the Licence for "such Dog or Dogs whenever so required by a Justice of the Peace, Officer, Head or other Constable of C[illegible] "or of the Dublin Metropolitan or other local Police Force, and in case of Refusal he shall, if licensed, be li[illegible] "Penalty not exceeding Five Shillings."

Dollard, Printinghouse, Dublin. P.

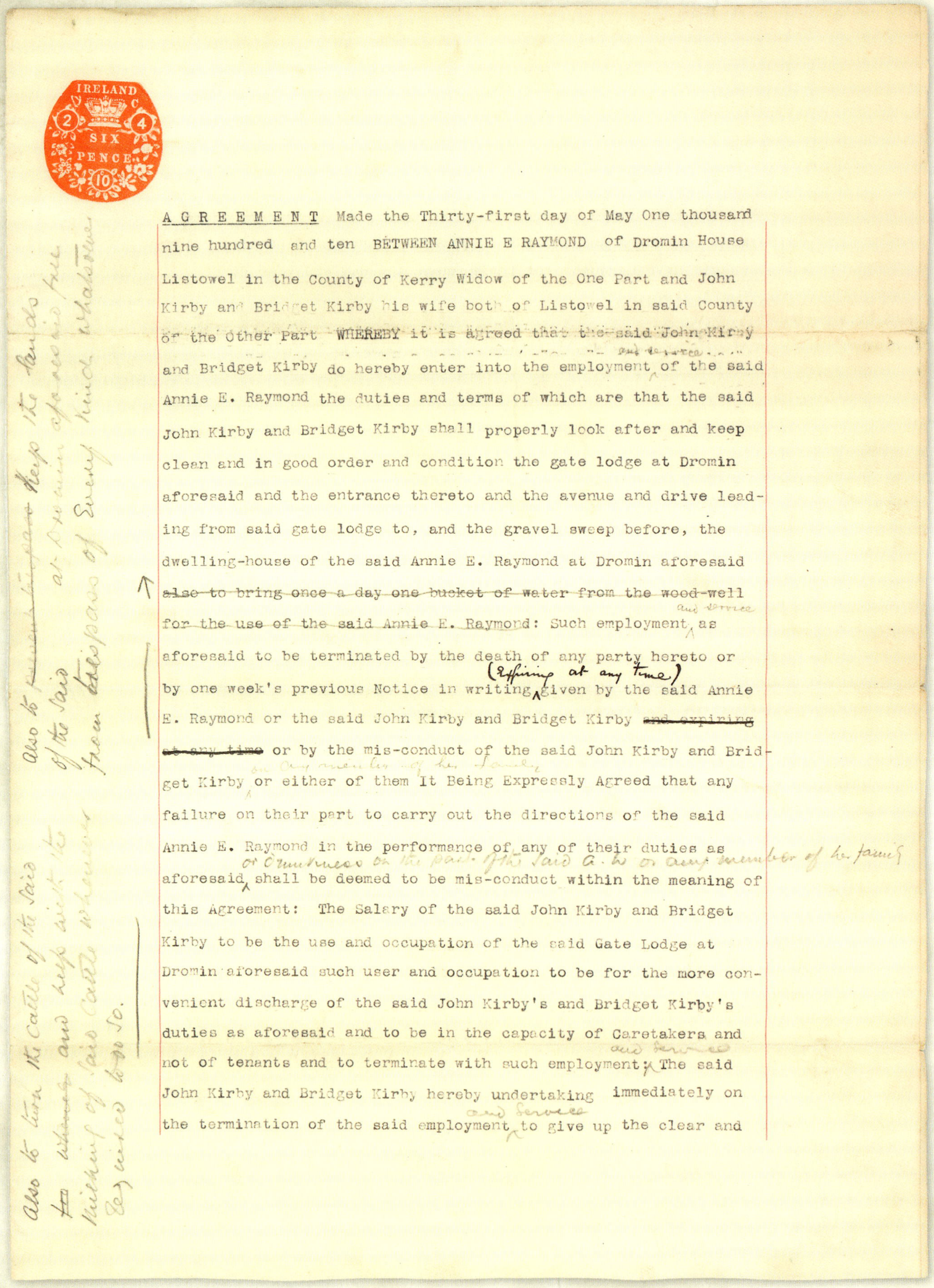

IRELAND SIX PENCE

A G R E E M E N T Made the Thirty-first day of May One thousand nine hundred and ten BETWEEN ANNIE E RAYMOND of Dromin House Listowel in the County of Kerry Widow of the One Part and John Kirby and Bridget Kirby his wife both of Listowel in said County of the Other Part WHEREBY it is agreed that the said John Kirby and Bridget Kirby do hereby enter into the employment and service of the said Annie E. Raymond the duties and terms of which are that the said John Kirby and Bridget Kirby shall properly look after and keep clean and in good order and condition the gate lodge at Dromin aforesaid and the entrance thereto and the avenue and drive leading from said gate lodge to, and the gravel sweep before, the dwelling-house of the said Annie E. Raymond at Dromin aforesaid ~~also to bring once a day one bucket of water from the wood-well for the use of the said Annie E. Raymond:~~ Such employment and service as aforesaid to be terminated by the death of any party hereto or by one week's previous Notice in writing (Expiring at any time) given by the said Annie E. Raymond or the said John Kirby and Bridget Kirby ~~and expiring at any time~~ or by the mis-conduct of the said John Kirby and Bridget Kirby or any member of the family or either of them It Being Expressly Agreed that any failure on their part to carry out the directions of the said Annie E. Raymond in the performance of any of their duties as aforesaid or drunkenness on the part of the said J. K. or any member of the family shall be deemed to be mis-conduct within the meaning of this Agreement: The Salary of the said John Kirby and Bridget Kirby to be the use and occupation of the said Gate Lodge at Dromin aforesaid such user and occupation to be for the more convenient discharge of the said John Kirby's and Bridget Kirby's duties as aforesaid and to be in the capacity of Caretakers and not of tenants and to terminate with such employment and service: The said John Kirby and Bridget Kirby hereby undertaking immediately on the termination of the said employment and service to give up the clear and

Also to keep the lands of the said ... free from trespass of every kind whatsoever. Also to turn the cattle of the said ... and keep out ... whenever required to do so.

A signed agreement between Anna Raymond and John & Bridget Kirby for the position of caretakers at the gate lodge. This was witnessed by James F. Raymond, who was then a solicitor's apprentice with H.J. Marshall of the Square, and Robert J. Tackaberry, who for many of years gave unstinting service to several of the town's solicitors as Law Clerk.

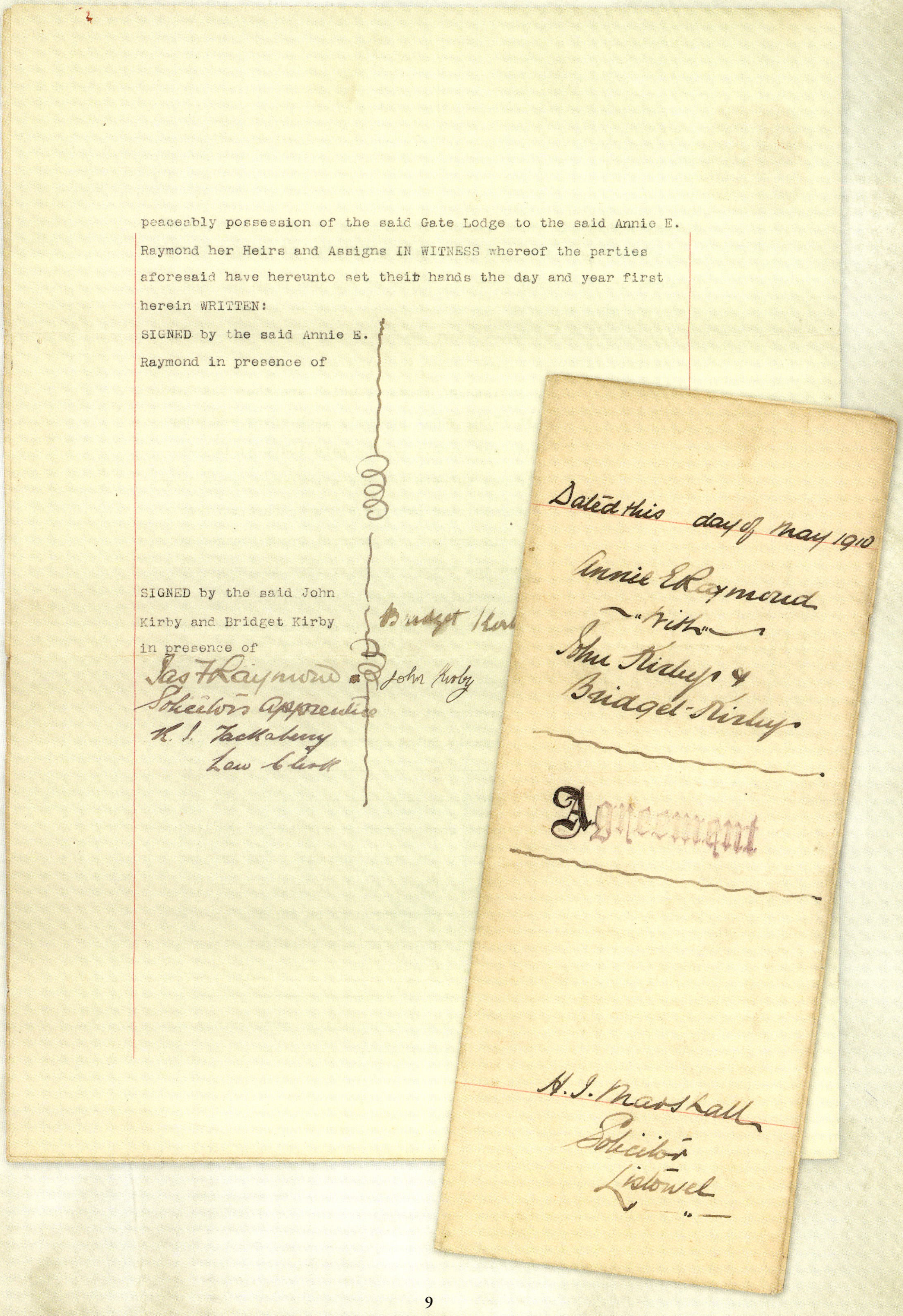

peaceably possession of the said Gate Lodge to the said Annie E. Raymond her Heirs and Assigns IN WITNESS whereof the parties aforesaid have hereunto set their hands the day and year first herein WRITTEN:

SIGNED by the said Annie E. Raymond in presence of

SIGNED by the said John Kirby and Bridget Kirby in presence of

Jas. F. Raymond
Solicitor's Apprentice
H. J. Tackaberry
Law Clerk

Bridget Kirby
John Kirby

Dated this day of May 1910
Annie E. Raymond
"with"
John Kirby &
Bridget Kirby

Agreement

H. J. Marshall
Solicitor
Listowel

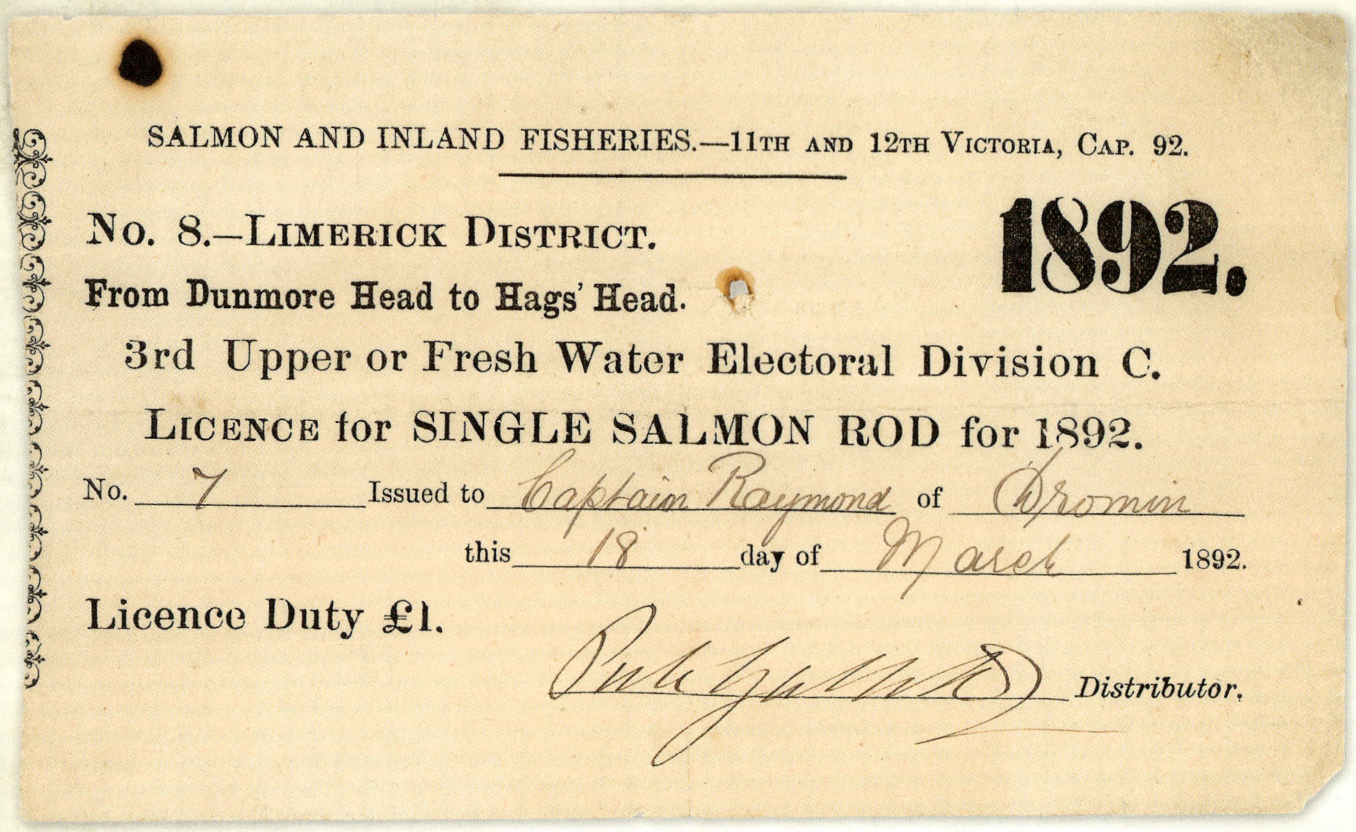

SALMON AND INLAND FISHERIES.—11TH AND 12TH VICTORIA, CAP. 92.

NO. 8.—LIMERICK DISTRICT. **1892.**

From Dunmore Head to Hags' Head.

3rd Upper or Fresh Water Electoral Division C.

LICENCE for SINGLE SALMON ROD for 1892.

No. 7 Issued to Captain Raymond of Dromin

this 18 day of March 1892.

Licence Duty £1.

[illegible] Distributor.

Salmon Licence dated March 18, 1892 issued to Captain Raymond.

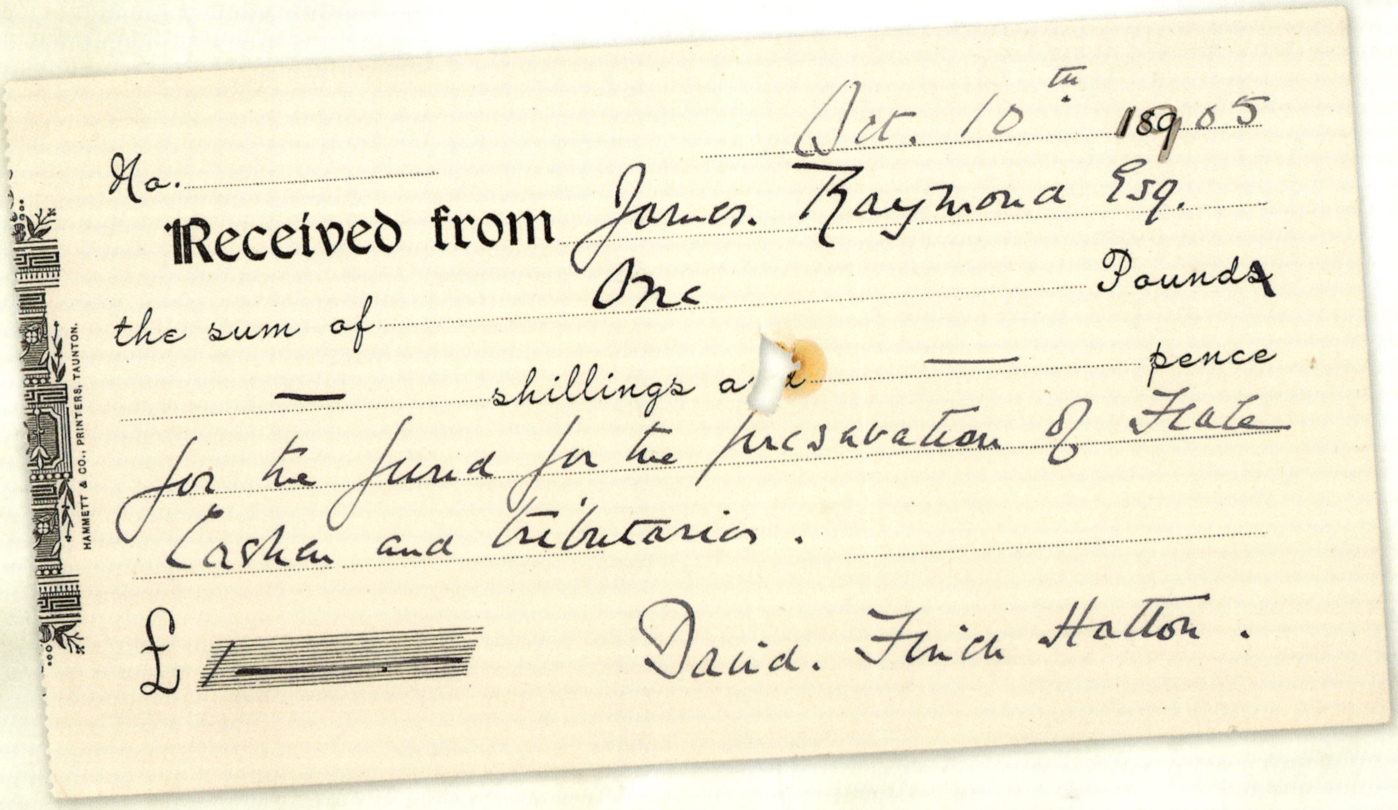

Oct. 10th 1905

No.

Received from James Raymond Esq.

the sum of One Pounds

— shillings and — pence

for the fund for the preservation of Feale Cashen and tributaries.

£1 —

David. Finch Hatton.

HAMMETT & CO., PRINTERS, TAUNTON.

Receipt dated October 10, 1905 for subscription towards the preservation of Feale/Cashen and tributaries.

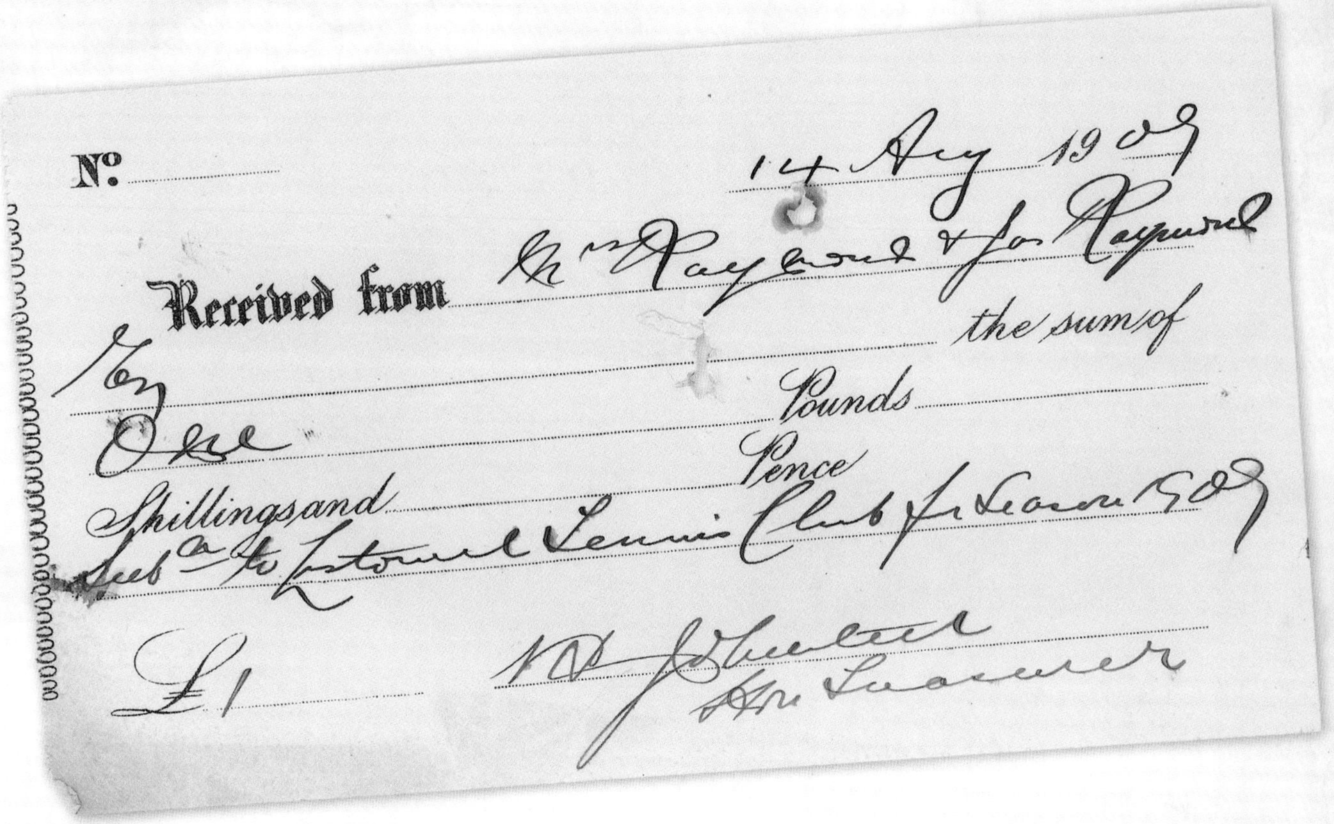

No.
14 Aug 1909
Received from Mrs Raymond & Jas Raymond
Esq the sum of
One Pounds
Shillings and Pence
Sub. to Listowel Tennis Club for season 1909
£1
[illegible]
Hon Treasurer

Receipt dated August 14, 1909 for membership subscription to Listowel Lawn Tennis Club.

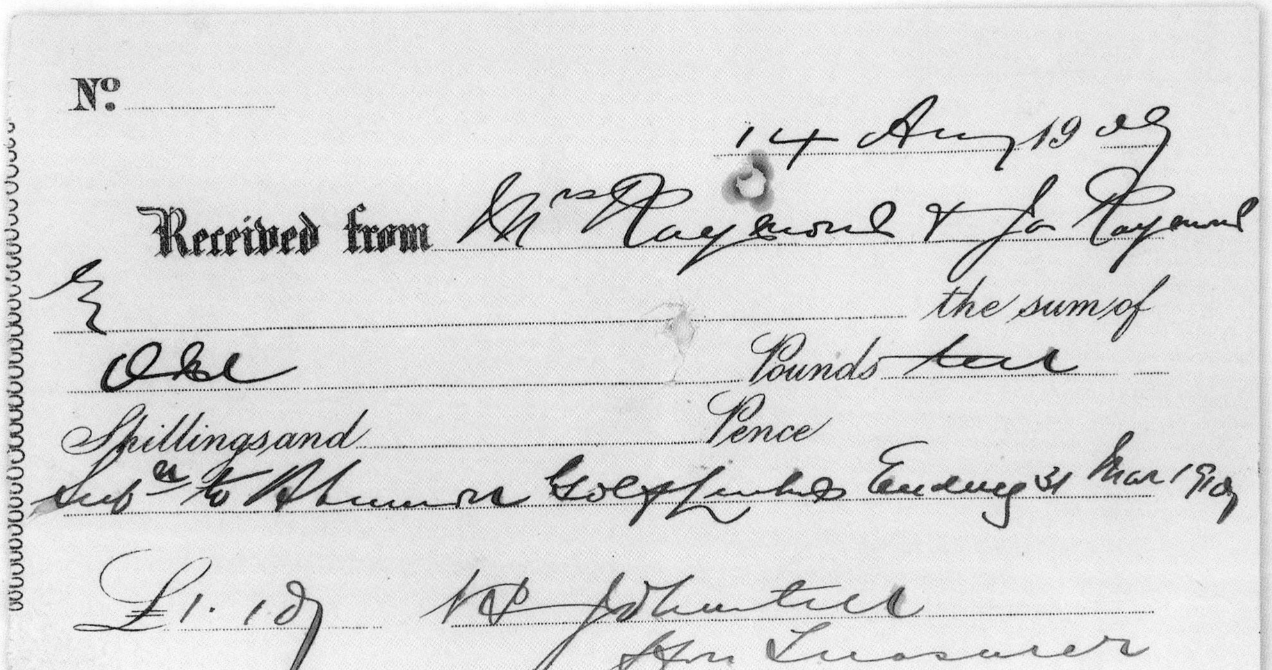

No.
14 Aug 1909
Received from Mrs Raymond & Jas Raymond
Esq the sum of
One Pounds ten
Shillings and Pence
Sub. to Ballybunion Golf Links Ending 31 Mar 1910
£1.10.0
[illegible]
Hon Treasurer

Receipt dated August 14, 1909 for membership subscription to Ballybunion Golf Links

Chapter 2

UPPER WILLIAM STREET

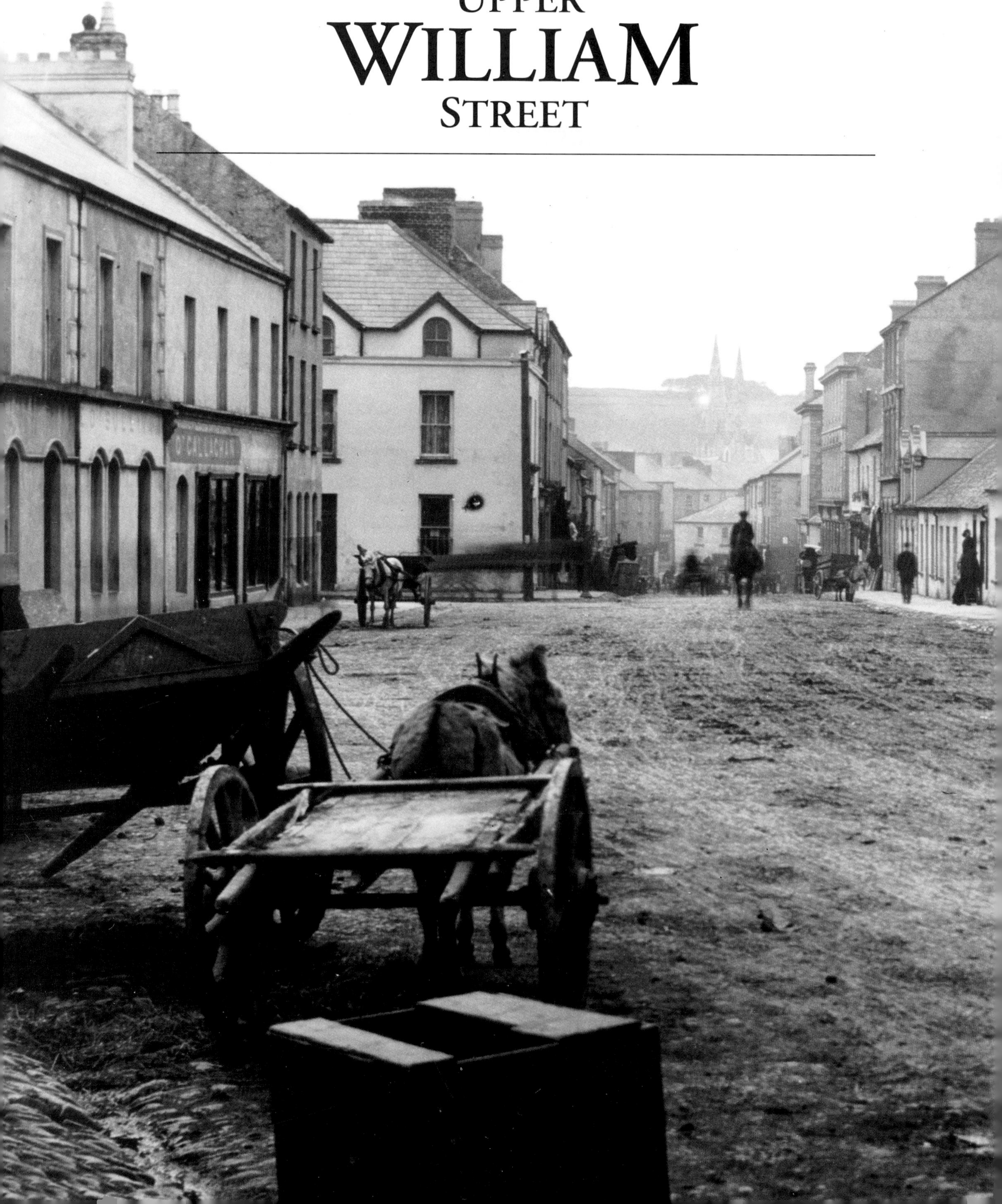

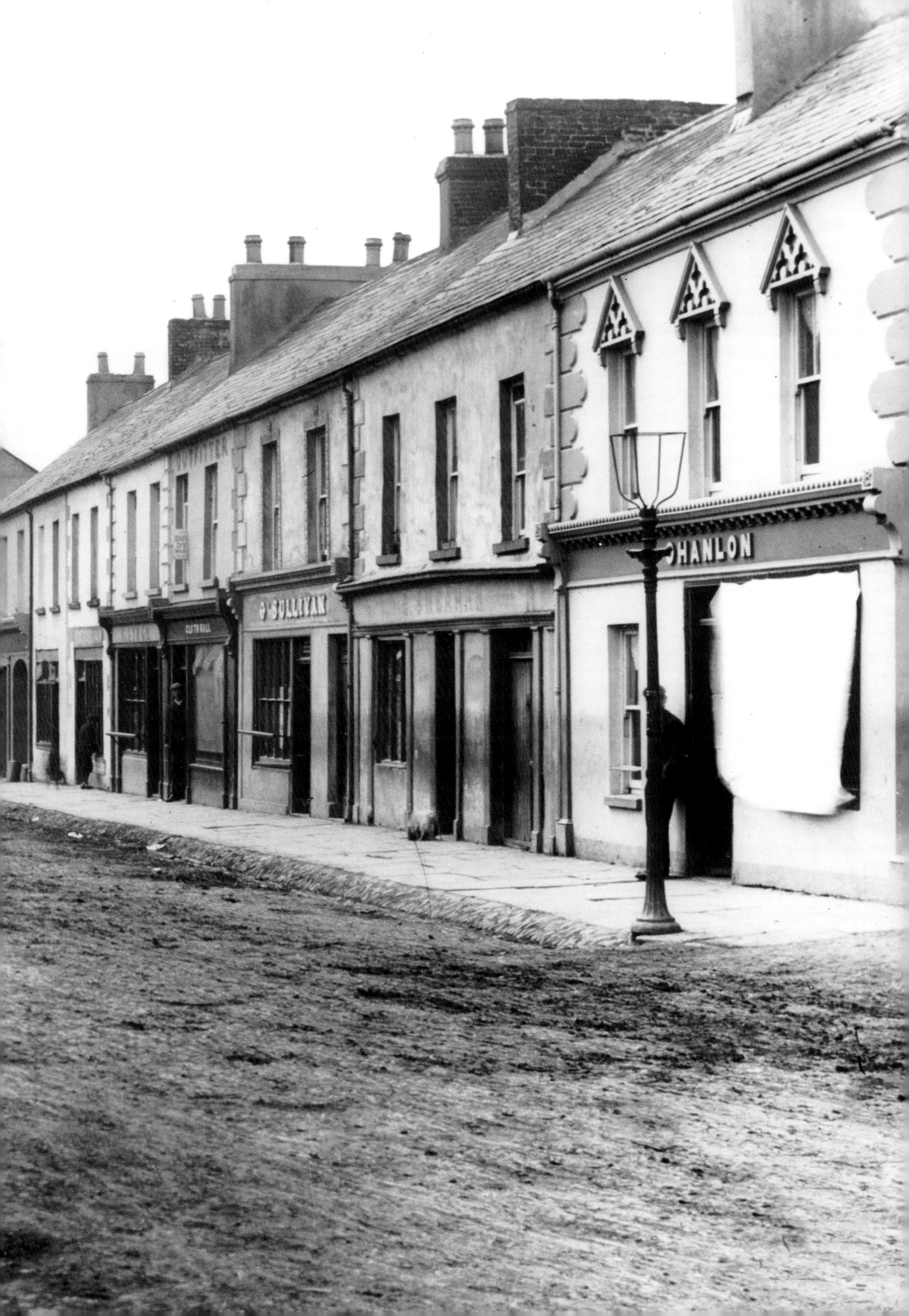

HANLON
SULLIVAN
CLOTH HALL

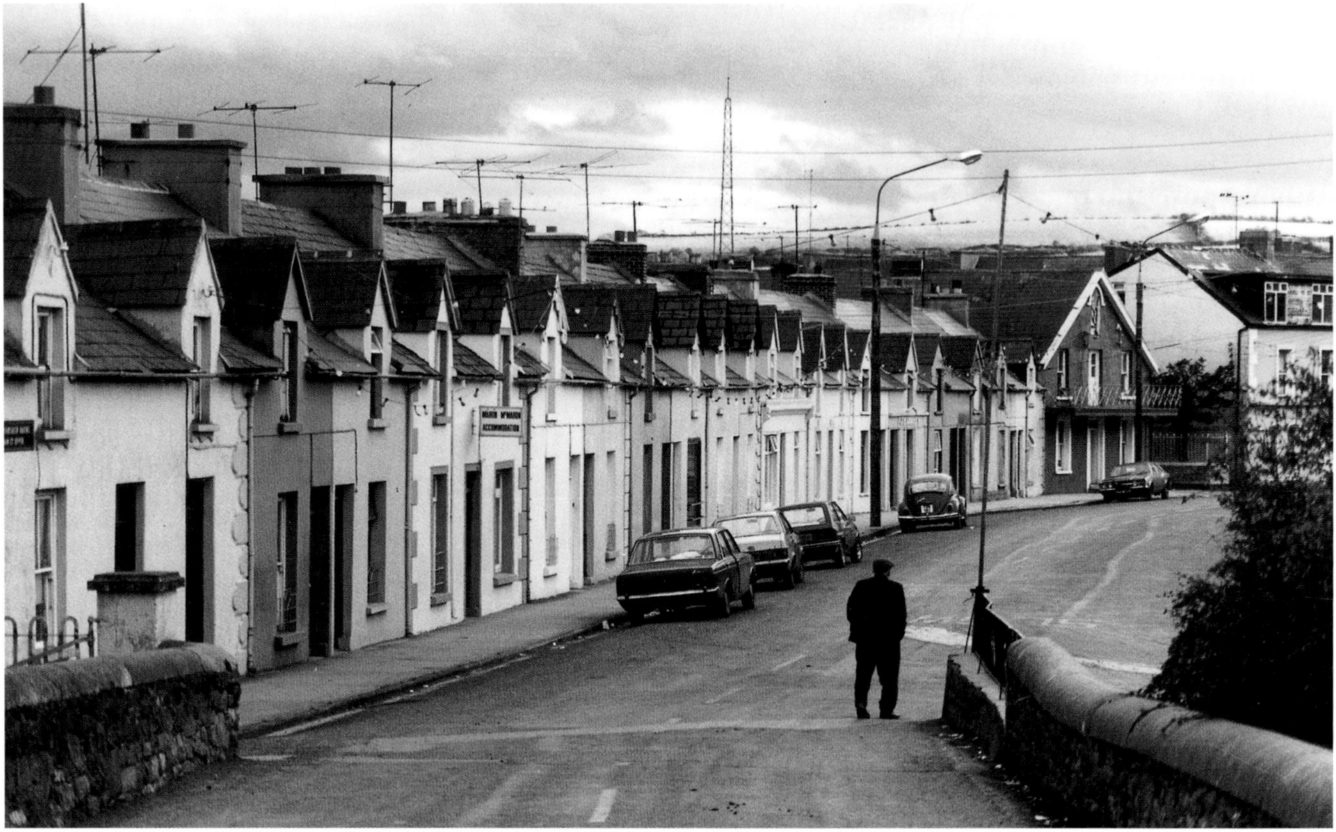

Above: This 1960s view of Upper William Street shows a unique and unspoilt row of dormer houses which would have been built from the 1880s onwards and completed by 1900. They replaced old thatched houses. Saint Patrick's Temperance Hall at the end of the row was built in 1893. The photograph was taken from the Railway Bridge which linked the street to Clieveragh.

Previous pages: This Lawrence photograph, taken from outside 25 Upper William Street, shows the lower half of the street. The carts at the kerbside on the left belonged to either the Hennessy or Carmody family. The four two-storey houses on the left had just been built, replacing thatched houses. The three-storey house at the end of the row was built by Lord Listowel for his agents. It also served as a registry office.

Across the road are Hanlon's butchers, Sheahan's and O'Sullivan's public houses, Kennelly's Cloth Hall, Lynch's public house, O'Sullivan's sweet shop, Kiely's shoemaking establishment and the public house of Edward R. Stack. The three-storey high house in the background was the Railway

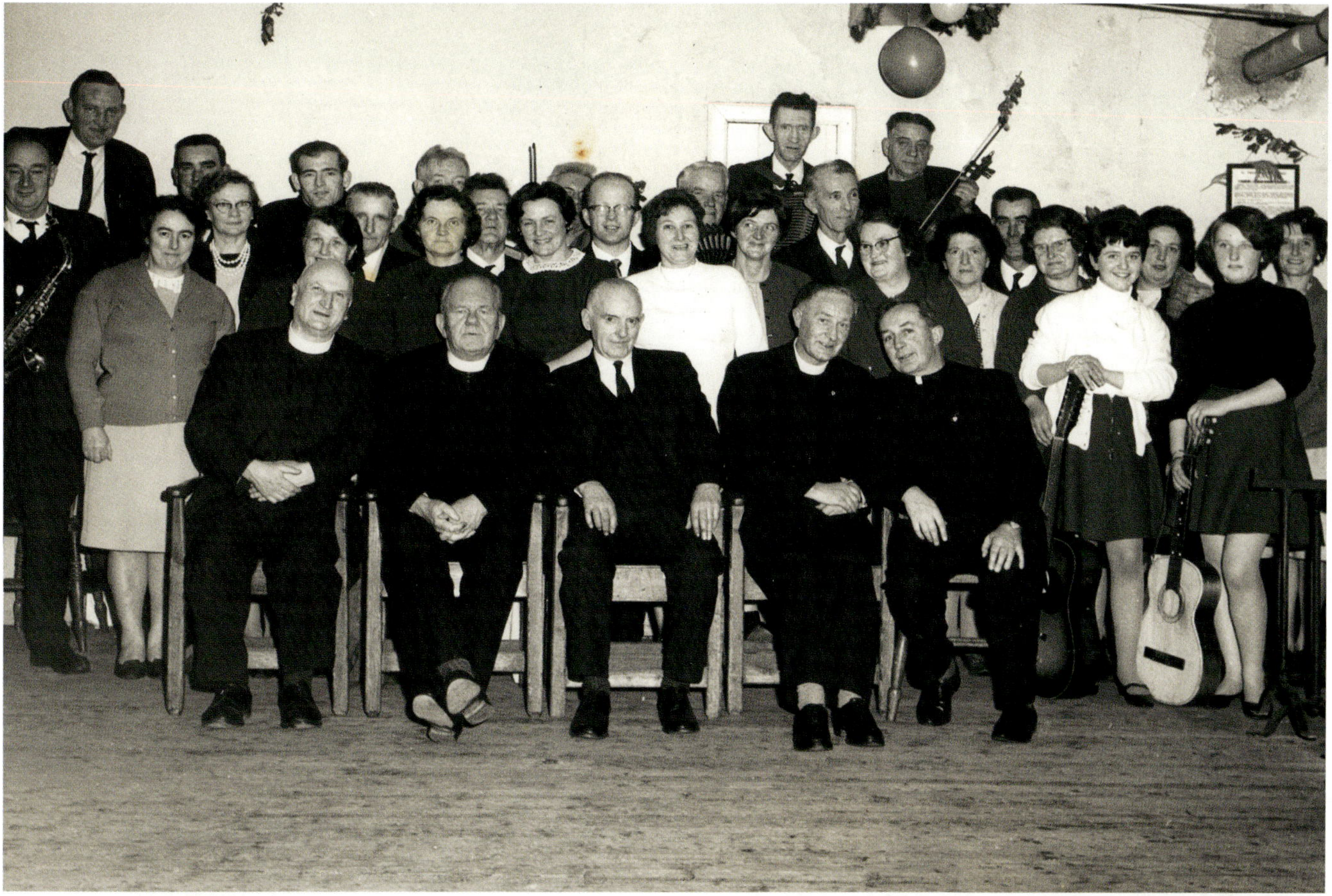

Saint Patrick's Hall Social, 1960s.
Front (l to r): Archdeacon Wallace, Canon O'Sullivan, Eddie Scanlon, Fr. Curtin and Fr. Galvin.
Back (l to r): T. Sullivan, E. Lawlor, Mary Relihan, S. Kenny, K. Stack, Mrs. Behan, J. Keane, J. Rohan, B. Moore, J. Larkin, J. Murphy, Mrs. Kenny, M. Regan, J. Griffin, M. Canty, T. Leahy, E. O'Connell, T. Brosnan, J. Flaherty, M. Burke, K. Medill, J.J. Kenny, Mrs. Rohan, A. Dowling, N. O'Connell, H. Lawlor, P. Lyons.

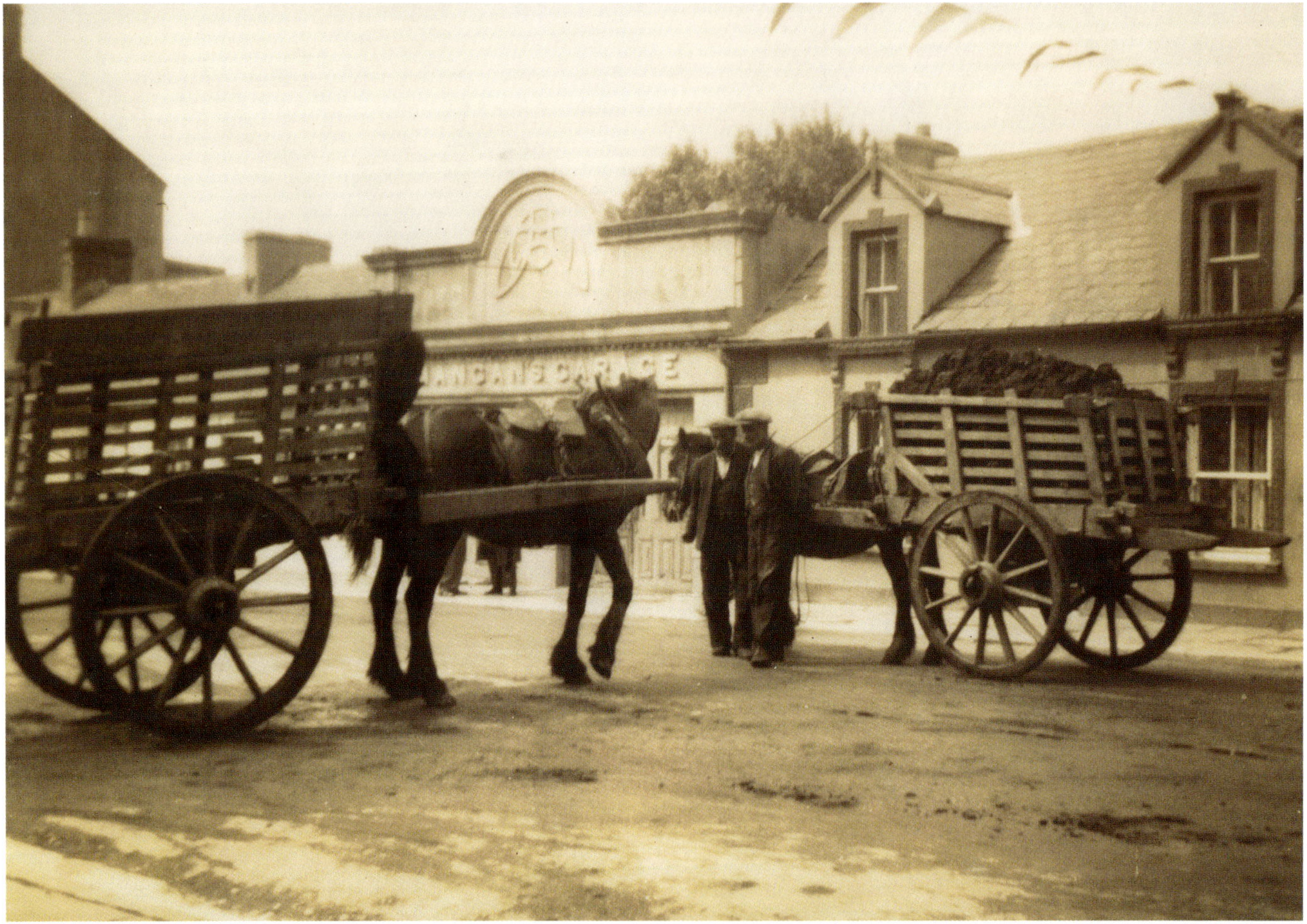

Above: Bringing home the winter fuel.

Top right: Mangan's garage, 1920s staff, with Peg Keane Stack (Mrs Barney Hanley) centre.

Opposite: Cranking up the engine on Charles Street with Mangan's Garage and Moriarty's cottage in background.

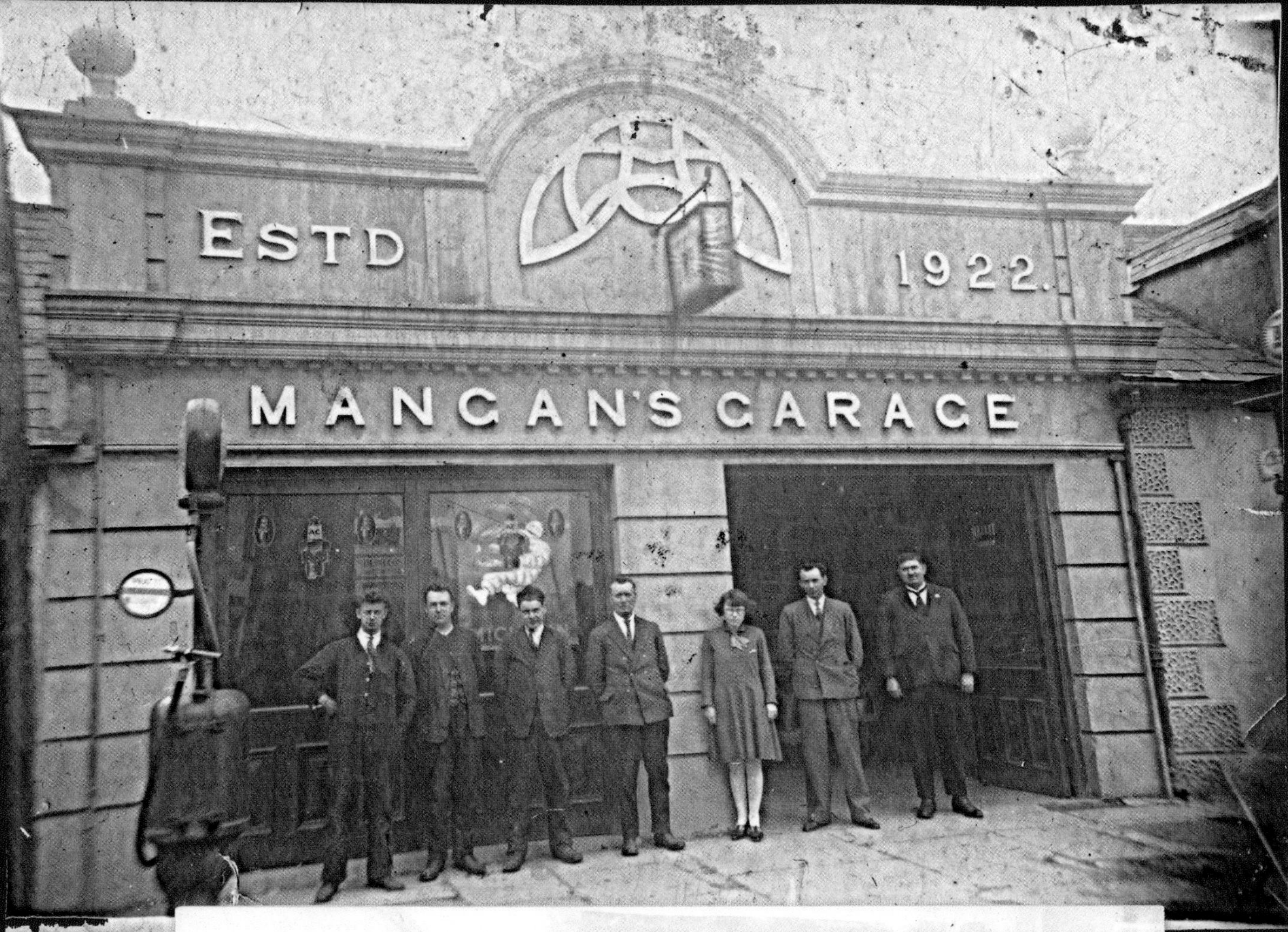
ESTD
1922.
MANGAN'S GARAGE

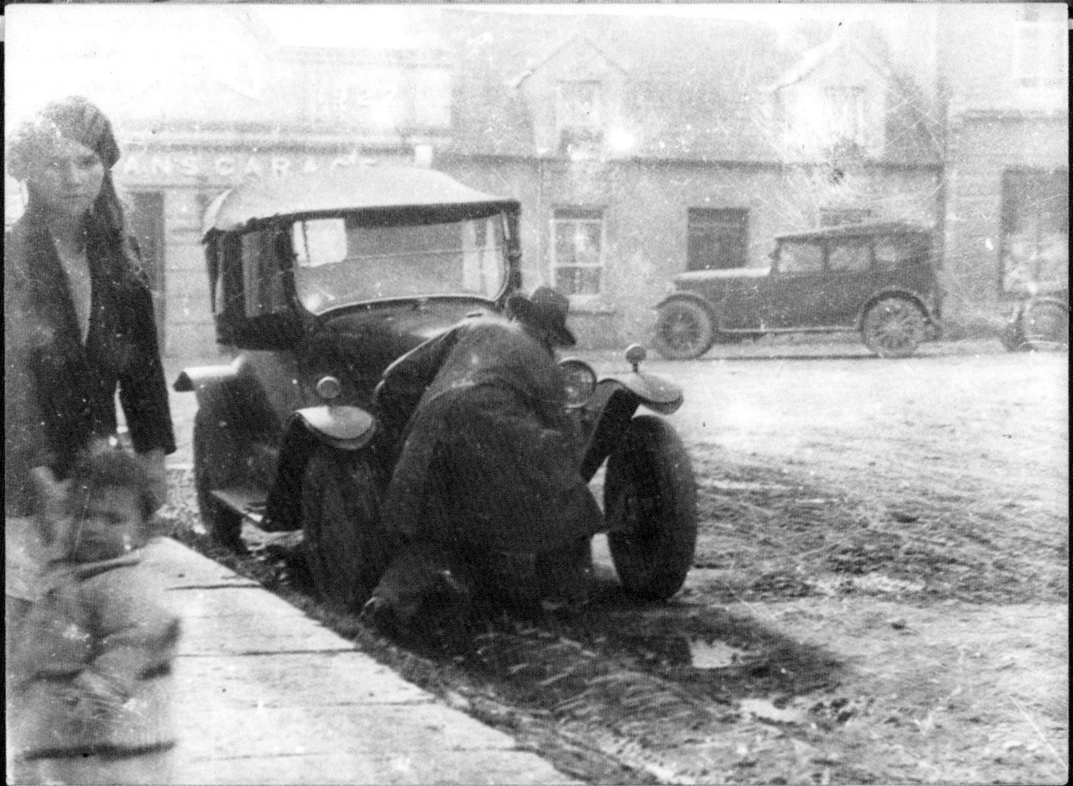
AN'S GARAGE

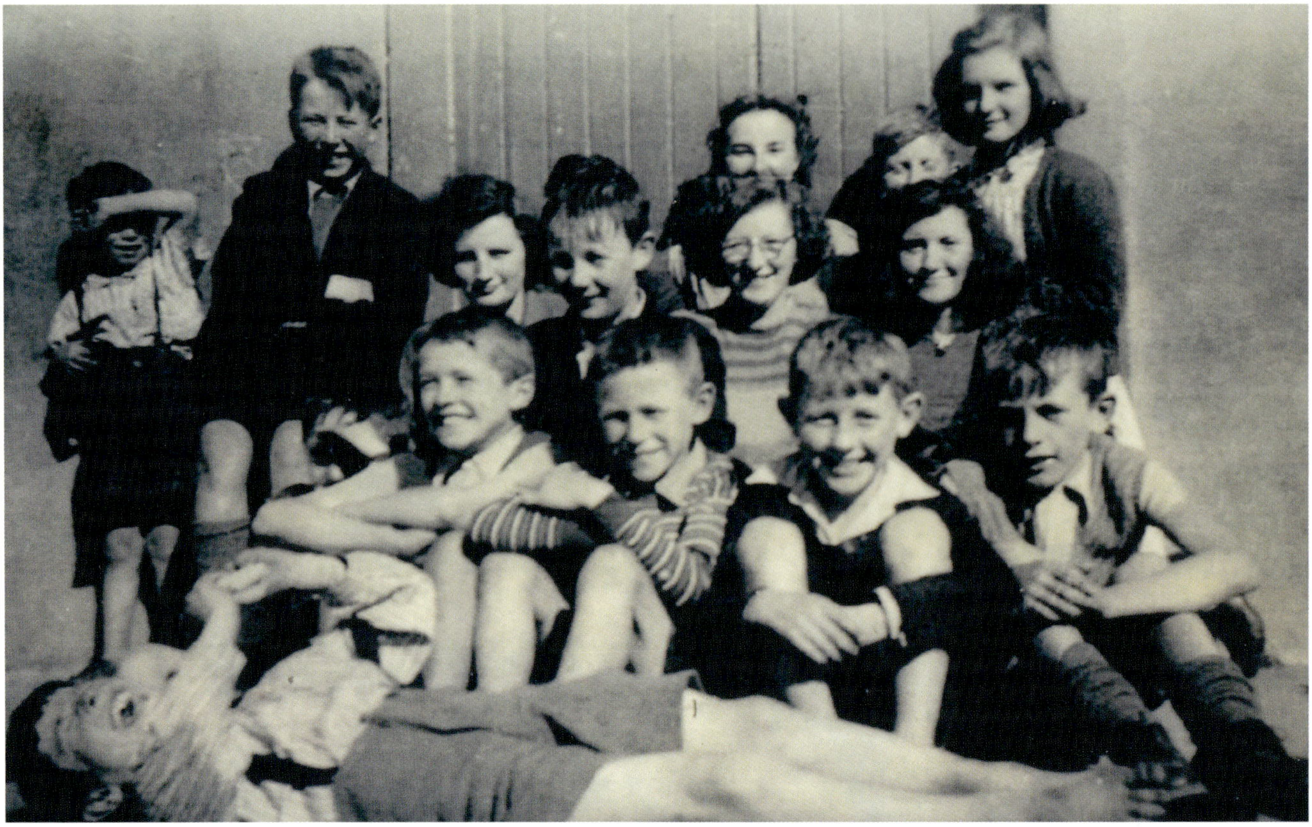

Above: A happy group of neighbours from Upper William Street seated on the steps of Saint Patrick's Hall circa early 1940s. Back (l to r): Patrick Buckley, Larry Buckley, Breda Quille, Donal Enright, Madge Sheahan. Middle: Maureen Sheahan, Jack Quille, Sheila Sheahan, Mai Enright. Front: Paschal Carmody, Johnny Buckley, John Enright, Maurice Kennelly. On the ground is Connie Buckley.

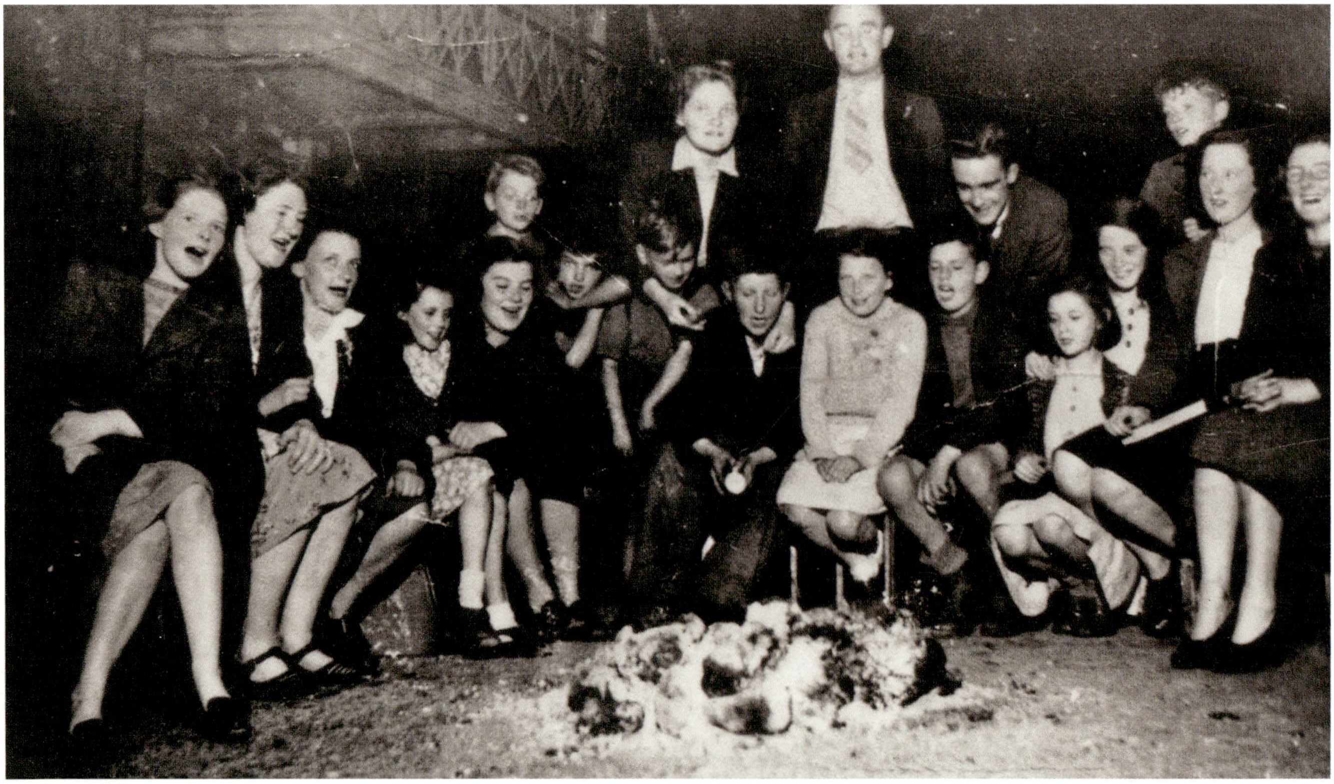

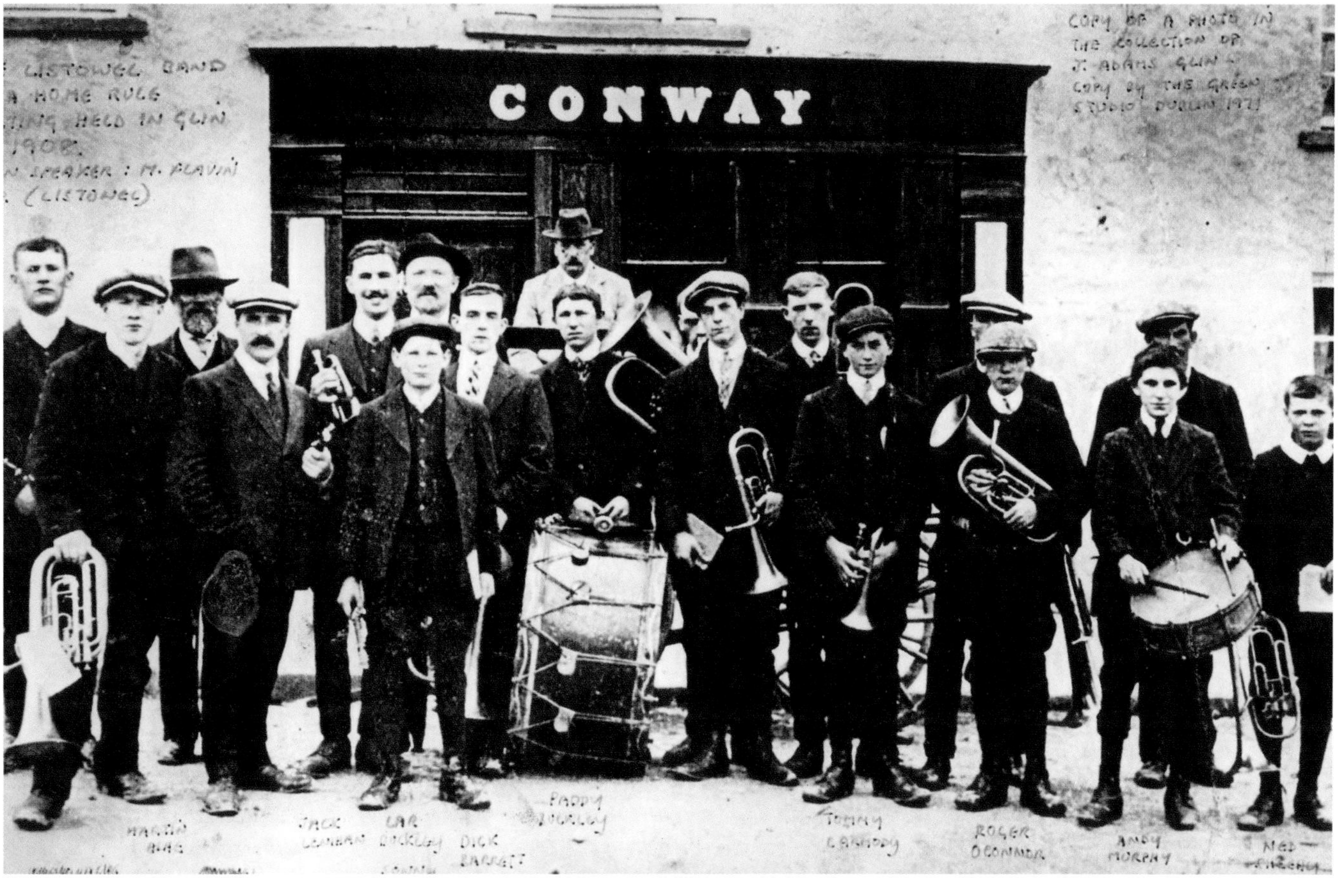

Above: The Saint Patrick's Temperance Band pictured at Glin, County Limerick in 1908. The occasion was a Home Rule meeting which was addressed by Michael J Flavin of Listowel. He was an early organiser of the Land League in North Kerry. Standing as an Anti-Parnellite candidate, he was first elected as a Member of Parliament in April 1896. He retired in 1918, having served the North Kerry constituency as Nationalist MP for 18 years.

Included in the photograph are Martin Ashe, Thomas J. Murphy, John (Jacko) Lenihan, Lar Buckley, Sonny Curtin, Dick Barrett, Paddy Buckley, Tommy Carmody, Roger O'Connor, Andy Murphy, Humphrey Kerins, Ned Sheehy.

Opposite: Bonfire night, outside Saint Patrick's Hall, June 23rd late 1940s. From left: Madge Sheahan, Joan Buckley, Theresa O'Connell, Ann O'Connell, Colette Quill, Moss Carmody, Charles Sheahan, Clem Sheahan, Donal Enright, Brenda O'Connell, Danny O'Connell, Cassie O'Connell, Mary McCarthy, Peggy Dore, Sheila Sheahan,
Back from left: Sheila Relihan, Michael Quille, Jimmy Murray.

The roadway outside the Temperance Hall was a traditional place for the lighting of a bonfire to commemorate Saint John's Eve. Turf would have been collected from the houses in Pound Lane. The turf, when collected, would be drawn down to the hall and when lit, street folk would sit around and engage in a sing song till late. Pound Lane was the original name of all of William Street until the 1860s. Up to then an animal pound existed where the Mermaids night club complex is today. William Street, upper and lower, were the new names given to the street. However, the original name is still retained and remembered by many of the older families in the Upper William Street area, as also is the name Patrick Street. Patrick Street originates from the 1920s when the names of the various streets in the town were changed to honour national heroes.

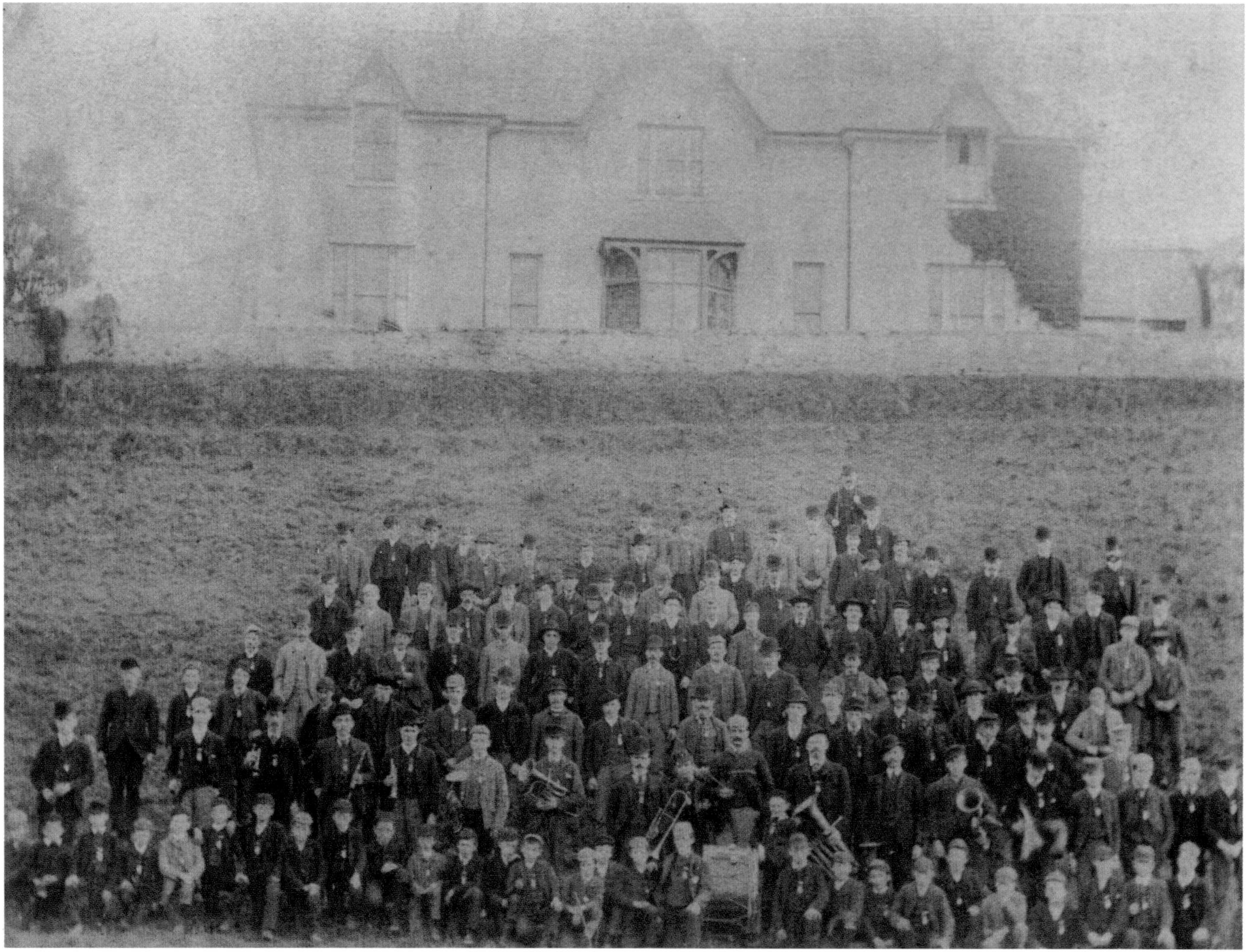

A rare photograph of The Temperance Band and supporters pictured in a field at the bottom of Ballygrennan Hill. Mount Rivers, home of Gerald McElligott, is in the background.

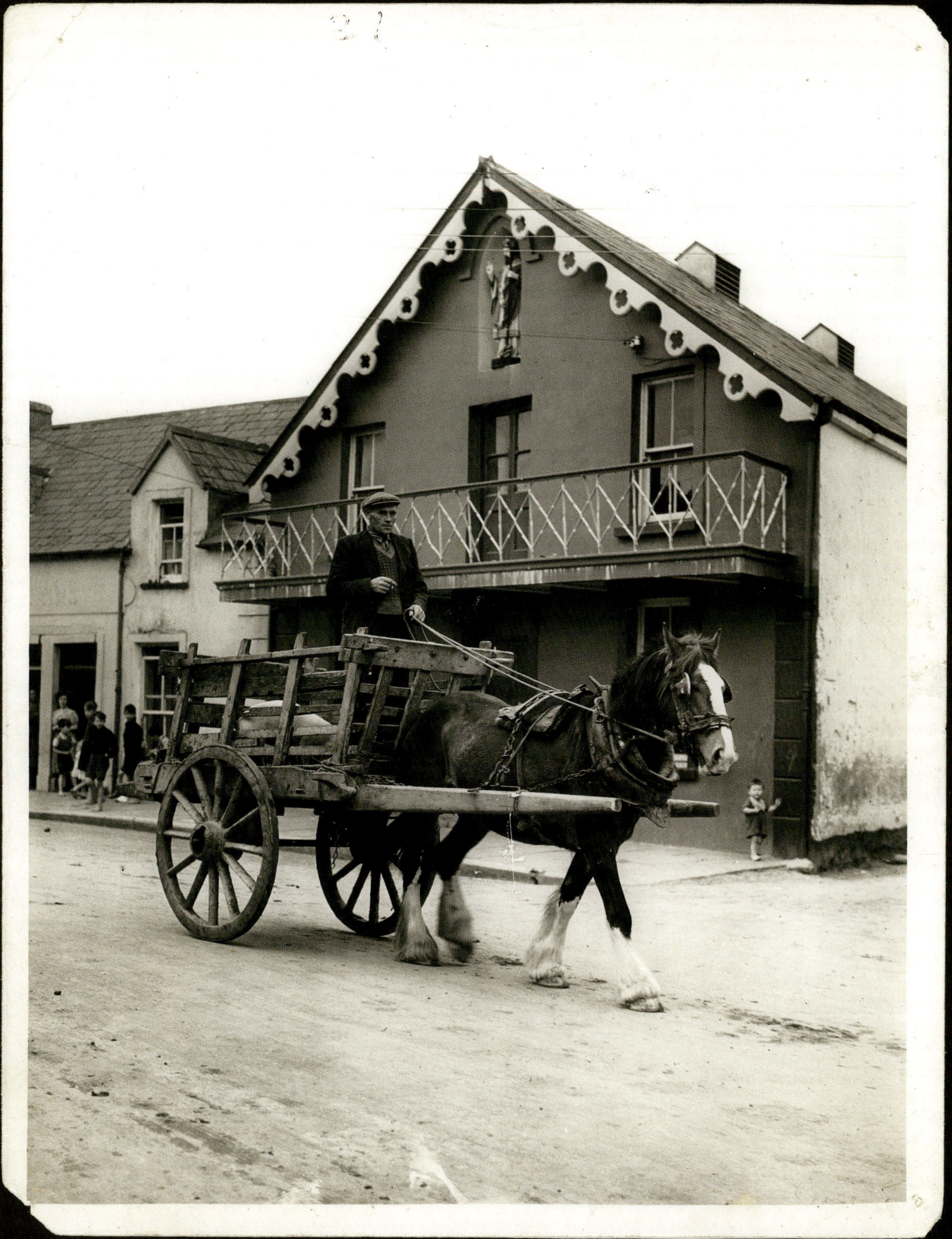

An early 1950s photograph of Michael Mason, Blanemore, Ballylongford, pictured on his way to the pig market, with Saint Patrick's Hall in background. The mainly shoeless boys outside O'Connor's house are playing a street game with glass marbles, and Mrs O'Connor is seen chatting to her next door neighbour Mae Sheehan (who is partly in picture).

1 & 3 Upper William Street,
Matthew J. Byrne, one-time solicitor to Lord Listowel, was born in Cork City. He ran his law practice from his office in Upper William Street. James Raymond, from whose home Dromin House many of the billheads and letterheads contained in this publication were located, was assistant to Matthew Byrne and succeeded him in the business. The corner where the office was located was known to townspeople as Bannatynes corner, as the Limerick milling company had a store at the rear of the solicitor's office. Another milling company, Ranks, used this store in later times. Their representatives in Listowel were the Macaulays of Ballygrennan.

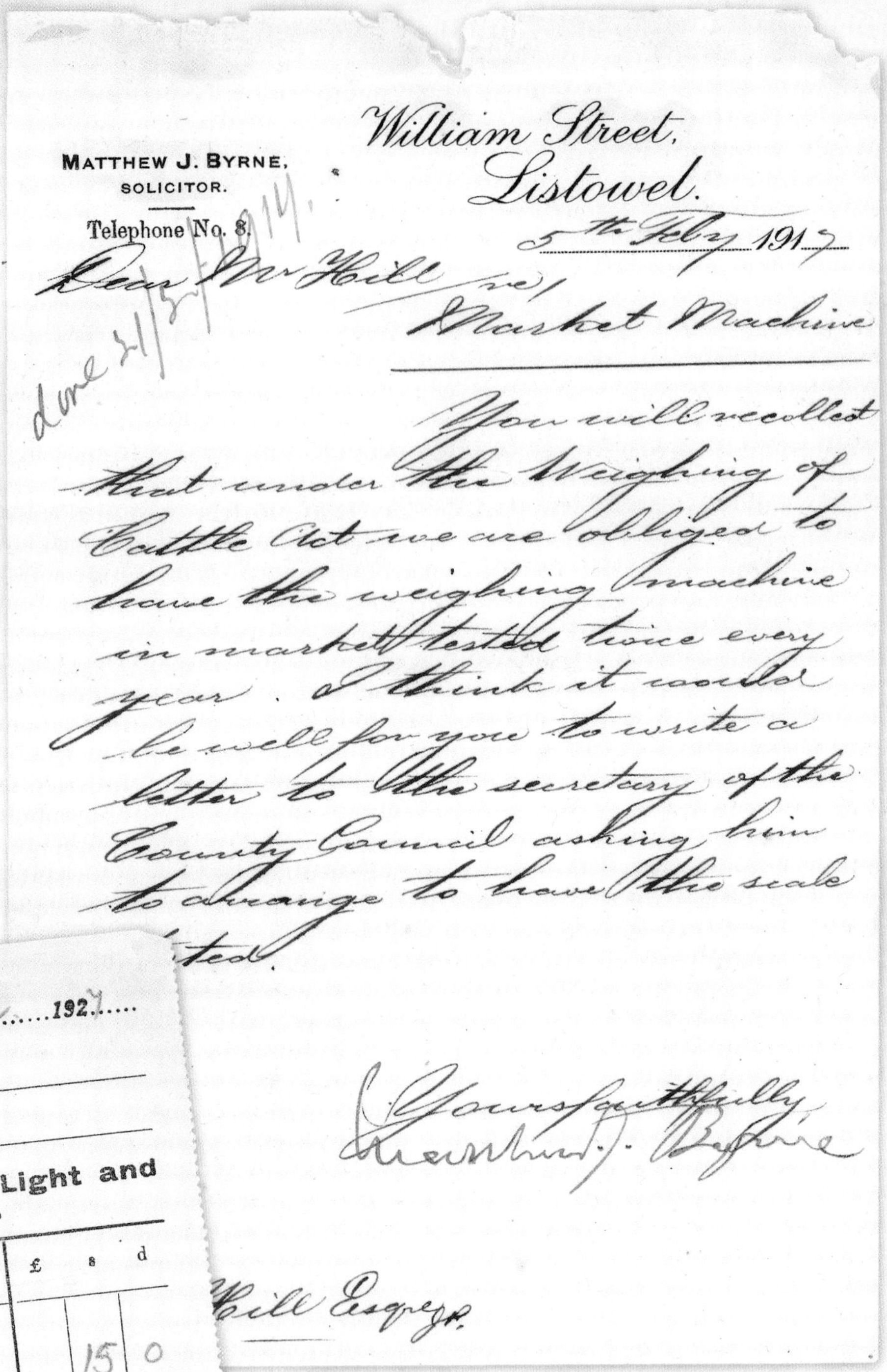

MATTHEW J. BYRNE,
SOLICITOR.
Telephone No. 8.

William Street,
Listowel.
5th Feby 1917

Dear Mr Hill re/
Market Machine

You will recollect that under the Weighing of Cattle Act we are obliged to have the weighing machine in market tested twice every year. I think it would be well for you to write a letter to the secretary of the County Council asking him to arrange to have the scale tested.

Yours faithfully
Matthew J. Byrne

Hill Esqre.

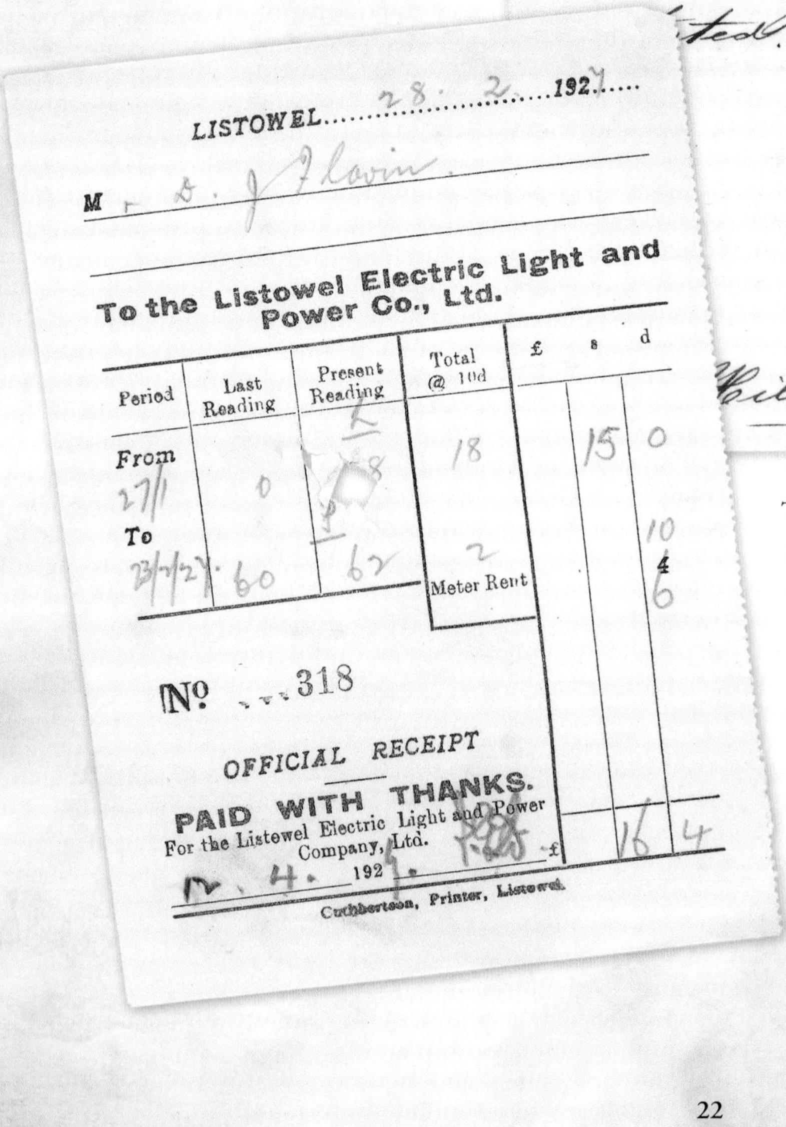

LISTOWEL 28. 2. 1927

M r D. J. Flavin

To the Listowel Electric Light and Power Co., Ltd.

Period	Last Reading	Present Reading	Total @ 10d	£	s	d
From 27/1 To 23/2/27	0 60	8 62	18 2		15	0 10
			Meter Rent			6
				£	16	4

Nº 318

OFFICIAL RECEIPT

PAID WITH THANKS.
For the Listowel Electric Light and Power Company, Ltd.
192

Cuthbertson, Printer, Listowel.

The letter above contains advice to Marshall Hill (Agent) on the necessity of getting the market weighing machine tested.

A private company, The Listowel Electric Light and Power Co., Ltd. was started in the town in the early 1900s. The company generated electricity from a large building which they built, known as the Power House, located at rear of the Upper William Street houses, on ground bought from the Hennessy family. The E.S.B., their successors, retained this building until their relocation to a new headquarters at Church Street in the early 1960s.

9 Upper William Street,

The Moore family were long-established blacksmiths in Listowel. John Moore, who was married to Eileen McMahon of Islandganiv, Listowel, is listed in Griffith's Valuation of the 1850s as having a forge in Pound Lane. He was followed in the trade by his son John (Johnsie) who was married to Ann Lawlor. Their son Val continued the trade. The forge closed on his retirement in the 1950s thus ending a century of 'a sound of the anvil'.

Photo: John and Annie Moore.

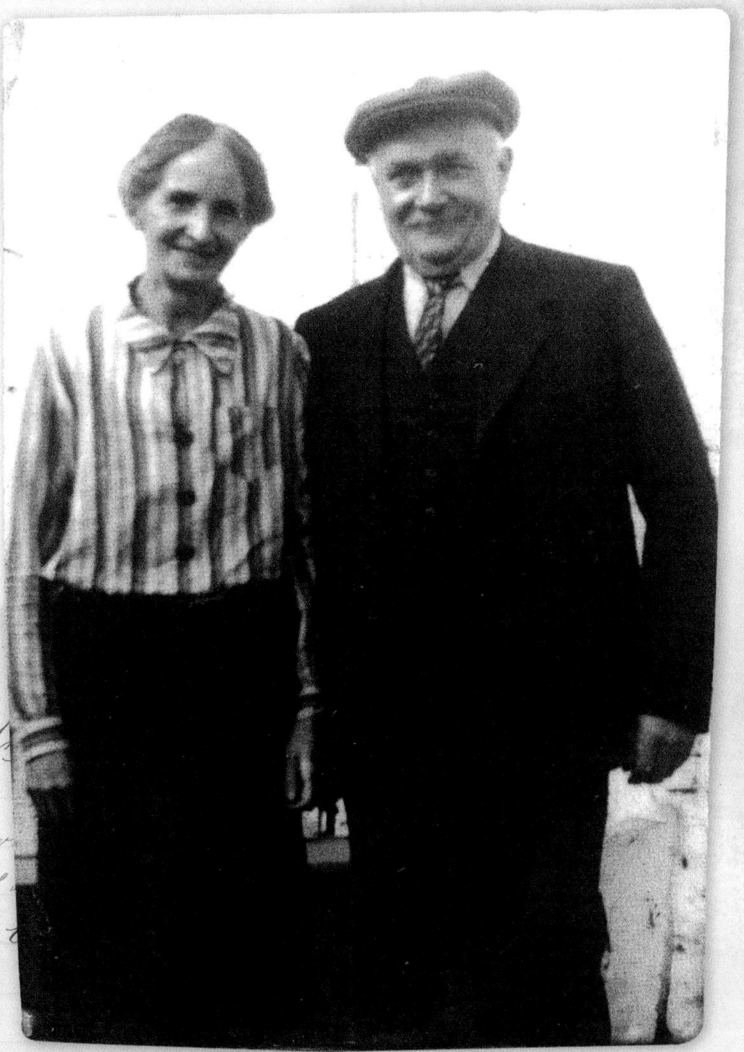

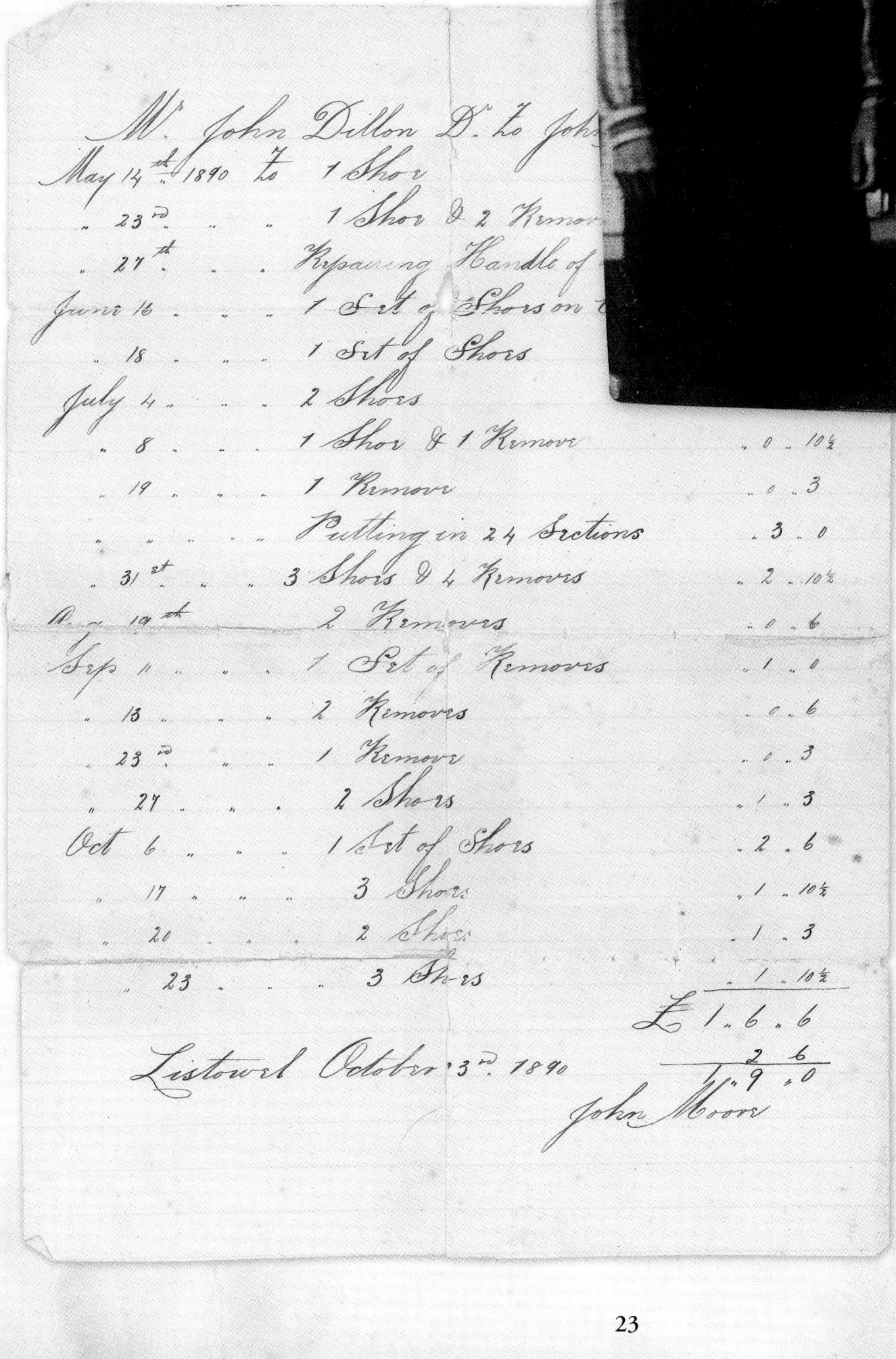

Mr. John Dillon Dr. to John

May 14th 1890 To 1 Shoe
" 23rd " " 1 Shoe & 2 Remov
" 27th . . Repairing Handle of
June 16 . . . 1 Set of Shoes on
" 18 . . . 1 Set of Shoes
July 4 . . . 2 Shoes
" 8 . . . 1 Shoe & 1 Remove . 0 . 10½
" 19 " " " 1 Remove . 0 . 3
" " " " Putting in 24 Sections . 3 . 0
" 31st " " 3 Shoes & 4 Removes . 2 . 10½
Aug 19th 2 Removes . 0 . 6
Sep 11 . . . 1 Set of Removes . 1 . 0
" 15 . . . 2 Removes . 0 . 6
" 23rd " " 1 Remove . 0 . 3
" 27 " . 2 Shoes . 1 . 3
Oct 6 " " " 1 Set of Shoes . 2 . 6
" 17 " " " 3 Shoes . 1 . 10½
" 20 . . . 2 Shoes . 1 . 3
" 23 . . . 3 Shoes . 1 . 10½

£1 . 6 . 6
2 6
1 . 9 . 0

Listowel October 3rd 1890

John Moore

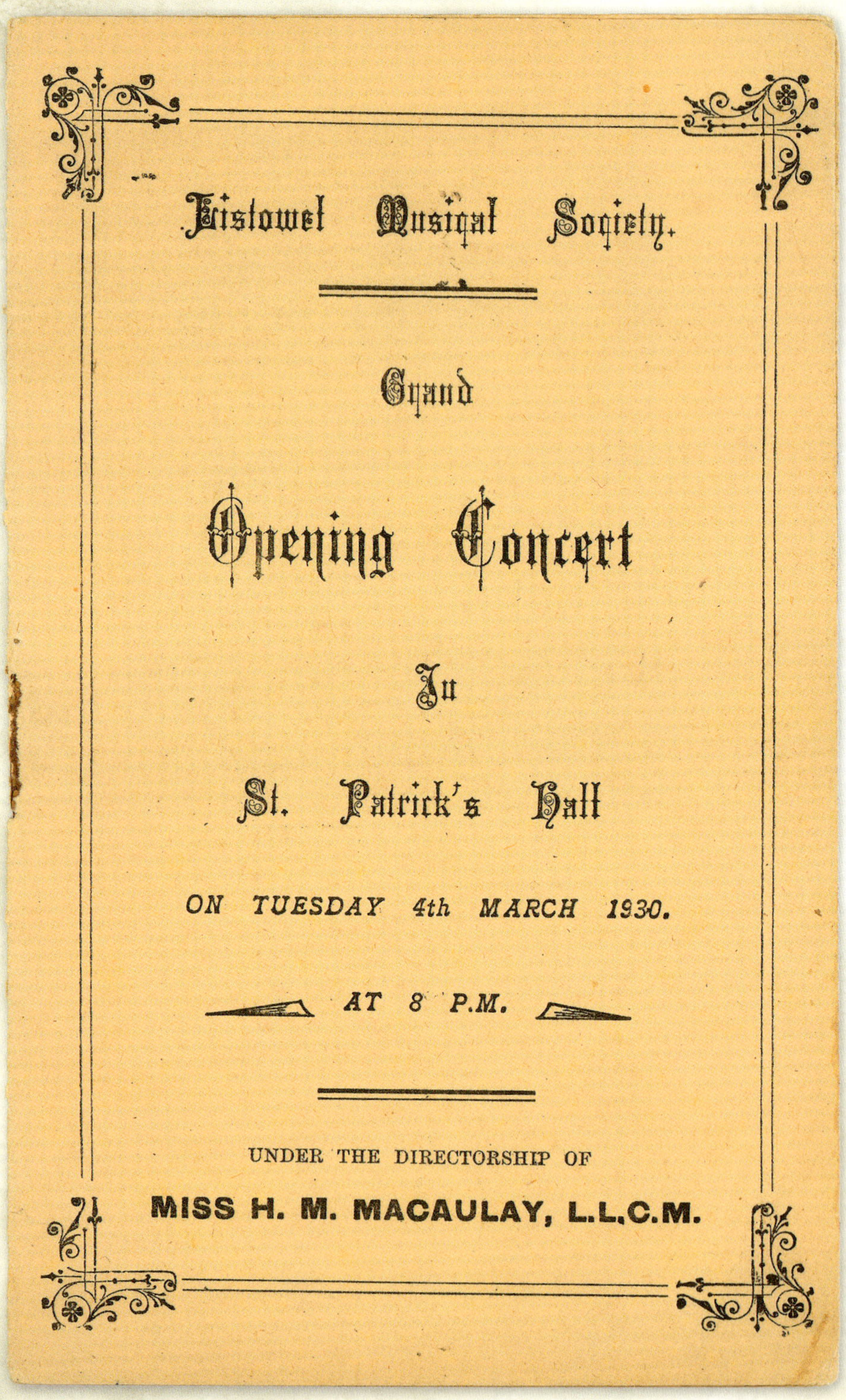

Saint Patrick's Temperance Hall

Saint Patrick's Hall was built at the behest of the local Temperance Society in 1893. It was a mecca for the young men of the town and it offered a variety of attractions. One of these was the newly-formed Brass and Reed Band. They quickly became very competent and were firm favourites at events locally and around the county. In 1895 the Society had the distinction of fielding one of two teams from the town in that year's County Senior Football Championship, entering under the name 'Saint Patricks'. History has recorded that in the second round, playing Tralee, the match was abandoned. Following a lengthy investigation the subsequent County Board meeting disqualified the Listowel 'Saint Patricks' team for 'bringing the game into disrepute'.

The Hall was very popular up until the 1960s. Because of new attractions and emigration, the Hall then went into decline. It closed as an active billiard and snooker hall, only to be used after this as an occasional youth club centre. However, a new committee formed in the 1990s began fundraising again and these funds along with the assistance of FÁS led to refurbishment and renovations between 1999 and 2002. It reopened again in 2002, and is now used extensively by a variety of groups and especially by members of the Listowel Active Retirement group.

Shown is the cover of the newly-formed Listowel Musical Society's programme of their opening concert, performed in the hall in 1930.

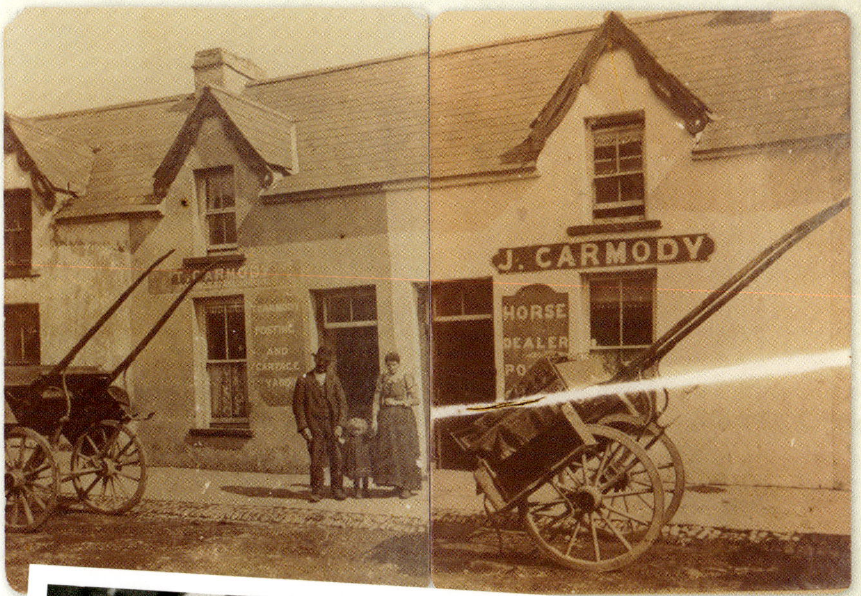

John and Nora Carmody,
Horse Dealers, 25 Upper William Street
John and Nora Carmody with daughter Bridie Mai, outside the front door of the family home around 1904. His brother Tom and wife Catherine lived next door. They were both sons of Maurice and Bridget. The Carmodys plied their trade in the horse-drawn car business, having long cars, side cars and wagonettes for hire. In 1907, John entered the Funeral Undertaking business when he purchased the goodwill from William McElligott, who was selling his business and emigrating to America. John's son, John Francis, had the first motor hackney car in Listowel. Vincent and Kathleen Carmody and John and Mary Carmody still reside in the respective family homes of their grandparents at 25 and 27 Upper William Street.

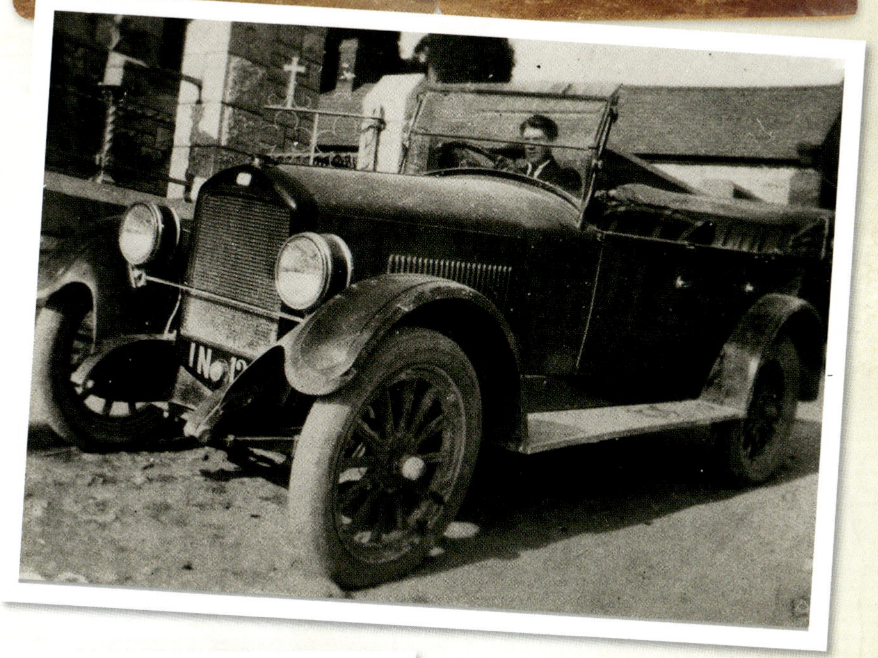

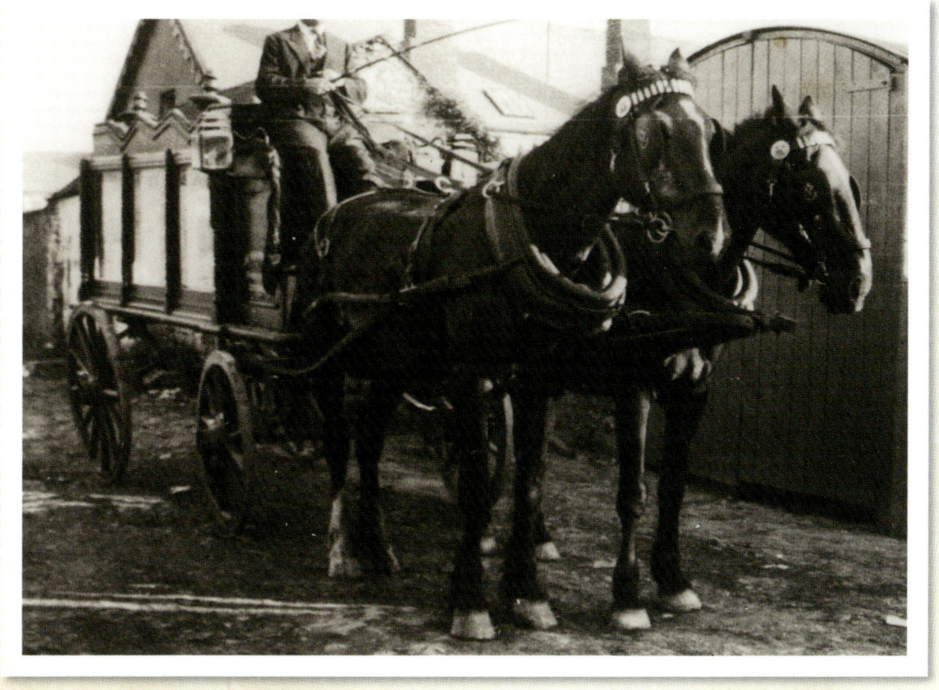

Above: John Francis is seen at Queenstown (Cobh), at the wheel of IN 12 in 1925.

Left: This photograph of the horse hearse was taken at the back of John Carmody's. The driver, not fully shown in the photograph, is Paddy James.

31 Upper William Street

Tailor John O'Connell trained in Bond Street in London. He ran a high-class tailoring business in Upper William Street from the 1880s. Many Listowel tailors served their apprenticeship under his watchful eye. John was followed into the trade by his son Jackie. With his demise, the tailor's shop, at 31 Upper William Street, closed.

Photo: John O'Connell on right with John O'Flaherty, who worked as a tailor at O'Connell's. Five of John O'Flaherty's sons subsequently became tailors.

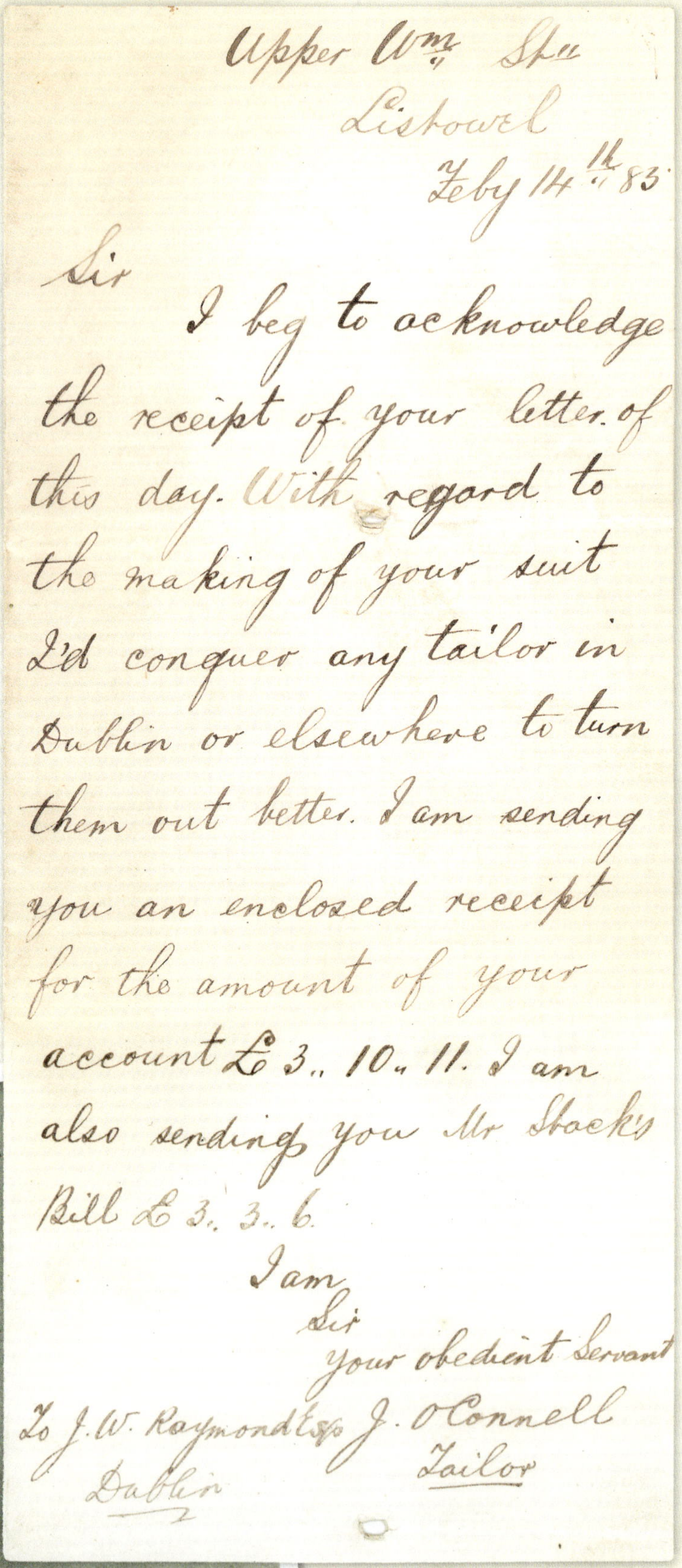
Upper Wm Stee
Listowel
Feby 14th 85

Sir

I beg to acknowledge the receipt of your letter of this day. With regard to the making of your suit I'd conquer any tailor in Dublin or elsewhere to turn them out better. I am sending you an enclosed receipt for the amount of your account £3.. 10.. 11. I am also sending you Mr Stack's Bill £3. 3. 6.

I am
Sir
your obedient Servant
J. O'Connell
Tailor

To J.W. Raymond Esq
Dublin

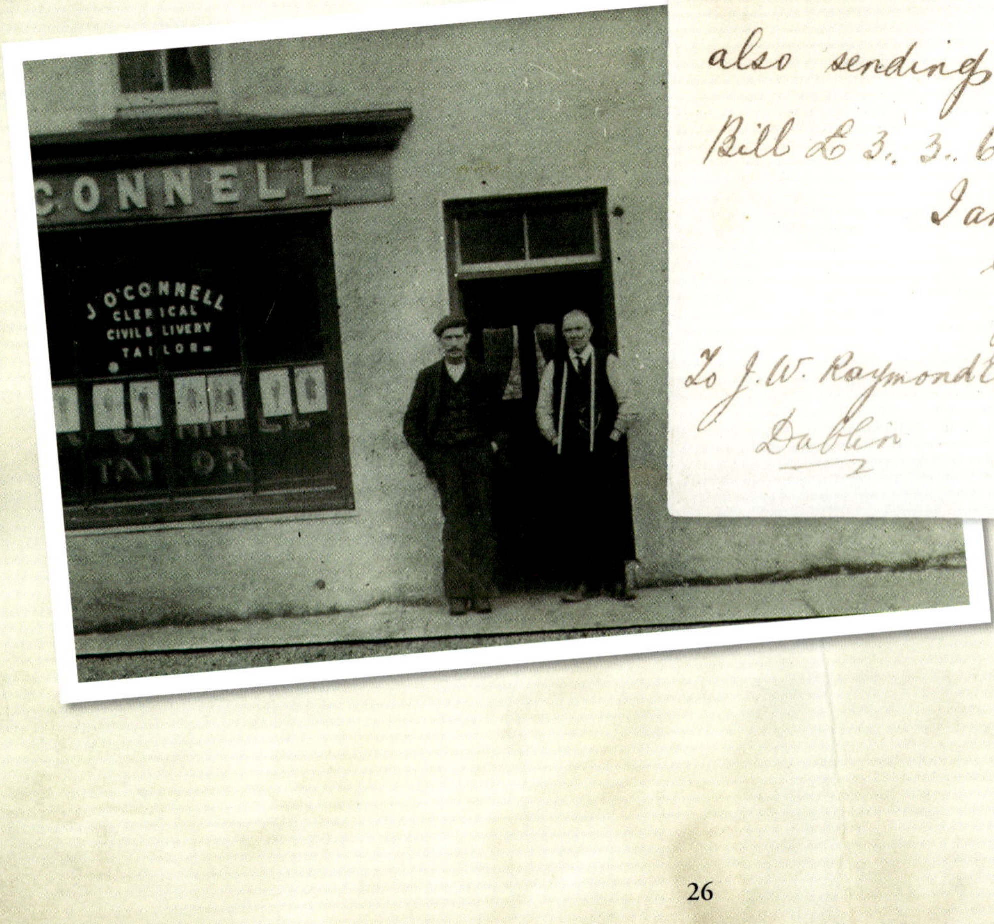

Memorandum.

From

Patrick D. O'Neill,

Egg and Poultry Exporter,

WILLIAM STREET.

Listowel, Feb 14th 1897

To Mrs Raymond

Received the sum of 14/7 amt due

(Dated 14th Feb 1897

P D O'Neill

LISTOWEL DRAMA GROUP.

President : Bryan MacMahon.
Hon. Treas. : Michael Kennelly.
Business Manager : R. I. Cuthbertson.
Hon. Sec. : Angela Collins.
Producer : Eamon Kelly.
Stage Manager : Wm. J. McDonnell.

PROUDLY PRESENT

"The Plough and the Stars"

A Tragedy in Four Acts by Sean O'Casey.

CAST :

Jack Clitheroe (Brick-Layer—Commandant in I.C Army.)		Kevin Donovan.
Nora Clitheroe	(His Wife.)	Vera McElligott.
Peter Flynn	(A Labourer—Nora's Uncle.)	John O'Flaherty.
Young Covey	(A Fitter—Clitheroe's Cousin.)	Brendan Carroll.
Bessie Burgess	(A Street Fruit Vendor.)	Kathleen Nicholson.
Mrs. Gogan	(A Charwoman.)	Kay O'Brien.
Mollser	(Her delicate child)	Sheila Keane.
Fluther Good	(A Carpenter)	Eamon Kelly.
Lieut. Langon	(Civil Servant— of Irish Volunteers.)	Bertie Conway.
Capt. Brennan	(Chicken Butcher— of I. C. Army.)	Wm. J. McDonnell.
Corp. Stoddart	(Of the Wiltshires.)	K. Kiely.
Sergt. Tinley	"	Bunny Dalton.
A Bar Tender		Michael Kennelly.
The Figure in the Window		Bryan MacMahon.

Production is by Eamon Kelly.

Act I.—The Living Room of the Clitheroe Flat in a Dublin Tenement.
Act II.—A Public House outside of which a Meeting is being held.
Act III.—The Street outside the Clitheroe Tenement.
Act IV.—The Room of Bessie Burgess.

Time : Acts I and II November 1915 ; Acts III and IV Easter Week, 1916.
A few days elapse between Acts III and IV.

THE STAGE SHALL NEVER DIE !

O'Neill's Poultry Store (now Sluagh Hall)

Patrick O'Neill, egg and poultry exporter, located his place of business at the top end of Upper William Street, by the side of the old railway bridge. The building was used, along with adjacent properties, as headquarters for the L.D.F. (Local Defence Force) during what was known as 'The Emergency', or the years of the Second World War. The post-war period saw the emergence of the F.C.A. (Fórsa Cosanta Áitiúil) and a refurbishment of the hall. It became known as the Sluagh Hall. It was equipped with a stage, and this served two purposes - to facilitate the mounting of a boxing ring and also a much sought after venue for the newly-formed Listowel Drama Group to stage their plays.

Included, along with O'Neill's letterhead, is a Drama Group programme of the 1940s. The Producer of the play was the famous seanchaí Eamon Kelly.

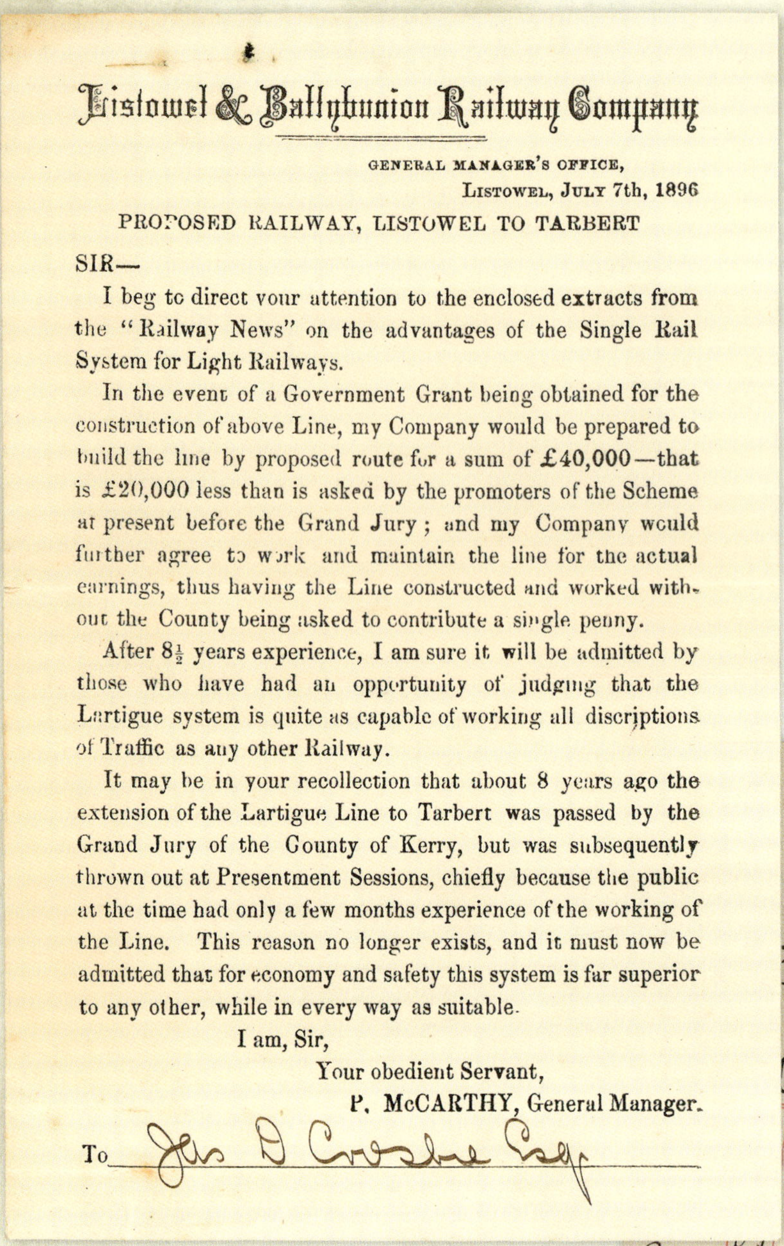

Listowel & Ballybunion Railway Company

GENERAL MANAGER'S OFFICE,
LISTOWEL, JULY 7th, 1896

PROPOSED RAILWAY, LISTOWEL TO TARBERT

SIR—

I beg to direct your attention to the enclosed extracts from the "Railway News" on the advantages of the Single Rail System for Light Railways.

In the event of a Government Grant being obtained for the construction of above Line, my Company would be prepared to build the line by proposed route for a sum of £40,000—that is £20,000 less than is asked by the promoters of the Scheme at present before the Grand Jury; and my Company would further agree to work and maintain the line for the actual earnings, thus having the Line constructed and worked without the County being asked to contribute a single penny.

After 8½ years experience, I am sure it will be admitted by those who have had an opportunity of judging that the Lartigue system is quite as capable of working all discriptions of Traffic as any other Railway.

It may be in your recollection that about 8 years ago the extension of the Lartigue Line to Tarbert was passed by the Grand Jury of the County of Kerry, but was subsequently thrown out at Presentment Sessions, chiefly because the public at the time had only a few months experience of the working of the Line. This reason no longer exists, and it must now be admitted that for economy and safety this system is far superior to any other, while in every way as suitable.

I am, Sir,

Your obedient Servant,

P. McCARTHY, General Manager.

To Jas D Crosbie Esq

The Lartigue Monorail

The world's first passenger-paying monorailway. It was invented and developed by Frenchman, Charles Lartigue. This unique rail system between Listowel and Ballybunion was built and opened in 1888. It was in use for 36 years until its closure in 1924. A dedicated committee was set up in the 1990s to investigate the possibility of building a replica engine and carriages and of restoring some of the track. This dream came to fruition when, after years of fundraising, the restored project was opened to the public in 2003. It is operated by a dedicated group of volunteers on a rota basis from May to September each year.

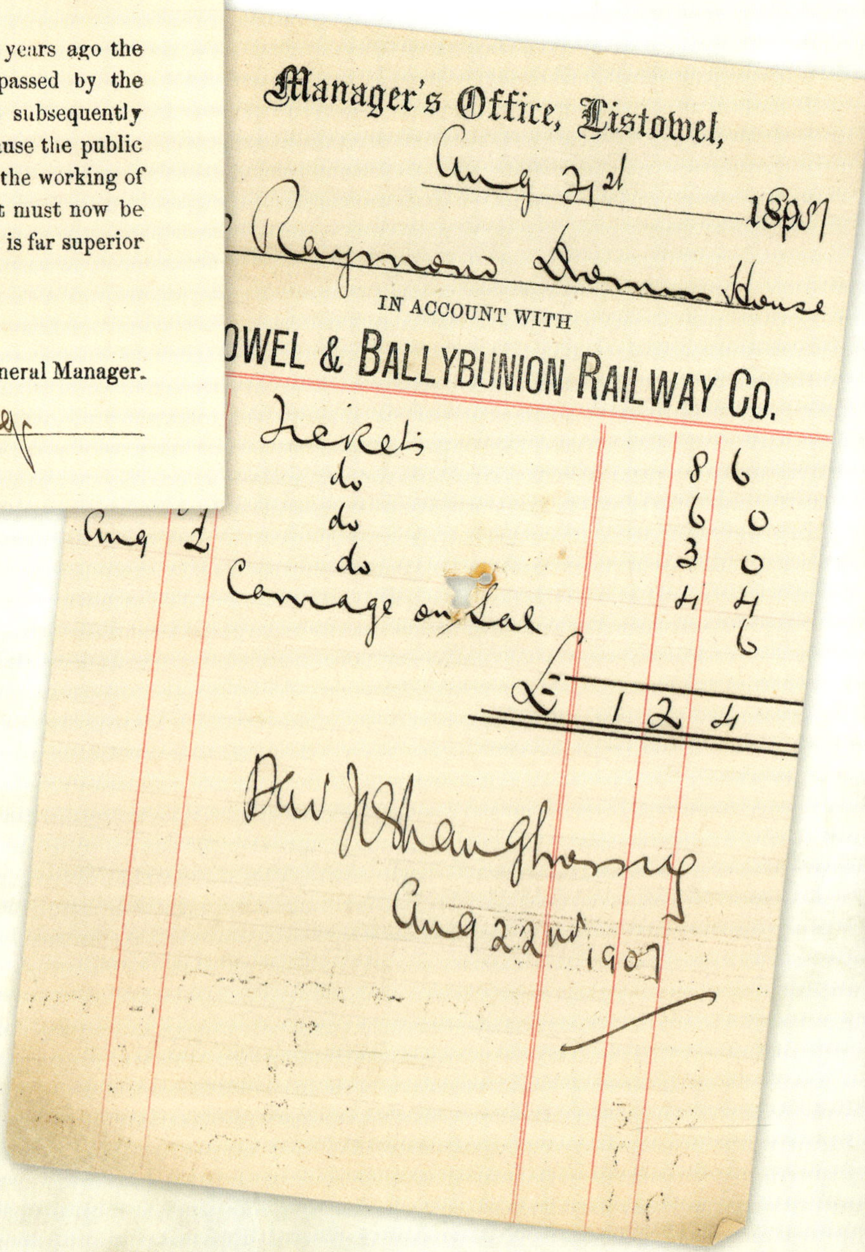

Manager's Office, Listowel,

Aug 21 1807

IN ACCOUNT WITH

OWEL & BALLYBUNION RAILWAY CO.

	Tickets	8	6
	do	6	0
Aug 2	do	3	0
	Carriage on Sal	4	4
			6
	£	1 2	4

Aug 22nd 1907

Above: Letter from Patrick McCarthy, General Manager, Lartigue Railway to Jas Crosbie, Agent to Lord Listowel, enlisting his support for a proposed new railway connection between Listowel and Tarbert.

Right: Letterhead of Lartigue Railway.

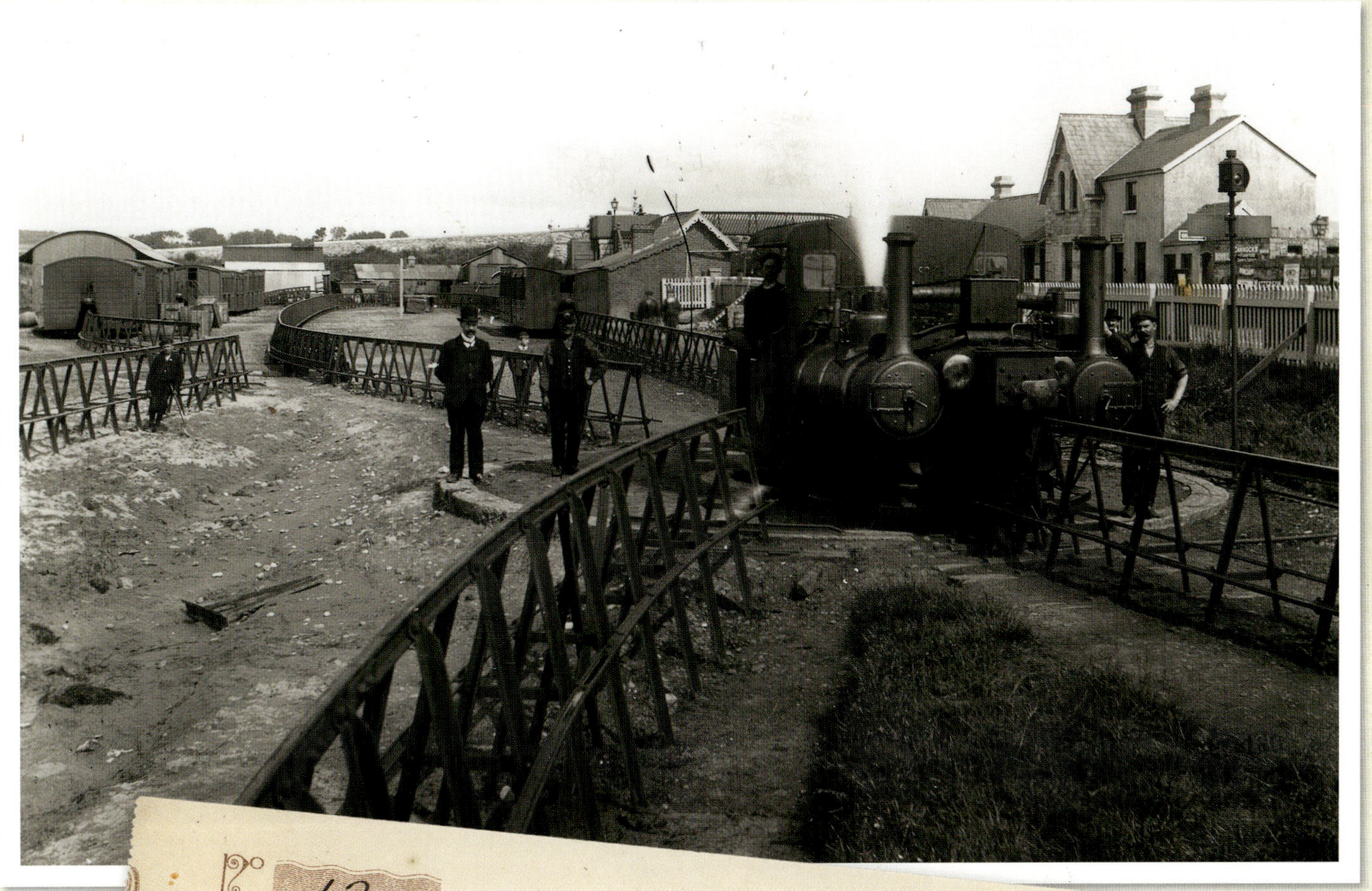

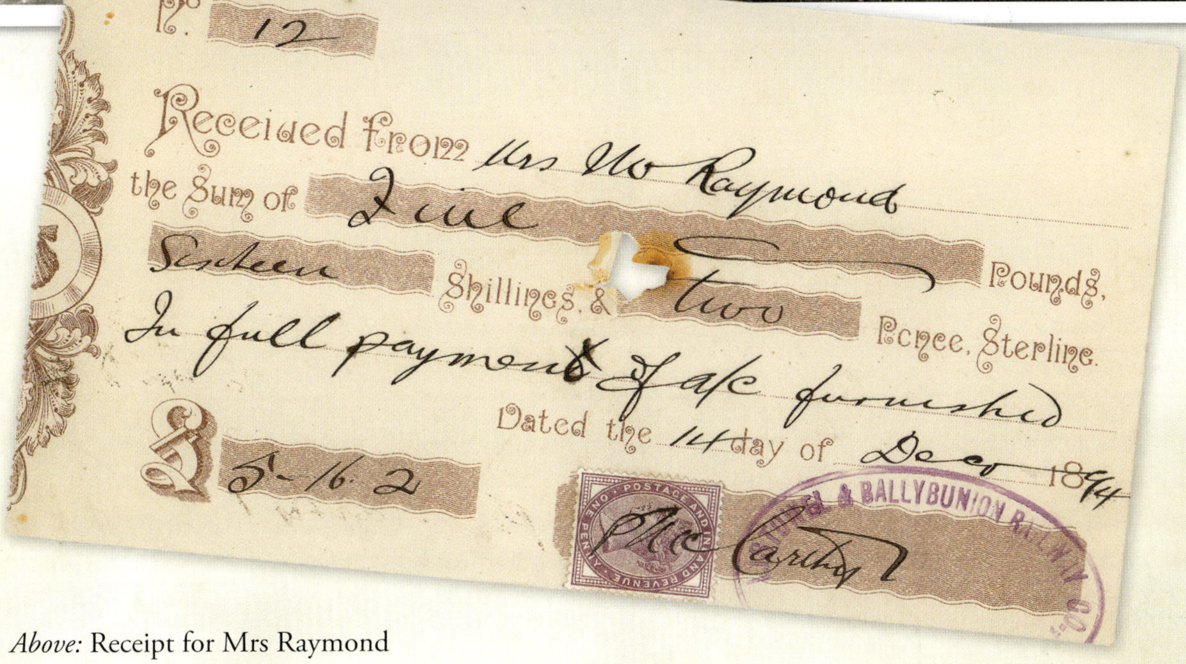

No. 12

Received from Mrs Wo Raymond

the Sum of Five Pounds,

Sixteen Shillings & two Pence, Sterling.

In full payment of a/c furnished

Dated the 14 day of Dec 1894

£5-16-2

BALLYBUNION R...

McCarthy

Above: Receipt for Mrs Raymond for travel on the railway.

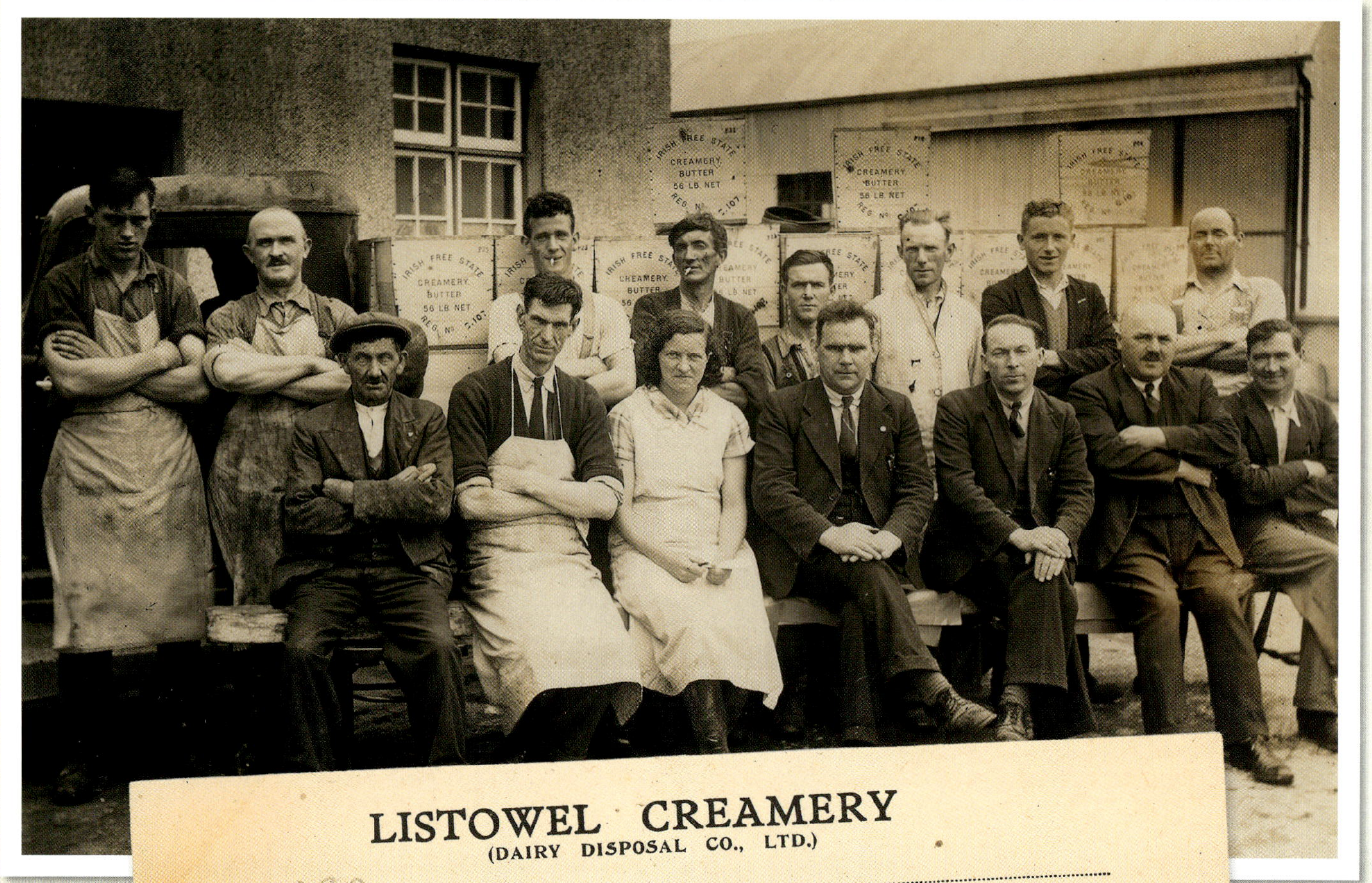

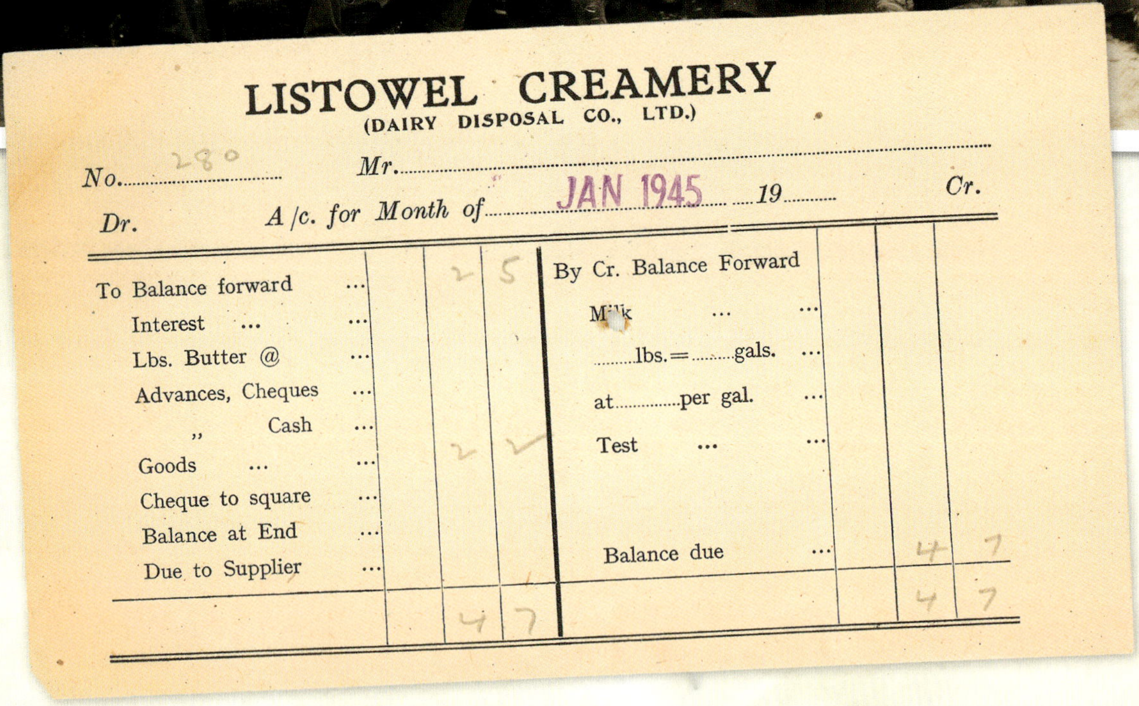

LISTOWEL CREAMERY
(DAIRY DISPOSAL CO., LTD.)

No. 280 Mr.

Dr. A/c. for Month of JAN 1945 19...... Cr.

To Balance forward ...	2	5	By Cr. Balance Forward		
Interest			Milk		
Lbs. Butter @ ...			.........lbs. = ...gals. ...		
Advances, Cheques ...			at.............per gal. ...		
" Cash ...	2	2	Test		
Goods					
Cheque to square ...					
Balance at End ...					
Due to Supplier ...			Balance due ...	4	7
	4	7		4	7

The arrival of the Dairy Disposal Company to Upper William Street in the late 1920s sounded the death knell to very many of the private and co-operative creameries which had been in place since the latter end of the nineteenth and the beginning of the twentieth centuries. The new creamery was set up in what was part of McDonnell's meadow. It soon became a hub of activity and brought a good deal of employment. Milk suppliers from the Listowel catchment area would queue each morning to deliver their milk, where first it would be separated, the cream used for butter production. Suppliers would avail of the separated milk to take home for feeding to calves or bread making. Small branch creameries were set up in the outlying areas. Lorries brought in the milk from these. The butter, which was made and packed in timber boxes, each containing 56lb net weight, was marketed under the trade name, 'Irish Free State Creamery Butter'. Each supplier received a monthly creamery book (a canvas-backed card) in which each day's delivery was marked and purchases were recorded.

Photo: Listowel Creamery staff, 1937. Back (l to r): (1) Ml. Galvin, (4) Jack Morrissey, (5) E. Murphy, (6) M. Enright. Front (l to r): (1) N. Murphy, (4) T. O'Sullivan, Manager, (5) P. Ryan, (6) M. Walsh, (7) Cecil McCarthy.

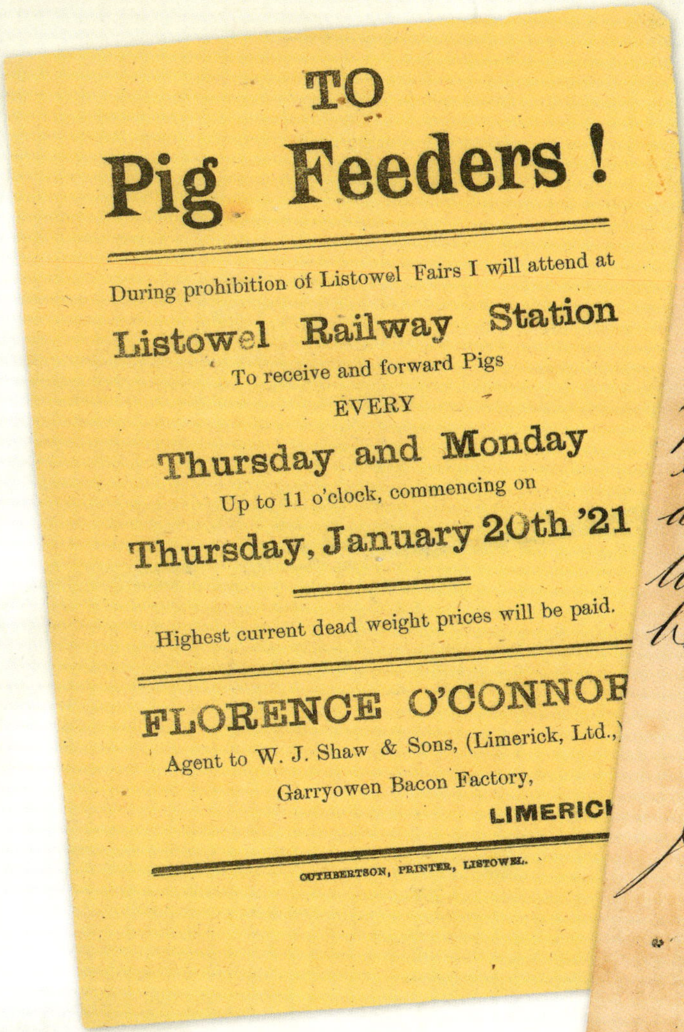

TO

Pig Feeders!

During prohibition of Listowel Fairs I will attend at

Listowel Railway Station

To receive and forward Pigs

EVERY

Thursday and Monday

Up to 11 o'clock, commencing on

Thursday, January 20th '21

Highest current dead weight prices will be paid.

FLORENCE O'CONNOR

Agent to W. J. Shaw & Sons, (Limerick, Ltd.,)

Garryowen Bacon Factory,

LIMERICK

CUTHBERTSON, PRINTER, LISTOWEL.

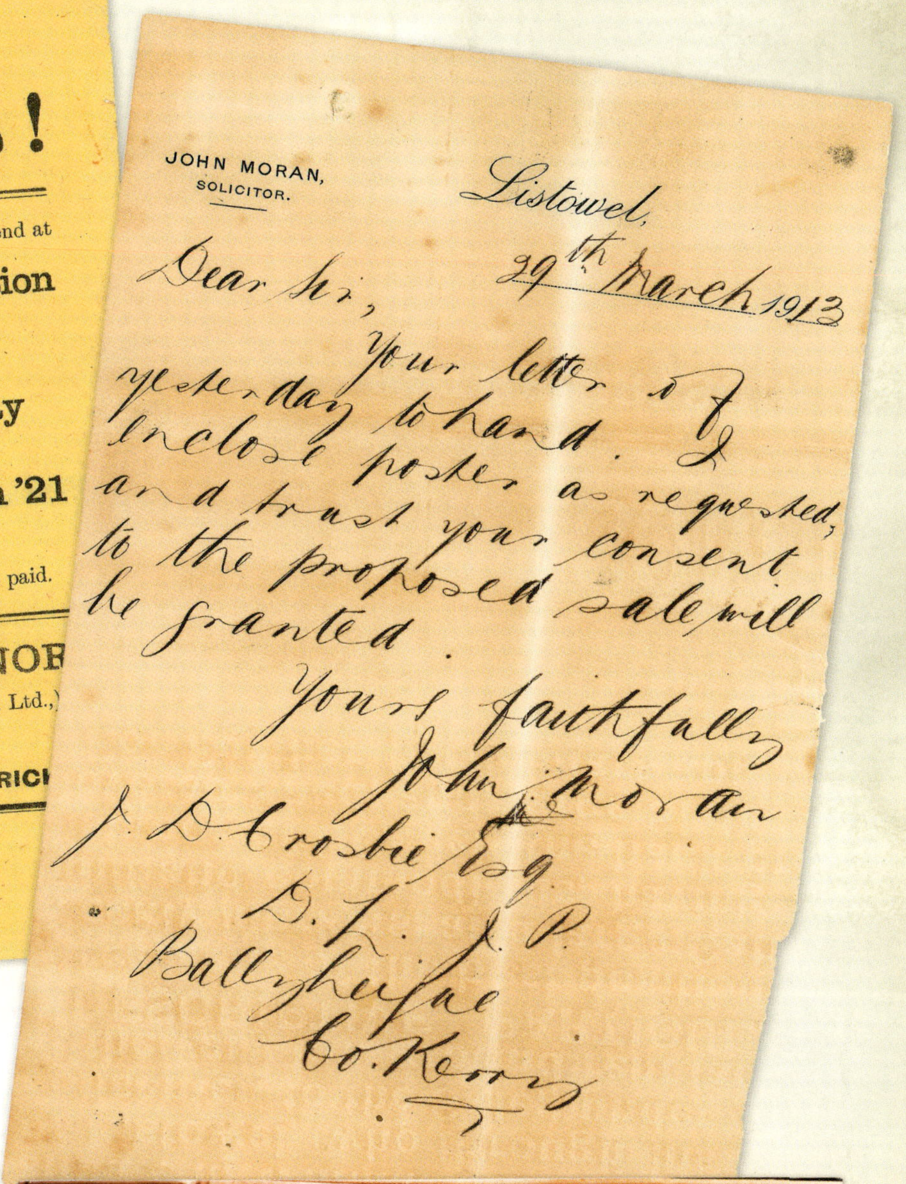

JOHN MORAN,
SOLICITOR.

Listowel,
29th March 1913

Dear Sir,

Your letter of yesterday to hand. I enclose poster as requested, and trust your consent to the proposed sale will be granted.

Yours faithfully
John Moran

J. D. Crosbie Esq.
D.L. J.P.
Ballyheigue
Co. Kerry

38 Upper William Street

Florence O'Connor, from Coolanonaugh, Tarbert, purchased this public house at the top of Upper William Street from John O'Neill. He was joined by his sisters Katie and Margaret who had been previously been running the Railway Hotel premises (later owned by M.J.Dillon and afterwards by Jack and Beatrice Carmody). Florence christened his public house 'The Railway Bar', due to its proximity to the railway station. Katie took charge of the bar and grocery, while Florence was an insurance agent and also acted as a buyer and agent for the Limerick Bacon Factory owners, Shaws. The business was bought by the Buckley family in the early 1970s. Subsequent owners were famous Kerry footballer Timmy Kennelly and his wife Nuala. It is now an Italian restaurant named Casa Mia.

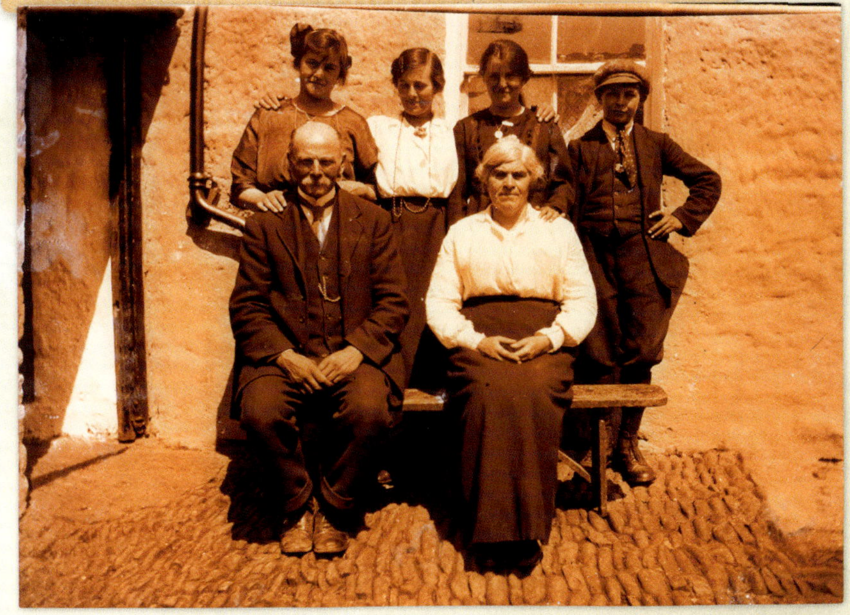

36 Upper William Street

John Moran practised as a solicitor from his home in Upper William Street. He was known locally as the Attorney Moran. He is pictured here with his wife Ellen and some members of his family.

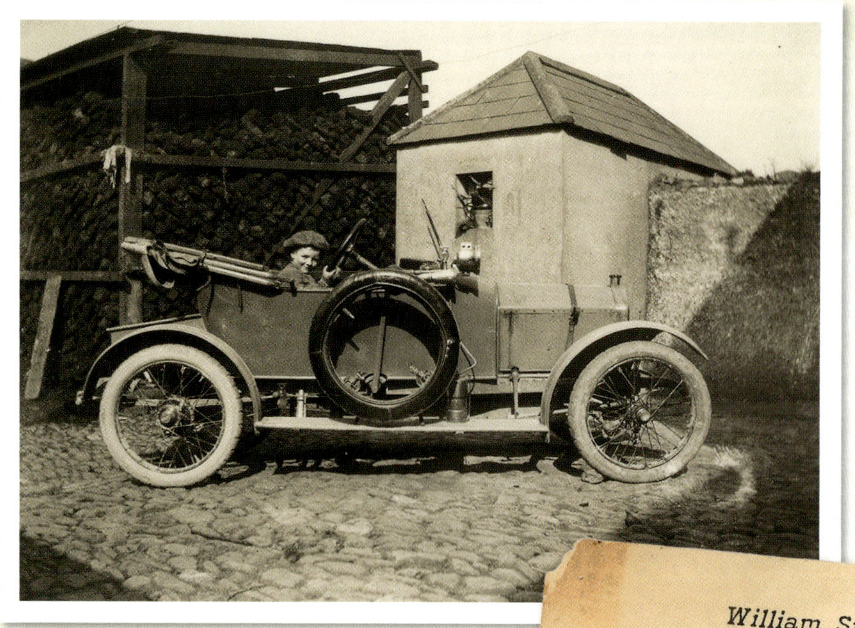

34 Upper William Street
John H. Pierse married Ellen Cussen in 1895; he set up his veterinary practice in what is now No. 34, Upper William Street.

Left: John Pierse's son, Richard, in his father's Swift car, taken in 1918 in the back yard of his house.

Lower left: John H. Pierse.

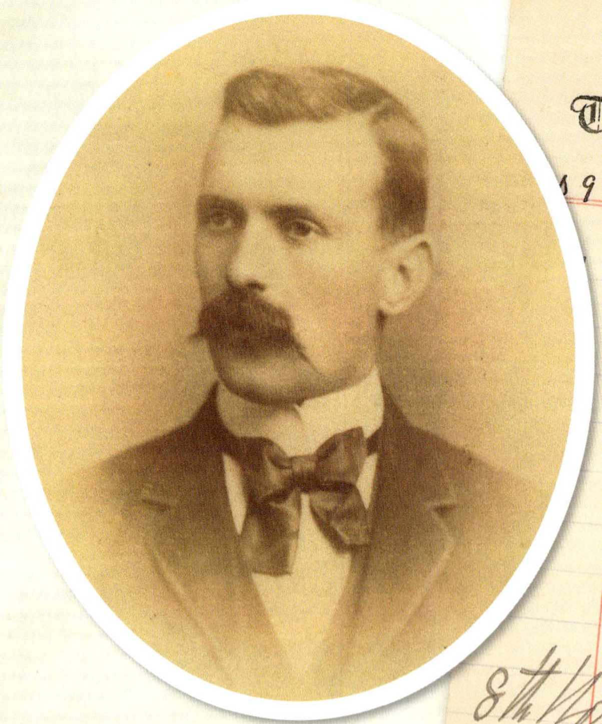

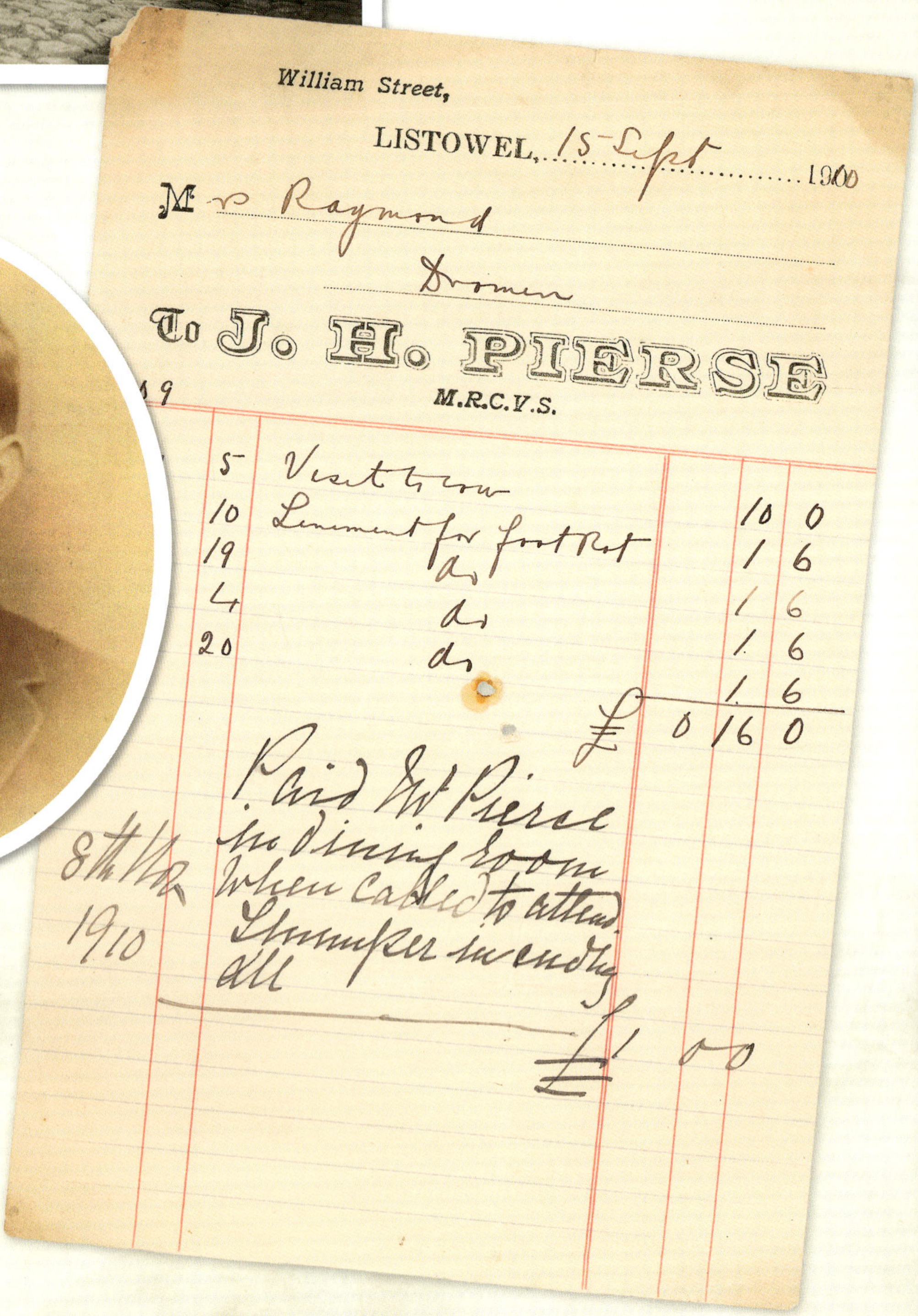

William Street,

LISTOWEL, 15 Sept 1900

Mrs Raymond

Dromin

To J. H. PIERSE

M.R.C.V.S.

5	Visit to cow			
10	Liniment for foot Rot		10	0
19	do		1	6
4	do		1	6
20	do		1	6
			1	6
		£ 0	16	0

Paid Mr Pierce in dining room when called to attend Stumper in ending all

8th Mar 1910

£1 0 0

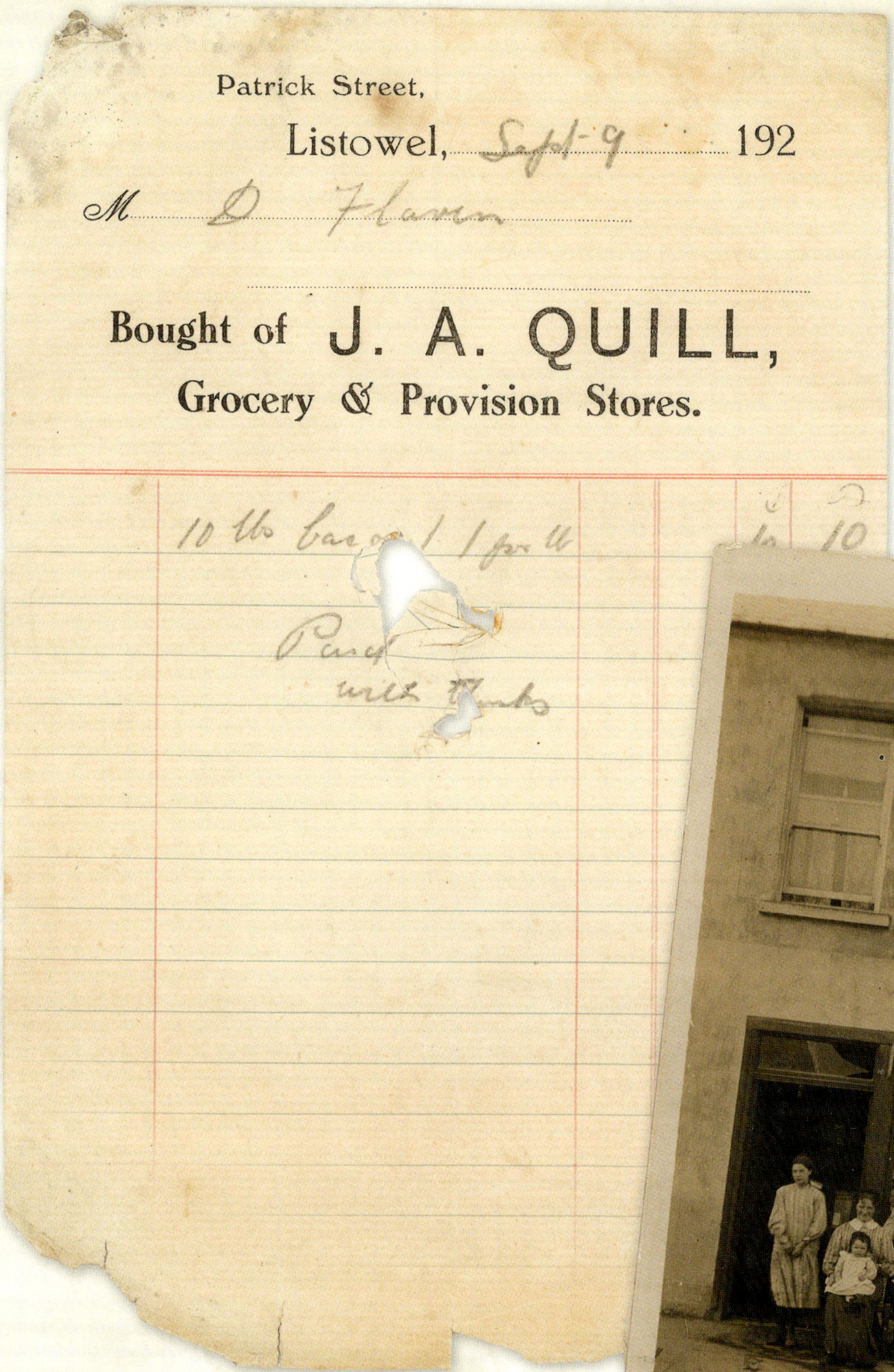

Patrick Street,

Listowel, Sept 9 192

M D Flavin

Bought of J. A. QUILL,

Grocery & Provision Stores.

10 lbs bacon 1/ [illegible] 10

Paid with thanks

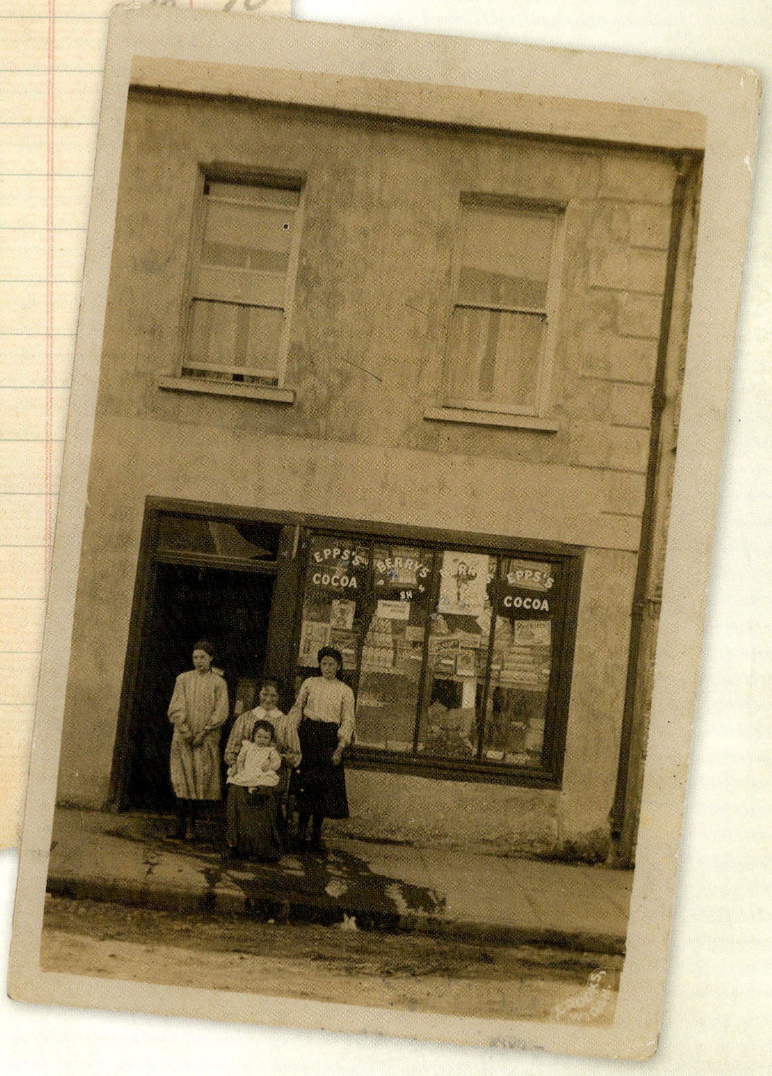

32 Upper William Street

Letterhead of the Grocery and Provision store belonging to Julia Ann Quill, wife of Denis Quill. Denis worked as a law clerk for the solicitor firm of Matthew J. Byrne. Both he and his brother Martin were very active during the War of Independence and spent many months on the run as members of the North Kerry flying column. Pictured, in 1914, outside the Quill shop front, is Mary Ann Relihan holding her daughter Bessie, with two of Mary Ann's younger sisters from Lacca West, Duagh. The Relihan family rented Quill's shop, eventually buying a public house further down the street. In a cluttered window, Epps's cocoa is well advertised; this was one of the prominent night caps of the nineteenth century.

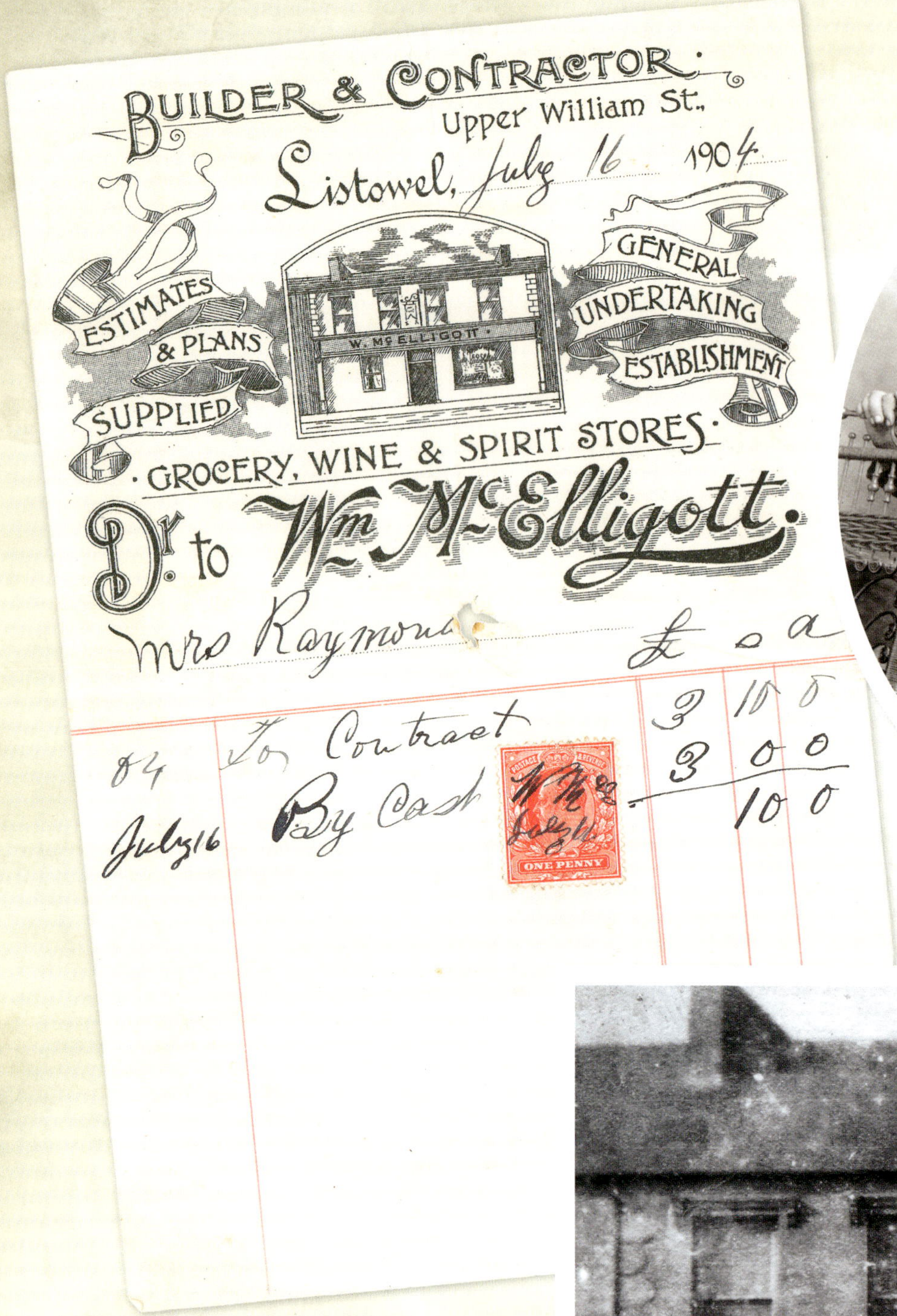
BUILDER & CONTRACTOR:
Upper William St.,
Listowel, July 16 1904
ESTIMATES & PLANS SUPPLIED
GENERAL UNDERTAKING ESTABLISHMENT
GROCERY, WINE & SPIRIT STORES.
Dr. to Wm McElligott.
Mrs Raymond

		£	s	d
04	To Contract	3	10	0
July 16	By Cash	3	0	0
			10	0

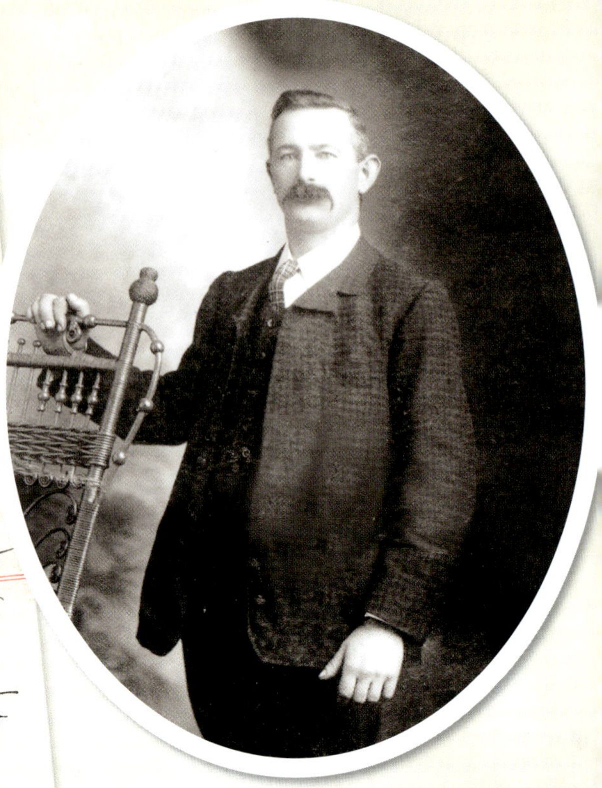

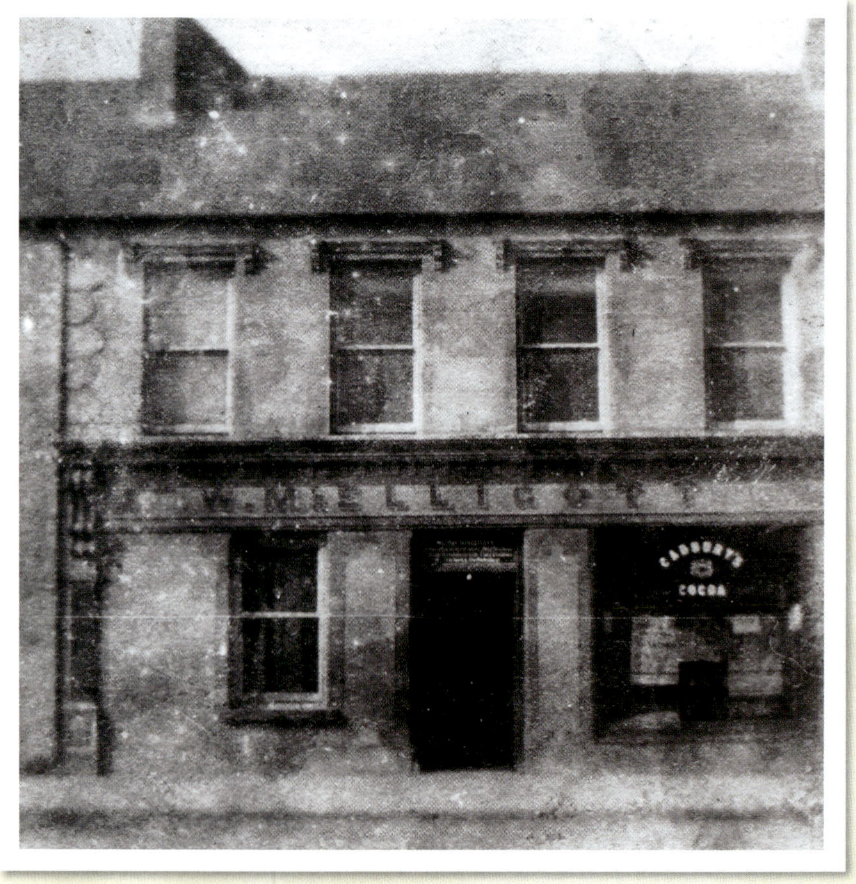

28 Upper William Street
The faded image of McElligott's shop front is more than compensated by a most artistic billhead. William McElligott built and ran an extensive business in Upper William Street from the 1880s. This encompassed a grocery, wine and spirit store, and a building contracting and undertaking establishment. The McElligotts sold their business to returned emigrants Michael and Kate O'Connor in 1907 and went to Sacramento, California. The O'Connors still run the public house and it is affectionately known as 'Mike the Pies'.

26 Upper William Street

Having served his time as a cooper in Kirby's of the Square, Lar Buckley first opened a business in Church Street, and in the 1890s he built two houses in the quickly developing Upper William Street area. Here his cooperage thrived. Lar died in 1933 and the business continued under his son Paddy, until his death in 1953. Lar and Patrick, pictured right, were the town's last coopers. It is worth mentioning that Lar Buckley's eldest daughter, Kathy, went to America in 1906. Prior to that she had worked as cook for the Huggard family at their hotel in Waterville.

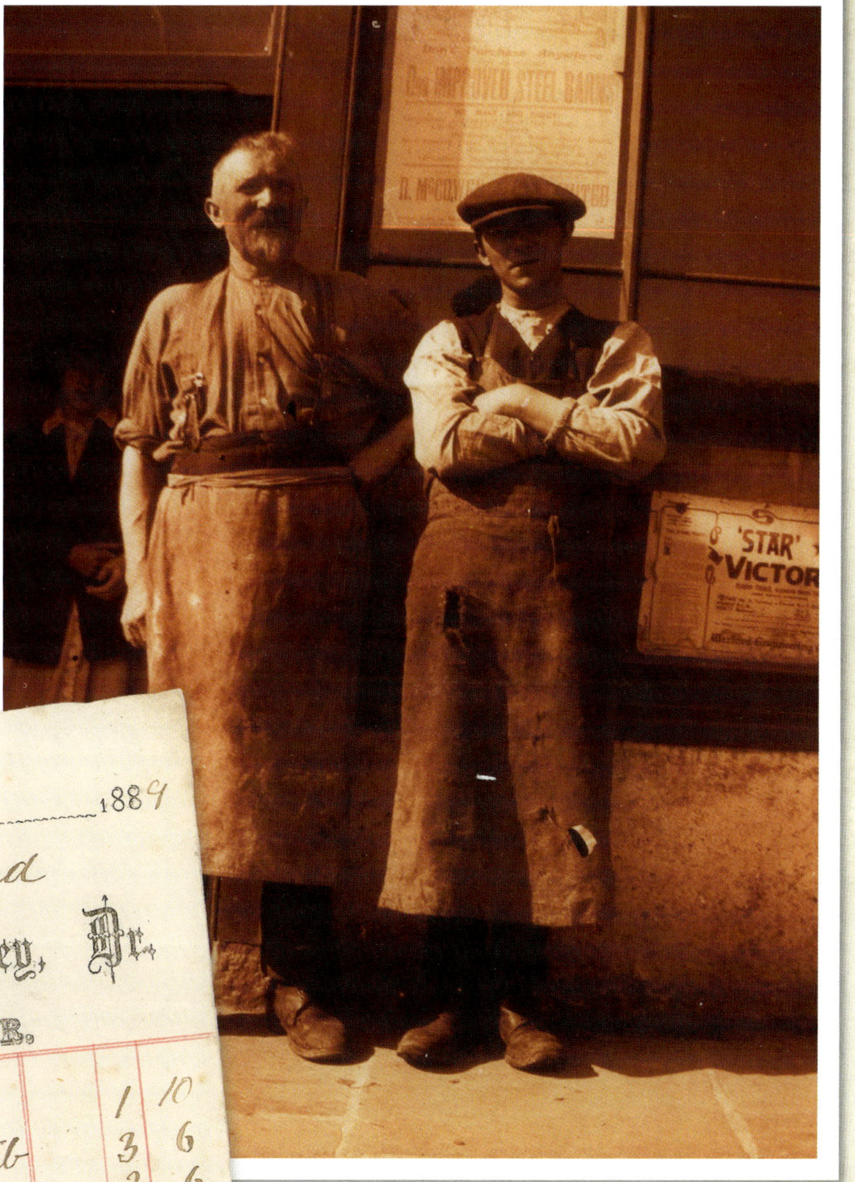

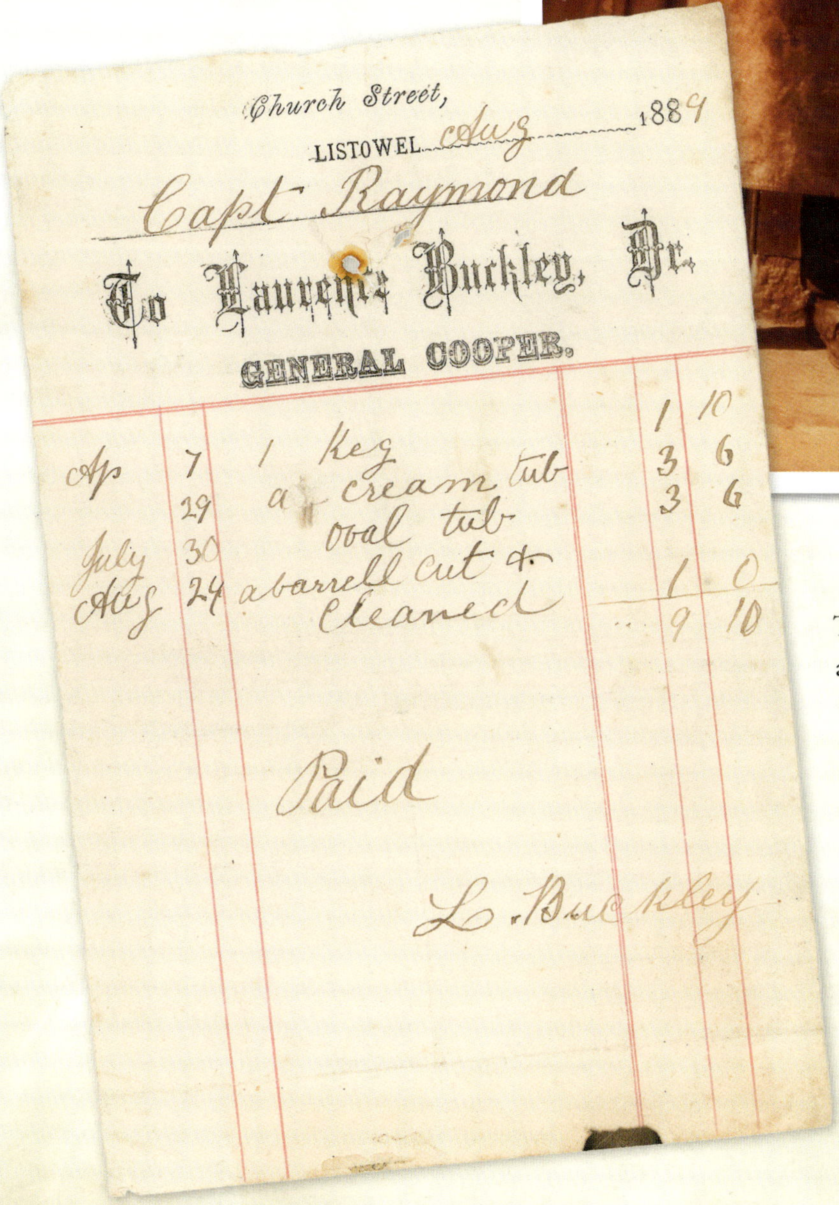

Church Street,
LISTOWEL Aug 1889
Capt Raymond
To Laurence Buckley, Dr.
GENERAL COOPER.

			1	10
Ap	7	1 keg	3	6
	29	a cream tub	3	6
July	30	oval tub		
Aug	24	a barrell cut & cleaned	1	0
			9	10

Paid

L. Buckley

That year, merchant banker, J.P. Morgan, and a group of friends had stayed at the hotel and had been so impressed with the cooking that he invited her to join his kitchen staff at his mansion at Hartford, Connecticut. Kathy was later invited by President Calvin Coolidge to take charge of the White House kitchens; she remained in this job during the later Presidencies of Hoover and Roosevelt.

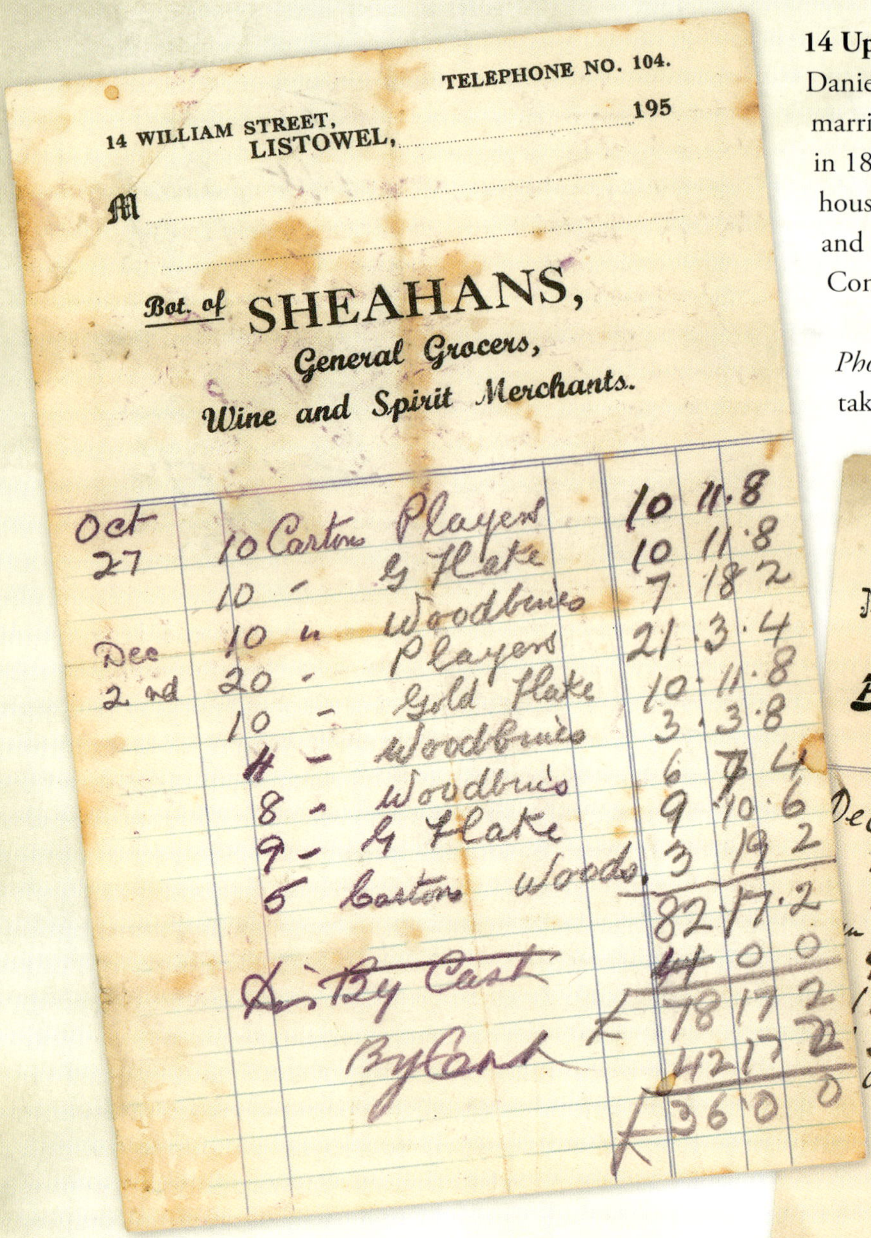
TELEPHONE NO. 104.
14 WILLIAM STREET, LISTOWEL, 195
M
Bot. of SHEAHANS,
General Grocers,
Wine and Spirit Merchants.

Oct 27	10 Cartons Players	10	11	8
	10 - G Flake	10	11	8
	10 " Woodbines	7	18	2
Dec 2nd	20 - Players	21	3	4
	10 - Gold Flake	10	11	8
	4 - Woodbines	3	3	8
	8 - Woodbines	6	7	4
	9 - G Flake	9	10	6
	5 Cartons Woods	3	19	2
		82	17	2
	~~By Cash~~	~~4~~	0	0
	£	78	17	2
	By Cash	42	17	2
		£36	0	0

14 Upper William Street

Daniel Sheahan from Ardagh, County Limerick, married Julia Murphy, daughter of Maurice Murphy, in 1896 and took over the running of the public house. The business was let to their son William and his wife Lena. It is now run by their grandson, Conor O'Doherty.

Photo: Sheahan's shop frontage with Mary Perryman, taken in the early 1950s.

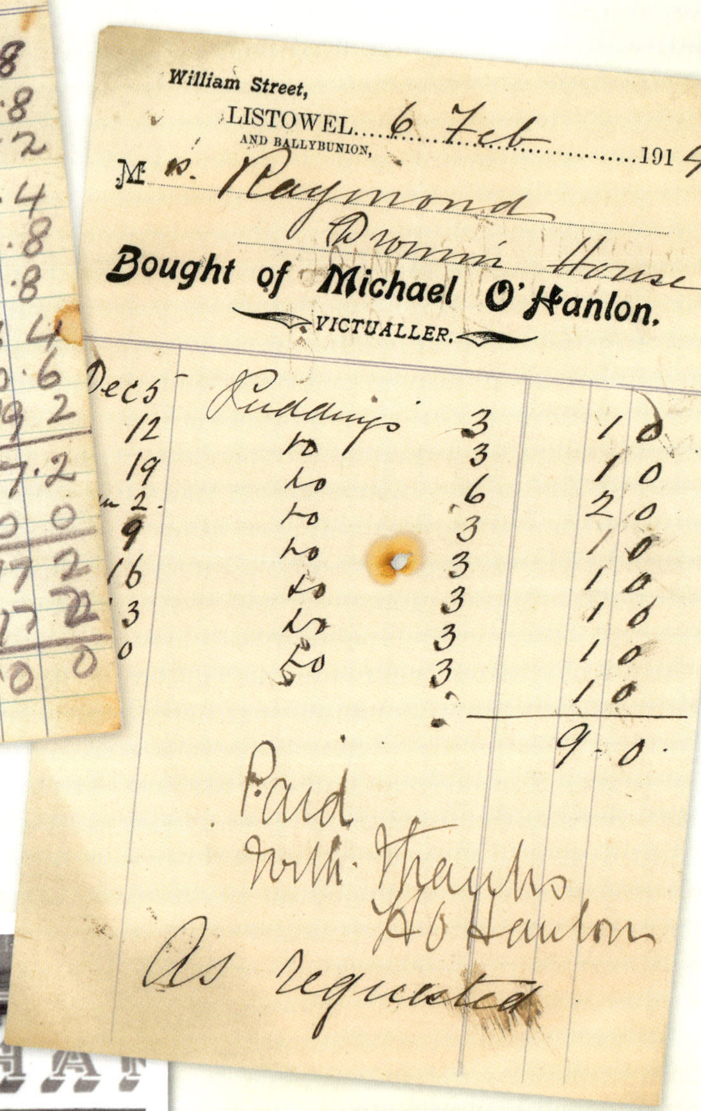
William Street,
LISTOWEL 6 Feb 1914
AND BALLYBUNION,
Mrs. Raymond Dromin House
Bought of Michael O'Hanlon.
VICTUALLER.

Dec 5	Puddings	3	1	0
12	do	3	1	0
19	do	6	2	0
Jan 2	do	3	1	0
9	do	3	1	0
16	do	3	1	0
23	do	3	1	0
30	do	3	1	0
			9	0

Paid with thanks
M O Hanlon
As requested

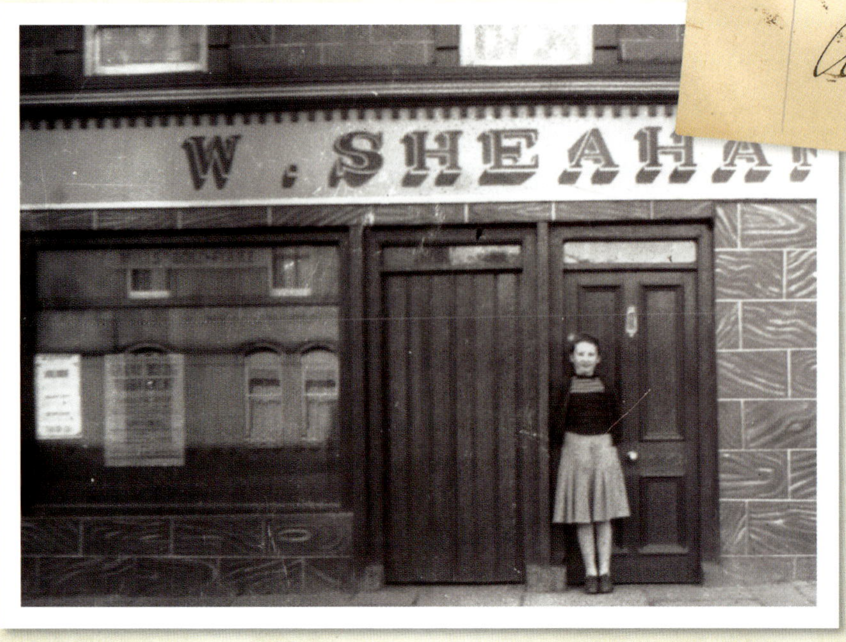

16 Upper William Street

Michael O'Hanlon followed his father Charles into the butchering business at his home at 16, Upper William Street. Michael's son, Michael Evangelist (he was known as Vangey) and grandson, also Michael, trained as dentists. They had their surgery in the family home. The practice closed when Michael Junior retired in 2009.

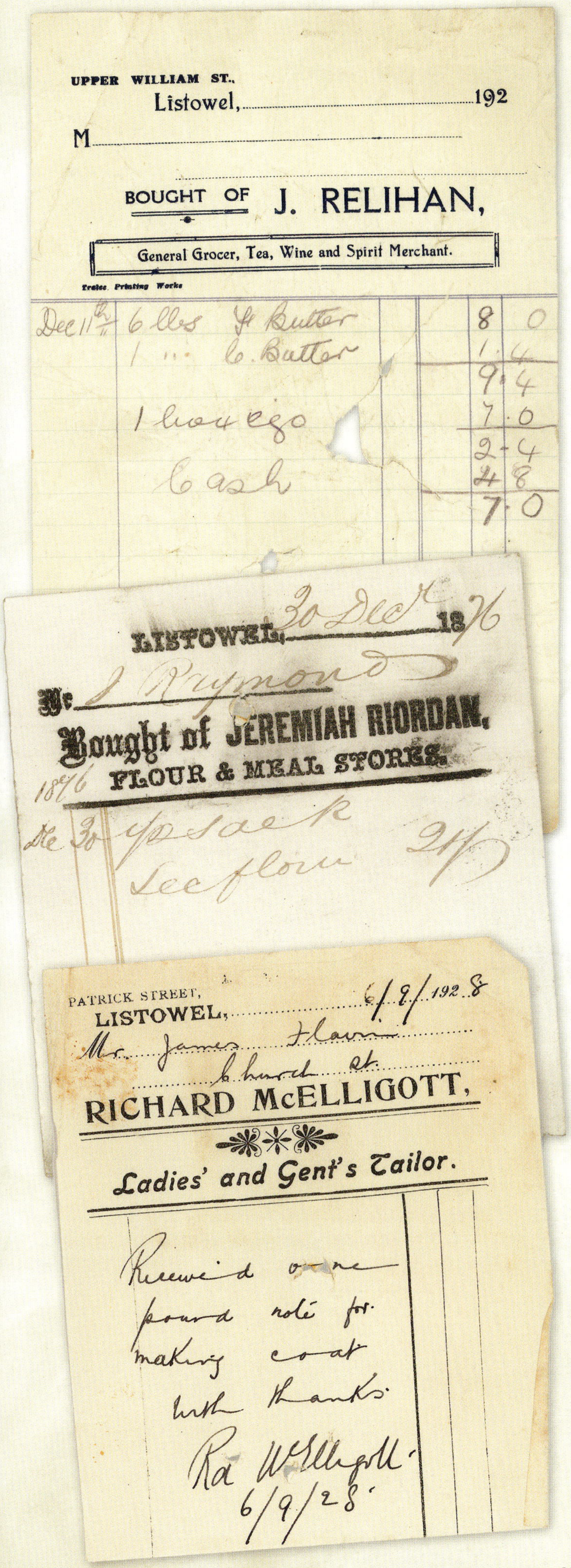

UPPER WILLIAM ST.,
Listowel, ...192
M..........

BOUGHT OF J. RELIHAN,

General Grocer, Tea, Wine and Spirit Merchant.

Tralee Printing Works

Dec 11	6 lbs F. Butter	8 0
	1 .. C. Butter	1 4
		9 4
	1 box eggs	7 0
		2 4
	Cash	4 8
		7 0

LISTOWEL, 30 Dec 1876

Mr J Raymond

Bought of JEREMIAH RIORDAN,
FLOUR & MEAL STORES.

1876 Dec 30 1/2 sack Sec flour 21/

PATRICK STREET,
LISTOWEL, 6/9/1928
Mr James Flavin
Church St.

RICHARD McELLIGOTT,
Ladies' and Gent's Tailor.

Received one pound note for making coat with thanks.
Rd McElligott
6/9/28

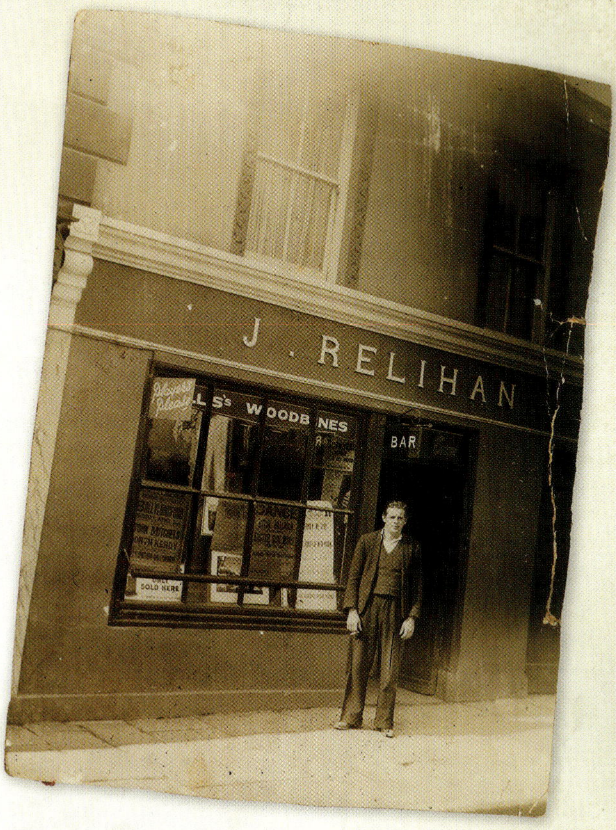

12 Upper William Street

A collage of billheads of various owners and occupiers of 12 Upper William Street.

The public house has had many owners since it was built over 150 years ago. Jeremiah Riordan founded his flour and meal store in 1876. Subsequently, Thomas Molyneaux, Tea, Wine & Spirit Merchant, owned the premises and after him came James O'Sullivan from Ballylongford. It was then purchased by John and Mary Ann Relihan. During their time, Richard McElligott, tailor (brother of Mary Ann's), later of the Bridge Road, had a room on the premises for his tailoring business. They were followed by Donie and Eve Finucane. Following extensive renovations it was sold to the Guinness Company. They put it forward as a prize in a marketing campaign in America. The winner, an American from New Jersey named Trevor O'Driscoll, retained it for a year before selling it to returned emigrants, Sean and Dara Costello.

Photo above: Jeremiah Reidy stands at the door in this 1950 image. The poster on the window presents us with a picture of the time. North Kerry are playing John Mitchels in the Senior County Championship, the Astor Cinema as well as showing films is hosting a dance on Easter Sunday Night; cigarette companies advertise, with Players, Woodbine and Gold Flake taking up space, while two Guinness signs tell us that Guinness only is sold here, and that the Guinness sold is direct from the wood.

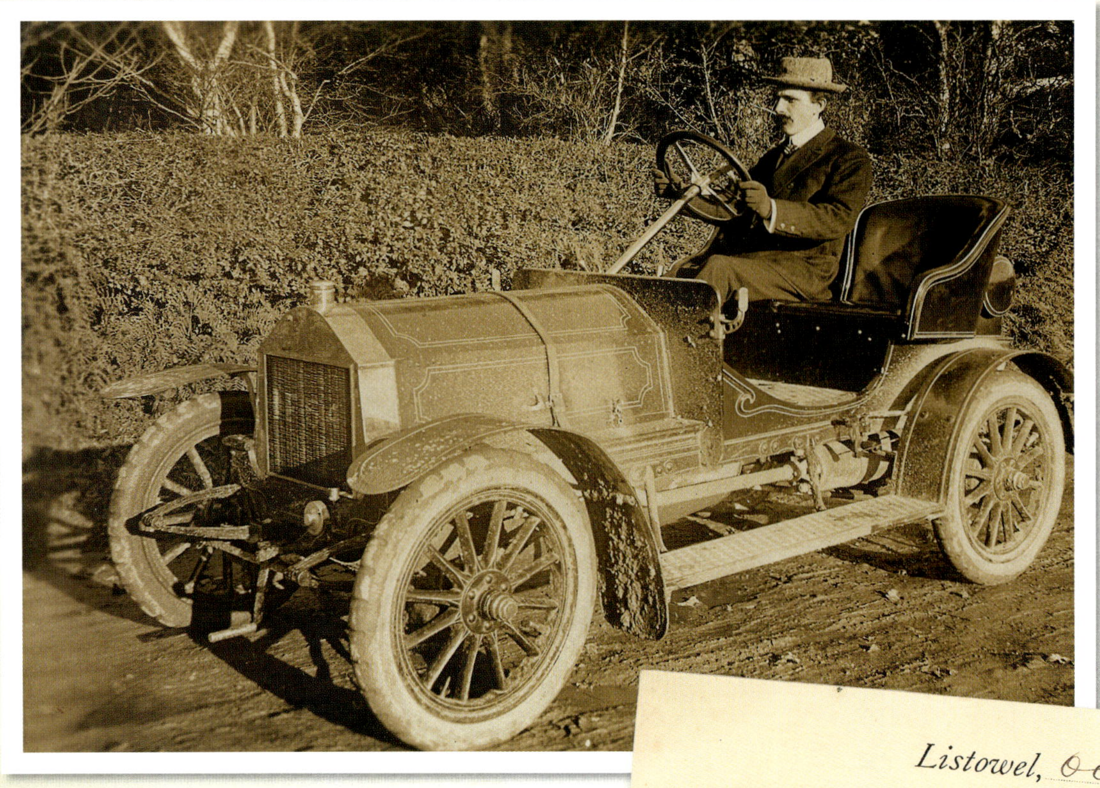

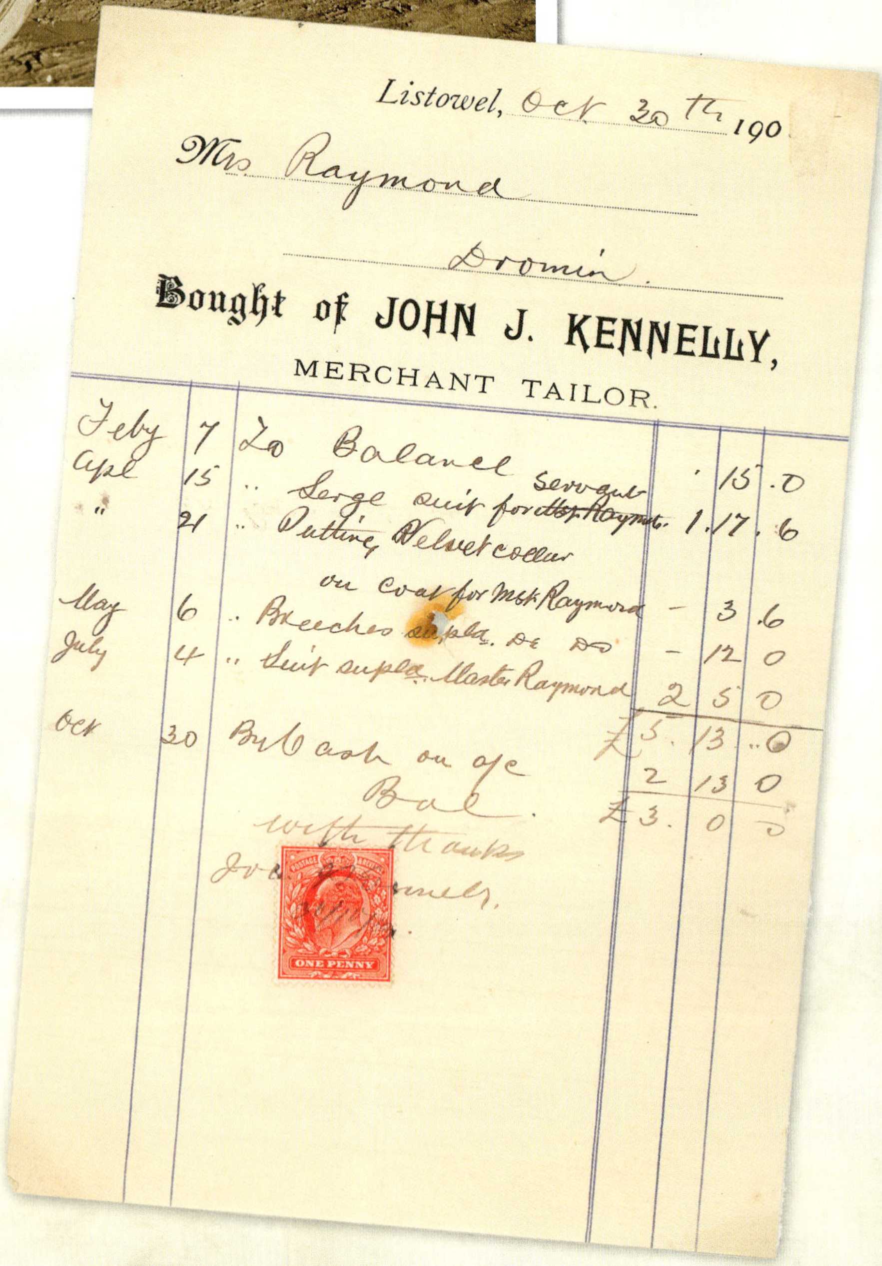

Listowel, Oct 20th 190

Mrs Raymond

Dromin.

Bought of JOHN J. KENNELLY,

MERCHANT TAILOR.

			£	s.	d.
Feby	7	To Balance servant		15	0
Apl	15	.. Serge suit for Mst Raymond	1	17	6
"	21	.. Putting Velvet collar on coat for Mst Raymond	-	3	6
May	6	.. Breeches supld. Do Do	-	12	0
July	4	.. Suit supld. Master Raymond	2	5	0
			£5	13	6
Oct	20	By Cash on a/c	2	13	0
		Bal.	£3	0	0

with thanks

Jo. J. Kennelly

ONE PENNY

10 Upper William Street

John J. Kennelly from Knockanure set up his tailoring business at 10 Upper William Street in 1897, naming it, 'The Cloth Hall'. A keen motor enthusiast, he had one of the first motor cars in Listowel. The drapery shop still operates, under the management of John's son Matt and his wife Nellie.

Photo: J.J. Kennelly at the wheel of an early Studebaker.

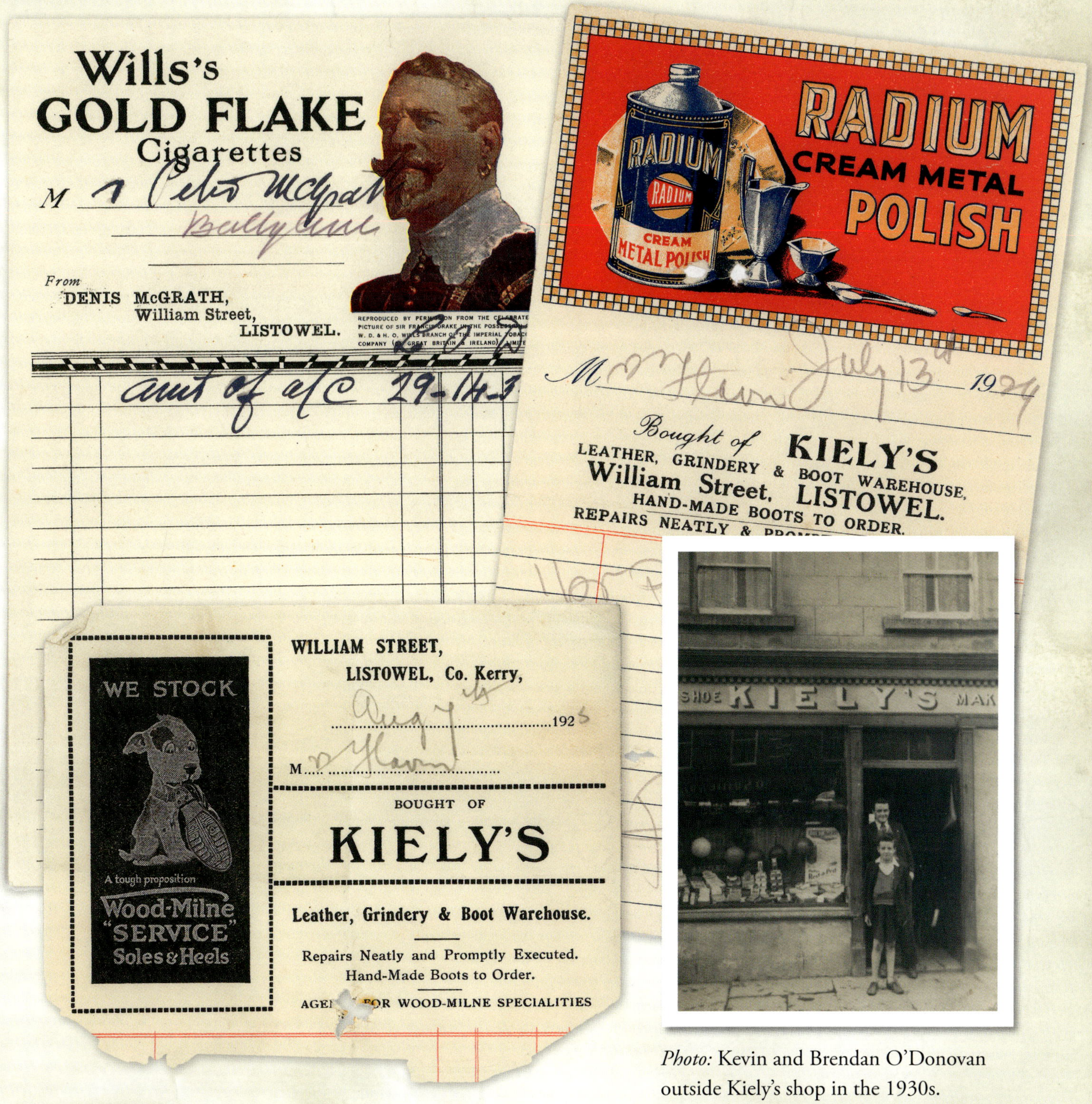
Wills's
GOLD FLAKE
Cigarettes

M

From
DENIS McGRATH,
William Street,
LISTOWEL.

REPRODUCED BY PERMISSION FROM THE CELEBRATED PICTURE OF SIR FRANCIS DRAKE IN THE POSSESSION OF W. D. & H. O. WILLS BRANCH OF THE IMPERIAL TOBACCO COMPANY (OF GREAT BRITAIN & IRELAND) LIMITED

amt of a/c 29-14-3

M July 13th 1924

Bought of KIELY'S
LEATHER, GRINDERY & BOOT WAREHOUSE,
William Street, LISTOWEL.
HAND-MADE BOOTS TO ORDER.
REPAIRS NEATLY & PROMPTLY

WILLIAM STREET,
LISTOWEL, Co. Kerry,

Aug 7th 1925

M

BOUGHT OF

KIELY'S

Leather, Grindery & Boot Warehouse.

Repairs Neatly and Promptly Executed.
Hand-Made Boots to Order.

AGENT FOR WOOD-MILNE SPECIALITIES

Photo: Kevin and Brendan O'Donovan outside Kiely's shop in the 1930s.

2 Upper William Street

Denis McGrath came from Coolaclarig, Listowel. He commenced work as a clerk in a shop owned by Patrick and Catherine Clancy, Lower William Street. Having gained sufficient experience in the trade he seized the opportunity to go into business himself, when the property of Edward R. Stack, The Arch Bar, Upper William Street came on the market. His daughter Bebe married Tom Stack of Cahirdown and their son, Martin, now operates an off licence at 2 Upper William Street.

4 Upper William Street

Michael Kiely, a master boot and shoemaker, started his business on the street in the latter part of the 1800s. He was assisted by his son John. His daughter Mary Ann left to train as a teacher in England where she met and married her husband Jim O'Donovan, a Welshman. Mary Ann came home to rear her family and assist in the running of the business. One son, Kevin, was involved in the business. When a downturn came in the shoe repair trade, Kevin started a news agency and bookshop. This business was developed further by his son Stephen. The shop closed in 2011.

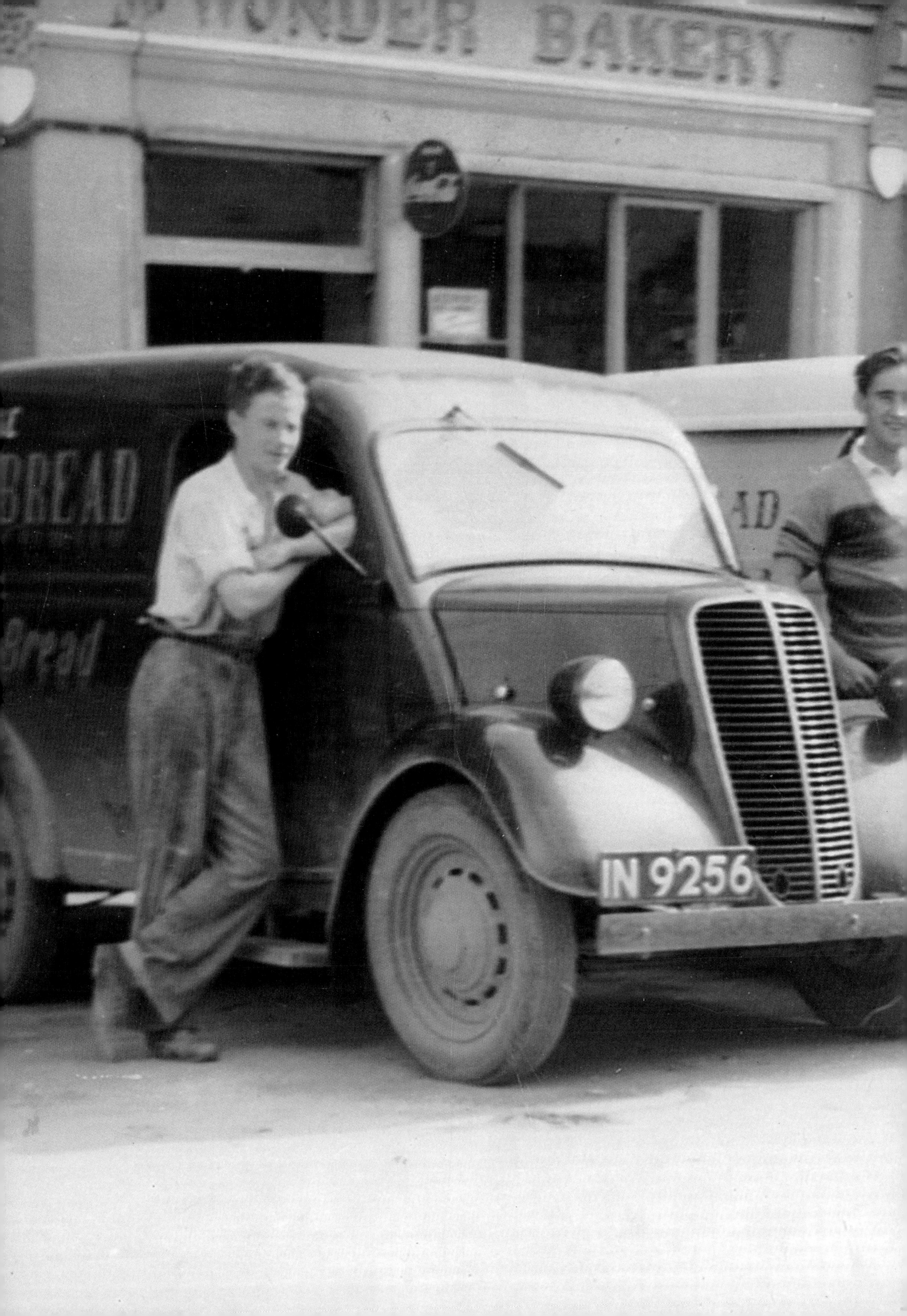
WONDER BAKERY
BREAD
Bread
IN 9256

Chapter 3

CHARLES STREET

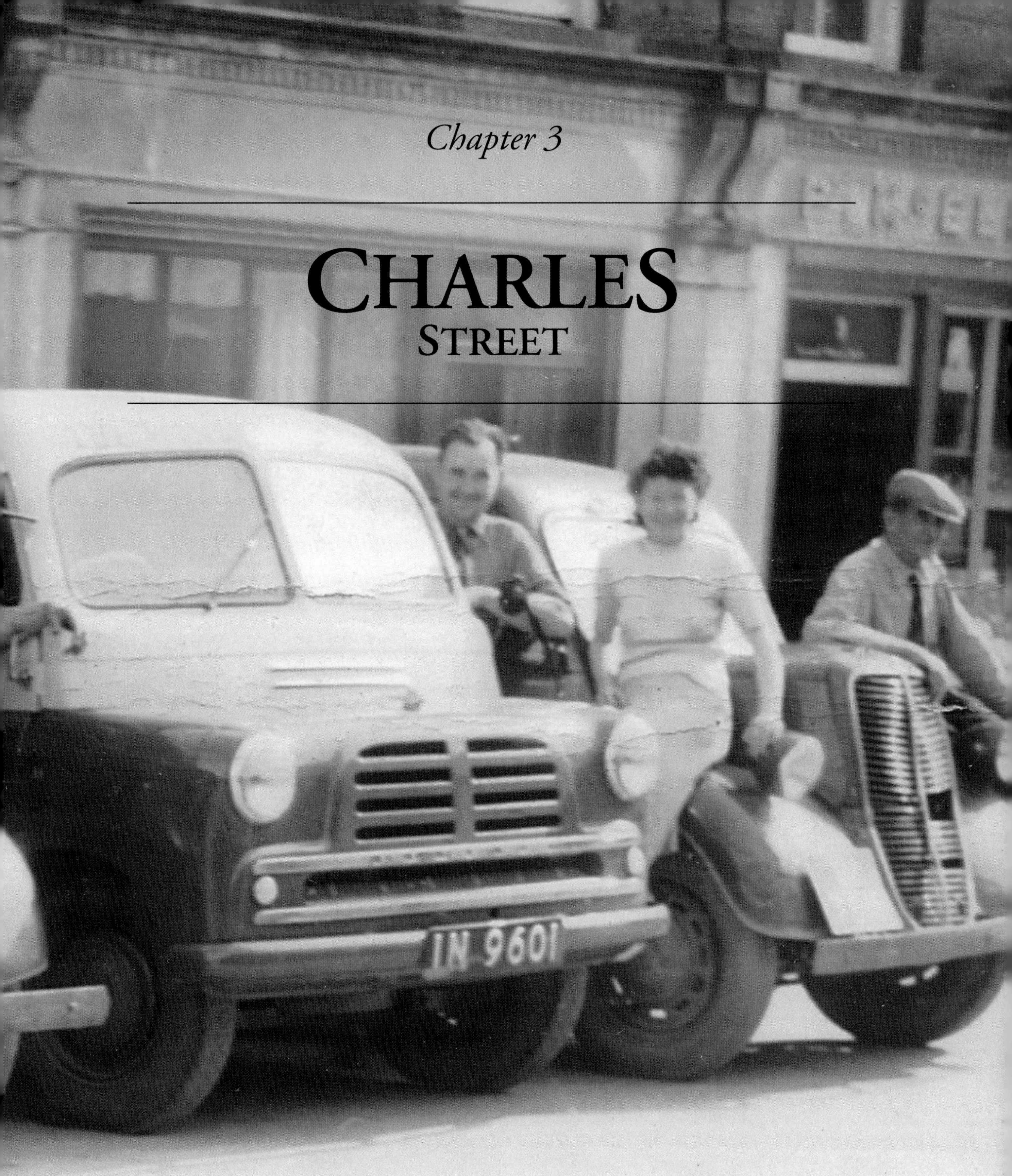

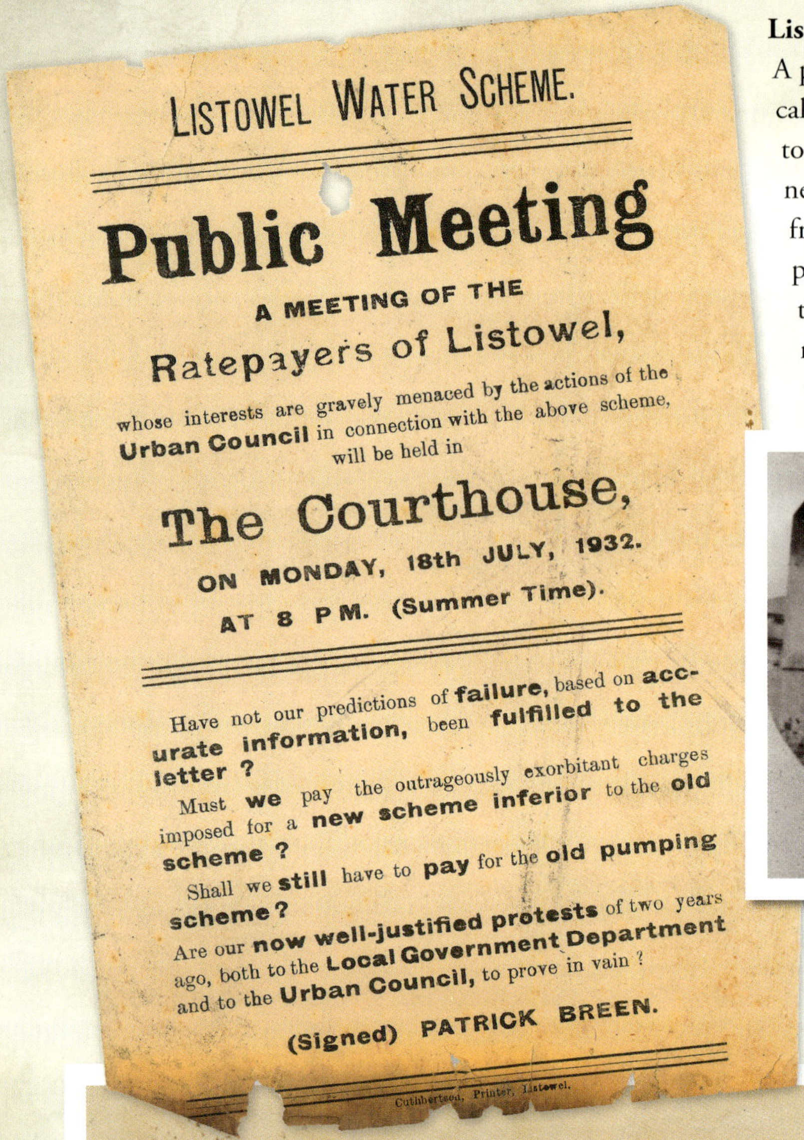

LISTOWEL WATER SCHEME.

Public Meeting

A MEETING OF THE

Ratepayers of Listowel,

whose interests are gravely menaced by the actions of the **Urban Council** in connection with the above scheme, will be held in

The Courthouse,

ON MONDAY, 18th JULY, 1932.

AT 8 P.M. (Summer Time).

Have not our predictions of **failure,** based on **accurate information,** been **fulfilled to the letter ?**

Must **we** pay the outrageously exorbitant charges imposed for a **new scheme inferior** to the **old scheme ?**

Shall we **still** have to **pay** for the **old pumping scheme?**

Are our **now well-justified protests** of two years ago, both to the **Local Government Department** and to the **Urban Council,** to prove in vain ?

(Signed) PATRICK BREEN.

Cuthbertson, Printer, Listowel.

Listowel Courthouse

A public meeting of the ratepayers of the Listowel was called by Patrick Breen, a Professor at St Michael's College, to voice their displeasure and concern over the proposed new water scheme, which had been planned to bring water from Lacca near Duagh to a new reservoir and treatment plant at Ballygrennan, Listowel by gravity flow and from there to supply purified water to the town. Considerable resentment had built up over this, and this was justified when the scheme was abandoned.

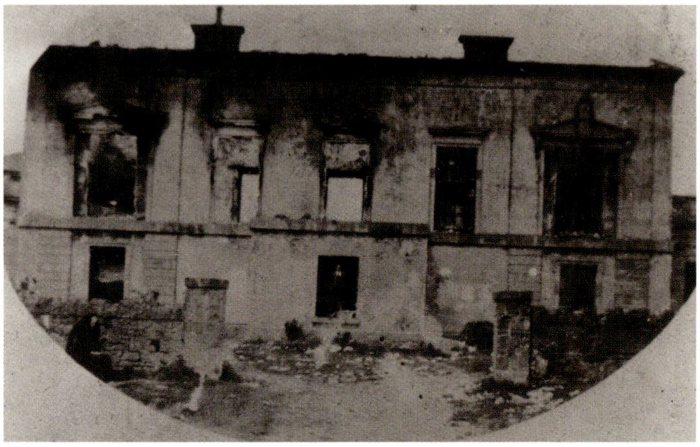

Photo below: The Courthouse which was built in the 1840s and, above, the burnt building in 1922 during the Civil War.

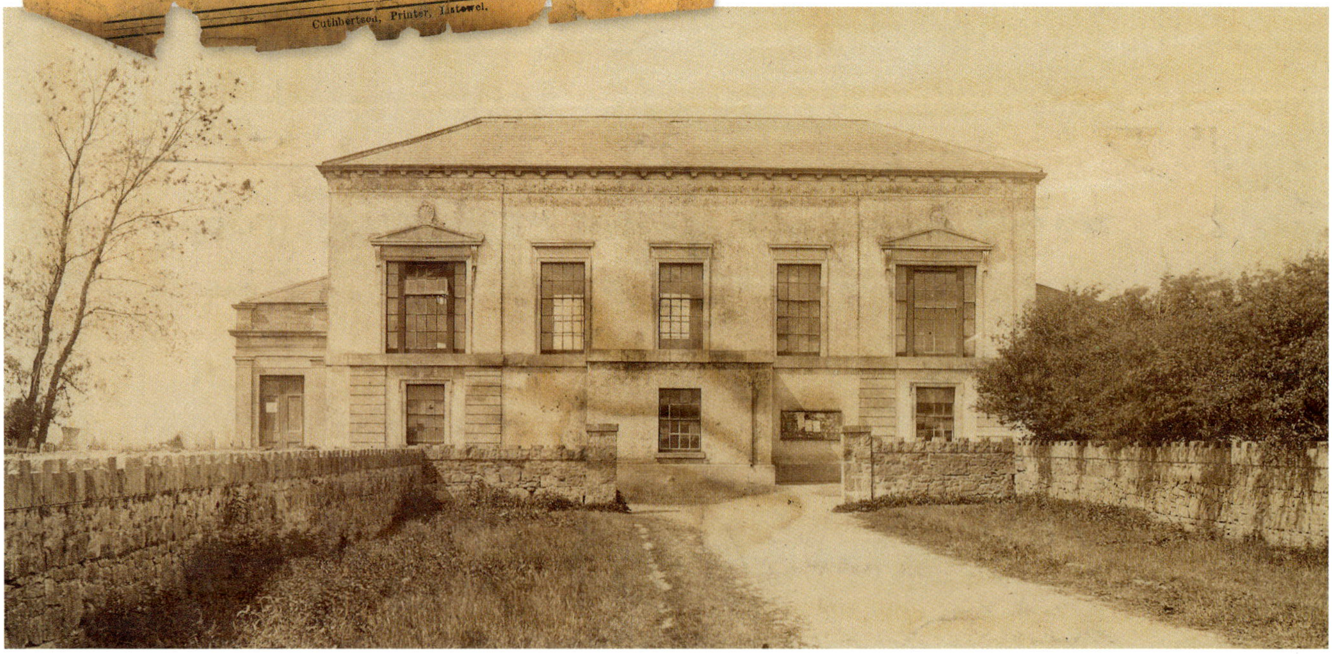

Previous pages: Paddy Carmody and his wife Margaret showed great enterprise when starting a bakery known as the 'Wonder Bakery' in their premises in Charles Street in the early 1950s. The house had previously been James Donoghue's Poultry store. The fleet of vans with sides emblazoned 'Make Wonder Bread your daily bread' traversed the roads of North Kerry and West Limerick for over a decade. The picture includes Maurice O'Connor, Vincent O'Carroll, Paddy & Margaret Carmody and Tom Carmody.

Tadhg Brennan, Colbert Street, blacksmith
Tadhg Brennan came from Lisselton to work for John Murphy at his blacksmith's business at Forge Lane in Listowel. Tadhg married Murphy's daughter Mae, and took over the running of the forge. He continued working at the business until his retirement in the early 1960s.

Below: Photograph of a Charles Street/Colbert Street group of the 1950s. Front (l to r): Michael Fitzgerald, John Horgan, Eleanor Dalton, Sheila Dillon, Ann Fitzgerald, Maura Brennan. Back (l to r): Mrs Catherine Fitzgerald, Paddy Dore & Marie Curtin, Margaret Horgan & Pat Horgan, Theresa Shine & Kathleen Shine, Lily Horgan, Joan O'Sullivan, Margaret Shine, On the window are Catherine McDonnell and Kay Hanrahan.

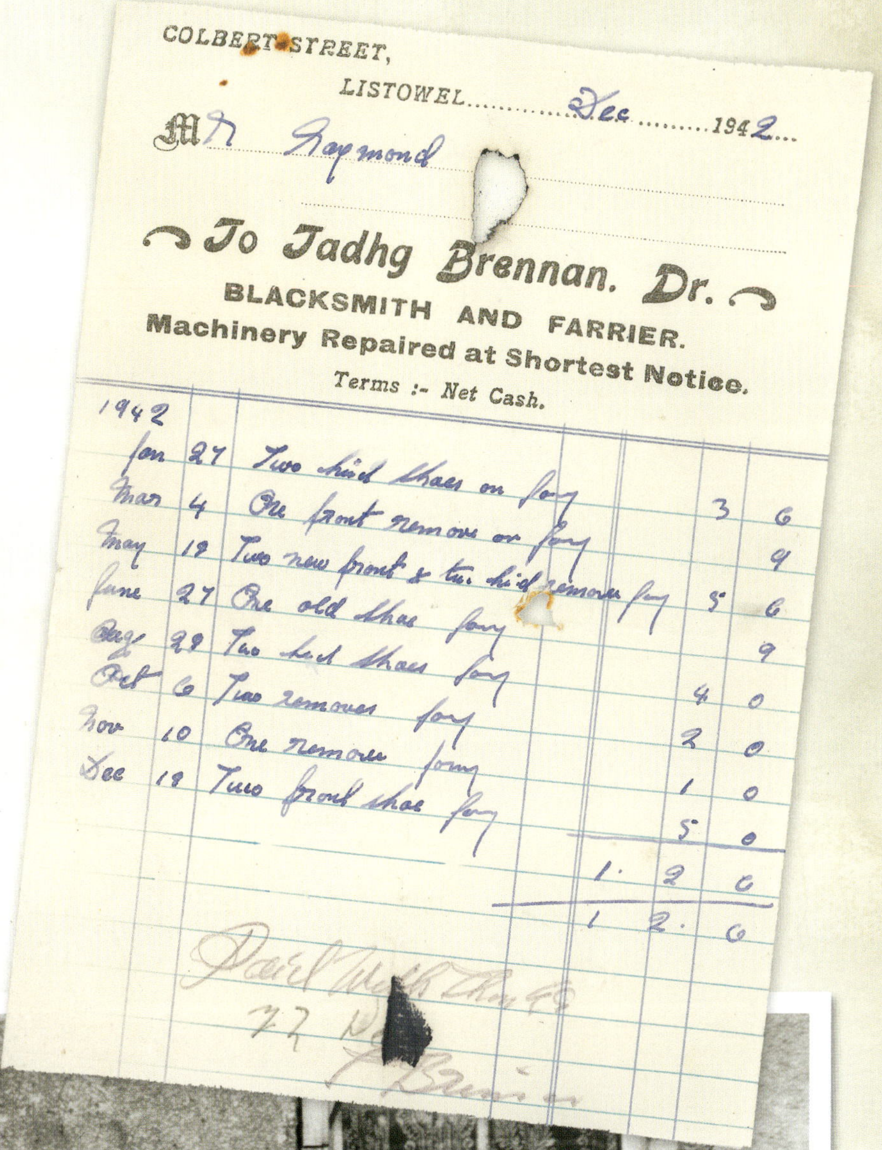
COLBERT STREET,
LISTOWEL .... Dec 1942
Mr Raymond

To Tadhg Brennan. Dr.
BLACKSMITH AND FARRIER.
Machinery Repaired at Shortest Notice.
Terms :- Net Cash.

1942				
Jan	27	Two hind shoes on fory	3	6
Mar	4	One front remove on fory		4
May	19	Two new front & two hind removes fory	5	6
June	27	One old shoe fory		9
Aug	29	Two hind shoes fory	4	0
Oct	6	Two removes fory	2	0
Nov	10	One remove fory	1	0
Dec	19	Two front shoes fory	5	0
			1. 2	0
			1 2.	0

Paid with thanks
22 Dec
T. Brennan

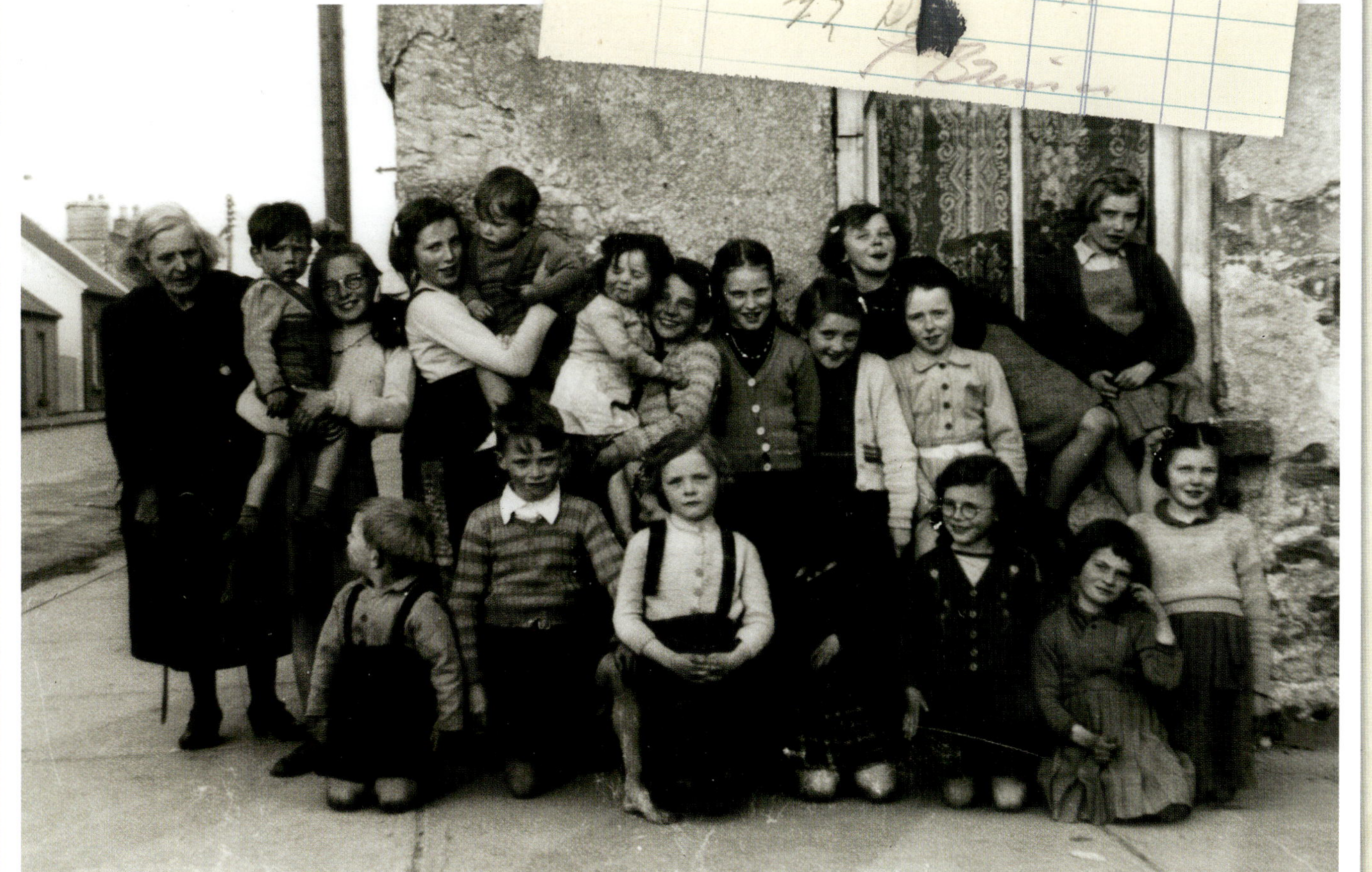

13 & 34 Charles Street

Timothy Mortell came to Listowel from County Cork in the early 1900s. He purchased premises in Charles Street which he converted into an egg store. He and his workmen travelled the roads of North Kerry in horse and car collecting eggs, fowl, animal hides, feathers and all kinds of scrap. In the 1930s a relation of Mortell's, James O'Donoghue came from America and bought the business from Mortell, who then moved to 34 Charles Street, where he continued trading on a much lesser scale.

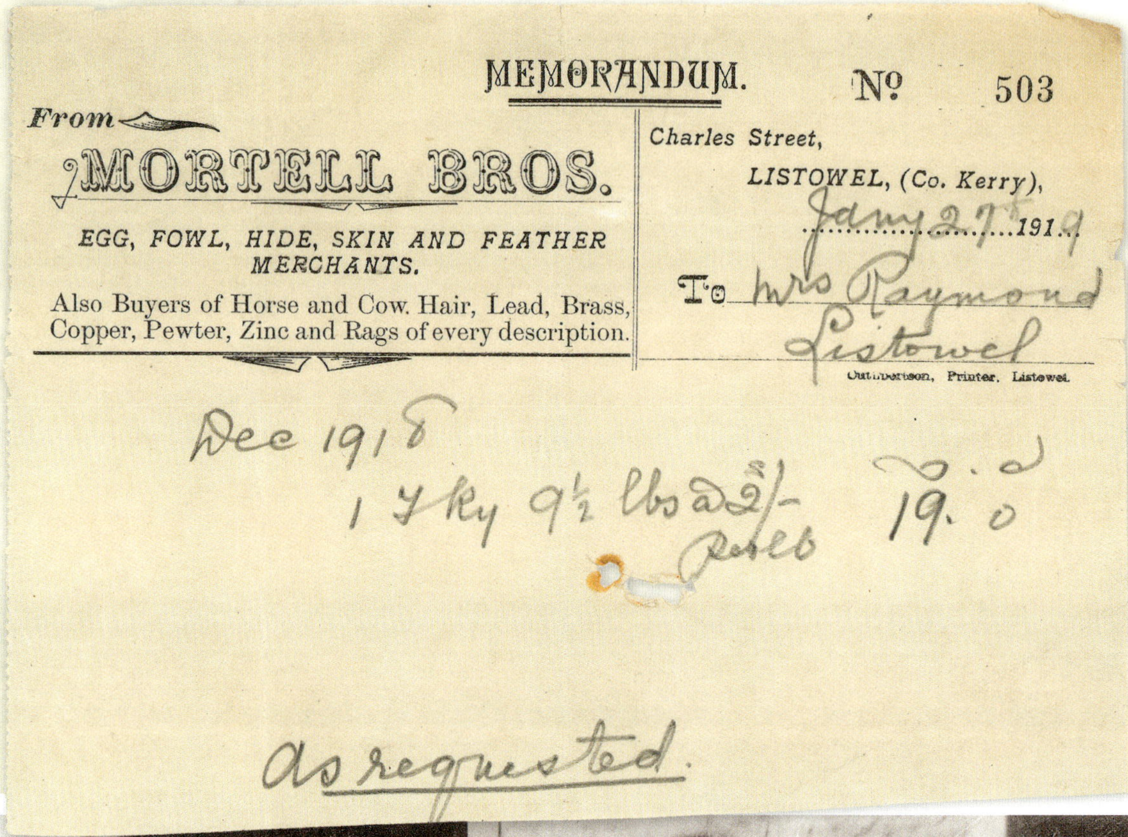
MEMORANDUM. № 503

From MORTELL BROS.

EGG, FOWL, HIDE, SKIN AND FEATHER MERCHANTS.

Also Buyers of Horse and Cow Hair, Lead, Brass, Copper, Pewter, Zinc and Rags of every description.

Charles Street,
LISTOWEL, (Co. Kerry),
Jany 27th 1919

To Mrs Raymond
Listowel

Cuthbertson, Printer, Listowel.

Dec 1918
1 7 ky 9½ lbs @ 2/- 19.0

As requested.

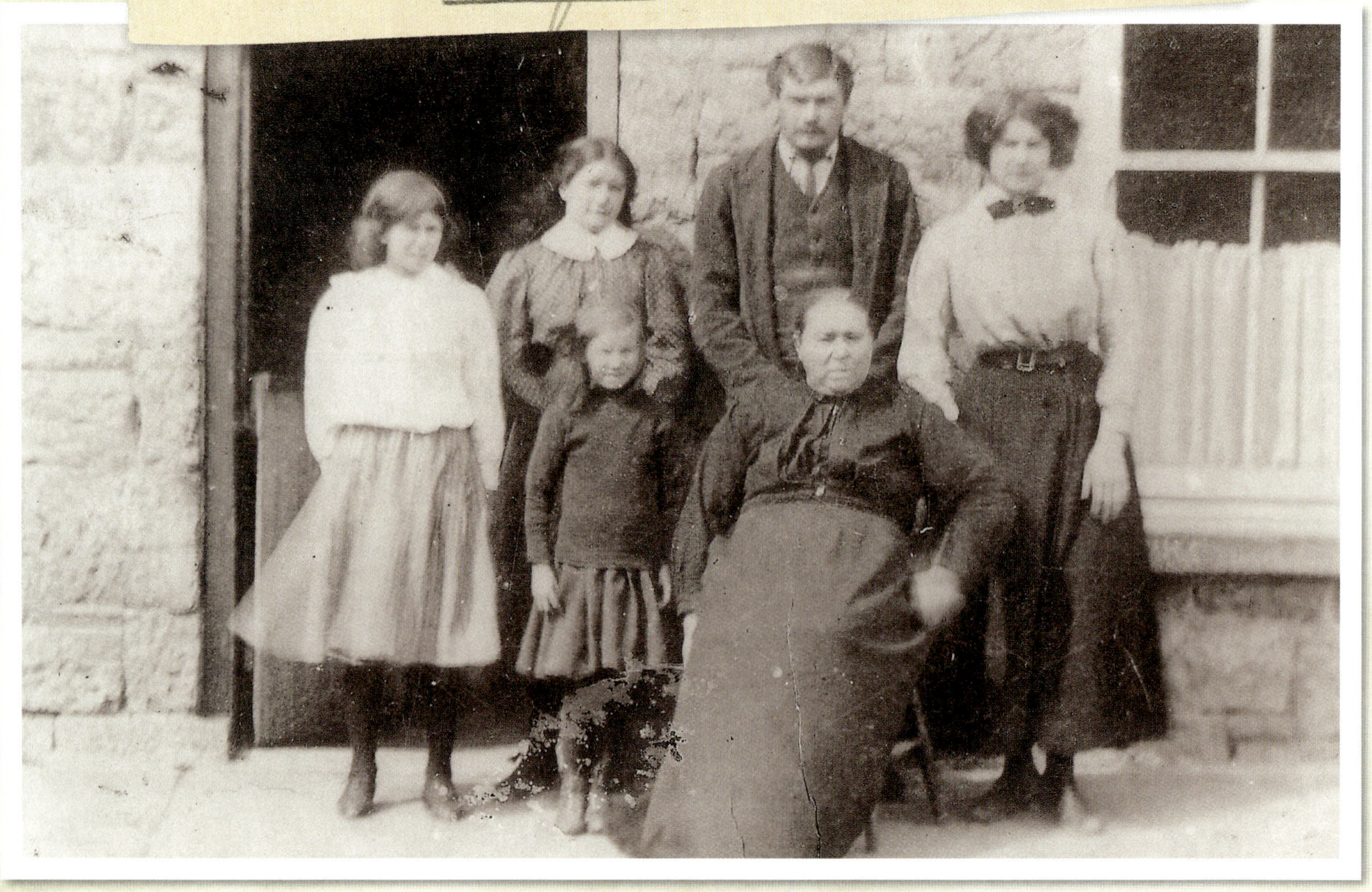

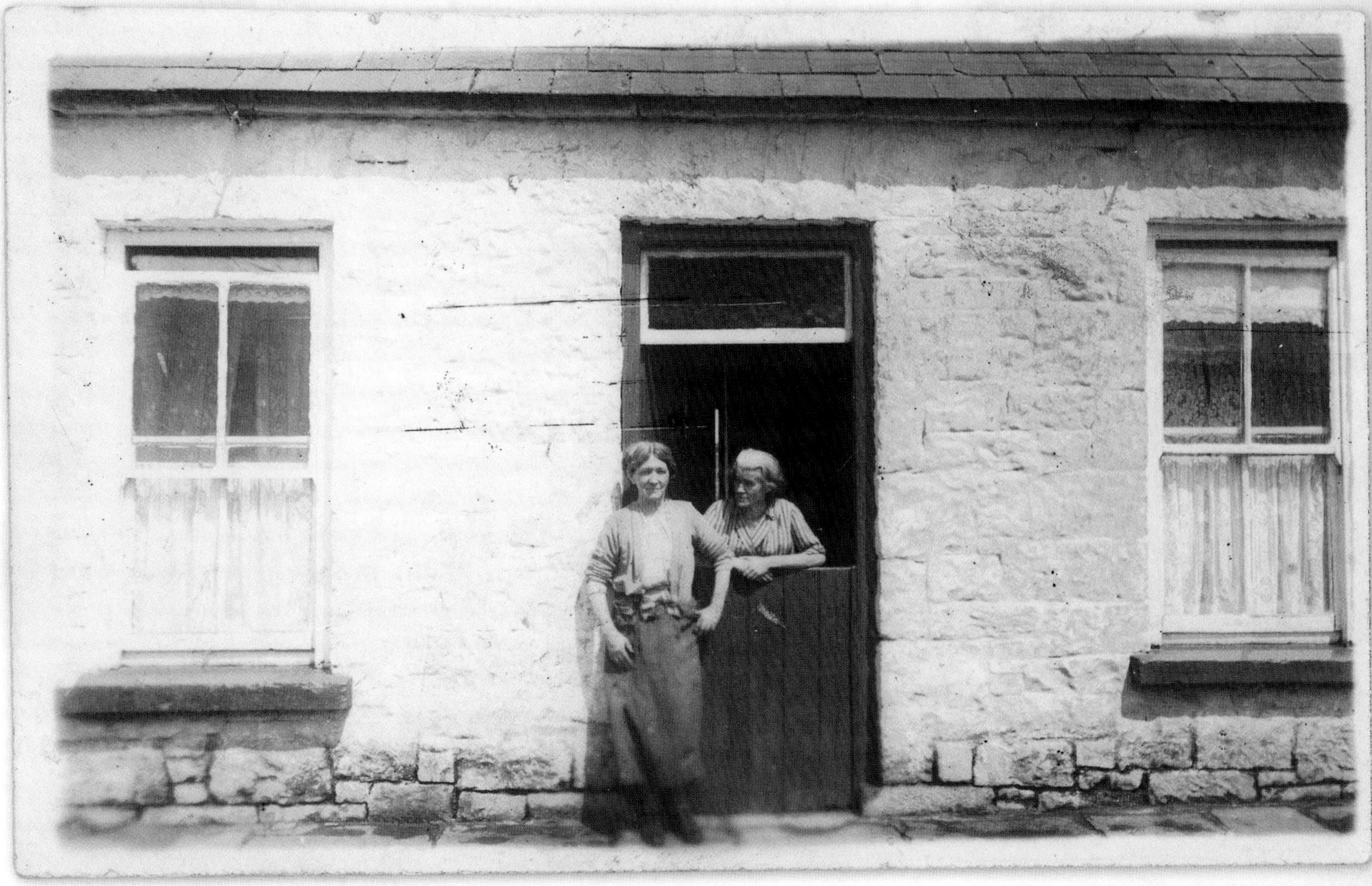

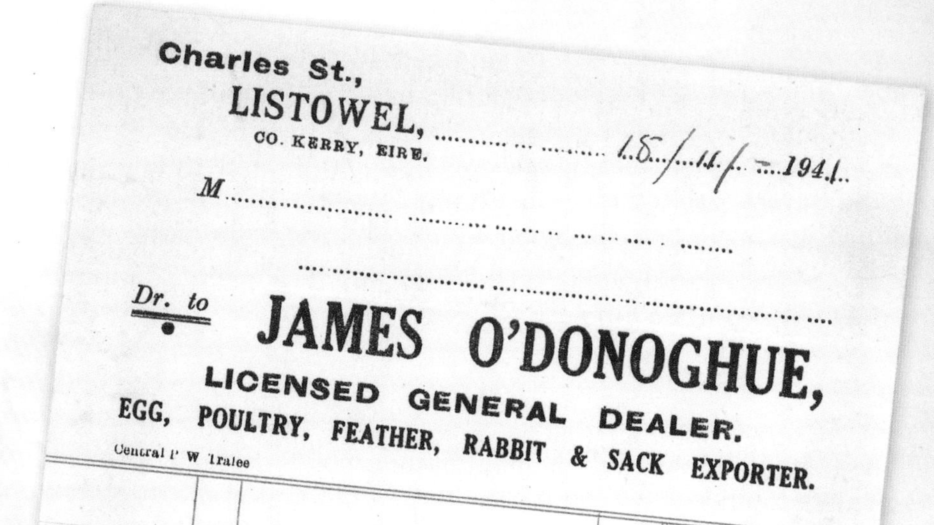

Charles St.,
LISTOWEL, ... 15/11/1941
CO. KERRY, EIRE.

M......................................

Dr. to **JAMES O'DONOGHUE,**
LICENSED GENERAL DEALER.
EGG, POULTRY, FEATHER, RABBIT & SACK EXPORTER.
Central P W Tralee

2	Rabbits @ 2/2	4	4

38 Charles Street
Mrs. Catherine Carmody, wife of John Carmody, plumber and tinsmith, with five of her children, circa 1911, outside the family home in Charles Street.

Photo left: Back (l to r): Eileen, Katherine, William and Margaret. Front: Genevieve (Jenny) and Catherine (sitting)

14 Charles Street
Mary and Pauline Scanlon (pictured above) outside the family home at 14 Charles Street, circa 1911. The house front was restored in 2010 to its original cut stone, and half door, by granddaughter Carmel Scanlon and husband Martin Griffin.

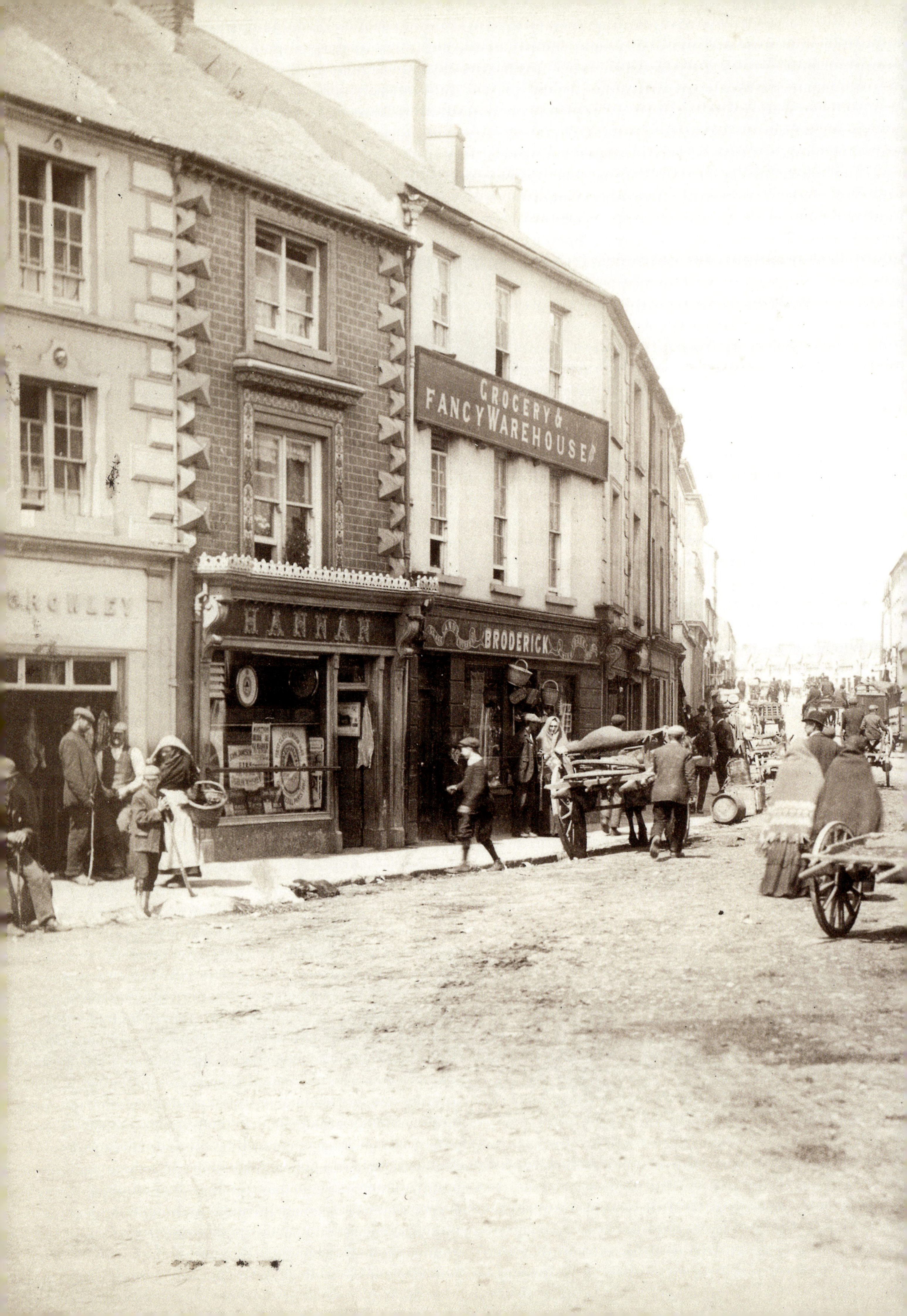
GROCERY &
FANCY WAREHOUSE
CROWLEY
HANNAN
BRODERICK

Chapter 4

LOWER WILLIAM STREET

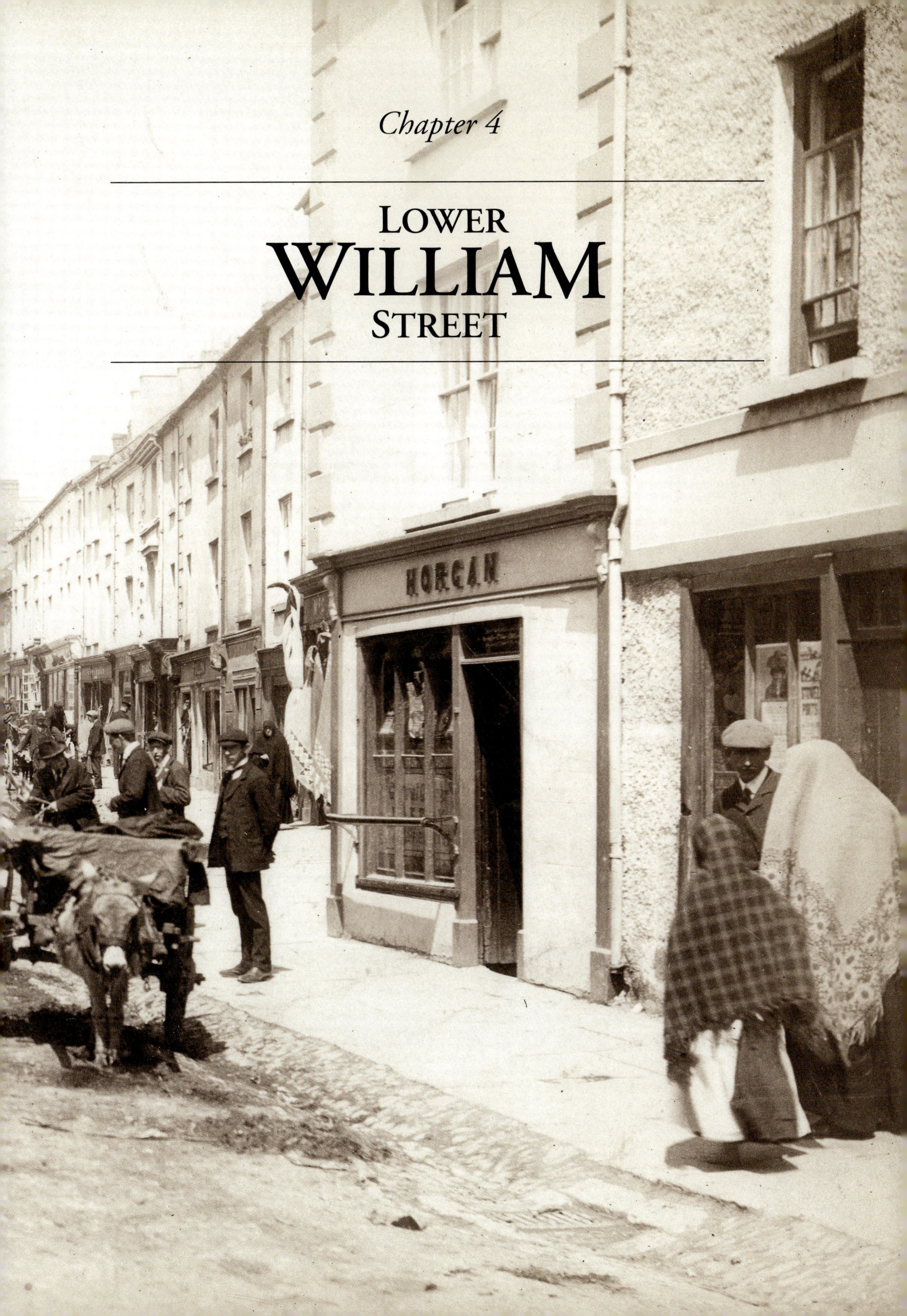

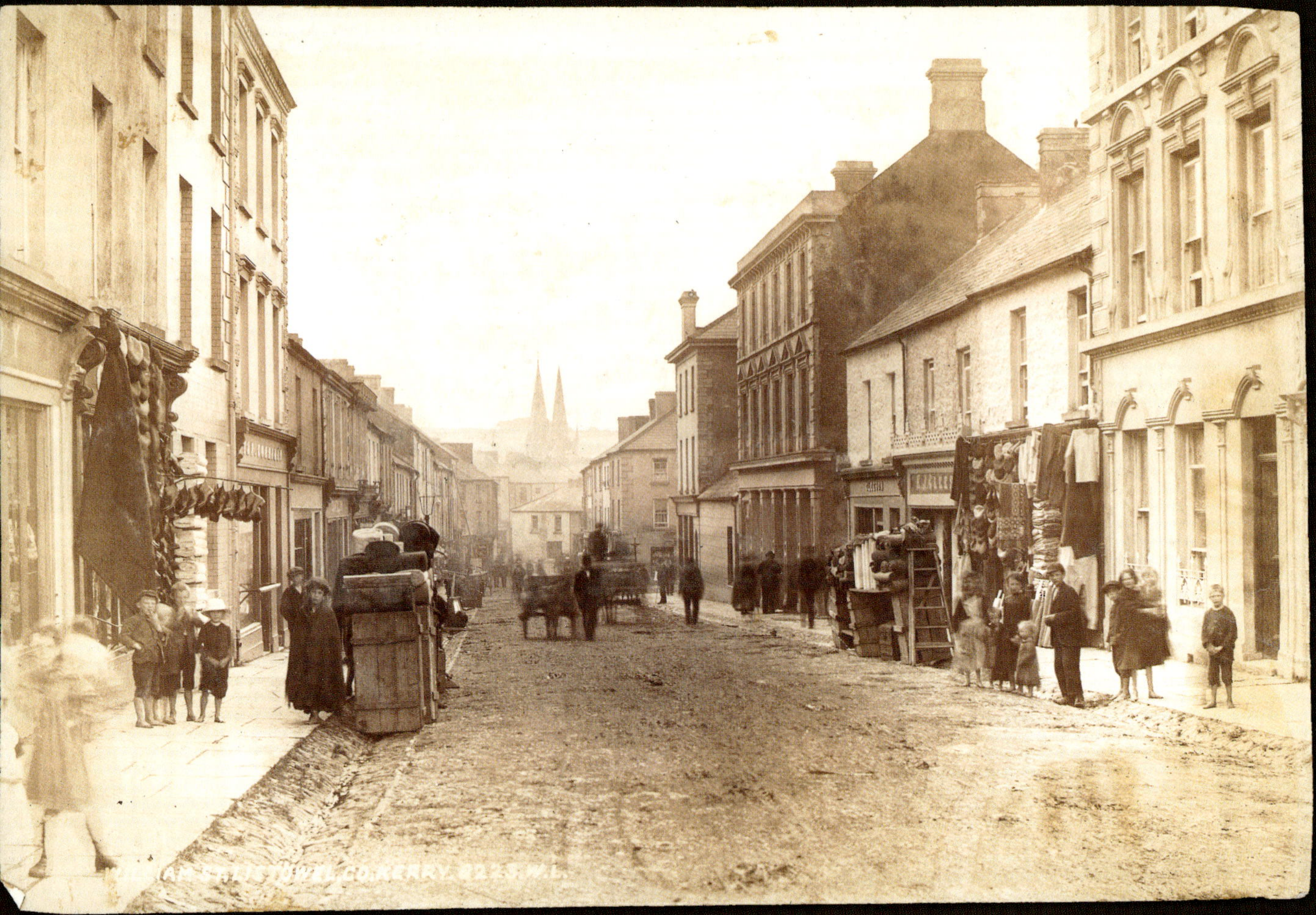

Above: What is most noticeable from this 1904 photograph, is the age-old custom of drapery shop owners hanging their wares off the fascia board and shop front and stacking surplus goods on top of boxes and crates on the roadside frontage. The onlookers pose, clearly impressed at the sight of the camera, many of them shoeless. The three-storey house on the extreme right belonged to Stacks of the Arcade; this was used as accommodation for their staff. It was afterwards to serve as Listowel Post Office for over thirty years. The other three-storey building further down the street was also the town's Post Office when it was run by the Peacock family. In between are the public house of Timothy and Joanna Gleeson, the fancy goods warehouse of their son Ned and the drapery shop of Ned McGrath. Cuthbertson's shop, the local printers can be partially seen on the left, the sweet shop of Reidy's just below (afterwards Davy Carroll's) and below that Tom Carroll's (afterwards Carroll-Henigans).

Previous pages: Market day in Listowel 1904, with men in their Sunday best and women wearing shawls of various hues and patterns. Outside Crowley's shop, a lady hawker sells trinkets from an oversize basket. Hannon's window carries a poster displaying a forthcoming auction, while a flitch of salted ling hangs from the door-jamb. Outside Broderick's (afterwards Fitzgibbon's) are an array of baskets, while overhead a plinth under the upper storey carries the legend 'Grocery, Fancy Warehouse'. Various forms of transport fill the roadway. On closer inspection one can see a cart with seat and guards and further up a sidecar as it makes its way up the street. Horgan's Bar & Grocery, then trading for over half a century, is on the right, while on its right is the one-time family home and newsagent's / stationery shop of D.C. Hennessy, the blind court reporter and poet.

Below: From a William Street postcard, produced by Thomas McAuliffe. A quieter street. However those around are aware of the camera. It is worth noting the group on the right outside Horgan's. From a school photograph of the time one can recognise four pupils from the Church of Ireland School in the Square. Two are wearing bibs and all have shoes. Mrs Lennox was their teacher. However, in marked contrast are the two children standing by the window, shoeless and partially covered with shawls. Across the road is probably Matt Hannon and daughter Mary Ann at the door of their highly decorated public house.

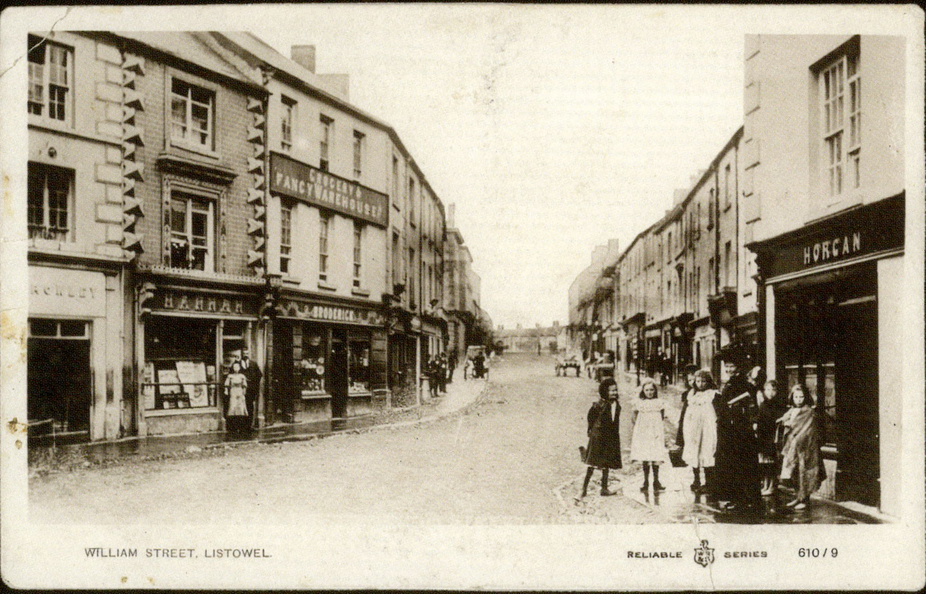

Below: William St Lower 1904. A summer scene in mid William Street. On the left is Cantillon's (afterwards Beechinor's and O'Connell's), now part of the Mermaids Complex. Below that is Faley's. You will notice the practice of hanging various items from the front of the shop. This was also practised by drapers. The building on the right had a variety of uses in its day - dance hall, post office, furniture store, toy store and draper shop.

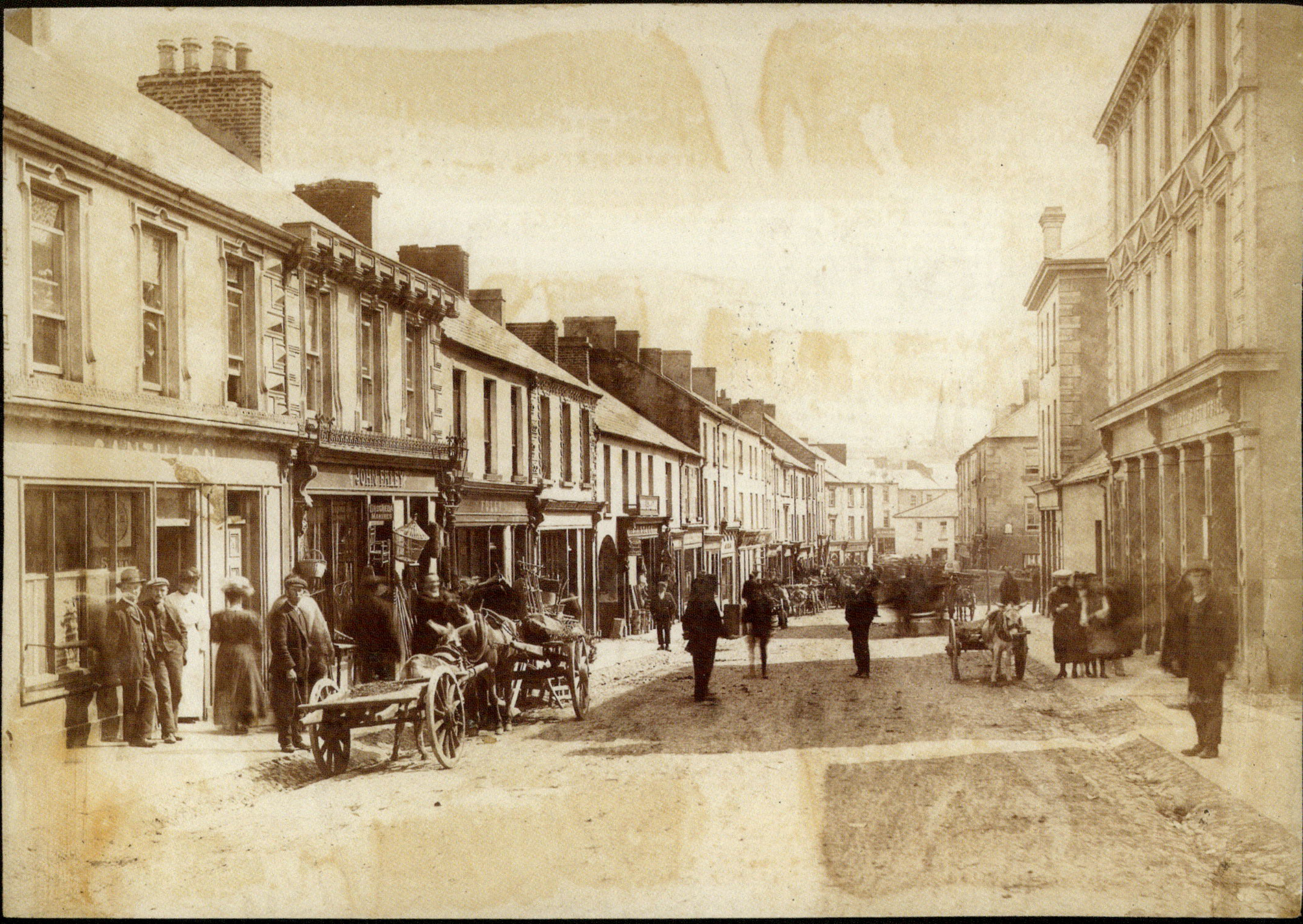

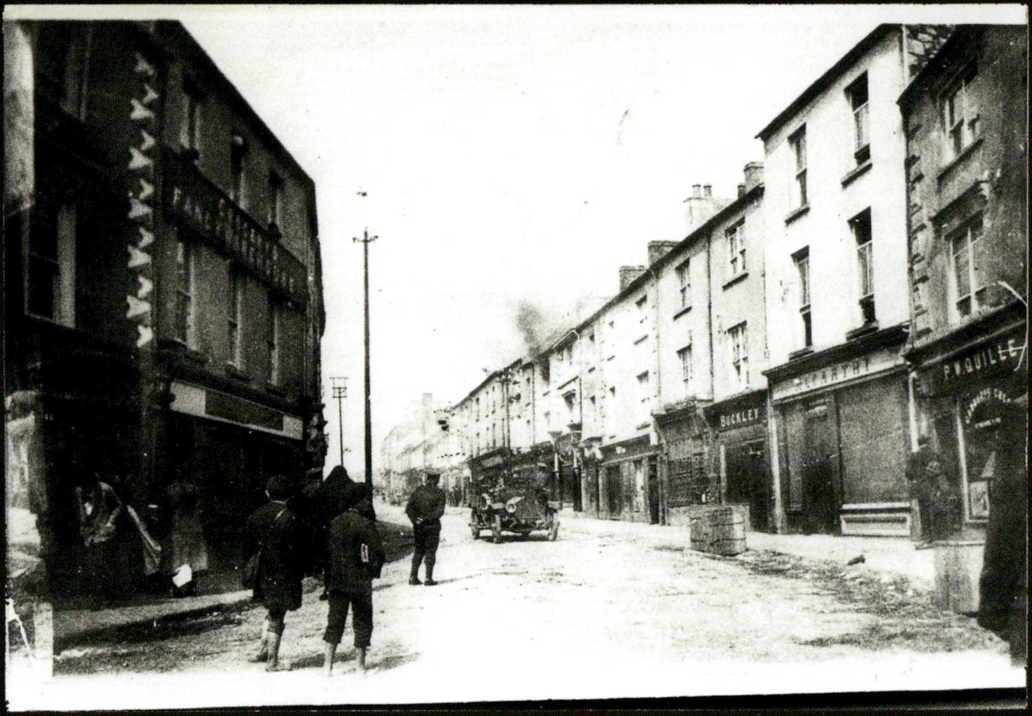

Above: The lunchtime scene of April 14th, 1921. Foley's shop further up on the right of the street is ablaze, having been set alight by the Black and Tans, seemingly in error. Faley's hardware store, further up the street, was thought to be the intended target, on account of it being the workplace of several very well-known Republican activists. On the right are the businesses of Quill (public house), McCarthy (draper) and Buckley (tailor).

Below: A lone horse and trap stands outside J.J. Galvin's shop front. When Italian tradesmen working for a Dublin building company were in Listowel doing mosaic work on the Church renovations they were contracted by John Galvin to put up the Irish version of the Galvin name in mosaic. The elaborate timber work and design was completed by a Mr. Reidy from Killarney. The Black and Tans took exception to the Gaelic wording and threatened to burn the house if it was not taken down. However, Galvin, with the Wisdom of Solomon, reemployed a carpenter to put up a new fascia board to cover the mosaic. It remained like this until the frontage was being refitted by Reidy's of Glin in the mid 1980s. When the timber was taken down, the mosaic reappeared, as clean and fresh as it was when fitted eighty years prior. Across the road are the homes of Barry's (J.D. Keane), Keane's and one of the local tinsmiths, Patrick Corbett.

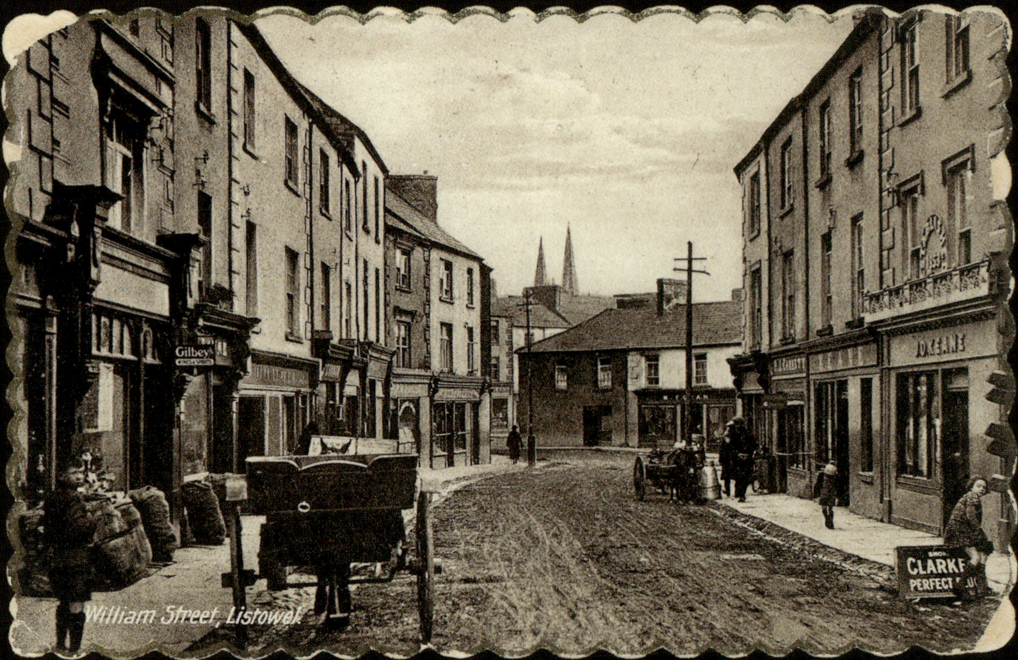

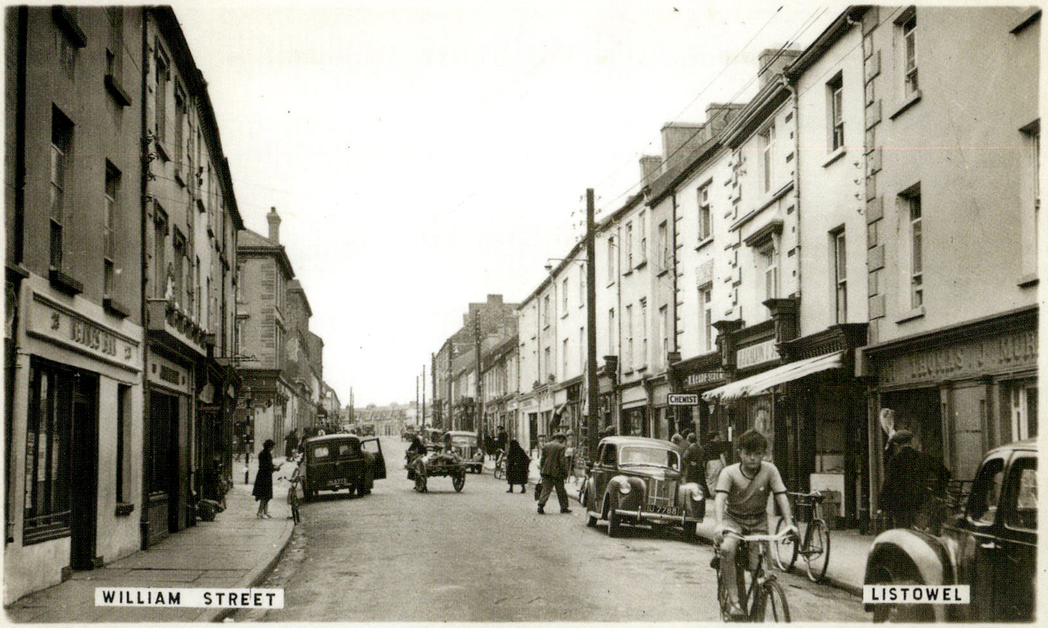

lbove: Women's shawls are fast disappearing in the 1950s, as are the number of horse and ass arts. The boy on the bike is Theo Hanley of Lower William Street.

Below: Motor cars have become more prominent in the 1950s. Con Guerin is now owner of The Long Bar'. Two of Fitzgibbon's staff are busy unpacking a crate which has been delivered y horse and long car from the railway.

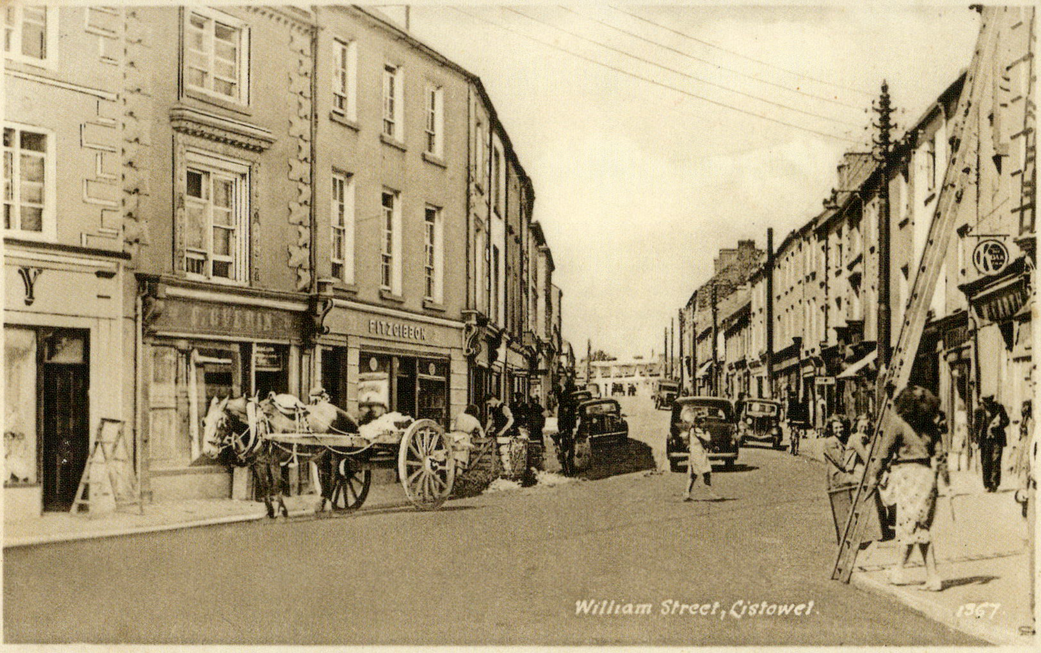

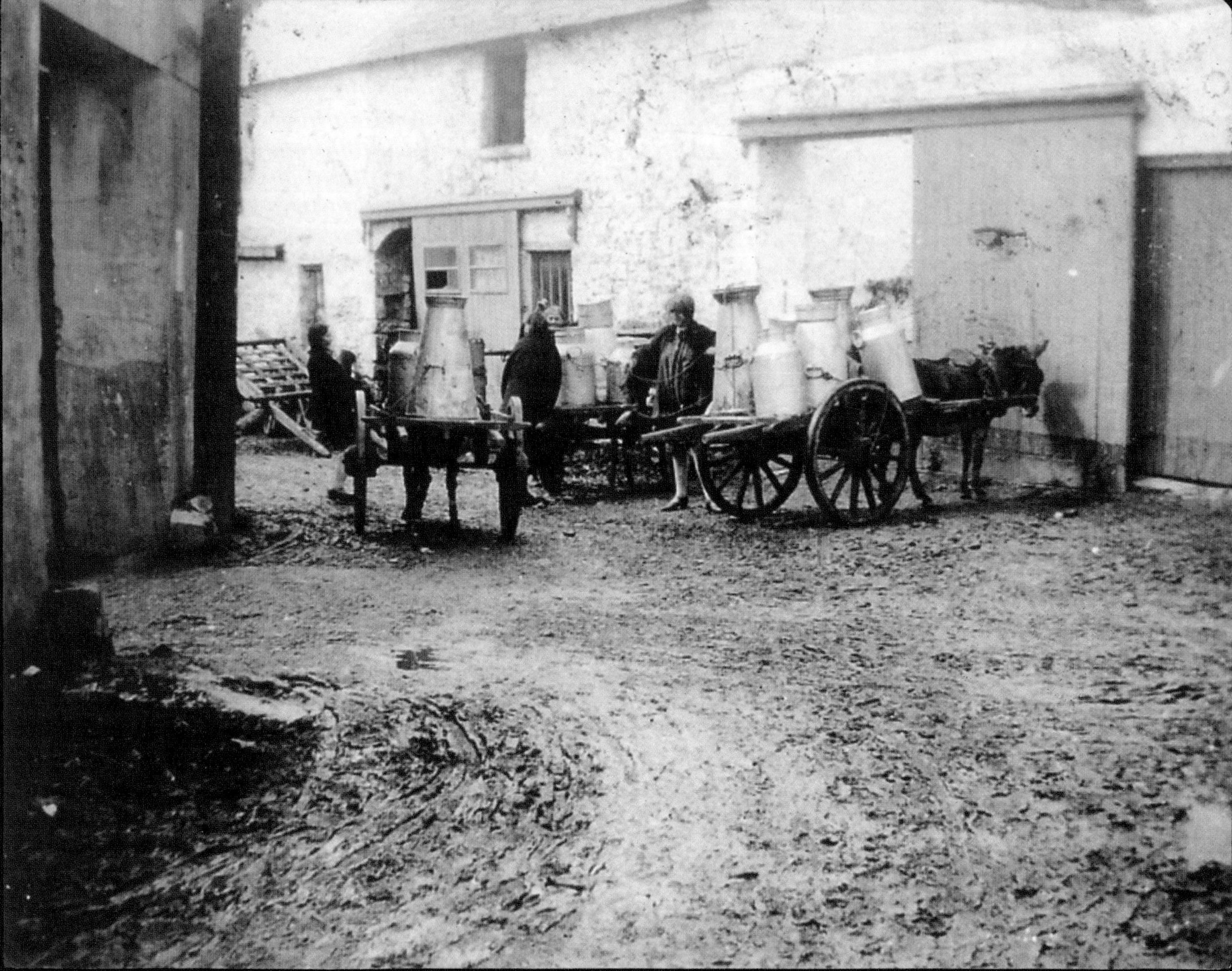

McKenna's had a private creamery in their yard at the back of William Street. This creamery had previously been operated by John Pierse Enright, a businessman with shops and yards on both Church Street and William Street in the late 1800s and early 1900s. The demise of McKenna's creamery came with the arrival and building of a new creamery by the Dairy Disposal Board in the 1930s in a greenfield site at the back of Upper William Street. Each supplier was given a number and book and each transaction was recorded for settlement at the end of each month.

Listowel Dairy Co. (McKenna's)

Milk Account with Mr. D. Flavin .... *No.* 246

For Month ending ...... 28 FEB 1930 ...... *19* ....

Date	New Milk	Sep. Milk	Butter-milk	Butter	REMARKS
1—					
2—					
3—					
4—					
5—					
6—					
7—					
8—					
9—					
10—					
11—					
12—					
13—					
14—					
15—					
16—					
17—					
18—					
19—					
20—					
21—					
22—					
23—					
24—					
25—					
26—					
27—	30	25			
28—	10	9			
29—	12	10		[illegible]	
30—					
31—	21	19			
Total	73			[illegible]	

ORMOND PRINTING CO., LTD., DUBLIN.

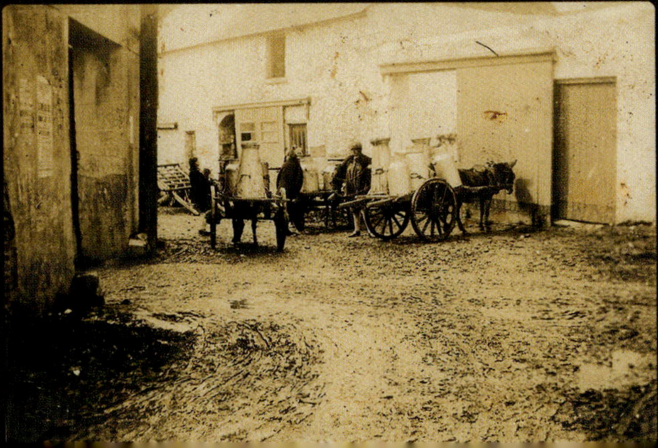

1 Lower William Street

David Spillane came from Limerick in the mid-1860s to manage a store for Hugh Kelter. In 1876 David married Johanna Enright from Listowel. With the demise of the Kelters' business in the 1880s, the Spillanes took over the running of the shop. In the colourful display of the billheads one can appreciate the range of goods which were carried in this shop.

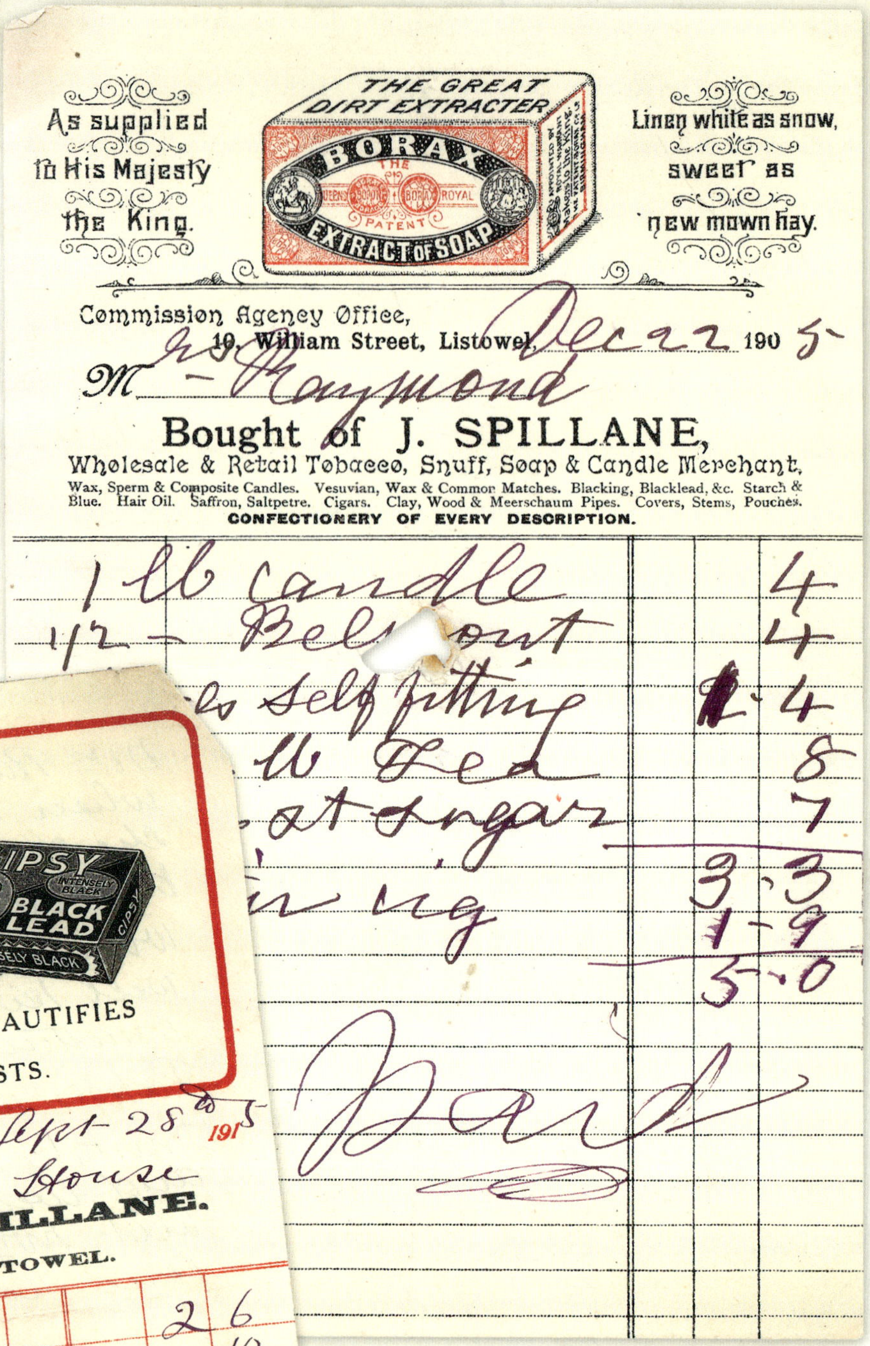

As supplied to His Majesty the King.

THE GREAT DIRT EXTRACTER

BORAX EXTRACT OF SOAP

Linen white as snow, sweet as new mown hay.

Commission Agency Office,
10, William Street, Listowel, Dec 22 1905

Mrs Raymond

Bought of J. SPILLANE,

Wholesale & Retail Tobacco, Snuff, Soap & Candle Merchant,

Wax, Sperm & Composite Candles. Vesuvian, Wax & Common Matches. Blacking, Blacklead, &c. Starch & Blue. Hair Oil. Saffron, Saltpetre. Cigars. Clay, Wood & Meerschaum Pipes. Covers, Stems, Pouches.

CONFECTIONERY OF EVERY DESCRIPTION.

1 lb candle		4
1/2 – Bell [illegible]		4
[illegible] self fitting	1	4
[illegible] lb Tea		8
[illegible] st sugar		7
	3	3
[illegible]	1	9
	5	0

Paid

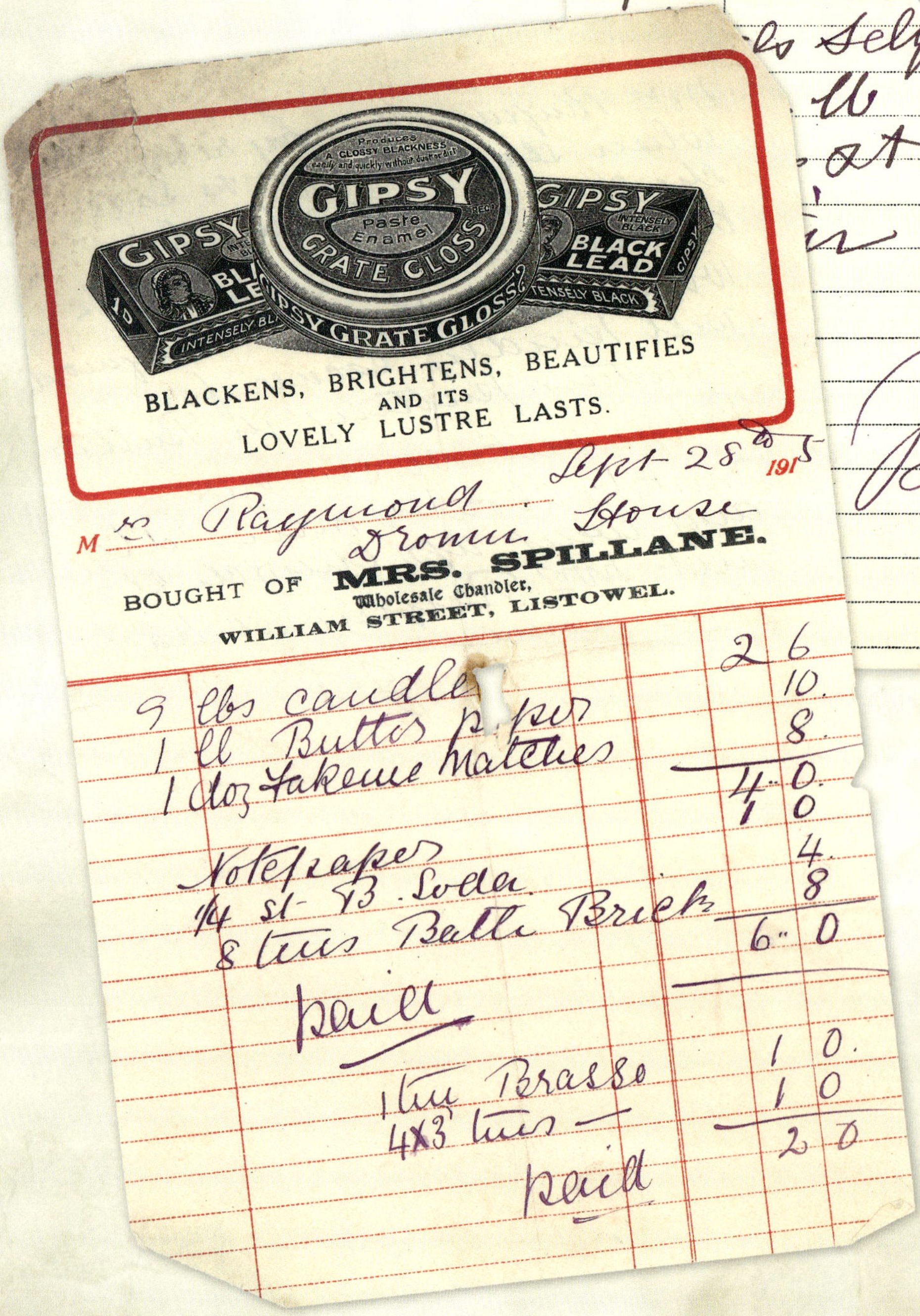

GIPSY GRATE GLOSS

BLACKENS, BRIGHTENS, BEAUTIFIES AND ITS LOVELY LUSTRE LASTS.

Mrs Raymond. Dromin House Sept 28 1915

BOUGHT OF MRS. SPILLANE.
Wholesale Chandler,
WILLIAM STREET, LISTOWEL.

	2	6
9 lbs candles		10
1 lb Butter paper		8
1 doz [illegible] Matches	4	0
	1	0
Notepaper		4
1/4 st [illegible] Soda		8
8 tins Bath Brick	6	0

Paid

1 tin Brasso	1	0
4x3 tins	1	0
	2	0

Paid

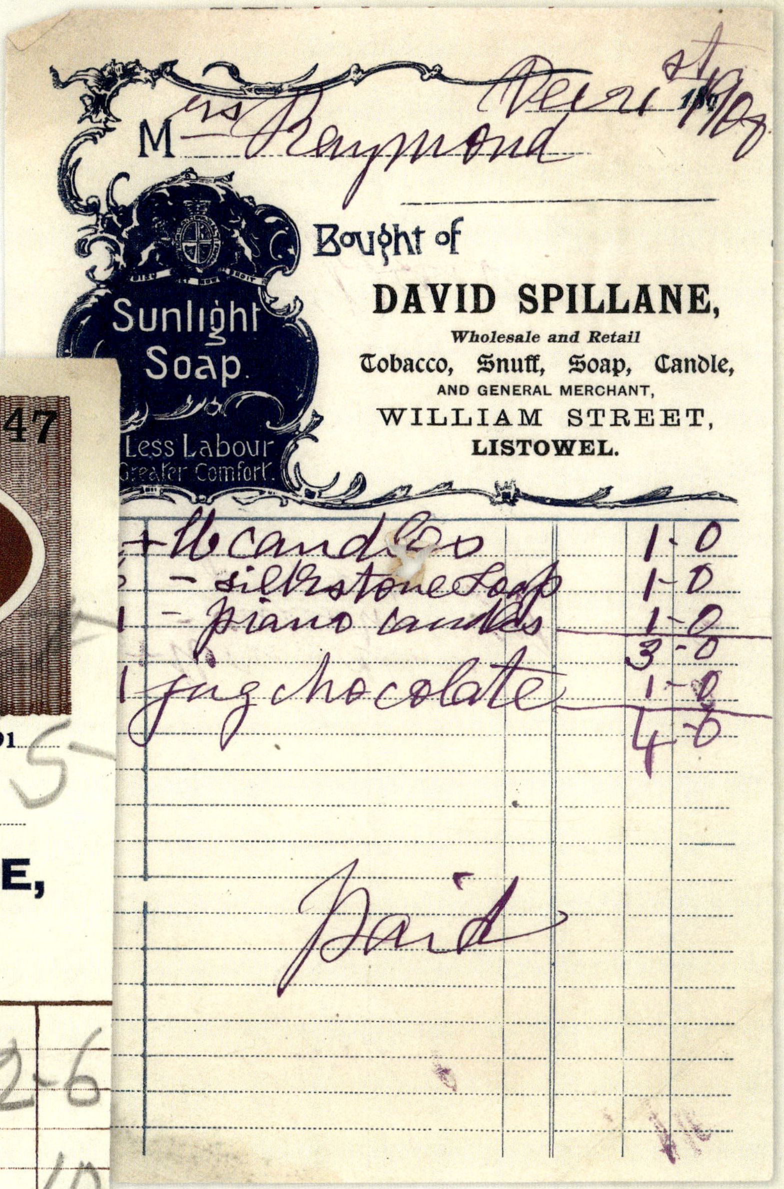

Mrs Raymond Dec 1st 1908

Bought of

DAVID SPILLANE,

Wholesale and Retail

Tobacco, Snuff, Soap, Candle,

AND GENERAL MERCHANT,

WILLIAM STREET,

LISTOWEL.

	lb candles	1-0
	silkstone soap	1-0
1	piano candles	1-0
		3-0
1	jug chocolate	1-0
		4-0

Paid

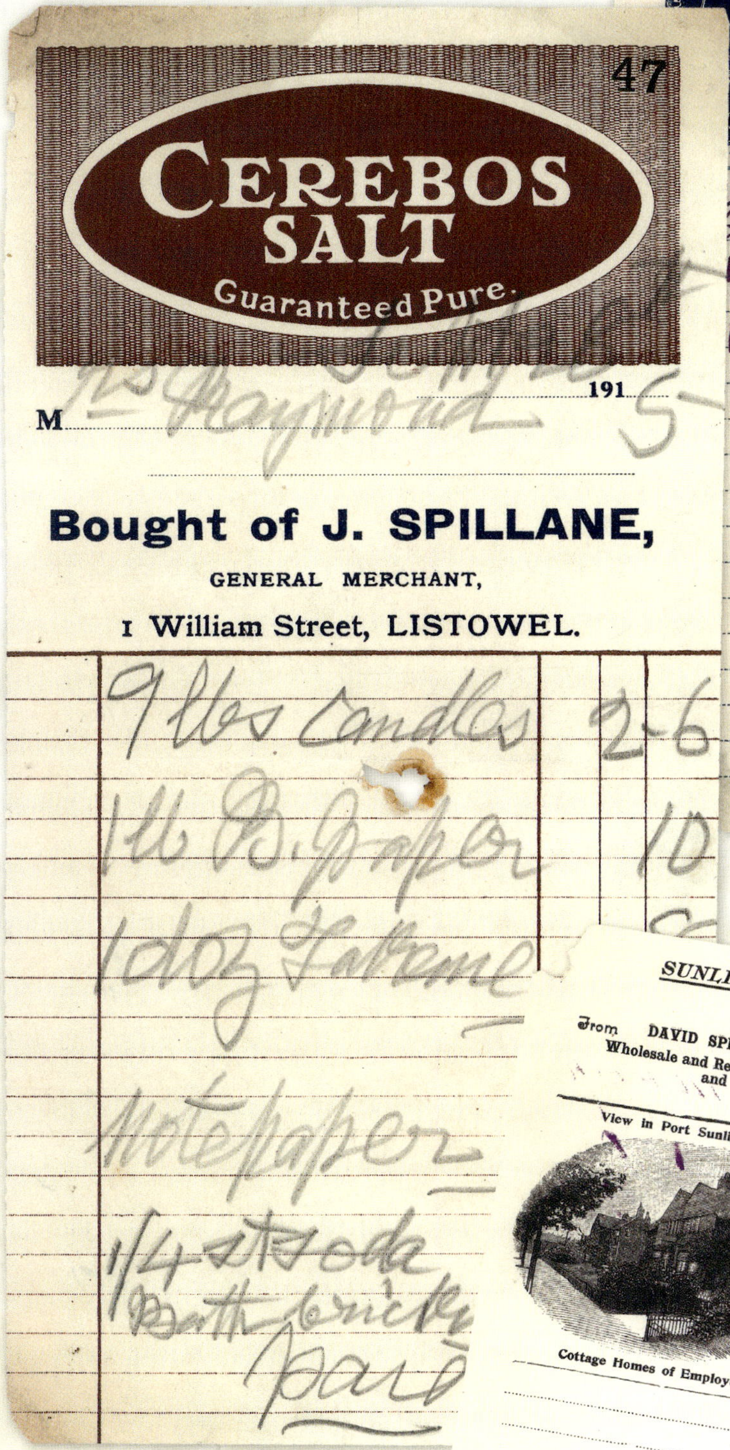

Mrs Raymond 191

Bought of J. SPILLANE,

GENERAL MERCHANT,

1 William Street, LISTOWEL.

9 lbs candles	2-6
1 lb B. paper	10
1 doz [illegible]	
Notepaper	
1/4 st soda	
Bath brick	

Paid

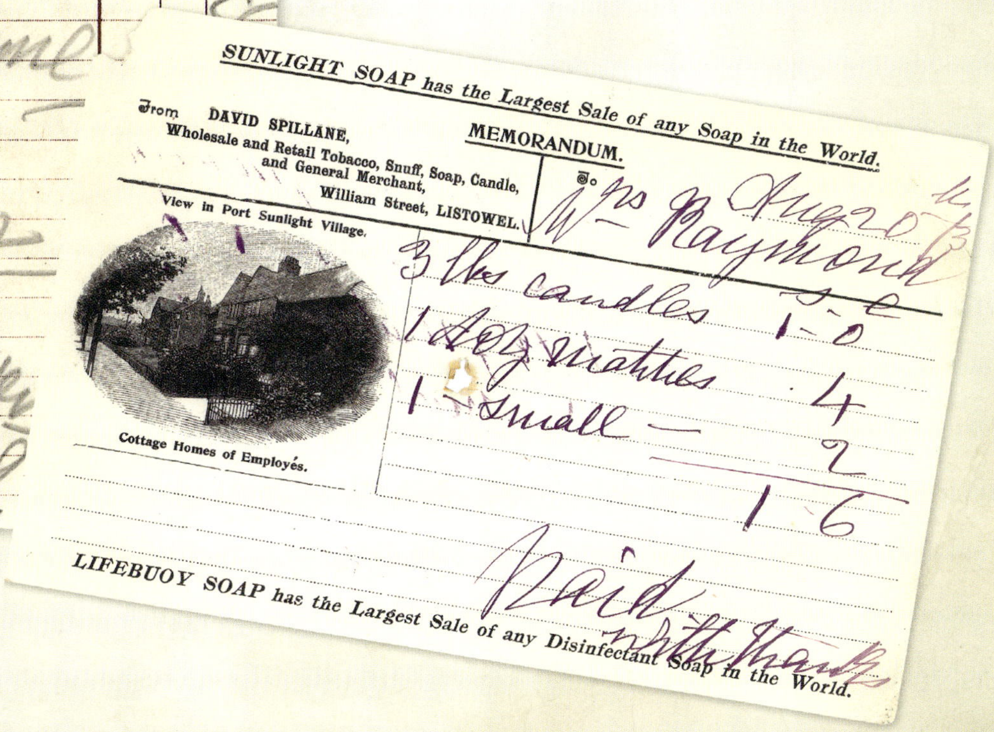

SUNLIGHT SOAP has the Largest Sale of any Soap in the World.

From DAVID SPILLANE,
Wholesale and Retail Tobacco, Snuff, Soap, Candle,
and General Merchant,
William Street, LISTOWEL.

MEMORANDUM.

To Mrs Raymond Aug 20 [illegible]

View in Port Sunlight Village.

Cottage Homes of Employés.

3 lbs candles	1-0
1 doz matches	4
1 small	2
	1-6

Paid with thanks

LIFEBUOY SOAP has the Largest Sale of any Disinfectant Soap in the World.

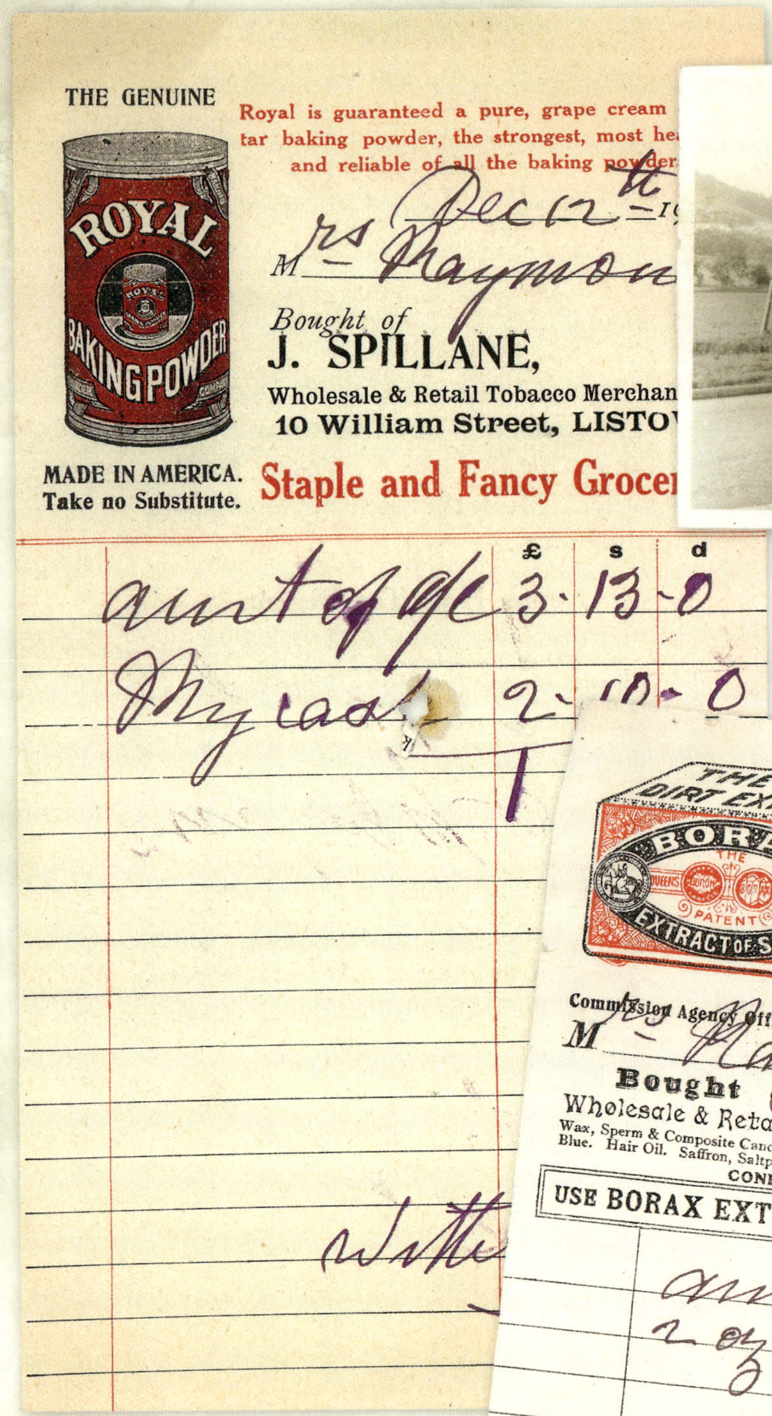
THE GENUINE

Royal is guaranteed a pure, grape cream
tar baking powder, the strongest, most he
and reliable of all the baking powder

Decr 12th 19
Mrs Raymond

Bought of
J. SPILLANE,
Wholesale & Retail Tobacco Merchan
10 William Street, LISTO

MADE IN AMERICA.
Take no Substitute.

Staple and Fancy Grocer

	£	s	d
amt of a/c	3	13	0
By cash	2	10	0
	1		

With

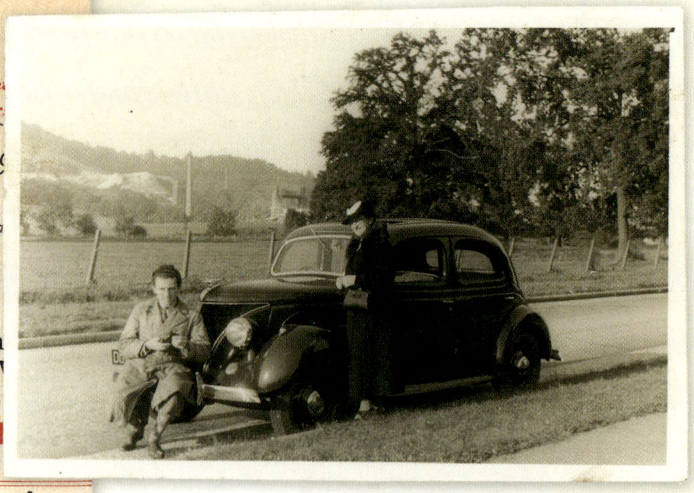

Photo: Nora Ann McCarthy (Spillane), daughter of David and Johanna, with her son Stanley.

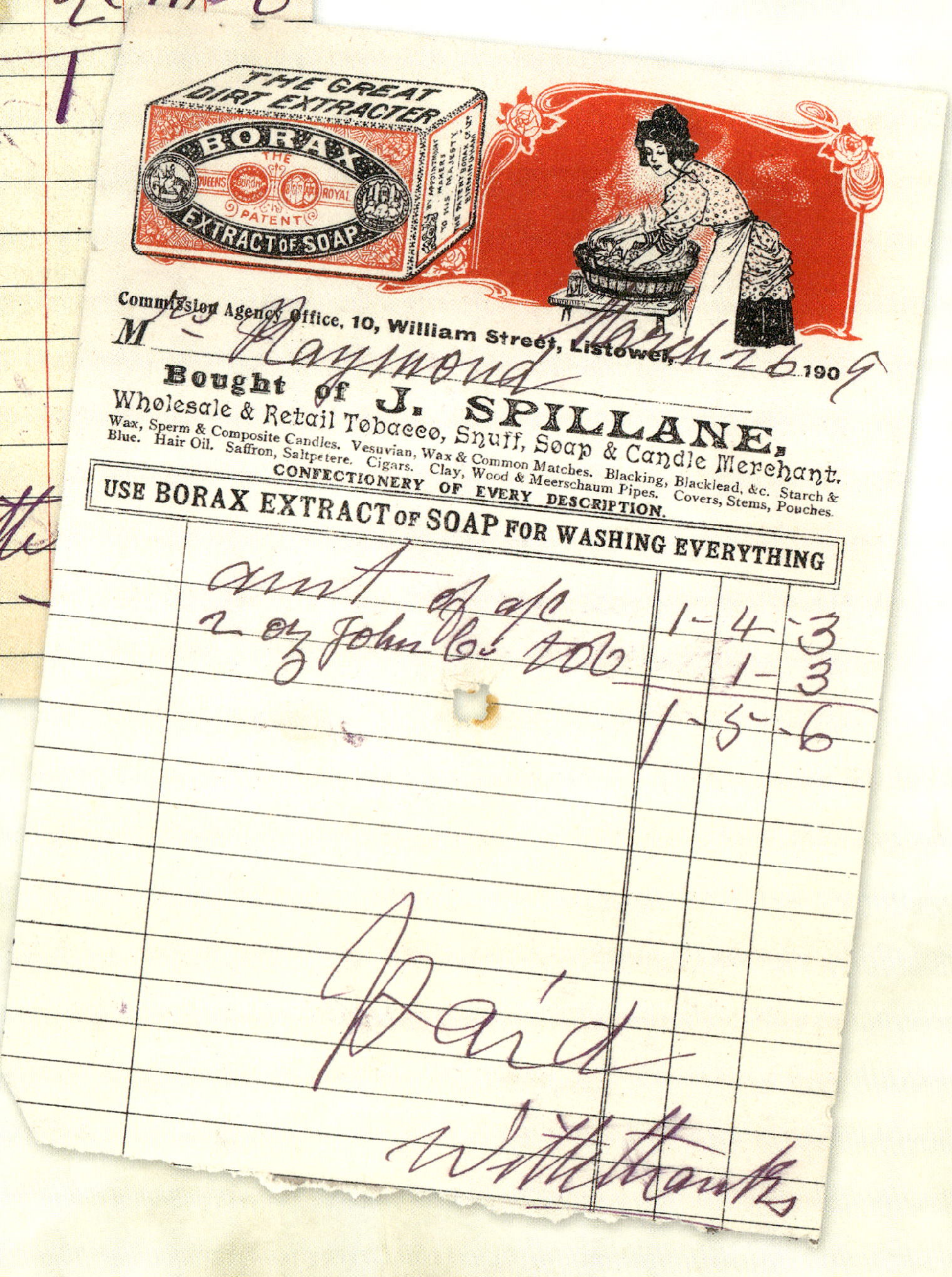
Commission Agency Office, 10, William Street, Listowel, March 26 1909

Mrs Raymond

Bought of J. SPILLANE,
Wholesale & Retail Tobacco, Snuff, Soap & Candle Merchant.
Wax, Sperm & Composite Candles. Vesuvian, Wax & Common Matches. Blacking, Blacklead, &c. Starch & Blue. Hair Oil. Saffron, Saltpetere. Cigars. Clay, Wood & Meerschaum Pipes. Covers, Stems, Pouches.
CONFECTIONERY OF EVERY DESCRIPTION.

USE BORAX EXTRACT OF SOAP FOR WASHING EVERYTHING

amt of a/c	1	4	3
2 oz John C. Tob		1	3
	1	5	6

Paid
With thanks

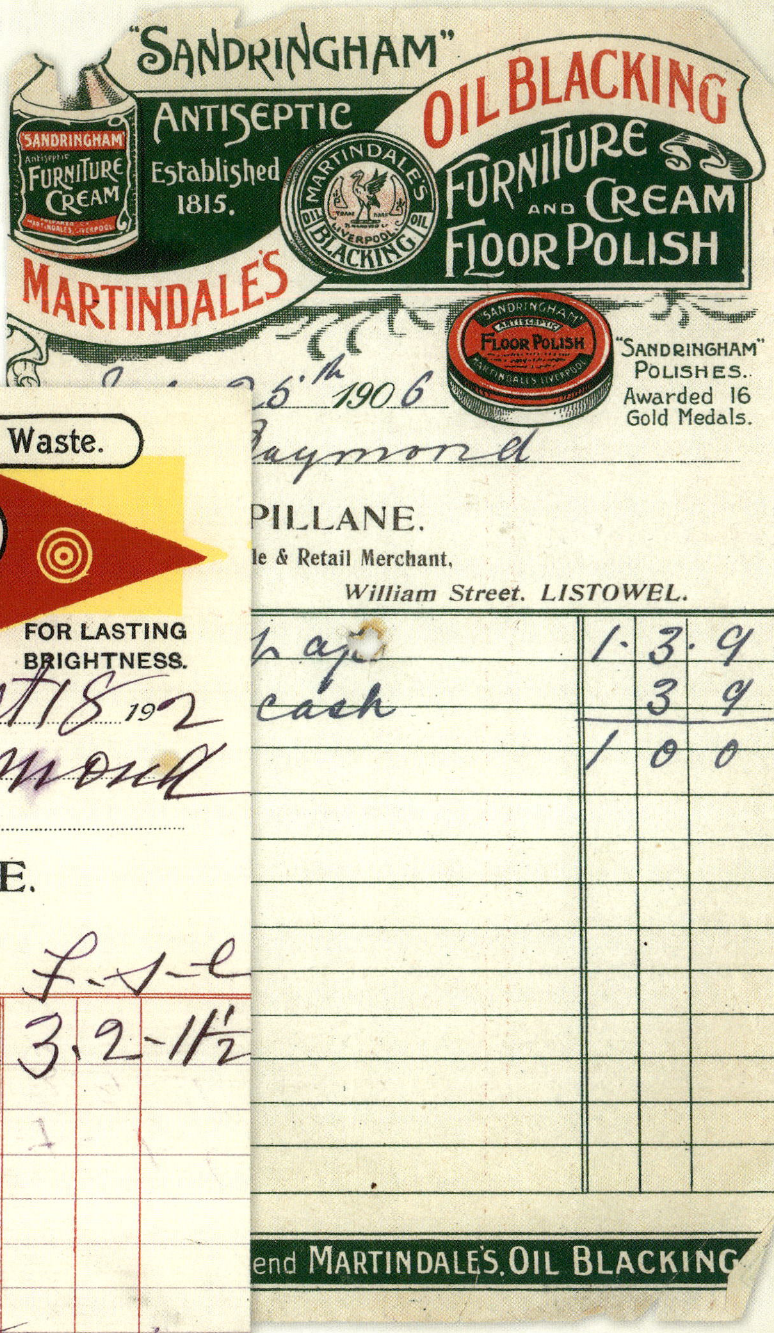
"SANDRINGHAM"
ANTISEPTIC
Established 1815.
OIL BLACKING
FURNITURE AND CREAM FLOOR POLISH
MARTINDALE'S
"SANDRINGHAM" POLISHES. Awarded 16 Gold Medals.
25th 1906
Raymond
SPILLANE.
le & Retail Merchant,
William Street. LISTOWEL.

a/c	1. 3. 9
cash	3 9
	1 0 0

end MARTINDALE'S OIL BLACKING

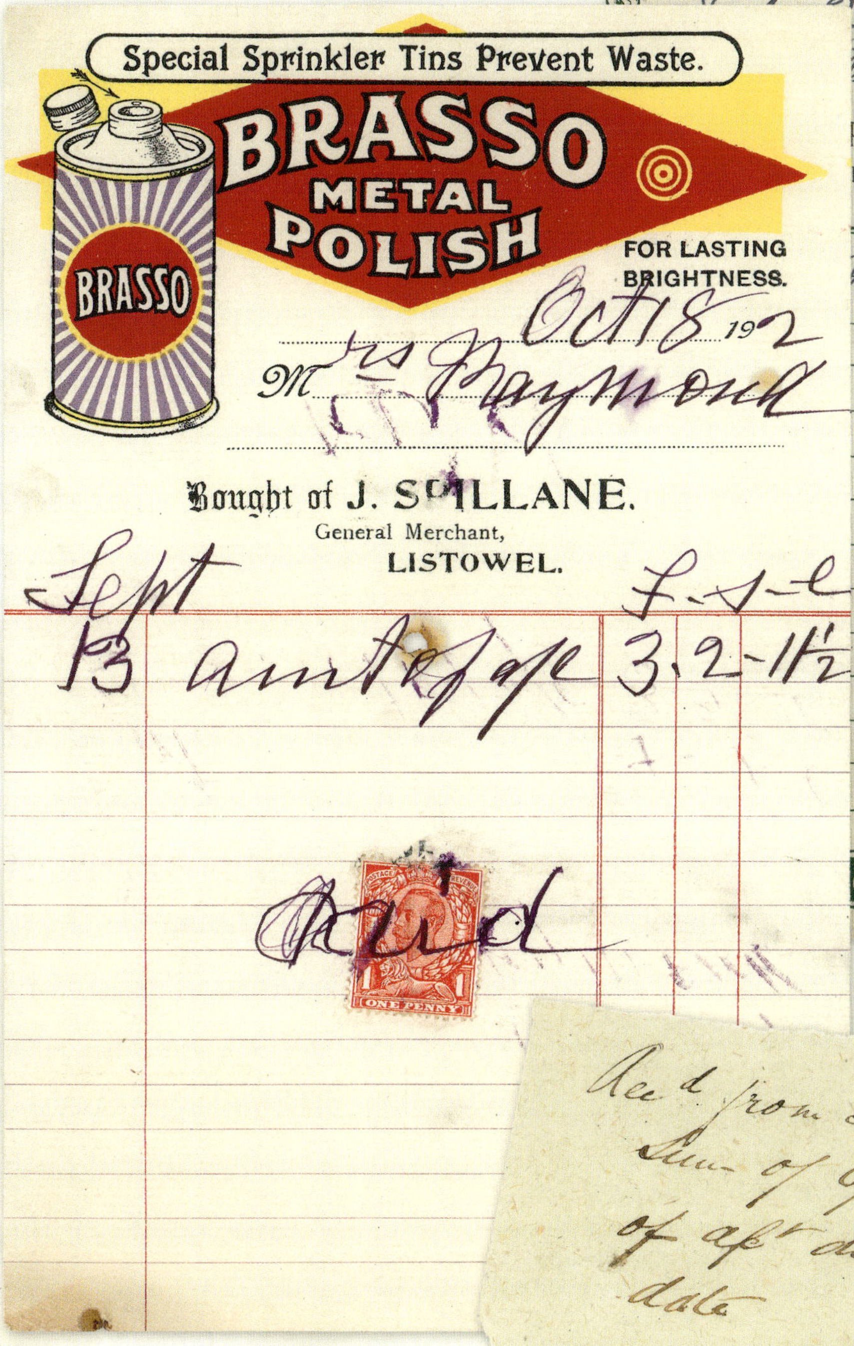
Special Sprinkler Tins Prevent Waste.
BRASSO METAL POLISH
FOR LASTING BRIGHTNESS.
Oct 18 192
Mrs Raymond
Bought of J. SPILLANE.
General Merchant,
LISTOWEL.

		£-s-d
Sept 13	amt of a/c	3. 2. 1½

Paid

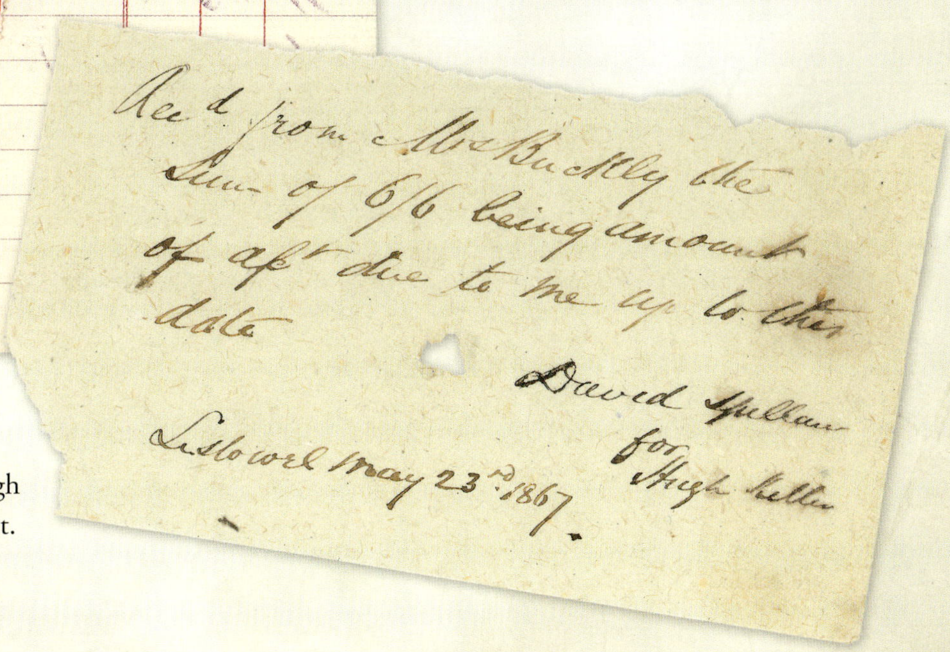
Rec^d from Mrs Buckley the sum of 6/6 being amount of a/c due to me up to this date

David Spillane for Hugh Kelter

Listowel May 23rd 1867.

Right: A receipt from D. Spillane of Hugh Kelter, to Mrs. Buckley of William Street.

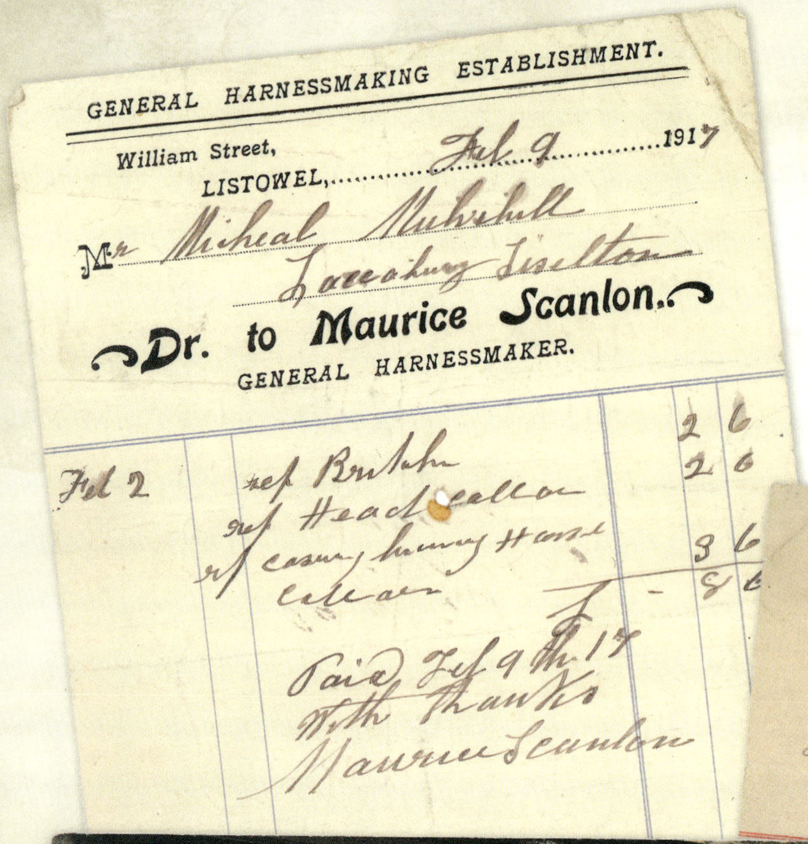
GENERAL HARNESSMAKING ESTABLISHMENT.

William Street,
LISTOWEL, Feb 9 1917

Mr Micheal Mulvihill

Dr. to Maurice Scanlon.
GENERAL HARNESSMAKER.

Feb 2

Paid Feb 9th 17
With thanks
Maurice Scanlon

3 Lower William Street

In the photograph below Moss Scanlon greets Paud Carey and his grandnephew Michael Greaney at the door of his harness-making shop in 1958. Scanlon served his apprenticeship to his father Maurice, who in turn acquired his harness-making skills from Dan Collins. Also in the photograph is John Nolan, long-time friend of the Scanlons.

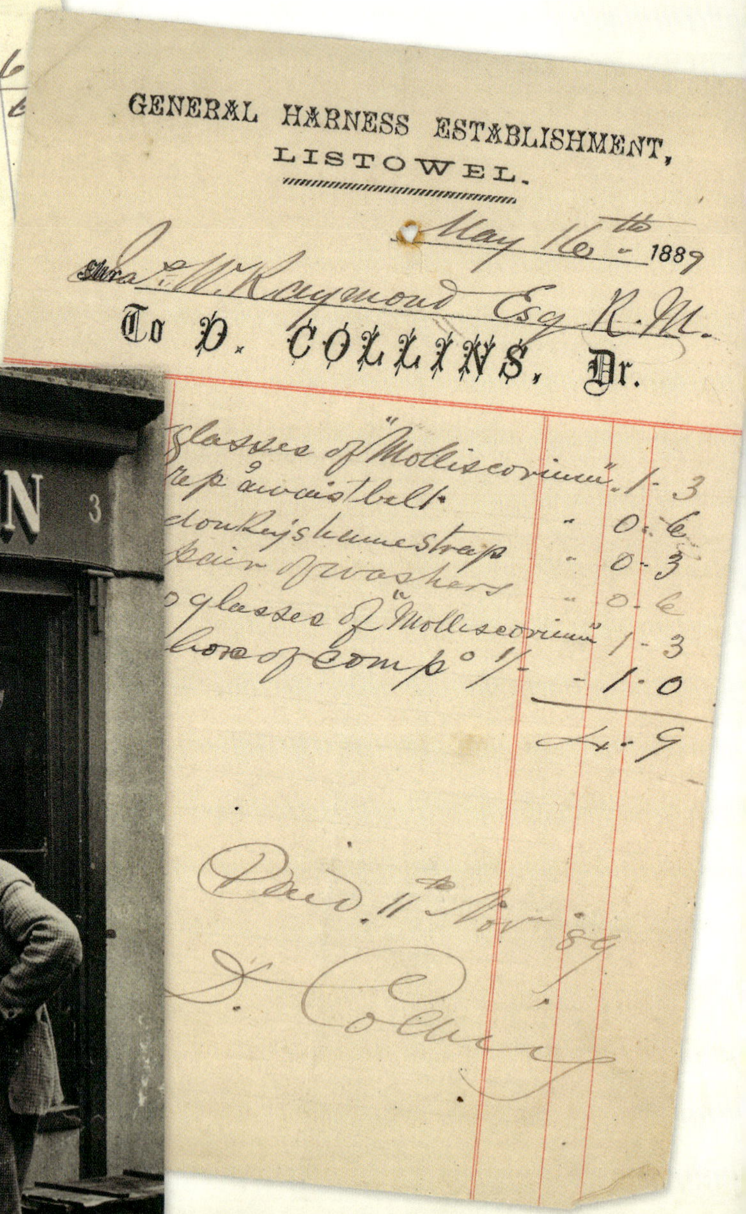
GENERAL HARNESS ESTABLISHMENT,
LISTOWEL.

May 16th 1889

To D. COLLINS, Dr.

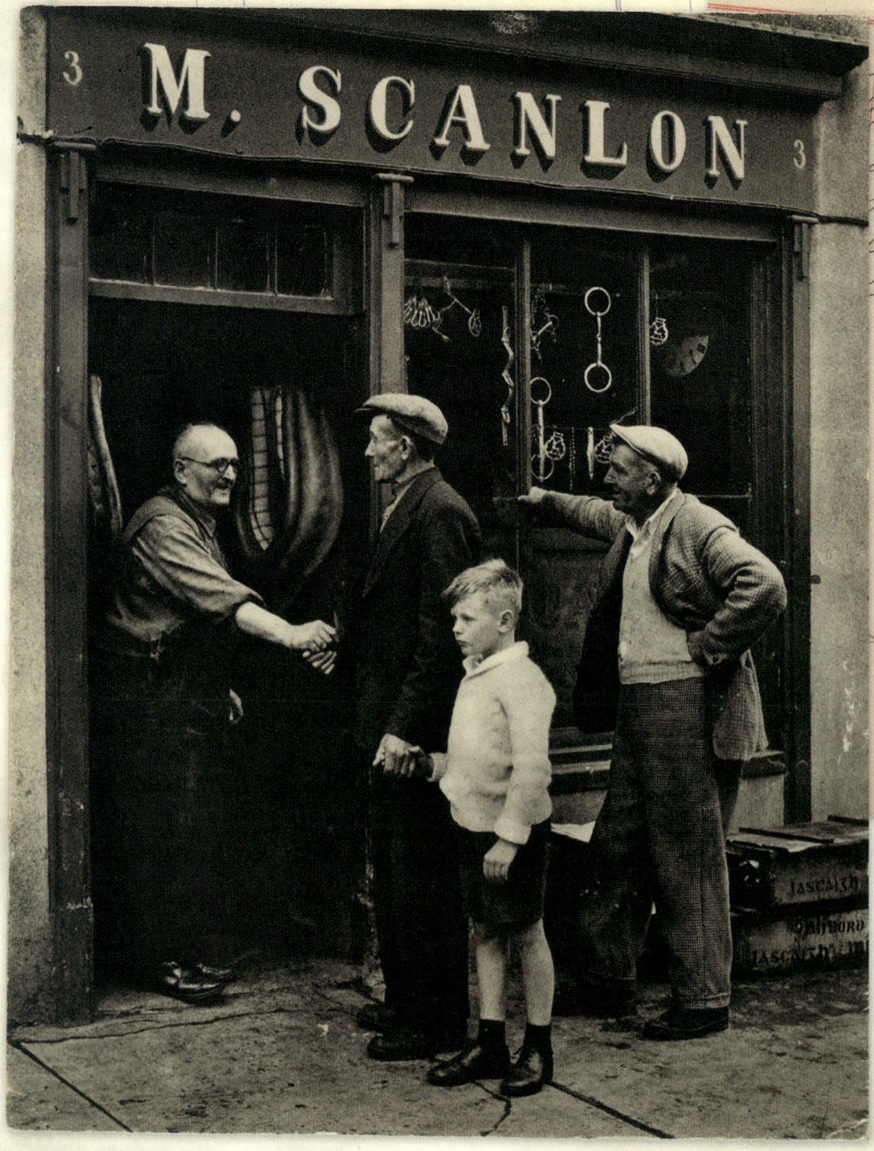

7 Lower William Street
Edward Cain was married to Hannah McElligott. They were shopkeepers and publicans in what is now No. 7 Lower William Street. He was the son of James Cain of Church Street.

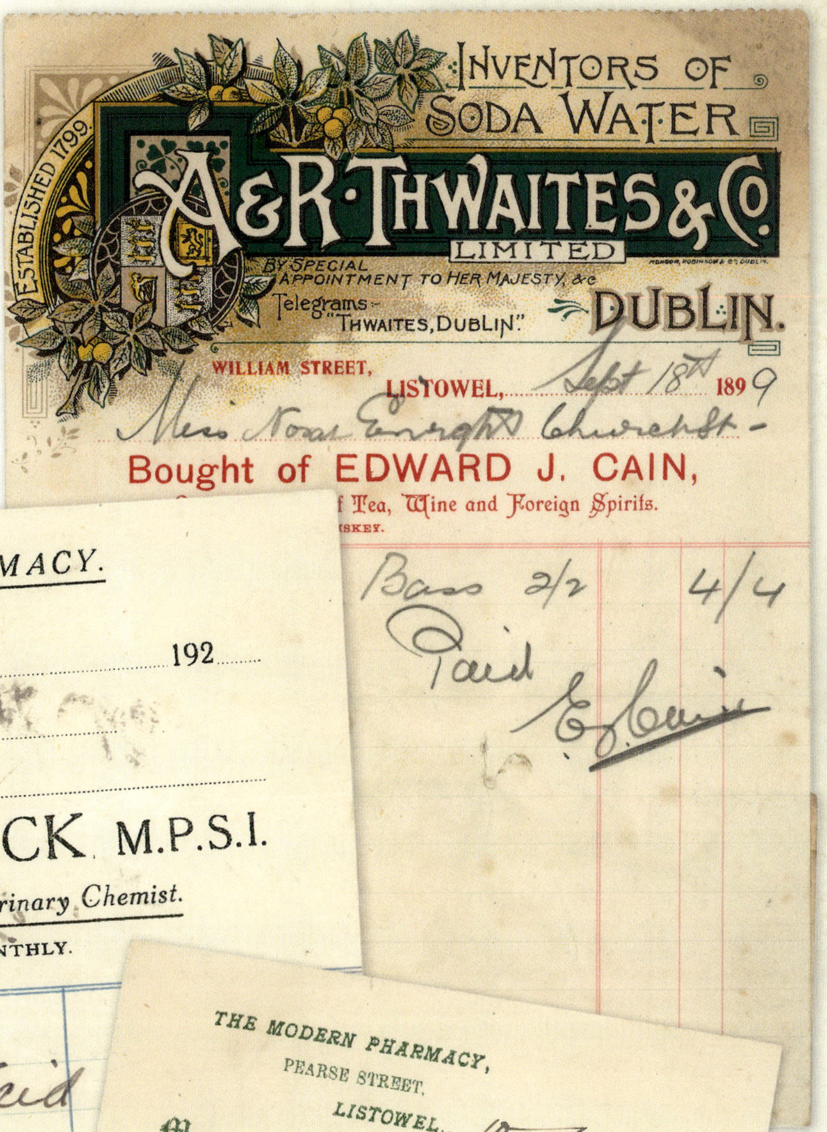
ESTABLISHED 1799.
INVENTORS OF SODA WATER
A&R·THWAITES & Co.
LIMITED
BY SPECIAL APPOINTMENT TO HER MAJESTY, &c
Telegrams - "THWAITES, DUBLIN."
DUBLIN.
WILLIAM STREET, LISTOWEL, Sept 18th 1899
Mess Norah Enright Church St -
Bought of EDWARD J. CAIN,
Tea, Wine and Foreign Spirits.
Bass 2/2 4/4
Paid
E J Cain

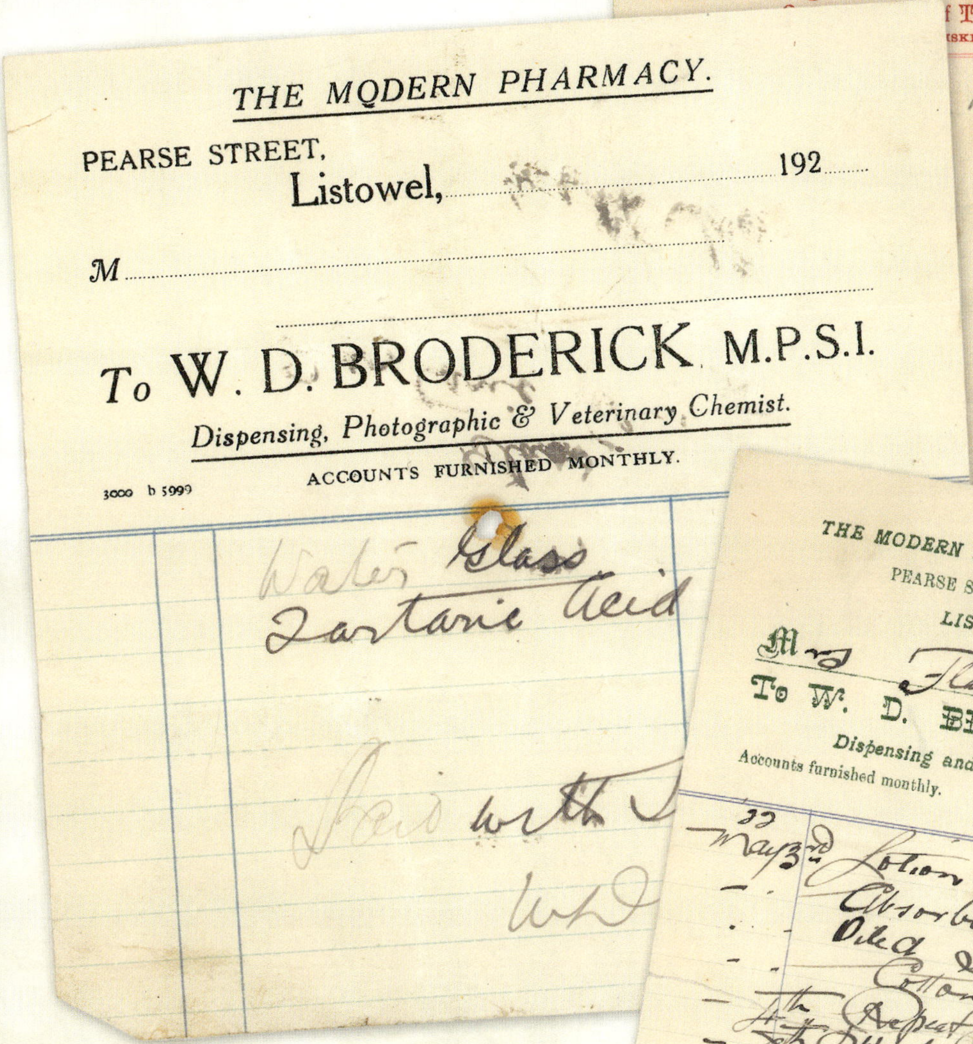
THE MODERN PHARMACY.
PEARSE STREET,
Listowel, 192
M
To W. D. BRODERICK M.P.S.I.
Dispensing, Photographic & Veterinary Chemist.
ACCOUNTS FURNISHED MONTHLY.
3000 b 5999
Water Glass
Tartaric Acid
Paid with T
WD

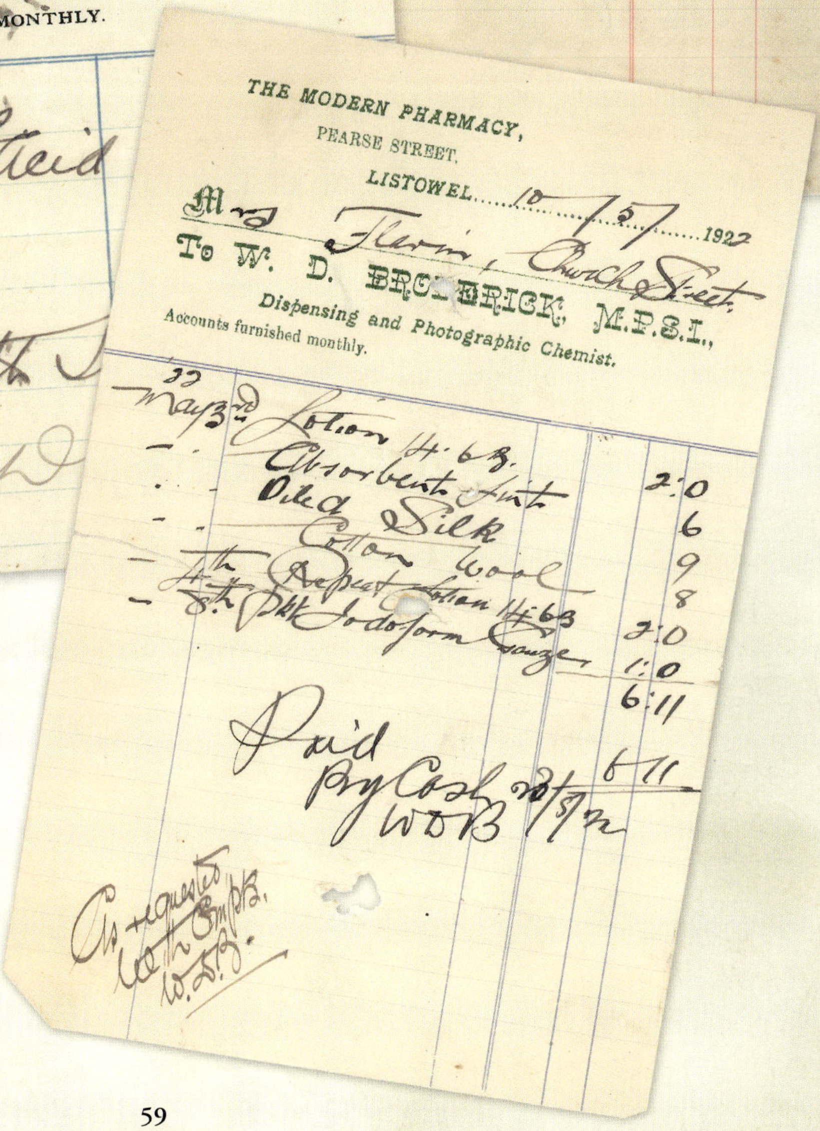
THE MODERN PHARMACY,
PEARSE STREET,
LISTOWEL 10/5/1922
Mrs Flavin, Church Street.
To W. D. BRODERICK, M.P.S.I.,
Dispensing and Photographic Chemist.
Accounts furnished monthly.

22 May 3rd	Lotion 4·6 oz.	
-	Absorbent Lint	2:0
-	Oiled Silk	6
-	Cotton Wool	9
- 4th	Repeat Lotion 4·6 oz	8
- 8th	Pkt Iodoform Gauze	2:0
		1:0
		6:11

Paid by Cash 10/5/22 WDB 6/11
As requested with Compts. W.D.B.

Having qualified as a chemist, William Broderick from Lisroe, Duagh, set up a business in the house when vacated by the Cain family. Today the premises remains as a chemist shop, trading as Broderick's and owned by Oonagh Harnett.

5 Lower William Street
The Hennessy family had part of Horgan's shop rented as a newsagent's shop and where they also sold stationery. D.C. Hennessy, who was blind, was a local court reporter and also was an accomplished poet. His book of poems *The Lays of North Kerry*, published in 1872, was republished by the North Kerry Literary Trust in 2001.

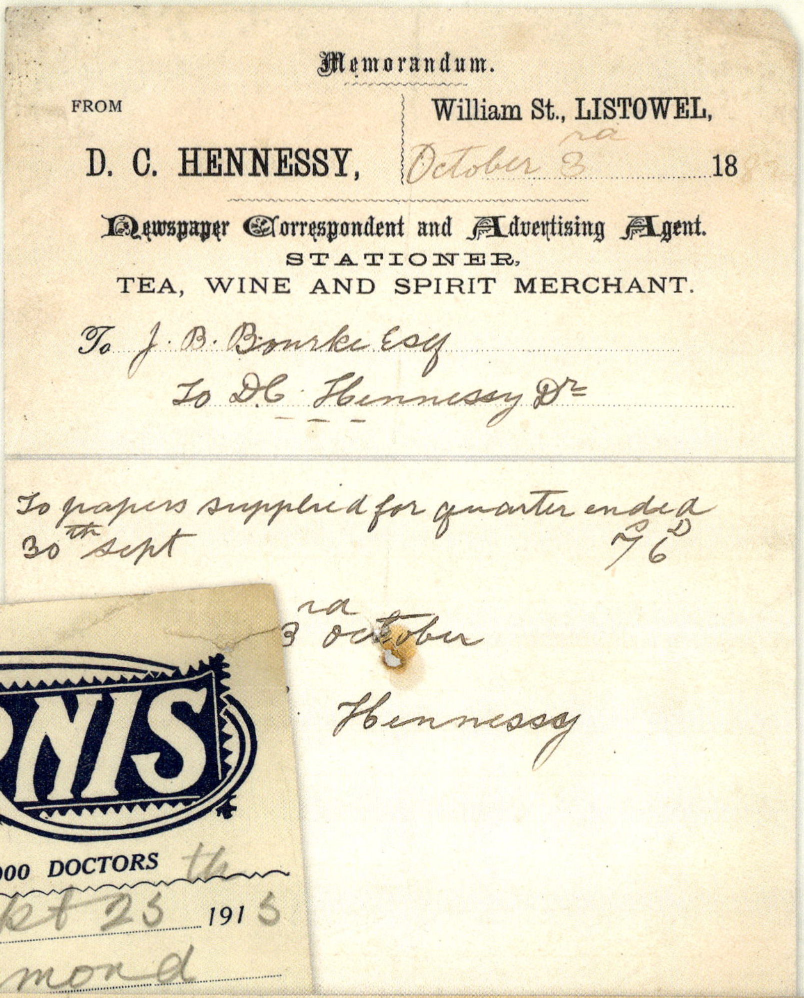
Memorandum.
FROM D. C. HENNESSY, William St., LISTOWEL, October 3rd 1882
Newspaper Correspondent and Advertising Agent.
STATIONER,
TEA, WINE AND SPIRIT MERCHANT.
To J. B. Bourke Esq
To DC Hennessy Dr
To papers supplied for quarter ended 30th Sept 7/6D
3rd October
Hennessy

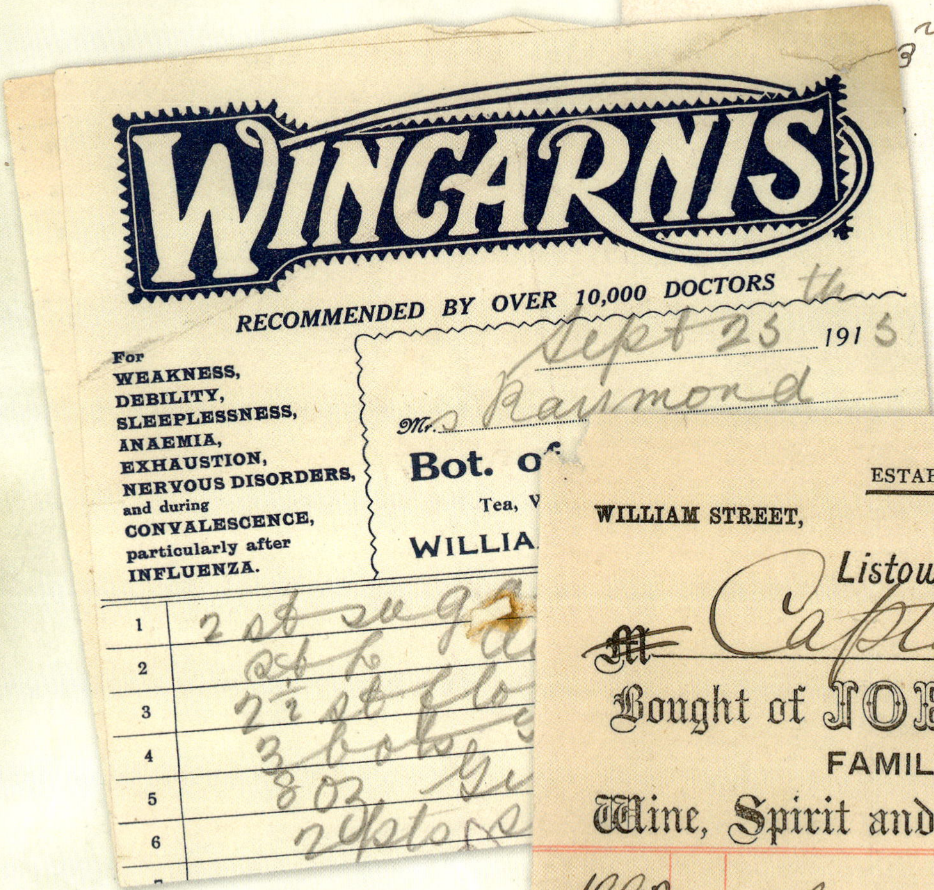

Sept 25th 1915
Mrs Raymond
Bot. o
Tea, V
WILLIA

1	2 st sug
2	st b
3	2½ st flo
4	3 bots
5	8 oz
6	2 st

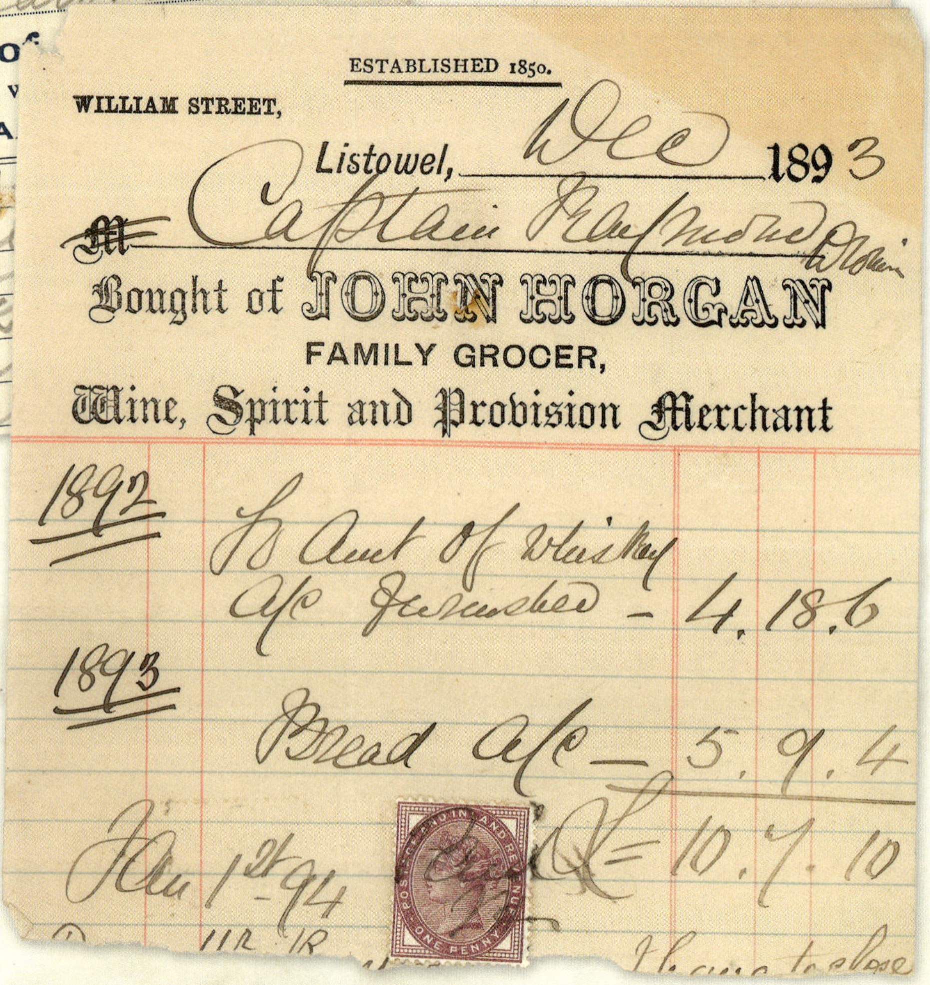
ESTABLISHED 1850.
WILLIAM STREET,
Listowel, Dec 1893
M Captain Raymond
Bought of JOHN HORGAN
FAMILY GROCER,
Wine, Spirit and Provision Merchant

1892	To Amt of Whiskey a/c furnished	4. 18. 6
1893	Bread a/c	5. 9. 4
Jan 1st 94		£ 10. 7. 10

5 Lower William Street
Horgan's, established in 1850, is now owned and operated by the Canty family. Their public house is called 'The Shebeen'. It previously had been owned by Patricia and William Kearney. This property was mentioned in *Griffith's Valuation* as having been formerly the site of an Auxiliary Workhouse.

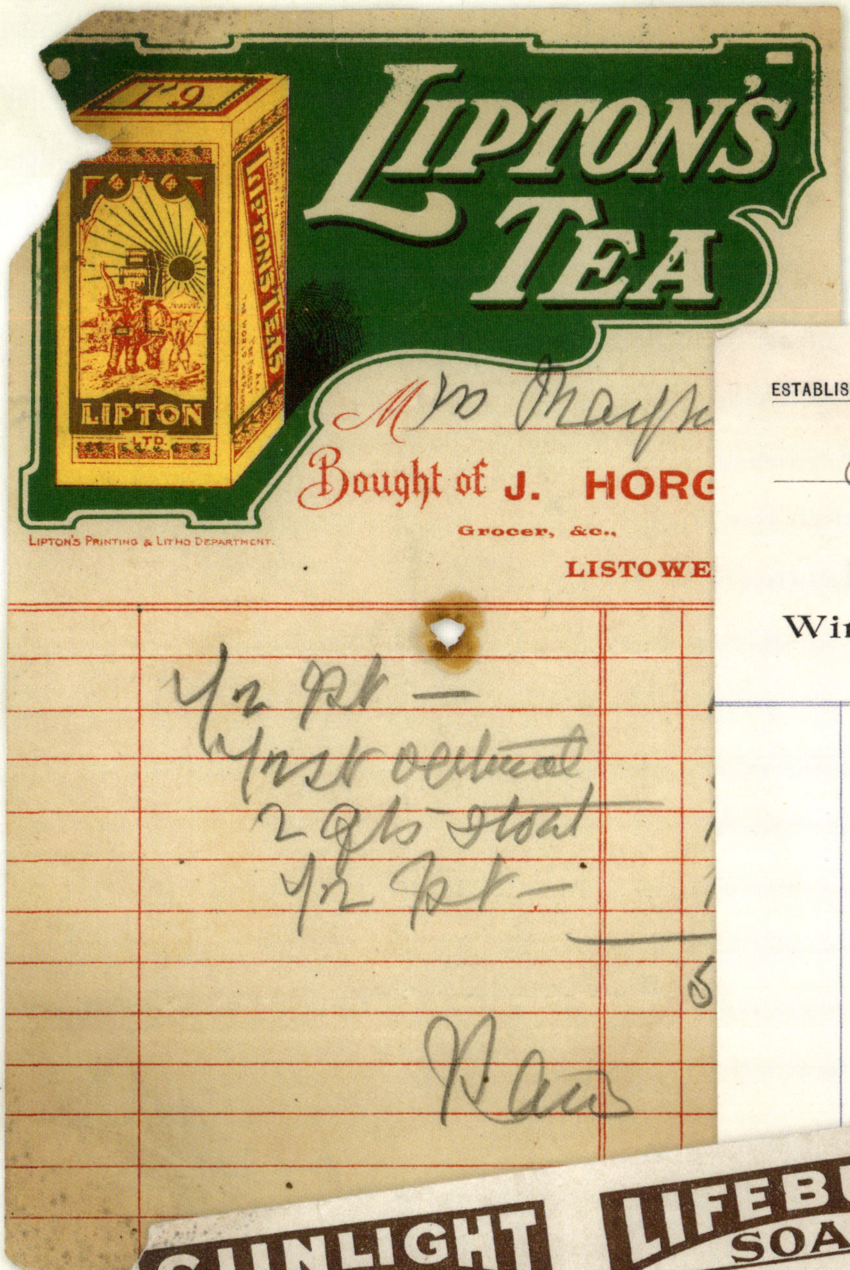

LIPTON'S TEA

Mrs Ray…

Bought of J. HORG…

Grocer, &c.,

LISTOWE…

LIPTON'S PRINTING & LITHO DEPARTMENT.

1/2 pt —
1 st oatmeal
2 qts stout
1/2 pt —

Paid

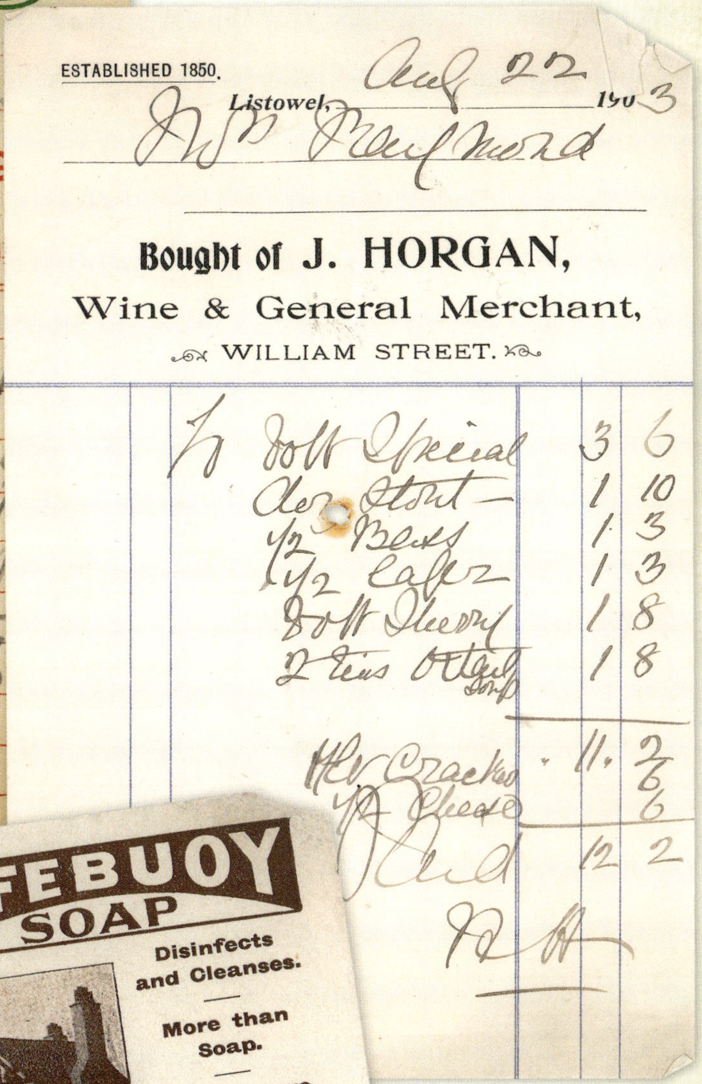

ESTABLISHED 1850. Listowel, Aug 22 1903

Mrs Raymond

Bought of J. HORGAN,
Wine & General Merchant,
WILLIAM STREET.

1/2 bott Special	3	6
doz Stout	1	10
1/2 Beef	1	3
1/2 cakes	1	3
bott Sherry	1	8
2 tins Oxtail soup	1	8
	11.	2
4lb Crackers		6
1/2 Cheese		6
Paid	12	2

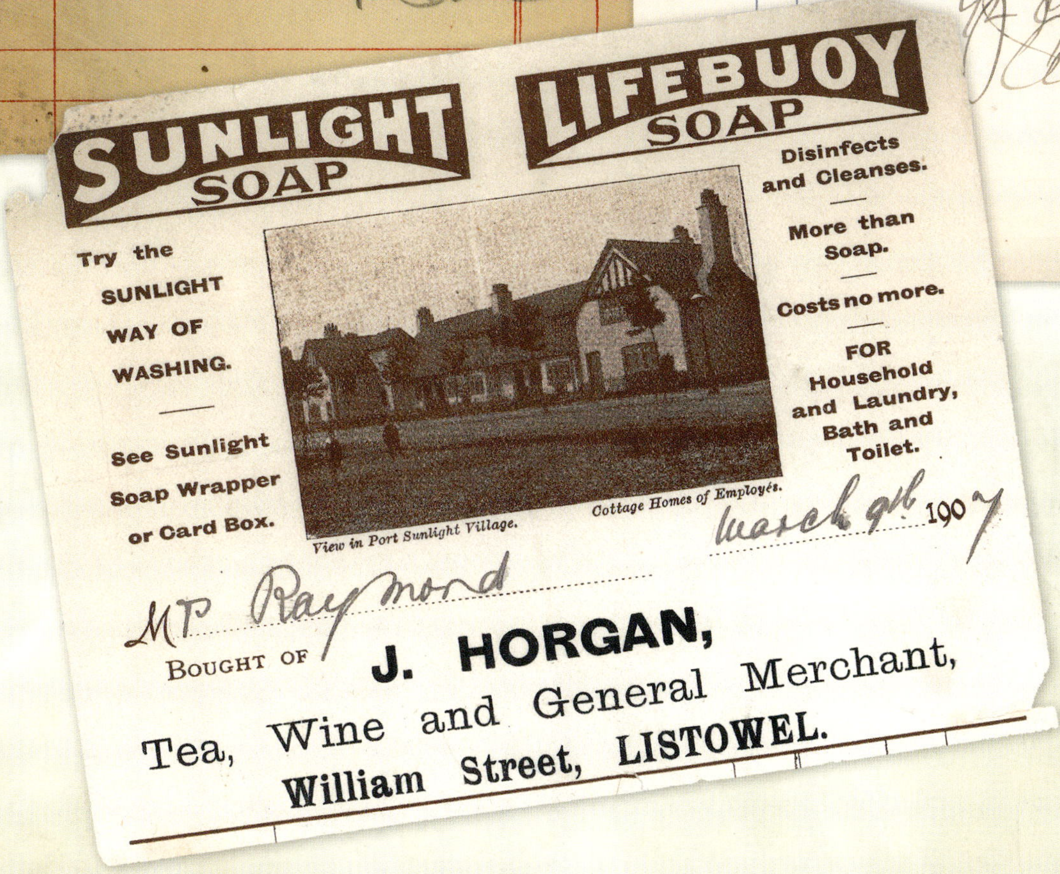

SUNLIGHT SOAP

LIFEBUOY SOAP

Try the SUNLIGHT WAY OF WASHING.

See Sunlight Soap Wrapper or Card Box.

Disinfects and Cleanses.

More than Soap.

Costs no more.

FOR Household and Laundry, Bath and Toilet.

View in Port Sunlight Village. Cottage Homes of Employés.

March 9th 1907

Mrs Raymond

BOUGHT OF **J. HORGAN,**
Tea, Wine and General Merchant,
William Street, LISTOWEL.

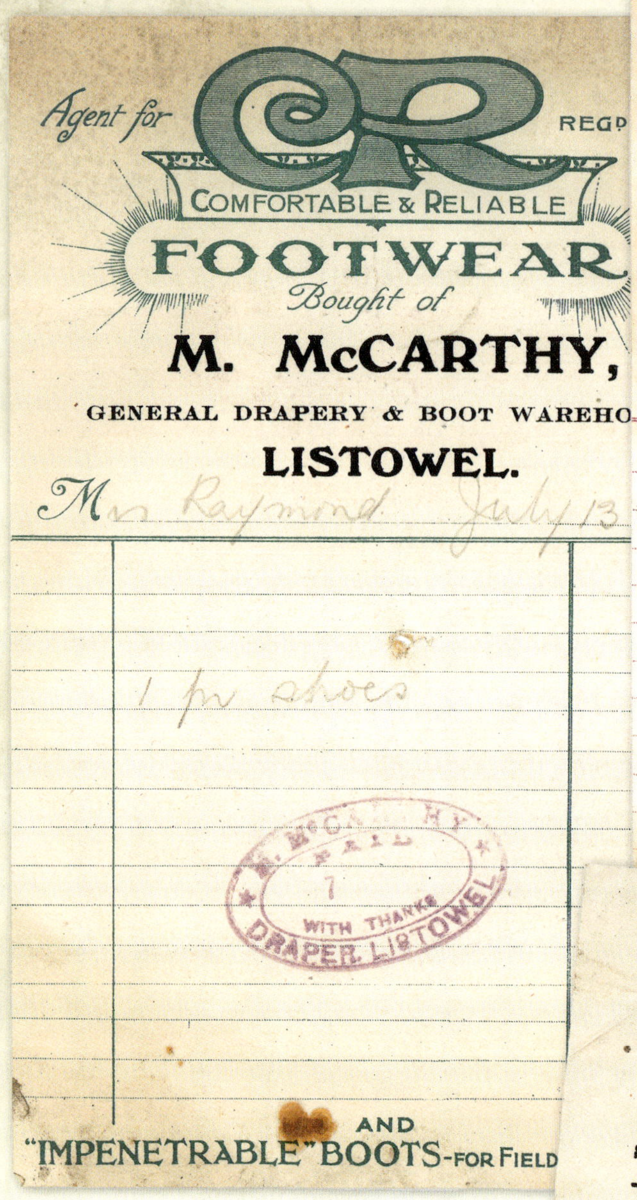

Agent for CR REGD

COMFORTABLE & RELIABLE

FOOTWEAR

Bought of

M. McCARTHY,

GENERAL DRAPERY & BOOT WAREHO

LISTOWEL.

Mrs Raymond July 13

1 pr shoes

M. McCARTHY PAID 7 WITH THANKS DRAPER LISTOWEL

AND

"IMPENETRABLE" BOOTS-FOR FIELD

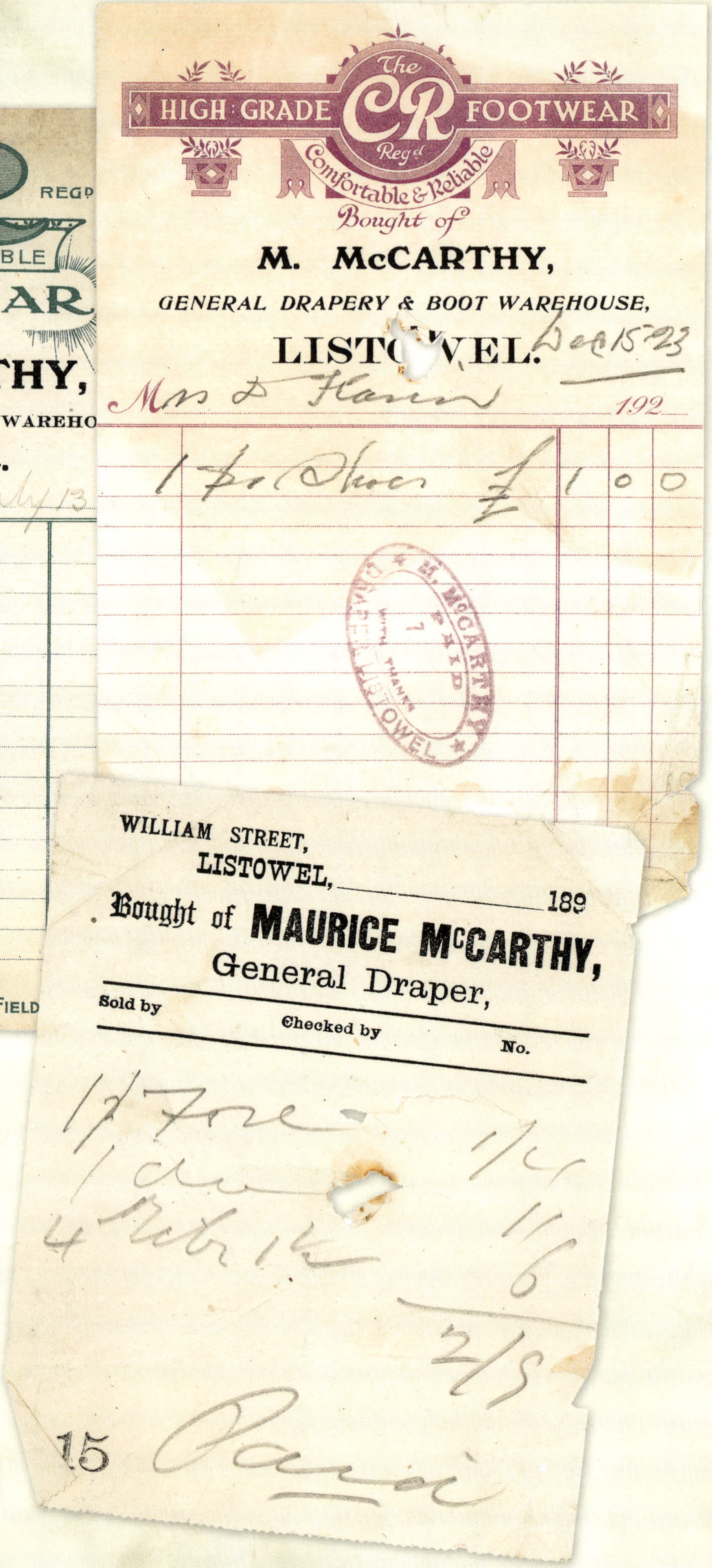

HIGH GRADE The CR Regd FOOTWEAR

Comfortable & Reliable

Bought of

M. McCARTHY,

GENERAL DRAPERY & BOOT WAREHOUSE,

LISTOWEL. Dec 15 '23

192

1 pr Shoes £ 1 0 0

M. McCARTHY PAID 7 WITH THANKS DRAPER LISTOWEL

WILLIAM STREET,

LISTOWEL, 189

Bought of MAURICE McCARTHY,

General Draper,

Sold by Checked by No.

1/4

1/6

6

2/8

15 Paid

11 Lower William Street

Maurice and Ellen McCarthy's General Drapery and Boot Store was at 11 Lower William Street. In 1901, McCarthy's employed three assistants in their shop.

17 Lower William Street

Thomas J Murphy (below), victualler and skin buyer, was known in Listowel as 'The Colonel'. He inherited the business around 1908 from the former owner Thomas Dillon, a relative, who operated as a hide and skin dealer and salt manufacturer for the previous 50 years.

Murphy's Pearse Street address was part of an unofficial movement to change the names of the streets during the late 1920s.

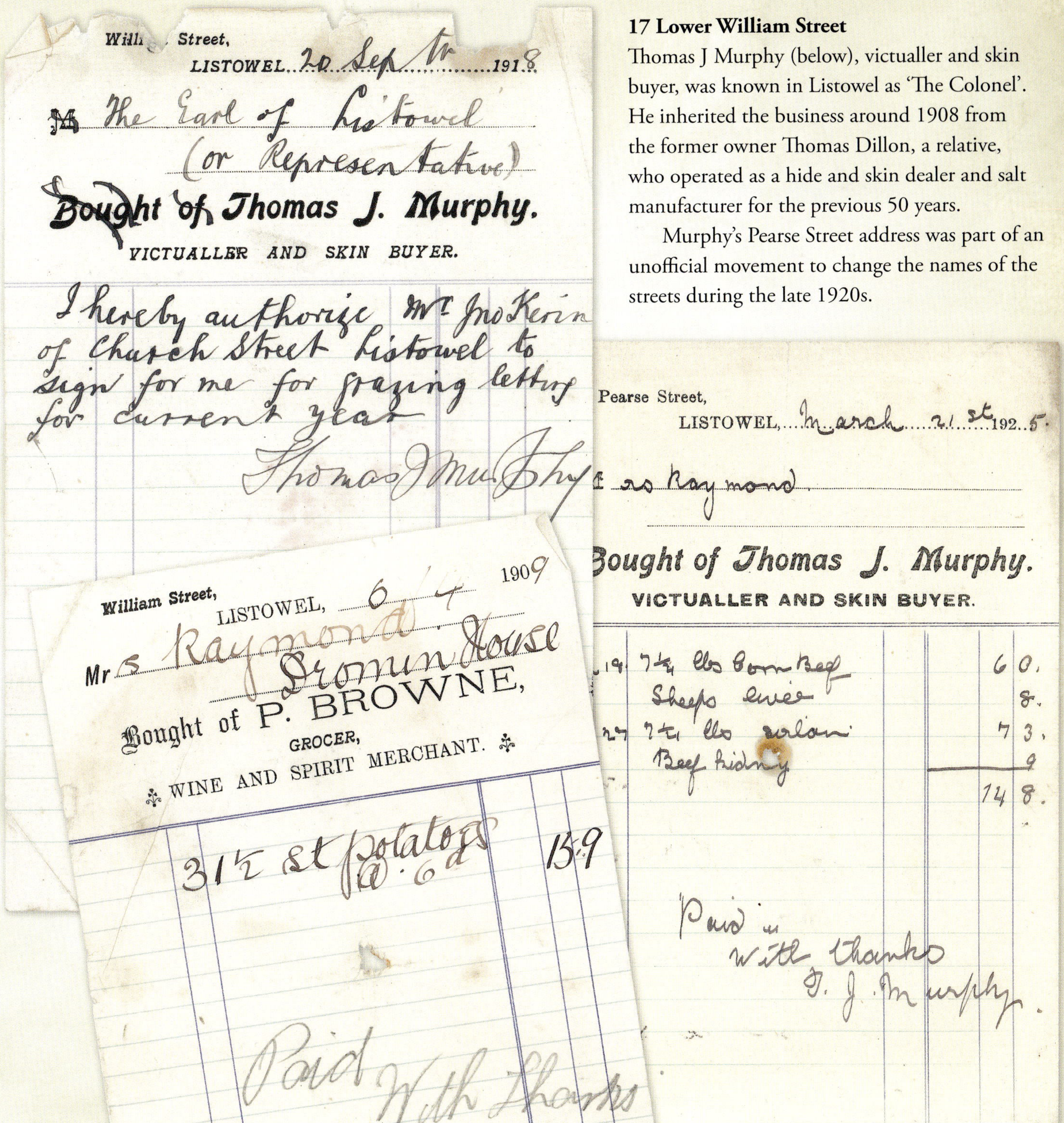

William Street,
LISTOWEL, 20 Sept 1918
M The Earl of Listowel
(or Representative)
Bought of Thomas J. Murphy.
VICTUALLER AND SKIN BUYER.
I hereby authorize Mr Jno Kerin of Church Street Listowel to sign for me for grazing letting for current year
Thomas J Murphy

Pearse Street,
LISTOWEL, March 21st 1925
Mrs Raymond
Bought of Thomas J. Murphy.
VICTUALLER AND SKIN BUYER.

19	7¼ lbs Corn Beef	6	0
	Sheeps liver		8
27	7¼ lbs sirloin	7	3
	Beef kidney		9
		14	8

Paid with thanks
T. J. Murphy

William Street,
LISTOWEL, 6/4 1909
Mrs Raymond
Dromin House
Bought of P. BROWNE,
GROCER,
WINE AND SPIRIT MERCHANT.

31½ st potatoes 10·6d	15/9

Paid With thanks
P Browne

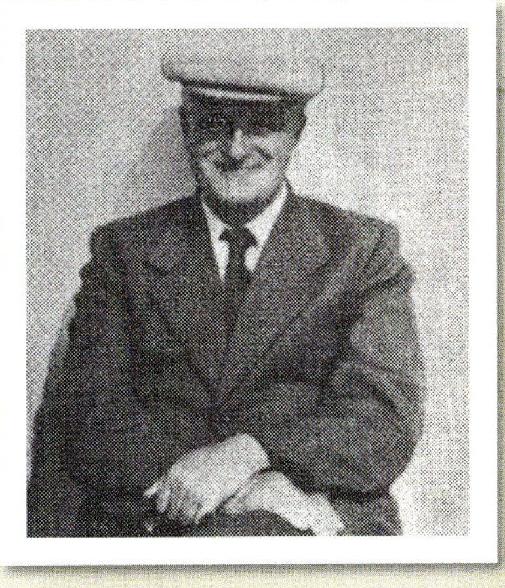

19 Lower William Street

Catherine Browne operated as a publican. Her son, Paddy, started a butcher's shop on the premises and also became a bookmaker. Paddy's great-grandson, Berkie, now runs a bookmaker's office in the house.

21 Lower William Street

J.J. Galvin commenced trading in the 1870s, dealing in an extraordinary range of commodities as is evident from the billhead top. A wine and spirit off-licence business continues today at the same location. The outstanding colourful billheads would have been presented by the oil companies, with whom the Galvin family dealt with in relation to their garage business in Market Street.

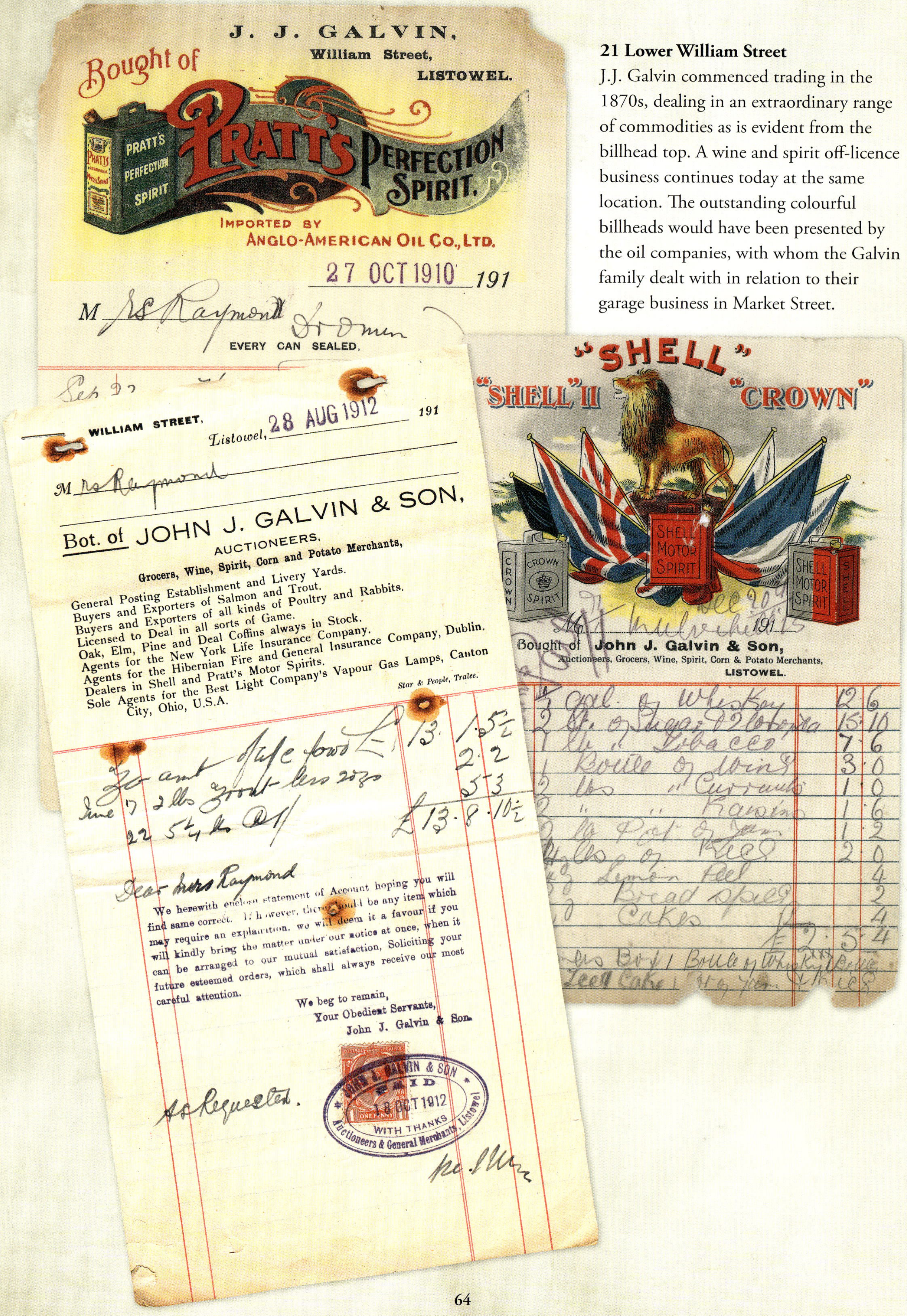

J. J. GALVIN,
William Street,
LISTOWEL.

Bought of
PRATT'S PERFECTION SPIRIT.
IMPORTED BY
ANGLO-AMERICAN OIL CO., LTD.

27 OCT 1910 191

M Rs Raymond

EVERY CAN SEALED.

WILLIAM STREET, Listowel, 28 AUG 1912 191

M rs Raymond

Bot. of JOHN J. GALVIN & SON,
AUCTIONEERS,
Grocers, Wine, Spirit, Corn and Potato Merchants,
General Posting Establishment and Livery Yards.
Buyers and Exporters of Salmon and Trout.
Buyers and Exporters of all kinds of Poultry and Rabbits.
Licensed to Deal in all sorts of Game.
Oak, Elm, Pine and Deal Coffins always in Stock.
Agents for the New York Life Insurance Company.
Agents for the Hibernian Fire and General Insurance Company, Dublin.
Dealers in Shell and Pratt's Motor Spirits.
Sole Agents for the Best Light Company's Vapour Gas Lamps, Canton City, Ohio, U.S.A.

Star & People, Tralee.

To amt as per acct £13. 1. 5½
June 7 2 lbs Trout less 2d 2. 2
22 5¼ lb @1/ 5. 3
£13. 8. 10½

Dear Mrs Raymond

We herewith enclose statement of Account hoping you will find same correct. If however, there should be any item which may require an explanation, we will deem it a favour if you will kindly bring the matter under our notice at once, when it can be arranged to our mutual satisfaction, Soliciting your future esteemed orders, which shall always receive our most careful attention.

We beg to remain,
Your Obedient Servants,
John J. Galvin & Son.

As Requested.

JOHN J. GALVIN & SON
PAID
18 OCT 1912
WITH THANKS
Auctioneers & General Merchants, Listowel

"SHELL"
"SHELL" II "CROWN"

SHELL MOTOR SPIRIT
CROWN SPIRIT

M 191

Bought of John J. Galvin & Son,
Auctioneers, Grocers, Wine, Spirit, Corn & Potato Merchants,
LISTOWEL.

½	Gal. of Whiskey	12	6
2	St. of Sugar	15	10
1	lb. Tobacco	7	6
1	Bottle of Wine	3	0
2	lbs Currants	1	0
2	Raisins	1	6
2	lb Pot of Jam	1	2
	Peel	2	0
	Lemon Peel		4
	Bread Spice		2
	Cakes		4
		£2. 5	4

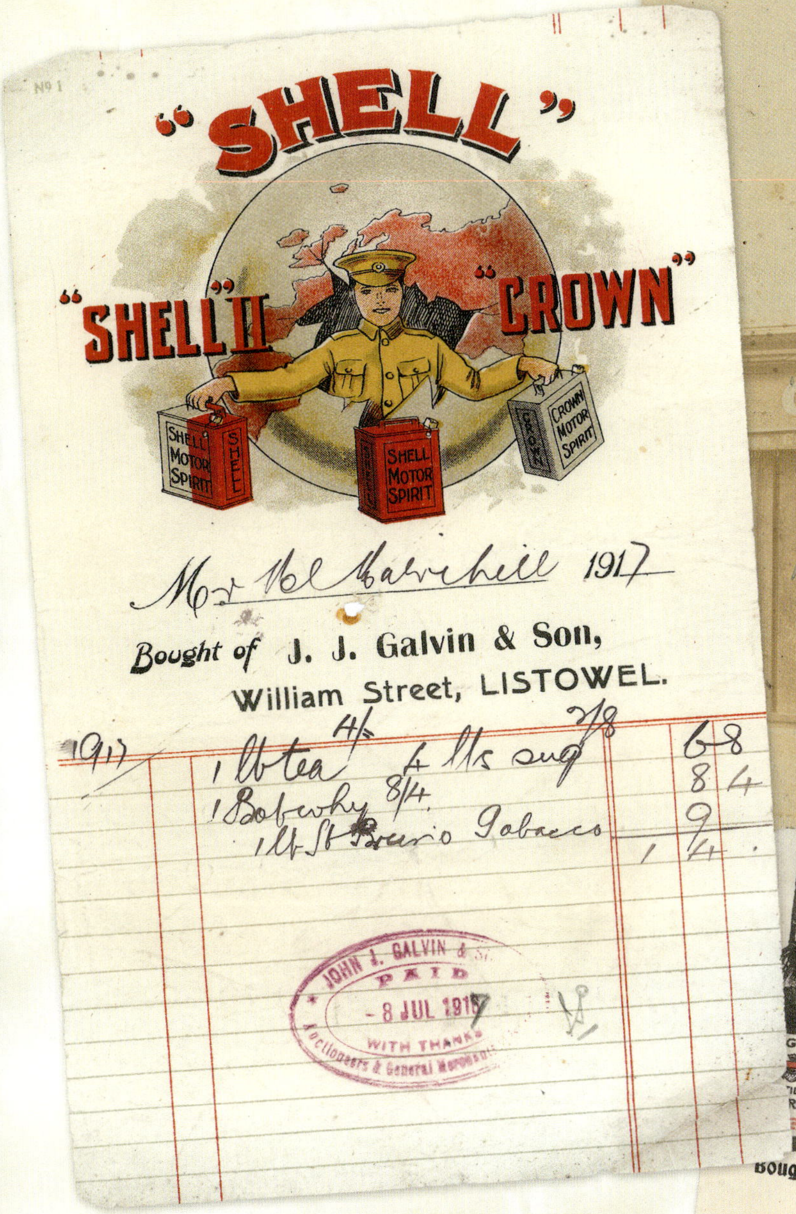
No 1

"SHELL"

"SHELL II" "CROWN"

SHELL MOTOR SPIRIT

CROWN MOTOR SPIRIT

Mr McMahon Hill 1917

Bought of J. J. Galvin & Son,
William Street, LISTOWEL.

1917	1 lb tea 4/- 4 lbs sug 2/8		6	8
	1 Bot why 8/4		8	4
	1 lb St Bruno Tobacco		9	
		1	4	

JOHN J. GALVIN & SON
PAID
- 8 JUL 1918
WITH THANKS
Auctioneers & General Merchants

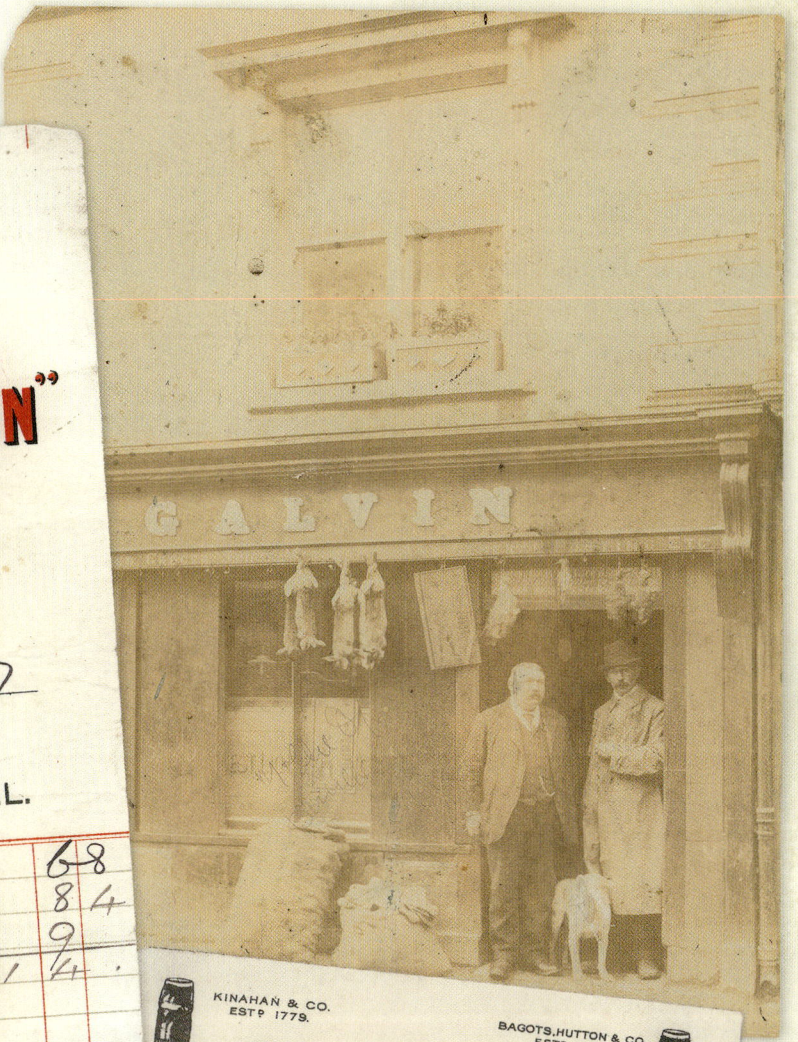

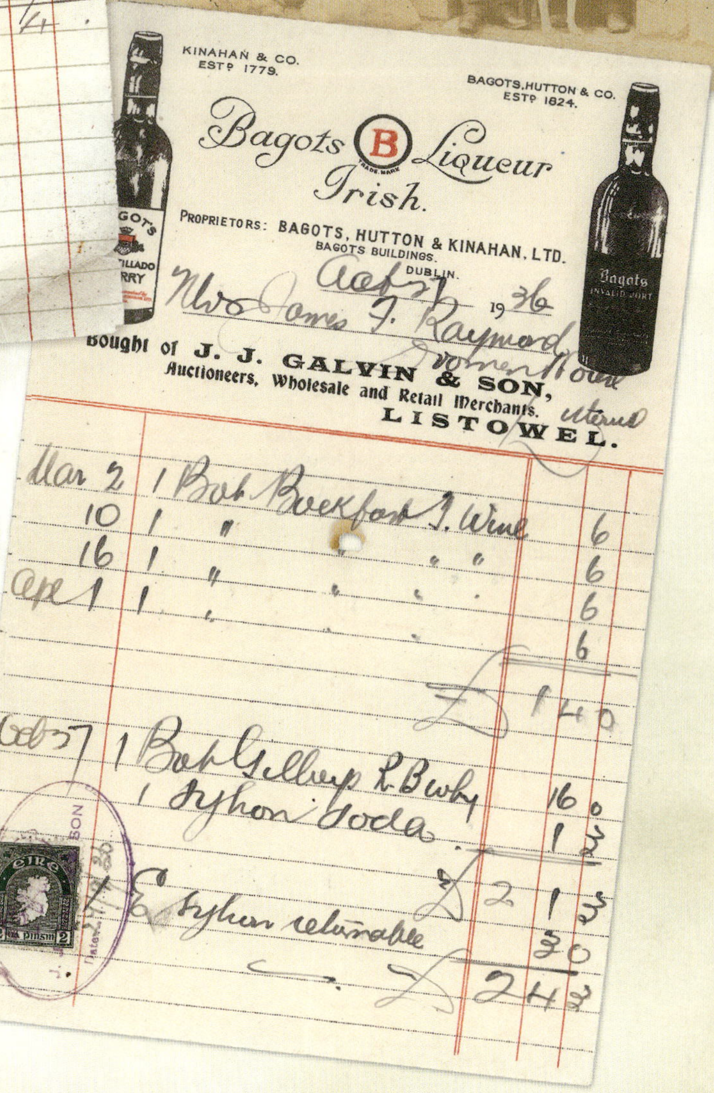
KINAHAN & CO.
ESTD 1779.

BAGOTS, HUTTON & CO.
ESTD 1824.

Bagots B Liqueur Irish.

PROPRIETORS: BAGOTS, HUTTON & KINAHAN, LTD.
BAGOTS BUILDINGS.
DUBLIN.

Bagots

Mrs James J. Raymond Octr 1936

Bought of J. J. GALVIN & SON,
Auctioneers, Wholesale and Retail Merchants,
LISTOWEL.

Mar 2	1 Bot Breakfast Wine		6
10	1 "		6
16	1 "		6
Apl 1	1 "		6
		£1	4 0
Octr 7	1 Bot Gilbeys L Whisky	16	0
	1 Syphon Soda	1	3
		£2	1 3
	Syphon returnable		2 0
		£2	4 3

EIRE 2

23 Lower William Street

William Keane-Stack was born at Dromin Lower, Listowel, in 1894. He qualified as a pharmaceutical chemist in 1920. He was married to Margaret McDermott from Indianapolis, Indiana, USA. He ran his pharmacy at 23 Lower William Street. The business shut in 1994. John B. Keane served for some time as a pharmaceutical assistant with the Keane-Stacks.

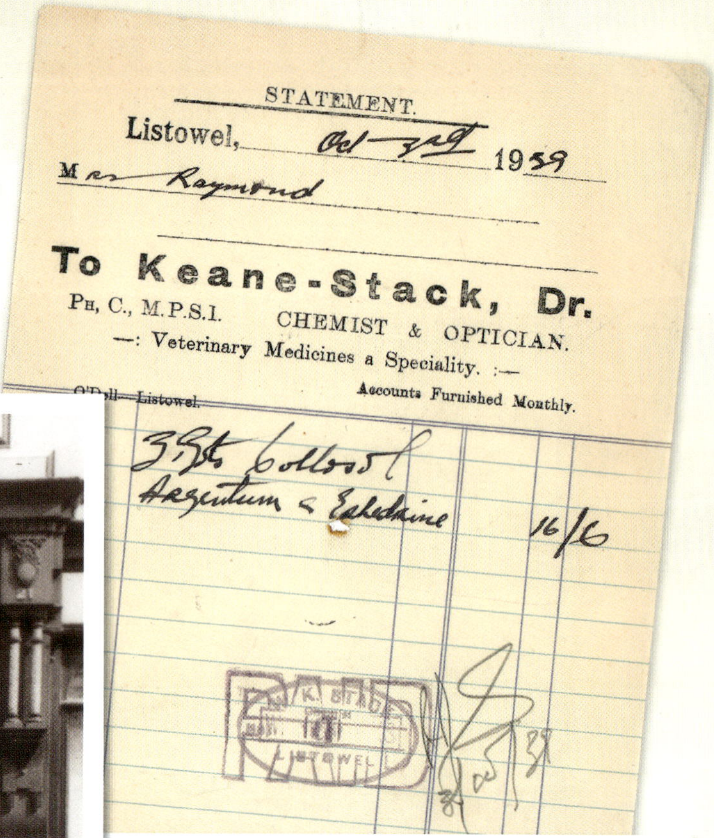

STATEMENT.

Listowel, Oct 3rd 1939

M rs Raymond

To Keane-Stack, Dr.

PH, C., M.P.S.I. CHEMIST & OPTICIAN.

—: Veterinary Medicines a Speciality. :—

Accounts Furnished Monthly.

3 Bts Collosol Argentum & Ephedrine 16/6

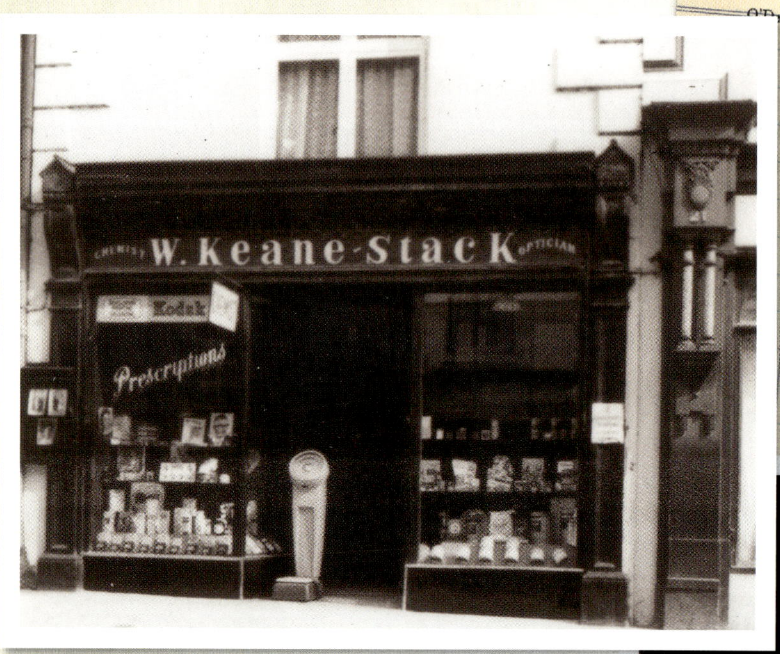

Below: William's brother Jim Keane-Stack (second from left) in a group outside the pharmacy, circa 1930s.

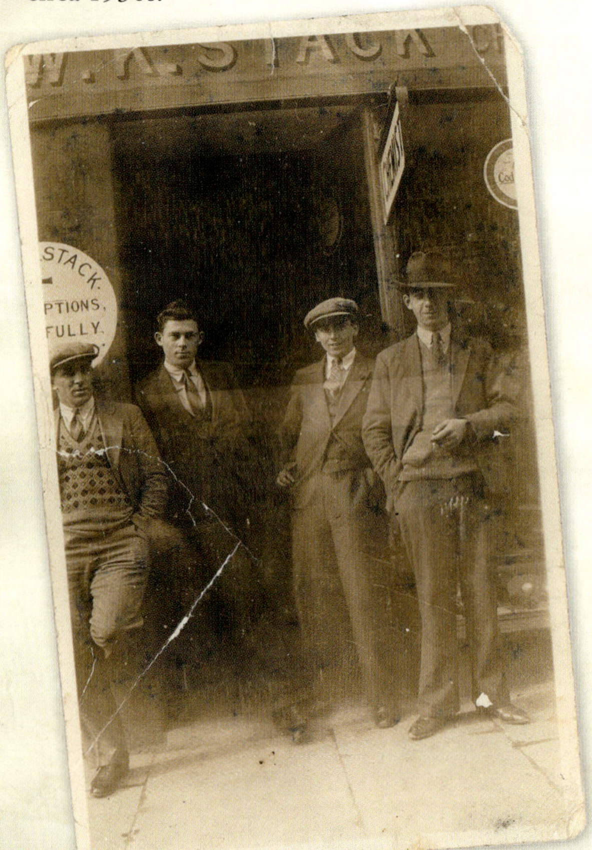

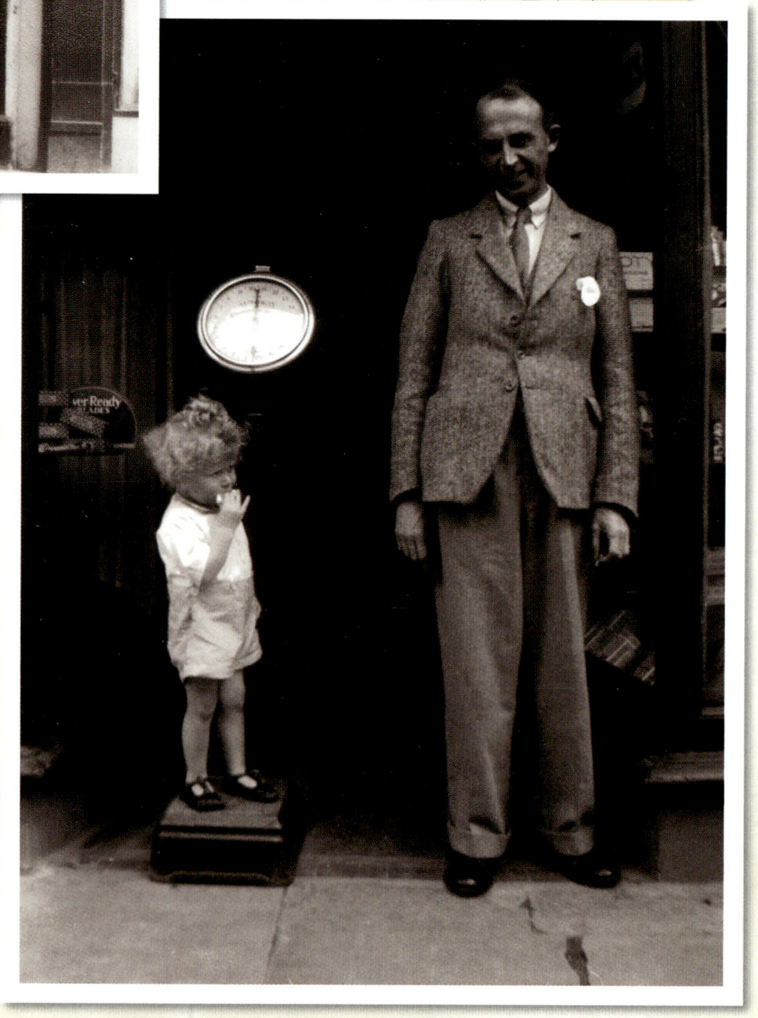

Above: William Keane-Stack and his son Stephen taken in the 1930s.

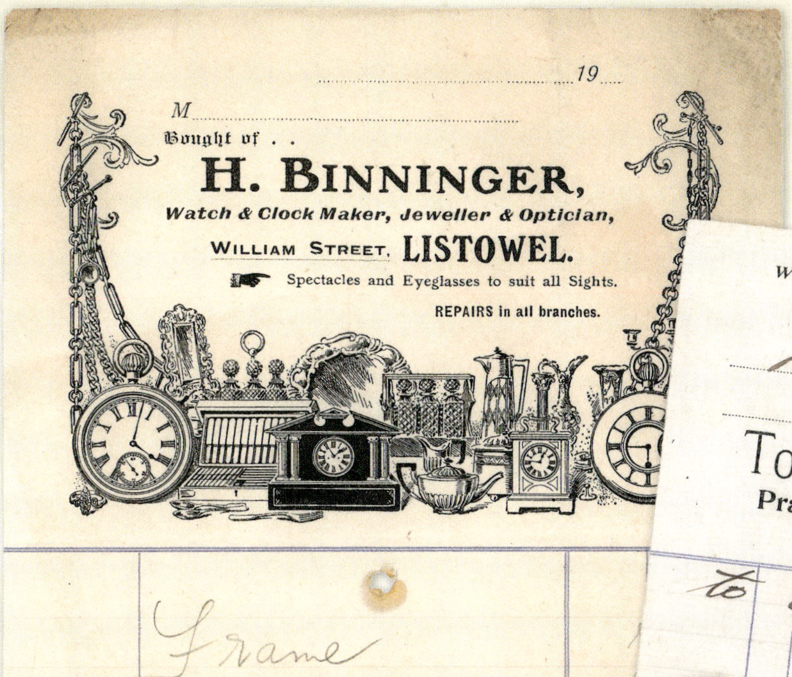

......19....

M.........

Bought of . .

H. BINNINGER,

Watch & Clock Maker, Jeweller & Optician,

WILLIAM STREET, LISTOWEL.

Spectacles and Eyeglasses to suit all Sights.

REPAIRS in all branches.

Frame

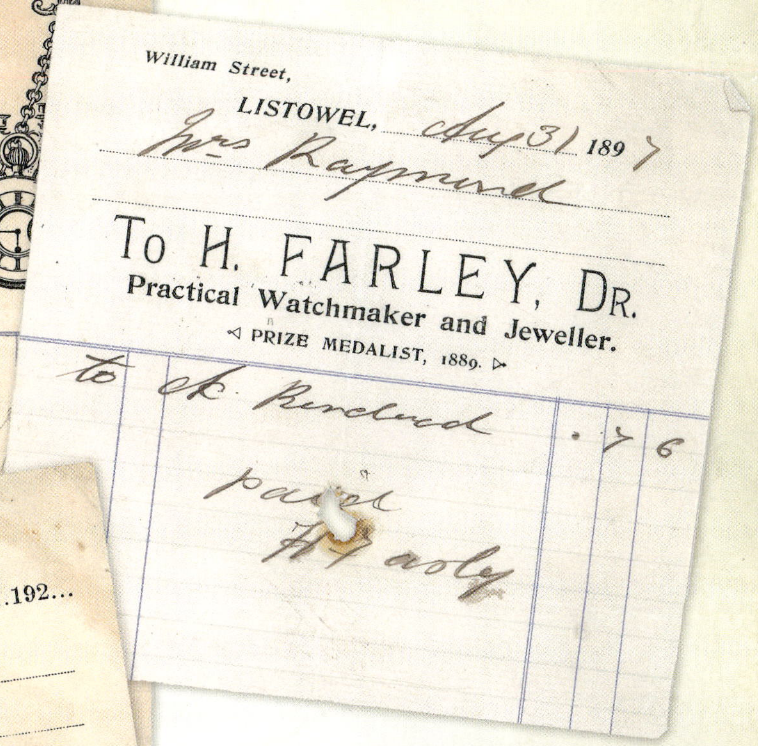

William Street,

LISTOWEL, Aug 31 1897

Mrs Raymond

To H. FARLEY, DR.

Practical Watchmaker and Jeweller.

◁ PRIZE MEDALIST, 1889. ▷

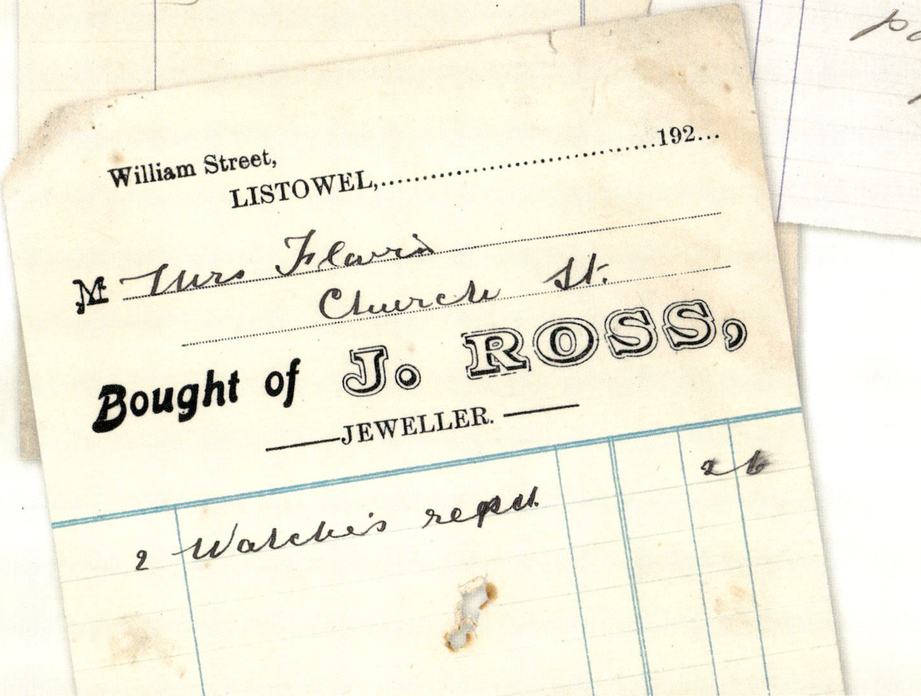

William Street,

LISTOWEL,......192...

M Mrs

Church St.

Bought of J. ROSS,

JEWELLER.

2 Watches repd.

Paid

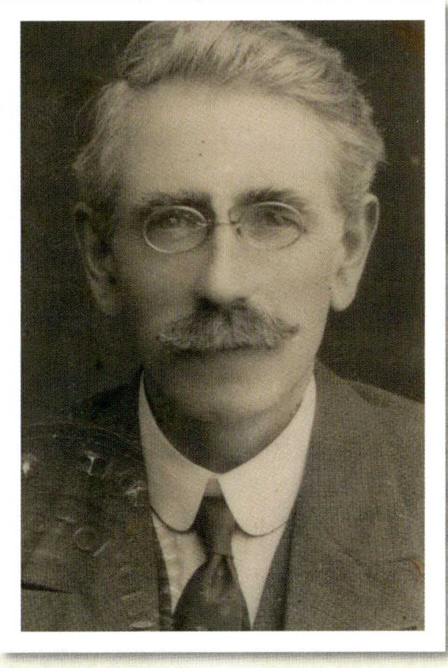

25 Lower William Street

The evolution of house and business changes is evident from the number of businesses that operated in what is now No. 25 Lower William Street. On these premises were jewellery businesses and also Dillon's Drapers. In the 1920s, John Ross (pictured left) came from Aberdeen to work with J. Farley. For a short period he had a jeweller's shop in Church Street, before moving back to William Street. He later moved to Tralee where the Ross family still have their business. Herman Binninger was a German whose business as a jeweller was complemented by his skills as an optician. Since the 1950s, the Sexton family have run their clothing shop from here.

27 Lower William Street

Matthew O'Connor from Derry Farm, Listowel, married Margaret Foran, daughter of Edmund Foran of Inch, Lisselton, at Ballybunion on November 26, 1889. They commenced business at Lower William Street. After Matthew's death in 1922, the house and business were bought and joined to those of T. F. Cronin in the adjoining house. Paddy Power bookmakers now operate a bookmaking business from this property.

Photo: Matthew and Margaret O'Connor.

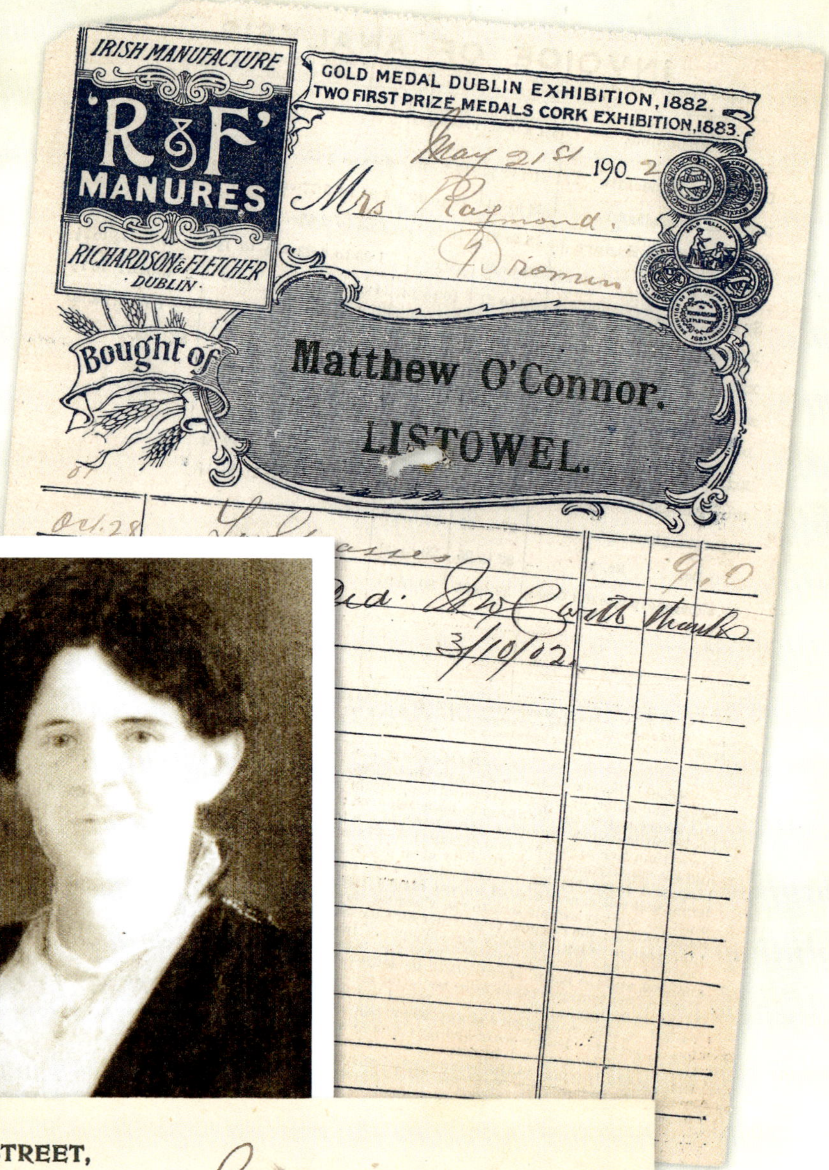

IRISH MANUFACTURE
'R&F'
MANURES
RICHARDSON & FLETCHER
DUBLIN

GOLD MEDAL DUBLIN EXHIBITION, 1882.
TWO FIRST PRIZE MEDALS CORK EXHIBITION, 1883

May 21st 1902
Mrs Raymond.
Dromin

Bought of Matthew O'Connor, LISTOWEL.

Oct 28 ... 9.0
Rcd. M O'C with thanks
3/10/02

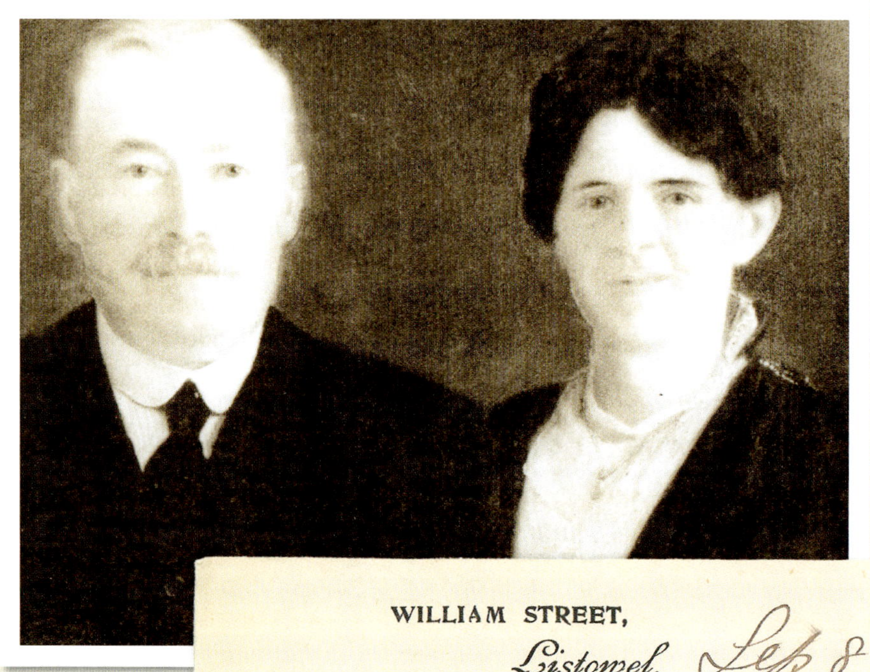

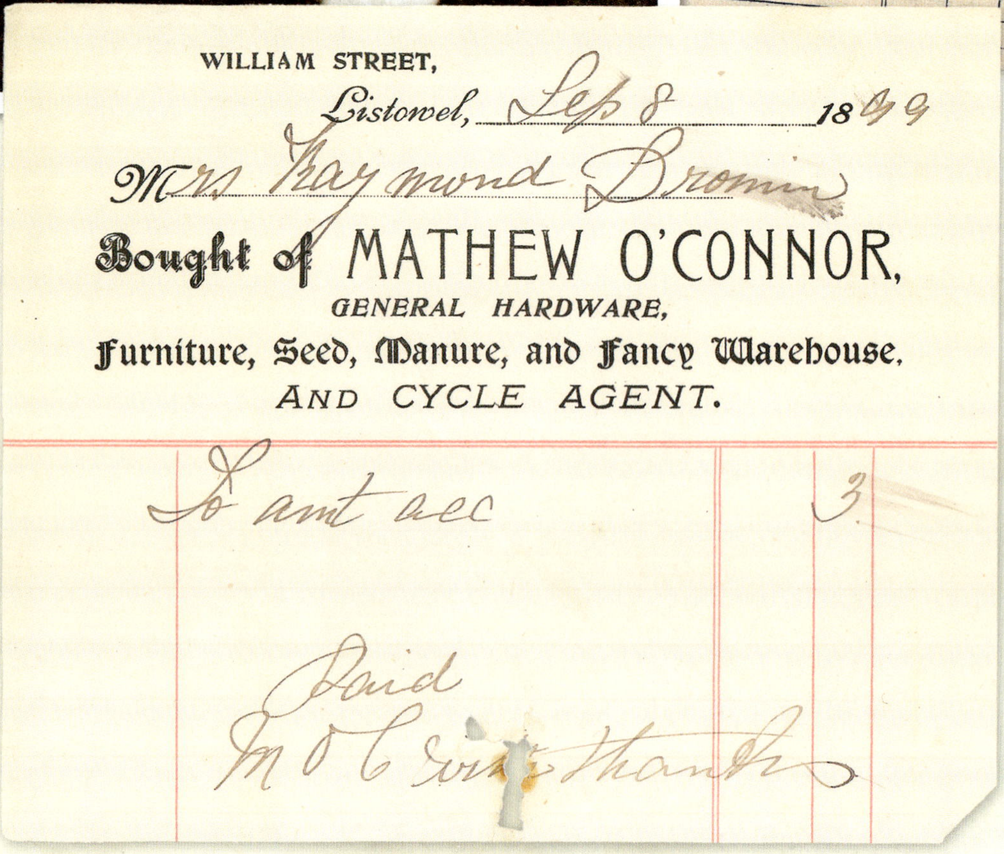

WILLIAM STREET,
Listowel, Sep 8 1899
Mrs Raymond Bromin

Bought of MATHEW O'CONNOR,
GENERAL HARDWARE,
Furniture, Seed, Manure, and Fancy Warehouse,
AND CYCLE AGENT.

To amt acc	3

Paid
M O'C with thanks

33 Lower William Street

Patrick and Catherine Clancy lived and carried out their business at 33 William Street. The business was inherited by a Nolan family who willed it to the Ahernes of Coolard. Subsequent owners were Daly's and Harris's. It is now a vegetable store run by Pat and Mary Whelan.

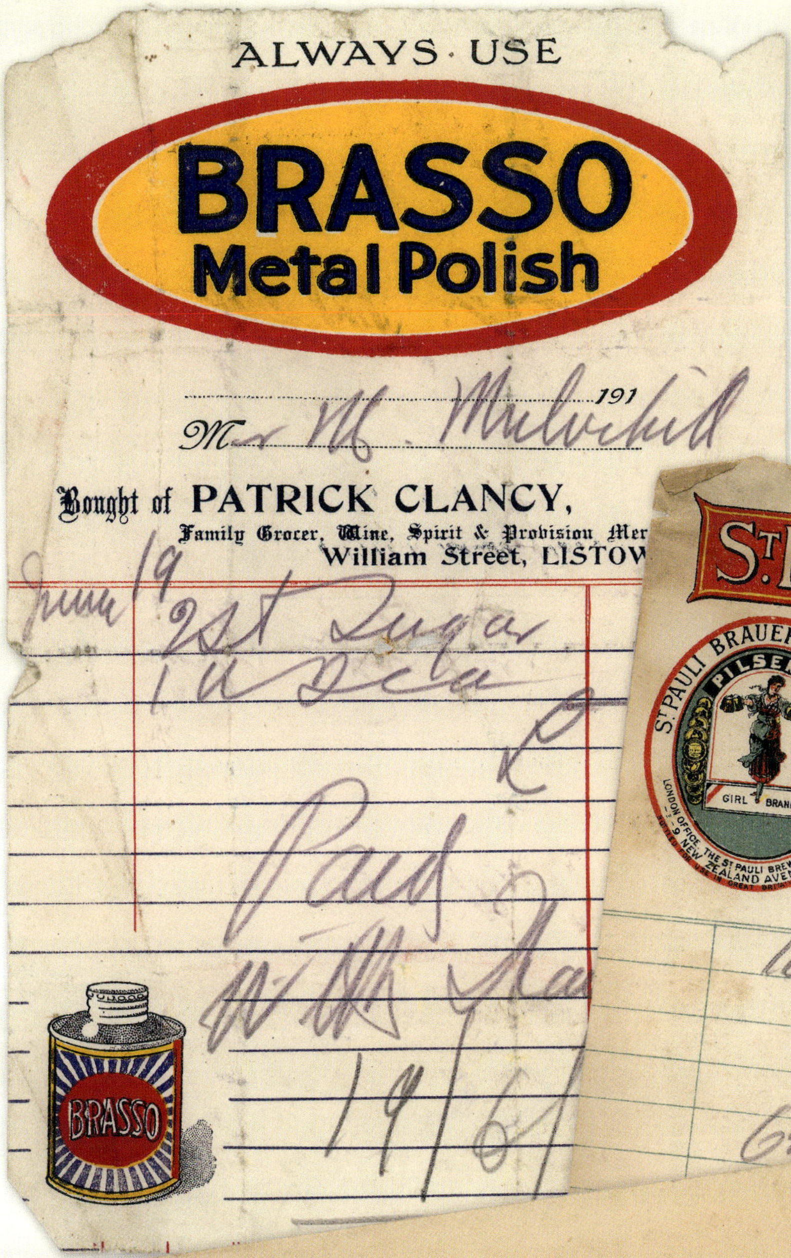
ALWAYS · USE
BRASSO
Metal Polish
191
Mr M. Mulvihill
Bought of PATRICK CLANCY,
Family Grocer, Wine, Spirit & Provision Mer
William Street, LISTOW
June 19 2st Sugar
Paid
19/6

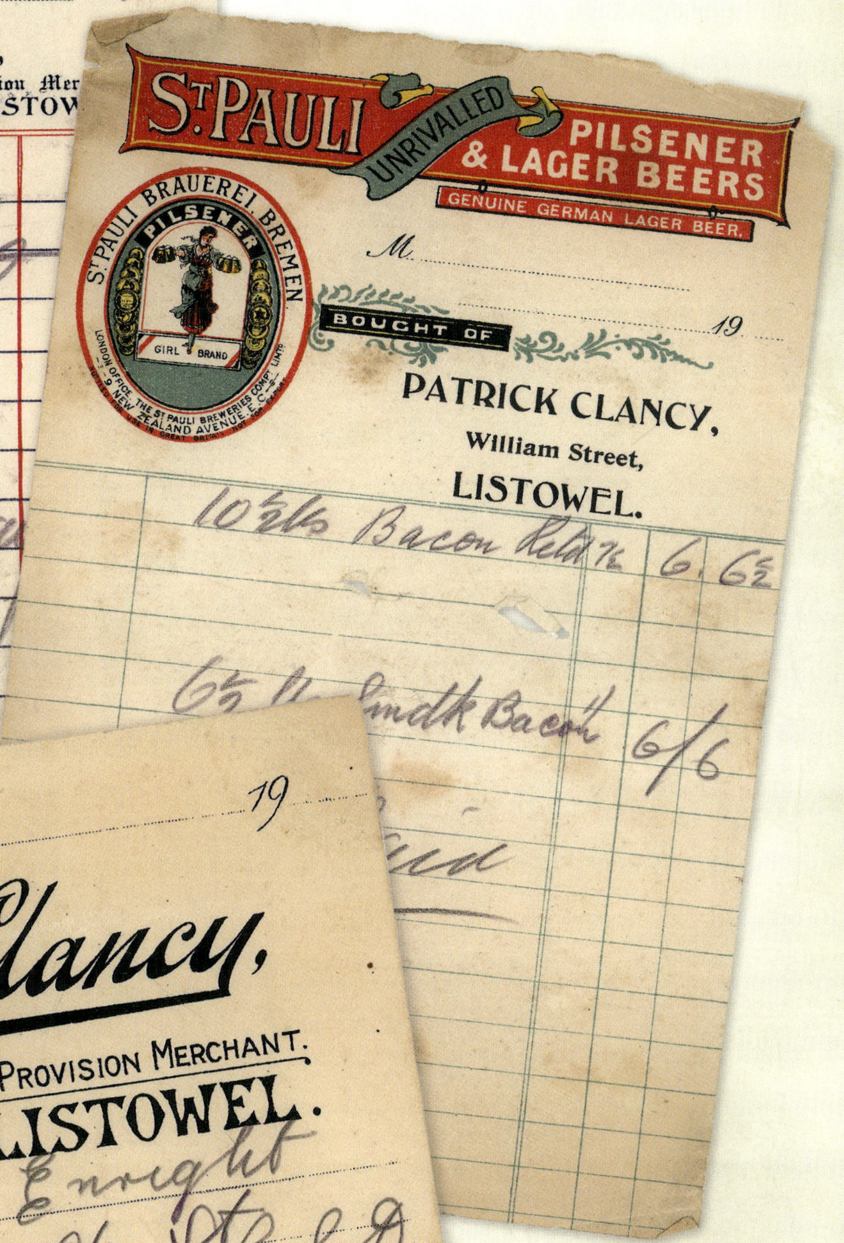

M.
19
BOUGHT OF
PATRICK CLANCY,
William Street,
LISTOWEL.

10½ lbs Bacon		6. 6½
6½ lbs Smk Bacon		6/6

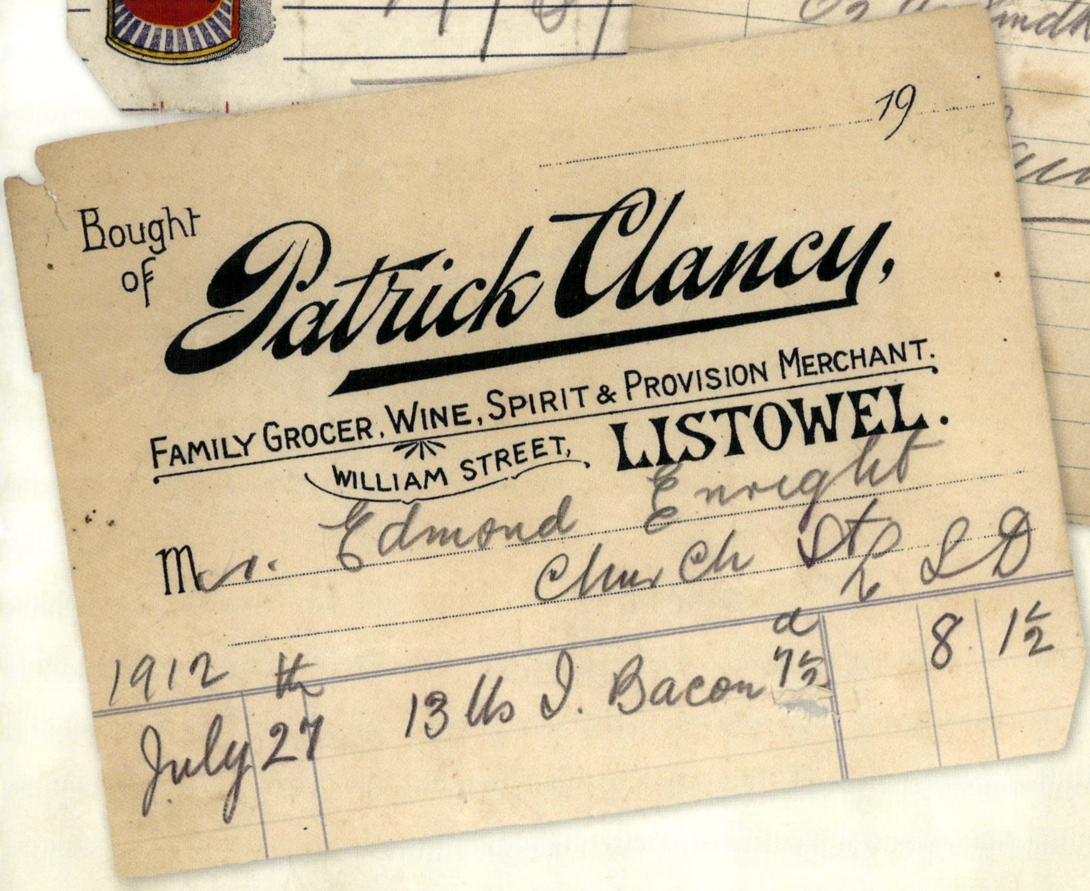
19
Bought of Patrick Clancy,
FAMILY GROCER, WINE, SPIRIT & PROVISION MERCHANT.
WILLIAM STREET, LISTOWEL.
Mr. Edmond Enright
Church St.

1912 July	27th	13 lbs J. Bacon 7½d	8	1½

29 Lower William Street

T. F. Cronin's centrally-located hardware shop, now No. 31 Lower William Street, at the intersection of William Street and Market Street, was a hive of activity for over 60 years. Thomas Cronin was from Cork and was married to Bridget Howard from County Clare. Cronin was a small, dapper man and it was said that when asked for something small he would usually search in his waistcoat pockets first.

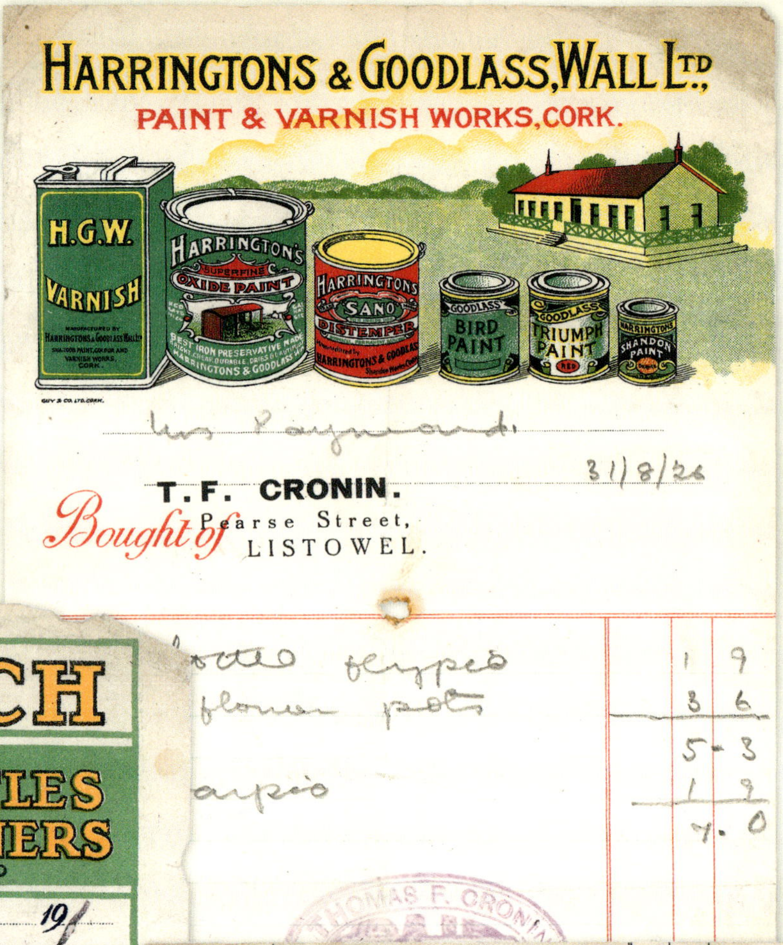

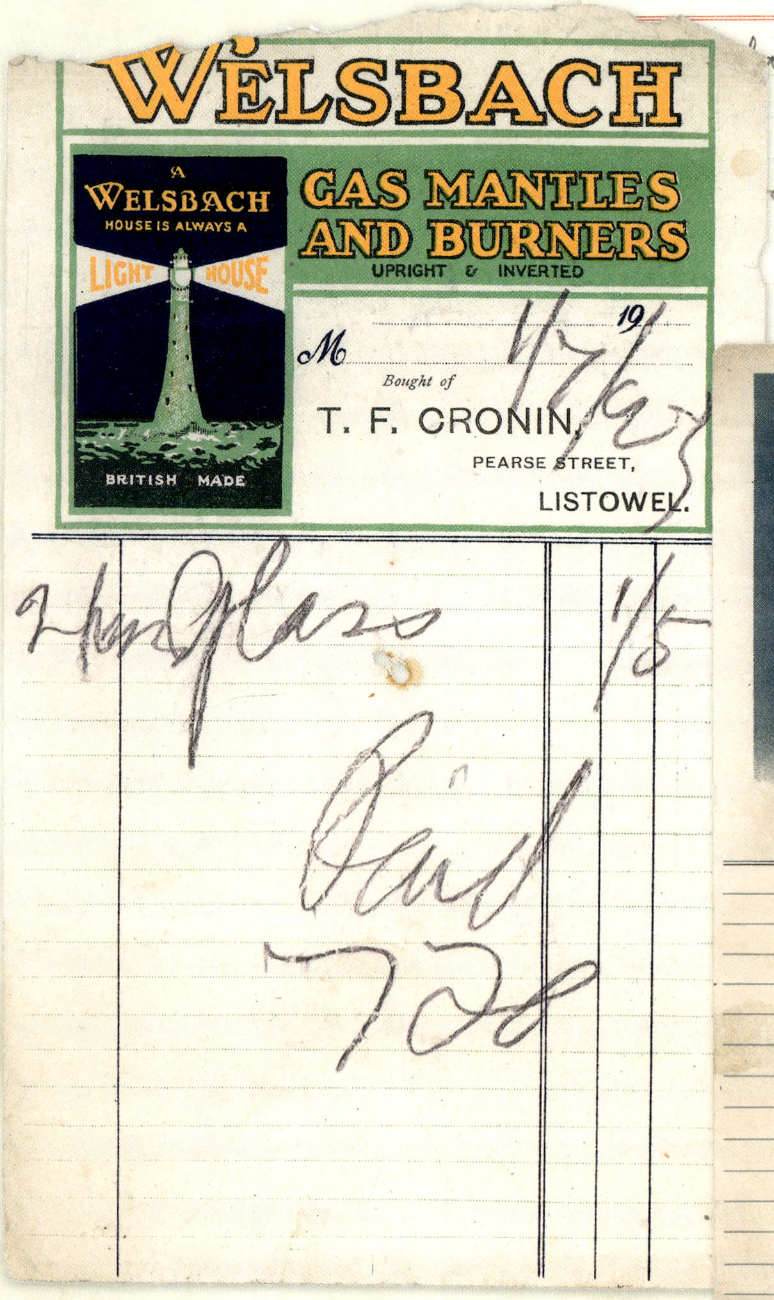

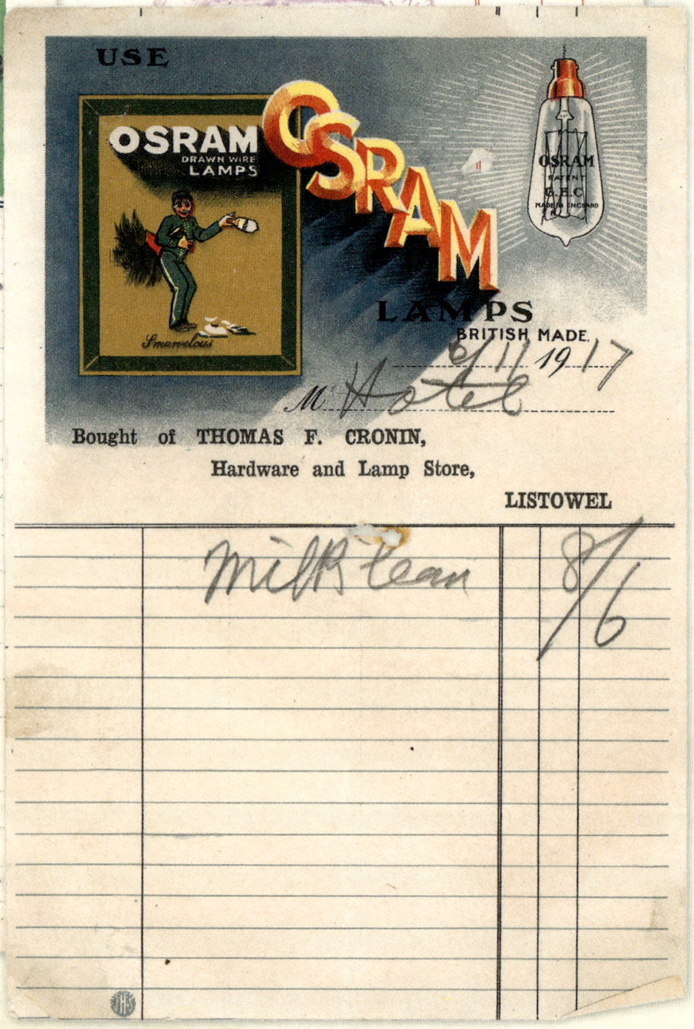

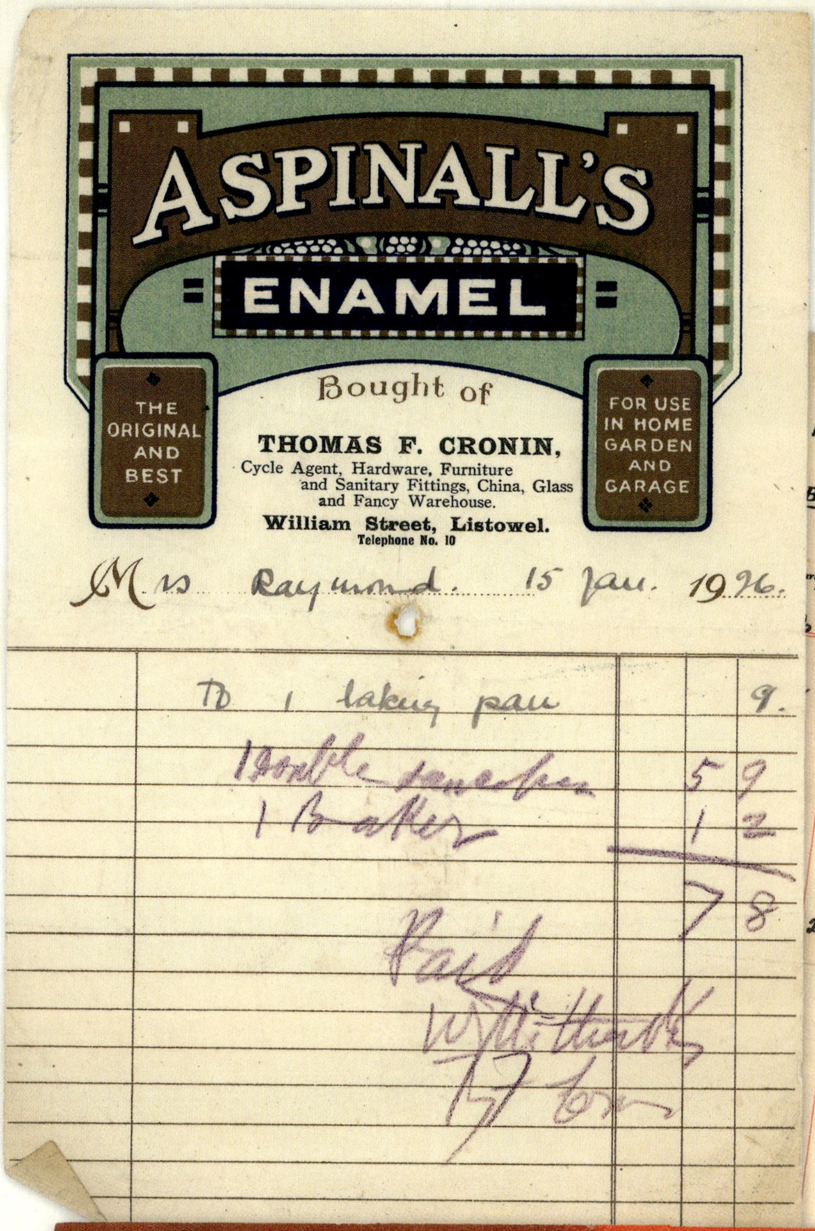
ASPINALL'S ENAMEL

THE ORIGINAL AND BEST

FOR USE IN HOME GARDEN AND GARAGE

Bought of

THOMAS F. CRONIN,
Cycle Agent, Hardware, Furniture and Sanitary Fittings, China, Glass and Fancy Warehouse.
William Street, Listowel.
Telephone No. 10

Mrs Raymond. 15 Jan. 1926.

To 1 baking pan			9
1 Double saucepan		5	9
1 Basket		1	2
		7	8

Paid with thanks

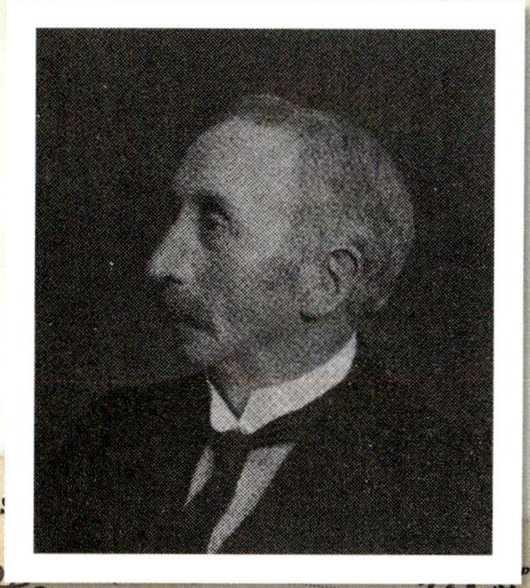

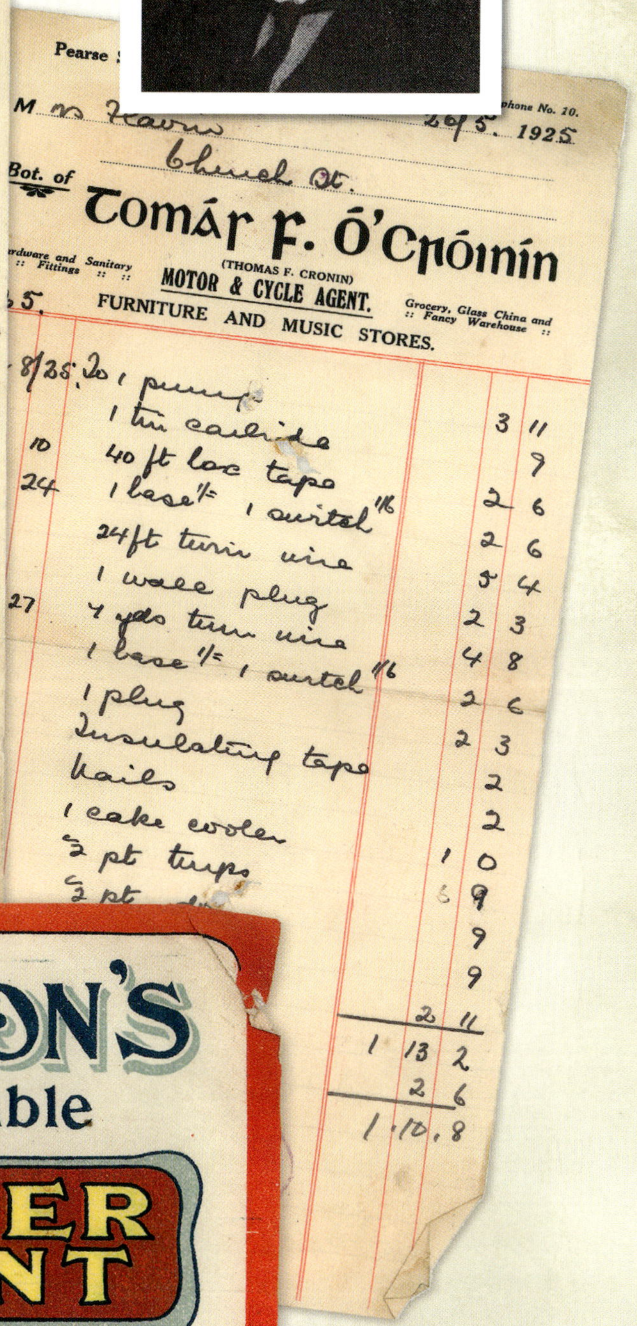
Pearse

Mrs Kearn 26/5. 1925
Church St.

Telephone No. 10.

Bot. of

Tomás F. Ó'Cróinín
(THOMAS F. CRONIN)
MOTOR & CYCLE AGENT.

Hardware and Sanitary Fittings

Grocery, Glass China and Fancy Warehouse

FURNITURE AND MUSIC STORES.

8/25	To 1 pump			
	1 tin carbide		3	11
10	40 ft lac tape			9
24	1 base 1/- 1 switch 1/6		2	6
	24 ft twin wire		2	6
	1 wall plug		5	4
27	4 yds twin wire		2	3
	1 base 1/- 1 switch 1/6		4	8
	1 plug		2	6
	Insulating tape		2	3
	Nails			2
	1 cake cooler			2
	3 pt tins		1	0
	3 pt		6	9
				9
				9
			2	11
		1	13	2
			2	6
		1	10	8

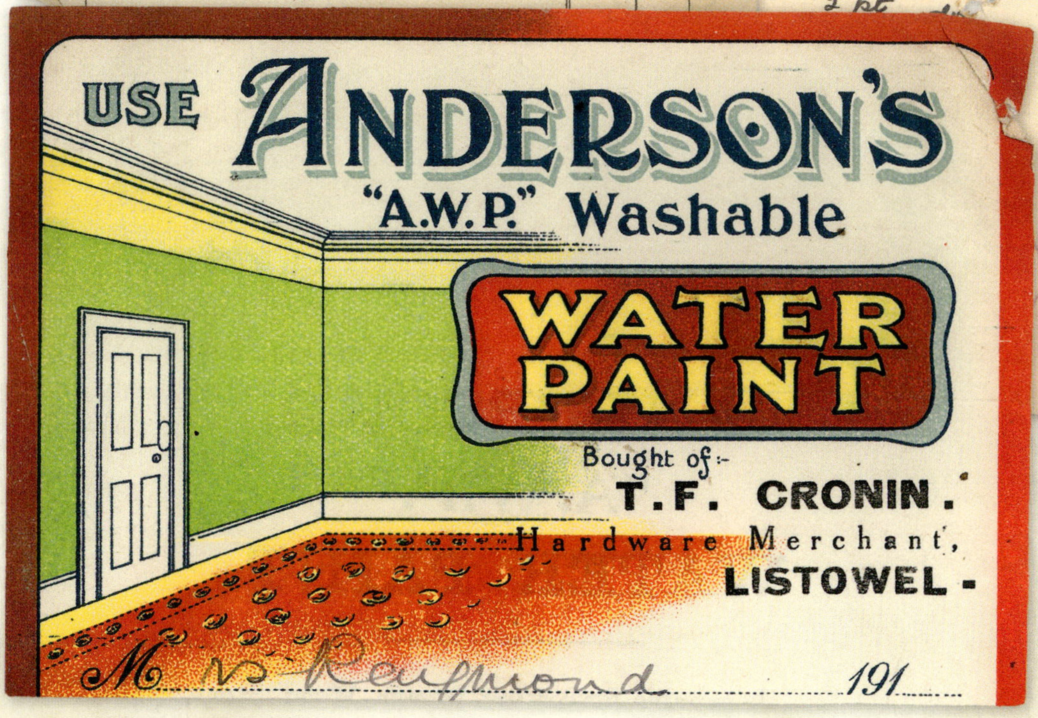
USE ANDERSON'S
"A.W.P." Washable
WATER PAINT

Bought of:-
T.F. CRONIN.
Hardware Merchant,
LISTOWEL.

Mrs Raymond 191

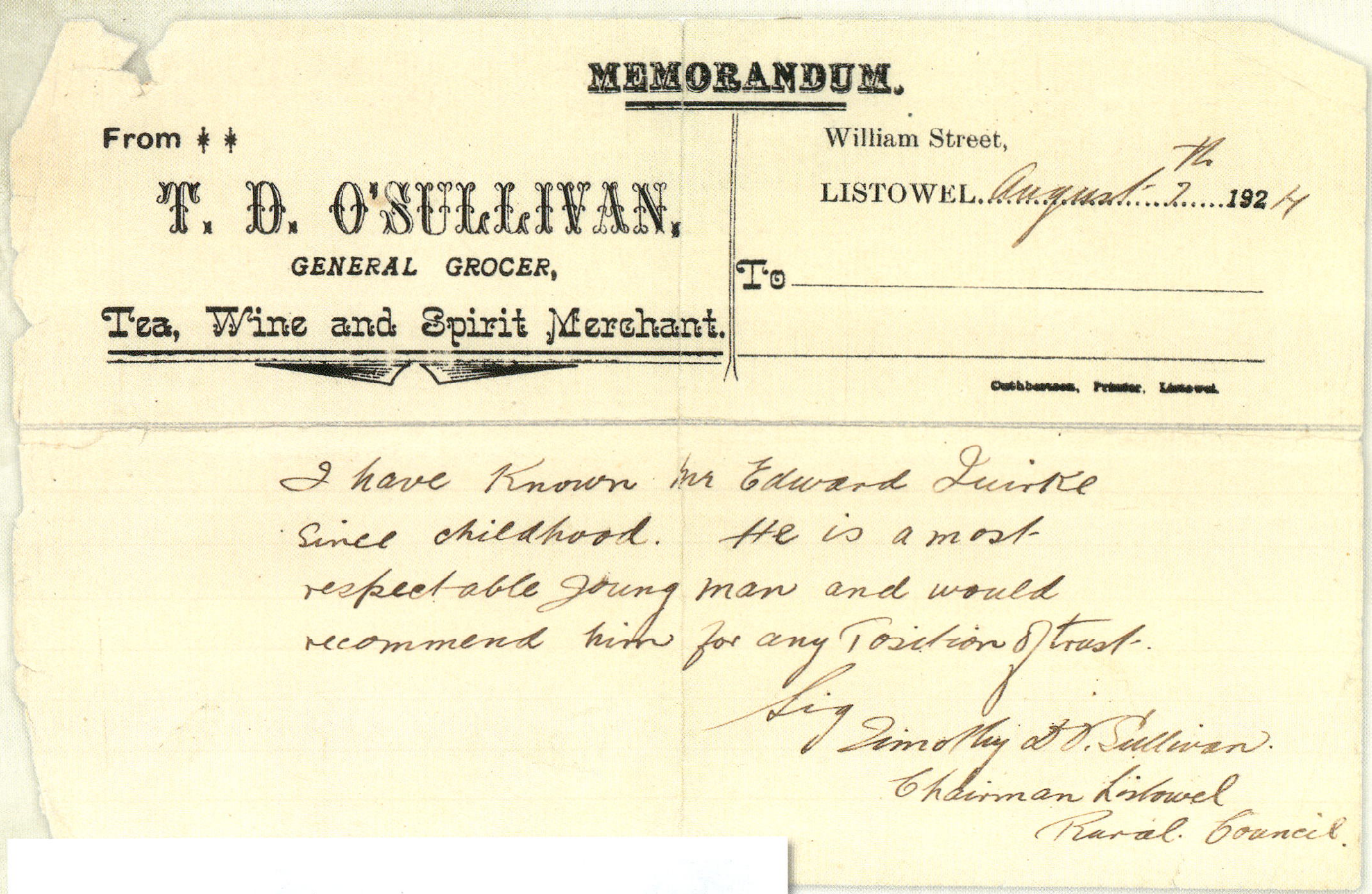

MEMORANDUM.

From
T. D. O'SULLIVAN,
GENERAL GROCER,
Tea, Wine and Spirit Merchant.

William Street,
LISTOWEL. August 7th 1924

To

Cuthbertson, Printer, Listowel.

I have Known Mr Edward Quirke since childhood. He is a most respectable young man and would recommend him for any Position of trust.

Sig Timothy D O'Sullivan.
Chairman Listowel
Rural Council

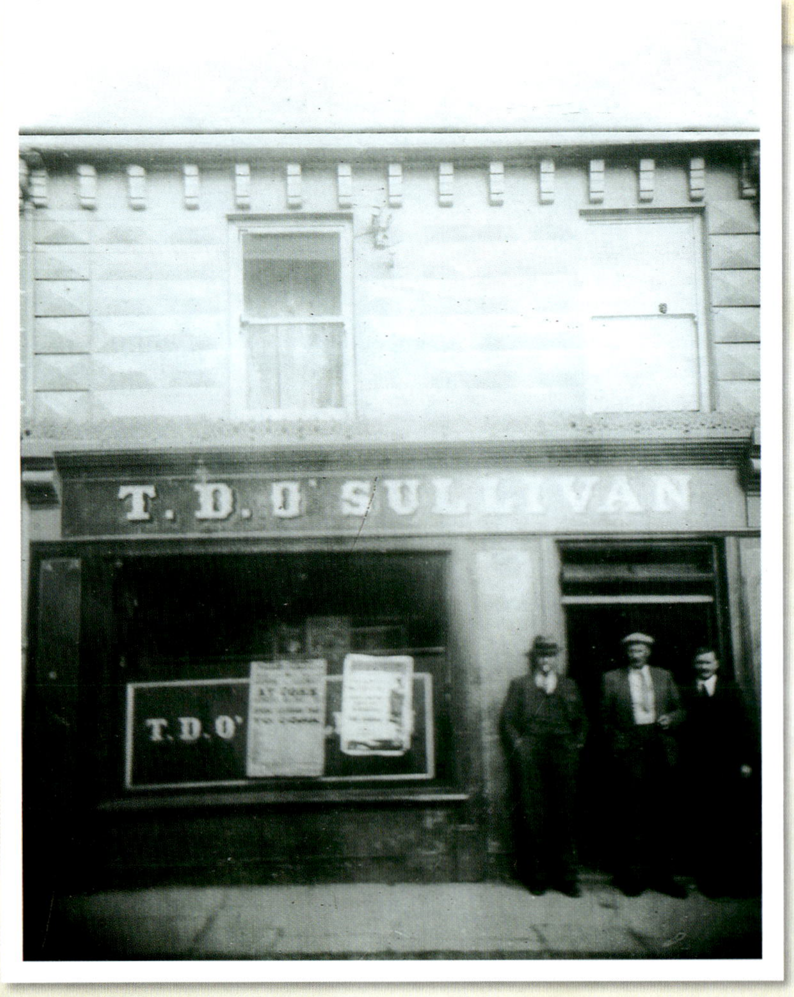

37 Lower William Street

T.D. O'Sullivan and his family rented and ran a public house at 37 Lower William Street for over 40 years. A noted coursing enthusiast, he named the bar 'The Greyhound Bar'. The business was bought by the newly-married John B. and Mary Keane in 1955. Here at night in the quiet hours after the pub closed, John B. would scribe his words. The plays and books which flowed from his pen would, for the next five decades, propel him to the forefront of the Irish literary world and made Keane a household name. The pub is still run by Mary Keane and their eldest son Billy.

T.D. O'Sullivan's letterhead contains a reference written by him in his capacity as Chairman of Listowel Rural Council for Edward Quirke of Dirha, Listowel, who was about to emigrate to America.

Photo left: The Greyhound Bar, T.D. O'Sullivan on right.

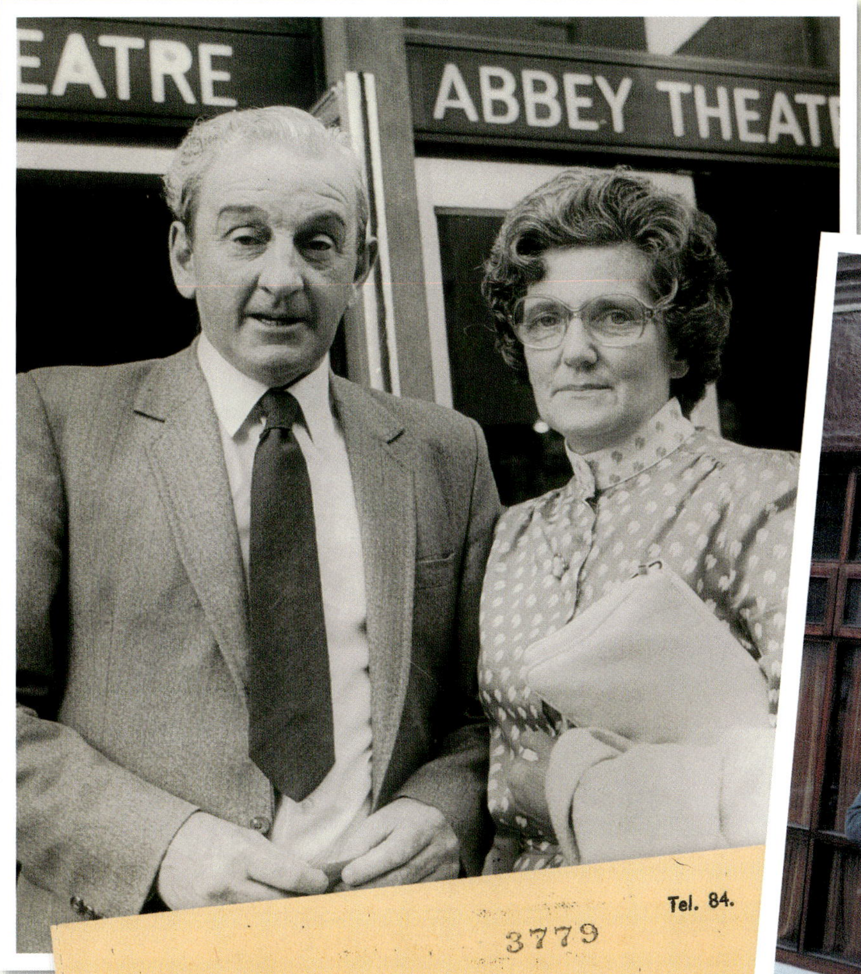

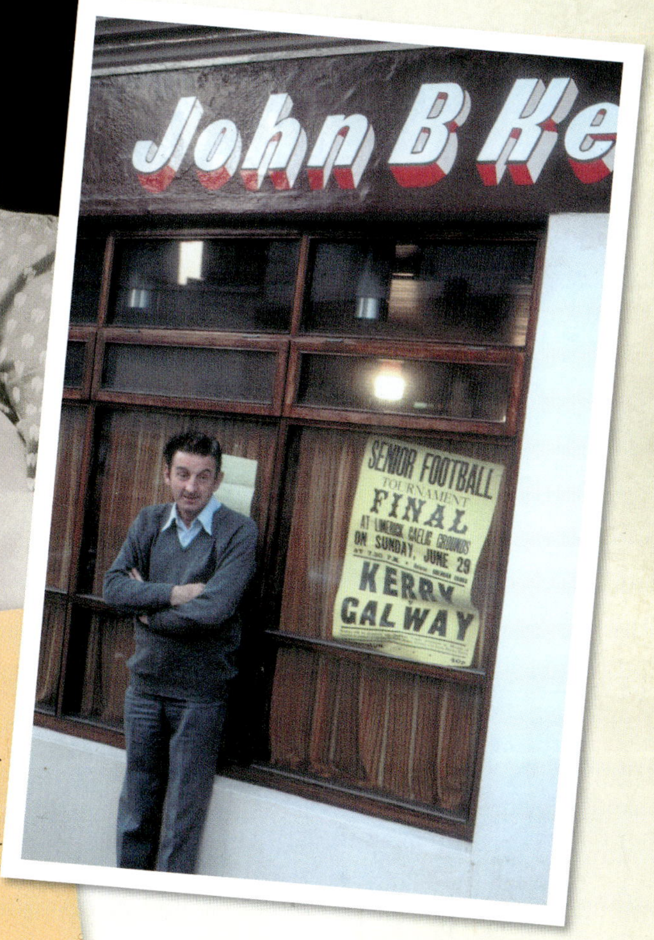

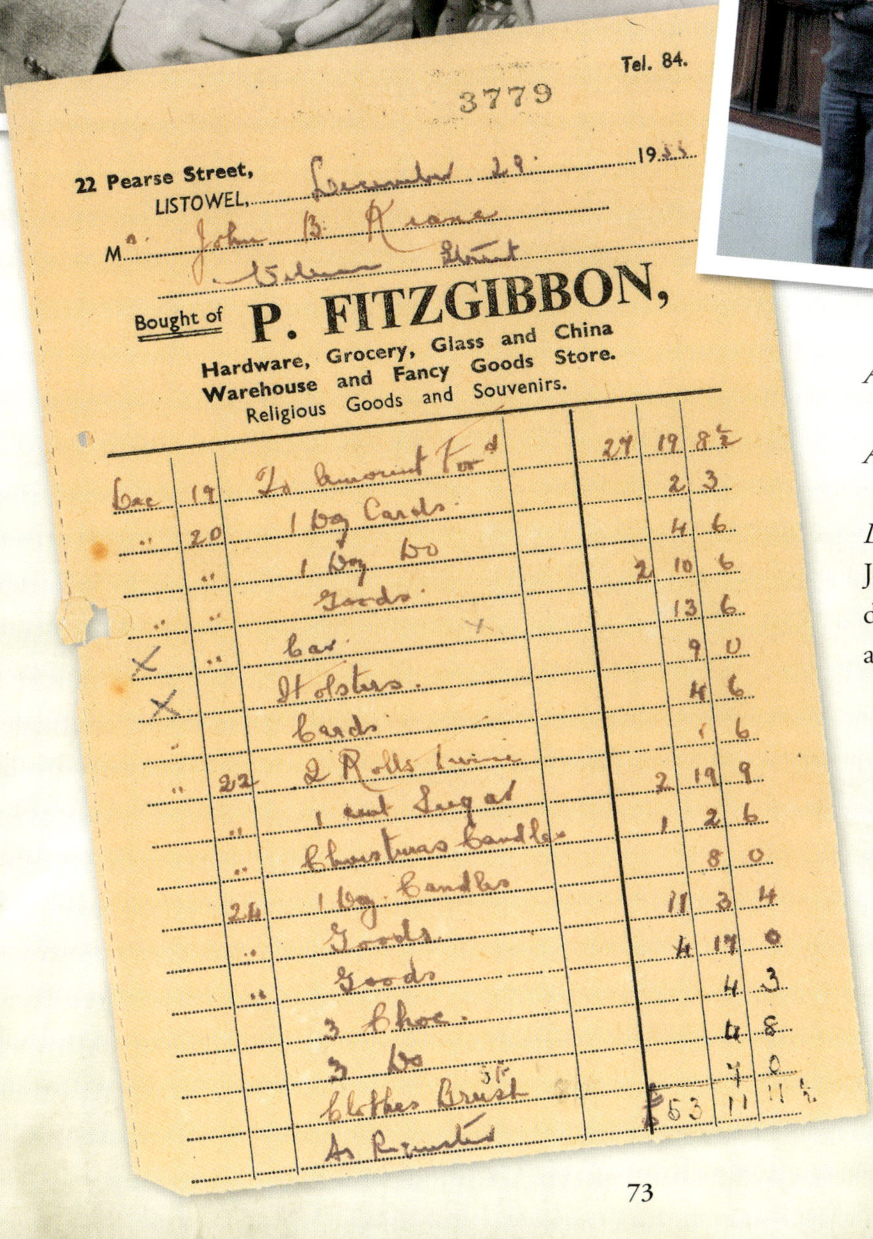
Tel. 84.

3779

22 Pearse Street,
LISTOWEL, December 29. 1955

Mr. John B. Keane
William Street

Bought of **P. FITZGIBBON,**
Hardware, Grocery, Glass and China
Warehouse and Fancy Goods Store.
Religious Goods and Souvenirs.

			£	s.	d.
		To Amount Fwd	27	19	8½
Dec	19	1 Doz Cards		2	3
..	20	1 Doz Do		4	6
	..	Goods	2	10	6
..	..	Car		13	6
..		Holsters		9	0
		Cards		4	6
..		2 Rolls Twine		1	6
..	22	1 cwt Sugar	2	19	9
	..	Christmas Candles	1	2	6
	..	1 Doz Candles		8	0
	24	Goods	11	3	4
	..	Goods	4	17	0
	..	3 Choc.		4	3
		3 Do		4	8
		Clothes Brush		7	0
			£53	11	11½
		As Rendered			

Above left: John B. and Mary Keane

Above: John B. outside his bar.

Left: A list of goods purchased by John B. Keane from Fitzgibbon's during the Christmas season and dated December 29, 1955.

41 Lower William Street

Edward J. Stack established in 1887 a very successful general drapery known as 'The Arcade' in William Street. This business drew customers from a wide area of North Kerry and West Limerick. His family subsequently ran a furniture business and now, 130 years since its founding, his great great granddaughter Jennifer Scanlan operates a ladies' boutique in part of the house. The furniture business is run today by Damian Stack, his mother Mary and wife Joan.

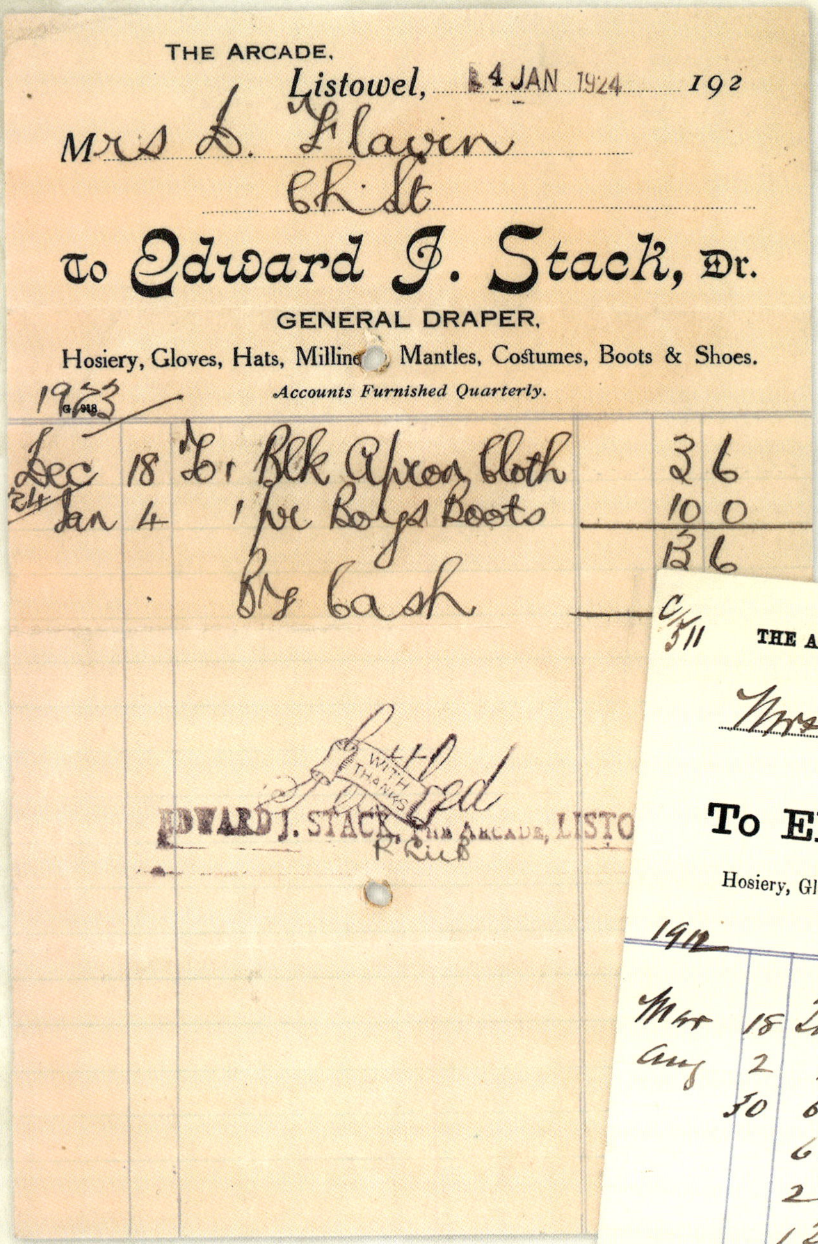
THE ARCADE.
Listowel, 14 JAN 1924 192
Mrs L. Flavin
Ch. St
To Edward J. Stack, Dr.
GENERAL DRAPER,
Hosiery, Gloves, Hats, Millinery, Mantles, Costumes, Boots & Shoes.
Accounts Furnished Quarterly.
1923
Dec 18 To, Blk Apron Cloth 3 6
1924 Jan 4 1 pr Boys Boots 10 0
13 6
By Cash
WITH THANKS
EDWARD J. STACK, THE ARCADE, LISTOWEL
Settled

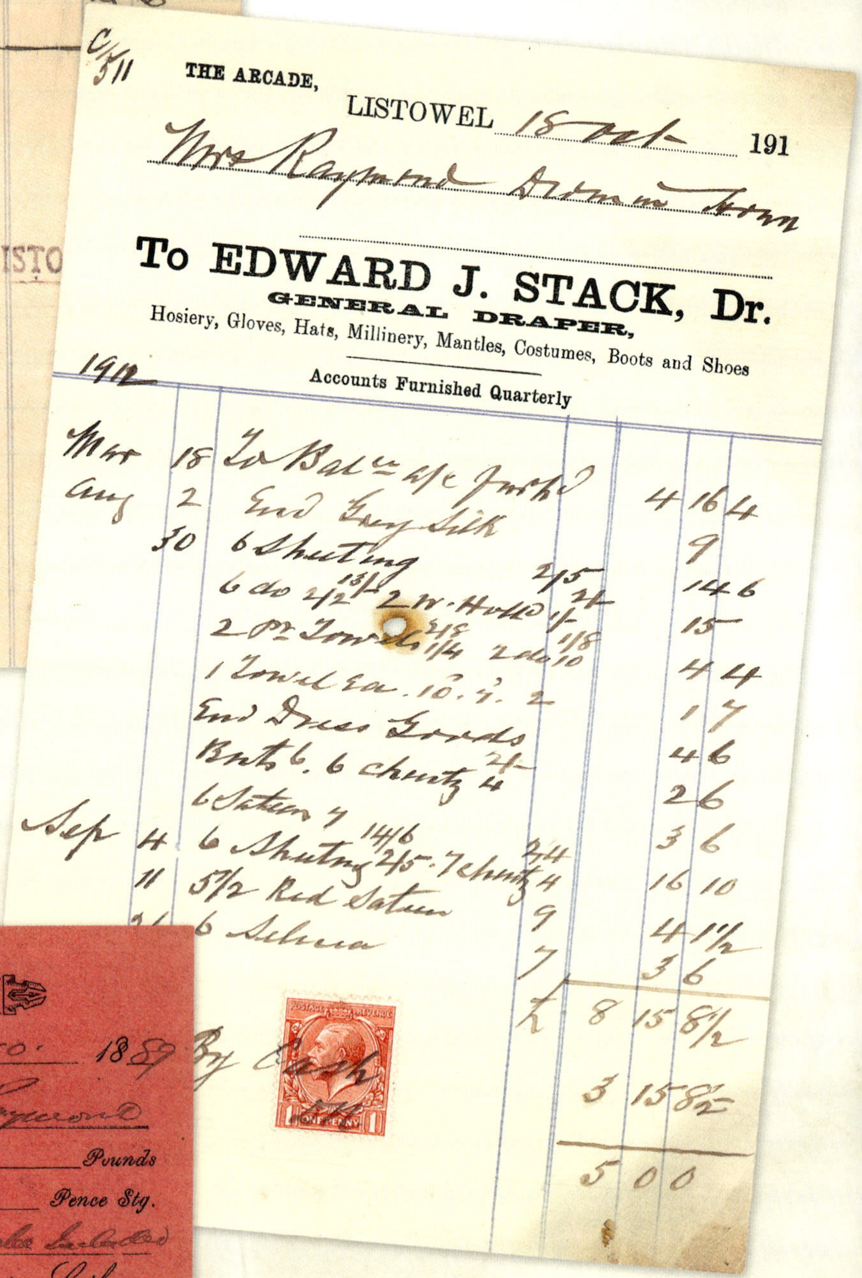
THE ARCADE,
LISTOWEL 18 Oct 191
Mrs Raymond
To EDWARD J. STACK, Dr.
GENERAL DRAPER,
Hosiery, Gloves, Hats, Millinery, Mantles, Costumes, Boots and Shoes
Accounts Furnished Quarterly
1912
Mar 18 To Bal a/c 4 16 4
Aug 2 End Grey Silk 9
30 6 Sheeting 14 6
Sep 4 6 Sheeting 3 6
11 5½ Red Sateen 16 10
8 15 8½
By Cash 3 15 8½
5 0 0

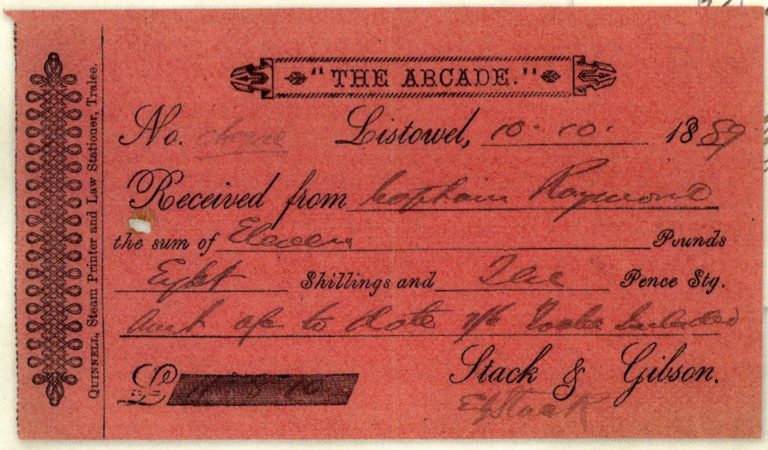
"THE ARCADE."
No. Listowel, 10. 10. 1889
Received from
the sum of Eleven Pounds
Eight Shillings and Ten Pence Stg.
Stack & Gilson.
QUINNELL, Steam Printer and Law Stationer, Tralee.

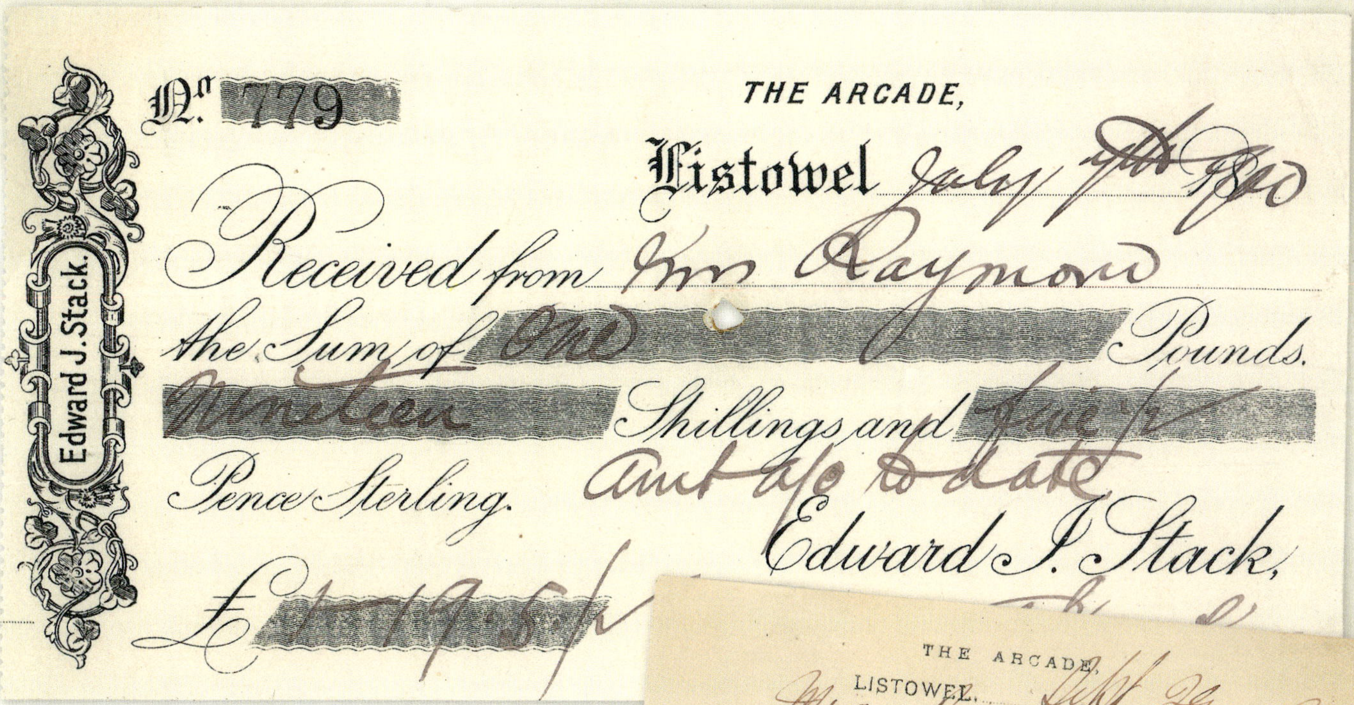

Edward J. Stack.

No. 779

THE ARCADE,

Listowel July 7th 1890

Received from Mrs Raymond

the Sum of One Pounds.

Nineteen Shillings and five p

Pence Sterling. Amt a/c to date

Edward J. Stack,

£ 1.19.5

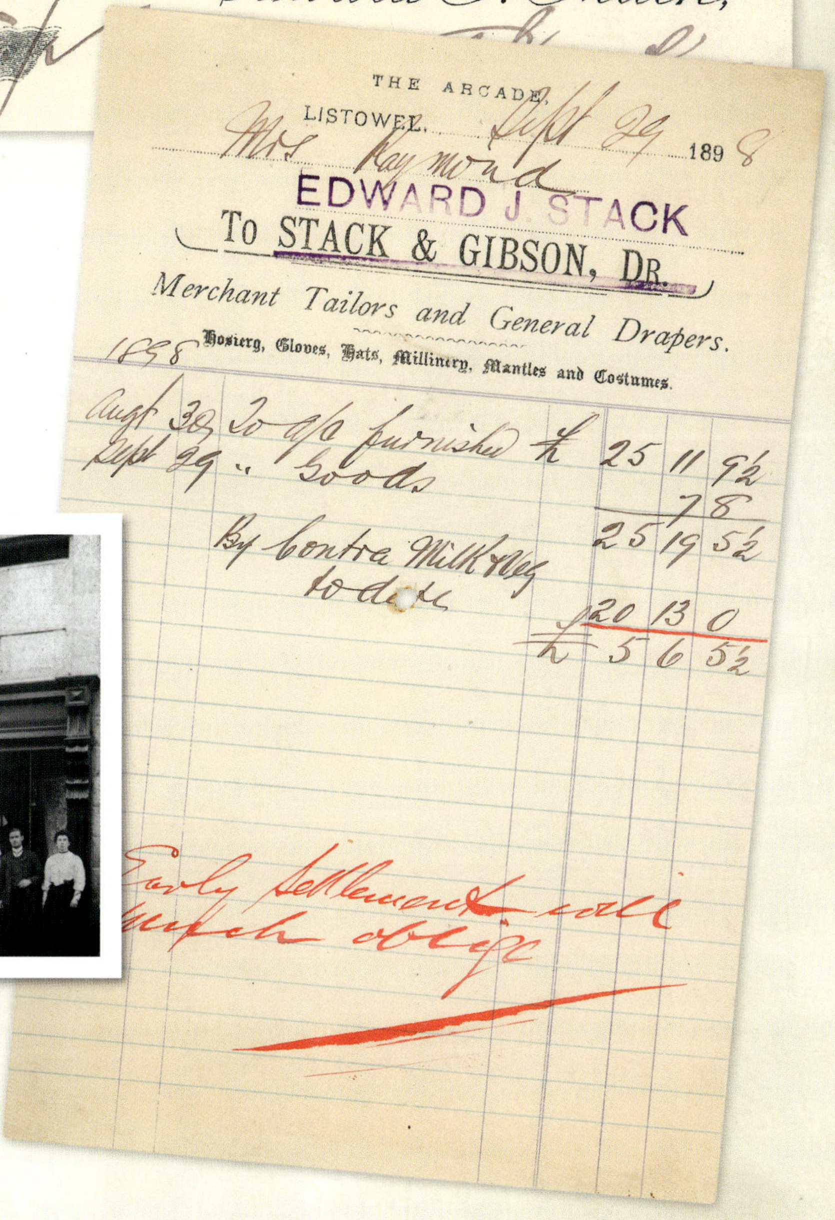

THE ARCADE,

LISTOWEL. Sept 29 1898

Mrs Raymond

EDWARD J. STACK

To STACK & GIBSON, DR.

Merchant Tailors and General Drapers.

Hosiery, Gloves, Hats, Millinery, Mantles and Costumes.

			£		
1898					
Augt 30	To a/c furnished	£	25	11	9½
Sept 29	" Goods			7	8
			25	19	5½
	By Contra Milk & Eggs to date	£	20	13	0
		£	5	6	5½

Early settlement will much oblige

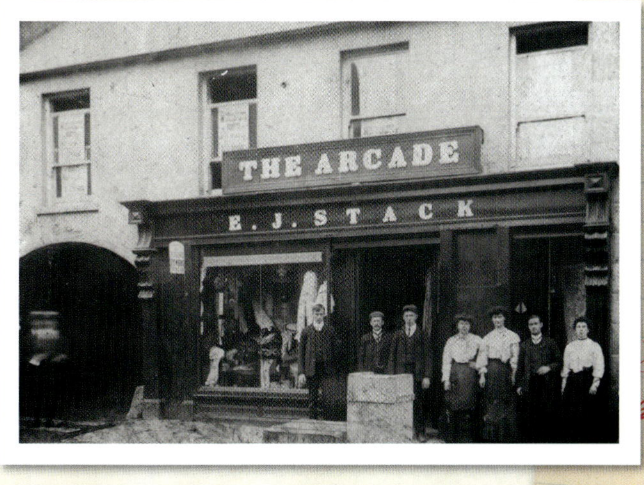

Stack's, The Arcade, circa 1910.

43 Lower William Street

Fitzgerald's of No. 43 William Street were general grocers, tea, wine and spirit merchants. They also operated a horse-drawn hackney service in the days before the advent of the motor car. The photograph, taken around 1910, shows two daughters, Catherine and Maryanne, with their aunt, Miss Kissane from Asdee.

McCarthy Insurance Services, owned by Con McCarthy, now operate from this house.

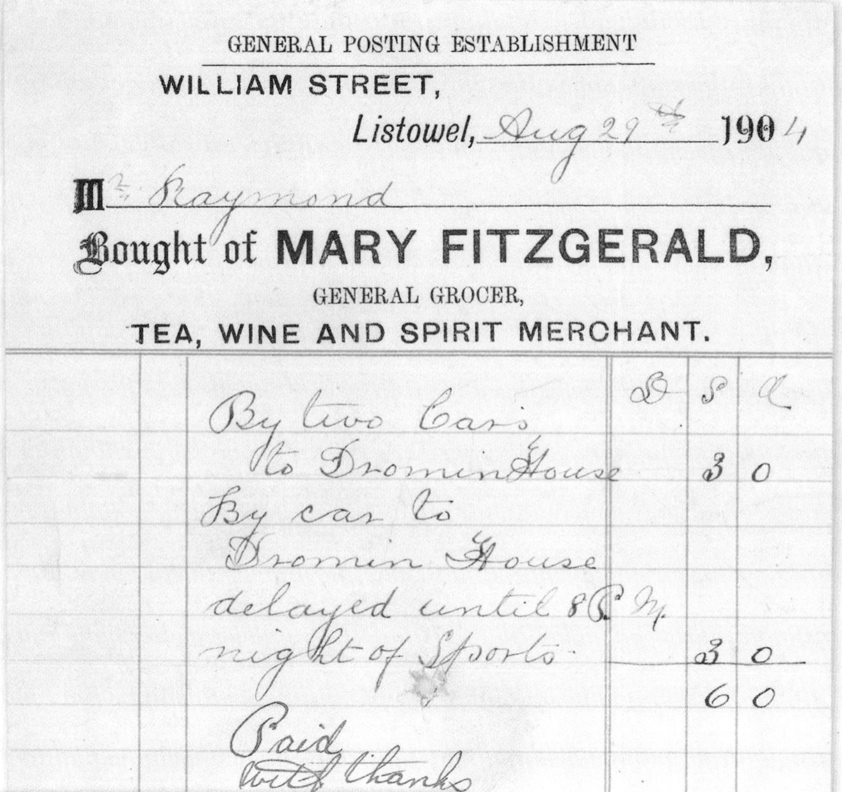

GENERAL POSTING ESTABLISHMENT

WILLIAM STREET,

Listowel, Aug 29th 1904

Mr Raymond

Bought of MARY FITZGERALD,

GENERAL GROCER,

TEA, WINE AND SPIRIT MERCHANT.

	£	s	d
By two Cars to Dromin House		3	0
By car to Dromin House delayed until 8 P.M. night of Sports		3	0
		6	0

Paid with thanks

...rald

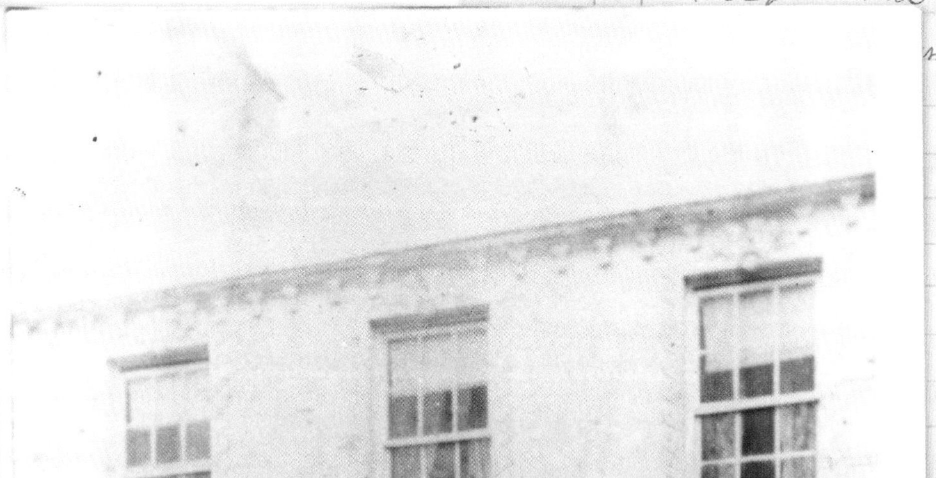

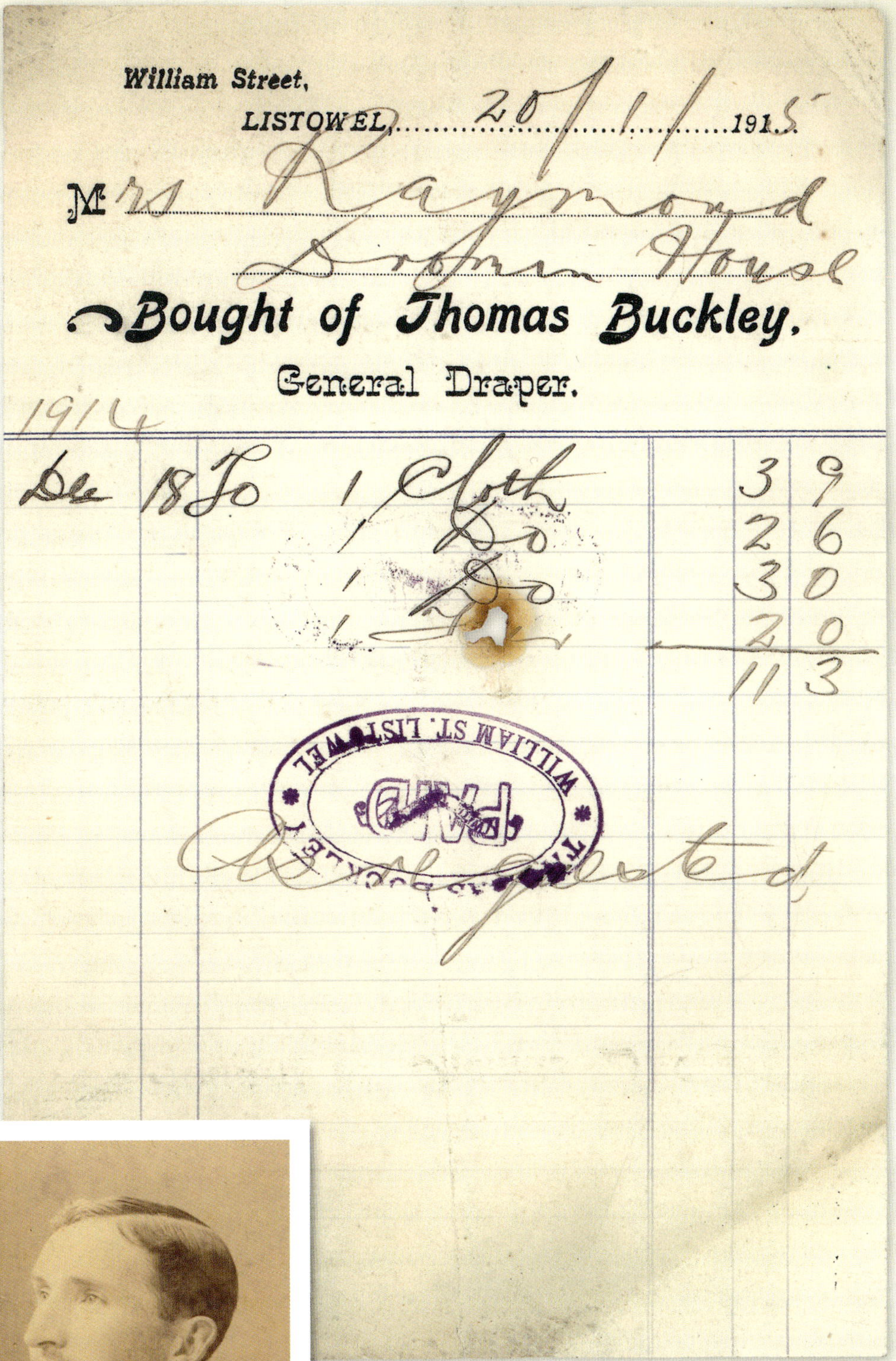

William Street,
LISTOWEL, 20/1/1915
Mrs Raymond
Drohan House
Bought of Thomas Buckley.
General Draper.

1914 Dec	18 To	1 Cloth	3	9
		1 Do	2	6
		1 Do	3	0
		1 Do	2	0
			11	3

PAID
WILLIAM ST. LISTOWEL

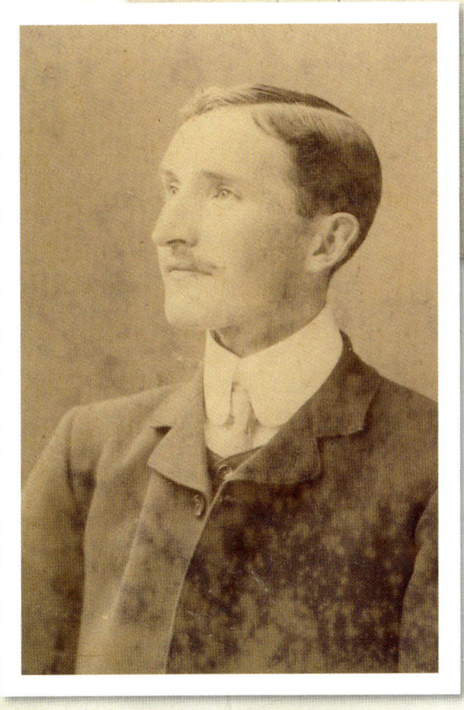

45 Lower William Street

Thomas Buckley was married to Ellen Moran, sister of Ned Moran of Market Street. They started a drapery shop in what was formerly a butcher and grocery shop owned by Timothy Foley. The business passed on to Tommy Buckley's niece and her husband, Eileen and Denis Moriarty, in 1949. Following Denis's death in 1980, the business was operated by his widow Eileen and son Ned. The family's association with the business ended in 2011.

Photo left: Thomas Buckley.

47 Lower William Street

Faley's hardware shop had a presence in William Street from the 1880s, until its closure in the mid 1950s. The Mermaids bar and nightclub, owned by Liam O'Flaherty, now occupies this site.

In the photograph below, taken around 1904, the shop frontage carries an array of household implements, with the Faleys proudly posing at the front door.

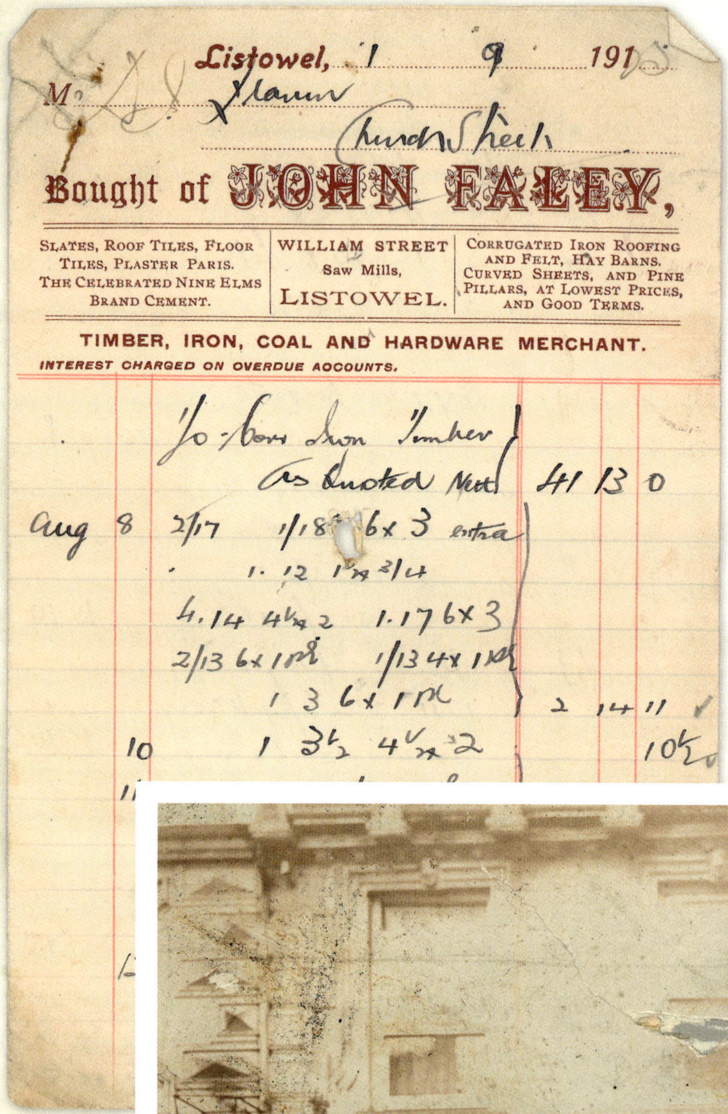
Listowel, 1 9 191
Mr
Bought of JOHN FALEY,

SLATES, ROOF TILES, FLOOR TILES, PLASTER PARIS. THE CELEBRATED NINE ELMS BRAND CEMENT.

WILLIAM STREET Saw Mills, LISTOWEL.

CORRUGATED IRON ROOFING AND FELT, HAY BARNS. CURVED SHEETS, AND PINE PILLARS, AT LOWEST PRICES, AND GOOD TERMS.

TIMBER, IRON, COAL AND HARDWARE MERCHANT.

INTEREST CHARGED ON OVERDUE ACCOUNTS.

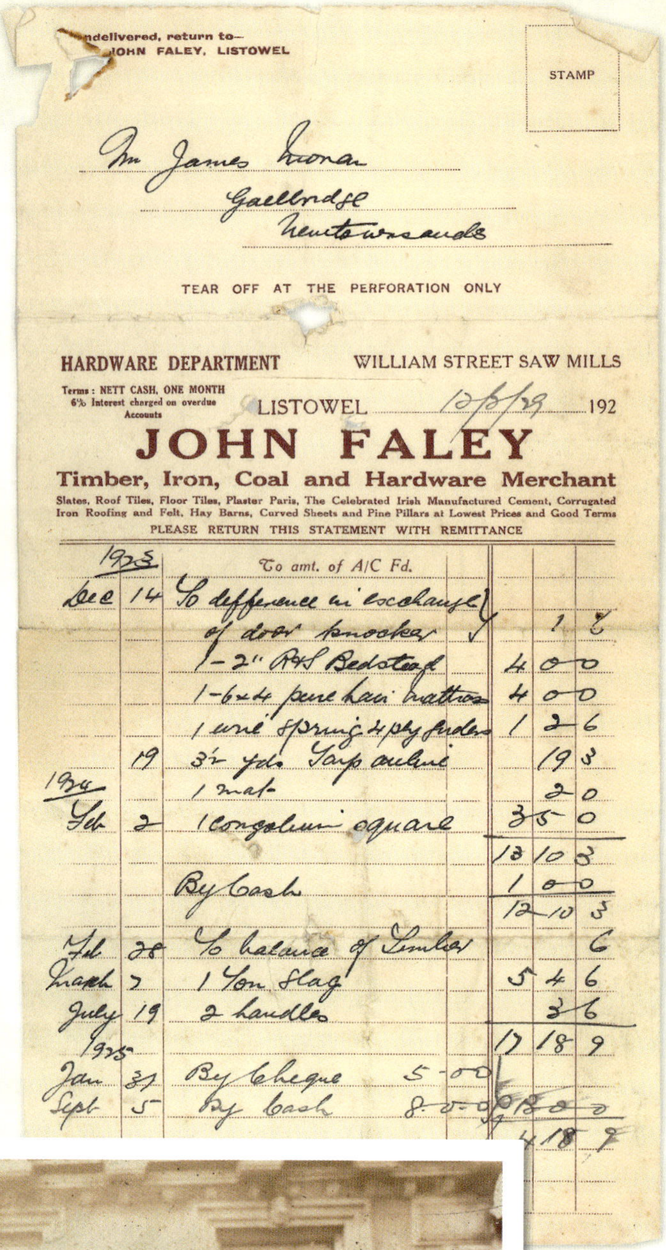
Undelivered, return to—
JOHN FALEY, LISTOWEL

STAMP

TEAR OFF AT THE PERFORATION ONLY

HARDWARE DEPARTMENT

WILLIAM STREET SAW MILLS

Terms: NETT CASH, ONE MONTH. 6% Interest charged on overdue Accounts

LISTOWEL 192

JOHN FALEY

Timber, Iron, Coal and Hardware Merchant

Slates, Roof Tiles, Floor Tiles, Plaster Paris, The Celebrated Irish Manufactured Cement, Corrugated Iron Roofing and Felt, Hay Barns, Curved Sheets and Pine Pillars at Lowest Prices and Good Terms

PLEASE RETURN THIS STATEMENT WITH REMITTANCE

To amt. of A/C Fd.

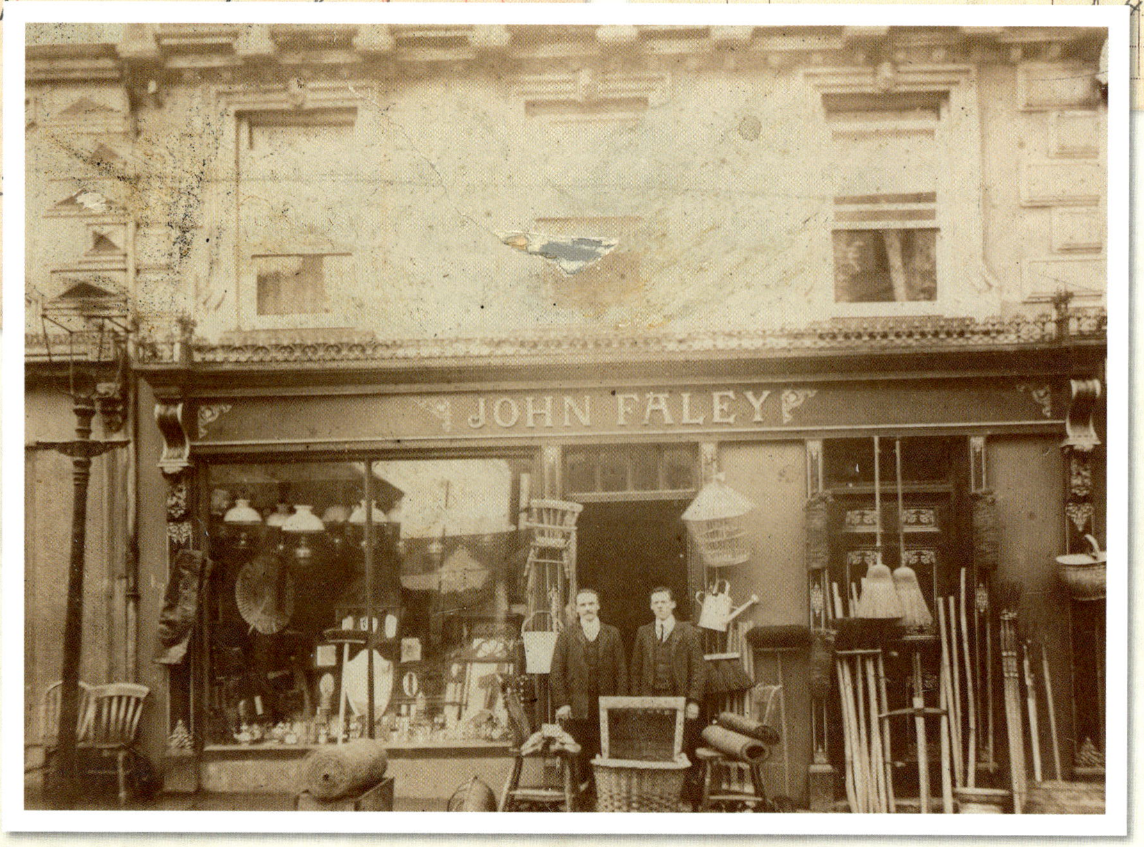

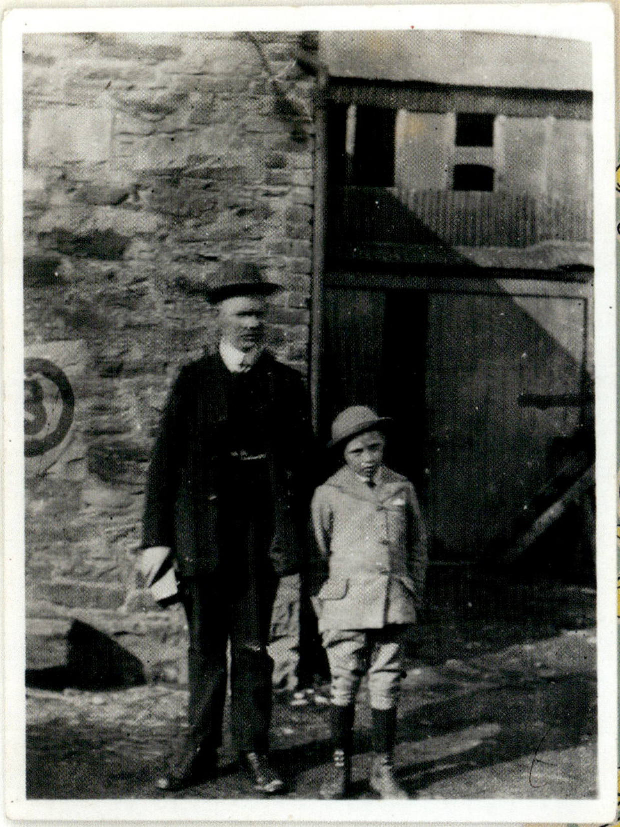

John and Edward Faley.

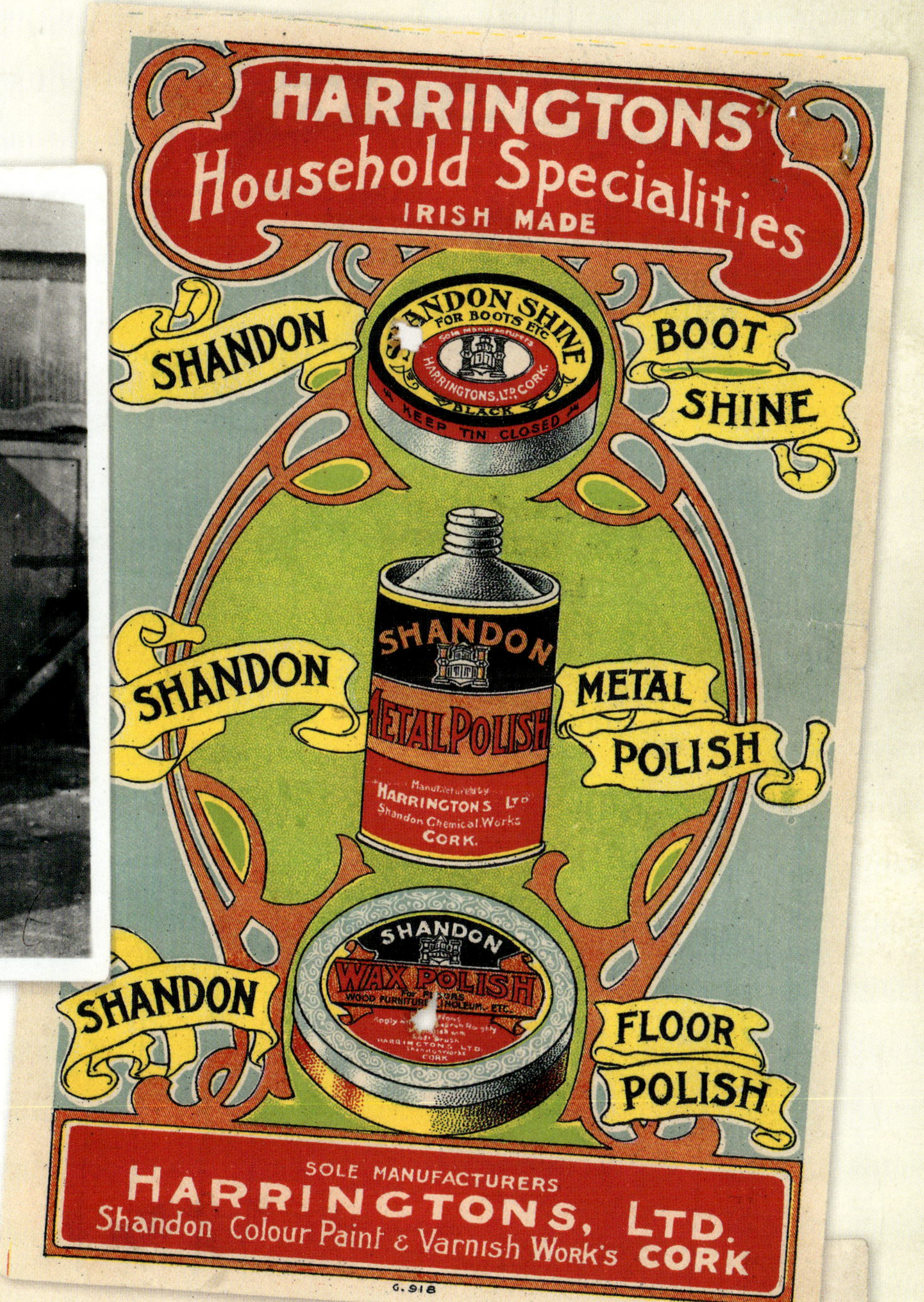

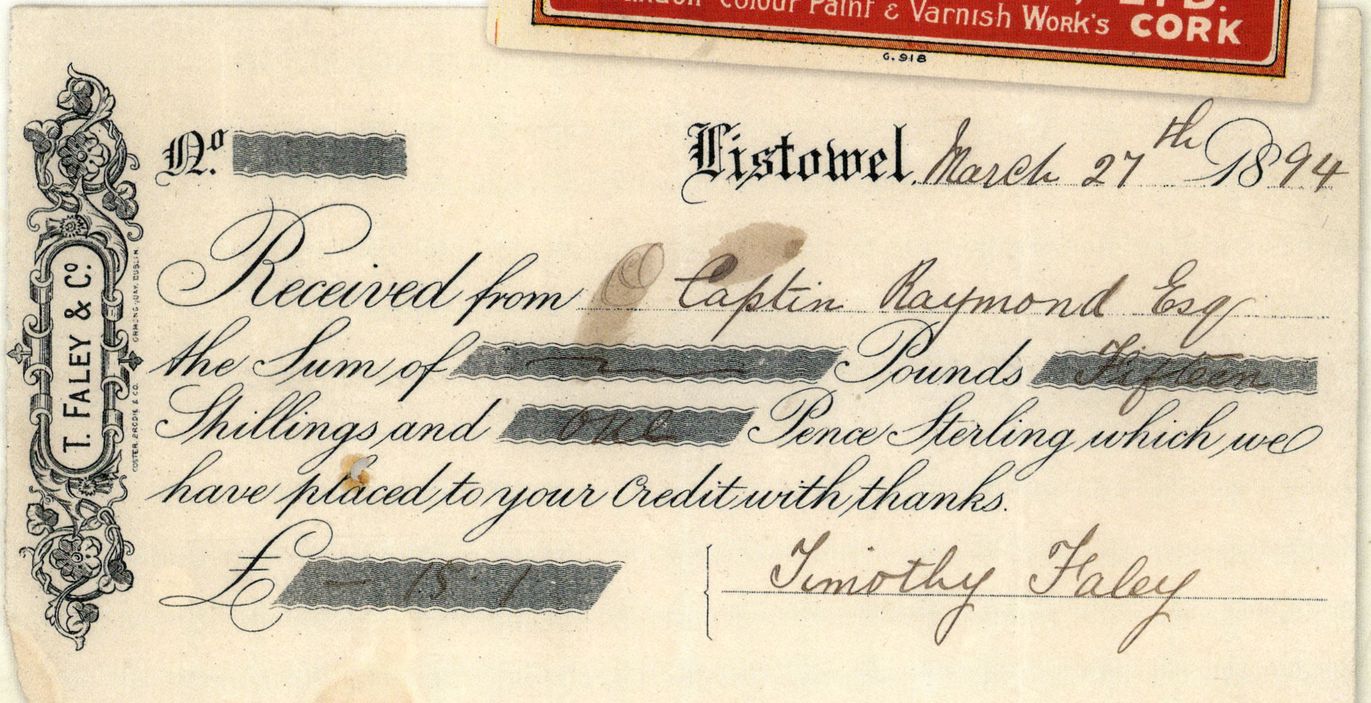

T. FALEY & Co.

No

Listowel March 27th 1894

Received from Captin Raymond Esq

the Sum of — Pounds Fifteen

Shillings and one Pence Sterling which we

have placed to your Credit with thanks.

£ — 15 . 1

Timothy Faley

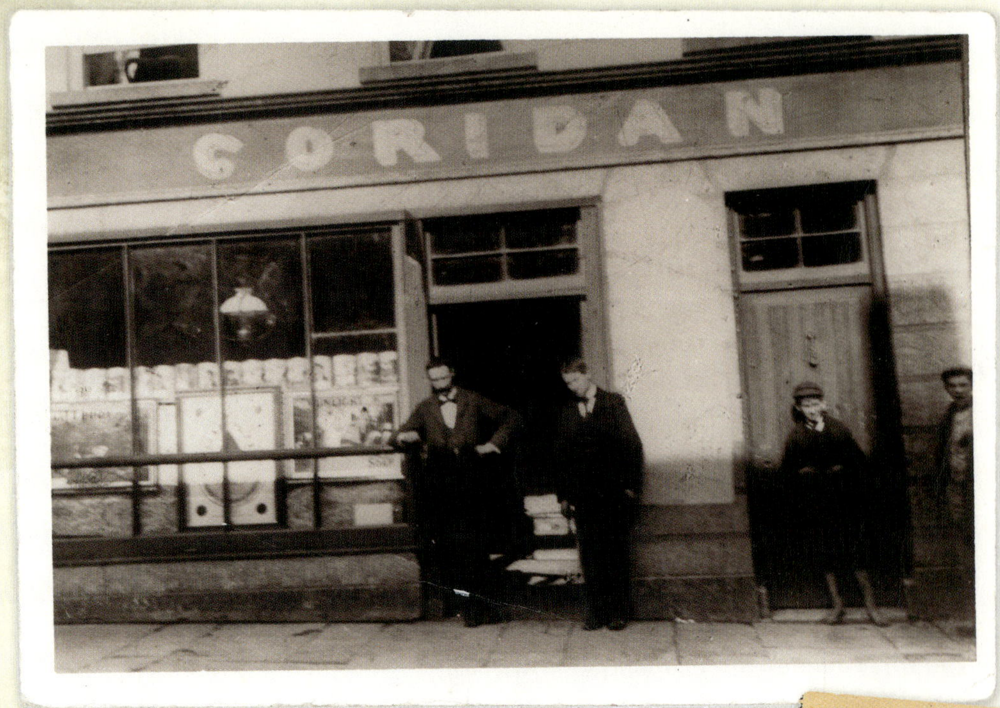

53 Lower William Street
The Corridan brothers, from Moyessa, Listowel, opened a shop in William Street. Enterprising businessmen, their shop thrived. Thomas remained in William Street, where he married in 1903. Patrick bought a bar and grocery in Main Street which had been vacated by Jeremiah Foran.

Photo: The Corridan brothers, Thomas and Patrick, at the front door of their shop. Note the misspelling of the name over the door.

51 Lower William Street
Patrick Stack and his brother Michael married two Fitzgerald sisters, Mary Ann and Catherine, from 'down the street'. Patrick conducted his cart-making business at the rear of his grocery shop. He was followed into the business by his son Thomas (Toss). This house is now part of the Mermaids complex owned by Liam O'Flaherty.

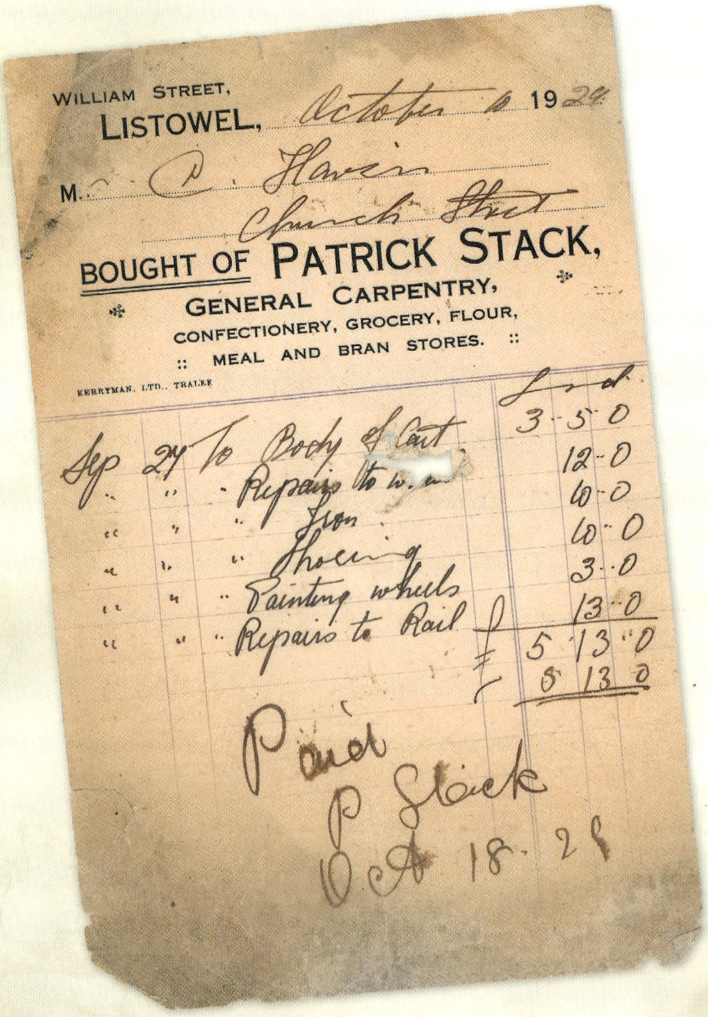

WILLIAM STREET,
LISTOWEL, October 6 1924
M. P. Haven
Church Street

BOUGHT OF PATRICK STACK,
GENERAL CARPENTRY,
CONFECTIONERY, GROCERY, FLOUR,
:: MEAL AND BRAN STORES. ::

KERRYMAN, LTD., TRALEE

			£ s d
Sep 24	To	Body of Cart	3-5-0
"	"	Repairs to ...	12-0
"	"	Iron	10-0
"	"	Shoeing	10-0
"	"	Painting wheels	3-0
"	"	Repairs to Rail	13-0
		£	5 13 0
		£	5 13 0

Paid
P Stack
Oct 18. 24

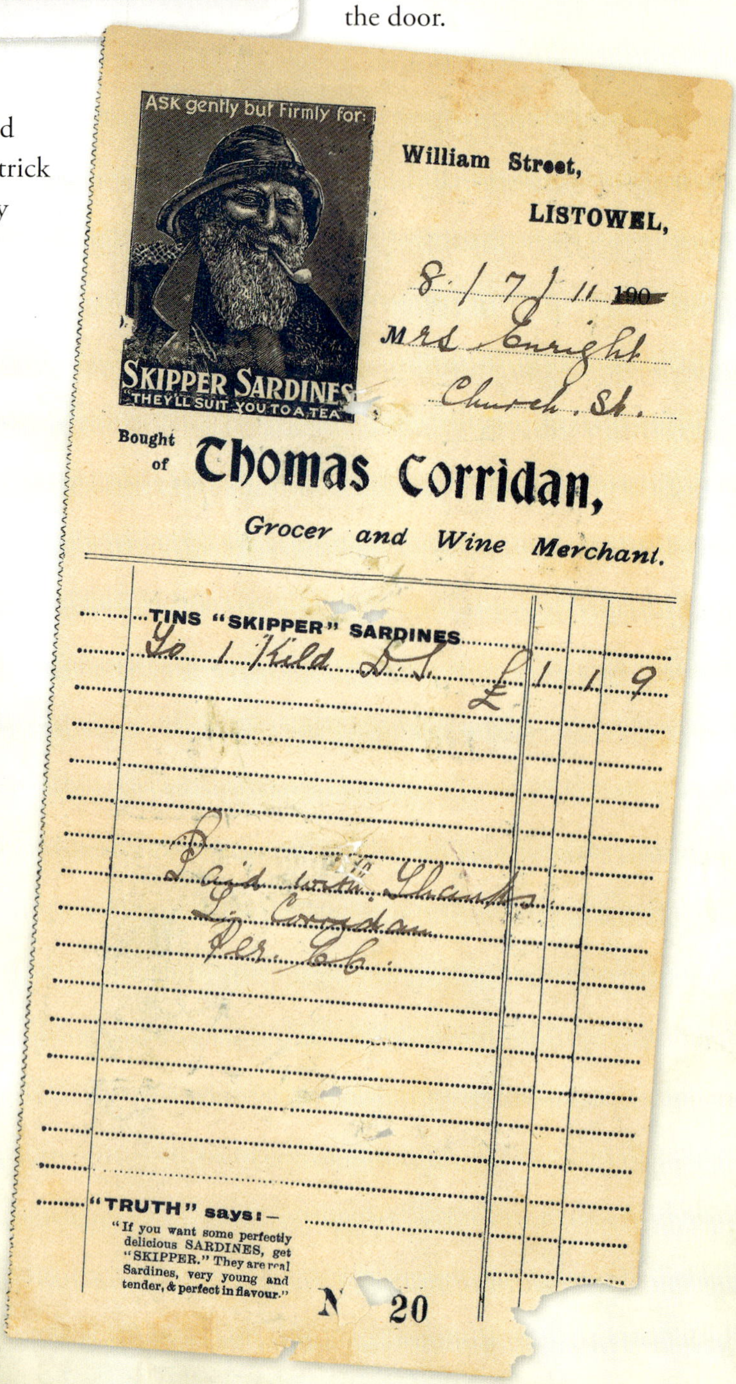

William Street,
LISTOWEL,
8/7/11 190
Mrs Enright
Church St.

Bought of **Thomas Corridan,**
Grocer and Wine Merchant.

TINS "SKIPPER" SARDINES
To 1 Kild ... £1.1.9

Paid with Thanks
T. Corridan
Per ...

"TRUTH" says:—
"If you want some perfectly delicious SARDINES, get "SKIPPER." They are real Sardines, very young and tender, & perfect in flavour."

№ 20

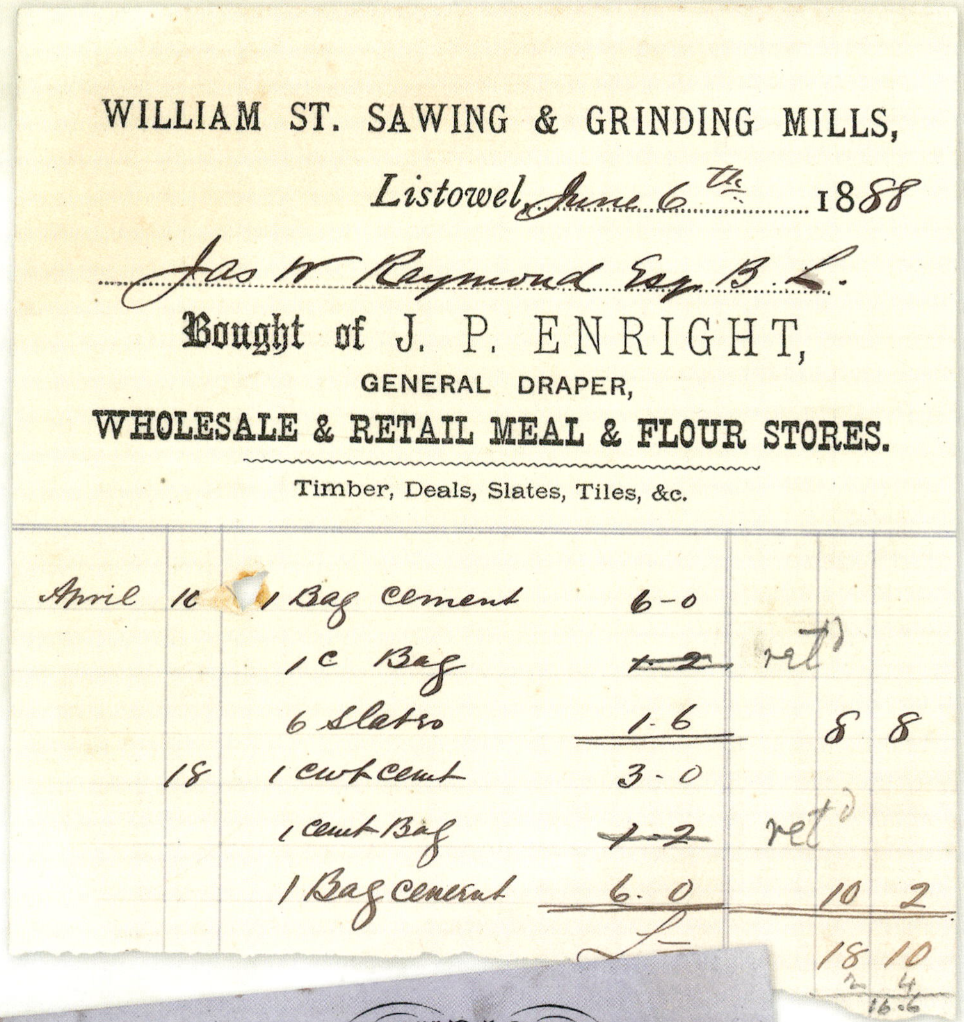

WILLIAM ST. SAWING & GRINDING MILLS,

Listowel, June 6th 1888

Jas W Raymond Esq B. L.

Bought of J. P. ENRIGHT,

GENERAL DRAPER,

WHOLESALE & RETAIL MEAL & FLOUR STORES.

Timber, Deals, Slates, Tiles, &c.

April	10	1 Bag cement	6-0		
		1 C Bag	~~1-2~~ ret^d		
		6 Slates	1-6	8	8
	18	1 cwt cement	3-0		
		1 Cement Bag	~~1-2~~ ret^d		
		1 Bag cement	6.0	10	2
		£		18	10
				2	4
				16.6	

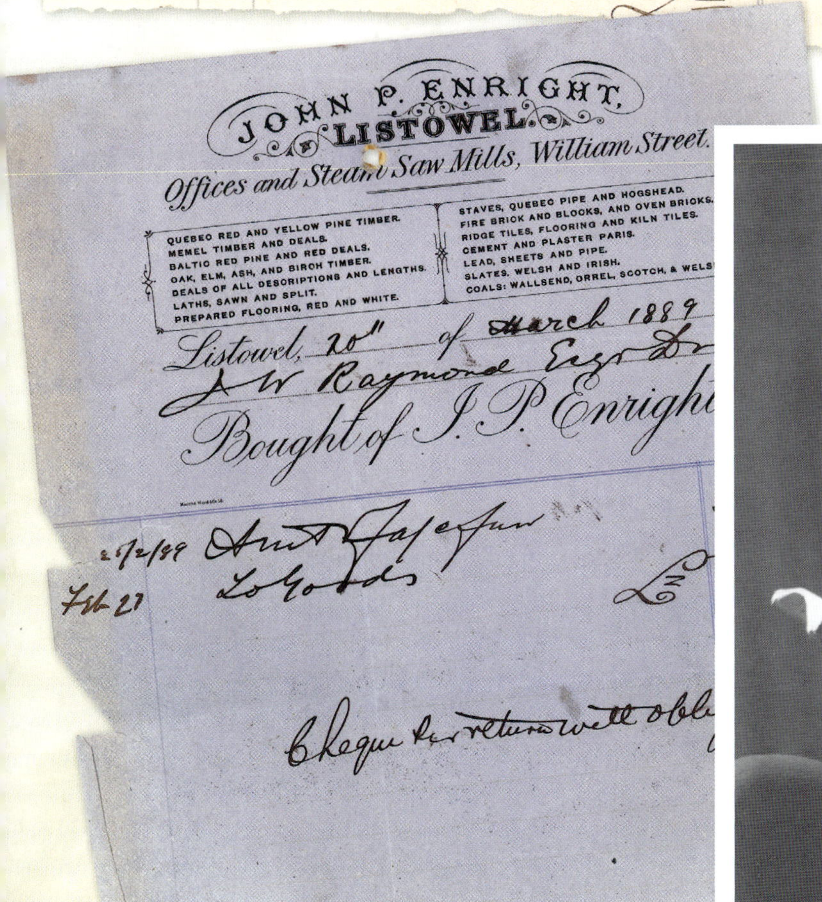

JOHN P. ENRIGHT,
LISTOWEL.
Offices and Steam Saw Mills, William Street.

QUEBEC RED AND YELLOW PINE TIMBER.
MEMEL TIMBER AND DEALS.
BALTIC RED PINE AND RED DEALS.
OAK, ELM, ASH, AND BIRCH TIMBER.
DEALS OF ALL DESCRIPTIONS AND LENGTHS.
LATHS, SAWN AND SPLIT.
PREPARED FLOORING, RED AND WHITE.

STAVES, QUEBEC PIPE AND HOGSHEAD.
FIRE BRICK AND BLOCKS, AND OVEN BRICKS.
RIDGE TILES, FLOORING AND KILN TILES.
CEMENT AND PLASTER PARIS.
LEAD, SHEETS AND PIPE.
SLATES, WELSH AND IRISH.
COALS: WALLSEND, ORREL, SCOTCH, & WELSH

Listowel, 20th of March 1889

J W Raymond Esq Dr

Bought of J. P. Enright

2/2/89 Amt of acc fur
Feb 27 Lo Goods £

Cheque per return will oblige

55 Lower William Street

John P. Enright could rightly be called an entrepreneur of his times. He had a store in Church Street in the 1870s. He then moved to William Street where he built several houses. With the development of the laneway at the back of the street, he availed of land which had previously been used as a pound. Here he built offices and a steam sawmill in the 1880s. In the 1900s he developed a private creamery in the yard. McKennas bought the yard from the Enrights.

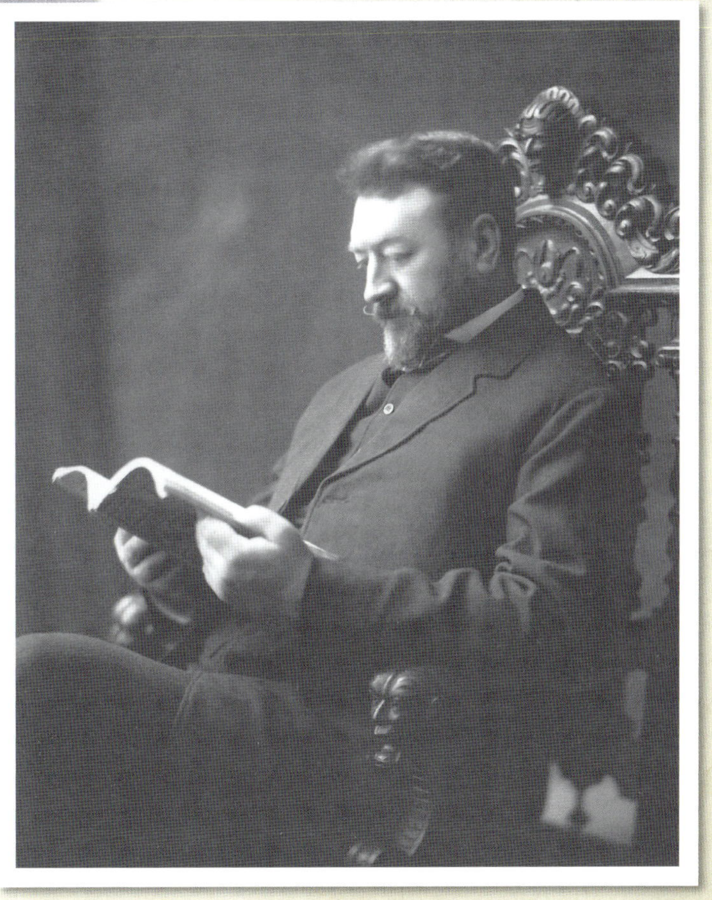

Photo: John P. Enright.

57 & 59 Lower William Street

Kate Kissane from Kilgarvan, Ballydonoghue, trained as draper in Clery's of Dublin. In 1893, she opened her own shop at No. 57 William Street. Kate married Thomas Carroll from Asdee. Their daughter, Mary Josephine, married Chas Henigan from Church Street. They ran their business as Carroll-Henigan. Michael, their son, continued running the drapery shop with his wife Sighle until it closed when they retired in 2003. The business, founded by Kate Kissane, continued uninterrupted for 110 years.

David Carroll, like Thomas Carroll, came from Asdee. He served his drapery apprenticeship with Kate and Thomas. Some years later when the adjoining shop, Reidy's, came on the market, David bought it and set up his own drapery business.

Photos: On left, Thomas Carroll's shop frontage with Thomas on right, David Carroll at centre. Below, Thomas and Kate Carroll, circa 1895.

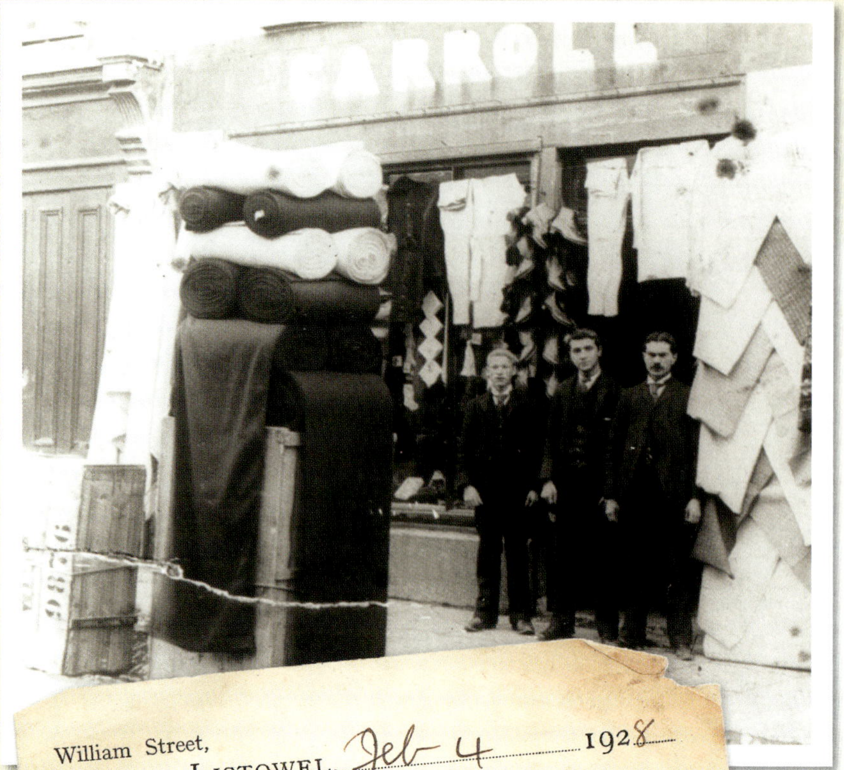

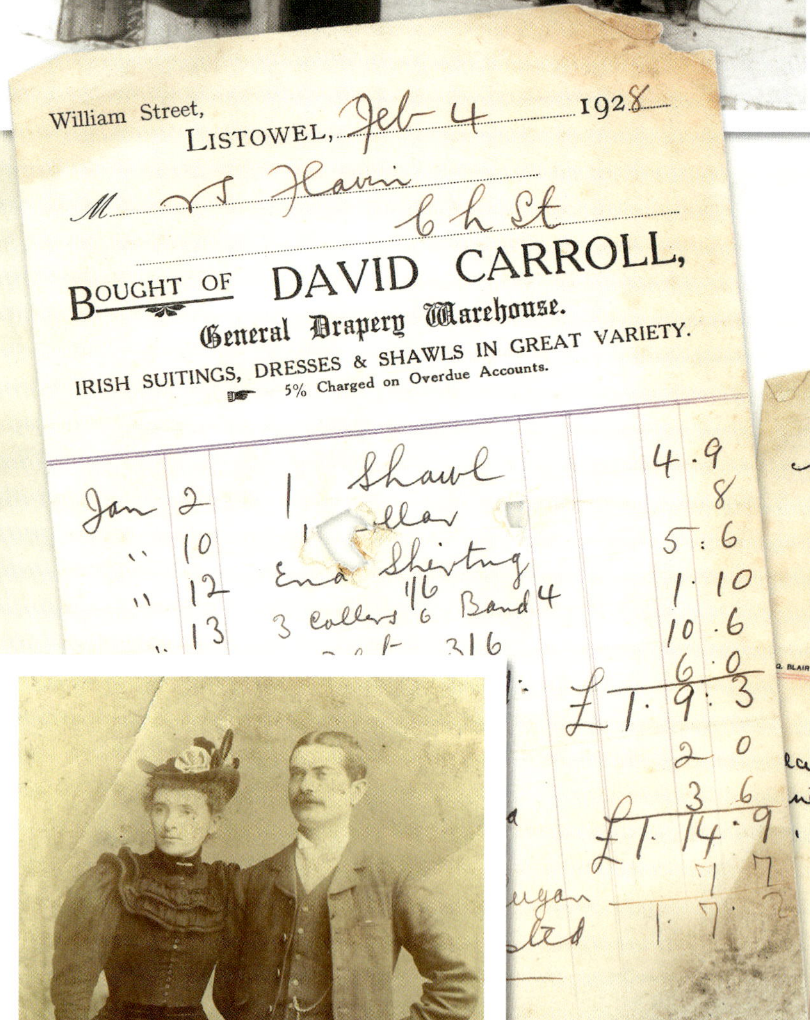

William Street,
LISTOWEL, Feb 4 1928

M. T. Flavin
Ch St

BOUGHT OF DAVID CARROLL,
General Drapery Warehouse.
IRISH SUITINGS, DRESSES & SHAWLS IN GREAT VARIETY.
5% Charged on Overdue Accounts.

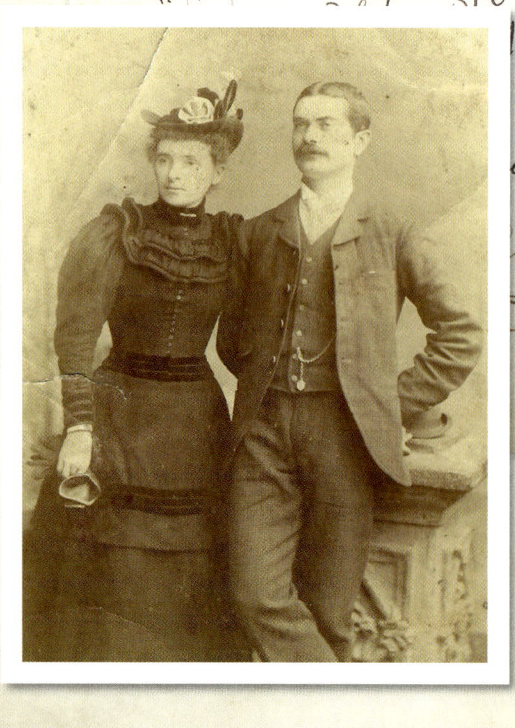

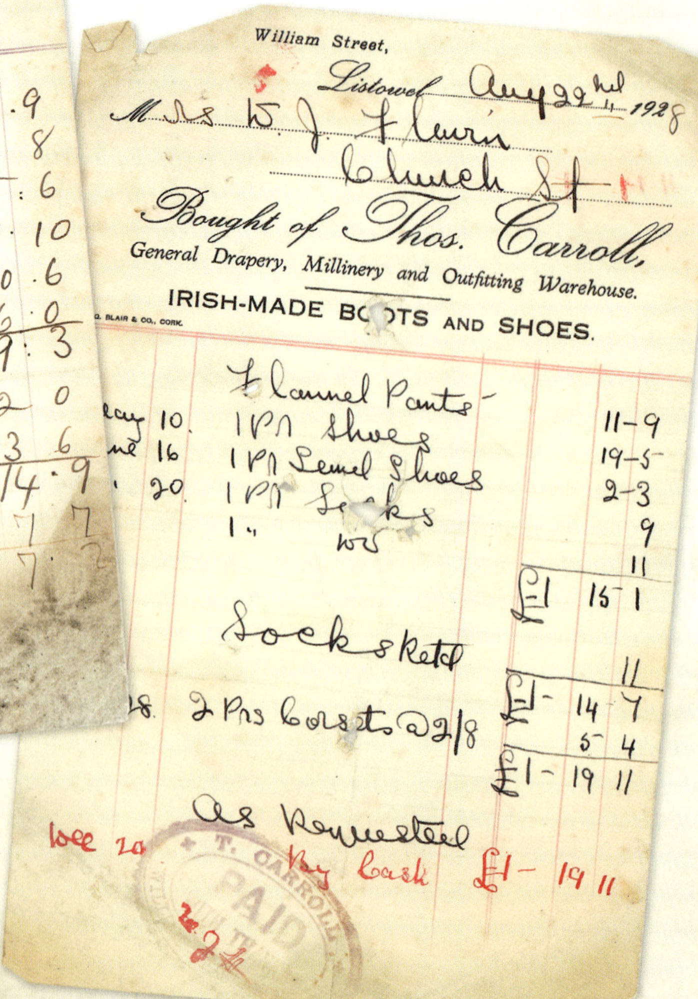

William Street,
Listowel Aug 22nd 1928

Mrs W. J. Flavin
Church St

Bought of Thos. Carroll,
General Drapery, Millinery and Outfitting Warehouse.
IRISH-MADE BOOTS AND SHOES.

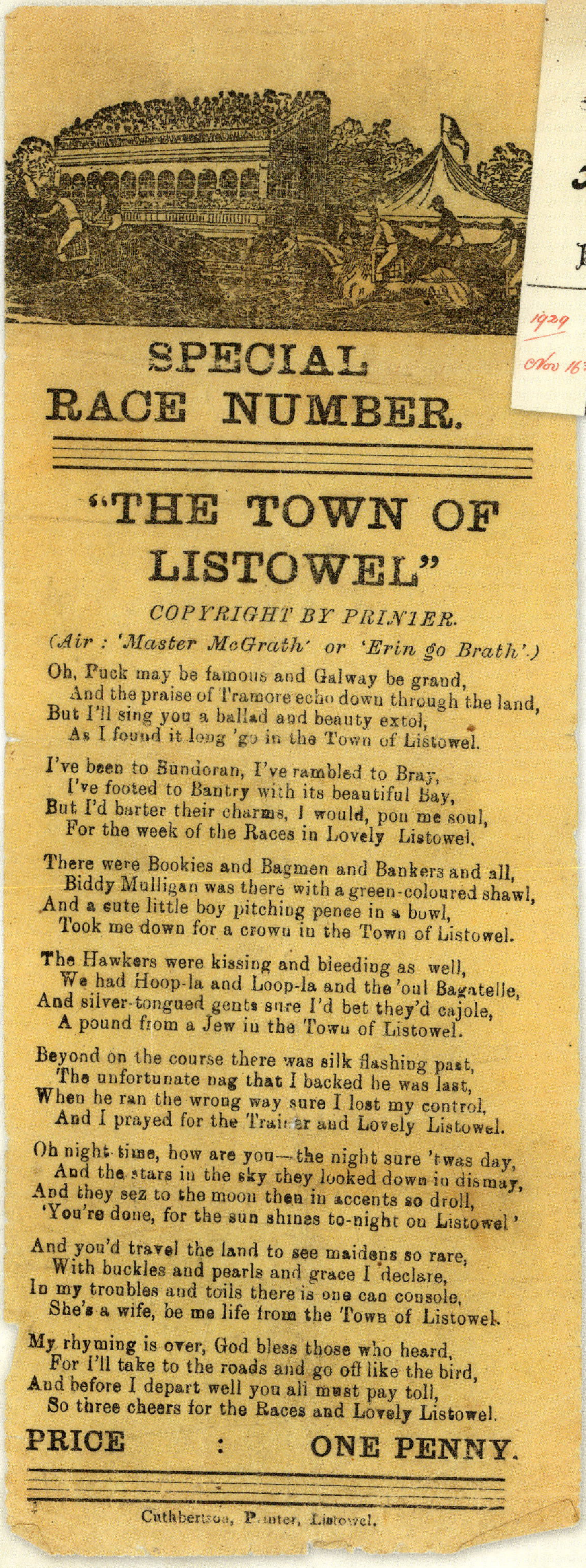

SPECIAL RACE NUMBER.

"THE TOWN OF LISTOWEL"

COPYRIGHT BY PRINTER.

(Air : 'Master McGrath' or 'Erin go Brath'.)

Oh, Puck may be famous and Galway be grand,
And the praise of Tramore echo down through the land,
But I'll sing you a ballad and beauty extol,
As I found it long 'go in the Town of Listowel.

I've been to Bundoran, I've rambled to Bray,
I've footed to Bantry with its beautiful Bay,
But I'd barter their charms, I would, pon me soul,
For the week of the Races in Lovely Listowel.

There were Bookies and Bagmen and Bankers and all,
Biddy Mulligan was there with a green-coloured shawl,
And a cute little boy pitching pence in a bowl,
Took me down for a crown in the Town of Listowel.

The Hawkers were kissing and bleeding as well,
We had Hoop-la and Loop-la and the 'oul Bagatelle,
And silver-tongued gents sure I'd bet they'd cajole,
A pound from a Jew in the Town of Listowel.

Beyond on the course there was silk flashing past,
The unfortunate nag that I backed he was last,
When he ran the wrong way sure I lost my control,
And I prayed for the Trainer and Lovely Listowel.

Oh night time, how are you—the night sure 'twas day,
And the stars in the sky they looked down in dismay,
And they sez to the moon then in accents so droll,
'You're done, for the sun shines to-night on Listowel'

And you'd travel the land to see maidens so rare,
With buckles and pearls and grace I declare,
In my troubles and toils there is one can console,
She's a wife, be me life from the Town of Listowel.

My rhyming is over, God bless those who heard,
For I'll take to the roads and go off like the bird,
And before I depart well you all must pay toll,
So three cheers for the Races and Lovely Listowel.

PRICE : ONE PENNY.

Cuthbertson, Printer, Listowel.

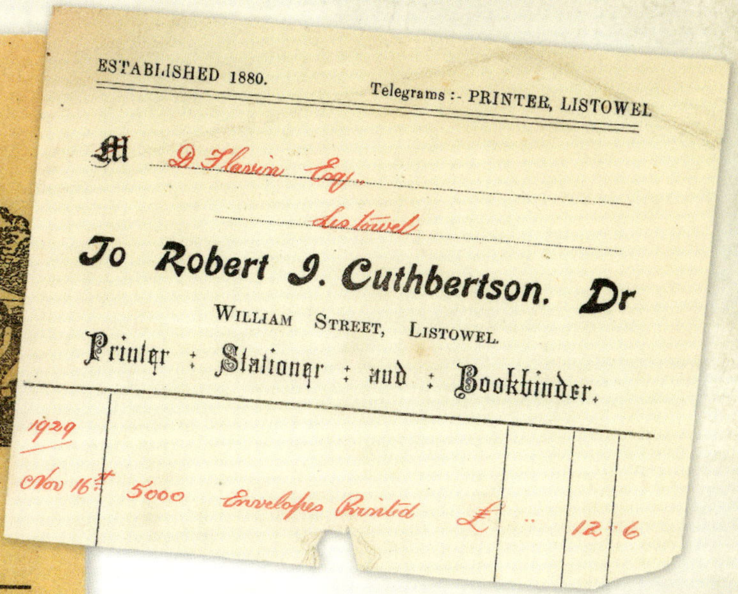

ESTABLISHED 1880. Telegrams :- PRINTER, LISTOWEL.

M D. Flavin Esq.
Listowel

To Robert J. Cuthbertson. Dr

WILLIAM STREET, LISTOWEL.

Printer : Stationer : and : Bookbinder.

1929
Nov 16th 5000 Envelopes Printed £ .. 12 6

61 Lower William Street

Robert Irvine Cuthbertson and his wife Ellen came from Ayrshire, Scotland, via Limerick to Listowel in the early 1880s. He rented a front room at Wilmot's in Church Street where he began his printing work. With his printing business expanding, he and his wife and young family moved to a house in William Street in the 1890s, which was rented from John P. Enright. Here the family stayed until the last of the family, Robert, died in 1960. Along with his general printing business, Robert (Bob Jnr) specialised in printing what was known as *The Penny Ballads*. With the help of his great friend Bryan MacMahon, who would write a ballad to commemorate an event or sporting occasion, Bob would then set ink on paper on the offcuts of used paper. These ballads along with the popular songs of the day would then be sold as ballad sheets. Travelling singers and musicians would buy sheafs of these for later singing at fairs and carnivals. Several generations of the Nolan family of Charles Street gave unstinting service working with the Cuthbertsons since John Nolan became the printing family's first apprentice.

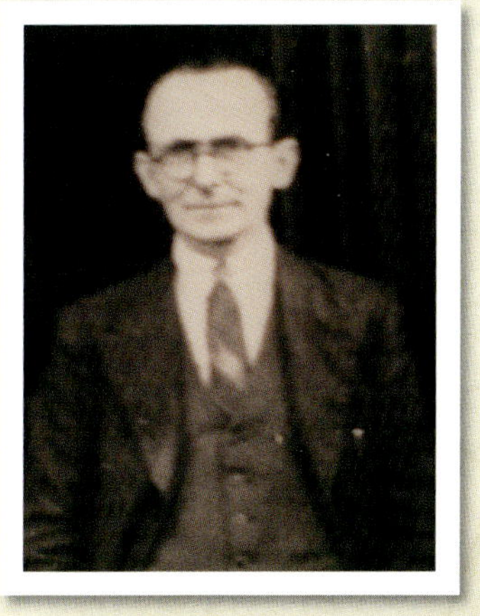

Photo: Robert (Bob) Cuthbertson.

63 Lower William Street

The Railway Hotel was situated at the corner of William Street and Charles Street. It was afterwards occupied by M.J. Dillon and is today occupied by Jackie and Beatrice Carmody. The richly-embellished hotel letterhead is complemented by one of M.J. Dillon's which is an advertising gem.

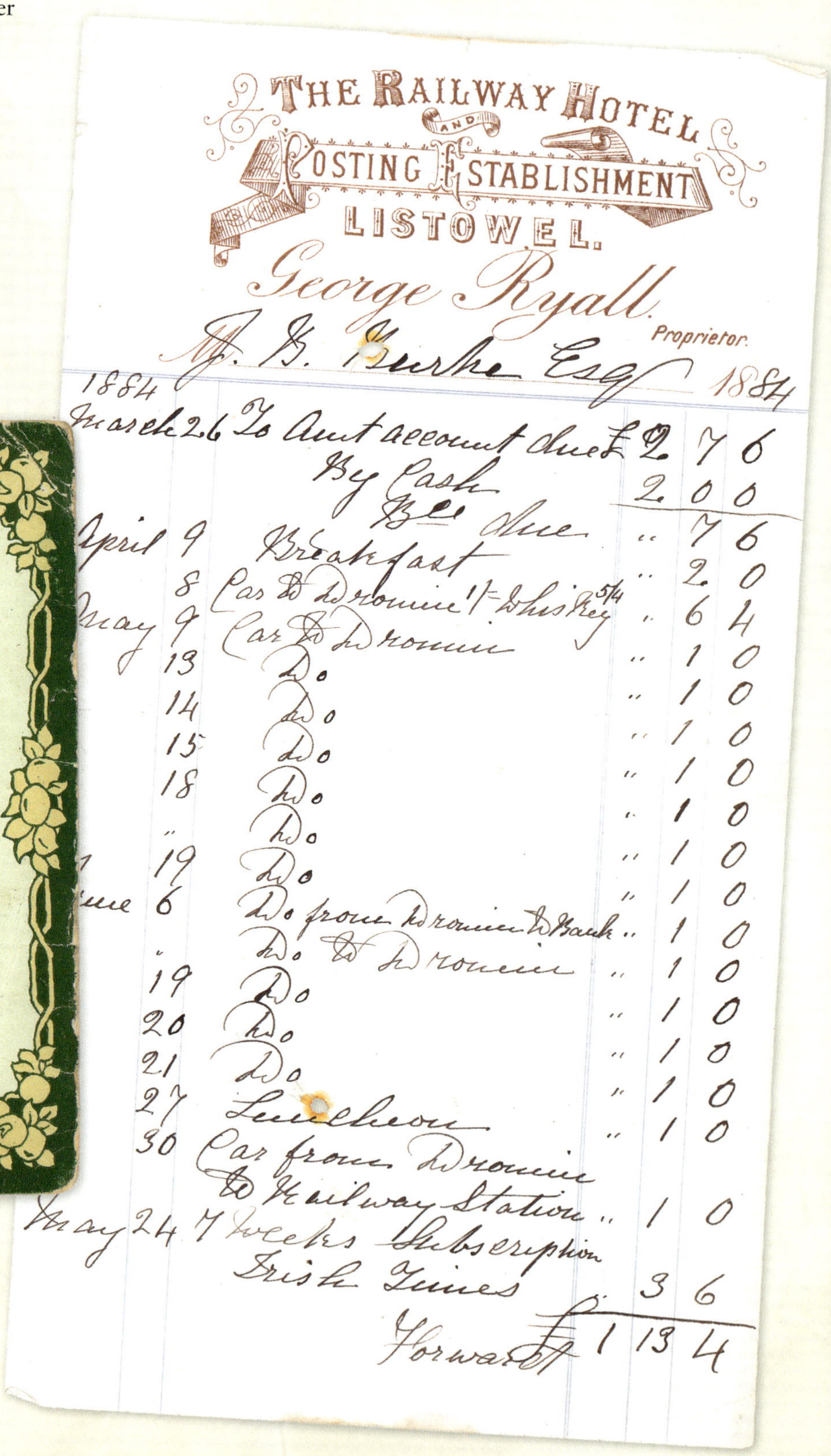
THE RAILWAY HOTEL
AND
POSTING ESTABLISHMENT
LISTOWEL.
George Ryall.
Proprietor.

M. B. Burke Esq 1884

1884			£	s	d
March	26	To Amt account due	2	7	6
		By Cash	2	0	0
		Bl. due	..	7	6
April	9	Breakfast	..	2	0
	8	Car to Dromin 1/- Whiskey 5/4	..	6	4
May	9	Car to Dromin	..	1	0
	13	Do	..	1	0
	14	Do	..	1	0
	15	do	..	1	0
	18	Do	..	1	0
	..	Do	..	1	0
	19	Do	..	1	0
June	6	Do from Dromin to Bank	..	1	0
	..	Do to Dromin	..	1	0
	19	Do	..	1	0
	20	Do	..	1	0
	21	Do	..	1	0
	27	Luncheon	..	1	0
	30	Car from Dromin to Railway Station	..	1	0
May	24	7 weeks Subscription Irish Times		3	6
		Forward	£1	13	4

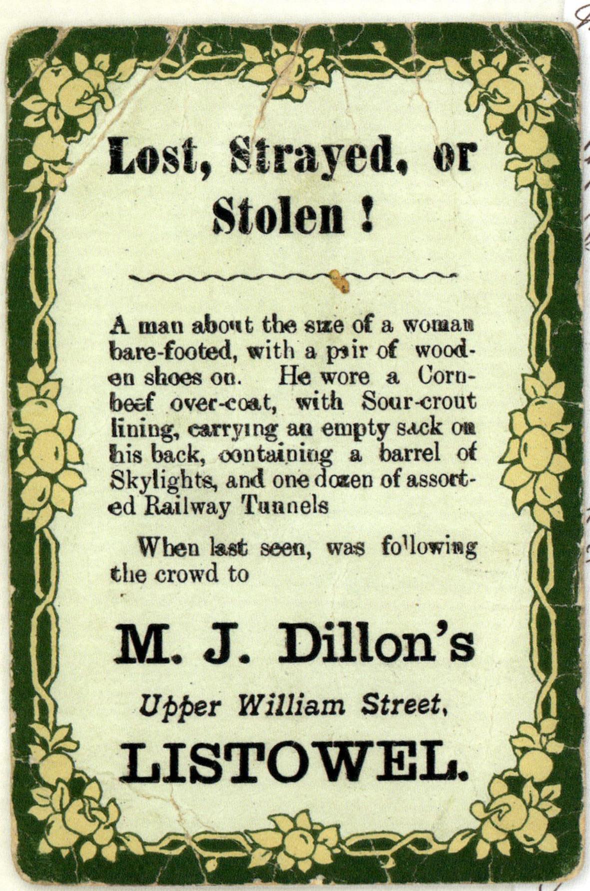

46 Lower William Street

Ned McGrath from Coolaclarig, outside Listowel, started a general drapery and fancy goods establishment in the early 1900s. He married Teresa Clarke from Barnstown, Co. Wexford, a trained milliner. The family continued with the business until the mid-1960s. The house at No. 46 William Street is now owned by Eamon McGrath.

Photo: Edward and Theresa McGrath with their eldest son Peter (Bobby) circa July 1914.

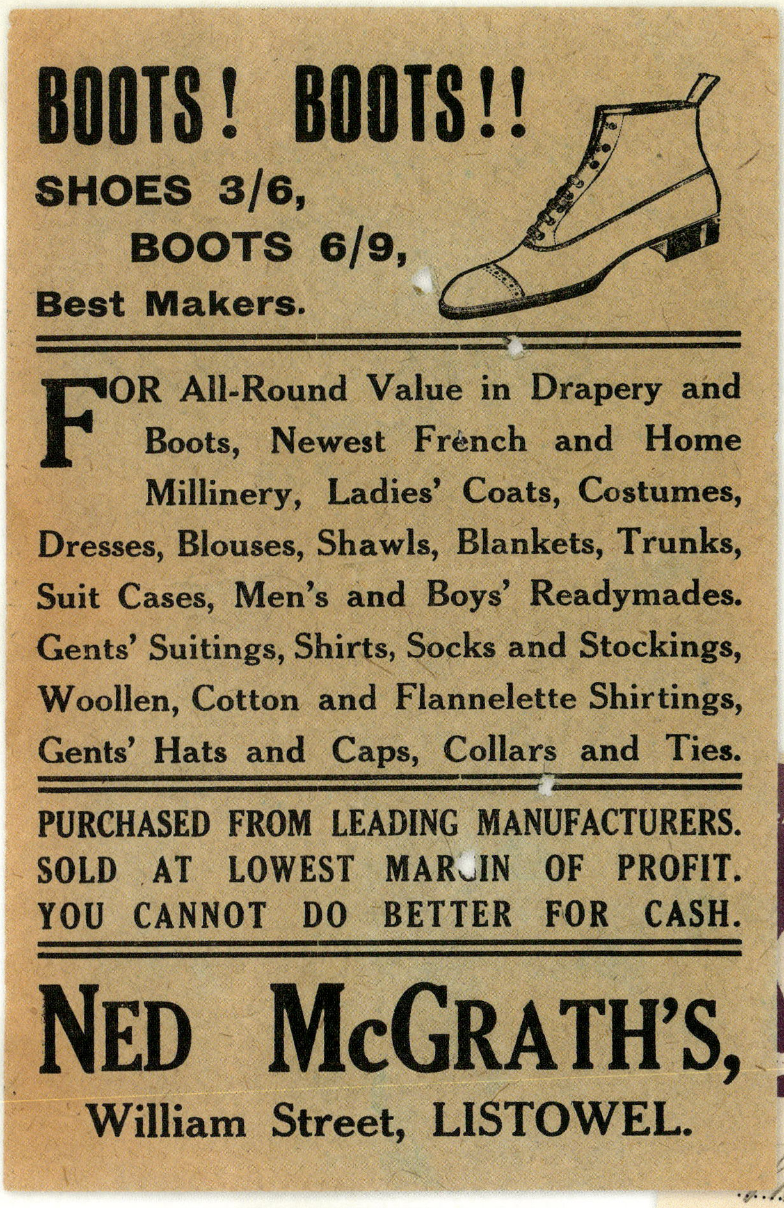

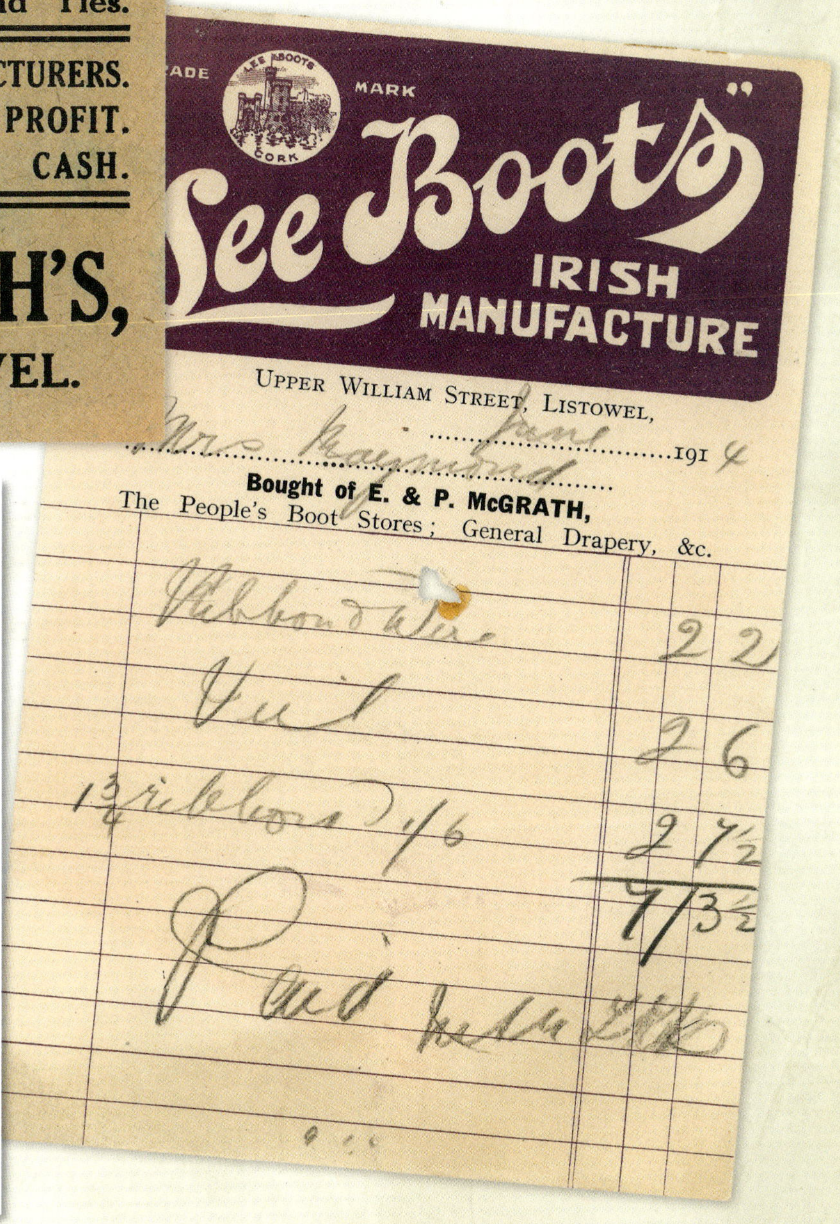

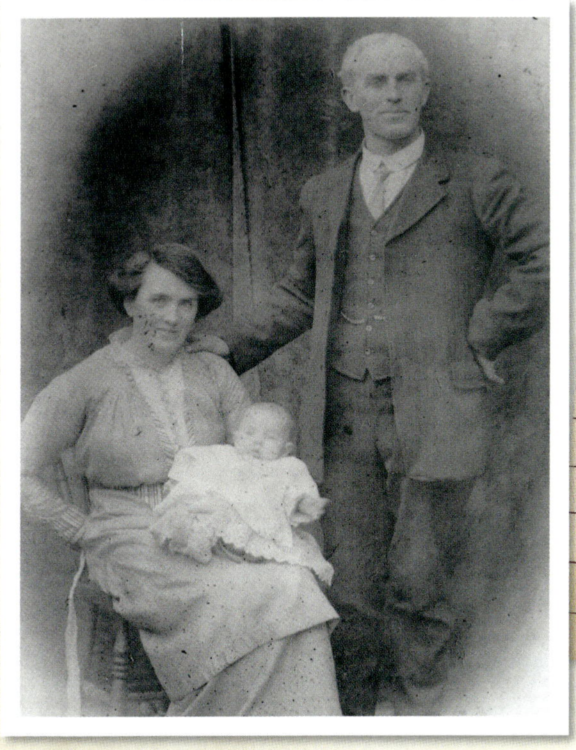

48 & 50 Lower William Street

The was the site of Listowel Post Office for over 30 years from the 1940s. Before that, the Post Office was situated at No. 40 Lower William Street. The accompanying letter from the Tralee postmaster to Marshall Hill (a land agent of Lord Listowel) is an apologetic reply for a delayed telegram. It is interesting to note that his excuse for the delay is the losing of his most skilled telegraph operators for the war effort in 1915, ie 'the front'.

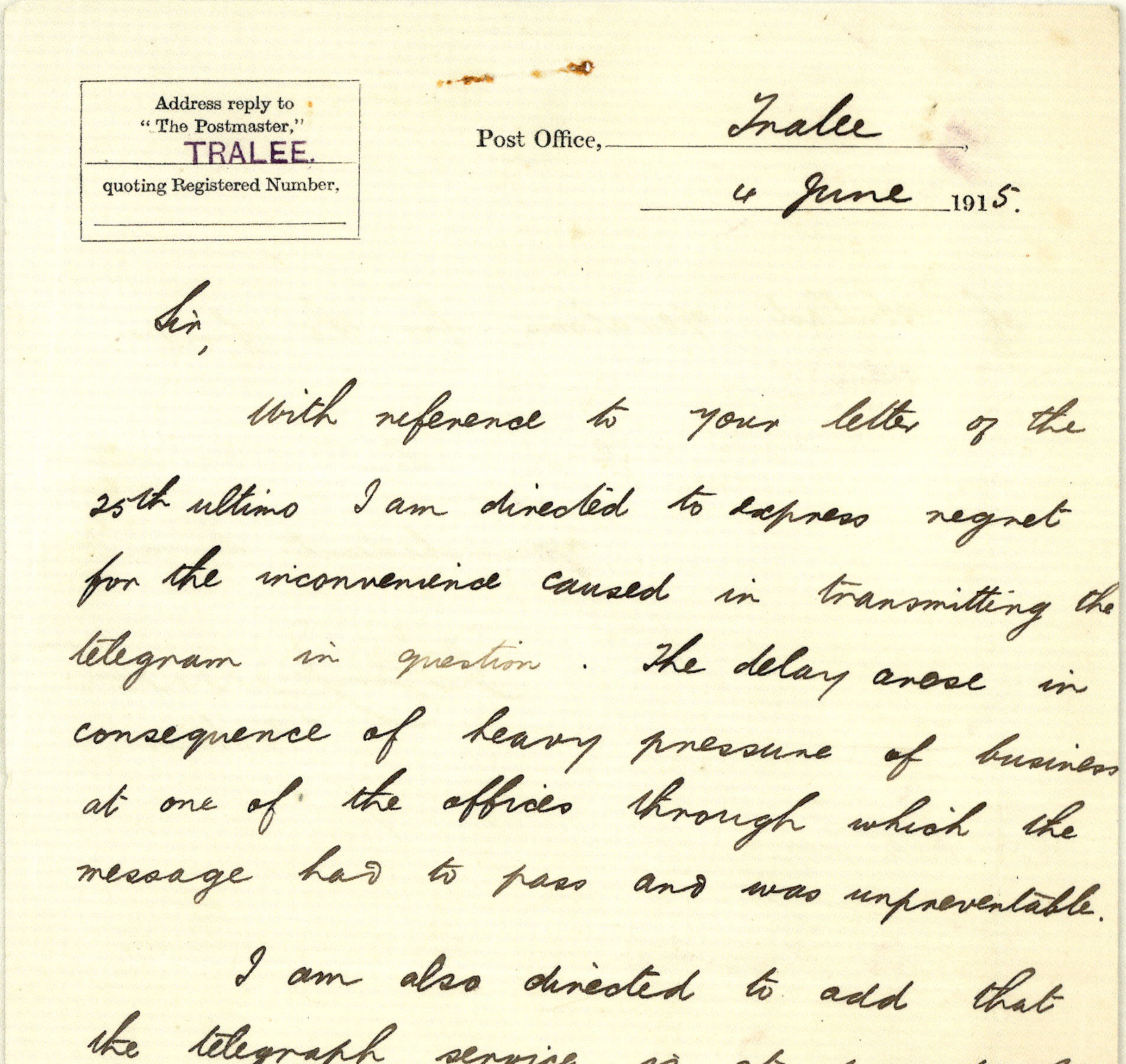

Address reply to
"The Postmaster,"
TRALEE.
quoting Registered Number,

Post Office, Tralee
4 June 1915.

Sir,

With reference to your letter of the 25th ultimo I am directed to express regret for the inconvenience caused in transmitting the telegram in question. The delay arose in consequence of heavy pressure of business at one of the offices through which the message had to pass and was unpreventable.

I am also directed to add that the telegraph service is at present being worked with a depleted and to some extent with a comparatively inexperienced staff in consequence of heavy withdrawals

Photo opposite: Listowel Postmen, late 1940s. Front (l to r): Paddy Moloney, Jack Carroll, Denis Carroll, Mick Enright. Back (l to r): Denis Horgan, unknown, John Joe Hartnett, Dick Broder, Denis Stack.

of skilled operators for the front.

I am, Sir,
your obedient servant

B. M. Senior
Bodmin

W Hill Esq

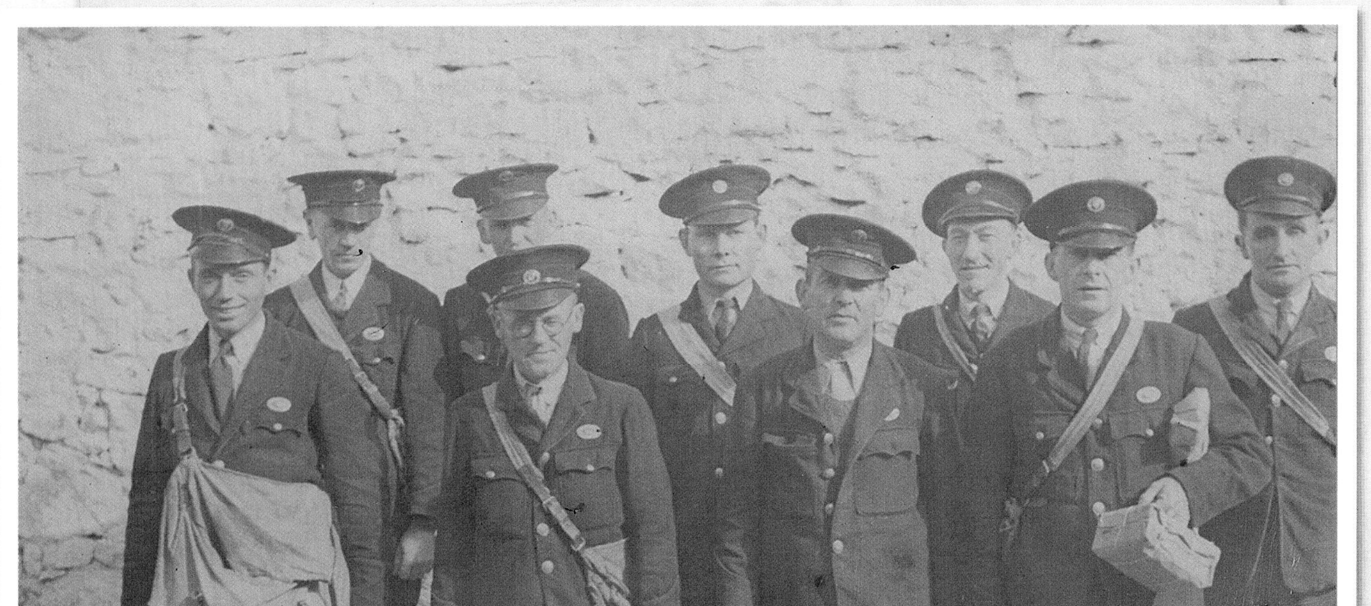

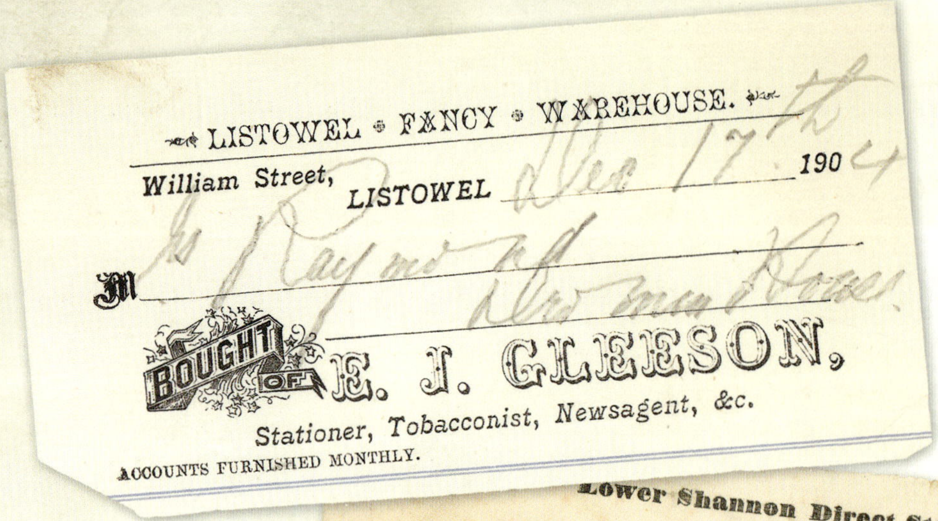

LISTOWEL • FANCY • WAREHOUSE.

William Street, LISTOWEL Dec 17th 1904

M

BOUGHT OF E. J. GLEESON,

Stationer, Tobacconist, Newsagent, &c.

ACCOUNTS FURNISHED MONTHLY.

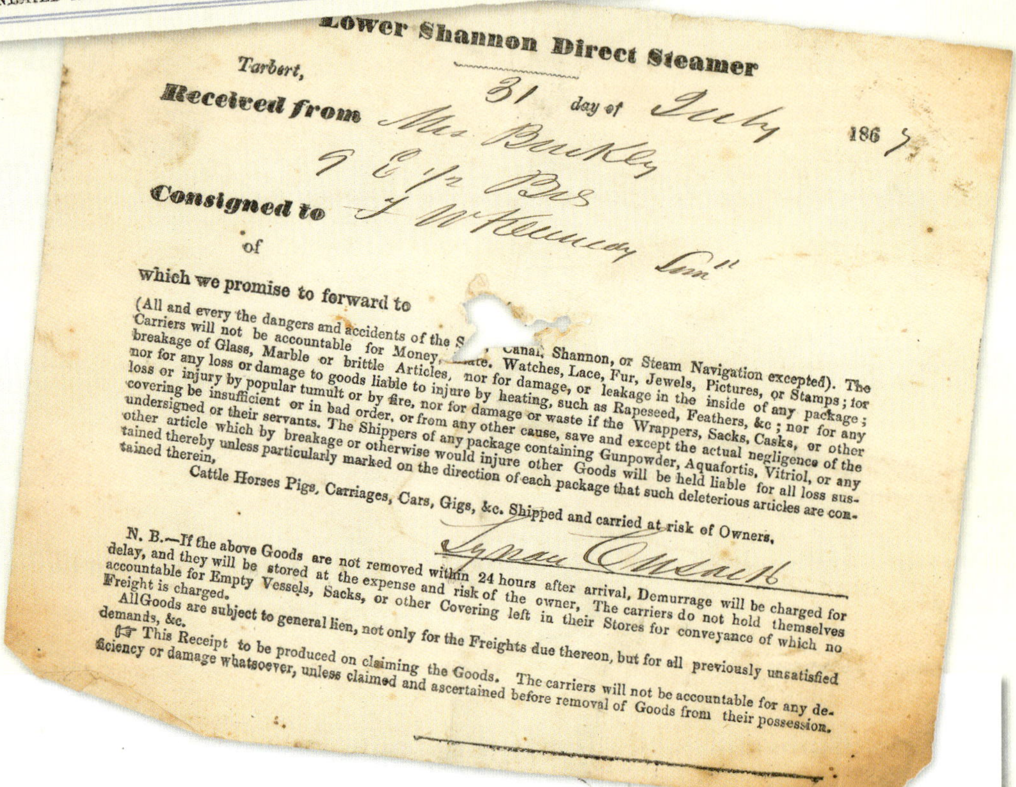

Lower Shannon Direct Steamer

Tarbert, 31 day of July 1867

Received from

Consigned to

of

which we promise to forward to

(All and every the dangers and accidents of the S[illegible] Canal, Shannon, or Steam Navigation excepted). The Carriers will not be accountable for Money, [illegible]ate. Watches, Lace, Fur, Jewels, Pictures, or Stamps; for breakage of Glass, Marble or brittle Articles, nor for damage, or leakage in the inside of any package; nor for any loss or damage to goods liable to injure by heating, such as Rapeseed, Feathers, &c; nor for any loss or injury by popular tumult or by fire, nor for damage or waste if the Wrappers, Sacks, Casks, or other covering be insufficient or in bad order, or from any other cause, save and except the actual negligence of the undersigned or their servants. The Shippers of any package containing Gunpowder, Aquafortis, Vitriol, or any other article which by breakage or otherwise would injure other Goods will be held liable for all loss sustained thereby unless particularly marked on the direction of each package that such deleterious articles are contained therein,

Cattle Horses Pigs, Carriages, Cars, Gigs, &c. Shipped and carried at risk of Owners.

N. B.—If the above Goods are not removed within 24 hours after arrival, Demurrage will be charged for delay, and they will be stored at the expense and risk of the owner, The carriers do not hold themselves accountable for Empty Vessels, Sacks, or other Covering left in their Stores for conveyance of which no Freight is charged.

AllGoods are subject to general lien, not only for the Freights due thereon, but for all previously unsatisfied demands, &c.

☞ This Receipt to be produced on claiming the Goods. The carriers will not be accountable for any deficiency or damage whatsoever, unless claimed and ascertained before removal of Goods from their possession.

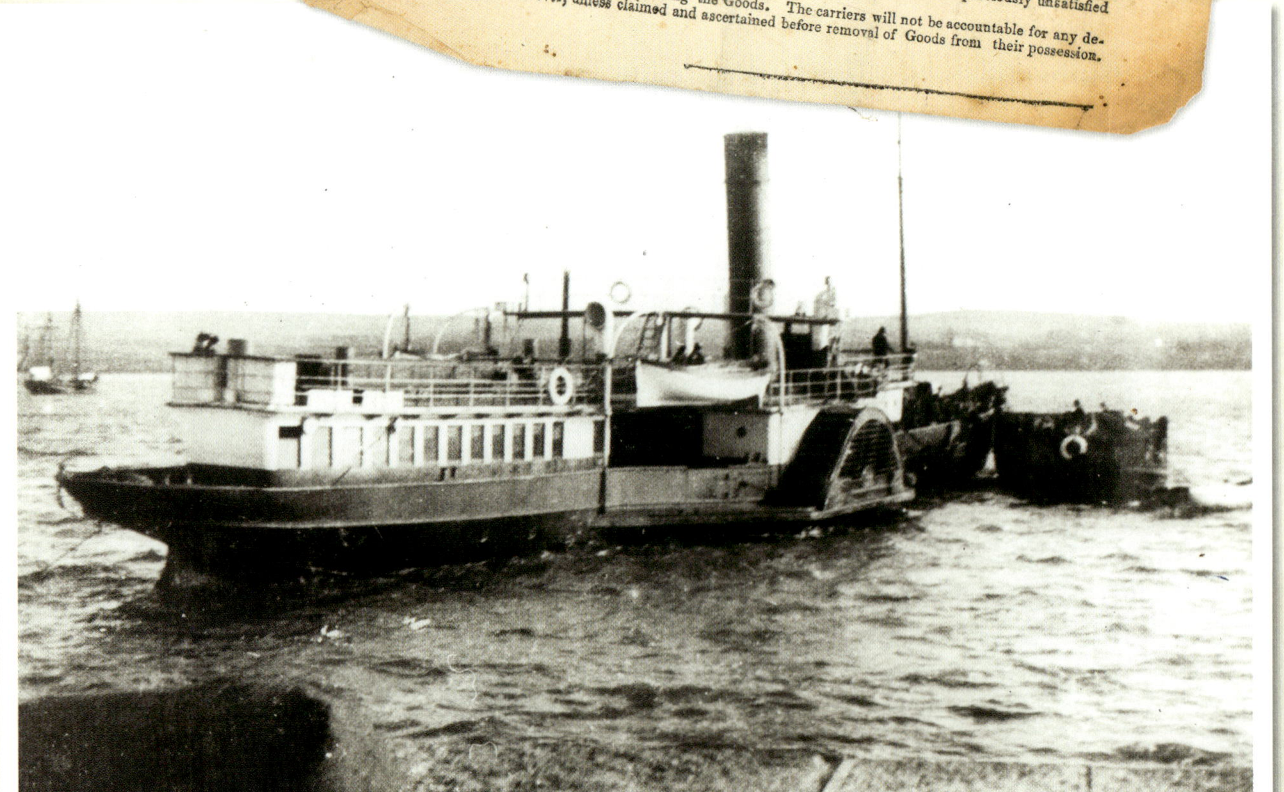

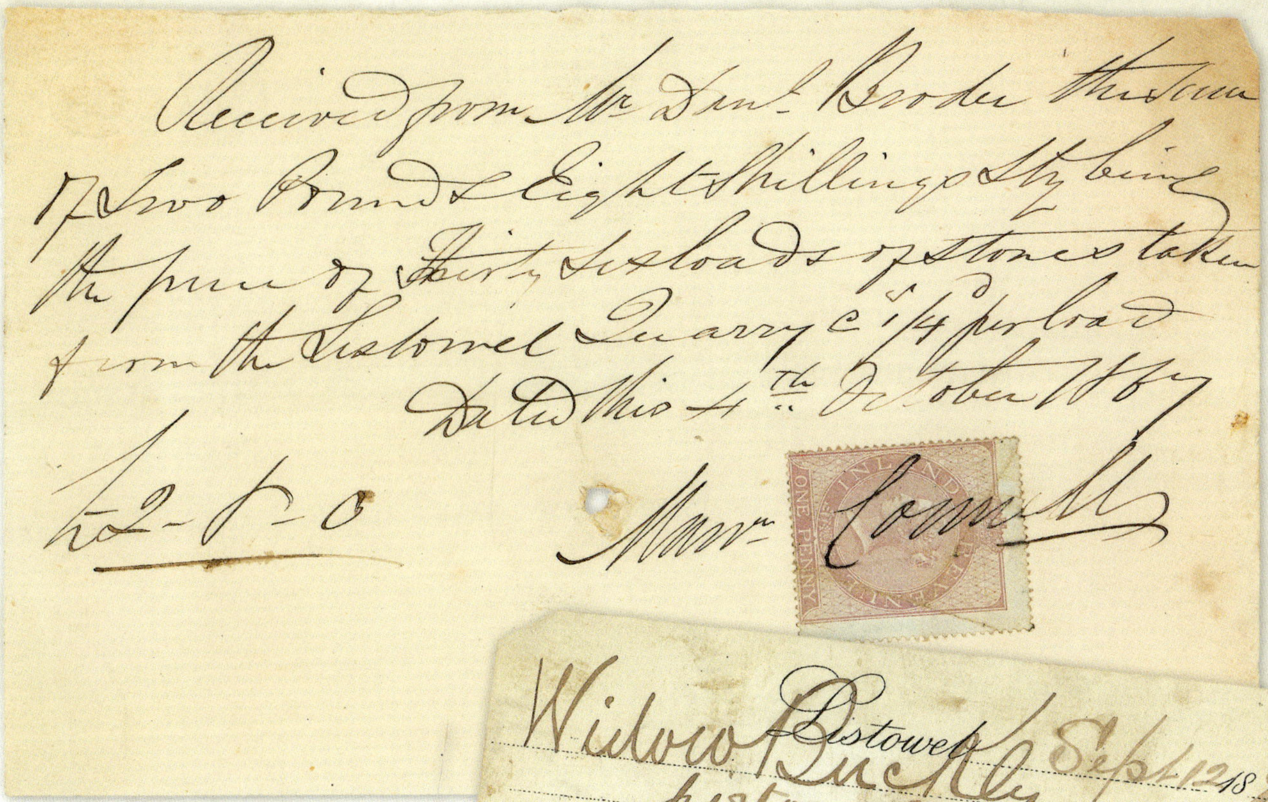
Received from Mr Danl. Broder this sum of Two Pounds & Eight Shillings Stg being the price of Thirty six loads of stones taken from the Listowel Quarry @ 1/4 per load
Dated this 4th October 1867
£2-8-0
Maur. Connell

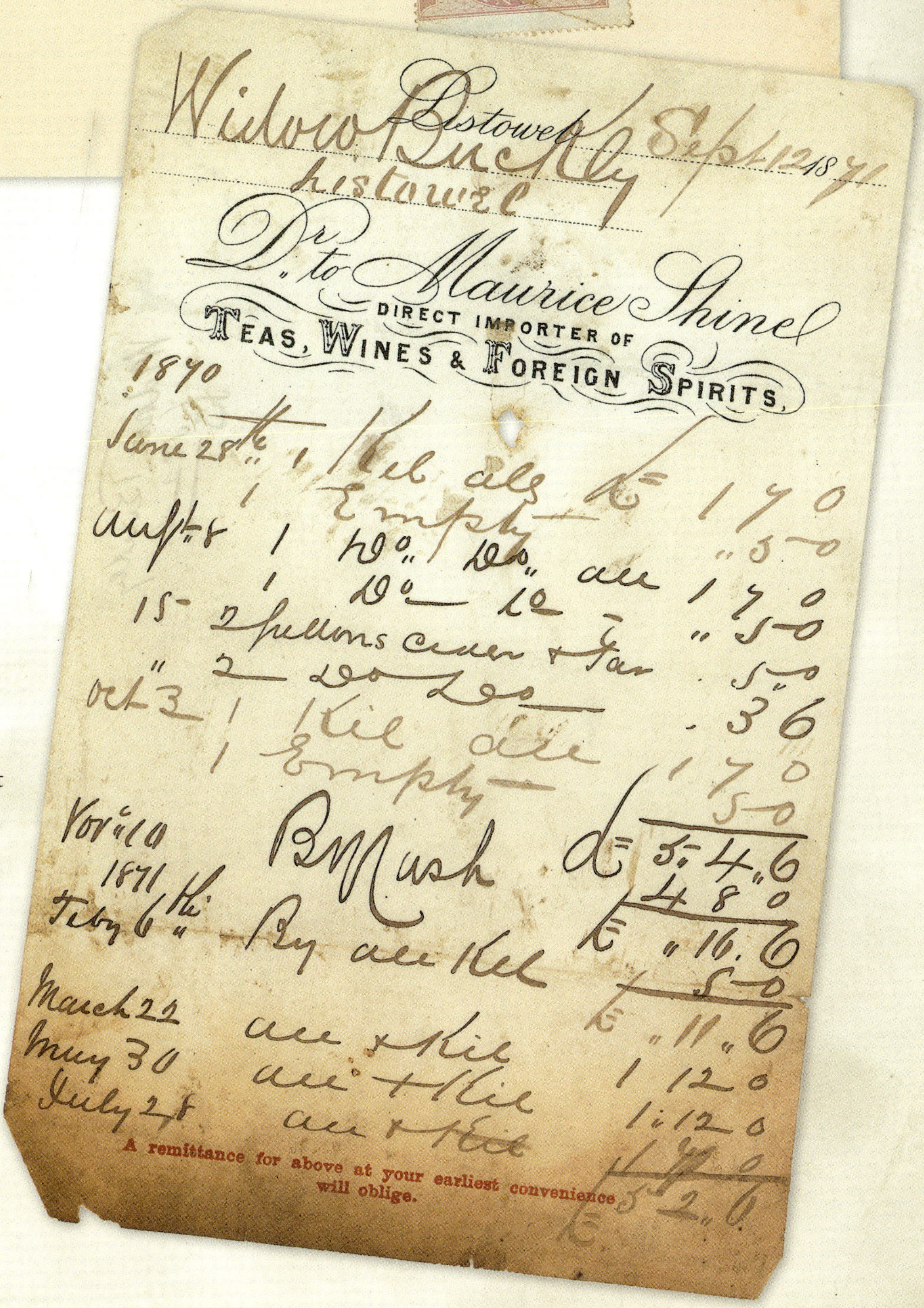
Widow Buckley Listowel Sept 12 1871
Listowel
Dr. to Maurice Shine
DIRECT IMPORTER OF
TEAS, WINES & FOREIGN SPIRITS.

1870		
June 28th	1 Kel ale	£1 7 0
	1 Empty	" 5 0
Augt 8	1 Do. Do. ale	1 7 0
	1 Do. Do.	" 5 0
15	2 gallons cider & Jar	. 5 0
"	2 Do. Do.	. 3 6
Oct 3	1 Kil ale	1 7 0
	1 Empty	5 0
Nov 10	By Cash	£5 4 6
		4 8 0
1871		£ " 16 6
Feby 6th	By ale Kel	5 0
		£ " 11 6
March 22	ale & Kil	1 12 0
May 30	ale & Kil	1 12 0
July 28	ale & Kil	1 7 0
		£5 2 6

A remittance for above at your earliest convenience will oblige.

42 & 44 Lower William Street
John and Johanna Buckley built a house at William Street in the 1860s, trading as a public house. John died shortly afterwards, and Johanna continued the business. She was known as 'the Widow Buckley'. Timothy Gleeson came to Listowel, from Tipperary, as a workman on the new Limerick to Tralee railway line. Johanna and Tim married on December 1st, 1871.

The house is now a restaurant called 'Jumbo's', owned by Dermot O'Mahony.

Included is a rare letterhead and photo of the Tarbert/Limerick lower Shannon ferry.

E.J. Gleeson receipt is from the shop next door, which he had rented.

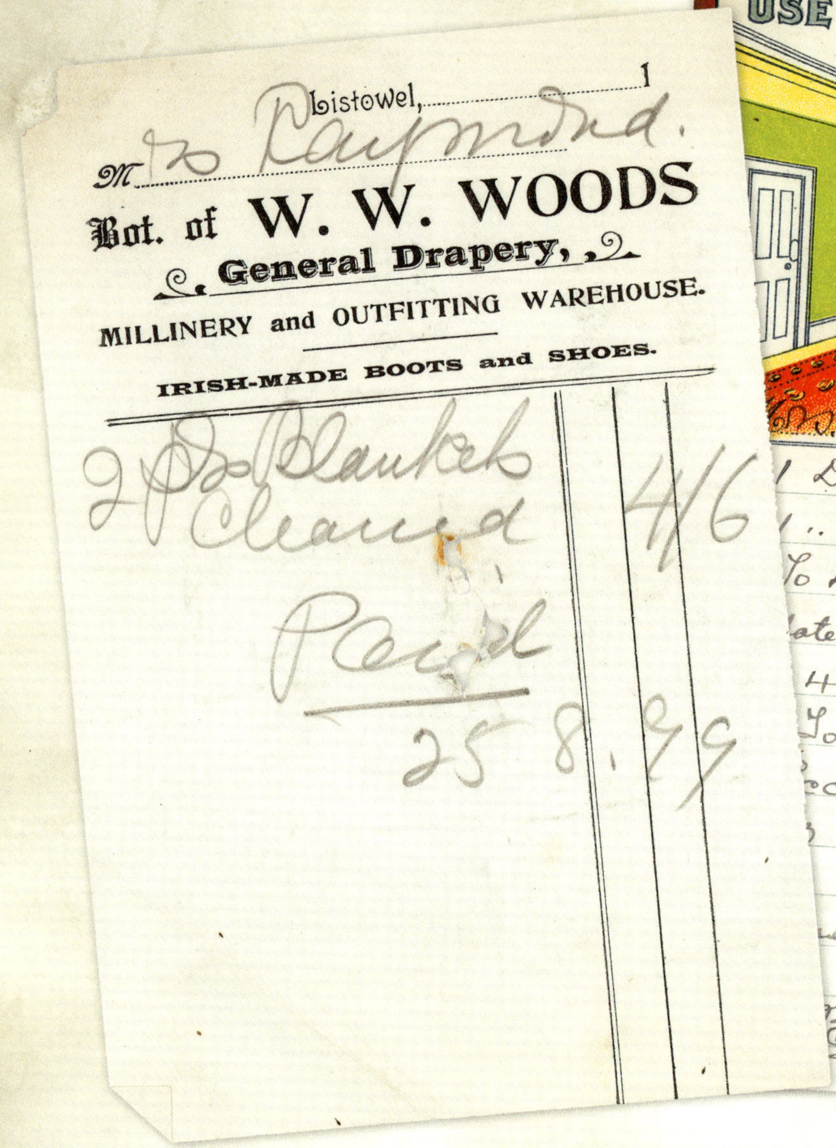
Listowel, 1
Mr. D. Raymond.
Bot. of W. W. WOODS
General Drapery,
MILLINERY and OUTFITTING WAREHOUSE.
IRISH-MADE BOOTS and SHOES.
2 Pr. Blankets Cleaned 4/6
Paid
25. 8. 99

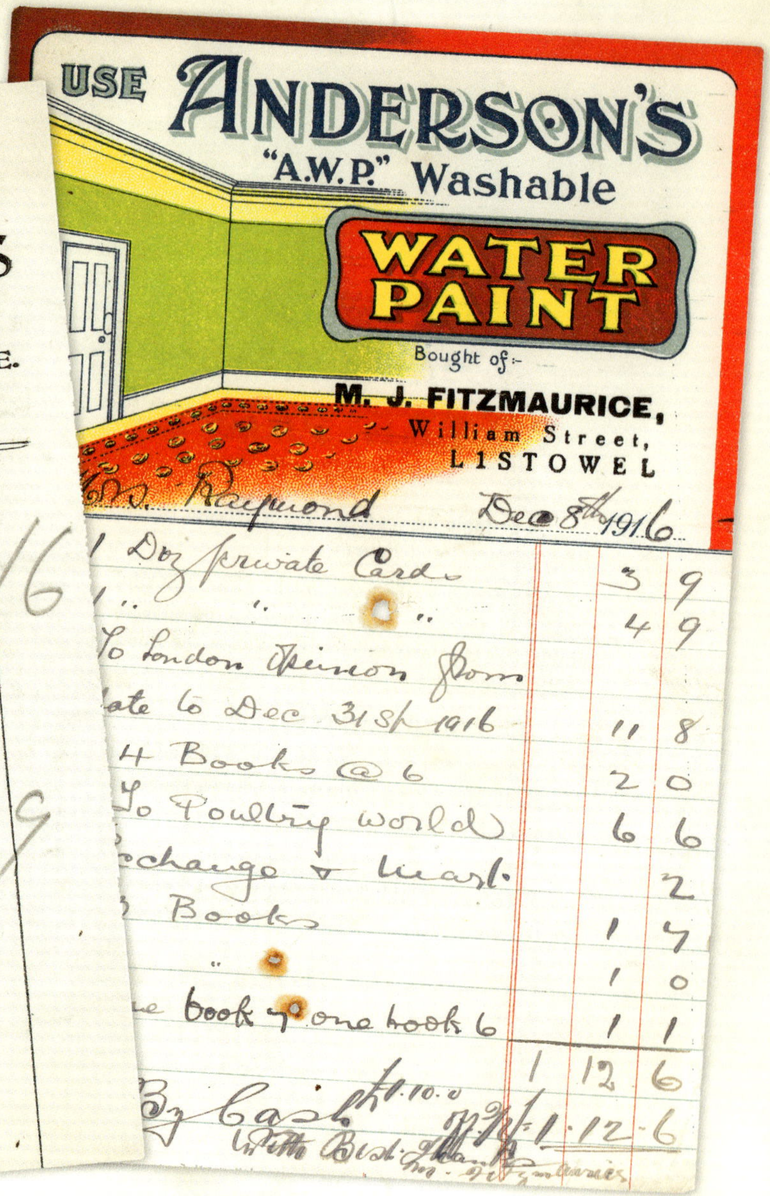

Bought of:-
M. J. FITZMAURICE,
William Street,
LISTOWEL
Mr. Raymond Dec 8th 1916

1 Doz private Cards	3	9
1 " " "	4	9
To London Opinion from		
date to Dec 31st 1916	11	8
4 Books @ 6	2	0
To Poultry world	6	6
Exchange & Mart		2
3 Books	1	7
"	1	0
One book & one book 6	1	1
	1 12	6
By Cash £1.10.0	1.12	6

With Best Thanks M. J. Fitzmaurice

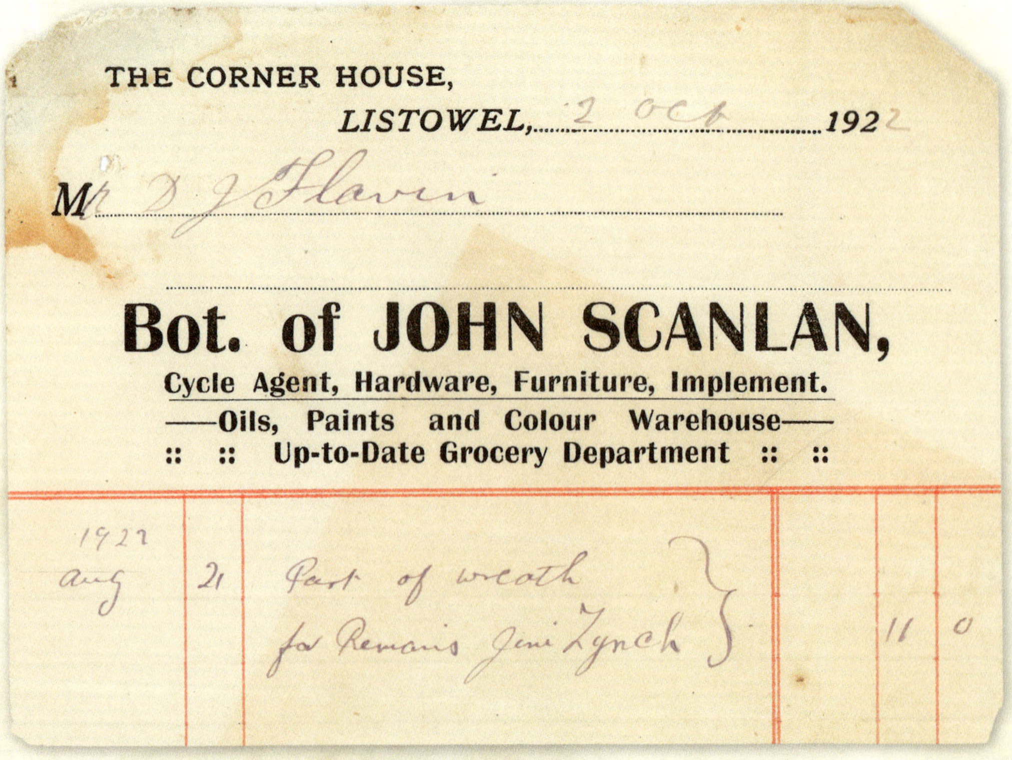
THE CORNER HOUSE,
LISTOWEL, 2 Oct 1922
Mr D J Flavin

Bot. of JOHN SCANLAN,
Cycle Agent, Hardware, Furniture, Implement.
—Oils, Paints and Colour Warehouse—
:: :: Up-to-Date Grocery Department :: ::

1922 Aug	21	Part of wreath for Remains Jim Lynch	11	0

36 Lower William Street
A trio of receipts from the corner house, No. 36 William Street. Along with the above, others who had a shop here were: Stack's, Shanahan's and at present Horan's.

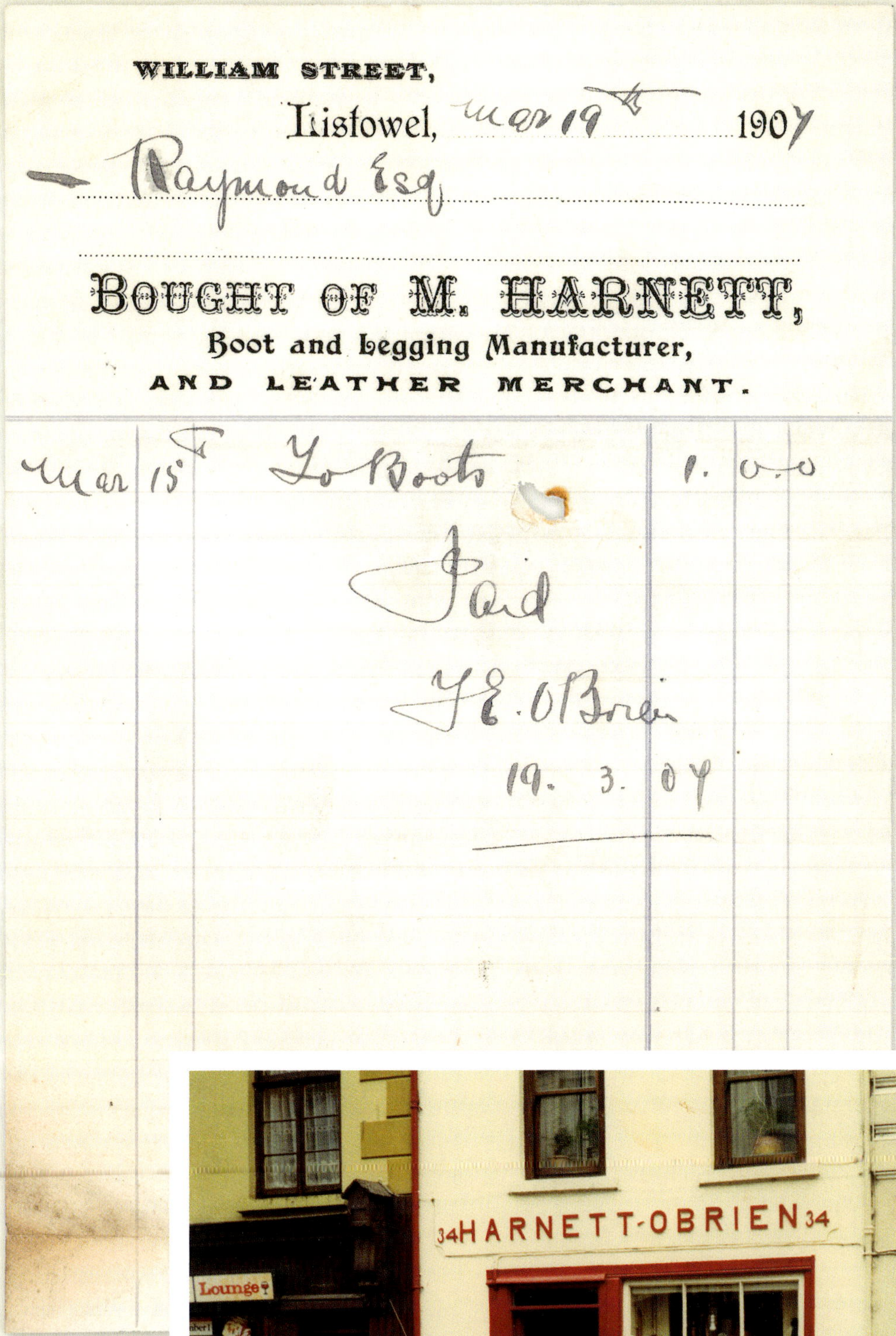
WILLIAM STREET,
Listowel, Mar 19th 1907
Raymond Esq
BOUGHT OF M. HARNETT,
Boot and Legging Manufacturer,
AND LEATHER MERCHANT.

Mar 15th	To Boots	1.	0. 0

Paid
T. E. O'Brien
19. 3. 07

34 Lower William Street
John and Johanna Harnett established a boot and shoe-making shop at their home in Lower William Street in the 1870s. After John's death, the business was continued by his daughter Mary. She was joined in the business in 1906 by her new husband Tim O'Brien from Mitchelstown. With the demise of boot and shoe-making, the shop continued as a leather shop run by Theresa O'Brien until its closure in the 1980s. Theresa is pictured below with her sister Josie and visitors in the 1980s. The premises is now the site of John Sexton's menswear business.

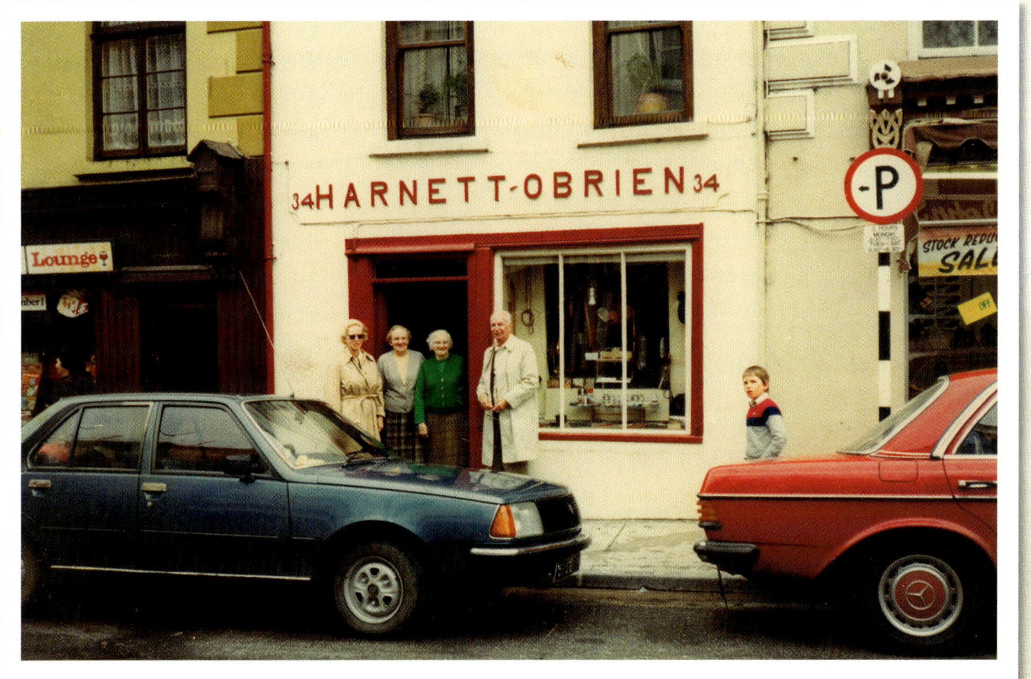

30 Lower William Street
In 1853, James D. Keane established a bar, grocery and cooperage at No. 30 Lower William Street. David Barry married James's daughter Bridget in 1888. The bar was operated for many years by their son John (Jack).

Photo below: John (Jack) Barry.

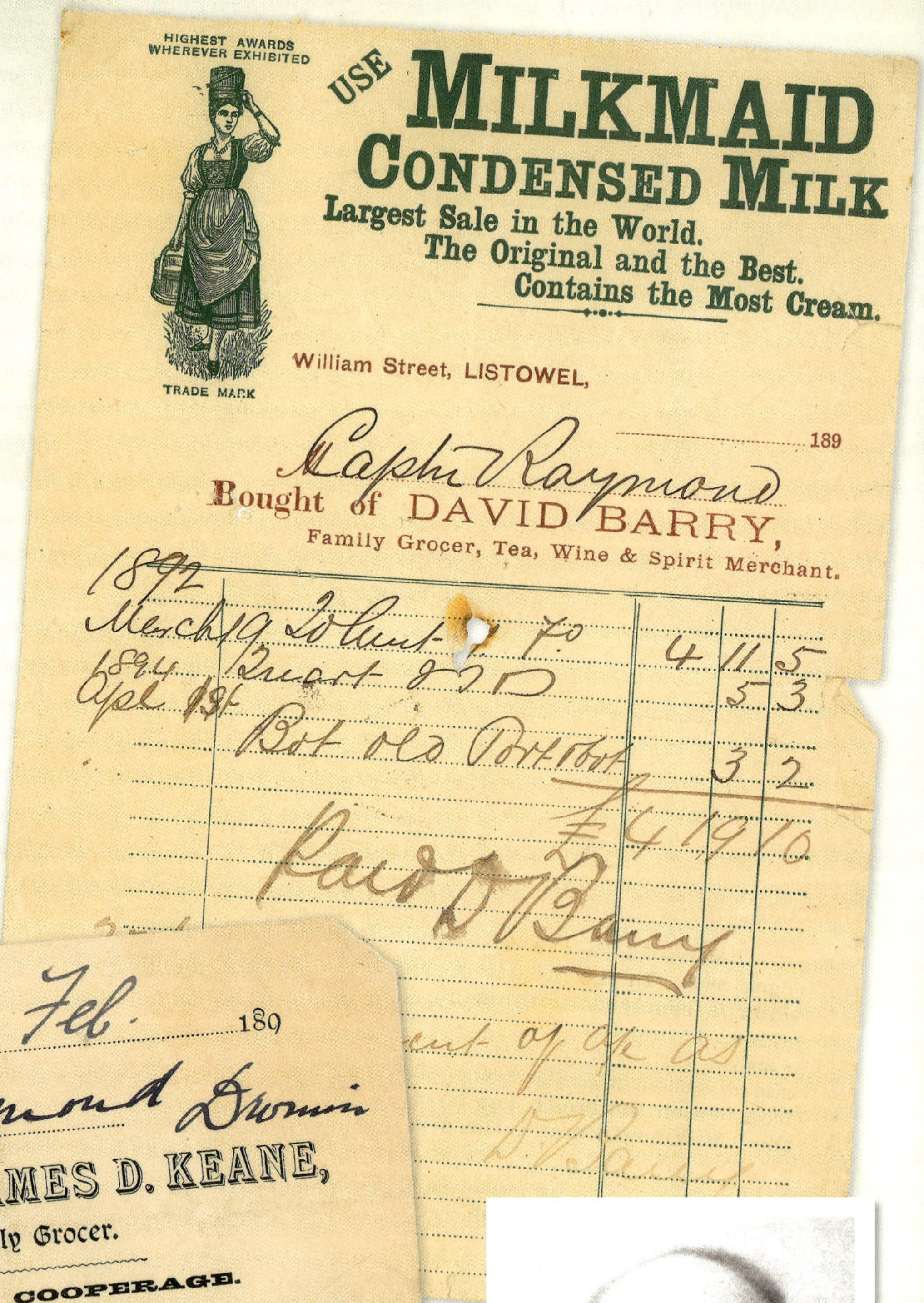
HIGHEST AWARDS WHEREVER EXHIBITED

TRADE MARK

USE MILKMAID CONDENSED MILK
Largest Sale in the World.
The Original and the Best.
Contains the Most Cream.

William Street, LISTOWEL, ...189

Captn Raymond

Bought of DAVID BARRY,
Family Grocer, Tea, Wine & Spirit Merchant.

1892 March 19	To Acct.	4	11	5
1894 Apl 1st			5	3
	Bot old Port		3	2
		£4	19	10

Paid D. Barry

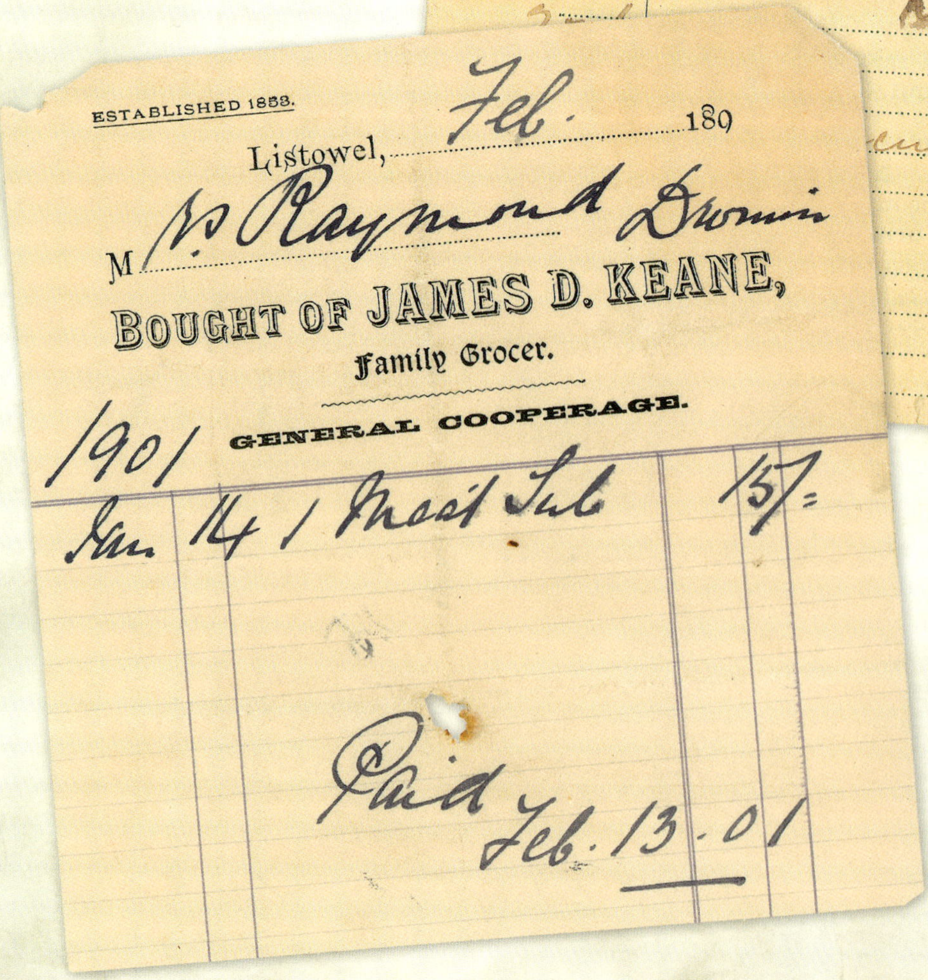
ESTABLISHED 1853.

Listowel, Feb. 1901

M Raymond

BOUGHT OF JAMES D. KEANE,
Family Grocer.
GENERAL COOPERAGE.

1901 Jan 14	1 Meat Tub	15/-

Paid Feb. 13. 01

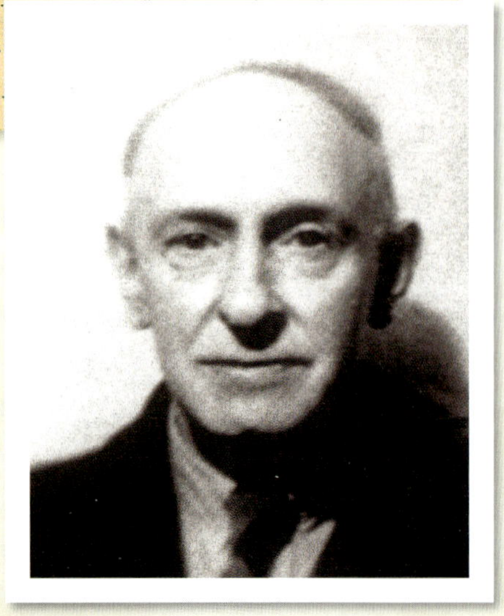

22 & 26 Lower William Street

Patrick Corbett, a tinsmith, from Tralee, was married to Mary Mulally from Tarbert, pictured. He opened his shop at No. 26 William Street in 1900. The business passed on through their daughter Sarah to the McGillicuddy family. The business was expanded by Jackie McGillicuddy, who purchased the adjoining Fitzgibbon shop in the 1970s. The business now operates as Corbett-Fitzgibbon. Fitzgibbon's was originally run by two Broderick sisters, one of whom, Hannie, married Patrick Fitzgibbon from County Limerick. They had a light hardware/fancy goods store for many years.

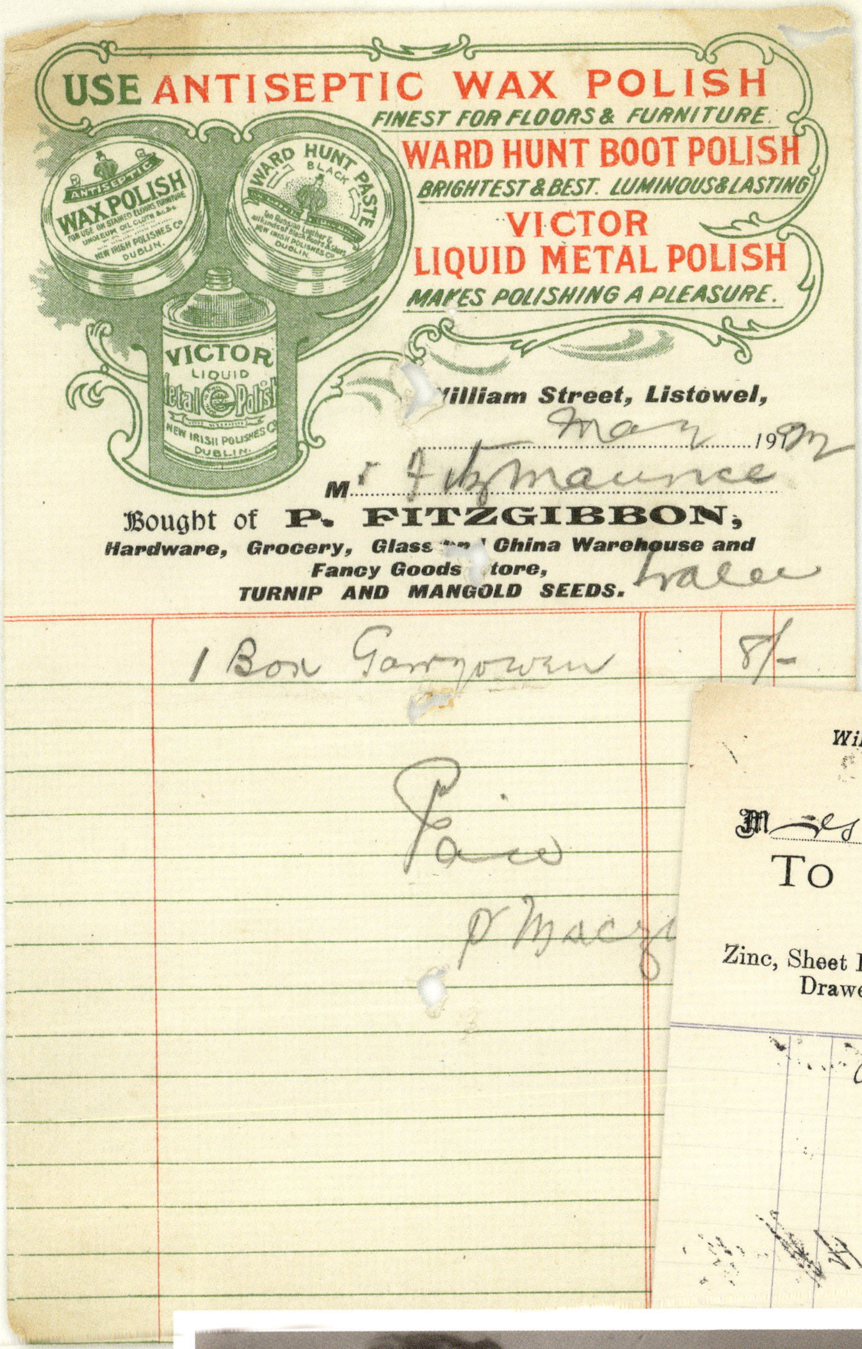
USE ANTISEPTIC WAX POLISH
FINEST FOR FLOORS & FURNITURE.
WARD HUNT BOOT POLISH
BRIGHTEST & BEST. LUMINOUS & LASTING
VICTOR
LIQUID METAL POLISH
MAKES POLISHING A PLEASURE.

William Street, Listowel, May 1902

Mr Fitzmaurice

Bought of P. FITZGIBBON,
Hardware, Grocery, Glass and China Warehouse and
Fancy Goods Store,
TURNIP AND MANGOLD SEEDS.

Tralee

1 Box Garryowen	8/-

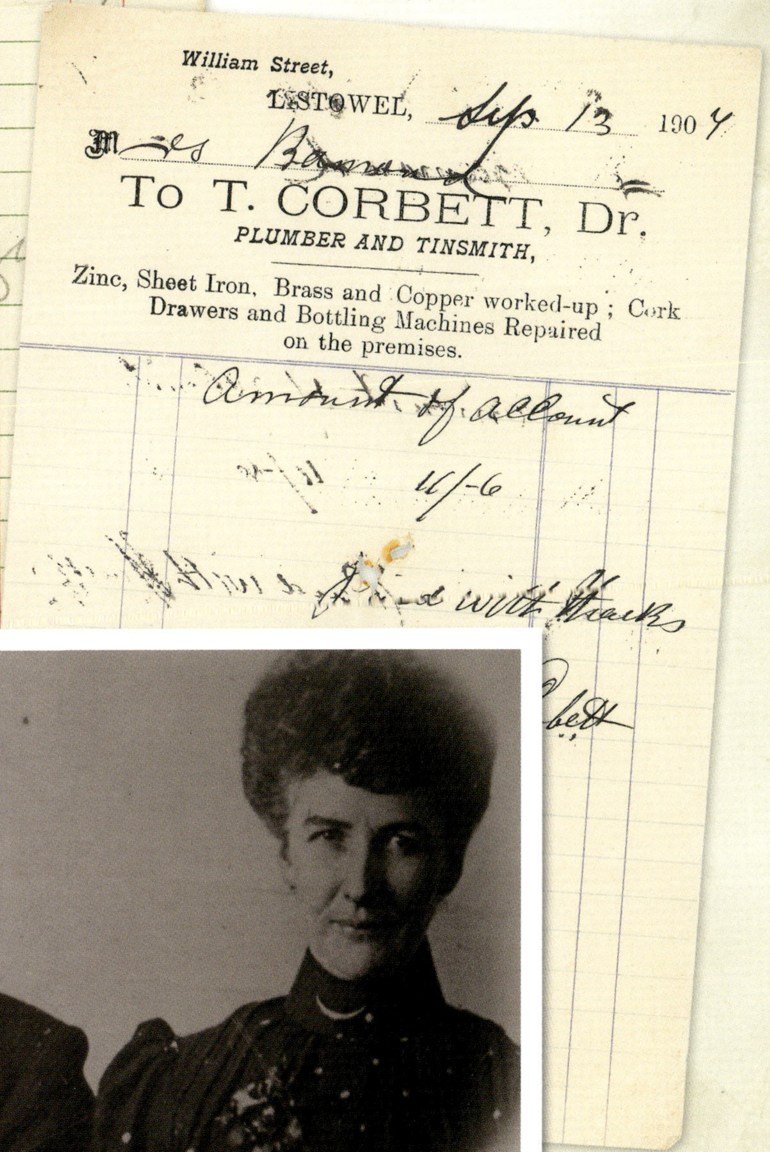
William Street,
LISTOWEL, Sep 13 1904

TO T. CORBETT, Dr.
PLUMBER AND TINSMITH,

Zinc, Sheet Iron, Brass and Copper worked-up; Cork Drawers and Bottling Machines Repaired on the premises.

Amount of account 11/-6

with thanks

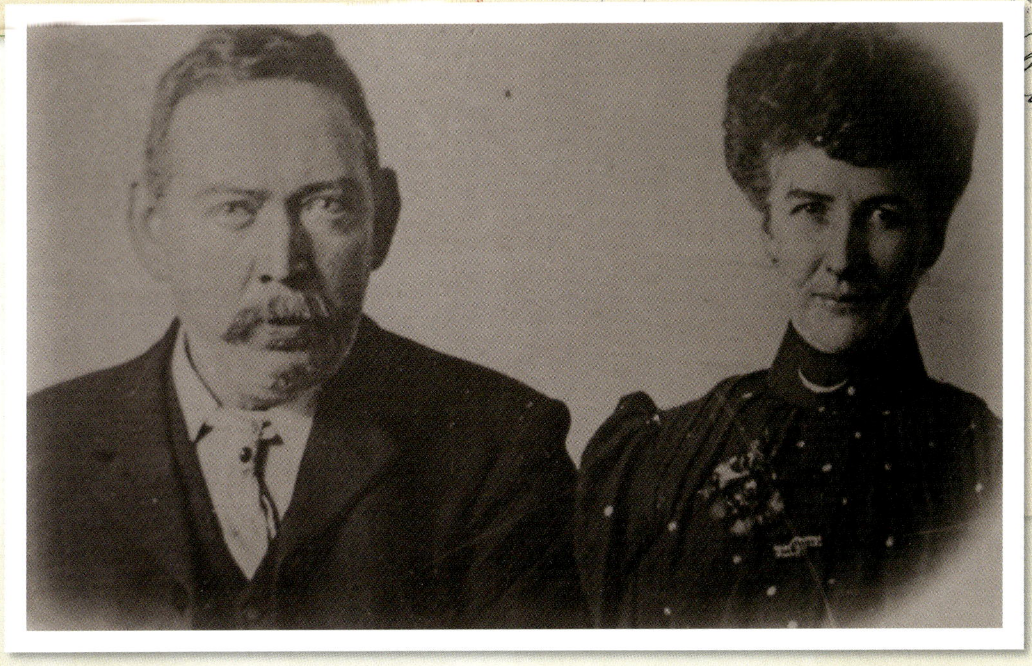

24 Lower William Street

Nolan's, a long-established William Street business, was inherited by Mai Fitzgerald who married Arthur Chute. It now operates as a restaurant called 'Mai Fitz's'.

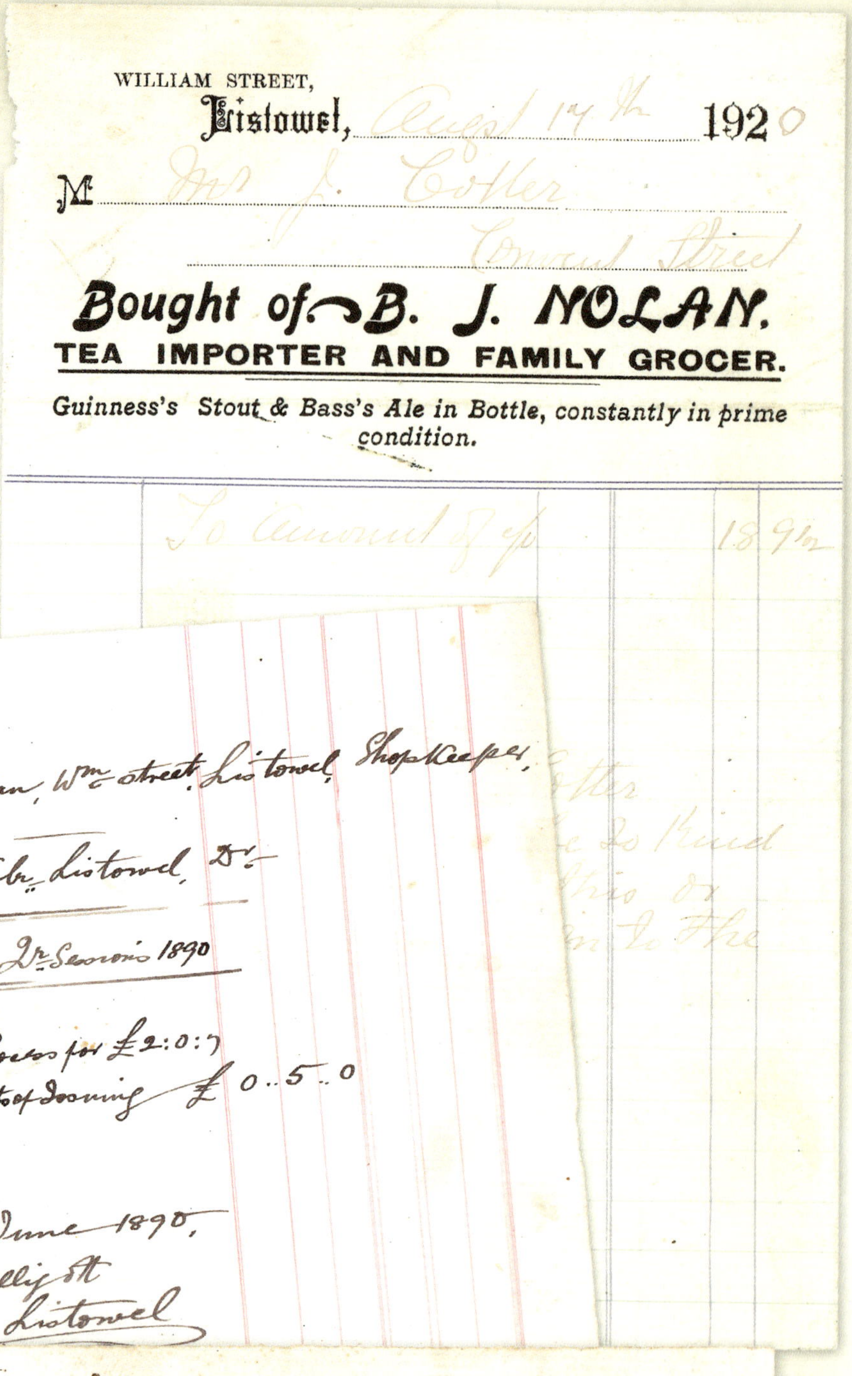
WILLIAM STREET,
Listowel, Aug 17th 1920
Mr J. Cotter
Convent Street
Bought of B. J. NOLAN.
TEA IMPORTER AND FAMILY GROCER.
Guinness's Stout & Bass's Ale in Bottle, constantly in prime condition.
To amount of a/c 18 9½

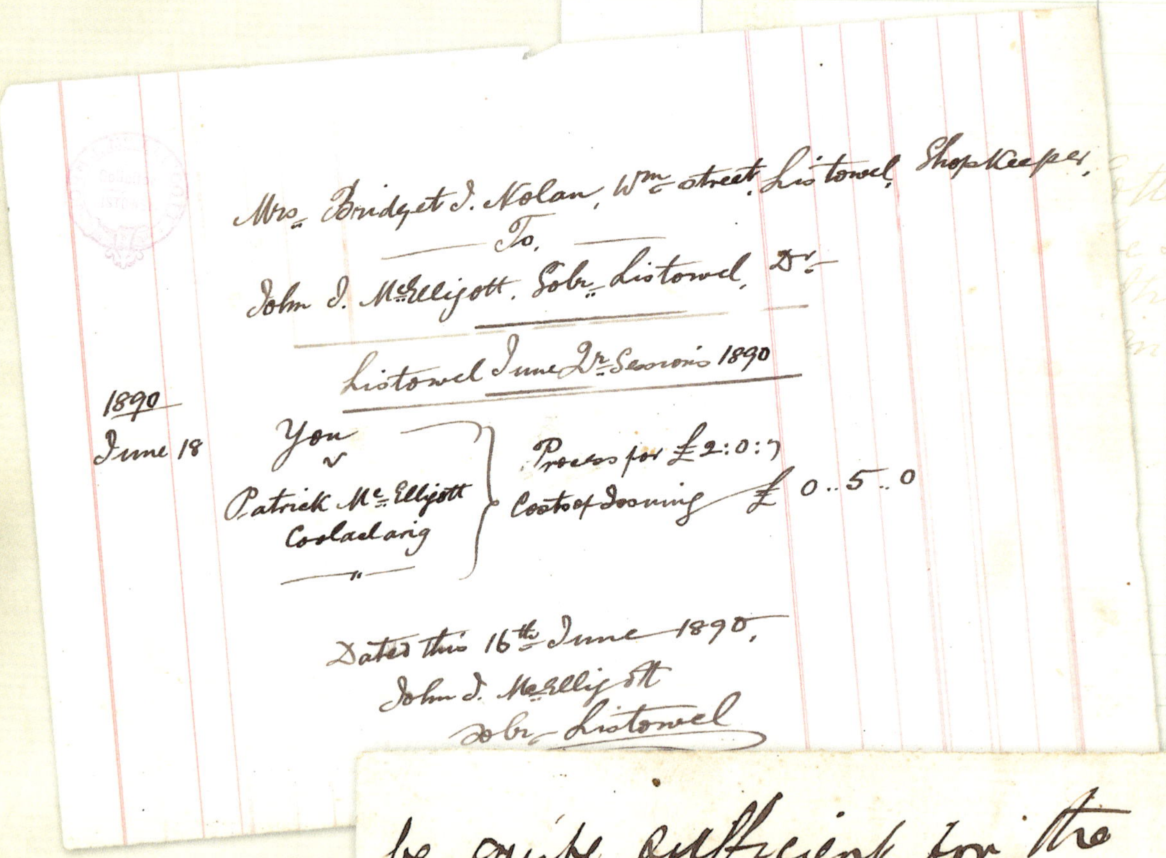
Mrs Bridget J. Nolan, Wm street Listowel Shopkeeper
To
John J. McElligott Solr Listowel Dr
Listowel June Qr Sessions 1890
1890 June 18 You v Patrick McElligott Coolaclarig
Process for £2:0:7
Costs of decreeing £0..5..0
Dated this 16th June 1890
John J. McElligott
Solr Listowel

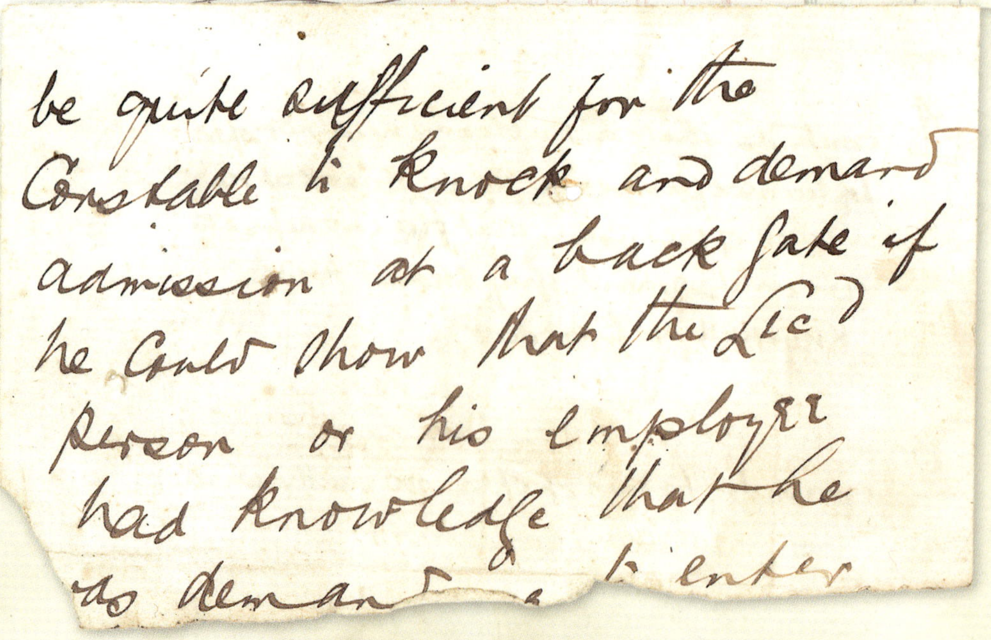
be quite sufficient for the
Constable to knock and demand
admission at a back gate if
he could show that the Lic'd
person or his employee
had knowledge that he
was demand... to enter

THE MUNSTER

Tea, Wine and Spirit Warehouse,

WILLIAM STREET

LISTOWEL, May 12th 1877

Mr Timothy Glavin [illegible] St Listowel

Bought of J. J. NOLAN

TEA IMPORTER & FAMILY GROCER.

Guinness's Stout and Bass's Ales in Bottle, constantly in prime condition.

2 lb [illegible]	1	2
[illegible] gallons pickle		7
	" 1	9

Paid 12/5/77

J Nolan

No. 1

View in Port Sunlight Village.

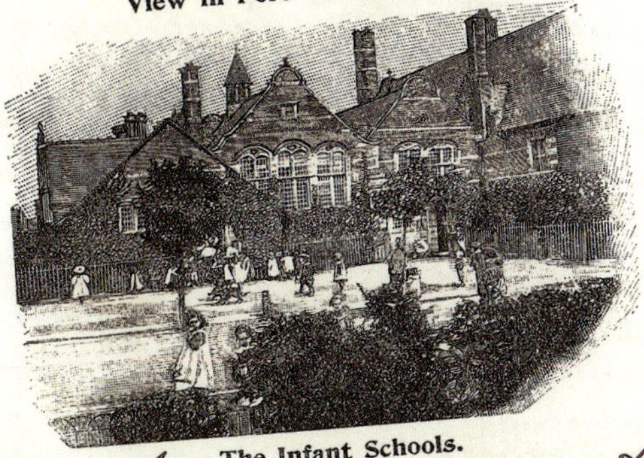

The Infant Schools.

SUNLIGHT SOAP : : Has the : Largest : Sale of any Soap in : The World.

LIFEBUOY : SOAP : : : Has the : : Largest : : Sale of any : Disinfectant : Soap in the : World.

Apr 27th 1907

Mr John Carmody Cash

BOUGHT OF B. J. NOLAN,

TEA IMPORTER AND FAMILY GROCER,

William Street, LISTOWEL.

Guinness's Stout and Bass's Ale in Bottle, constantly in Prime Condition.

1906		£	s	d
Dec 7	To Drink		1	8
	Do		2	8
" 12	" Cash & Drink			4
" 17	" Drink			4
" 18	" Do			7
" 20	" Do		10	0
" 21	" Cash Lent		1	0
" 22	" Do			5
" 29	" Drink		3	0
1907 Jan 16	" Cash 2/- Drink 1/-			
" 26		£ 1	0	6

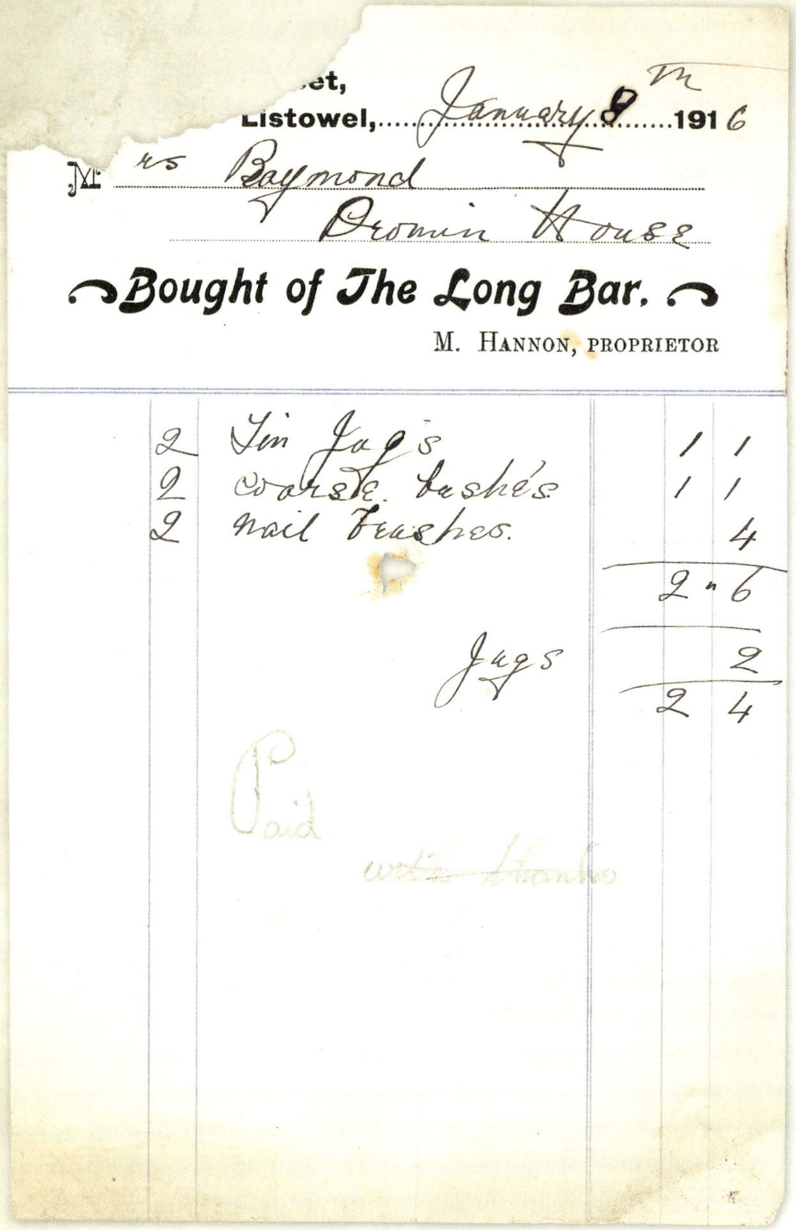
...et,
Listowel, January 8th 1916
Mrs Raymond
Dromin House
Bought of The Long Bar.
M. HANNON, PROPRIETOR

2	Tin Jugs	1	1
2	coarse brushes	1	1
2	nail brushes		4
		2	6
	Jugs		2
		2	4

Paid
with thanks

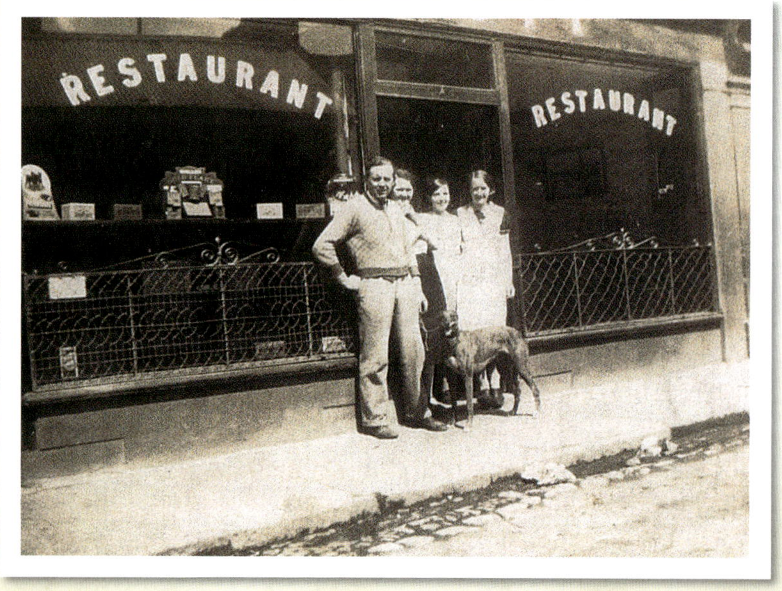

16 & 18 Lower William Street
Crowley's General Grocery & Bacon Store
This imposing frontage originally consisted of two houses. The near one being occupied by the Potter family, pawnbrokers, in the late 1800s, while the more decorative upper building was the original Crowley homestead.

20 Lower William Street
Matt and Margaret Hannon (*Photo opposite*).

Photo opposite below: Amadee Crowley, posing on right, with hand on hips in the 1940s.

Matthew and Margaret (née McElligott) Hannon owned the public house called 'The Long Bar'. They also had two other houses in Lower William Street, the Horseshoe Bar and the end house bought subsequently by Sandy Fitzgerald. Matthew operated a cinema known as 'the crooked cinema' in the Market, adjacent to Tay Lane. This was the oldest cinema in Listowel, and possibly Kerry. The projector was located at the back of the screen, mainly for two reasons, to alleviate brightness and to counteract the shape of the building which had been built with a slight curve. The screen used be painted by linseed oil. When the oil dried out the surface contained thousands of hardened crystals which gave an outstanding clear picture without any blinding effect on the audience. This procedure was the brainchild of Matt Hannon's son, also Matt. He became a doctor and was a keen inventor all his life. The interior of this cinema was destroyed by the Black and Tans who set fire to it when Matt Hannon disregarded a warning from them not to show a certain film.

Photo left: Fitzgerald's Restaurant, Tay Lane, built by Matt Hannon. In its time it served as a Technical School, Garda Station and a Labour Exchange. It was bought and opened as a restaurant by Sandy Fitzgerald from Castlegregory on his return from America in the 1930s. The building now houses the Tae Lane Boutique.

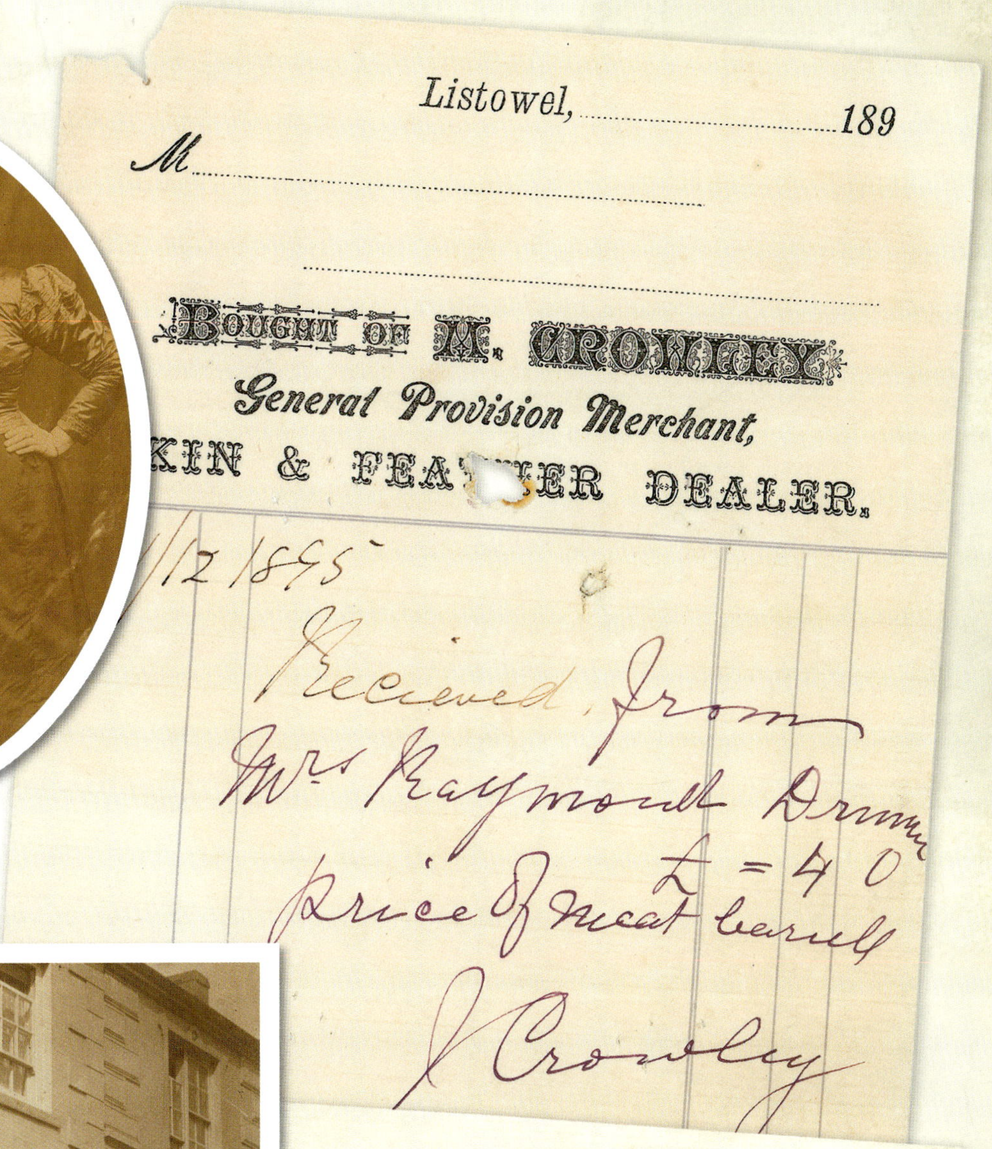

Listowel, ... 189

M ....

BOUGHT OF M. CROWLEY.

General Provision Merchant,

[S]KIN & FEA[TH]ER DEALER.

[1]/12 1895

Recieved from

Mrs Raymond Drum[...]

£ = 4 0

price of meat barrell

J Crowley

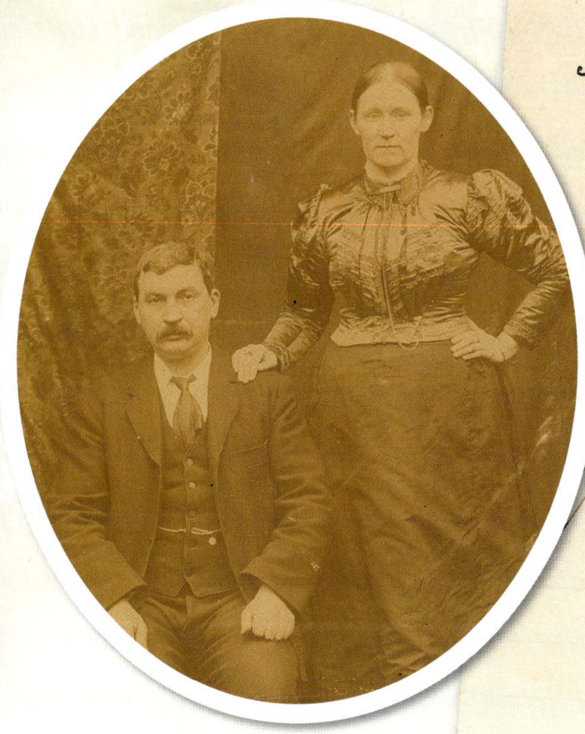

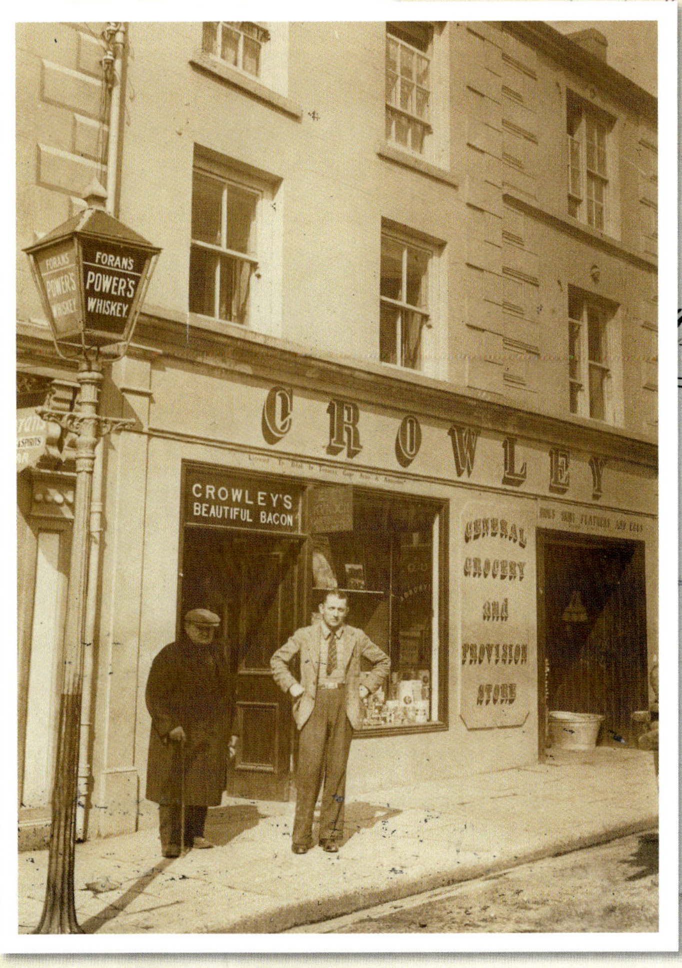

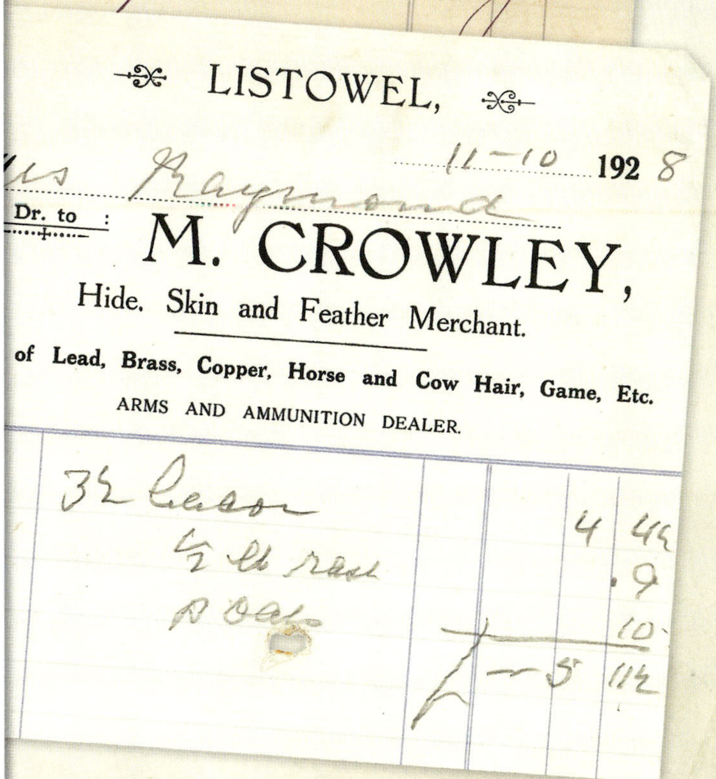

LISTOWEL, 11-10 1928

[...]s Raymond

Dr. to: M. CROWLEY,

Hide. Skin and Feather Merchant.

[...] of Lead, Brass, Copper, Horse and Cow Hair, Game, Etc.

ARMS AND AMMUNITION DEALER.

3½ bacon	4 4½
½ lb rash	.9
	10
	£ - 5 11½

14 Lower William Street

The bar, which was originally called 'The Northern Star', was bought by Jeremiah and Bibanna Foran in 1901. They renamed it 'The Horseshoe Bar'. Following the Forans' retirement to Ballybunion, it was bought by Mathew Hannon for his daughter Margaret who had married Batty McElligott from Ardfert. Liam Woulfe purchased the business from the McElligotts and ran the public house with his wife Frances. Their son Kevin, a qualified chef, renovated the premises and established a popular restaurant. It was sold to Jerry Behan from Lisselton in 2005; he has since bought the adjoining property of No. 12 and has, through extensive reconstruction and renovation, delivered a state-of-the-art dining and bar facility.

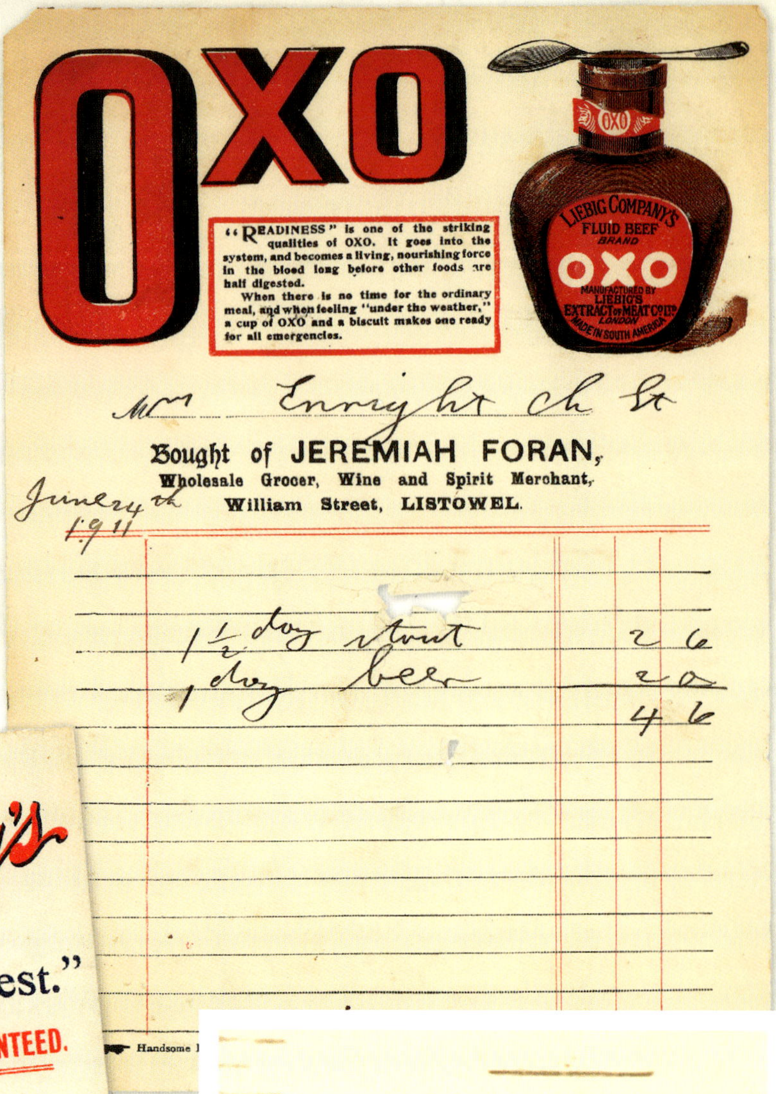
OXO

"READINESS" is one of the striking qualities of OXO. It goes into the system, and becomes a living, nourishing force in the blood long before other foods are half digested. When there is no time for the ordinary meal, and when feeling "under the weather," a cup of OXO and a biscuit makes one ready for all emergencies.

LIEBIG COMPANY'S FLUID BEEF BRAND OXO MANUFACTURED BY LIEBIG'S EXTRACT of MEAT Co LTD LONDON MADE IN SOUTH AMERICA

Mrs Enright Ch St

Bought of JEREMIAH FORAN,
Wholesale Grocer, Wine and Spirit Merchant,
William Street, LISTOWEL.

June 24th 1911

1½ doz stout		2	6
1 doz beer		2	0
		4	6

Handsome

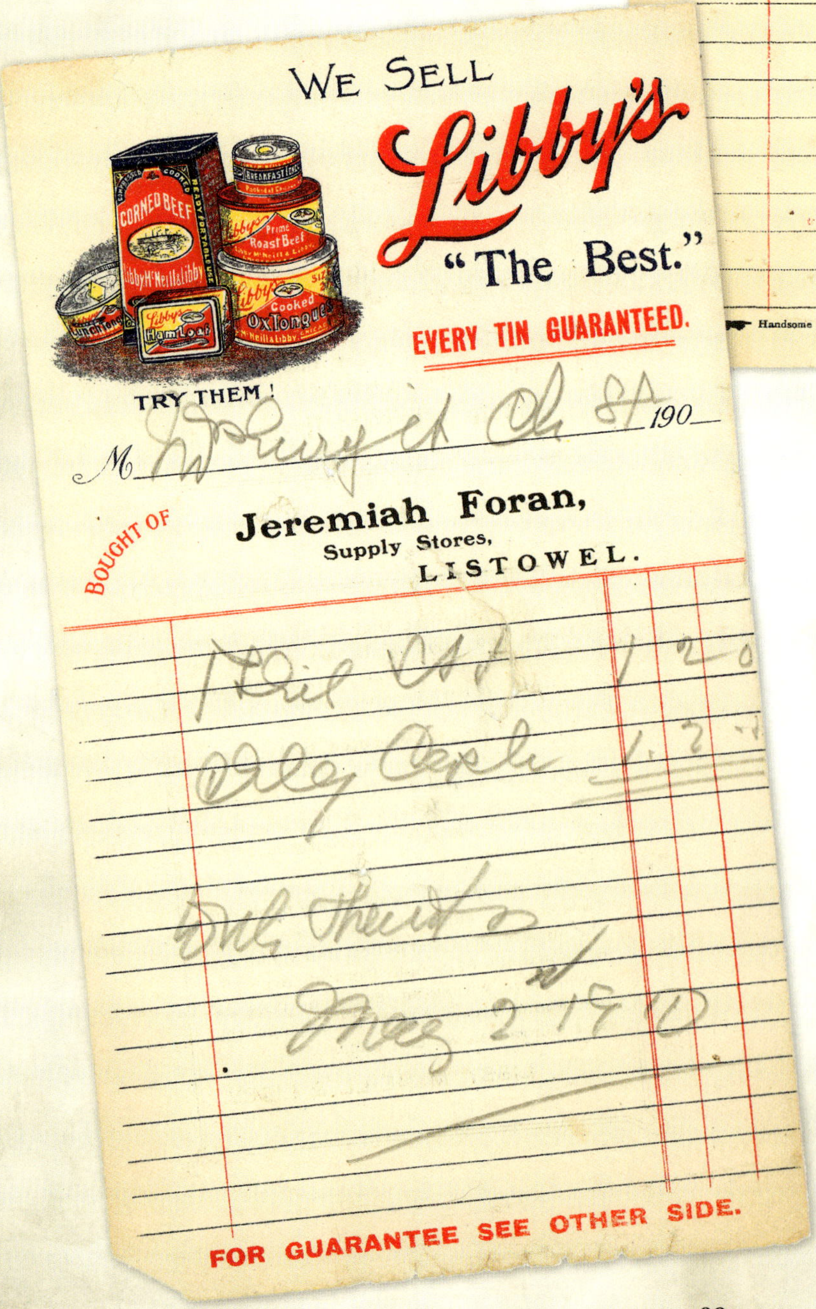
WE SELL Libby's "The Best."

EVERY TIN GUARANTEED.

TRY THEM!

M. ________ 190__

BOUGHT OF Jeremiah Foran,
Supply Stores,
LISTOWEL.

FOR GUARANTEE SEE OTHER SIDE.

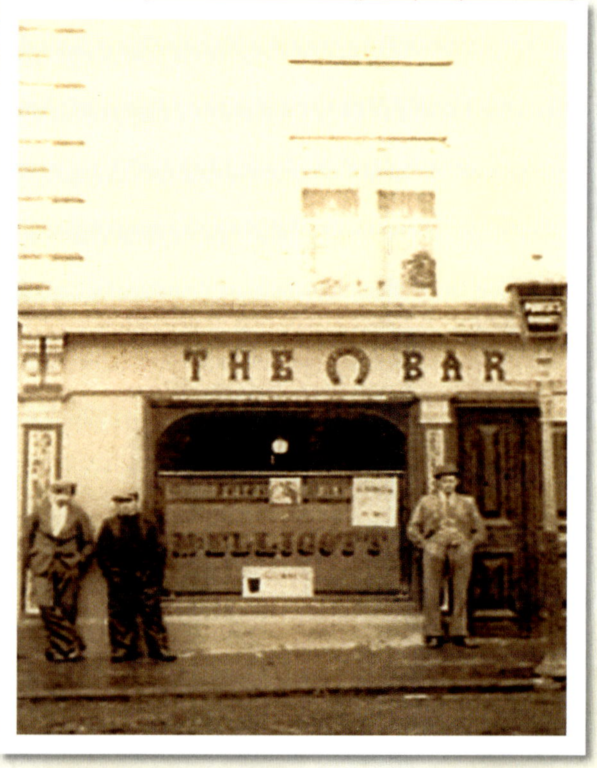

Photo above:
Horseshoe Bar frontage in the 1930s.

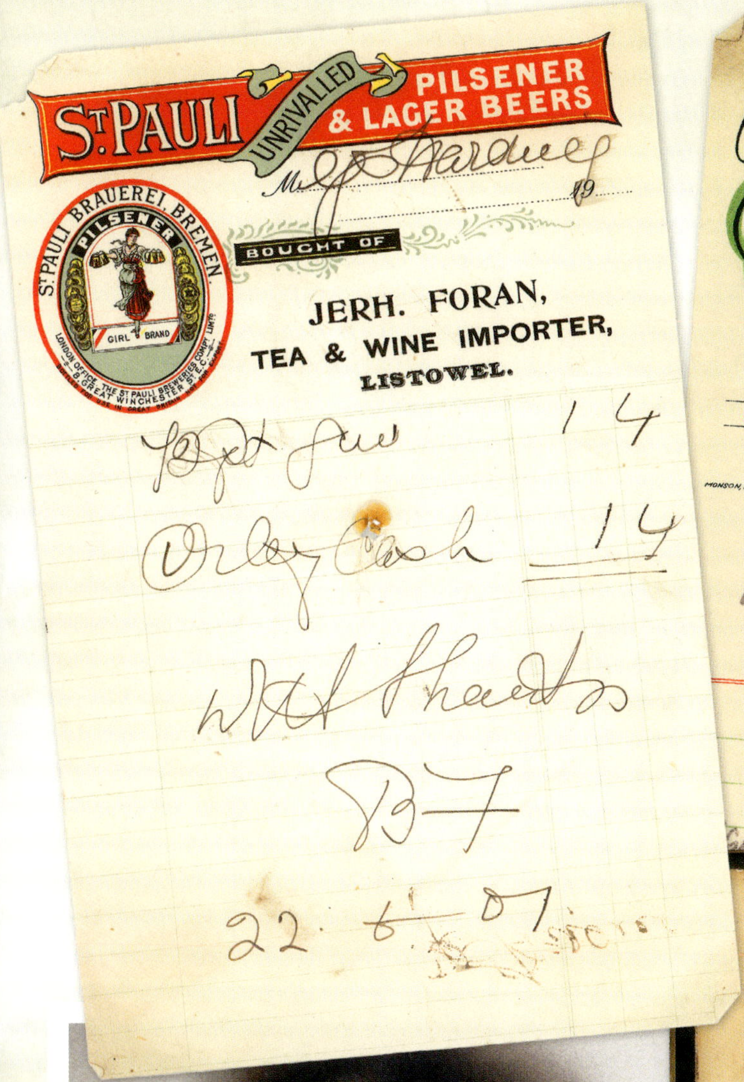
ST. PAULI UNRIVALLED PILSENER & LAGER BEERS

ST. PAULI BRAUEREI BREMEN

PILSENER

GIRL BRAND

BOUGHT OF

JERH. FORAN,

TEA & WINE IMPORTER,

LISTOWEL.

Orley Cash 1 4

22. 6. 07

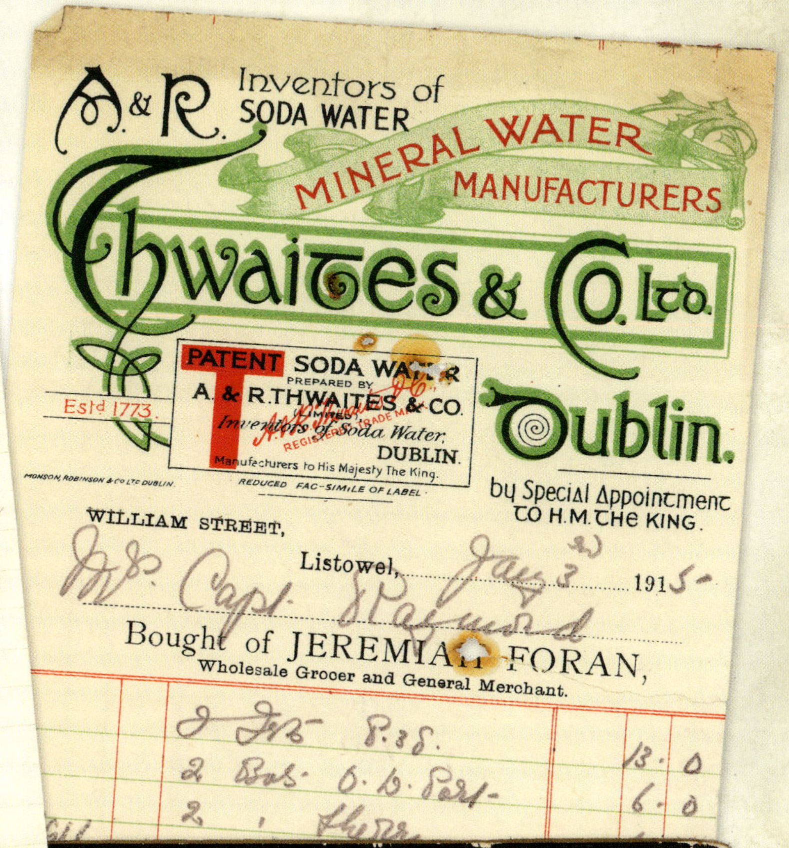
A & R. Inventors of SODA WATER

MINERAL WATER MANUFACTURERS

Thwaites & Co. Ltd.

Dublin.

Estd 1773.

PATENT SODA WATER PREPARED BY A. & R. THWAITES & CO. Inventors of Soda Water. DUBLIN. Manufacturers to His Majesty The King.

REDUCED FAC-SIMILE OF LABEL

by Special Appointment to H.M. The King.

WILLIAM STREET,

Listowel, Jan 3 1915

Bought of JEREMIAH FORAN,

Wholesale Grocer and General Merchant.

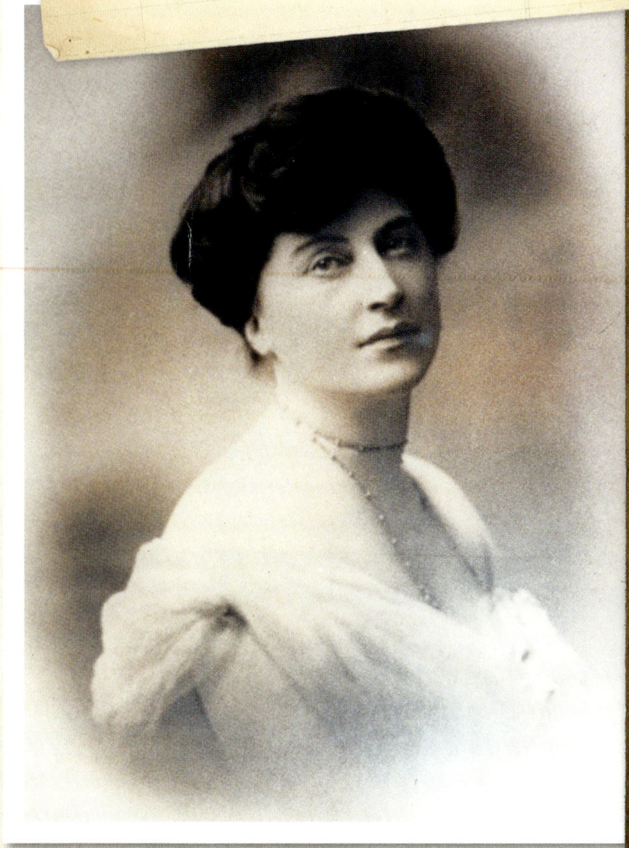

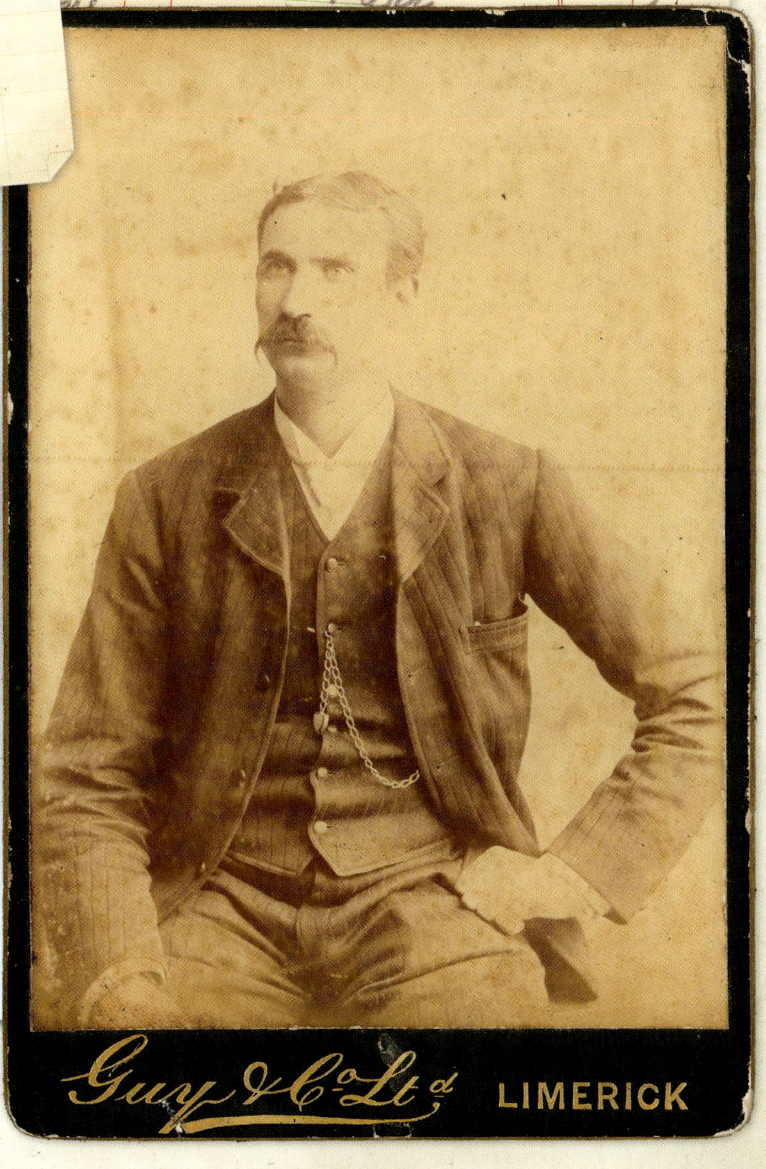

Photos: Bibianna Foran and Jeremiah Foran.

12 Lower William Street
Located in an area known as Tay Lane, the Walsh family ran a very popular bar and grocery business here. In later years it was known as 'John Josie's'. Note the advertising on the bag of tea below which would have been filled on the premises.

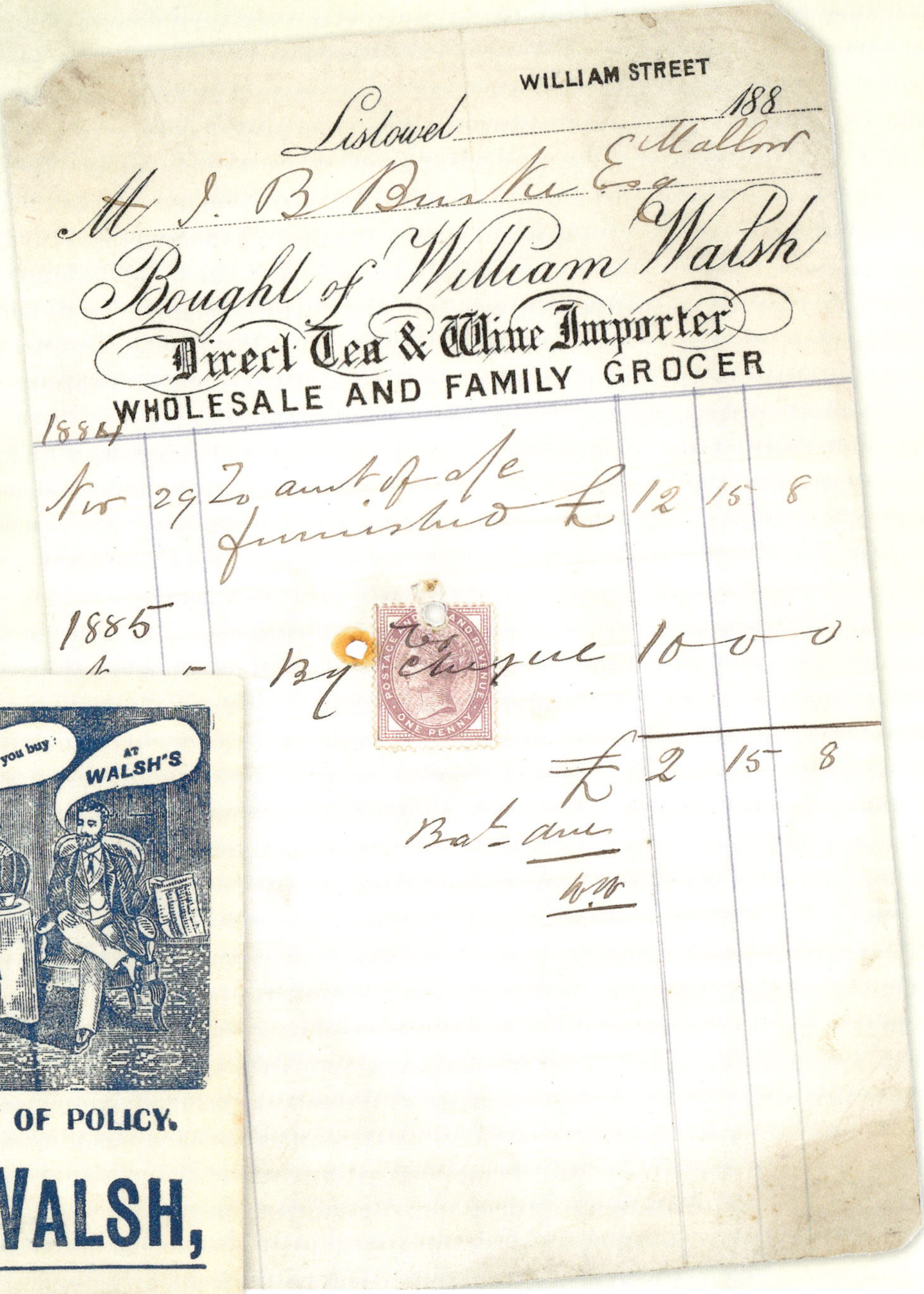
WILLIAM STREET

Listowel 188

Mr J. B Burke Esq Mallow

Bought of William Walsh

Direct Tea & Wine Importer

WHOLESALE AND FAMILY GROCER

1884					
Nov	29	To amt of a/c furnished	£12	15	8
1885					
		By cheque	10	0	0
			£2	15	8
		Bal. due £			

W.W.

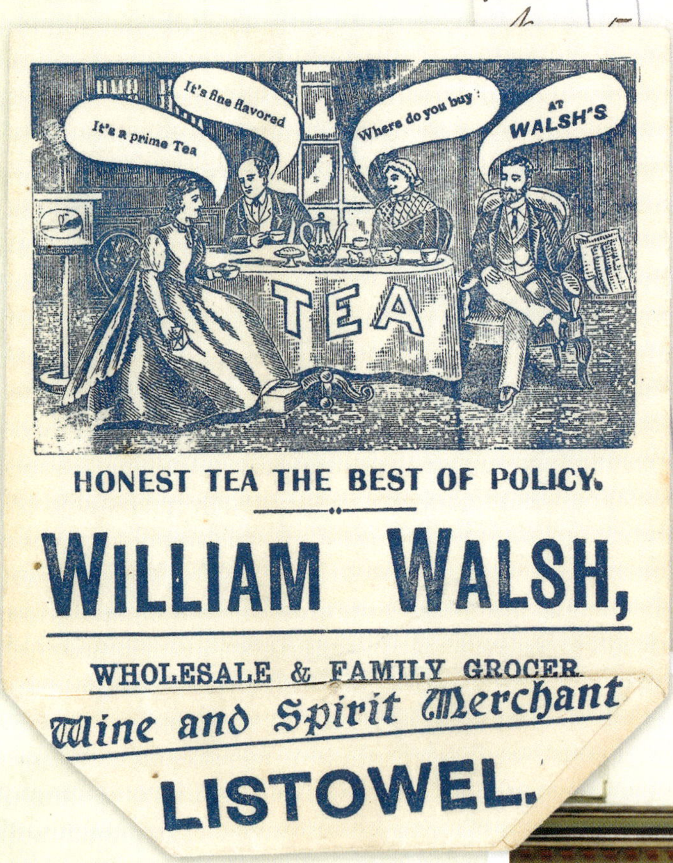

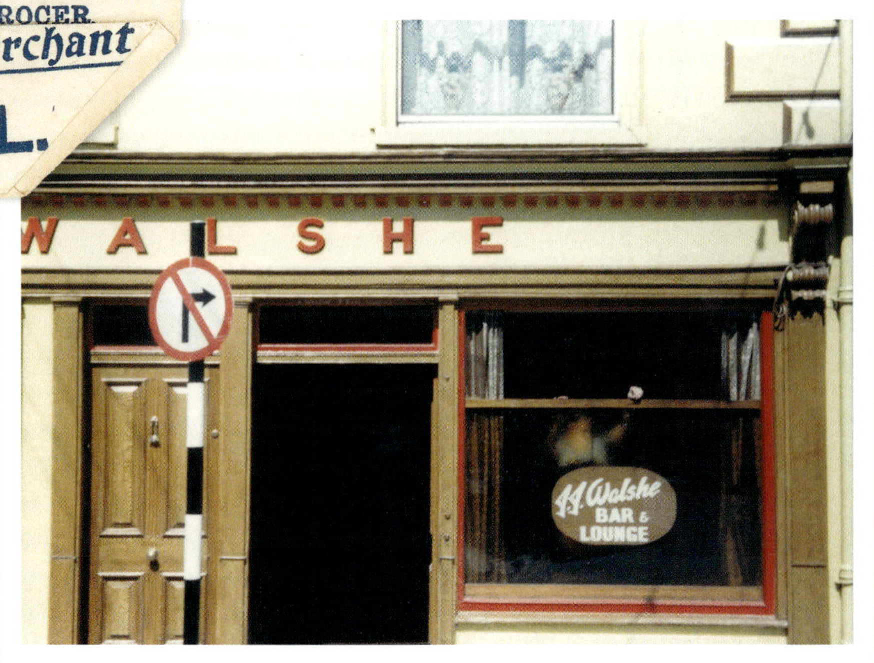

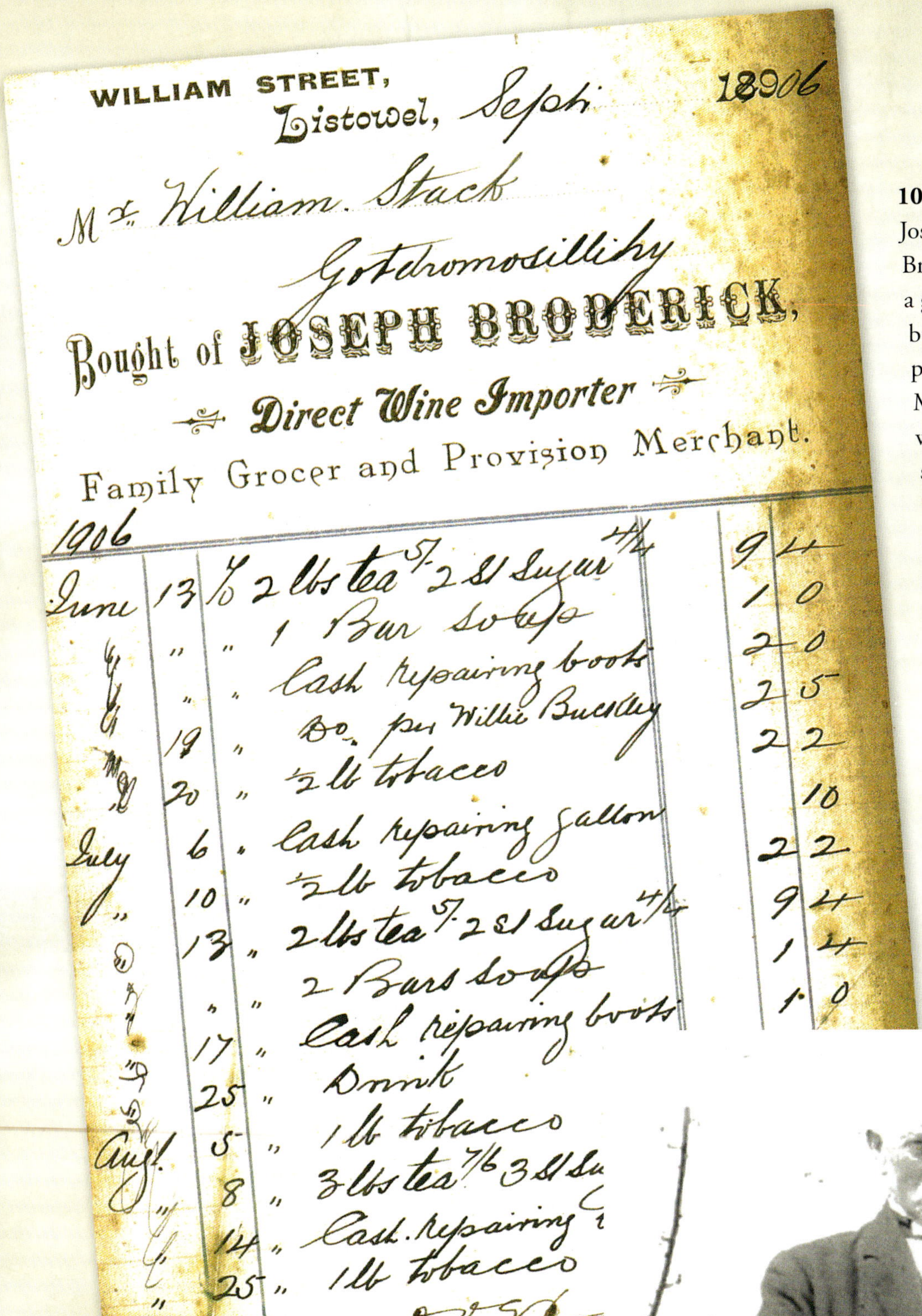

WILLIAM STREET, Listowel, Sept 1906

Mr. William Stack
Gortdromosillihy

Bought of JOSEPH BRODERICK,
Direct Wine Importer
Family Grocer and Provision Merchant.

1906				
June	13	½	2 lbs tea 5/- 2 st Sugar 4/4	9 4
	"	"	1 Bar soap	1 0
	"	"	Cash repairing boots	2 0
	"	"	Do. per Willie Buckley	2 5
	19	"	½ lb tobacco	2 2
	20	"		10
July	6	"	Cash repairing gallon	2 2
	10	"	½ lb tobacco	9 4
	13	"	2 lbs tea 5/- 2 st Sugar 4/4	1 4
	"	"	2 Bars soap	1 0
	17	"	Cash repairing boots	
	25	"	Drink	
Aug.	5	"	1 lb tobacco	
	8	"	3 lbs tea 7/6 3 st Su	
	14	"	Cash. repairing	
	25	"	1 lb tobacco	

10 Lower William Street
Joseph (pictured below) and Brigid Broderick operated a grocery and public house business from 1889 in a premises that was rented from Matt Hannon. The business was subsequently run by their son Jeremiah and his wife Hannah. Jeremiah bought the premises from the Hannons in the 1950s. The same business is now run by Jeremiah's son Joe, his wife Mary and their two sons Seanie and Diarmuid.

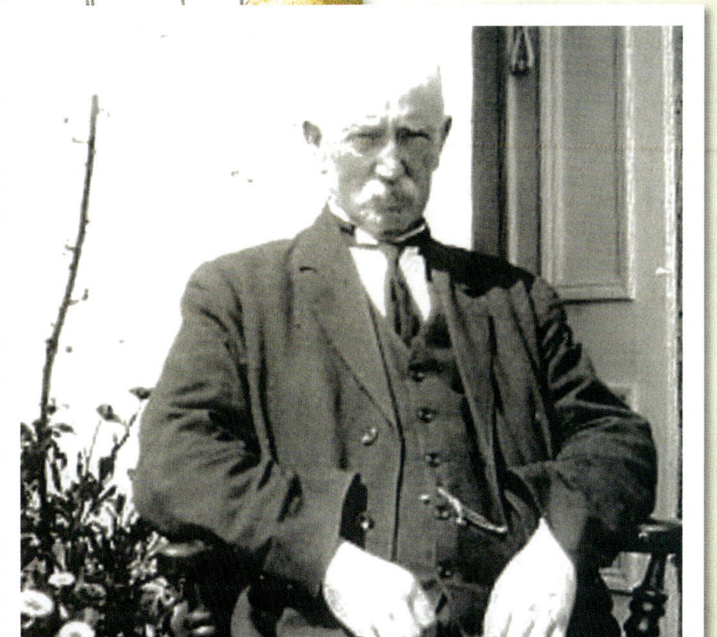

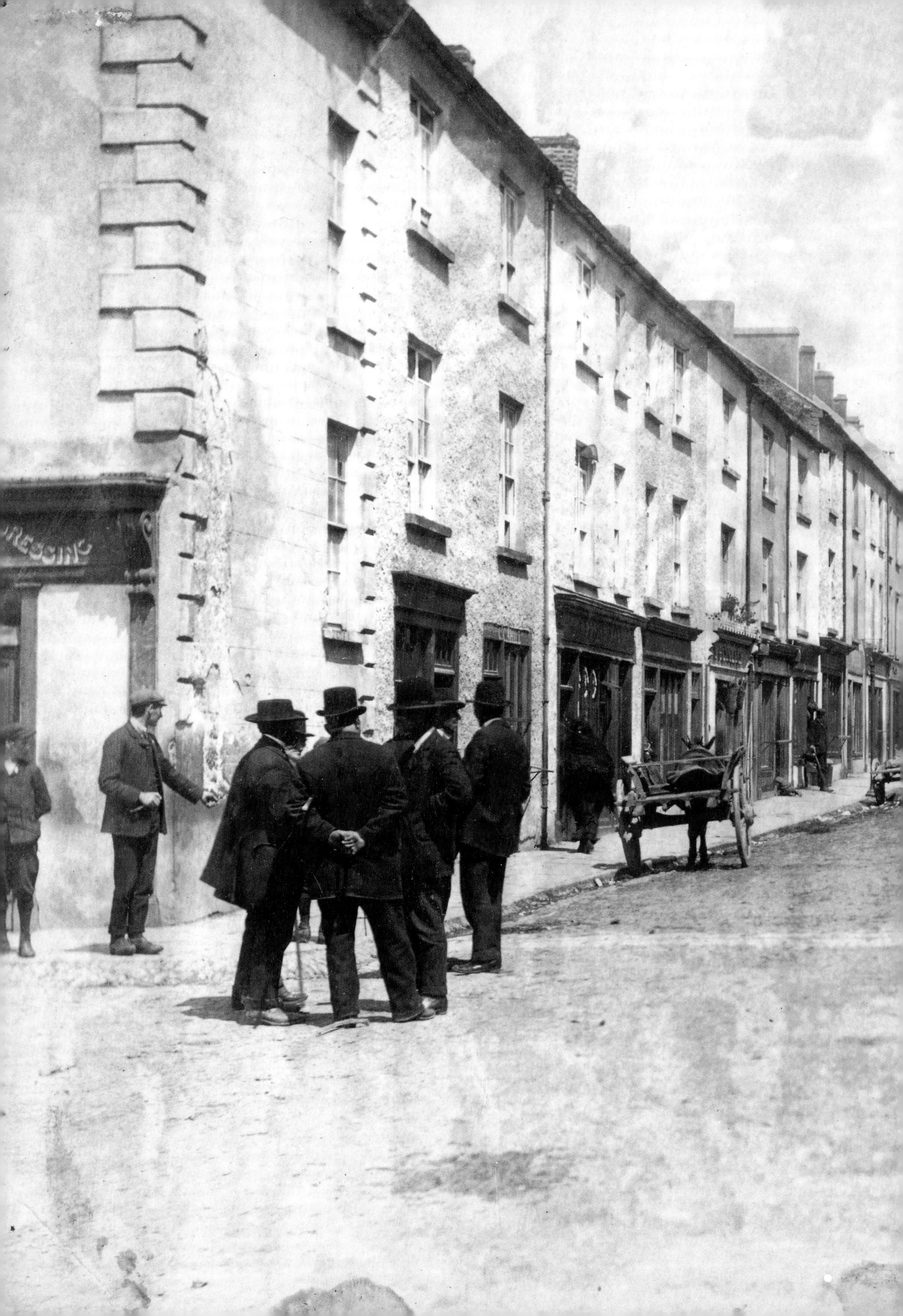
RESSING

Chapter 5

CHURCH STREET

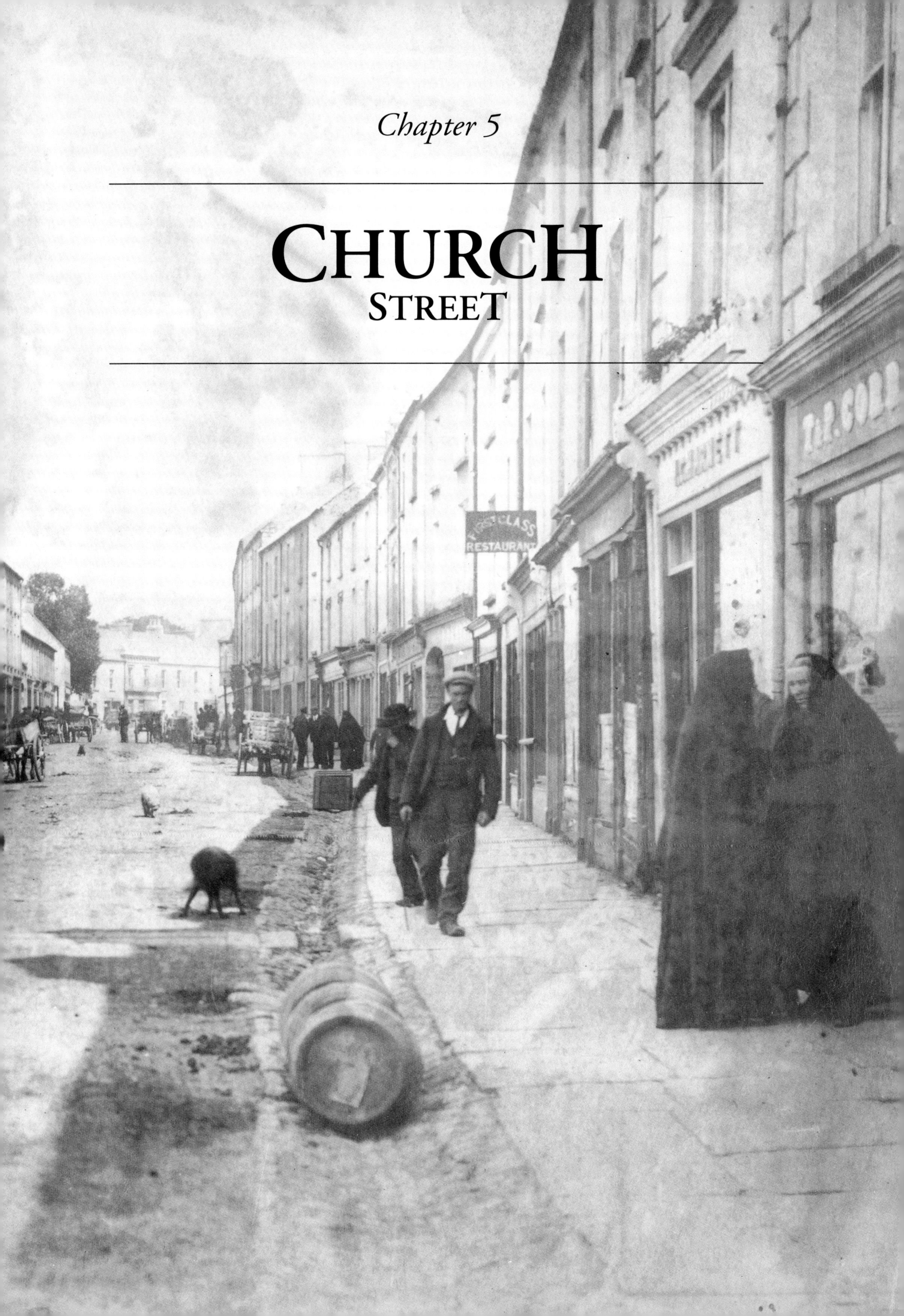

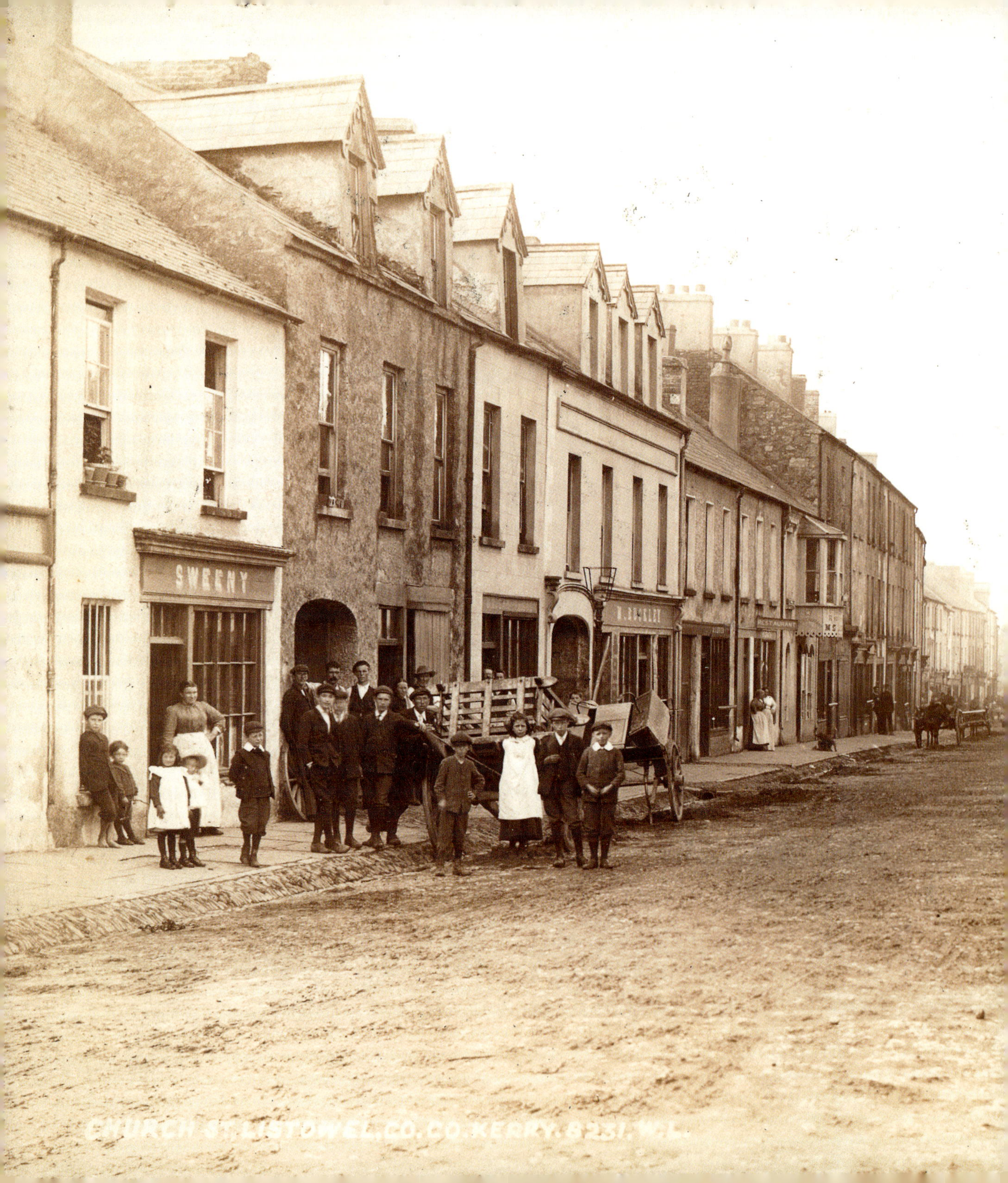
SWEENY
RESTAURANT
CHURCH ST. LISTOWEL. CO. CO. KERRY. 8231. W.L.

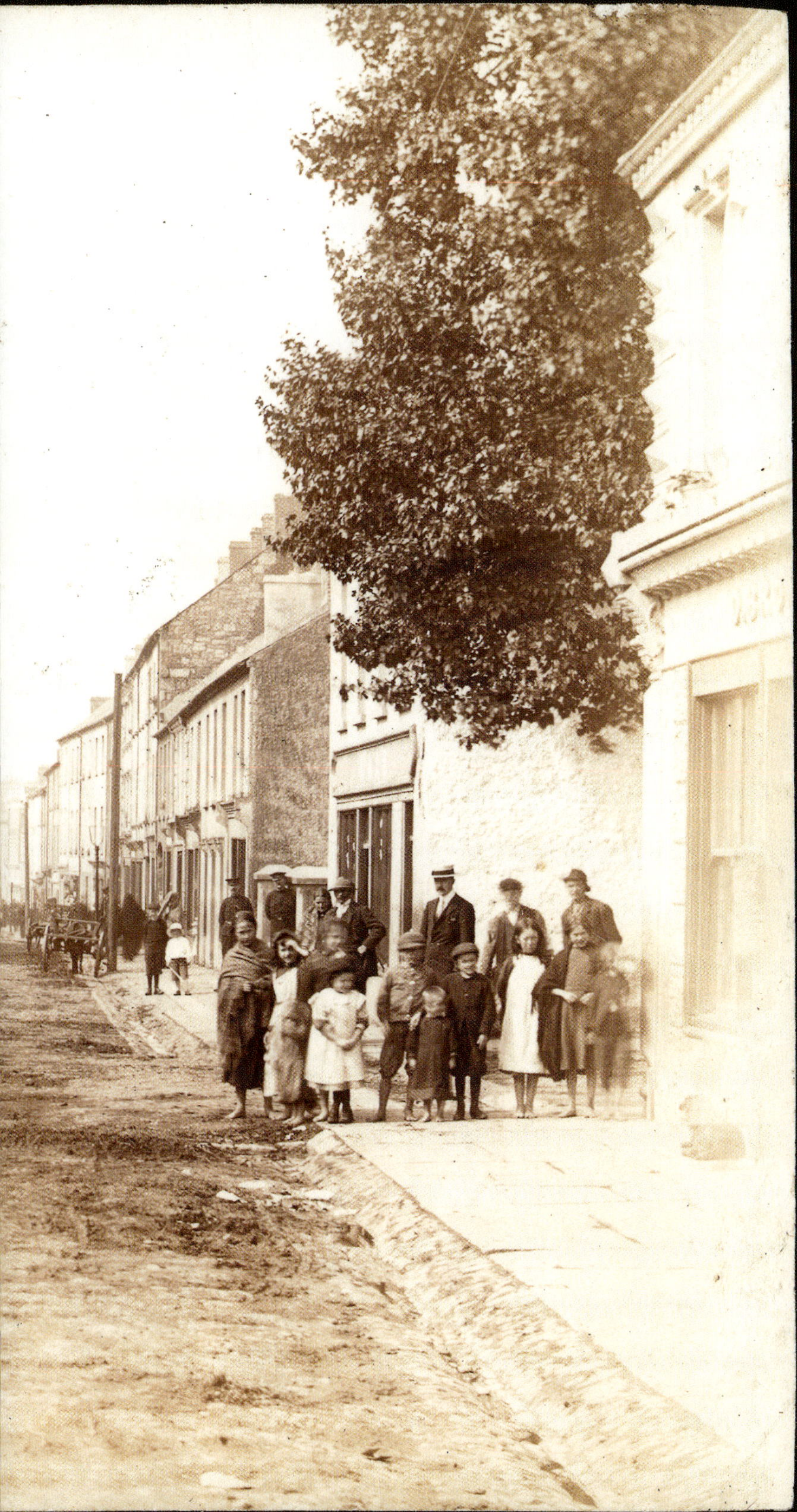

Left: An iconic photograph from the Lawrence Collection of 1904. Local residents, many of whom would never have seen a camera before, are posing for the photographer. On the left is a group outside Sweeney's house, and outside the archway leading to the workshop of cart-maker Michael Quill. On the right is another group, probably from Forge Lane/Bridewell Lane area. The house at the corner, behind the tree, was once the home of Cains, keepers of Listowel Bridewell. Outside the barracks, further down, are some RIC officers.

Previous pages: A group of men in Sunday best congregate at Cotter's Corner, no doubt discussing the affairs of the day in 1904, while on the right two shawled women, outside T & P Corridan's, are more than likely talking about more mundane housekeeping affairs. Empty porter firkins lay awaiting collection on the paved channel. Dogs, asses and carts populate the roadway.

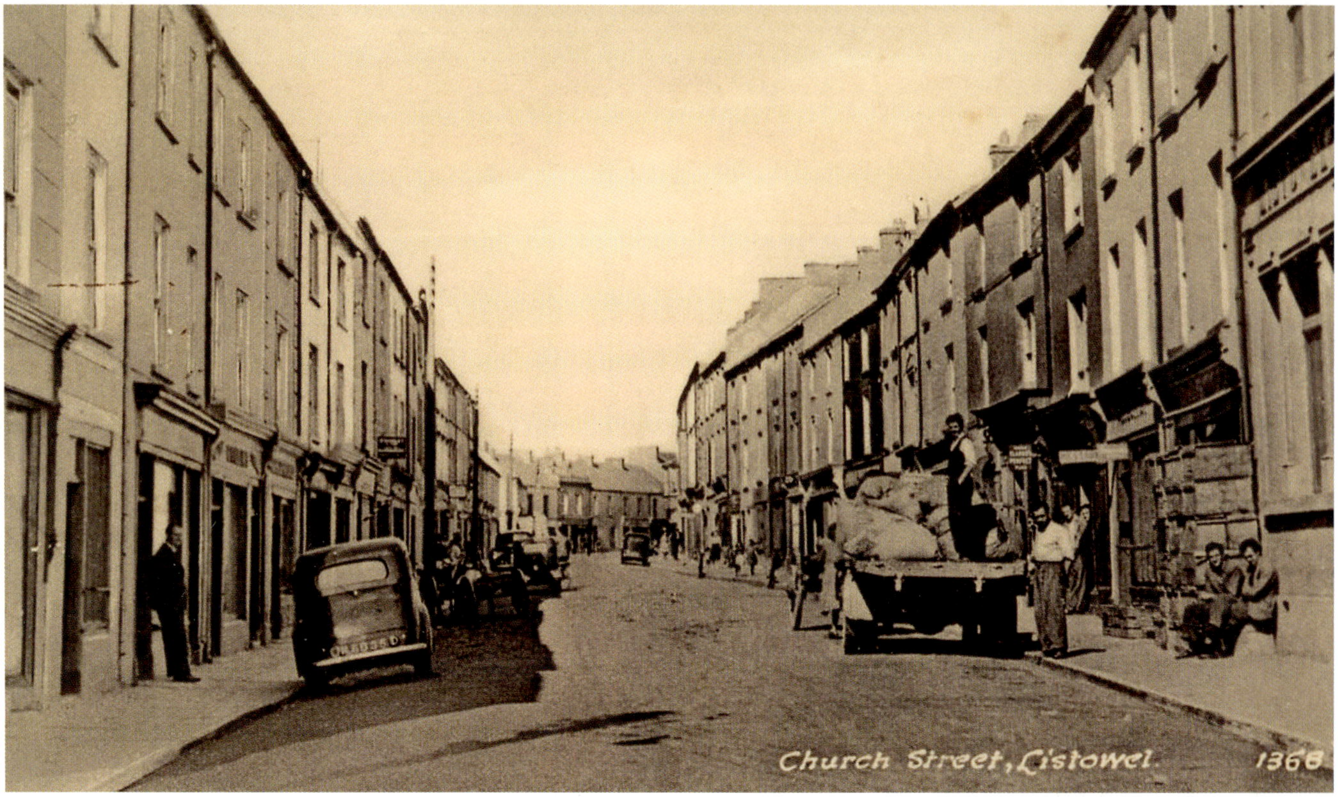

Above: This 1950 image of the street shows a tarred roadway. Up the street, on the right, Fitzpatrick's egg store is a hive of activity with feathers being loaded and fowl being boxed. One of those sitting down, relaxing, is a young John B. Keane. Resting at the doorway on the left is Paddy Vaughan, Manager of McGuire's Chemist Shop. On the extreme right is part of the town's Technical School.

Below: This 1930s photograph records early motor traffic as well as the more mundane forms of transport at the time. Shawls are still in vogue. A group of people standing at the corner with the civic guards are no doubt posing for the lens. Public lighting in a limited capacity can be seen. The buildings, which had stood prior to this on the right, had been demolished to make way for the new Technical School. Footpaths are of flagstones and the channels are paved.

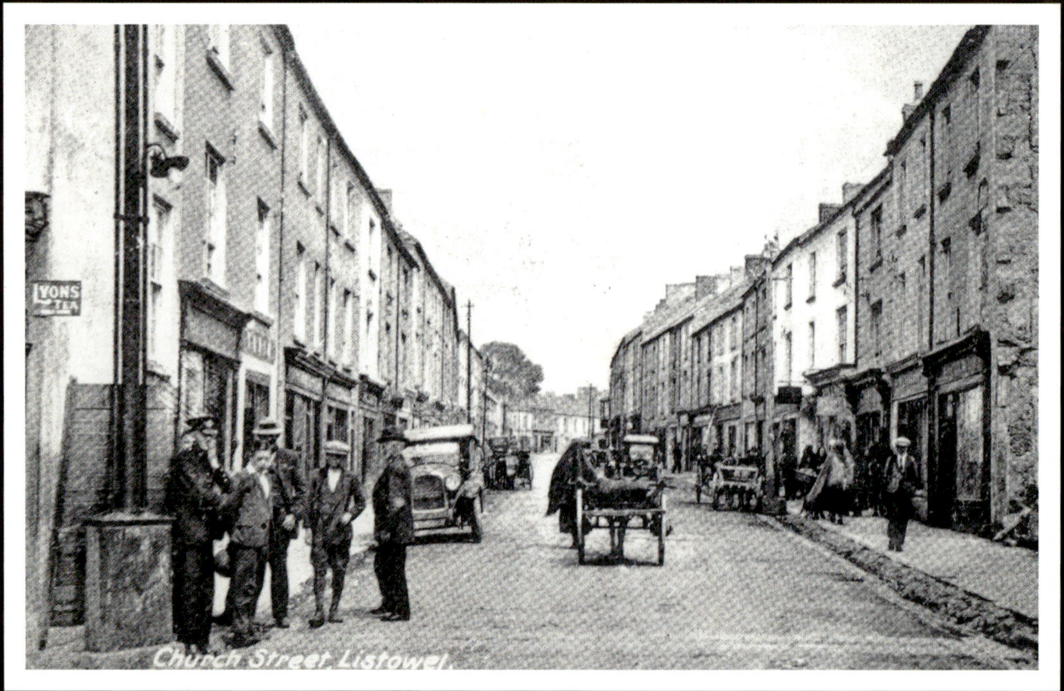

Below: McCarthy's photograph of 1910 shows on left, Farrell's harness-making establishment, while on the street below stand two women outside the thatched house of Barry the Weaver. Children pose on the muddy roadway. On the right, from top, Breen's, Naylor's, Lane/Dillon's and Brown's.

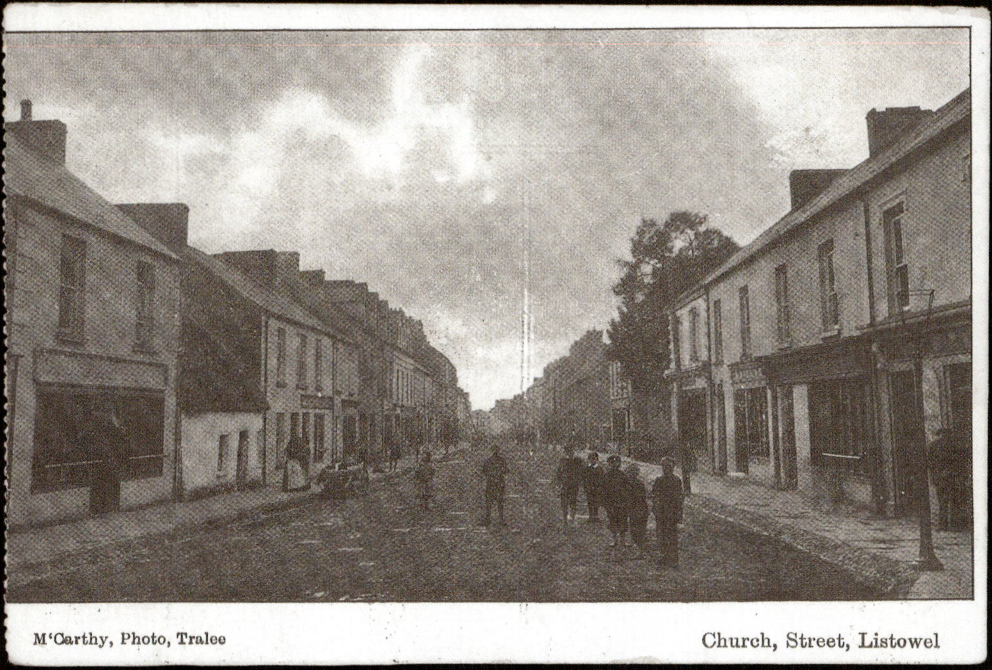

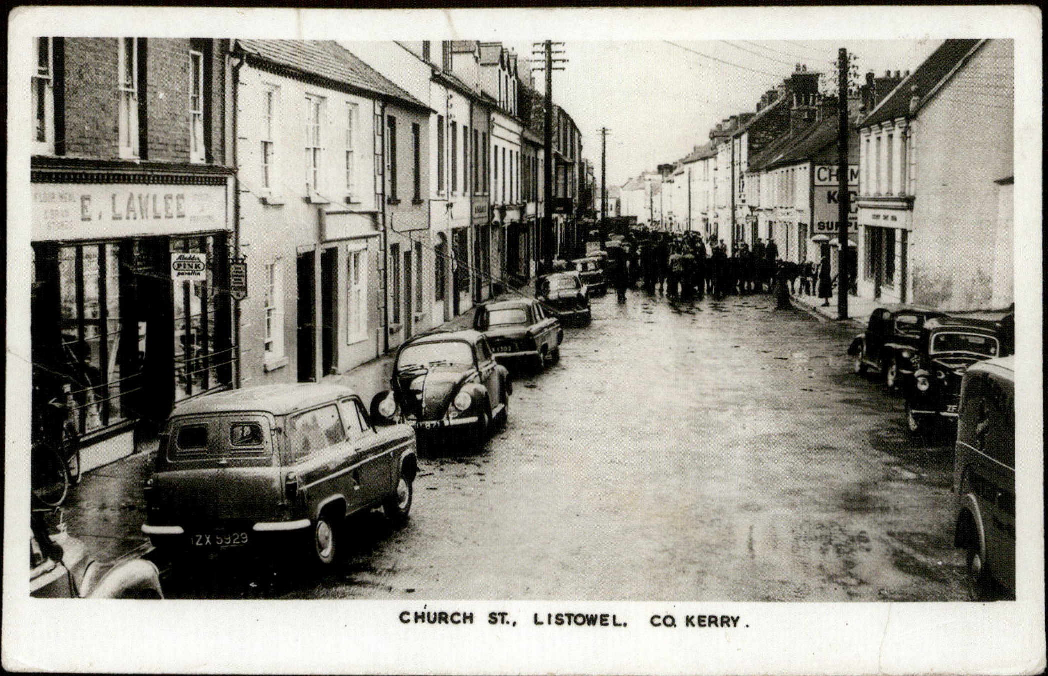

Above: Pádraig Kennelly's photograph of the 1960s shows the overspill of cattle from the Square, stretching up as far as Upper Church Street. Lawlee's brick-fronted house now occupies the space where Barry the Weaver's thatched house once stood. Motor transport now rules the road.

2 & 4 Church Street

Nora Hayes sold high-class millinery and mantles from the house which is now occupied by Chic Boutique. Her father, Patrick, was a boot and shoemaker and also a local councillor. Her brother, Jim, was a teacher at the local boys' National School.

Kirby's had a long-established drapery business in what is now No. 4 Church Street.

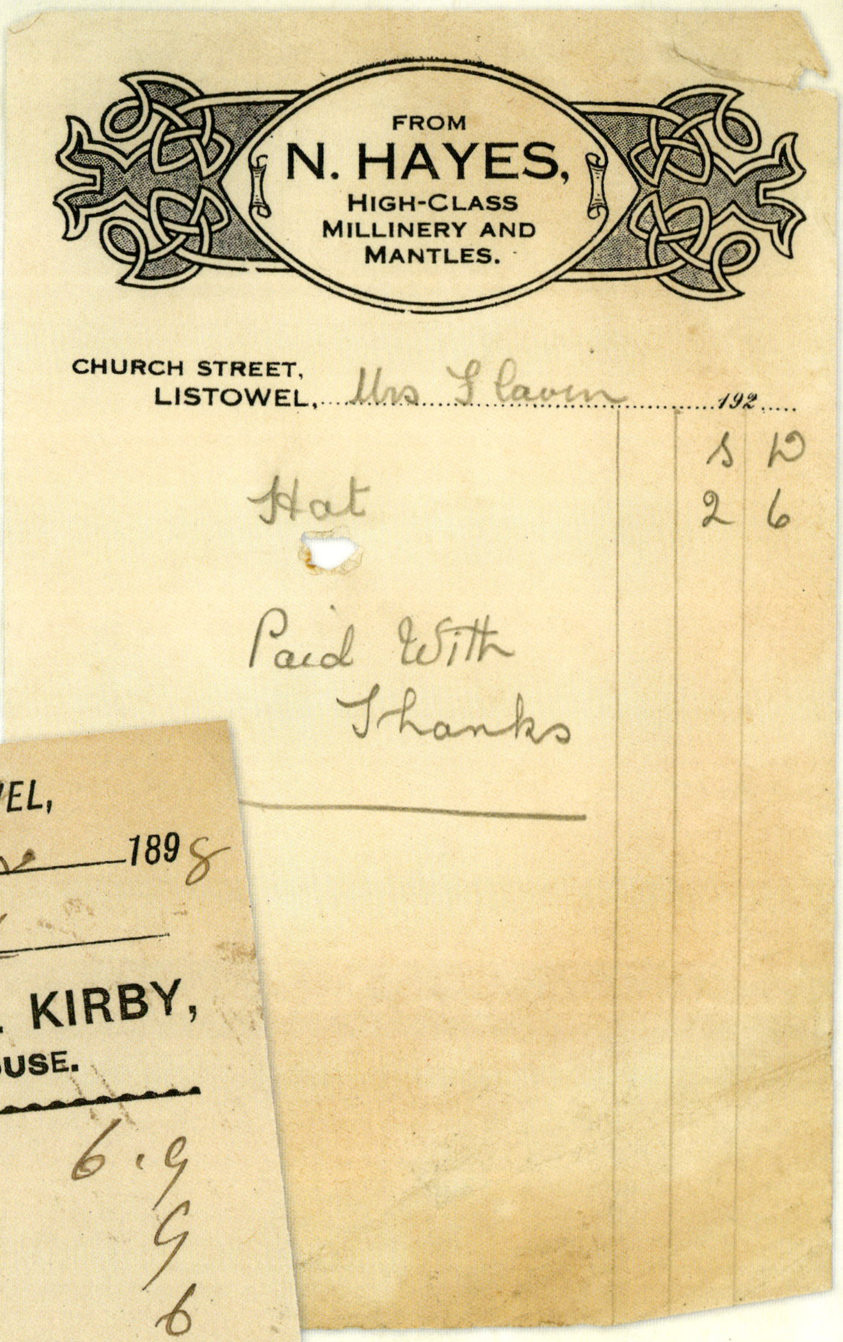

FROM
N. HAYES,
HIGH-CLASS
MILLINERY AND
MANTLES.

CHURCH STREET,
LISTOWEL, ...192.....

	s	d
Hat	2	6

Paid With Thanks

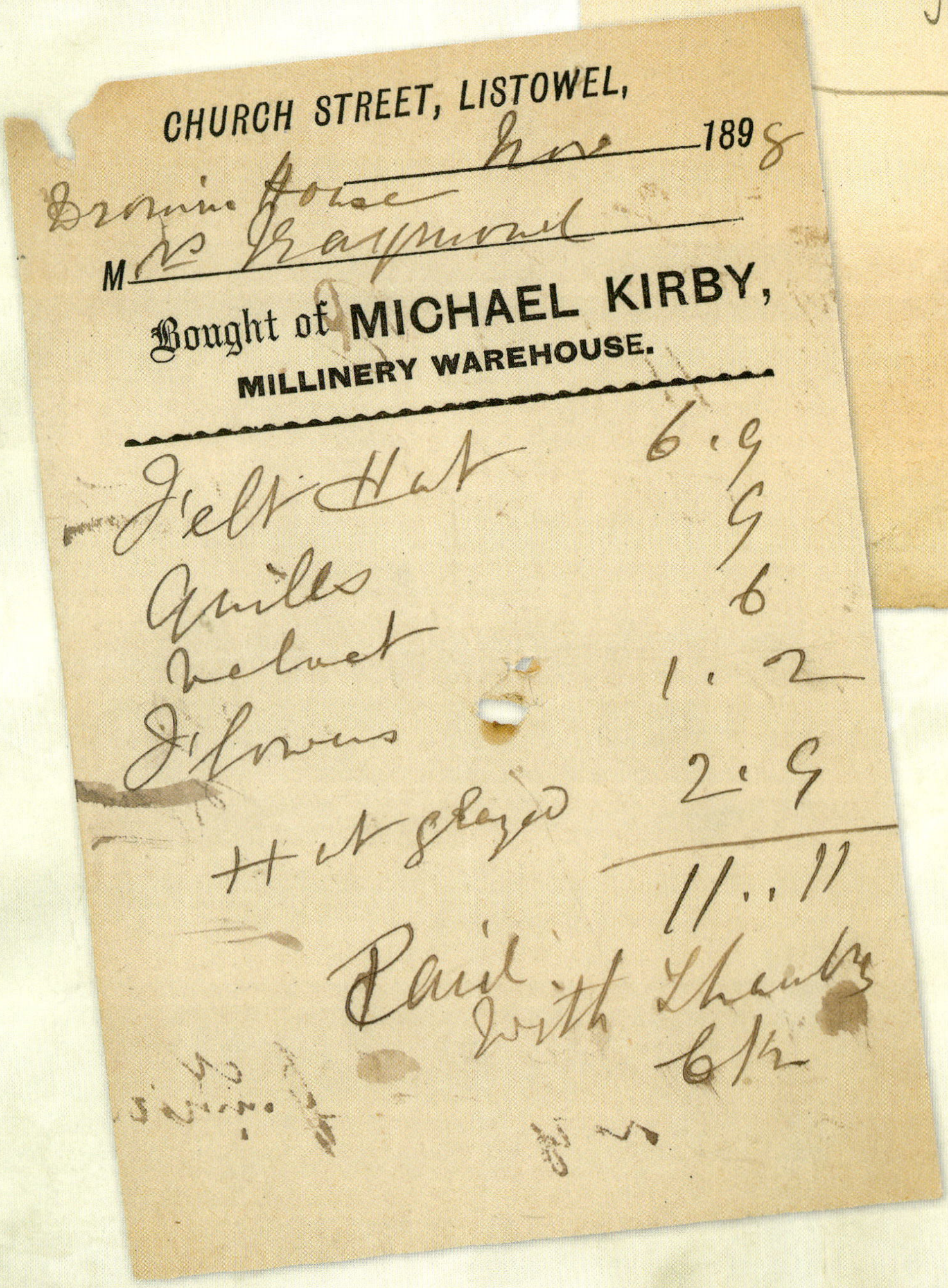

CHURCH STREET, LISTOWEL,
Nov 1898

Bought of MICHAEL KIRBY,
MILLINERY WAREHOUSE.

Felt Hat	6.9
	9
Quills	6
Velvet	1.2
Flowers	2.9
	11..11

Paid with Thanks

6 Church Street

The McGuires were a long-time Listowel medical family. John F. McGuire opened his Chemist Shop in the Medical Hall in Church Street in 1890. Prior to this the Pharmacy was operated by a Raymond Roche.

Included in this page is a billhead to Captain Raymond from the Veterinary Establishment of J.M. Canty, M.R.C.V.S. Nothing is known of who Canty was or where his practice was located. However, he was Listowel's first recorded veterinary surgeon.

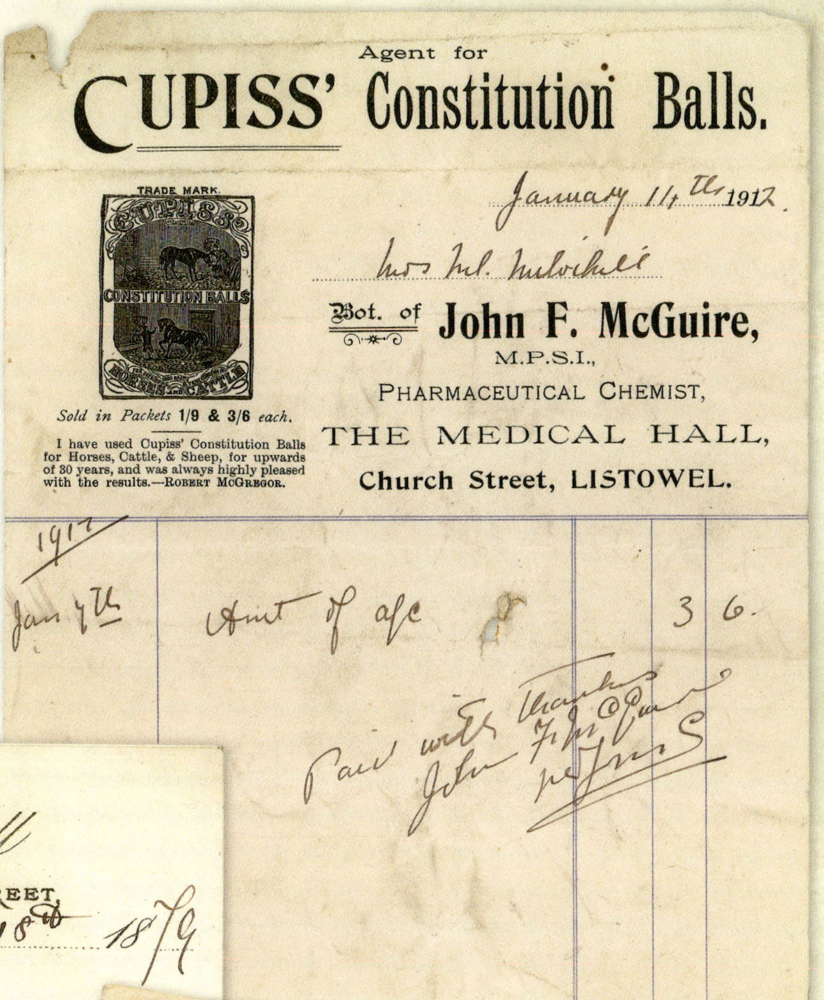

Agent for
CUPISS' Constitution Balls.

TRADE MARK
CONSTITUTION BALLS

Sold in Packets 1/9 & 3/6 each.

I have used Cupiss' Constitution Balls for Horses, Cattle, & Sheep, for upwards of 30 years, and was always highly pleased with the results.—ROBERT MCGREGOR.

January 11th 1912

Bot. of John F. McGuire,
M.P.S.I.,
PHARMACEUTICAL CHEMIST,
THE MEDICAL HALL,
Church Street, LISTOWEL.

1912
Jan 7th Amt of a/c 3 6.

Paid with thanks
John F. McGuire

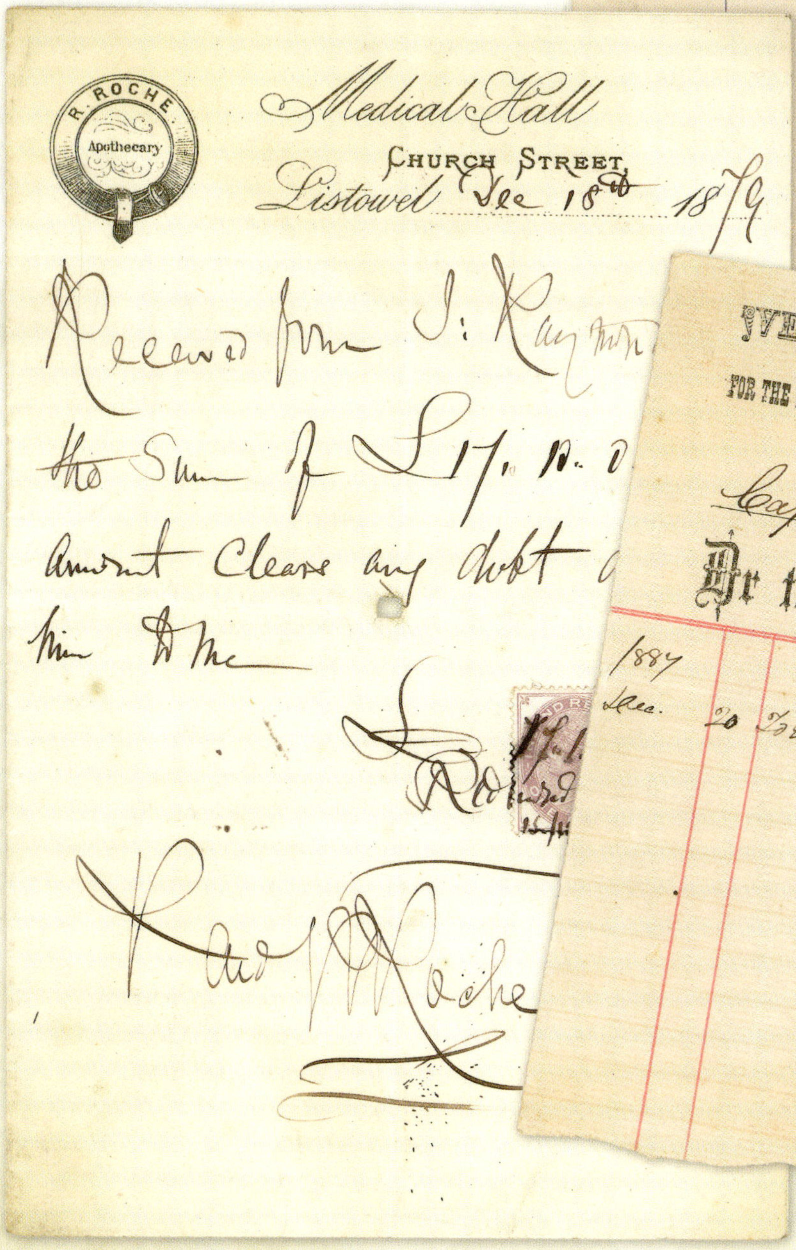

R. ROCHE
Apothecary

Medical Hall
CHURCH STREET,
Listowel Dec 18th 1879

Received from J. Raymond
the Sum of £17. 0. 0
Amount Clears any debt
him to me

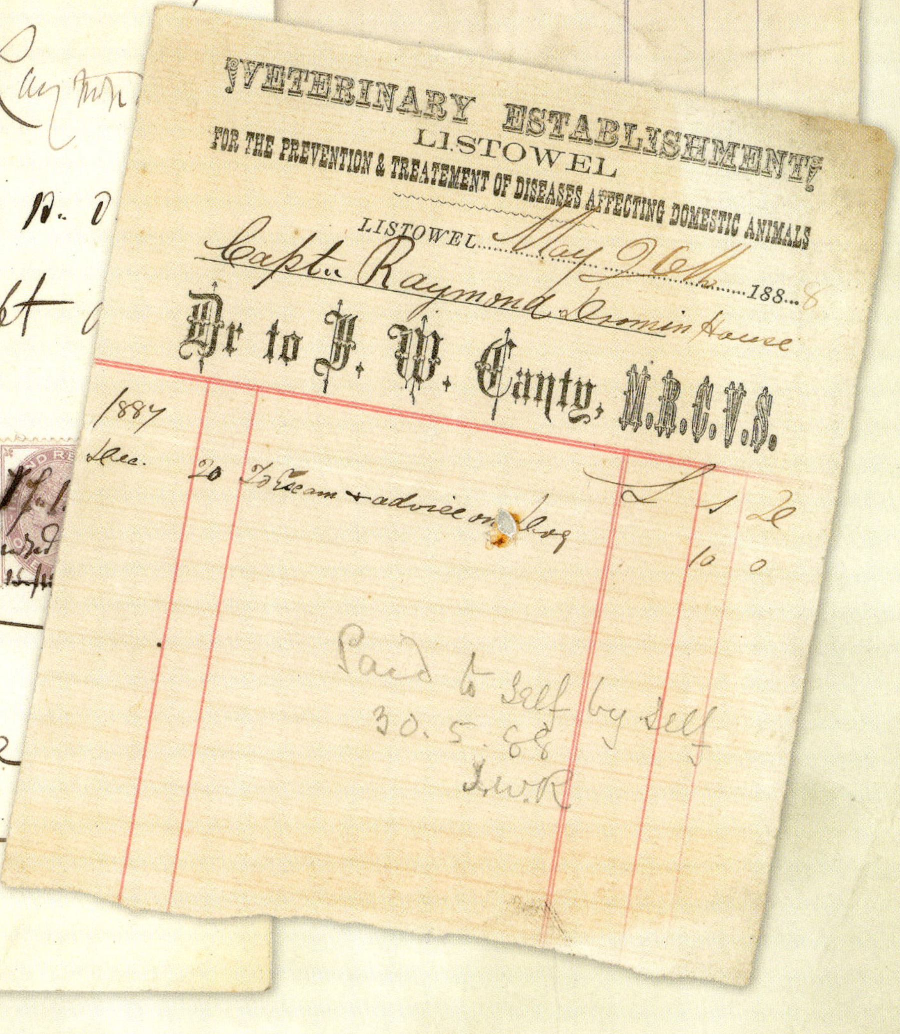

VETERINARY ESTABLISHMENT
LISTOWEL
FOR THE PREVENTION & TREATEMENT OF DISEASES AFFECTING DOMESTIC ANIMALS

LISTOWEL May 26th 1888

Capt. Raymond

Dr to J. W. Canty, M.R.C.V.S.

1887 Dec. 20 To team + advice on dog £ s d 10 0

Paid to Self by Self
30.5.88

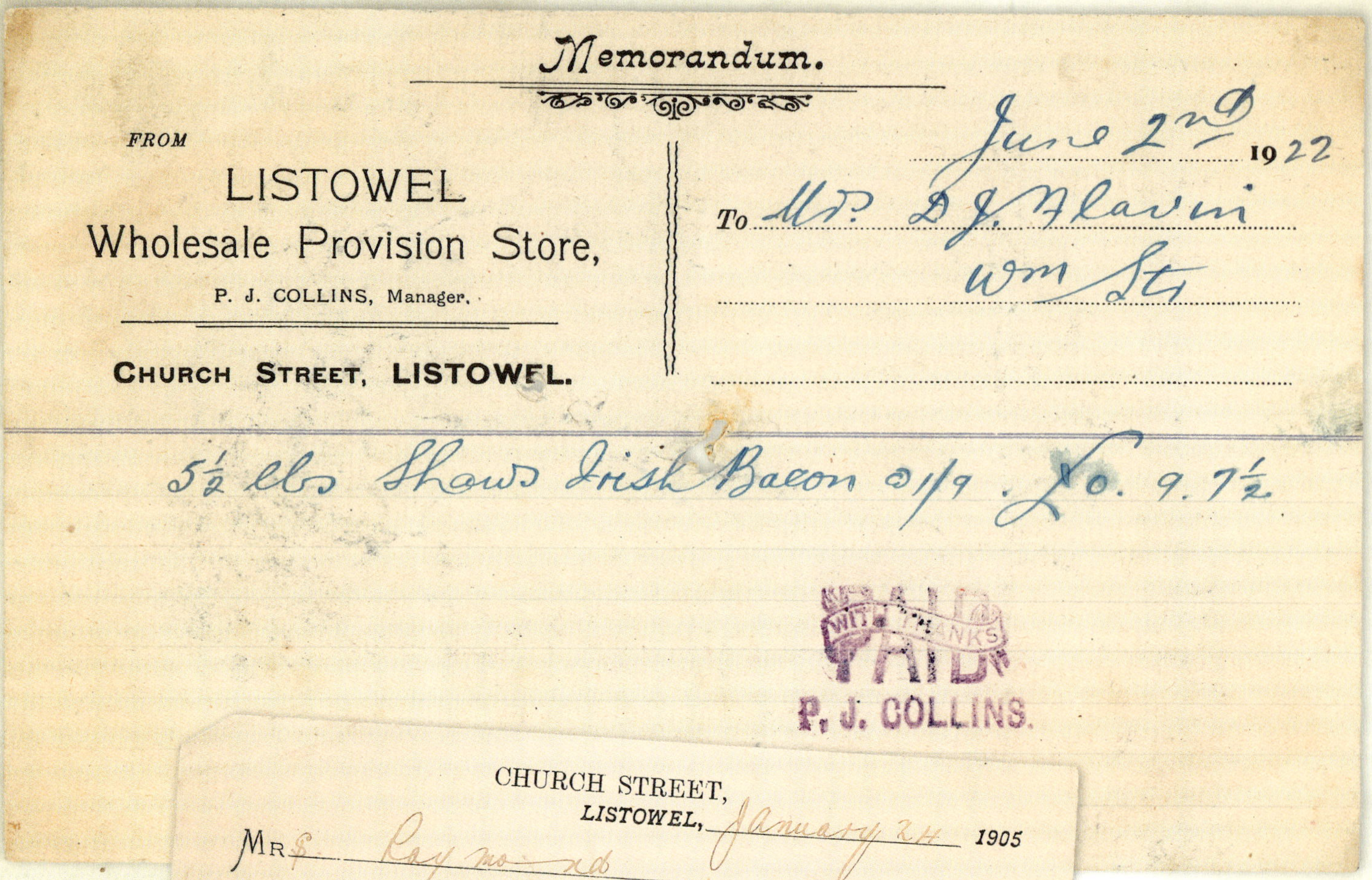

Memorandum.

FROM

LISTOWEL
Wholesale Provision Store,
P. J. COLLINS, Manager.

CHURCH STREET, LISTOWEL.

June 2nd 1922

To Mr. D. J. Flavin
Wm St.

5½ lbs Shaws Irish Bacon 1/9 . £0. 9. 7½

PAID WITH THANKS
P. J. COLLINS.

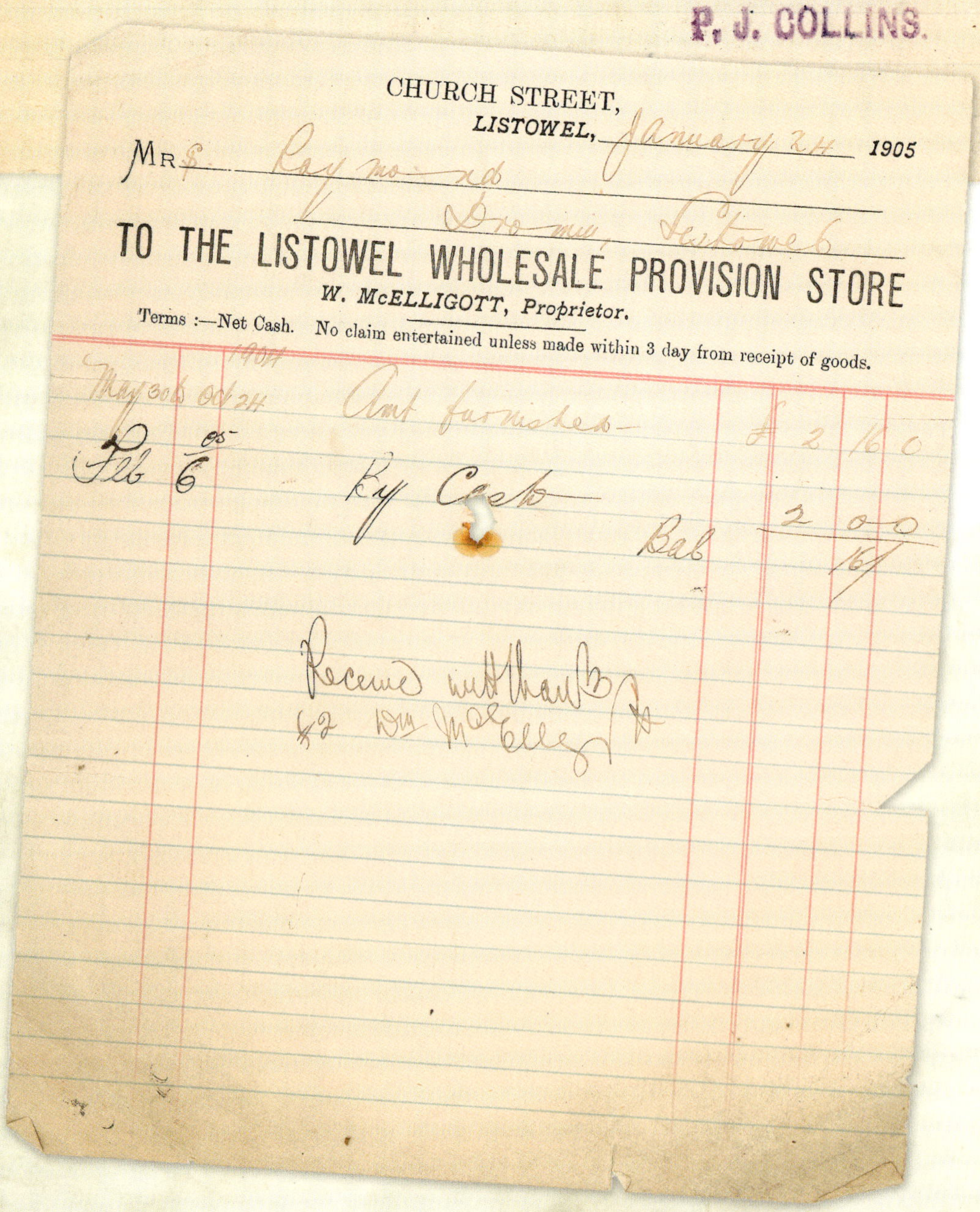

CHURCH STREET,
LISTOWEL, January 24 1905

Mrs Raymond
Dromin, Listowel

TO THE LISTOWEL WHOLESALE PROVISION STORE
W. McELLIGOTT, Proprietor.

Terms :—Net Cash. No claim entertained unless made within 3 day from receipt of goods.

1904 May 30th Oct 24	Amt furnished	£ 2 16 0
Feb 6 05	By Cash	2 0 0
	Bal	16/

Received with thanks
£2 Wm McElligott

8 Church Street

A wholesale provision store, supplying mainly bacon, salt and butter, was opened at Church Street by William McElligott in the 1890s. This was in the building which was called 'The Old Listowel Inn', owned and managed by the McElligotts in the 1870s and 1880s. P.J. Collins came to manage the provision store and eventually bought the business from the McElligotts.

Photo: P.J. Collins outside his provision store in Church Street.

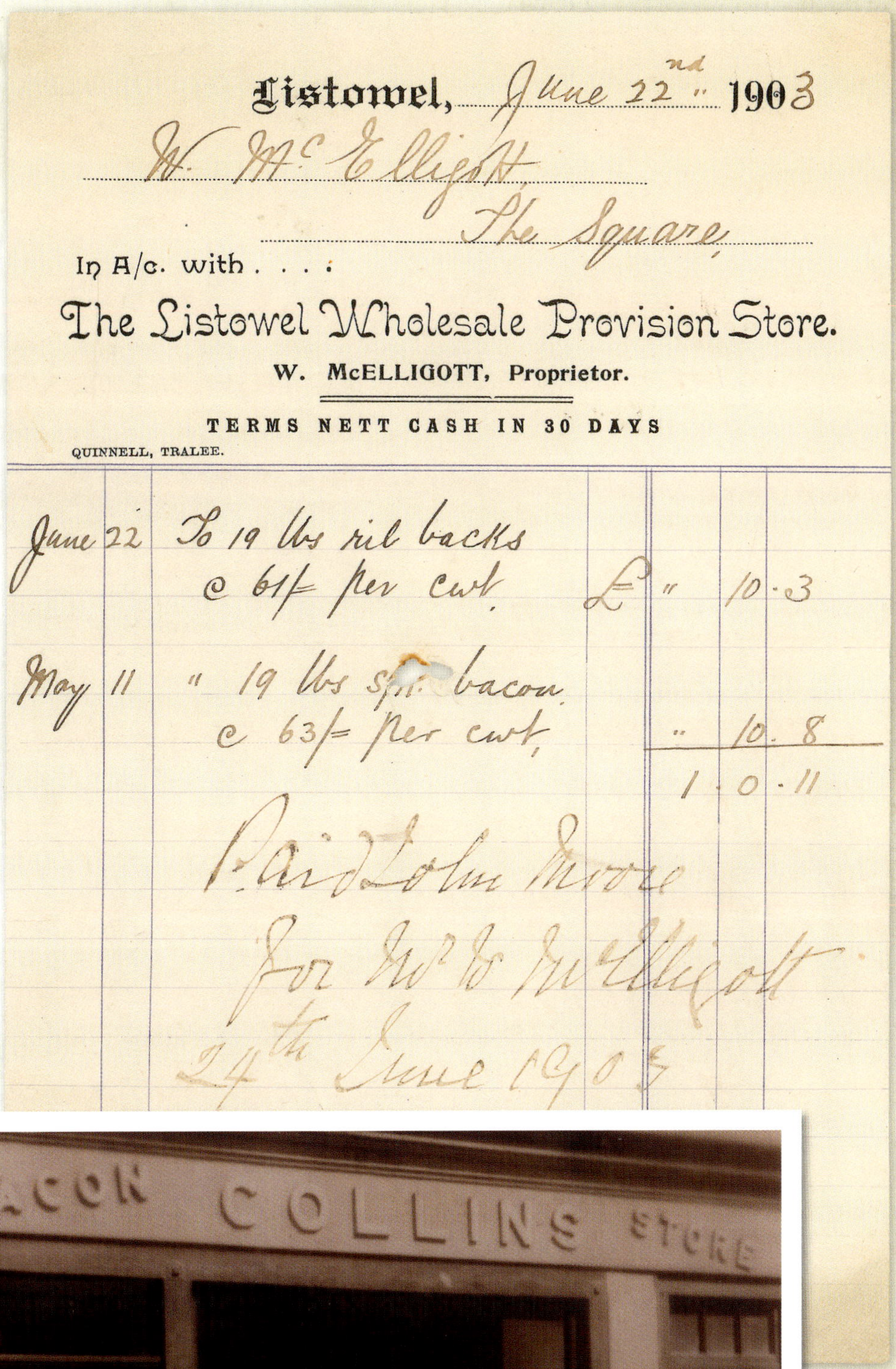
Listowel, June 22nd 1903

W. McElligott,

The Square

In A/c. with . . . :

The Listowel Wholesale Provision Store.

W. McELLIGOTT, Proprietor.

TERMS NETT CASH IN 30 DAYS

QUINNELL, TRALEE.

June	22	To 19 lbs rib backs @ 61/- per cwt	£	"	10	3
May	11	" 19 lbs sp... bacon @ 63/- per cwt		"	10	8
				1	0	11

Paid John Moore

For Mrs W McElligott

24th June 1903

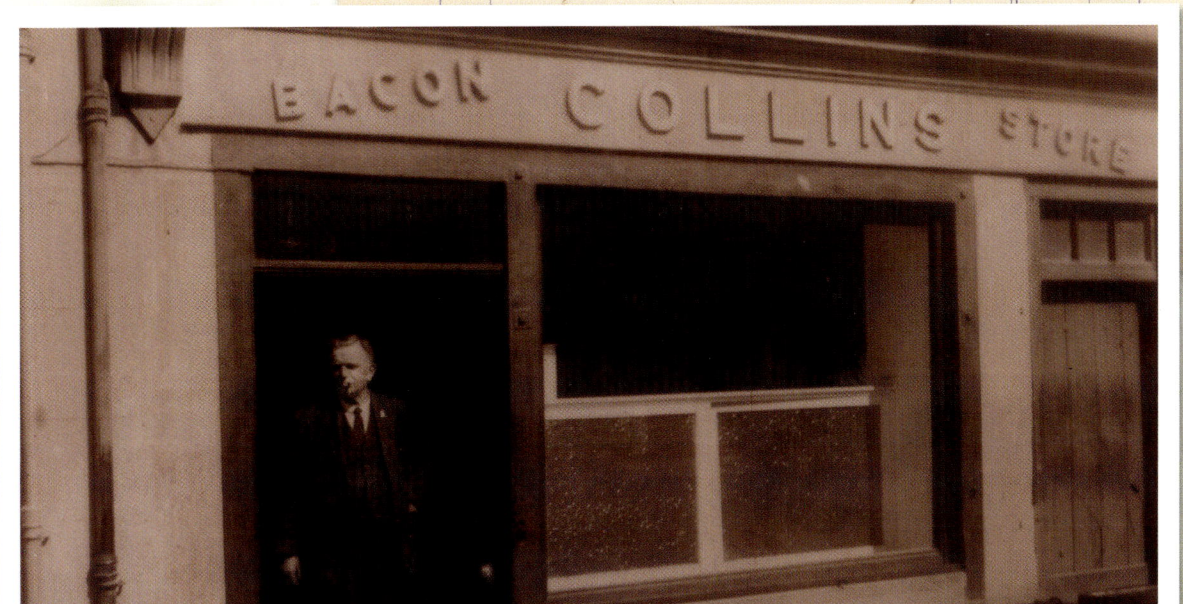

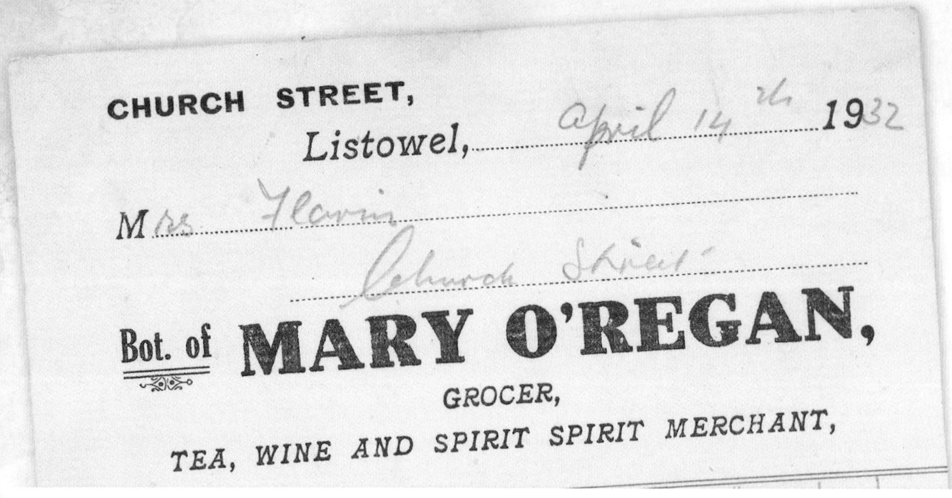
CHURCH STREET,
Listowel, April 14th 1932
Mrs Flavin
Church Street
Bot. of MARY O'REGAN,
GROCER,
TEA, WINE AND SPIRIT SPIRIT MERCHANT,

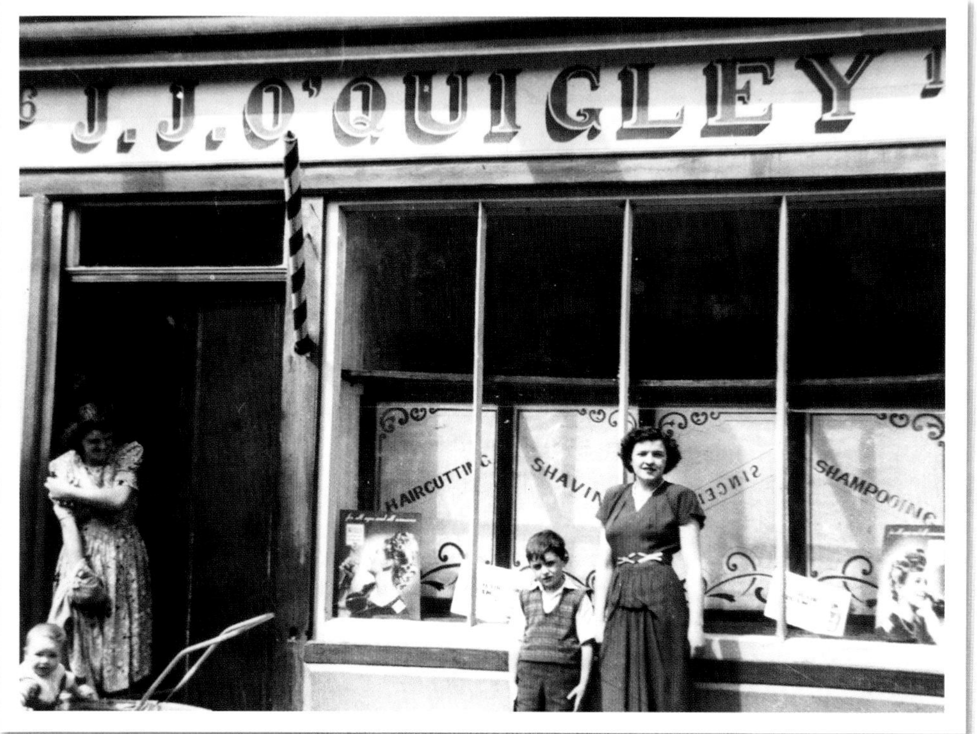

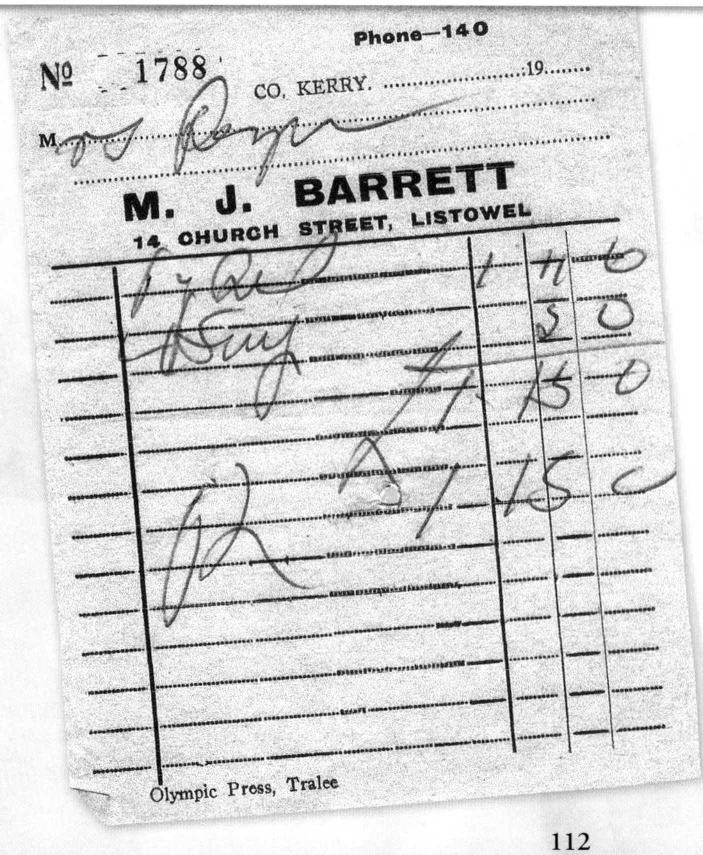
Phone—140
№ 1788 CO. KERRY. ....19......
M..........
M. J. BARRETT
14 CHURCH STREET, LISTOWEL
Olympic Press, Tralee

12, 14 & 16 Church Street
O'Regans & Barretts, two of Listowel's many small businesses which flourished trading in the town up to the demise of that type of business in the 1970s. These businesses included a grocery section in front and usually a curtained-off bar to the rear. A partitioned snug to facilitate discreet drinkers, womenfolk or those wanting a private conversation was usually inside the front door with easy access to counter service.

J.J. O'Quigley from Dublin opened a barber's saloon in a room rented from Reidy's in William Street in 1911. He had previously worked both in Tralee and Abbeyfeale. In 1912, J.J. bought the goodwill of the business and leased the house that had been vacated by Galway-born barber, Michael Hurley, at 16 Church Street. J.J. was succeeded in the business by his son Martin. The barber shop is still open and celebrated its century in 2012 under the management of Margaret Coffey.

Photo: The frontage of O'Quigley's barber shop from the 1950s includes Joan, wife of barber Martin O'Quigley, two of her children Martin (Junior) in pram and Jimmy, and her sister from Charles Street, Anna Moore. Anna worked as a hair stylist with Philomena Chute in an upstairs salon.

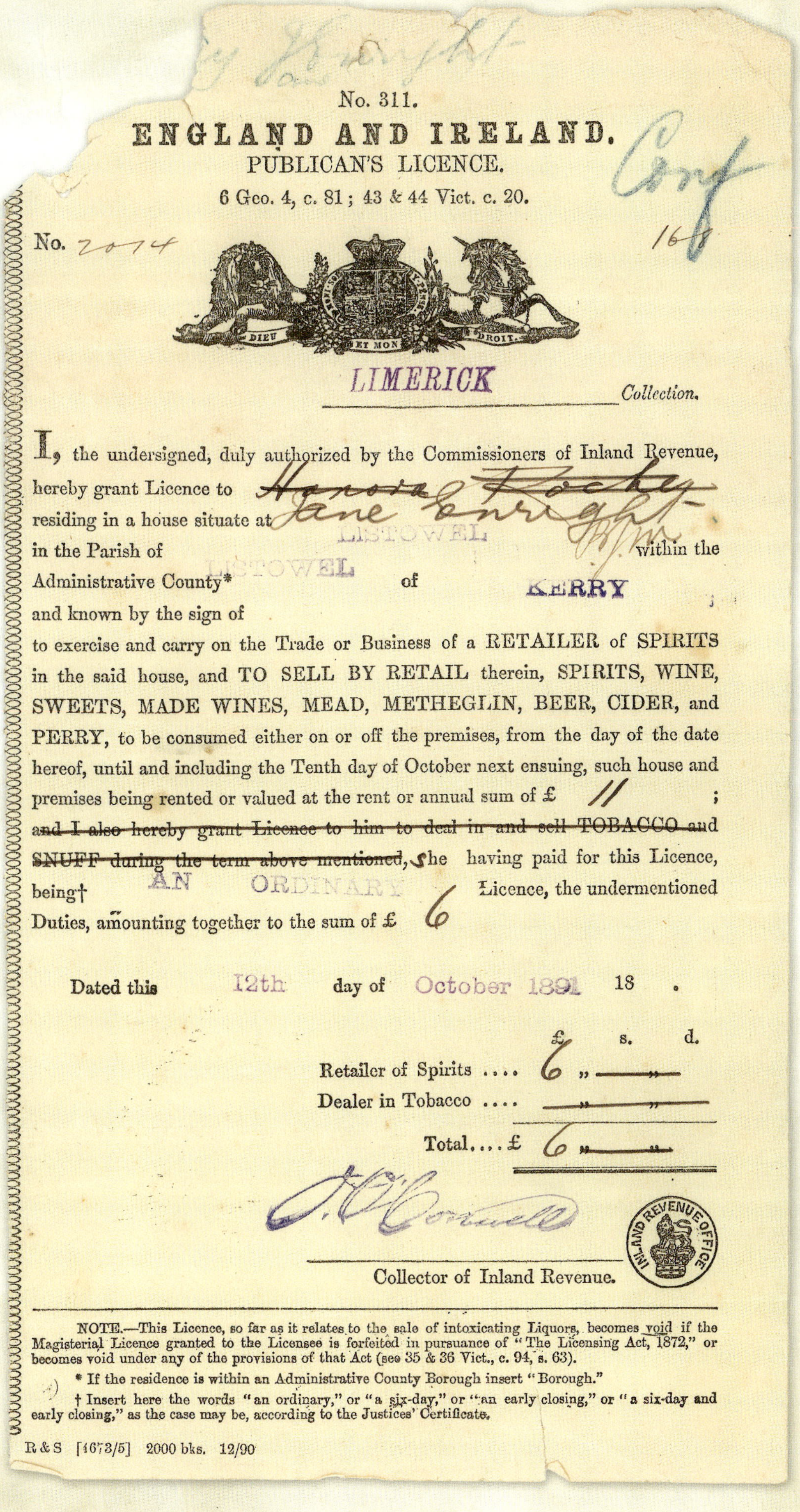

No. 311.

ENGLAND AND IRELAND.

PUBLICAN'S LICENCE.

6 Geo. 4, c. 81; 43 & 44 Vict. c. 20.

No. 2074 | 168

LIMERICK Collection.

I, the undersigned, duly authorized by the Commissioners of Inland Revenue, hereby grant Licence to ~~Honora Rocky~~ Jane Enright residing in a house situate at LISTOWEL in the Parish of LISTOWEL within the Administrative County* of KERRY and known by the sign of to exercise and carry on the Trade or Business of a RETAILER of SPIRITS in the said house, and TO SELL BY RETAIL therein, SPIRITS, WINE, SWEETS, MADE WINES, MEAD, METHEGLIN, BEER, CIDER, and PERRY, to be consumed either on or off the premises, from the day of the date hereof, until and including the Tenth day of October next ensuing, such house and premises being rented or valued at the rent or annual sum of £ 11 ; ~~and I also hereby grant Licence to him to deal in and sell TOBACCO and SNUFF during the term above mentioned~~, she having paid for this Licence, being† AN ORDINARY Licence, the undermentioned Duties, amounting together to the sum of £ 6

Dated this 12th day of October 1891 18 .

	£	s.	d.
Retailer of Spirits	6	"	"
Dealer in Tobacco	"	"	"
Total.... £	6	"	"

J. O'Connell

Collector of Inland Revenue.

INLAND REVENUE OFFICE

NOTE.—This Licence, so far as it relates to the sale of intoxicating Liquors, becomes void if the Magisterial Licence granted to the Licensee is forfeited in pursuance of "The Licensing Act, 1872," or becomes void under any of the provisions of that Act (see 35 & 36 Vict., c. 94, s. 63).

* If the residence is within an Administrative County Borough insert "Borough."

† Insert here the words "an ordinary," or "a six-day," or "an early closing," or "a six-day and early closing," as the case may be, according to the Justices' Certificate.

R & S [4673/5] 2000 bks. 12/90

22 Church Street
Jean Enright was widow of John Enright. She had her public house at Church Street. Her husband worked as a clerk at Listowel Railway Station. After his death, his position was filled by his son Edmond.

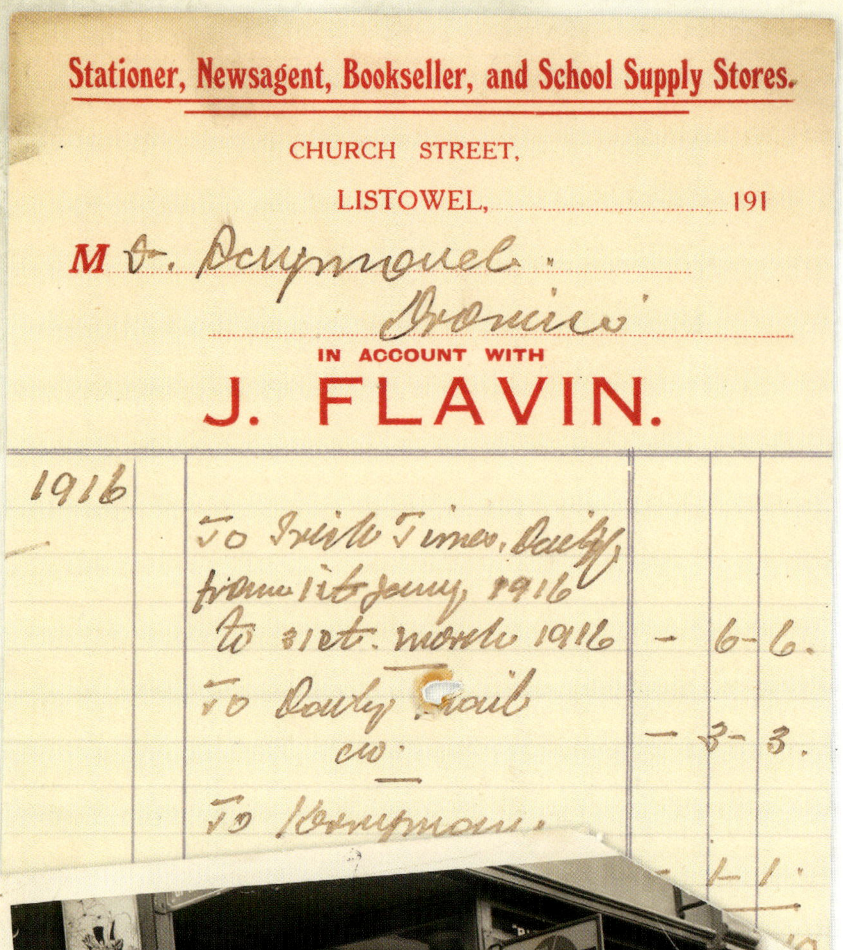

Stationer, Newsagent, Bookseller, and School Supply Stores.

CHURCH STREET,

LISTOWEL, ... 191

M ....

IN ACCOUNT WITH

J. FLAVIN.

1916	To Irish Times, Daily from 1st Jany 1916 to 31st March 1916	- 6 - 6.
	To Daily Mail do	- 3 - 3.
	To Freeman	- 1 - 1

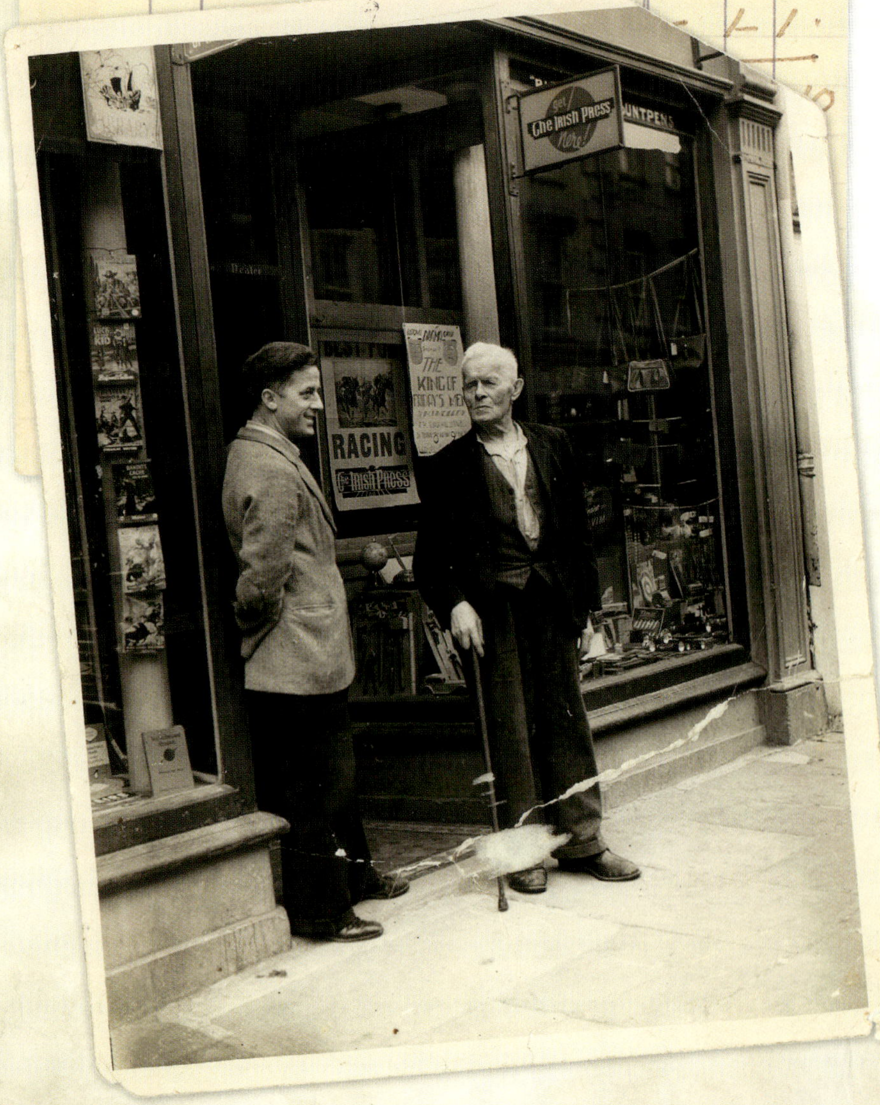

30 Church Street

Photo: Micheál Flavin and his father Danny Flavin at the door of their newsagent's and bookshop in the 1950s.

Flavin's, for many years, maintained a well-stocked lending library. The shop was frequented by a great number of well known Irish Literary figures over the years. In *Streets of Listowel*, Bryan MacMahon called it "A University of the People". The business is still operated by the Flavin family. The house was one of a number of businesses which were targeted by British Forces during the troubles, and burnt down. The Flavin family then relocated and ran a newspaper shop at No. 2 Upper William Street until their house was rebuilt. As can be seen from the letter opposite, Danny Flavin was a friend of Pádraig Ó Siochfhradha who wrote under the pen name 'An Seabhac'. The book which he refers to is *Jimín Mháire Thaidhg*. This was a text-book in Irish schools for many years. The letter also contains an offer to use 'his good offices' and this would have been in relation to the rebuilding of Flavin's house. 'An Seabhac' was clearly a man of influence.

Photo: M.J. Flavin, MP for North Kerry from 1896 to 1918, who was Danny Flavin's brother. In 1901, he and eleven other Nationalist MPs were ejected from the parliament at Westminster while demanding justice for Ireland. While five policemen were removing him, Flavin sang defiantly:

"God save Ireland,' say we proudly,
'God save Ireland,' say we all,
If upon the scaffold high
Or the Commons floor we die,
Oh, what matter then for Erin dear we fall"

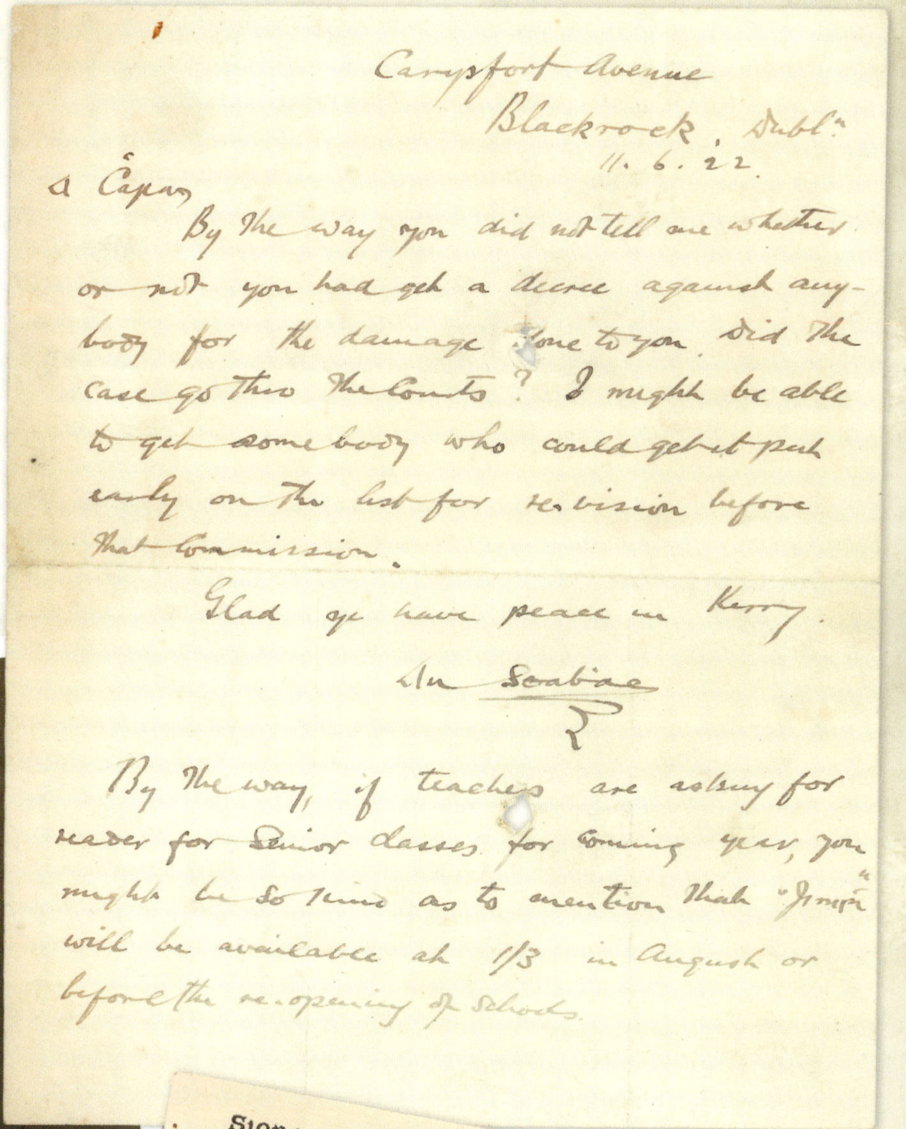
Carysfort Avenue
Blackrock, Dubl.
11. 6. 22.

A Ċara

By the way you did not tell me whether or not you had got a decree against anybody for the damage done to you. Did the case go thro' the Courts? I might be able to get somebody who could get it put early on the list for revision before that Commission.

Glad ye have peace in Kerry.

An Seabac

By the way, if teachers are asking for reader for Senior classes for coming year, you might be so kind as to mention that "Jimín" will be available at 1/3 in August or before the re-opening of Schools.

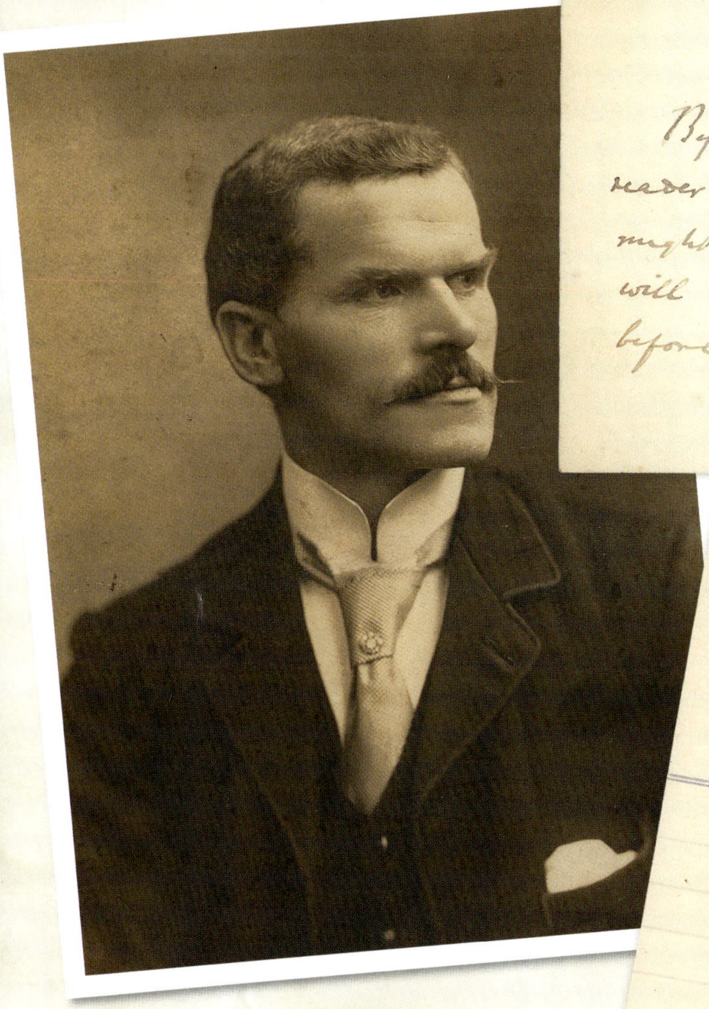

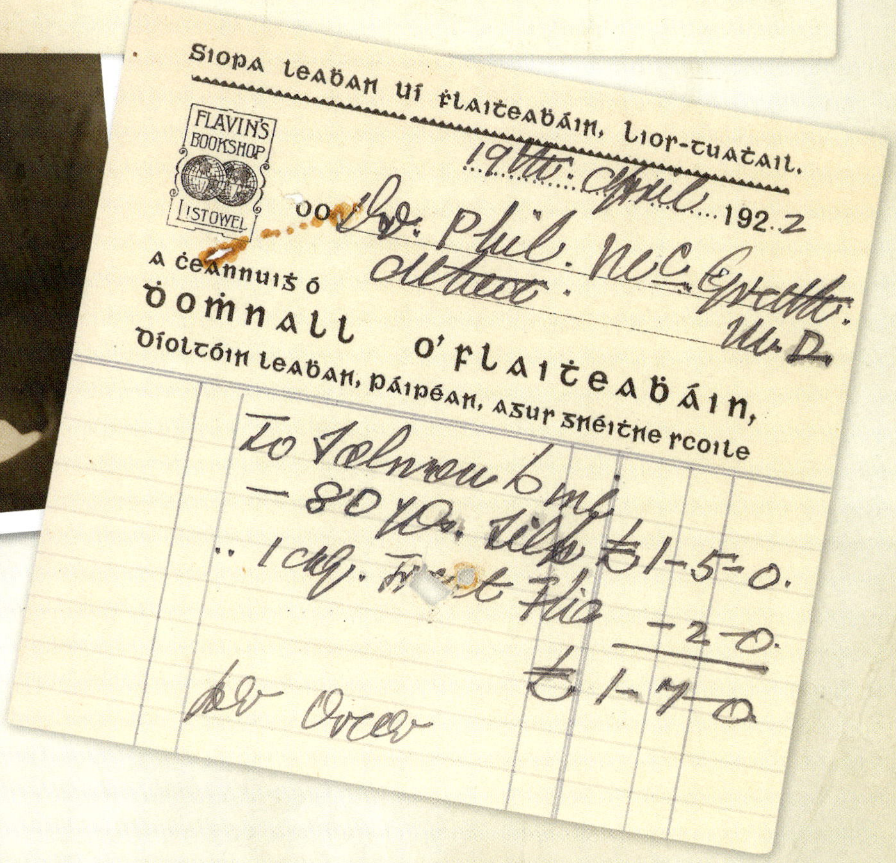
Siopa Leabar Uí Flaiteabáin, Lios-Tuatail.

FLAVIN'S BOOKSHOP LISTOWEL

19th April 1922

Dr. Phil. McC... M.D.

A Ceannuiġ ó
Domnall O'Flaiteabáin,
Díoltóir Leabar, Páipéar, agus Sneíte Scoile

To ... 80 ... £1-5-0.
.. 1 cop. ... -2-0.
£1-7-0

See Over

34 Church Street

James (Jim) O'Donovan (pictured below) was born 1869 at Kilcox, Lisselton. He emigrated to Chicago in the late 1890s. He returned to Ireland and lived in the family home at Kilcox. Some time around 1916 he purchased No. 34 Church Street, Listowel where he ran a grocery shop for several years.

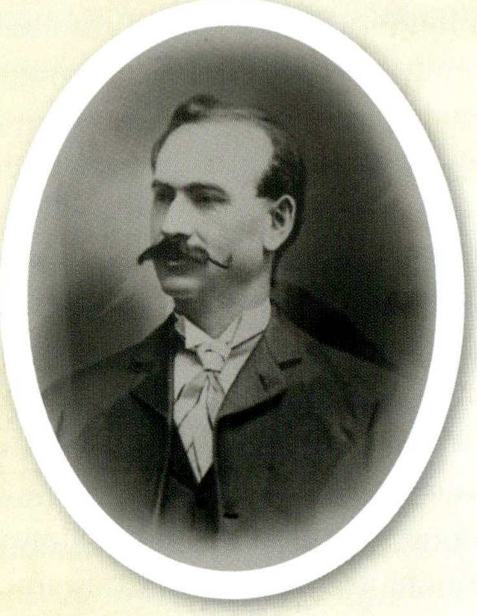

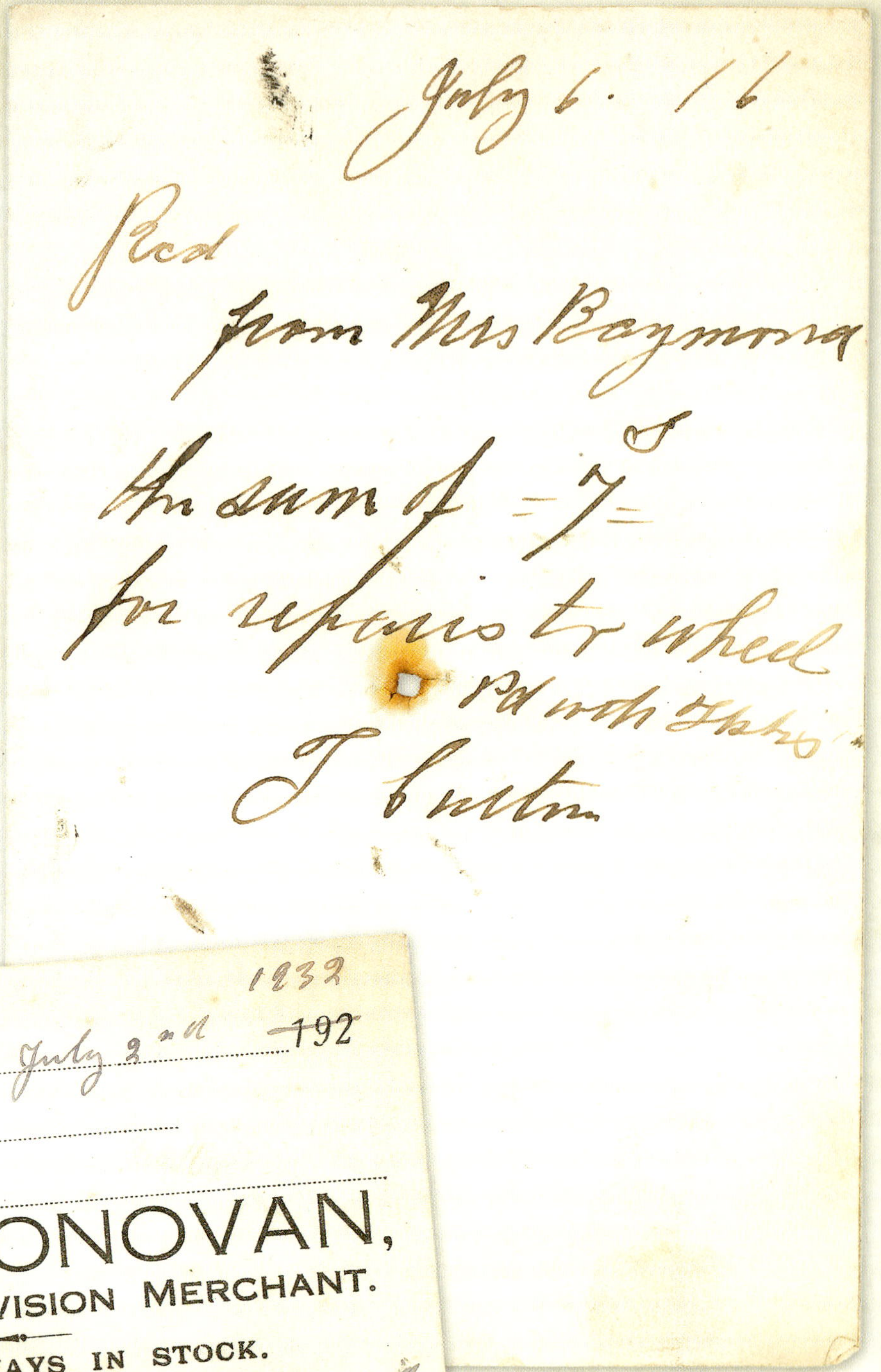

July 6. 16

Recd from Mrs Raymond the sum of 7s for repairs to wheel

Pd with thanks

T Curtin

The Curtins were wheelwrights on the premises.

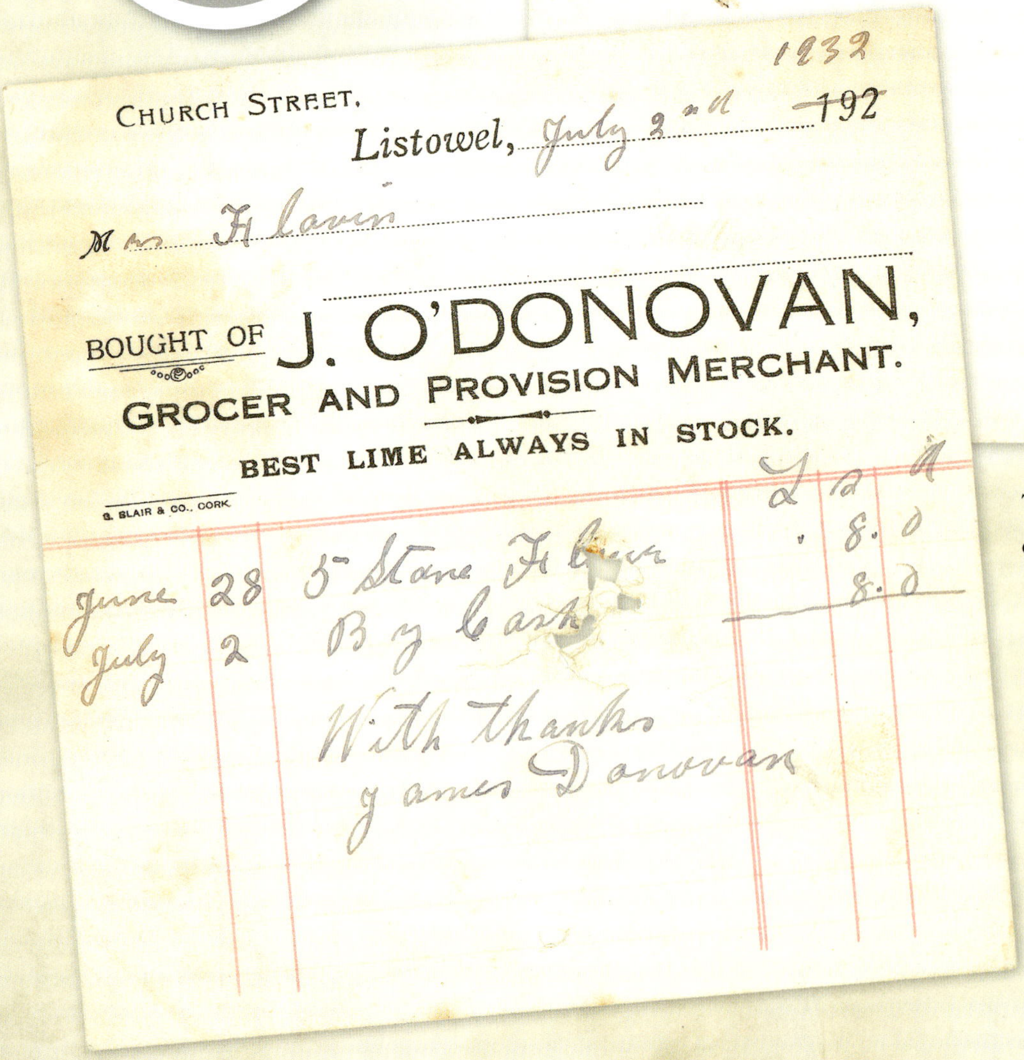

CHURCH STREET,

Listowel, July 2nd 1932

Mrs Flavin

BOUGHT OF J. O'DONOVAN,

GROCER AND PROVISION MERCHANT.

BEST LIME ALWAYS IN STOCK.

G. BLAIR & CO., CORK.

			£	s	d
June	28	5 Stone Flour		8	0
July	2	By Cash		8	0

With thanks
James Donovan

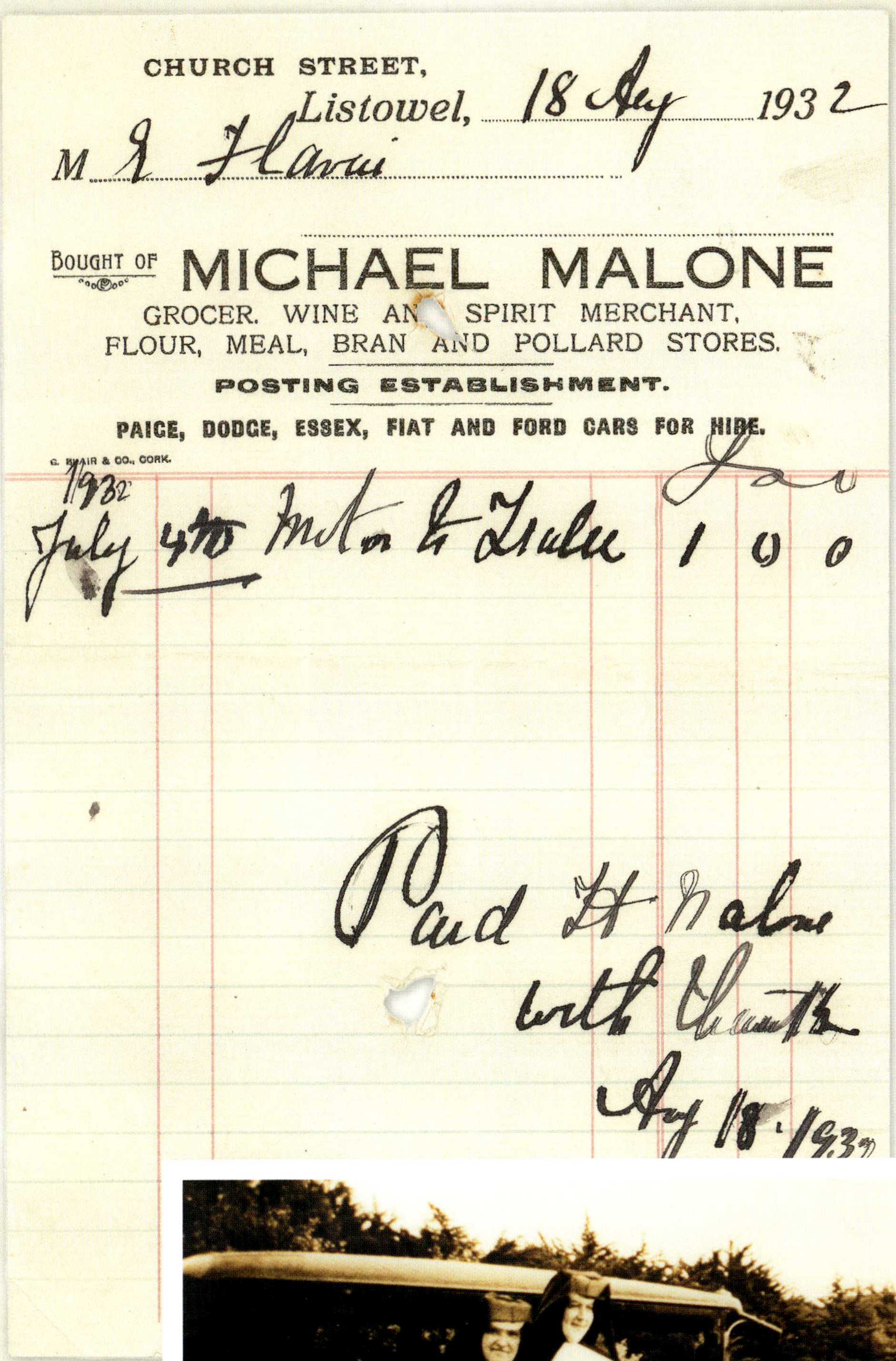

CHURCH STREET,
Listowel, 18 Aug 1932
M J Flavin

BOUGHT OF MICHAEL MALONE
GROCER, WINE AN SPIRIT MERCHANT,
FLOUR, MEAL, BRAN AND POLLARD STORES.
POSTING ESTABLISHMENT.
PAIGE, DODGE, ESSEX, FIAT AND FORD CARS FOR HIRE.
G. BLAIR & CO., CORK.

			£	s	d
1932 July	4th	Motor to Tralee	1	0	0

Paid H Malone
with thanks
Aug 18. 1932

36 Church Street

Michael Malone, an RIC man from Co. Laois, retired from the force and married Johanna Lyons from Derry, outside Listowel. They bought a public house in Church Street. They also carried on a trade with side car, long car, and trap hire. With the advent of the motor car the Malones started a lucrative car hire and hackney trade. The business closed in the 1950s.

Subsequently, the house was bought by Finbarr McAuliffe. As well as running the public house, he also had a fish shop and wholesale salmon business.

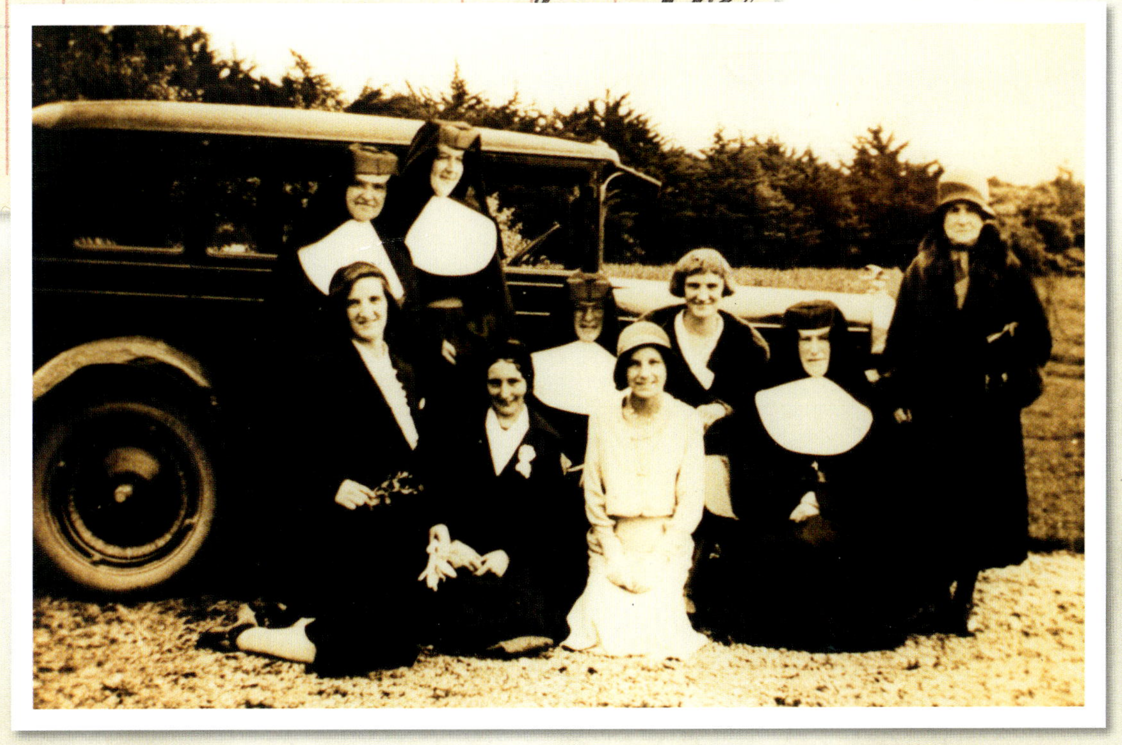

Photo: Mrs. Malone and friends entertaining some nuns from The Presentation Convent, Listowel.

38 Church Street

James Crowley M.R.C.V.S. was elected as a Sinn Féin member of the first two Dáils in 1919 and 1921. He was re-elected again to the third Dáil in 1922 also as a Sinn Féin member, taking his place in the pro-Treaty side. In the fourth, fifth and sixth Dáils, in 1923, 1927 and again in 1927, he was re-elected as a member of Cumann na nGaedhael. Noel Crowley, James's son, set up a general printing business in the family home in the 1930s.

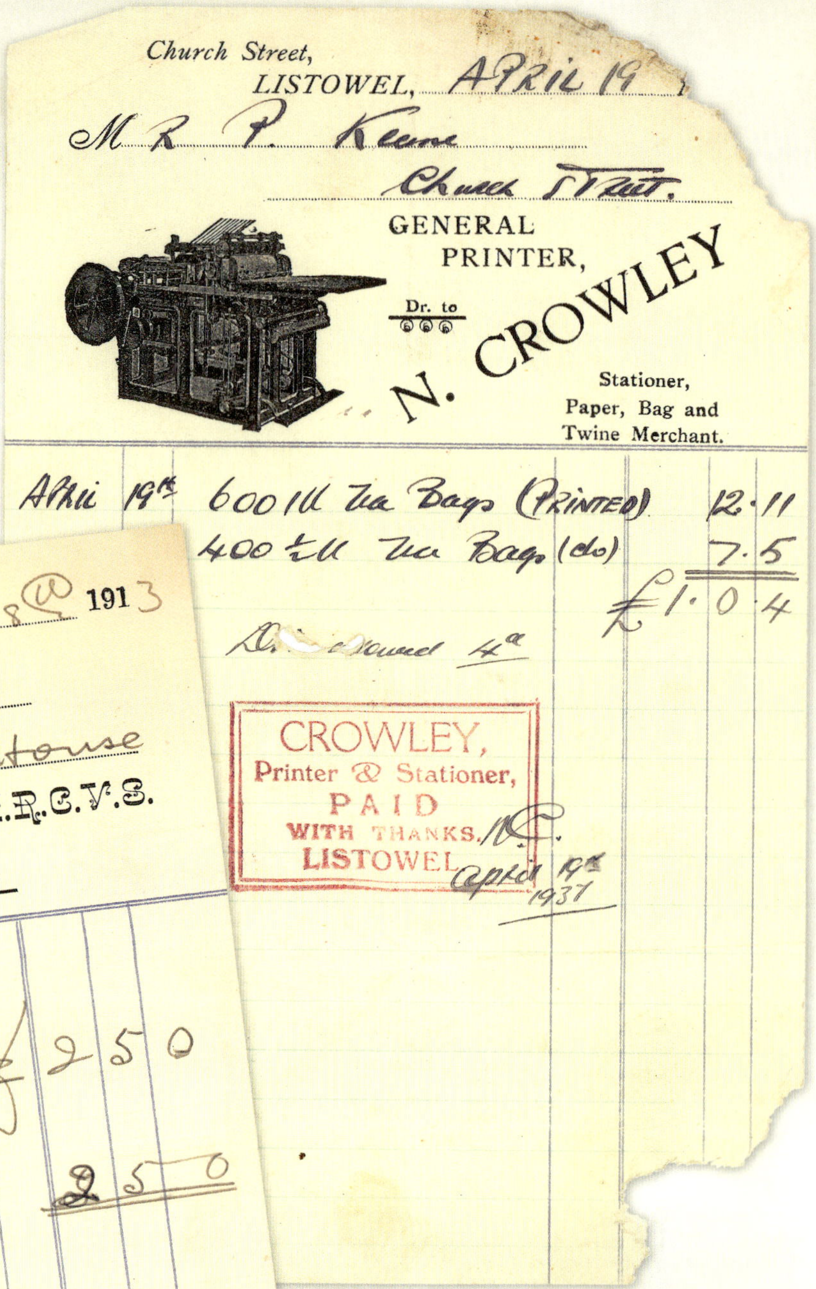
Church Street,
LISTOWEL, April 19
Mr P. Keane
Church Street.
GENERAL PRINTER,
Dr. to
N. CROWLEY
Stationer, Paper, Bag and Twine Merchant.

April 19th 600 ½lb Tea Bags (Printed) 12.11
400 ¼lb Tea Bags (do) 7.5
£1.0.4
D[illegible] allowed 4d

CROWLEY, Printer & Stationer, PAID WITH THANKS, LISTOWEL
N.C.
April 19th 1937

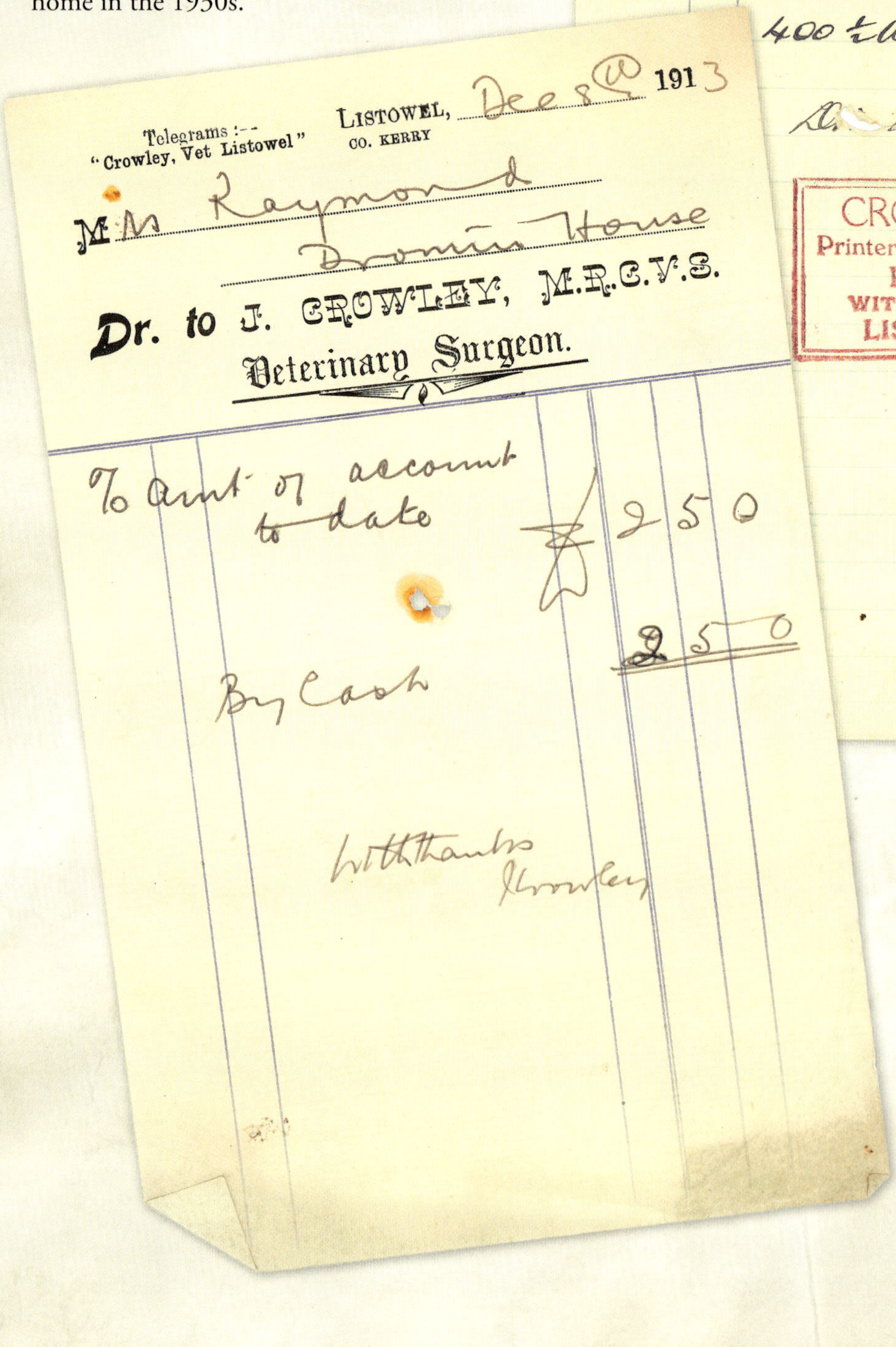
Telegrams :— "Crowley, Vet Listowel"
LISTOWEL, Dec 8th 1913
CO. KERRY
Mrs Raymond
Dromin House
Dr. to J. CROWLEY, M.R.C.V.S.
Veterinary Surgeon.

To amt of account to date £2 5 0
By Cash 2 5 0
With thanks
J Crowley

Opposite: Bryan MacMahon (teacher, short story writer, playwright and ballad-maker) purchased the Crowley house in 1936 and lived there until his death in 1998. Together with his wife Kitty, he ran a bookshop from the house for a number of years until it closed in 1948. In Bryan MacMahon's own words, he did this to make some additional money with which to educate his increasing family of sons.

Photo: Bryan and Kitty MacMahon.

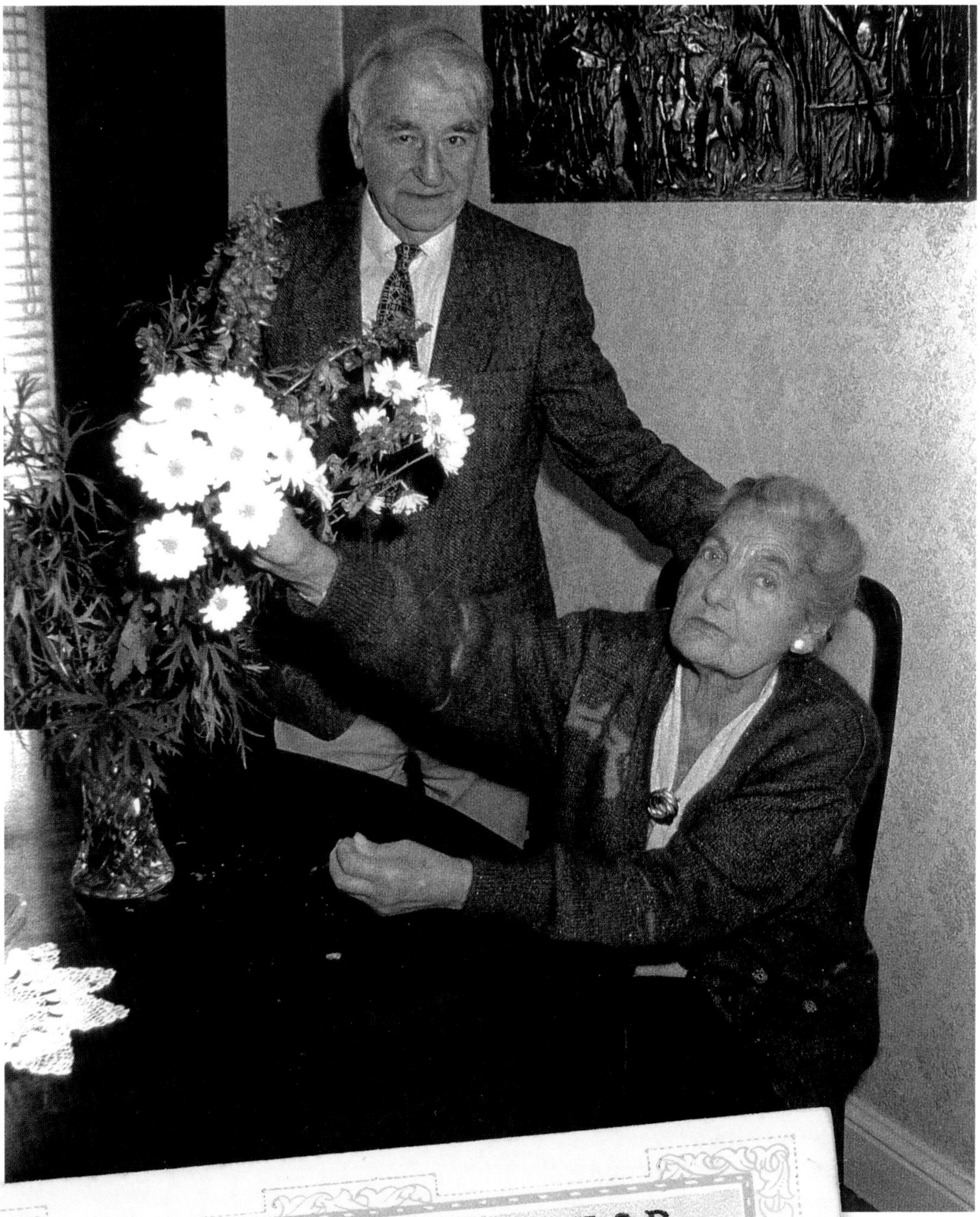

McMAHON'S BOOKSHOP,
(Prop. K. McMAHON)
Agent: Educational Co. of Ireland, Ltd.,
Browne & Nolan, Ltd., Etc.

ASHE STREET, LISTOWEL,
Co. Kerry, ______________19___

A Chara,
I thank you very sincerely for your esteemed order and assure you that it shall have my immediate attention.

Very faithfully yours,
(Mrs.) Kathleen McMahon.

Auction of HOUSE PROPERTY

IN CHURCH-ST. in the Town of Listowel

On Thursday 30th April

AT THE LISTOWEL ARMS HOTEL,

AT ONE O'CLOCK

Messrs WM McCARTHY, Senior and Junior have instructed Subscriber to put up and Sell, by Public Auction as above, all their Right, Title, and Interest in that

LICENSED HOUSE AND PREMISES,

as at present in the occupation of one of the Vendors, and in which he has carried on business for some years, in as large and ample a manner as same is held by Lease from and under the Right Honourable, the Earl of Listowel, on a Lease of 99 years, from the 25th day of March, 1870 at the small yearly ground rent of £1 18s 6d-

The House is in First-class repair, and is well fitted for a Licensed House, having a frontage of over 18ft, and a depth of 115ft, with an enclosed yard, and entrance from a back road that runs at the rere,

The Vendors will give immediate possession on the purchase being approved of by the Right Hon the Earl of Listowel, and all further information on application to FRANCIS CREAGH, Esq., Solicitor or to

GERALD M'ELLIGOTT, Auctioneer

Listowel, April 7th, 1885

ROBERT I. CUTHBERTSON, Printer, Listowel.

House for sale by Gerald McElligott, Auctioneer and owner of the Listowel Arms Hotel.

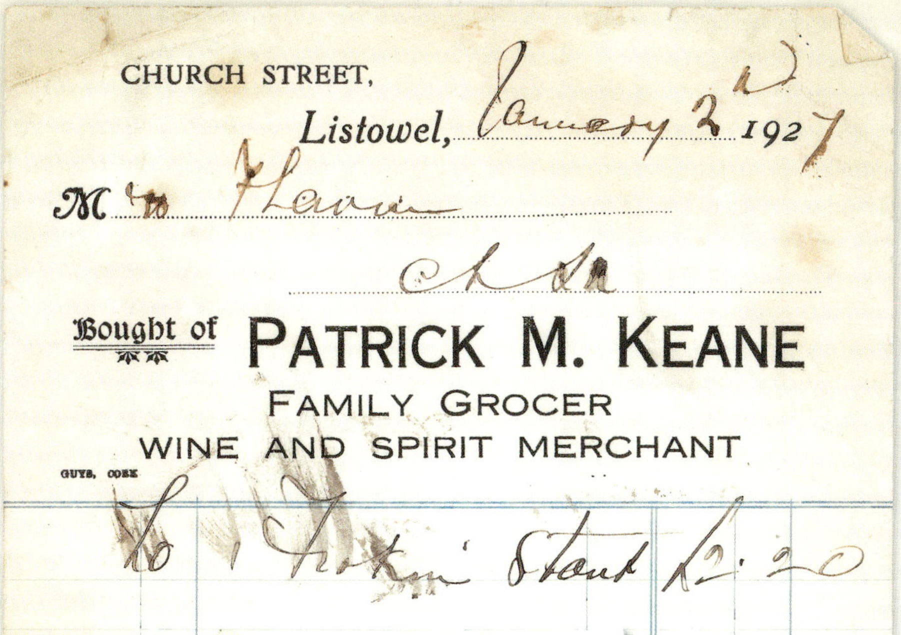
CHURCH STREET,
Listowel, January 2nd 1927
M
Bought of PATRICK M. KEANE
FAMILY GROCER
WINE AND SPIRIT MERCHANT

44 Church Street
Willie Keane stands outside his family's public house at 44 Church Street in the 1930s. This frontage, known as 'The Harp and Lion', was richly decorated by Listowel's master craftsman, Pat McAuliffe, around 1910. The plaster work on the first floor depicts a lion standing on a plinth over a harp enclosed by mouldings bearing legends in three languages: *Erin go Bragh* – Ireland Forever; *Maison de Villa* – House in the Town; *Spes Mea in Deo* – My hope is in God.

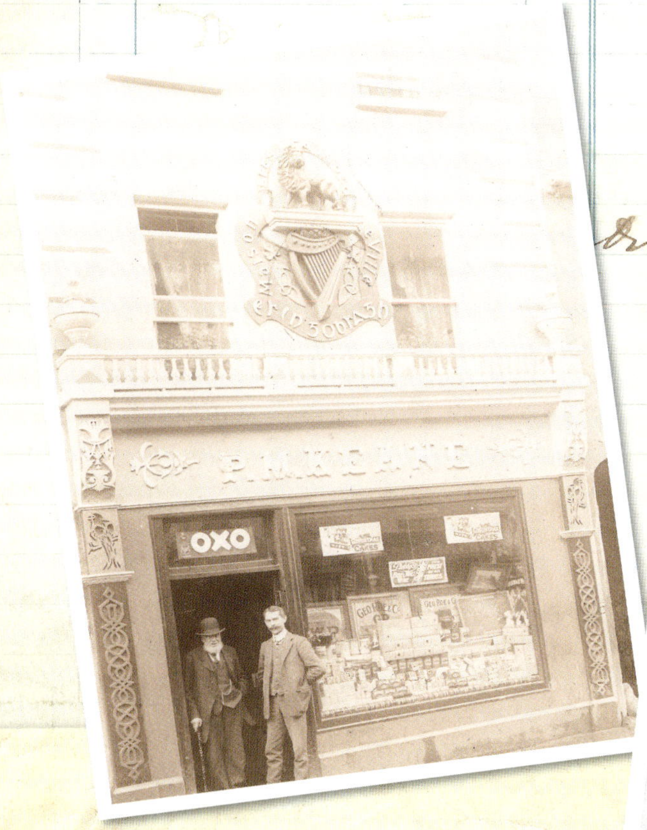

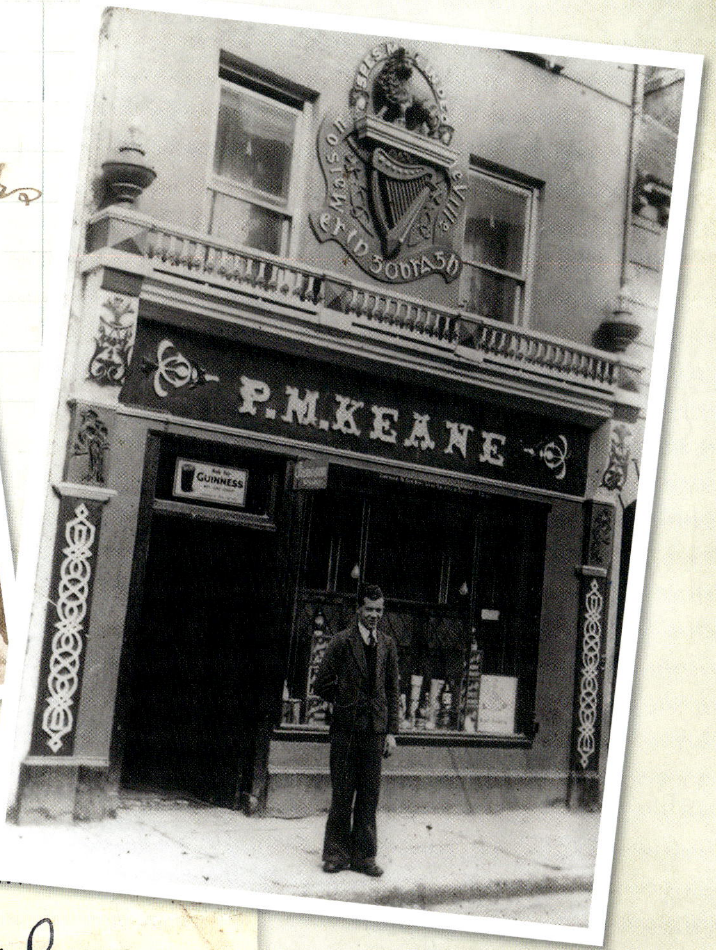

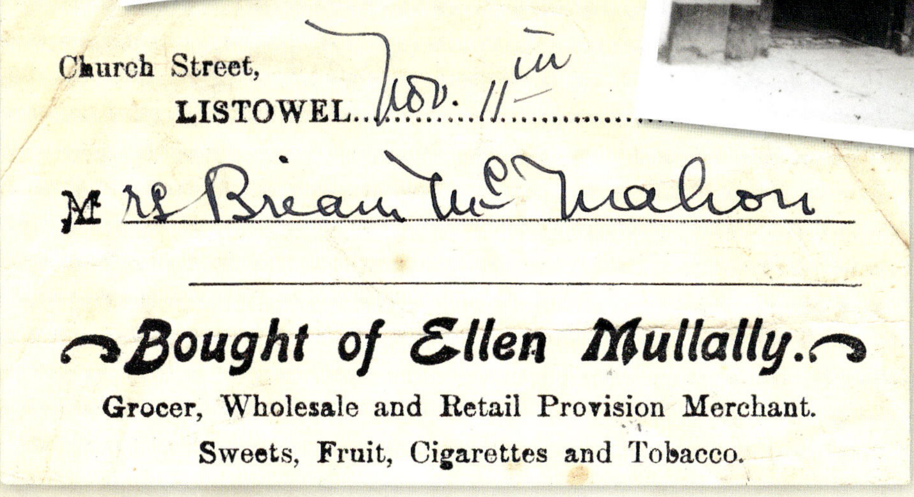
Church Street,
LISTOWEL. Nov. 11th
M
Bought of Ellen Mullally.
Grocer, Wholesale and Retail Provision Merchant.
Sweets, Fruit, Cigarettes and Tobacco.

42 Church Street
The Mullallys were lifelong De Valera supporters. Once in their shop as a young boy I offered my penny for mixed sweets. Lena threw three sweets on the counter and said "there you are, mix them yourself".

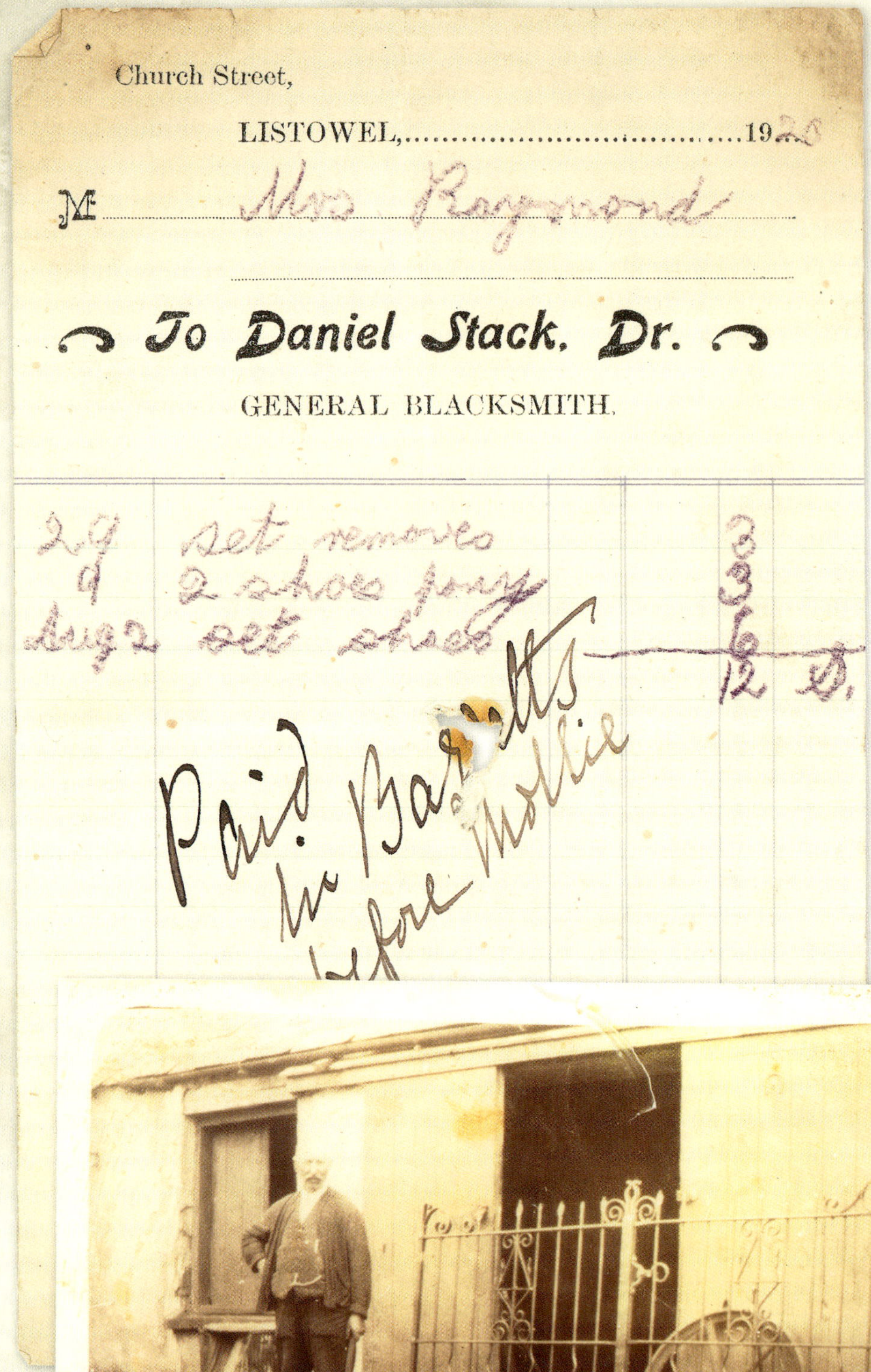

Church Street,

LISTOWEL,..................................19 20

M Mrs Raymond

To Daniel Stack, Dr.

GENERAL BLACKSMITH.

2.9	set removes	3
9	2 shoes pony	3
Aug 2	set shoes	6
		12 S.

Paid Mc Barretts before Mollie

Dan Stack, General Blacksmith, originally from Ballybunion, set up a forge at the rear of Church Street. His brother, John, served his time with the Bunyan brothers of Market Street, before joining in the business with his brother Dan. John's son, Alfie, later worked at the forge. It closed in 1960.

Photo: John and Alfie Stack outside their forge.

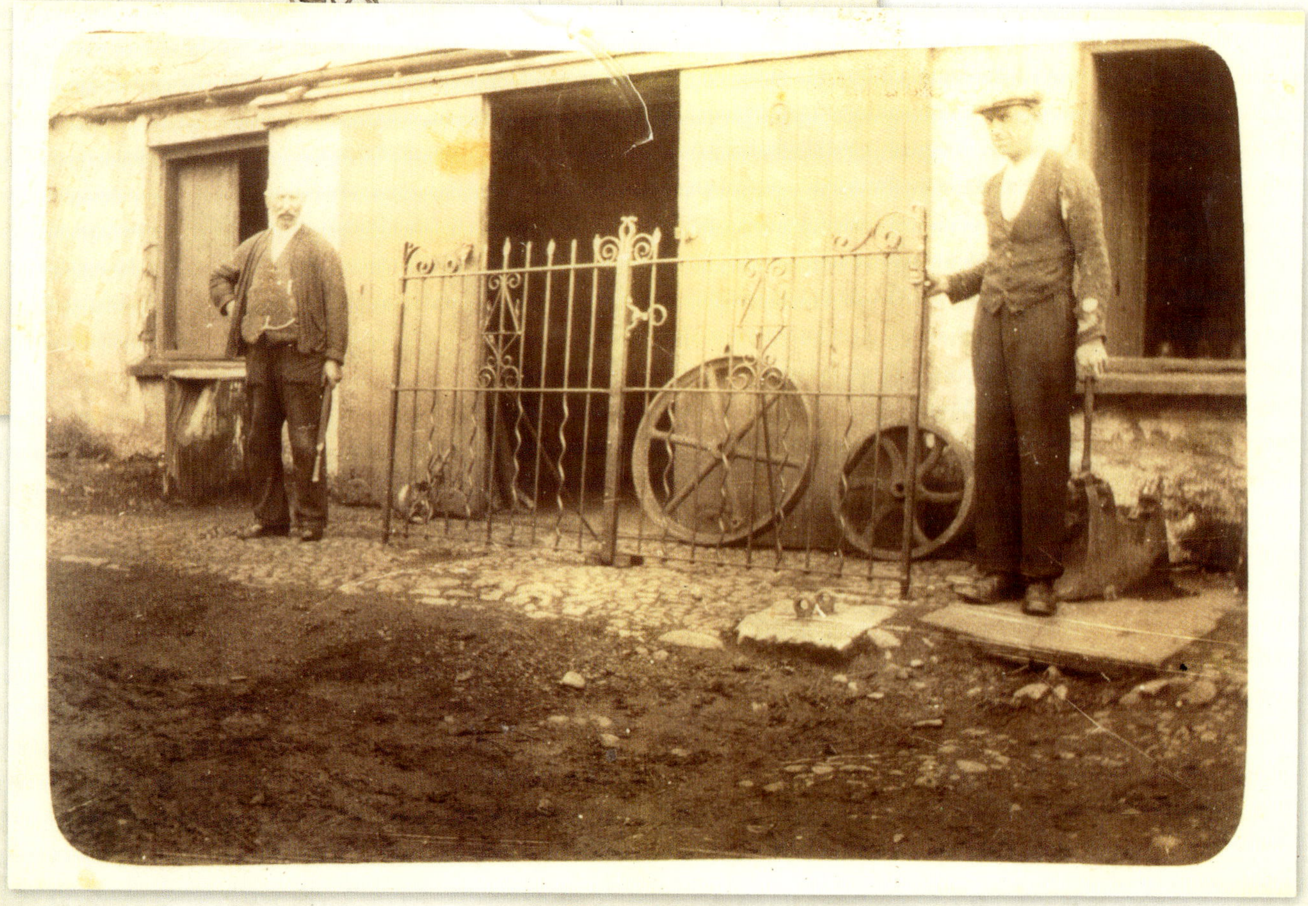

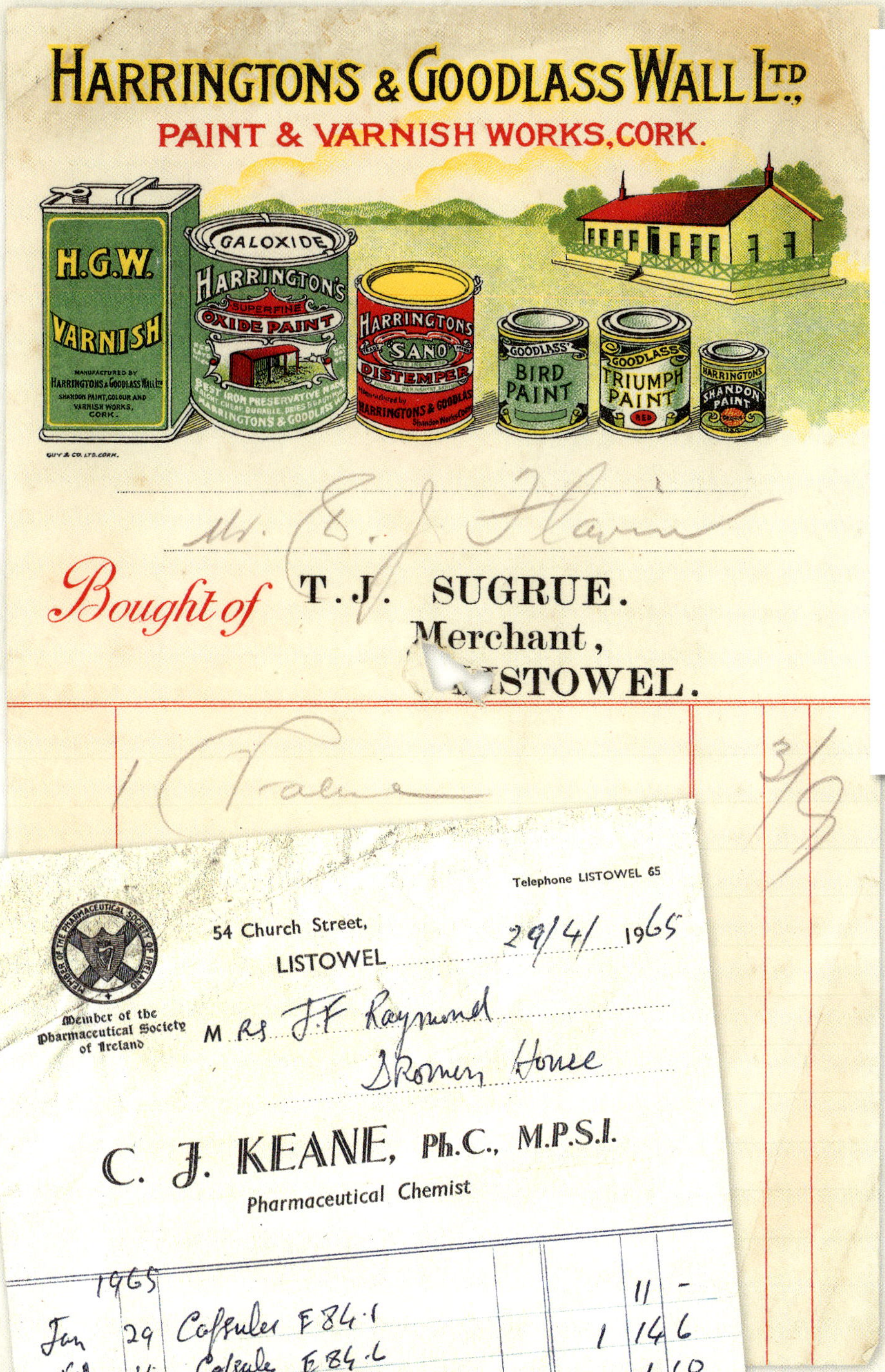
HARRINGTONS & GOODLASS WALL LTD.
PAINT & VARNISH WORKS, CORK.

Mr. E. J. Flavin
Bought of T. J. SUGRUE.
Merchant,
LISTOWEL.
1 Trale 3/9

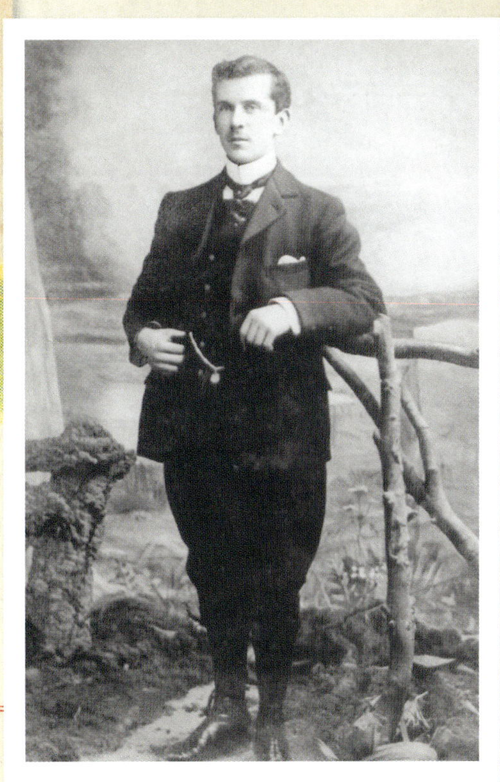

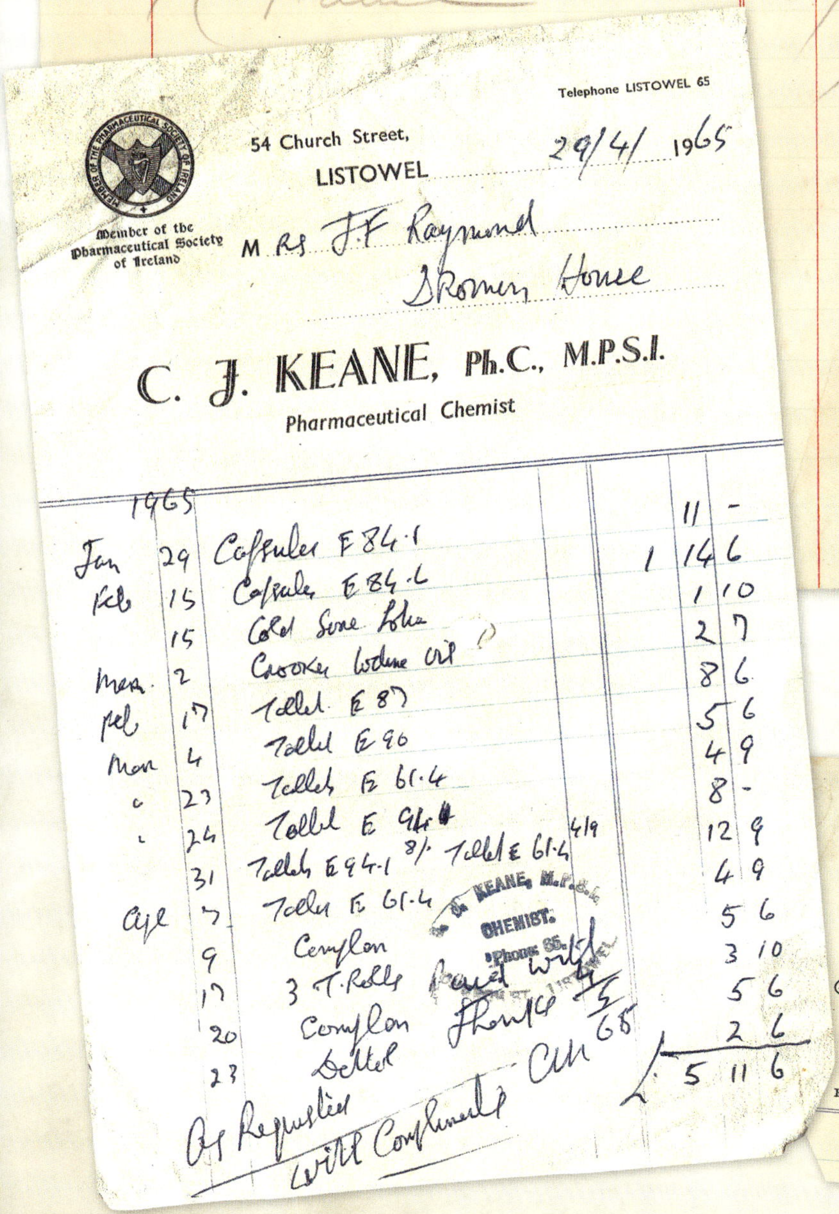
Telephone LISTOWEL 65
54 Church Street,
LISTOWEL 29/4/ 1965
Member of the Pharmaceutical Society of Ireland
MRS J F Raymond
Skomen House
C. J. KEANE, Ph.C., M.P.S.I.
Pharmaceutical Chemist

1965				11 -
Jan	29	Capsules E 84.1	1	14 6
Feb	15	Capsules E 84.2		1 10
	15	Cold Sore Lotion		2 7
Mar	2	Crookes Iodine Oil		8 6
Feb	17	Tablet E 87		5 6
		Tablet E 90		4 9
Mar	4	Tablets E 61.4		8 -
"	23	Tablet E 94		12 9
"	24	Tablets E 94.1 8/- Tablet E 61.4 4/9		
	31	Tablets E 61.4		4 9
Apl	7	Tablets E 61.4		5 6
	9	Complan		3 10
	17	3 T. Rolls		5 6
	20	Complan		2 6
	23	Dettol	£	5 11 6

As Requested
with Compliments
Paid with thanks 5/5/65 CJK
C. J. KEANE, M.P.S.I. CHEMIST Phone 65

50 Church Street
Paddy Griffin had a public house as well as an egg, butter, and bacon store at Church Street. His sisters, Nora, a milliner, and Hannah lived with him.

54 Church Street
T.J. Sugrue from Tralee (pictured above) operated a light hardware shop at Church Street. He was married to Margaret Kennelly from Knockanure, a sister of J.J. Kennelly (tailor) of Upper William Street. Sugrue won a county football championship medal with Tralee Mitchels in 1902.

C.J. Keane had a chemist shop on this premises from the mid 1940s until the late 1960s.

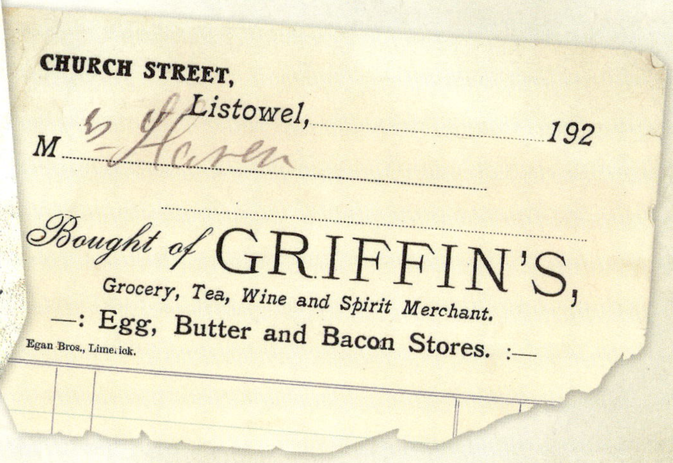
CHURCH STREET,
Listowel, 192
M. J. Haren
Bought of GRIFFIN'S,
Grocery, Tea, Wine and Spirit Merchant.
—: Egg, Butter and Bacon Stores. :—
Egan Bros., Limerick.

56 Church Street

The barracks of the Royal Irish Constabulary was in Church Street on the site of the old Bridewell. The picture shows the burnt shell of the barracks in 1922. Two years earlier, the barracks was the scene of the infamous Listowel police mutiny led by Constable Jeremiah Mee.

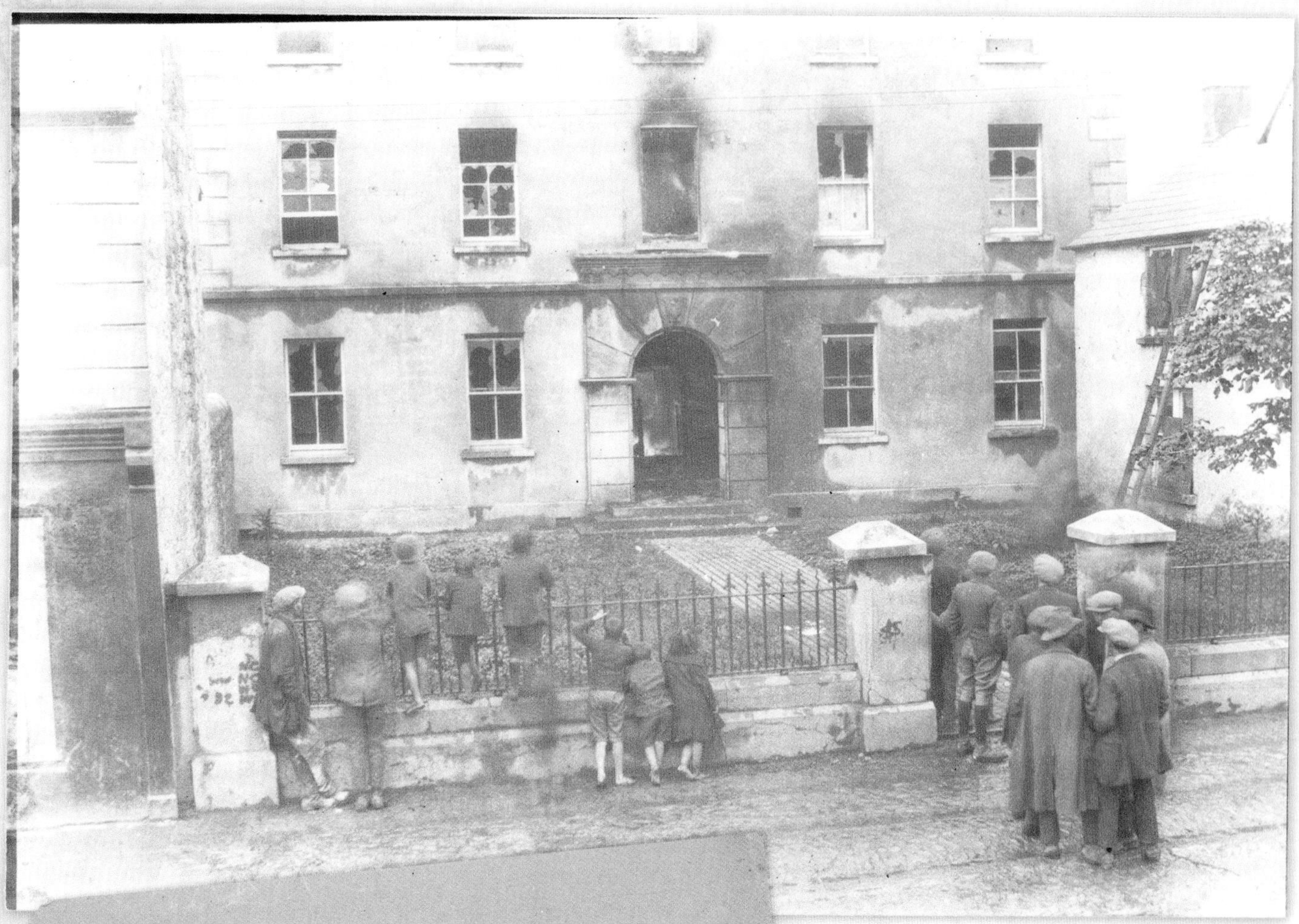

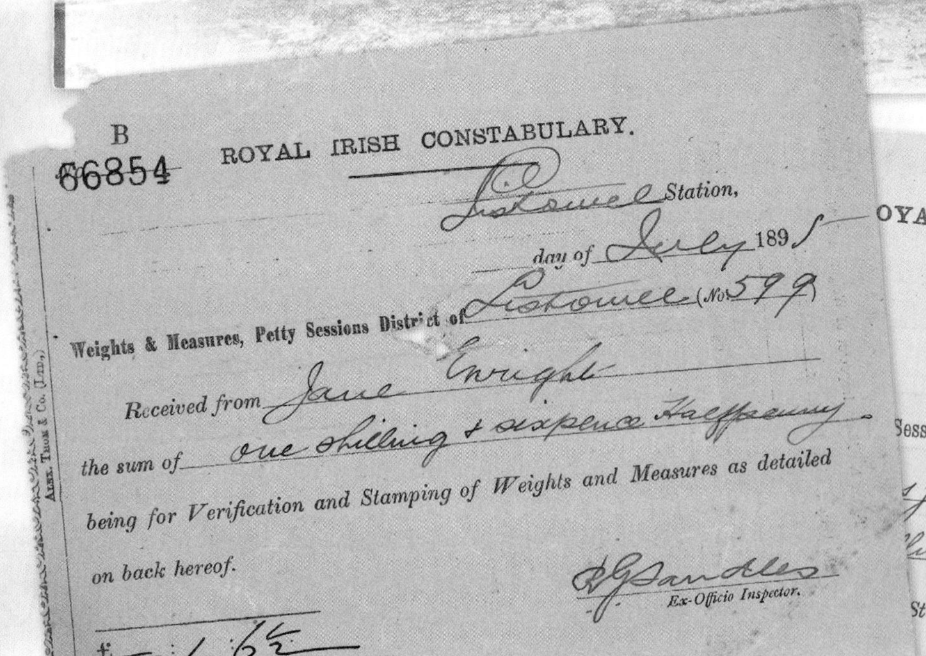

B

66854 ROYAL IRISH CONSTABULARY.

Listowel Station,

day of July 1895

Weights & Measures, Petty Sessions District of Listowel (No. 599)

Received from Jane Enright

the sum of one shilling + sixpence Halfpenny

being for Verification and Stamping of Weights and Measures as detailed

on back hereof.

Ex-Officio Inspector.

£ -:1:6½

Alex. Thom & Co. (Ltd.)

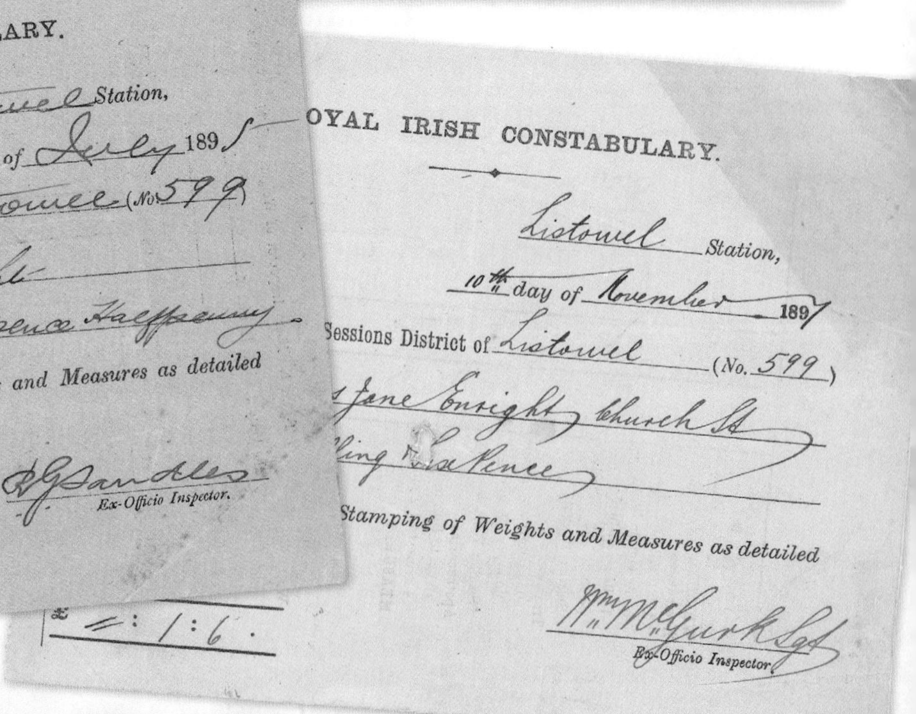

ROYAL IRISH CONSTABULARY.

Listowel Station,

10th day of November 1897

Sessions District of Listowel (No. 599)

Jane Enright Church St

lling & Sixpence

Stamping of Weights and Measures as detailed

Wm McGurk Sgt

Ex-Officio Inspector

£ -:1:6.

Above left: The receipt, dated 1895, is from the Inspector of Weights and Measures to Jane Enright, Publican, Church Street.

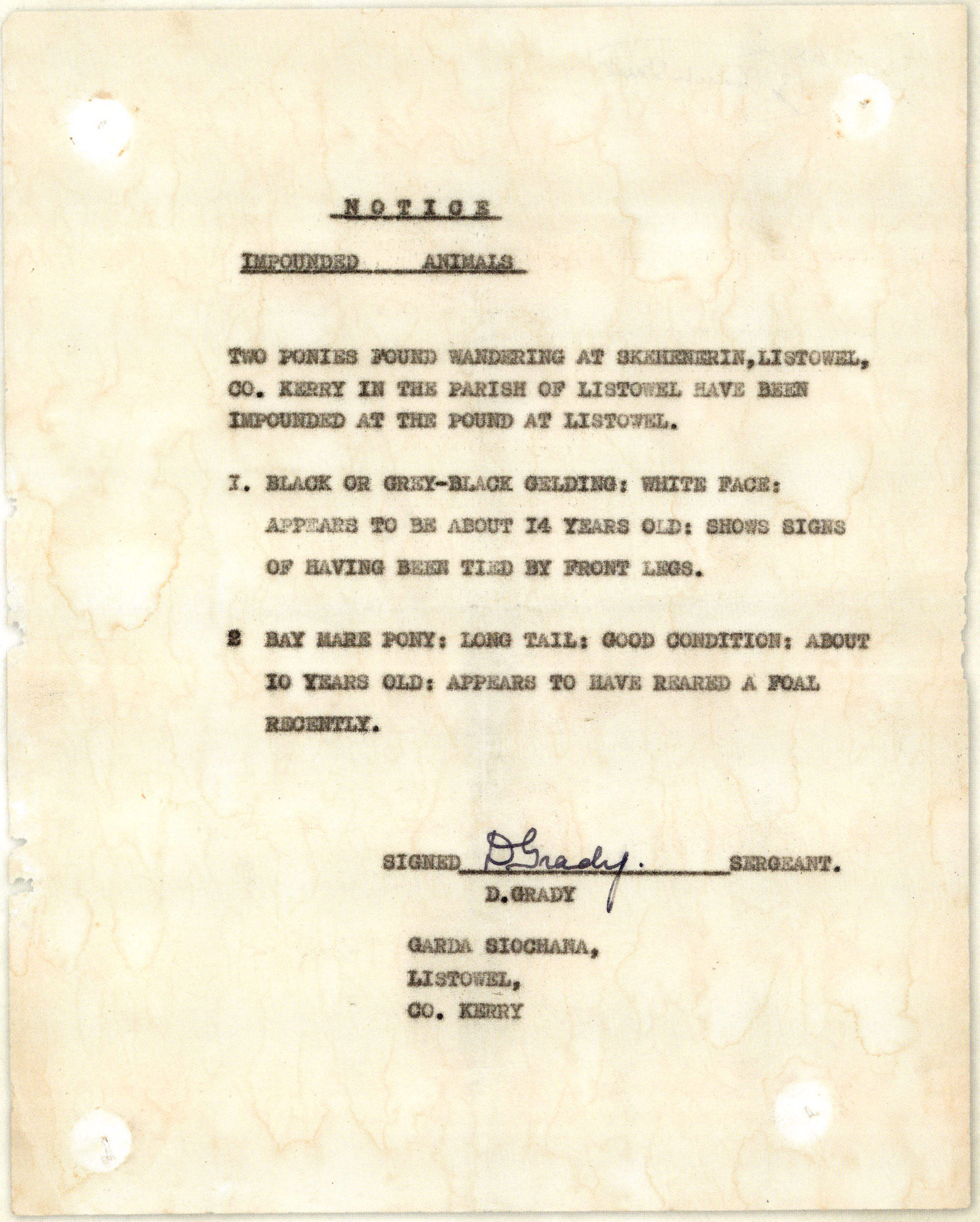

NOTICE

IMPOUNDED ANIMALS

TWO PONIES FOUND WANDERING AT SKEHENERIN,LISTOWEL, CO. KERRY IN THE PARISH OF LISTOWEL HAVE BEEN IMPOUNDED AT THE POUND AT LISTOWEL.

I. BLACK OR GREY-BLACK GELDING: WHITE FACE: APPEARS TO BE ABOUT I4 YEARS OLD: SHOWS SIGNS OF HAVING BEEN TIED BY FRONT LEGS.

2 BAY MARE PONY: LONG TAIL: GOOD CONDITION: ABOUT IO YEARS OLD: APPEARS TO HAVE REARED A FOAL RECENTLY.

SIGNED D.Grady. SERGEANT.
D.GRADY

GARDA SIOCHANA,
LISTOWEL,
CO. KERRY

An undated Garda Síochána public notice from the 1930s informing the general public of the impounding of two horses found wandering at Skehenerin, Listowel.

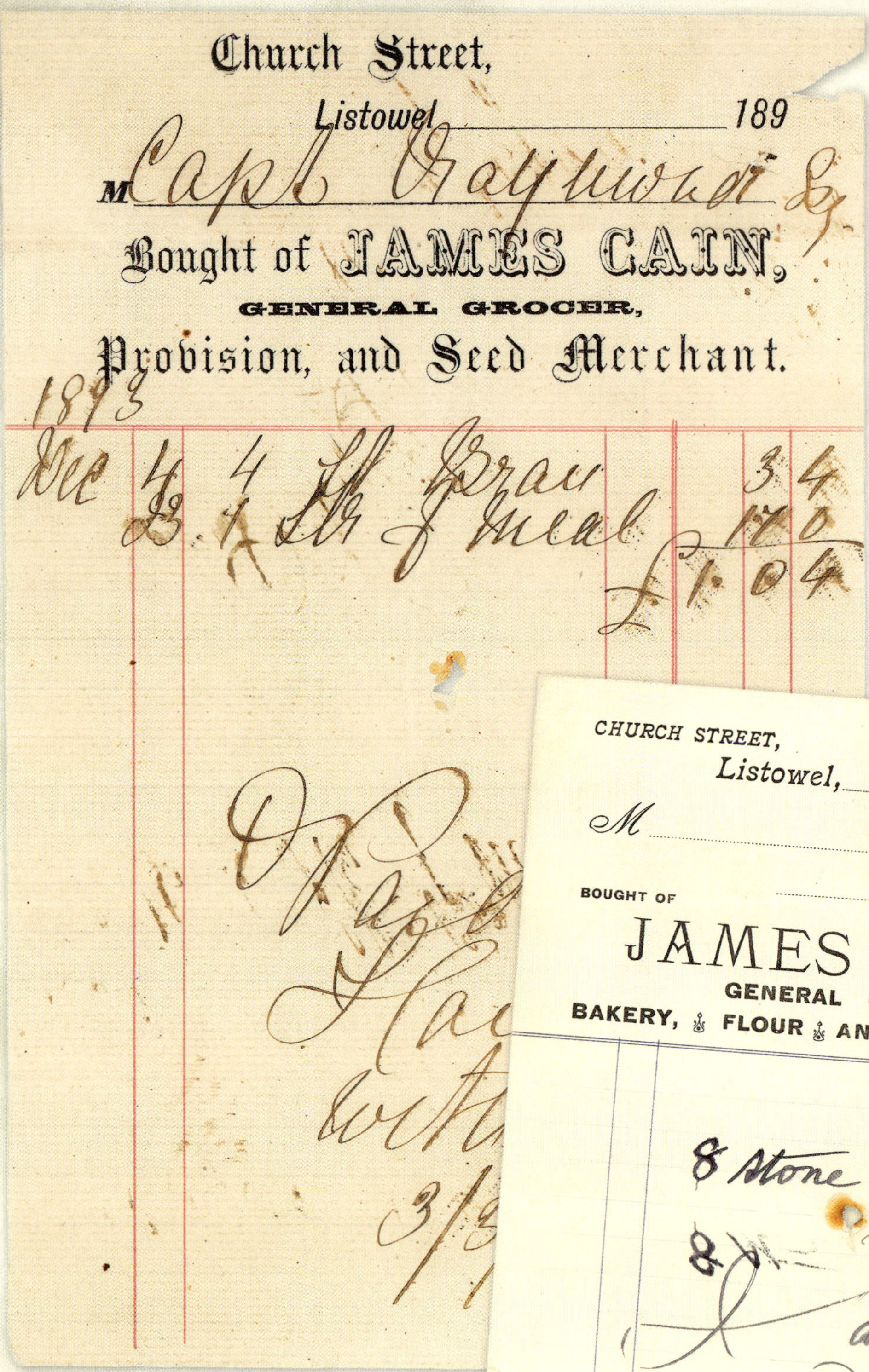

Church Street,

Listowel 189

M

Bought of JAMES CAIN,

GENERAL GROCER,

Provision, and Seed Merchant.

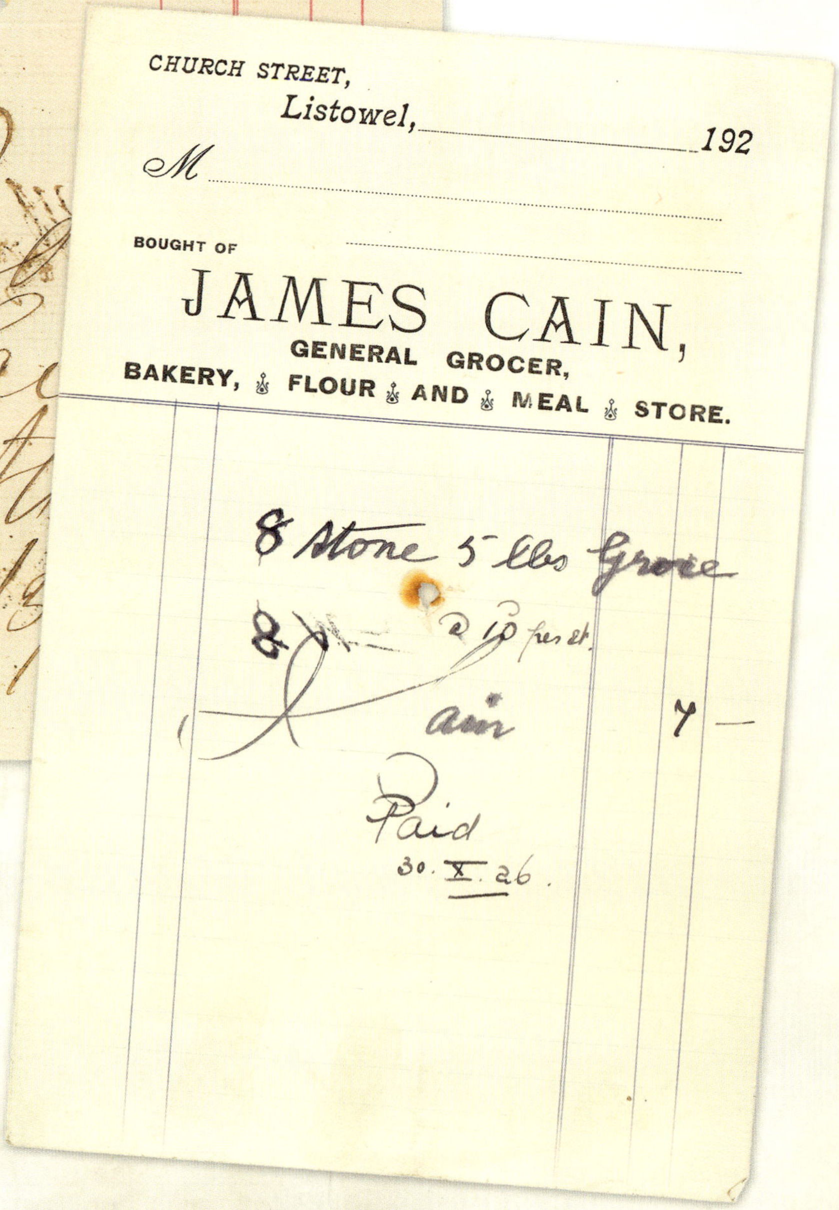

CHURCH STREET,

Listowel, 192

M

BOUGHT OF

JAMES CAIN,

GENERAL GROCER,

BAKERY, FLOUR AND MEAL STORE.

Paid

30. X. 26

58 Church Street

The Cain family, whose house was at the corner of Church Street and Forge Lane, were known to generations of Listowel people as Cains of the Bridewell. Edward Cain and his son James were long-time keepers of the Bridewell in the 1800s. The Bridewell would have been located in the area presently occupied by the Garda Station. After the Barracks was built for the RIC, the Cain family commenced a business at the corner house where they sold general groceries, flour and meal and also ran a bakery.

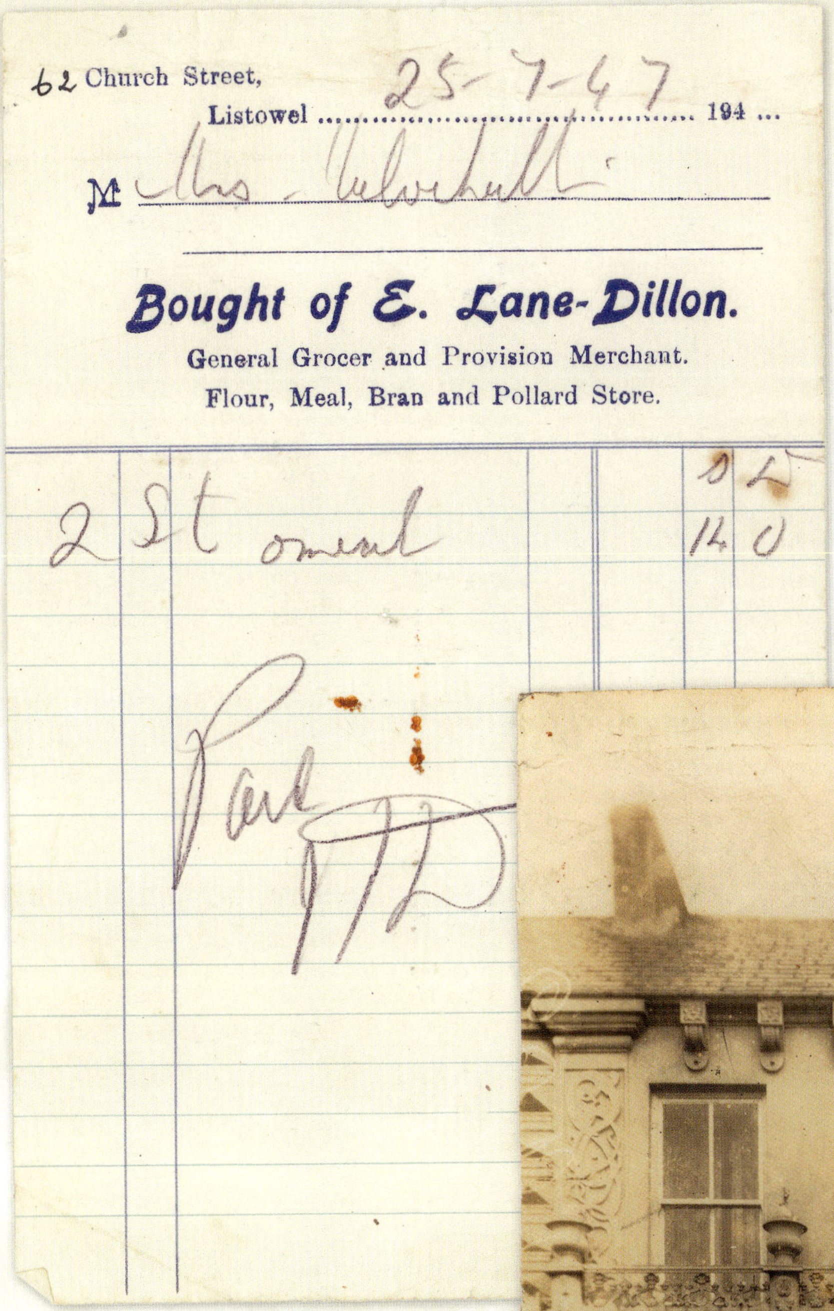
62 Church Street,
Listowel 25-7-47 194 ...
M Mrs

Bought of E. Lane-Dillon.
General Grocer and Provision Merchant.
Flour, Meal, Bran and Pollard Store.

2 St omeal 14 0

Paid

62 Church Street
Daniel Lane, native of Islandanny, Kilmorna, built his Church Street residence circa 1875. He had three daughters, Elizabeth, Ann and Mary Ann. Elizabeth inherited the house and she in turn left it to her niece, Eileen Lane from Kilmorna. Eileen married John J. Dillon who ran a grocery, flour and meal store. Liam Dillon, son of John J., ceased trading there in 1993.

Photo: Eileen (Lane) Dillon, on right, with a friend.

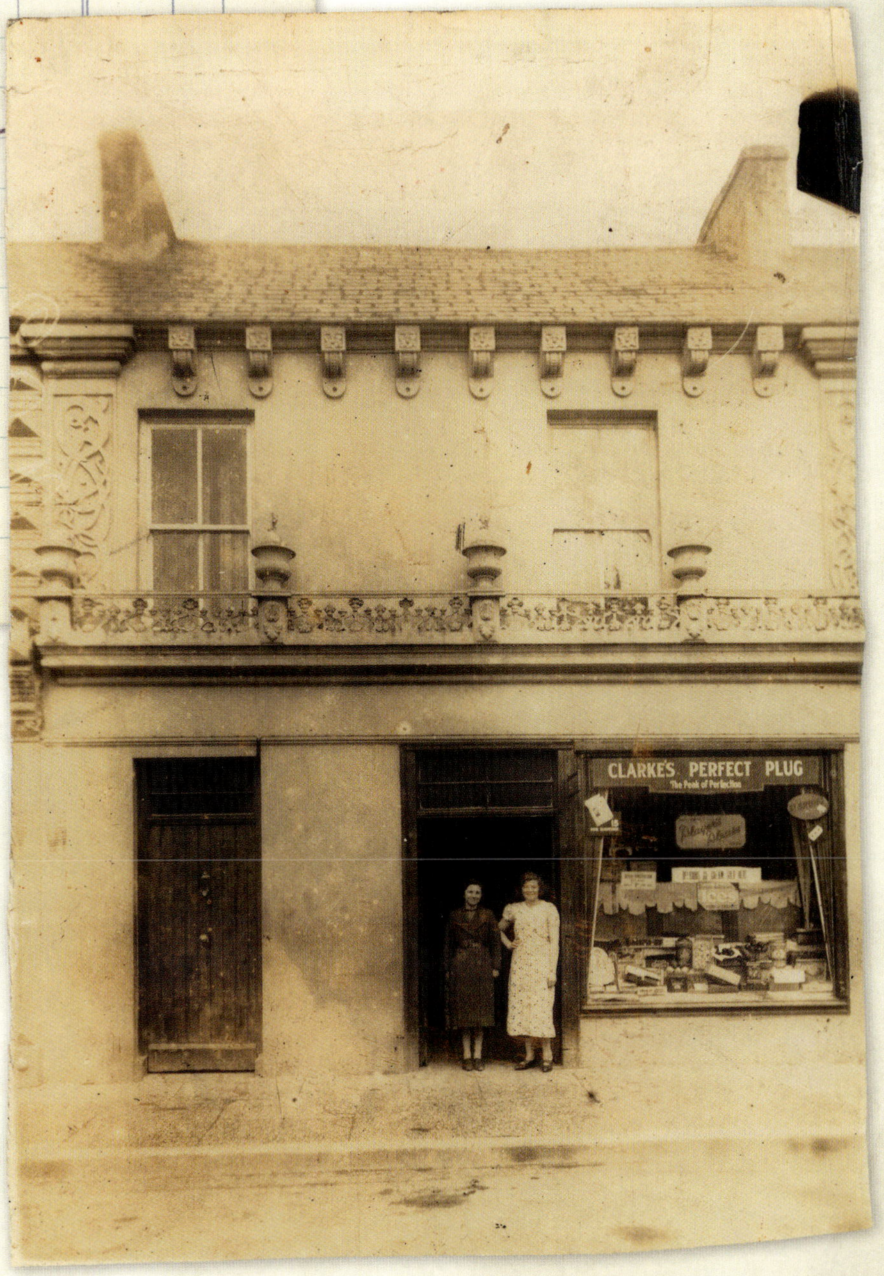

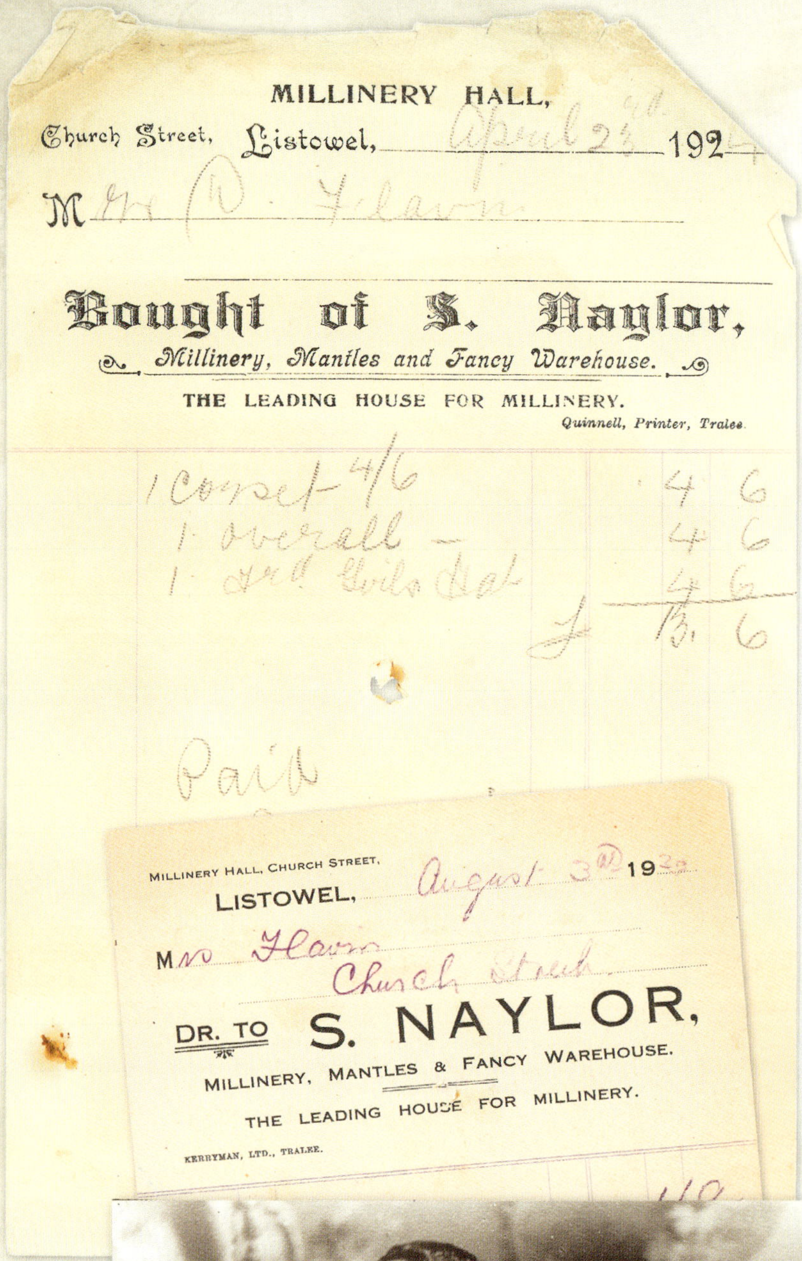

64 Church Street

Sarah Naylor (née Quaid) came from Dromcollogher, County Limerick. She married Henry Naylor, RIC officer, a Protestant from Hillsborough, County Down, on the first day of October 1898 at St. Michael's Church, Limerick. By 1906, they had moved to Listowel where Sarah opened the Millinery Hall, 64 Upper Church Street. Sarah was an uncompromising and resolute woman. Proof of this, if proof were needed, was that she married an RIC officer, a Protestant from Northern Ireland, at a time when Republican rumblings were rife and 'mixed marriages' were taboo. Henry was dishonorably discharged from the RIC because of his fondness for 'the water of life' (not the Biblical connotation). Sarah then had to rear a young family by the sweat of her brow, often working through the night, when her sons were being put through college. Her daughters had to stay at home, learning their craft, contributing to the meagre family coffers.

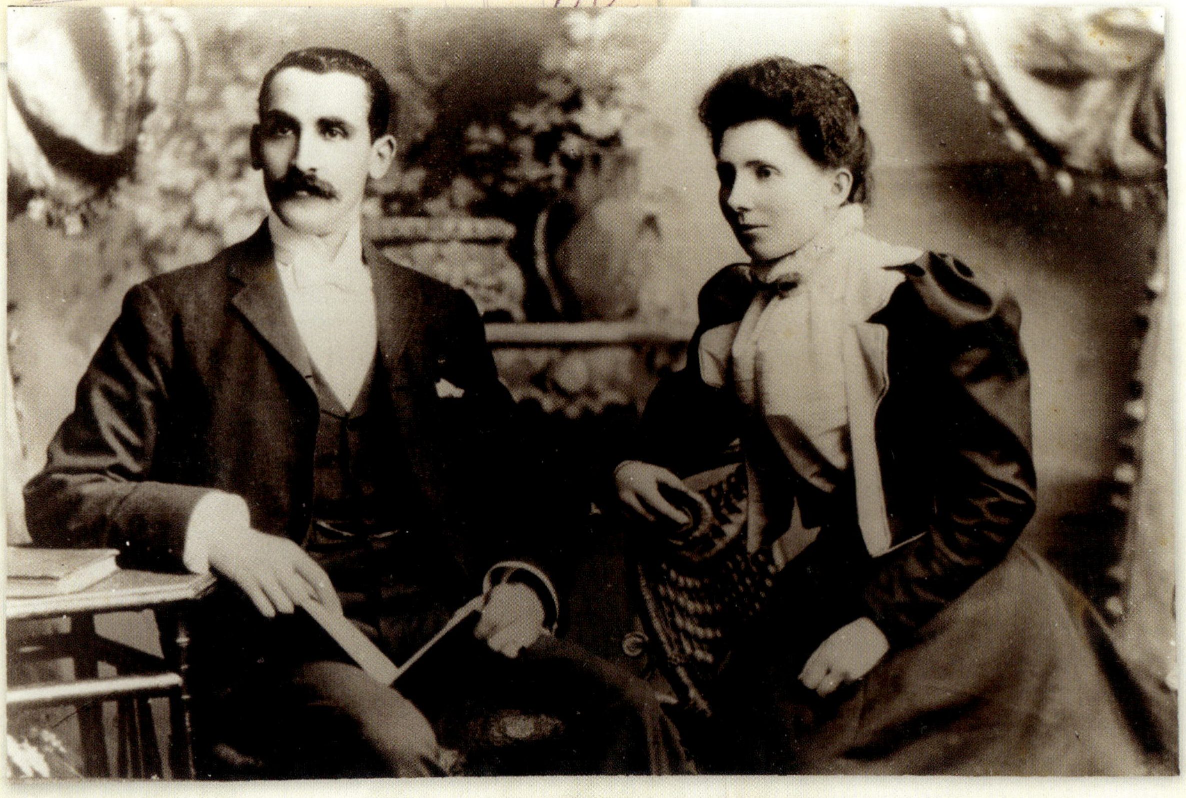

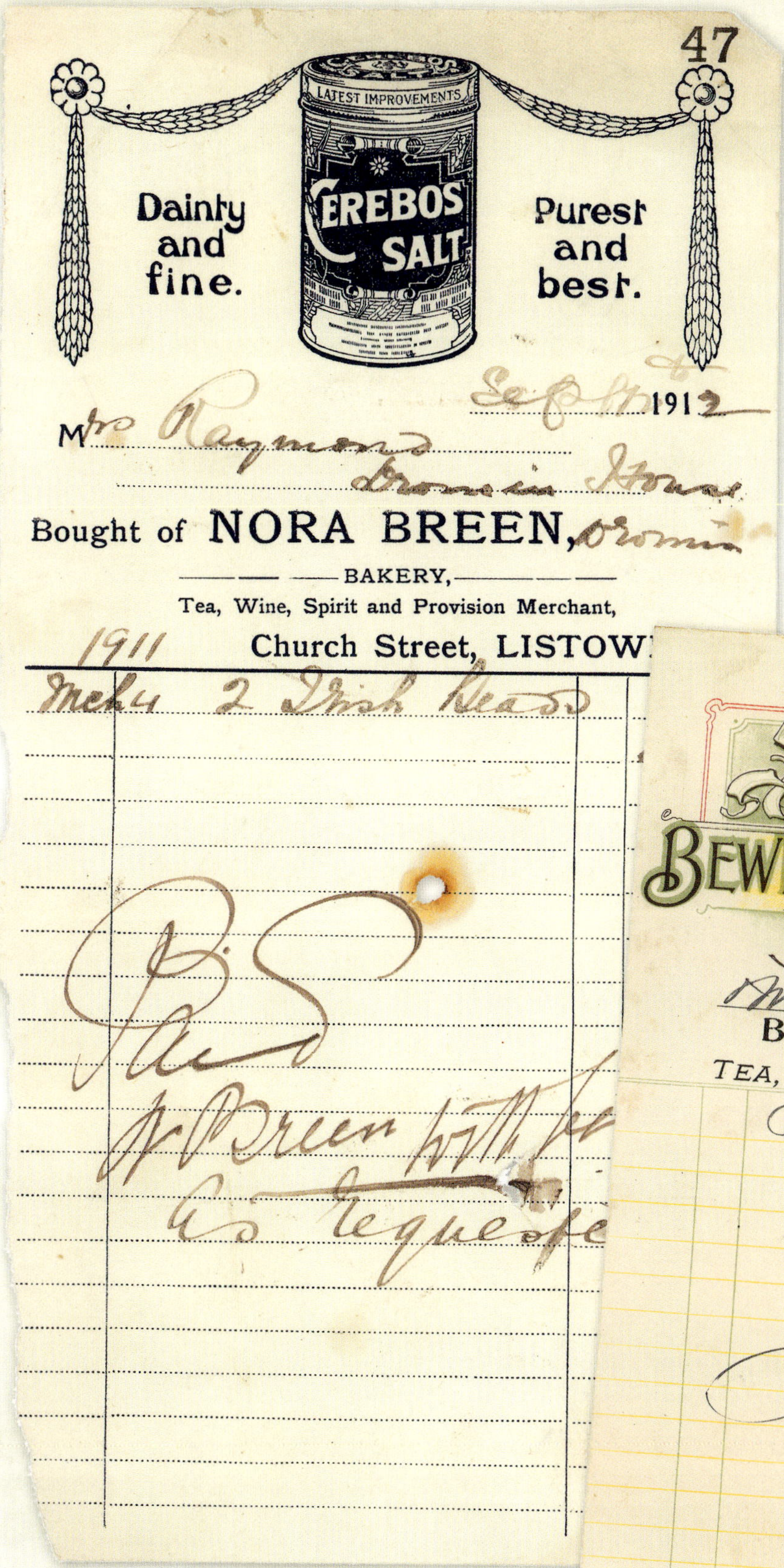
47

Dainty and fine.

LATEST IMPROVEMENTS

CEREBOS SALT

Purest and best.

191

M

Bought of NORA BREEN,

BAKERY,

Tea, Wine, Spirit and Provision Merchant,

Church Street, LISTOW

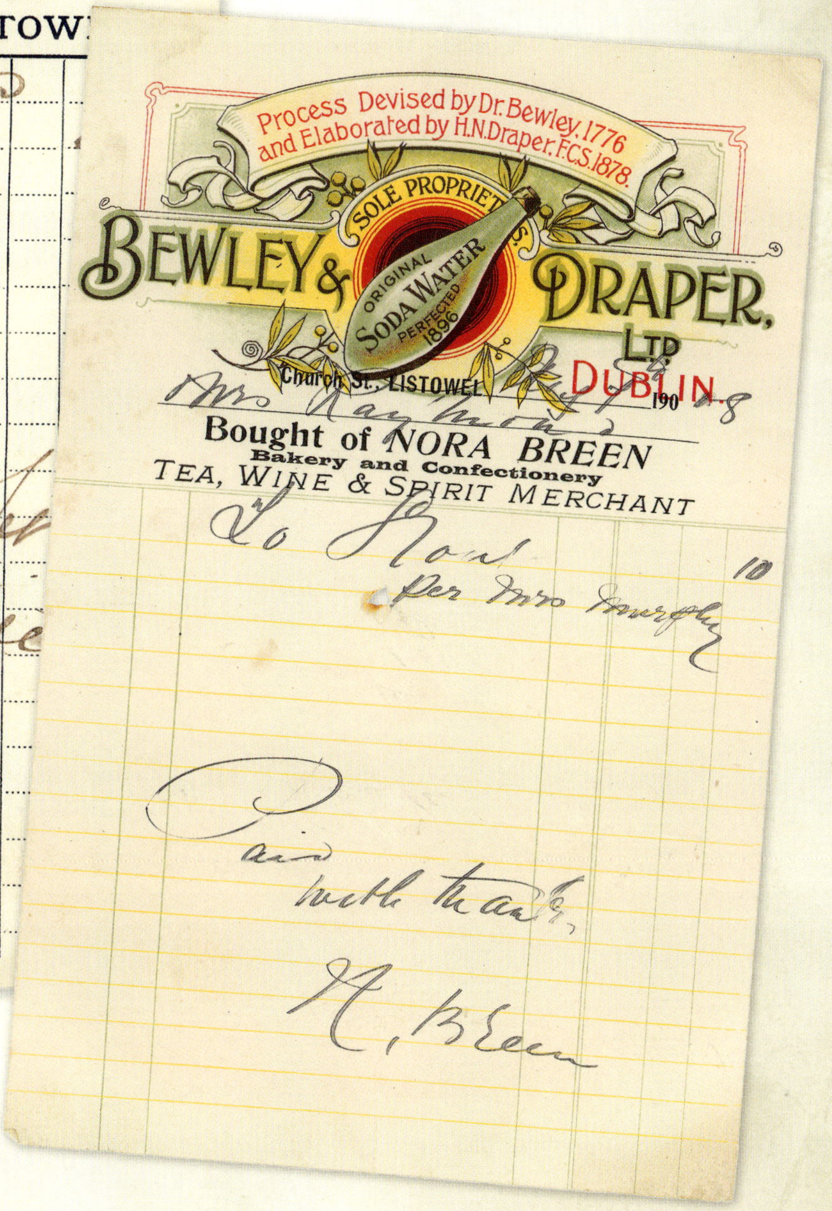
Process Devised by Dr. Bewley, 1776 and Elaborated by H.N. Draper. F.C.S. 1878.

BEWLEY & DRAPER, LTD DUBLIN.

SOLE PROPRIETORS

ORIGINAL SODA WATER PERFECTED 1896

Church St., LISTOWEL 190

Bought of NORA BREEN

Bakery and Confectionery

TEA, WINE & SPIRIT MERCHANT

66 Church Street

The Breen family had an extensive business in Upper Church Street. Nora ran the shop. Her husband Paddy was a teacher of the classics in nearby St. Michael's College. By coincidence, when the house was being sold in the 1940s, it was bought by another Breen, Michael, a Tipperary man, who had been living in Killarney. The premises is now 'The Grape & Grain' restaurant run by Paudie and Martina O'Connor.

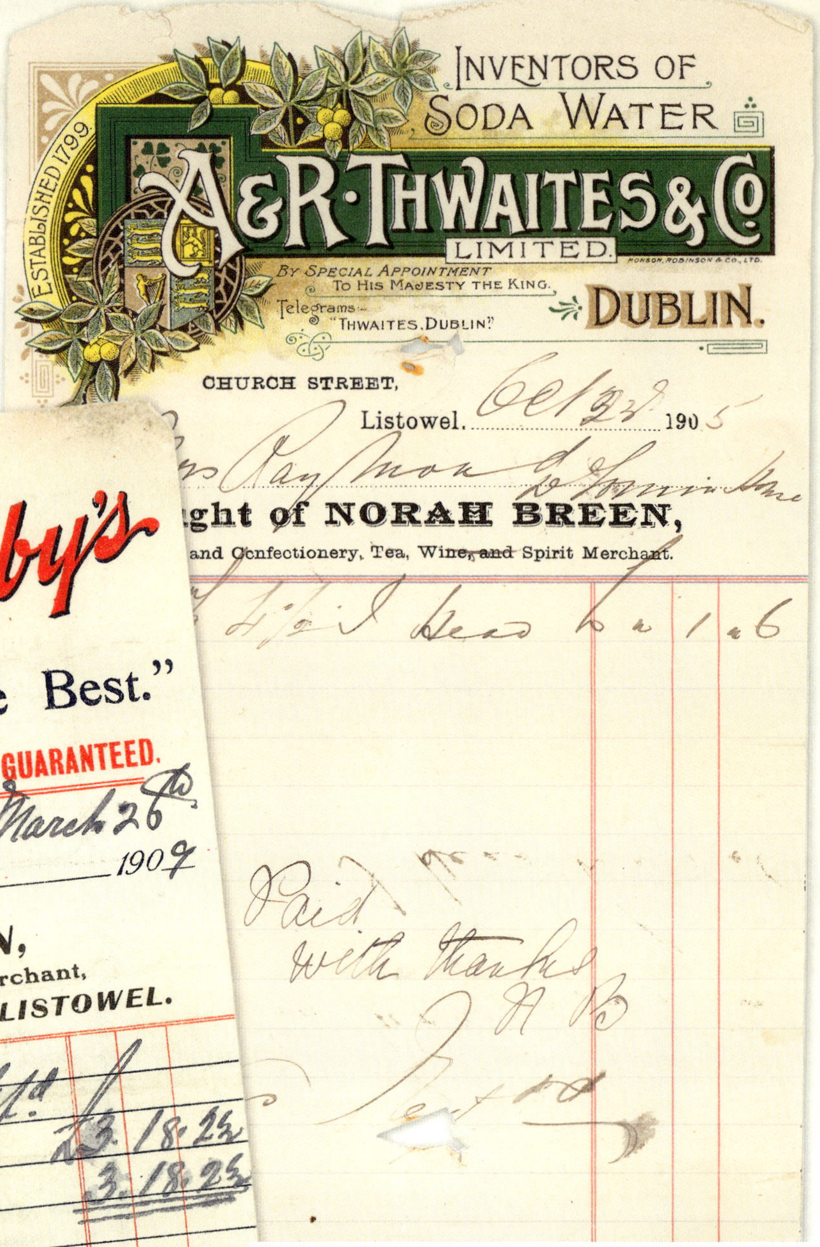

INVENTORS OF SODA WATER

ESTABLISHED 1799

A&R. THWAITES & Co LIMITED.

BY SPECIAL APPOINTMENT TO HIS MAJESTY THE KING.

Telegrams:- "THWAITES, DUBLIN."

DUBLIN.

CHURCH STREET,

Listowel. Oct 23rd 1905

...ght of NORAH BREEN,

...and Confectionery, Tea, Wine, and Spirit Merchant.

Paid with thanks

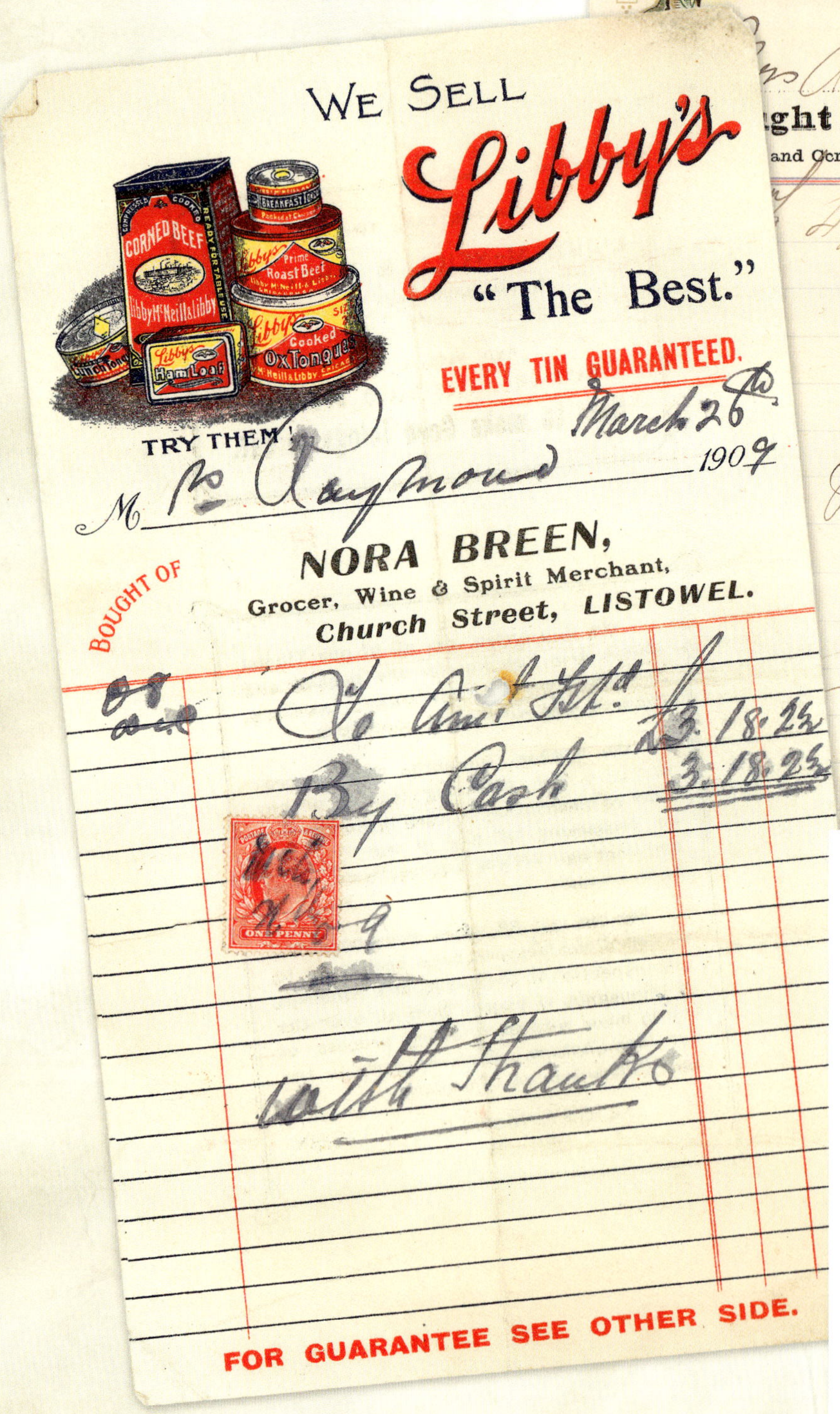

WE SELL Libby's "The Best."

EVERY TIN GUARANTEED.

TRY THEM!

March 26th 1907

M Raymond

BOUGHT OF

NORA BREEN,

Grocer, Wine & Spirit Merchant,

Church Street, LISTOWEL.

To Amt	£3. 18. 2½	
By Cash	3. 18. 2½	

with thanks

FOR GUARANTEE SEE OTHER SIDE.

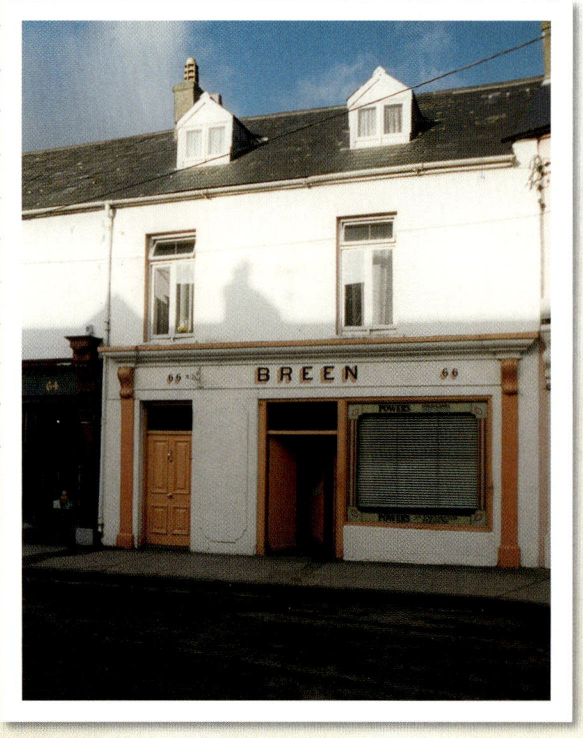

Photo: Frontage of Breen's circa 1950s.

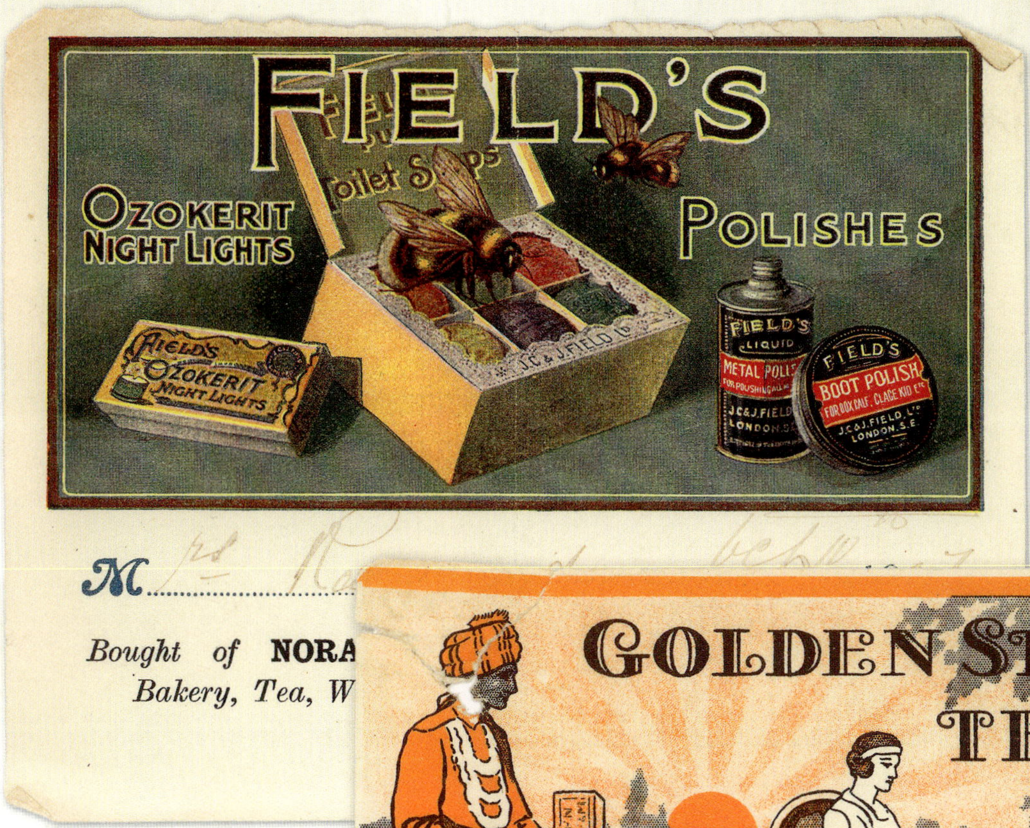
FIELD'S
Toilet Soaps
OZOKERIT NIGHT LIGHTS
POLISHES
FIELD'S OZOKERIT NIGHT LIGHTS
FIELD'S LIQUID METAL POLISH
FIELD'S BOOT POLISH
M
Bought of NORA
Bakery, Tea, W

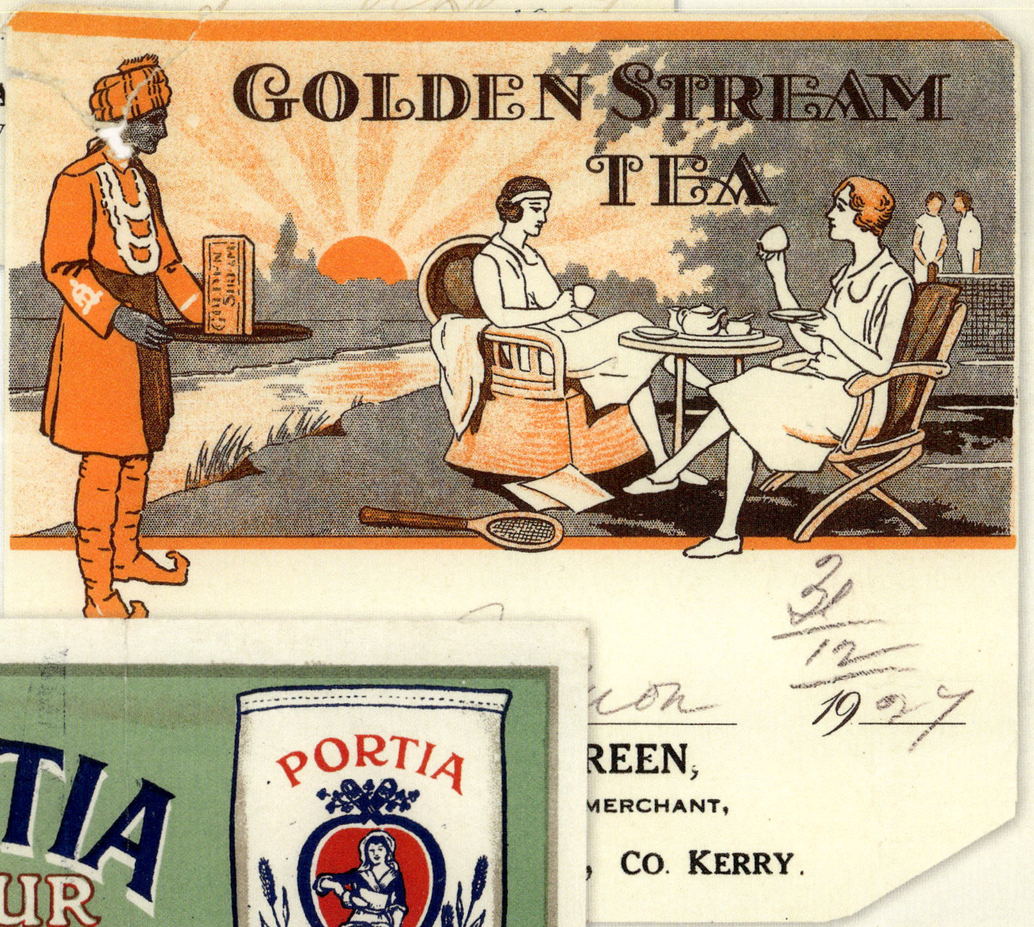
GOLDEN STREAM TEA
GOLDEN STREAM
REEN,
MERCHANT,
CO. KERRY.

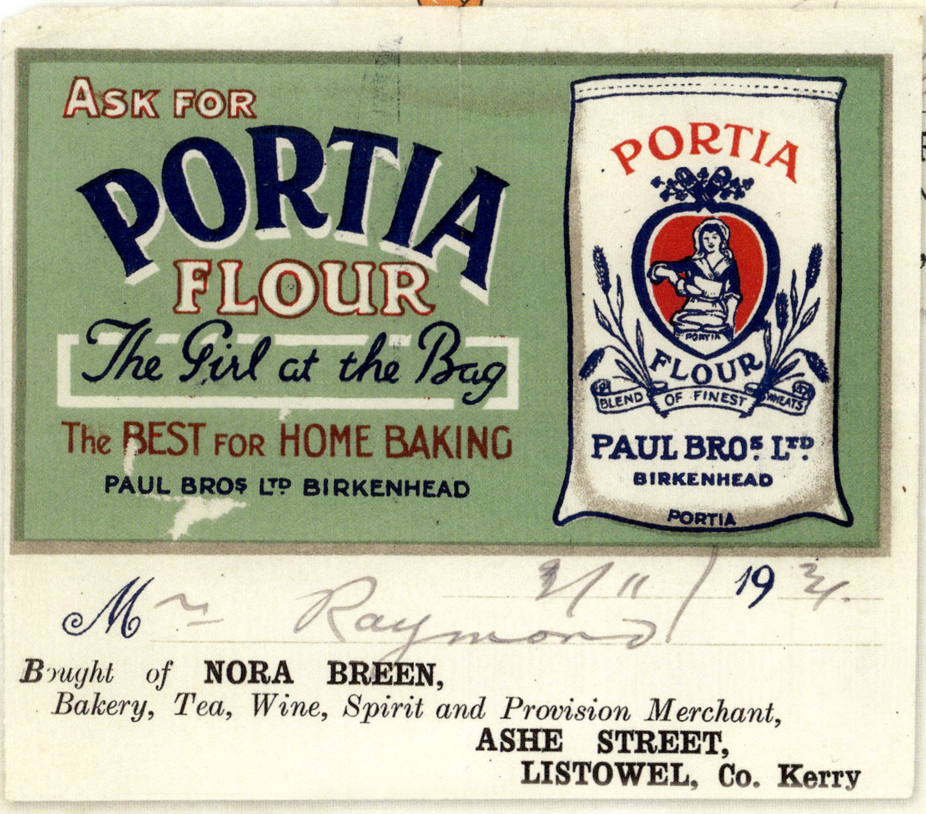
ASK FOR
PORTIA FLOUR
The Girl at the Bag
The BEST FOR HOME BAKING
PAUL BROS LTD BIRKENHEAD
PORTIA
FLOUR
BLEND OF FINEST WHEATS
PAUL BROS. LTD.
BIRKENHEAD
PORTIA
M
Bought of NORA BREEN,
Bakery, Tea, Wine, Spirit and Provision Merchant,
ASHE STREET,
LISTOWEL, Co. Kerry

68 Church Street

The Wilmots were a long-time Church Street family of blacksmiths. The letter presented was written to Mrs. Raymond, Dromin House, by Edward (Ned) Wilmot expressing concern for an unsettled debt. The basic English in his letter would have been in sharp contrast to the levels of academic achievement of his son Séamus who was to become Registrar of the National University of Ireland. The remains of the Wilmot forge are on the laneway at the rear of the house, off Forge Lane. A first cousin of Edward Wilmot, Joseph Wilmot, was also a blacksmith; his forge off the laneway at Upper Church Street is now incorporated into the grounds of Listowel Garden Centre.

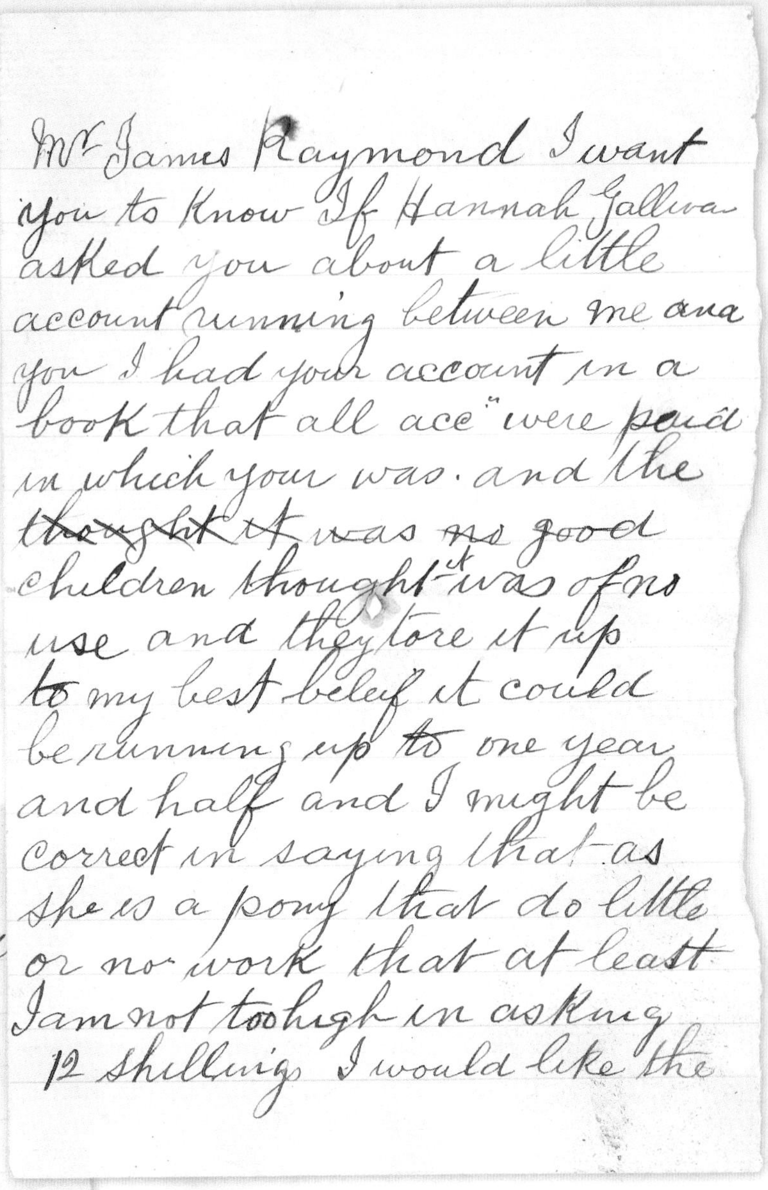

Mr James Raymond I want
you to Know If Hannah Gallivan
asked you about a little
account running between me and
you I had your account in a
book that all accts were paid
in which your was. and the
~~thought it~~ was ~~no good~~
children thought it was of no
use and they tore it up
to my best belief it could
be running up to one year
and half and I might be
correct in saying that as
she is a pony that do little
or no work that at least
I am not too high in asking
12 shillings I would like the

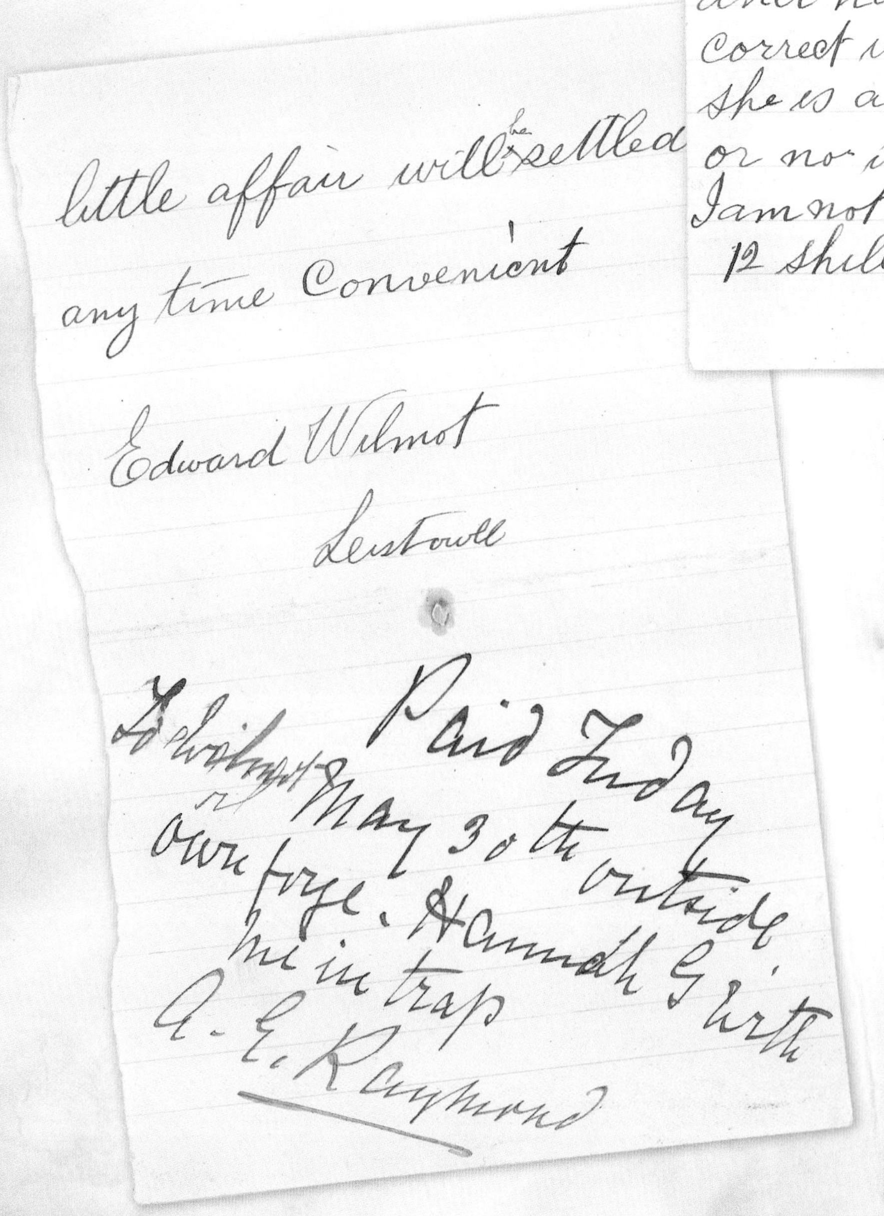

little affair will be settled
any time Convenient

Edward Wilmot
Listowell

[illegible] Paid Friday
May 30th outside
our forge. Hannah G[illegible]
in trap
A. E. Raymond

Photo top: Conferring of an Honorary Degree to President John F. Kennedy in 1963, Iveagh House, Dublin. *Front:* President John F. Kennedy, President UCD Michael Tierney, Chancellor NUI Eamon De Valera, Registrar NUI Dr. Séamus Wilmot. Back: Leader of the Labour Party Brendan Corish TD, Seán McEntee TD, Taoiseach Seán Lemass TD, John Kelly TD, Foreign Minister Frank Aiken TD.

Photo bottom: The Wilmot family in 1943. Dr. Séamus Wilmot and his wife May with family, from left, Conal, Ronan, Ann and Brendan.

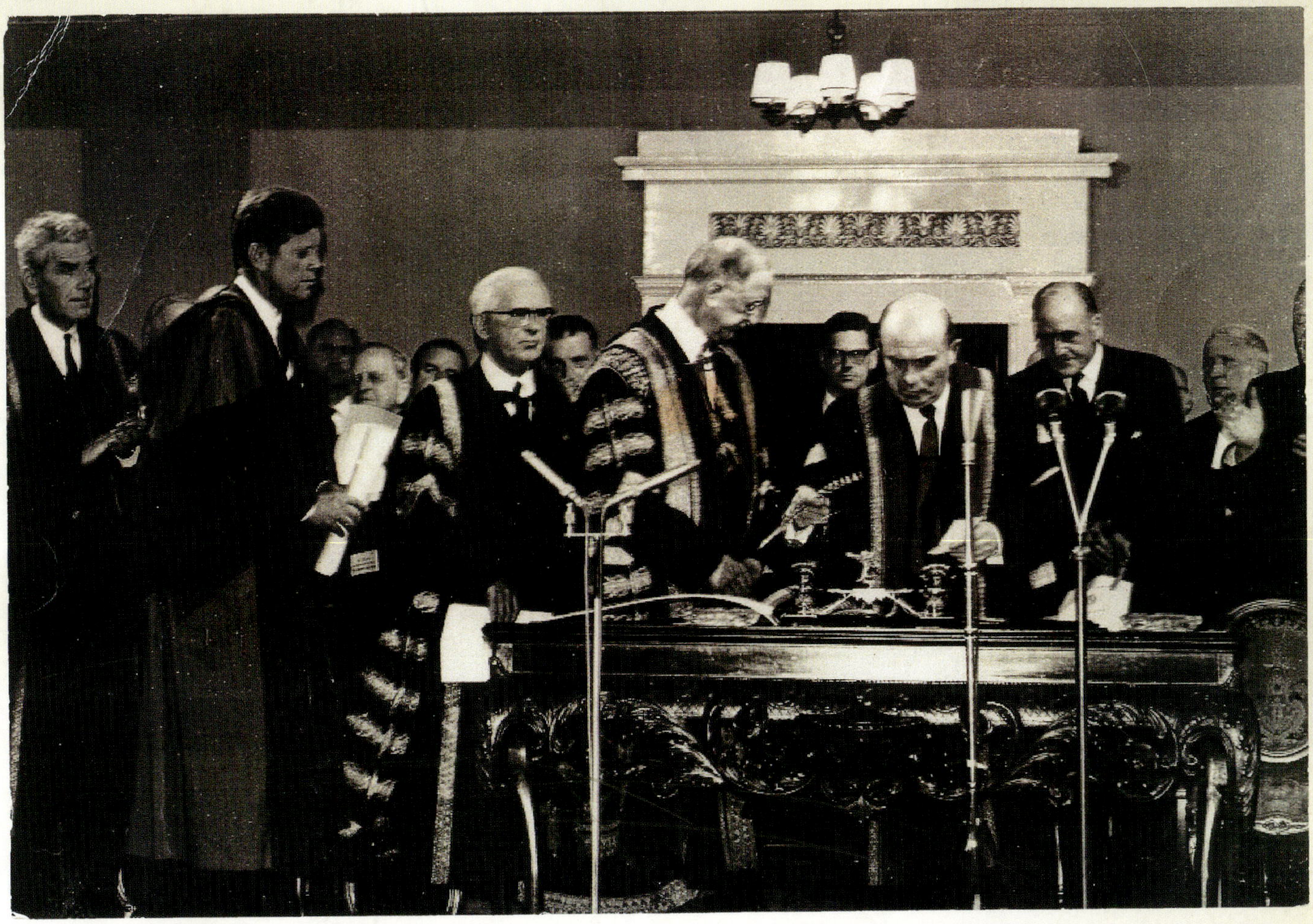

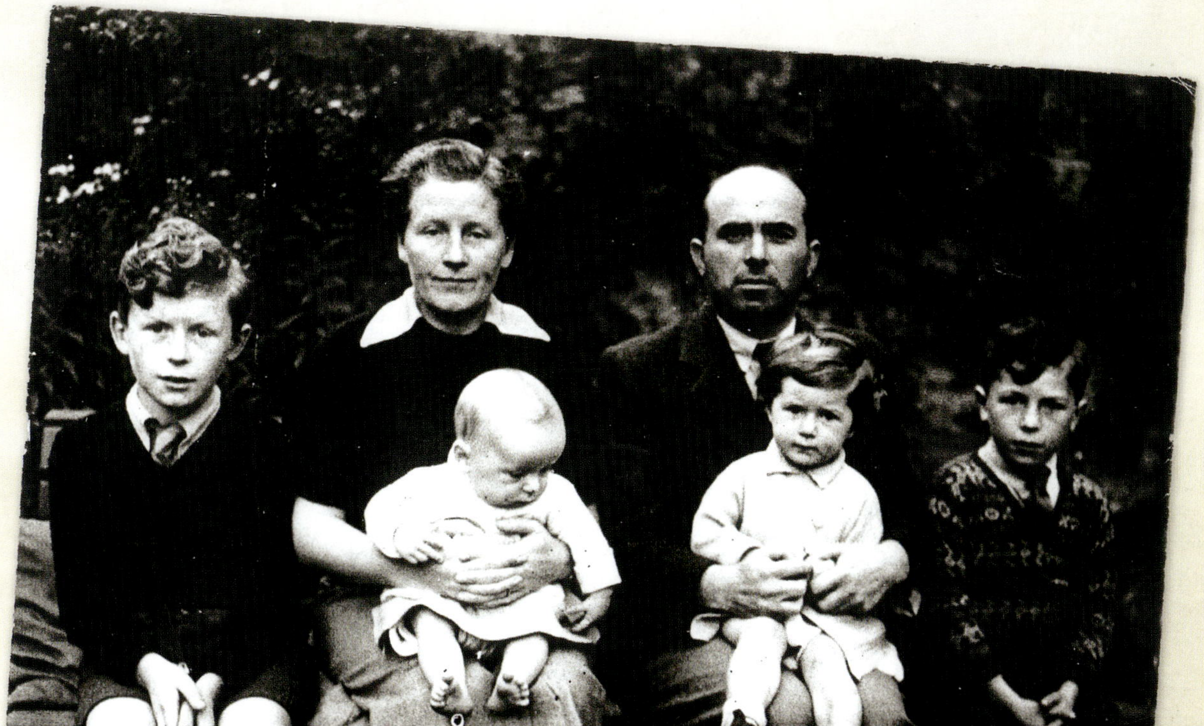

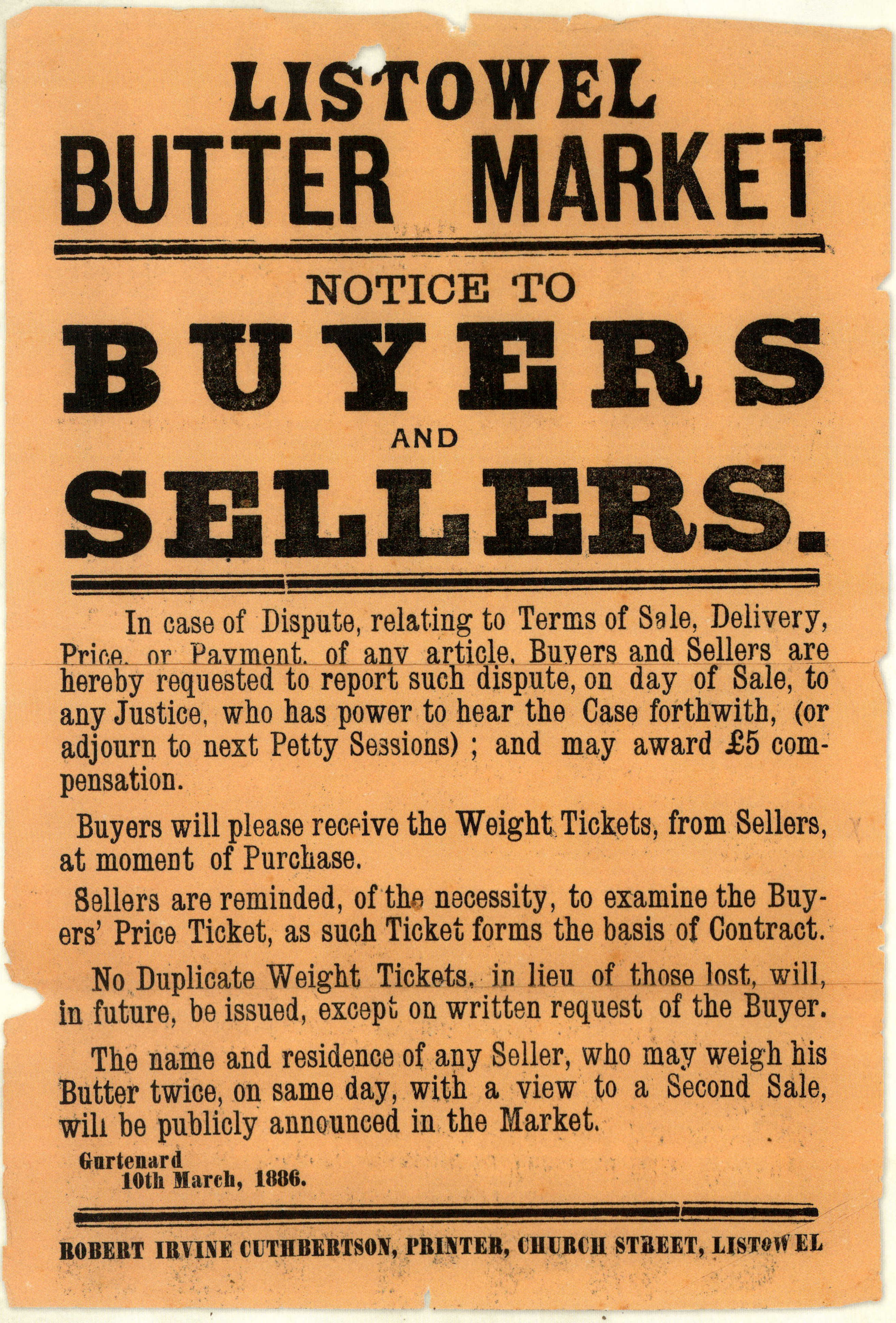

LISTOWEL
BUTTER MARKET

NOTICE TO

BUYERS
AND
SELLERS.

In case of Dispute, relating to Terms of Sale, Delivery, Price, or Payment, of any article, Buyers and Sellers are hereby requested to report such dispute, on day of Sale, to any Justice, who has power to hear the Case forthwith, (or adjourn to next Petty Sessions) ; and may award £5 compensation.

Buyers will please receive the Weight Tickets, from Sellers, at moment of Purchase.

Sellers are reminded, of the necessity, to examine the Buyers' Price Ticket, as such Ticket forms the basis of Contract.

No Duplicate Weight Tickets, in lieu of those lost, will, in future, be issued, except on written request of the Buyer.

The name and residence of any Seller, who may weigh his Butter twice, on same day, with a view to a Second Sale, will be publicly announced in the Market.

Gurtenard
10th March, 1886.

ROBERT IRVINE CUTHBERTSON, PRINTER, CHURCH STREET, LISTOWEL

Cuthbertson Poster 1886
Poster of Listowel Butter Market of 1886. This is the only known poster which signifies that the Cuthbertson family had a business in Church Street. The Cuthbertsons were tenants of the Wilmot family and operated their print shop out of the front room of that house. They opened a new printing works when they moved to William Street in the late 1880s. Here they remained until their business closed in 1960.

70 Church Street
The Hennessys ran a public house, grocery and provision store at the turn of the century. They also had a cooperage at the rear of the business. They retired from the business and took up farming in Lisselton in the early 1900s. The business was afterwards rented to Mary Namock and later still to John R. Walsh from Ballyhahill, County Limerick, who was creamery manager of both Ballylongford and Moyvane Creameries. Due to his active involvement in Sinn Féin affairs, Walsh's home at No. 70 Church Street was one of those targeted for burning in 1921. The house was subsequently bought by Joseph, son of John R., in the 1940s.

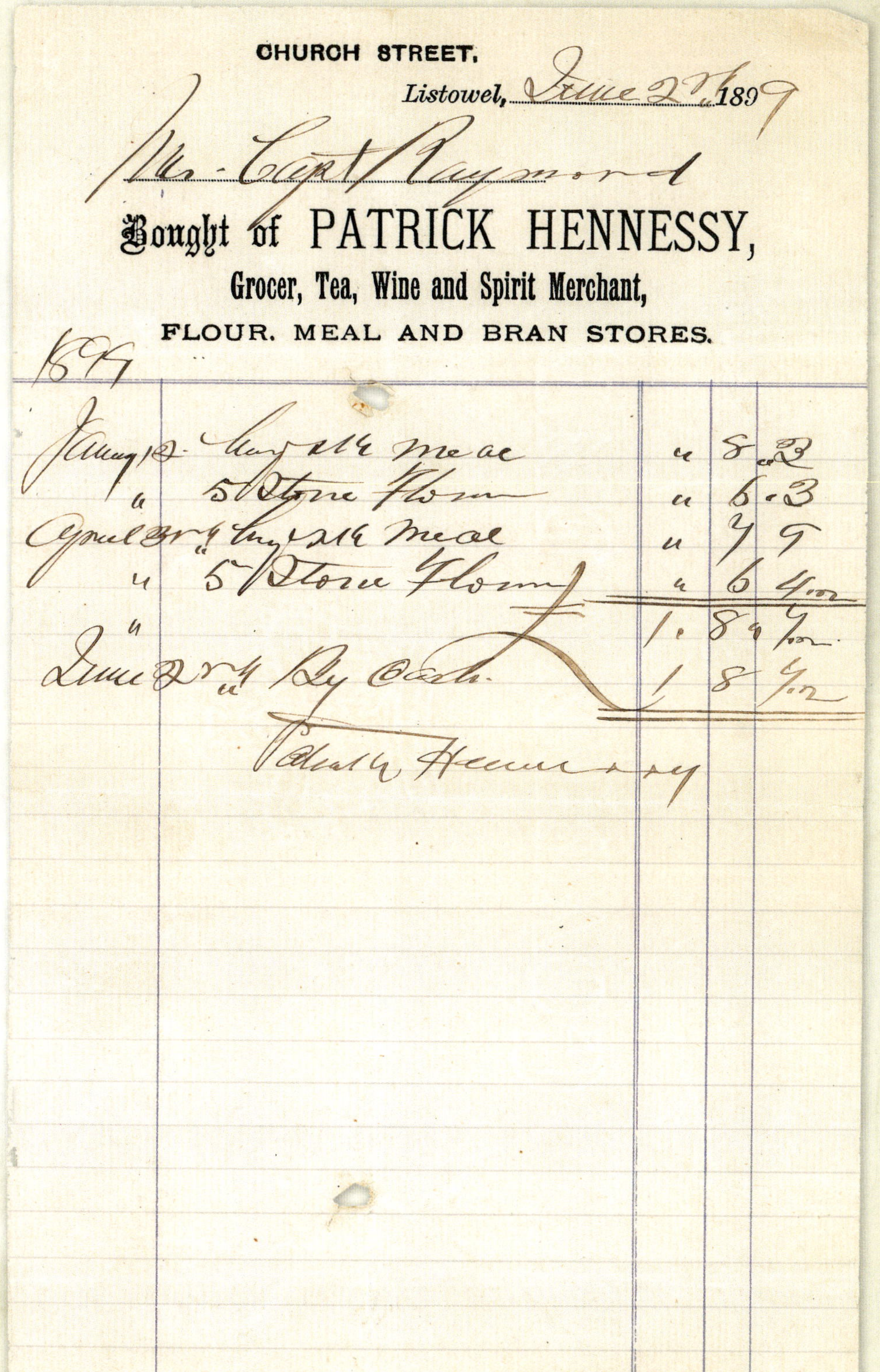
CHURCH STREET,
Listowel, June 27th 1899
Mr Capt Raymond
Bought of PATRICK HENNESSY,
Grocer, Tea, Wine and Spirit Merchant,
FLOUR, MEAL AND BRAN STORES.

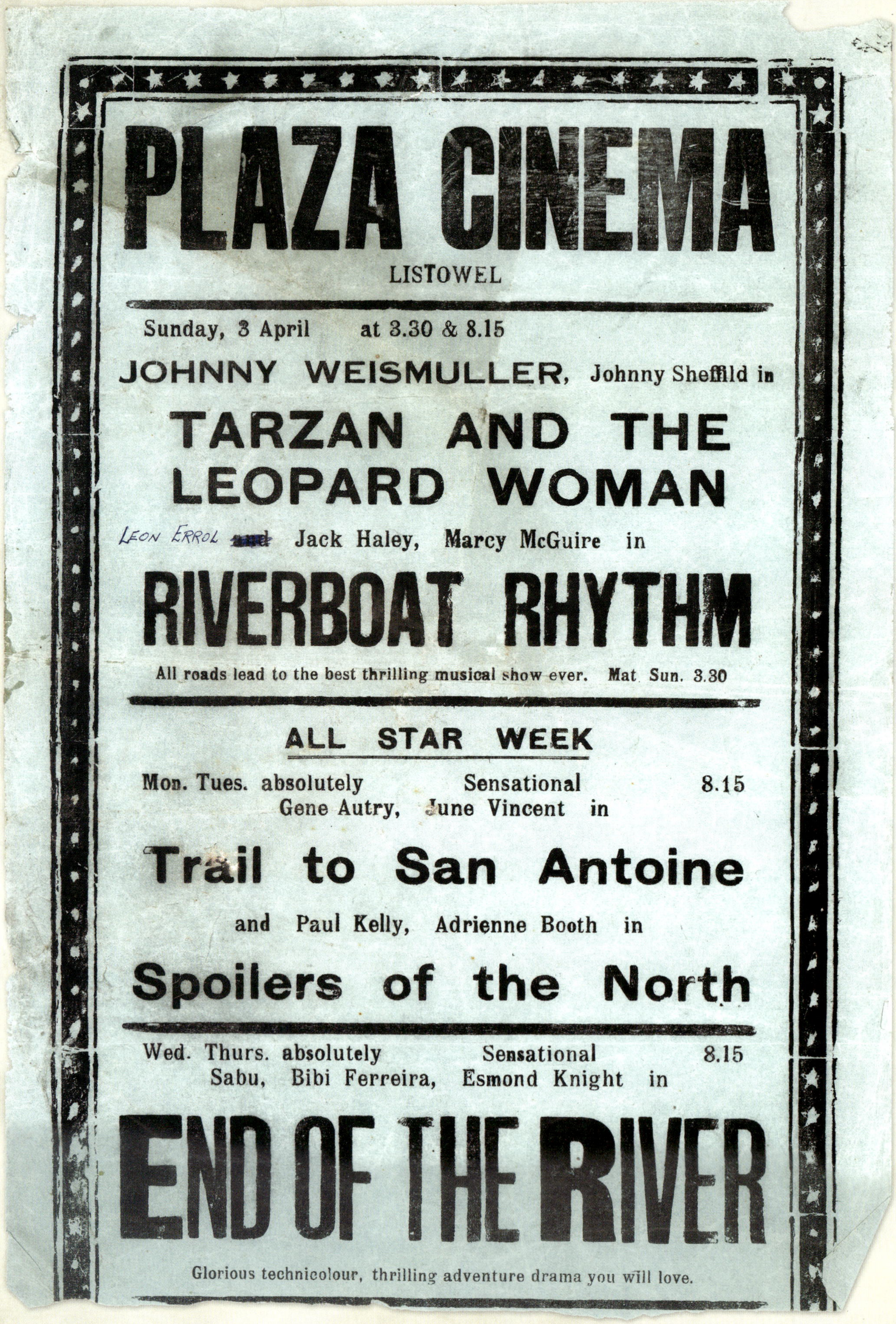
PLAZA CINEMA
LISTOWEL
Sunday, 3 April at 3.30 & 8.15
JOHNNY WEISMULLER, Johnny Sheffild in
TARZAN AND THE LEOPARD WOMAN
LEON ERROL and Jack Haley, Marcy McGuire in
RIVERBOAT RHYTHM
All roads lead to the best thrilling musical show ever. Mat Sun. 3.30
ALL STAR WEEK
Mon. Tues. absolutely Sensational 8.15
Gene Autry, June Vincent in
Trail to San Antoine
and Paul Kelly, Adrienne Booth in
Spoilers of the North
Wed. Thurs. absolutely Sensational 8.15
Sabu, Bibi Ferreira, Esmond Knight in
END OF THE RIVER
Glorious technicolour, thrilling adventure drama you will love.

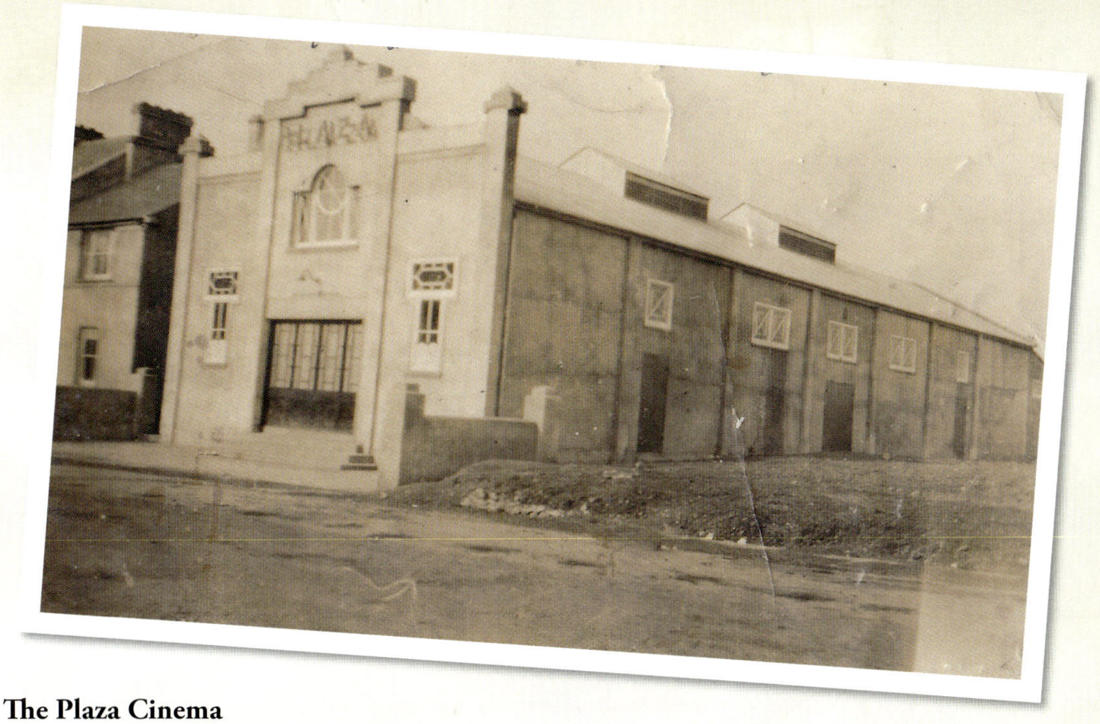

The Plaza Cinema

The Plaza Cinema was built for Trevor Chute by Jackie Hannon of the Bridge Road in the late 1930s. There had been two previous cinemas in Listowel prior to this. One was situated off Tay Lane and the other was Pa Cooney's, which was located in an annex to Michael Quill's in Church Street. Many Listowel people had memories of attending and watching silent movies at Cooney's where the accompanying music was performed by Gertie O'Connor, pianist, from Main Street and her future husband, Fred Mann, who played the violin.

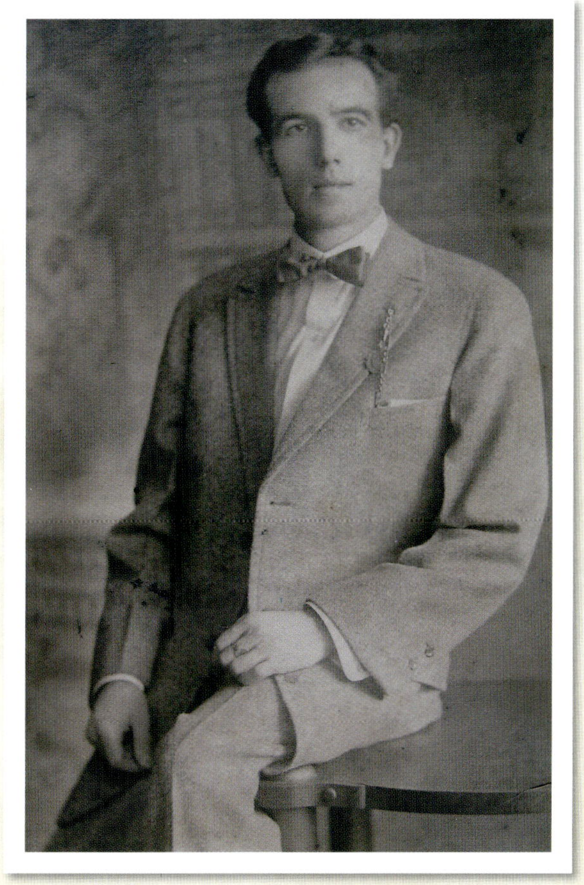

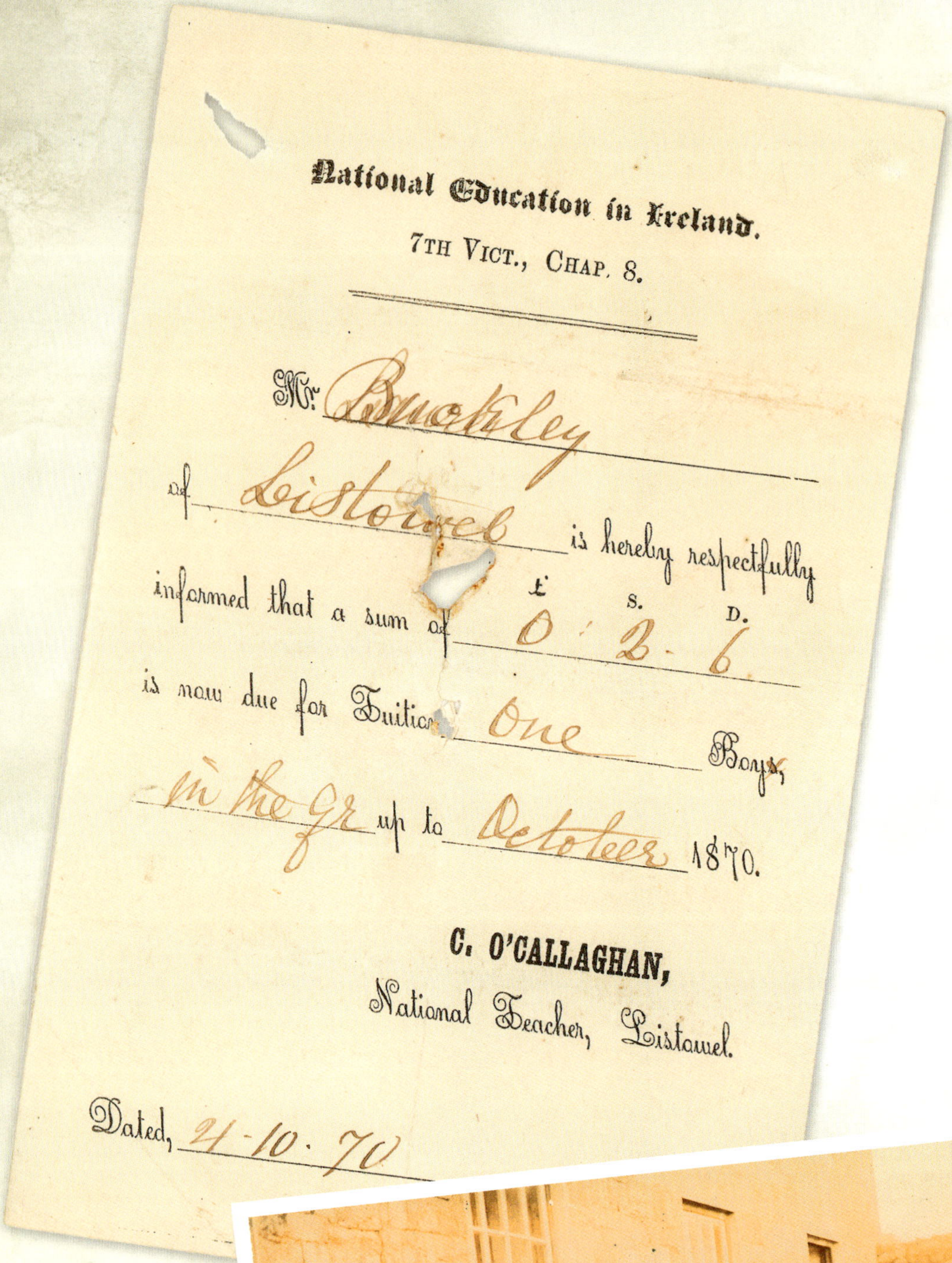
National Education in Ireland.

7TH VICT., CHAP. 8.

Mr. Buckley

of Listowel is hereby respectfully

informed that a sum of £ 0 : s. 2 : D. 6

is now due for Tuition One Boys,

in the Qr up to October 1870.

C. O'CALLAGHAN,

National Teacher, Listowel.

Dated, 21-10-70

Boys' National School
This reminder, from 1870, to Mr. Buckley, from Callaghan O'Callaghan, National Teacher, Listowel for the sum of half a crown was for the tuition of one boy in the quarter up to October. In those days, up until 1892, National School education had to be paid for.

Below: This sepia image may be the earliest remaining photo of a boys' national school in Listowel and was taken in the early 1900s.

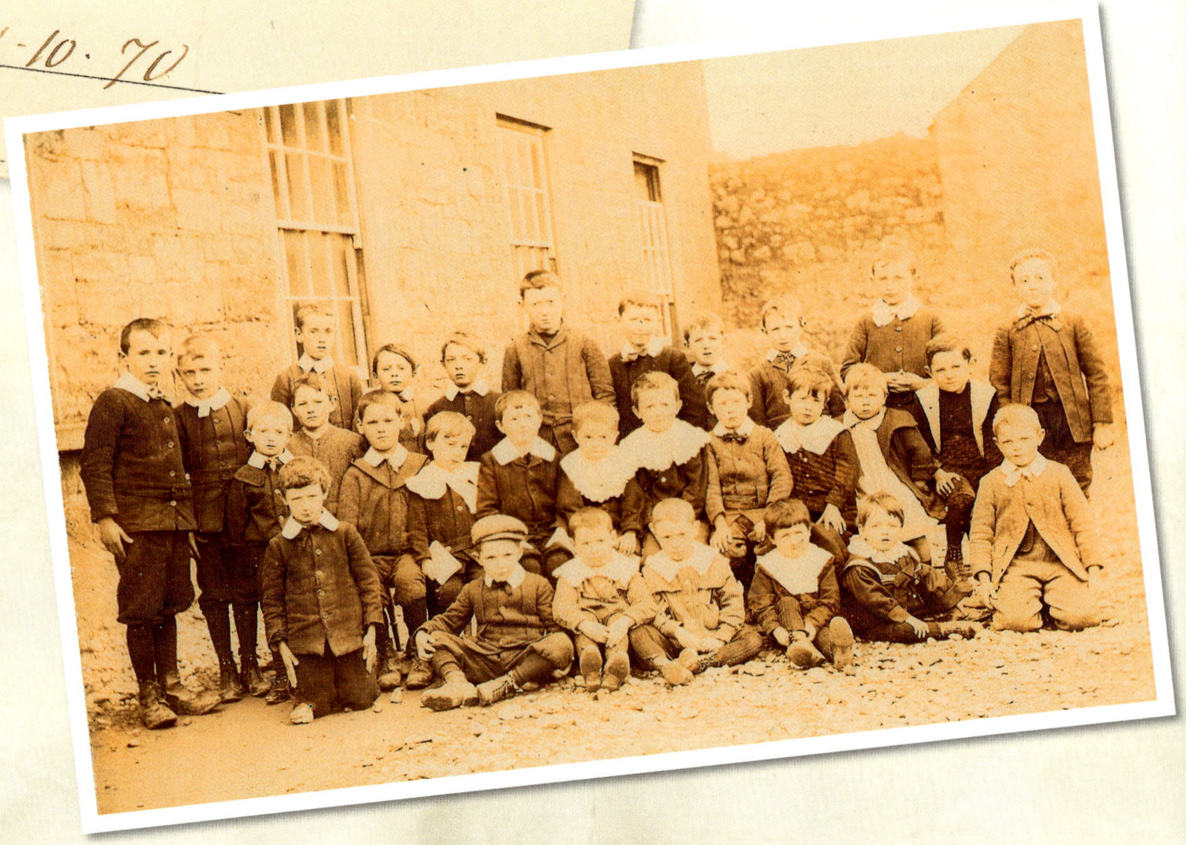

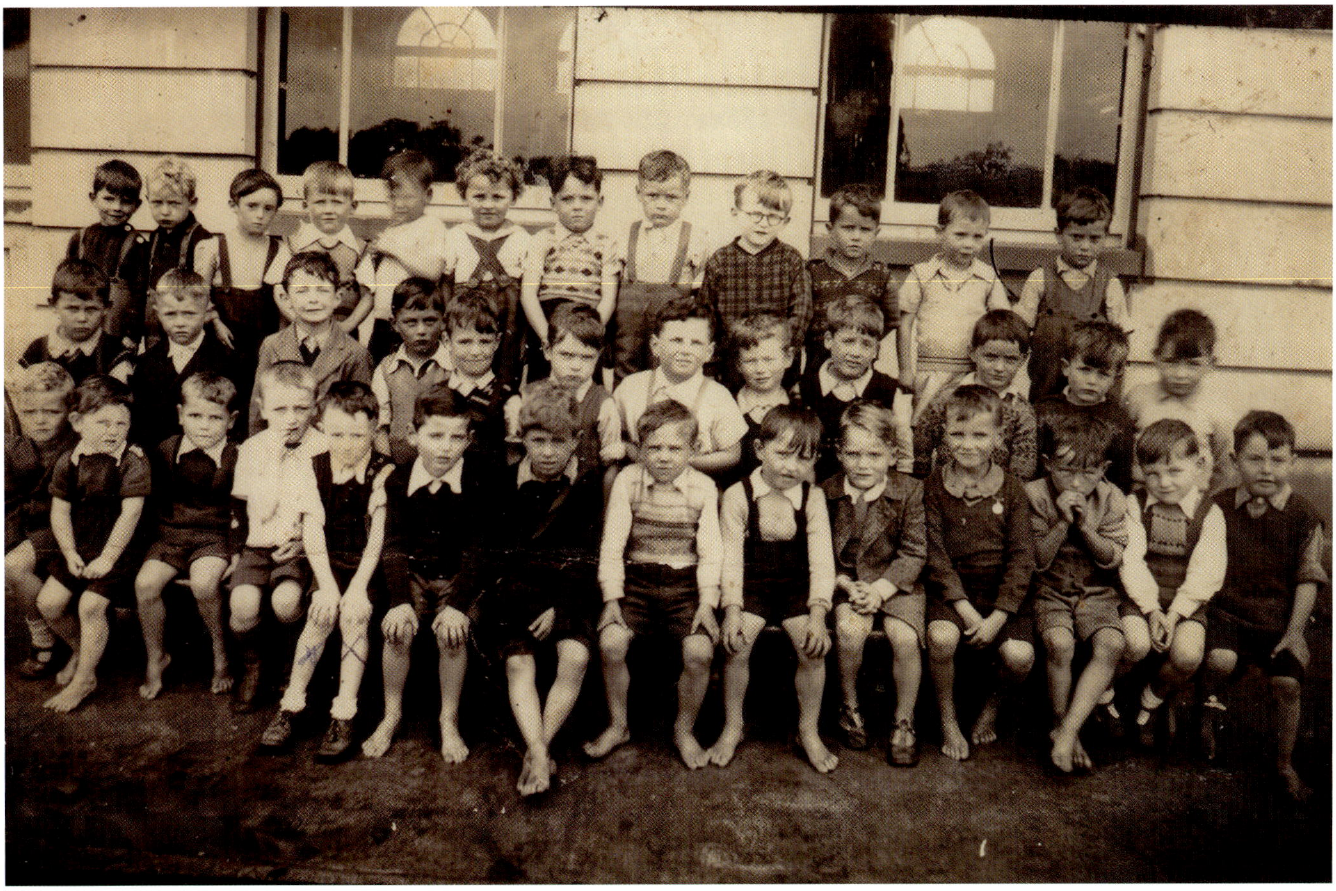

Above: This photo was taken outside the Carnegie Library. It is of a 'babies' class taught by Mrs Scanlon circa 1949/1950.

Front (l to r): Unknown, Pat Baynam, Michael Flaherty, Patsy Lyons, Junior Prendeville, John Fitzgerald, Liam Nolan, Pat Galvin, Tom Roche, Johnny Horgan, Danny Carroll, Danny Murphy, Tony Stack, Liam Healy.

Middle (l to r): Teddy Moloney, Tony Barrett, Paddy Fitzgibbon, Ml (Mickeen) Sheehy, Sean Leahy, Xavier McAuliffe, Charlie Hanlon, Johnny Guerin, Vincent Carmody, Vincent Savage, Pat Browne, Patsy Browne.

Back row (l to r): Unknown, Unknown, Roly Chute, PJ O'Connor, Unknown, Paddy Moloney, Alf Neville, Dominic Stack, Terence Stack, Tommy Behan, Paddy Keane, Eddie Flaherty.

ENTRY FORM.

NORTH KERRY AGRICULTURAL & INDUSTRIAL SOCIETY.

Show will be held Thursday June 3rd, 1926

ENTRIES CLOSE WITH SECRETARY ON SATURDAY, MAY 22nd. 1926

No of Class in Prize List.................. Name of animal..

Colour.......................... Date of Birth.................................... Tattoo Marks (if any)..................

Pedigree ____

____

____

____

____

If Exhibit is a Dairy Shorthorn Bull or Heifer out of a Registered Cow

State also : Registered No. of Dam.................... Yield of milk on which Dam was Registered............ lbs. in .... weeks. Butterfat yield (percentages or lbs) .... Age of Cow at commencement of this milking period.......... years. Subsequent yield accepted for entry in Department's Register ....lbs in............ weeks. Age of Cow at commencement of this subsequent period.............. years No of G. Dam.................. Yield of G Dam if Registered.............. lbs in..........weeks Butterfat........

If Sire is a Registered Dairy Bull, give following particulars :—

No. of Dam of Sire.................... Milk yield on which Dam of Sire was registered.................. lbs. in ....weeks Butterfat................... Age of Cow at commencement of period ....years Subsequent yield of Dam of Sire accepted for entry in Department's Register.................. lbs. in .... weeks Butterfat.................... Age of Cow at commencement of this period....................years.

If Exhibit is a Registered Shorthorn Cow, state the following :—

Registered No....................Yield on which registered.................. lbs. in............weeks. Butterfat .... Age of Cow at commencement of period.............. years. Subsequent yield accepted for entry in Department's register.................... lbs in .... weeks. Age of cow at commencement of this period..............years. Date of last calving..

Very Important—This Entry Form must be accurately and fully filled in otherwise the Department will disqualify the Exhibit.

The contents of this certificate are true and I hereby agree to conform to the Rules and Regulations of the North Kerry Agricultural and Industrial Society.

Signature of Exhibitor or his Agent ______________________________

Dated ______________________ 1926

Amount of Entry Fee enclosed £ : s d Subscription £ : s d

No Entry accepted unless accompanied by Fee.

See Prize List for Particulars of Entry Fee and Special Conditions Governing Registered Dairy Shorthorn classes.

This Certificate of Entry, accurately filled in every particular and signed by Exhibitor or his Agent must be lodged on or before May 22nd, 1926 with

MICHAEL GRIFFIN, *Secretary, LISTOWEL*

N.B.—1. In the Registered Dairy Shorthorn Classes the above information must be given correctly.
2. In the Butter and Egg Classes you need state only number of Class with signature of Exhibitor

Cuthbertson, Printer, Listowel.

The North Kerry Agricultural and Industrial Society First Annual Show
This show was held on Tuesday, 24th June 1913. The annual show, which was held in the Sportsfield, was equal to a day of the races for the local economy. There was show jumping, all types of animal displays and competitions. Cake and home-made bread judging took place in the adjacent St. Michael's College. The show continued to be held on various dates in June most years after that. On the night of the show a dance would be held. The monies from this would enable the committee to clear debts and start anew the following year. However, in the mid 1950s, due to falling attendances and a lack of general interest, allied with a dismal attendance at the show dance, the committee of the day took the decision to cancel plans for any future show. So ended a 50-year-old tradition.

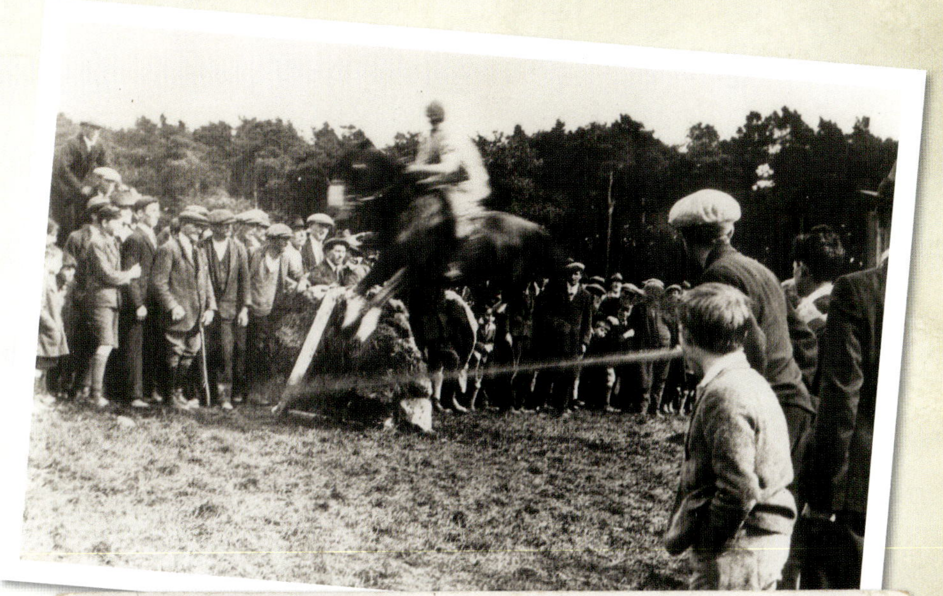

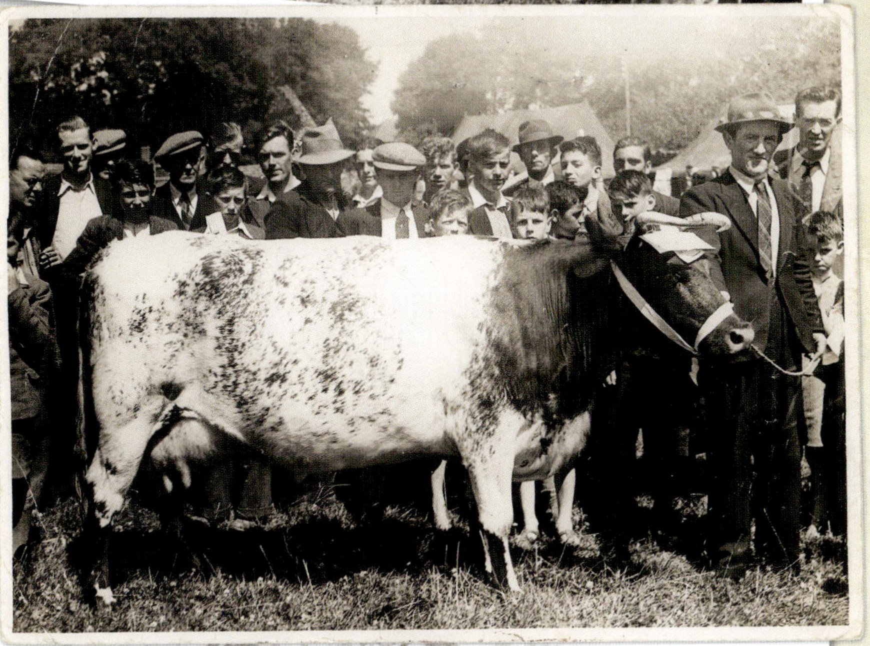

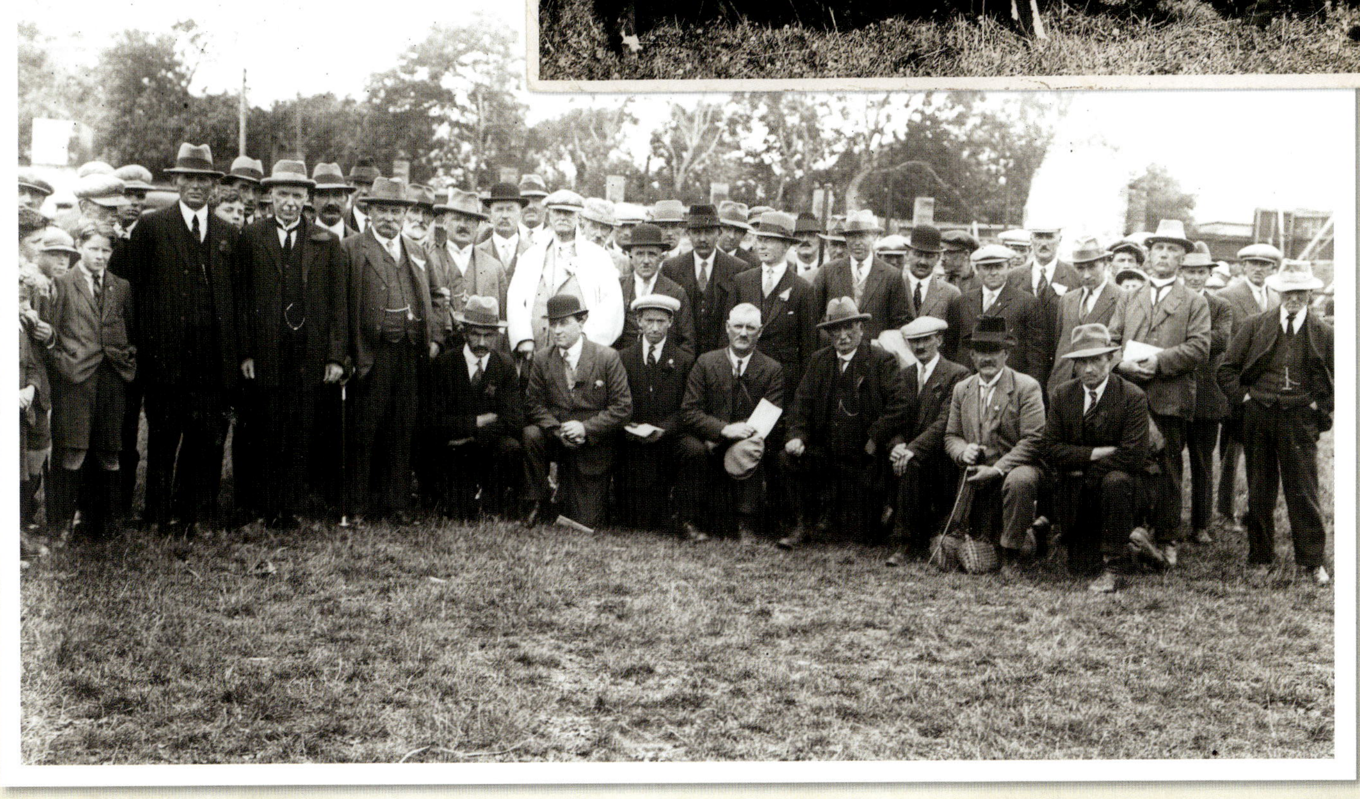

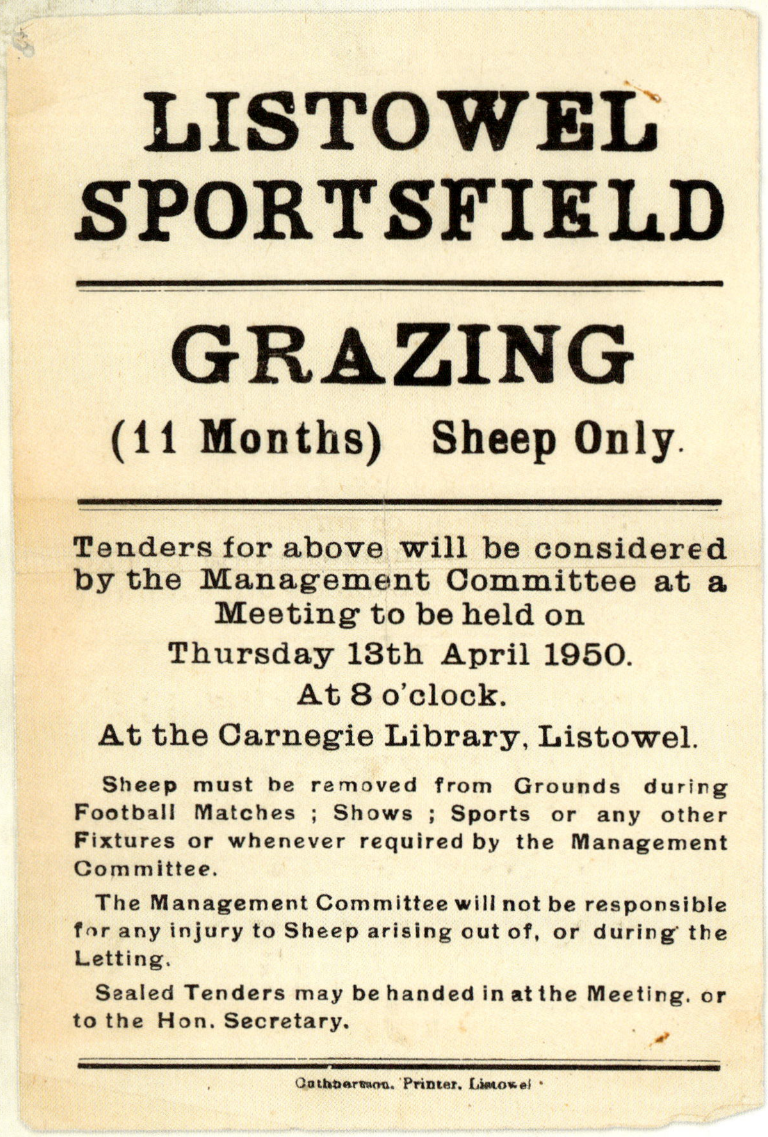

LISTOWEL SPORTSFIELD

GRAZING

(11 Months) Sheep Only.

Tenders for above will be considered by the Management Committee at a Meeting to be held on Thursday 13th April 1950. At 8 o'clock. At the Carnegie Library, Listowel.

Sheep must be removed from Grounds during Football Matches ; Shows ; Sports or any other Fixtures or whenever required by the Management Committee.

The Management Committee will not be responsible for any injury to Sheep arising out of, or during the Letting.

Sealed Tenders may be handed in at the Meeting, or to the Hon. Secretary.

Cuthbertson, Printer, Listowel

The Sportsfield

Now Frank Sheehy Park, the Sportsfield had a vibrant committee in the early 1900s. It had a cinder running track around the perimeter of the pitch and a wooden stand. In 1904, the committee built a modern gymnasium costing £250. This hall also doubled as a centre for the town's entertainment, with drama, opera, and travelling shows held there throughout the year. An article in the 1960 field re-opening programme by John Molyneaux recalled from records an insight into usage of the hall...

'The activities in the Hall were varied and remunerative, and provide us with an interesting insight into the fullness of social life at the turn of the century. Listed among the functions held in the Hall were dances organised by the Hockey club, Ladies' club, O'Shaughnessy club, Tennis club, Bachelors' club, Harrier club, Badminton club, Volunteers, Camogie club, Terrier coursing club. Concerts were promoted by Town Clock Fund, Fuel Fund, Temperance Society, Altar Society, Confraternity and other events also took place in the hall such as Dancing Lessons by Mr. Roche, St. Patrick's Night Boxing, T.B. Exhibition, various Silent Picture companies, and a Carpet auction. Charges for meetings ranged from 5/- to £1. The Hall's equipment included Horizontal Bar, Parallel Bars, Dumb-Bells, Trapeze, Ropes and Hooks, Trapeze Bar, Punching Ball, Vaulting Horse, Springboard, Ring apparatus, Boxing gloves and Ropes.'

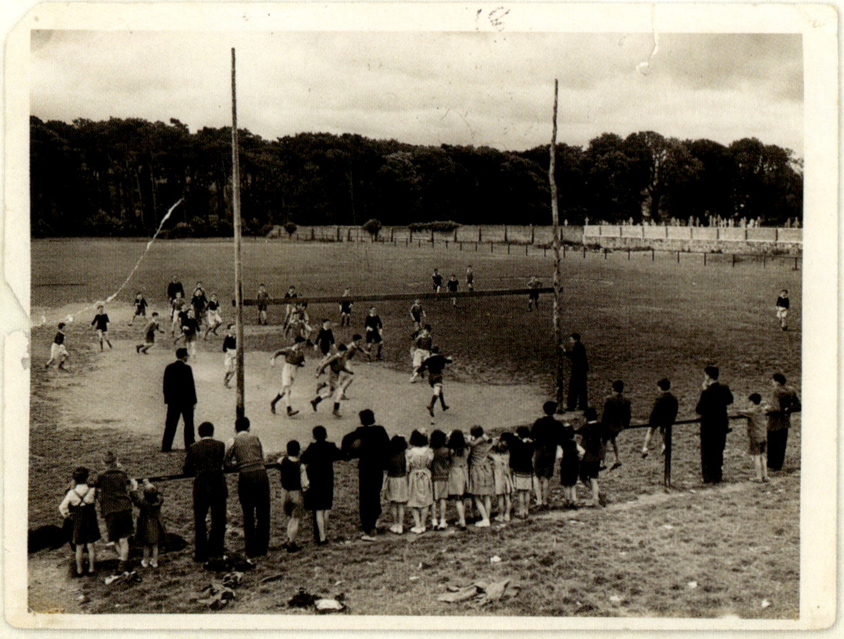

Photo: Listowel sportsfield in the 1950s. The pitch was surrounded by railings from the old Lartigue railway.

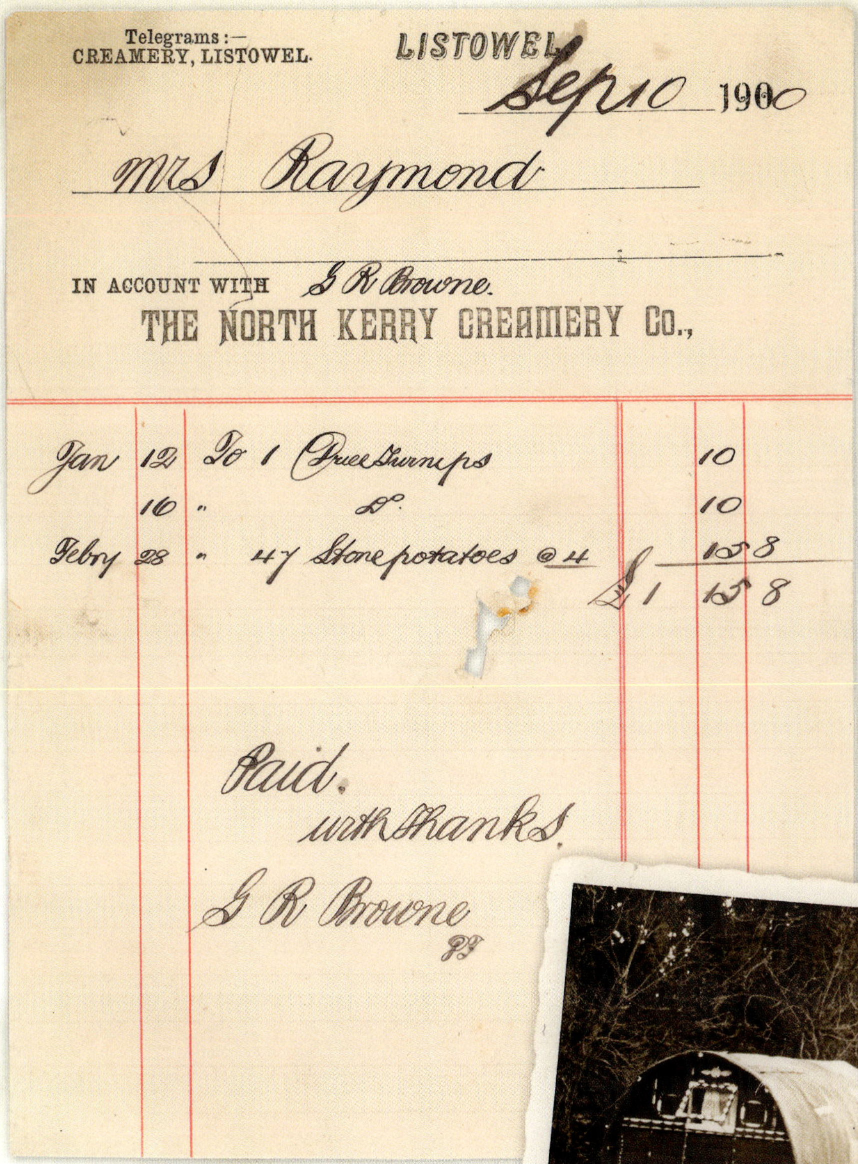

Telegrams :—
CREAMERY, LISTOWEL.

LISTOWEL Sep 10 1900

Mrs Raymond

IN ACCOUNT WITH G R Browne.
THE NORTH KERRY CREAMERY Co.,

Jan	12	To 1 [illegible]		10
	16	" do		10
Febry	28	" 47 Stone potatoes @ 4		15 8
			£1	15 8

Paid.
with thanks
G R Browne

Creamery Pioneer

George R. Browne, creamery pioneer and owner of the North Kerry Creamery which was located at Cahirdown. Browne was the instigator, along with others, of the many private creameries which opened in North Kerry in the late 1800s and early 1900s. Many Swedish men worked in the installation of the creamery plant. One of these, Lars Larson, died as a young man while in Listowel. He is buried in a marked grave next to the resting place of Browne in St. Michael's Cemetery.

Below: A speed trap from the 1950s at lower Cahirdown. A traveller's caravan is pictured at the side of the road with a vigilant Garda on duty.

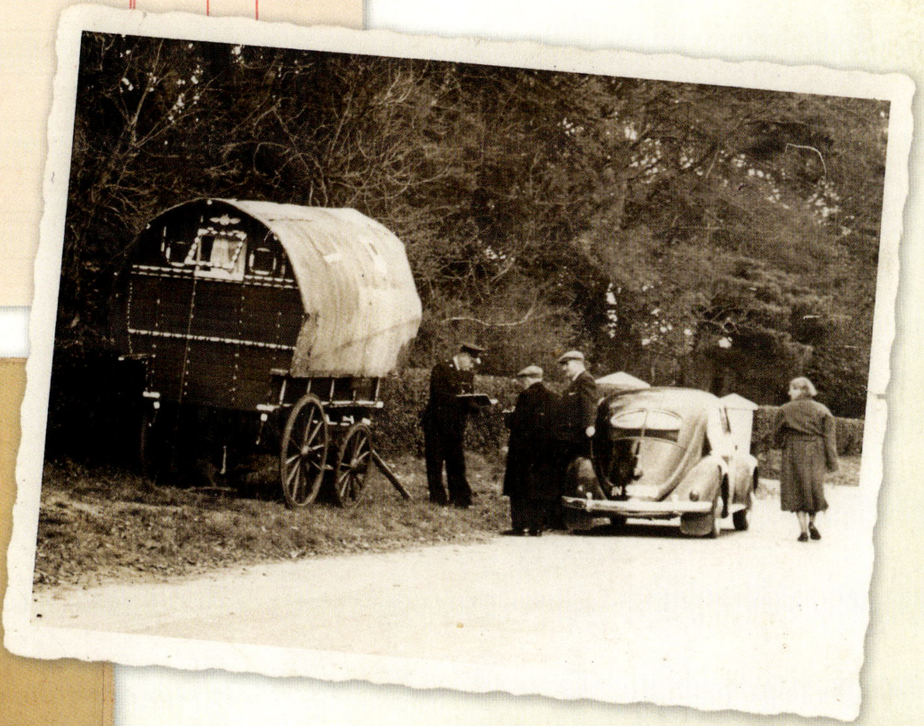

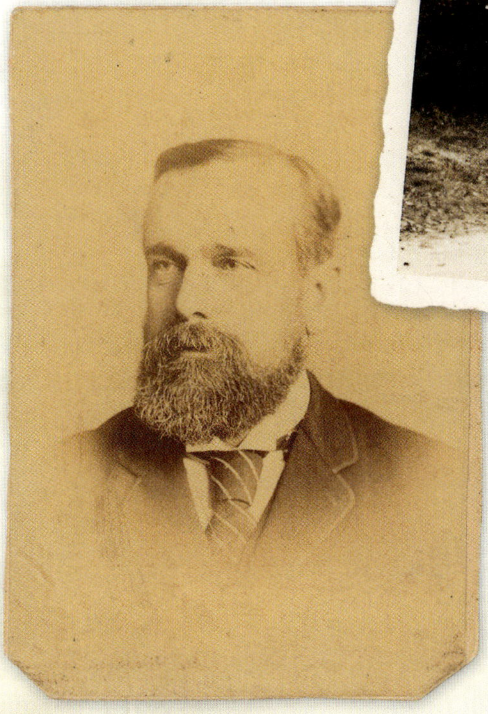

Left: George R. Browne.

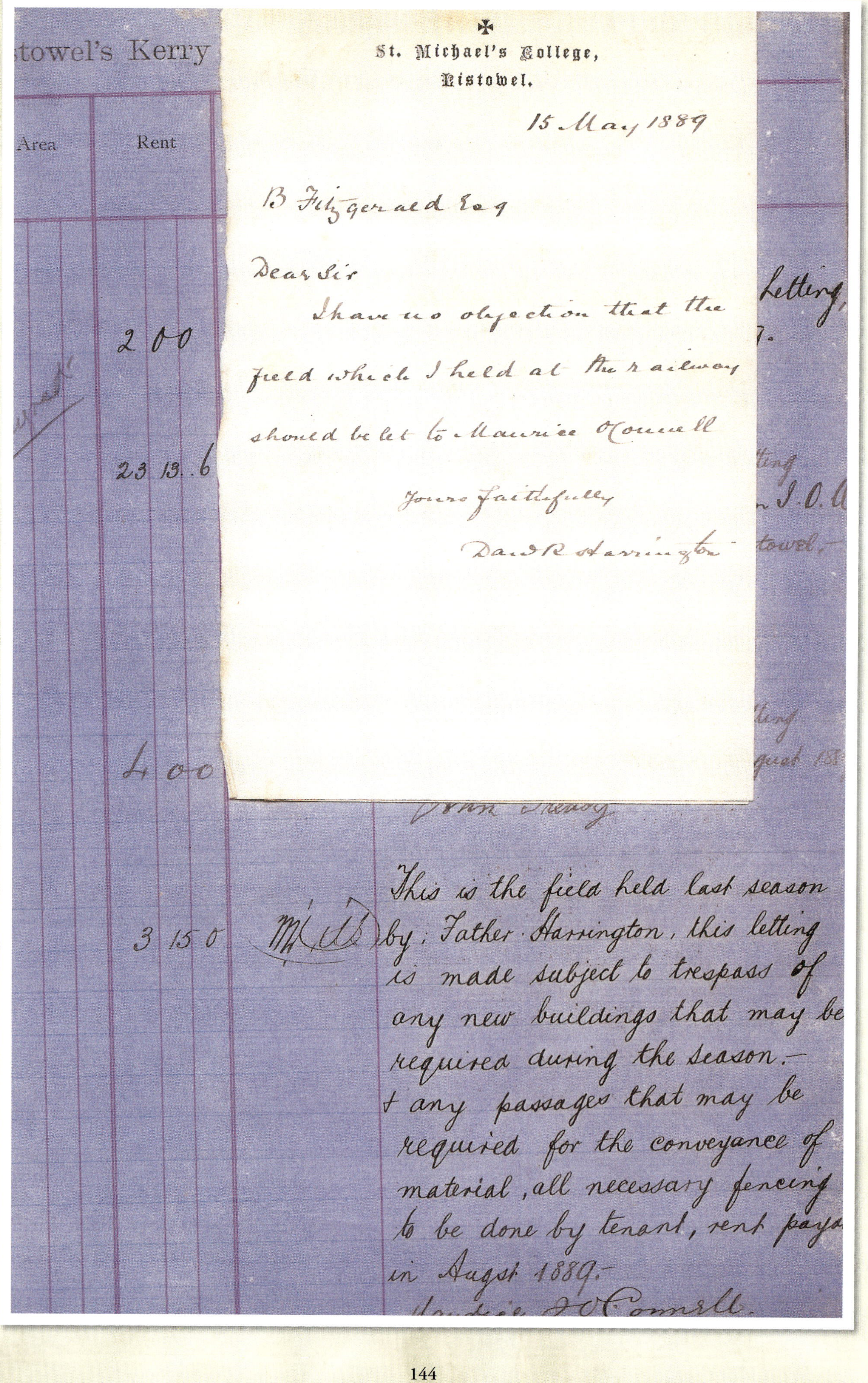

St. Michael's College,
Listowel.

15 May 1889

B Fitzgerald Esq

Dear Sir

I have no objection that the field which I held at the railway should be let to Maurice O'Connell

Yours faithfully

David R Harrington

Area	Rent	
	2 0 0	
	23 13 6	
	4 0 0	
	3 15 0	This is the field held last season by Father Harrington, this letting is made subject to trespass of any new buildings that may be required during the season. & any passages that may be required for the conveyance of material, all necessary fencing to be done by tenant, rent paya[ble] in Augst 1889. Maurice O'Connell.

St. Michael's College

Originally the District Fever Hospital, St. Michael's College opened as a Boys' Secondary School in 1879. Since that time it has seen many changes and extensions.

The letter to Brinsley Fitzgerald, Lord Listowel's agent, is to confirm Father Harrington's agreement to the letting of a field which he previously had rented at the top of Upper William Street to one of the teachers at the college, Maurice O'Connell. Also included is the signed agreement and letting arrangements entered into by O'Connell from Lord Listowel's Kerry Rental Book.

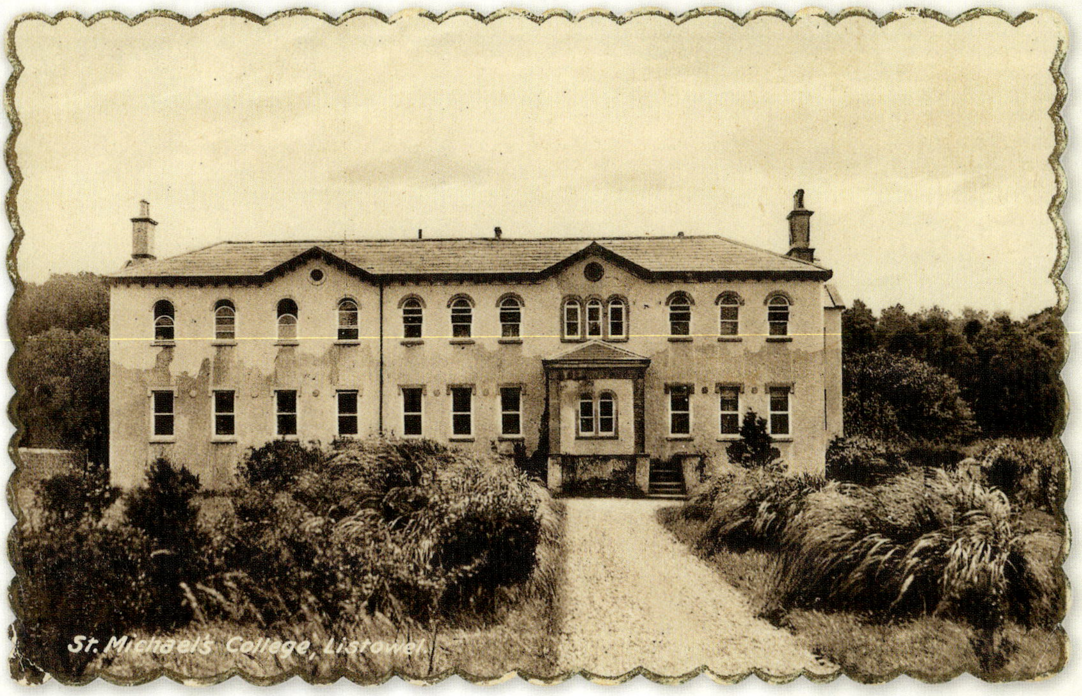

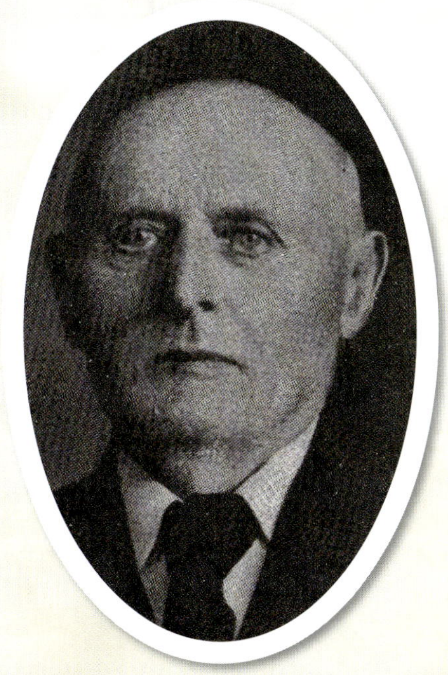

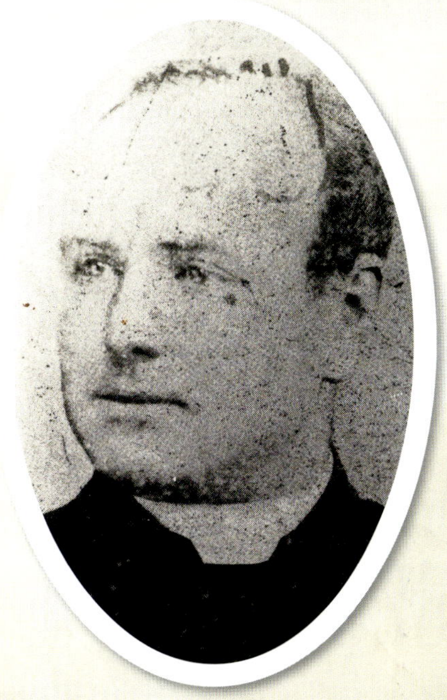

Above left: Maurice J. O'Connell (1857-1940), the longest serving teacher at St. Michael's.
Above right: Fr. Daniel J. Harrington (1850-1928), first president of St. Michael's.

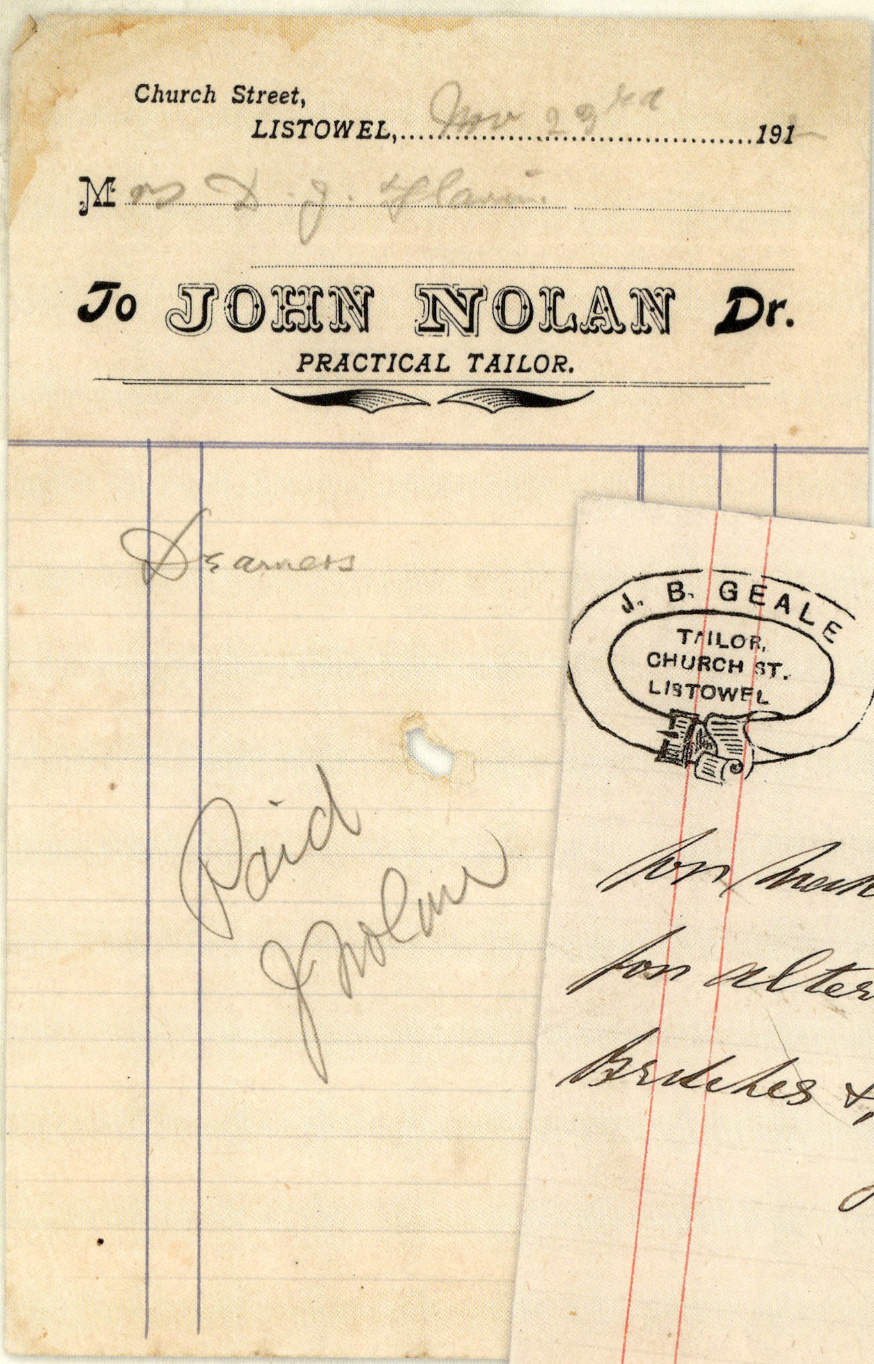
Church Street,
LISTOWEL, Nov 29th 191
M
To JOHN NOLAN Dr.
PRACTICAL TAILOR.

Paid
J Nolan

101 Church Street

John Nolan, Master Tailor, was born in Coilbee, Listowel and served his apprenticeship in both Castleisland and Tralee. He set up his tailoring business in the early 1900s at his home in Upper Church Street. He specialised in the making of Garda uniforms.

Below: Tailor J.B. Geale's billhead from a Church Street of earlier times.

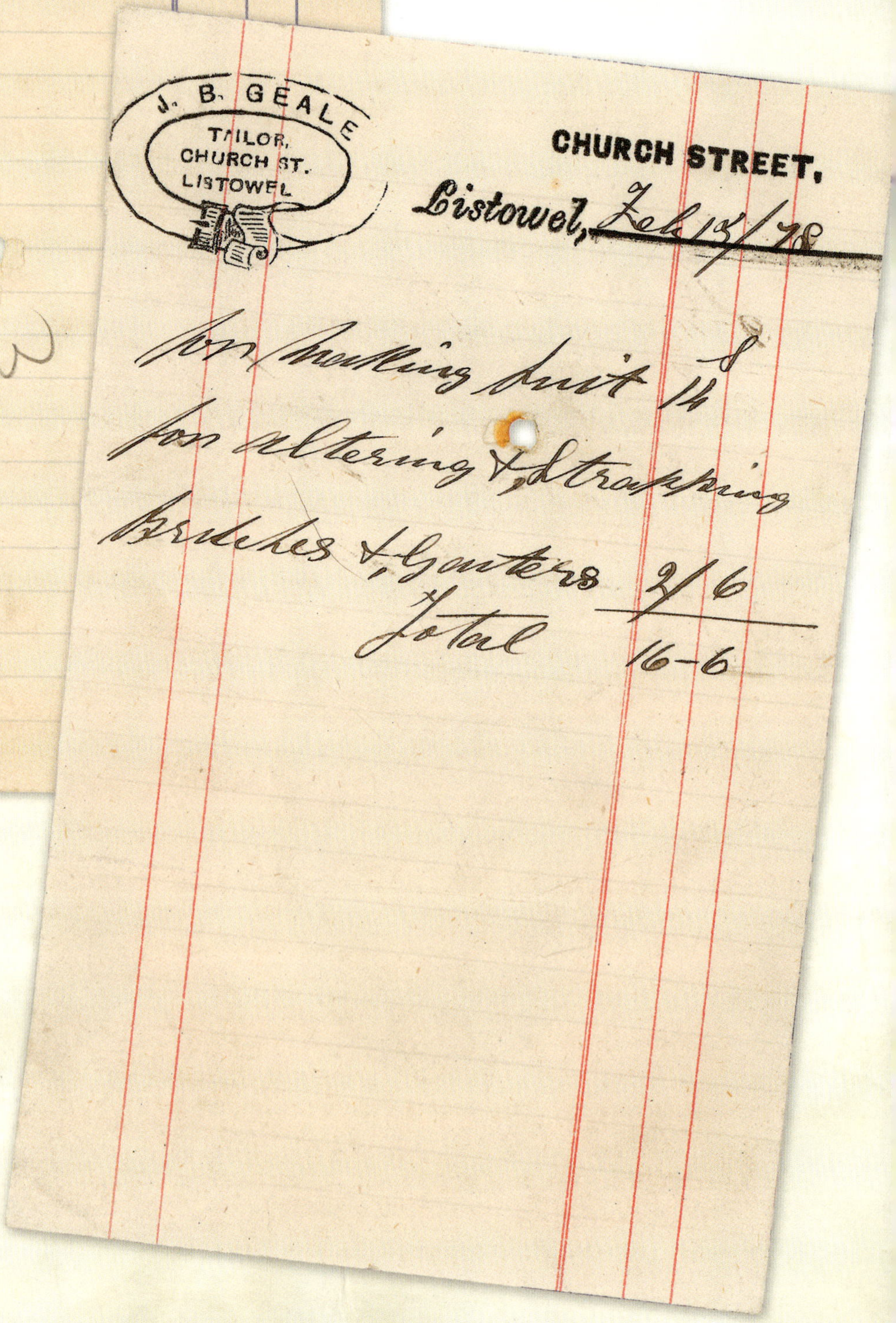
J. B. GEALE
TAILOR,
CHURCH ST.
LISTOWEL

CHURCH STREET,
Listowel, Feb 15/78

For making suit 14
for altering & strapping
breeches & gaiters 2/6
Total 16-6

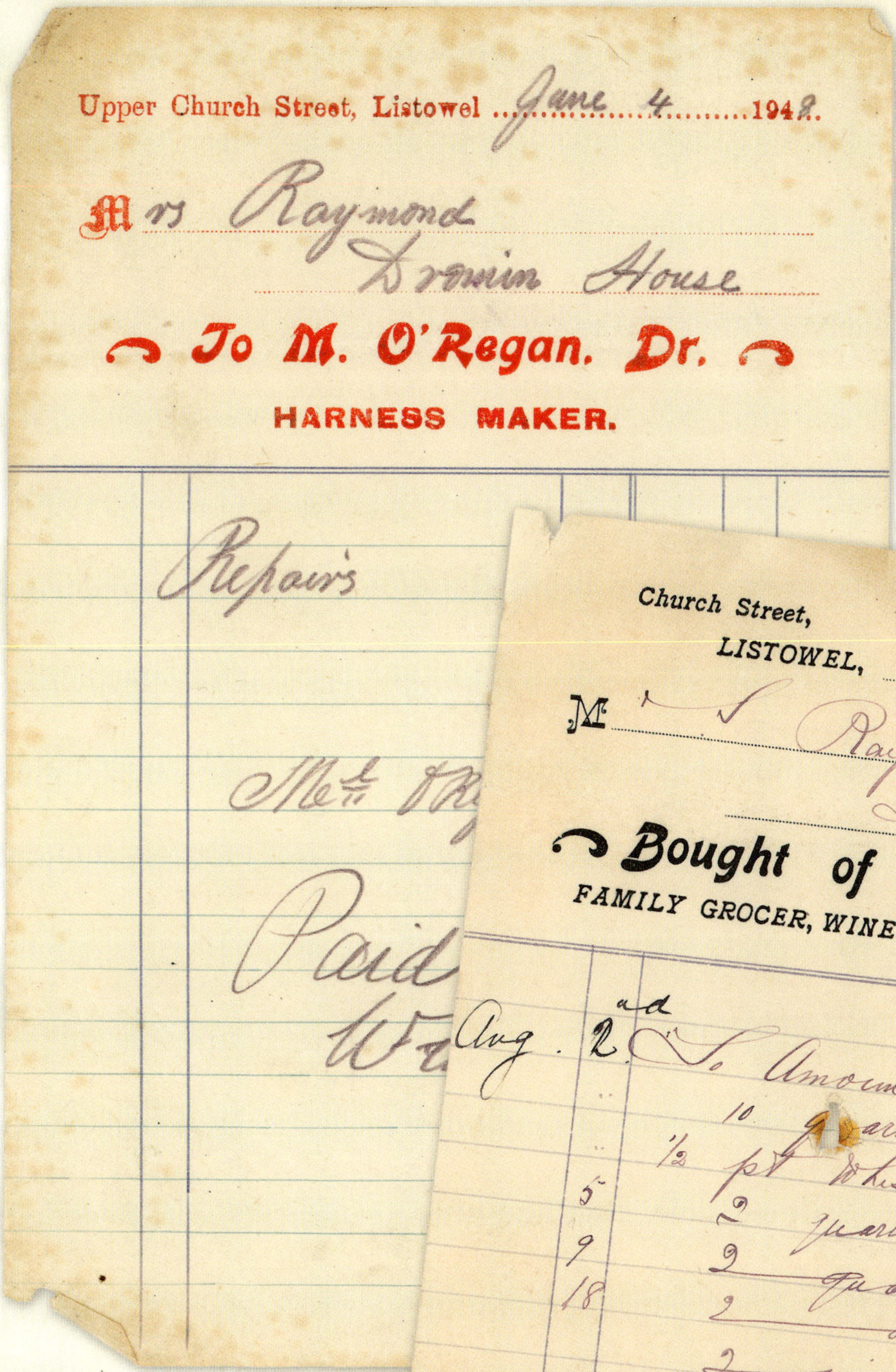

Upper Church Street, Listowel ...June 4.........1918.

Mrs Raymond
Dromin House

To M. O'Regan. Dr.

HARNESS MAKER.

Repairs

Paid

89 Church Street
Michael Regan, Harness Maker, plied his trade at his home in Upper Church Street. His home, now demolished, was opposite the Church Street Junction with Courthouse Road. Michael was born in Knockane, Listowel.

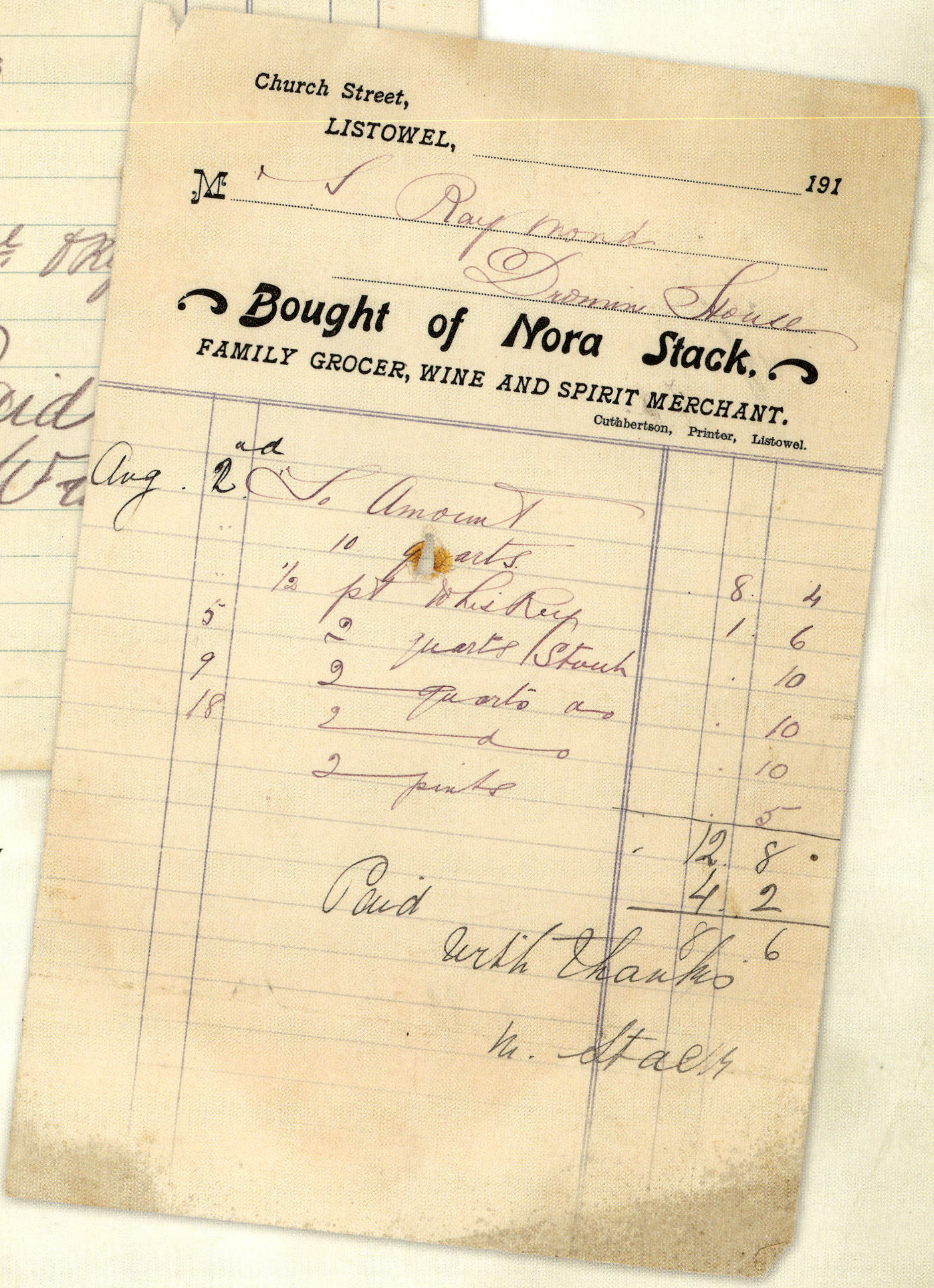

Church Street,
LISTOWEL, ...191

M ... Raymond
Dromin House

Bought of Nora Stack.

FAMILY GROCER, WINE AND SPIRIT MERCHANT.

Cuthbertson, Printer, Listowel.

Aug. 2nd	To Amount			
	10 quarts			
	½ pt whiskey		8.	4
5	2 quarts Stout		1.	6
9	2 quarts do		.	10
18	2 do		.	10
	2 pints		.	10
			.	5
			12.	8
	Paid		4.	2
			8.	6

With thanks
N. Stack

83 Church Street
Nora Stack had a family grocery and public house some doors down the street from Regan's. The bar was known as 'The Star and Garter'. On the 19th January 1921, during the War of Independence, District Inspector Tobias O'Sullivan of the Royal Irish Constabulary was shot dead outside the front door of the pub. Nora Stack was from Coilbee, Listowel.

79 Church Street

Elizabeth Gaire, from Duagh, married Tommy McAuliffe of Listowel. They set up home in Church Street. Elizabeth had trained in tailoring at her family home in Duagh, where the Gaires were well-known tailors. She continued her profession as a costumier until retirement.

Photo: Tommy and Elizabeth McAuliffe.

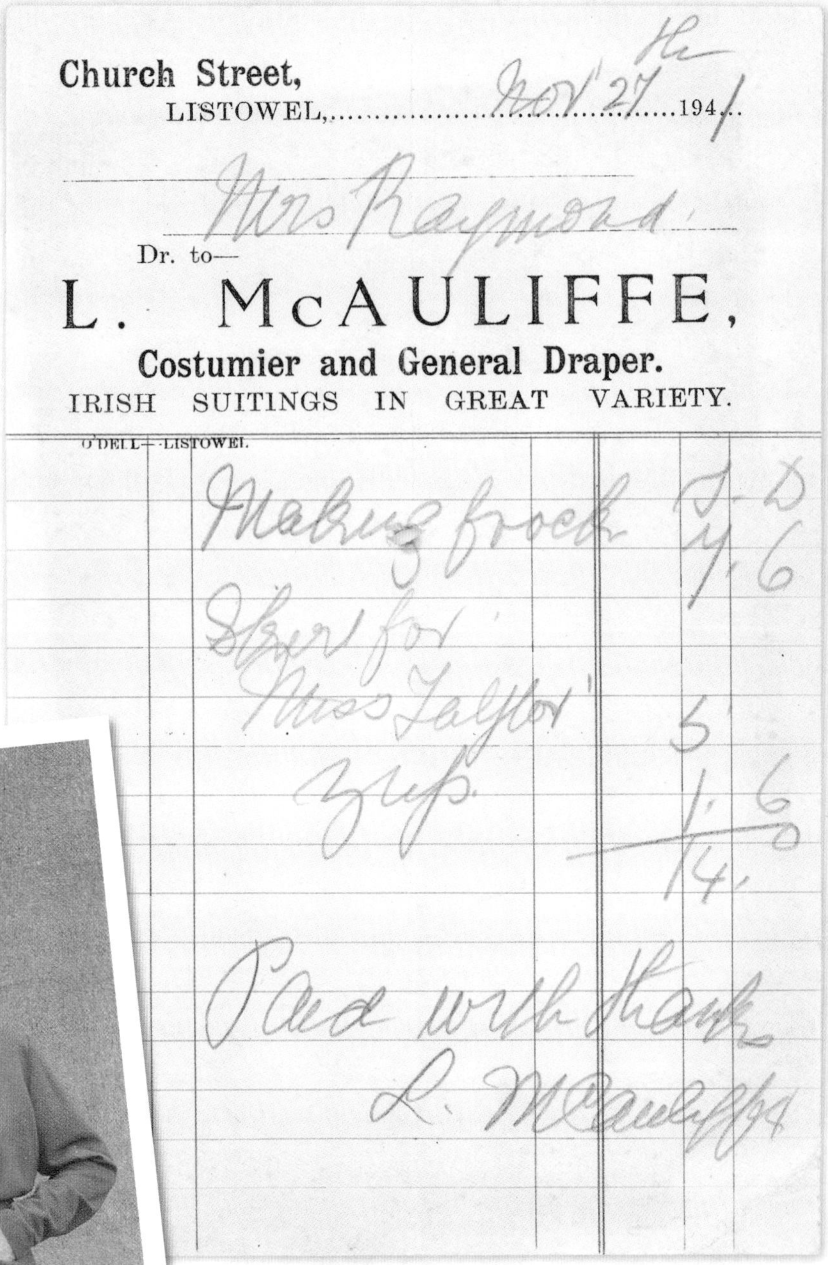

Church Street,
LISTOWEL, Nov 27 1941

Mrs Raymond

Dr. to—

L. McAULIFFE,

Costumier and General Draper.

IRISH SUITINGS IN GREAT VARIETY.

O'DELL—LISTOWEL.

	S.	D.
Making frock	7	6
Skirt for Miss Taylor	5	
Zip	1	6
	14	0

Paid with thanks
L. McAuliffe

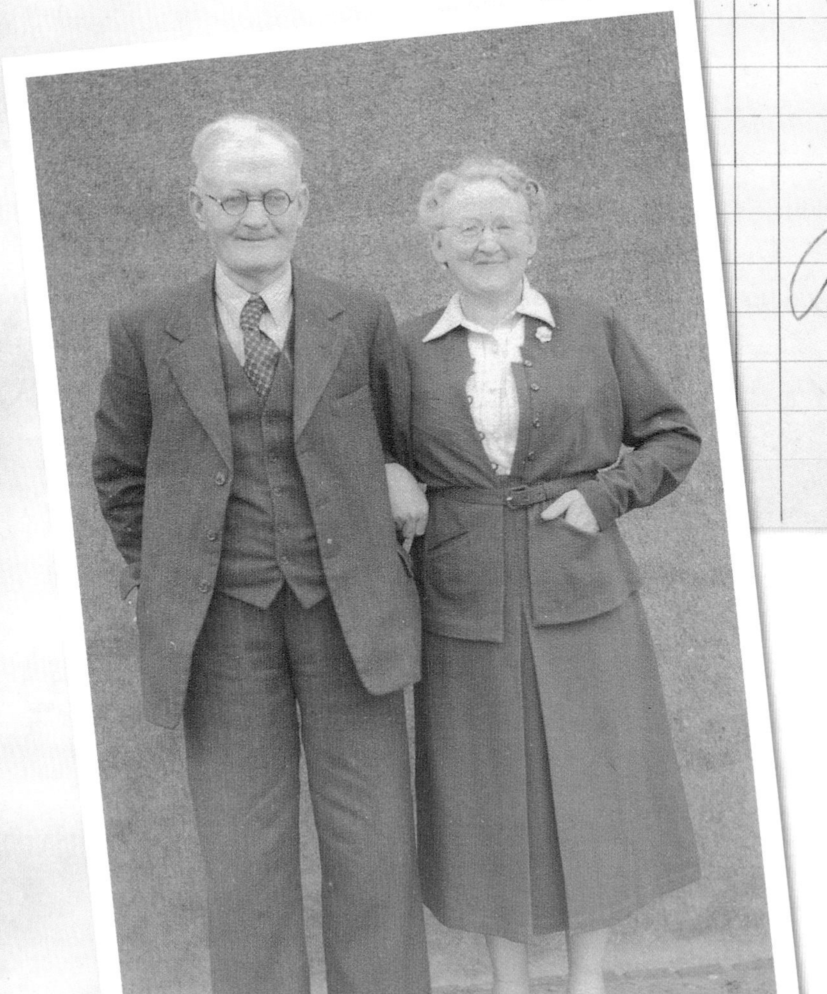

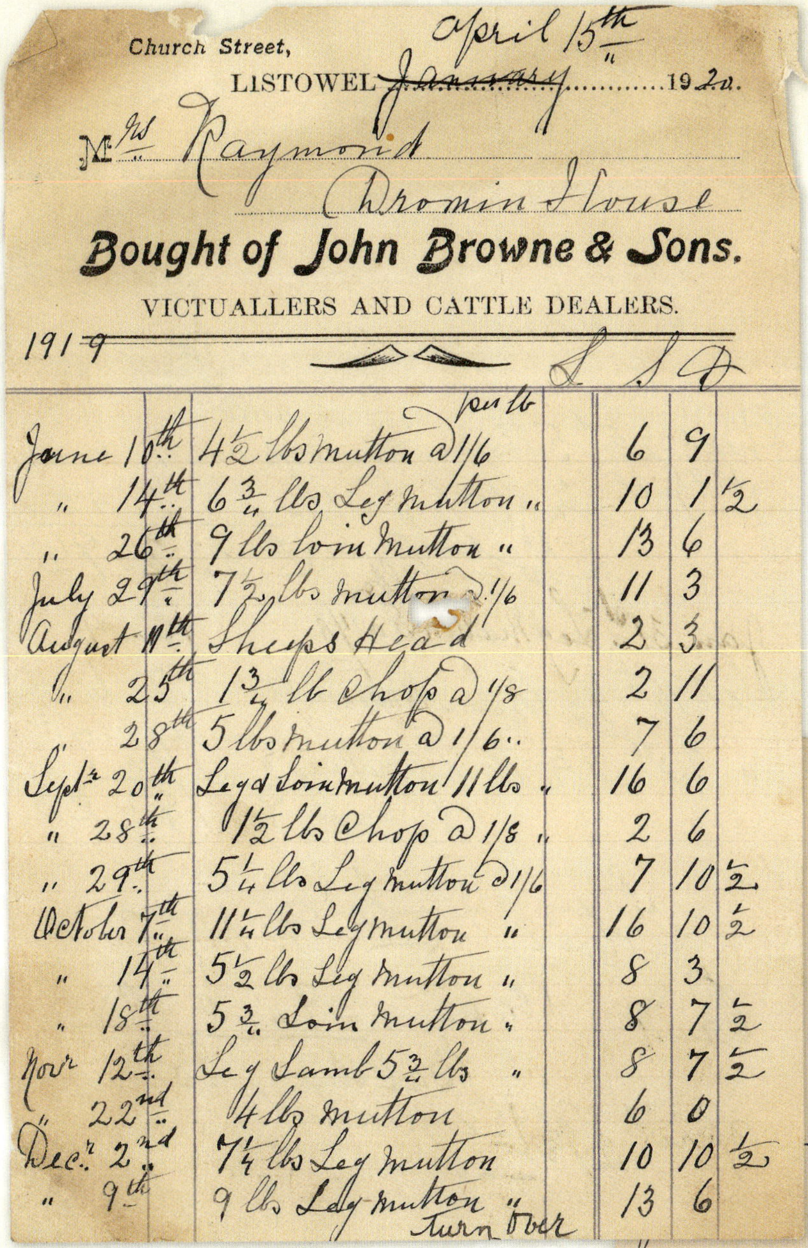

Church Street,
LISTOWEL ~~January~~ April 15th 1920.

Mrs Raymond
Dromin House

Bought of John Browne & Sons.

VICTUALLERS AND CATTLE DEALERS.

1919		£	S	D
June 10th	4½ lbs mutton @1/6 per lb		6	9
" 14th	6¾ lbs Leg mutton "		10	1½
" 26th	9 lbs loin mutton "		13	6
July 29th	7½ lbs mutton @1/6		11	3
August 11th	Sheeps Head		2	3
" 25th	1¾ lb Chop @1/8		2	11
28th	5 lbs mutton @1/6		7	6
Sept 20th	Leg & Loin mutton 11 lbs "		16	6
" 28th	1½ lbs Chop @1/8 "		2	6
" 29th	5¼ lbs Leg mutton @1/6		7	10½
October 7th	11¼ lbs Leg mutton "		16	10½
" 14th	5½ lbs Leg mutton "		8	3
" 18th	5¾ Loin mutton "		8	7½
Nov 12th	Leg Lamb 5¾ lbs "		8	7½
22nd	4 lbs mutton		6	0
Dec 2nd	7¼ lbs Leg mutton		10	10½
" 9th	9 lbs Leg mutton "		13	6

turn over

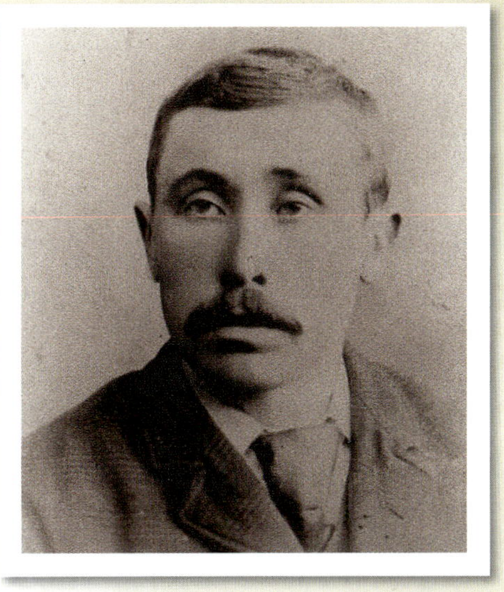

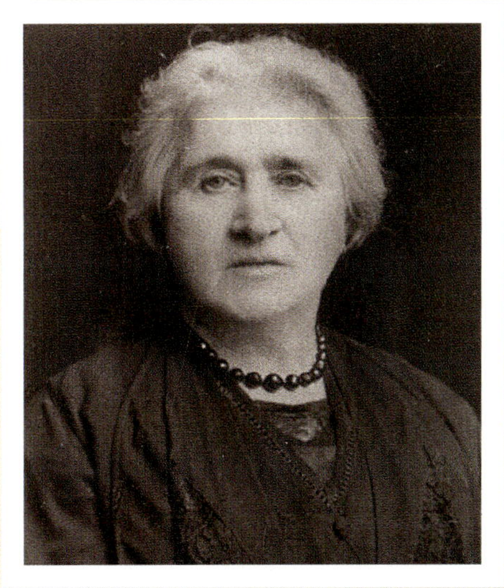

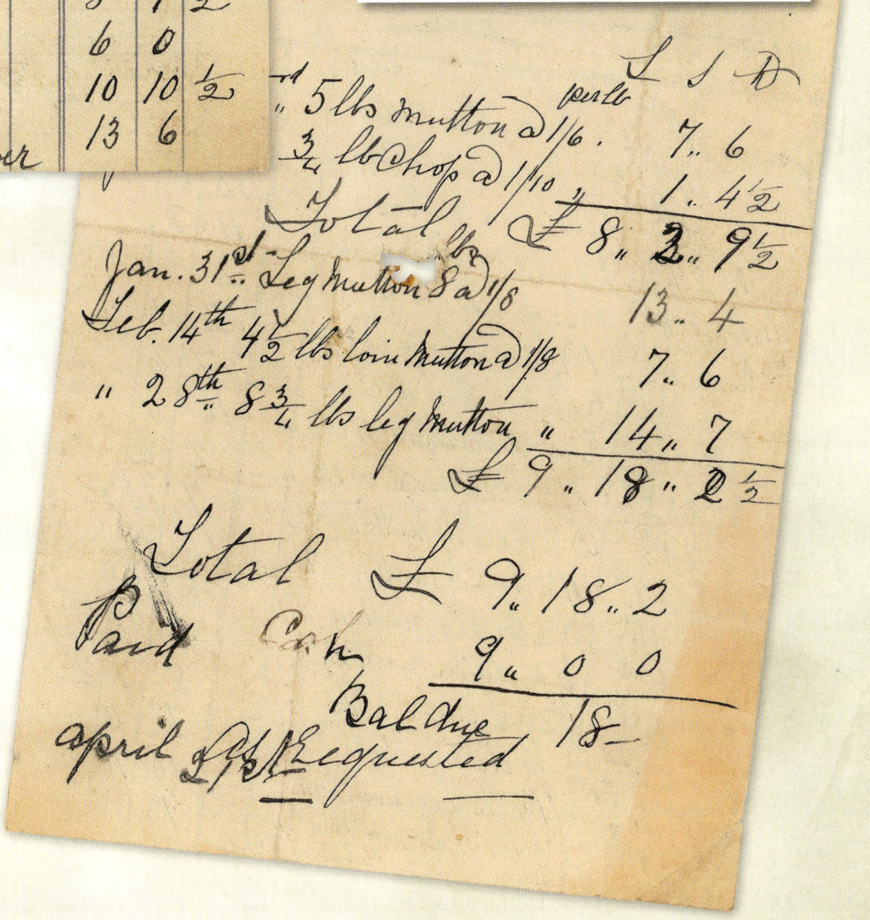

	£	S	D
" 5 lbs mutton @1/6 per lb		7.	6
¾ lb Chop @1/10		1.	4½
Total £	8.	2.	9½
Jan. 31st Leg mutton 8 @1/8		13.	4
Feb. 14th 4½ lbs loin mutton @1/8		7.	6
" 28th 8¾ lbs leg mutton "		14.	7
£	9.	18.	2½

Total £ 9. 18. 2
Paid Cash 9. 0. 0
Bal due 18–
April £18 Requested

77 Church Street
Browne's butchers operated their business in their cottage-style house in Church Street which had been vacated by cooper Lar Buckley. The business thrived over the years with one son, Jack, opening another butcher's shop in Ballybunion.

Photos: John and Catherine Browne.

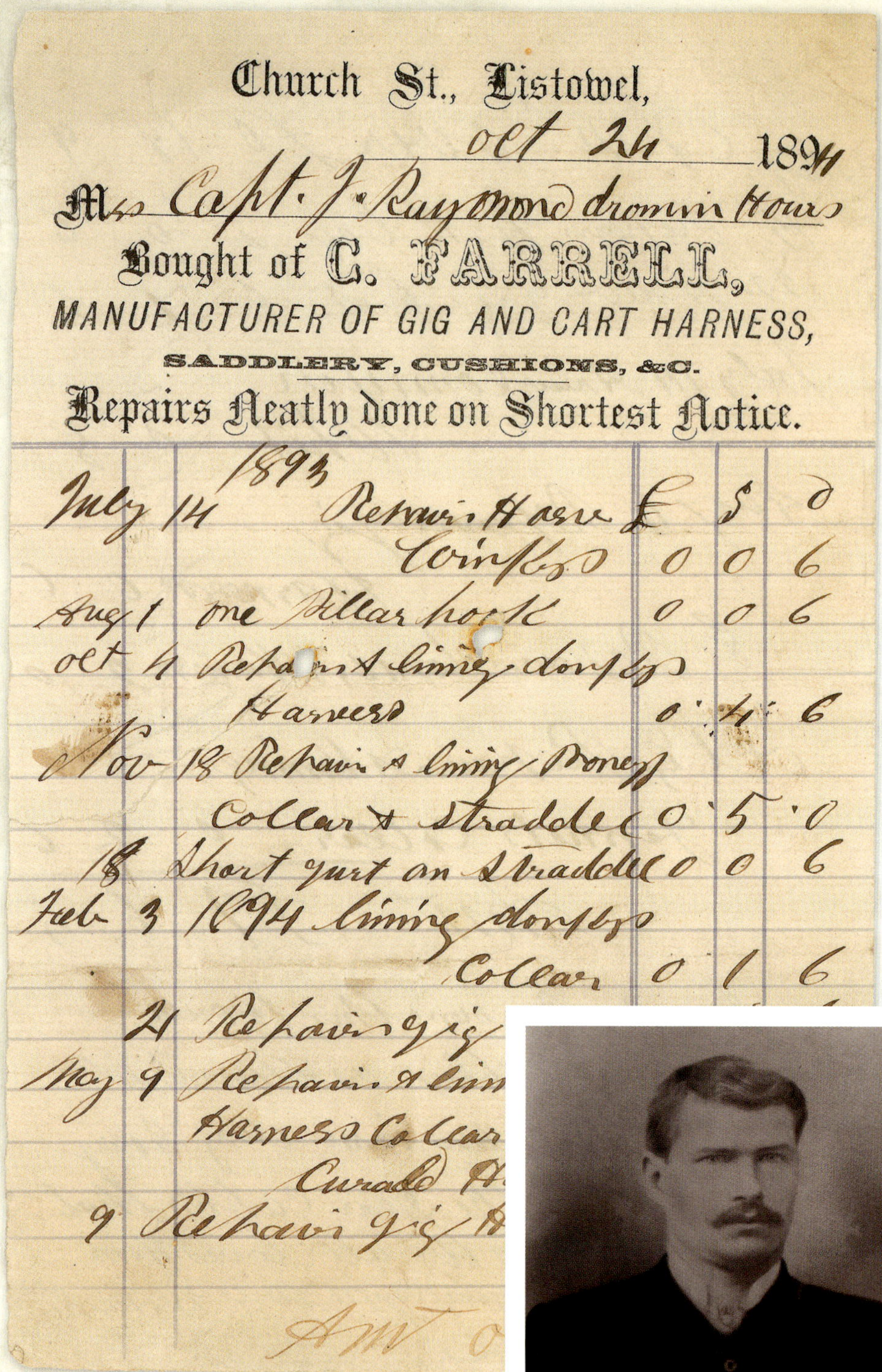

Church St., Listowel,
Oct 24 1894

Mrs Capt. J. Raymond Dromin House

Bought of C. FARRELL,

MANUFACTURER OF GIG AND CART HARNESS,

SADDLERY, CUSHIONS, &C.

Repairs Neatly done on Shortest Notice.

			£	s	d
1893 July	14	Repairs Horse			
		Girths	0	0	6
Aug	1	one Pillar hook	0	0	6
Oct	4	Repairs & lining double			
		Harness	0	4	6
Nov	18	Repairs & lining Money			
		Collar & straddle	0	5	0
	18	Short girt on Straddle	0	0	6
Feb	3	1894 lining double			
		Collar	0	1	6
	21	Repairing gig			
May	9	Repairs & lin			
		Harness Collar			
		Curade H			
	9	Repairs gig H			

Amt o

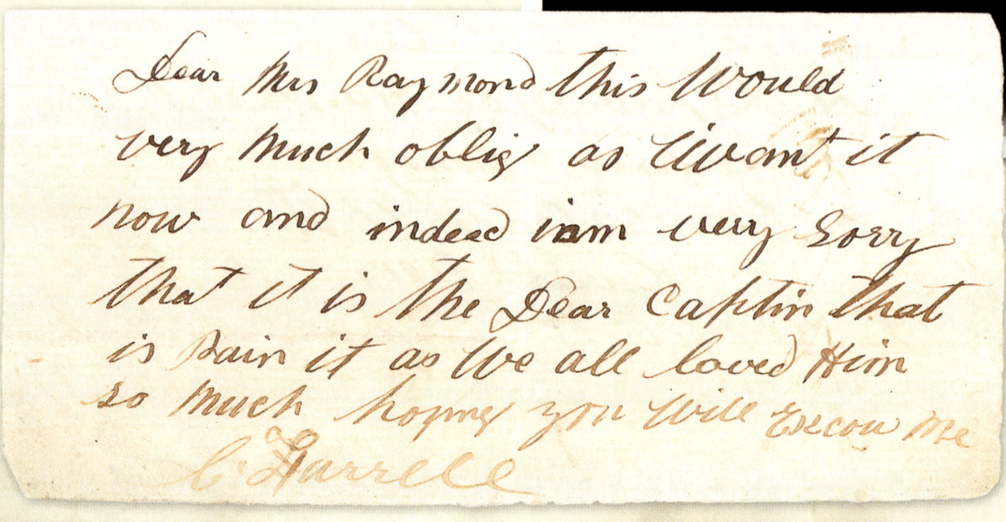

Dear Mrs Raymond this would very much oblige as I want it now and indeed I am very sorry that it is the Dear Captain that is pain it as we all loved Him so much hoping you will excuse me

C. Farrell

75 Church Street

Con Farrell worked at his harness-making trade from his thatched home in Church Street from 1880. In 1894, he reconstructed his house by raising it one storey and slating it. The billhead from Con Farrell to Mrs. Capt. J.W. Raymond, Dromin House, carries an itemised bill up until October 5th. On a note at the bottom, Con Farrell requests the settling of the debt. In the note there is a line "we all loved him so much". This is a reference to the death of Captain Raymond which occurred the previous month on September 5, 1894.

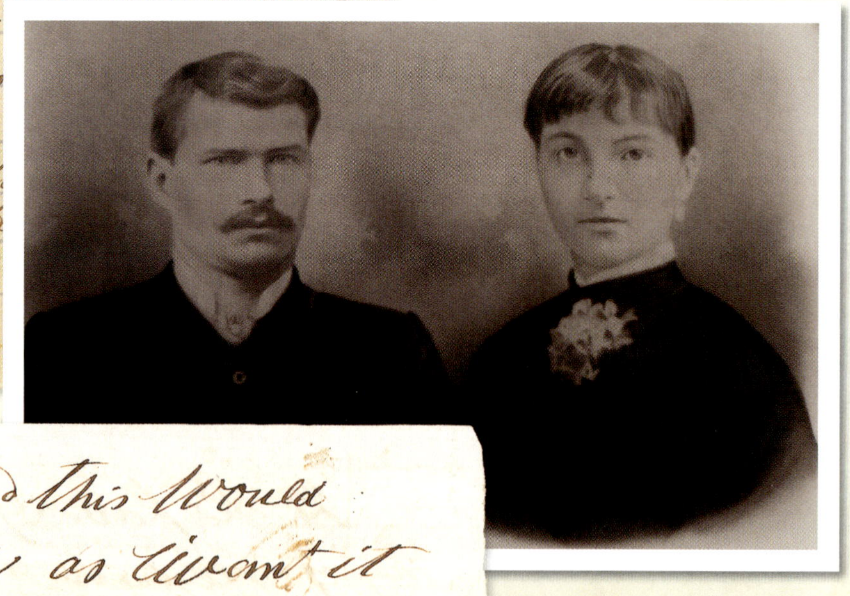

Photo: Con and Honora Farrell.

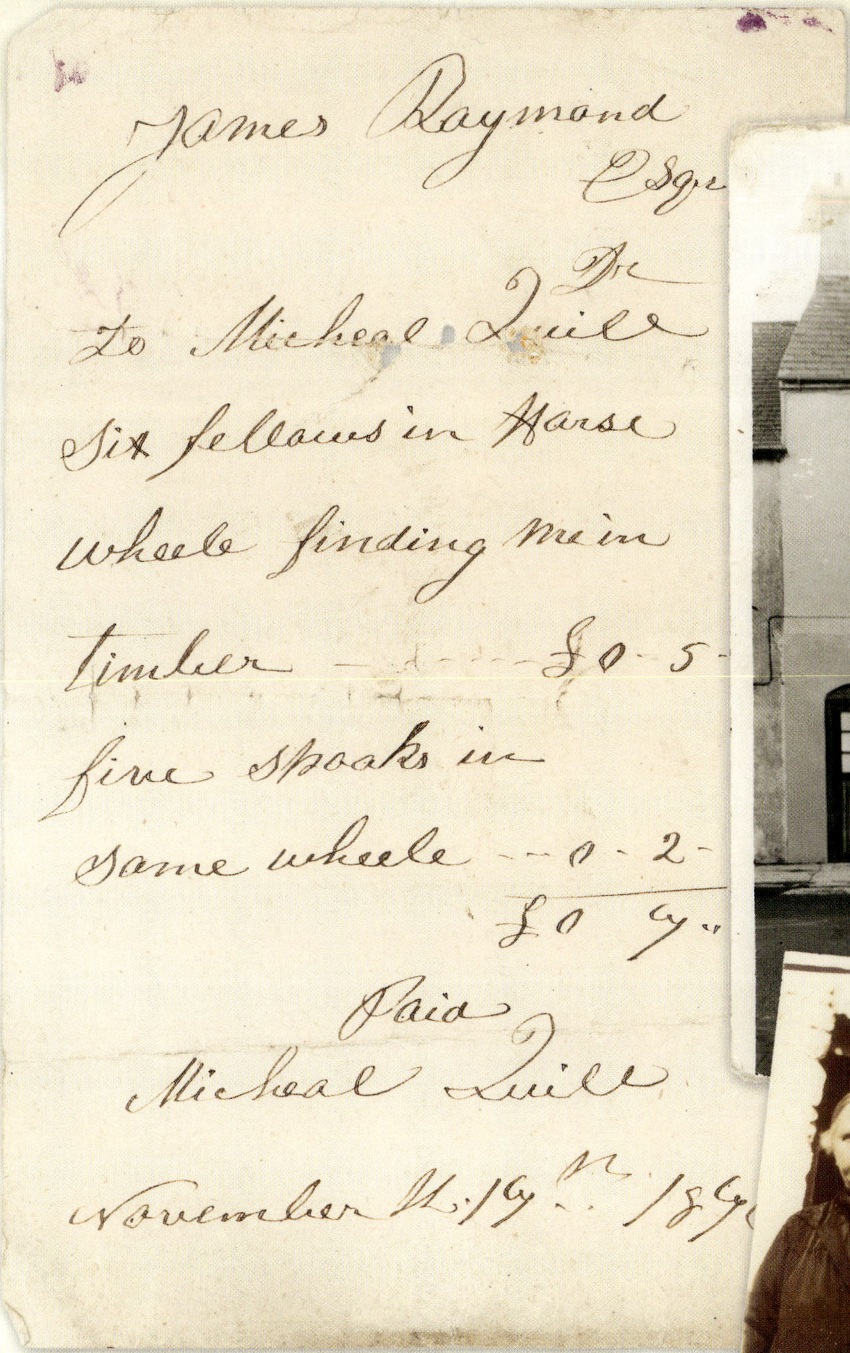

James Raymond
Esqr

Dr
To Micheal Quill

Six fellows in Horse wheele finding me in timber — £0-5-

five spoaks in same wheele — 0-2-

£0 7-

Paid
Micheal Quill
November th 19th 189

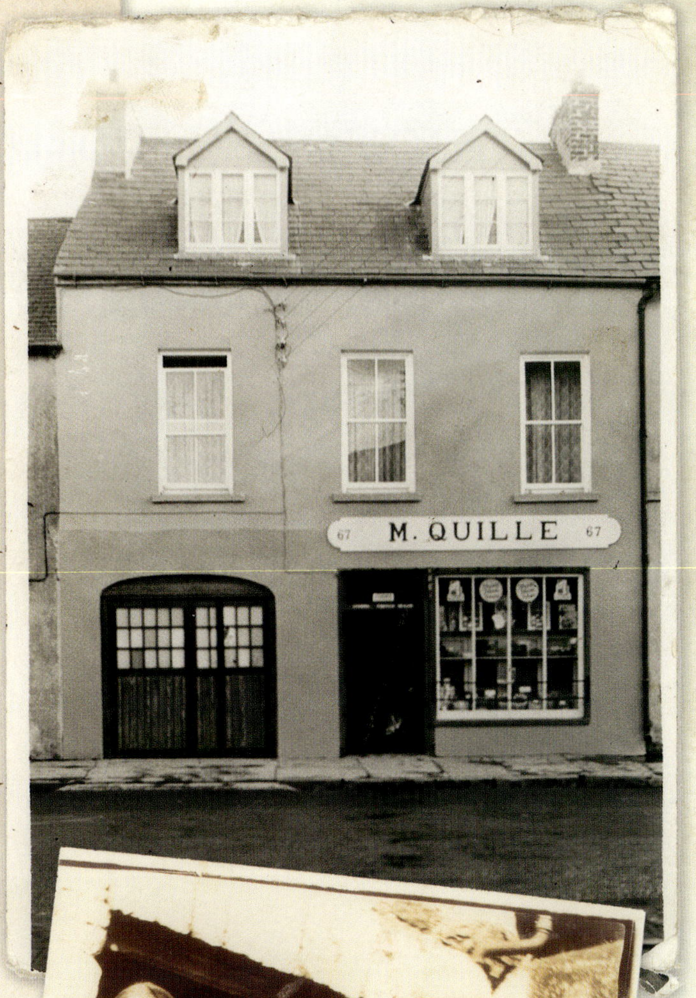

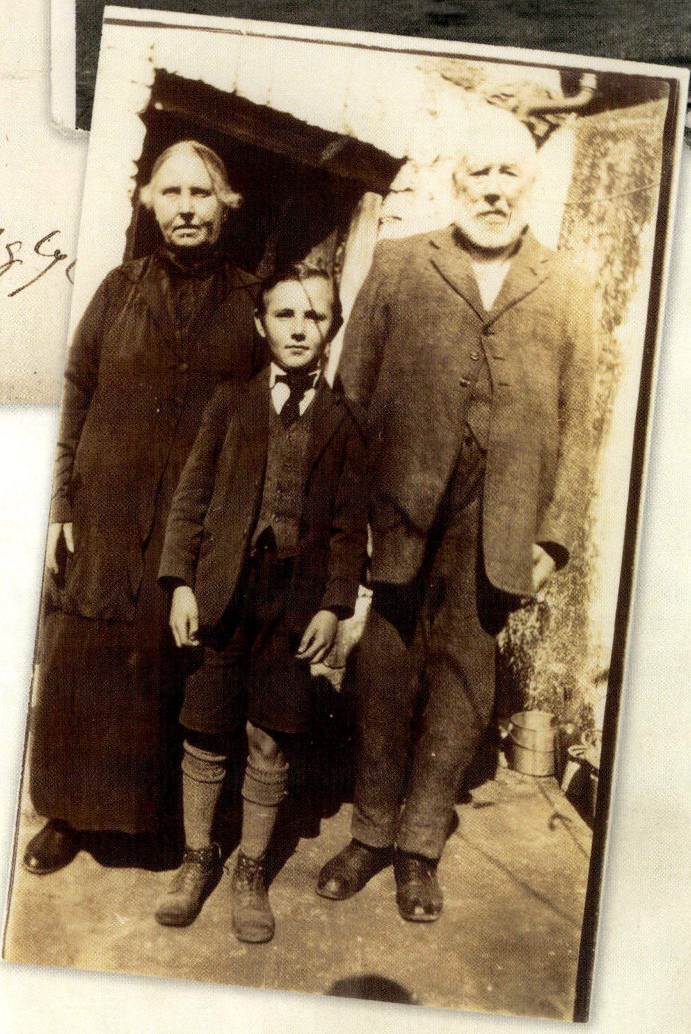

67 Church Street

Michael Quill, pictured here circa 1930 with his wife Ellen and grandson Michael, worked as a cartmaker and wheelwright at his house in Church Street for over fifty years. In later years part of the house was used as a location for a cinema where, under the management of Pa Cooney, silent films were shown. The house is now known as 'The North County Guesthouse' and is operated by Brian and Monica Quill.

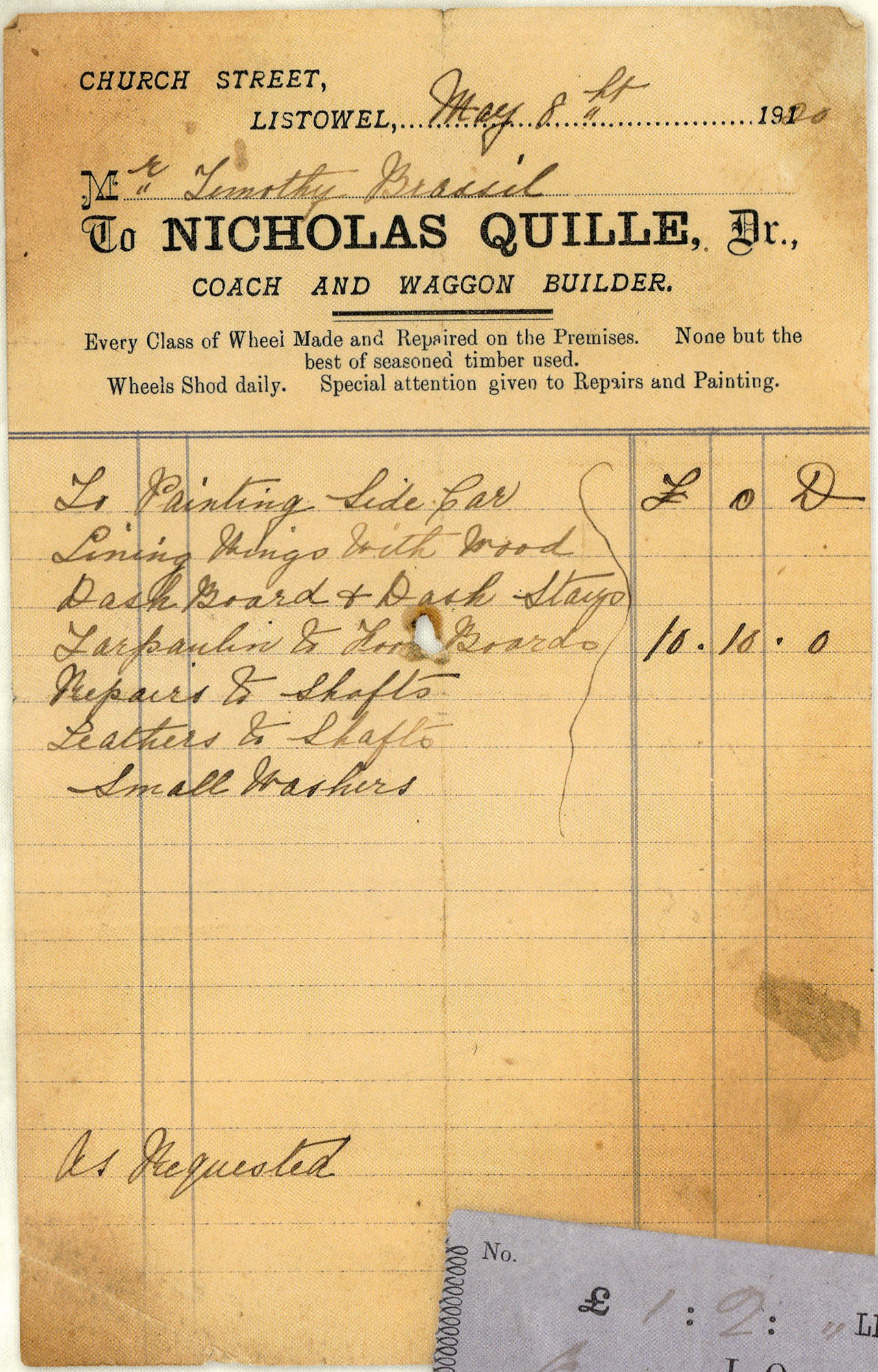

CHURCH STREET,
LISTOWEL, May 8th 1920

Mr Timothy Brassil

To NICHOLAS QUILLE, Jr.,

COACH AND WAGGON BUILDER.

Every Class of Wheel Made and Repaired on the Premises. None but the best of seasoned timber used.
Wheels Shod daily. Special attention given to Repairs and Painting.

	£	s	D
To Painting Side Car			
Lining Wings with Wood			
Dash Board & Dash Stays			
Tarpaulin & Foot Boards	10	10	0
Repairs to Shafts			
Leathers to Shafts			
Small Washers			
As Requested			

Left: A bill presented to Timothy Brassil of Lislaughtin, Ballylongford by Nicholas Quille, coach and wagon builder, for payment for work completed. Quille's workshop was at the rear of Upper Church Street.

Below: From Church of Ireland records we know the McCowen family had four children baptised in Listowel, from 1866 to 1871. McCowen of Church Street is mentioned in various directories as a glass and earthenware dealer, ironmonger and hardware merchant, seed and guano merchant, an agent and shoemaker. In Guys directory of 1886, a Mrs. McCowen, William Street, is mentioned as a bookseller, stationer and earthenware dealer. We do not know if there was any connection between the Tralee and Listowel McCowens.

The receipt shown is an IOU from Johanna Buckley of William Street to McCowen.

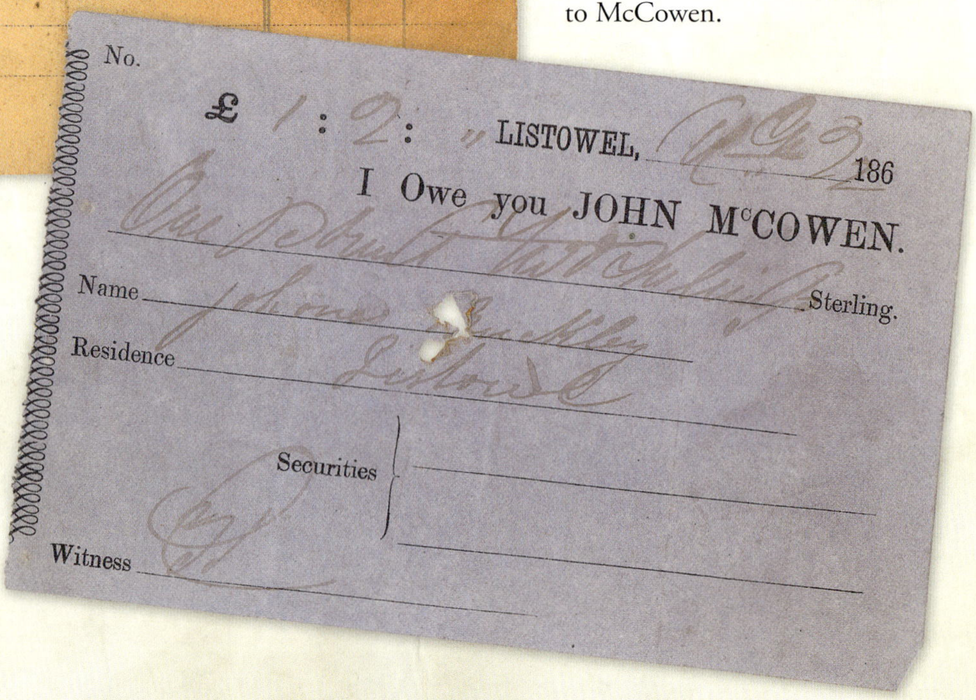

No.

£ 1 : 2 : " LISTOWEL, 186

I Owe you JOHN McCOWEN.

Sterling.

Name Johanna Buckley

Residence Listowel

Securities

Witness

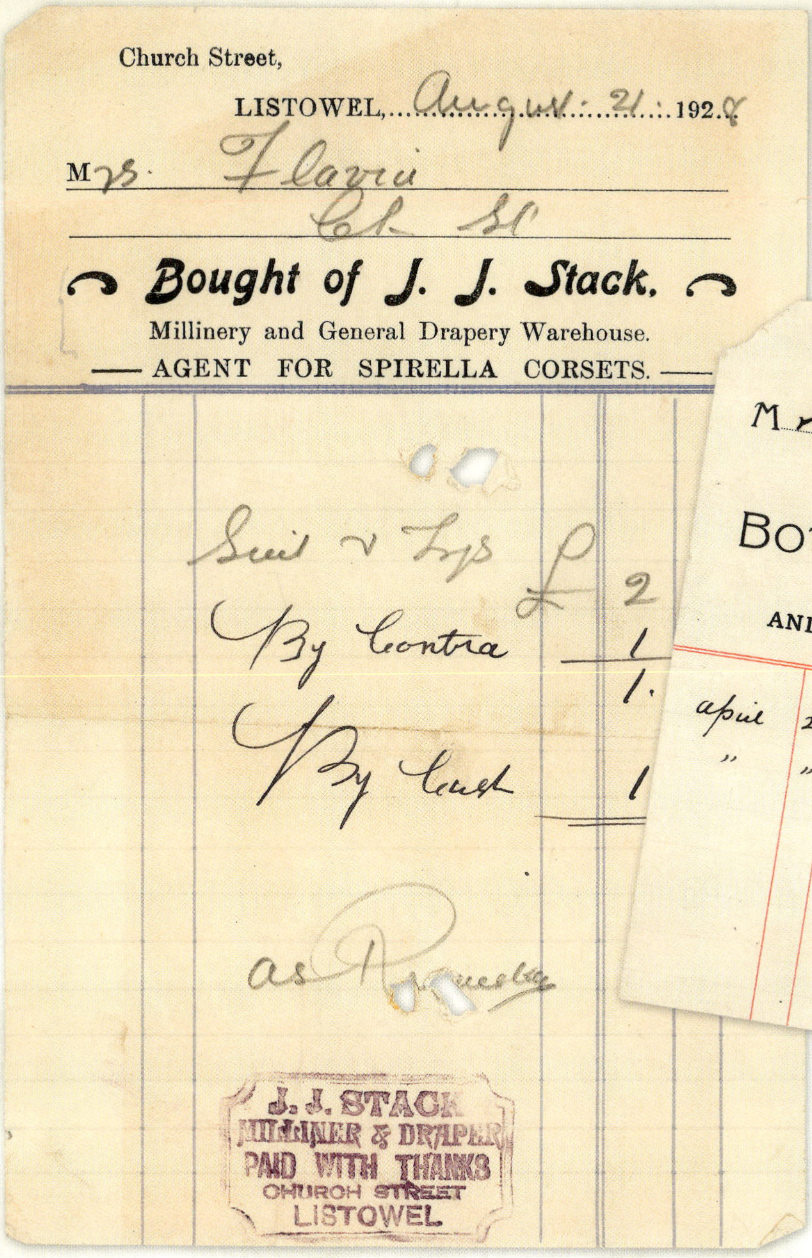
Church Street,

LISTOWEL, August 21 192 8

Mrs. Flavin

Ch St

Bought of J. J. Stack.

Millinery and General Drapery Warehouse.

— AGENT FOR SPIRELLA CORSETS. —

Suit & Tops £ 2

By Contra 1

1.

By Cash 1

as Requested

J. J. STACK
MILLINER & DRAPER
PAID WITH THANKS
CHURCH STREET
LISTOWEL

47 Church Street

John Joseph and Bridie Stack owned a millinery and general drapery.

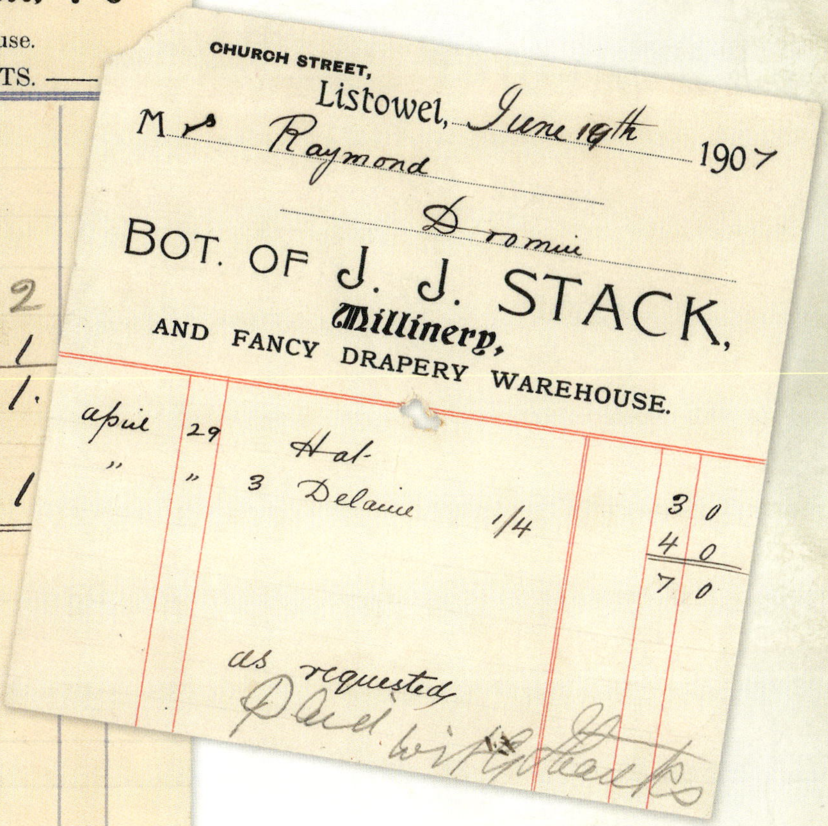
CHURCH STREET,

Listowel, June 19th 1907

Mrs Raymond

BOT. OF J. J. STACK,

Millinery,

AND FANCY DRAPERY WAREHOUSE.

april	29	Hat		3 0
"	"	3 Delaine	1/4	4 0
				7 0

as requested

Paid with thanks

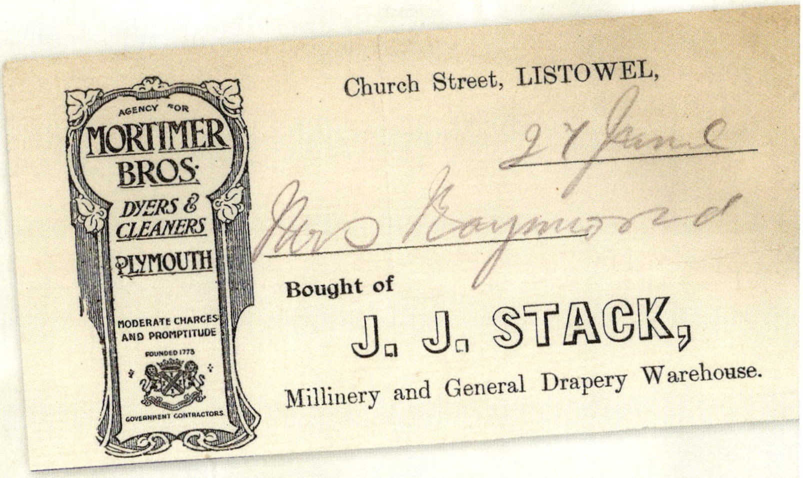
AGENCY FOR
MORTIMER BROS
DYERS & CLEANERS
PLYMOUTH
MODERATE CHARGES AND PROMPTITUDE
FOUNDED 1775
GOVERNMENT CONTRACTORS

Church Street, LISTOWEL,

27 June

Mrs Raymond

Bought of

J. J. STACK,

Millinery and General Drapery Warehouse.

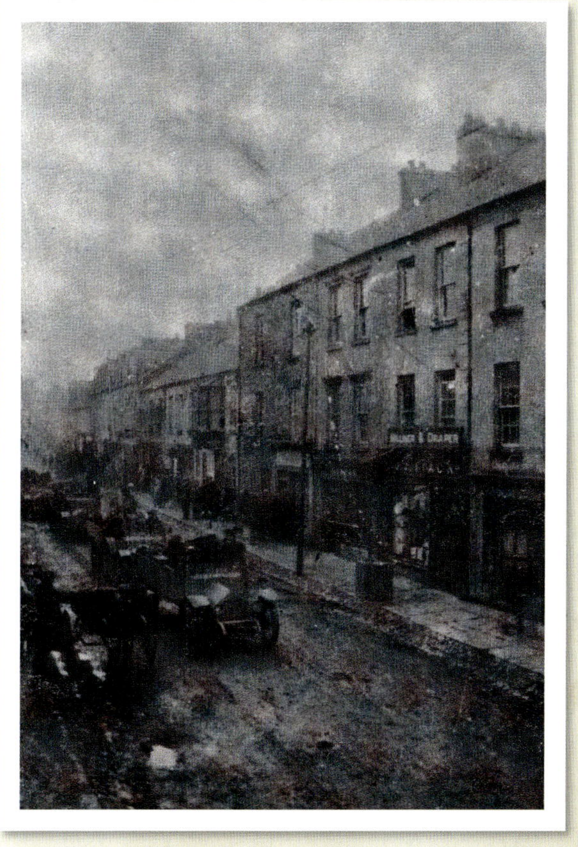

Right: J.J. Stack's drapery shop is seen as the backround to a historic day in the town's history, 14 February 1922, when the Black and Tans left Listowel.

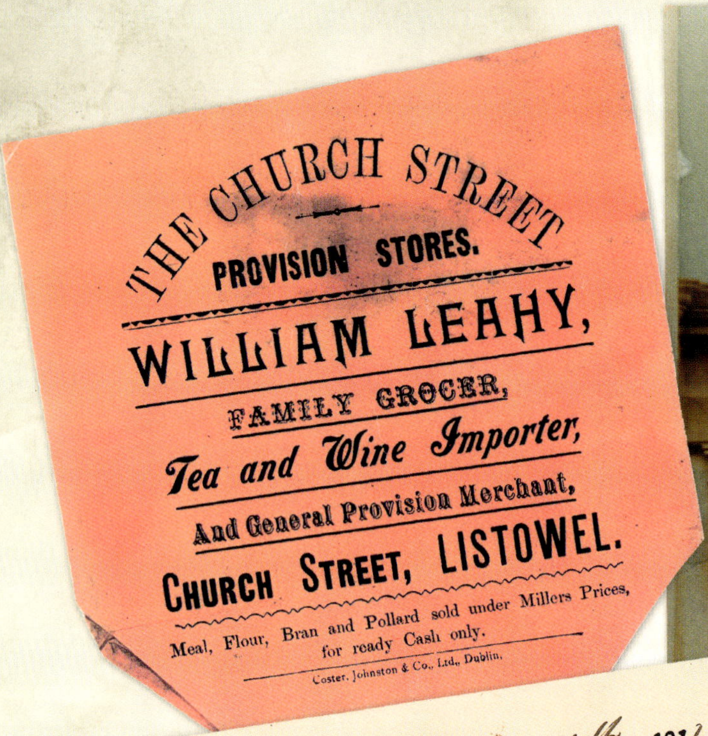
THE CHURCH STREET
PROVISION STORES.
WILLIAM LEAHY,
FAMILY GROCER,
Tea and Wine Importer,
And General Provision Merchant,
CHURCH STREET, LISTOWEL.
Meal, Flour, Bran and Pollard sold under Millers Prices, for ready Cash only.
Coster, Johnston & Co., Ltd., Dublin.

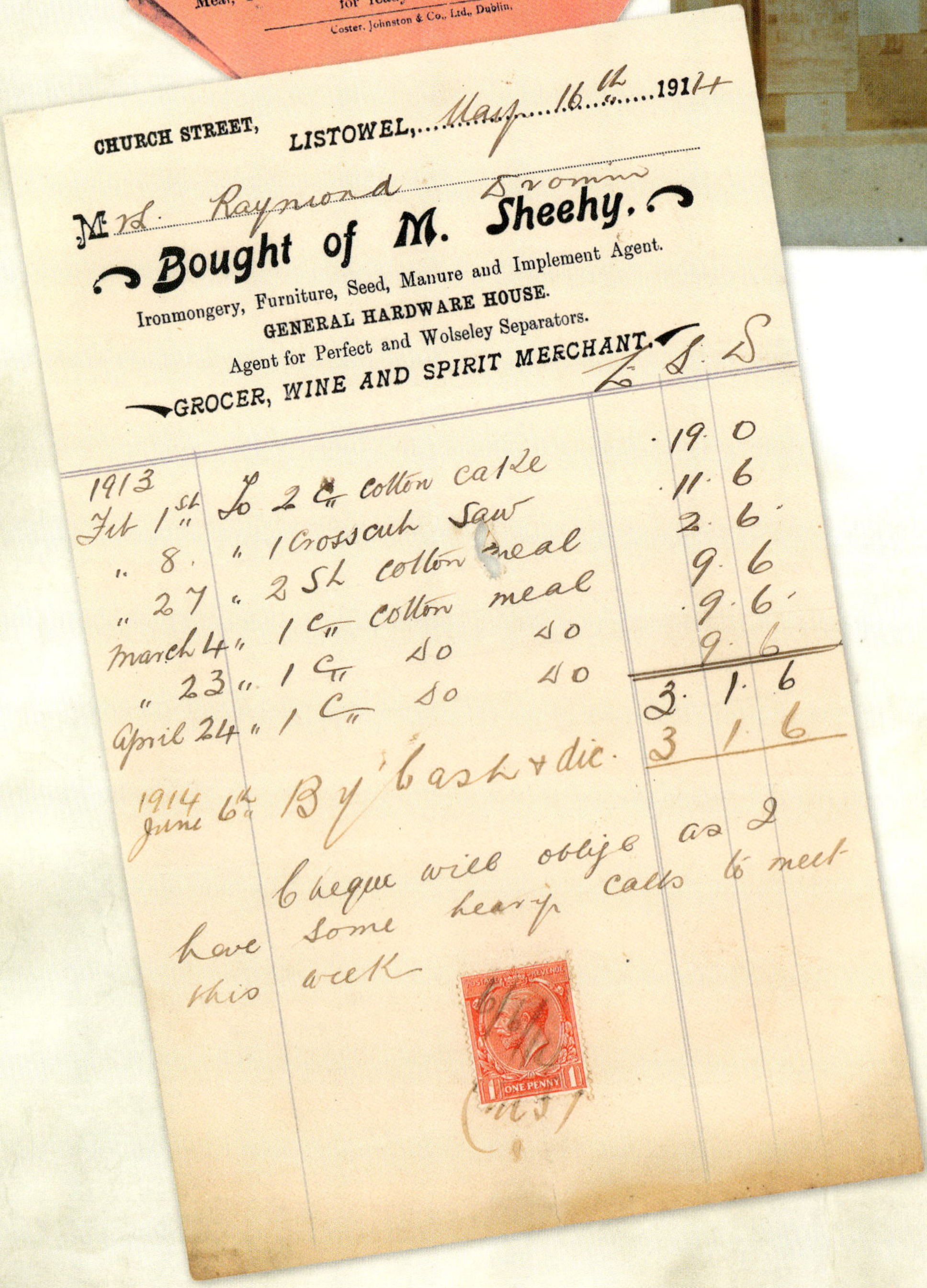
CHURCH STREET, LISTOWEL, May 16th 1914

Mr Raymond [illegible]

Bought of M. Sheehy.
Ironmongery, Furniture, Seed, Manure and Implement Agent.
GENERAL HARDWARE HOUSE.
Agent for Perfect and Wolseley Separators.
GROCER, WINE AND SPIRIT MERCHANT.

		£	S.	D.
			19	0
1913 Feb 1st	To 2 Cwt cotton cake		11	6
" 8	" 1 Crosscut Saw		2	6
" 27	" 2 St cotton meal		9	6
March 4	" 1 Cwt cotton meal		9	6
" 23	" 1 Cwt do do		9	6
April 24	" 1 Cwt do do	3	1	6
1914 June 6th	By Cash & dic	3	1	6

Cheque will oblige as I have some heavy calls to meet this week

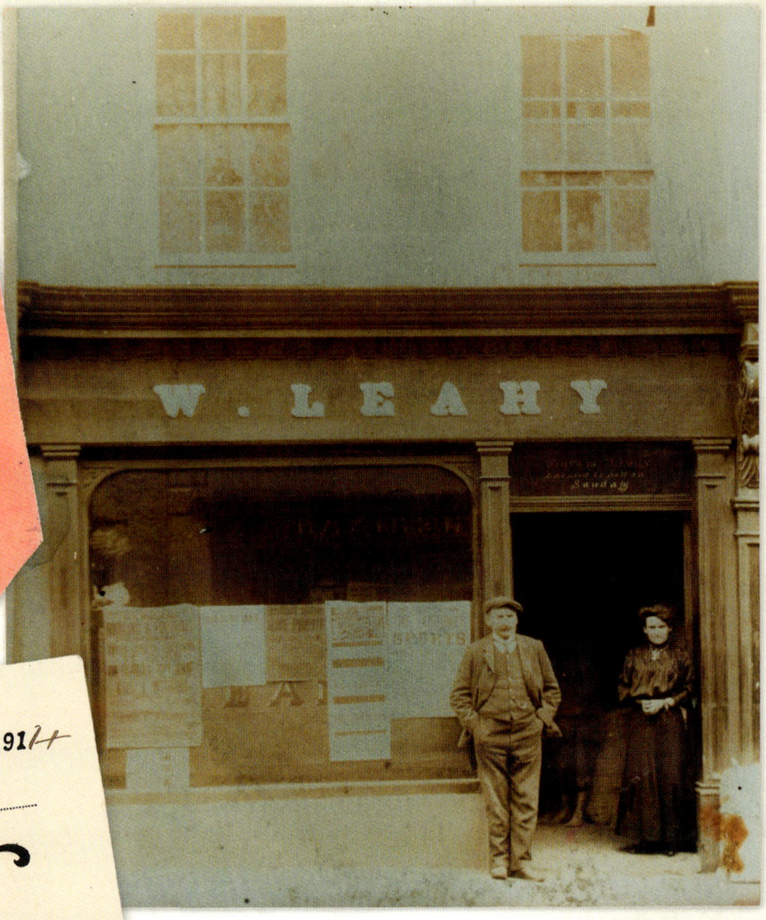

41 & 43 Church Street
William Leahy, a native of Carhooearagh, Moyvane, ran a very successful provision store and bar for many years. The business was inherited by his daughter Mary, who married Morgan Sheehy from Scrahan, Duagh. Sheehy had been indentured to John McKenna and had served his time in the hardware business. He opened a hardware shop in the adjoining house No. 43. This was in operation until the 1930s.

Photo: William and his wife Mary Leahy pose outside the door of their public house at 41 Church Street in 1904.

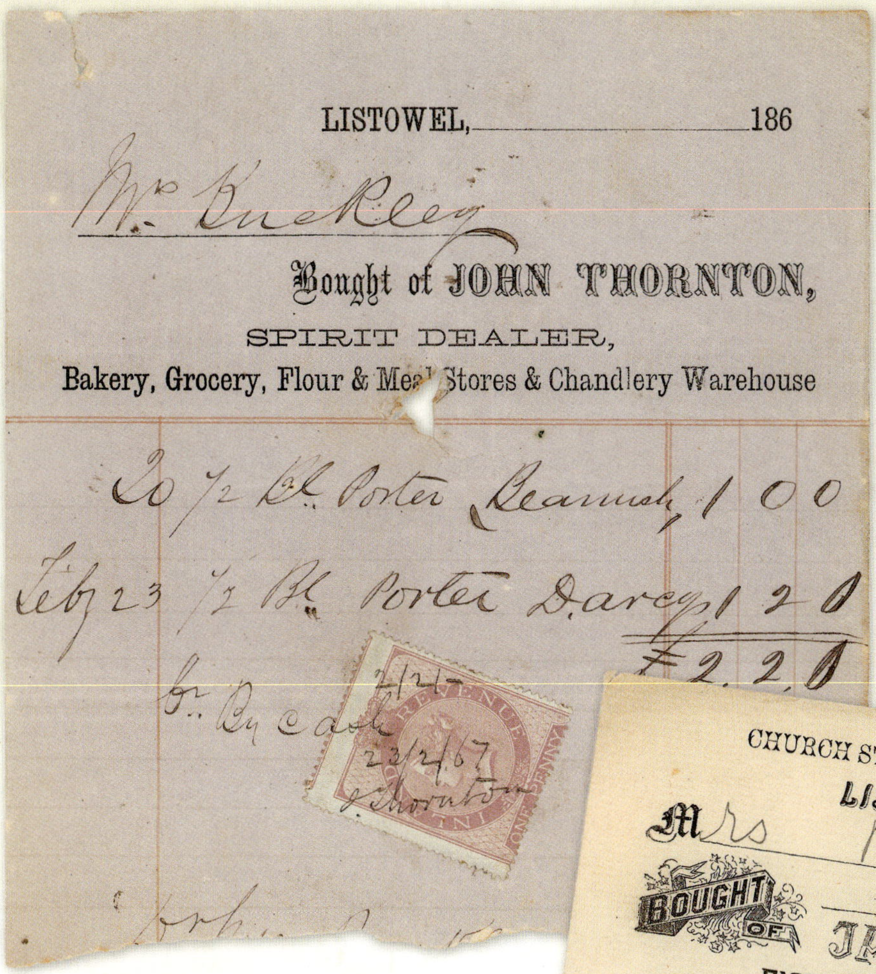
LISTOWEL, ______________ 186

Mr Buckley

Bought of JOHN THORNTON,

SPIRIT DEALER,

Bakery, Grocery, Flour & Meal Stores & Chandlery Warehouse

20 ½ Bl. Porter Dearnish		1	0	0
Feby 23 ½ Bl. Porter D.arcy		1	2	0
		£2	2	0

Br. By cash 22/2/67 J Thornton

John Thornton and Margaret Kissane, both from Lisselton, were married on February 16, 1863. They settled in Church Street, where they had an extensive business, including Bakery, Spirit Dealer's, Flour and Meal Store. In later years the family had a shop in William Street. One of the sons, Jack, had a sweet shop at the Convent Cross as well as some fields where a section of the Feale Drive housing estate is built today.

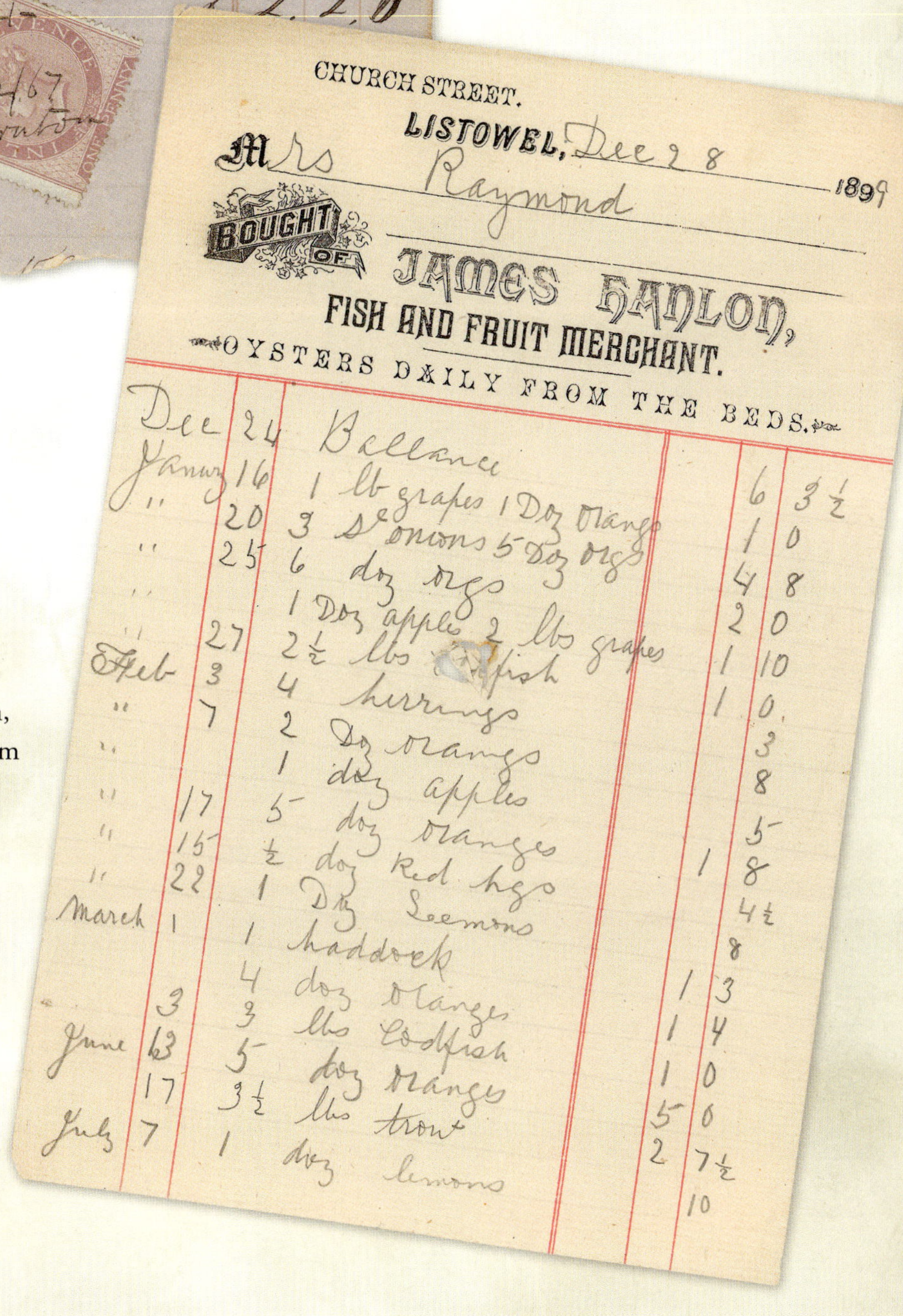
CHURCH STREET.

LISTOWEL, Dec 28 1899

Mrs Raymond

BOUGHT OF JAMES HANLON,

FISH AND FRUIT MERCHANT.

OYSTERS DAILY FROM THE BEDS.

Dec	24	Ballance		6	3½
Janry	16	1 lb grapes 1 Doz Oranges		1	0
"	20	3 st onions 5 Doz eggs		4	8
"	25	6 doz eggs		2	0
"		1 Doz apples 2 lbs grapes		1	10
"	27	2½ lbs Codfish		1	10
Feb	3	4 herrings		1	0
"	7	2 Doz oranges			3
"		1 doz apples			8
"	17	5 doz oranges			5
"	15	½ doz Red figs		1	8
"	22	1 Doz Lemons			4½
March	1	1 haddock			8
		4 doz oranges		1	3
	3	3 lbs Codfish		1	4
June	13	5 doz oranges		1	0
	17	3½ lbs trout		5	6
July	7	1 doz lemons		2	7½
					10

31 Church Street

James O'Hanlon from County Louth, and his wife, Bridget O'Mahoney from Moyvane, were proprietors of a Fish and Fruit shop at No. 31 Church Street. James was known locally as 'Jumping Alive' because of his standard reply when asked about the freshness of his fish stock. "My fish are so fresh, they're jumping alive".

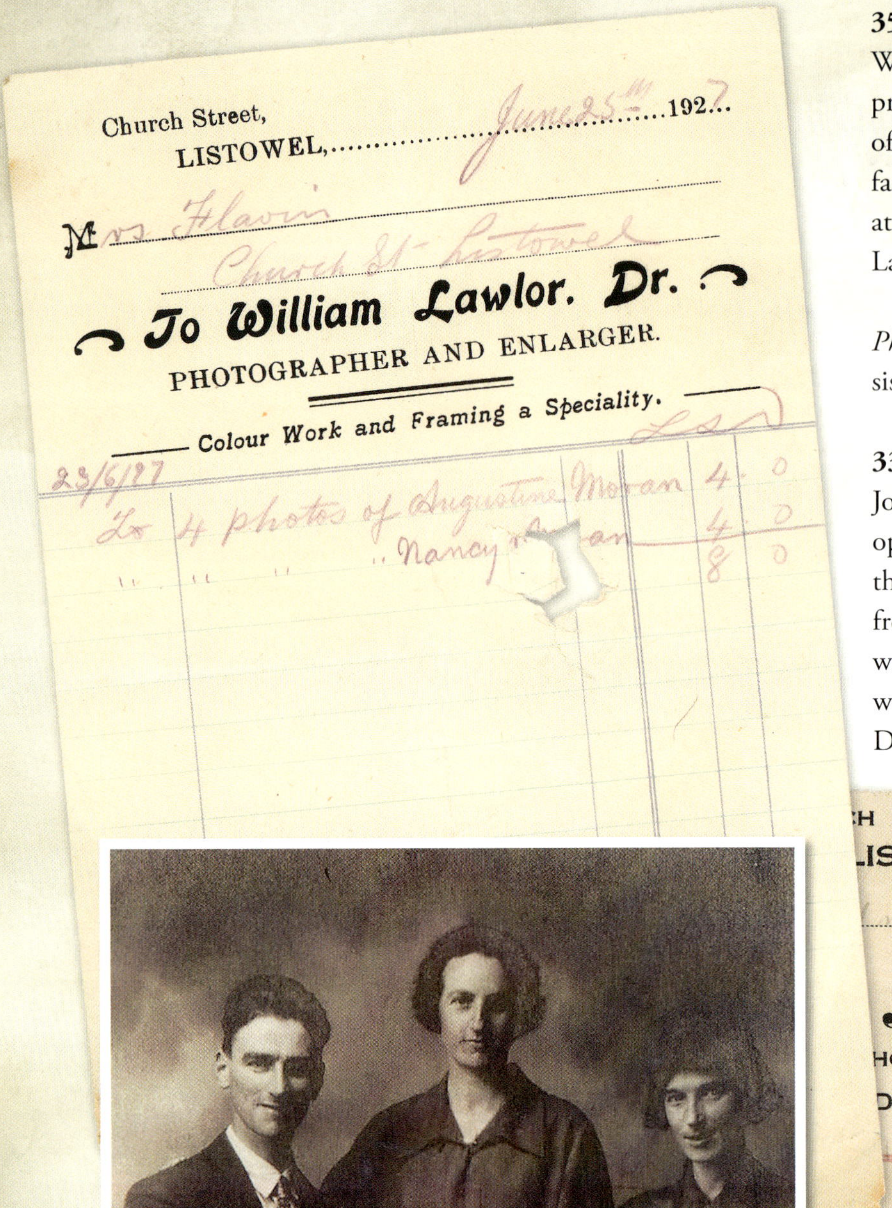
Church Street,
LISTOWEL, June 25th 1927
Mrs Flavin
Church St- Listowel
To William Lawlor. Dr.
PHOTOGRAPHER AND ENLARGER.
Colour Work and Framing a Speciality.

		£ s d
23/6/27	To 4 photos of Augustine Moran	4 0
	" " " Nancy Moran	4 0
		8 0

35 Church Street

William Lawlor was one of the first local professional photographers in Listowel. Many of his photographs turn up occasionally in old family albums. He lived in the family home at 35 Church Street, which was known as Lawlor's Hotel and Restaurant.

Photo: William Lawlor pictured with his sisters, Julia and Mary.

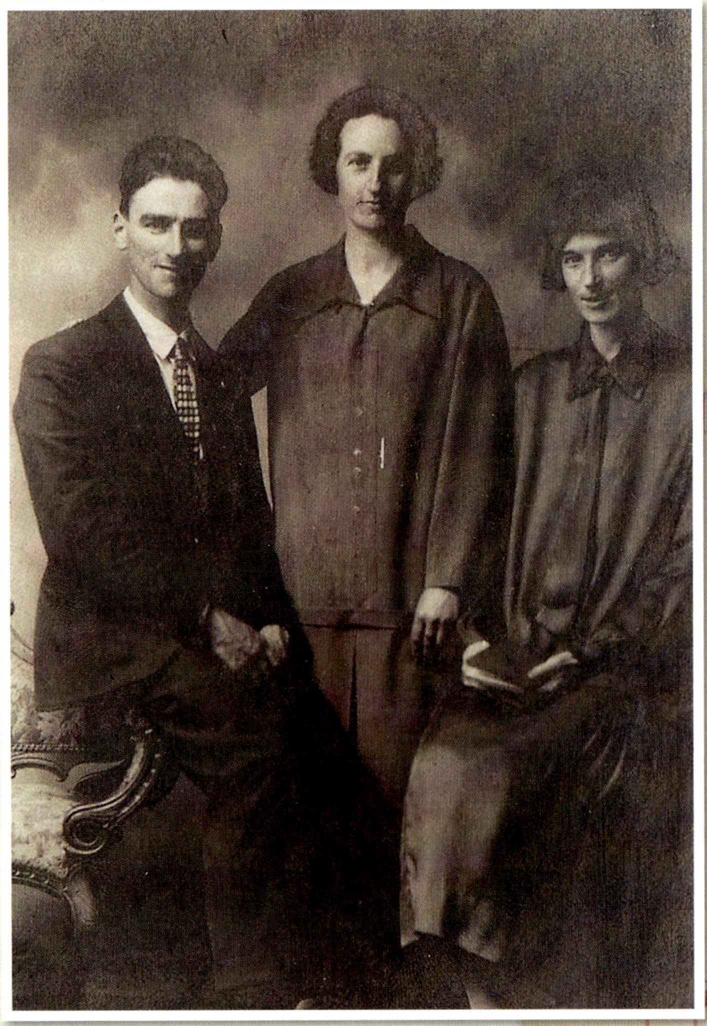

33 Church Street

John O'Dwyer came from Limerick. He opened a shop at 33 Church Street. Following the death of his wife, who was a Sheehan from Ballygrennan, he remarried. His second wife, Hannah, also from Limerick, had worked previously with the Raymonds of Dromin House.

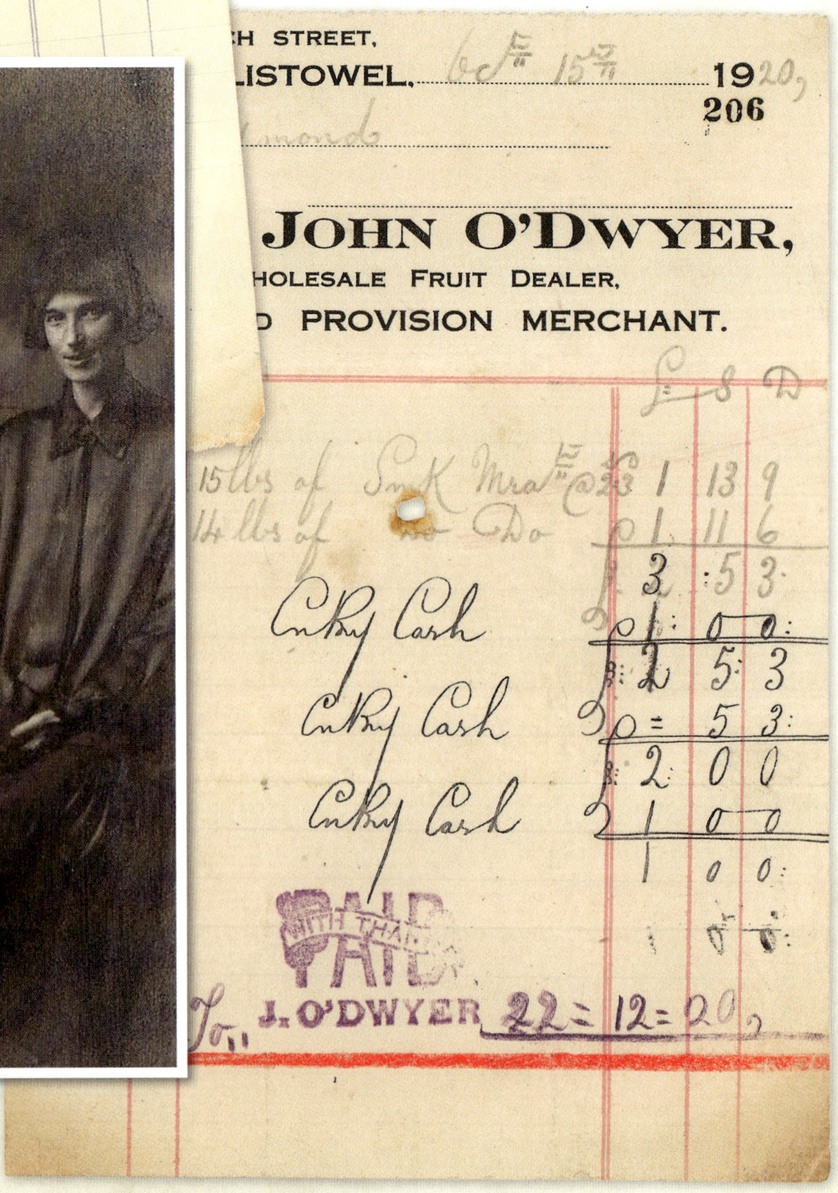
H STREET,
LISTOWEL, Oct 15th 1920
206
JOHN O'DWYER,
HOLESALE FRUIT DEALER,
D PROVISION MERCHANT.
£ S D
15 lbs of Smk Meat @ 1 13 9
14 lbs of Do 1 11 6
3 5 3
Cr by Cash 1 0 0
2 5 3
Cr by Cash 5 3
2 0 0
Cr by Cash 1 0 0
1 0 0
PAID WITH THANKS
J. O'DWYER 22=12=20

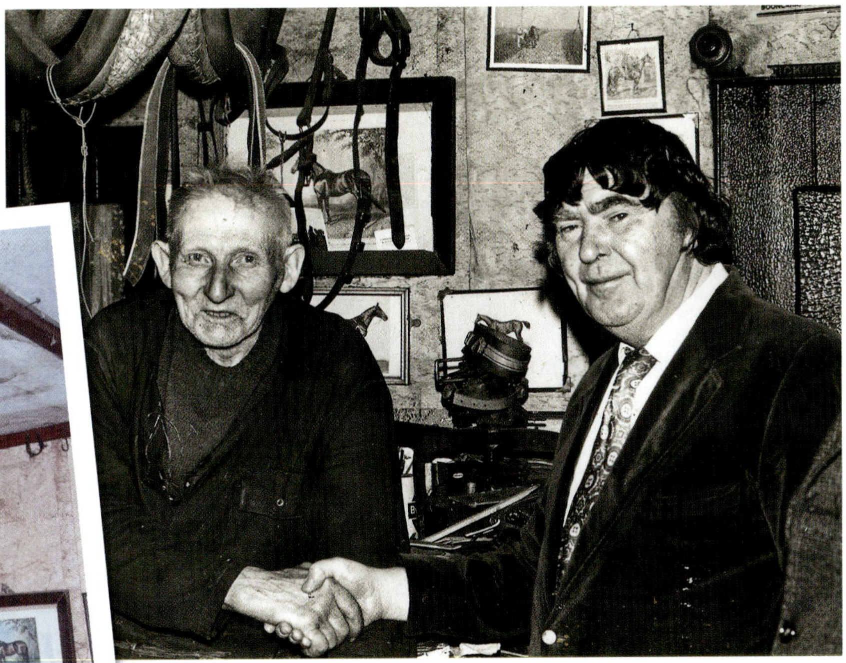

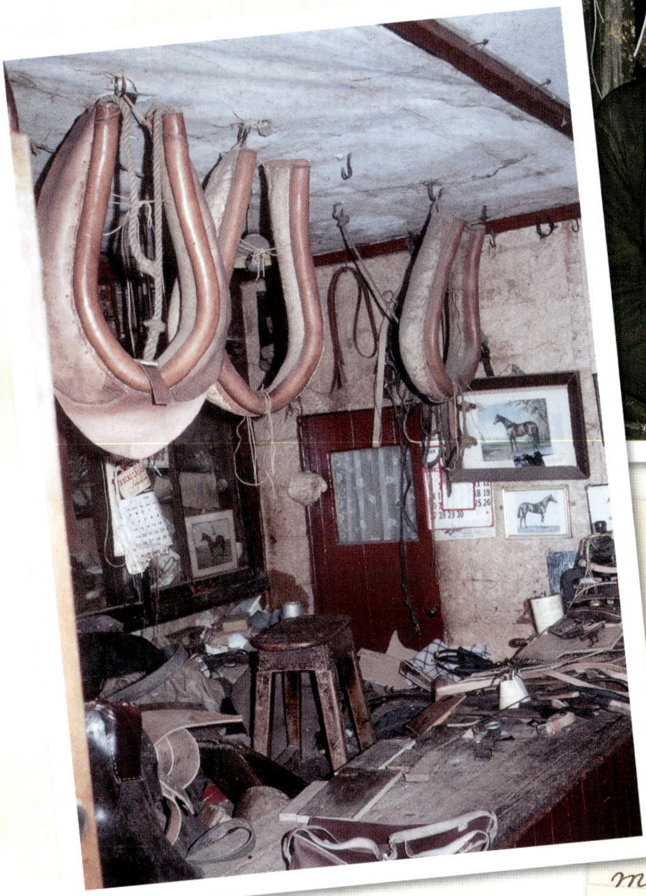

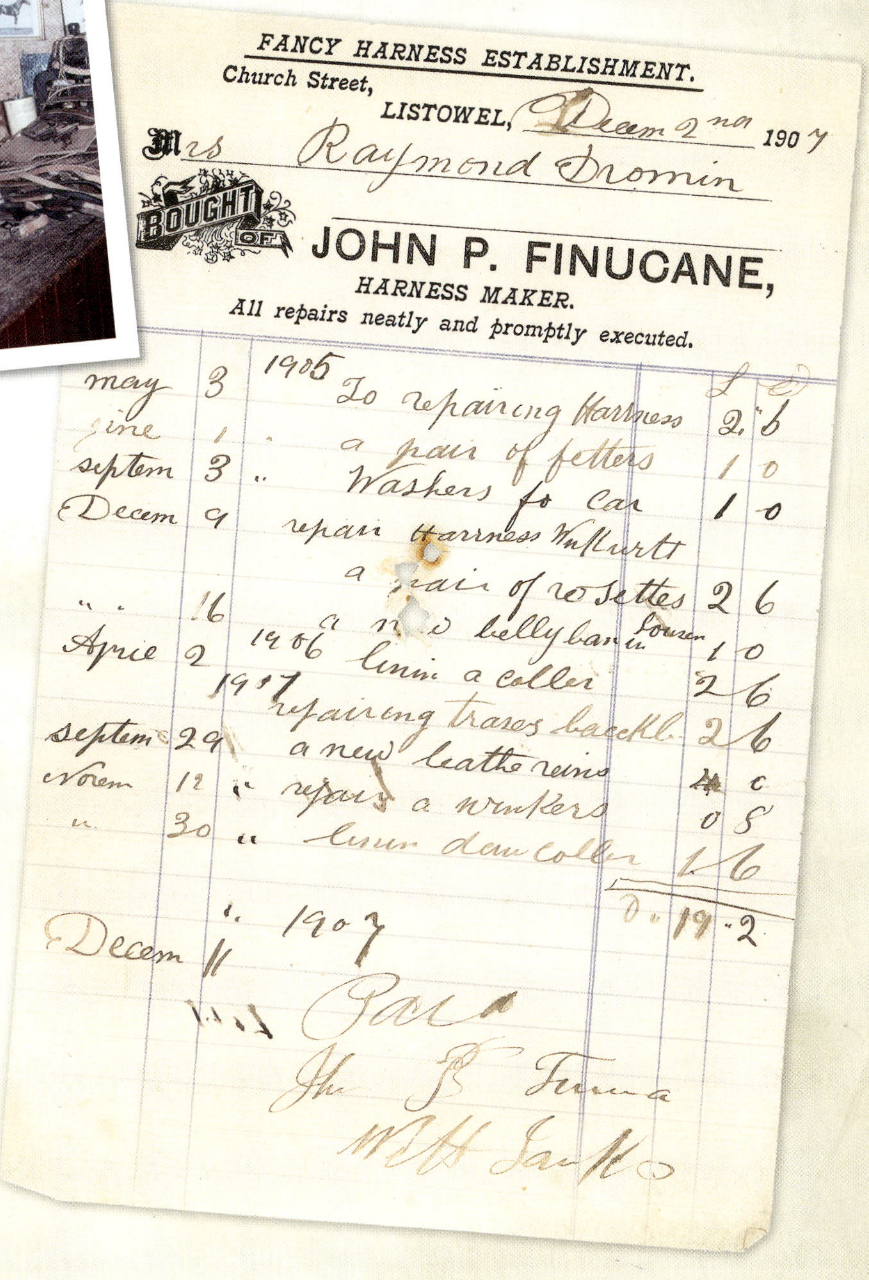
FANCY HARNESS ESTABLISHMENT.
Church Street,
LISTOWEL, Decem 2nd 1907
Mrs Raymond Dromin
BOUGHT OF JOHN P. FINUCANE,
HARNESS MAKER.
All repairs neatly and promptly executed.

			£	s d
may	3	1905 To repairing Harness		2 6
june	1	" a pair of fetters		1 0
septem	3	" Washers for car		1 0
Decem	9	repair Harness		
		a pair of rosettes		2 6
"	16	a new bellyband		1 0
Aprie	2	1906 linin a coller		2 6
		1907 repairing traces buckle		2 6
septem	29	a new leather reins		4 0
Novem	12	" repair a winkers		0 5
"	30	" linin draw coller		1 6
			0	19 2

Decem 11 1907

Paid

J. P. Finucane

W. H. Jack

25 Church Street

Finucane's harness-making business was established by John P. Finucane in the 1880s. The business continued for nearly a century. The shop interior changed little during this time, as the early 1980 photograph shows. The second photograph shows the last harness-maker, Paddy Finucane, greeting local balladeer and songwriter, Seán McCarthy.

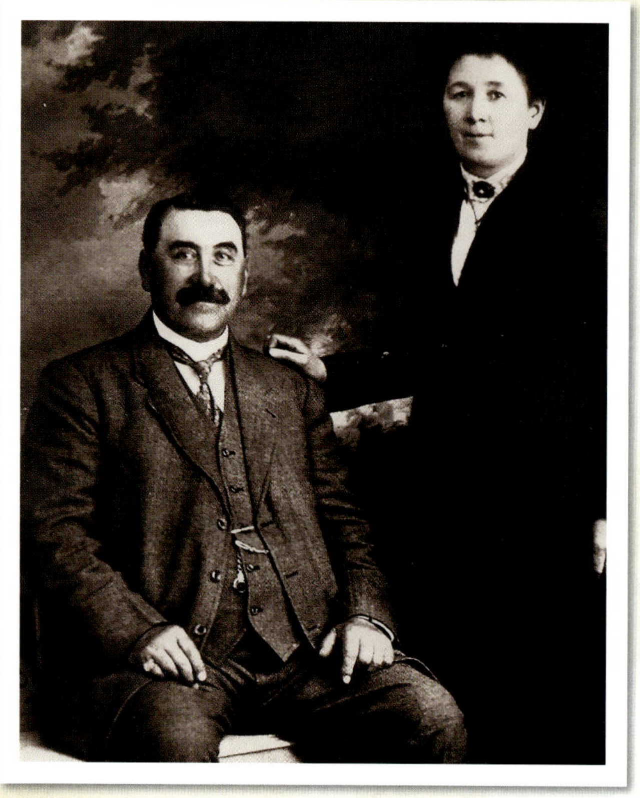

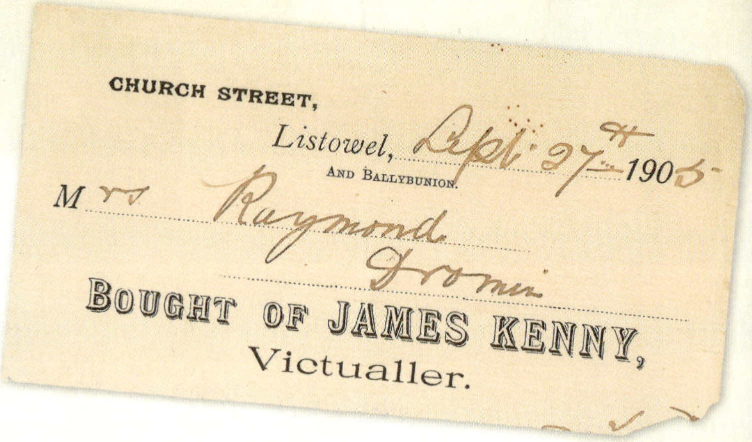
CHURCH STREET,
Listowel, Sept. 27th 1905
AND BALLYBUNION.
Mrs Raymond
Dromin
BOUGHT OF JAMES KENNY,
Victualler.

21 Church Street

James and Elizabeth Kenny, parents of fourteen children, ran a butcher's shop at Church Street. Two of their sons followed into the business, Pat at the home shop, and John Joe, who opened a butcher's shop in the Square in part of what was Danaher's house.

Photo left: James and Elizabeth Kenny.

15 Church Street

The Stack family came from Carhooearagh, Moyvane. One of a number of families of the same name in the locality, they were distinguished by the prefix Morrisin Tom. Their predecessors in the Church Street house were Timothy and Mary Molyneaux. Mary was a relative of the Stacks. Shortly after becoming tenants, the Stacks commissioned local plaster artist, Pat McAuliffe, to remodel the house frontage. What he achieved has stood the test of time and is recognised as one of his finest works. Mae Quillinan inherited the house from her aunt Bridget Stack. Mae died in the 1990s. The Emporium is now owned by the Lynch family.

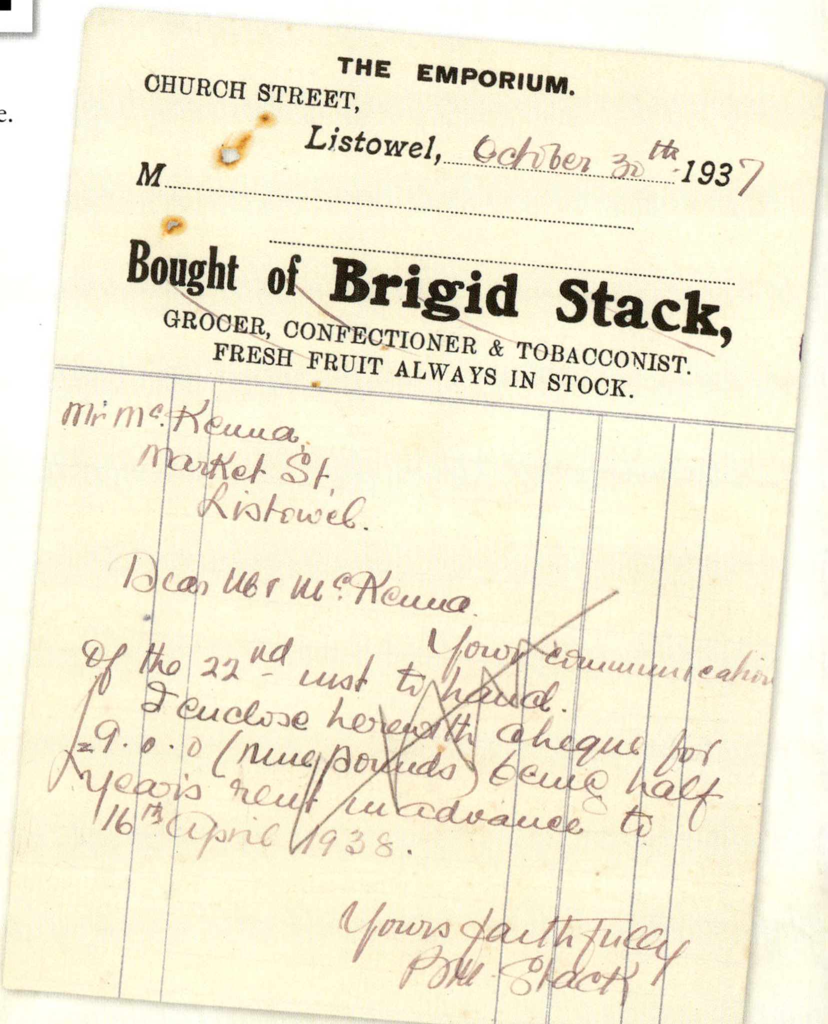
THE EMPORIUM.
CHURCH STREET,
Listowel, October 30th 1937
M
Bought of Brigid Stack,
GROCER, CONFECTIONER & TOBACCONIST.
FRESH FRUIT ALWAYS IN STOCK.

Mr McKenna,
Market St,
Listowel.

Dear Mr McKenna.
Your communication of the 22nd inst to hand.
I enclose herewith cheque for £9.0.0 (nine pounds) being half year's rent in advance to 16th April 1938.

Yours faithfully
B M Stack

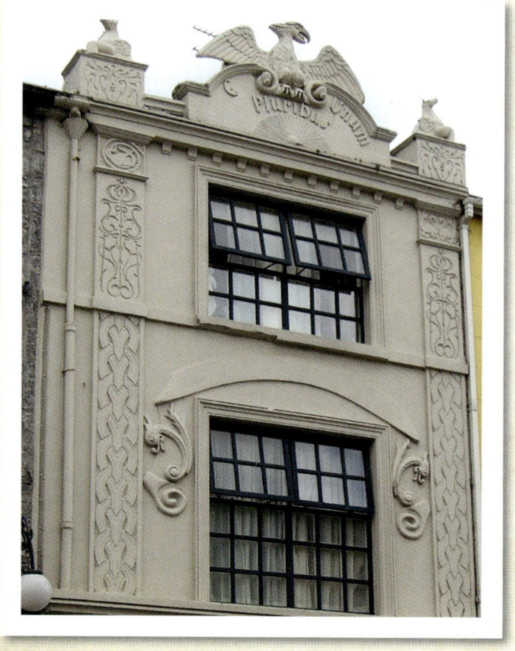

Photo: The artistry of plaster worker Pat McAuliffe is seen to great effect in this photograph by Seán Lynch.

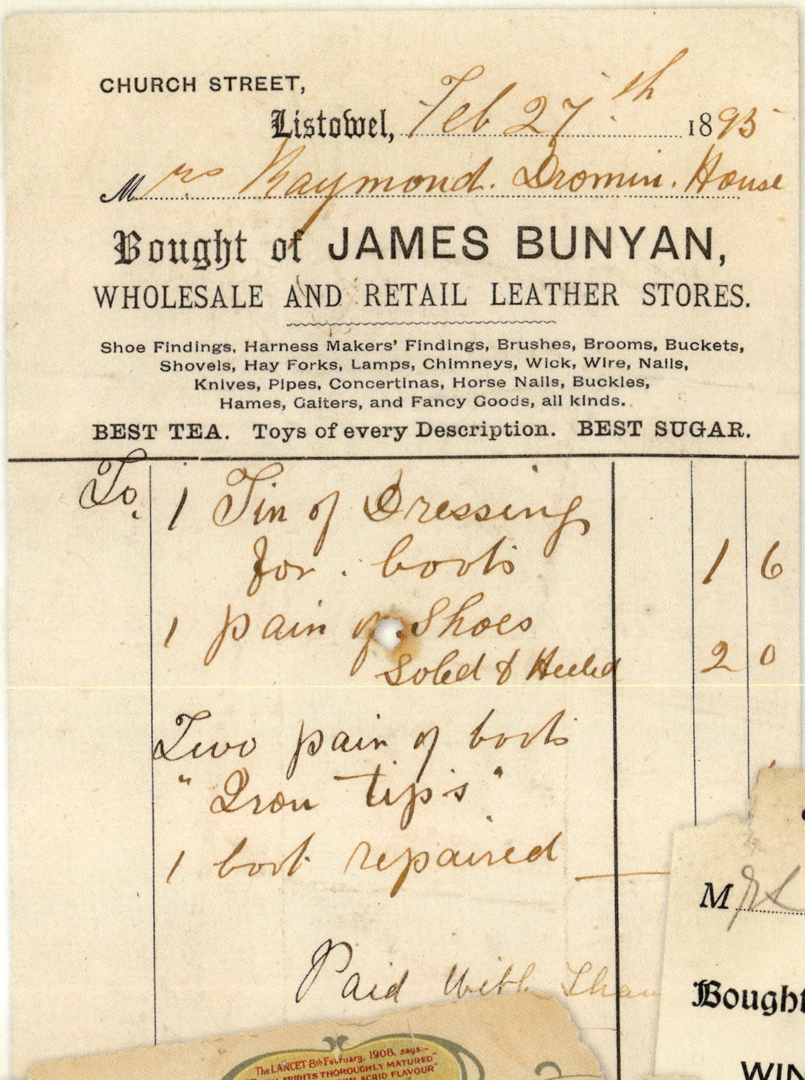

CHURCH STREET,
Listowel, Feb 27th 1895
Mrs Raymond. Dromin House
Bought of JAMES BUNYAN,
WHOLESALE AND RETAIL LEATHER STORES.
Shoe Findings, Harness Makers' Findings, Brushes, Brooms, Buckets, Shovels, Hay Forks, Lamps, Chimneys, Wick, Wire, Nails, Knives, Pipes, Concertinas, Horse Nails, Buckles, Hames, Gaiters, and Fancy Goods, all kinds.
BEST TEA. Toys of every Description. BEST SUGAR.

To 1 Tin of Dressing for boots 1 6
1 pair of Shoes Soled & Heeled 2 0
Two pair of boots "Iron tips"
1 boot repaired
Paid with Thanks

13 Church Street

James Bunyan had a long-established leather store at 13 Church Street. James was married to Margaret Horgan of Ballyduff. The receipt shows the comprehensive range of goods available at the shop.

John J. Forde ran the bar previously owned by Martin Mulvihill. There is a local legend that a coffin was once being shouldered down Church Street on its way to the Church. Those shouldering the coffin, being friendly with Forde, decided to call into his bar, leaving the coffin under the archway at the side of the house. Glasses were raised in respect to the dearly departed. It was said that later that night the mourners went to their homes one by one, and the coffin was left unattended under the arch.

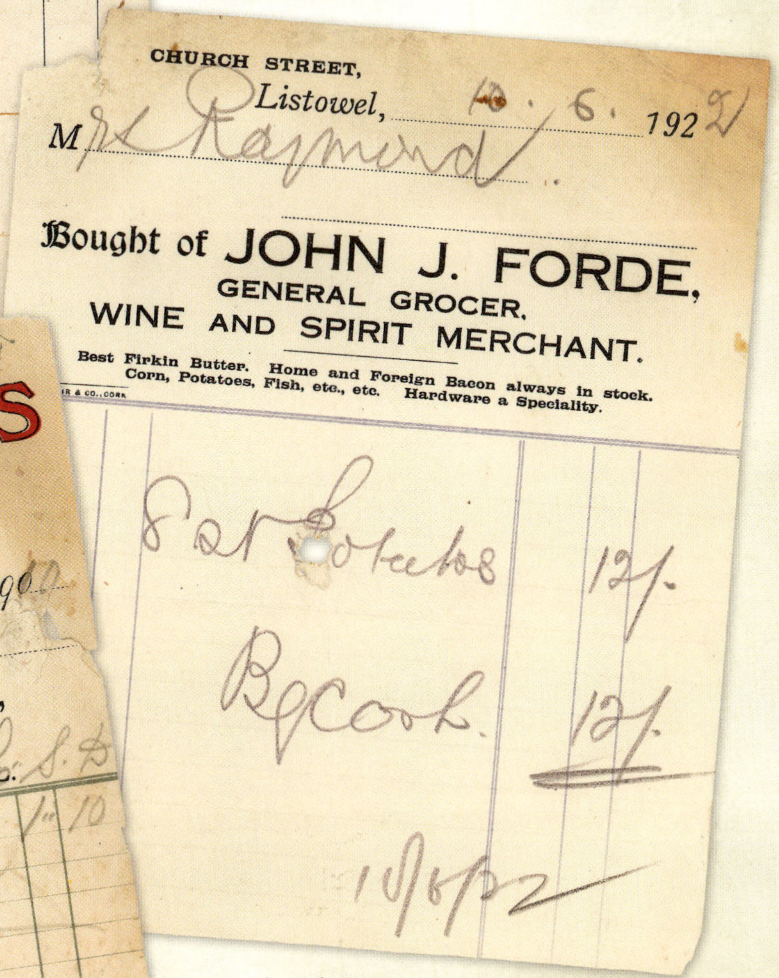

CHURCH STREET,
Listowel, 10. 6. 1921
Mrs Raymond
Bought of JOHN J. FORDE,
GENERAL GROCER,
WINE AND SPIRIT MERCHANT.
Best Firkin Butter. Home and Foreign Bacon always in stock.
Corn, Potatoes, Fish, etc., etc. Hardware a Speciality.

Potatoes 12/-
12/-

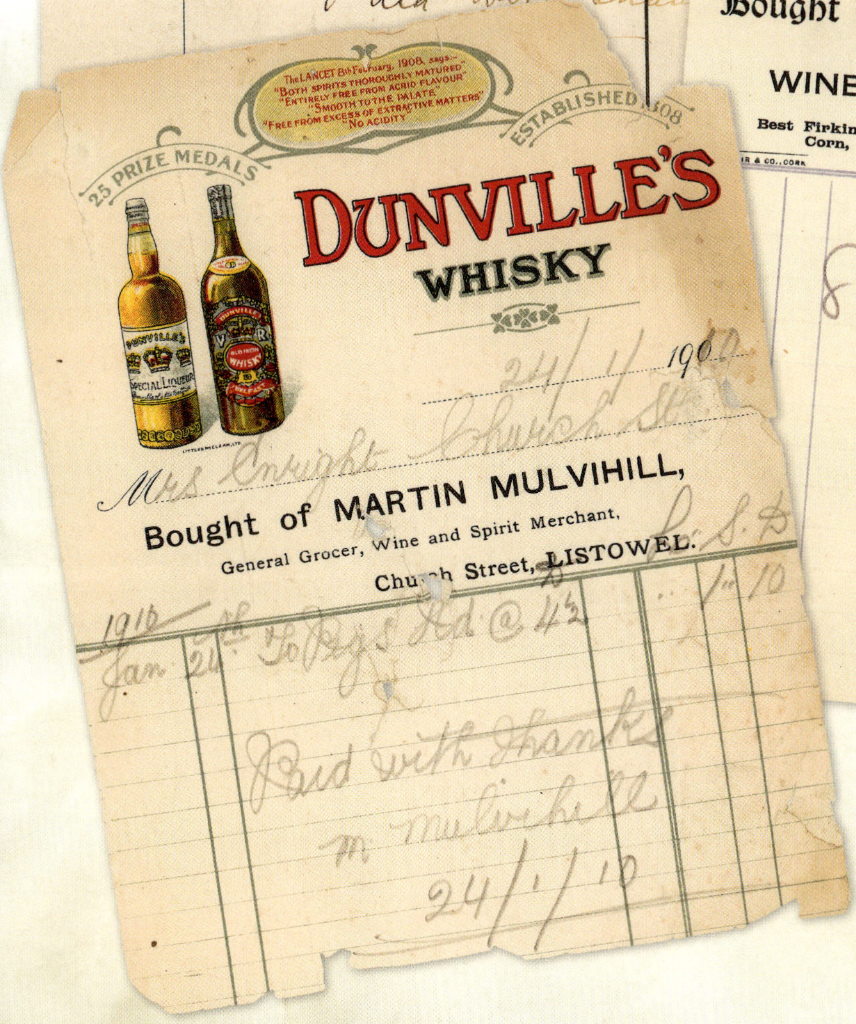

The LANCET 8th February, 1906, says—
"Both spirits thoroughly matured"
"Entirely free from acrid flavour"
"Smooth to the palate"
"Free from excess of extractive matters"
"No acidity"
25 PRIZE MEDALS
ESTABLISHED 1808
DUNVILLE'S
WHISKY
24/1/1910
Mrs Enright Church St.
Bought of MARTIN MULVIHILL,
General Grocer, Wine and Spirit Merchant,
Church Street, LISTOWEL.
£ s. d.
1910 Jan 24th 1 10
Paid with thanks
M Mulvihill
24/1/10

11 Church Street

Martin and Ellen Mulvihill ran a public house in what is now 11 Church Street. Martin was known as 'Head Mulvihill', due to his participation as a Constable during the Belfast riots of 1886.

11 Church Street
J.J. Cronin was born in Finuge. He married Catherine Phelan from Ballyragget, County Kilkenny. She had served her time in the Munster Warehouse in Tralee. Their business was at 11 Church Street, where Mulvihill and Forde had been previous to that. It was later purchased from the Cronins by Michael Kearney of Moyvane.

Photo: Catherine (Phelan) Cronin.

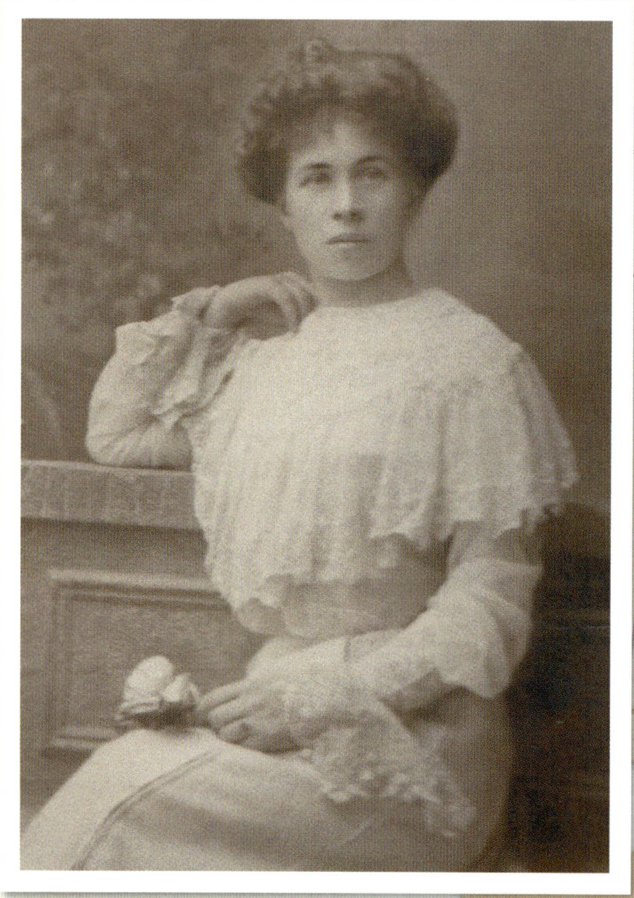

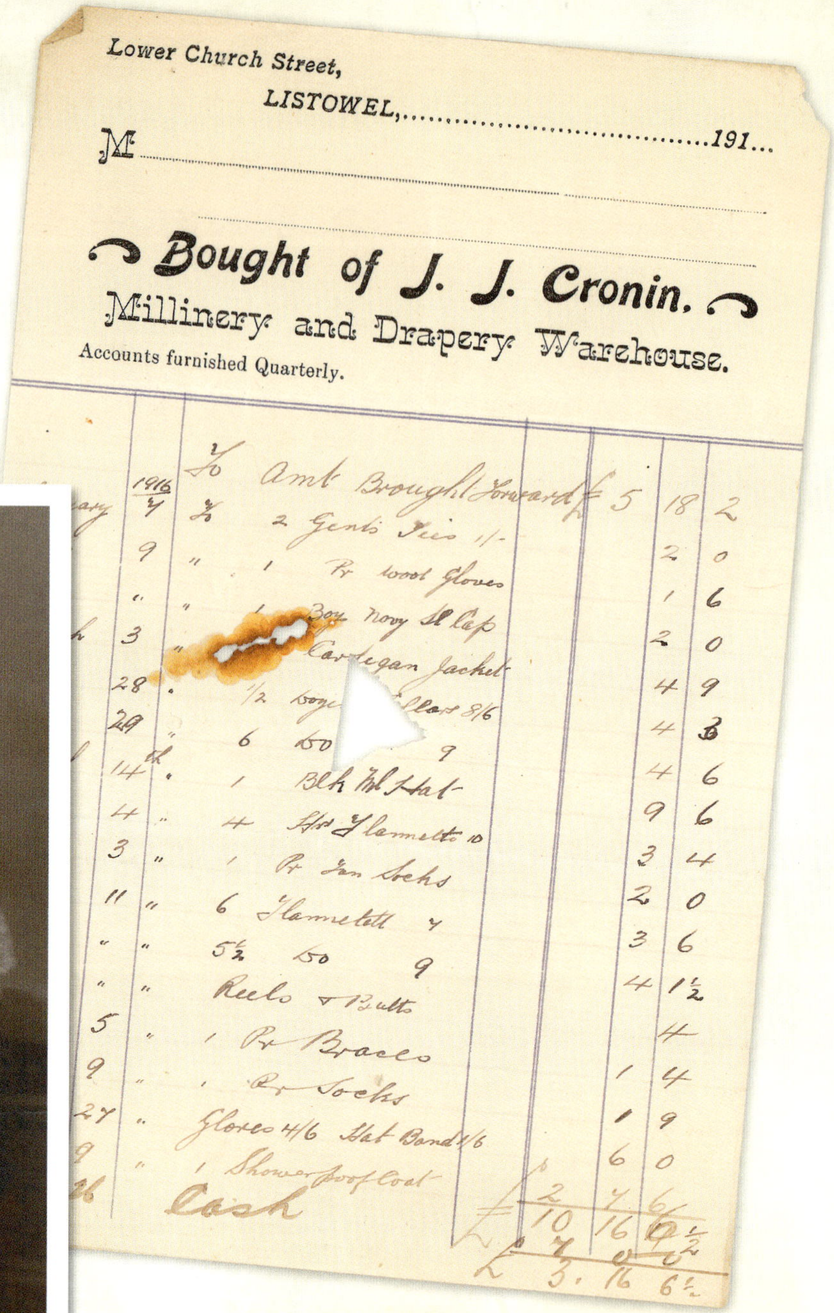

Lower Church Street,
LISTOWEL,..............................191...
M..............................

Bought of J. J. Cronin.
Millinery and Drapery Warehouse.
Accounts furnished Quarterly.

			£	s.	d.
1916		Amt Brought Forward	5	18	2
7	"	2 Gents Ties 1/-		2	0
9	"	1 Pr wool gloves		2	0
"	"	1 Boy Navy Sl Cap		1	6
3		Cardegan Jacket		2	0
28		½ doz ... 8/6		4	9
29		6 do 9		4	3
14		1 Blk ... Hat		4	6
4	"	4 ... Flannette 10		9	6
3	"	1 Pr ... Socks		3	4
11	"	6 Flannette 4		2	0
"	"	5½ do 9		3	6
"	"	Reels & Butts		4	1½
5	"	1 Pr Braces			4
9	"	1 Pr Socks		1	4
27	"	Gloves 4/6 Hat Band 1/6		1	9
9	"	1 Shower proof Coat		6	0
			2	7	6
			10	16	0½
26		Cash	7	0	0
			3	16	6½

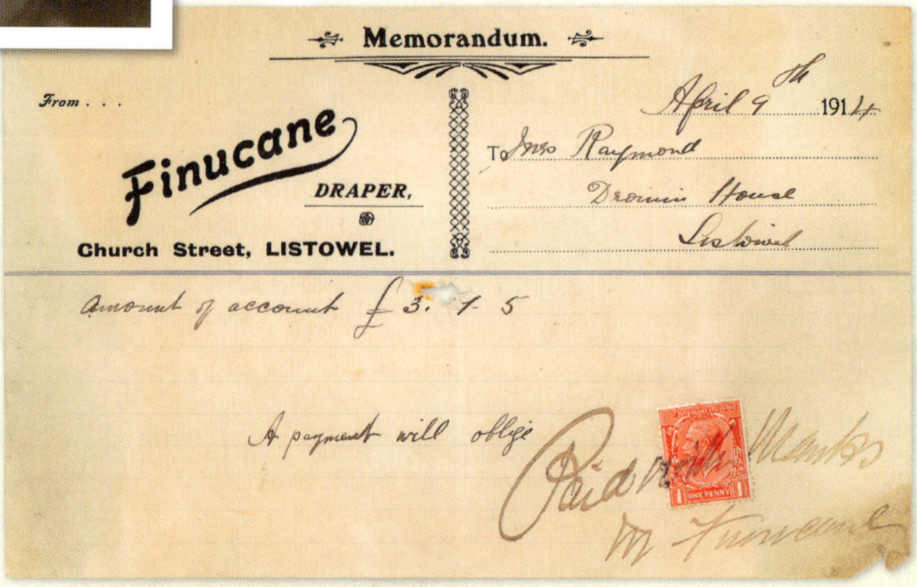

Memorandum.

From . . .
Finucane
DRAPER,
Church Street, LISTOWEL.

April 9th 1914
To Mrs Raymond
Dromin House
Listowel

Amount of account £3. 1. 5

A payment will oblige

Paid with thanks
M Finucane

9 Church Street
Finucane's was a drapery shop in 9 Lower Church Street for over fifty years. After a fire gutted the premises in the 1950s, it never reopened for business. Later, the ground floor served as a science room for the nearby overcrowded Technical School. It was afterwards bought by P.J. Maher. It is now, together with No. 11, part of the extended Listowel Printing Works/Eason complex which has been developed by P.J. Maher's son Barry.

5 Church Street

Number five Church Street, now owned by the Scully family, was used as an egg and poultry store by Fitzpatricks of Kanturk. Their lorries and vans would traverse the North Kerry countryside daily collecting eggs, fowl and feathers.

The Loughnane and Hunt premises were demolished to facilitate the building of the Technical School in the 1930s.

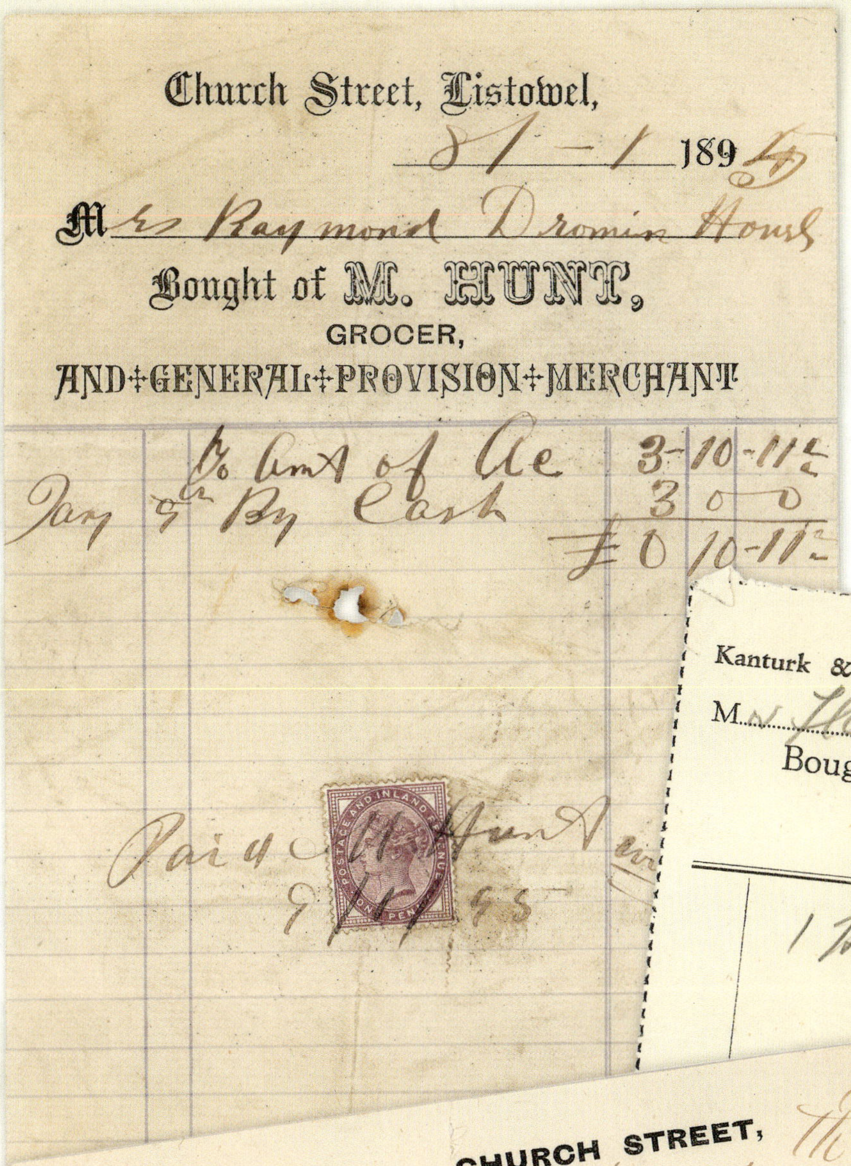
Church Street, Listowel, 31-1-1895

Mrs Raymond Dromin House

Bought of M. HUNT,

GROCER,

AND GENERAL PROVISION MERCHANT

To amt of Ac 3-10-11½

Jany 5th By Cash 3 0 0

£0 10-11½

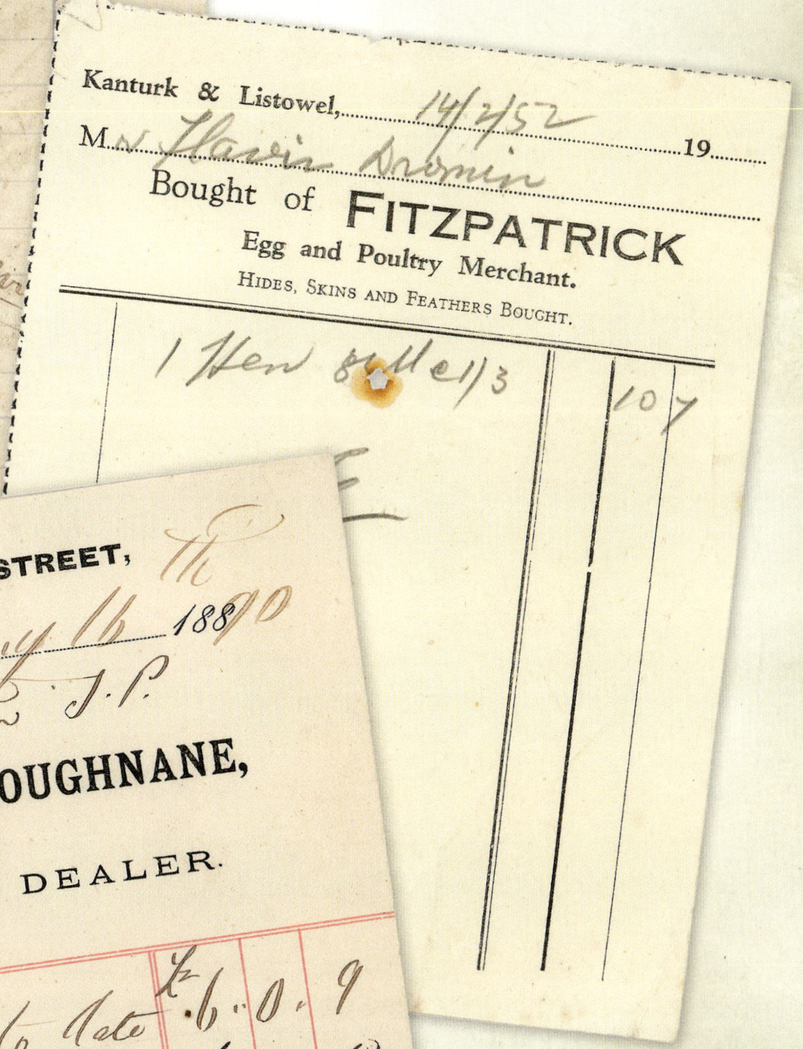
Kanturk & Listowel, 14/2/52 ....19........

M. Flavin Dromin

Bought of FITZPATRICK

Egg and Poultry Merchant.

HIDES, SKINS AND FEATHERS BOUGHT.

1 Hen 8lb @ 1/3 10 7

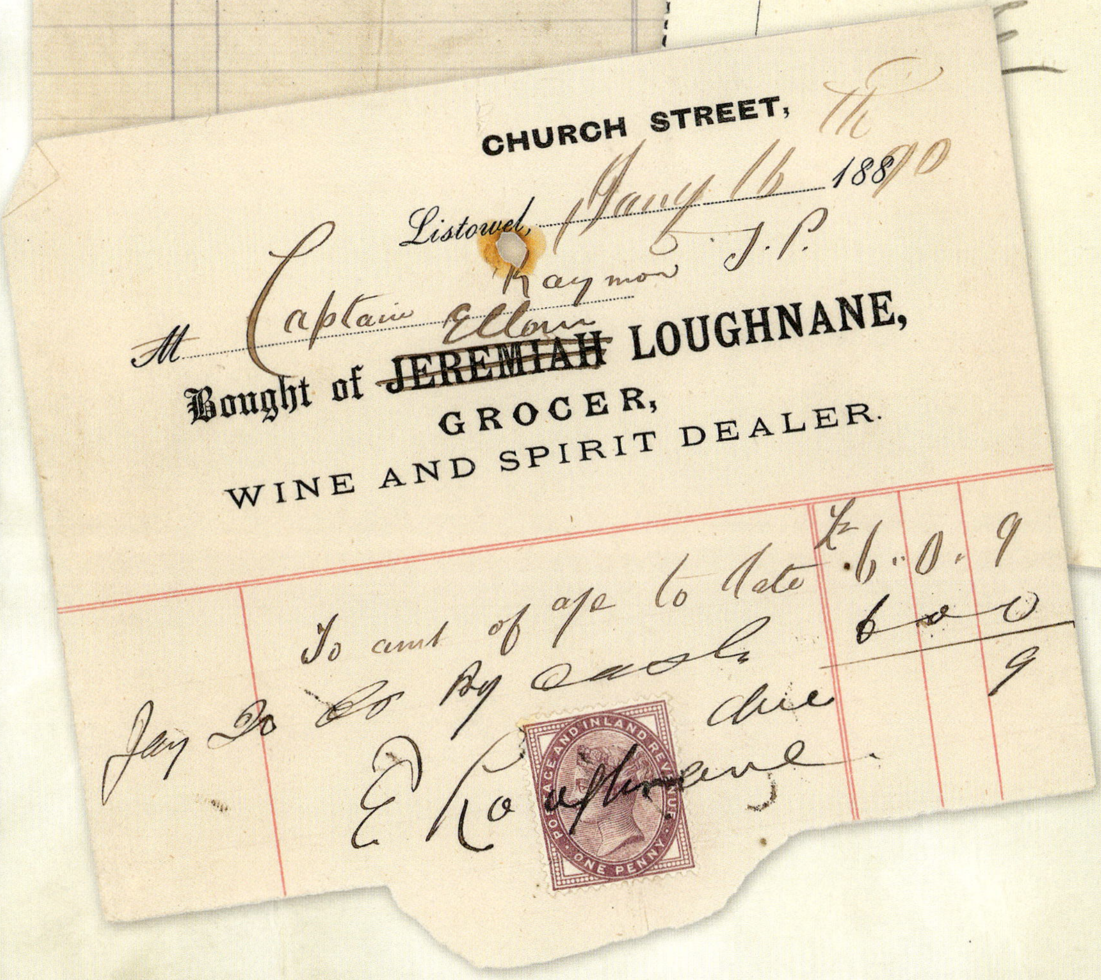
CHURCH STREET,

Listowel, Jany 16th 1890

M Captain Raymond J.P.

Bought of ~~JEREMIAH~~ LOUGHNANE,

GROCER,

WINE AND SPIRIT DEALER.

To amt of a/c to date £6.0.9

Jany 20 By cash 6 0 0

due 9

Chapter 6

MAIN STREET

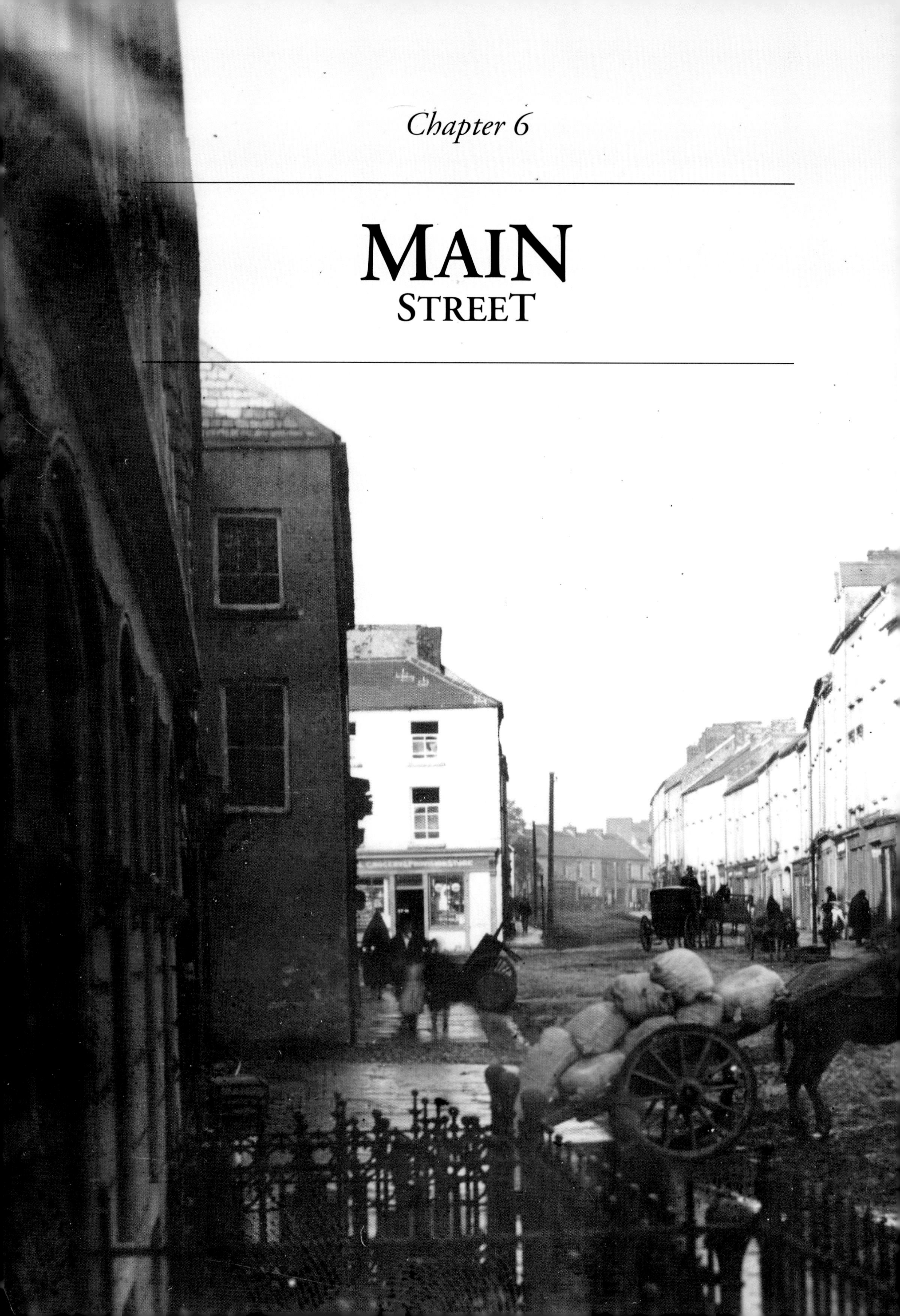

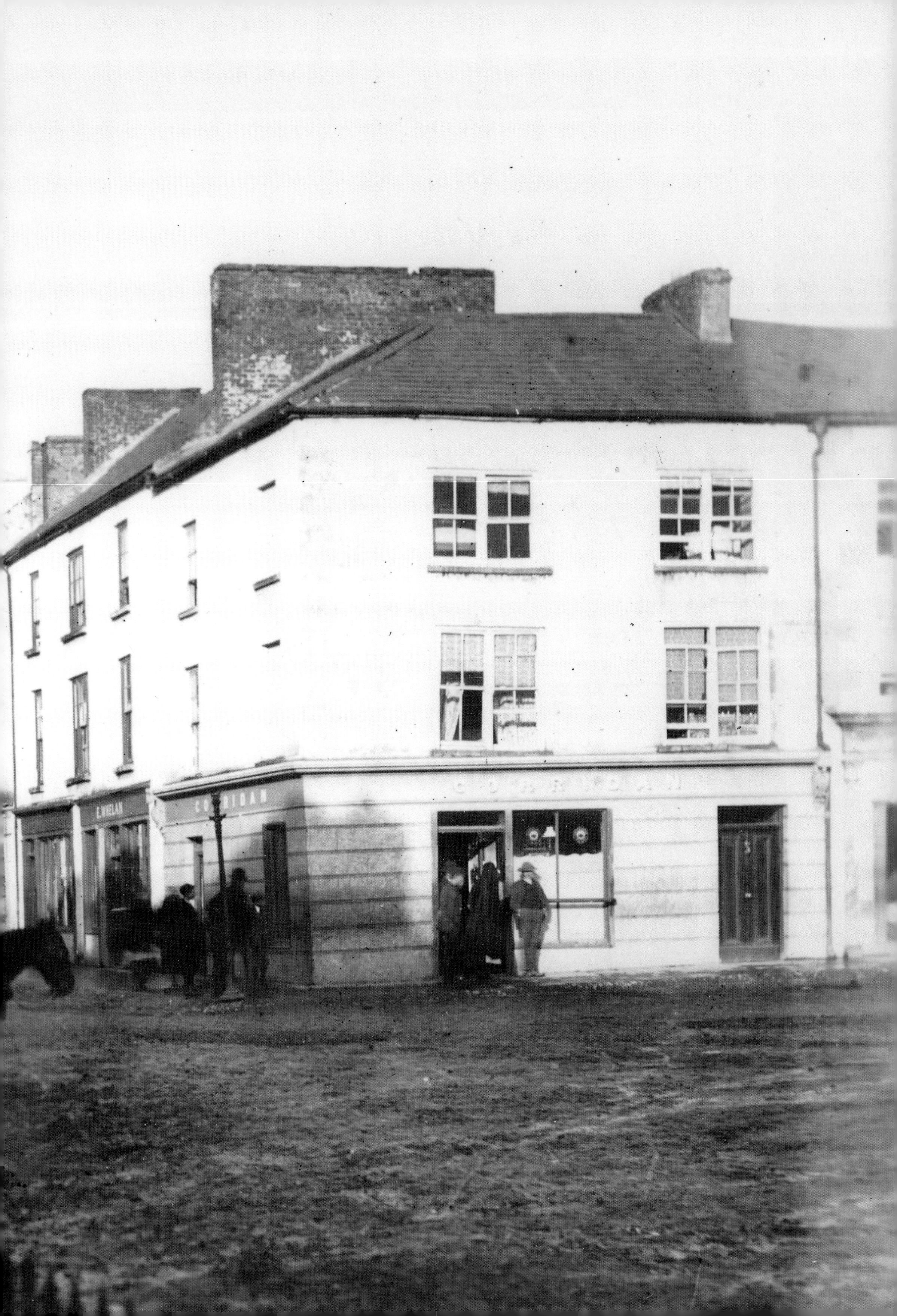
E. WHELAN

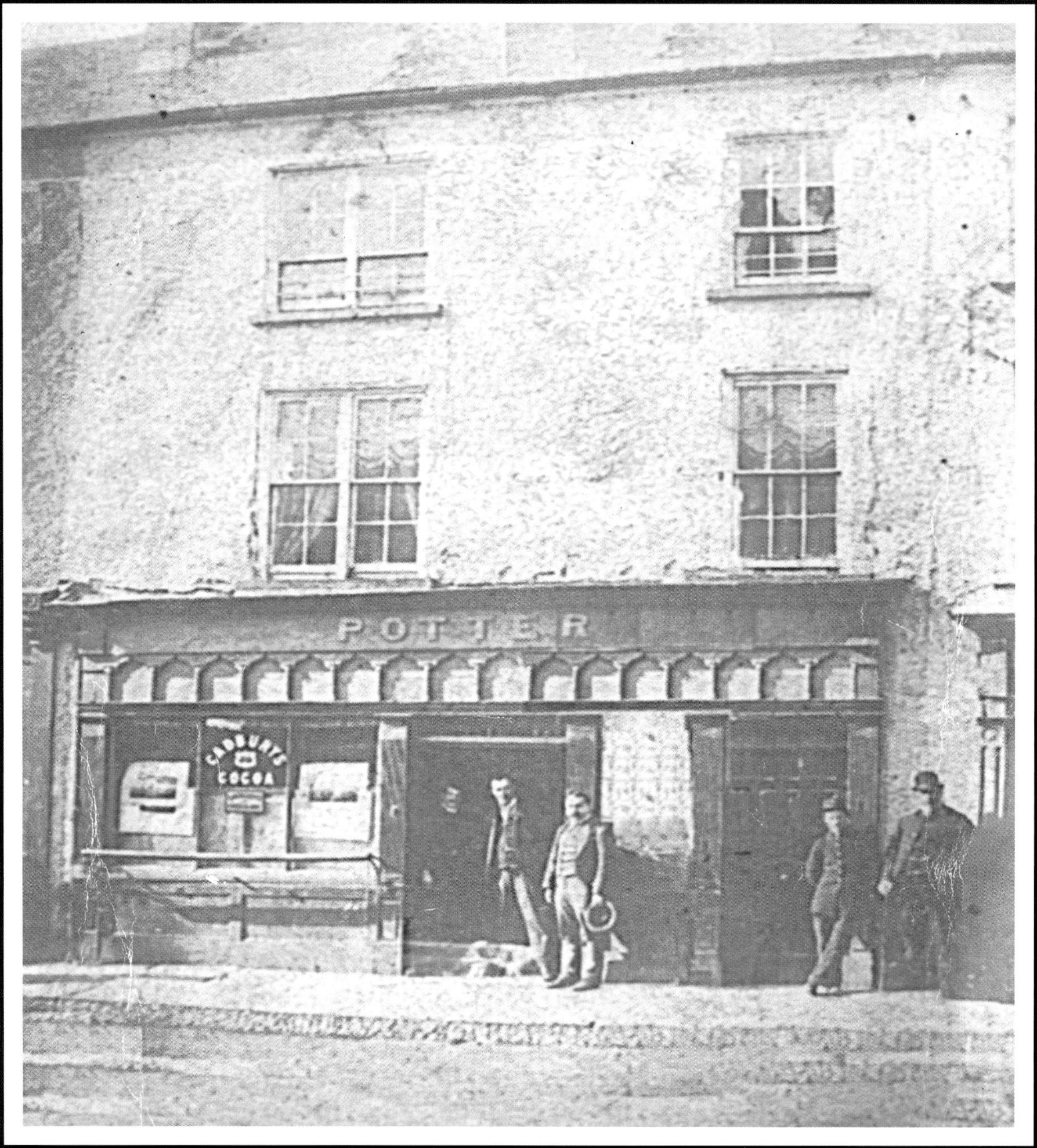

Above: Potter's Shop, Main Street, now the Maid of Erin, was originally the home of Maurice Shine and later his son Daniel. The Potter family also had a pawn shop in William Street. The photograph was taken in the mid 1890s. Miss Eleanor McGuire was postmistress and stamp distributor. Her post office was located in the house to the right of Potter's at No. 13 Main Street. The smaller of the two men on the right would appear to be a postman. Cadbury's Cocoa is well advertised.

Previous pages: A glimpse of part of Main Street from the 1890s. The rented shop of Corridan's, known as The Corner House, on the right at the entrance to Main Street, was once the home of Edmond O'Callaghan, who had served under Admiral Horatio Nelson at Cape St Vincent in 1797. It was said that he brought back considerable prize money from his adventures and his house was reputed to have been the first slated house in the Square. One of his daughters, Elizabeth, married James Sheehan who was the proprietor of a woollen and linen drapery shop located in the Square. Behind the house are the refreshment rooms of Ellen Whelan. Windows are seen at the corner, opposite Corridan's – these were blocked up in later years. In the foreground is a heavily-laden horse cart. Up at the corner of Church Street is the house later to be known in different generations as 'Cotters' and 'Scully's Corner'. A coach is positioned at the entrance to Church Street.

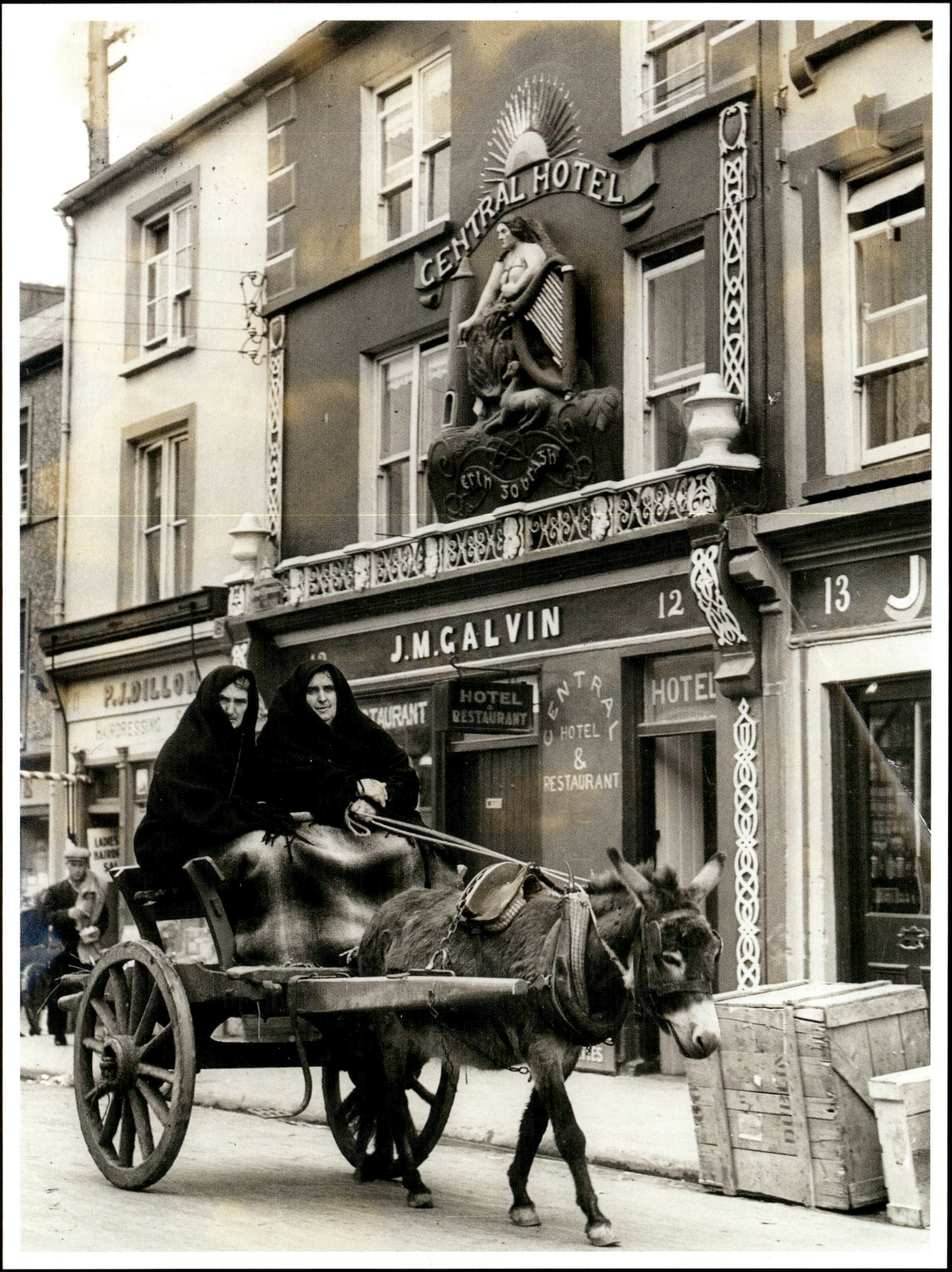

In this well-known mid 1950s photograph, Mrs Hayes and Mrs Lawlee were snapped as they made their way from the Square. Galvin's Central Hotel is adorned by McAuliffe's iconic 'Maid of Erin'. Sometime after the plasterwork of the bare-breasted maid had been completed, a rather pious parishioner approached Canon Davis to register a protest over the nudity. In an effort to pacify the lady, the broad-minded Canon retorted: "Madame, well in the event of a famine, she will suckle the town."

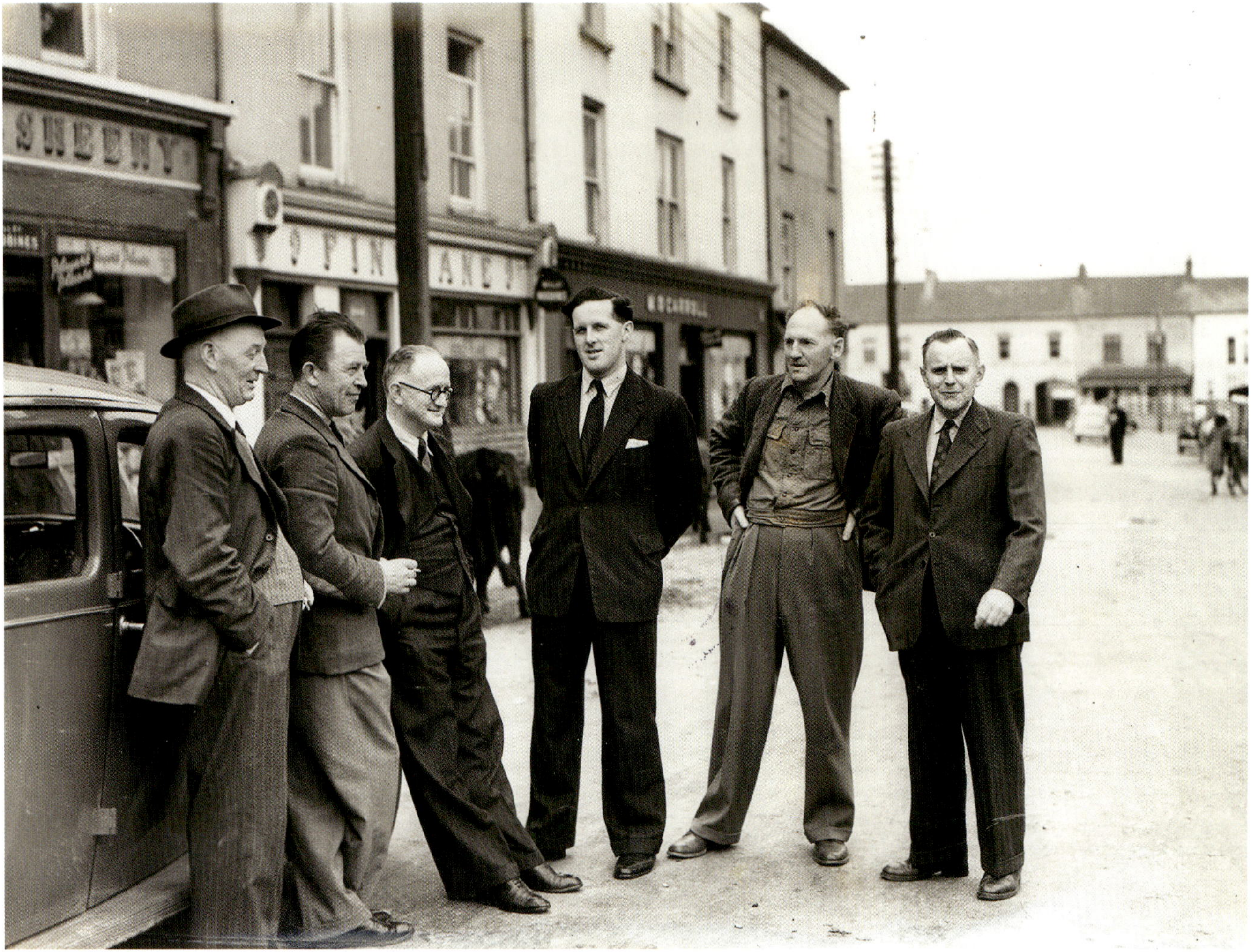

Main Street meeting in the 1950s

An Impromptu Gathering. Pictured left to right: Jack Lynch, Frank Sheehy, Louis O'Connell, Vincent Walsh, Gerard McElligott, and Michael Keane.

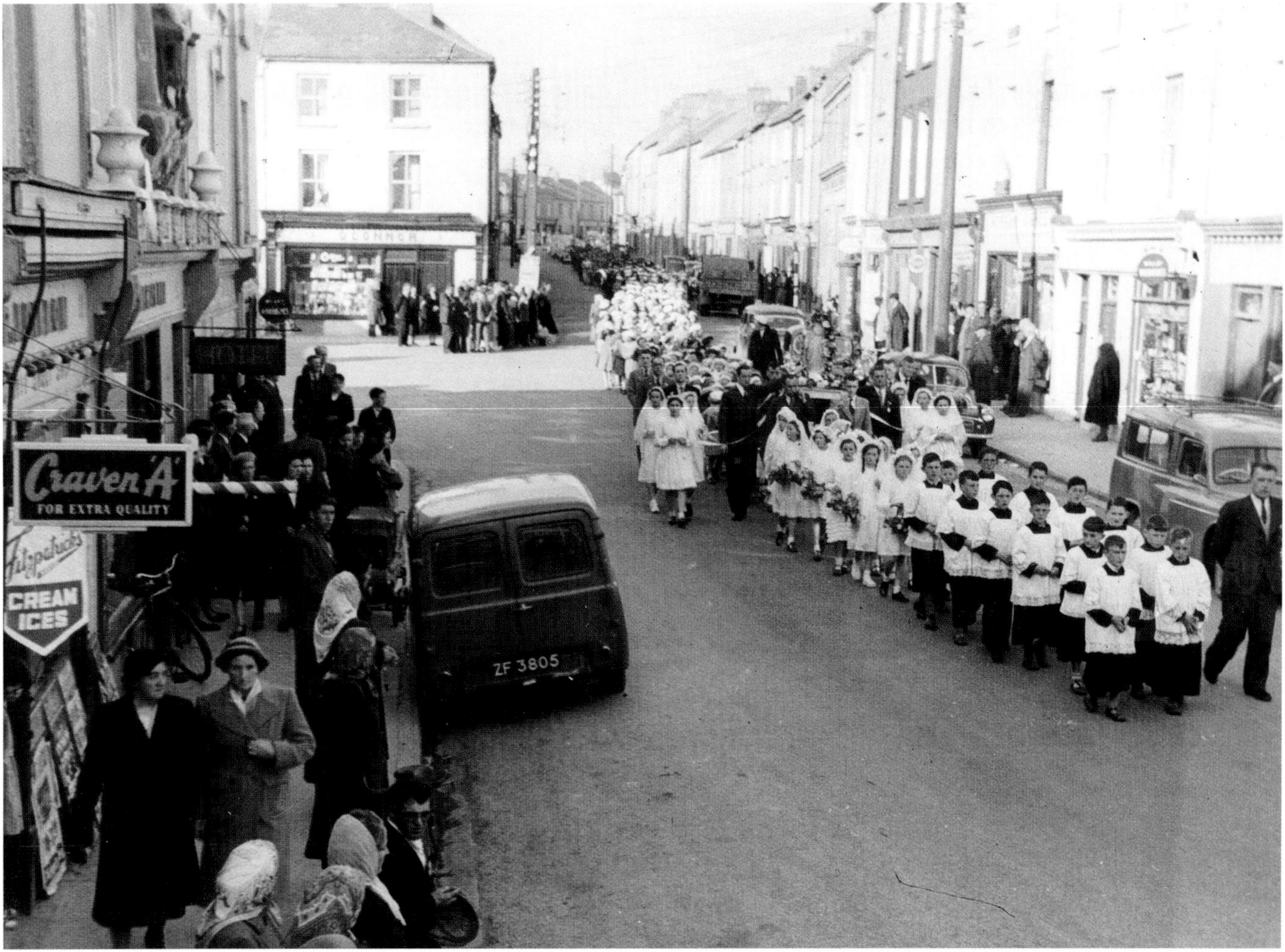

Sunday 29 May 1954

Marian Year procession winds its way down Church Street and Main Street on its way to the Church. Frank Sheehy is walking in front with the altar boys. The Moore sisters from William Street are on the left outside Dillon's shop. A crowd of interested spectators is watching from outside O'Connor's shop.

Doodle Rally, Small Square, June 1951

An idea conceived by a group of young townsmen in the back room of Curly Connor's public house in Church Street back in the early spring of 1951 has now entered into the realms of local folklore, legend and history. This idea was the formation of a fictitious political party called the Independent Coulogeous Party under its leader Tom Doodle. Listowel at this point in time still retained much of the bitterness which spilled over in the aftermath of the Civil War and the invention of this fictitious politician was an effort by those young men, who themselves came from various political traditions, to defuse and poke a bit of fun at the underlying political tensions.

Having invented the Politician, the executive of the Doodle Party, as they had come to be known, decided that they would advertise him as a candidate in the forthcoming General Election of that year. But who could play the part of Doodle? In a piece written by John B. Keane for the *Shannonside Annual* in 1958, he recalled, "To find the right man, not an easy task – but where there is a will there is a way. The will was ever present, the way followed suit. We found our man. Call it destiny, call it what you will, he was born to fill the role. Never was a part played with such subtle distinction. He literally was to live the short few hours of his only appearance".

Within weeks placards appeared, attached to telephone poles bearing the legend Vote Number One: Tom Doodle

Use your Noodle,
Vote for Doodle,
Doodle on the ball,
Next stop the Dáil.

Shortly afterwards, on a memorable June night they brought Doodle to town. Accompanied by fellow members of the Executive he arrived at the Listowel Railway Station on the six o'clock train. From *North Kerry Camera*, Fr. Kieran O'Shea recalled, "At the station a thousand curious people had already gathered. Eventually the train arrived. All heads turned expectantly wondering what would happen next. A door opened and out stepped a man dressed in black, swallow-tailed coat, top hat, side whiskers and beard. Doodle was here."

He then climbed into a waiting lorry which was led by a guard of honour and two bands, the lorry followed by the vast crowd. So began Doodle's triumphal journey through the streets and on to his Field of Dreams in the town's Small Square. In another recollection, John B. recalled "Everywhere we went, enthusiastic crowds lined the footpaths. Dogs howled unceremoniously, children bawled and old men held up their sticks in salute. Matrons held their children aloft to witness the advent of the great man. Even the Guards holding back their smiles, saluted stiff backed as the cavalcade moved through the streets. It was one of those scenes that never comes about by forethought. It was just the right blend of personality and atmosphere and time"

It was said afterwards that a bed-ridden elderly woman from Church Street was brought to her front door on a stretcher to view the procession and on seeing Doodle she cried aloud "Parnell, my boy, you're back again".

Finally, it is worth remembering John B's memories of the rally. "In the Small Square a makeshift platform had been erected outside Fred W Mann's 'jewelers'. Fred had obligingly installed a microphone free of charge. Here the crowd was enormous. A great sea of faces was upturned expectantly towards the platform where we now found ourselves. Here too, was our President, Michael Gulliver Stack, in full regalia, replete from side-whiskers to spats. "I started forward nervously to say a few words but no sound came from my throat. The hush that followed was adamantine, undeniable. I shall never know what I said. All I remember now is that Michael Gulliver Stack was giving his immortal introductory speech to Doodle. Stack's

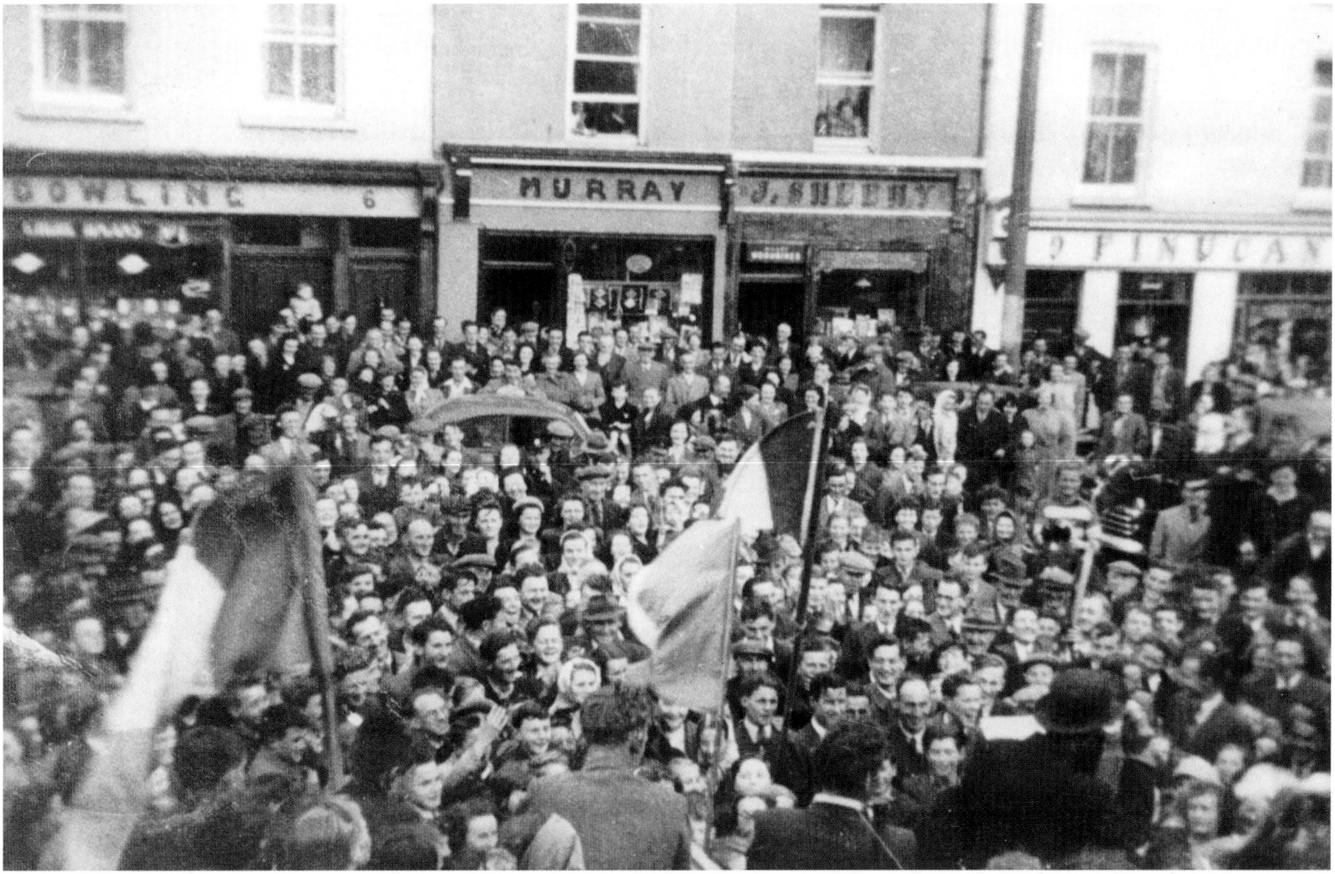

final sentence was drowned in a mountainous wave of laughter and shouting, and then Doodle was before the people. His speech is too well known to bother outlining it here. What is important is that he held three thousand suspicious North Kerrymen in the throes of laughter for nearly an hour. He began by stressing the importance of his five-point plan. Here are the points:

1. To plough the Rocks of Bawn;
2. To build a factory for shaving the hair from gooseberries;
3. To develop the periwinkle industry;
4. To give free treatment for sick heads;
5. To salvage the skins of black puddings after the contents had been eaten.

"He went on to speak of the necessity of humour in everyday life, of laughing in the face of odds and last of all, of the guiding policy of the Independent Coulogeous Party, i.e. to put community before oneself.

Before people were aware that his speech was finished, he had vanished - spirited away to parts unknown in Willy O'Connor's motor car, and he has not been seen nor has his identity been disclosed to this day".

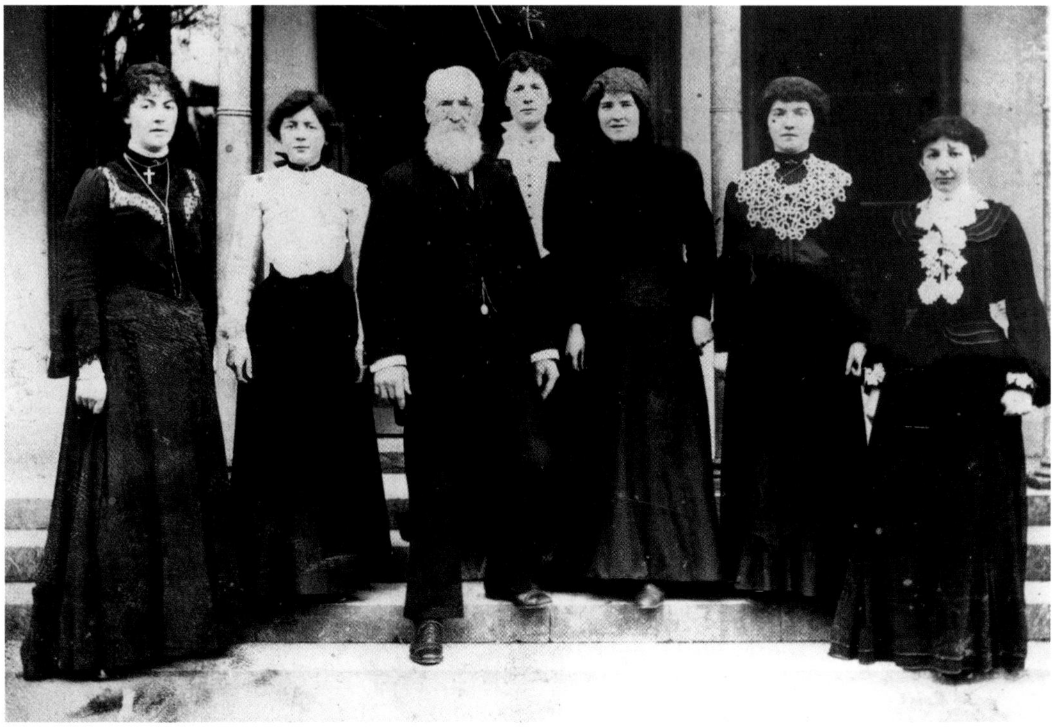

1 Main Street

J.J. Dillon was a draper, who, when he bought his house at 1 Main Street, became a confectioner. His daughter, Mary Josephine, married John Scully from Co. Cork, who had come to Listowel as an agricultural instructor. Sean Scully, son of John Scully, inherited the house in Main Street. In 1954, he acquired the house at No. 2 Main Street. In subsequent years, the Scullys extended their shop into this house.

The photograph above was taken outside Gurtinard House in the early 1900s. Pictured from left: Josephine Dillon, Annie O'Connell, J.J. Dillon, Unknown, Johanna Corridan, Mrs. Finucane, Catherine O'Connor.

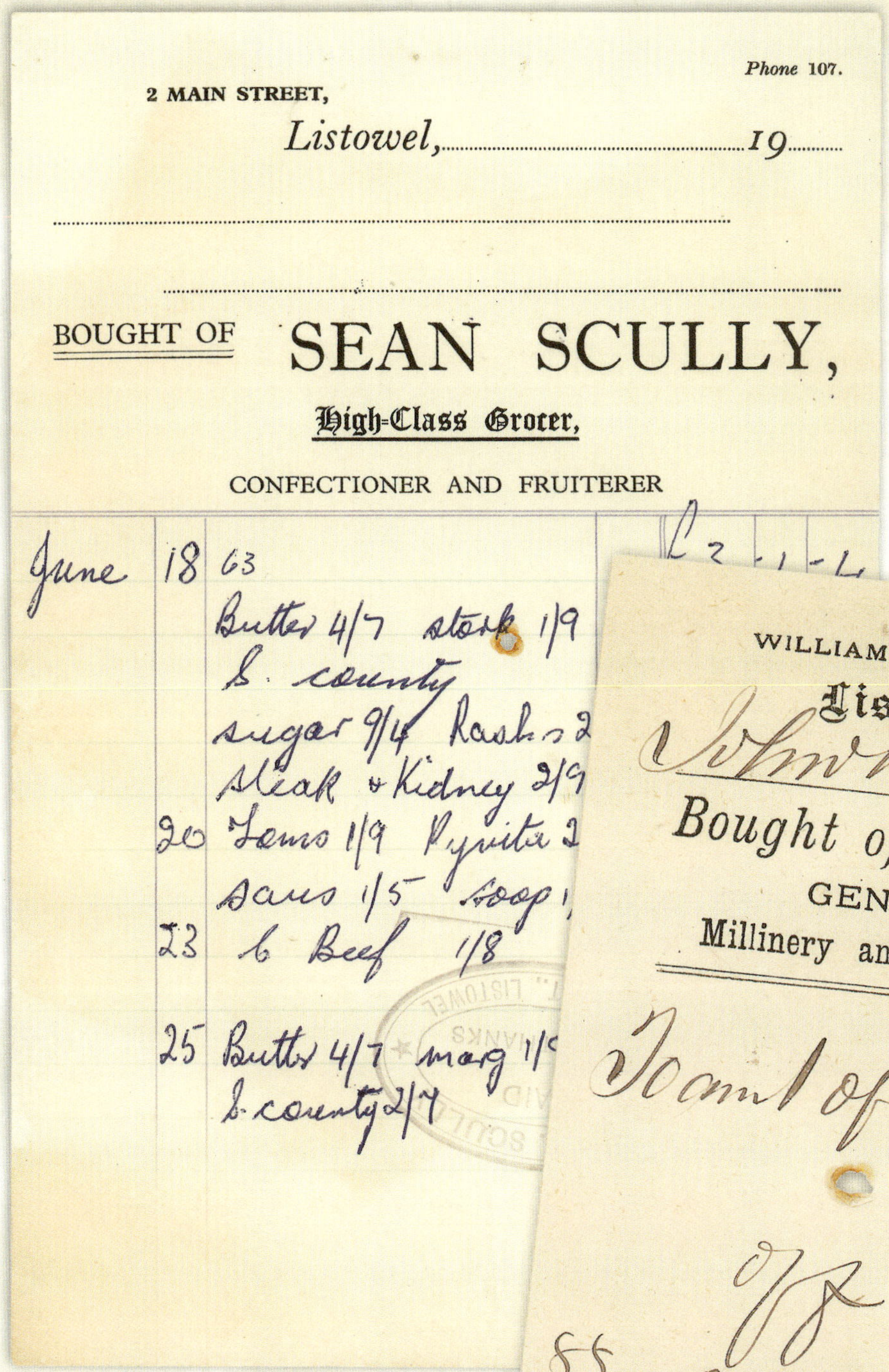

Phone 107.

2 MAIN STREET,

Listowel, ... 19........

BOUGHT OF **SEAN SCULLY,**

High-Class Grocer,

CONFECTIONER AND FRUITERER

June	18	63	£ 3 . 1 . 4
		Butter 4/7 stock 1/9	
		S. county	
		sugar 9/4 Rashers 2	
		Steak & Kidney 2/9	
	20	Toms 1/9 Ryvita 2	
		saus 1/5 soap	
	23	6 Beef 1/8	
	25	Butter 4/7 marg 1/	
		S. county 2/7	

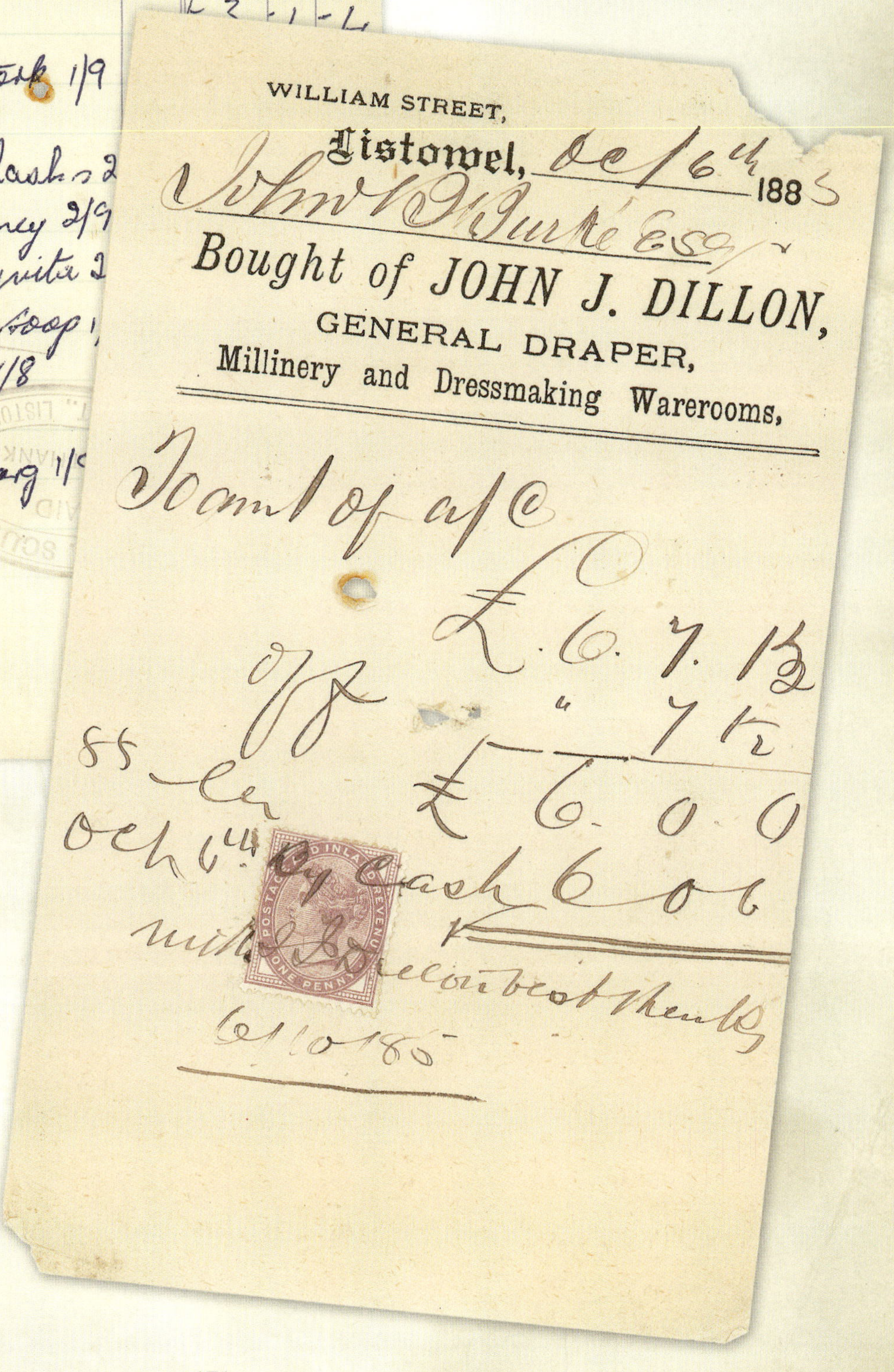

WILLIAM STREET,

Listowel, Oc 16th 1885

John W. Burke Esq

Bought of JOHN J. DILLON,

GENERAL DRAPER,

Millinery and Dressmaking Warerooms,

To amt of a/c

£ 6 . 7 . 1½

off " 7½

85 £ 6 . 0 . 0

Oct 6th By Cash 6 0 0

with ... best thanks

6/10/85

2 Main Street

An interesting mix of billheads from the corner house of Main Street and Church Street which is now owned by the Scully family. Pre-1900, one of the occupiers was Michael McDonnell, butcher. His family also had a butcher's shop in Market Street. McDonnell and his wife Annie lived in Bedford House after it had been vacated by the wife and family of Parson Fitzmaurice following his death in the mid 1890s. A watchmaker and jeweller by the name of Edward Isaac Jones from Galway, who guaranteed all watches bought over £1, also operated from the premises.

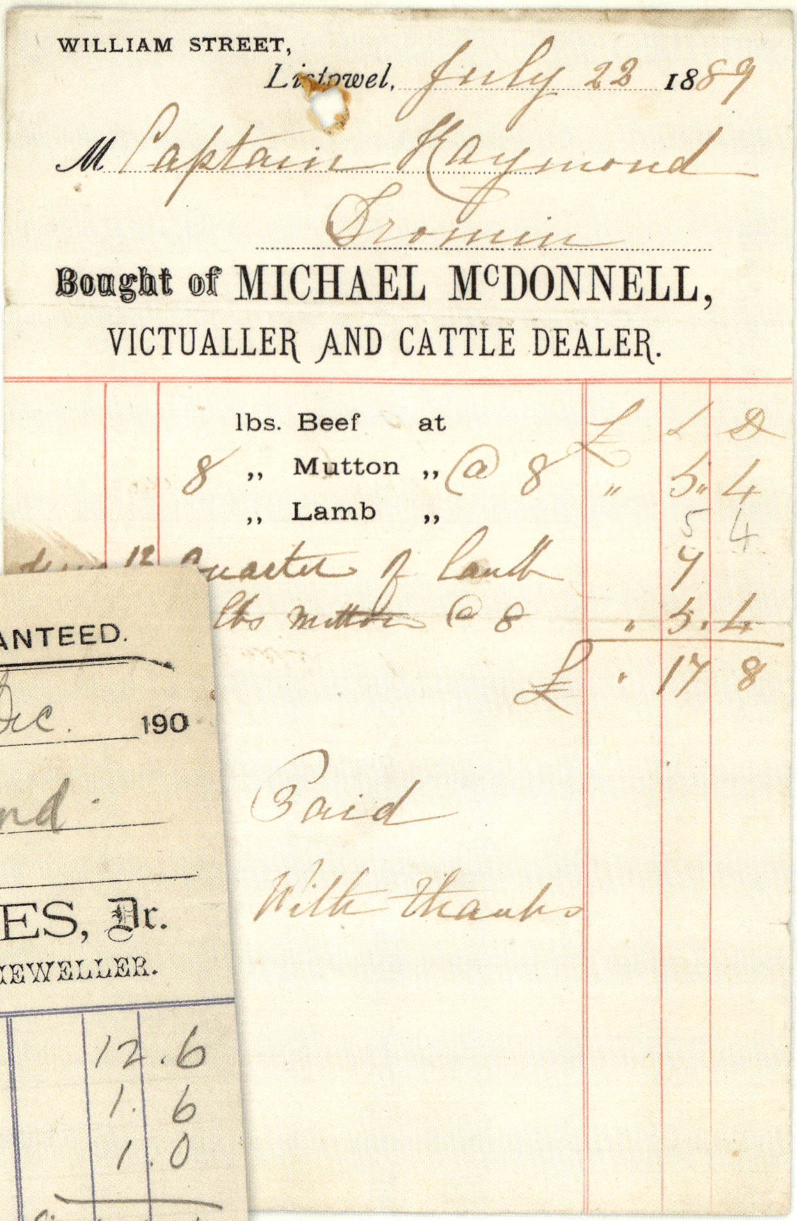

WILLIAM STREET,
Listowel, July 22 1889

M Captain Raymond
Gromin

Bought of MICHAEL McDONNELL,
VICTUALLER AND CATTLE DEALER.

	lbs. Beef at	£	s	d
	8 ,, Mutton ,, @ 8	"	5.	4
	,, Lamb ,,		5	4
12	Quarter of Lamb		7	
	lbs mutton @ 8	.	5.	4
		£ .	17	8

Paid
With thanks

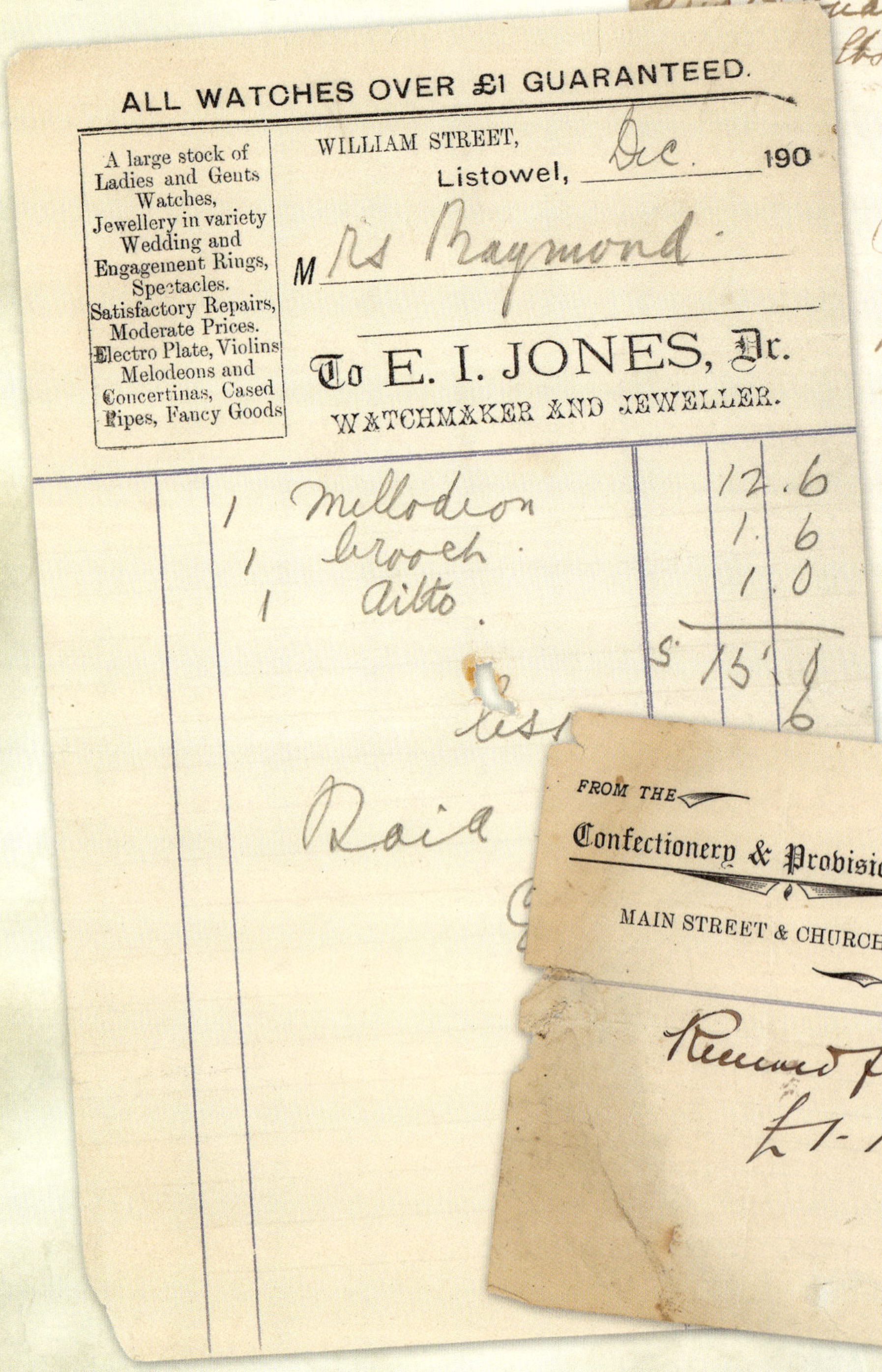

ALL WATCHES OVER £1 GUARANTEED.

A large stock of Ladies and Gents Watches, Jewellery in variety Wedding and Engagement Rings, Spectacles. Satisfactory Repairs, Moderate Prices. Electro Plate, Violins Melodeons and Concertinas, Cased Pipes, Fancy Goods

WILLIAM STREET,
Listowel, Dec 190

M rs Raymond

To E. I. JONES, Dr.
WATCHMAKER AND JEWELLER.

1	mellodeon	12	6
1	brooch	1	6
1	ditto	1	0
		15	0
	disc		6

Paid

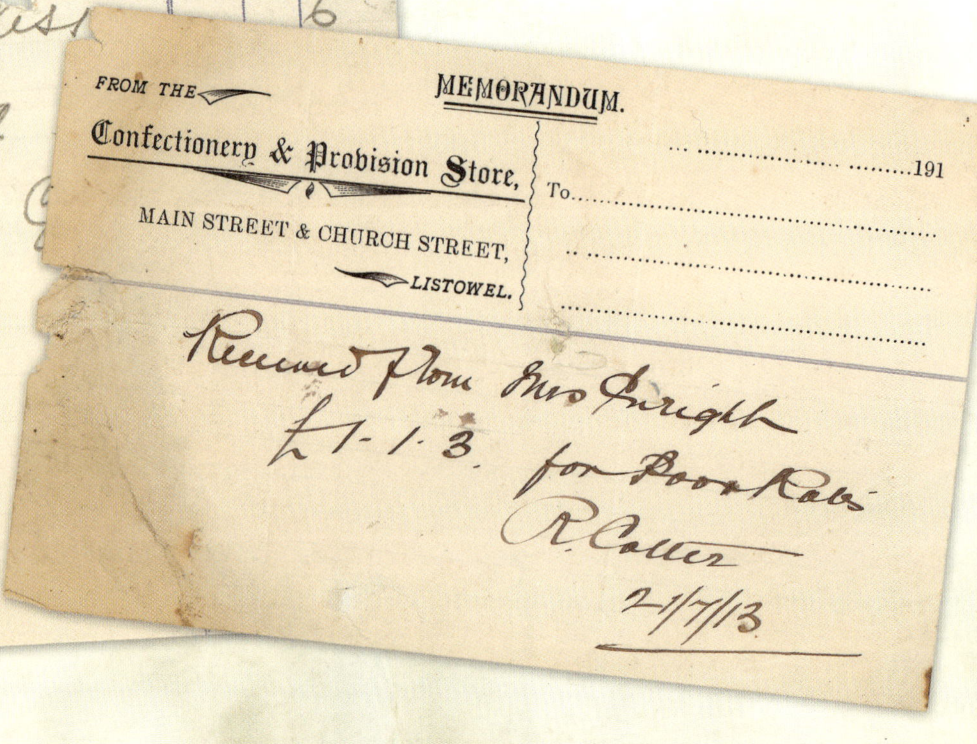

FROM THE Confectionery & Provision Store,
MAIN STREET & CHURCH STREET,
LISTOWEL.

MEMORANDUM.

........................191
To...................................

Received from Mrs Enright
£1-1-3. for Poor Rate
R. Collier
2/7/13

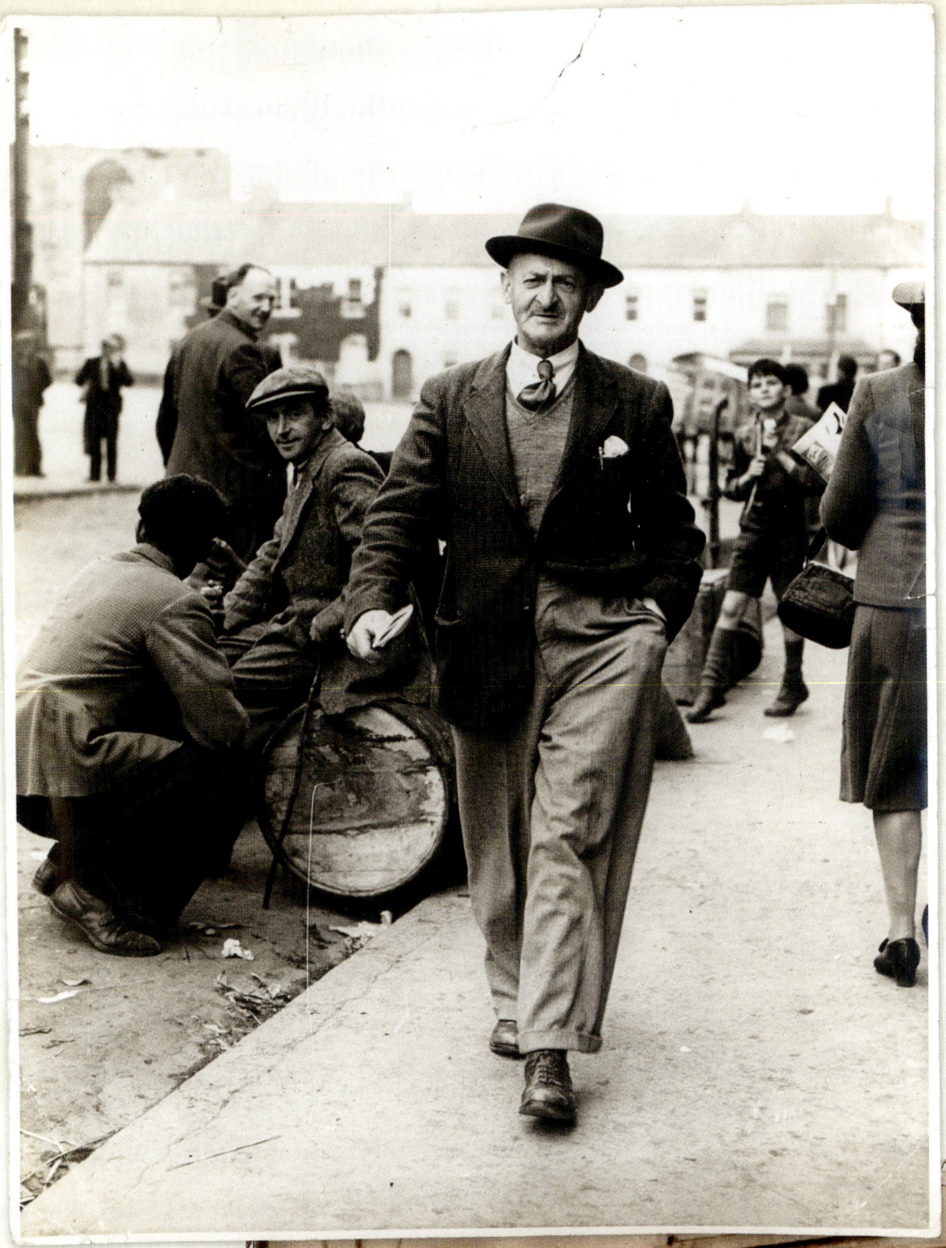

The Cotter family had a confectionary and provision store here for many years. One of this family was Timothy F. Cotter, one of Listowel's great characters, locally known as 'Tasty'.

Photo left: Timothy F. Cotter, walking up Main Street.

Photo below: Michael McDonnell pictured at the door of his butcher shop in Main Street. An assistant, his cousin, John Quirke, is at the window.

The house was bought from the O'Connor family by Sean Scully.

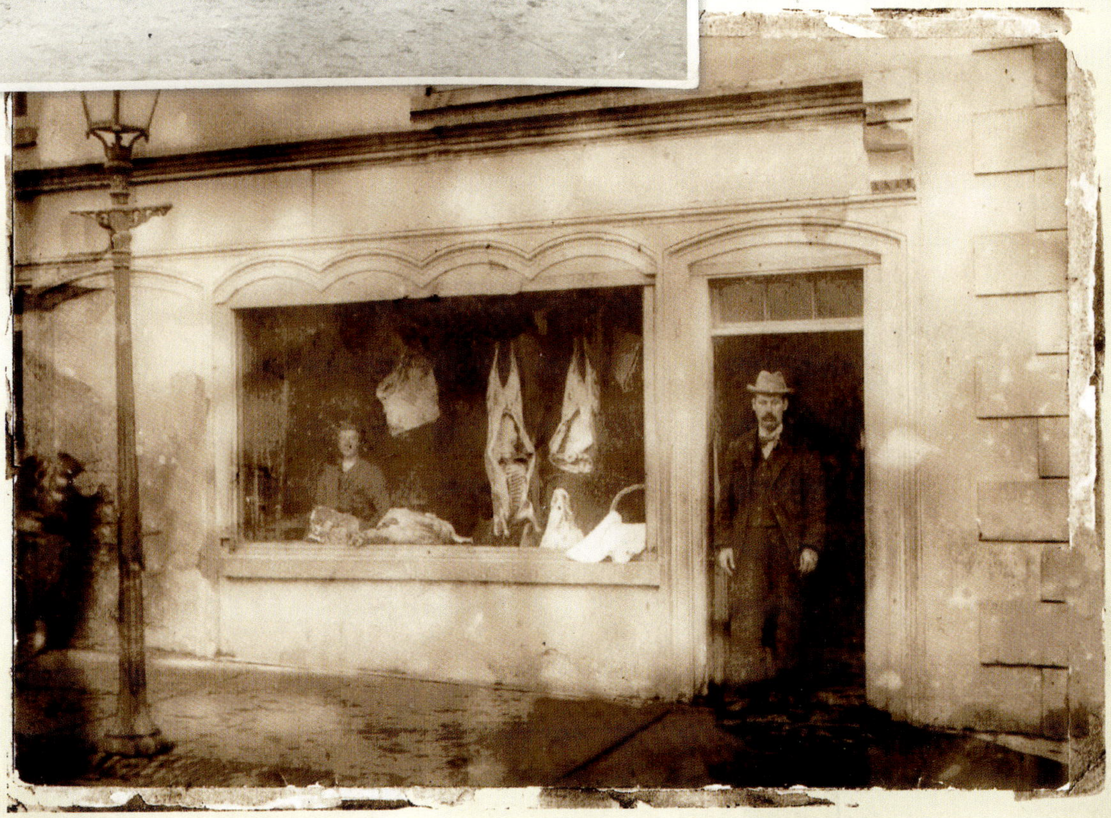

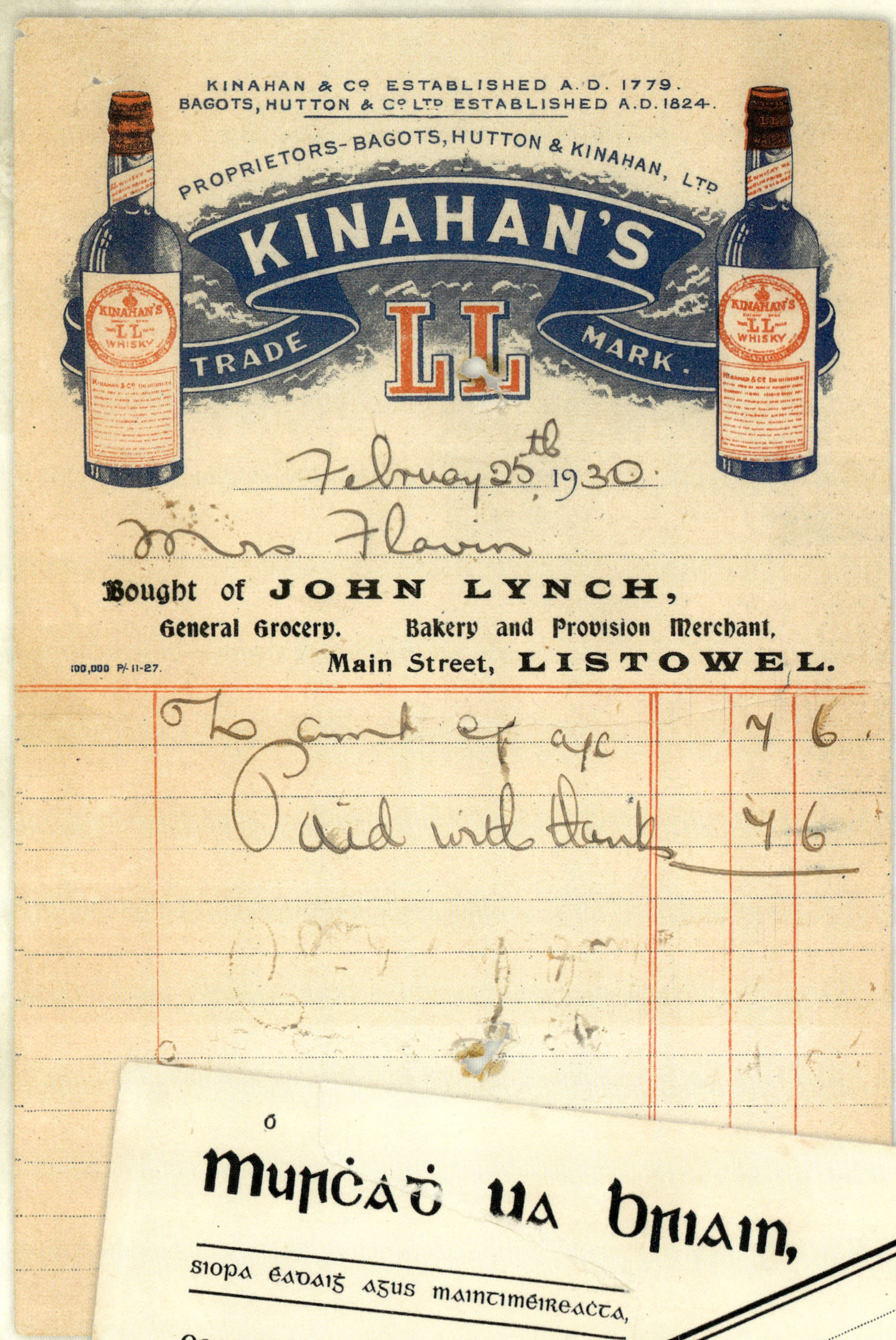
KINAHAN & Co ESTABLISHED A.D. 1779.
BAGOTS, HUTTON & Co LTD ESTABLISHED A.D. 1824.
PROPRIETORS - BAGOTS, HUTTON & KINAHAN, LTD
KINAHAN'S
TRADE LL MARK.

February 25th 1930
Mrs Flavin

Bought of JOHN LYNCH,
General Grocery. Bakery and Provision Merchant,
100,000 P/- 11-27. Main Street, LISTOWEL.

To amt of a/c	7	6
Paid with thanks	7	6

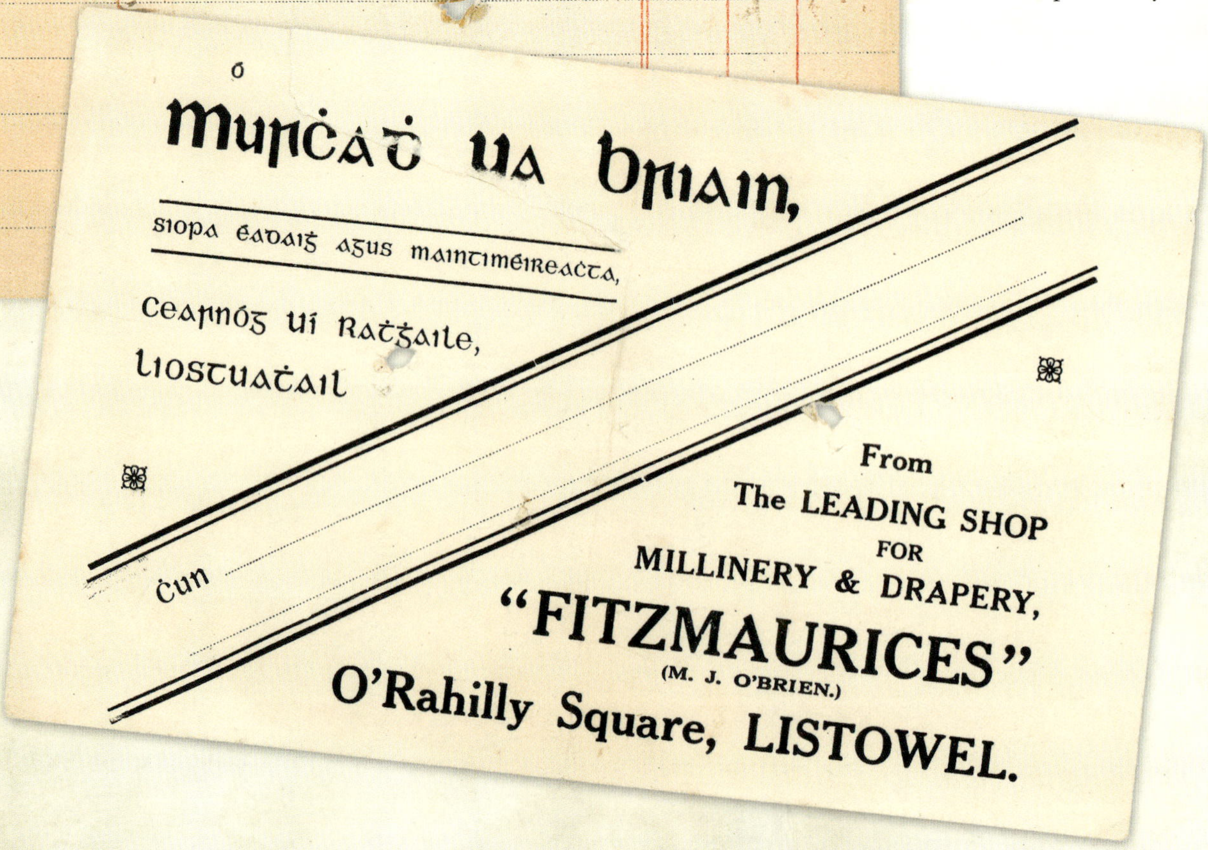
ó
Murċaḋ ua Briain,
Siopa éadaiġ agus maintiméireacta,
Cearnóġ Uí Raṫġaile,
Liostuaṫail

Ċun

From
The LEADING SHOP
FOR
MILLINERY & DRAPERY,
"FITZMAURICES"
(M. J. O'BRIEN.)
O'Rahilly Square, LISTOWEL.

18 Main Street
John Lynch, from the Stack's Mountains, ran a very successful business with wife Kathleen and sister-in-law Julie Mary. This business continued to flourish when they moved to a location in the Square. The Lynch family now run a home bakery and tearooms/coffee shop in what were Lynch's and Morgan O'Brien's premises.

17 Main Street
O'Brien's had an interesting bilingual letterhead with street name, *Cearnóg Uí Rathghaile*, O'Rahilly Square.

There was an ongoing local campaign in the late 1920s to rename the town streets after the names of our dead patriots. This found some local favour. However, the names never became official as the necessary plebiscites were never enacted.

Now part of Lynch's coffee shop.

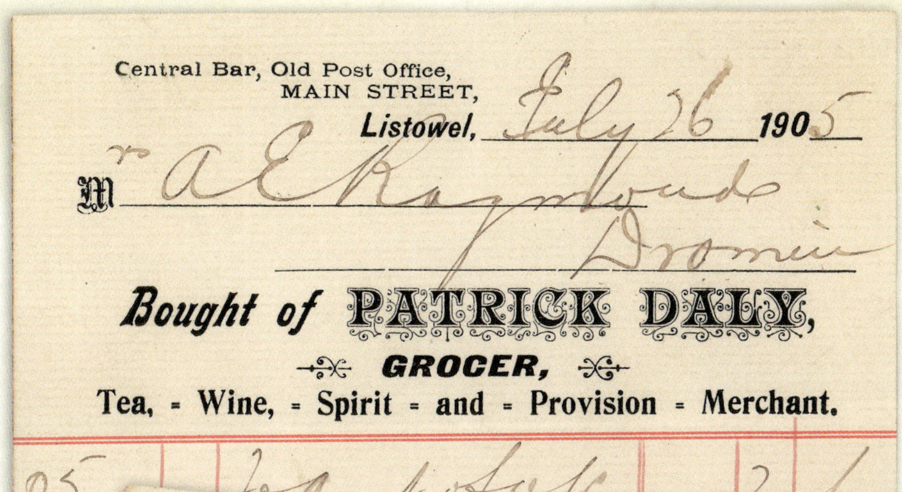
Central Bar, Old Post Office,
MAIN STREET,
Listowel, July 26 1905

Mr A E Raymonds
Dromin

Bought of PATRICK DALY,
GROCER,
Tea, - Wine, - Spirit - and - Provision - Merchant.

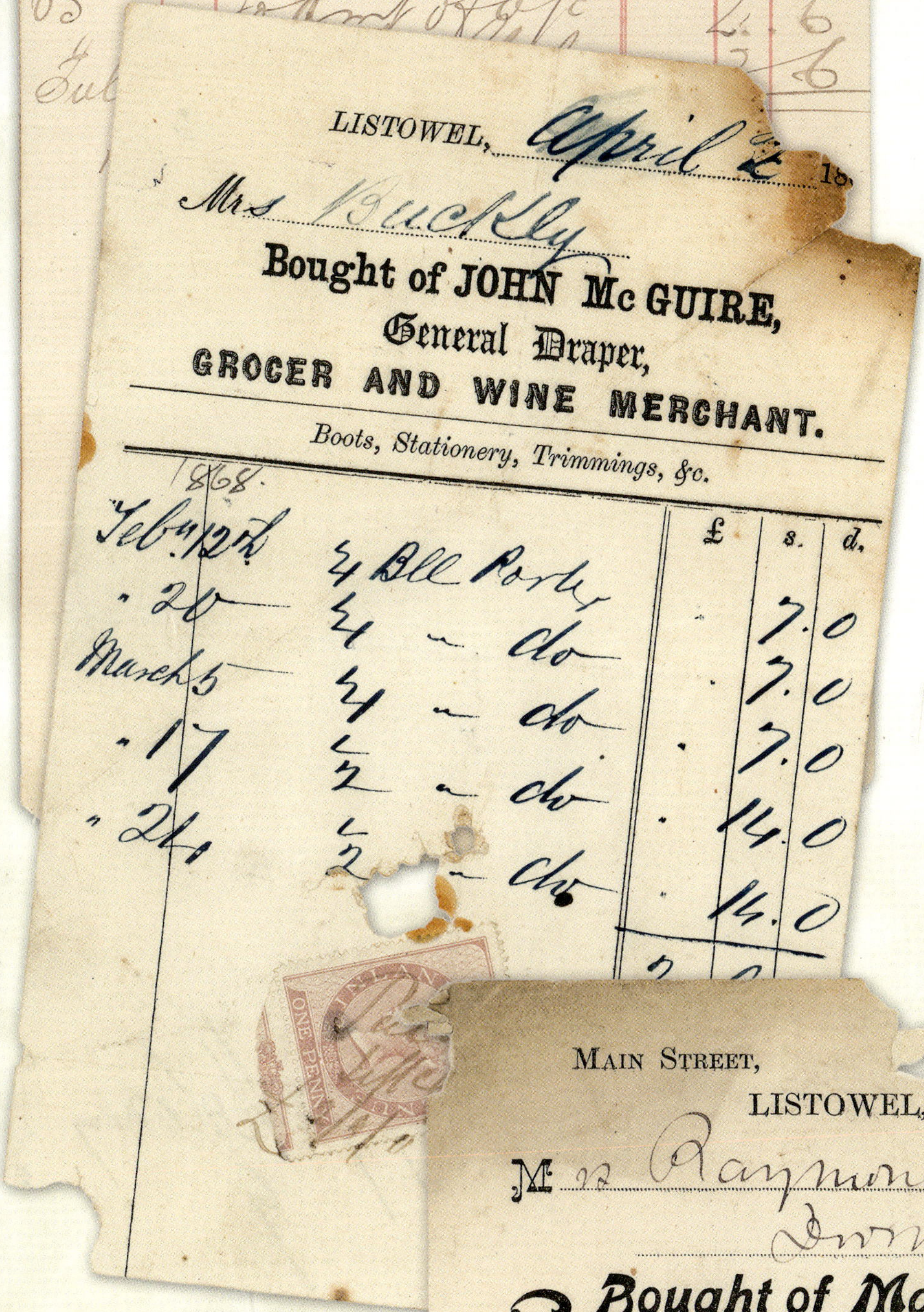
LISTOWEL, April 2 18

Mrs Buckly

Bought of JOHN Mc GUIRE,
General Draper,
GROCER AND WINE MERCHANT.
Boots, Stationery, Trimmings, &c.

1868		£	s.	d.
Feby 12th	4 Btl Porter		7	0
" 20	4 — do		7	0
March 5	4 — do		7	0
" 17	2 — do		14	0
" 24	2 — do		14	0

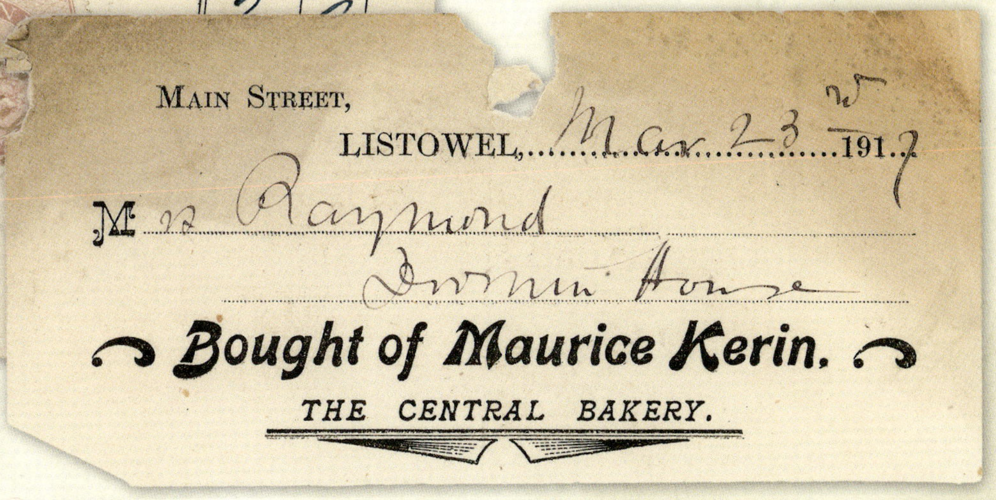
MAIN STREET,
LISTOWEL, Mar 23 1917

Mrs Raymond
Dromin House

Bought of Maurice Kerin.
THE CENTRAL BAKERY.

14 Main Street

Maurice Kerin from Limerick opened a bakery and restaurant in 1903 at his well-located house at 14 Main Street. Following Maurice's death, his daughter Agnes ran the bakery shop. Paddy Sharry from Forge Lane and Paddy (Bán) O'Connor of Church Street were the bakers, while Peter Murphy sold the bread from a horse-drawn bread van. The bakery closed in 1953.

13 Main Street

John McGuire married Margaret McElligott, daughter of Gerard McElligott, in 1858. They opened an extensive business in what is now 15 Main Street. John also became postmaster in succession to the Stokes family. His daughter Eleanor, who married Thomas Beary from Co. Cork, Creamery Manager, succeeded her father as Post Office Manager. On Eleanor McGuire's retirement, the post office was transferred to William Street.

Patrick Daly succeeded the McGuires and Bearys. The letterhead is interesting. He has named his bar 'The Central Bar, Old Post Office'. The Dalys were succeeded by J. P. Kennelly.

12 Main Street

The Shine family were one of Listowel's most important business families in the early to mid 1800s. They also had much property and land around the town. They were succeeded at this address by the Potter family. Mary Potter married Jeremiah Galvin. They established a hotel in the house, which they renamed 'The Central Hotel'.

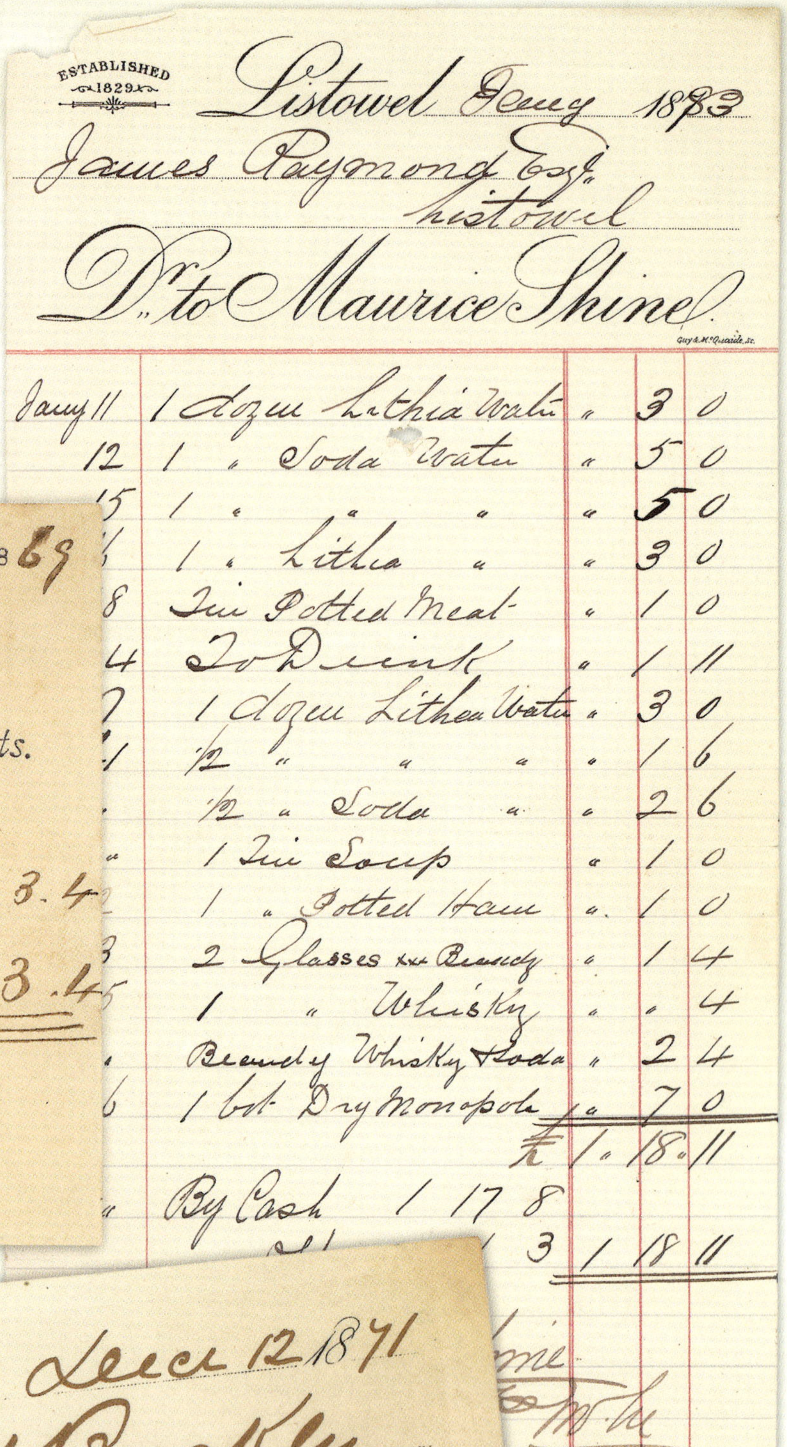
ESTABLISHED 1829

Listowel Jany 1883

James Raymond Esq.
Listowel

Dr. to Maurice Shine

Jany 11	1 dozen Lithia Water		3	0
12	1 " Soda Water		5	0
15	1 " " "		5	0
	1 " Lithia "		3	0
8	Tin Potted Meat		1	0
4	To Drink		1	11
7	1 dozen Lithea Water		3	0
1	½ " " "		1	6
	½ " Soda		2	6
	1 Tin Soup		1	0
	1 " Potted Ham		1	0
	2 Glasses xx Brandy		1	4
	1 " Whisky			4
	Brandy Whisky & Soda		2	4
6	1 bot. Dry Monopole		7	0
		£1	18	11
	By Cash 1 17 8			
	3	1	18	11

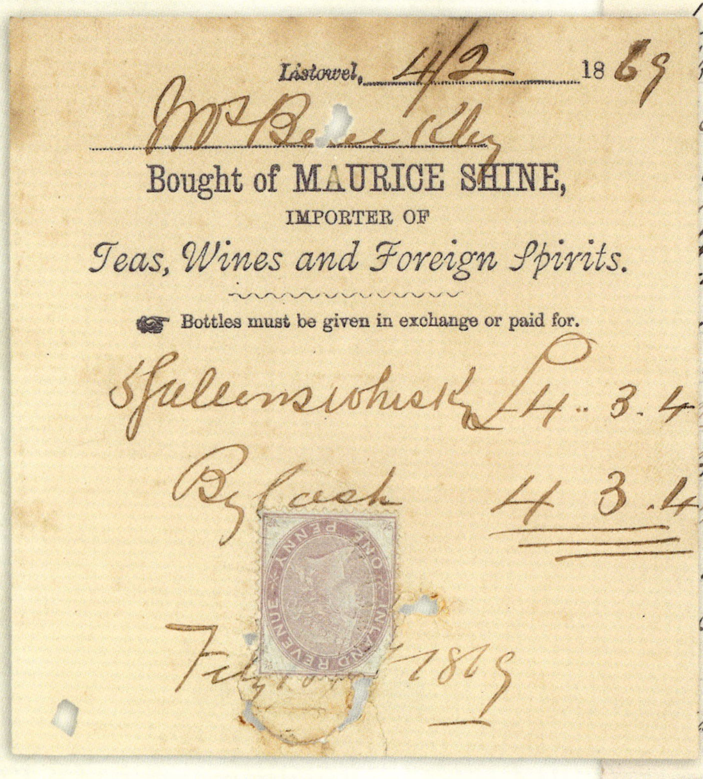
Listowel, 4/2 1869

Mrs Buckley

Bought of MAURICE SHINE,
IMPORTER OF
Teas, Wines and Foreign Spirits.

Bottles must be given in exchange or paid for.

5 gallons whisky £4.. 3. 4

By cash 4 3. 4

Feby 1869

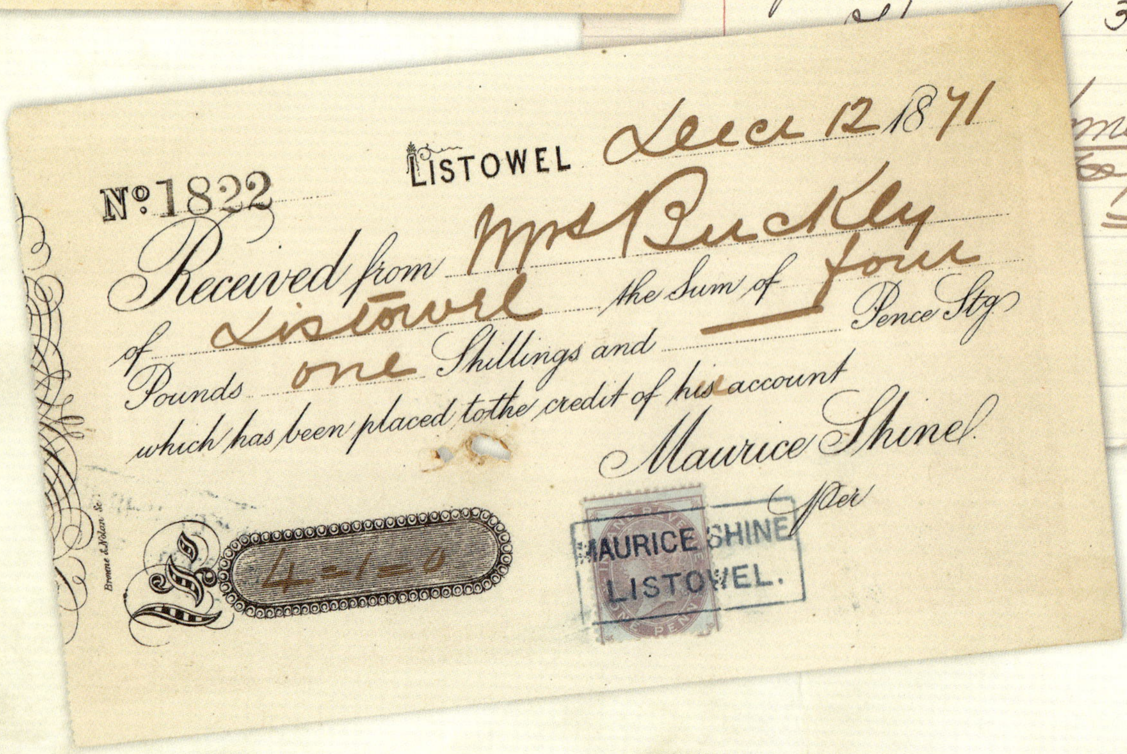
No 1822 LISTOWEL Decr 12 1871

Received from Mrs Buckley of Listowel the Sum of four Pounds one Shillings and Pence Stg which has been placed to the credit of his account

Maurice Shine
Per

£4-1-0

MAURICE SHINE
LISTOWEL.

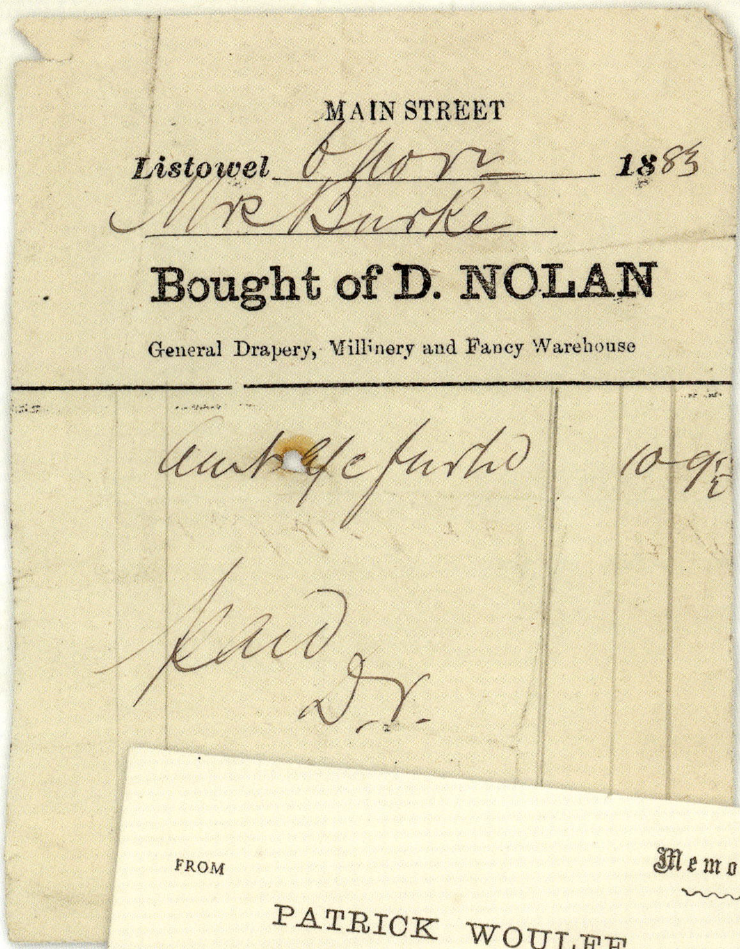
MAIN STREET
Listowel 6 Nov 1883
Mr Burke
Bought of D. NOLAN
General Drapery, Millinery and Fancy Warehouse

10-9½

Paid D.N.

Dan Nolan had a drapery at Main Street. He was succeeded by Patrick and Sarah Woulfe. In the letterhead of 1885, which Sarah writes, she thanks Mrs. Bourke for her payment of £4.0.0, and tells her that her husband Patrick (who must not have been in good health) was going for a change of air to Queenstown.

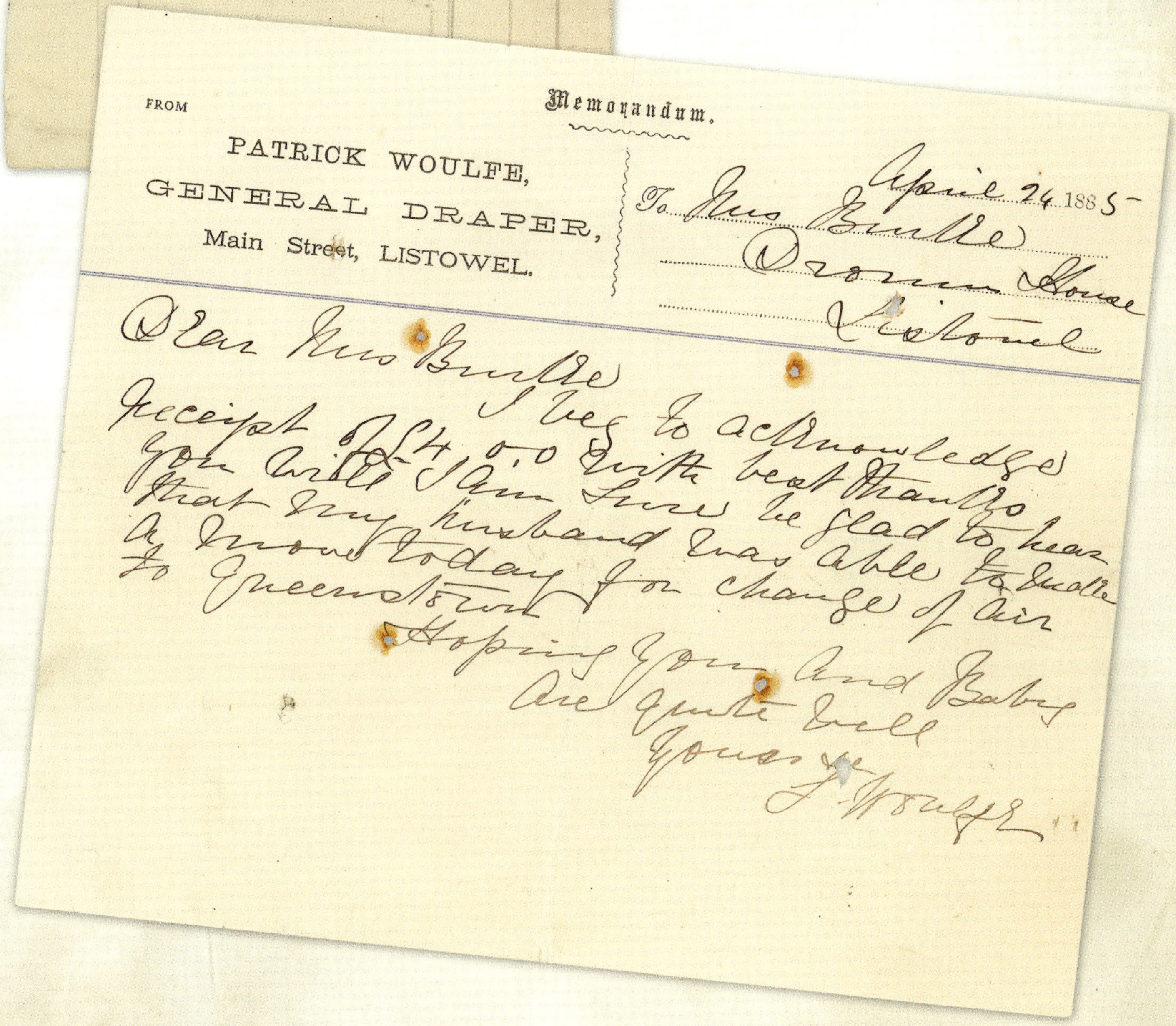
FROM

Memorandum.

PATRICK WOULFE,
GENERAL DRAPER,
Main Street, LISTOWEL.

April 24 1885
To Mrs Burke
Dromin House
Listowel

Dear Mrs Burke
I beg to acknowledge receipt of £4.0.0 with best thanks.
You will I am sure be glad to hear that my husband was able to make a move today for change of air to Queenstown.
Hoping you and Baby are quite well
Yours &c
S. Woulfe

9 Main Street

Molly Finucane's shop was at 9 Main Street. Cigarette companies took advantage of a method of free advertising by presenting shopkeepers with sheaves of blank billheads containing their company logo. The shopkeeper would then go to the local printer and have their own name and address printed on them. In this case in the billheads of the 1920s, Molly had inserted 'Main Street' on some, and 'O'Rahilly Square' on others.

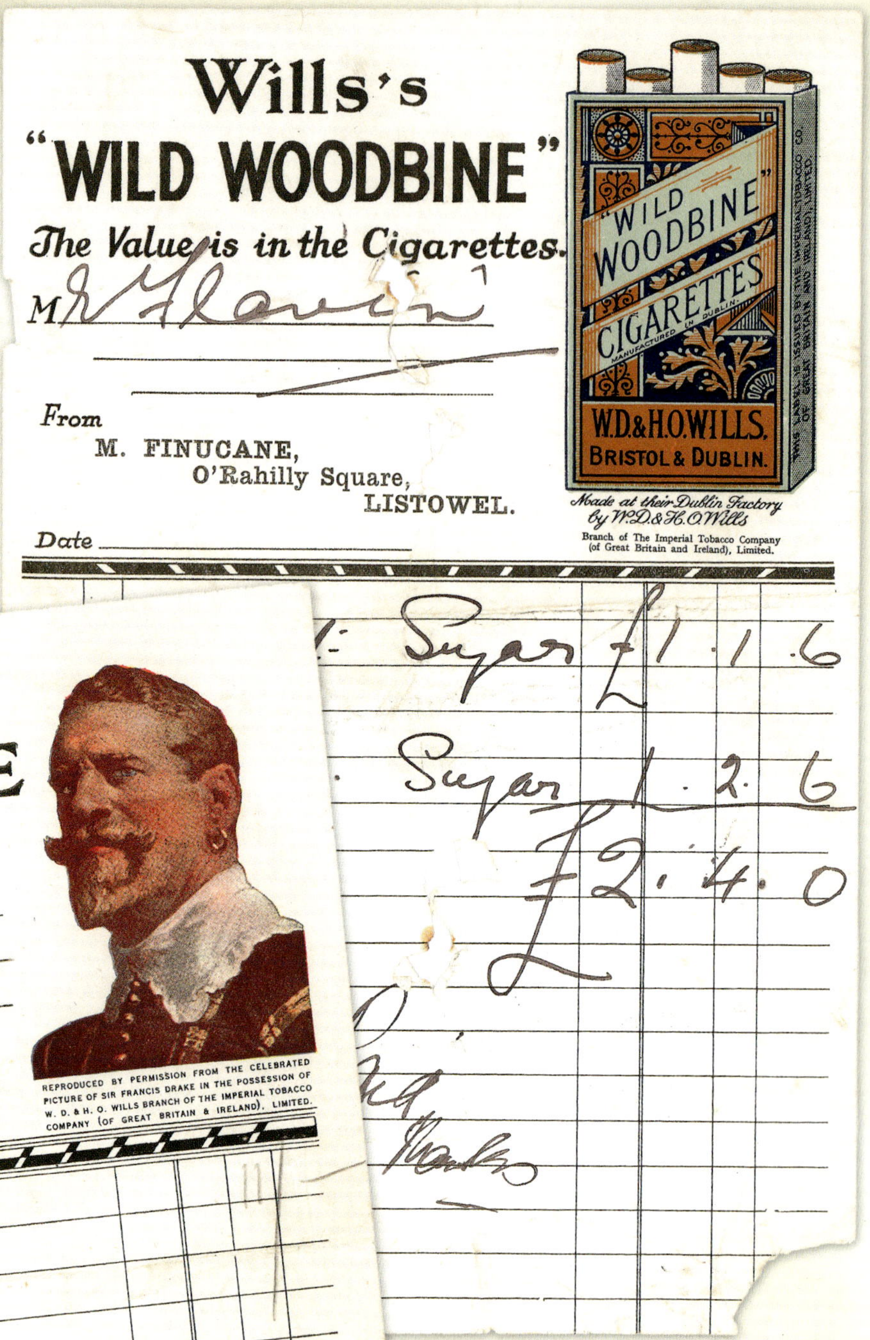

Wills's

"WILD WOODBINE"

The Value is in the Cigarettes.

M Flavin

From

M. FINUCANE,
O'Rahilly Square,
LISTOWEL.

Date

Sugar £1.1.6

Sugar 1.2.6

£2.4.0

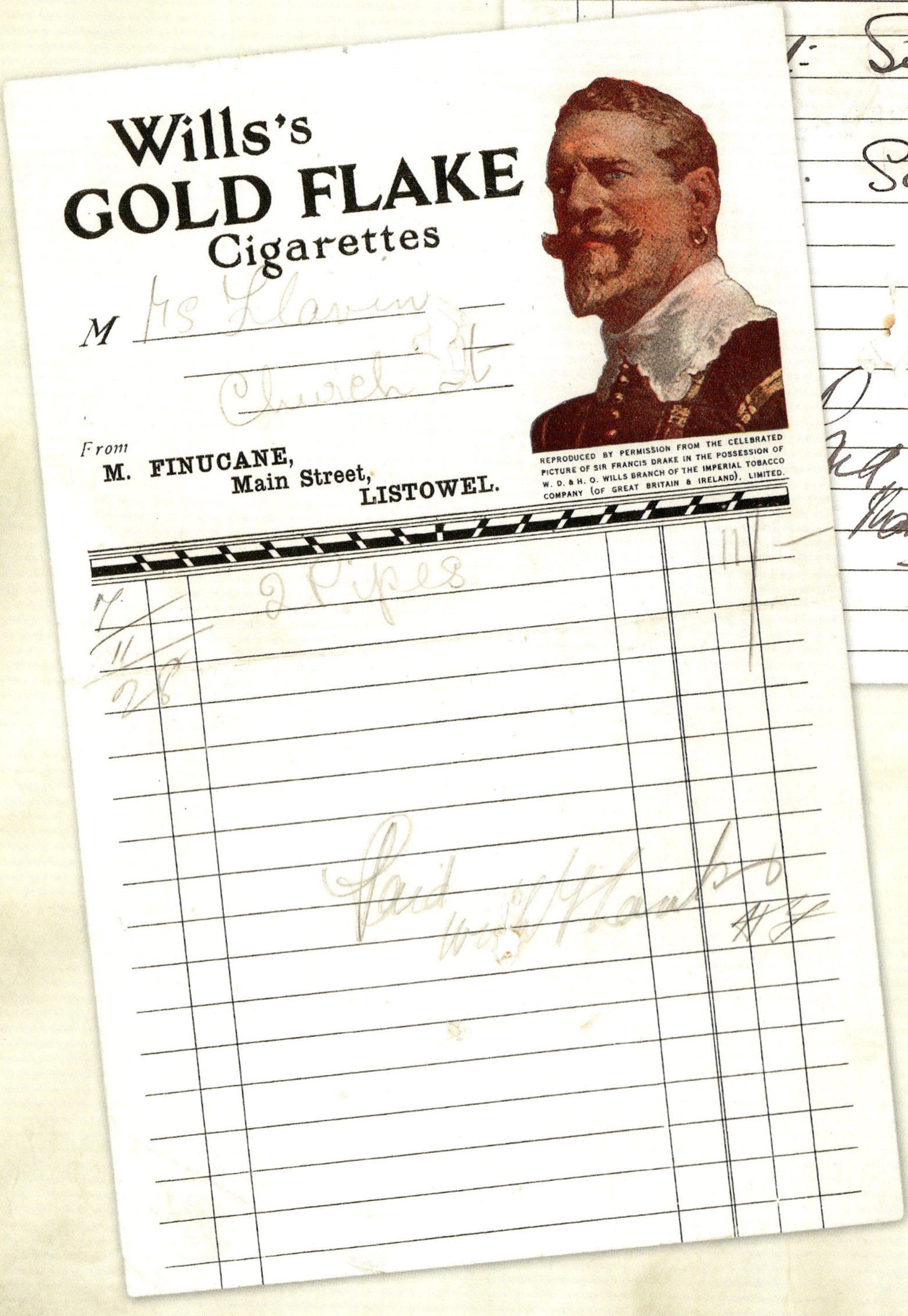

Wills's
GOLD FLAKE
Cigarettes

M Ms Flavin
Church St

From
M. FINUCANE,
Main Street,
LISTOWEL.

REPRODUCED BY PERMISSION FROM THE CELEBRATED PICTURE OF SIR FRANCIS DRAKE IN THE POSSESSION OF W. D. & H. O. WILLS BRANCH OF THE IMPERIAL TOBACCO COMPANY (OF GREAT BRITAIN & IRELAND), LIMITED.

7/11/28 2 Pipes

Paid with thanks

Thomas Cronin

In Henry & Coughlan's County Kerry Directory of 1867, Thomas Cronin, Main Street, is listed as having an emigration agency and grocery. He was also an insurance agent. As the receipt shows, he was also an agent for M. Butler and Co., Brewers of Castle Desmond Brewery, which was located at Ballymullen, Tralee. The Bill contains the account of Mrs. Johanna Buckley, who ran a public house in William Street, where Jumbo's Restaurant is now. The letterhead dates from 1868.

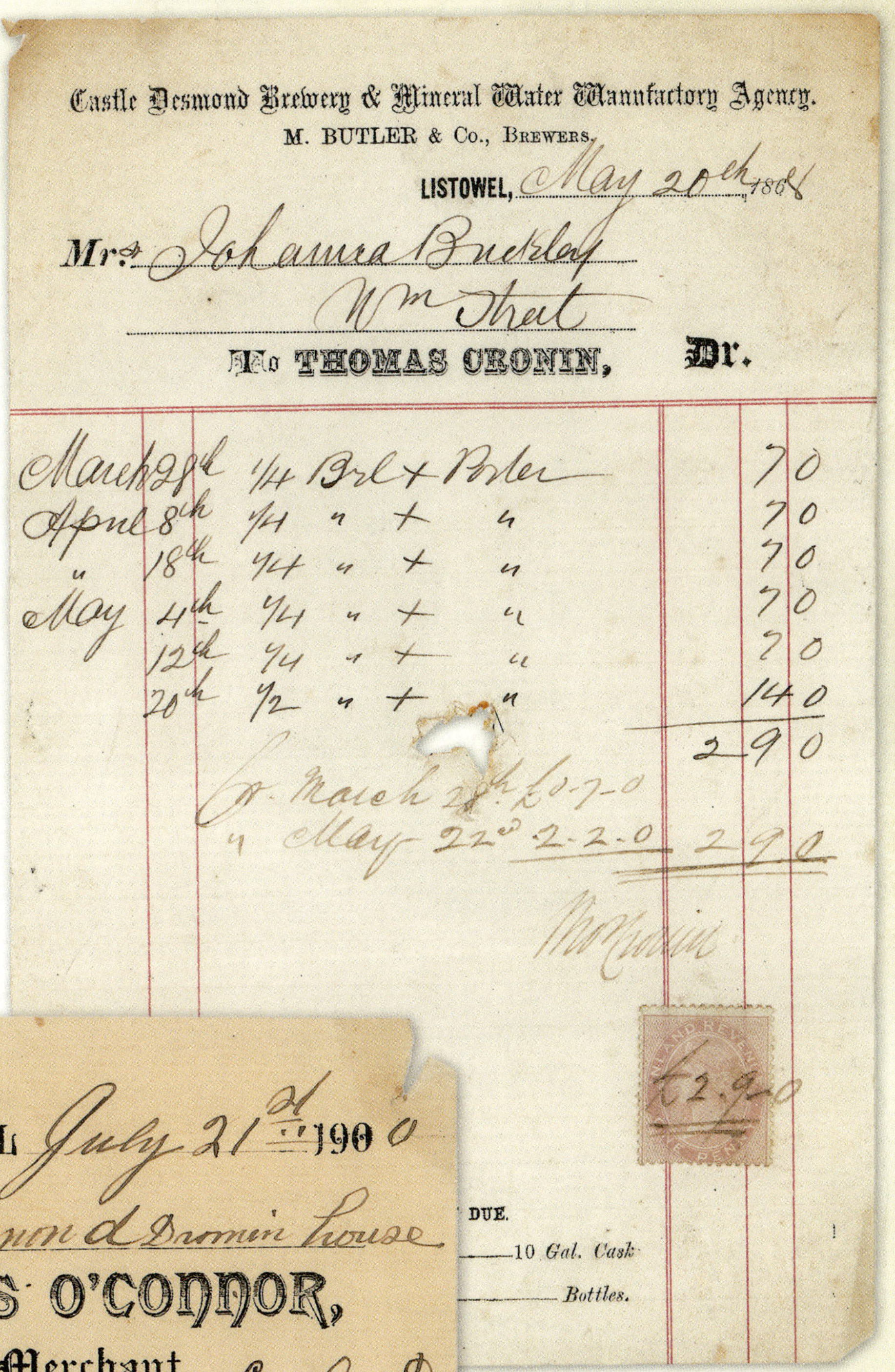

Castle Desmond Brewery & Mineral Water Manufactory Agency.
M. BUTLER & Co., BREWERS.

LISTOWEL, May 20th 1868

Mrs Johanna Buckley
Wm Street

To THOMAS CRONIN, Dr.

March 28th	1/4 Brl + Porter		7 0
April 8th	1/4 " + "		7 0
" 18th	1/4 " + "		7 0
May 4th	1/4 " + "		7 0
12th	1/4 " + "		7 0
20th	1/2 " + "		14 0
		2	9 0
	Cr. March 28th £0-7-0		
	" May 22d 2-2-0	2	9 0

T. Cronin

£2-9-0

DUE.
10 Gal. Cask
Bottles.

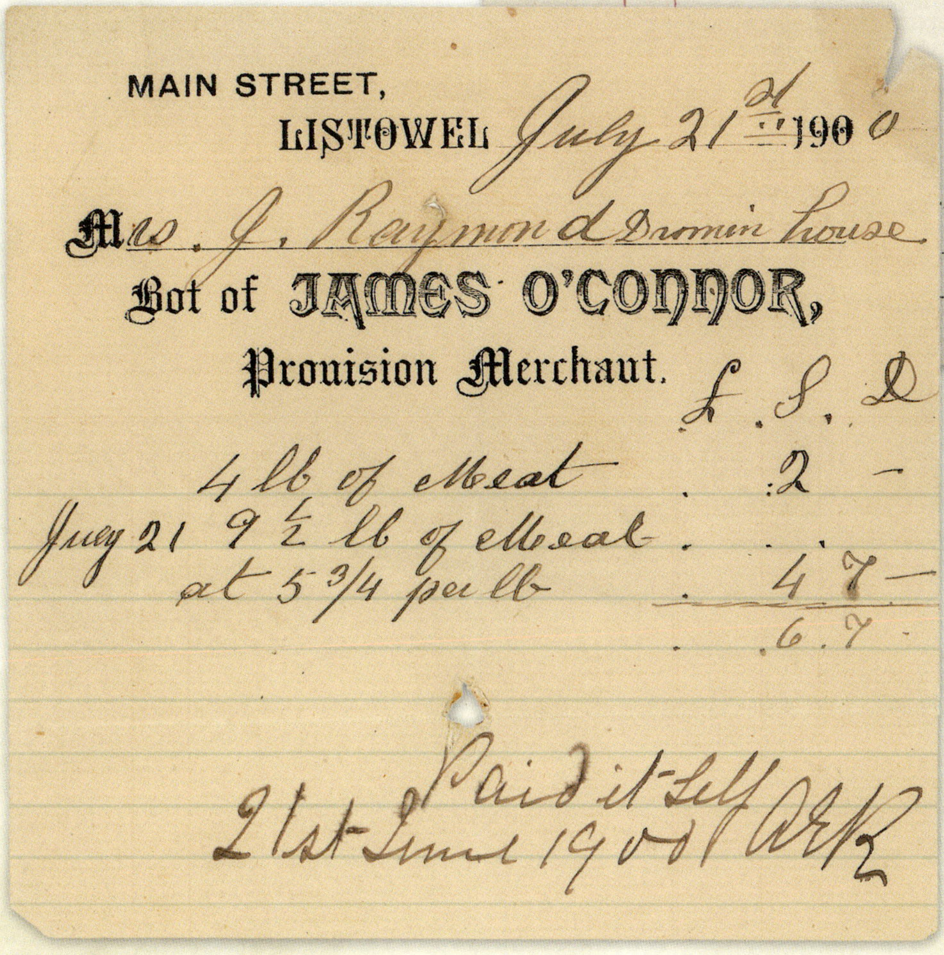

MAIN STREET,
LISTOWEL July 21st 1900

Mrs. J. Raymond Dromin house

Bot of JAMES O'CONNOR,
Provision Merchant.

	£	S.	D
4 lb of Meat	.	2	-
July 21 9 1/2 lb of Meat at 5 3/4 per lb	.	4	7
	.	6	7

Paid it self
21st June 1900

7 Main Street

James O'Connor, Provision Merchant, resided at 7 Main Street. The house was subsequently owned by the Murray family. The Murrays specialised in selling religious goods in their shop and especially at Church Missions and Retreats, when they would operate from a stall in the church grounds.

6 Main Street

Thomas McAuliffe, a bookseller and newsagent, also had a fancy warehouse. When Robert French of the photographic firm, William Lawrence, came to Listowel in 1904 on his mission to record the various towns and cities, McAuliffe was his guide. It was he who directed French to the most advantageous places to photograph. McAuliffe can be seen posing in a cameo role in some of the Listowel images. The photographs were also sold in the shop. Mamie McAuliffe (daughter of Thomas, pictured far right) married E.J. Boylan. He converted the house next to McAuliffe's into an automobile showroom and office. For many years after, the remains of an old petrol pump stood on the street.

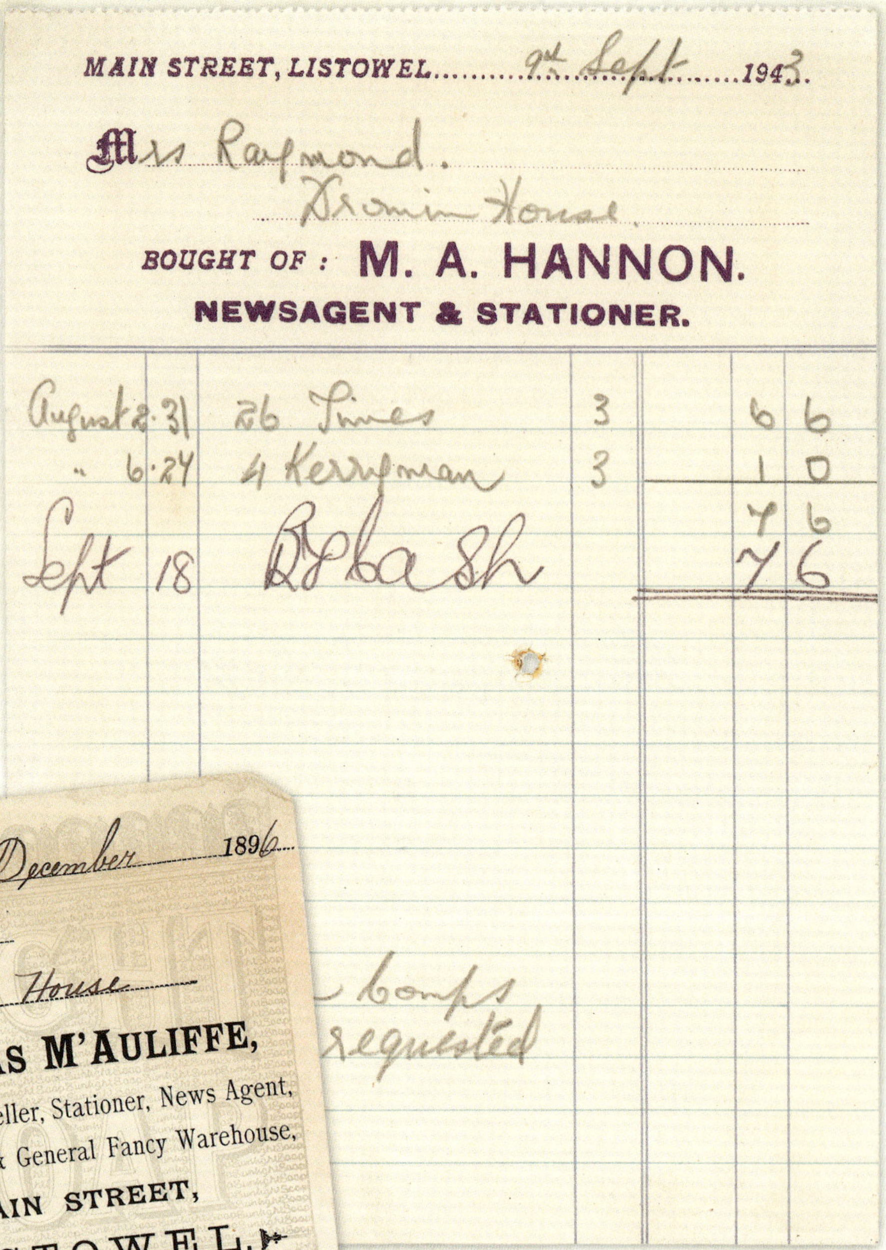
MAIN STREET, LISTOWEL........9th Sept........1943.

Mrs Raymond.
Dromin House.

BOUGHT OF : M. A. HANNON.
NEWSAGENT & STATIONER.

August	2-31	26 Times	3	6	6
"	6-24	4 Kerryman	3	1	0
				7	6
Sept	18	By Cash		7	6

...comps
...requested

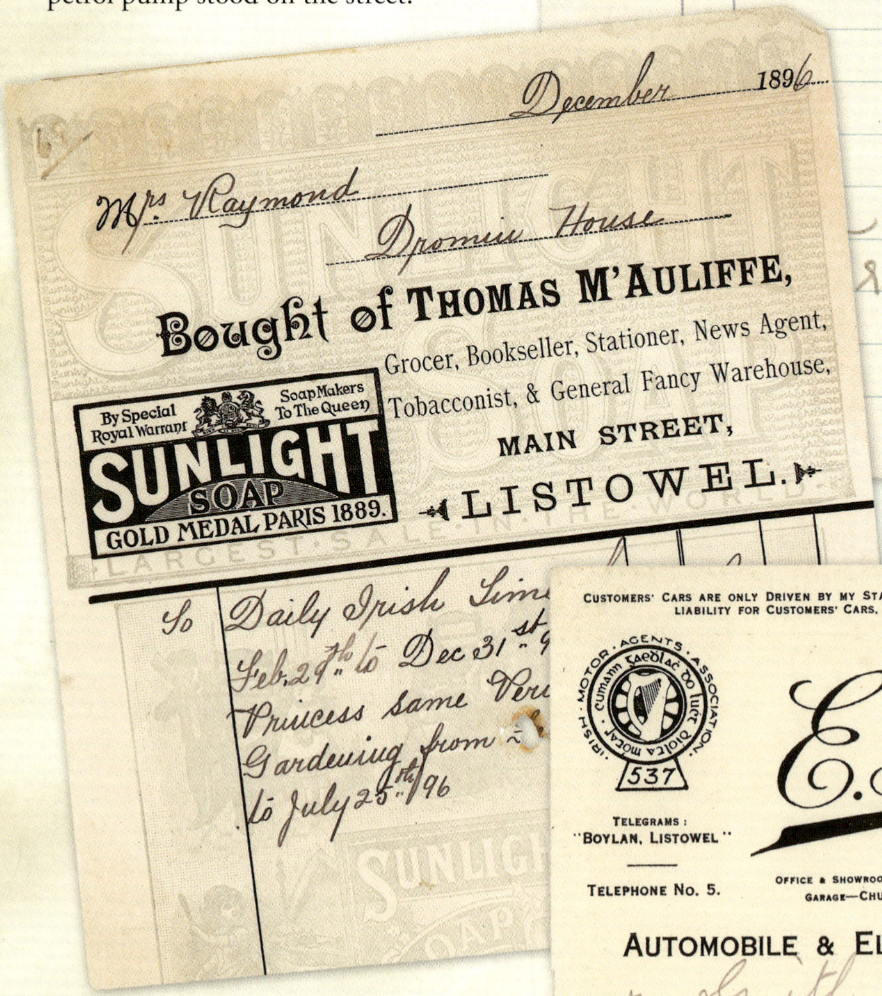
December 1896

Mrs Raymond
Dromin House

Bought of THOMAS M'AULIFFE,
Grocer, Bookseller, Stationer, News Agent,
Tobacconist, & General Fancy Warehouse,
MAIN STREET,
LISTOWEL.

To Daily Irish Times
Feb. 27th to Dec 31st...
Princess same...
Gardening from...
to July 28th 96

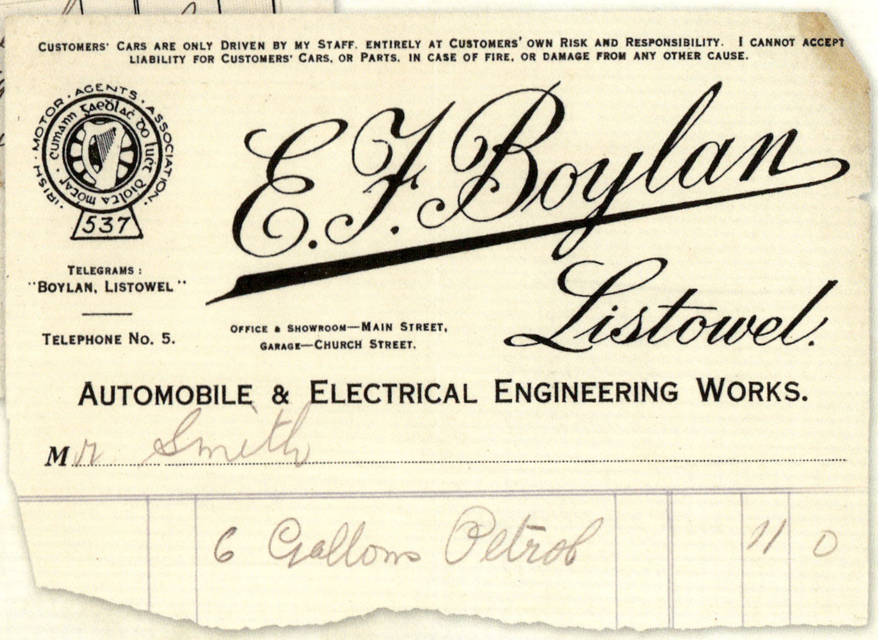
CUSTOMERS' CARS ARE ONLY DRIVEN BY MY STAFF, ENTIRELY AT CUSTOMERS' OWN RISK AND RESPONSIBILITY. I CANNOT ACCEPT LIABILITY FOR CUSTOMERS' CARS, OR PARTS, IN CASE OF FIRE, OR DAMAGE FROM ANY OTHER CAUSE.

E. J. Boylan
Listowel.

TELEGRAMS : "BOYLAN, LISTOWEL"

TELEPHONE No. 5.

OFFICE & SHOWROOM—MAIN STREET,
GARAGE—CHURCH STREET.

AUTOMOBILE & ELECTRICAL ENGINEERING WORKS.

Mr Smith

6 Gallons Petrol 11 0

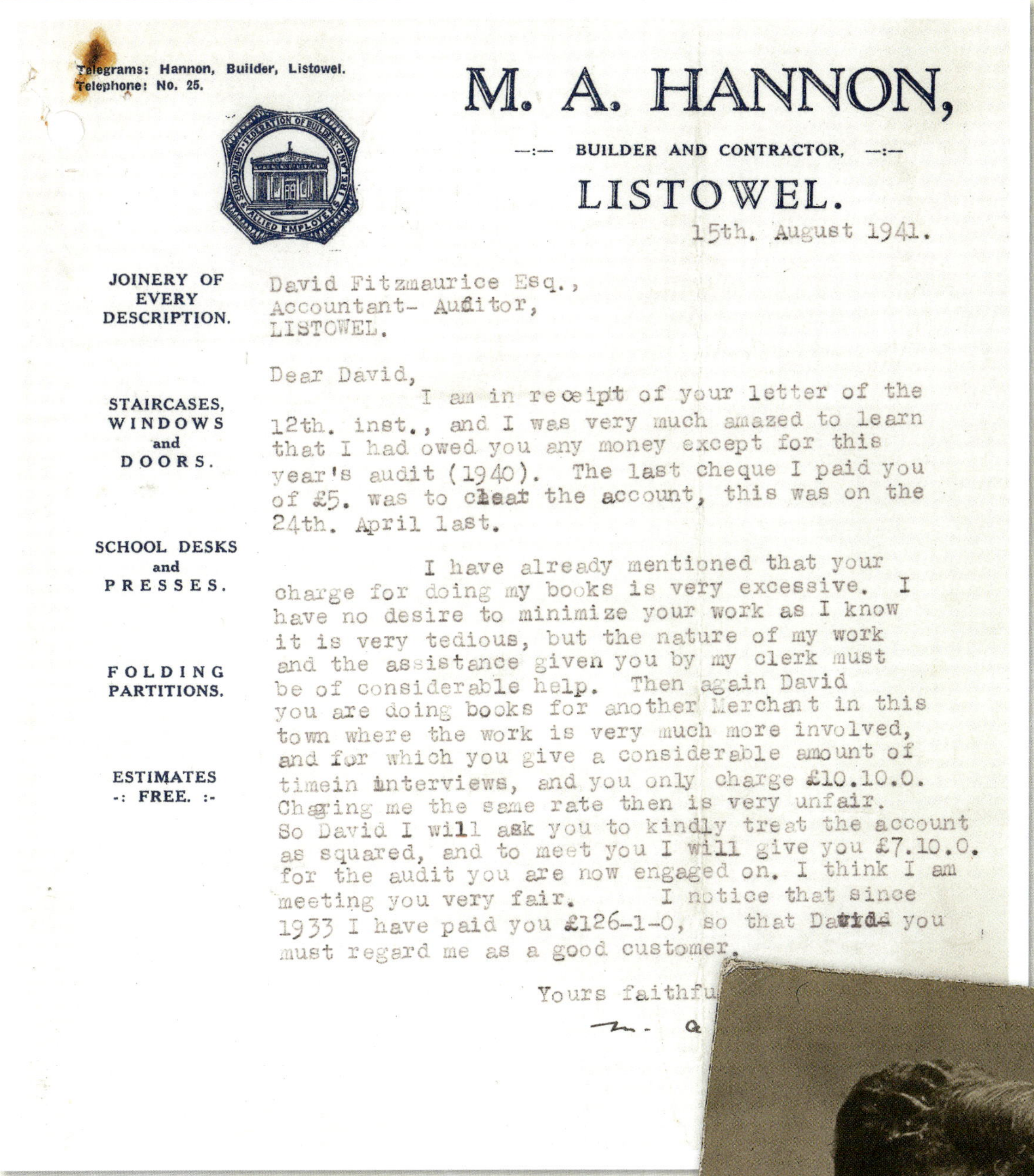

Telegrams: Hannon, Builder, Listowel.
Telephone: No. 25.

M. A. HANNON,

—:— BUILDER AND CONTRACTOR, —:—

LISTOWEL.

JOINERY OF EVERY DESCRIPTION.

STAIRCASES, WINDOWS and DOORS.

SCHOOL DESKS and PRESSES.

FOLDING PARTITIONS.

ESTIMATES -: FREE. :-

15th. August 1941.

David Fitzmaurice Esq.,
Accountant- Auditor,
LISTOWEL.

Dear David,

I am in receipt of your letter of the 12th. inst., and I was very much amazed to learn that I had owed you any money except for this year's audit (1940). The last cheque I paid you of £5. was to clear the account, this was on the 24th. April last.

I have already mentioned that your charge for doing my books is very excessive. I have no desire to minimize your work as I know it is very tedious, but the nature of my work and the assistance given you by my clerk must be of considerable help. Then again David you are doing books for another Merchant in this town where the work is very much more involved, and for which you give a considerable amount of timein interviews, and you only charge £10.10.0. Charging me the same rate then is very unfair. So David I will ask you to kindly treat the account as squared, and to meet you I will give you £7.10.0. for the audit you are now engaged on. I think I am meeting you very fair. I notice that since 1933 I have paid you £126-1-0, so that David you must regard me as a good customer.

Yours faithfu

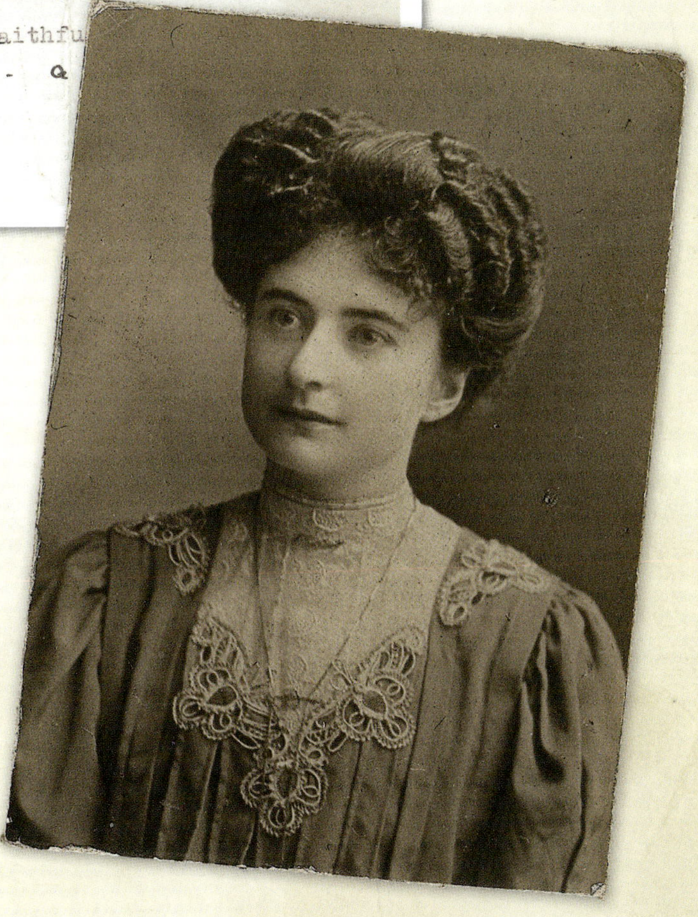

6 Main Street

M.A. Hannon had a successful construction company in Listowel. He bought the McAuliffe business in the late 1930s and continued as newsagent and stationer. Some years later, he sold the shop to Rita Dowling from Coolard. In 1980, M.A. Hannon's son, Danny, repurchased the business from Rita Dowling's nephew, Buddy O'Connor.

The letter above is from Moss Hannon to David Fitzmaurice, Accountant, looking for a reduction in his annual accounts bill.

4 Main Street
Brothers Tom and Pat Corridan (pictured below) purchased this business in Main Street when previous owners, Jeremiah and Bibianna Foran, relocated to Lower William Street in the 1890s. Tom subsequently bought a bar and grocery in William Street. Pat retained the Main Street shop until 1954. This is now the premises of Listowel artist Olive Stack.

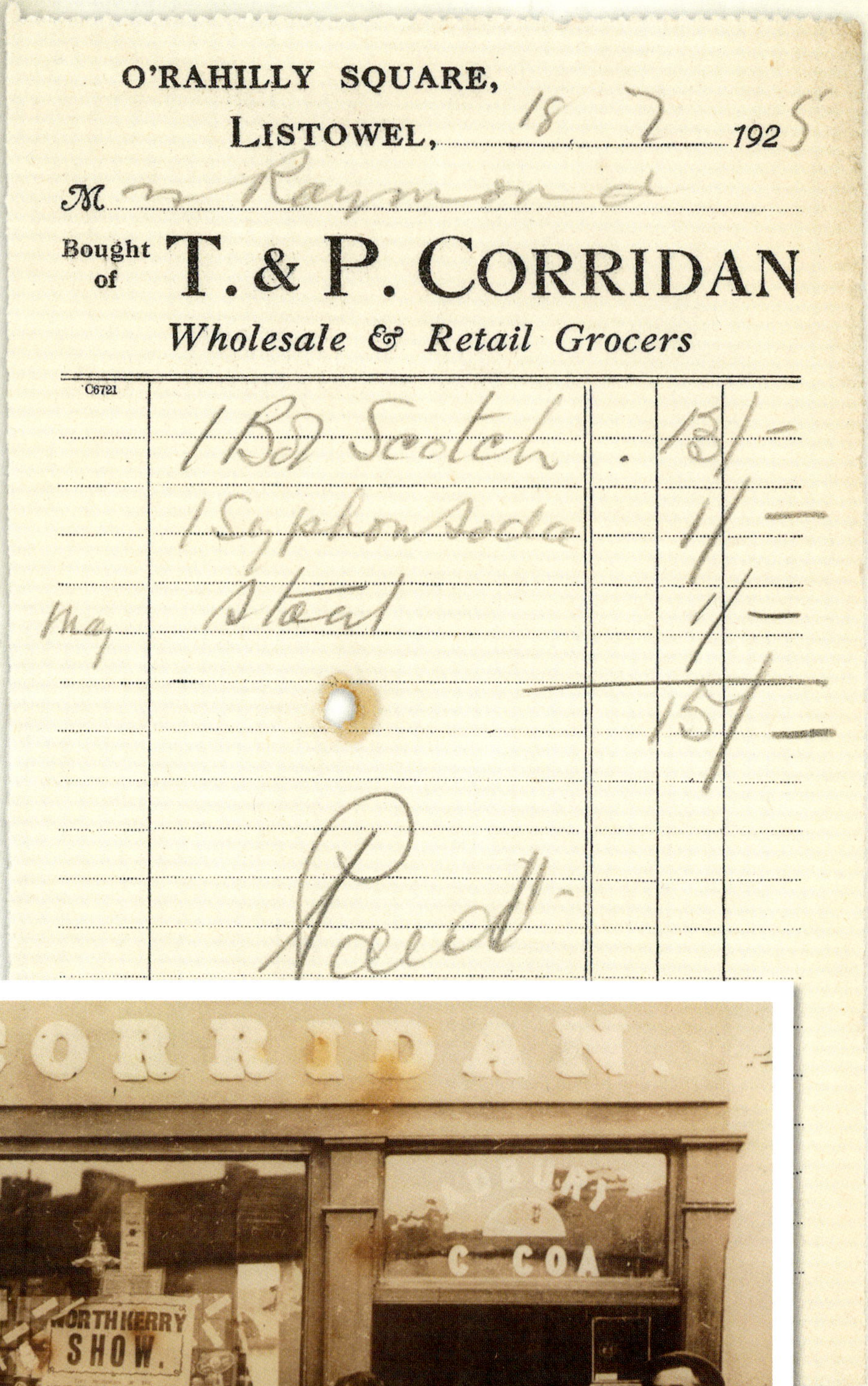
O'RAHILLY SQUARE,
LISTOWEL, 18 7 1925
M r Raymond

Bought of **T. & P. CORRIDAN**
Wholesale & Retail Grocers

C6721

1 Bot Scotch		13/-
1 Syphon Soda		1/-
Stout		1/-
		15/-

Paid

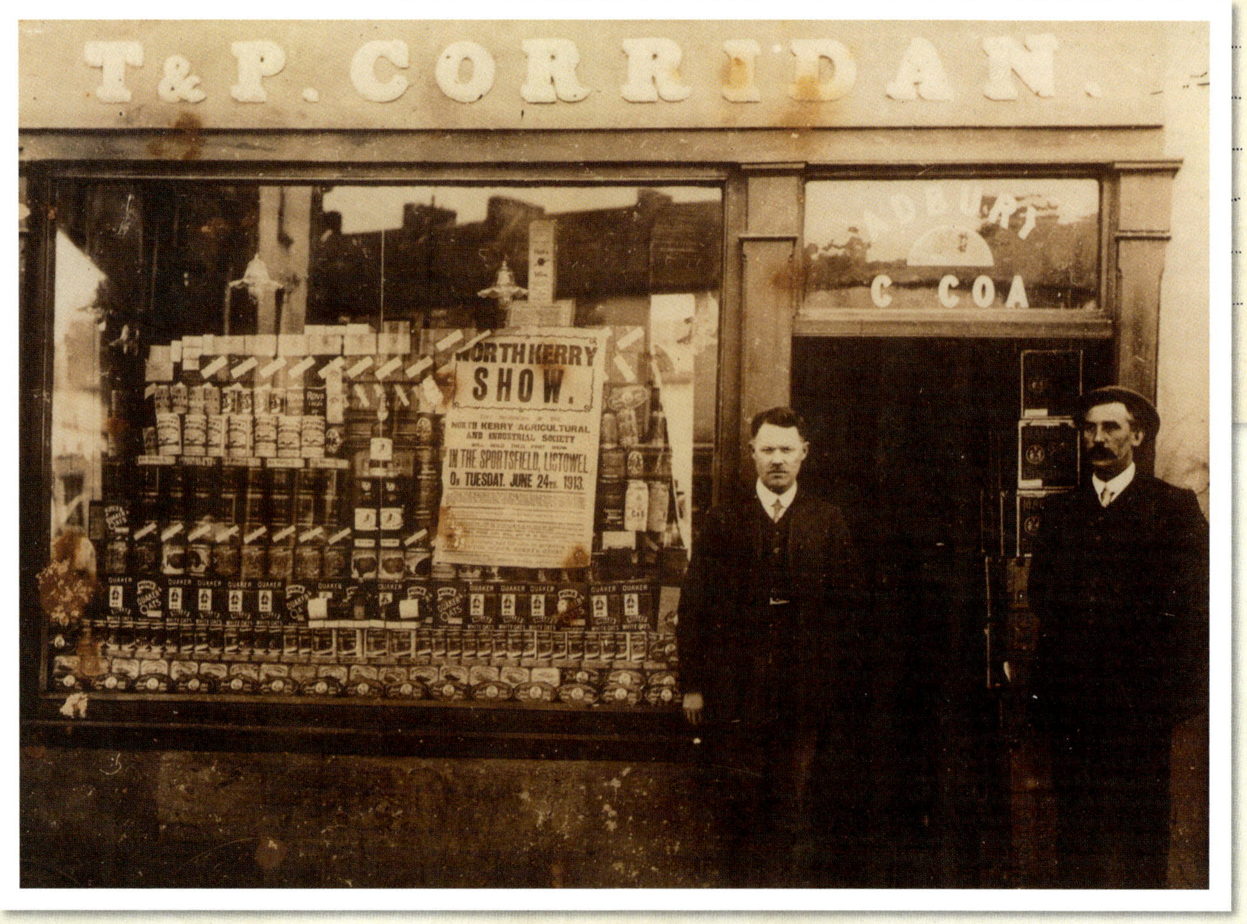

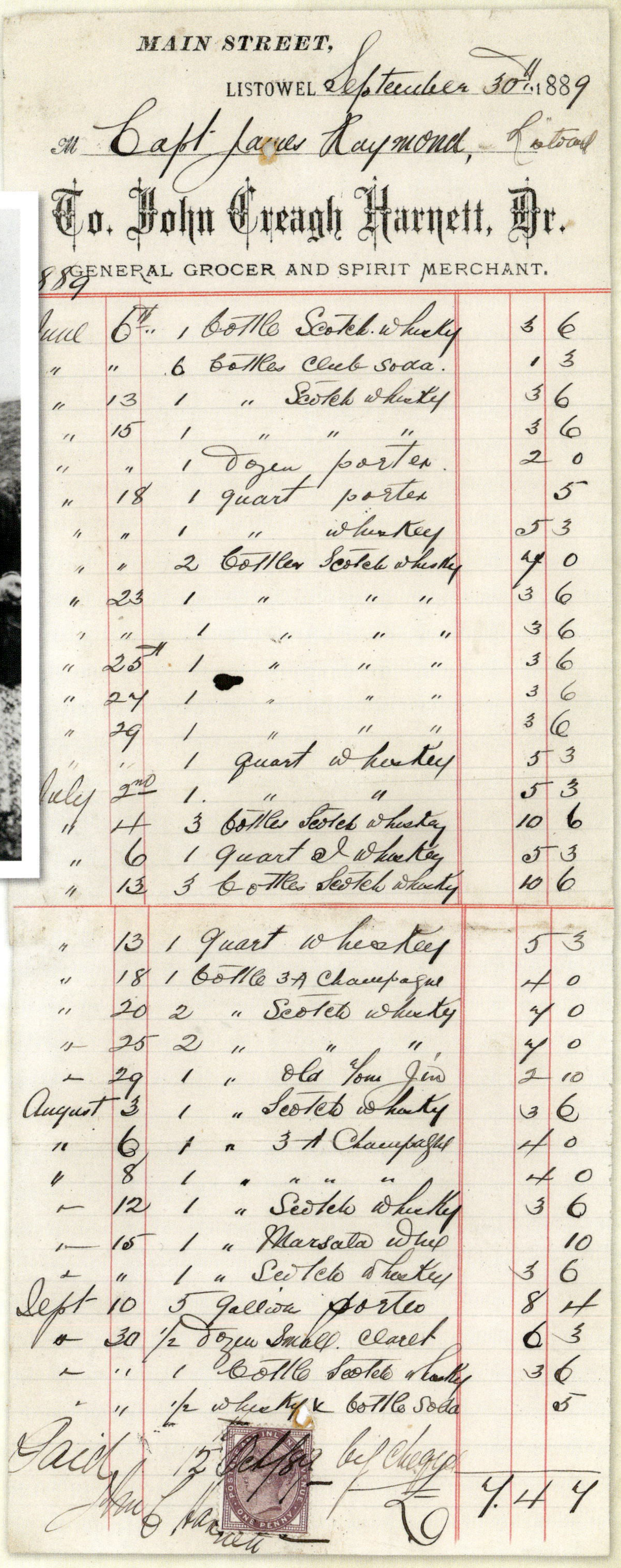

MAIN STREET,
LISTOWEL September 30th 1889

M Capt James Raymond, Listowel

To. John Creagh Harnett, Dr.

GENERAL GROCER AND SPIRIT MERCHANT.

1889

June	6th	1 bottle Scotch whisky	3	6
"	"	6 bottles Club soda.	1	3
"	13	1 " Scotch whisky	3	6
"	15	1 " " "	3	6
"	"	1 dozen porter.	2	0
"	18	1 quart porter		5
"	"	1 " whiskey	5	3
"	"	2 bottles Scotch whisky	7	0
"	23	1 " " "	3	6
"	"	1 " " "	3	6
"	25th	1 " " "	3	6
"	27	1 " " "	3	6
"	29	1 " " "	3	6
"	"	1 quart whiskey	5	3
July	2nd	1. " "	5	3
"	4	3 bottles Scotch whisky	10	6
"	6	1 quart I whiskey	5	3
"	13	3 bottles Scotch whisky	10	6
"	13	1 quart whiskey	5	3
"	18	1 bottle 3A Champagne	4	0
"	20	2 " Scotch whisky	7	0
"	25	2 " " "	7	0
"	29	1 " Old Tom Jin	2	10
August	3	1 " Scotch whisky	3	6
"	6	1 " 3A Champagne	4	0
"	8	1 " " "	4	0
"	12	1 " Scotch whisky	3	6
"	15	1 " Marsala wine		10
"	"	1 " Scotch whisky	3	6
Sept	10	5 gallon porter	8	4
"	30	1/2 dozen small claret	6	3
"	"	1 bottle Scotch whisky	3	6
"	"	1/2 whisky & bottle soda		5

Paid 12 Octbr by cheque £9.4.4

John C Harnett

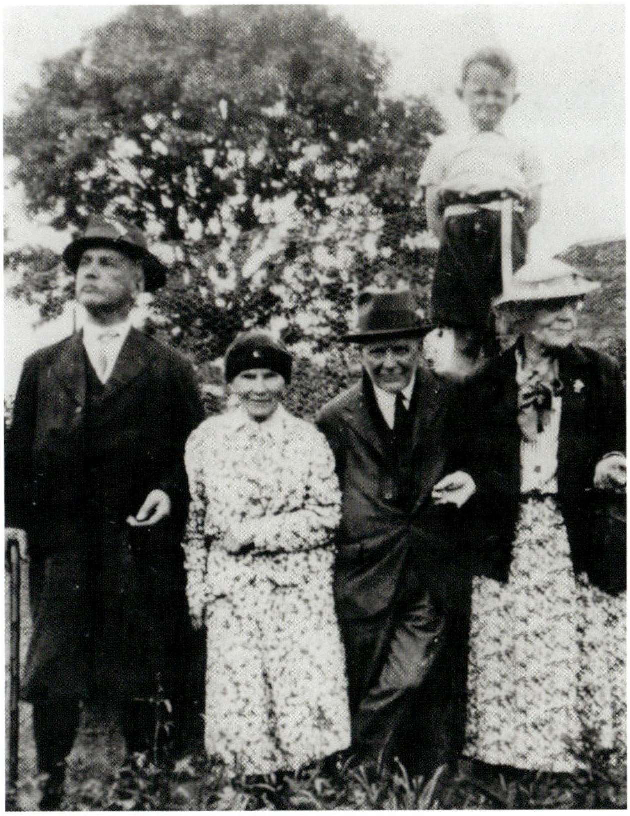

3 Main Street
John Creagh Harnett had a general grocery and public house at Main Street. Harnett was a man of great wealth. He had a large house and 200 acres of land at Moynsha, Abbeyfeale. Much of this land is now owned by the Byrne brothers, John and Patsy, of Coolanelig, Duagh.

Photo above: Taken circa 1930 includes from left: John Creagh Harnett, Georgina Fitzmaurice (playwright's sister), George Fitzmaurice (playwright) and other individuals unknown.

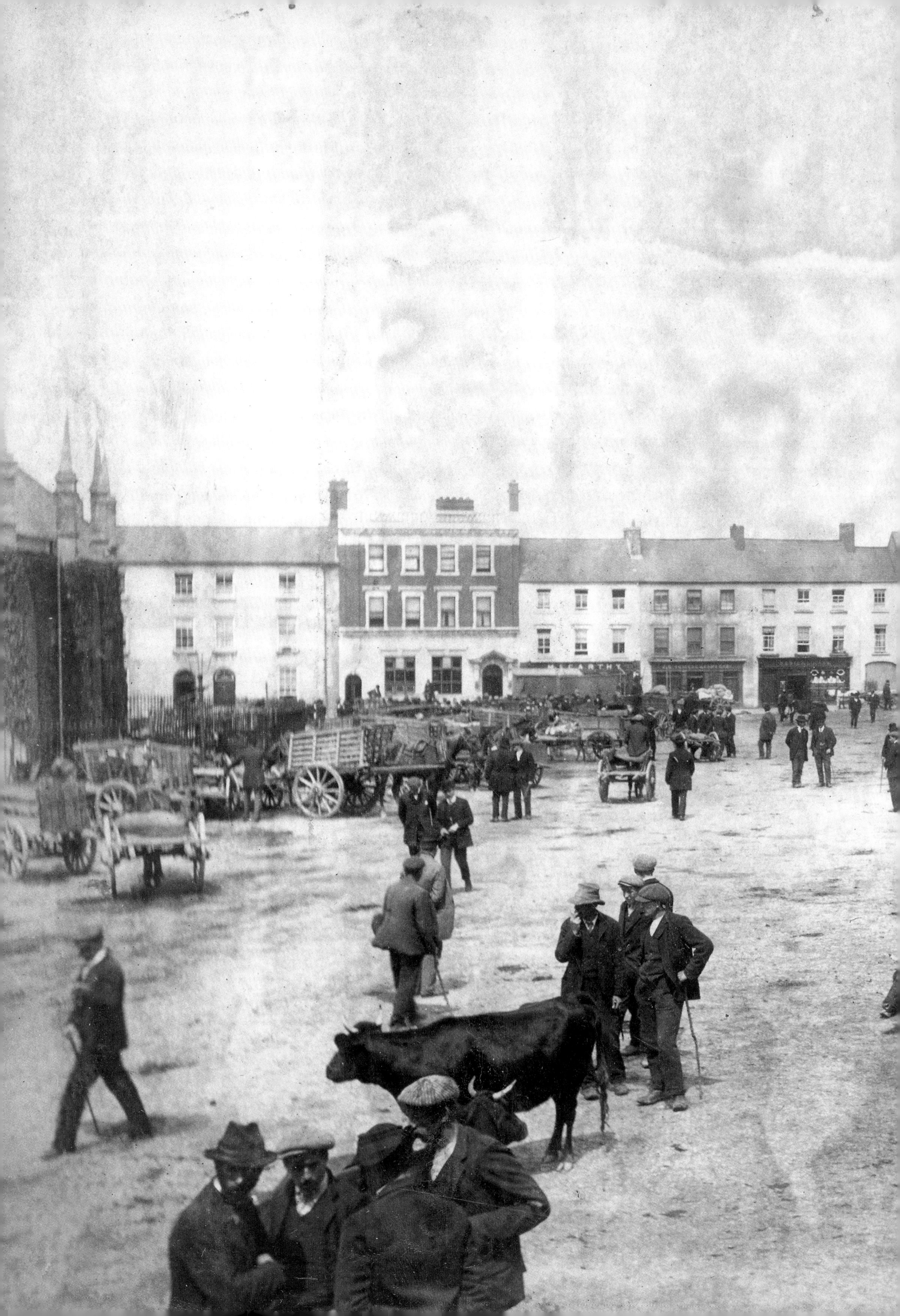

Chapter 7

THE SQUARE

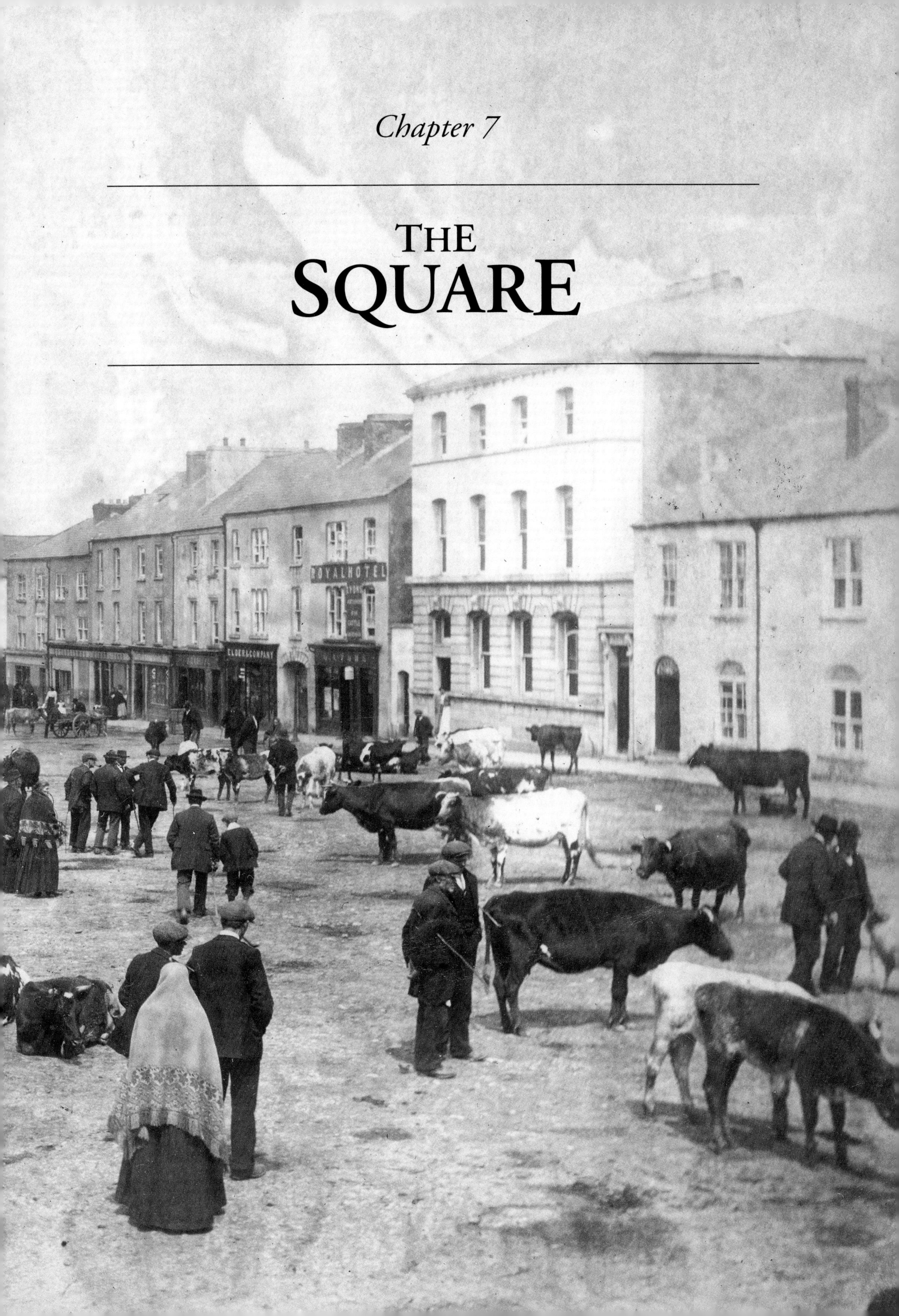

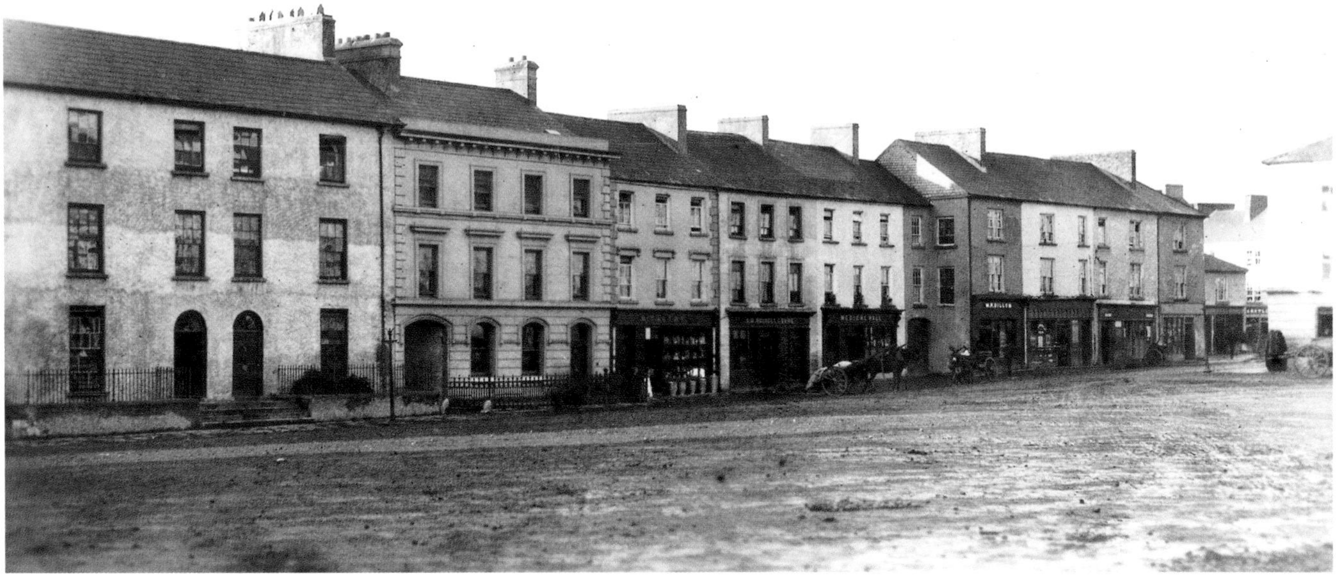

Above: Early 1880s/1890s view of the western side of the Square. This is one of a number of photographs taken by Captain J.W. Raymond of Dromin House and reproduced on glass. The house on the extreme left was the residence of Thomas F. O Rahilly. Third house from the left is now the Allied Irish Bank and was previously the Provincial Bank. Before this it had served as a medical hall and as the town's post office. To the right of the bank are three businesses: McCarthy's, Russell's and Woulfe's Medical Hall. Further up on Main Street, the upper frontage of Potter's shop was still awaiting the adornment of Pat McAuliffe's masterpiece 'The Maid of Erin'.

Previous pages: Cattle fair in Listowel Square, 1904. It's clear from this photograph that the Square was the commercial hub of the town in those days. The Bank of Ireland and the Provincial Bank dominate the Square's northern and western sides. Next to the Bank on Ireland on the right is the Royal Hotel, while McCarthy's hardware store is situated next to the Provincial Bank.

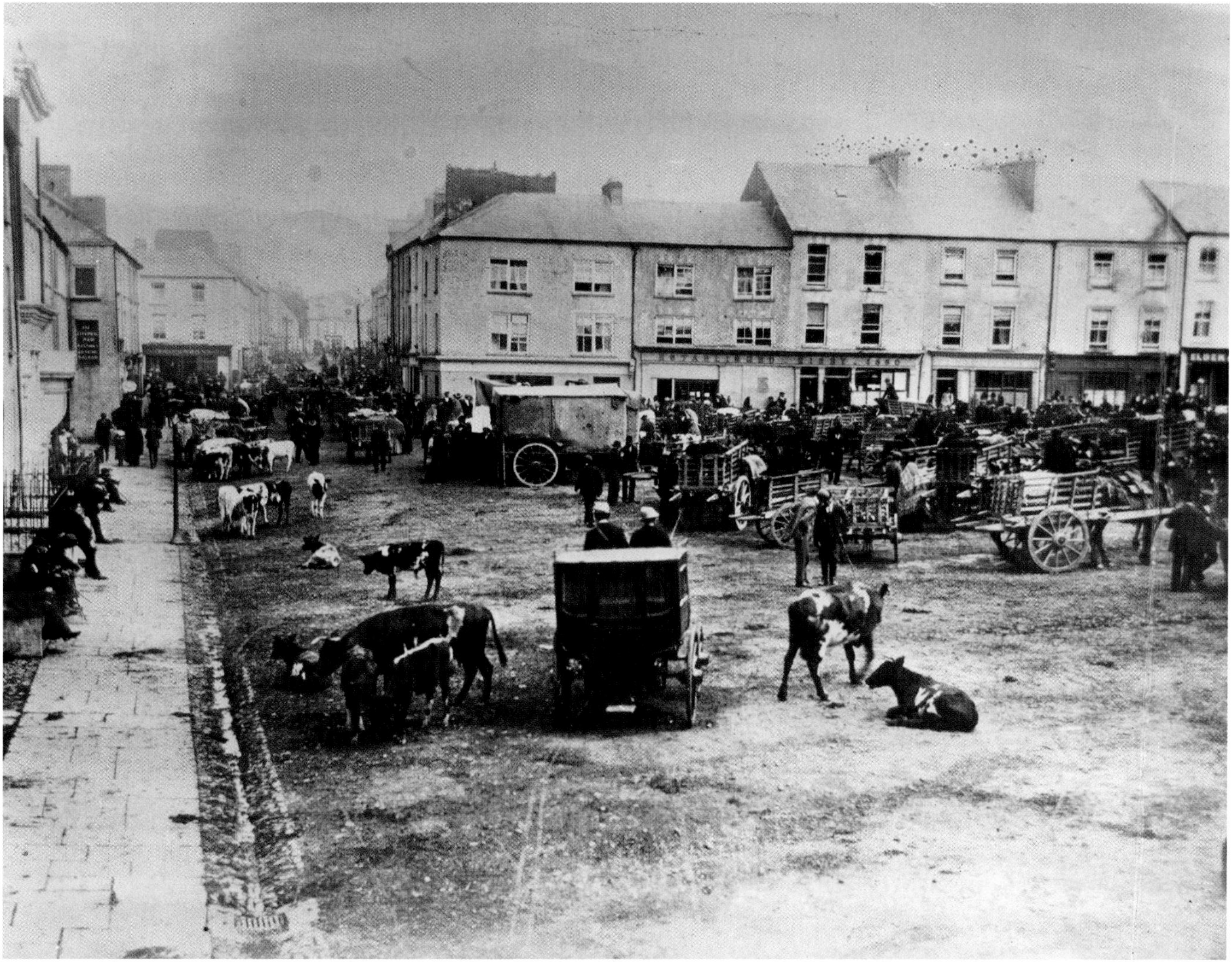

A bustling day of commerce on a market day of 1904. Ordinary cattle fairs were held on alternate weeks. Three Big Fairs were held annually in May, July and October. The building of the cattle mart in 1960 brought an end to the street fairs. Two interesting features in the photograph are the horse-drawn police wagon on patrol in the Square, and (further up in mid picture) a large hawker's caravan which would have sold clothes, harnesses and light farm implements.

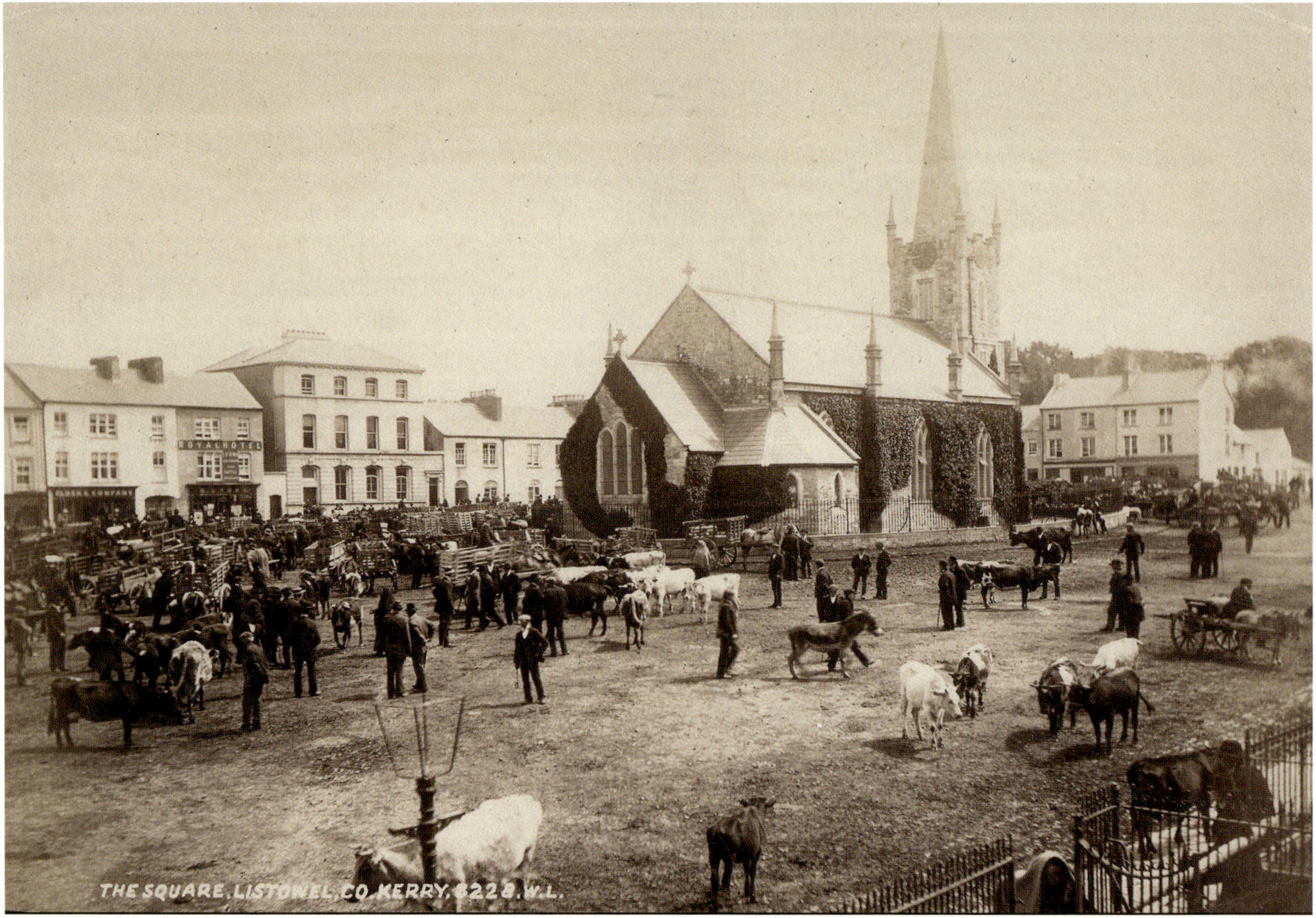

Listowel Square, showing part of the northern and southern side, 1904. The Square was the focal point of fair day activity; livestock would be driven on foot from the very early morning to the town from all over the North Kerry countryside. Tolls were taken up at various entry points to the town by Lord Listowel's agents. In relation to the Square, a point of entry from the Bridge Road was locally known as the Custom Gap. The corner house at this point of entry was owned by the Collopy family from where they ran a public house and hotel.

Below: A photograph taken of the funeral procession of Private Edward (Sac) Sheehy, a Free State soldier who was the first casualty in Listowel during the Civil War. He was killed at the rear of the Workhouse, where he and his comrades were stationed. An unusual aspect of the cortège, which was led by the Listowel Brass and Reed band, was the appearance of both factions, Republican and Free State, marching side by side in honour of the young man who had died.

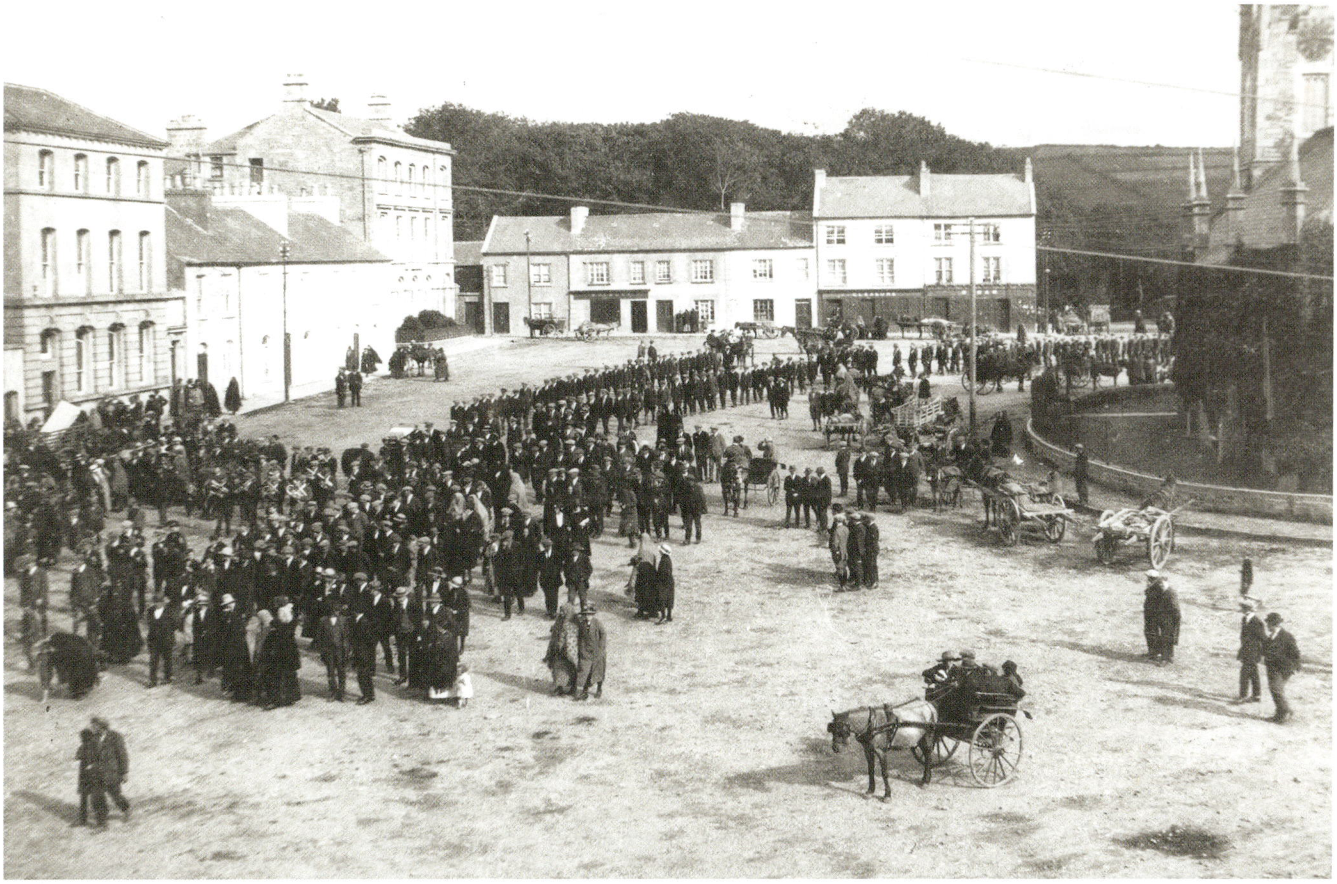

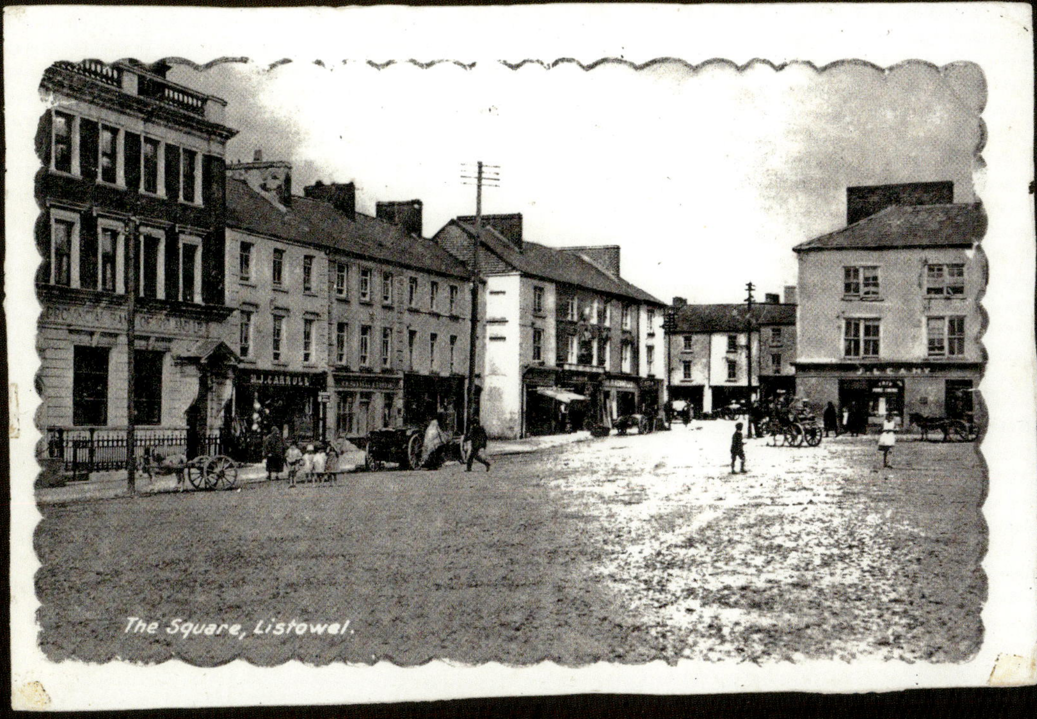

Right: The Square in the 1920s. Motor transport is still a rare commodity. Women in shawls of various hues are prominent. Donkeys and carts are in abundance.

Right: General Eoin O'Duffy, leader of the Blueshirt movement, speaking from the elevated position of a horse's cart outside Saint John's in 1934.

Below: A scene from a Blueshirt meeting in the Square. On close inspection one can see the large number of Gardaí in attendance on the periphery of the crowd. Trouble was a frequent visitor to the town during this period due to tensions between the followers of the Blueshirts and local Republicans.

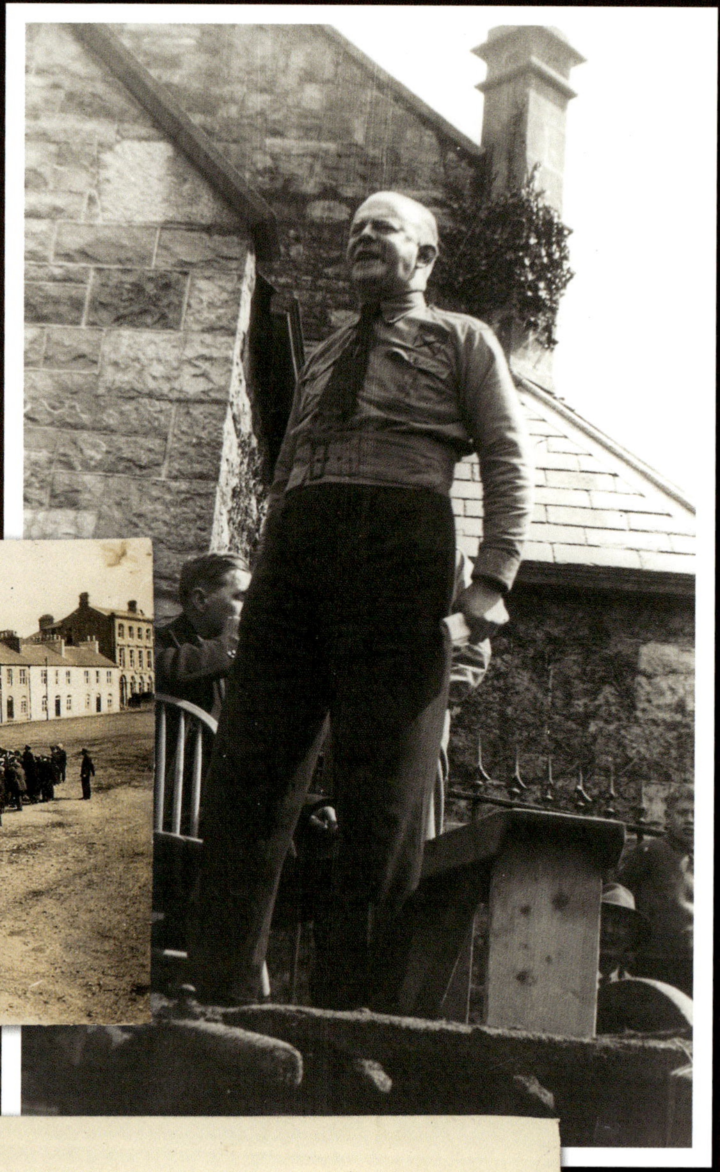

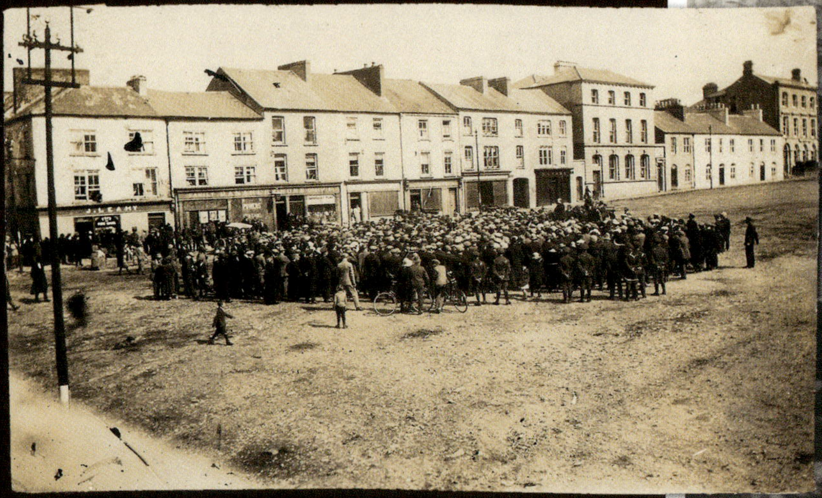

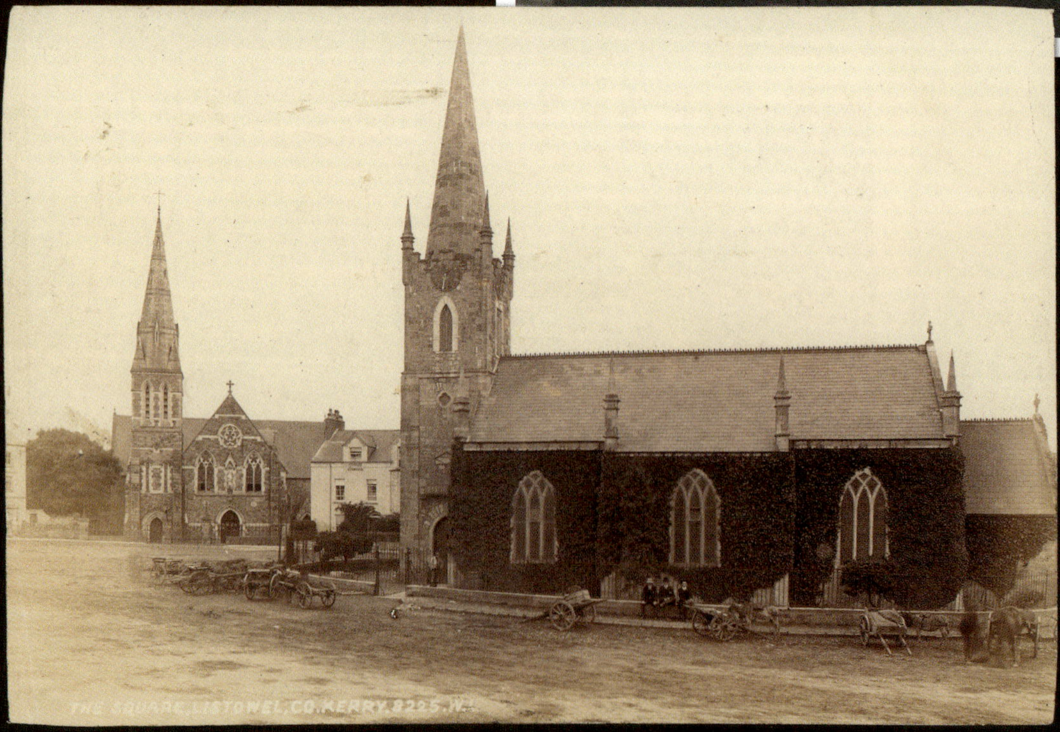

Saint John's Church of Ireland, built in 1819, is the centrepiece of Listowel Square. Once surrounded by a low wall topped with high railings, these became hitching posts for the ass and carts of many doing a day's shopping in the town.

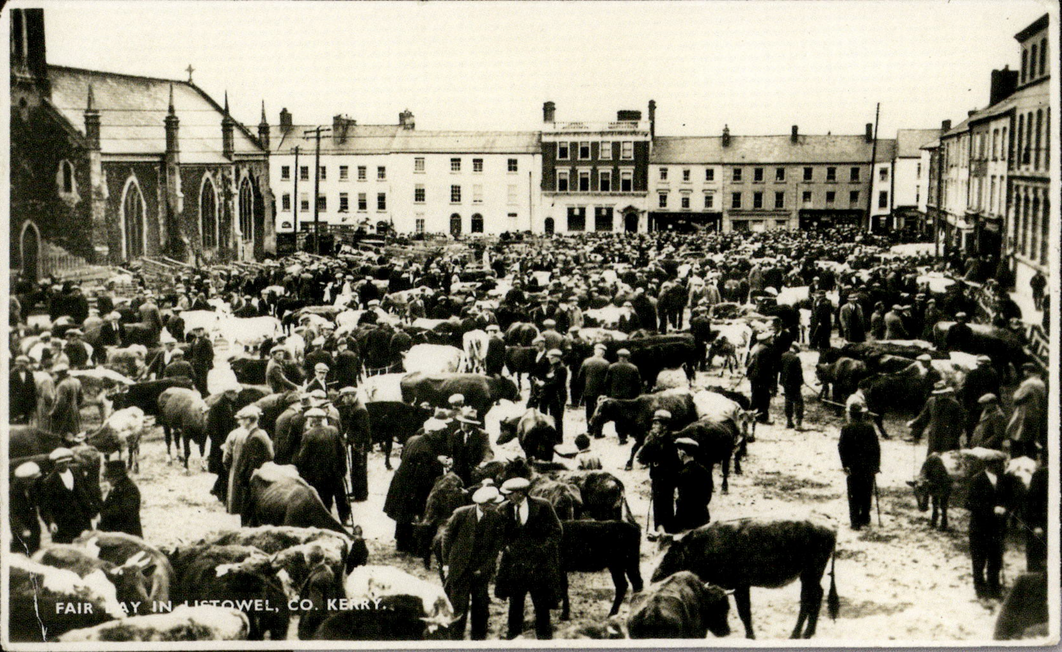

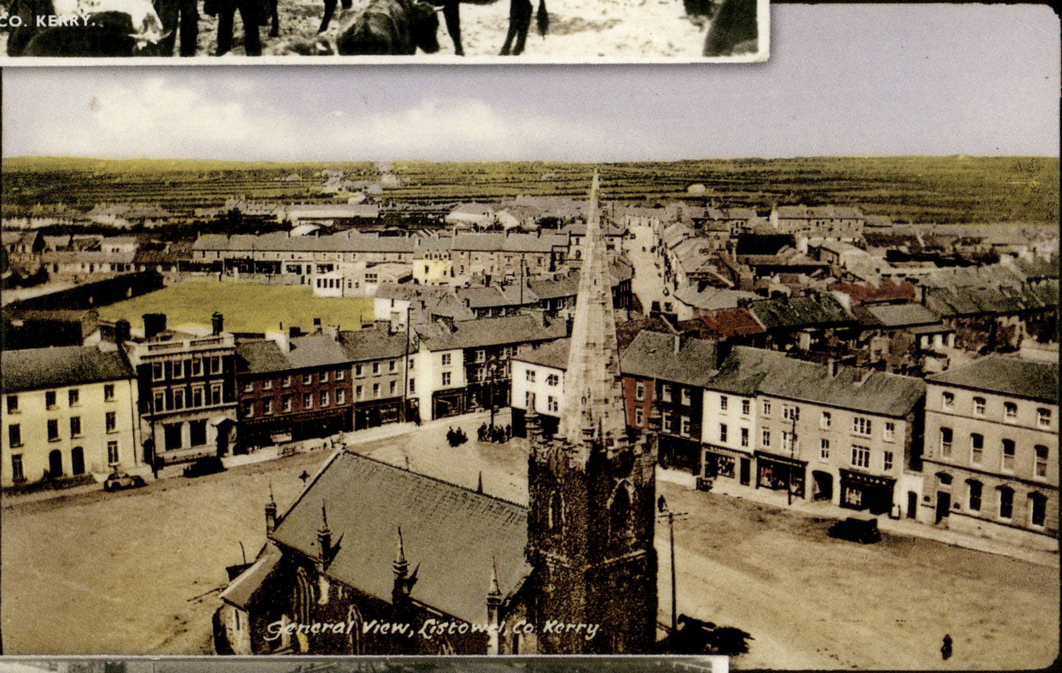

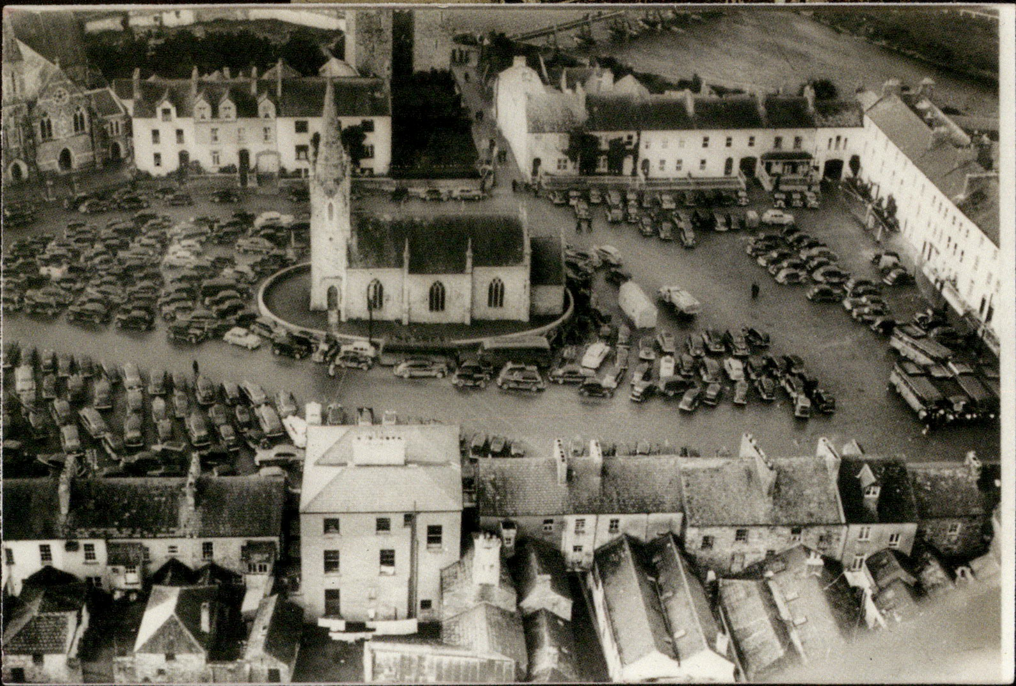

A photo collage of the Square.
Top: Big Fair Day, late 1940s.
Middle: Photograph taken by David Lawlor (Parish Clerk) from the spire of Saint Mary's Church in the 1930s.
Bottom: Aerial picture, taken on a race day in the 1950s.

41 The Square

The proprietor of the Square's medical hall in the 1880s and 1890s was P.J. Woulfe. The family also ran a drapery in Main Street. Dinny Leane, having qualified as a chemist, commenced practising at the turn of century (1900). He was an active member of Listowel Race Company and its long-time secretary. For many years meetings of the company were held in an office above Leane's Pharmacy. Listowel Urban Council also had a temporary office here after the burning of their offices at the Carnegie Library in the Bridge Road during the War of Independence. Subsequently, the pharmacy was owned by Bridget Ross (née Harnett) and is now run by Gerry Lynn.

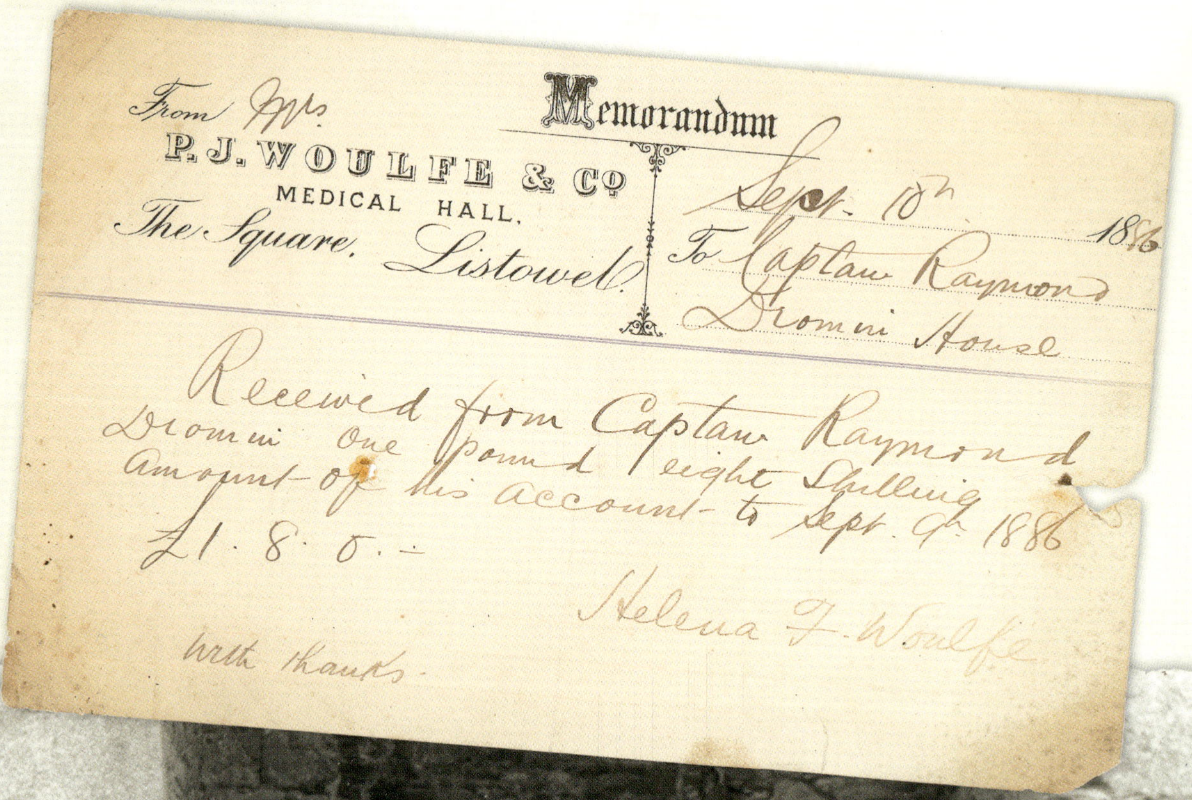

From Mrs
P.J. WOULFE & Co
MEDICAL HALL,
The Square, Listowel.

Memorandum

Sept. 10th 1886
To Captain Raymond
Dromin House

Received from Captain Raymond
Dromin One pound eight Shilling
amount of his account to Sept. 9th 1886
£1. 8. 0.-

Helena F. Woulfe

With thanks.

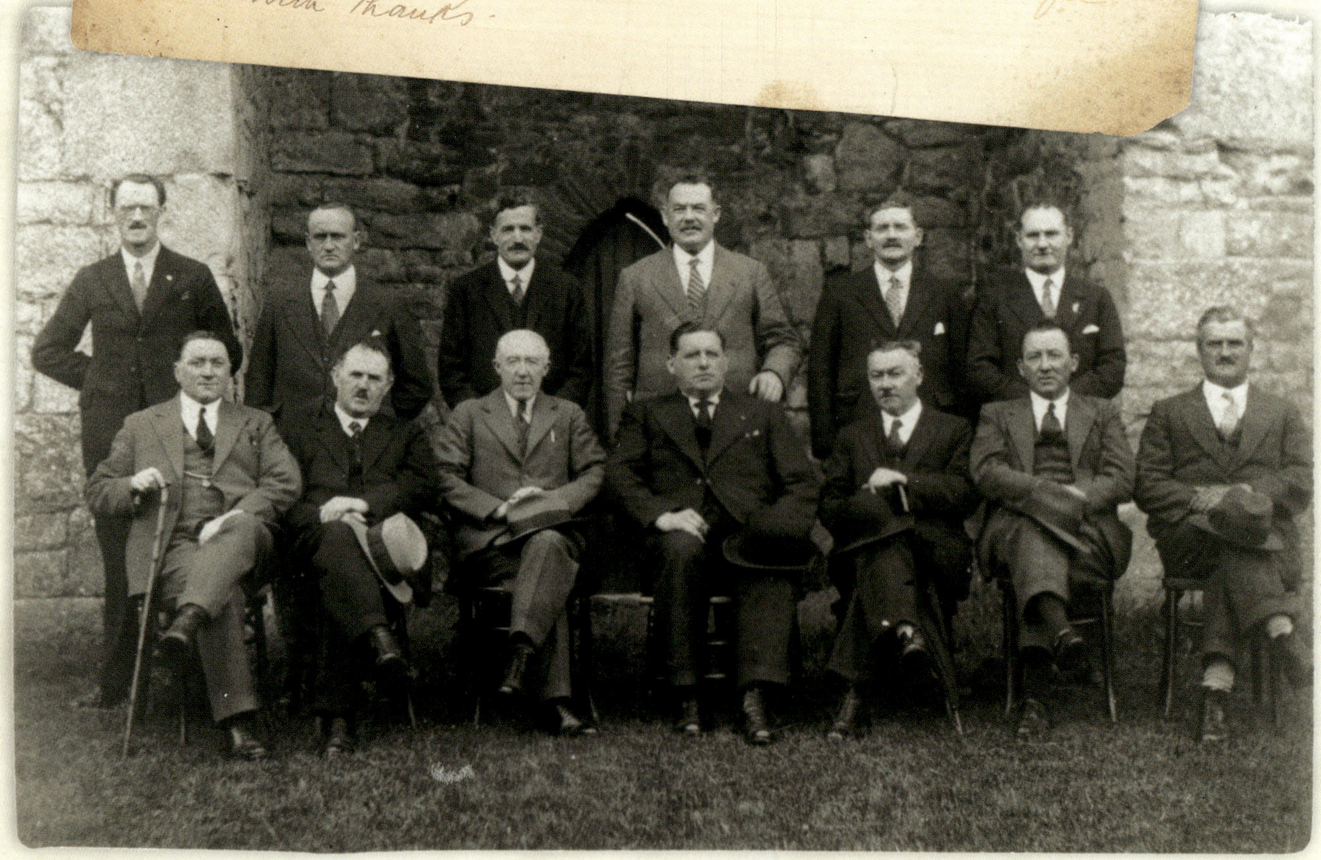

Photograph of Race Directors of 1923 outside Listowel Castle. Front: Morgan Sheehy, Ned Gleeson, Dinny Leane, Tom Walsh, John Stack, Jim Crowley, Thomas Murphy. Back: John Moran (Ass. Sec), Tom O'Connell, Florence O'Connor, John R.Walsh, T. D. O'Sullivan, Jack O'Sullivan.

40 The Square

Andrew Stephens, from County Wexford, acted as North Kerry agent for the Limerick flour milling company, Russell's. Their flour and meal store was situated where the upper section of O'Carroll's Hardware is today. Charles Egan was a one-time occupier of the house prior to Russell's. The early 1890s photograph includes Andrew Stephens and his daughters, Eva, Winifred and Anna, his father as well as two of his staff.

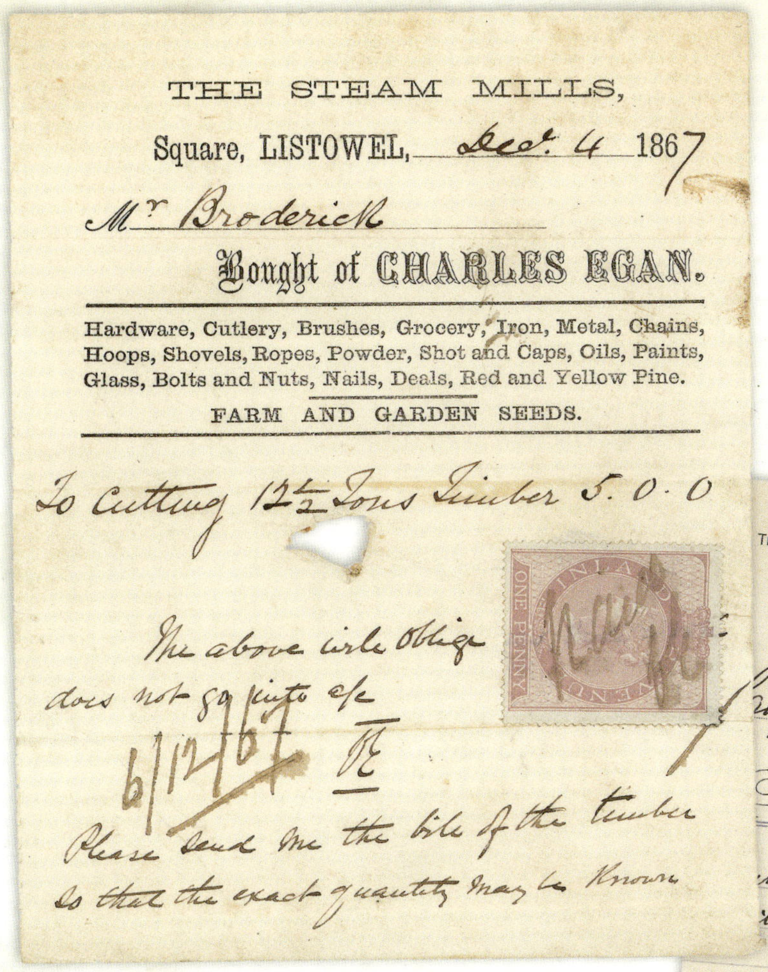

THE STEAM MILLS,

Square, LISTOWEL, Decr 4 1867

Mr Broderick

Bought of CHARLES EGAN.

Hardware, Cutlery, Brushes, Grocery, Iron, Metal, Chains, Hoops, Shovels, Ropes, Powder, Shot and Caps, Oils, Paints, Glass, Bolts and Nuts, Nails, Deals, Red and Yellow Pine.

FARM AND GARDEN SEEDS.

To Cutting 12½ Tons Timber 5. 0. 0

INLAND REVENUE ONE PENNY

The above will oblige

does not go into a/c

6/12/67

Please send me the bill of the timber so that the exact quantity may be known

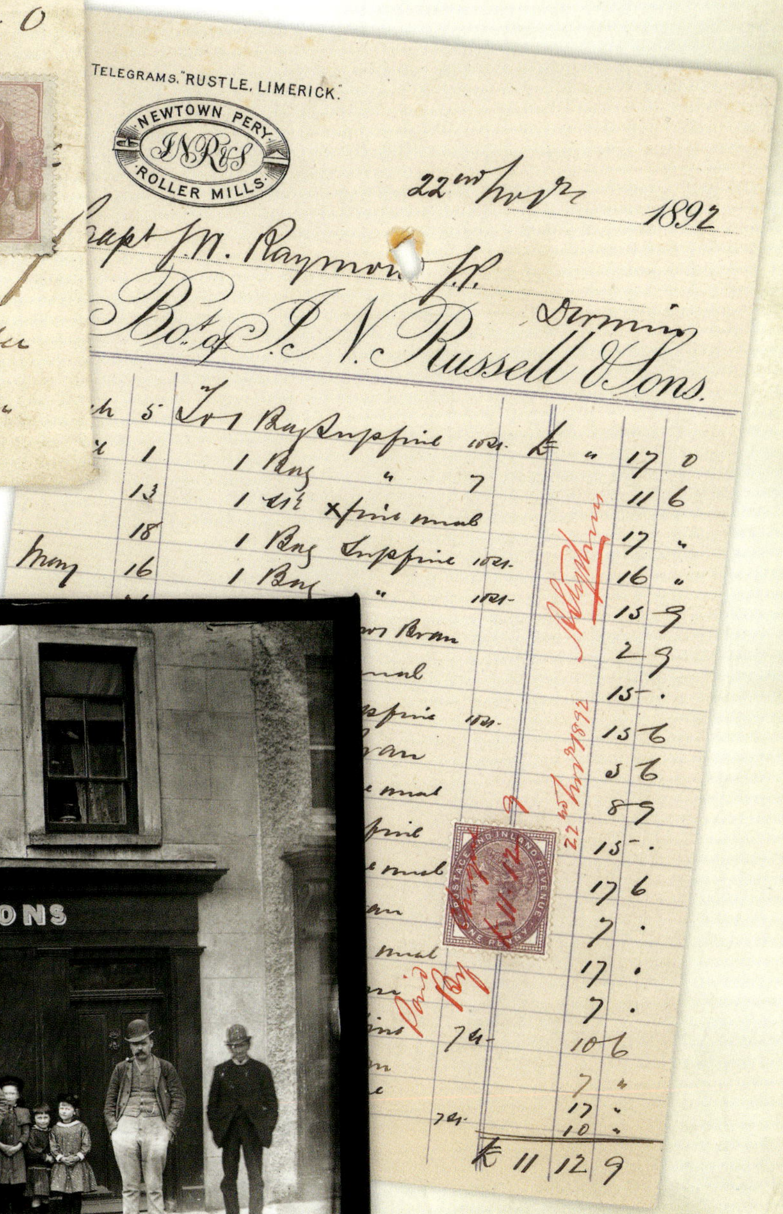

TELEGRAMS. "RUSTLE, LIMERICK."

NEWTOWN PERY JNR&S ROLLER MILLS.

22nd Novr 1892

Capt J.W. Raymond J.P.

Bot of J. N. Russell & Sons.

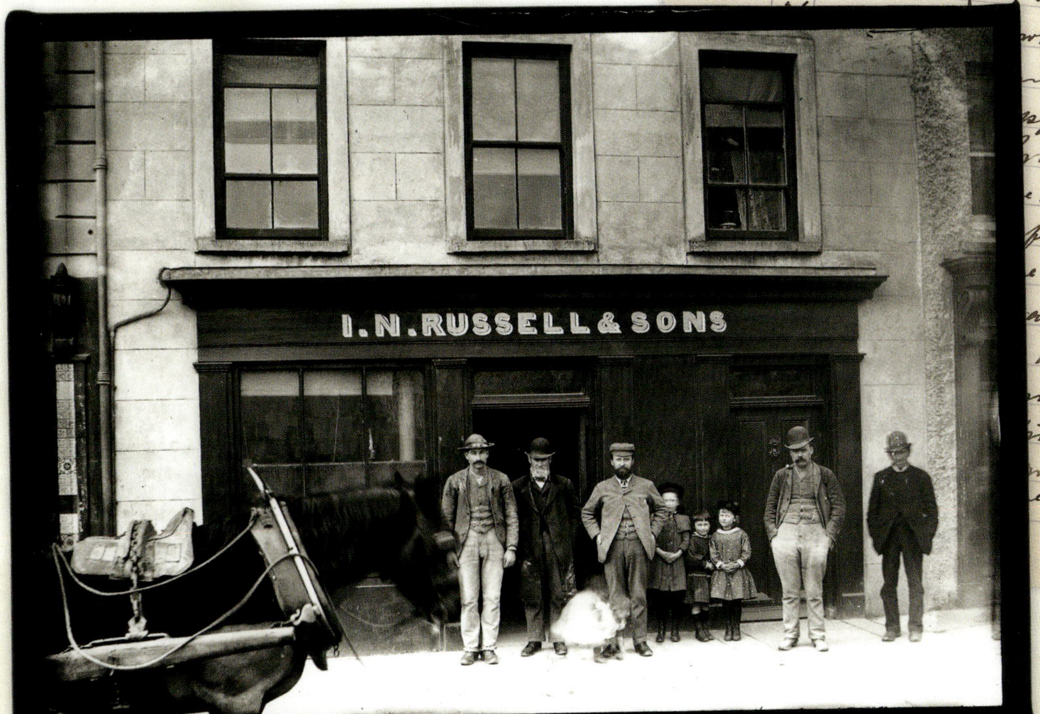

39 The Square

Carroll's Hardware is trading in the Square since 1908. The present shop is a combination of two houses, the lower, now number 40, next to the AIB bank, was the original shop. This house was formerly occupied in the early 1800s by James Sheehan, where he had a woollen and linen warehouse. The Sheehans vacated this premises and moved to the Corner House, No. 1 the Square, after Sheehan's death, where the business was continued by Mrs Sheehan. This latter house had belonged to Edmond O'Callaghan, Elizabeth Sheehan's father. Afterwards, it was taken over by P.D. Griffin. Following Sheehan's departure from the original house at No. 39, it was bought by Richard McCarthy, and he opened a hardware shop (the billhead on top gives a glimpse of the vast array of goods carried). The McCarthy family also had a house and land, known as the Glebe, in a townland called Inchymagilleragh West, outside Listowel.

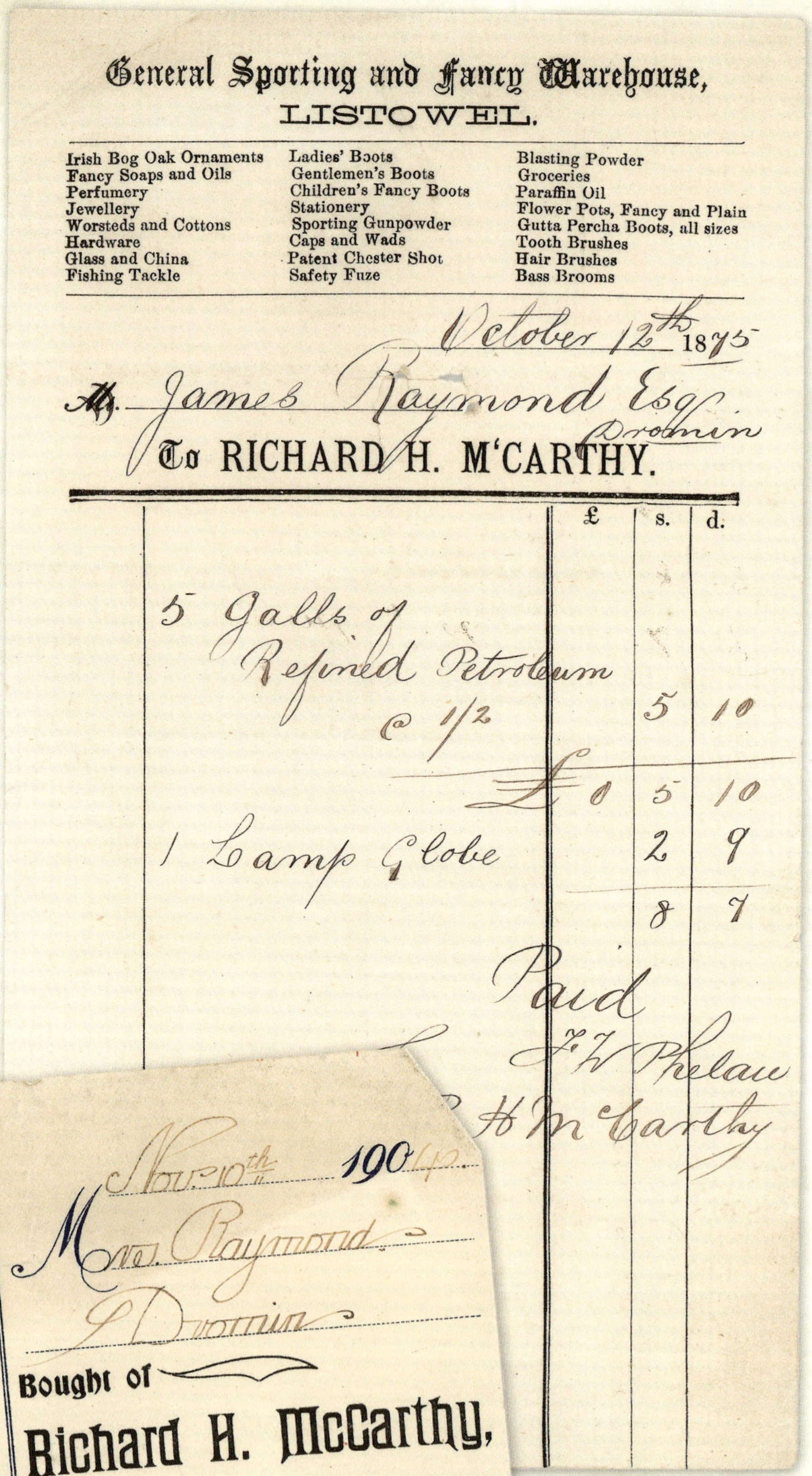

General Sporting and Fancy Warehouse,
LISTOWEL.

Irish Bog Oak Ornaments	Ladies' Boots	Blasting Powder
Fancy Soaps and Oils	Gentlemen's Boots	Groceries
Perfumery	Children's Fancy Boots	Paraffin Oil
Jewellery	Stationery	Flower Pots, Fancy and Plain
Worsteds and Cottons	Sporting Gunpowder	Gutta Percha Boots, all sizes
Hardware	Caps and Wads	Tooth Brushes
Glass and China	Patent Chester Shot	Hair Brushes
Fishing Tackle	Safety Fuze	Bass Brooms

October 12th 1875

Mr. James Raymond Esq. Dromin

To RICHARD H. M'CARTHY.

	£	s.	d.
5 Galls of Refined Petroleum @ 1/2		5	10
	£ 0	5	10
1 Lamp Globe		2	9
		8	7

Paid
J. W. Phelan
R H McCarthy

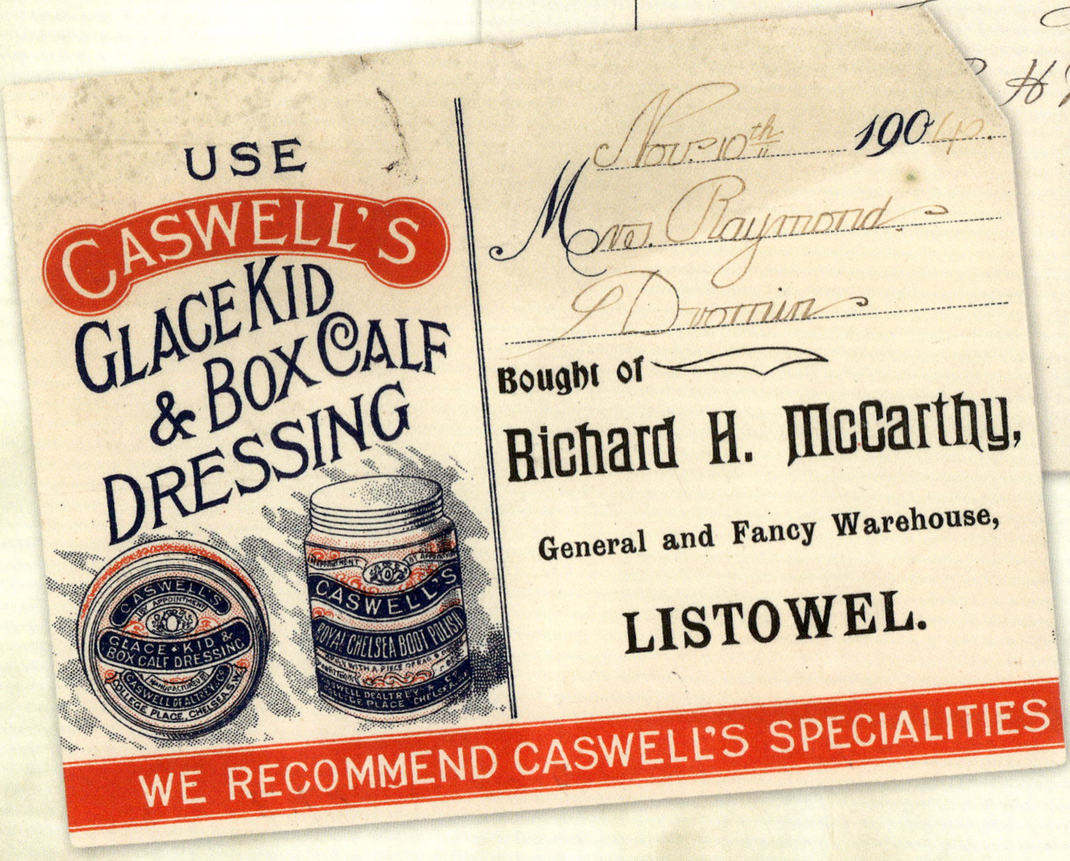

Nov. 10th 1904
Mrs Raymond
Dromin

Bought of
Richard H. McCarthy,
General and Fancy Warehouse,
LISTOWEL.

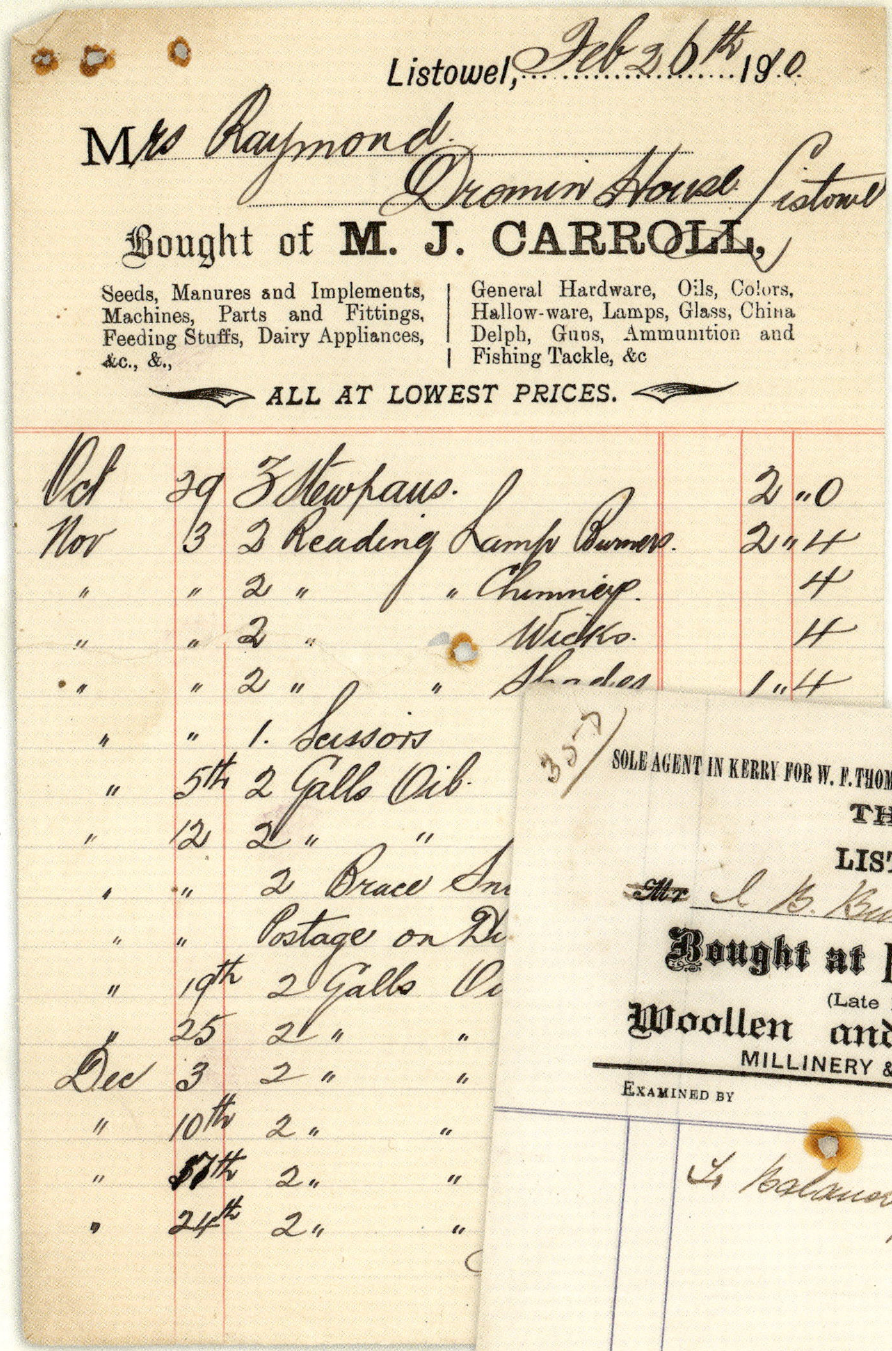

Listowel, Feb 26th 1910

Mrs Raymond

Dromin House Listowel

Bought of M. J. CARROLL,

Seeds, Manures and Implements, Machines, Parts and Fittings, Feeding Stuffs, Dairy Appliances, &c., &c., | General Hardware, Oils, Colors, Hallow-ware, Lamps, Glass, China Delph, Guns, Ammunition and Fishing Tackle, &c

ALL AT LOWEST PRICES.

Oct	29	3 Stewpans	2 " 0
Nov	3	2 Reading Lamp Burners	2 " 4
"	"	2 " " Chimneys	4
"	"	2 " " Wicks	4
"	"	2 " " Shades	1 " 4
"	"	1. Scissors	
"	5th	2 Galls Oil	
"	12	2 " "	
"	"	2 Brace Sn[illegible]	
"	"	Postage on D[illegible]	
"	19th	2 Galls Oi[illegible]	
	25	2 " "	
Dec	3	2 " "	
"	10th	2 " "	
"	17th	2 " "	
"	24th	2 " "	

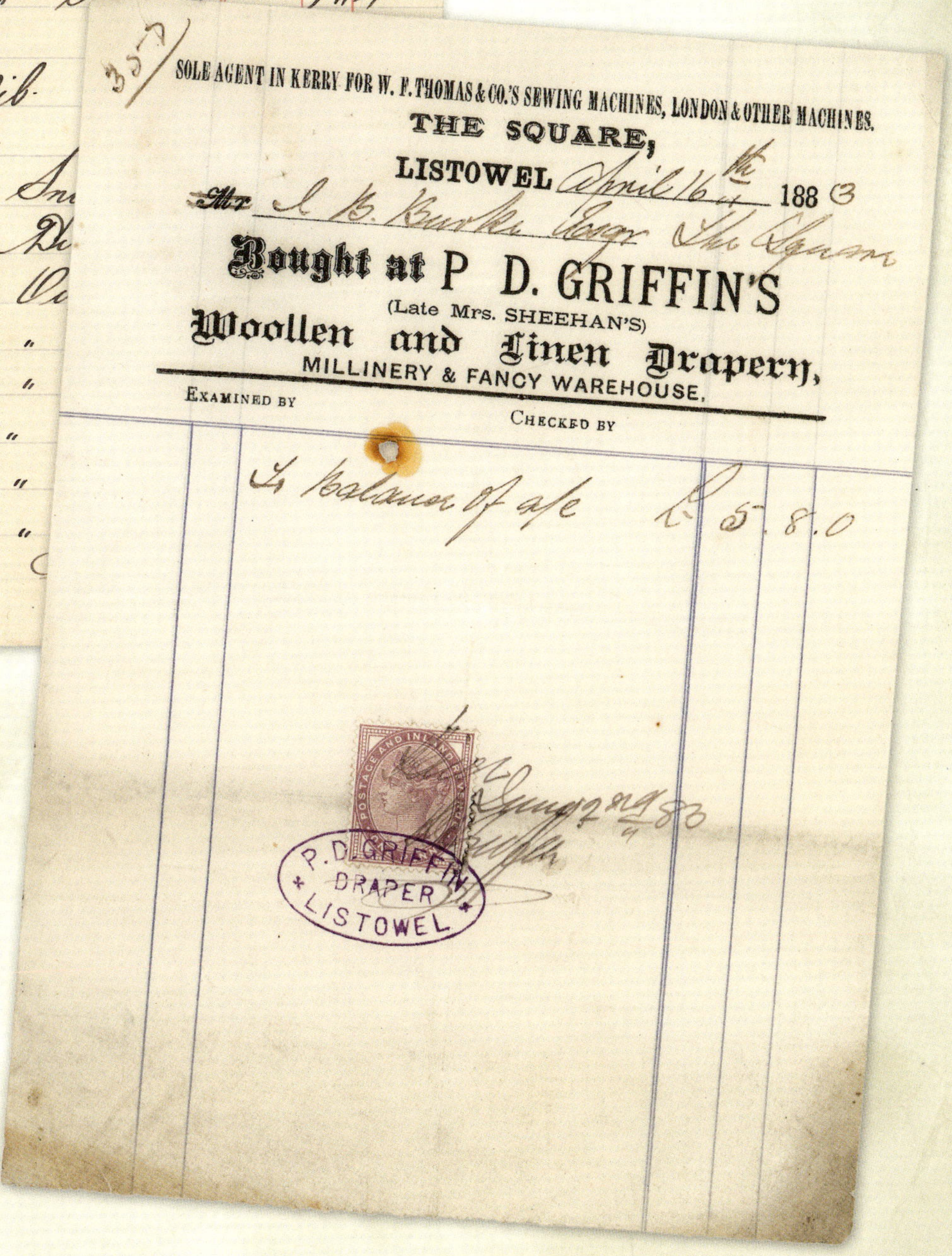

357

SOLE AGENT IN KERRY FOR W. F. THOMAS & CO.'S SEWING MACHINES, LONDON & OTHER MACHINES.

THE SQUARE,

LISTOWEL April 16th 1883

~~Mr~~ J. B. Burke Esqr The Square

Bought at P D. GRIFFIN'S

(Late Mrs. SHEEHAN'S)

Woollen and Linen Drapery,

MILLINERY & FANCY WAREHOUSE.

EXAMINED BY CHECKED BY

To Balance of a/c £ 5. 8. 0

June 2nd /83

P. D. GRIFFIN

DRAPER

LISTOWEL

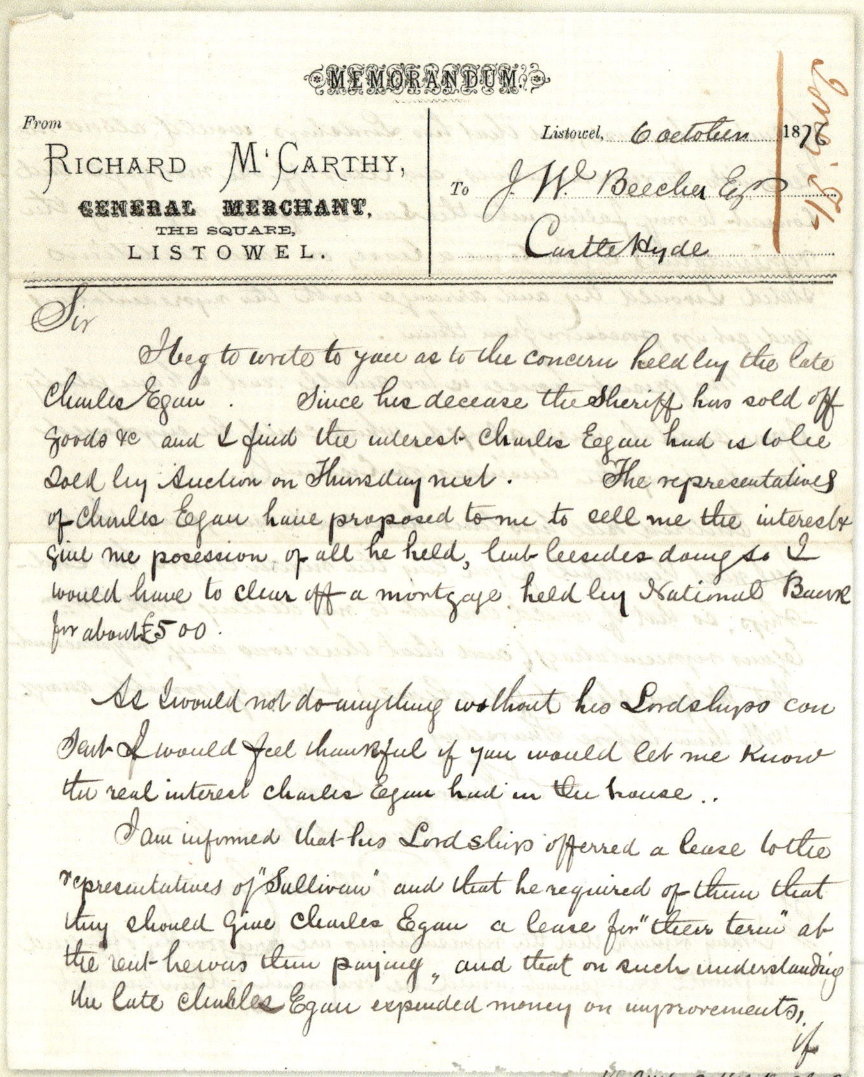
MEMORANDUM

From
RICHARD M'CARTHY,
GENERAL MERCHANT,
THE SQUARE,
LISTOWEL.

Listowel, 6 October 1876

To J W Beecher Esq
Castlehyde

Sir

I beg to write to you as to the concern held by the late Charles Egan. Since his decease the Sheriff has sold off goods &c and I find the interest Charles Egan had is to be sold by Auction on Thursday next. The representatives of Charles Egan have proposed to me to sell me the interest & give me possession of all he held, but besides doing so I would have to clear off a mortgage held by National Bank for about £500.

As I would not do anything without his Lordships consent I would feel thankful if you would let me know the real interest Charles Egan had in the house.

I am informed that his Lordship offered a lease to the representatives of "Sullivan" and that he required of them that they should give Charles Egan a lease for "their term" at the rent he was then paying, and that on such understanding the late Charles Egan expended money on improvements. If

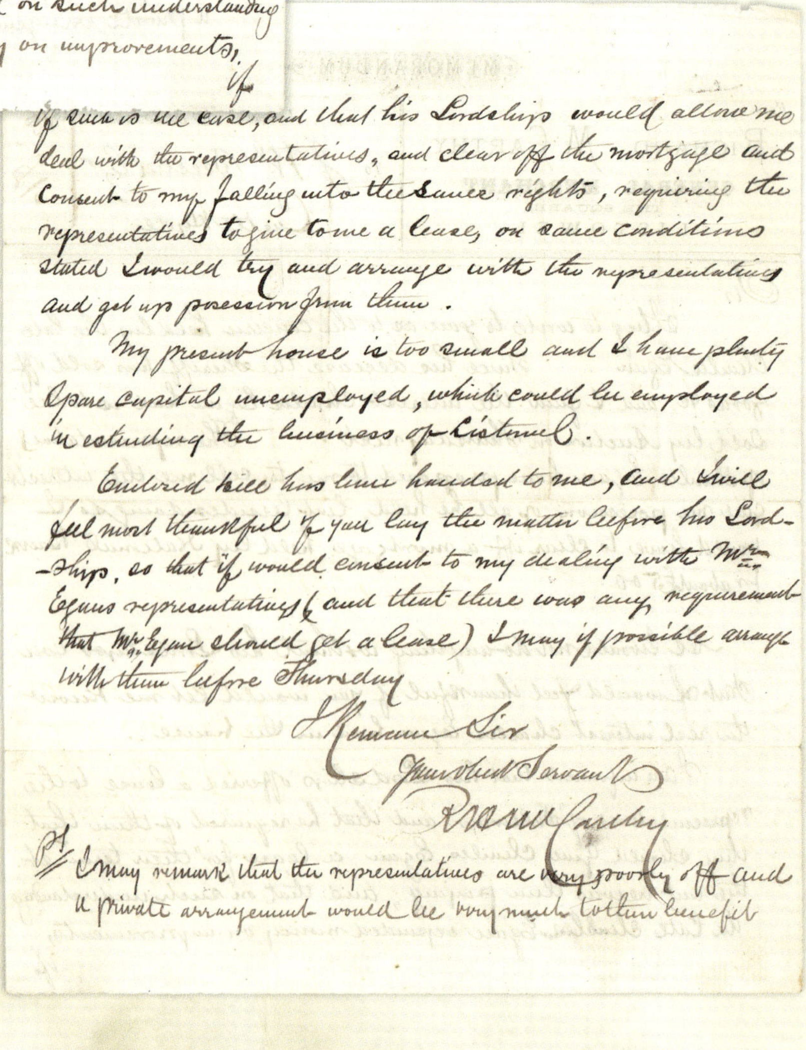
If such is the case, and that his Lordship would allow me deal with the representatives, and clear off the mortgage and consent to my falling into the same rights, requiring the representatives to give to me a lease, on same conditions stated I would try and arrange with the representatives and get up possession from them.

My present house is too small and I have plenty spare capital unemployed, which could be employed in extending the business of Listowel.

Enclosed bill has been handed to me, and I will feel most thankful if you lay the matter before his Lordships, so that if would consent to my dealing with Mr Egans representatives (and that there was any requirement that Mr Egan should get a lease) I may if possible arrange with them before Thursday

I Remain Sir
Your obedt Servant
R McCarthy

PS I may remark that the representatives are very poorly off and a private arrangement would be very much to their benefit

39 The Square

Richard McCarthy was eager to expand his business into the adjoining house, as can be seen from his October 1876 letter to Mr. Beecher, agent to Lord Listowel who was living at Castlehyde, County Cork. In this letter he is clearly intent on leaving no stone unturned, as he says, "I have plenty of spare capital unemployed, which could be employed extending the business of Listowel".

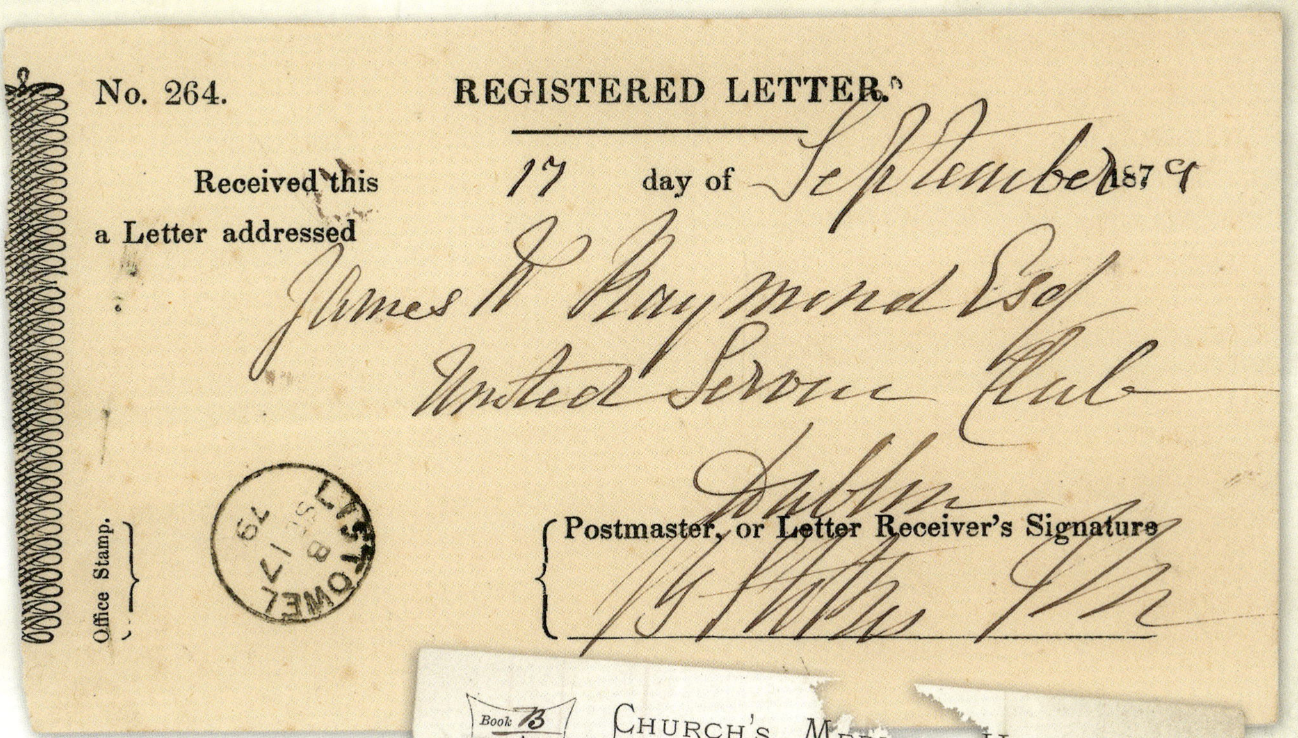
No. 264. **REGISTERED LETTER.**

Received this 17 day of September 1879

a Letter addressed

James W Raymond Esq

United Service Club

Dublin

Office Stamp. LISTOWEL SE 17 79

Postmaster, or Letter Receiver's Signature [illegible]

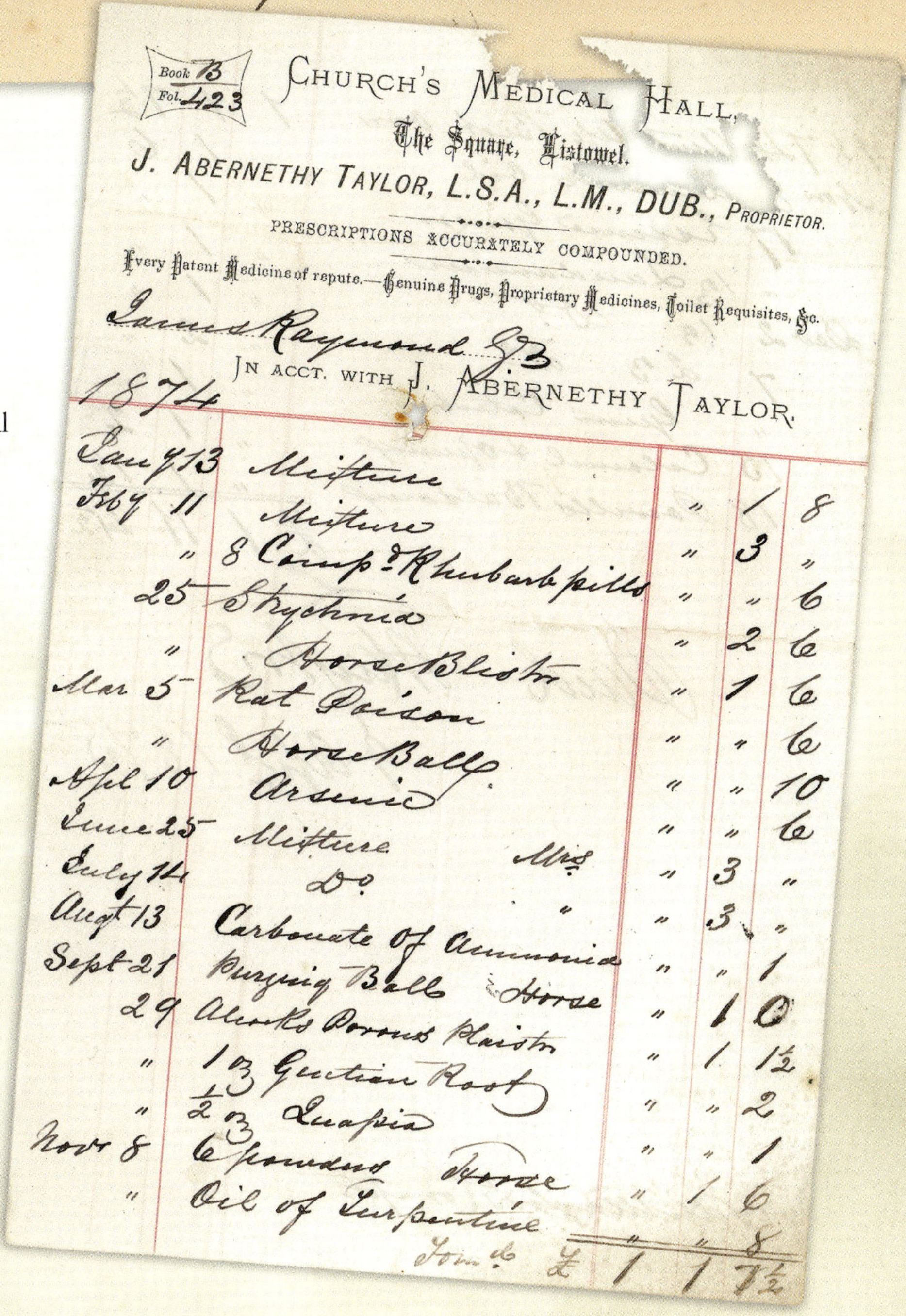
Book 13 Fol. 423

CHURCH'S MEDICAL HALL,

The Square, Listowel.

J. ABERNETHY TAYLOR, L.S.A., L.M., DUB., PROPRIETOR.

PRESCRIPTIONS ACCURATELY COMPOUNDED.

Every Patent Medicine of repute.—Genuine Drugs, Proprietary Medicines, Toilet Requisites, &c.

James Raymond Esq

IN ACCT. WITH J. ABERNETHY TAYLOR.

1874		£	s	d
Jany 13	Mixture	"	1	8
Feby 11	Mixture	"	3	"
"	8 Comp^d Rhubarb pills	"	"	6
25	Strychnia	"	2	6
"	Horse Blister	"	1	6
Mar 5	Rat Poison	"	"	6
"	Horse Balls	"	"	10
Apl 10	Arsenic	"	"	6
June 25	Mixture	"	3	"
July 14	Do. Mrs	"	3	"
Augt 13	Carbonate of Ammonia "	"	"	1
Sept 21	Purging Balls Horse	"	1	0
29	Allcock's Porous Plaister	"	1	1½
"	1 oz Gentian Root	"	"	2
"	½ oz Quassia	"	"	1
Novr 8	6 powders Horse	"	1	6
"	Oil of Turpentine	"	"	8
	Towd £	1	1	7½

38 The Square

The AIB bank, under its former name in Listowel, The Provincial Bank of Ireland, first opened on Saturday 25th of October 1879. Prior to this it served as Church's Medical Hall. George Church is mentioned in Pigot's Directory of 1824 as having an apothecary. By 1846 he had been replaced by John Church, who was also the town's postmaster. Following Church's death in 1864, he was succeeded as a pharmacist by James Abernethy Taylor and the post office duties were taken over by Catherine Stokes.

36 The Square

Correspondence from Thomas F. Rahilly, Clerk of the Petty Sessions, to Capt. James Raymond, Dromin House, in relation to summonses he had issued. O'Rahilly, originally from Ballylongford, lived at 36 The Square. He was the father of a large family who all achieved academic distinction. Alfred was long-time President of University College Cork, and in later life was ordained a priest and was subsequently appointed a Monsignor. Thomas F., a Celtic scholar, succeeded Bergin to become second Director for the school of Celtic Studies in the Institute for Advanced Studies. Cecile, a Celtic scholar, also worked at the Institute for Advanced Studies.

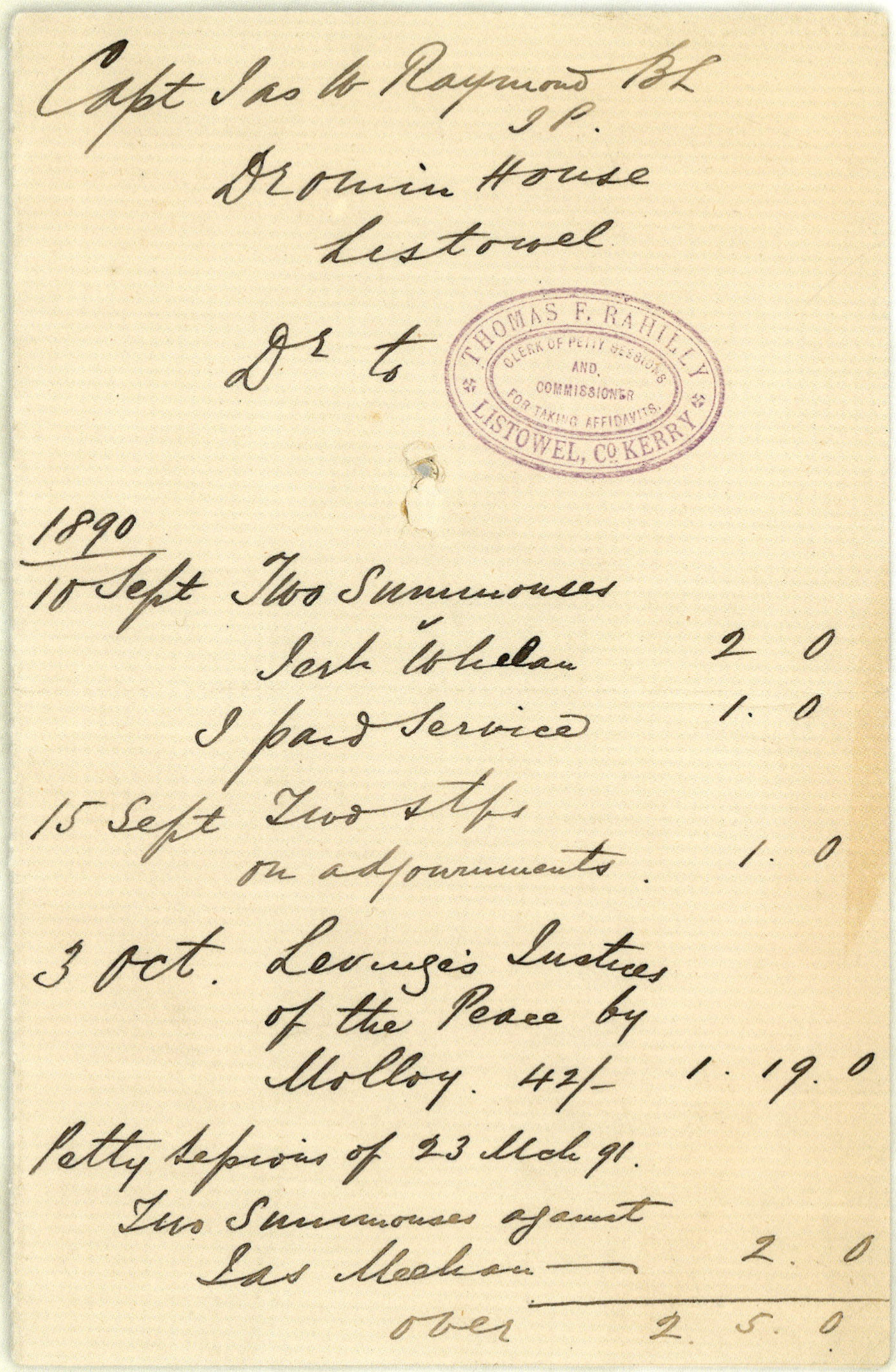
Capt Jas W Raymond BL JP.
Dromin House
Listowel

Dr to

THOMAS F. RAHILLY
CLERK OF PETTY SESSIONS AND COMMISSIONER FOR TAKING AFFIDAVITS.
LISTOWEL, CO KERRY

1890		
10 Sept	Two Summonses Jerh Whelan	2 0
	I paid Service	1. 0
15 Sept	Two stps on adjournments.	1. 0
3 Oct.	Levinge's Justices of the Peace by Molloy. 42/-	1. 19. 0
	Petty Sessions of 23 Mch 91. Two Summonses against Jas Meehan —	2. 0
	over	2. 5. 0

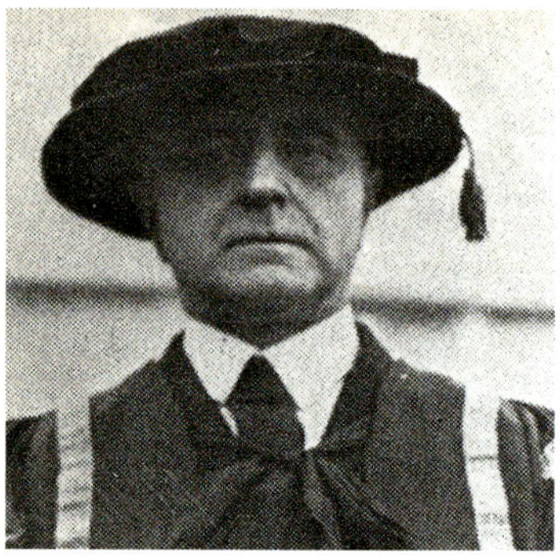
Dr (later Monsignor) Alfred O'Rahilly, President of UCC.

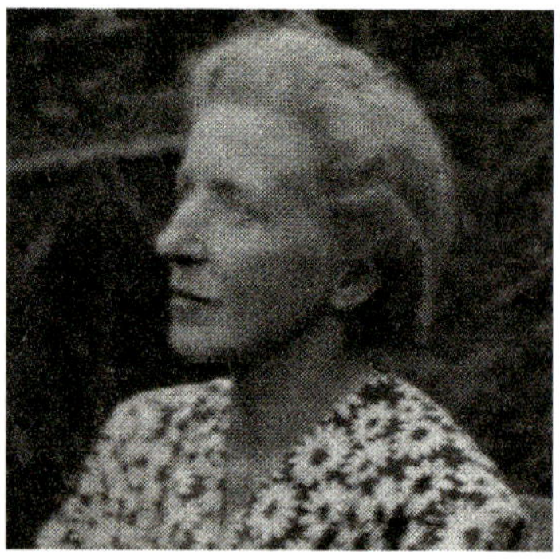
Professor Cecile O'Rahilly.

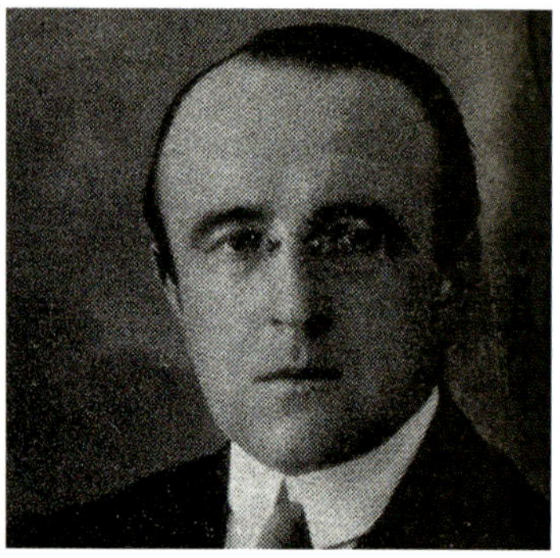
Professor Thomas F. O'Rahilly.

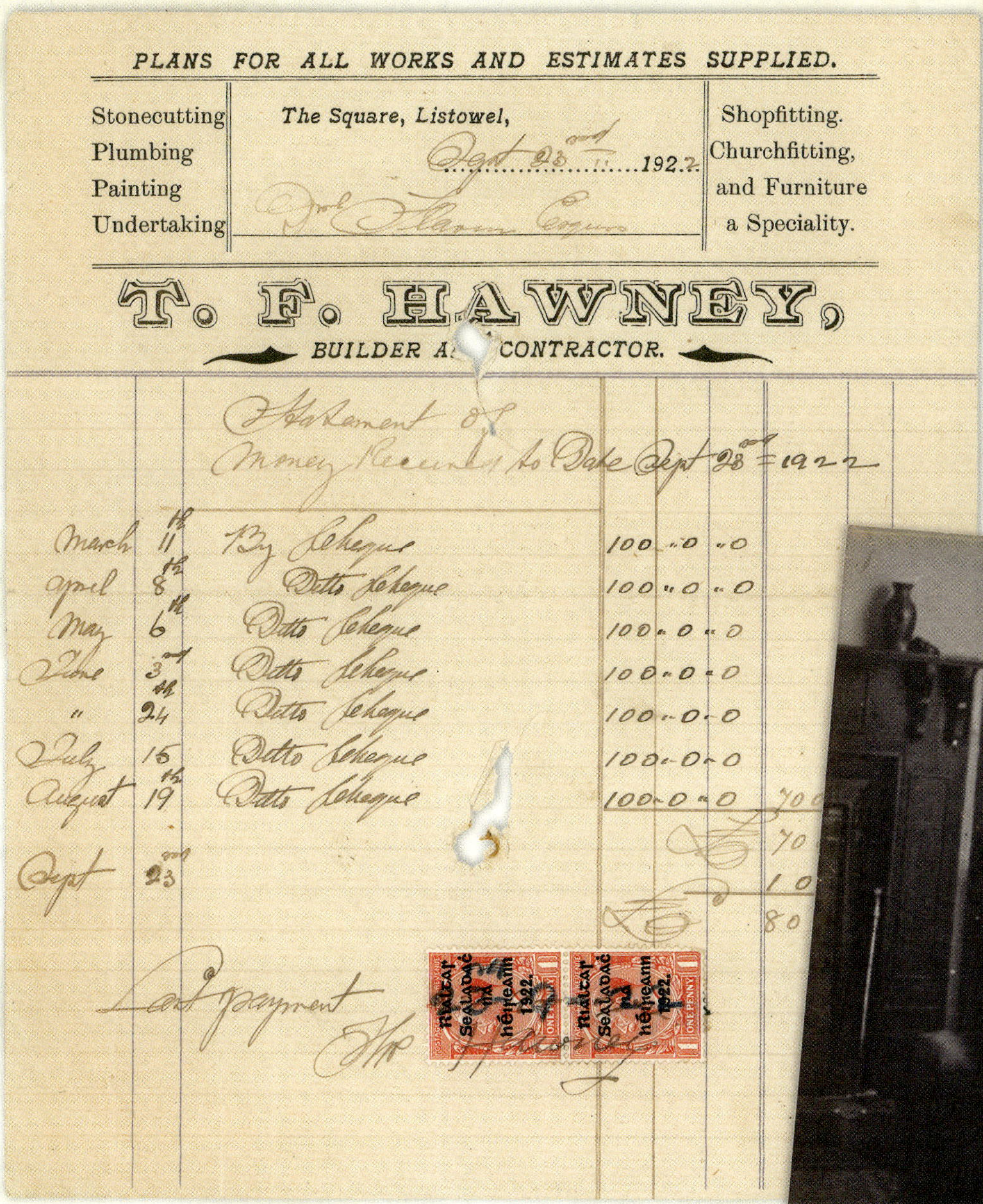

PLANS FOR ALL WORKS AND ESTIMATES SUPPLIED.

Stonecutting Plumbing Painting Undertaking	The Square, Listowel, Sept 23rd 1922 Dnl Flavin Esqre	Shopfitting. Churchfitting, and Furniture a Speciality.

T. F. HAWNEY,

BUILDER AND CONTRACTOR.

Statement of Money Received to Date Sept 23rd 1922

March	11th	By Cheque	100 .. 0 .. 0
April	8th	Ditto Cheque	100 .. 0 .. 0
May	6th	Ditto Cheque	100 .. 0 .. 0
June	3rd	Ditto Cheque	100 .. 0 .. 0
"	24th	Ditto Cheque	100 .. 0 .. 0
July	15	Ditto Cheque	100 .. 0 .. 0
August	19th	Ditto Cheque	100 .. 0 .. 0
			£700
Sept	23rd		£100
			£800

Last payment
T. F. Hawney

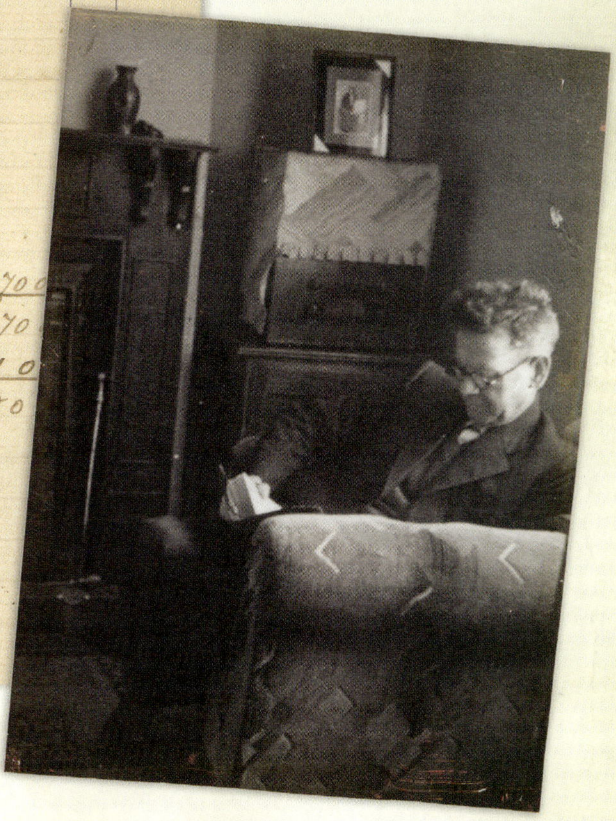

33 The Square

Thomas F. Hawney had returned from Africa in the early 1900s and set up a business as a builder and contractor, working out of a workshop in the Square at the rear of what are now the offices of Louis McDonough, solicitor, and David Fitzmaurice, accountant. He, his wife, South African-born Elizabeth, and family lived at 43 Church Street. They moved to Ballybunion, where they had a hotel on the main street called 'The West End'. Thomas Hawney's time in Africa influenced his work and he introduced to Ballybunion the colonial style of open verandah. These were to be seen outside the 'West End' and also McCarthy's 'Central Hotel'.

Joe Power, born 1888, son of Thomas and Catherine Power, from the Red Cottages, Cahirdown, served his apprenticeship with Hawney and in time worked for himself as a carpenter from the same workshop.

This correspondence is from T.F. Hawney to Daniel Flavin, acknowledging full payment of £800. This was for the rebuilding of Flavin's house in Church Street which had been burned down the previous year by British Forces.

Photo: Joseph Power is seen relaxing with a book at his home in Clieveragh, Listowel.

32 The Square

The Listowel Arms Hotel was in the ownership of the McElligott family for over a century. Gerald McElligott married Elizabeth Adams, daughter of the previous owner, John Adams, in 1854. McElligott was a very successful business man, acting as Land Agent, and having a large auctioneering practice. He built the family home, Mount Rivers, around this time. His son William succeeded him. The well-known tenor, Joseph Locke, bought the hotel from William's son, Gerald, in the 1960s, and he ran it for a short period. During this time it was renamed 'The White Horse Inn'. It changed ownership several times after this. It was purchased by Bernie and Josie O'Callaghan in 1995.

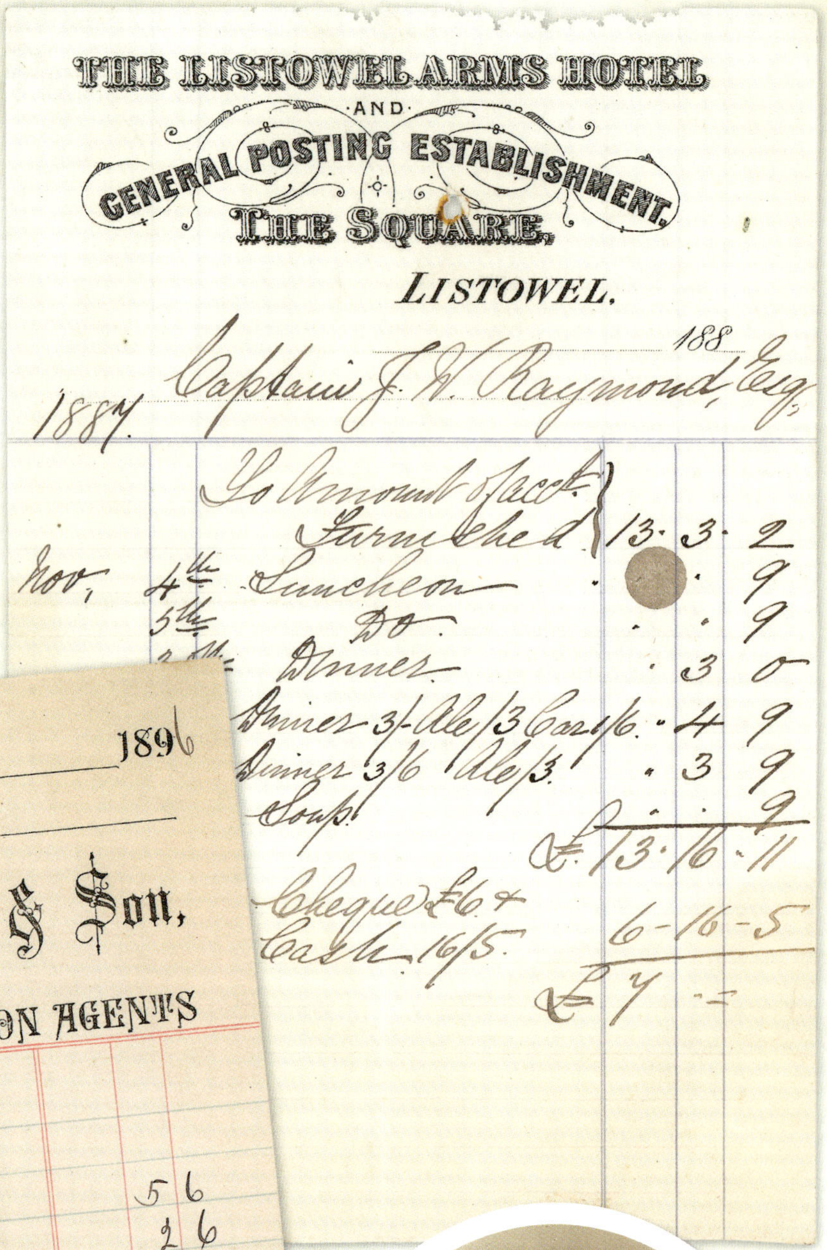

THE LISTOWEL ARMS HOTEL
AND
GENERAL POSTING ESTABLISHMENT,
THE SQUARE,
LISTOWEL.

188

1887 Captain J. W. Raymond, Esq.

		To Amount of acct. furnished	13	3	2
Nov.	4th	Luncheon	.	.	9
	5th	Do	.	.	9
		Dinner	.	3	0
		Dinner 3/- Ale /3 Car 1/6	.	4	9
		Dinner 3/6 Ale /3	.	3	9
		Soap	.	.	9
			£13	16	11
		Cheque £6 + Cash 16/5	6	16	5
			£7	-	-

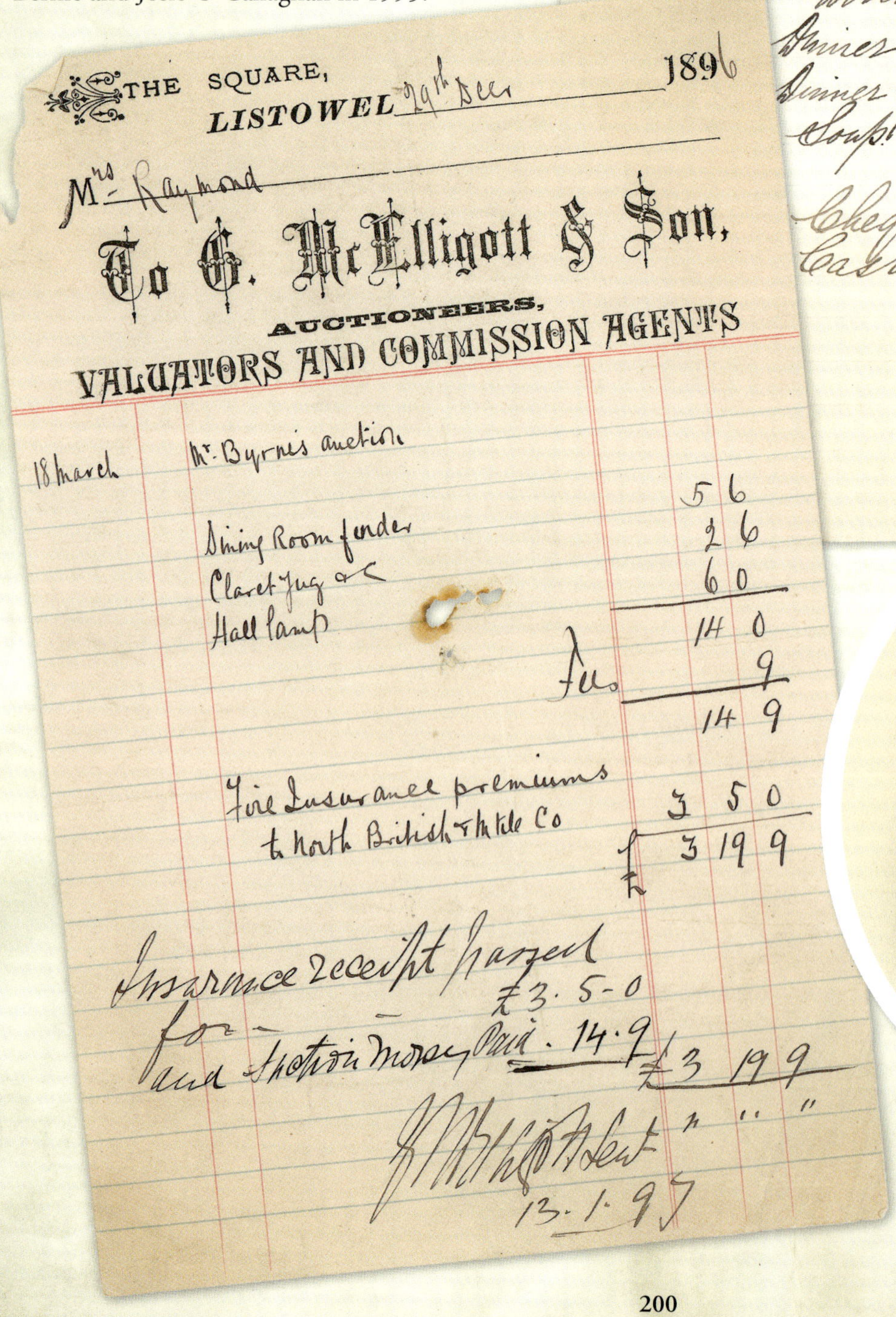

THE SQUARE, LISTOWEL 29th Decr 1896

Mrs Raymond

To G. McElligott & Son,
AUCTIONEERS,
VALUATORS AND COMMISSION AGENTS

18 March	Mr. Byrne's auction		
		5	6
	Dining Room fender	2	6
	Claret Jug &c	6	0
	Hall lamp	14	0
	Fees		9
		14	9
	Fire Insurance premiums to North British & Mile Co	3 5	0
		£ 3 19	9

Insurance receipt passed for £3-5-0
and Auction money Paid . 14 . 9
£3 19 9

13.1.97

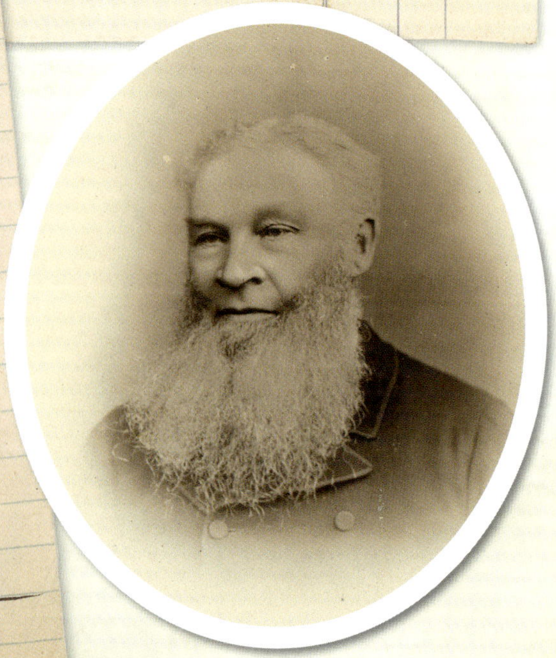

Gerald McElligott,
1828-1910

Charles Stewart Parnell made his third-last public speech from a window of the hotel on Sunday, September 13, 1891. He concluded his address with the now-famous words: "No man has the right to set a boundary on the march of a nation… No man has the right to limit the aspiration of our people". Not everyone was impressed by his stirring speech. Gerald McElligott recorded in his unpublished diary: "As far as Listowel and district is concerned, he got no support and judging from the entire demonstration, his cause is a lost one." McElligott's diary entry for October 6, 1891 read: "Poor Parnell died in Brighton."

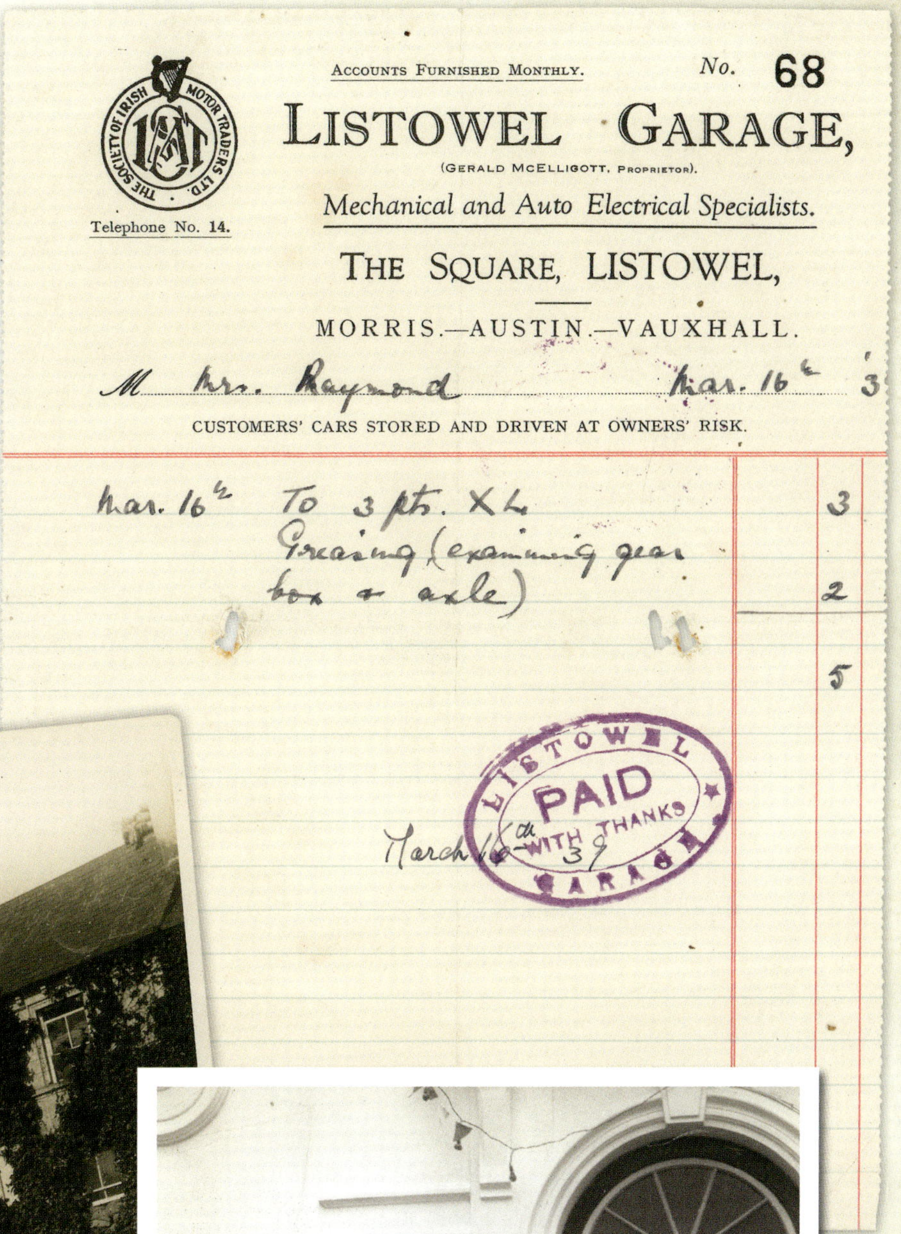

THE SOCIETY OF IRISH MOTOR TRADERS LTD.

Telephone No. 14.

ACCOUNTS FURNISHED MONTHLY.

No. 68

LISTOWEL GARAGE,

(GERALD MCELLIGOTT, PROPRIETOR).

Mechanical and Auto Electrical Specialists.

THE SQUARE, LISTOWEL,

MORRIS.—AUSTIN.—VAUXHALL.

M Mrs. Raymond Mar. 16th 3

CUSTOMERS' CARS STORED AND DRIVEN AT OWNERS' RISK.

Mar. 16th	To 3 pts. XL	3
	Greasing (examining gear box & axle)	2
		5

LISTOWEL GARAGE PAID WITH THANKS

March 16th 39

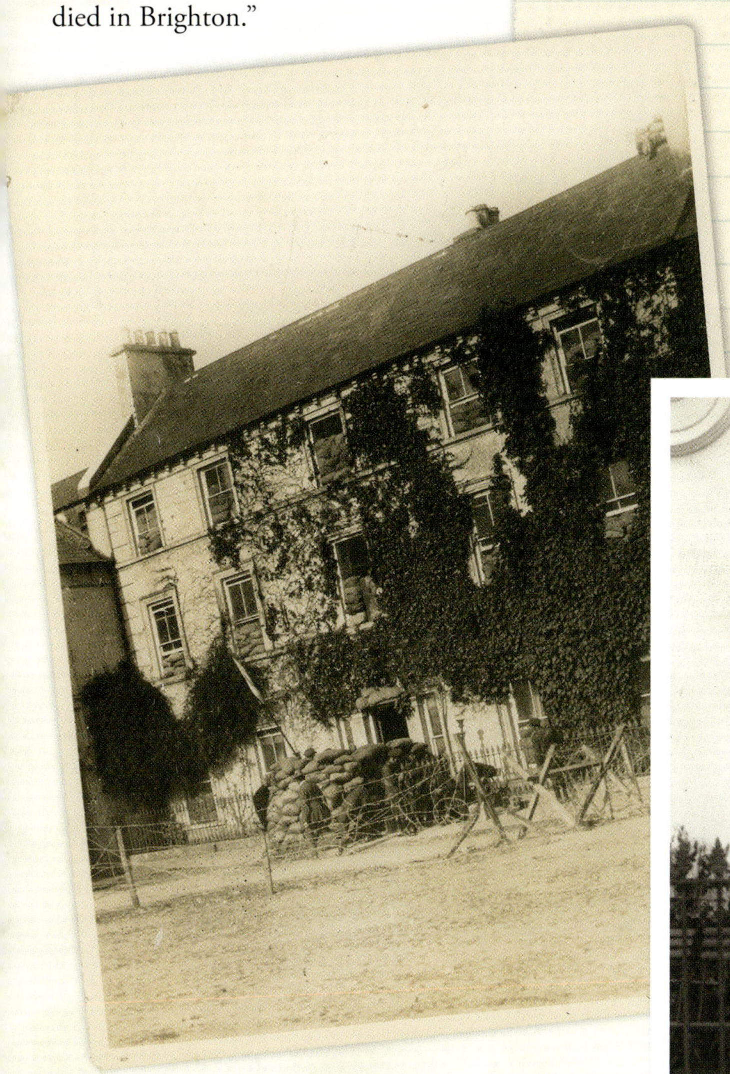

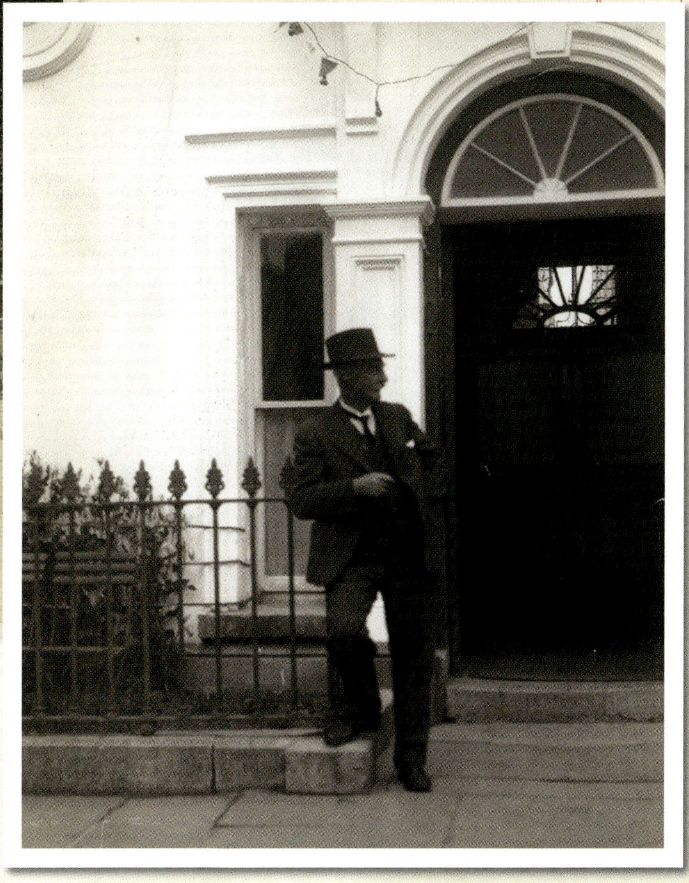

Photo above: The hotel when it was occupied by Free State soldiers during the Civil War.

Photo right: William McElligott, 1871-1941, outside the hotel front door in the 1930s.

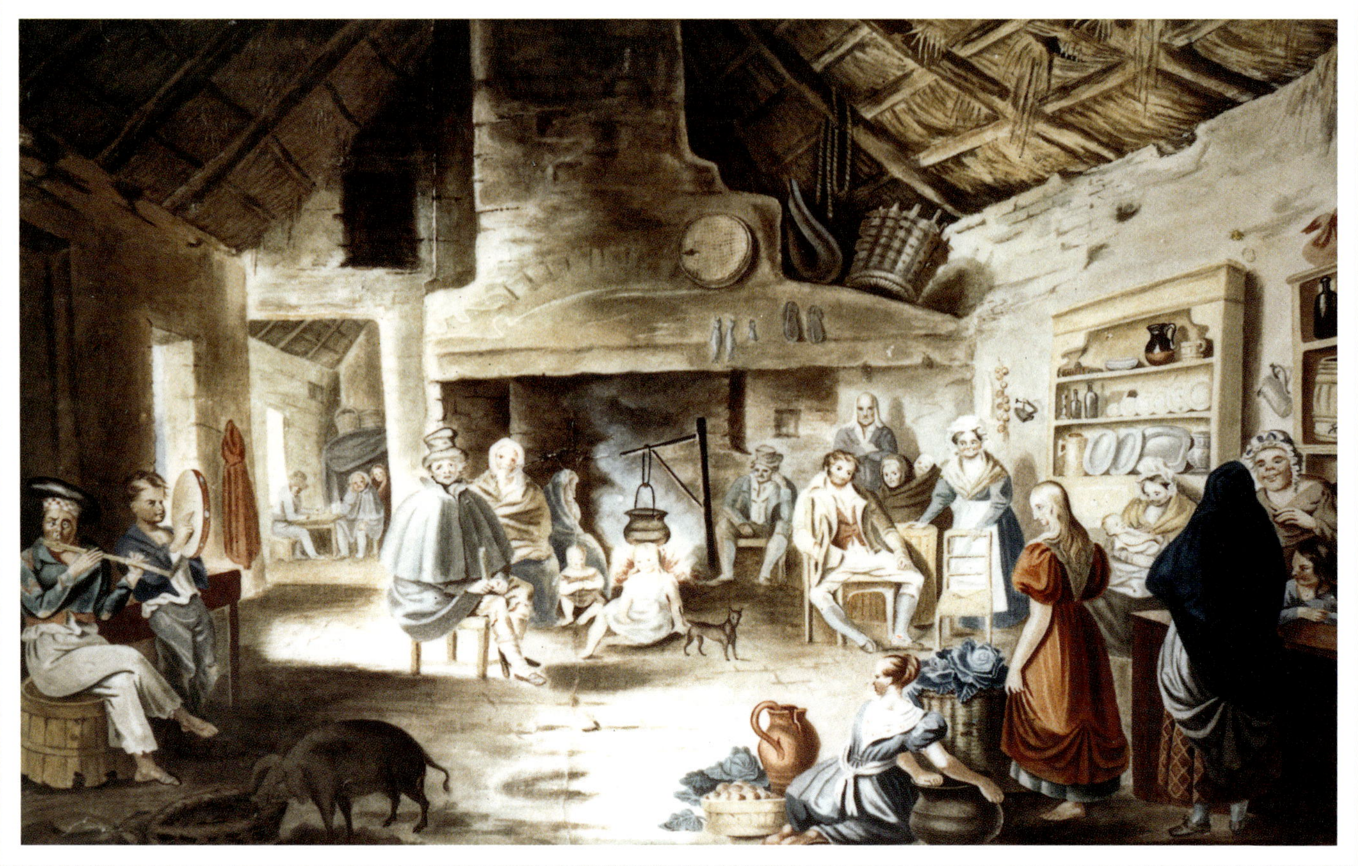

A local squire being entertained in a Listowel inn about 1842

This watercolour, which now hangs in the offices of Listowel UDC, was painted by Bridget Maria FitzGerald (1817-1905), who lived in the Castle House in the Square which is now the Seanchaí Centre.

The other persons in the picture include, from left, the musicians, one playing a fife, the other beating a bodhrán; three customers drinking 'up in the room'; behind the squire and around the fire, an old woman, a woman probably nursing a sick infant, two young children, the 'man of the house', another member of the 'quality', who seems to be slightly inebriated, an old woman, a young woman carrying a child papoose-fashion and the 'woman of the house'; in the right-hand corner of the picture, two girls preparing a meal, a young woman nursing an infant, two women chatting, one of whom is seemingly in charge of the drink, a young girl listening intently to the music.

In the left foreground is a pig eating probably potatoes and potato-skins, and in front of the fire is a mongrel. A variety of food is to be seen in the picture: three fish and two small chunks of bacon are curing on the chimney-breast, some onions are hanging up to dry on the wall to the right of the fire, drink is stored in the area to the right of the picture, where some cakes, tied up in a cloth, are also to be seen, and in the foreground are potatoes, cabbage and probably a cauliflower.

The picture is particularly informative with regard to the quality, style and colour of clothes worn by people at that time. There are a number of other interesting items, such as a child's cot, an iron pot, an iron pot-hanger, a griddle, a donkey's collar and pannier, a milk-churn, a súgán chair, a well-filled dresser and a counter in that part of the kitchen in which the drink is kept.

Also worth noting are the stone flags on the floor, the entrance to the left of the chimney-breast, access to which was gained by a ladder and where the 'boy' usually slept at night, and the hole to the right of the fire, where salt and, later, tea and sugar were kept.

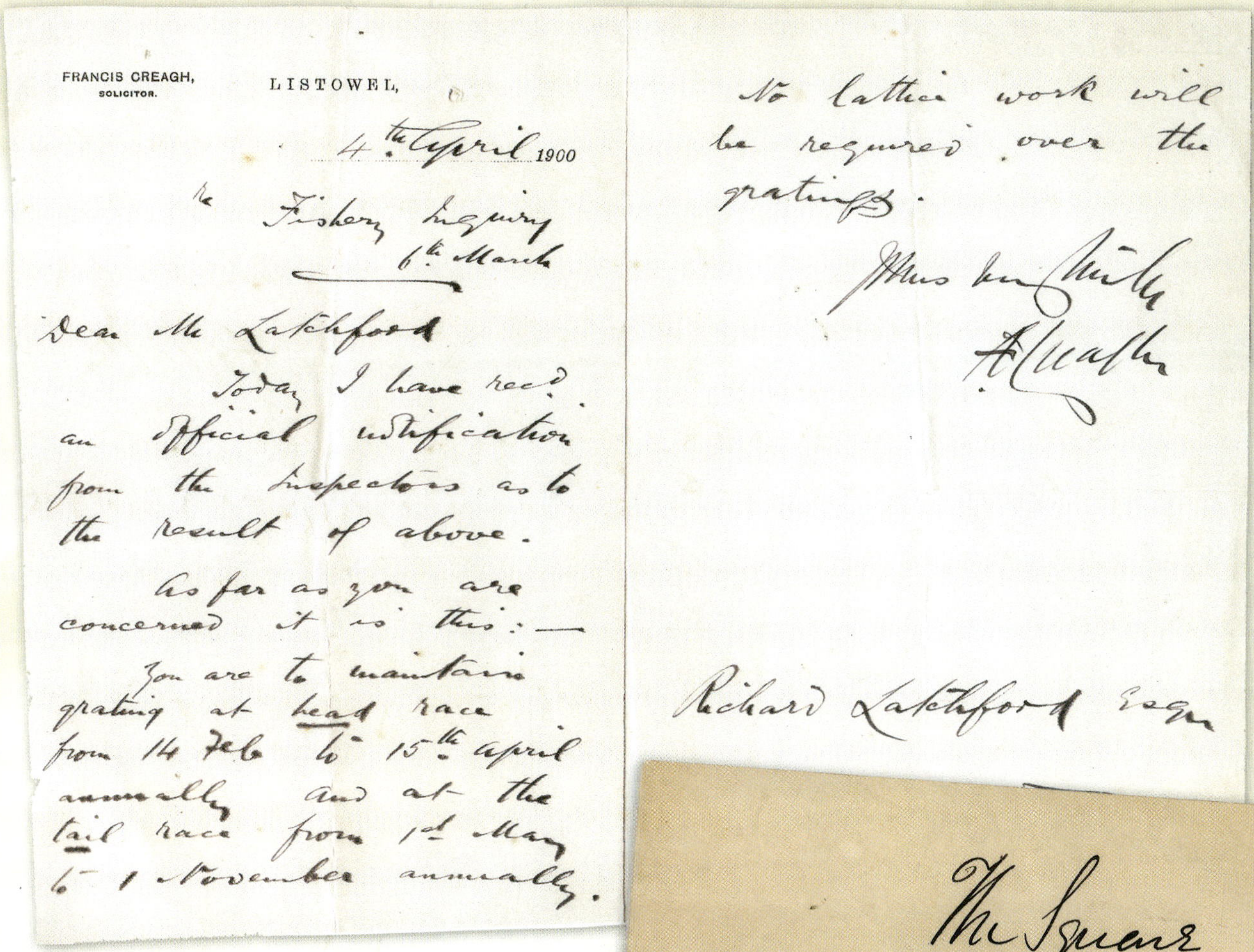

FRANCIS CREAGH,
SOLICITOR.

LISTOWEL,

4th April 1900

re Fishery Inquiry
6th March

Dear Mr Latchford

Today I have recd. an official notification from the Inspectors as to the result of above.

As far as you are concerned it is this:—

You are to maintain grating at head race from 14 Feb to 15th April annually and at the tail race from 1st May to 1 November annually.

No lattice work will be required over the gratings.

Yours very truly
F. Creagh

Richard Latchford Esqr

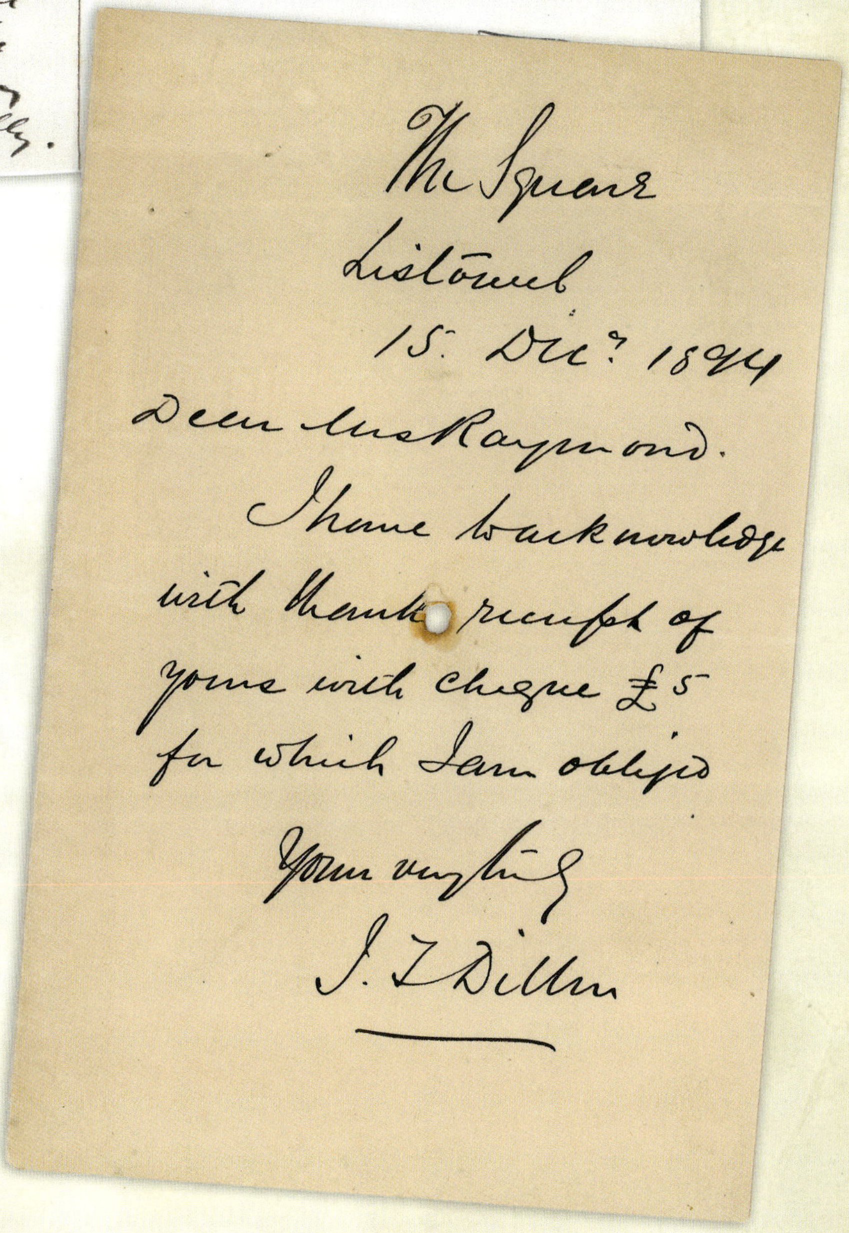

The Square
Listowel
15th Dec. 1894

Dear Mrs Raymond.

I have to acknowledge with thanks receipt of yours with cheque £5 for which I am obliged

Yours very truly
J. J. Dillon

24 The Square

Francis Creagh, Solicitor, and Doctor John J. Dillon were married to two De Courcy sisters of Dooncaha Lodge, Tarbert, Ellen and Ann Margaret, and lived near each other in the Square. Francis and Ellen's children included Bertha (1878-1944) and Mabel Creagh (1890-1936). Bertha Beatty is the author of *Kerry Memories* first published in 1939, reprinted 2007, an account of growing up in an Ascendancy family in Listowel. Mabel Creagh was one of the earliest woman golfers in Ballybunion. Among the Dillon family was Elizabeth (Lily or Lillian) Dillon (1880-1963), an internationally famous airwoman.

Shown are: Doctor Dillon's receipt to Mrs. Raymond and Francis Creagh's letter to Richard Latchford, re: fishing inquiry.

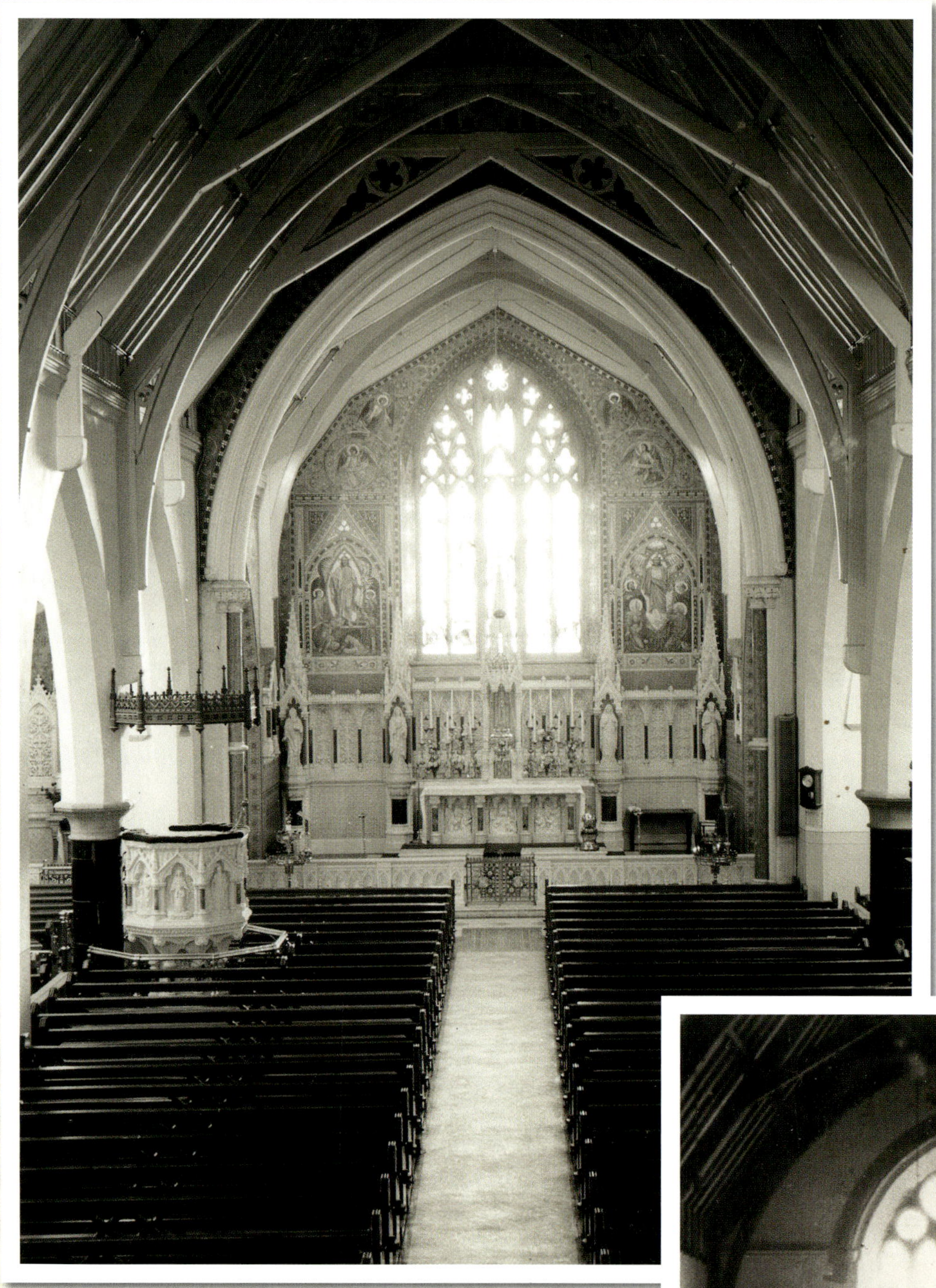

Saint Mary's Catholic Church

The town's church was built in 1829, and the bell tower and spire was added in 1865. However, major work in 1910, under the direction of Canon Davis, transformed the building to what you can see today. Galleries which had flanked the Sacristy were taken down. The back wall of the Church was removed and an additional fifty feet added to the building. New side aisles were also constructed. Pews were also installed. Previous to this the nave of the church contained no seating.

Above: Stephen Keane-Stack's study of the Church interior, circa 1960.

Right: A rare photograph of the interior of Saint Mary's Church prior to renovations in 1910. A gallery can be seen on the right-hand side of the Sacristy. Wooden railings top the elevated altar area. A coffin sits in the centre of the floor.

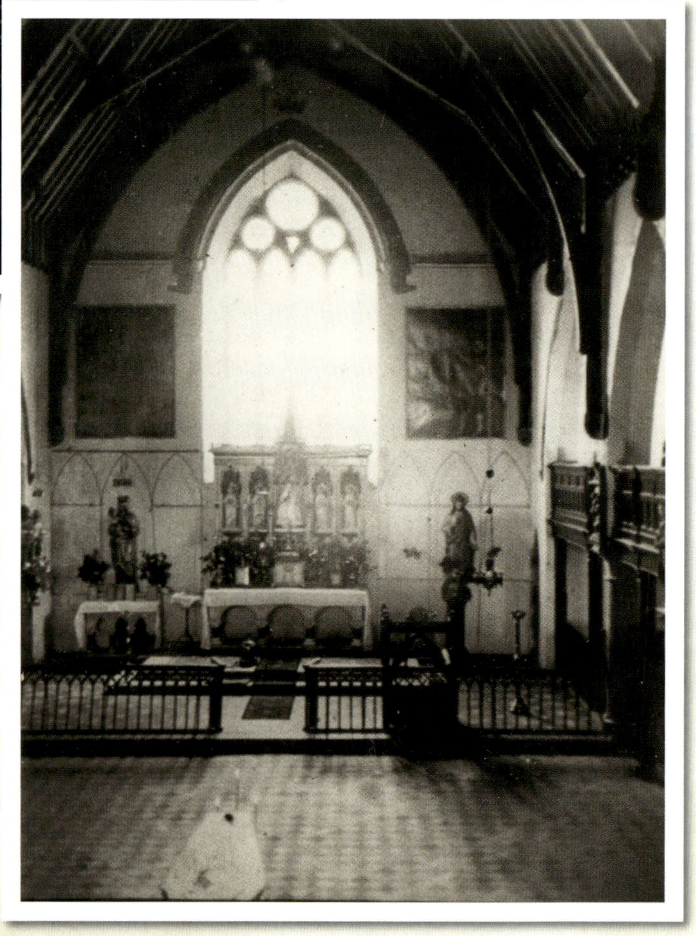

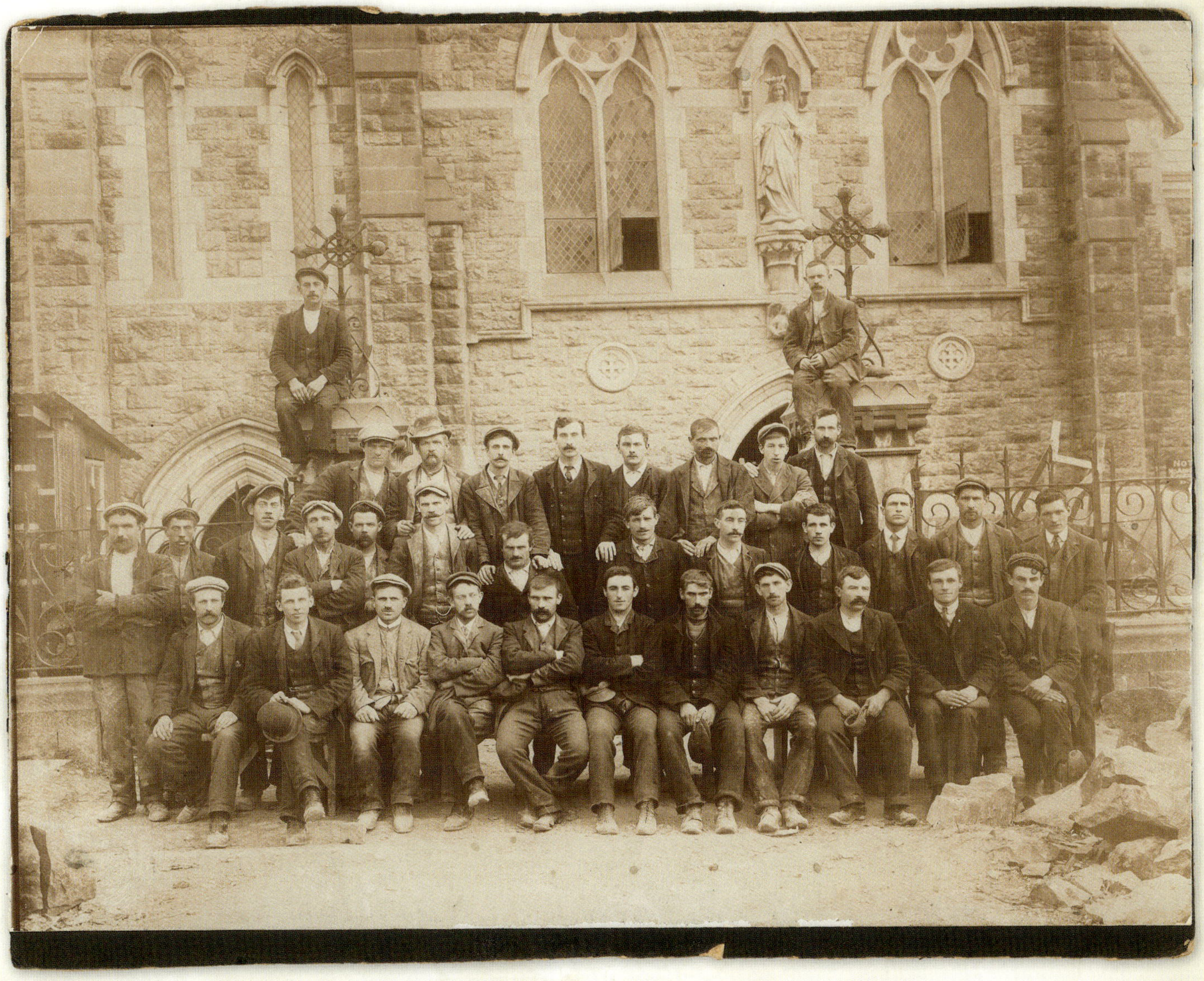

Some of those who worked on the Church reconstruction of 1910.
Front (l to r): P. Ring, J. Murphy, J. Cronin, S. Coyle, J. Murphy. M. O'Connor, P. Stack, J. Lynch, B. Triggs, J. Gould, J. Cotter. Middle (l to r): J. Granville, P. Mulvihill, J. Russell, T. King, P. Murphy, J. Martin, J. Lynch, J. Seward, P. Coyle, T. Hourigan, T. Murphy. T. Ring, T. Clohessy. Back row (l to r): S. Dore, M. Clohessy, P. Ring, M. Browne, T. Hannon, J. Callaghan, T. Bell, M. Healy. Men on Piers: M. Ashe, P. Murphy.

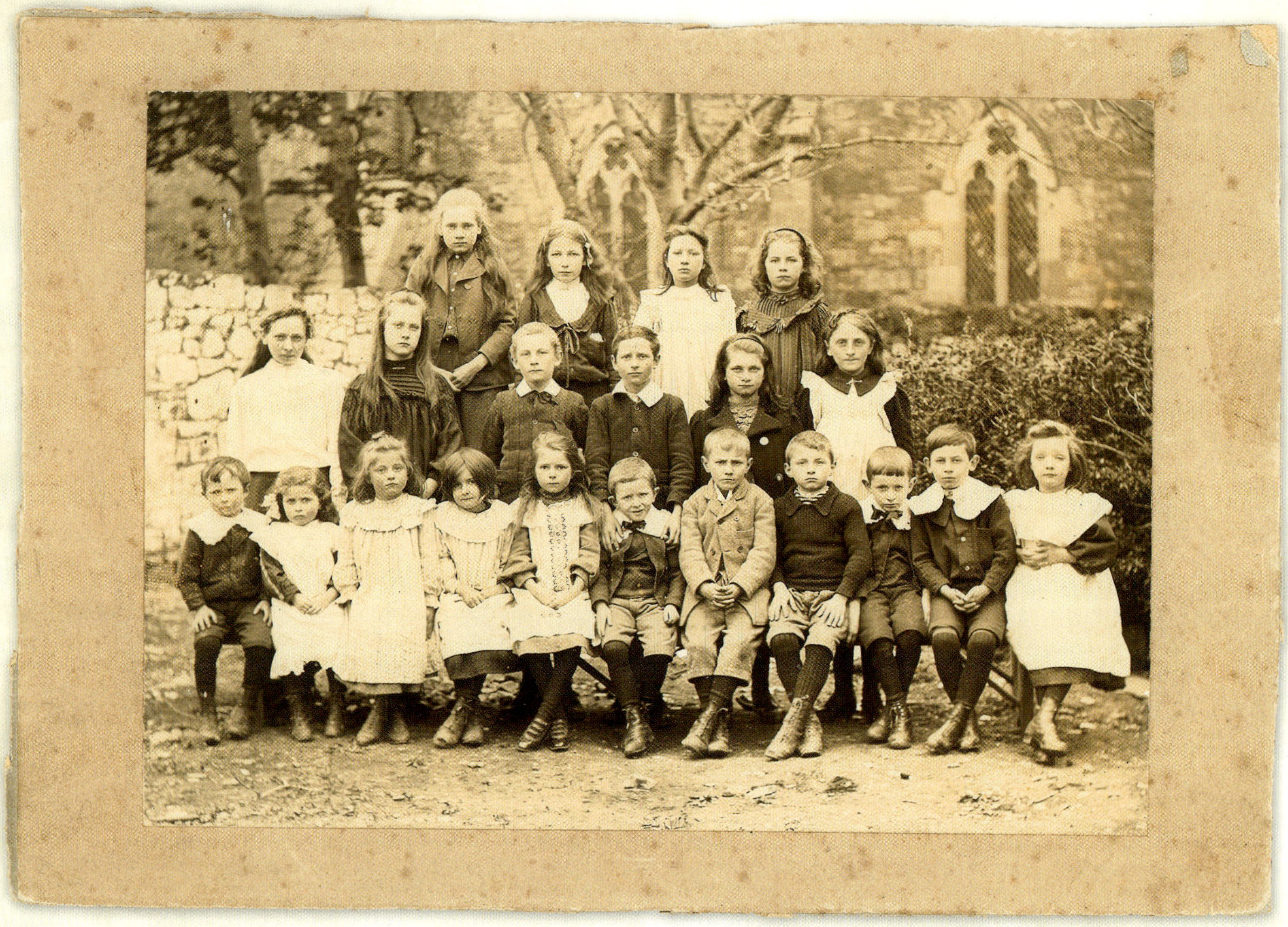

21 The Square

The Church of Ireland National School had a presence in the Square for nearly one hundred years, 1840-1933. This photograph circa 1907 was taken in the yard of the school. The location is now 21 The Square, home of the Sheahan family. Saint Mary's Catholic Church is in the backround.

Old Carnegie Library, Bridge Road
A letter from Mrs A. Gleeson, clerk of Listowel Urban Council, to Edward O'Brien, Lord Listowel's agent. The address is interesting. This was the first Carnegie Library to be built in Listowel. It was located on the Bridge Road and it was burnt down in March 1921. Confusion existed over who did the burning. Local Sinn Féin blamed the Black and Tans and they in turn blamed Sinn Féin.

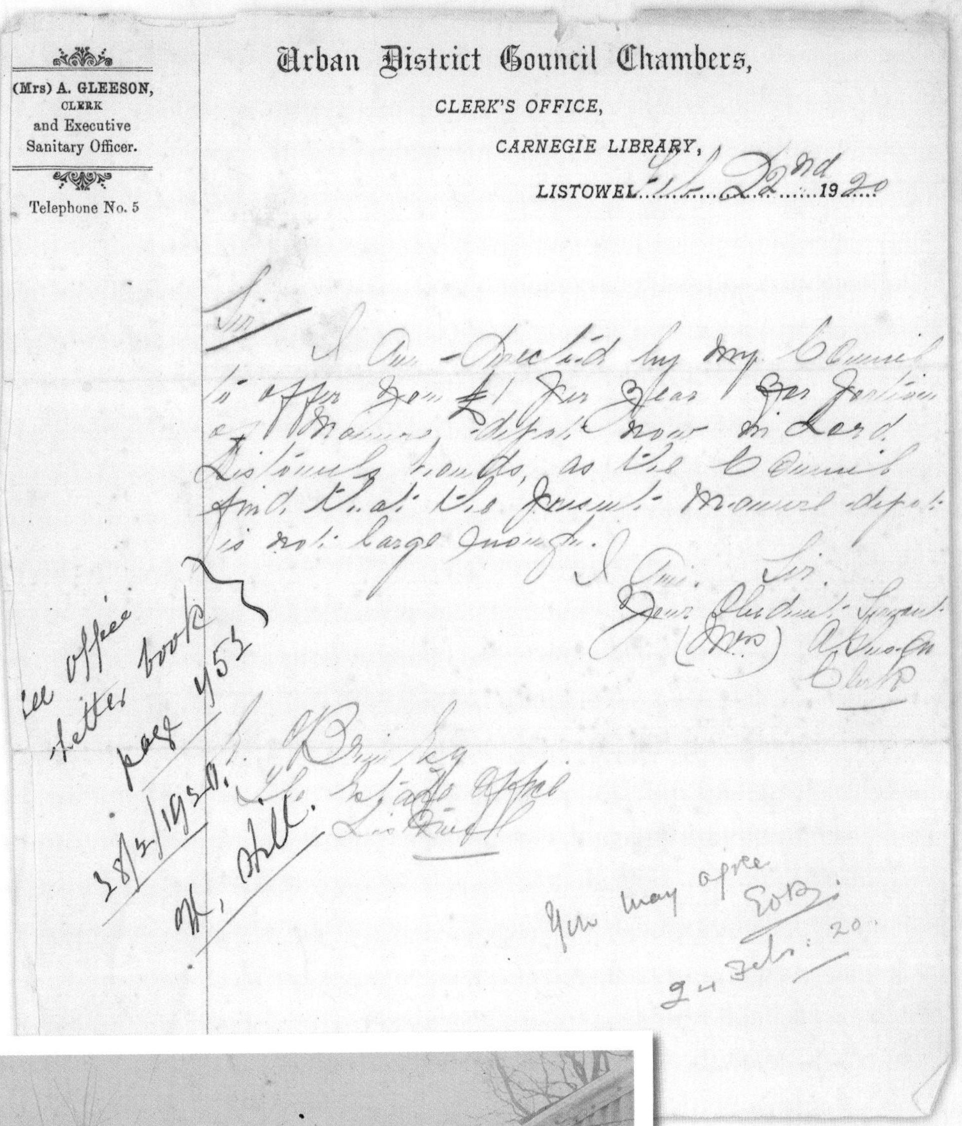

(Mrs) A. GLEESON,
CLERK
and Executive
Sanitary Officer.

Telephone No. 5

Urban District Council Chambers,
CLERK'S OFFICE,
CARNEGIE LIBRARY,
LISTOWEL Feb 22nd 1920

Sir
I am directed by my Council to offer you £1 per year per portion of Manure depot near Lord Listowel's lands, as the Council find that the present manure depot is not large enough.
I am, Sir,
Your obedient Servant
(Mrs) A Gleeson
Clerk

See office letter book page 453

28/2/1920.

E. O'Brien Esq
The Estate Office
Listowel

You may approve
EOB
24 Feb: 20

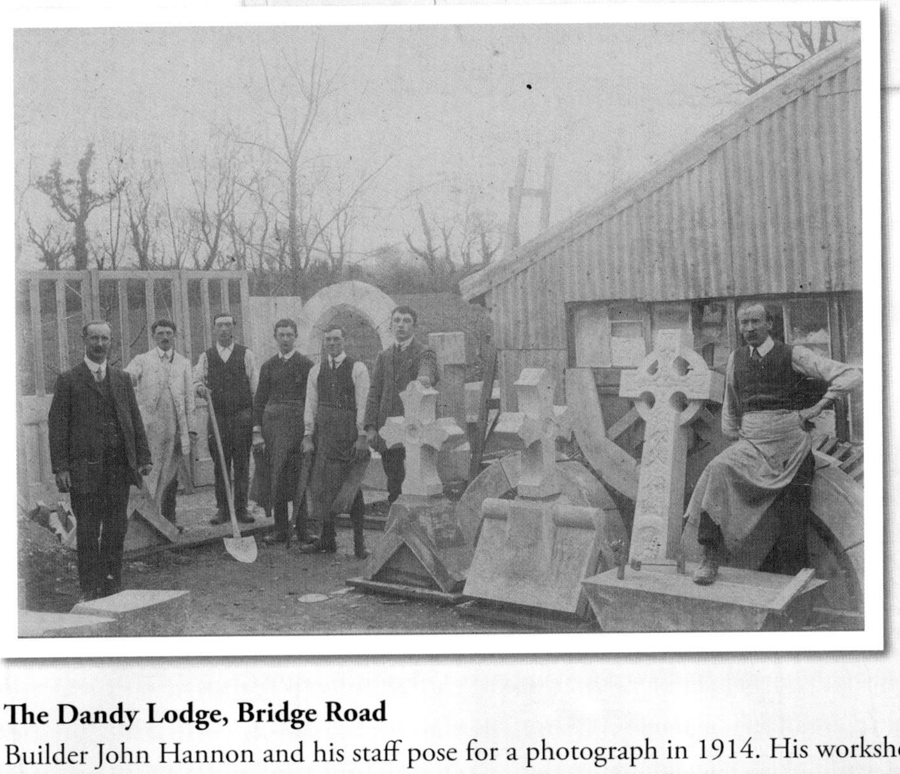

The Dandy Lodge, Bridge Road
Builder John Hannon and his staff pose for a photograph in 1914. His workshop was at the Bridge Road and he lived in the adjoining house, which was known as The Dandy Lodge. This was once a gate lodge to Gurtinard House. In the 1990s, the Lodge was knocked and rebuilt as a heritage project on a site in Listowel Town Park.

From left: John Hannon, Paddy Whelan (known locally as the 'Cement God'), Tom Fitzmaurice, Tom Hannon, Moss Hannon, Jer. Hannon, Jack Hannon (Scarriff, Co. Clare).

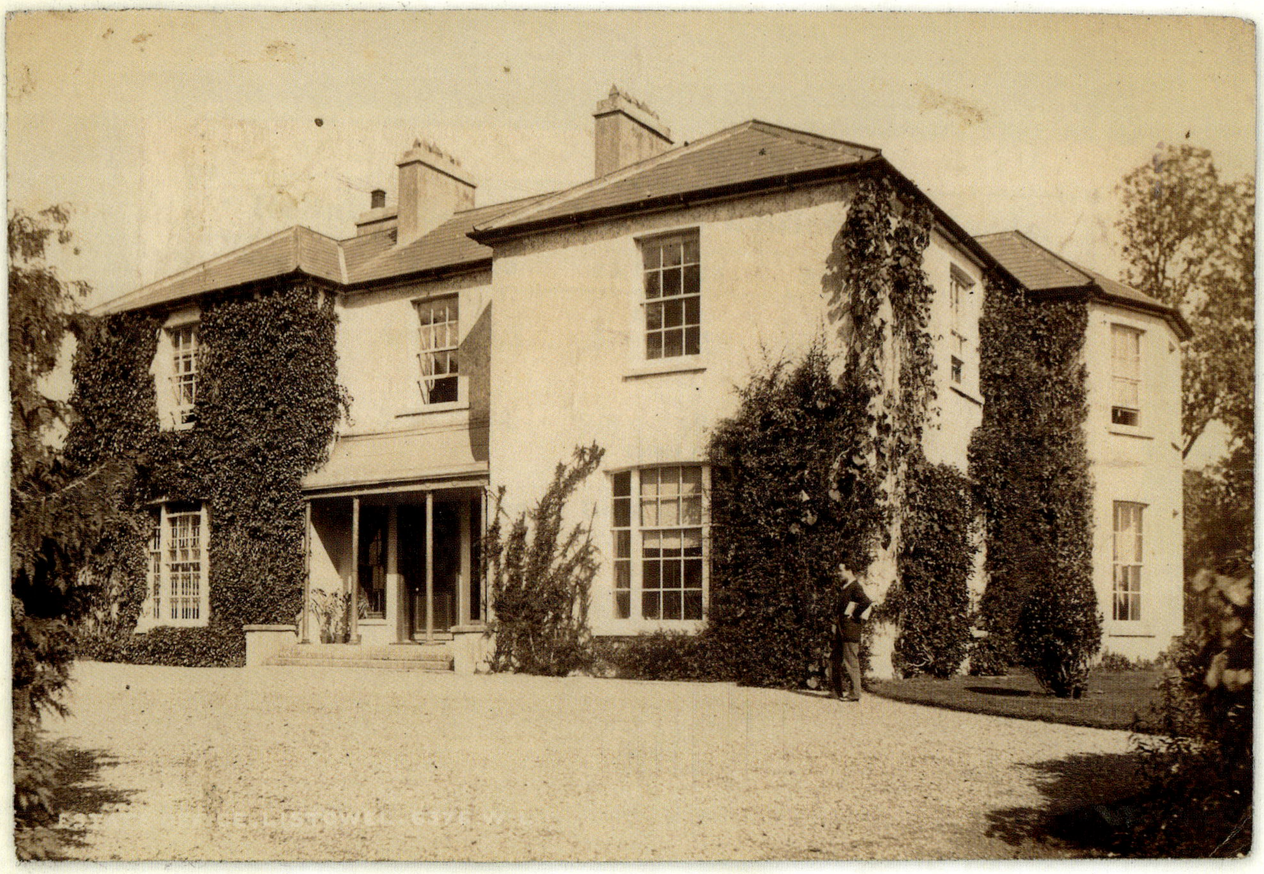

Gurtinard House, Bridge Road

In an effort to secure the land around Gurtinard House for the townspeople, the local Sinn Féin club agitated as The Listowel Sinn Féin Food Committee. Many of its members were committed to jail. When the land was eventually secured, the committee sought out interested townspeople who would invest the required monies to pay for the land. One of these was Laurence Buckley, cooper of William Street. Gurtinard House was built for Lord Listowel. It also served as the Estate Office.

In a printed notice, Edward O'Brien, agent, announces that tenants who wished to do so could now purchase their own holding.

RECEIVED from *Laurence Buckley* the sum of *Eighty pounds* by way of fine or premium for privilege to graze and milch cow during the months of *May June July August September October November December & January.* in each year on the lands of Gurtenard until said sum of *Eighty pounds* (without interest) be repaid to him, subject to the provisions contained in deed as to grazing of Gurtenard dated

Dated this *26th* day of *December 1919*

For THE LISTOWEL FOOD COMMITTEE

ESTATE OFFICE,

LISTOWEL,

30th June, 1917.

Dear Sir (or Madam,)

Lord Listowel has decided to dispose of his Fee Simple Estate, in the Town of Listowel, and Lands adjoining, but before proceeding with arrangements for Sale, to outsiders, wishes to give his own Tenants the first offer, and is prepared to receive Proposals, from each, for Purchase of his own holding, in Fee Simple.

Accordingly no steps will be taken to sell, to outsiders, until the expiration of a month, from this date, and meantime any tenant, wishing to purchase, can ascertain terms, and conditions, of Sale by an enquiry at this Office.

Yours truly,

EDWARD O'BRIEN,

Agent to Lord Listowel

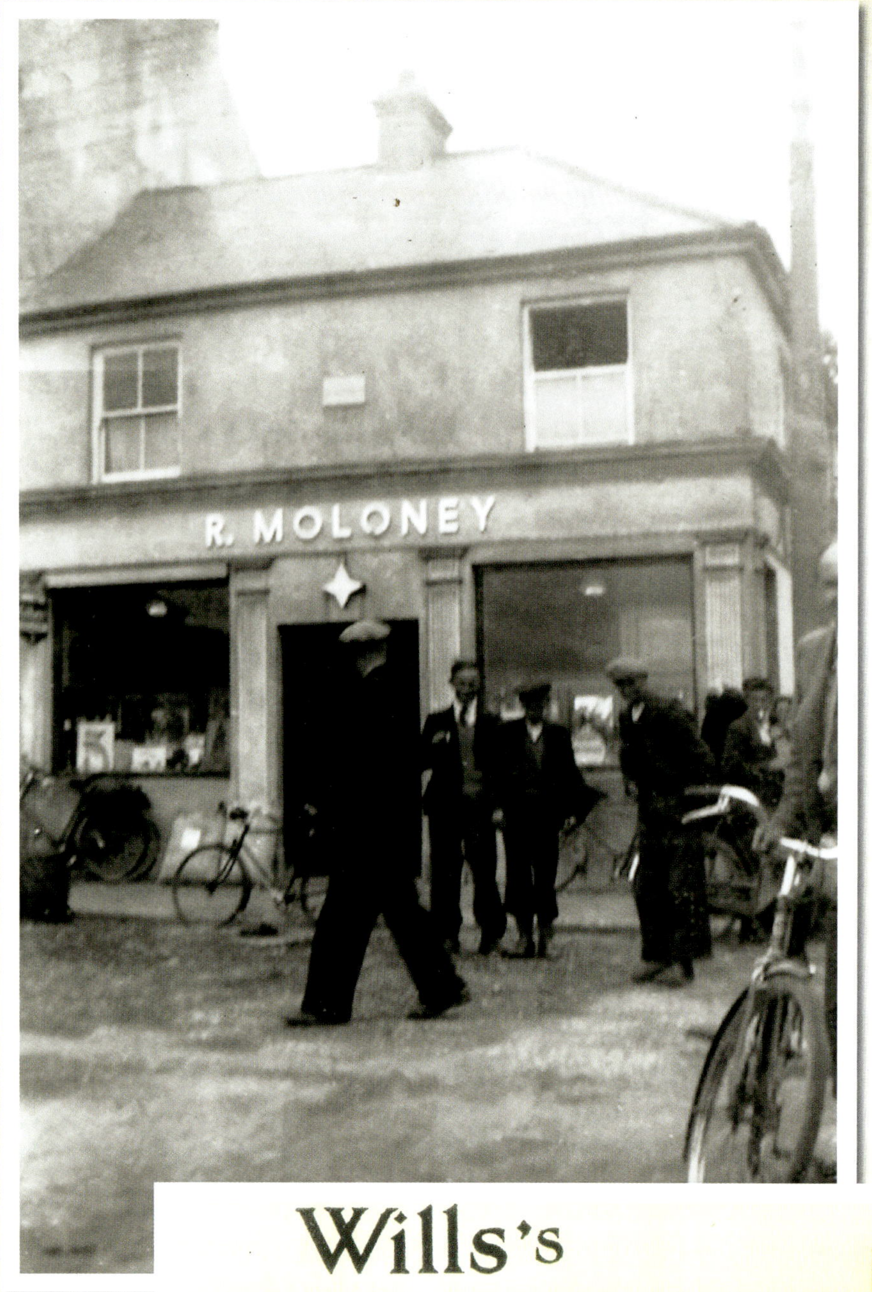

18 The Square

Matthew Behan of Lixnaw married Honora Mary Collopy in 1893. Together they ran the public house in what was formerly Collopy's Hotel at the corner of The Square and Bridge Road. This corner was also called the Custom Gap, as tolls were collected at this place by agents of Lord Listowel on fair days. It was bought by the Macauley family in the 1930s. Shortly after the purchase, the house burnt to the ground. When reconstructed it was rebuilt as a two-storey house. Robert Moloney became the owner in the 1940s. He renamed it 'The Southern Star'. A plaque on the upper storey commemorates the building of the original house in 1819 and the reconstructed house in 1939.

Photo: The Southern Star front.

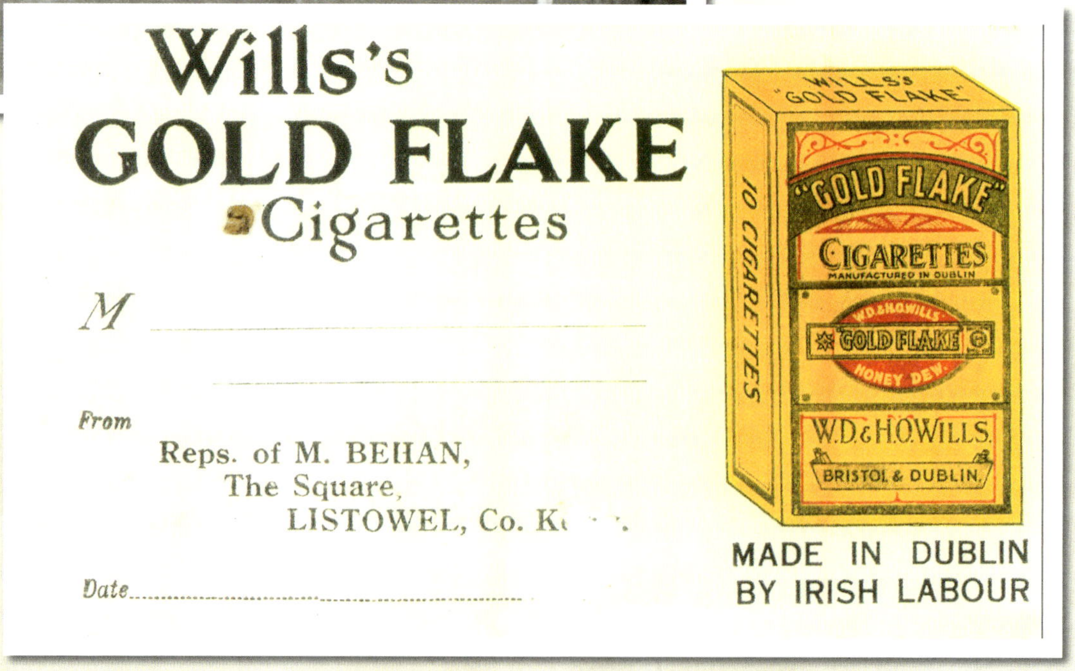

Public announcements once required the use of a Town Crier. In the 1880s, Listowel had one of rare quality, Michael Lane, a bell ringer. Many of his pronouncements were cried out in verse. One which has survived is as follows:

"Lost, but not found,
From Collopy's corner up to the Pound,
A hole in the middle,
And furry all round".

What was lost was a lady's muff, which was a cylindrical fur or cloth cover, open at both ends, in which the hands were placed to keep them warm. 'The Pound' in the verse refers to the public cattle pound which was at the upper end of William Street.

Photo: Michael Lane, town crier and billposter.

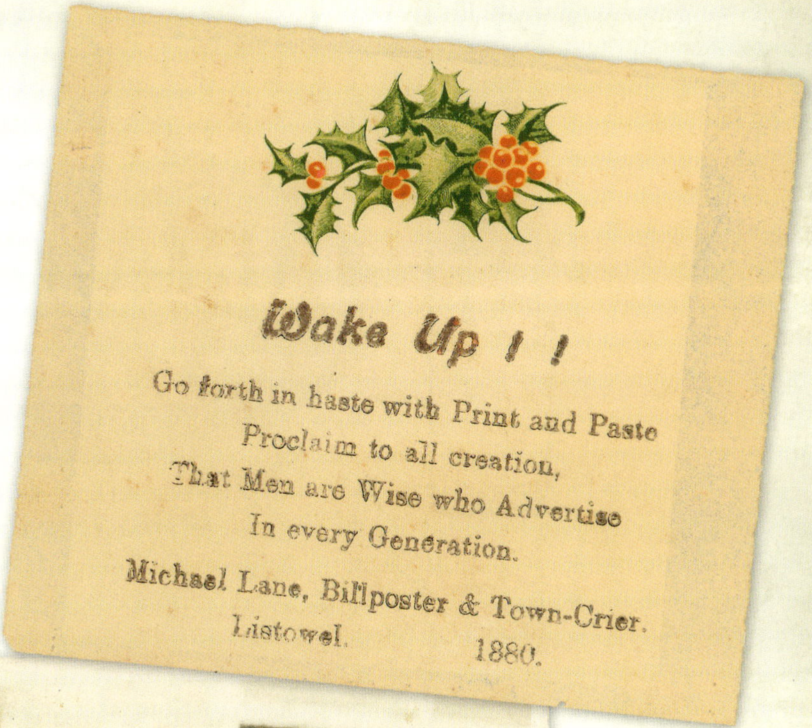

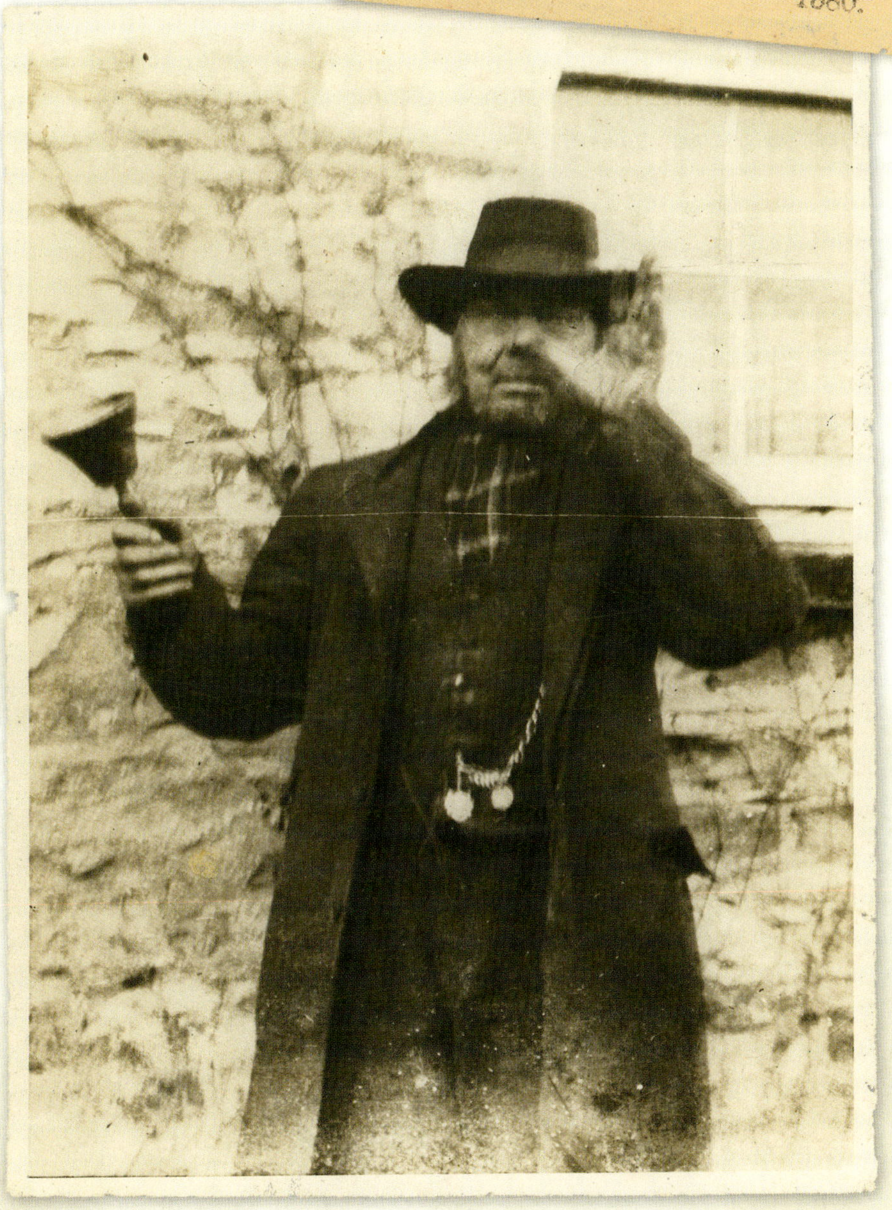

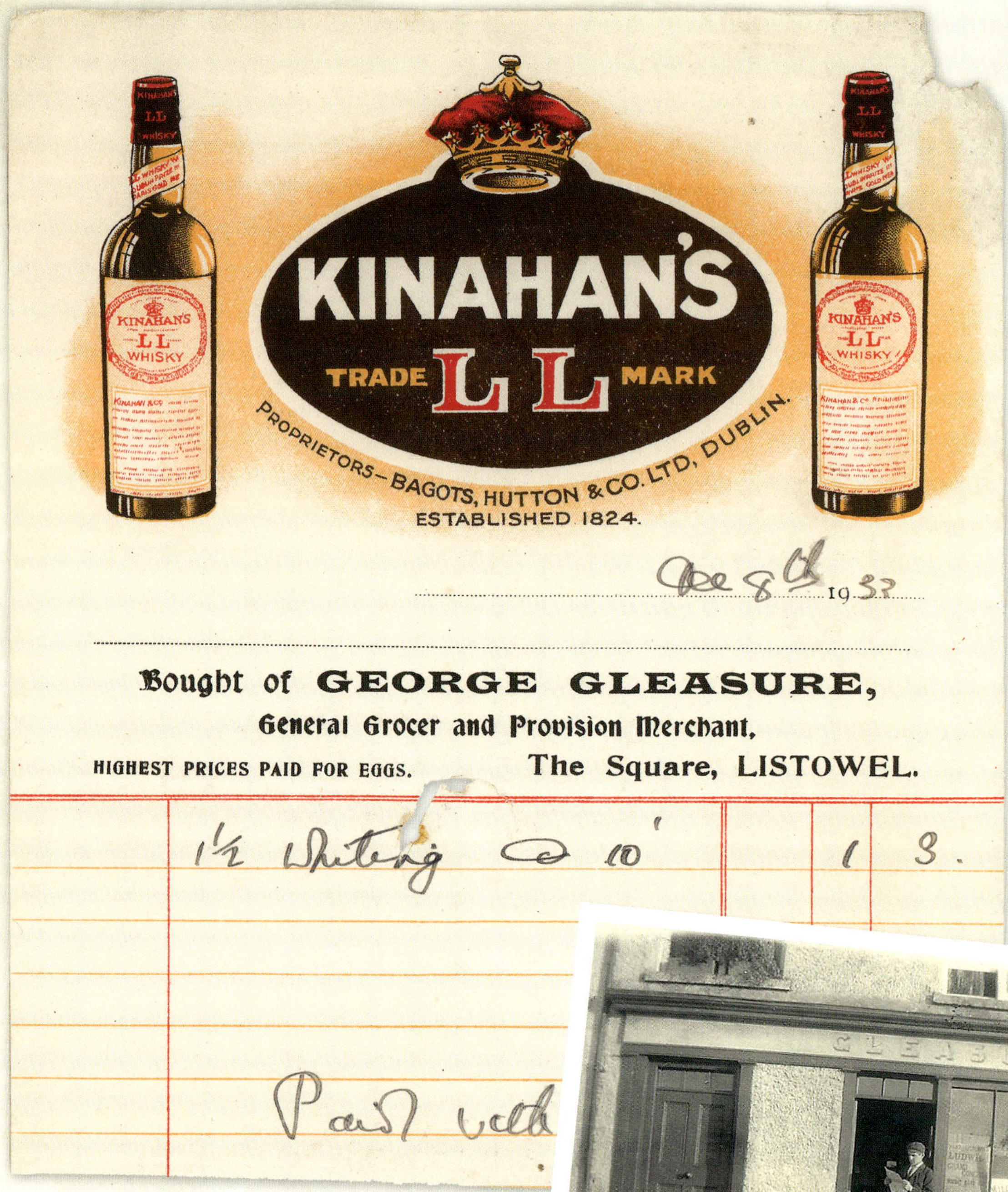
KINAHAN'S
TRADE L L MARK
PROPRIETORS–BAGOTS, HUTTON & CO. LTD, DUBLIN.
ESTABLISHED 1824.

Dec 8th 19

Bought of GEORGE GLEASURE,
General Grocer and Provision Merchant,
HIGHEST PRICES PAID FOR EGGS. The Square, LISTOWEL.

1½ Whiting @ 10 | 1 | 3.

Paid with

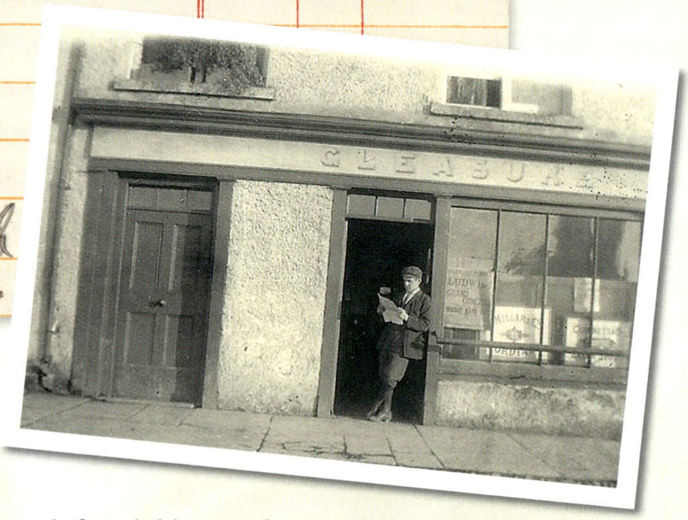

16 The Square

George Gleasure returned from Boston as a widower with five children in the 1890s.

He bought a public house and also the adjoining house. His eldest son, Frank, returned to Boston in the early 1900s and he was followed by his younger brother Joe (pictured) in 1907. However, tragedy soon followed and on December 19th of that year, Joe was killed by a shunting train. The Gleasures continued trading under George's stewardship until his death in the early 1920s. His youngest son, George, inherited the business and together with his wife, Eva, continued in business until their retirement years, which they spent in Ballybunion.

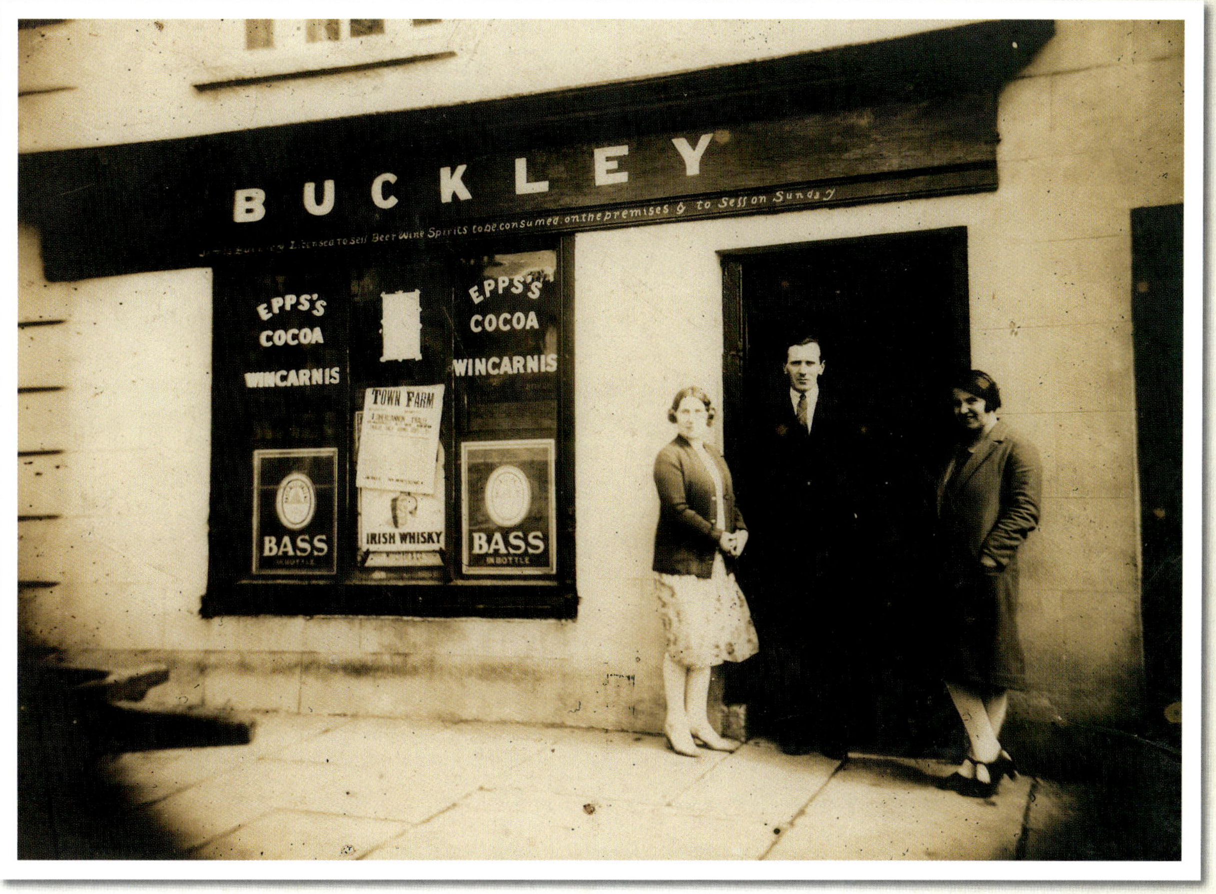

14 The Square

The Buckley family (above) ran a public house, locally known as 'The Well'. The name was derived from the fact that a Constabulary Force had a barracks or Bridewell there in the 1850s. The public house is today run by Christy Walsh, a descendent of the Buckleys.

13 The Square

Miss Stack *(billhead right)* gave piano lessons at the house she shared with her cousins, the Marshall family, at 13 The Square.

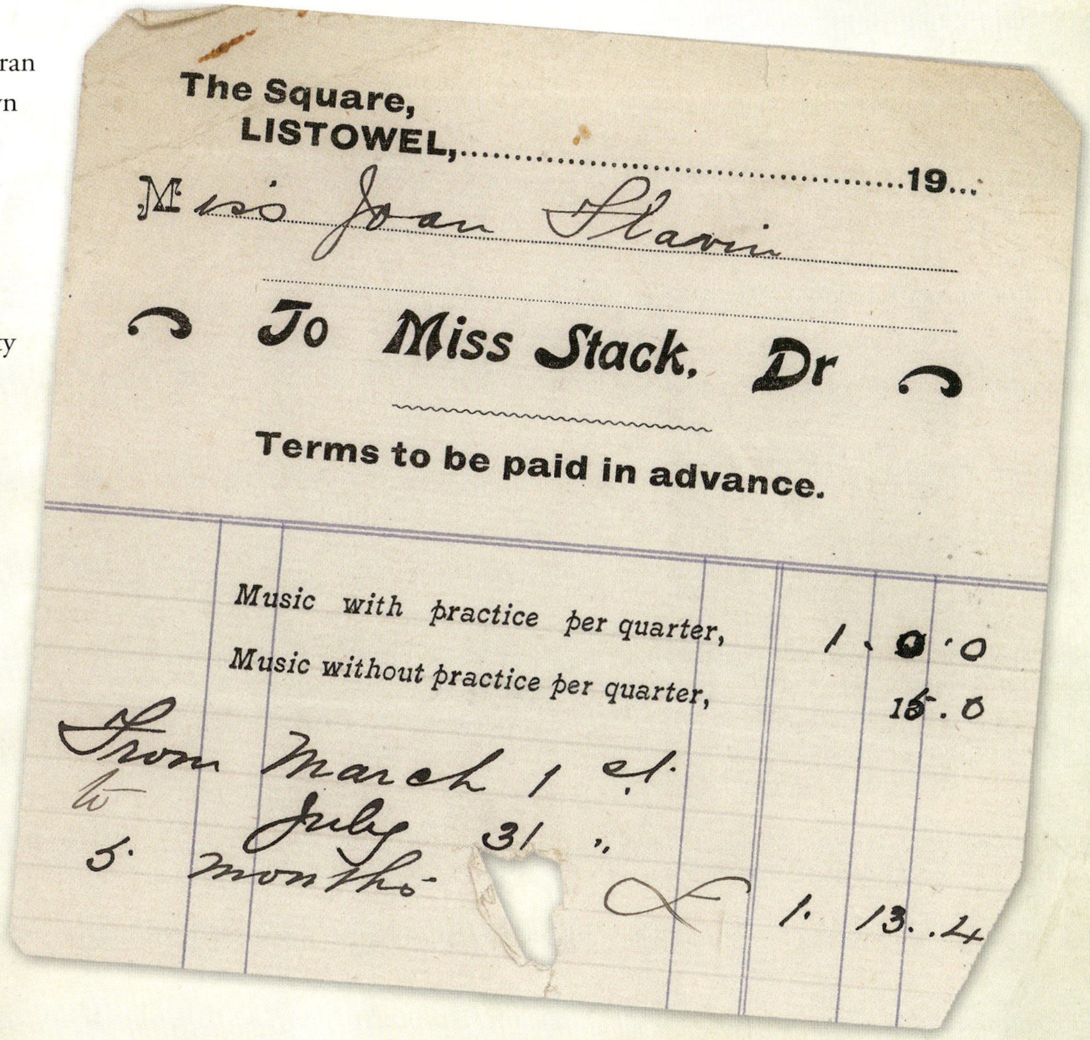

The Square,
LISTOWEL,..........................19...

Miss Joan Flavin

To Miss Stack, Dr

Terms to be paid in advance.

Music with practice per quarter,	1.0.0
Music without practice per quarter,	15.0
From March 1st to July 31 " 5 months	£1.13.4

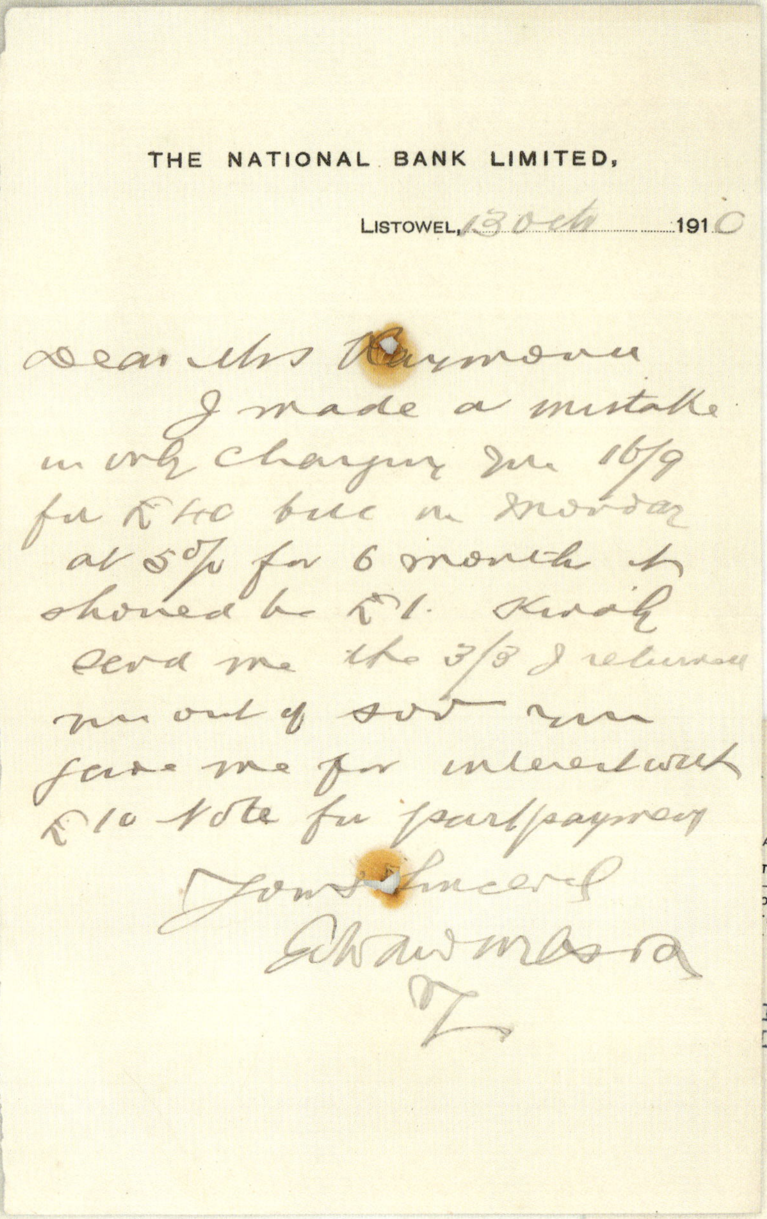

THE NATIONAL BANK LIMITED,

LISTOWEL, 13 Oct 1910

Dear Mrs Raymond
I made a mistake in my charging you 16/9 for £40 bill on Monday at 5% for 6 months it should be £1. Kindly send me the 3/9 I returned you out of £0? you gave me for interest with £10 note for part payment

Yours Sincerely
Edward Moran

12 The Square

The National Bank was built at the northern corner of the Square in the early 1800s. Before the bank was built, part of the site contained a Tannery.

Left: Letter from bank employee to Mrs Raymond.

Below: Letter from Henry Marshall to Dan Flavin.

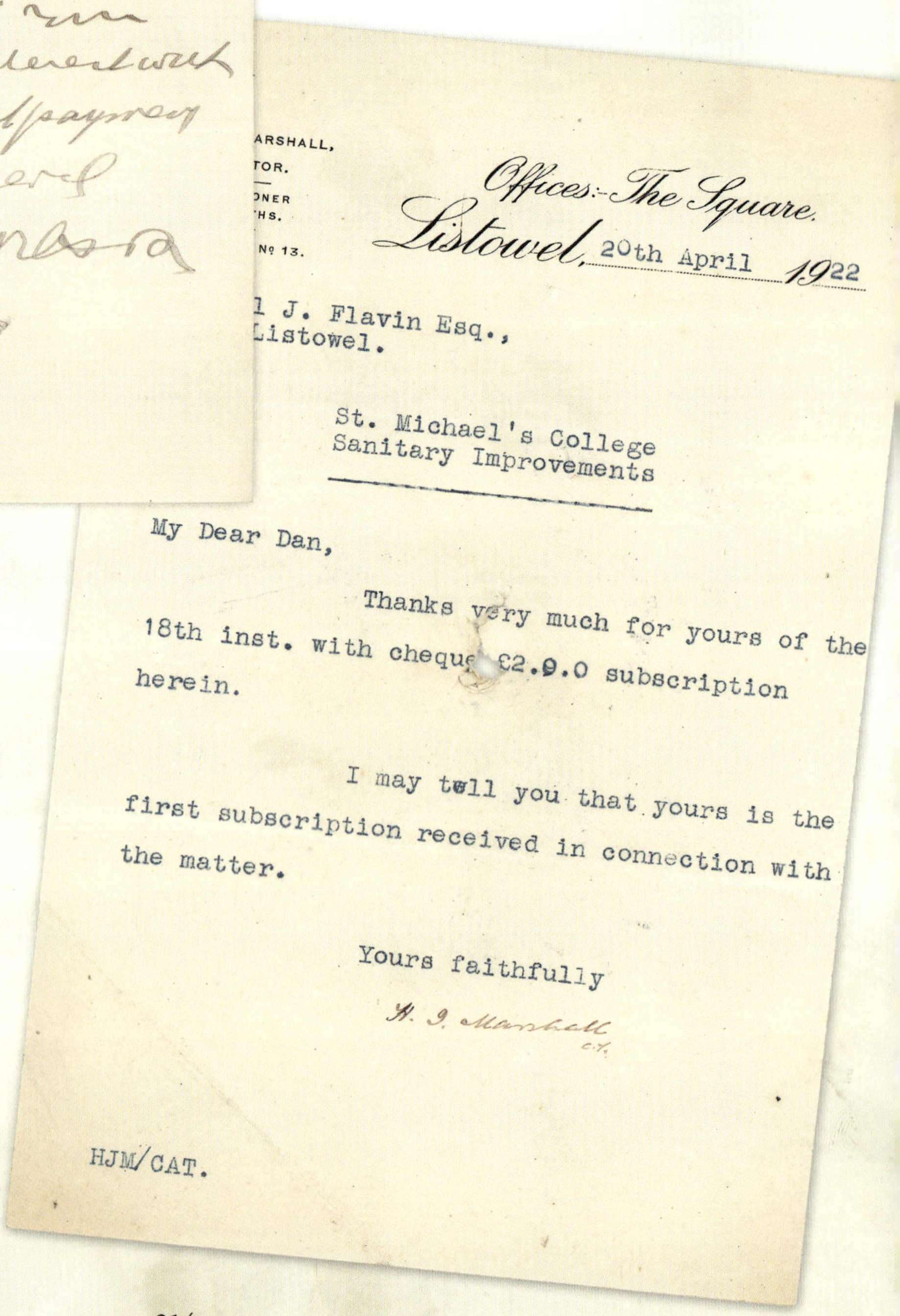

ARSHALL,
TOR.
ONER
THS.
No 13.

Offices:- The Square.
Listowel, 20th April 1922

1 J. Flavin Esq.,
Listowel.

St. Michael's College
Sanitary Improvements

My Dear Dan,

Thanks very much for yours of the 18th inst. with cheque £2.9.0 subscription herein.

I may tell you that yours is the first subscription received in connection with the matter.

Yours faithfully

H. J. Marshall

HJM/CAT.

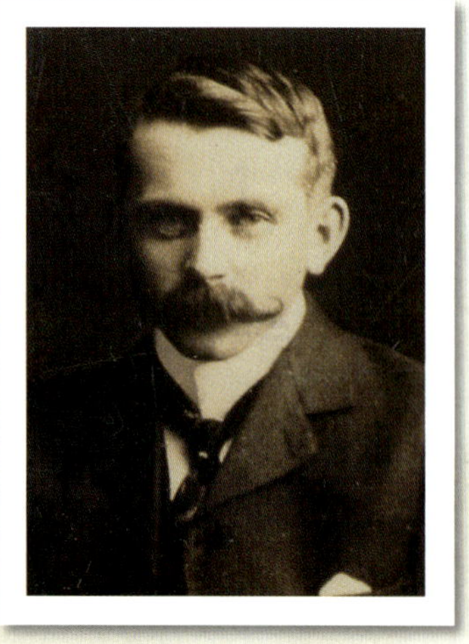

Henry Joseph Marshall, Solicitor of 9 The Square.

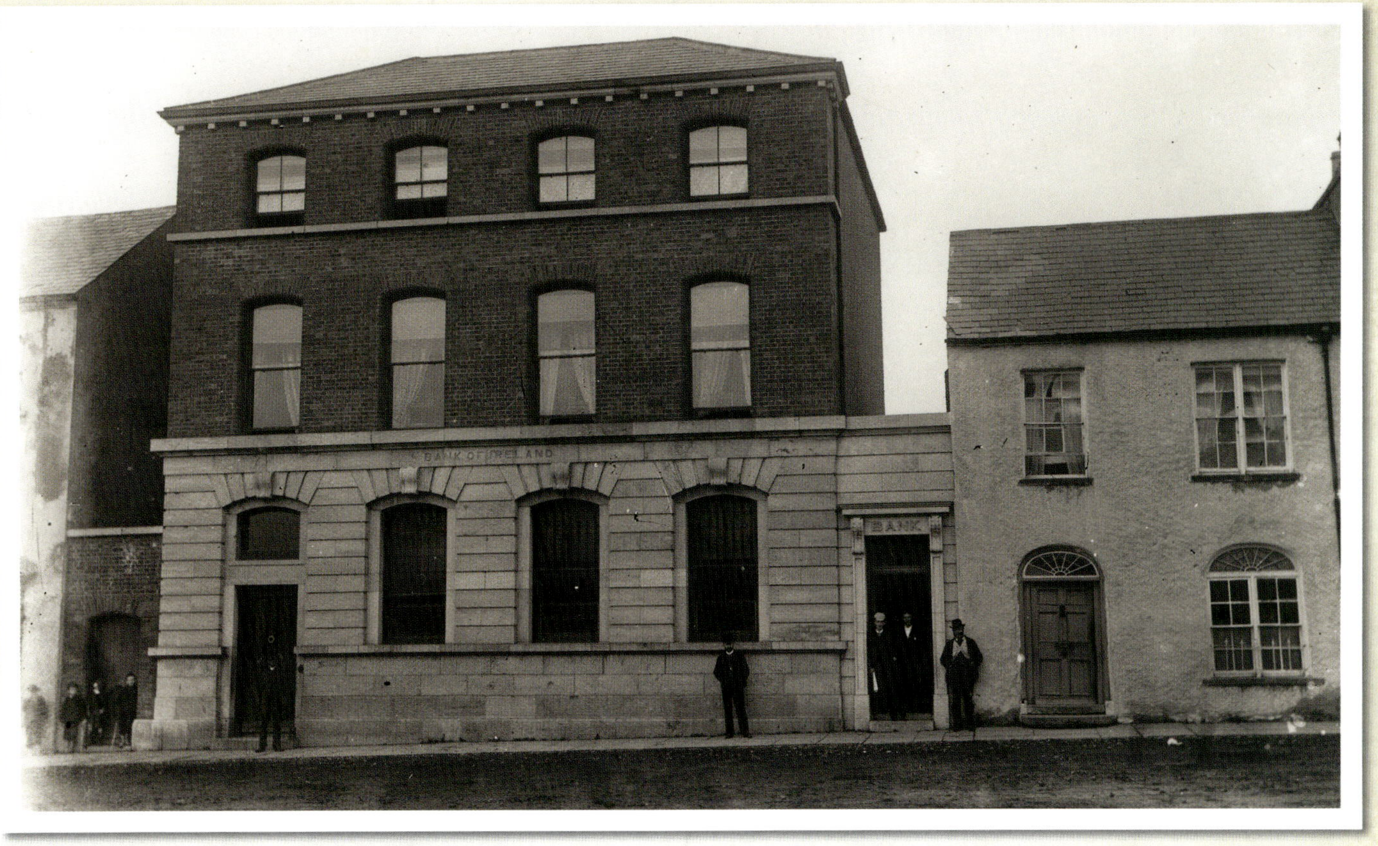

8 The Square
Early photograph of The Bank of Ireland *(above)*. On the right is the office of Henry J. Marshall, solicitor.

Below: 1927 receipt from Bank of Ireland to James F. Raymond acknowledging the deposit of a locked wooden box.

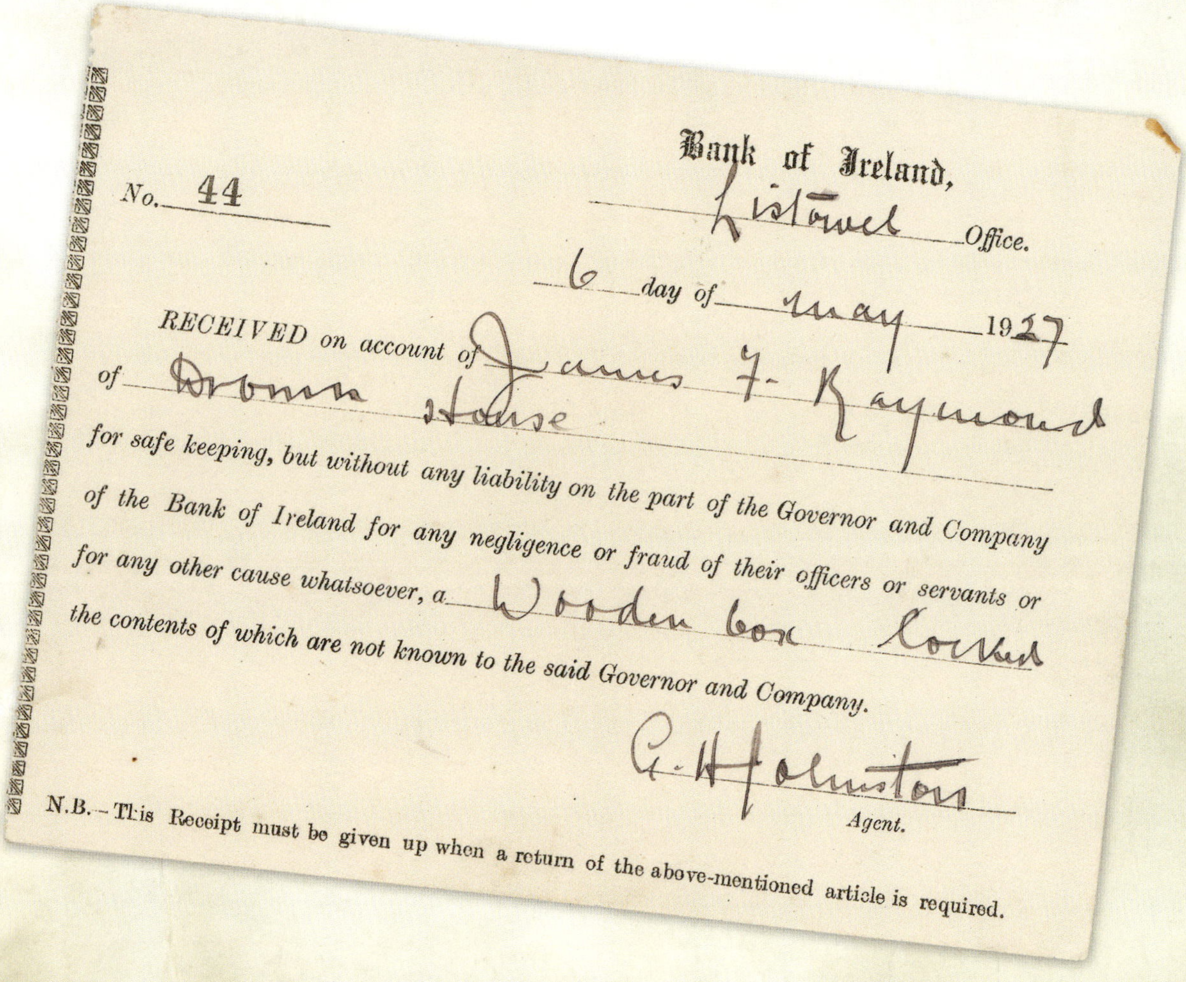

Bank of Ireland,

No. 44

Listowel *Office.*

6 *day of* May 1927

RECEIVED on account of James F. Raymond

of Dromin House

for safe keeping, but without any liability on the part of the Governor and Company of the Bank of Ireland for any negligence or fraud of their officers or servants or for any other cause whatsoever, a Wooden box Locked

the contents of which are not known to the said Governor and Company.

G. H. Johnston
Agent.

N.B.–This Receipt must be given up when a return of the above-mentioned article is required.

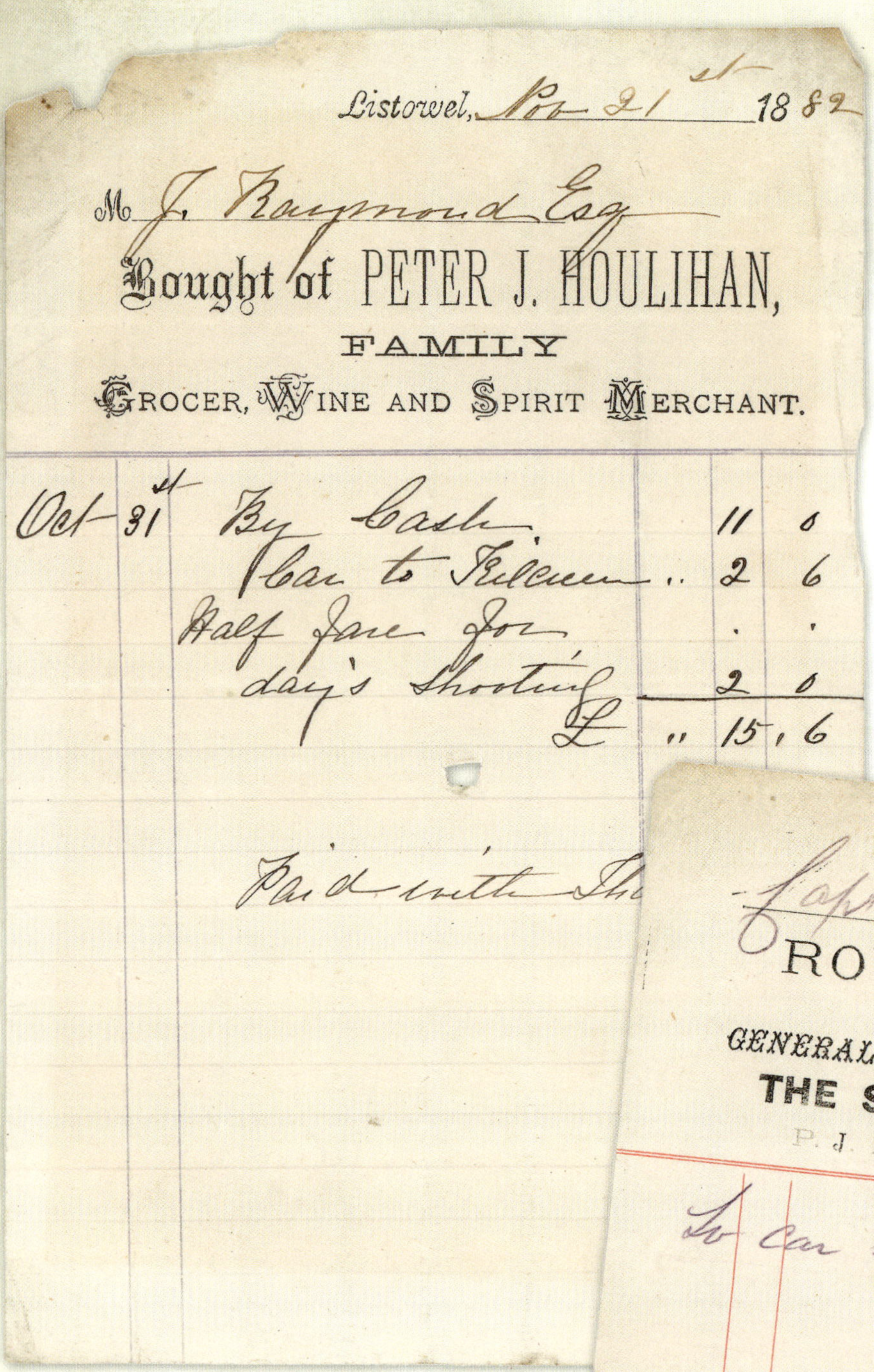
Listowel, Nov 21st 1882

M J. Raymond Esq

Bought of PETER J. HOULIHAN,

FAMILY

GROCER, WINE AND SPIRIT MERCHANT.

Oct 31st	By Cash	11	0
	Car to Kilcenn ..	2	6
	Half fare for day's Shooting	2	0
	£ ..	15	6

Paid with Th

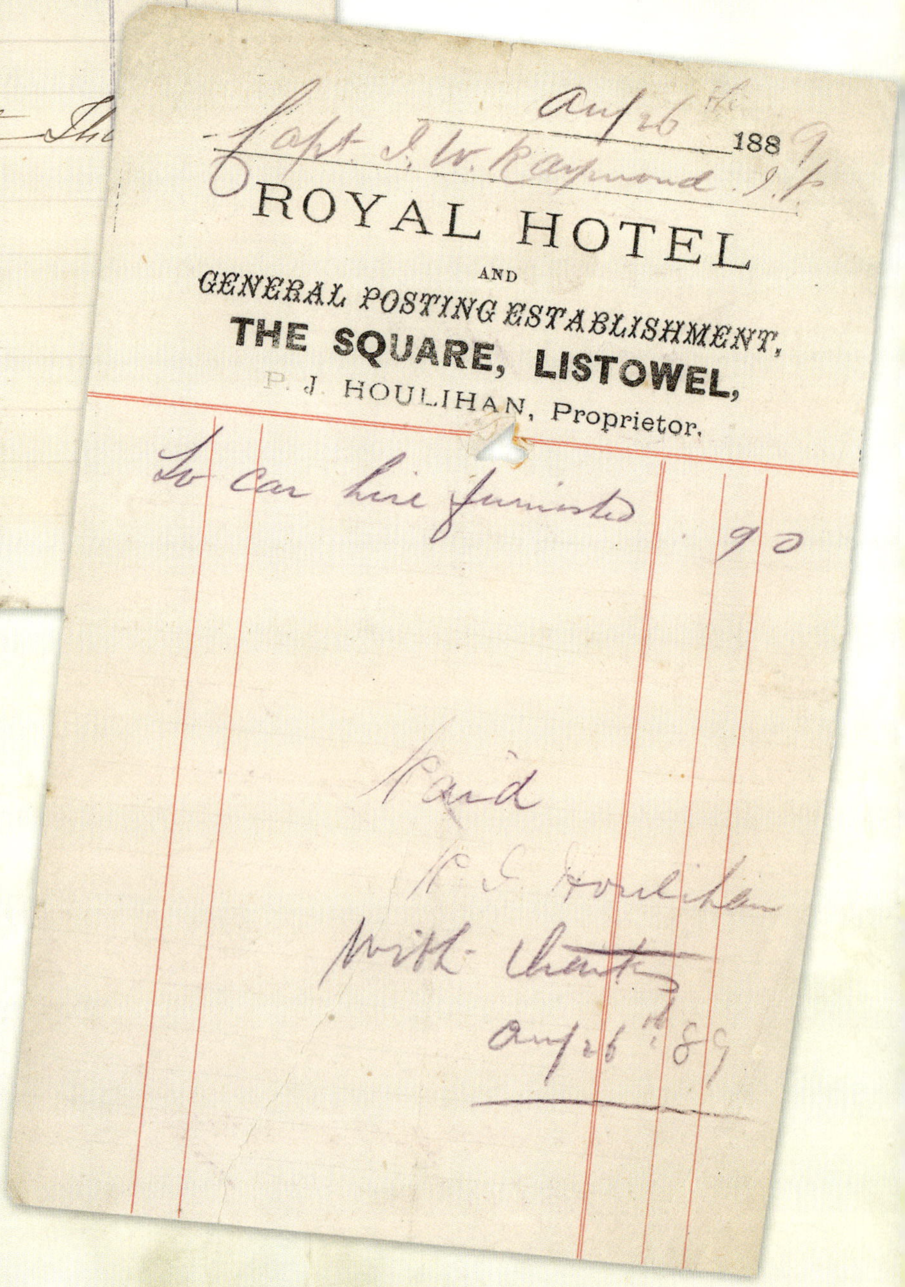
Capt. J. W. Raymond J.P. Aug 26th 1889

ROYAL HOTEL

AND

GENERAL POSTING ESTABLISHMENT,

THE SQUARE, LISTOWEL,

P. J. HOULIHAN, Proprietor.

To car hire furnished 9 0

Paid

P. J. Houlihan

With thanks

Aug 26th 89

7 The Square

Peter Houlihan and his wife Ellen Freeman from Tralee ran the Royal Hotel and Posting Establishment from a prime location in the Square in the 1880s.

6 The Square

A branch of Hogg and Company was based here, circa 1900.

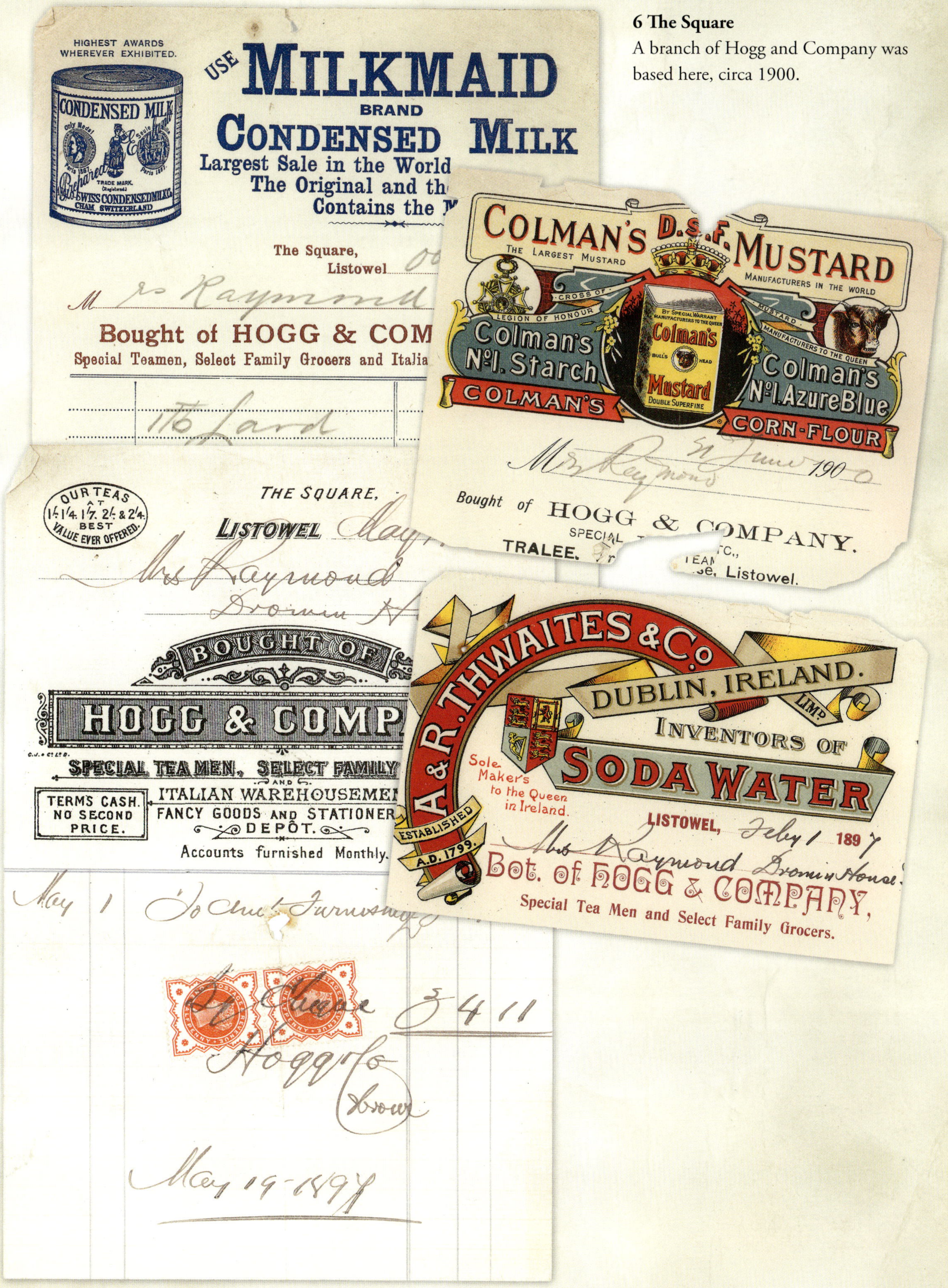

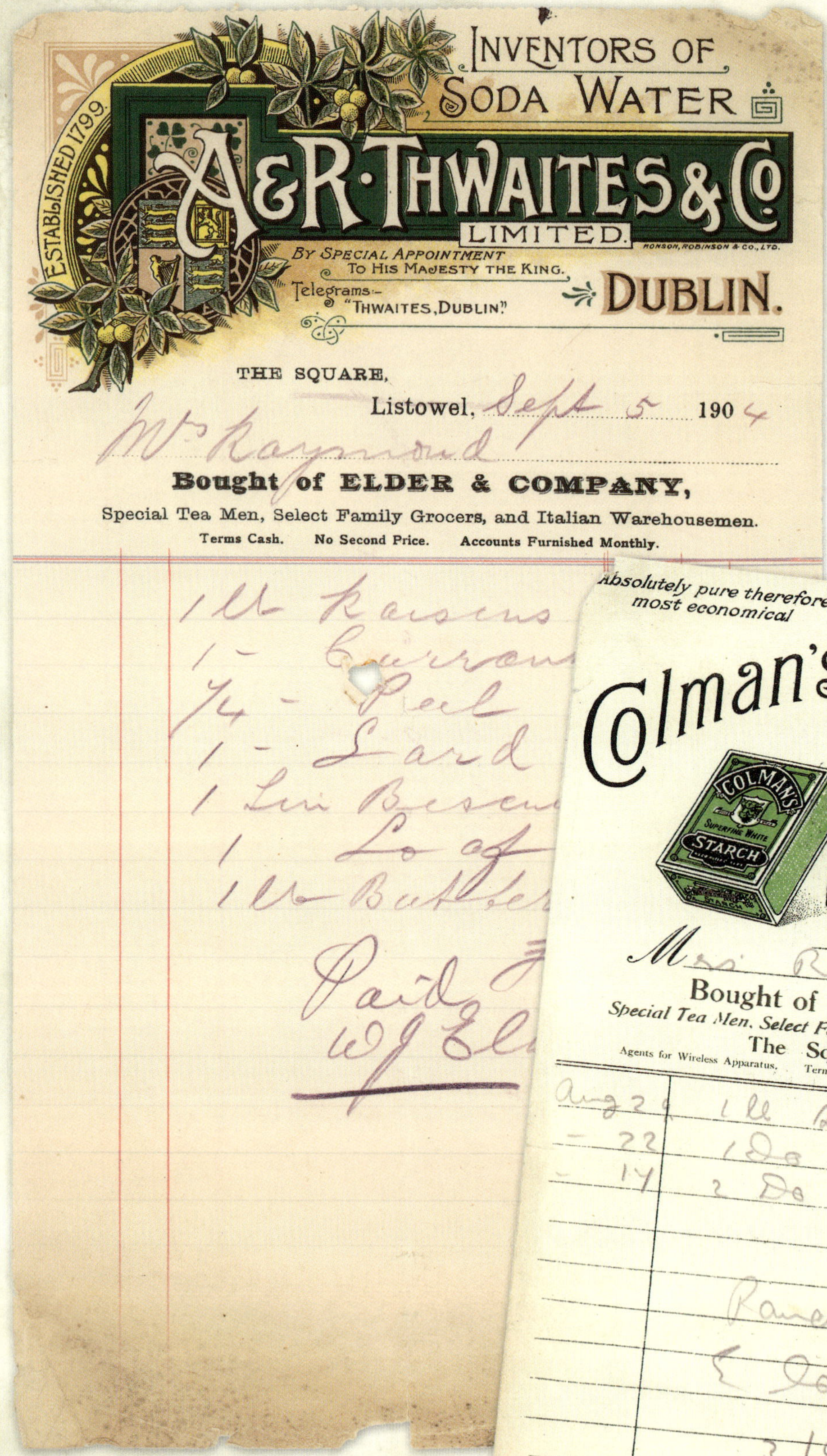
Established 1799
Inventors of Soda Water
A&R Thwaites & Co
Limited.
By Special Appointment To His Majesty the King.
Telegrams:- "Thwaites, Dublin."
Dublin.

The Square,
Listowel, Sept 5 1904
Mrs Raymond
Bought of ELDER & COMPANY,
Special Tea Men, Select Family Grocers, and Italian Warehousemen.
Terms Cash. No Second Price. Accounts Furnished Monthly.

1 lb Raisins
1 - Currants
1/4 - Peel
1 - Lard
1 Tin Biscuits
1 Loaf
1 lb Butter

Paid
W J El

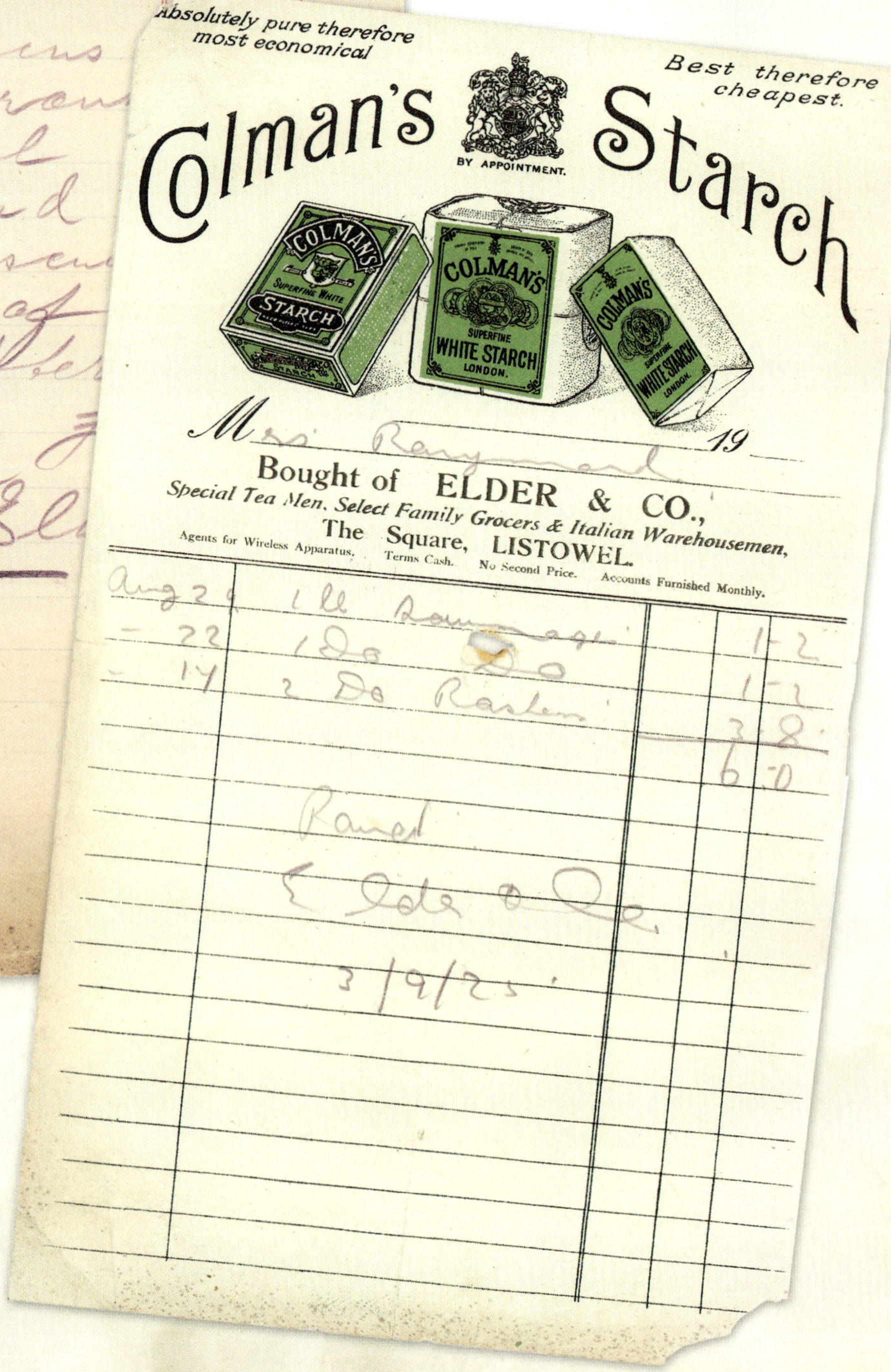
Absolutely pure therefore most economical
Best therefore cheapest.
Colman's Starch
By Appointment.

Mrs Raymond 19
Bought of ELDER & CO.,
Special Tea Men. Select Family Grocers & Italian Warehousemen,
The Square, LISTOWEL.
Agents for Wireless Apparatus. Terms Cash. No Second Price. Accounts Furnished Monthly.

Aug 2	1 lb Rashers		1-2
22	1 Do Do		1-2
14	2 Do Rashers		3-8
			6-0

Recd
E Elder & Co
3/9/25

6 The Square

William J. Elder succeeded Hogg and Company at 6 The Square. It was said that once when Elder was seeking a new clerk for the shop, he put a notice on the front window which read, "Clerk wanted, no Catholic need apply". The following morning across the shop window was scrawled, "no Catholic will apply".

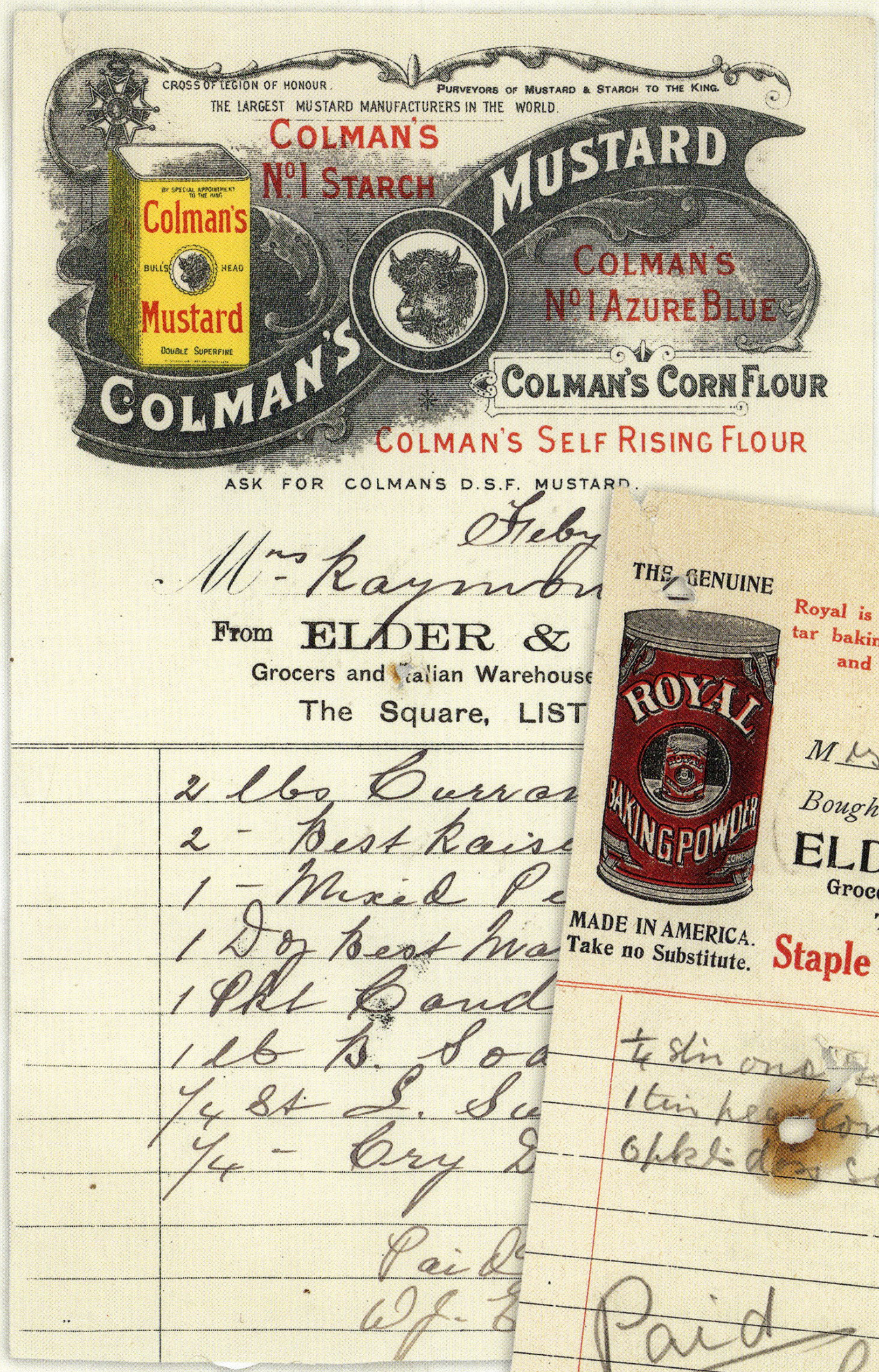
CROSS OF LEGION OF HONOUR. PURVEYORS OF MUSTARD & STARCH TO THE KING.
THE LARGEST MUSTARD MANUFACTURERS IN THE WORLD.
COLMAN'S No 1 STARCH
MUSTARD
Colman's Mustard
COLMAN'S No 1 AZURE BLUE
COLMAN'S
COLMAN'S CORN FLOUR
COLMAN'S SELF RISING FLOUR
ASK FOR COLMANS D.S.F. MUSTARD.

Feby

Mrs Raymon…

From ELDER & …

Grocers and Italian Warehouse…

The Square, LIST…

2 lbs Curran…
2 - Best Raisi…
1 - Mixed Pe…
1 Doz Best Ma…
1 Pkt Cand…
1 lb B. Soa…
1/4 St L. Su…
1/4 - Cry D…

Paid
W.J. E…

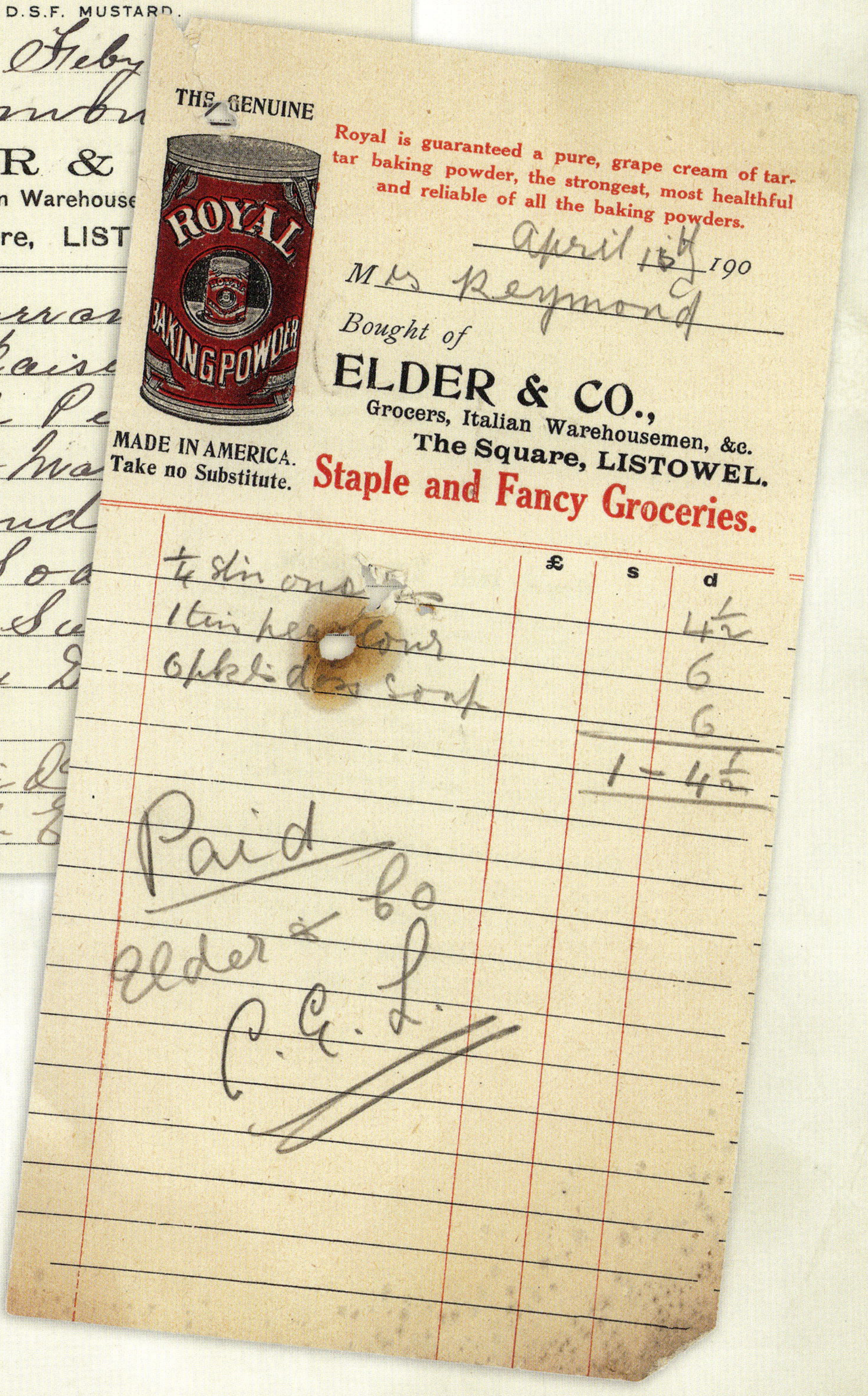
THE GENUINE

ROYAL BAKING POWDER

MADE IN AMERICA.
Take no Substitute.

Royal is guaranteed a pure, grape cream of tartar baking powder, the strongest, most healthful and reliable of all the baking powders.

April 16th 190

Mrs Raymond

Bought of

ELDER & CO.,
Grocers, Italian Warehousemen, &c.
The Square, LISTOWEL.
Staple and Fancy Groceries.

	£	s	d
¼ st onions			½
1 tin pea flour			4½
6 pkts … soap			6
			6
		1	4½

Paid
Elder & Co
C.G.L.

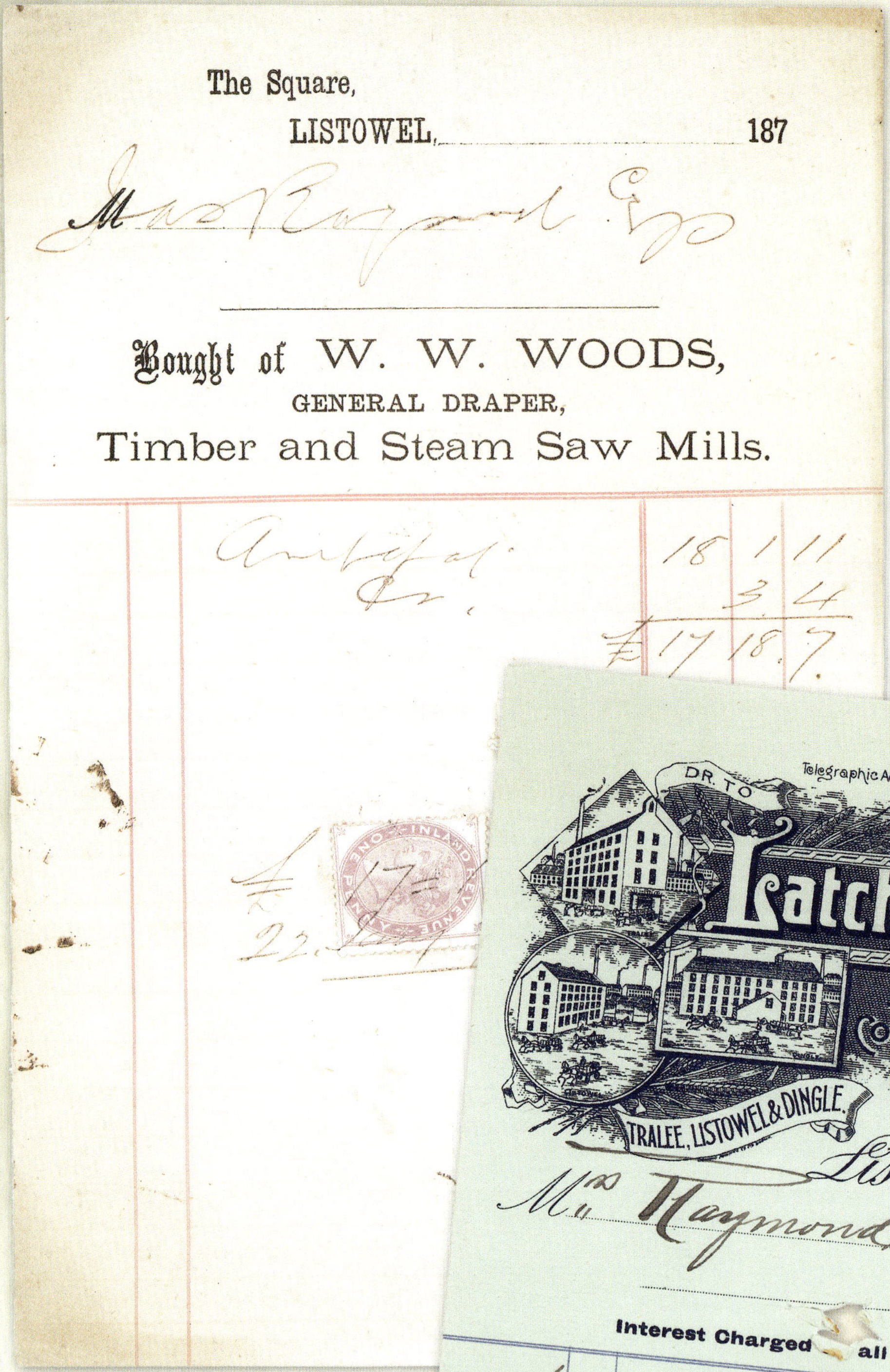
The Square,
LISTOWEL, 187

Bought of W. W. WOODS,
GENERAL DRAPER,
Timber and Steam Saw Mills.

18 1 11
3 4
£17 18 7

6 The Square (rear)
W.W. Woods ran a diverse business at 6 The Square as draper and timber merchant. He occupied the premises later occupied by Hogg, Elder and the grocery/bakery of John Lynch.

4 The Square
John Latchford of Tralee established a water-powered Flour Mill at a site in Greenville in the early 1860s. Previous to this he had endeavoured to secure a closed mill at the rear of the Castle which had been owned by the Church and Leonard families.

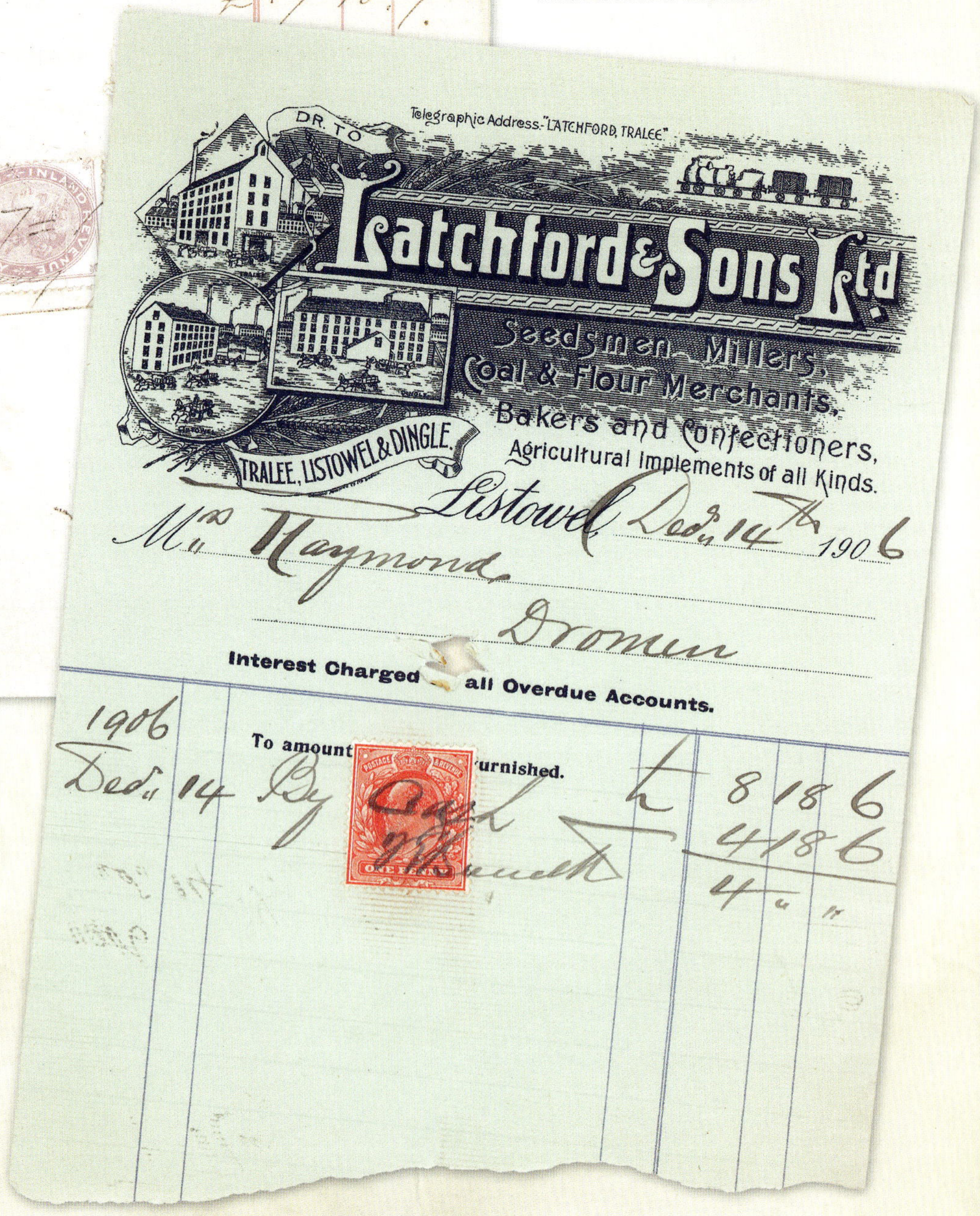
DR. TO
Telegraphic Address: "LATCHFORD, TRALEE."
Latchford & Sons Ltd
Seedsmen Millers,
Coal & Flour Merchants,
Bakers and Confectioners,
Agricultural Implements of all Kinds.
TRALEE, LISTOWEL & DINGLE.
Listowel, Dec 14th 1906
Mr Raymond
Dromin
Interest Charged on all Overdue Accounts.
To amount furnished.
1906 Dec 14 By Cash £ 8 18 6
4 18 6
4 " "

When many of the mainly Limerick-based milling companies saw the potential for trade in Listowel, they opened branch offices and appointed agents to handle their affairs. The Shamrock Steam Mills were owned by McCowens of Tralee.

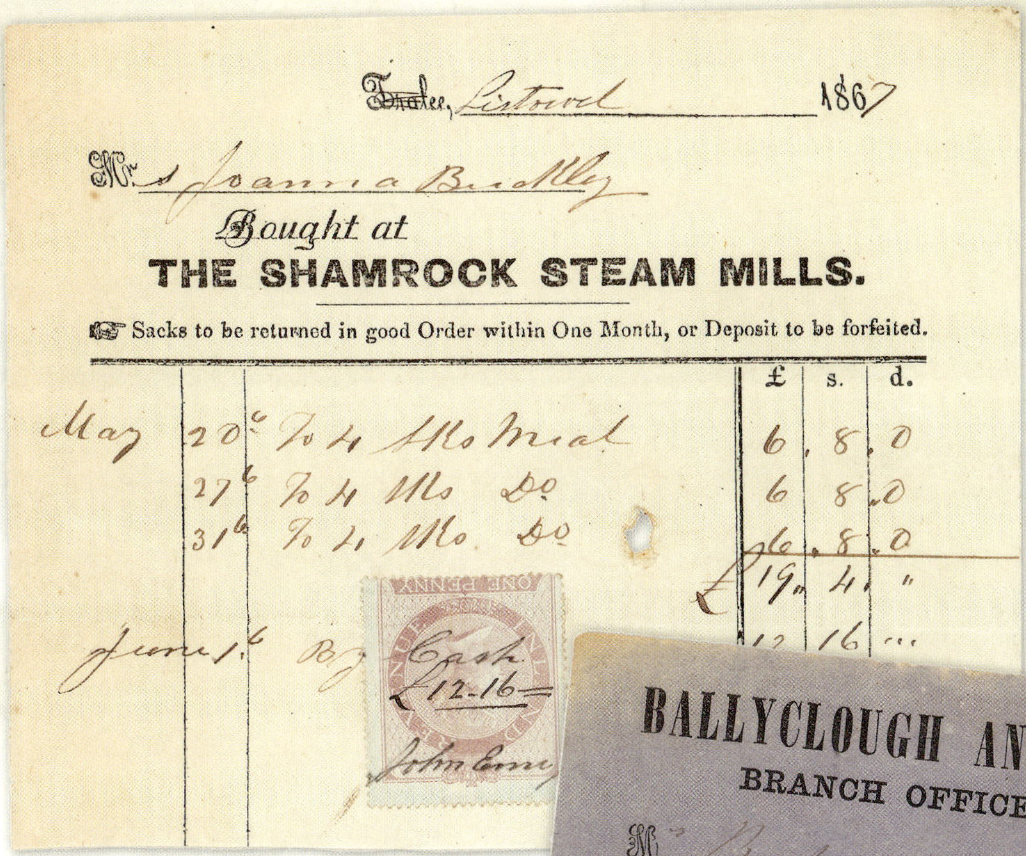
~~Tralee~~, Listowel 1867

Mrs Joanna Buckley

Bought at

THE SHAMROCK STEAM MILLS.

Sacks to be returned in good Order within One Month, or Deposit to be forfeited.

			£	s.	d.
May	20th	To 4 Slks Meal	6	8	0
	27th	To 4 Slks Do	6	8	0
	31st	To 4 Slks Do	6	8	0
			£ 19	4	"
June	1st	By Cash	12	16	"

ONE PENNY

£12-16

Shown here are billheads of three of these companies: The Shamrock Steam Mills, May 1867; Ballinclough and Ennis Mills, J. Bannatyne, December 6th, 1866; Croom Mills Office of 23rd October 1866.

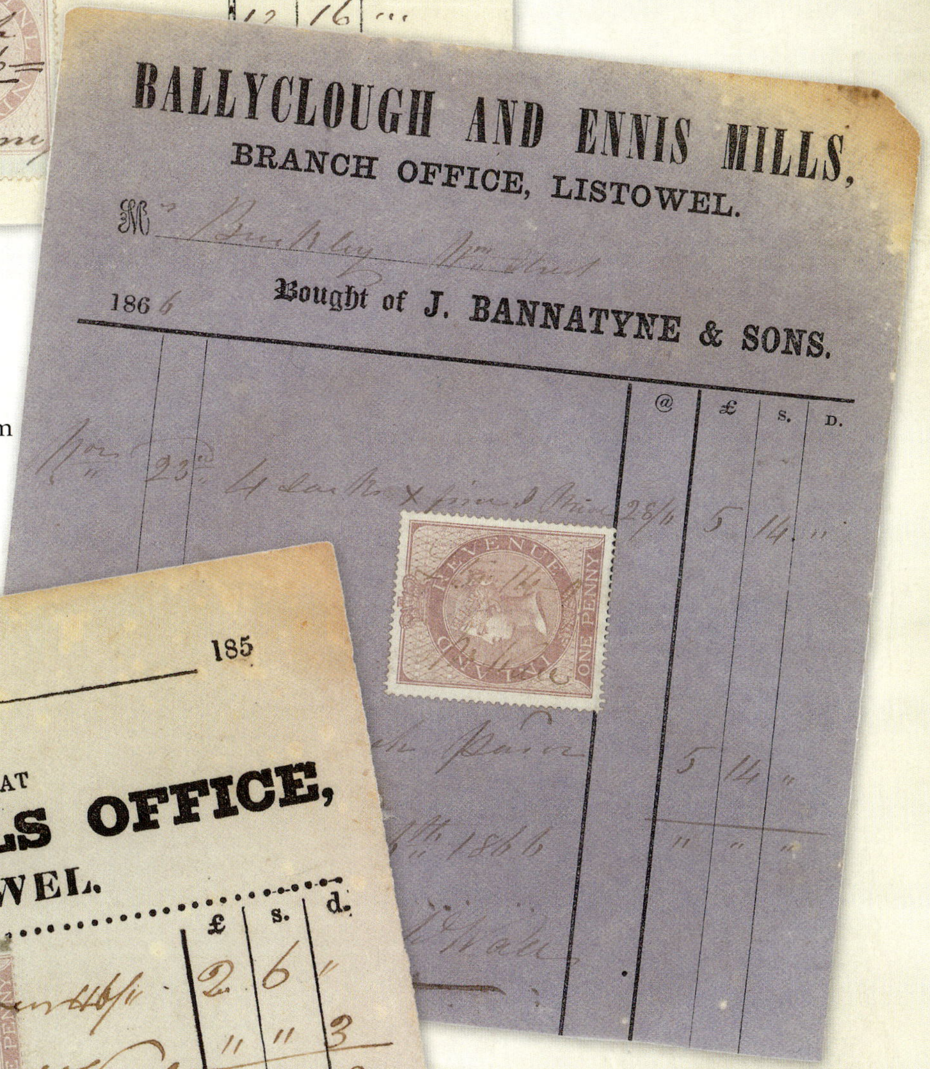
BALLYCLOUGH AND ENNIS MILLS,

BRANCH OFFICE, LISTOWEL.

Mr Buckley

1866 Bought of J. BANNATYNE & SONS.

			@	£	s.	D.
	23rd	4 sacks	28/6	5	14	"
				5	14	"
		1866		"	"	"

REVENUE ONE PENNY

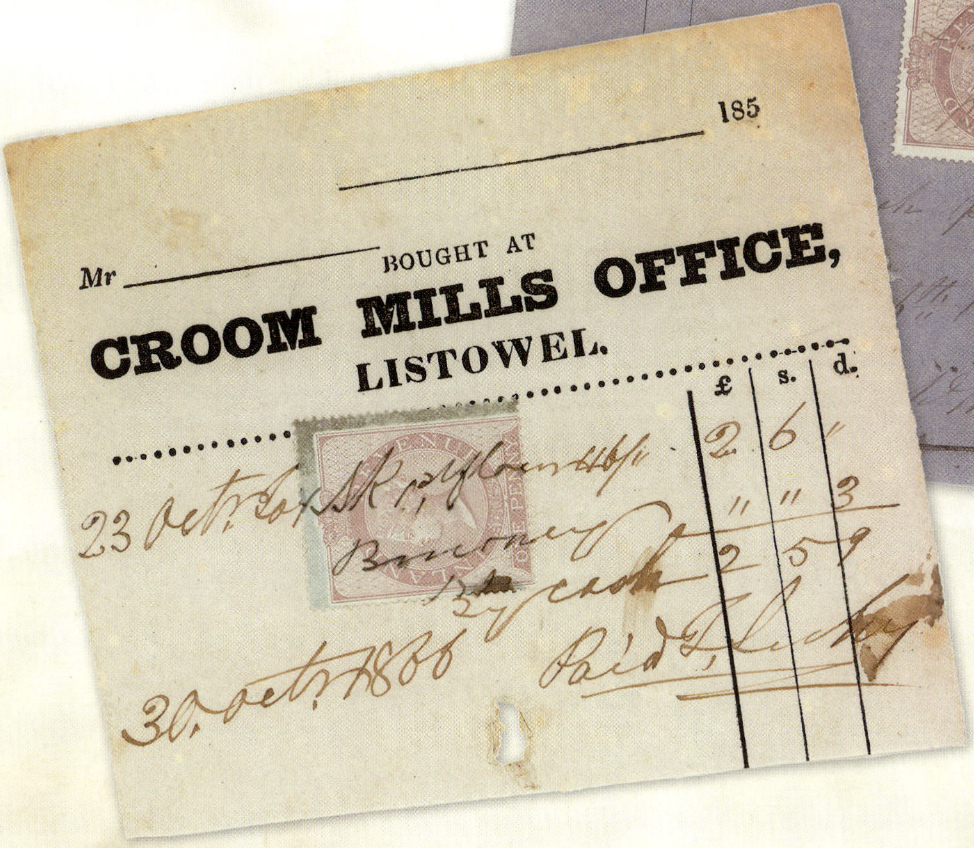
185

Mr BOUGHT AT

CROOM MILLS OFFICE,

LISTOWEL.

	£	s.	d.
23 Oct	2	6	"
	"	"	3
	2	5	9
30 Oct 1866 Paid			

REVENUE ONE PENNY

2 & 3 The Square

Patrick Kirby from Duagh began trading in The Square in 1860. His large shop was located in two houses, now Nos 2 and 3 The Square. Here, he and his family ran a public house, bakery, cooperage, grocery and dealt in flour and meal.

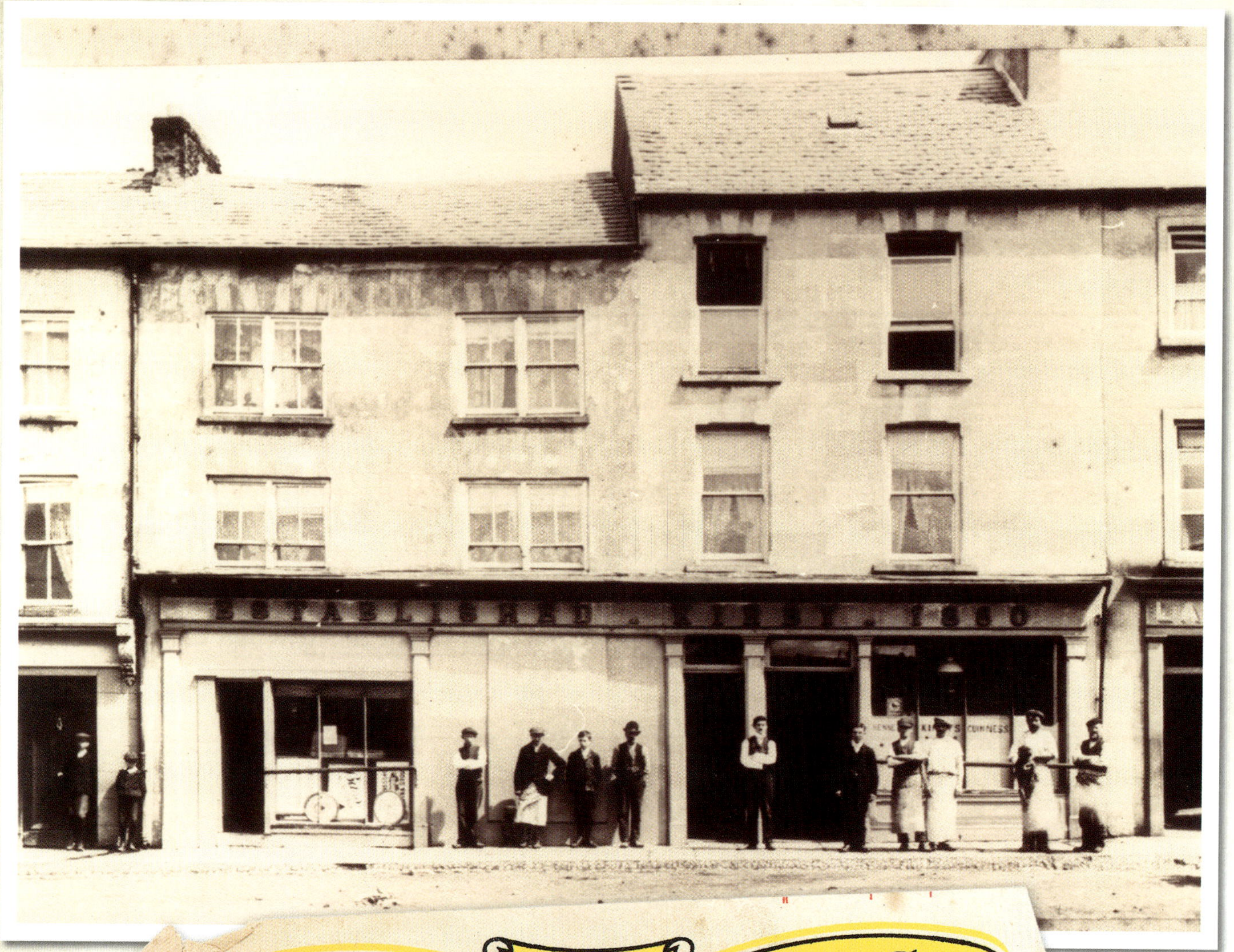

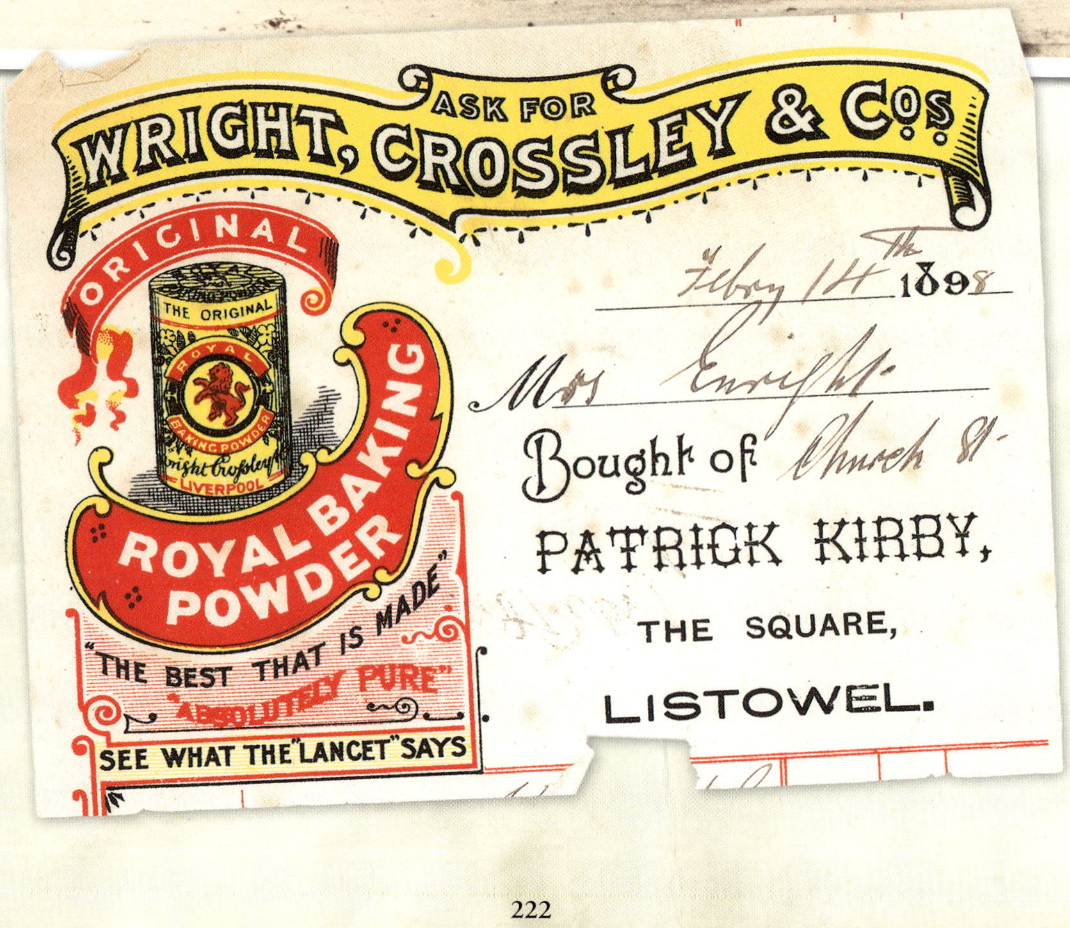

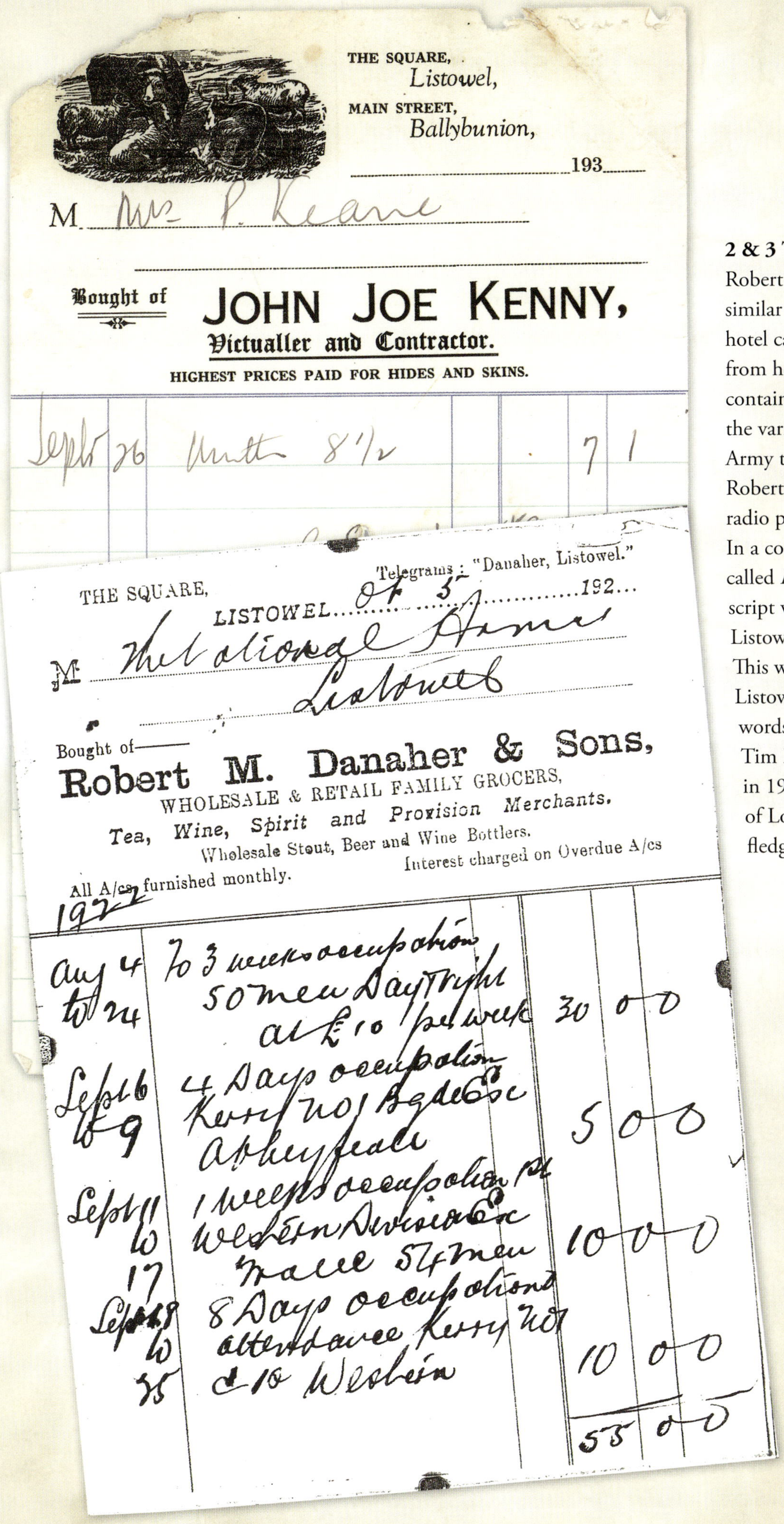
THE SQUARE,
Listowel,
MAIN STREET,
Ballybunion,
193

M. Mrs P. Keane

Bought of
JOHN JOE KENNY,
Victualler and Contractor.
HIGHEST PRICES PAID FOR HIDES AND SKINS.

Sept	26	Mutton 8½	7	1

Telegrams: "Danaher, Listowel."
THE SQUARE,
LISTOWEL Oct 5 192
M The National Army
Listowel

Bought of
Robert M. Danaher & Sons,
WHOLESALE & RETAIL FAMILY GROCERS,
Tea, Wine, Spirit and Provision Merchants.
Wholesale Stout, Beer and Wine Bottlers.
All A/cs furnished monthly.
Interest charged on Overdue A/cs

1922

Aug 4 to 24	To 3 weeks occupation 50 men Day & Night at £10 per week	30	0	0
Sept 6 to 9	4 Days occupation Kerry No 1 Bgde Esc Abbeyfeale	5	0	0
Sept 11 to 17	1 week occupation for Western Division Esc Tralee 54 men	10	0	0
Sept 18 to 25	8 Days occupation attendance Kerry No 1 & 10 Western	10	0	0
		55	0	0

2 & 3 The Square

Robert Danaher from Athea had a similar business to Kirby's. A small hotel called 'Hotel Brendan' operated from here. The bill, with letterhead, contains details of his account with the various sections of the National Army that were based in Listowel. Robert's son, Tim, became a notable radio producer with Radio Éireann. In a contribution to a radio series called *Hometown*, Tim penned a script which was narrated by another Listowel man, Eamon Keane. This was called *A Gift of Ink* - a Listowel man's tribute to the fellow wordsmiths of his native town. Tim Danaher was one of those who in 1971, under the chairmanship of Louis Murphy, founded the fledgling Writers' Week.

Chapter 8

MARKET STREET

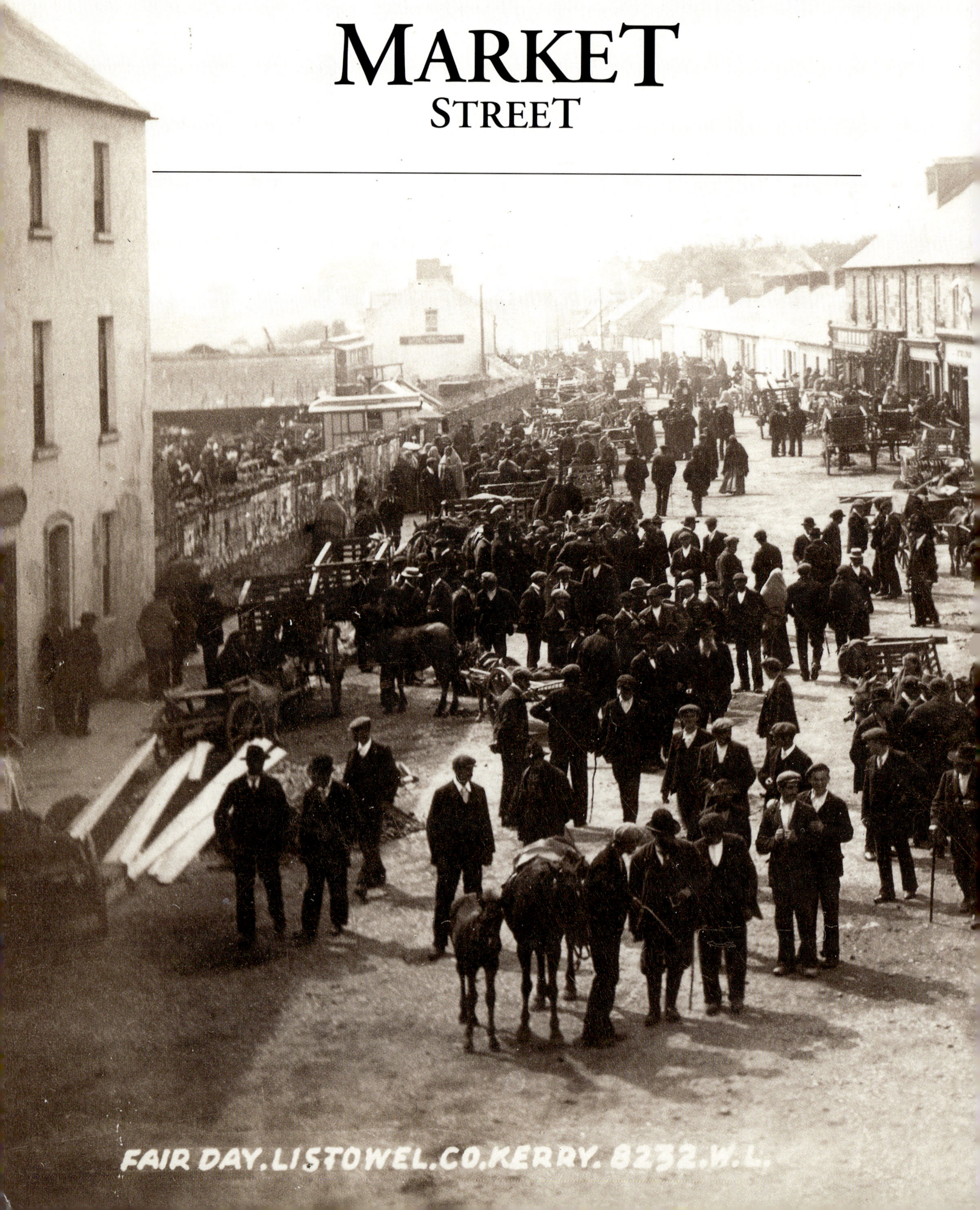

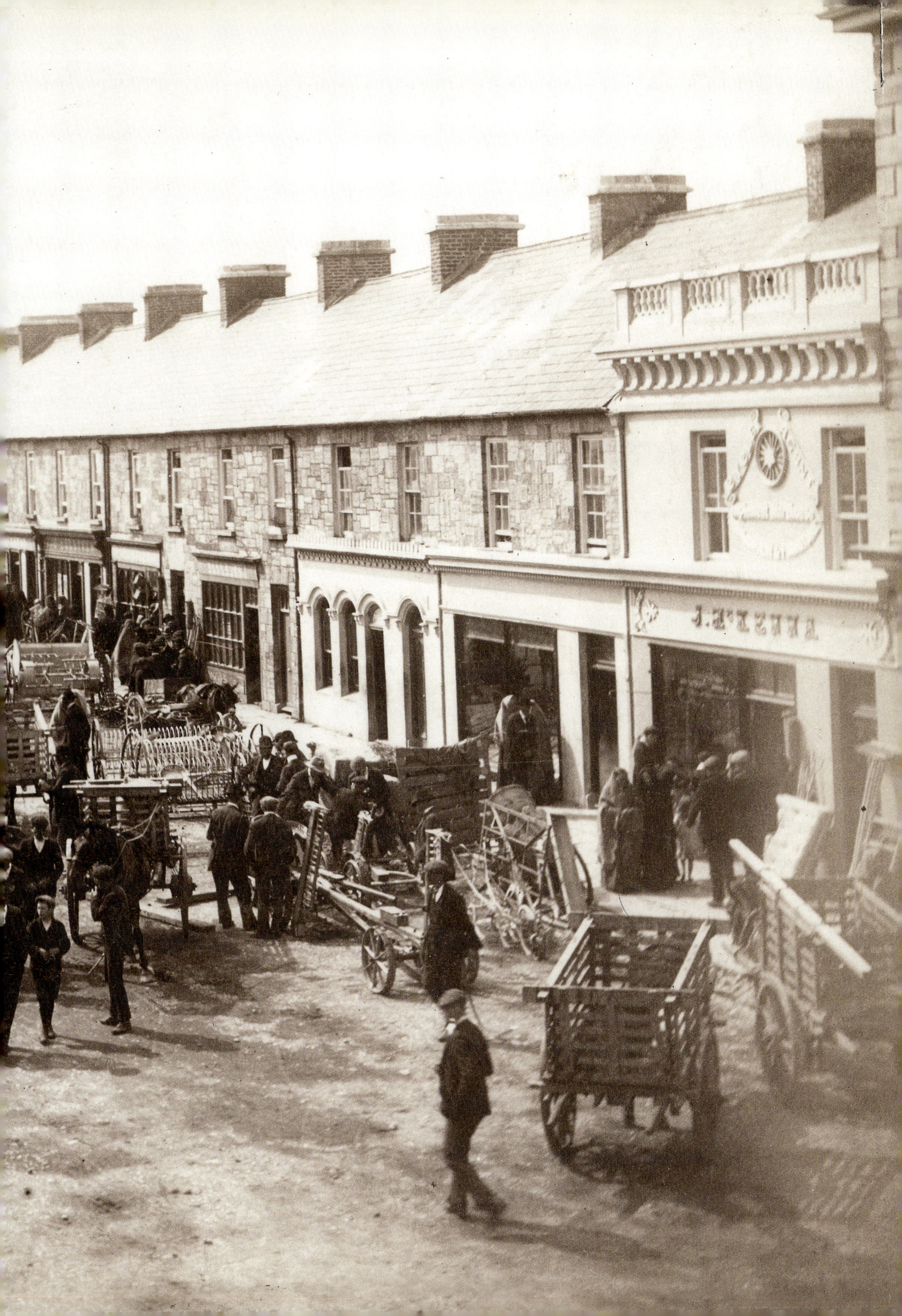

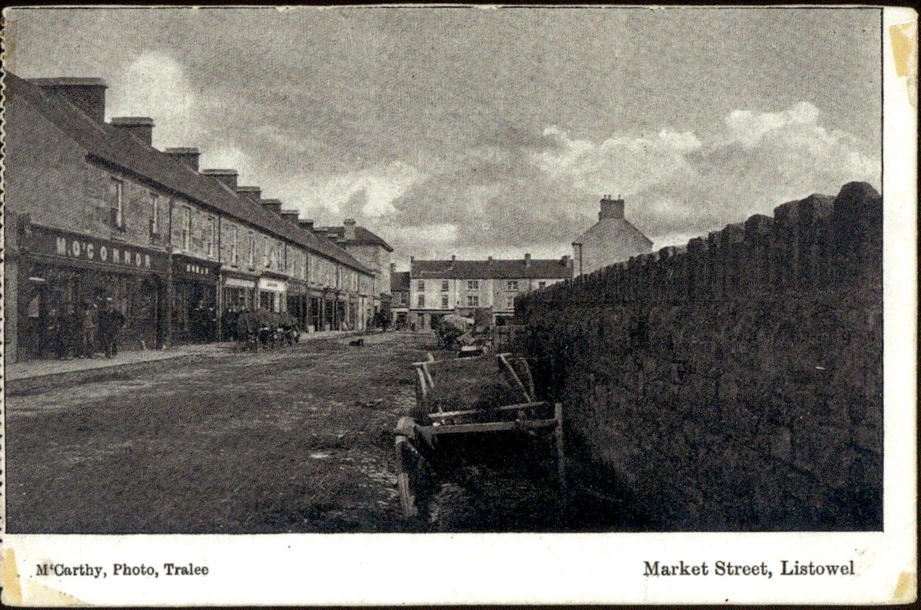

Left: Photograph circa 1910 of Market Street looking back towards William Street. Michael O'Connor's commercial hotel is on the left and the extended market wall is to the right. The original market wall was built in 1854 to enclose the new market place; it was extended in the 1890s to incorporate the addition of the new back market yard.

Previous pages: A 1904 bustling Market Street scene. The street had undergone many changes from when it was first known as the Ennismore Road and Glanaphuca. With the knocking of old thatched cottages on the right, the widening of the street, the rebuilding of houses with cut stone and the presence of a new market place, at first it was renamed 'New Street' later 'Market Street'. Note McAuliffe's workmanship over McKenna's. Various pieces of machinery on the roadway outside McKenna's are being scrutinised by prospective customers.

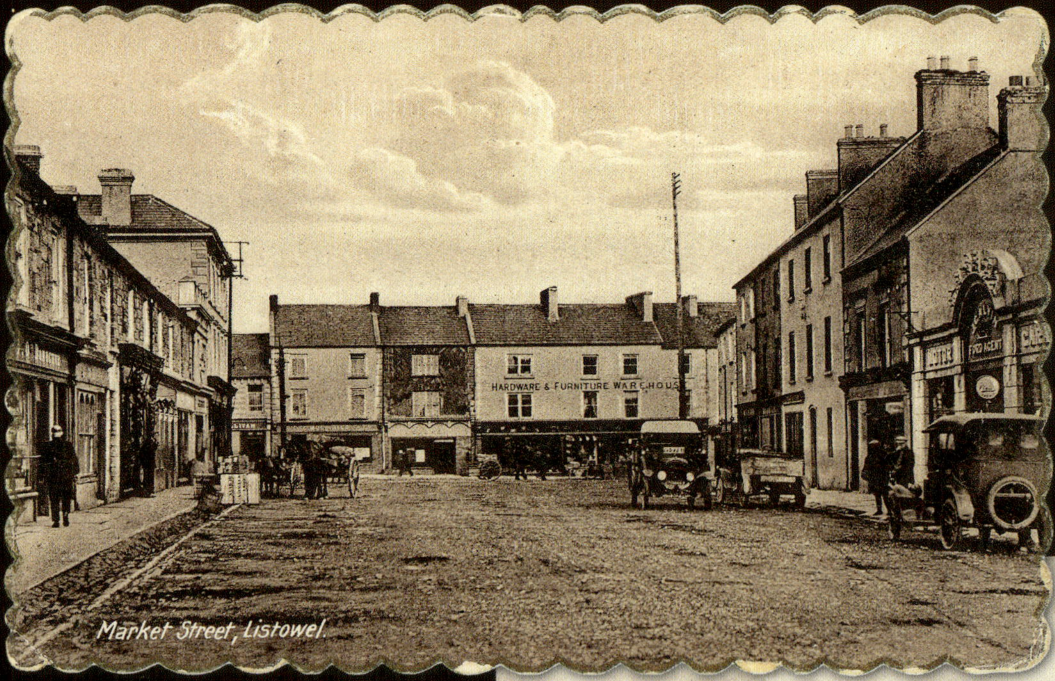

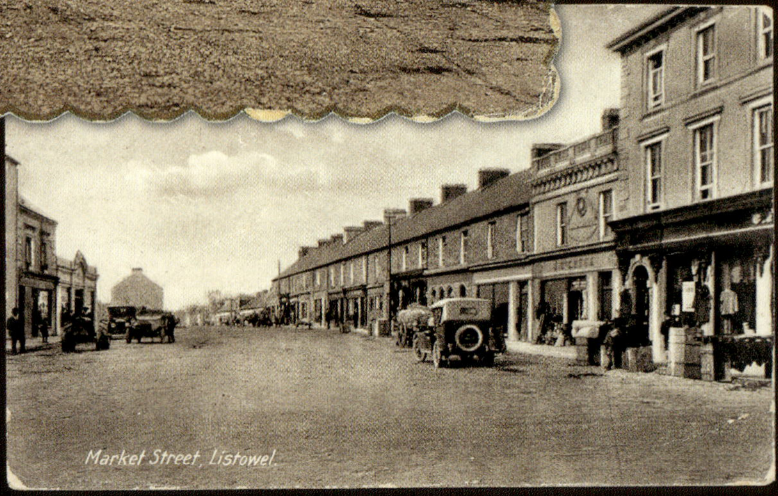

Two photographs of Market Street from the 1920s/1930s are in contrast to the 1904 photo of a Market Day. Looking towards William Street, above, one can see the frontages of part of T.D. O'Sullivan's, Con Mulvihill's, Clancy's and the extensive property of T.F. Cronin. Galvin's name still fronts the garage on the right, and cars have got more plentiful. Right: Looking towards Convent Street, Walsh's two-storey shop is on the right next to McKenna's.

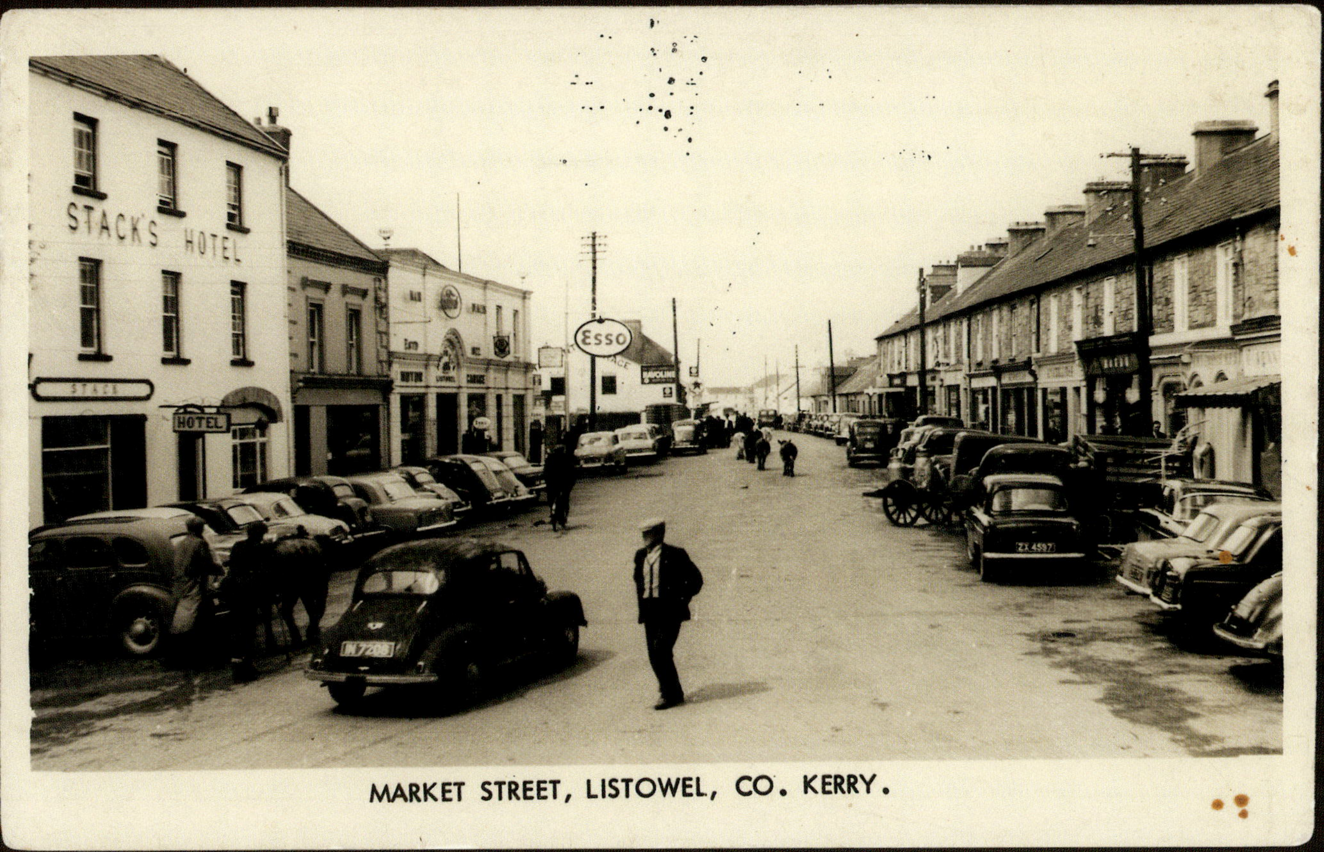

Above: A Fair Day scene from the 1950s. Some cattle are in evidence, clearly coming from The Square. Cars have become very plentiful. Stack's Hotel is on the left and further on the Esso sign outside Moloney's Garage is very prominent. Further back, beyond the Market Wall, is Tarrant's Garage, fronted by its Caltex sign.

Below: Convent Street of the 1930s with thatched cottages lining the river side.

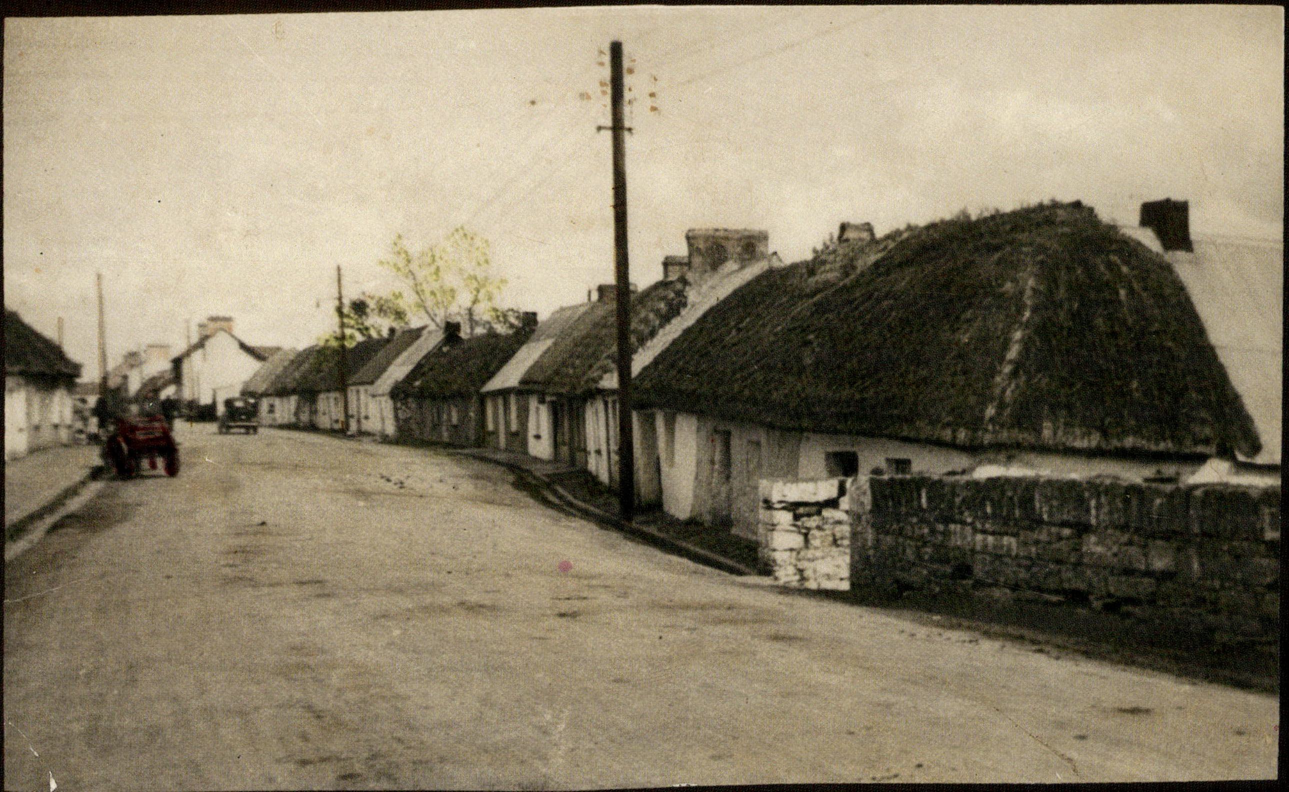

1 Market Street
Contrasting billheads: Note the different names of the street. When nationalistic fervour swept the town in the 1920s, the street names were changed without a plebiscite. Emmet Street in this billhead for T.J. Walsh is now called Market Street, while Pearse Street is today's Lower William Street.

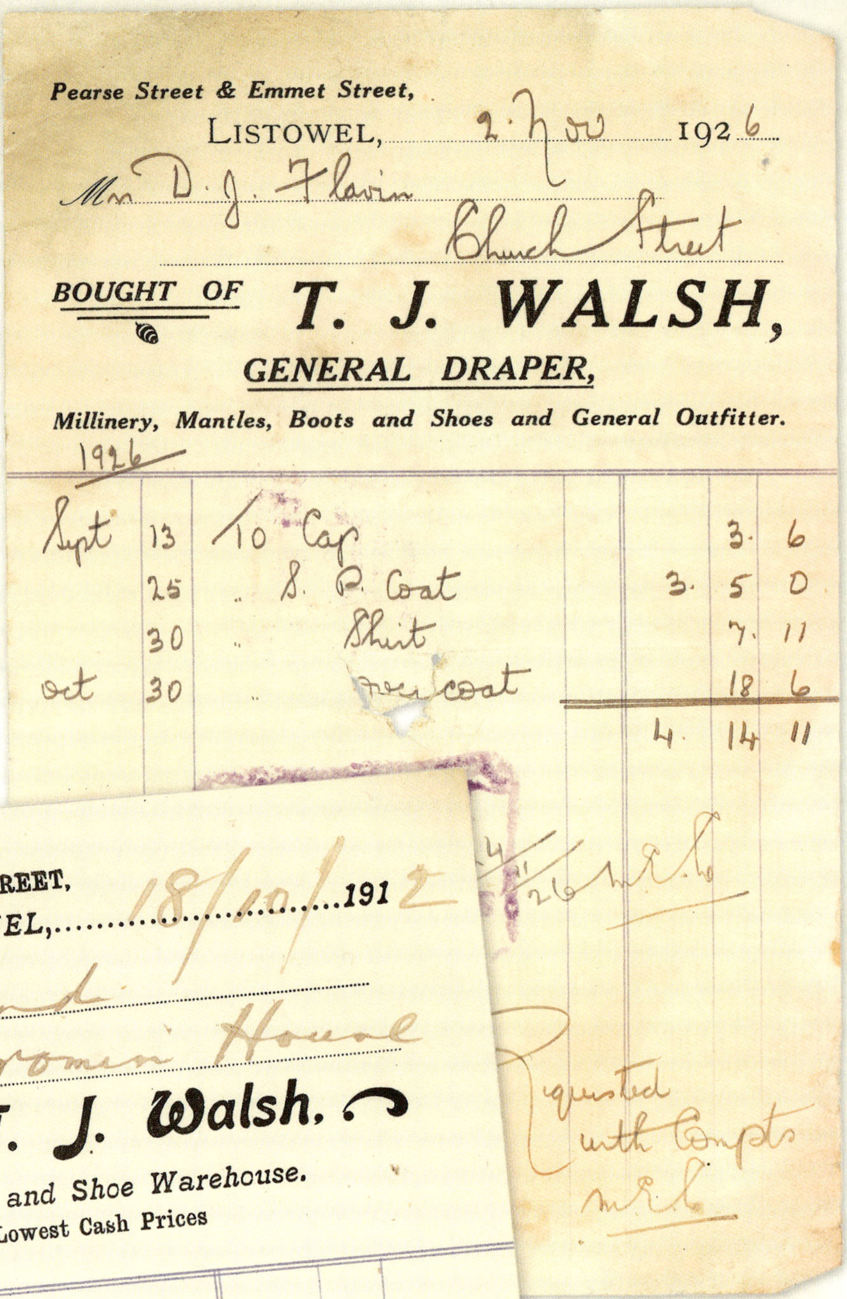
Pearse Street & Emmet Street,
LISTOWEL, 2 Nov 1926
Mr D. J. Flavin
Church Street
BOUGHT OF T. J. WALSH,
GENERAL DRAPER,
Millinery, Mantles, Boots and Shoes and General Outfitter.

1926

Sept	13	10 Cap		3	6
	25	S. P. Coat	3	5	0
	30	Shirt		7	11
Oct	30	Overcoat		18	6
			4	14	11

Requested with Compts M.E.C.

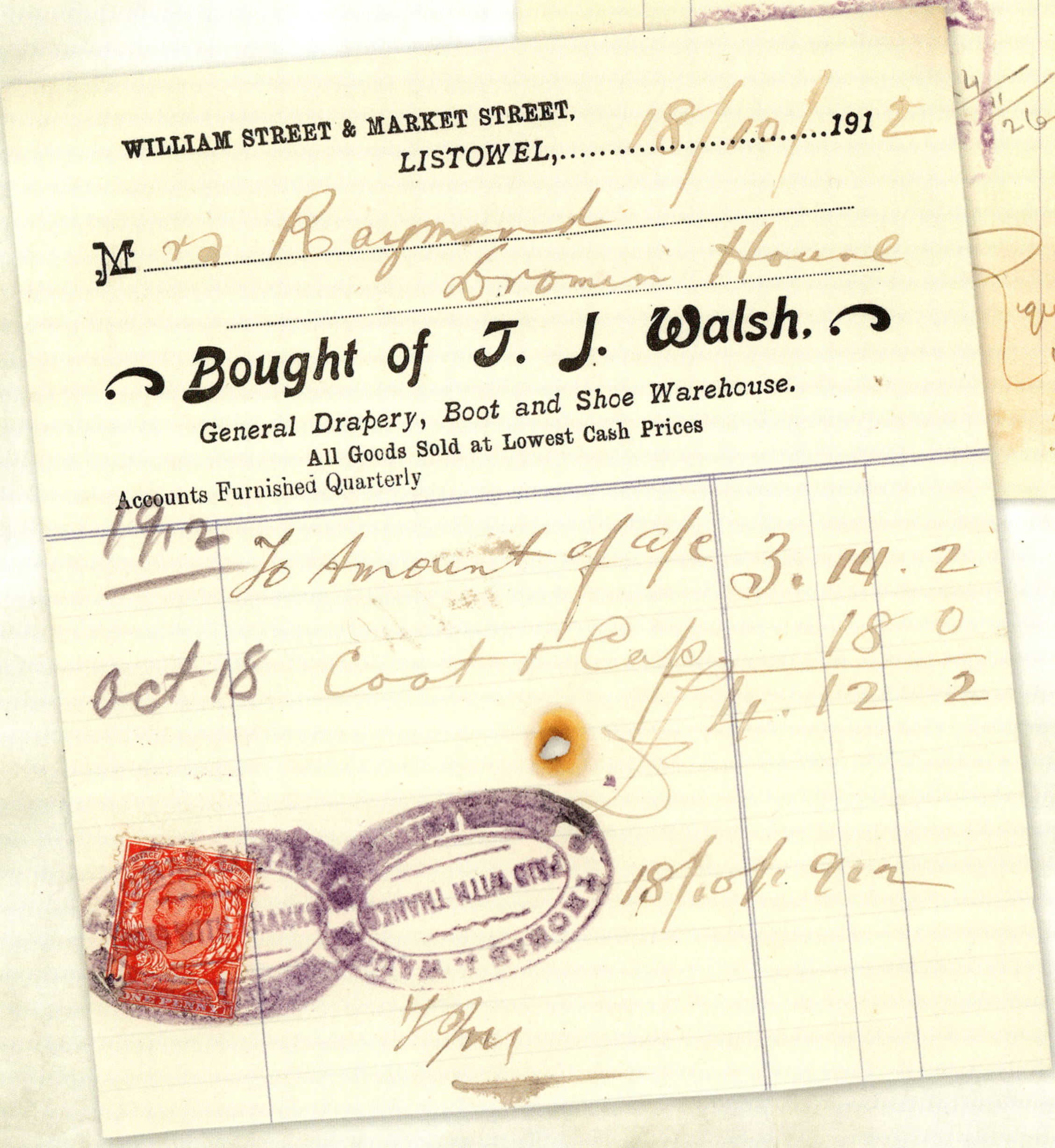
WILLIAM STREET & MARKET STREET,
LISTOWEL, 18/10/1912
Mrs Raymond
Bromin House
Bought of J. J. Walsh.
General Drapery, Boot and Shoe Warehouse.
All Goods Sold at Lowest Cash Prices
Accounts Furnished Quarterly

1912	To Amount of a/c	3. 14. 2
Oct 18	Coat & Cap	18 0
		£4. 12 2

PAID WITH THANKS THOMAS J. WALSH

18/10/1912

1 Market Street
John Stack (1845-1897), who traded at this address, was an Irish Nationalist politician. Stack was Member of Parliament for North Kerry from 1885 to 1892.

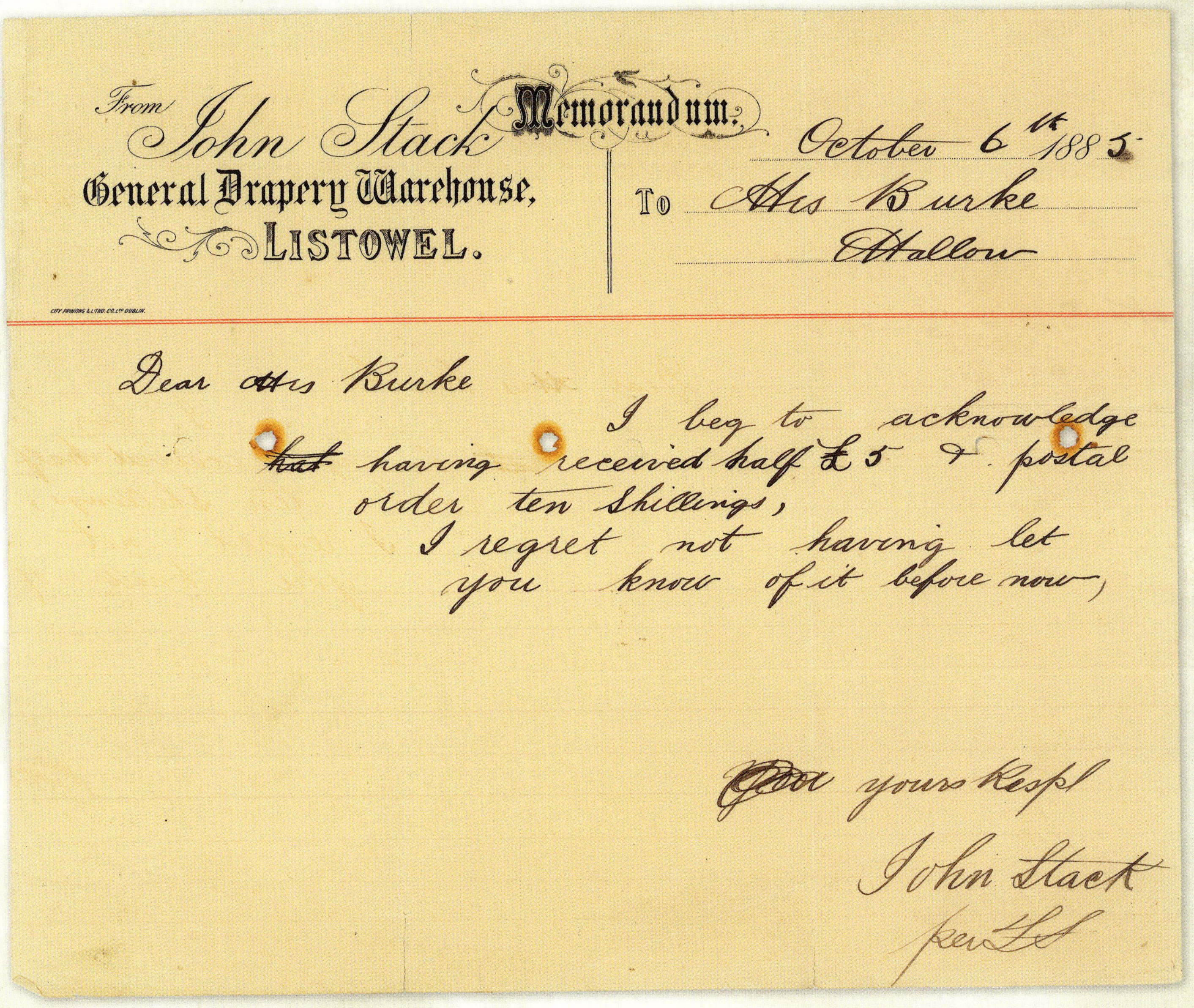

From John Stack
General Drapery Warehouse,
LISTOWEL.

Memorandum.

October 6th 1885

To Mrs Burke
Hallow

City Printing & Litho. Co. Ltd Dublin.

Dear Mrs Burke

I beg to acknowledge ~~hav~~ having received half £5 & postal order ten Shillings,

I regret not having let you know of it before now,

yours Respt
John Stack
per

5 Market Street

John McDonnell practised as a victualler, assisted by his wife Bridget, at his shop in Market Street. This shop was afterwards incorporated into McKenna's. McDonnell had a brother, Michael, who had a butcher's shop in Main Street / Church Street.

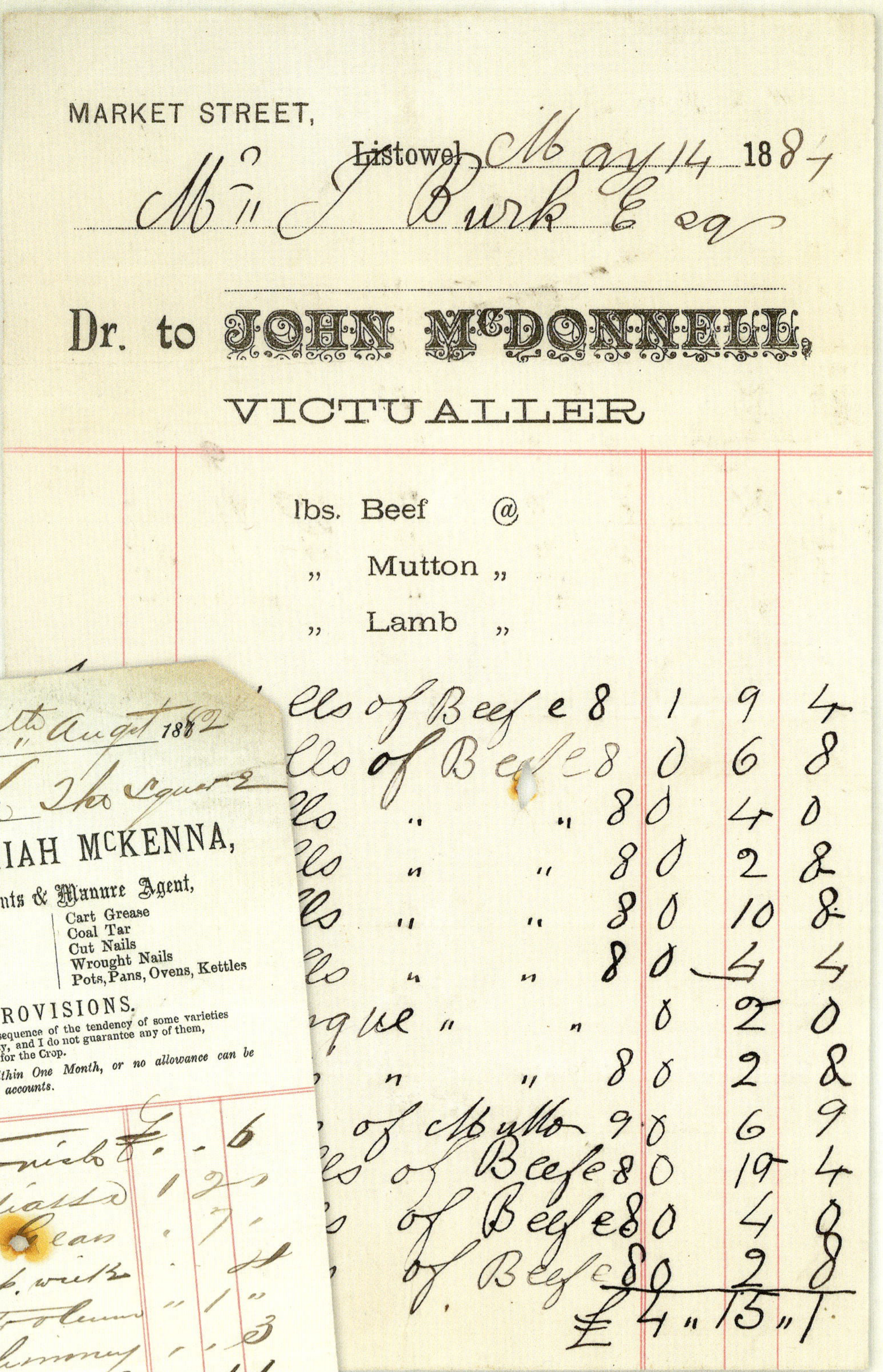
MARKET STREET,

Listowel May 14 1884

Mr J Burk Esq

Dr. to JOHN McDONNELL,

VICTUALLER

lbs. Beef @				
„ Mutton „				
„ Lamb „				
...lls of Beef e 8	1	9	4	
...lls of Beef e 8	0	6	8	
...lls „ „ 8	0	4	0	
...lls „ „ 8	0	2	8	
...lls „ „ 8	0	10	8	
...lls „ „ 8	0	4	4	
...ngue „ „	0	2	0	
... „ „ 8	0	2	8	
... of Mutton 9	0	6	9	
...lls of Beef e 8	0	19	4	
... of Beef e 8	0	4	0	
... of Beef e 8	0	2	8	
	£4	15	1	

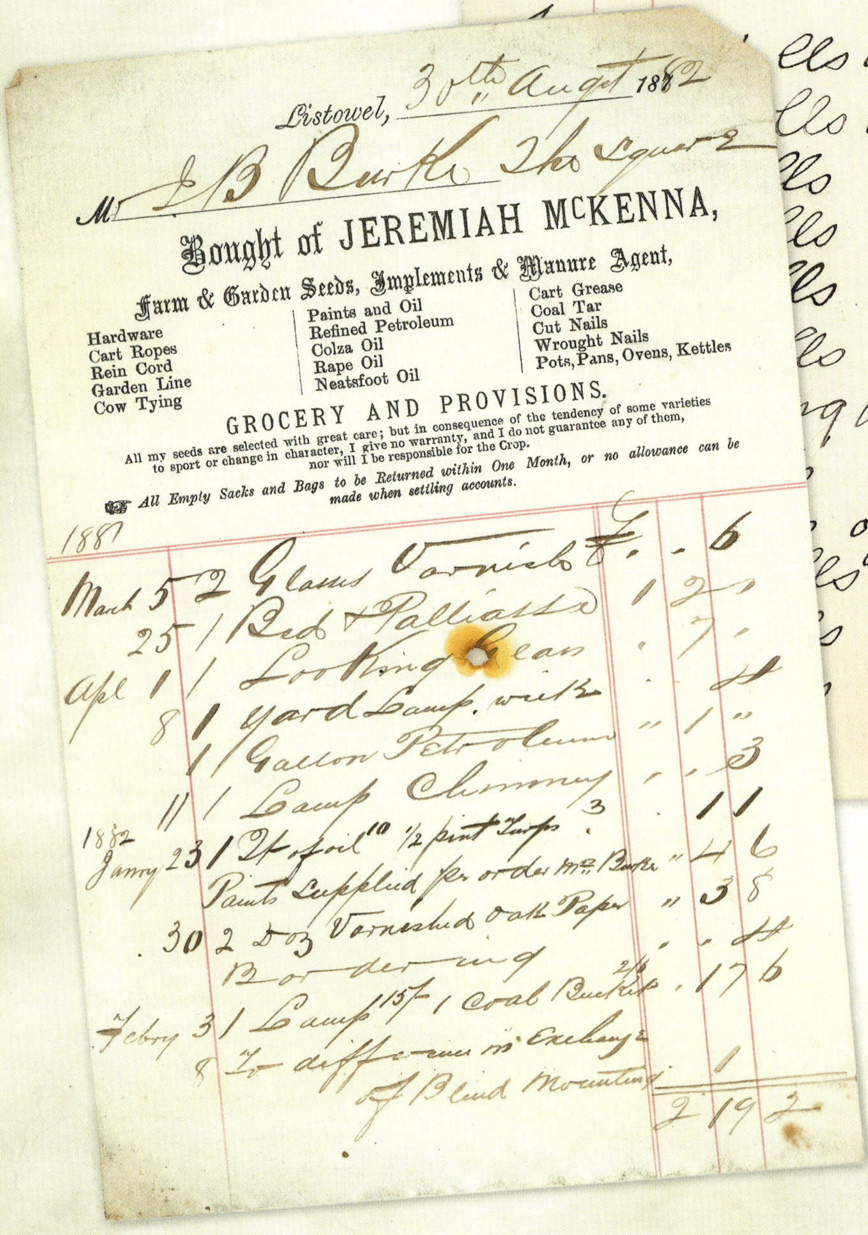
Listowel, 30th Augst 1882

Mr J B Burke Esq

Bought of JEREMIAH McKENNA,

Farm & Garden Seeds, Implements & Manure Agent,

Hardware, Cart Ropes, Rein Cord, Garden Line, Cow Tying | Paints and Oil, Refined Petroleum, Colza Oil, Rape Oil, Neatsfoot Oil | Cart Grease, Coal Tar, Cut Nails, Wrought Nails, Pots, Pans, Ovens, Kettles

GROCERY AND PROVISIONS.

All my seeds are selected with great care; but in consequence of the tendency of some varieties to sport or change in character, I give no warranty, and I do not guarantee any of them, nor will I be responsible for the Crop.

All Empty Sacks and Bags to be Returned within One Month, or no allowance can be made when settling accounts.

1881

		£	s	d
March 5	2 Glass Varnish			6
25	1 Bed & Palliass		12	
Apl 1	1 Looking Glass		7	
8	1 yard Lamp wick			4
	1 Gallon Petroleum		1	
	1 Lamp Chimney			3
11	1 Lamp Chimney		1	1
1882 Jany 23	1 Pt oil 10 ½ pint Turps 3		4	6
	Paints supplied per order Mrs Burke		3	8
30	2 Doz Varnished Oak Paper			4
	Bordering 2/6		17	6
Febry 3	1 Lamp 15/- 1 Coal Bucket			
8	To difference in Exchange of Blind Mounting		1	
		2	19	2

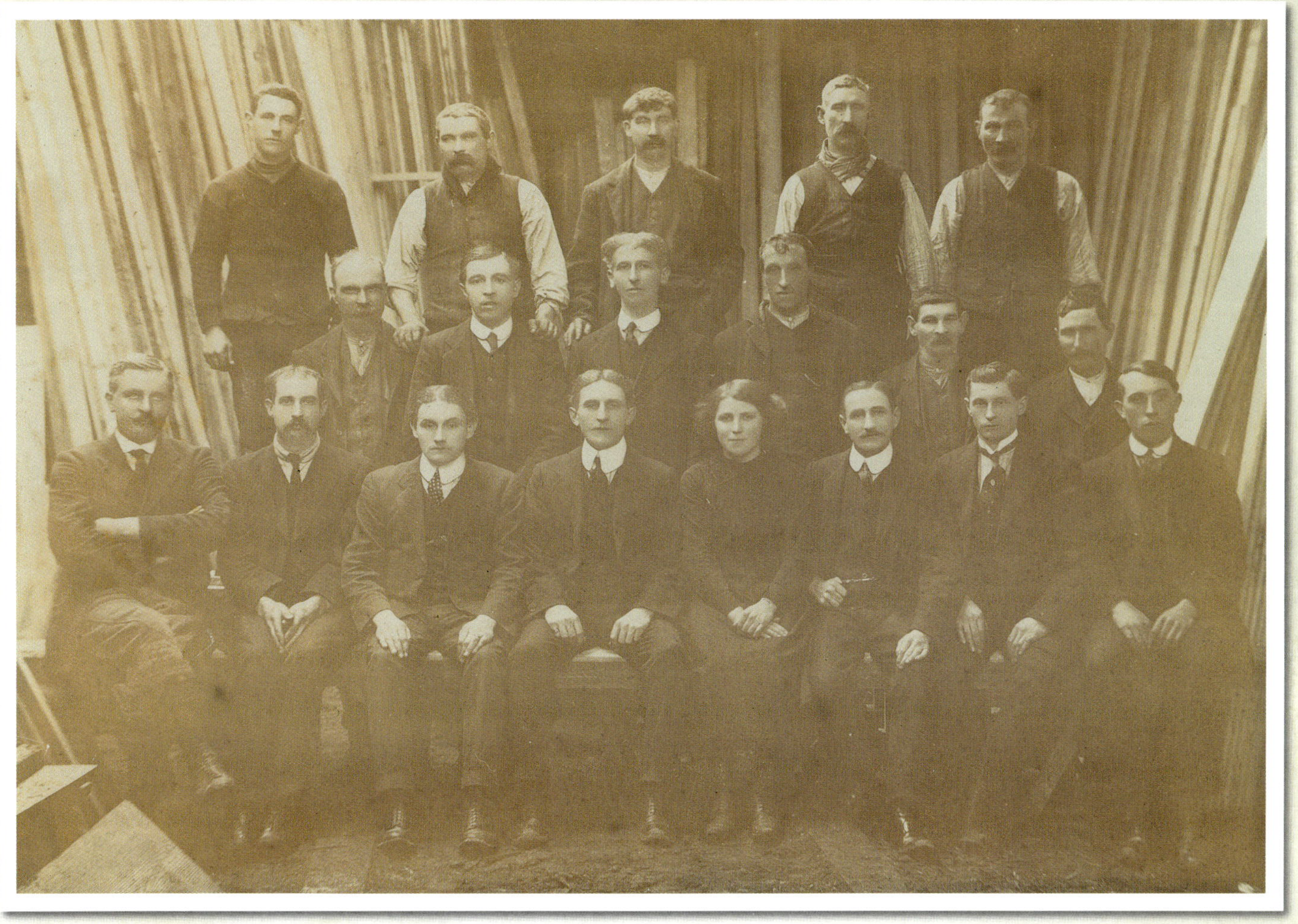

3 Market Street

Jeremiah McKenna and Johanna Horgan both worked at Ennismore House for George Hewson. They married on October 17, 1871. Shortly afterwards, they opened a shop in Market Street. Here they first sold vegetables and groceries. The vegetables were grown by the McKennas on their land on the Ballybunion Road. Jeremiah died in 1880 leaving his wife Johanna to run the business. Her son John, who was born in 1879, succeeded his mother. He extended the shop to incorporate McDonnell's next door, dispensed with the grocery and stocked a much larger range of hardware and farm implements. Further expansion, which nearly doubled the shop size, took place under the stewardship of John's son, John G. (Jack), with the acquisition of Walsh's corner drapery store next door. The mill department, bought in 1910 from J. P. Enright and located at the rear of Charles Street/William Street, was sold in the 1980s and moved to a greenfield site on the Ballybunion Road which was adjacent to Jeremiah McKenna's original vegetable garden.

The staff photo above from 1914/15 features Jeremiah McKenna, fourth from left in the front row. Also included are, front (l to r): Ml Horgan, Bob Hawley, (?) Keenan, J. McKenna, Nell Deenihan, Patk Hennessy, Pat Griffin, Jack Sullivan. Middle row (l to r): Mick Fitzgerald, Ml Lyons, William Horgan, Unknown, (?) Curtin, Unknown. Back row (l to r): Harry Reidy, Tom Carey, Ned Murphy, John Sullivan, Mick Connor. The photo was taken before Michael Horgan left to join the British Army during the early part of the First World War.

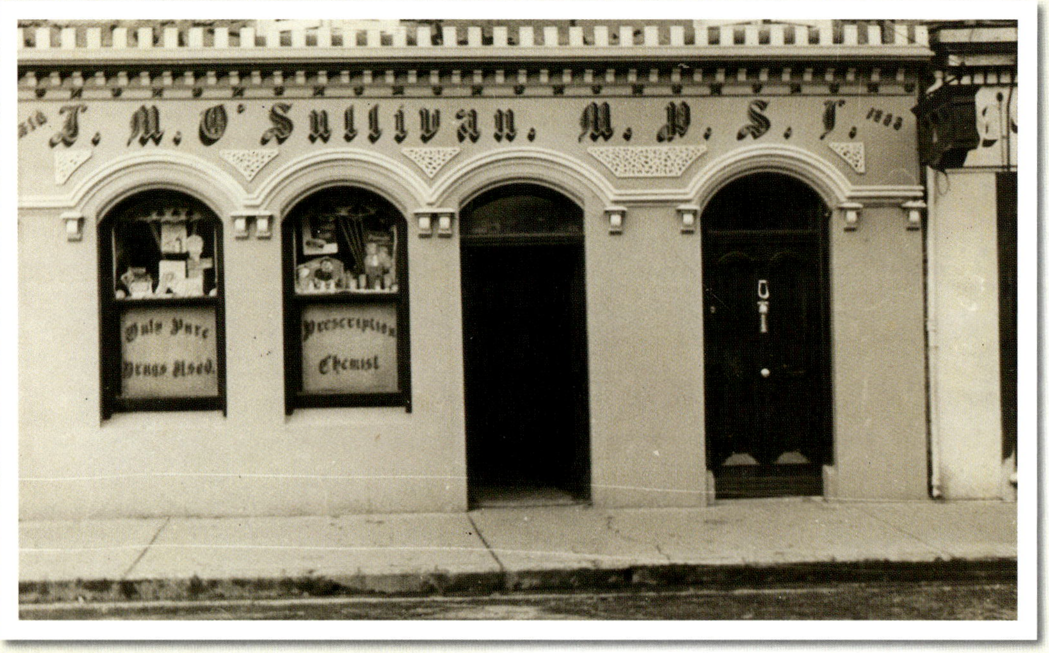

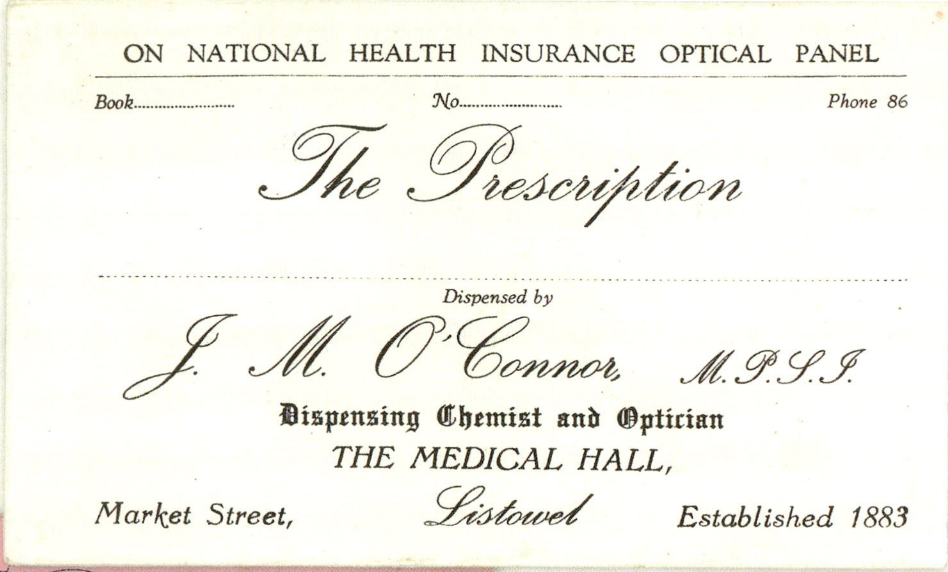
ON NATIONAL HEALTH INSURANCE OPTICAL PANEL

Book........................ No........................ Phone 86

The Prescription

Dispensed by

J. M. O'Connor, M.P.S.I.

Dispensing Chemist and Optician

THE MEDICAL HALL,

Market Street, *Listowel* Established 1883

7 Market Street

Gerard Leahy Stack married Sarah Ann Hilliard of Billerough in 1884. The previous year he had opened his pharmacy in the street. He was succeeded by John O'Sullivan from Athea, Co. Limerick and he in turn was followed by John O'Connor from Knockanure. The pharmacy is now owned by Jerry O'Connor.

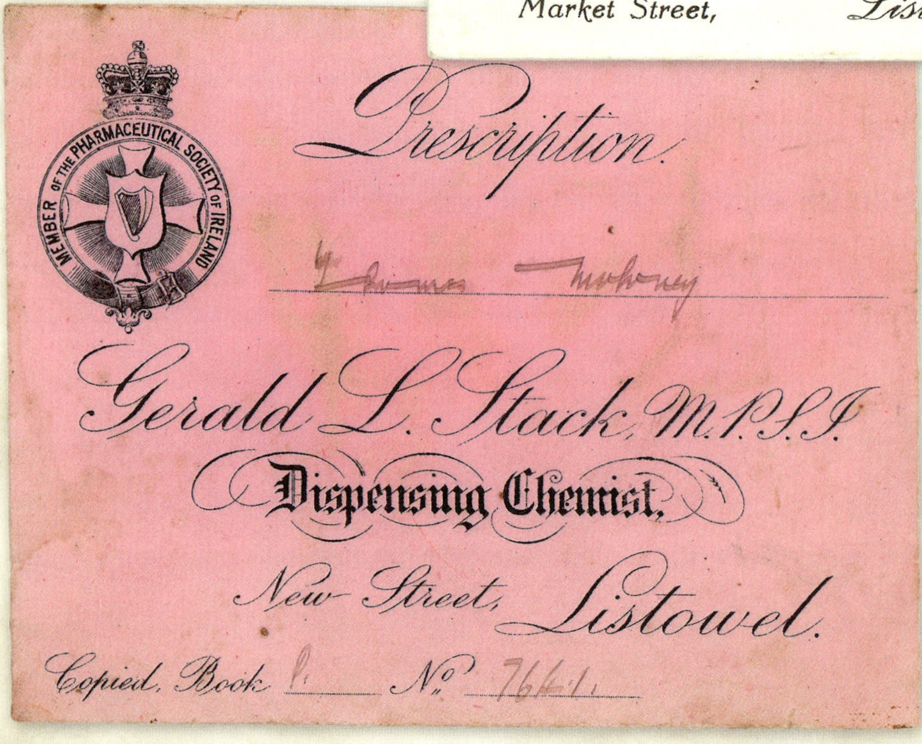
MEMBER OF THE PHARMACEUTICAL SOCIETY OF IRELAND

Prescription.

Gerald L. Stack, M.P.S.I.

Dispensing Chemist,

New Street, Listowel.

Copied, Book ______ *No.* ______

Gerard Stack's prescription envelope (left) is interesting. It bears the name 'New Street'. This name was only used for a short period, prior to it becoming 'Market Street'.

The photo above shows the highly decorative shop front with the two unusual small shop windows.

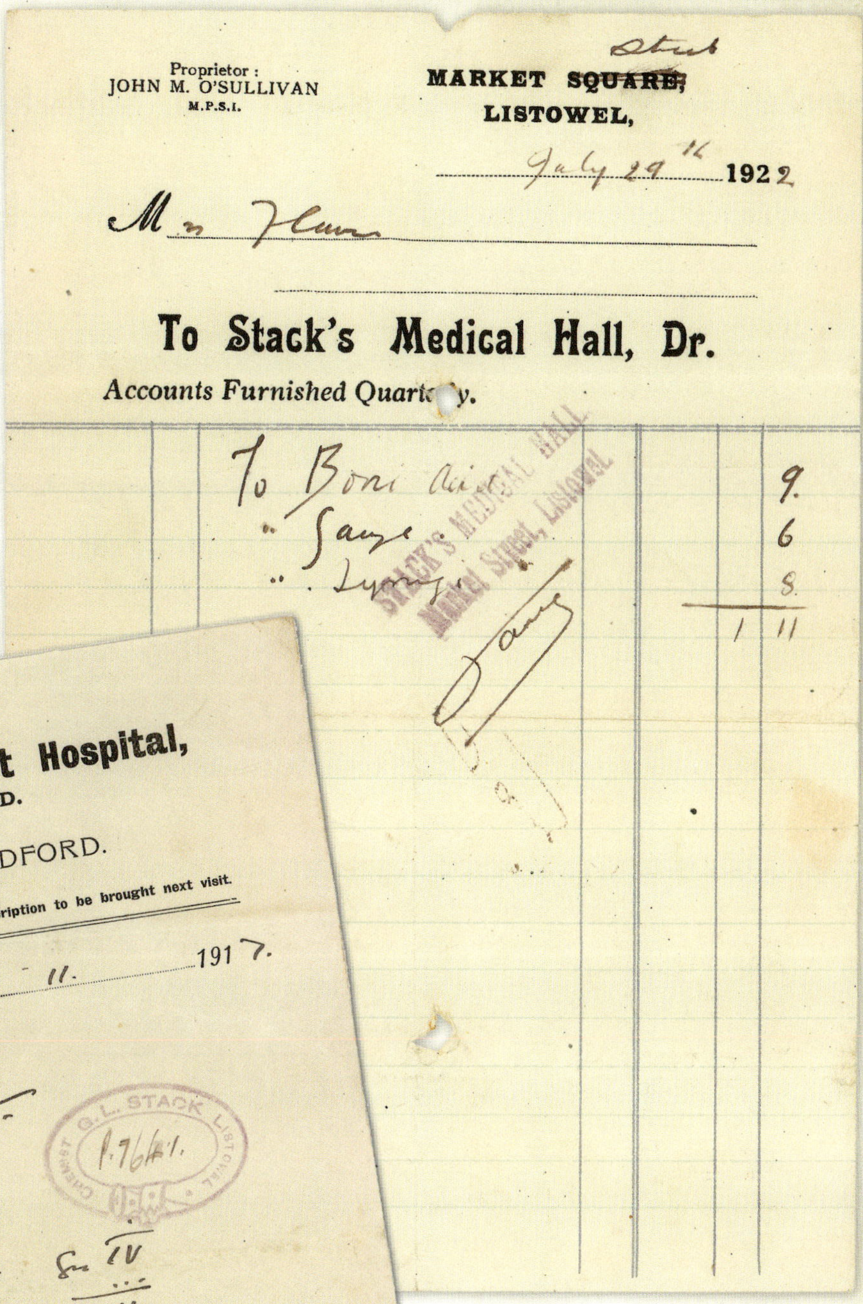
Proprietor:
JOHN M. O'SULLIVAN
M.P.S.I.

MARKET ~~SQUARE~~ Street
LISTOWEL,

July 29th 1922

To Stack's Medical Hall, Dr.

Accounts Furnished Quarterly.

To Boric Acid	9
" Gauze	6
" Syringe	8
	1 11

STACK'S MEDICAL HALL, Market Street, Listowel.

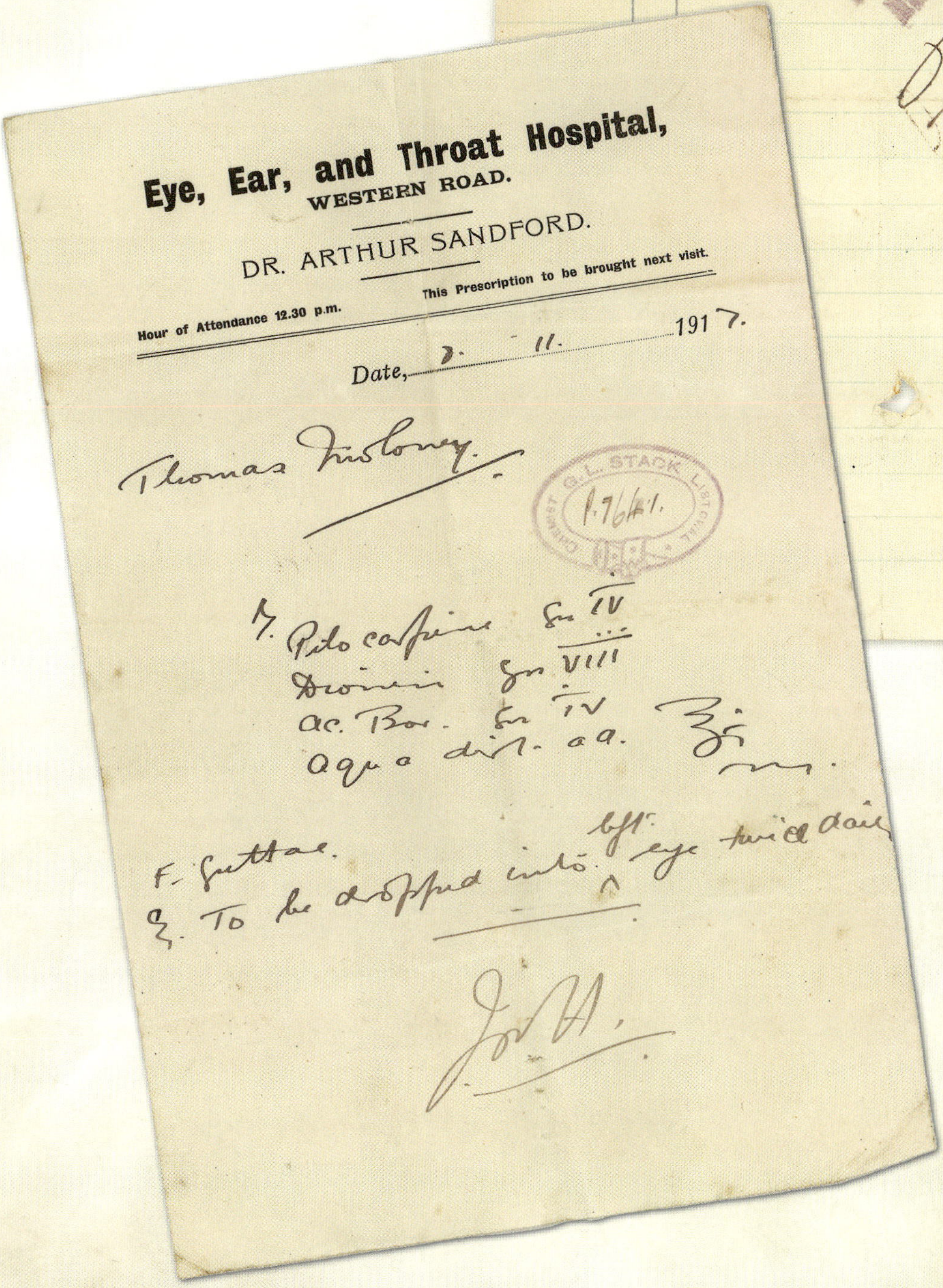
Eye, Ear, and Throat Hospital,
WESTERN ROAD.

DR. ARTHUR SANDFORD.

Hour of Attendance 12.30 p.m. This Prescription to be brought next visit.

Date, 3. 11. 1917.

Thomas Moloney.

CHEMIST G.L. STACK LISTOWEL

℞ Pilocarpine gr iv
Dionin gr viii
Ac. Bor. gr iv
Aqua dist. ad. ℥i

F. guttae.
S. To be dropped into left eye twice daily

11 Market Street
Timothy Kennelly came from Knockanure to open his general grocery and hardware shop in 11 Market Street. Following his death, the business passed to his nephew, John Murphy. In 1936, the business was bought by Jack O'Sullivan who relocated from 4 Market Street which was in turn bought by Michael Kennelly who then opened a travel agency there.

9 Market Street
Ned Moran was a successful business man with a drapery shop and shoe shop in Market Street, He left the shoe shop to his nephew John (Jack) Whelan from Irremore. This shop operates today under the management of Con Whelan, Jack Whelan's grandson.

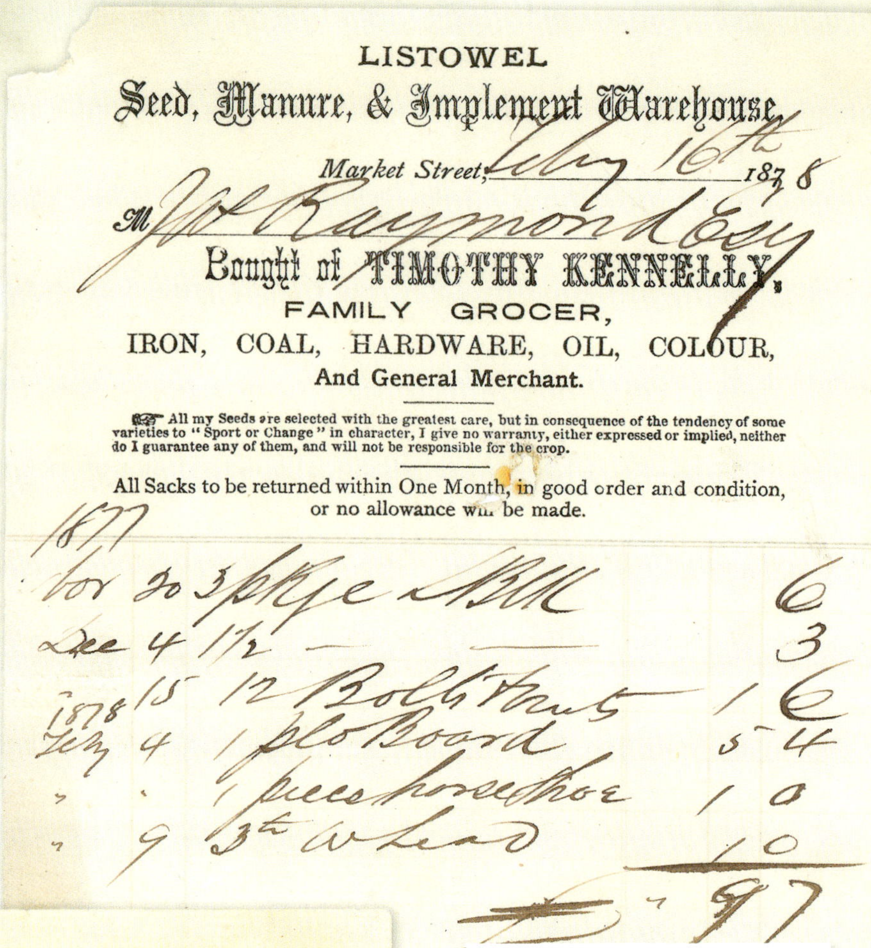
LISTOWEL
Seed, Manure, & Implement Warehouse,
Market Street, Feby 16th 1878
M Wm Raymond Esq
Bought of TIMOTHY KENNELLY,
FAMILY GROCER,
IRON, COAL, HARDWARE, OIL, COLOUR,
And General Merchant.

All my Seeds are selected with the greatest care, but in consequence of the tendency of some varieties to "Sport or Change" in character, I give no warranty, either expressed or implied, neither do I guarantee any of them, and will not be responsible for the crop.

All Sacks to be returned within One Month, in good order and condition, or no allowance will be made.

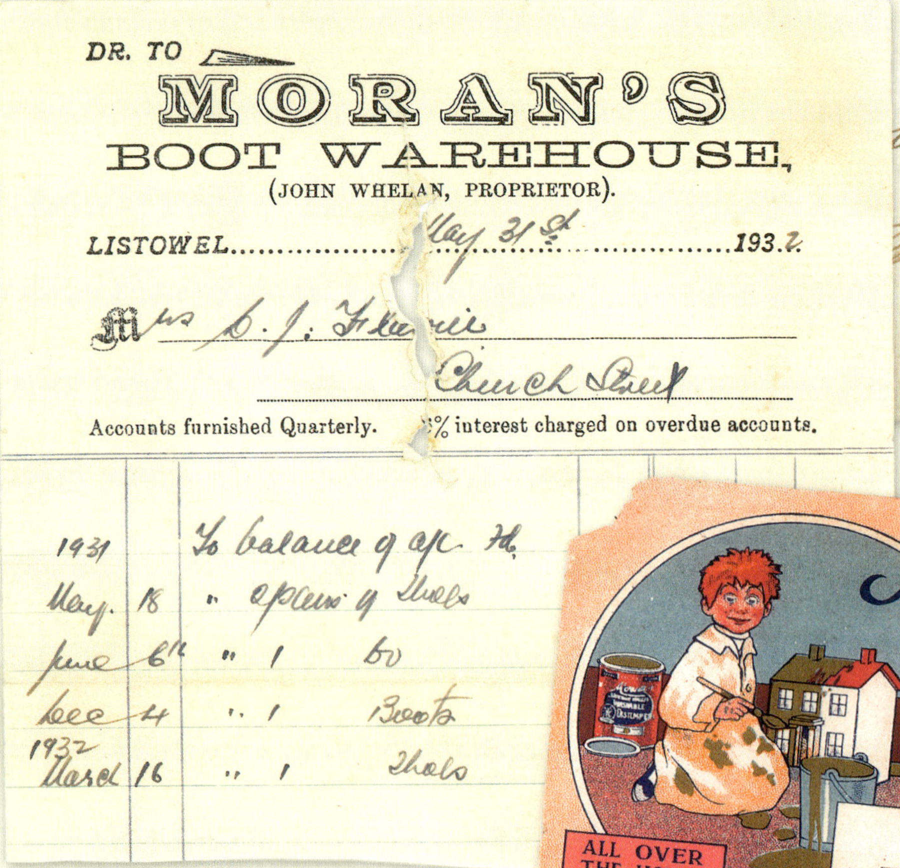
DR. TO
MORAN'S
BOOT WAREHOUSE,
(JOHN WHELAN, PROPRIETOR).
LISTOWEL........May 31st........193.2
Mrs C. J. Fitzmaurice
Church Street
Accounts furnished Quarterly. % interest charged on overdue accounts.

1931		To balance of a/c	
May.	18	" a pair of Shoes	
June	6th	" 1 do	
Dec	4	" 1 Boots	
1932 March	16	" 1 Shoes	

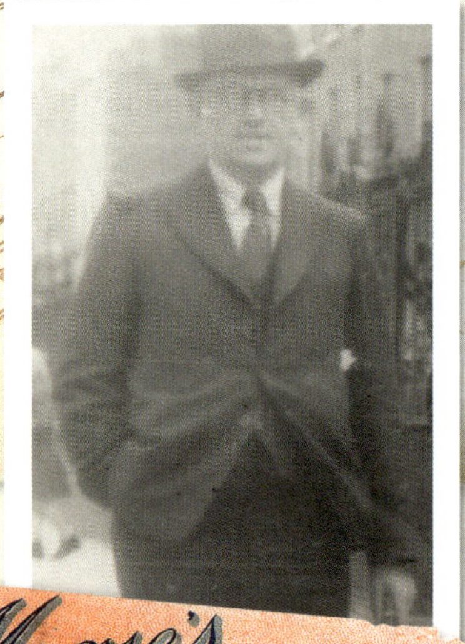

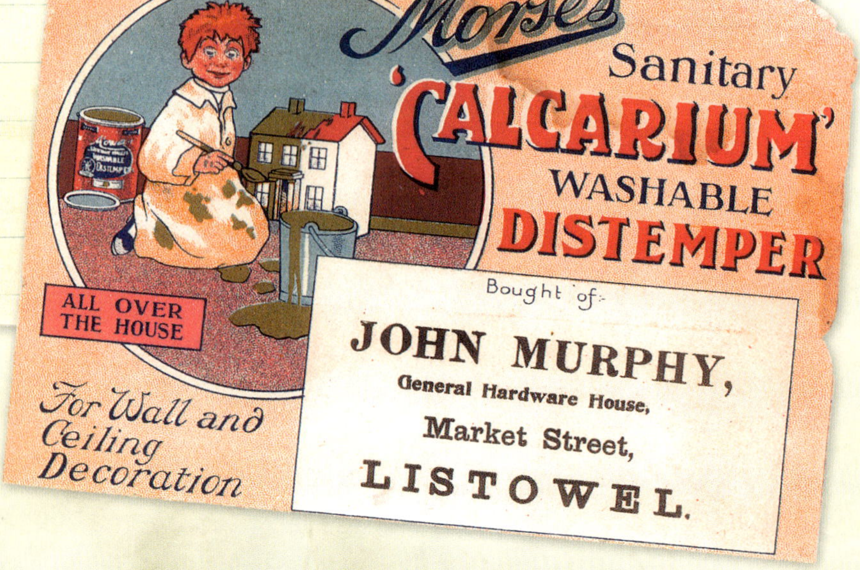

Photo right: Jack Whelan in Dublin in the 1940s.

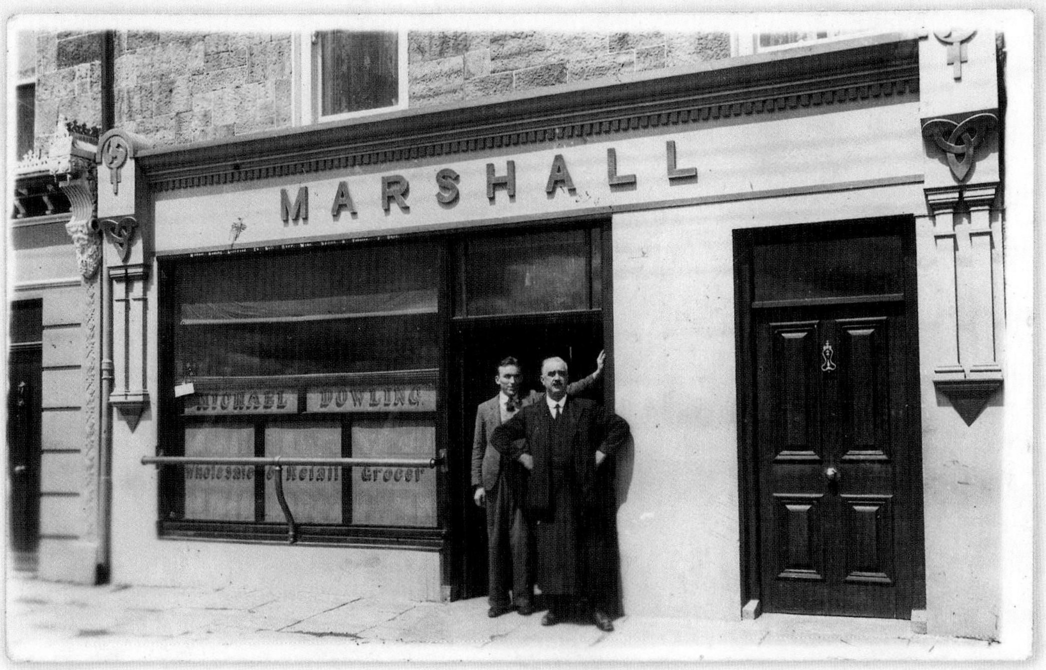

17 Market Street

Thomas Marshall married Johanna Corridan in 1868. They commenced trading in Market Street in 1870. Their house was one of 12 cut-stone houses built by Denis McMahon and his son William in the mid 1850s. These were built to enable business people to avail of the new potential in the street with the coming of the market place in 1854. Henry Joseph Marshall, a son of the Marshalls, became a solicitor. In later years he was the senior partner in the firm Marshall & Macauley in the Square.

Michael Dowling from Tralee purchased the business in the late 1890s.

Advertising was not lost on people in those days. Marshall even had his shop details on tea bags as seen below.

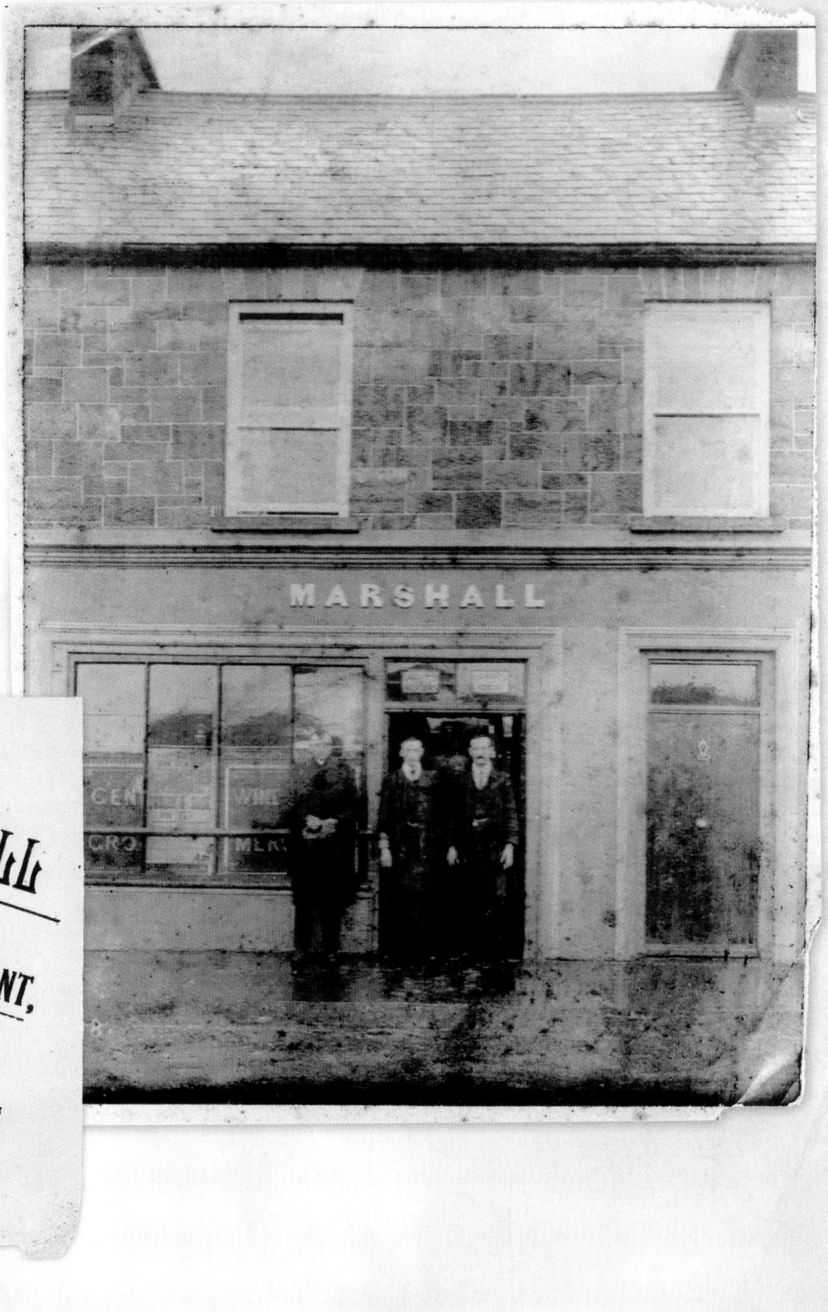

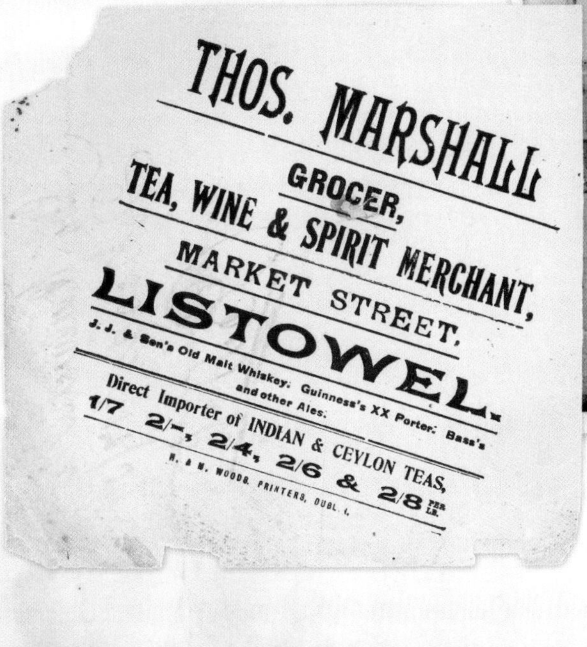

J.M. Thomas advertised his jewellery business with the most decorative billheads. He also traded in cartridges and fishing tackle. Mr. Raymond must have been a keen sportsman.

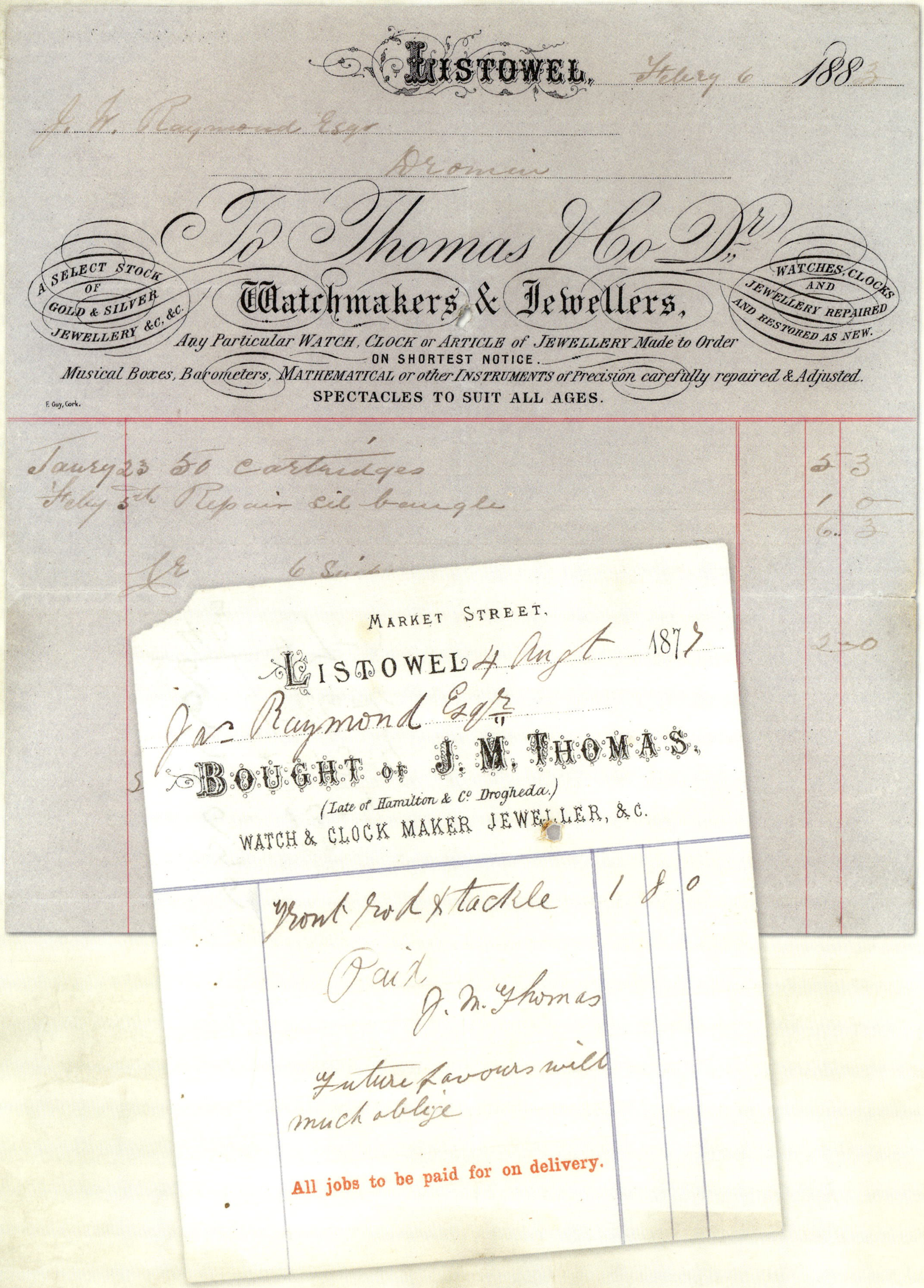

LISTOWEL, Febry 6 1883

J. W. Raymond Esqr

Dromin

To Thomas & Co Dr

A SELECT STOCK OF GOLD & SILVER JEWELLERY &C. &C.

Watchmakers & Jewellers,

WATCHES, CLOCKS AND JEWELLERY REPAIRED AND RESTORED AS NEW.

Any Particular WATCH, CLOCK or ARTICLE of JEWELLERY Made to Order
ON SHORTEST NOTICE.

Musical Boxes, Barometers, MATHEMATICAL or other INSTRUMENTS of Precision carefully repaired & Adjusted.

SPECTACLES TO SUIT ALL AGES.

F. Guy, Cork.

Janry 23 50 cartridges	5	3
Febry 5th Repair sil bangle	1	0
	6	3
Cr 6 Sui…	2	0

MARKET STREET,

LISTOWEL 4 Augt 1877

Jas Raymond Esqr

BOUGHT of J. M. THOMAS,

(Late of Hamilton & Co Drogheda.)

WATCH & CLOCK MAKER JEWELLER, &C.

Trout rod & tackle	1	8	0

Paid
J. M. Thomas

Future favours will
much oblige

All jobs to be paid for on delivery.

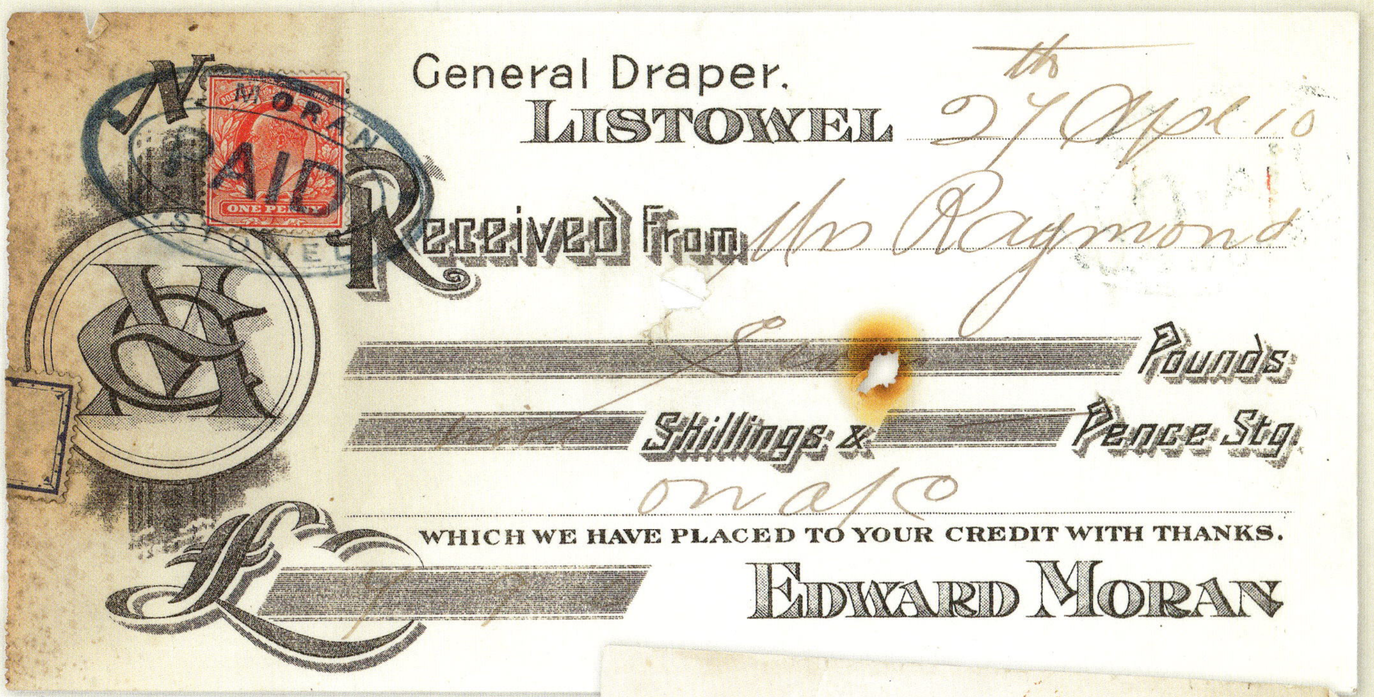
General Draper.
LISTOWEL 27th Apl 10
Received From Mr Raymond
Pounds
Shillings & Pence Stg.
on a/c
WHICH WE HAVE PLACED TO YOUR CREDIT WITH THANKS.
EDWARD MORAN

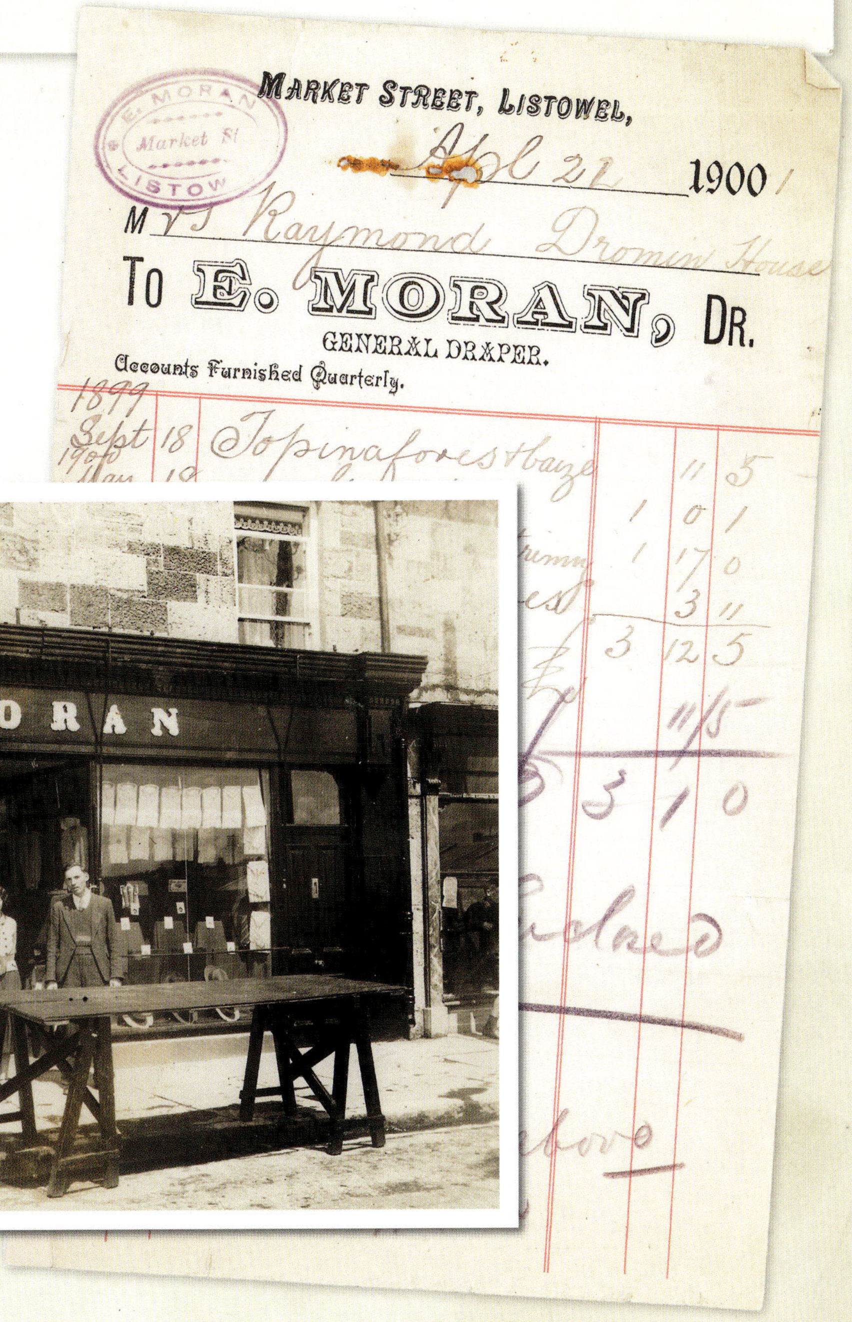
MARKET STREET, LISTOWEL, Apl 21 1900
Mr Raymond Dromin House
To E. MORAN, DR.
GENERAL DRAPER.
Accounts Furnished Quarterly.

23 Market Street
Moran's shop, pictured in the 1940s. It was owned and run at this time by Edward Leahy, a nephew of Ned Moran. The billhead is from year 1899/1900 and the receipt from 1910.

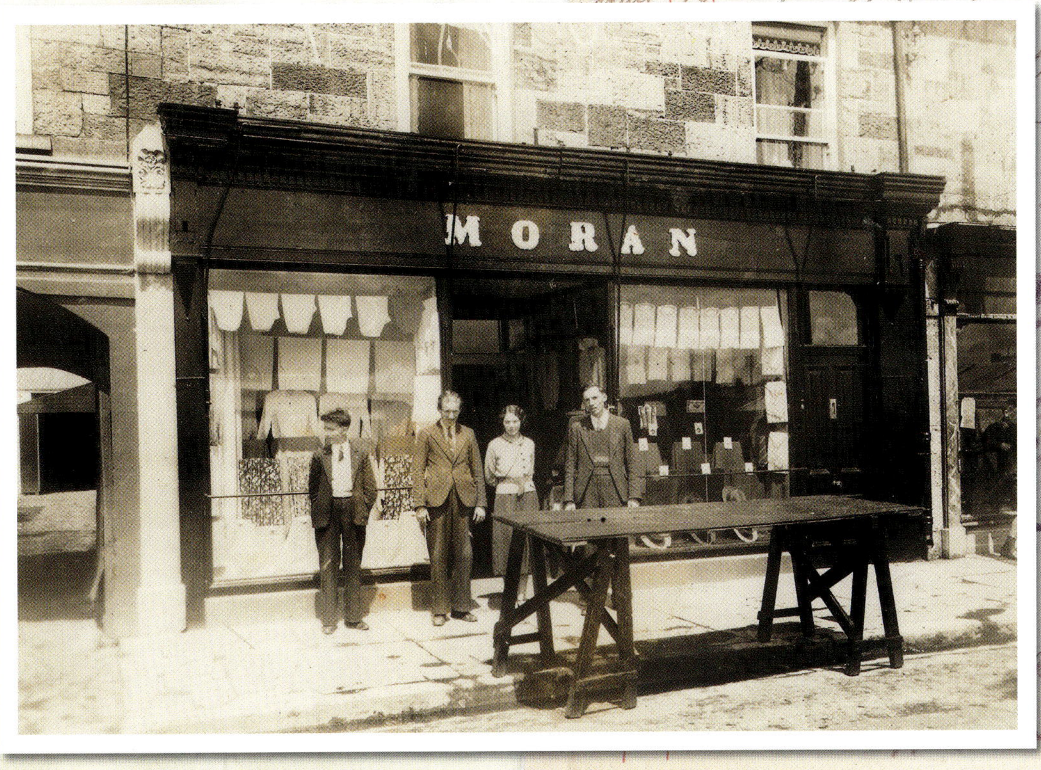

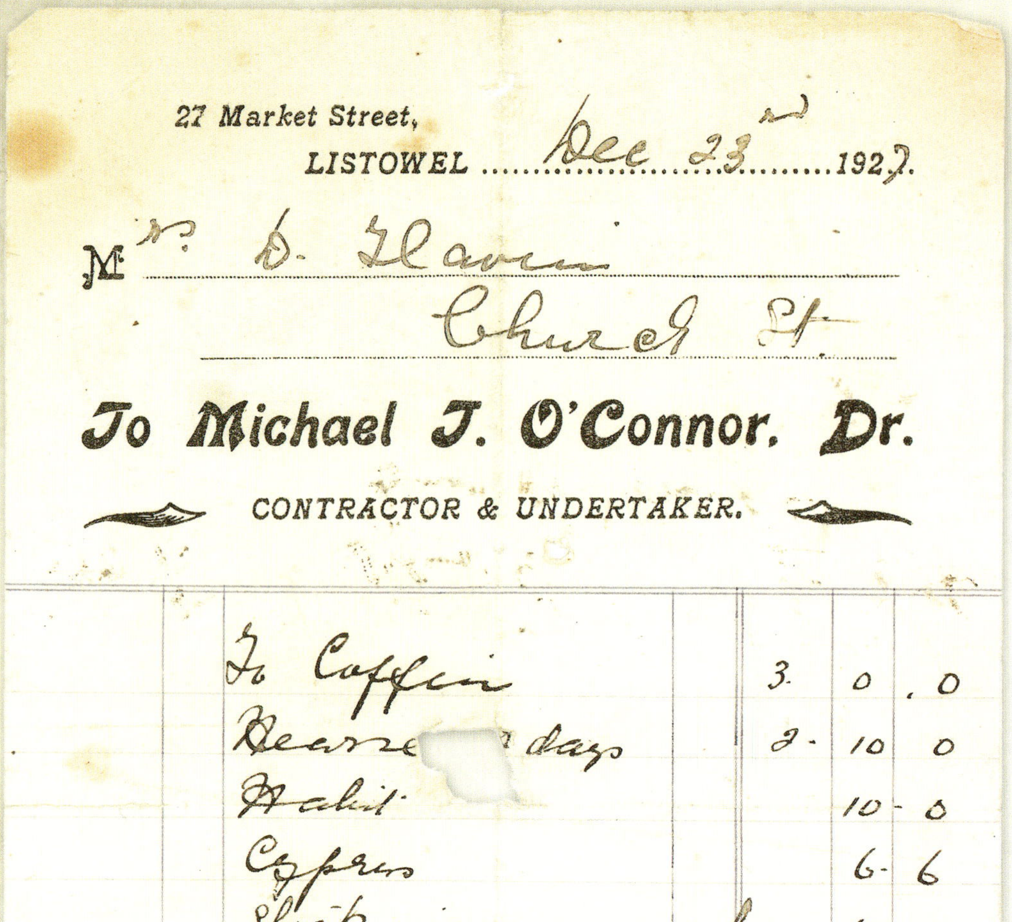

27 Market Street,
LISTOWEL ....Dec 23rd....1927.

Mrs D. Havern
Church St

To Michael J. O'Connor. Dr.

CONTRACTOR & UNDERTAKER.

To Coffin	3. 0. 0
Hearse .. days	2. 10 0
Habit	10 - 0
Crepes	6 - 6
Stockings	1 - 0
	£6 . 7 . 6

Jan 1/12 Paid

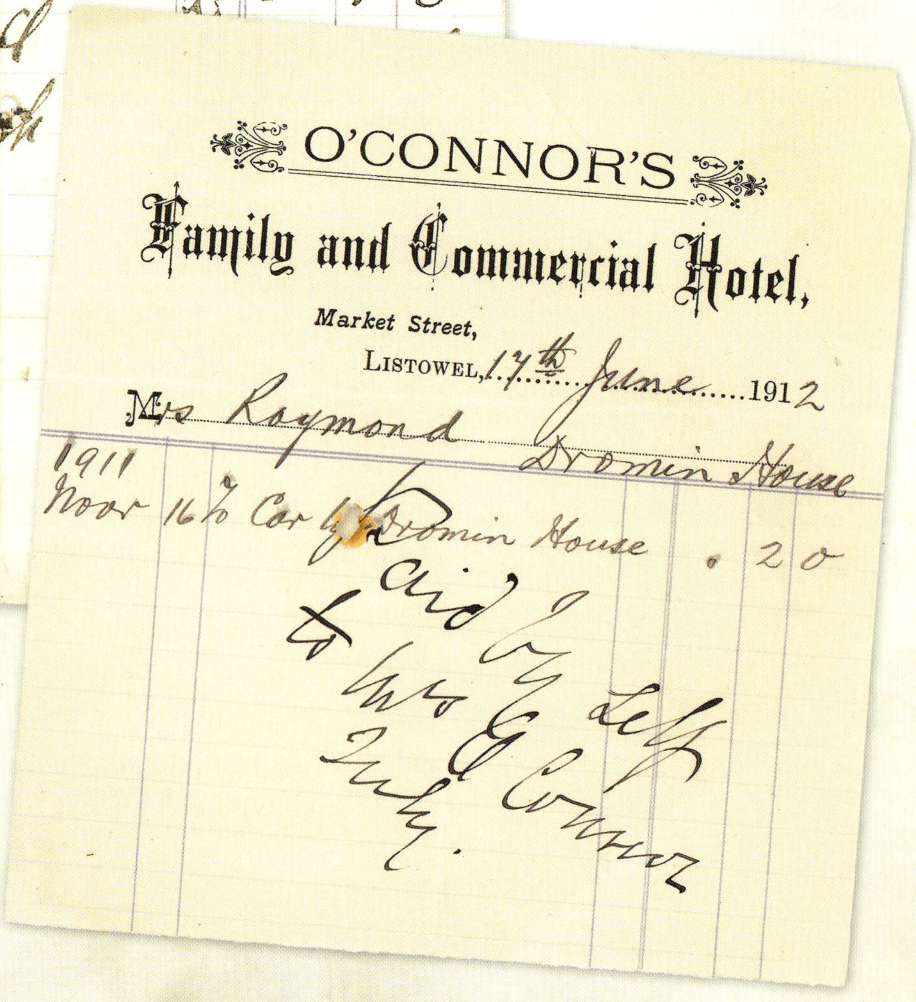

O'CONNOR'S
Family and Commercial Hotel,
Market Street,
LISTOWEL, 17th June 1912

Mrs Raymond Dromin House

1911 Nov 16	To Car to Dromin House	. 2 0

Paid by ... Self ... J. O'Connor

25 Market Street
Michael O'Connor ran the hotel, 'Family and Commercial Hotel', at his home in Market Street. He also was a contractor and undertaker. Richard Pierse M.R.C.V.S. bought the house in the late 1930s and from there he ran a very successful veterinary practice which was continued by his son Thomas until his retirement. The house is now part of the building which houses the Pierse & Fitzgibbon legal practice.

25 Market Street
The Tackaberrys commenced trading in the 1850s. They were located in the house later occupied by O'Connor's Hotel. The photograph of the Tackaberry Family was taken in the back yard of the house pre 1900. Pictured at back are Bob, and Jack and front from left are Con, Mary and May.

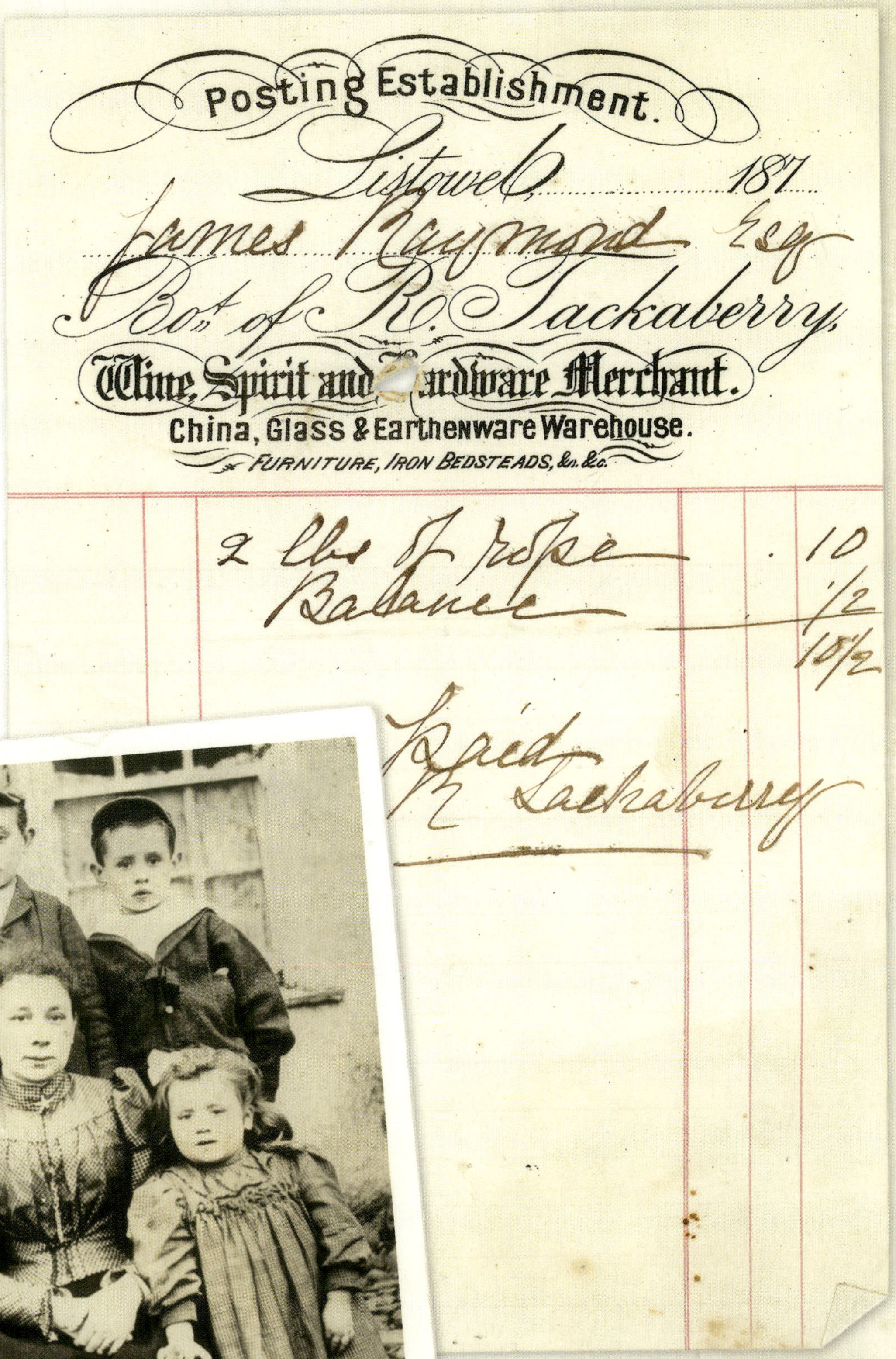
Posting Establishment.
Listowel 187
James Raymond Esq
Bot. of R. Tackaberry.
Wine, Spirit and [illegible]ardware Merchant.
China, Glass & Earthenware Warehouse.
FURNITURE, IRON BEDSTEADS, &c. &c.

2 lbs of rope	. 10
Balance	1/2
	10/2

Paid
R. Tackaberry

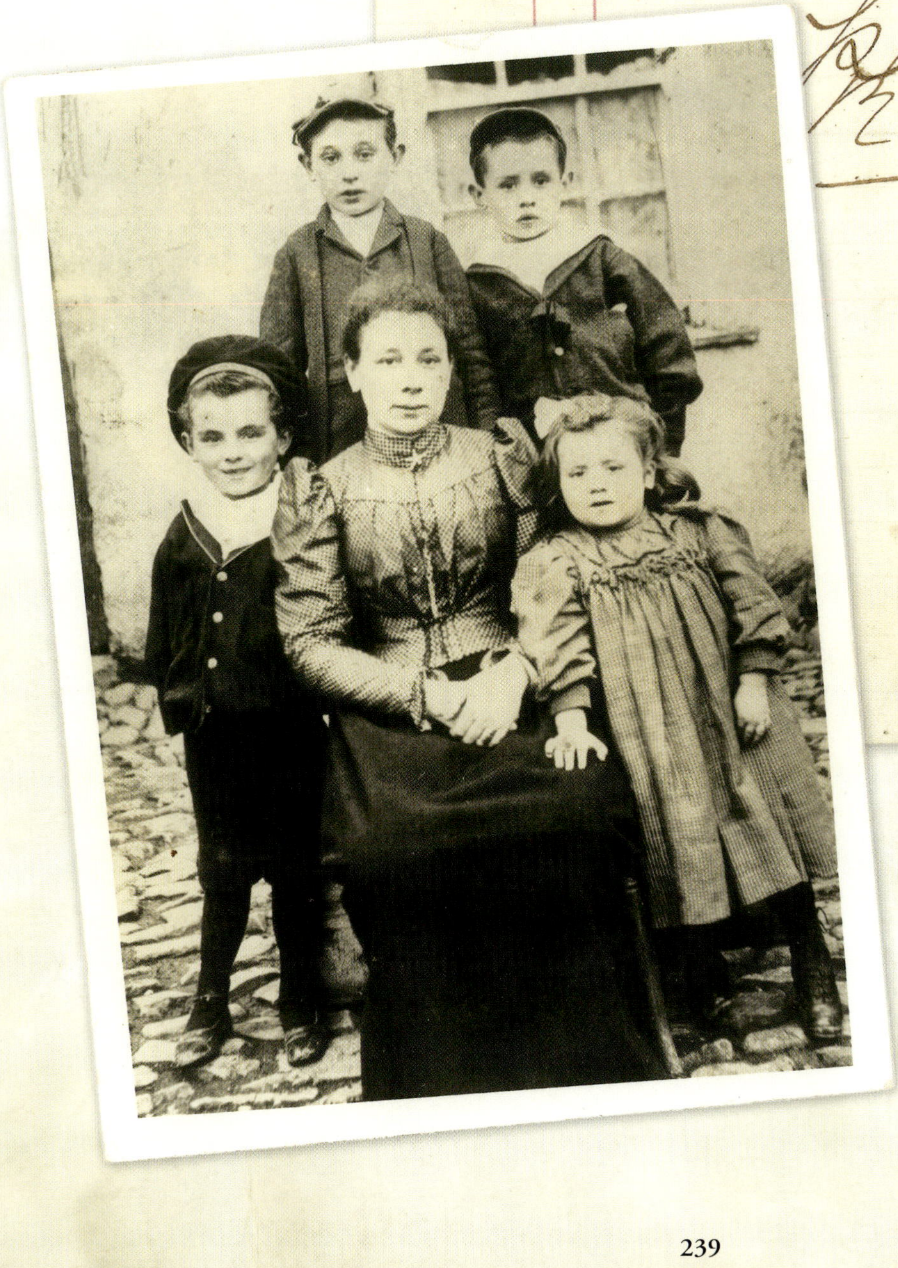

NORTH KERRY FARMERS
ASSOCIATION.

LISTOWEL, December 30th 1911

Dear Sir,

A Meeting of the above will be held on Wednesday, next, in the Technical Class Rooms, Market Street, at One o'Clock.

Kindly attend.

Yours faithfully,

R. WOULFE, } Hon.
J. SCULLY, } Secs.

35 Market Street (rear)
This building housed the first Technical School prior to its relocation to Church Street. The classrooms were used by many organisations for meetings including the local boy scouts.

Photo: A school group from 1931.

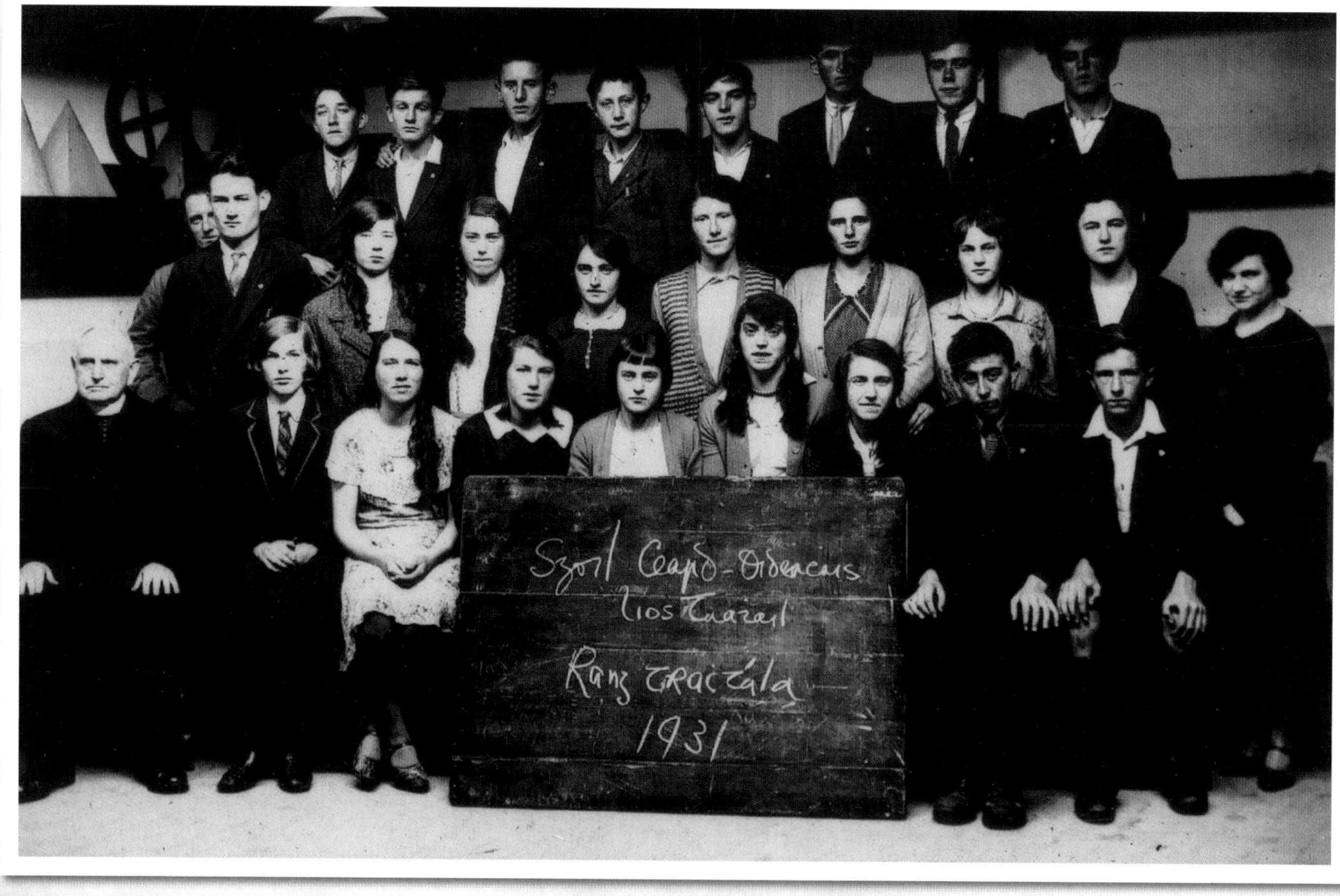

16 Market Street
When Edward O'Sullivan married Hannah Barrett (pictured below), he left his rented house in Upper William Street to continue his tailoring business in his new house in Market Street. The temporary change of Market Street to Emmet Street occurred in the 1920s, and Edward proudly called his location, Emmet Place.

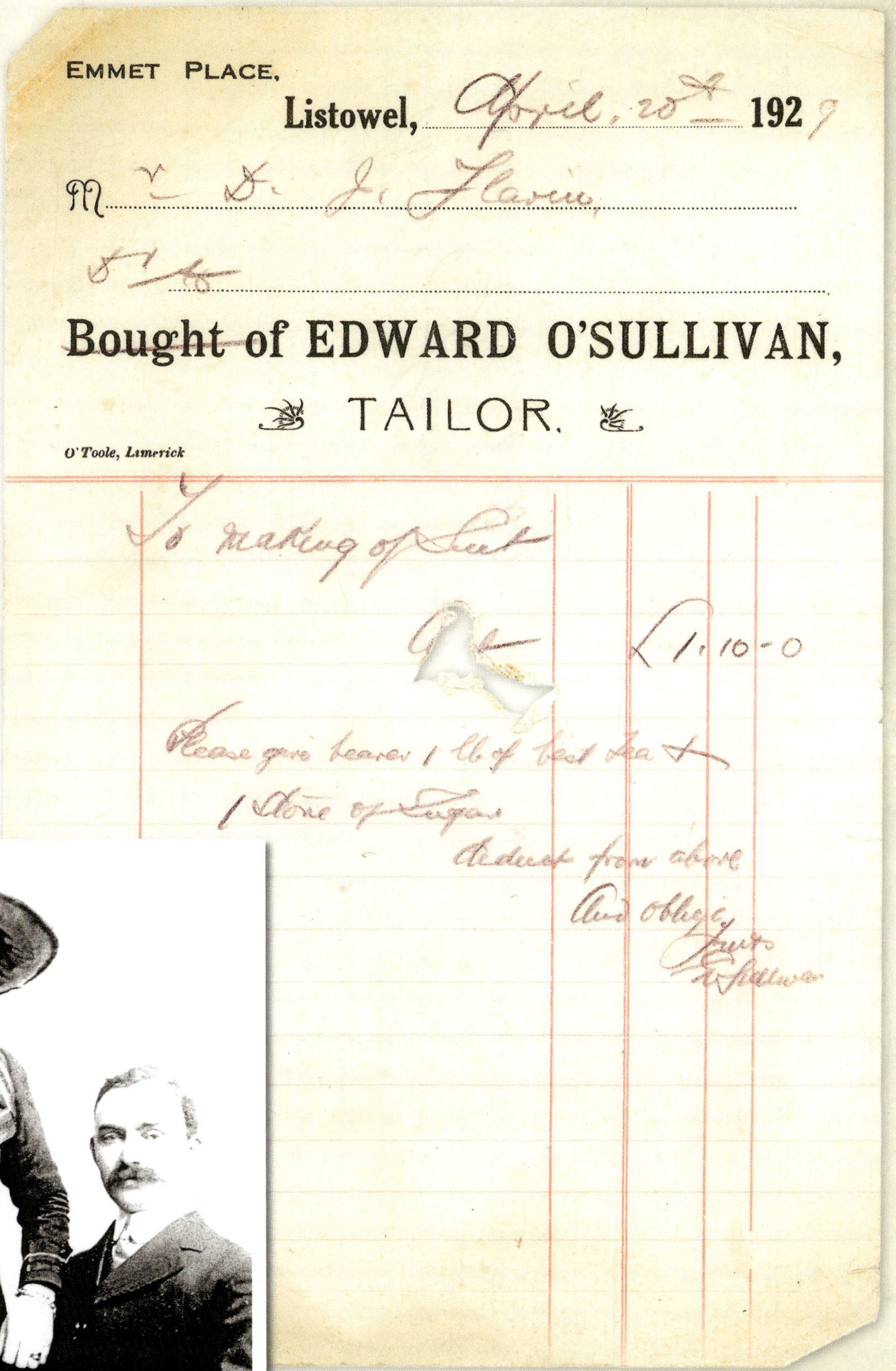

EMMET PLACE,
Listowel, April 20th 1929
Mr D. J. Flavin,

Bought of EDWARD O'SULLIVAN,
TAILOR.

O'Toole, Limerick

To making of Suit

£1.10-0

Please give bearer 1 lb of best tea &
1 stone of sugar
deduct from above
And oblige
Yours
E. O'Sullivan

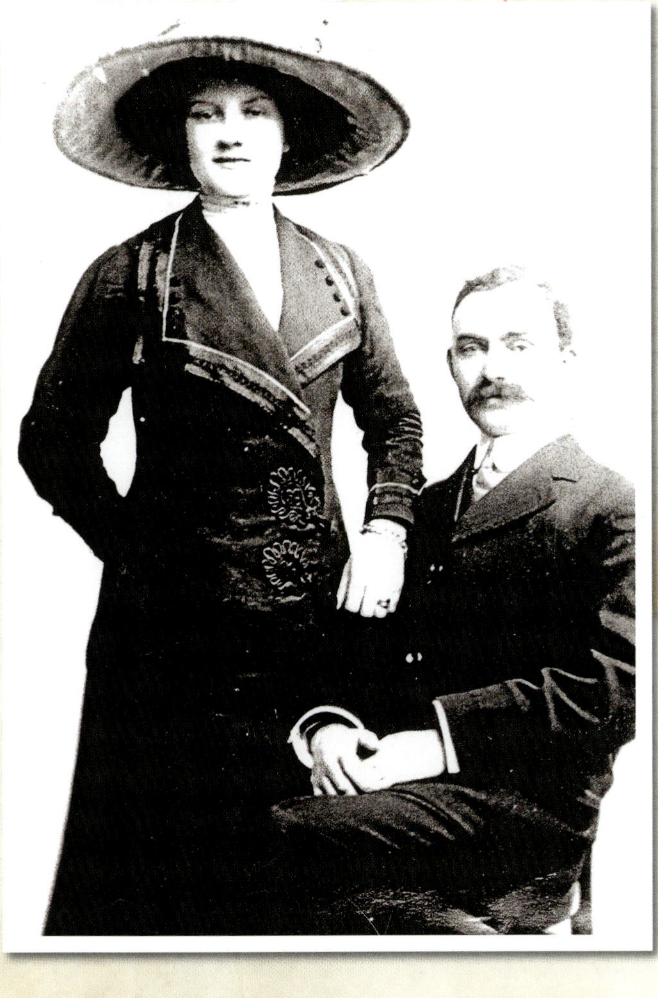

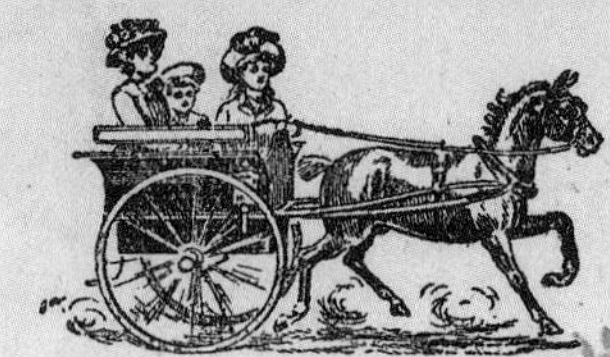

NEW STREET, ~~Killarney~~ ...May 25th... 192 3
(and Market St., Listowel)

M. M. Hill Esq
Estate Offices
Listowel

Bought of P. TARRANT,
HARNESSMAKER.

Cart and Gig Harness of every description at shortest notice, Car Cushions Saddles, Bridles. Coachbuilding in all its branches. Painting, Rubber Tyres put on. Second-hand Cars and Harness always in stock,

Killarney Printing Works.

Sir,
While we are negotiating about the plot in the market you'd do me a great favour by giving me permission to use about 10 ft of ground outside my shed for the purpose of putting down a concrete flag for shoeing wheels. I wouldnt require it longer than three months. Hoping you can see your way to grant me this privelege. Your ffully

P. Tarrant

Patrick Tarrant came from New Street, Killarney. In the 1920s he started his first business, a trap and coach-making establishment in Market Street. Subsequently, he got an extra site in the back market yard which he operated as a harness-making store. This is now closed. However, his grandson, Diarmuid, runs a garage on the original site in Market Street.

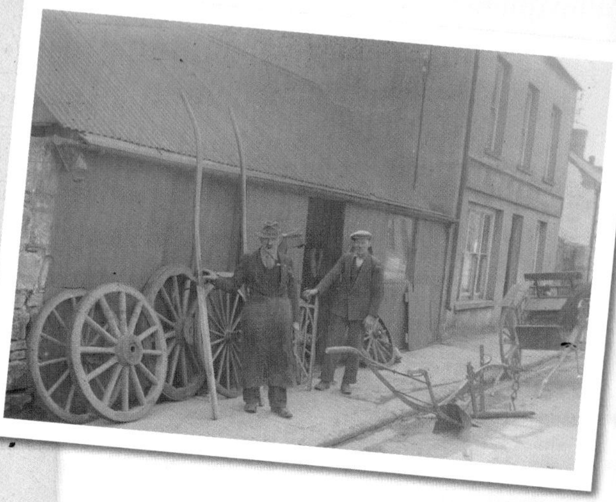

Two early photographs of the Tarrant workshop in Market Street. The house shown above was the tailoring shop of Edward O'Sullivan

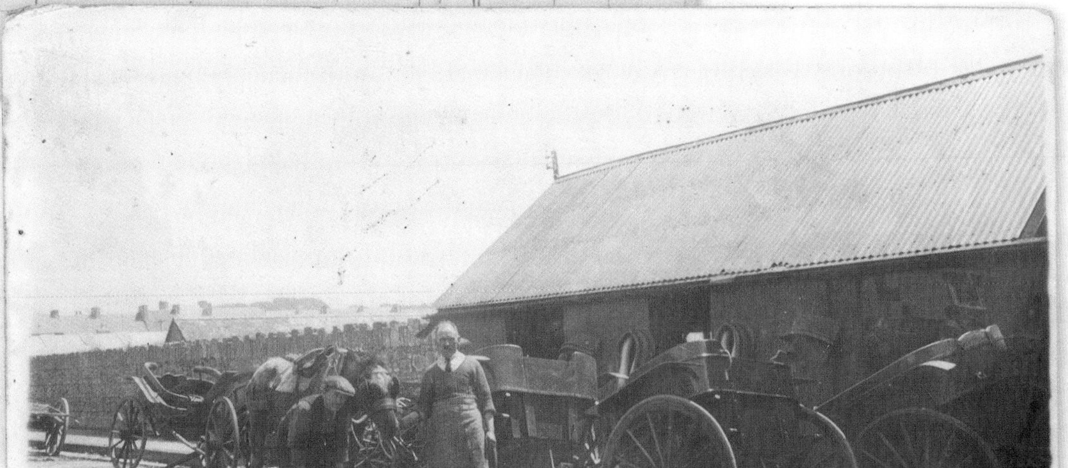

Salted [illegible], Salted Fish, Potatoes, Milk, Vegetables, Fruit, Turf and Goods or Wares of every description which may be offered for sale, and all Stalls or Standings for exhibiting the same for sale, or carrying on any trade or business in the Squares, Streets or Lanes of Listowel, to be removed therefrom, and to point out to the owners of all such animals, goods, stalls, or standings, who may not find it convenient to expose their goods for sale, or carry on their trades or occupations in their own premises, the New Market Place, which, with the concurrence of the proprietor thereof, subject to the payment of the Fees specified in Resolution No. 3, is hereby appointed, as the place where such animals and goods may be offered for sale or such trade and occupations carried on."

RESOLVED 3rd—"That as the Proprietor of the New Market Place, in addition to accommodation offered there under cover to Butchers in particular, and to the public in general, having through his Agent engaged, to provide Beams, Scales, Weights and Measures; to cause the same to be kept clean, especially the measures for Milk, and to cause the Market Place and approaches thereto, not being public streets or roads, to be kept clean, and the dirt created by the markets to be removed at least once a week on Saturdays, and the dirt created by Fairs to be removed immediately after each fair day, if fees according to the annexed list be paid on pigs, goods, stalls or standings, when not liable to Toll or Custom under the Proprietor's Patent Right; we consider the same to be just and fair, and when practicable that the fees should be demanded from the owners of pigs and goods on entering the Market Place:—

LIST OF FEES.

Potatoes, every 5s. worth sold,	1½d.	Carts containing Slips,	1d.
Milk, per Can,	0½d.	Butter, a Single Firkin carried by Hand into the Market Place,	0½d.
do. per Churn,	1d.	do. for every Cart containing over Four Firkins,	1½d.
do. per Barrel,	2d.	do. for every Cart containing Four Firkins and under,	1d.
Turf, per Horse Load,	0½d.	Carts with Turnips, Cabbage, Straw or other goods not already mentioned, per diem,	1d.
or for One Horse and Cart, per Week,	2d	Cobbler's Bulks, per Week,	1d.
do. per Ass Load,	0¼d.	Calves, each,	0½d.
or for One Ass and Cart, per Week,	1d.	Sheep, each,	0½d.
Turnips, for every 5s. worth sold,	1d.	Herring Barrels, per Week,	1d.
Oats, per 8 stone and under,	0½d.	If with a Standing,	0d.
Cabbages, per Cleeve, per Week,	0½d.	Butchers, per week,	3d.
Single Large Pigs,	1d.	Standings, per week,	1d.
Single Small Pigs,	0½d.		

RESOLVED 4th—"That as the Patent and Fortnightly Fairs of the Town of Listowel, have been held in the principal Square thereof, for a period long previous to the existence of any of the present house property of the Town of Listowel, although we are of opinion that such Fairs ought to be removed therefrom, we hesitate to interfere with them further than by appointing the New Market Place, during such Fairs for the sale of pigs, until authorised by further legislation relative to fairs, or until sufficient accommodation be provided in a Fair Green. Meanwhile the Proprietor of the Tolls and Customs of those Fairs has engaged to cause all dirt and nuisance created by them to be removed from the public thorough fares of the Town."

RESOLVED 5th—"That as the narrow passage to the Market Place under Scanlon's House is intended for Foot Passengers only, persons carrying bulky goods liable to obstruct it, and beasts of all kinds, are prohibited from using it."

RESOLVED 6th—"That as the foregoing Resolutions have been entered into on an agreement with the Proprietor's Agent, and are intended as an experiment, they are to hold good for one year, only from this date, subject to any alteration it may be necessry to make in them during that time."

RESOLVED 7th—"That the Constabulary be requested to put the 2nd Resolution in force, beginning on Monday, the 11th Instant, as regards everything specified in that Resolution, except Butter, and as regards that article on Friday, the 22nd September, and that these Resolutions be printed and posted up in the usual places for posting notices in Listowel, as soon as possible, and that a Copy be given to the Sub-Inspector of Constabulary, stationed in Listowel."

T. SANDES, Chairman.

The Market

A special meeting of the Listowel Magistrates took place at the Listowel Courthouse on September 2, 1854. This was held because of the public concern over unregulated fairs and markets on the streets of the town. As a result of this meeting, resolutions were passed for the purposes of regulating the markets. It was agreed that the new market place would be suitably prepared and properly walled. While those present were of the opinion that all markets and fairs should take place within this area, it was felt that the fortnightly cattle fairs should remain on the streets due to the limitations of space in the new market. After this, all pig fairs took place there. Fees or tolls were established and these were collected by Lord Listowel's agents at the entrance gates. Sheds were erected on one side of the market place and weighing scales were put in place. In the 1880s, an unused field at the rear of the market yard was added to give additional space. A butter market was also held here. The butter was supplied by the local farming families. Most of this butter when sold was transported to the butter market in Cork. The above notice is part of a poster outlining the resolutions passed at the meeting in September 2, 1854.

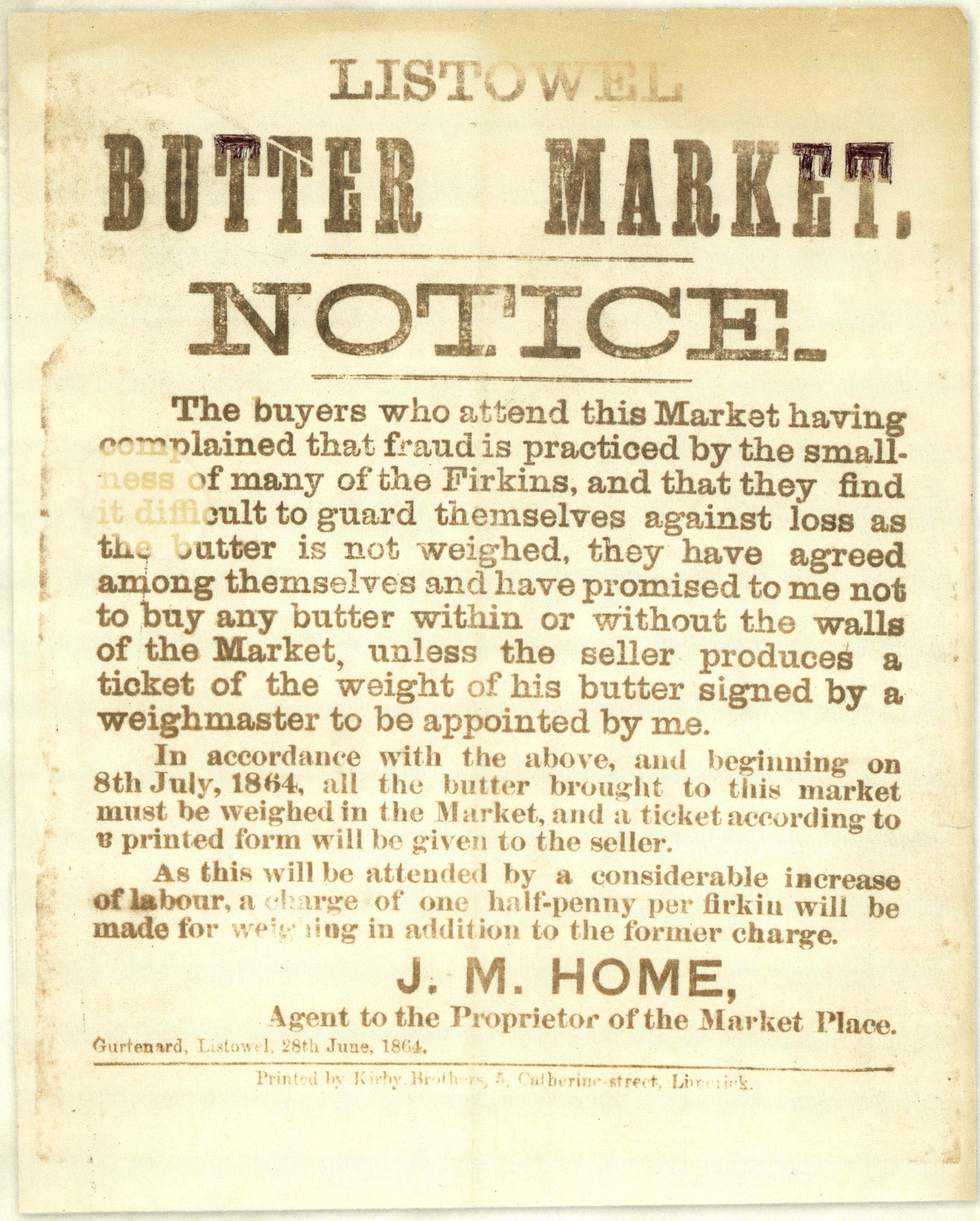

LISTOWEL

BUTTER MARKET.

NOTICE.

The buyers who attend this Market having complained that fraud is practiced by the smallness of many of the Firkins, and that they find it difficult to guard themselves against loss as the butter is not weighed, they have agreed among themselves and have promised to me not to buy any butter within or without the walls of the Market, unless the seller produces a ticket of the weight of his butter signed by a weighmaster to be appointed by me.

In accordance with the above, and beginning on 8th July, 1864, all the butter brought to this market must be weighed in the Market, and a ticket according to a printed form will be given to the seller.

As this will be attended by a considerable increase of labour, a charge of one half-penny per firkin will be made for weighing in addition to the former charge.

J. M. HOME,

Agent to the Proprietor of the Market Place.

Gurtenard, Listowel, 28th June, 1864.

Printed by Kirby Brothers, 5, Catherine-street, Limerick.

A notice above published by J.M. Home, agent to Lord Listowel, in 1864, outlining the rules of the Butter Market.

Right top: A letter detailing the acquisition of the new market field and the plans for its extension.

Right: Receipt for sand and gravel from River Feale in 1909.

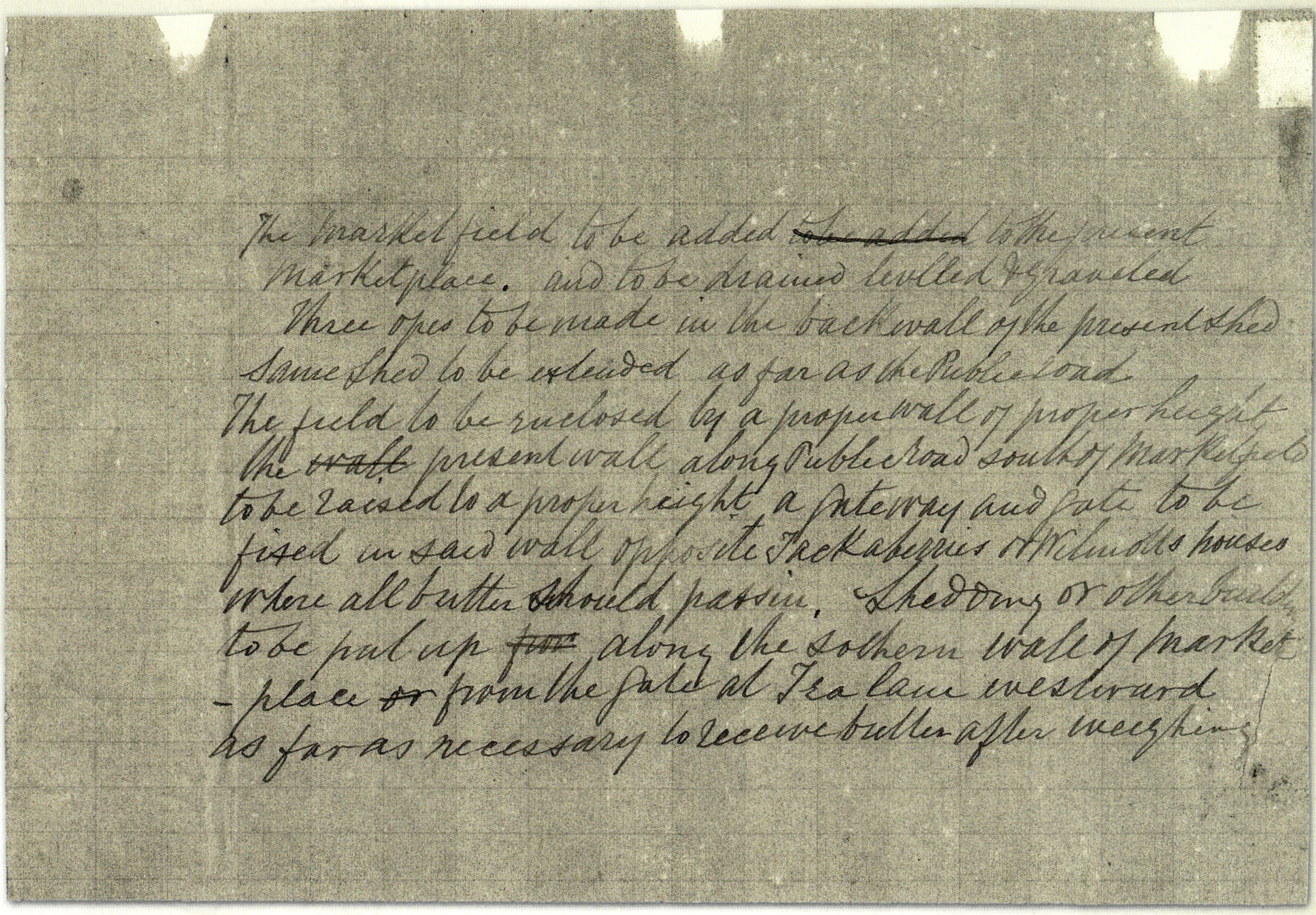

The Market field to be added ~~to be added~~ to the present Marketplace. and to be drained levelled & gravelled

Three opes to be made in the back wall of the present shed. Same shed to be extended as far as the Public road.

The field to be enclosed by a proper wall of proper height the ~~wall~~ present wall along Public road south of Market field to be raised to a proper height, a gateway and gate to be fixed in said wall opposite Thos Kabergies or Wilmotts houses where all butter ~~should~~ should pass in. Shedding or other building to be put up ~~for~~ along the sothern wall of Market-place ~~or~~ from the gate at Tea lane westward as far as necessary to receive butter after weighing

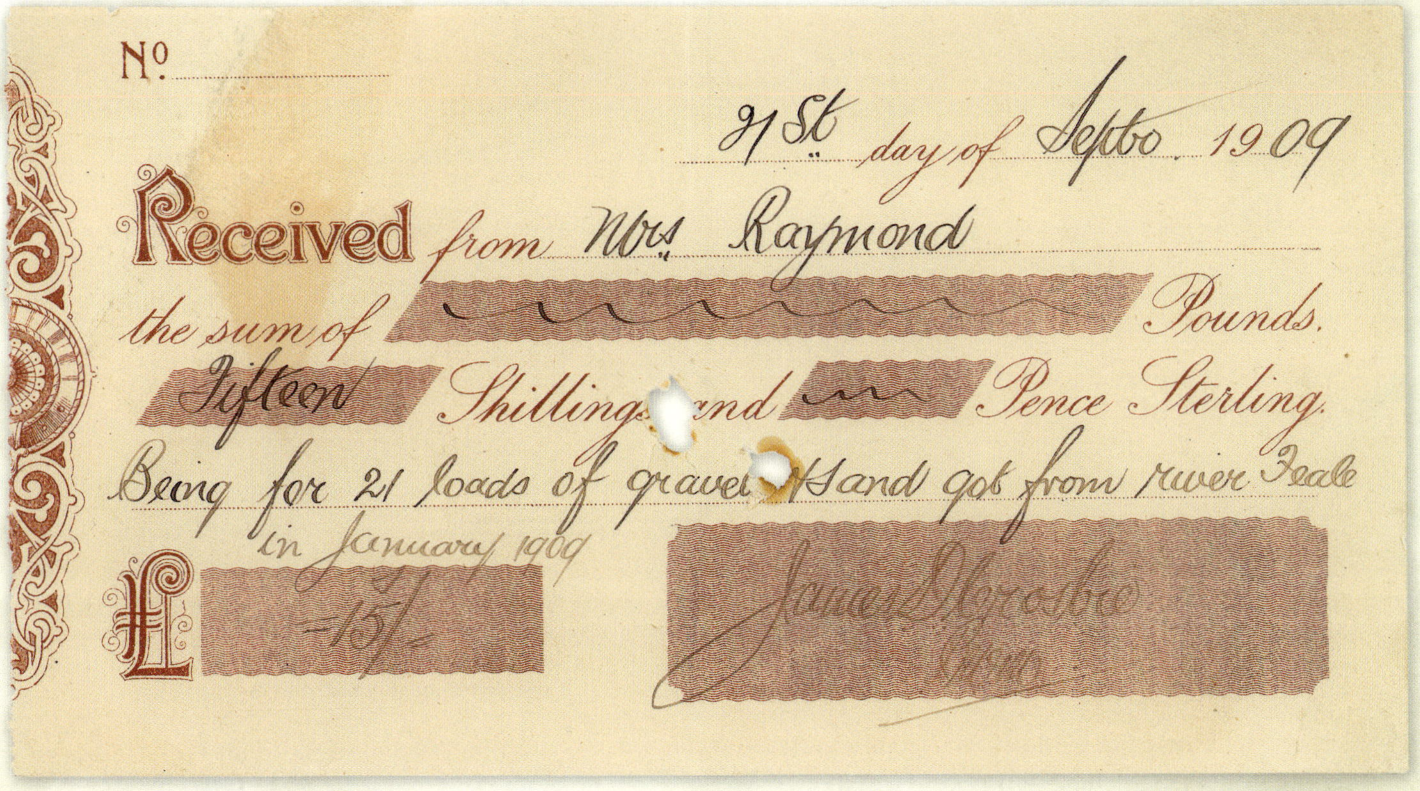

No. ....

21st day of Septbr 1909

Received from Mrs Raymond

the sum of ~~ Pounds.

Fifteen Shillings and ~~ Pence Sterling.

Being for 21 loads of gravel & sand got from river Feale in January 1909

£ -15/-

James D Crosbie
[illegible]

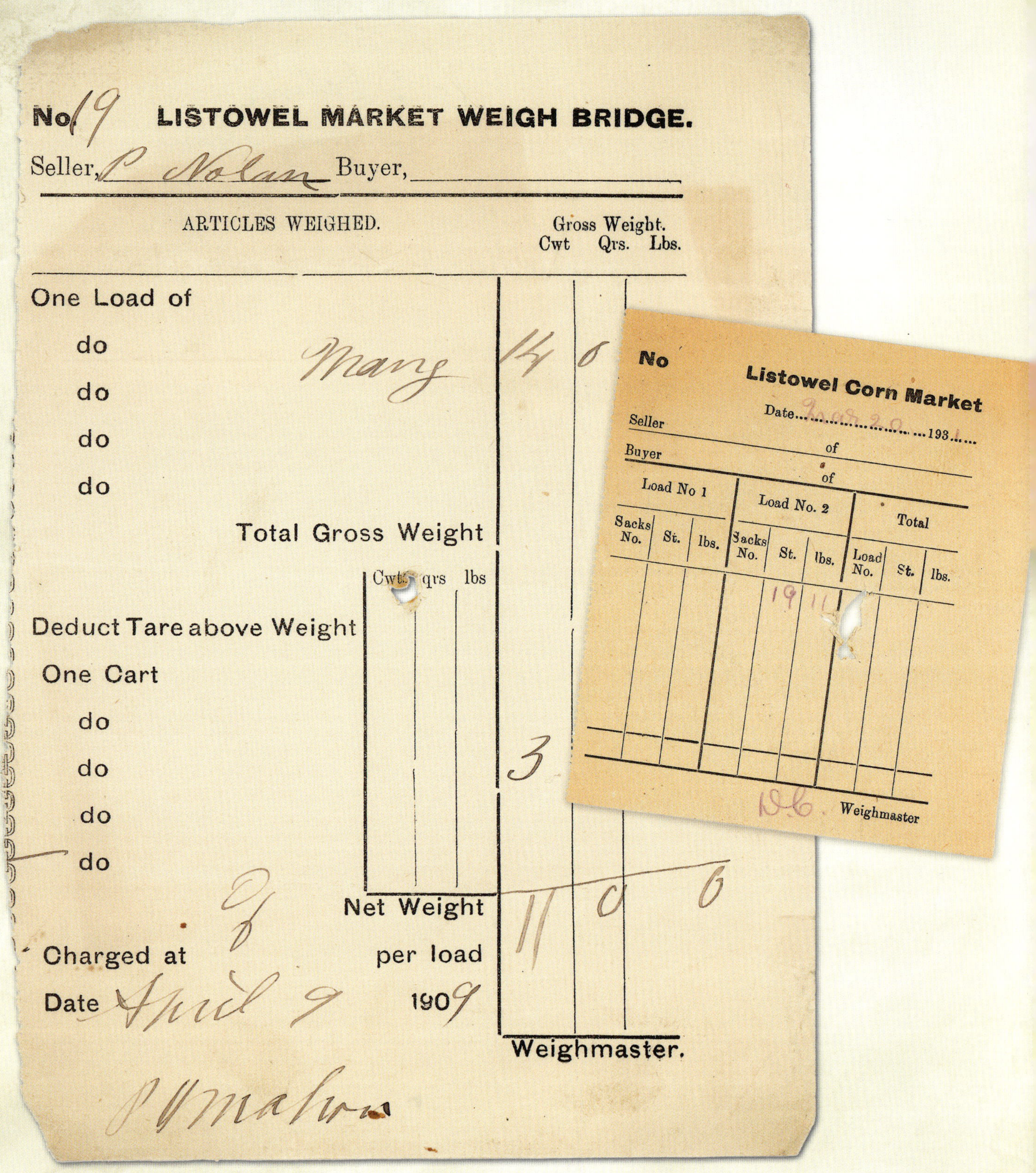

No. 19 **LISTOWEL MARKET WEIGH BRIDGE.**

Seller, P. Nolan Buyer, ______

ARTICLES WEIGHED.	Gross Weight. Cwt	Qrs.	Lbs.
One Load of			
do	14	6	
do			
do			
do			
Total Gross Weight			
Deduct Tare above Weight (Cwt. qrs lbs)			
One Cart			
do			
do	3		
do			
do			
Net Weight per load	11	0	6

Charged at

Date April 9 1909

Weighmaster.

P. McMahon

No

Listowel Corn Market

Date.................193....

Seller of

Buyer of

Load No 1			Load No. 2			Total		
Sacks No.	St.	lbs.	Sacks No.	St.	lbs.	Load No.	St.	lbs.
				19	11			

Weighmaster

This page: Receipts from the Market weigh bridge and corn market. Receipt from weigh bridge is signed by P. McMahon, grandfather of Bryan MacMahon.

Opposite: Letter from W. & G. Baird seeking the dates of fairs to be held in Listowel in 1909.

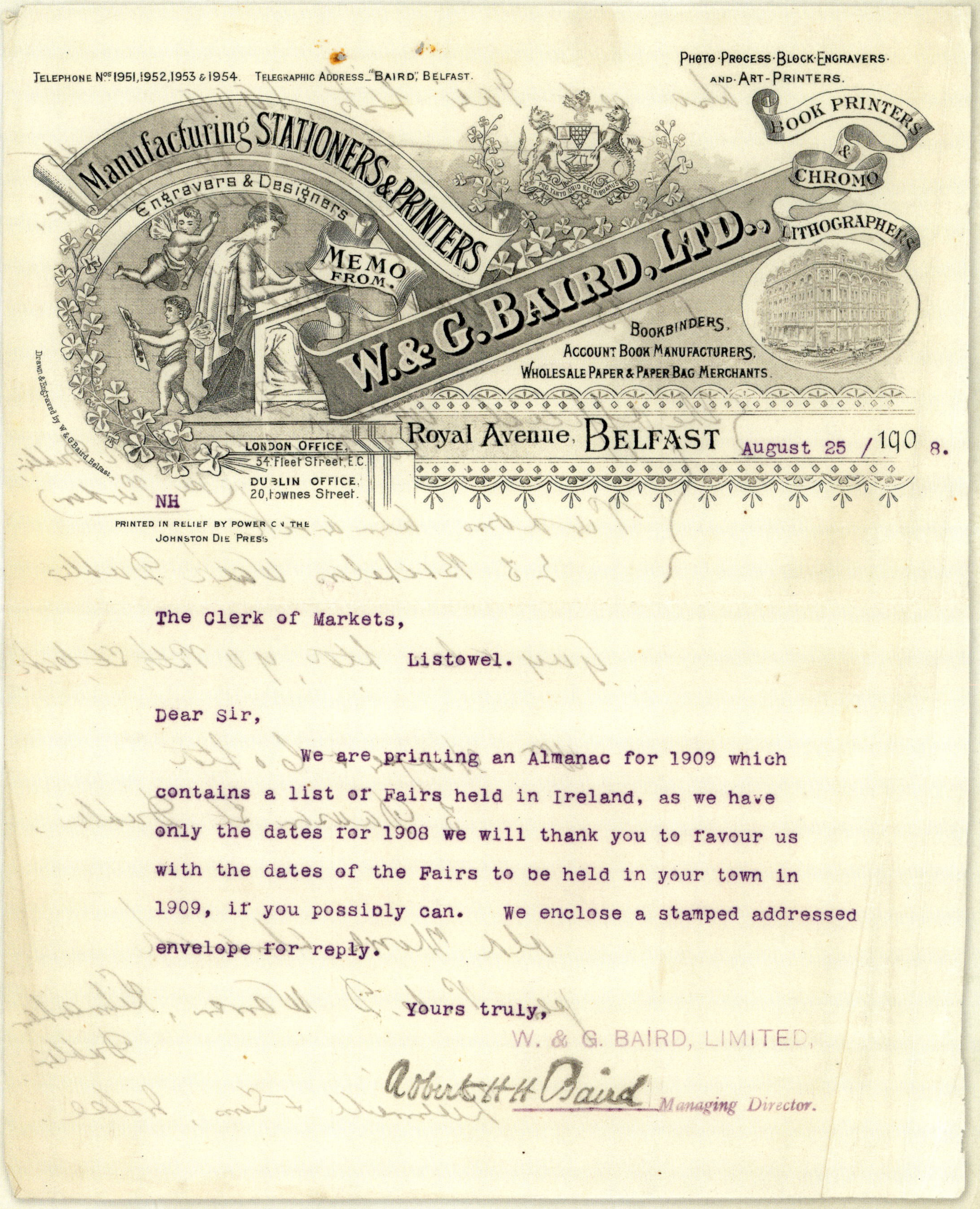

TELEPHONE N°s 1951, 1952, 1953 & 1954. TELEGRAPHIC ADDRESS "BAIRD," BELFAST.

PHOTO·PROCESS·BLOCK·ENGRAVERS· AND·ART-PRINTERS.

Manufacturing STATIONERS & PRINTERS

Engravers & Designers

MEMO FROM.

W. & G. BAIRD, LTD.

BOOK PRINTERS & CHROMO LITHOGRAPHERS

BOOKBINDERS,
ACCOUNT BOOK MANUFACTURERS,
WHOLESALE PAPER & PAPER BAG MERCHANTS.

Royal Avenue, BELFAST August 25 /1908.

LONDON OFFICE, 54 Fleet Street, E.C.
DUBLIN OFFICE, 20, Townes Street.

NH

PRINTED IN RELIEF BY POWER ON THE JOHNSTON DIE PRESS

The Clerk of Markets,

Listowel.

Dear Sir,

We are printing an Almanac for 1909 which contains a list of Fairs held in Ireland, as we have only the dates for 1908 we will thank you to favour us with the dates of the Fairs to be held in your town in 1909, if you possibly can. We enclose a stamped addressed envelope for reply.

Yours truly,

W. & G. BAIRD, LIMITED,

Robert H H Baird

Managing Director.

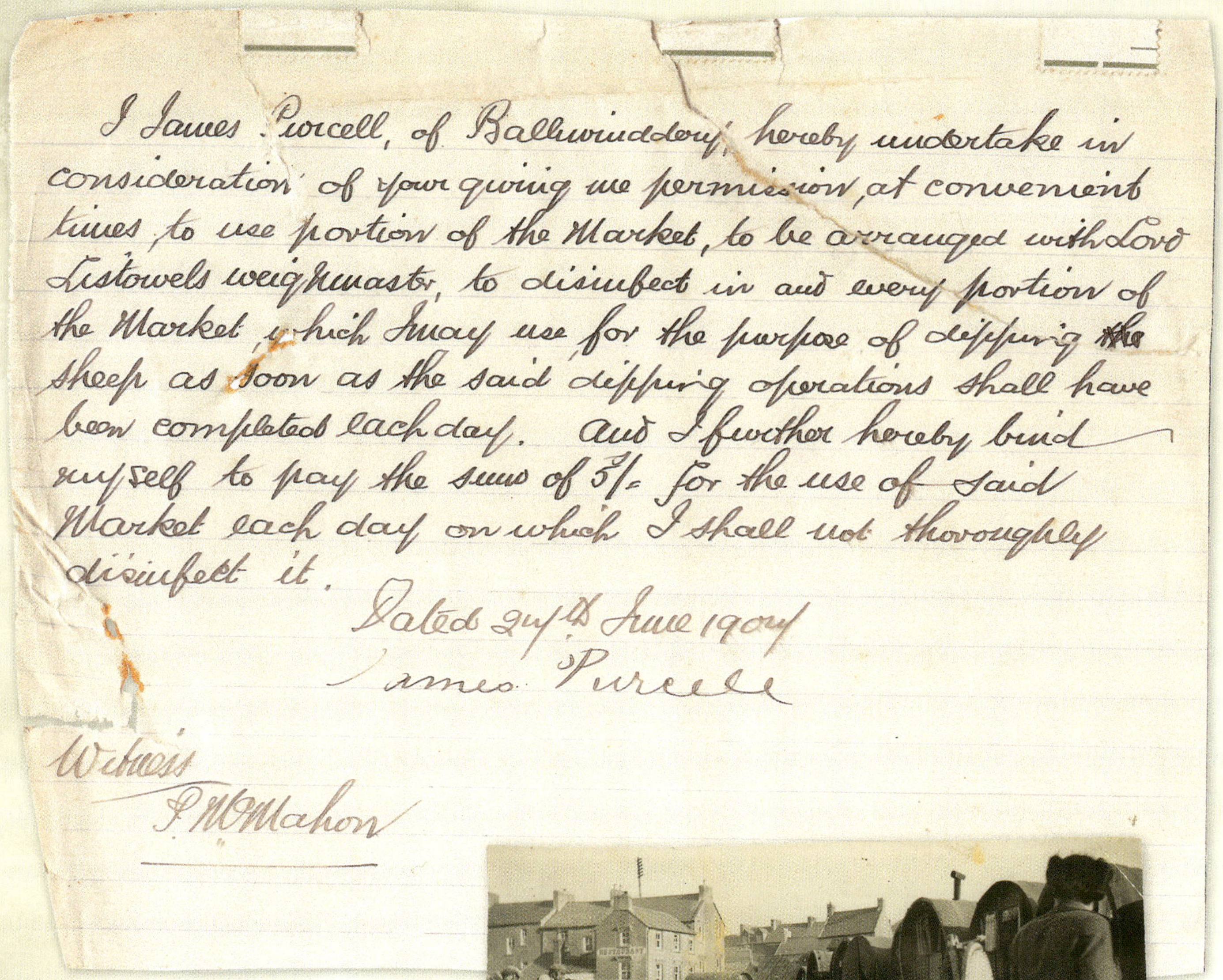

I James Purcell, of Ballinruddery, hereby undertake in consideration of your giving me permission, at convenient times, to use portion of the Market, to be arranged with Lord Listowels weighmaster, to disinfect in and every portion of the Market which I may use for the purpose of dipping the sheep as soon as the said dipping operations shall have been completed each day. And I further hereby bind myself to pay the sum of 5/- for the use of said Market each day on which I shall not thoroughly disinfect it.

Dated 24th June 1904
James Purcell

Witness
P. McMahon

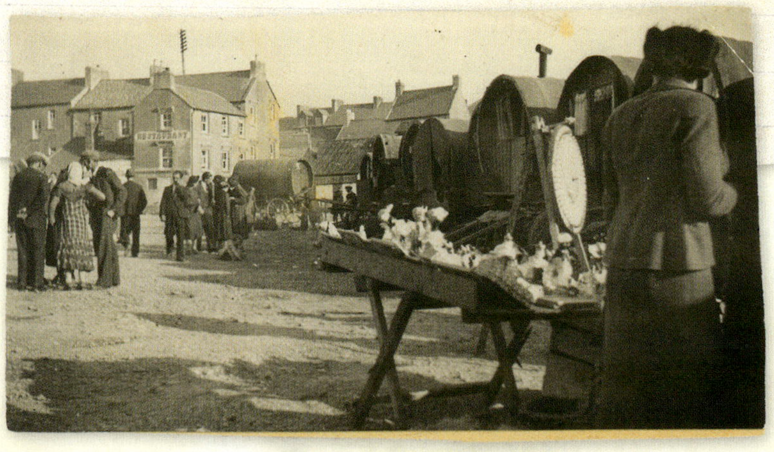

Letter above from James Purcell, Ballinruddery seeking permission to dip sheep in the Market.

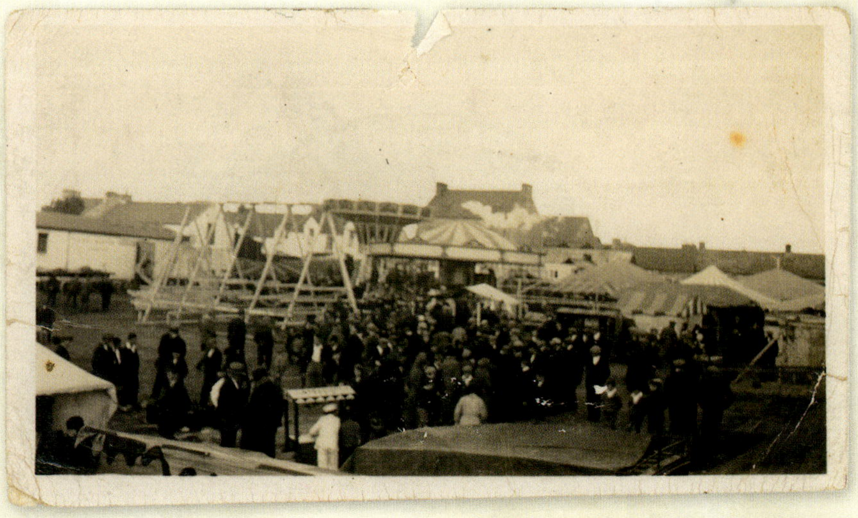

Above: Scene from Market during Listowel race week with travellers' caravans lining the rear wall.

Left: Carnival amusements in the Market from the 1930s.

LISTOWEL CALF MARKET

RE-OPENING DAY, TUESDAY 8th MARCH, 1892.

AND EVERY SUCCEEDING TUESDAY DURING THE SEASON.

Farmers will again find it their interest to support this Calf Market which last season proved so successful.

Some of the Principal Buyers of the South of Ireland have promised to attend.

BRINSLEY FITZGERALD} Agent to The Earl of Listowel

Gurtenand, Listowel.

Cuthbertson, Printer, William Street, Listowel.

LISTOWEL
BUTTER
MARKET

The attention of Sellers of Butter in this Market is called to Rule, dated 14th April, 1893, viz :-

"On no account shall WEIGH-MASTER weigh any Firkin which is not clearly branded with the name and townland of the Seller cut, or burned in deep letters into the timber, and on which the tar is not legibly marked by an author ized Cooper."

The foregoing rule will be strictly inforced from this date.

J. D. CROSBIE,
Agent to the Earl of Listowel.

9th April, 1894.

Cuthbertson, Printer, William Street, Listowel.

LISTOWEL
PIG & CATTLE
FAIRS.

The usual Pig Market which would be held on Tuesday the 25th Inst. WILL NOT be held on that day, in consequence of its being Christmas Day; and the Cattle Fair which in the ordinary course would be held on the 26th Inst., will not be held on that day in consequence of its being St. Stephen's Day.

The PIG and CATTLE FAIRS will therefore be held on the following days and no other :-

PIG FAIR

TUESDAY 11th and 18th DEC. 1906,
and 1st January, 1907,

and thenceforward on Tuesdays as advertized.

CATTLE FAIR

WEDNESDAY 12th DEC. 1906, and
2nd JANUARY, 1907,

And thenceforward fortnightly as advertized.

By Order. JAMES D. CROSBIE.

5th Dec. 1906.

Cuthbertson, Printer, Listowel.

NOTICE.

LISTOWEL MARKET.

SALE OF

CABBAGE PLANTS

For the convenience of buyers and sellers it has long been the custom of this Market to sell Cabbage Plants in bundles called "hundreds," and it is well understood that each such bundle is warranted by the seller to contain 120 SOUND plants suitable for planting.

Sellers should bear this in mind, and, if their bundles do not contain 120 such plants, should notify purchaser of the actual number in each bundle sold, otherwise they will be liable, according to the custom of this Market, to an action for misdescription and deceit, the purchaser being entitled to assume that each bundle contains 120 plants.

By order,

EDWARD O'BRIEN,

Agent to the Earl of Listowel.

Estate Office, Listowel,
20th April, 1916.

Cuthbertson, Printer, Listowel.

ENNISMORE

SALE

OF

TURBARY.

McELLIGOTT & SON are instructed to receive proposals for the purchase of 4 acres Statute of Turbary at Ennismore, the property of Doctor Davidge.

This turbary is of the very best quality, thoroughly drained and of exceptional depth. It has the great advantage of adjoining the Ennismore Black road, so ensuring that regardless of weather conditions it can be ricked on the roadside at any time.

It is offered for sale in lots of one, two, three or four Statute acres—held in Fee Simple—FREE OF RENT.

Further particulars from

McElligott & Son, Auctioneers

LISTOWEL

Cuthbertson, Printer, Listowel

10 Market Street

Listowel's first motor garage was built by the Galvin brothers. The garage was subsequently run by the Mangan and Moloney families. Later it was bought by Denis O'Sullivan for use as a supermarket. He then sold it to Ambrose Sheridan. It is now being operated by Ger Greaney.

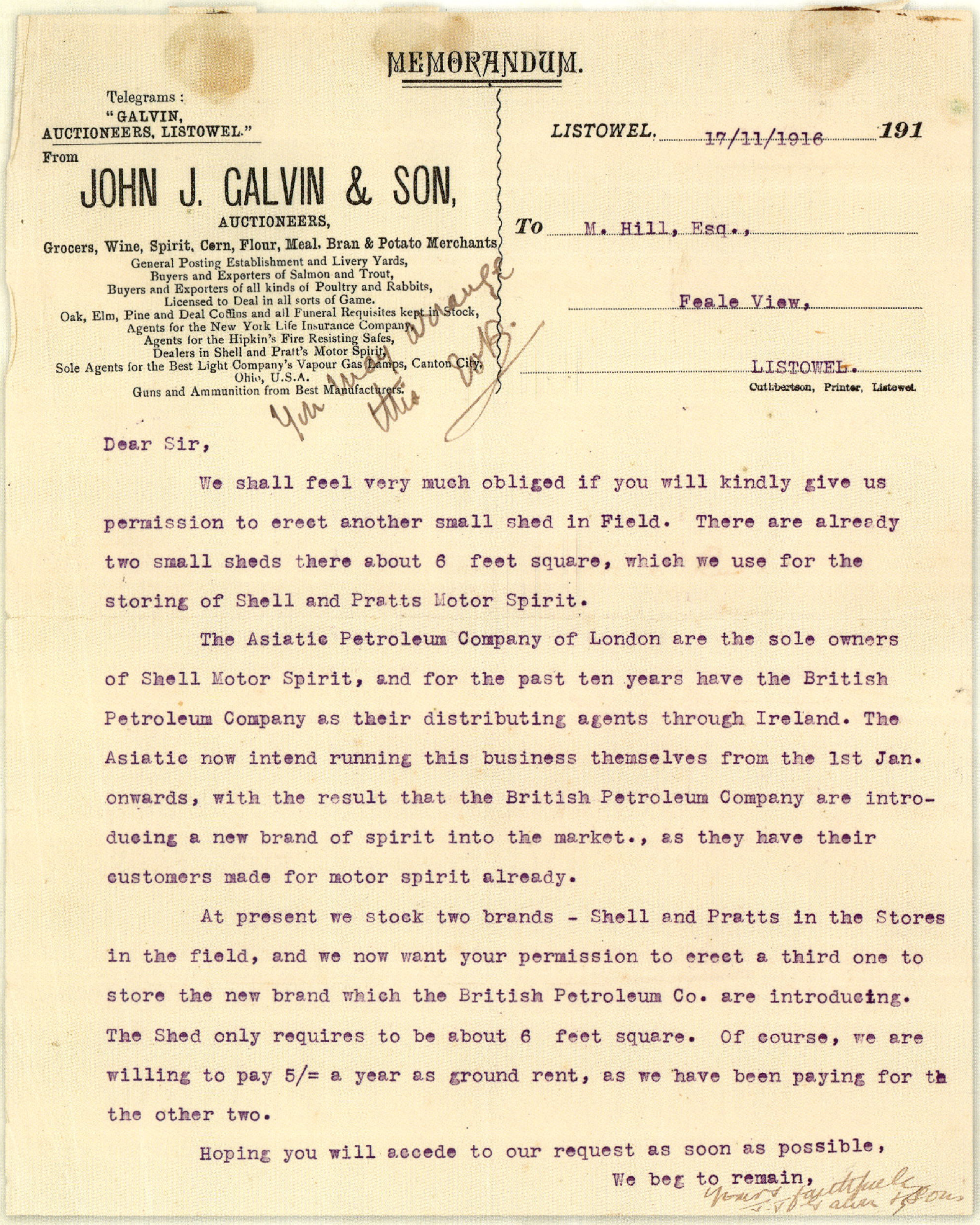

MEMORANDUM.

Telegrams:
"GALVIN,
AUCTIONEERS, LISTOWEL."

From

JOHN J. GALVIN & SON,

AUCTIONEERS,

Grocers, Wine, Spirit, Corn, Flour, Meal, Bran & Potato Merchants
General Posting Establishment and Livery Yards,
Buyers and Exporters of Salmon and Trout,
Buyers and Exporters of all kinds of Poultry and Rabbits,
Licensed to Deal in all sorts of Game.
Oak, Elm, Pine and Deal Coffins and all Funeral Requisites kept in Stock,
Agents for the New York Life Insurance Company,
Agents for the Hipkin's Fire Resisting Safes,
Dealers in Shell and Pratt's Motor Spirit,
Sole Agents for the Best Light Company's Vapour Gas Lamps, Canton City, Ohio, U.S.A.
Guns and Ammunition from Best Manufacturers.

LISTOWEL, 17/11/1916 191

To M. Hill, Esq.,

Feale View,

LISTOWEL.

Cuthbertson, Printer, Listowel.

Dear Sir,

We shall feel very much obliged if you will kindly give us permission to erect another small shed in Field. There are already two small sheds there about 6 feet square, which we use for the storing of Shell and Pratts Motor Spirit.

The Asiatic Petroleum Company of London are the sole owners of Shell Motor Spirit, and for the past ten years have the British Petroleum Company as their distributing agents through Ireland. The Asiatic now intend running this business themselves from the 1st Jan. onwards, with the result that the British Petroleum Company are intro-dueing a new brand of spirit into the market., as they have their customers made for motor spirit already.

At present we stock two brands - Shell and Pratts in the Stores in the field, and we now want your permission to erect a third one to store the new brand which the British Petroleum Co. are introducing. The Shed only requires to be about 6 feet square. Of course, we are willing to pay 5/= a year as ground rent, as we have been paying for th the other two.

Hoping you will accede to our request as soon as possible,

We beg to remain,
Yours faithfully
J. J. Galvin & Son

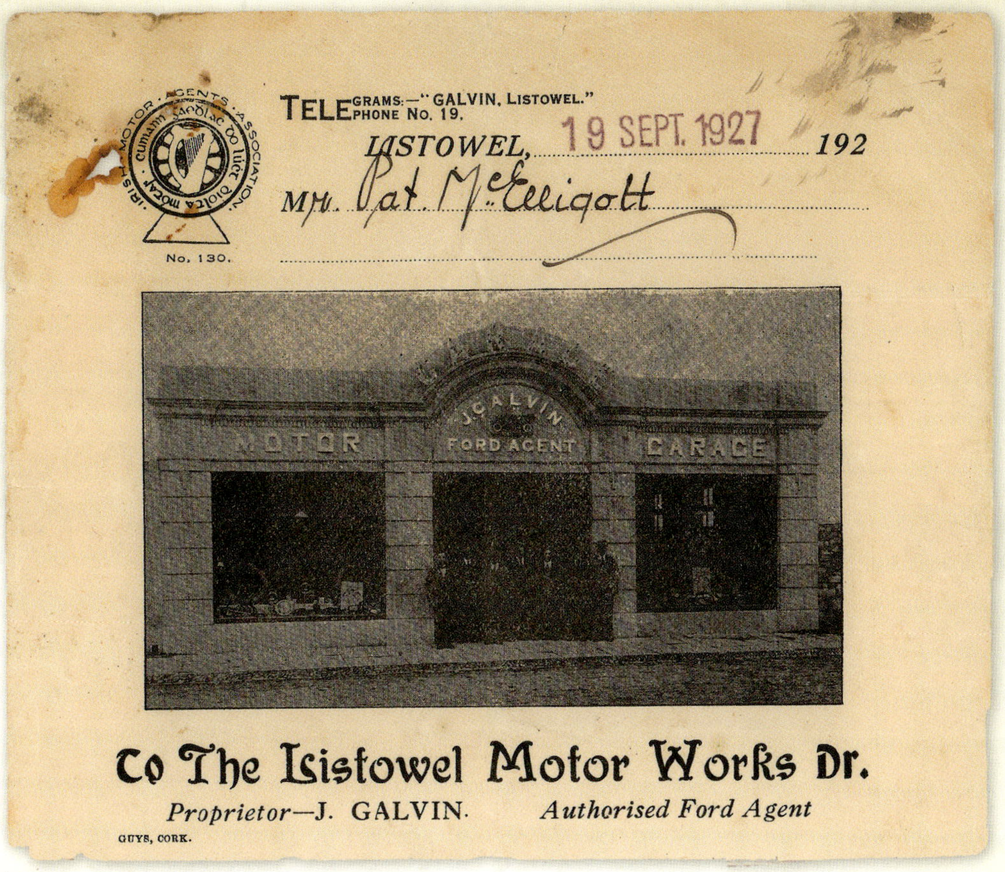

TELEGRAMS:—"GALVIN, LISTOWEL."
TELEPHONE No. 19.

No. 130.

LISTOWEL, 19 SEPT. 1927 192

Mr. Pat McElligott

To The Listowel Motor Works Dr.

Proprietor—J. GALVIN. *Authorised Ford Agent*

GUYS, CORK.

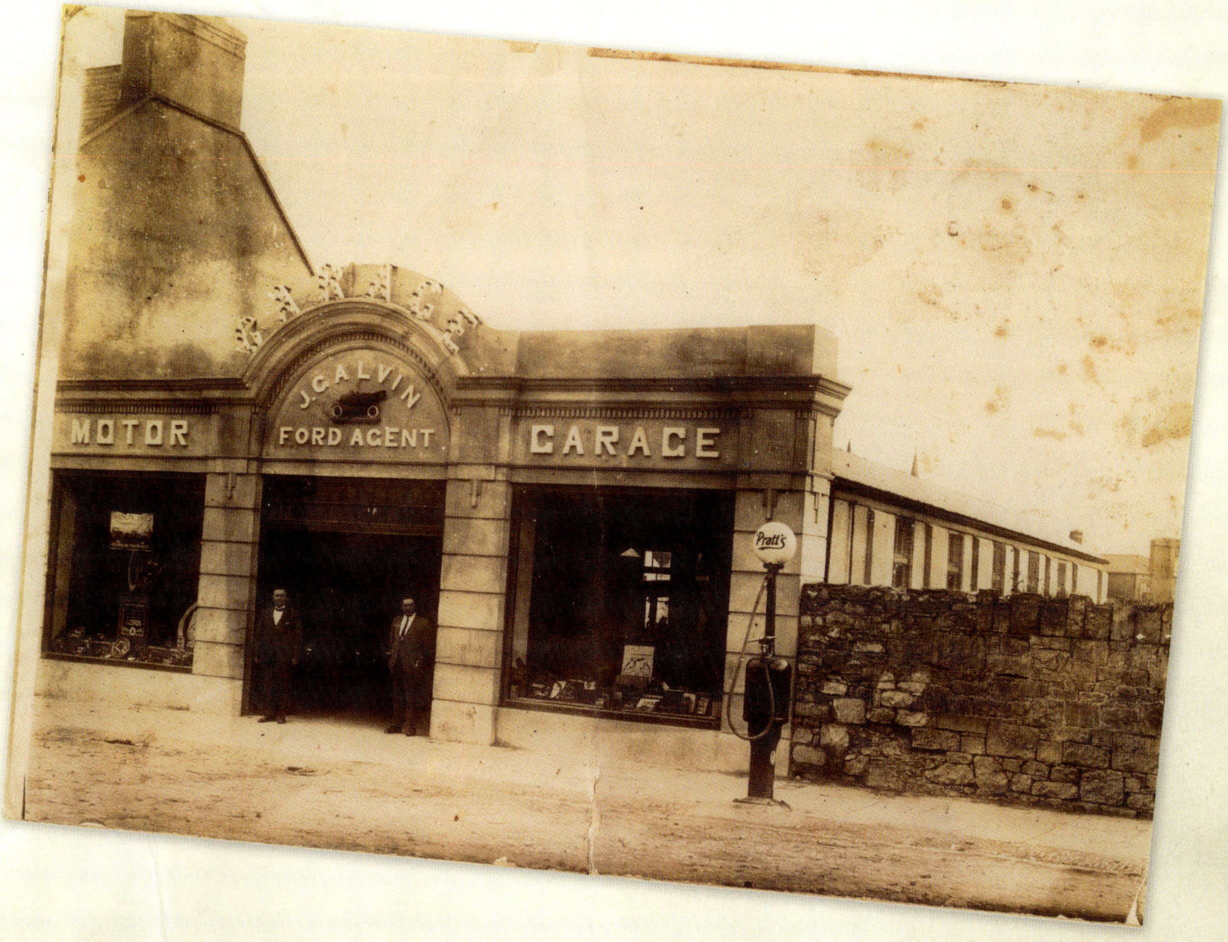

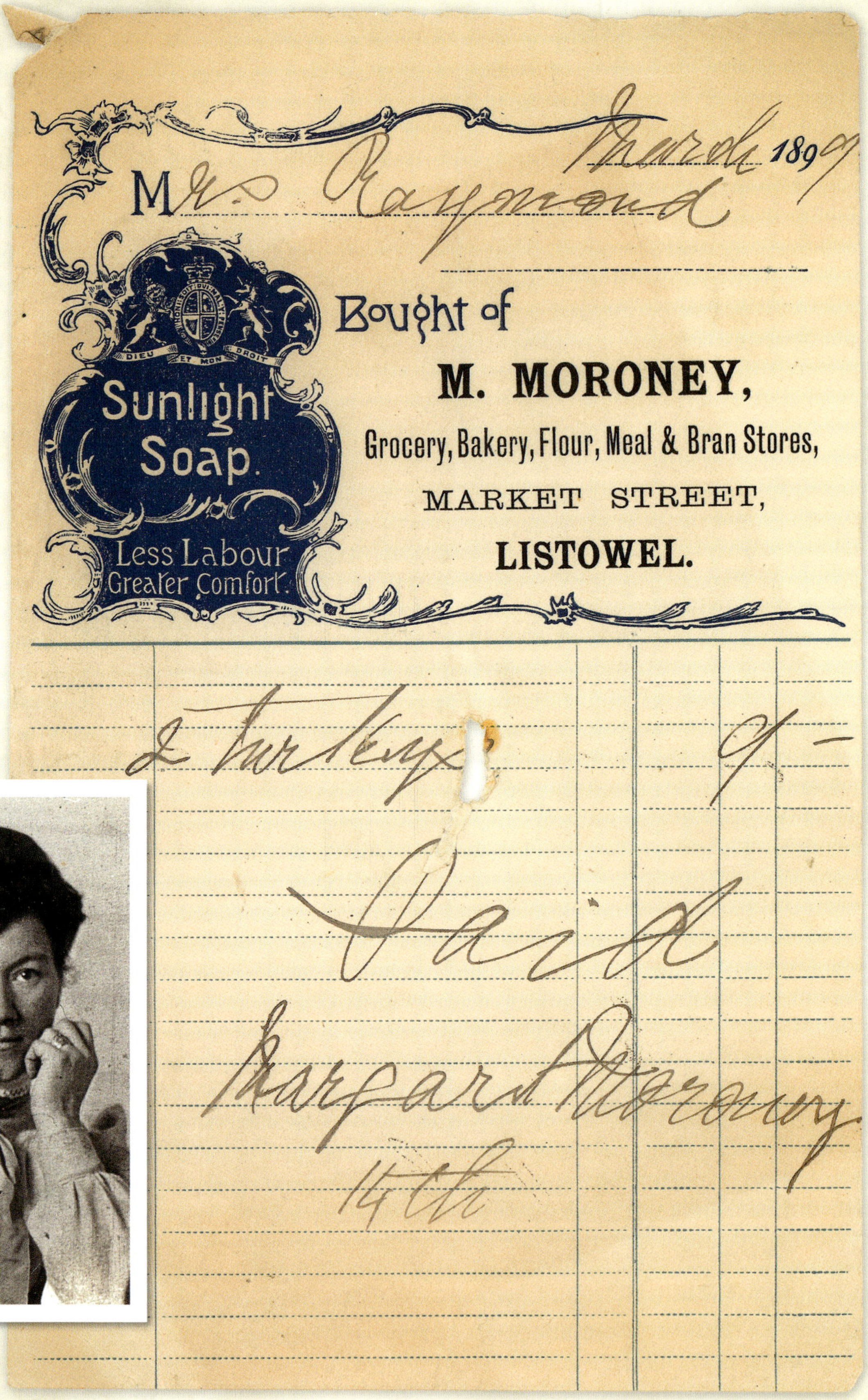

March 189[illegible]

Mrs Raymond

Bought of

M. MORONEY,

Grocery, Bakery, Flour, Meal & Bran Stores,

MARKET STREET,

LISTOWEL.

2 Turkeys 9/-

Paid

Margaret Moroney

14th

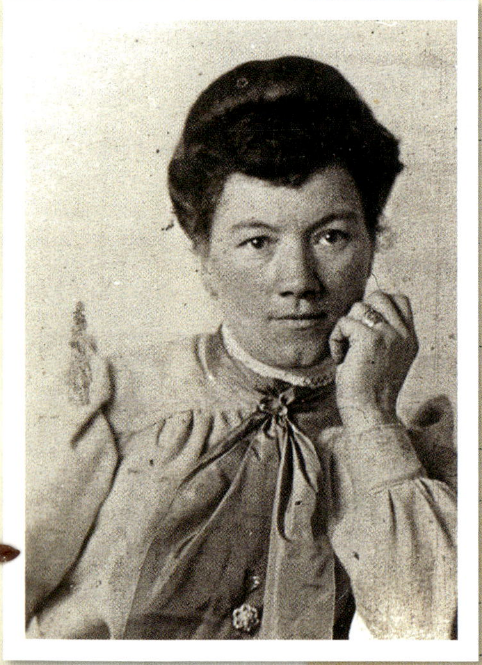

2 Market Street

Margaret Moroney, a widow, lived at 2 Market Street with her father Daniel O'Neill (a retired shopkeeper from Co Limerick). Margaret ran a grocery store here where she also had a bakery and flour and meal store. Margaret's stepdaughter, Emily (pictured above), married Michael Dalton in 1895. The Daltons resided in Charles Street.

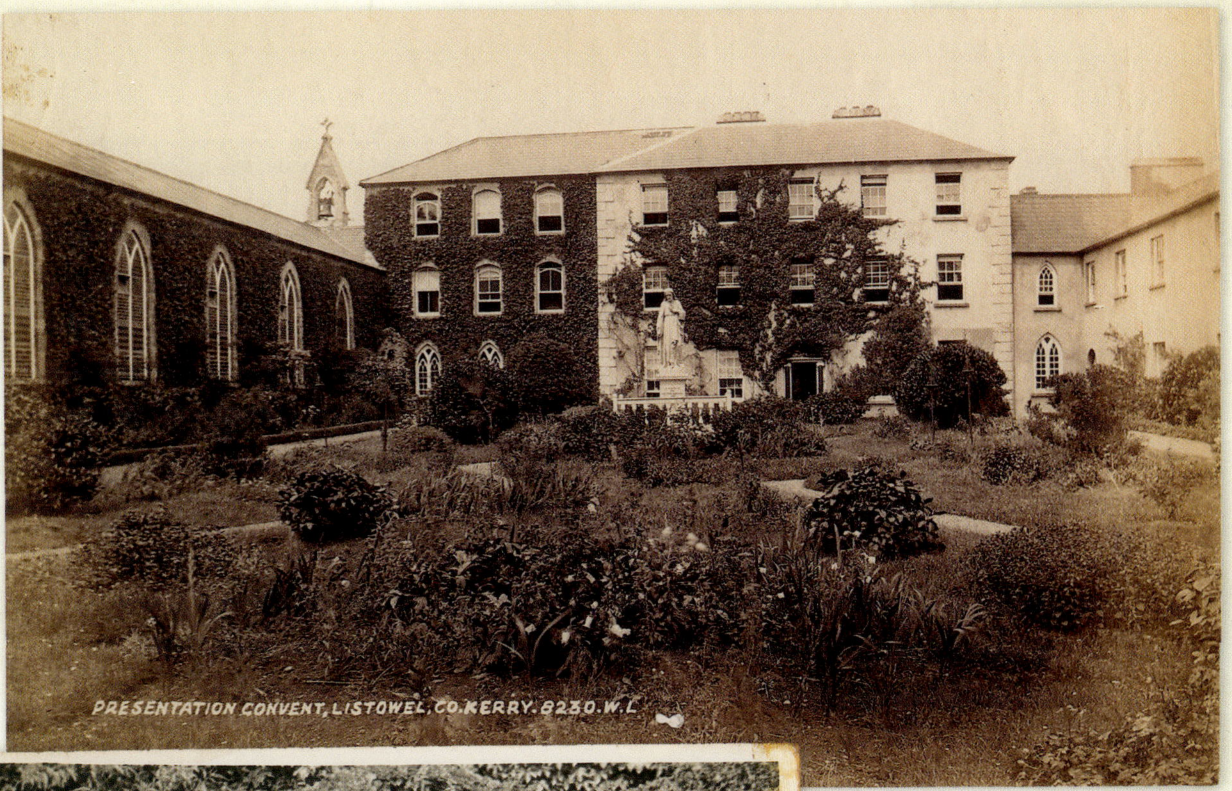

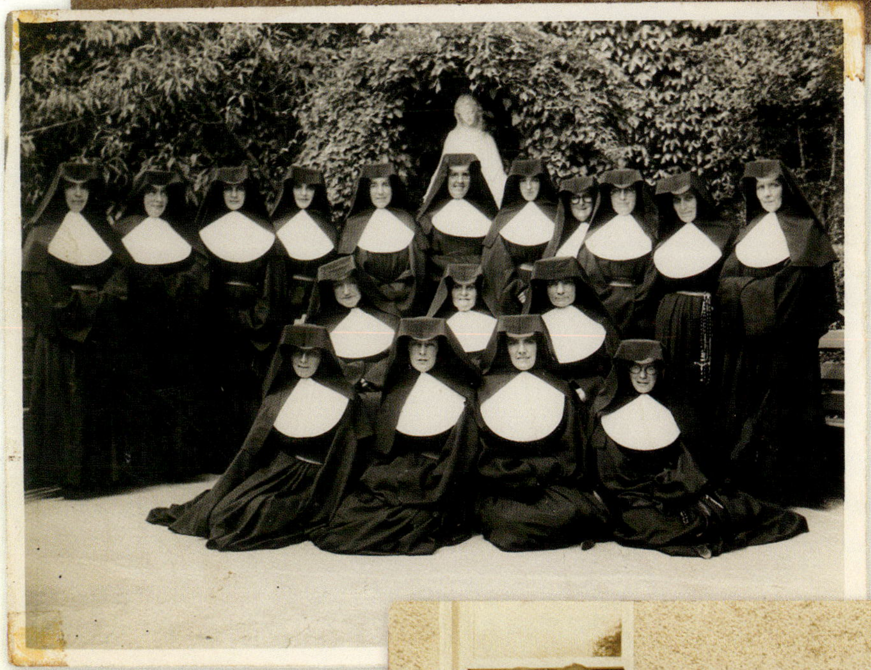

Presentation Convent

The Presentation Sisters came to Listowel at the invitation of PP Fr. Jeremiah (Darby) Mahony in 1844. They first catered for the primary education of the town's girls before the secondary school opened in the 1940s. In 1994, Bishop Diarmuid O'Sullivan celebrated the Sisters' 150 years in the town. While the schools are still thriving, the Convent itself closed in recent years. Picture: A fifth class group from the 1930s.

Above: Top row, left to right: Srs. de Pazzi, Gemma, Cyril, Patricia, Dympna, Michael, Aquinas, Francis, Philomena, Bernadette, Louis.
Middle Row: Mother Joseph, Mother Margaret, Mother Berchmans
Front: Srs. Colette, Jude, Austin, Clare.

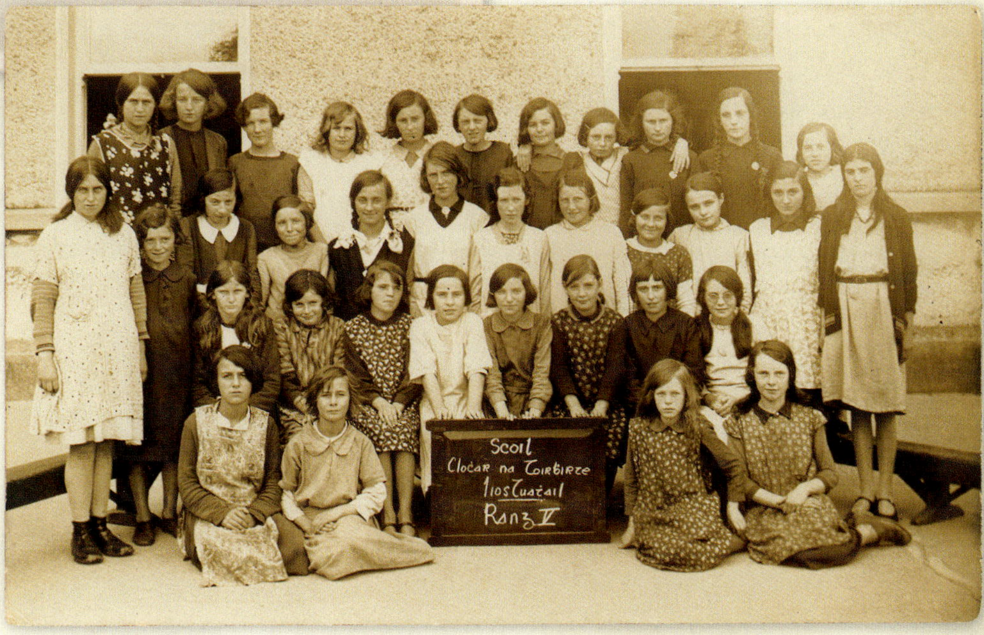

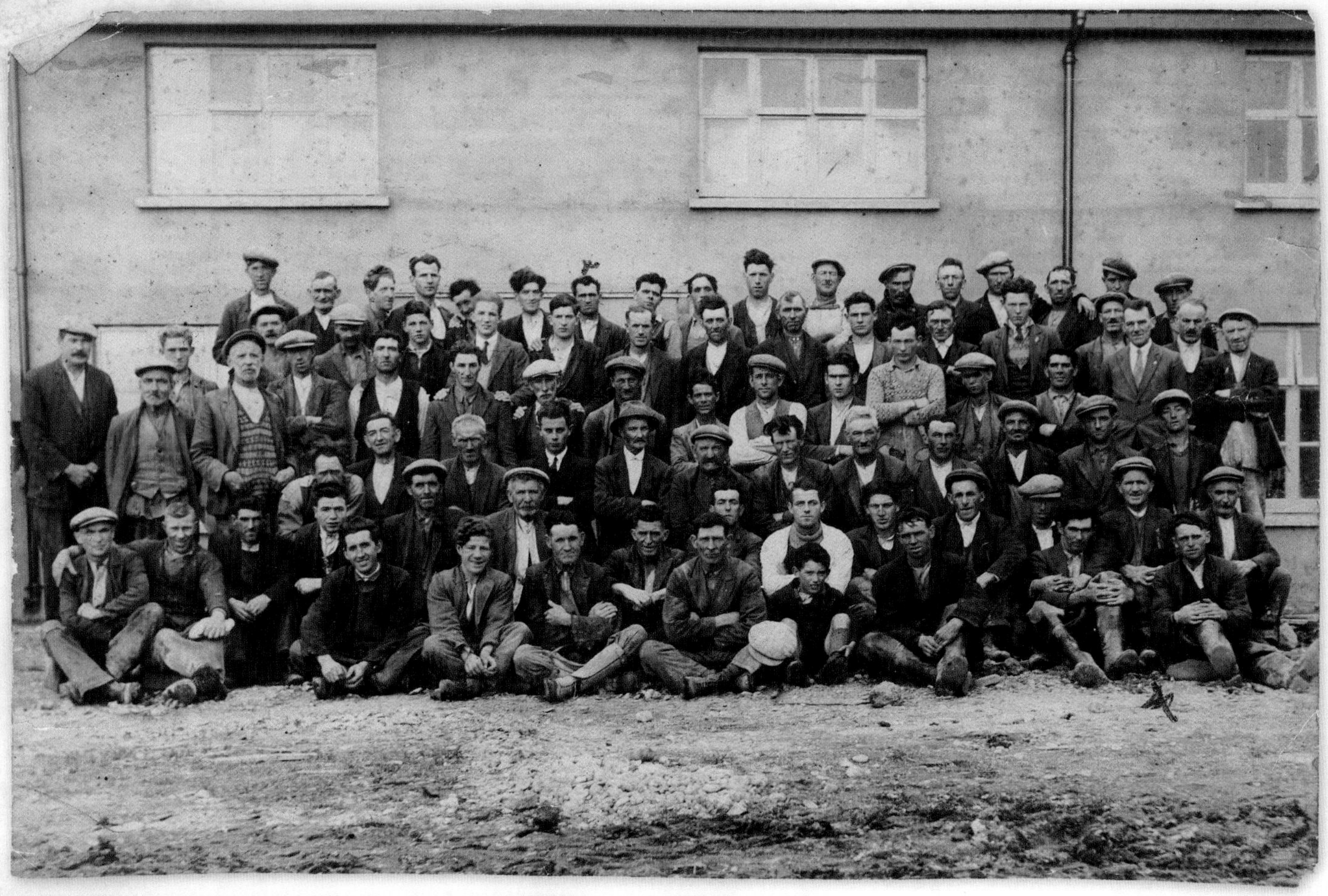

O'Connell's Avenue

The town had a serious lack of housing in the late 1920s. Many young families lived in rented rooms, while others had to make do with unsuitable accommodation in back houses in the many laneways. The urban council of the day, in conjunction with local government, made the decision to the build 104 new houses in the fields near the railway known as McDonnell's Meadows. This was, at the time, one of the largest local housing contracts in the fledgling Free State. The contract for building the houses went to local contractor M.A. Hannon. Site work started in 1932. As this was the year of the Eucharistic Congress in Dublin, 'Congress Avenue' was the name first ventured as a name for the new estate. However, this was later changed to O'Connell's Avenue, in honour of the Liberator, Daniel O'Connell. At a time when unemployment countrywide was high, it was a welcome boost to the skilled and unskilled workmen of the town. When work was completed in the mid-1930s, it was opened by the Minister of Local Government of the day, Seán T. O'Kelly (later President) and T.J. Walsh representing the U.D.C., pictured right.

Photo above: The workers who were employed in building the Avenue.

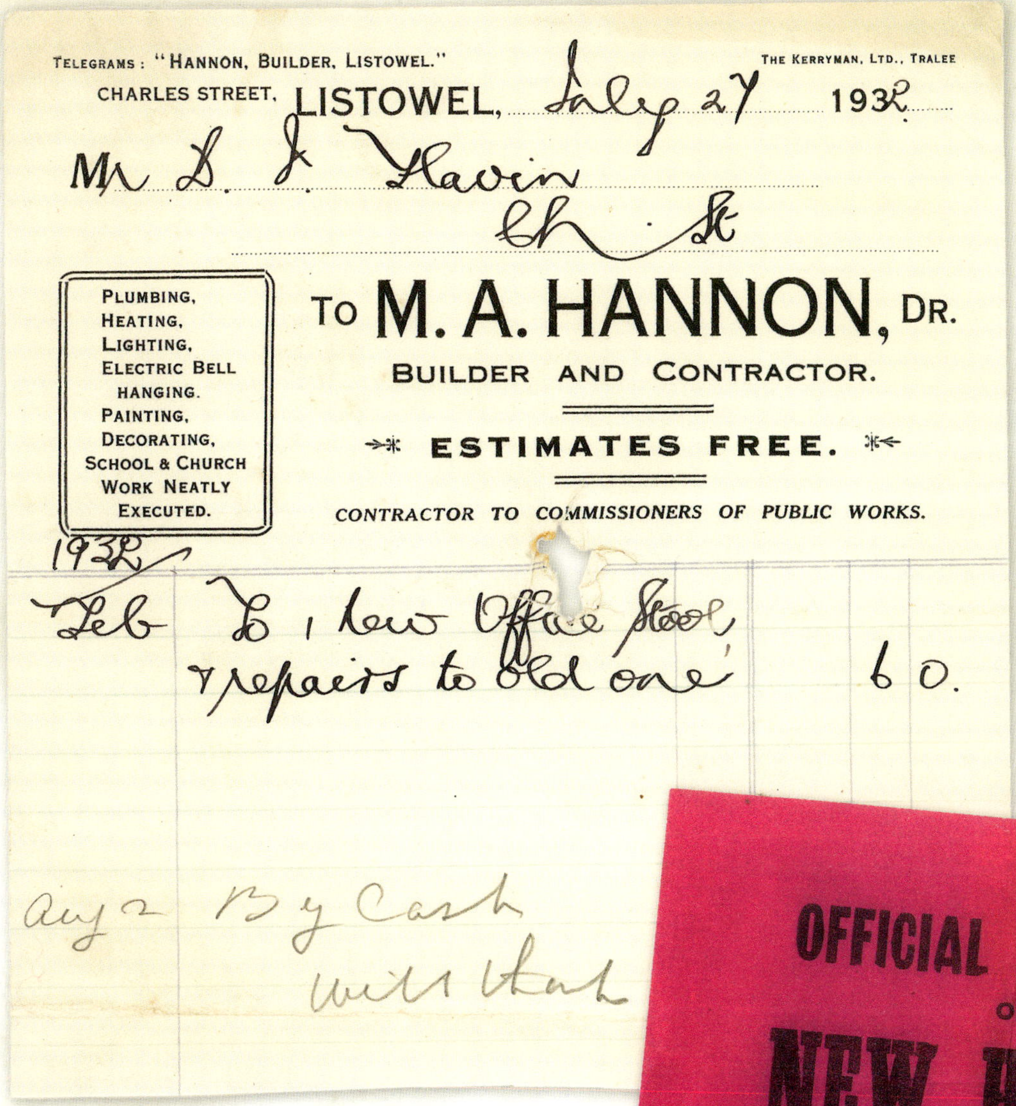

TELEGRAMS : "HANNON, BUILDER, LISTOWEL." THE KERRYMAN, LTD., TRALEE

CHARLES STREET, LISTOWEL, July 27 1932

Mr D. J. Flavin

Ch. St

PLUMBING, HEATING, LIGHTING, ELECTRIC BELL HANGING. PAINTING, DECORATING, SCHOOL & CHURCH WORK NEATLY EXECUTED.

TO M. A. HANNON, DR.

BUILDER AND CONTRACTOR.

ESTIMATES FREE.

CONTRACTOR TO COMMISSIONERS OF PUBLIC WORKS.

1932 Feb	To 1 new Office Stool, & repairs to old one	6 0.
Aug 2	By Cash With thanks	

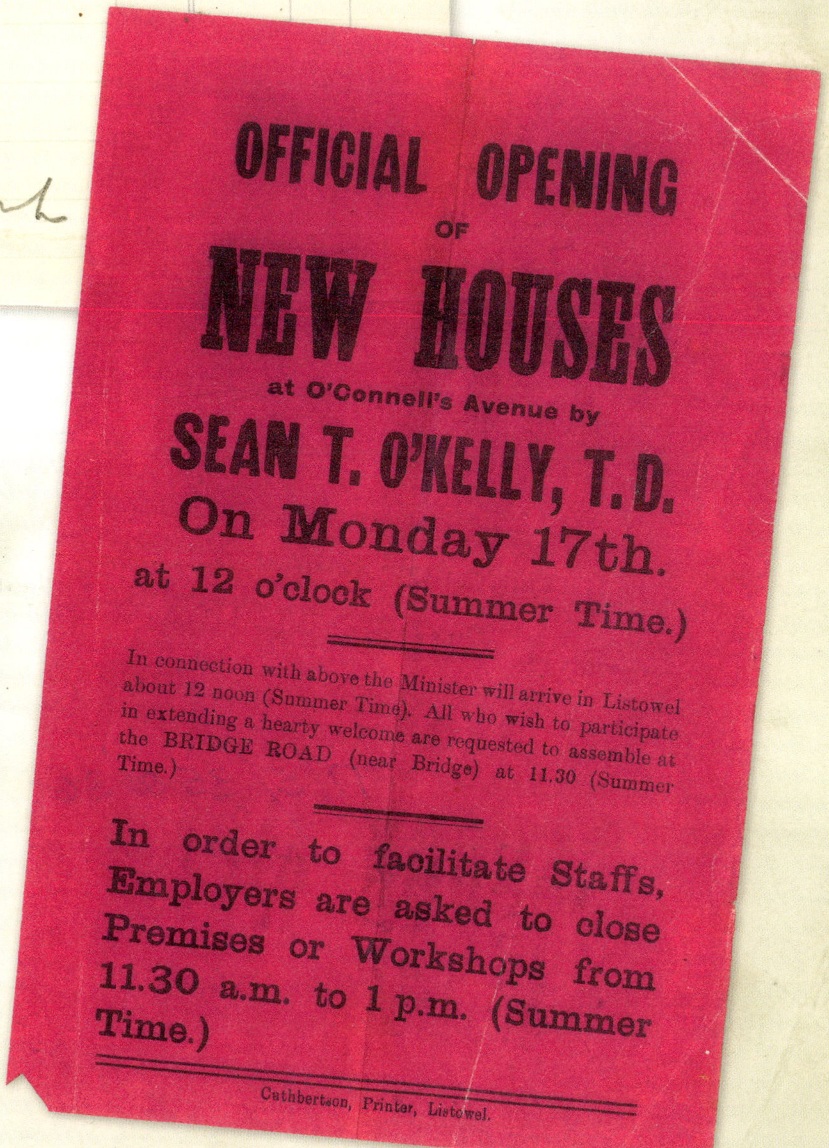

OFFICIAL OPENING

OF

NEW HOUSES

at O'Connell's Avenue by

SEAN T. O'KELLY, T.D.

On Monday 17th.

at 12 o'clock (Summer Time.)

In connection with above the Minister will arrive in Listowel about 12 noon (Summer Time). All who wish to participate in extending a hearty welcome are requested to assemble at the BRIDGE ROAD (near Bridge) at 11.30 (Summer Time.)

In order to facilitate Staffs, Employers are asked to close Premises or Workshops from 11.30 a.m. to 1 p.m. (Summer Time.)

Cuthbertson, Printer, Listowel.

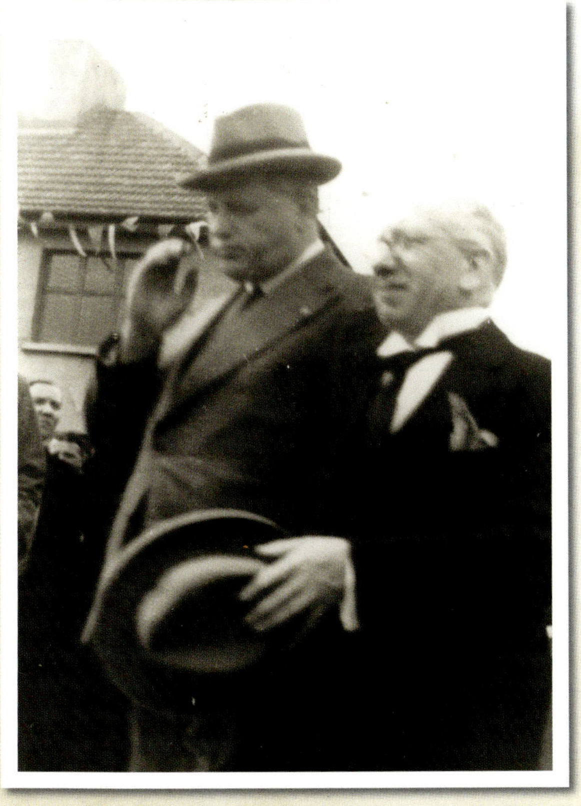

SPONSORS

I wish to thank the following whose financial contributions greatly assisted in the production of this book, particularly the Byrne Bros, Duagh & London, the major sponsors.

Jim and Mary Cogan, Cherrytree Drive, Listowel
J.G. McKenna, Greenville, Listowel
John Given, Listowel and Dublin
Seamus Given, Listowel and Dublin
Hugh Friel, Tralee
Listowel UDC
Listowel Livestock Mart
Listowel Arms Hotel
Allman Bros, Banemore
Patricia Regan, Newtown Anner Stud, Clonmel
Seán Moriarty, Dental Surgeon, The Square
Con McCarthy Insurance, Listowel
David Fitzmaurice, Accountant, The Square
Pat Corridan, Birmingham and Listowel
John J. Galvin and Son Ltd
The Sheahan family, William Street
Philip O'Carroll, Cahirdown and California
Joseph Walsh, Dublin and Listowel
Martin Stack, William Street
Tadhg and Nicole Kennelly, Sydney and Listowel
Robert Corridan, New York and Listowel
Pierse & Fitzgibbon Solicitors
Danny and Eileen Hannon, The Square
Seán and Dara Costello, William Street
Eamon and Mary O'Connor, Gurtinard
Michael and Anne Enright, Cahirdown
John Sexton, William Street
Jerry O'Connor, Market Street
Kieran and Anne Moloney, The Square
Jerry Behan, William Street
Liam O'Flaherty, William Street
Dermot O'Mahony, William Street
Helen Lucey, Marshall and Macauley Solicitors
Listowel Race Company
Jerry Kennelly, tweak.com
Kerry Group
Éamonn Dillon, Church Street
Jackie O'Connell, Bray, Co Wicklow
Con Whelan, Market Street
Michael Sheehy, New York and Main Street
Joe, Mary, Seanie & Diarmuid Broderick, William Street
M.J. Carroll Ltd, The Square
Ned Morkan, Asdee

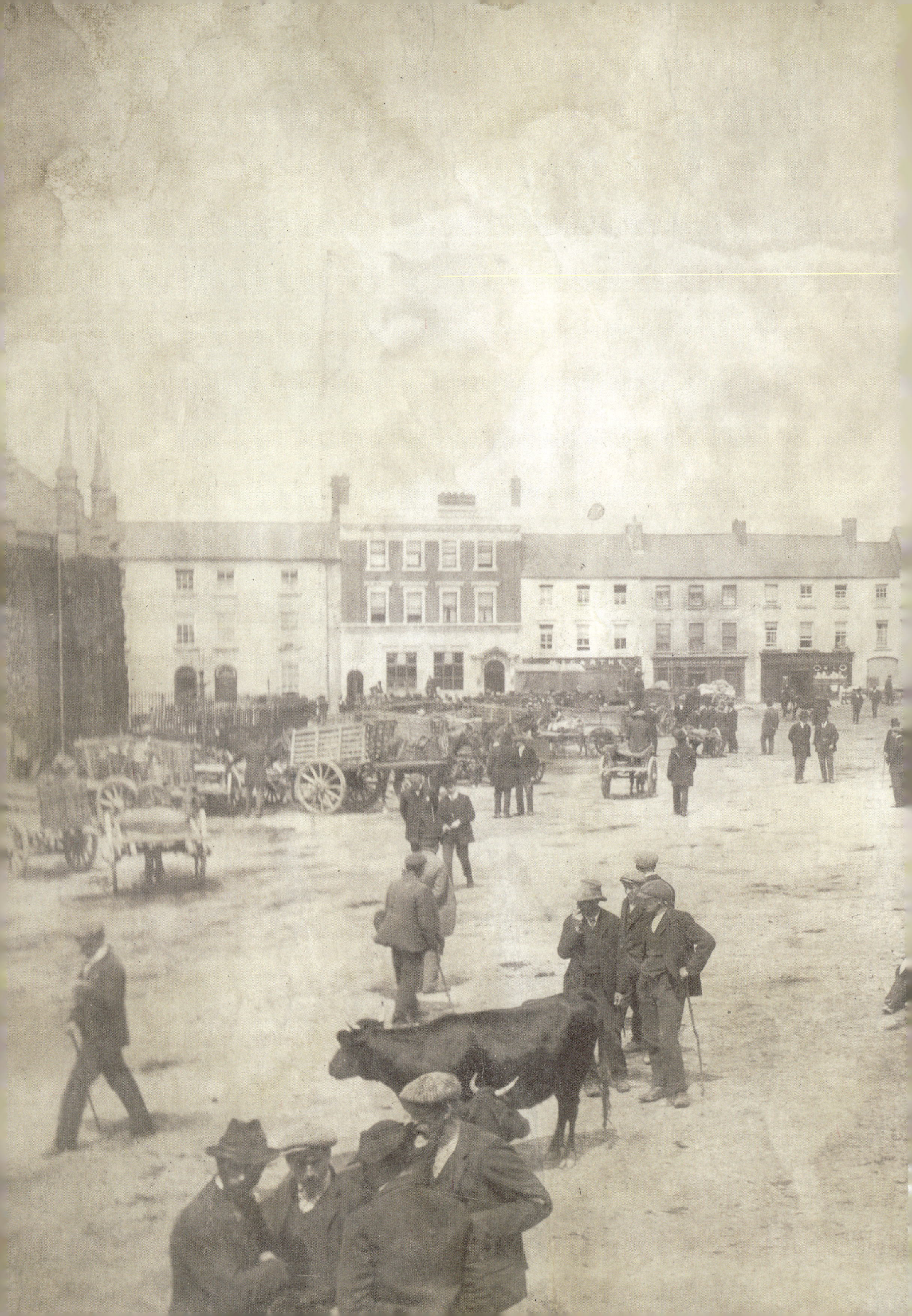